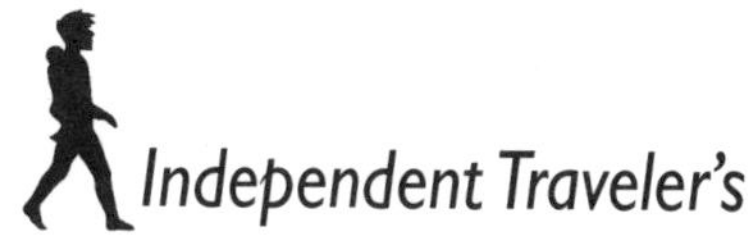

EUROPE 2000

Forthcoming titles in this series include:

Independent Traveler's USA 2000
The Budget Travel Guide

Independent Traveler's Australia 2000
The Budget Travel Guide

Independent Traveler's New Zealand 2000
The Budget Travel Guide

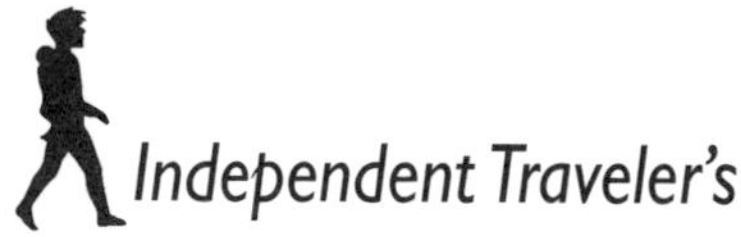

EUROPE 2000

THE BUDGET TRAVEL GUIDE

Edited by Tim Locke

Guilford, Connecticut

Published by Thomas Cook Publishing
The Thomas Cook Group Ltd
PO Box 227, Thorpe Wood
Peterborough PE3 6PU
United Kingdom
email: books@thomascook.com

The Globe Pequot Press
PO Box 480
Guilford, Connecticut USA
06437

ISBN 0-7627-0672-4

Library of Congress Cataloging-in-Publication Data is available

Publisher: Stephen York
Commissioning Editor: Deborah Parker
Map Editor: Bernard Horton
Text Design and Layout: Tina West

Cover Design by Pumpkin House
Copy editors: Leyla Davies, Anne O'Rorke
Proofreaders: Merle Read, Steve Cox
Route maps: Pixel Cartography
City maps updated by RJS Associates

Text typeset in Book Antiqua and Gill Sans using QuarkXPress
Picture research: Image Select International
Imagesetting: Z2 Reprographics, Thetford
Printed in Spain by GraphyCems, Navarra

HELP IMPROVE THIS GUIDE

This guide is updated each year. However, the information given may change and we would welcome reports and comments from our readers. Similarly we want to make this guide as practical and useful as possible and are grateful for any comments, criticisms and suggestions for improving future editions.

A free copy of this guide will be sent to all readers whose information or ideas are incorporated in the next edition. Please send all contributions to the Editor, Independent Traveller's USA, Thomas Cook Publishing at the address/email address given at the top of this page.

Written and researched by:

Ethel Davies
Sevil Delin
Jane Foster
Will Hardie
Dr Annie Kay
Susie Lunt
Jennifer Morris
Caroline Oldfield
Jeremy Smith
Dan Taylor
Mark Thomas
Wendy Wood
Barry Worthington

Additional research:
Geoff Hurst
Dr Atila Nagy
The compilers of the *Thomas Cook European Timetable*

Book Editor:

Tim Locke

NORTH AMERICA RESIDENTS

So you are in the US or Canada and are planning your trip of a lifetime. You have your plane ticket, your bags are packed and now all you need are your rail passes. Look no further - all you have to do is to contact one of the agents below who will assist you.

EUROPRAIL: Phone: **1-888-667-9734** Fax: **(519) 645 0682** Email: europrail@eurail.on.ca
See advert on inside of front cover.
FORSYTH TRAVEL LIBRARY: Phone: **1-800-367-7984** Fax: **(914) 681-7251** Email: forsythtrav@Aol.com
See advert on inside of back cover.

AUSTRALIA & NEW ZEALAND RESIDENTS

Getting your Eurail & Europasses down under couldn't be easier. Simply fill in the following application form and take it to your local licenced ATFA or TAANZ accredited travel agent or forward it to one of the General Sales Agents shown.

RAIL PLUS: Lvl 3, 459 Little Collins Street, Melbourne Vic 3000
Phone: (03) 9642 8644 Fax: (03) 9642 8403 Email: info@railplus.com.au
RAIL PLUS: Lvl 6, 76 Symonds Street, Aukland
Phone: (09) 303 2484 Fax: (09) 303 2355 Email: info@railplus.com.nz

EURAIL & EUROPASS ORDER FORM

1. Surname:	Initials:	Title:
Date of Birth:	Nationality:	
2. Surname:	Initials:	Title:
Date of Birth:	Nationality:	
3. Surname:	Initials:	Title:
Date of Birth:	Nationality:	
Contact Address:	Phone (home):	
	Phone (work):	

All prices are subject to change without notice.

	ADULT 1ST CLASS			1ST CLASS (2-5 passengers together)			YOUTH 2ND CLASS (under 26)		
Eurail Pass - Valid in 17 Countries (Consecutive Day Use)									
Per Person	AUD	NZD	QTY rqd	AUD	NZD	QTY rqd	AUD	NZD	QTY rqd
15 Day	923	1186		783	1007		647	833	
21 Day	1197	1535		1017	1305		832	1069	
1 Month	1483	1901		1260	1616		1038	1333	
2 Month	2100	2688		1787	2288		1470	1884	
3 Month	2597	3322		2207	2824		1815	2324	
Eurail Flexipass - Valid in 17 Countries (Use within 2 months)									
10 Day	1090	1398		927	1190		763	981	
15 Day	1437	1841		1220	1564		998	1281	
Europass - Base pass valid in France, Germany, Switzerland, Italy and Spain (Use within 2 months)									
5 Day	580	747		493	637		388	503	
6 Day	613	790		523	675		422	545	
8 Day	747	960		637	820		522	673	
10 Day	880	1130		1033	1326		855	1098	
15 Day	1213	1556		1033	1326		855	1098	
Additional Supplement									
1 country	100	135		87	118		75	103	
2 countries	167	220		143	190		130	173	
Circle additional countries required (1 or 2 only as selected): BENELUX - GREECE - PORTUGAL - AUSTRIA/HUNGARY (combined)									
Child 4 - 11 years inclusive pays half of Adult (or Saverpass if accompanied) fare (1st class only)									
Calculate your total pass price here:				Qty	Price	Total			
				Qty	Price	Total		**Total Cost**	

The Authors

Tim Locke is an editor and guidebook writer with a passion for places, rail travel, hiking and scenery, having journeyed over much of Europe including backpacking over the Alps and cycling in France. He is the author of several walking and general guides to Britain, as well as guides to Germany, New England and Thailand. He wishes to dedicate this guide to Ronald Locke (1921–1999) who enthused him with his passion for rail travel and discovering new places.

Ethel Davies is a freelance photographer and journalist who makes her living travelling around the globe. Rail travel remains one of her favourite modes of getting around.

Sevil Delin is an Oxford graduate working as a writer in Istanbul. A contributor to previous Thomas Cook guides, she can ask directions to the train station fluently in five languages.

Jane Foster lives on the Dalmatian coast where she works as an English teacher and freelance travel writer. Her special interests are Italy and the countries of former Yugoslavia. She is Croatian correspondent for *Colours* magazine.

Will Hardie has travelled through the Indian subcontinent and the Americas as well as extensively in Europe, where he wrote the Spain and Portugal sections of a previous Thomas Cook guide. He is now a reporter at Reuters news agency.

Dr Annie Kay, freelance travel writer and journalist specialising in Bulgaria. Winner of the Bulgarian Rose International Award for Journalists. Organiser of special tours to Bulgaria.

Susie Lunt is a freelance writer based in Prague, where she has lived off and on since 1991. She specialises in writing about Central and East European travel and culture and has travelled extensively throughout the region.

Jennifer Morris studied at Oxford where she edited a number of student publications including *Oxford Student* and *Isis*. She has travelled widely throughout Europe and America and has worked in France for several years. She winters in the Alps as a ski representative.

Caroline Oldfield has travelled extensively throughout Europe, edited student publications before gaining BA (Hons) Journalism, written for various publications; and is currently a Trinity Newspapers reporter and travel writer.

J J Smith and Dan Taylor were recently released from university and survived in the wild by preying on doughnuts. They now haunt the Oxford Media Underground. Dan would like to express no thanks at all to the Mannekin-Pis.

Mark Thomas took a year-out from managing his own PR consultancy to tour Europe with his family. The former journalist is also a freelance travel writer.

Wendy Wood studied at Oxford and has travelled extensively in Europe, most recently France and Spain. She has contributed to several Thomas Cook publications and revised the *Thomas Cook European Travel Phrasebook*.

Barry Worthington, lecturer in Tourism at Bolton Institute of Higher Education, travelled extensively over the last few years in the Baltic States and is in the process of completing a doctoral thesis on the Estonian Tourism Industry. He is a rail enthusiast.

The authors and Thomas Cook Publishing would like to thank the following for their help during the production of this book:

Alenka Rebec, Ljubljana Promotion Centre; Barry Fiedler; Beatrice at the Hotel Miramar in Cap d'Ail; and Leszek Butowski; Bernd Buhmann; Caroline Horton; Clare Ring; Deborah Emeny; Elizabeth Harney; Eva Draxler, Vienna tourist board; Hitesh Mehta and Charles Page, Rail Europe; Hotel Ibis, Krakow; Janina Pizlo, Krakow tourist information; Jaroslav Flak, Torun tourist board; Jela Faltanyova, Slovak tourist board; Klara Burianova; Natascha Kompatzki; Ognian Avgarski, Balkania Travel Ltd; Personnel (official and non official) involved in the tourist industry of the Baltic States; Peter Kozyrev of the *St. Petersburg Times*; Sara Malamunic, Split and Dalmatia County Tourist Board; the exceptionally helpful tourist office in Nice; the Romanian National Tourist Office; and tourist offices at Brno, Czech Rep; Dresden; Innsbruck; Kitzbuhel; Linz, Salzburg, Austria; Zakopane, Poland and throughout Europe.

The following are thanked for supplying the photographs (and to who the copyright belongs):

Colour section p. 32–33 all Neil Setchfield except (i) Eurostar train, Waterloo, Ethel Davies; (ii) Arc de Triomphe, Paris, Image Select International/Chris Fairclough Colour Library; (iii) Palombaggio, Corsica, Ethel Davies; Alpine scenery, John Heseltine. Pages 160–161 all Neil Setchfield except (i) Barbara Rogers; (ii) Alex Kouprianoff. Pages 288–289 all Neil Setchfield except (i) Jungfraujoch, Interlaken, Ethel Davies; Gornergrat, Chris Woodcock; (iii) Siena, Sara Kawasug. Pages 416–417 all Neil Setchfield except (i) Oslo–Bergen route, Ethel Davies; (iii) John Heseltine; (iv) Robert Harding Picture Library.

Contents

Reference Section

Introduction

Travel in Europe tends to breed an insatiable curiosity to see more. The incredible variety of this group of countries belies its relative compactness. For instance it's only a few hours by air from Spain, in the south-west corner, to Scandinavia, in the north-east, but the two nations could hardly be more different in their culture, people, buildings, scenery and climate. And within countries are astonishing differences – in Italy for example the Dolomites are snowy-capped Alps abutted by wildflower-flecked pastures and Austrian-looking chalets, while Sicily has a rugged, almost desert-like interior beyond the menacingly smouldering form of Mount Vesuvius.

Rail travel encapsulates much of the best of this continent. The network across Europe is still impressively dense, and the passes on offer make extended rail travel a great bargain. Trains are excellent for meeting other travellers, and generally safe and more comfortable than buses; they're also useful in that they get you right into city centres (and often the cheapest places to stay are gathered round the station). Some of the world's most scenic rail journeys are here (and feature in this book) – such as the routes north of Oslo in Norway, through the Swiss Alps or along the French and Italian rivieras. The *Thomas Cook Rail Map of Europe* highlights the most spectacular lines in green, while the *Thomas Cook European Timetable* (published monthly) will help you get to most places by rail or ferry.

Even if you're using a rail pass, don't rule out bus travel, particularly in Greece, Spain and other parts of southern Europe where it can be more convenient for certain journeys. It tends to be inexpensive and often gets you to places not on the rail network. If time is short, you might prefer flying within Europe and focusing on one or two countries. London's a good place to start, with plenty of inexpensive flights on offer through travel agencies advertising in newspapers and elsewhere (your money's safeguarded if the agency is bonded with an agency such as ABTA and goes bust; it's also worth paying for tickets with a credit card, as the credit card company effectively suffers any loss over £100 in the event of bankruptcy). Business-only destinations tend to be less good value than holiday areas; for instance Malaga is the main airport for the Costa del Sol, one of Spain's biggest package holiday destinations – you might not want to linger on the coast, but Malaga itself is the start of our tour of the great cities of Andalucía.

If you're starting from London and intend to hire a car elsewhere in Europe, you may get the best deals by booking from Britain (it pays to phone around). Check you're insured if the car gets damaged, and inspect the vehicle thoroughly before you drive off; some Mediterranean resorts have a notorious reputation for dodgy vehicles. The same goes for motor bikes (some hirers won't give you any insurance cover at all). Driving laws, standards and styles vary greatly within Europe. Britain, for example is often congested, and traffic drives on the left; Belgium is reasonably relaxed in the countryside, but Brussels can be terrifying, with poor lane discipline and frequent minor collisions; Spain's Costa del Sol has Europe's most accident-ridden road; France is generally pleasant, with long, empty roads, good toll autoroutes and clear signposting; and German Autobahns (motorways) are extremely fast.

Parts of Europe are ideal for travelling under your own steam. The Alps, Pyrenées, Tatras and Picos de Europa have stern peaks that are the preserves of the dedicated mountaineer, but there are also plenty of superb easier routes from villages or between idylically huts where you can overnight in often very convivial surroundings. France is criss-crossed by long-distance paths of varying difficulty, while England and Wales have a unique system of public rights of way that cross private land but are open to all, and the Germanic countries are particularly geared towards walkers. Cycling, too, has huge scope, though remember that not all trains will take cycles, and sometimes they have to be booked ahead; however you can hire cycles at some major stations.

Tim Locke

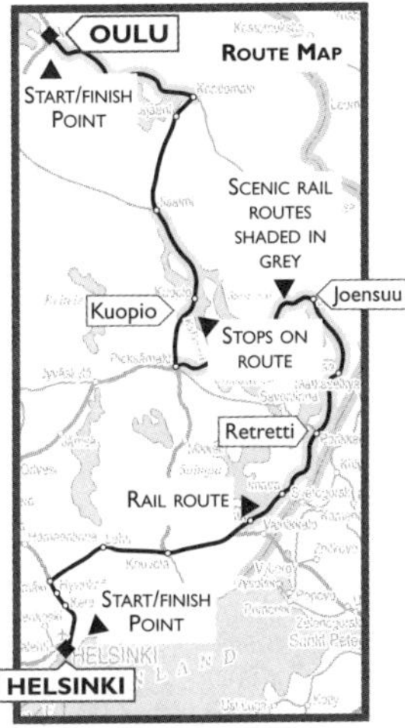

ROUTE DETAIL		
Helsinki–Oulu		ETT table 790
Type	Frequency	Journey Time
Train	5 daily	7 hrs 15 mins
Helsinki–Parikkala		ETT table 795
Type	Frequency	Journey Time
Train	4 daily	4 hrs

ROUTE DETAIL

Helsinki–Oulu: direct journey details

Helsinki–Parikkala: point to point information

Mode of travel, journey time, frequency of service and *ETT* table numbers are given.

KEY TO ICONS

- Telephone
- Bus
- Rail Stations
- Public Transport
- Ferry Services
- Airports
- Information
- Accommodation
- Food and Drink

Independent Traveller's Europe is divided into country, city and route chapters. City and route chapters fall within sections that cover one county, or a group of countries where we link areas of Europe e. g. Spain and Portugal, South-eastern Europe.

Many travellers will start their journey in London and head to Paris and beyond, and the format of this guide reflects this. So, the United Kingdom is followed by France, Spain, Portugal, Central Europe, Scandinavia, the Baltic States, Eastern Europe and finally South-East Europe. The routes are chosen for their interest and do not all link together, but using suggestions in this book and a copy of the *European Timetable*, they form a menu from which you can plan a rail tour.

Country introductory sections concentrate on accommodation and food and drink within that country. Each Country introduction ends with Editor's Choice, listing some of the best areas to head for if time is limited, and Beyond the Border, giving you pointers to train trips into adjacent countries. Country-specific details, national rail information and local rail passes are given within the **Directory**, pp. 540–569. **City chapters** cover the major centres within each country section. The 'Highlights' featured are just that – a selective choice of attractions, rather than an exhaustive listing of sights to see.

Route chapters start with a map plotting the route and possible stopping points (featured within that chapter), combined with route details and any 'notes' that may help the rail traveller. Places given in a plain type (rather than bold) in the route details are included as a transfer point en route, and not featured in the chapter. The type of transport is also indicated — usually train, but some routes may include ferry or bus travel.

Within route and city chapters, *day trips* are suggested. *Where Next?* features further places and attractions to explore, or links to other routes.

The **route map** on pp. 12–13 gives a summary of the routes covered in this book; **Travelling around Europe** gives basic travel advice, **Rail Passes** and **Rail Travel** concentrate on aspects of rail touring. **International Routes** details journeys that will take you across the continent. And, at the back of this guide is a selection of colour city and transport maps.

Travellers are strongly recommended to purchase the *Thomas Cook European Timetable* – referred to as the *ETT* – which is published monthly (see page 22). You will see ETT table numbers quoted throughout this guide, but please note that table numbers do change and services are altered. Don't forget also to check local station timetables as you travel, as the ETT doesn't have the room to show every short-distance rail service.

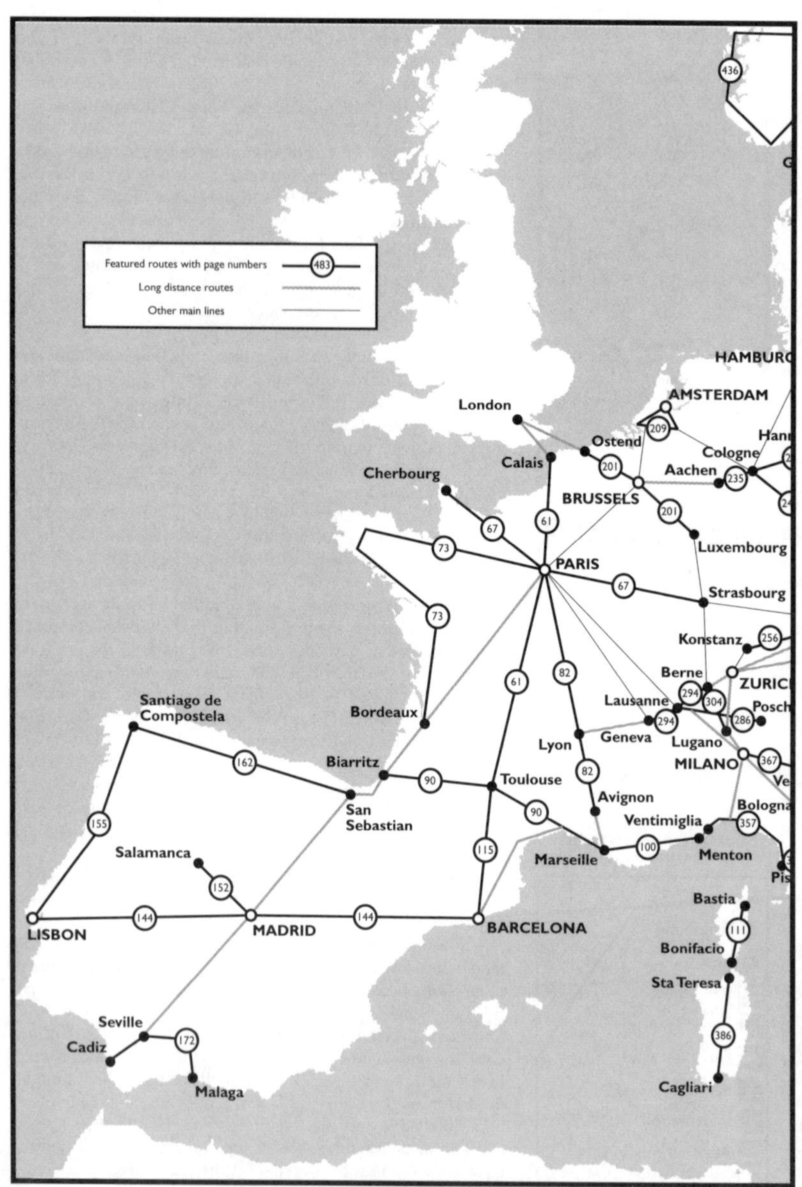
Featured routes with page numbers
483
Long distance routes
Other main lines
436
AMSTERDAM
209
London
Ostend
Cologne
Calais
201
Aachen
235
Cherbourg
BRUSSELS
61
201
67
Luxembourg
73
PARIS
67
Strasbourg
73
Konstanz
256
Berne
61
82
294
304
Santiago de Compostela
Lausanne
Bordeaux
294
286
Geneva
Lugano
Lyon
162
MILANO
367
Biarritz
82
90
Toulouse
Avignon
Bologna
San Sebastian
90
Ventimiglia
357
155
115
100
Menton
Marseille
Salamanca
152
Bastia
144
144
111
LISBON
MADRID
BARCELONA
Bonifacio
Sta Teresa
Seville
172
386
Cadiz
Malaga
Cagliari

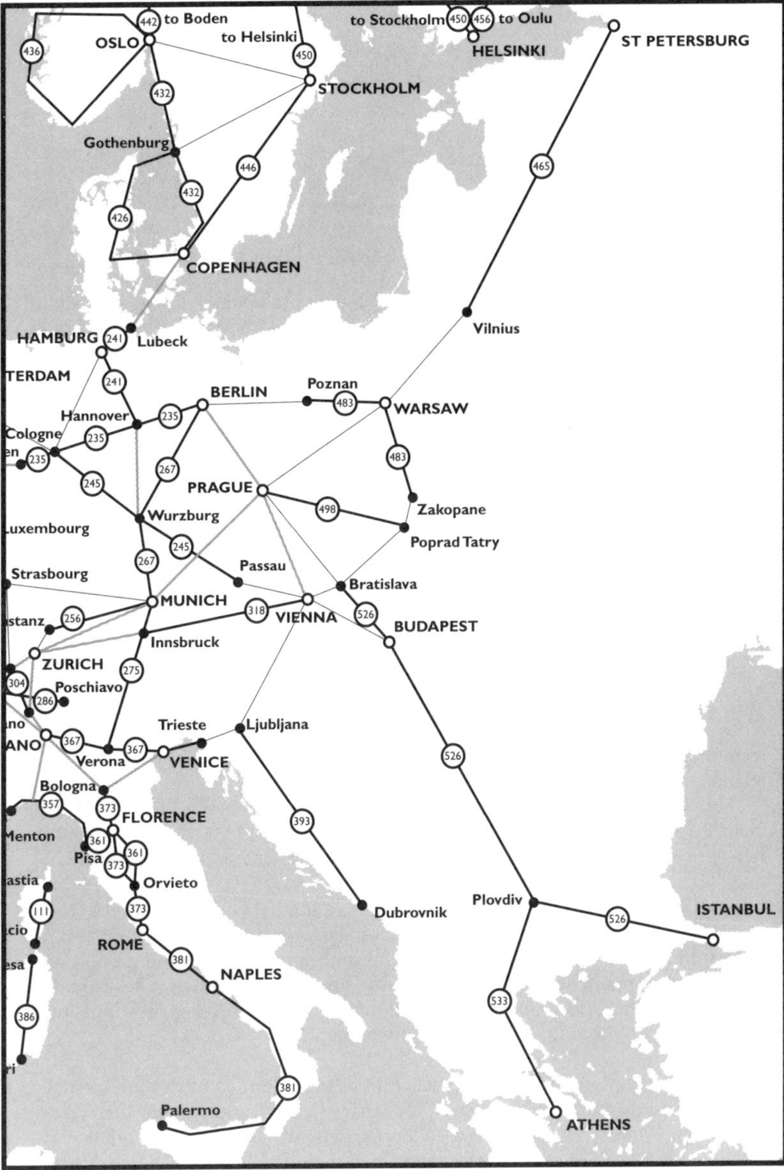
to Boden
OSLO
to Helsinki
to Stockholm
to Oulu
HELSINKI
ST PETERSBURG
STOCKHOLM
Gothenburg
COPENHAGEN
HAMBURG
Lubeck
Vilnius
BERLIN
Poznan
WARSAW
Hannover
Cologne
PRAGUE
Zakopane
Wurzburg
Poprad Tatry
Strasbourg
Passau
Bratislava
MUNICH
VIENNA
BUDAPEST
Innsbruck
ZURICH
Poschiavo
Trieste
Ljubljana
Verona
VENICE
Bologna
FLORENCE
Menton
Pisa
Orvieto
ROME
NAPLES
Dubrovnik
Plovdiv
ISTANBUL
Palermo
ATHENS

Travelling Around Europe

This chapter is full of helpful tips for anyone planning to travel around Europe. For information covering specific countries, see under individual countries in the Directory section (p. 540–p. 569).

Accommodation

Europe offers an excellent choice, from five-star hotels to room only. Your main problem may lie in finding something to suit your budget. Rooms in private houses are often a good, inexpensive and friendly option (local tourist offices often have lists), but you may be expected to stay for more than one night. The quality of cheaper hotels in Eastern Europe may still be less than inspiring and you could do better with a private room. Local tourist offices are almost always your best starting point if you haven't pre-booked. If they don't handle bookings themselves (there's usually a small charge), they will re-direct you to someone who does and/or supply you with the information to do it yourself – tell them your price horizons.

Hostels: For those on a tight budget, the best bet is to join HI (Hostelling International); there's no age limit. Membership of a national association will entitle you to use over 5000 HI hostels in 60 different countries and, apart from camping, they often provide the cheapest accommodation. The norm is dormitory-style, but many hostels also have single and family rooms. Many offer excellent-value dining and many have self-catering and/or laundry facilities. Some hostels are open 24 hours, but most have lock-out times and reception's hours are usually limited – check what they are and advise them if you are arriving out of hours. Reservation is advisable – especially in summer, when many hostels fill well in advance and even those with space are likely to limit your stay to three nights if you just turn up without booking. In winter (except around Christmas) you may be able to get special price deals. Buy the HI's directory Europe, which lists hostel addresses, contact numbers, locations and facilities; the HI website is http://www.iyhf.org. For information, to join, and to book international accommodation in advance: Australia, ☎(02) 9261 1111; Canada, ☎1 (800) 663 5777; England (and Wales), ☎(01727) 845047 (information only); Republic of Ireland, ☎(01) 830 1766; New Zealand, ☎ (09) 379 4224; Northern Ireland, ☎ (01232) 324 733; Scotland, ☎(0141) 332 3004; South Africa, ☎(021) 242 511; USA,☎(0202) 783 6161. Wherever we have given hostel details, the hostels are HI unless stated otherwise.

Camping: This is obviously the cheapest accommodation if you're prepared to carry the equipment. There are campsites right across Europe, from basic (just toilets and showers) to luxury family-oriented sites with dining-rooms, swimming pools and complexes of permanent tents. The drawback is that sites are often miles from the city centres. There's no really good pan-European guide to campsites, but most tourist offices can provide a directory for their country.

Borders

Land borders between the EU (European Union) countries are virtually non-existent and it's only if you arrive/leave by air or sea that you're likely to encounter any formalities. Checks between the EU and other West European countries are seldom more than perfunctory. Most former Eastern bloc countries, however, still go through the full routine and you should be prepared for delays when crossing between East and West.

CHILDREN Most children find train travel a great novelty and thoroughly enjoy themselves. However, they can get bored on long journeys. Most tourist destinations in Europe are reasonably well adapted for children and babysitters are not hard to find (ask at the local tourist office). Many hotels offer family rooms or provide a cot in a normal double. Many sights and forms of transport accept babies for free, and children under 12 for half price. For useful reading try: Maureen Wheeler, *Travel with Children* (Lonely Planet).

CLIMATE The climate in Europe is affected by three main factors: latitude (Scandinavia is colder than Spain); altitude (the Alps are colder than Belgium); and distance from the sea (the central European countries, such as the Czech Republic, can suffer surprisingly harsh winters and unexpectedly hot summers). That said, most of Europe has a relatively gentle climate. Rain is common throughout the year, except along some stretches of the Mediterranean. The summer temperature rarely exceeds 28°C (see the climate chart, for centigrade and fahrenheit equivalents on p. 570), except in the far south (the Mediterranean area), where it can be agonisingly hot (occasionally even 40°C) in high summer. Winter tends to be grey and wet, with temperatures hovering around -5/+5°C and relatively little snow, except in Scandinavia, the high mountains and parts of central Europe. In the far north, midsummer is the best time to travel, to take advantage of the ultra-long days. Almost everywhere else, May and September are the best months, and have the added advantage of avoiding school holiday crowds.

CONSULAR SERVICES/EMBASSIES Most embassies/consulates/high commissions will lend a helping hand if their nationals have real problems – and charge a small fee for any services rendered. Help should be available if: your passport is stolen (or a travel document that will get you home); if there's a death or serious accident (advice on procedures, next of kin notified – probably also sympathetic help); if you go to jail – don't expect sympathy, nor direct intervention, but they will explain your rights and tell you how to get a lawyer. Should something happen to make the area dangerous (an act of God, local rebellion, etc), contact your embassy to register your presence and ask for advice. In case of real financial trouble, embassies may agree to make a small loan or contact next of kin with a request for help, but they do not look kindly on people who have simply overspent. Do not expect them to act as surrogate travel agents, banks, interpreters, etc. If your own country has no representation, get advice from one with which it has ties, e.g. Commonwealth citizens can try the British Embassy.

CURRENCY Most European countries place no limit on the import/export of currencies. However, almost all the former Eastern bloc countries state that the amount taken out must not exceed the amount taken in, making allowance for the amount spent while there (and checks are made on your departure), so always declare large amounts of cash on arrival.

Carry credit cards (which can be used in cash machines, but don't rely too heavily on them) and travellers' cheques (usually best in the local currency; if you're travelling through several countries, cheques in sterling or US dollars will probably suffice; keep the counterfoil separate from the cheques, as you can be reimbursed if you lose the cheques; record which cheques you have cashed). The Thomas Cook offices listed in this book will cash any type of Eurocheque/travellers' cheque and will replace Thomas Cook Travellers Cheques if yours are lost/stolen. Eurocheques are only semi-useful: many establishments charge a hefty fee for dealing with them, and others don't take them at all.

Though it's obviously risky to carry wads of banknotes, you should always try to obtain some local currency before you enter a new country. If you are unable to do so and arrive outside banking hours, the best bet (albeit an expensive option) is to ask the receptionist at a big hotel to change some for you. Try to ensure you always carry one or two coins of each denomination for use in slot machines.

Although technically illegal, many travellers in Bulgaria and Romania find it useful to carry a few small-denomination German notes and coins. There is no black market in currency in Western Europe. You may find people eager to trade in some Eastern European countries, but you could face heavy penalties if caught. You may also be ripped off by those making the exchange, or lay yourself open to muggers working with them.

In border towns and on cross-border transport, you can almost always use either of the relevant currencies (a good way to dispose of excess coins), but you generally pay less if you choose the one in which prices are marked.

CUSTOMS Importing narcotics and offensive weapons is banned throughout Europe, and pornography is banned in many countries. Never carry luggage across borders for other people. If you have to take a prescribed drug on a regular basis, carry a doctor's letter to prove it's legitimate.

There are often restrictions on the import and export of plants and fresh foodstuffs (particularly meat and meat products), as well as certain souvenirs (such as those made of tortoiseshell) and you might be asked to abandon them at borders.

CUSTOMS ALLOWANCES IN THE EU European Union member states (Austria, Belgium, Denmark, Finland, France, Germany, Greece, the Republic of Ireland, Italy, Luxembourg, the Netherlands, Portugal, Spain, Sweden and the UK) have set the purchase of tobacco, alcohol and perfume at the same basic allowance for each country, and the tobacco and alcohol allowances apply to anyone aged 17 or over.

There are no restrictions between the EU countries for goods bought in ordinary shops and including local taxes, but you may be questioned if you have excessive amounts. Allowances are:

800 cigarettes, 200 cigars, 400 cigarillos and 1 kg tobacco
+ 90 litres wine (maximum 60 litres sparkling)
+ 10 litres alcohol over 22% volume (e.g. most spirits)
+ 20 litres alcohol under 22% volume (e.g. port and sherry)
+110 litres beer.

The allowances for goods bought outside the EU are:

200 cigarettes or 50 cigars or 100 cigarillos or 250 g tobacco*
+ 2 litres still table wine
+ 1 litre spirits or 2 litres sparkling or fortified wine
+ 8 litres Luxembourg wine if imported via the Luxembourg frontier
+ 50 g/60 ml perfume
+ 0.5 l/250 ml toilet water.

*Some EU countries have more generous tobacco allowances for non-Europeans arriving from outside Europe, so check in the duty-free shop or with your carrier.

Allowances for those returning home:

Australia: goods to the value of Aust$400 (half for those under 18) plus 250 cigarettes or 250 g tobacco and 1 litre alcohol.

Canada: allowances apply to anyone aged 19 or more (a year younger if you are entering AL, MN or QU). You are allowed 50 cigars and 200 cigarettes and 400 g tobacco plus 1.1 litre alcohol or 24 x 355 ml bottles/tins beer, as well as gifts not exceeding Can$60 each in value.

New Zealand: goods to the value of NZ$700. Anyone over 17 may also take 200 cigarettes or 250 g tobacco or 50 cigars or a combination of tobacco products not exceeding 250 g in all plus 4.5 litres of beer or wine and 1.125 litres spirits.

South Africa: goods to a total value of 500 Rand. Those aged 18 or more are allowed 400 cigarettes and 50 cigars and 250 g tobacco plus 2 litres wine and 1 litre spirits plus 50 ml perfume and 250 ml toilet water.

Republic of Ireland and UK: standard EU regulations apply (see foregoing notes and above).

USA: goods to the value of US$400 as long as you have been out of the country for at least 48 hrs and only use your allowance once every 30 days. Anyone over 21 is also allowed 1 litre alcohol plus 100 (non-Cuban) cigars and 200 cigarettes and a reasonable quantity of tobacco.

DISABILITIES, TRAVELLERS WITH

Usually only the more modern trains and more upmarket hotels cater for travellers with disabilities, who need to reserve and ensure there is someone on hand to help. The amount of advance warning required for trains varies; Austrian State Railways ask for three days' notice, while the ever-efficient Swiss need only one day. In many European stations the platforms are quite low and passengers have to climb steep steps to board trains. Once aboard, only the more modern carriages provide space for a wheelchair; otherwise, space will be provided in the baggage car. Express services, such as the French TGV and the Spanish AVE, have good facilities, while some Scandinavian trains have adapted hydraulic lifts, accessible toilets and spacious compartments. Some national rail offices and tourist offices have leaflets about rail travel for the disabled. A few national networks offer discount passes for the disabled. The best routes to travel include the main lines in Scandinavia, Switzerland, Germany, the Netherlands (Dutch information line ☎(00 31 30) 235 55 55) and France. The worst facilities are in Turkey, Spain, Hungary, Greece, Bulgaria, the Czech Republic and Slovakia. UK information: **RADAR**, UNIT 12, CITY FORUM, 250

CITY RD, LONDON EC1V 8AF; ☎(020) 7250 3222, publish the annual guide *European Holidays and Travel* (£5 including postage), aimed at disabled travellers. US information: **SATH** (Society for the Advancement of Travel for the Handicapped), 347 5TH AVE, SUITE 610, NEW YORK NY 10016; ☎(212) 447 7284. For useful reading try: Susan Abbott and Mary Ann Tyrrell's *The World Wheelchair Traveller* (AA Publishing, £3.95); and Alison Walsh's *Nothing Ventured: A Rough Guide Special (Penguin, £7.99).*

DISCOUNTS In many countries reductions are available on public transport and on entrance fees for senior citizens, students and the young. Carry proof of your status, e.g. an official document that shows your age or an International Student Identity Card (ISIC) from your student union or travel agents such as, STA and Campus Travel. Some destinations offer (for a small fee) a book of discount vouchers covering anything from museums to restaurants. Many discount passes for tourists, including some rail passes, must be purchased before you leave home as they are not available in the country itself.

DRIVING If you want to hire a motor vehicle while you are away, check requirements with the AA/RAC, or your own national motoring organisation, well before you leave, so that you have time to get any necessary documentation and additional insurance cover. To hire a vehicle (except a moped), you usually have to be over 21, with two years' driving experience. In most European countries your national licence is valid for up to six months, but you may need a translation as well and it can be easier to get an international licence. Always check that the vehicle is in good condition before you set out, with special attention to brakes, lights and tyres (including the spare). Most road signs are standardised throughout Europe, but the quality of signposting varies dramatically, as do speed limits. Check for local peculiarities before you set out. Except in the British Isles, Europeans drive on the right. There is a network of motor-rail services across Europe, for those who wish to take their own cars across Europe by train.

ELECTRICITY With a few exceptions (notably the UK, which uses 230/240V), the European countries use 220V. The shape of plugs varies and, if you are taking any sort of electrical gadget, you should take a travel adaptor.

HEALTH There are no compulsory vaccination requirements. However, it is always advisable to keep your tetanus protection up to date and vaccination against typhoid and hepatitis A is also a good idea. You must be able to produce a certificate against yellow fever if you have been in a yellow fever endemic zone in the six days before entering Europe. UK citizens should fill in Form E111(available free from post offices) before leaving, allowing access to treatment across most of Europe (you may have to pay up-front and reclaim the cost when you return home). It's worth visiting a pharmacy before consulting a doctor: European pharmacists tend to be well trained and may well save you medical bills by prescribing something that solves your problem.

Although most of Europe is temperate, there is a definite risk of sunburn in the south and in high mountain areas. Don't spend hours outdoors without using a high-factor sunblock. If casual sex is your scene, fine, but do take precautions against AIDS and other unpleasant sexually-transmitted diseases; bring condoms with you if travelling to Eastern Europe. Rabies risk is very small, but be wary of stray and wild animals. Lyme disease – caught from ticks in undergrowth – is present in Central European forests (long trousers and long-sleeved shirts are a useful method of avoidance); symptoms are similar to arthritis and if they show up within three months of possible exposure ask your doctor for a blood test – early treatment is nearly always effective.

Most tap water in Western Europe is safe. Boil or sterilise all tap water (including the water you use to brush your teeth) if you think there may be cause for concern.

HITCHHIKING What used to be fun and a good way to meet local people is now too risky. However, in a few countries, such as Poland, there are official schemes for getting drivers and hitchers together, so that both can feel safe.

INSURANCE Take out travel insurance that covers your health as well as your belongings. It should also give cancellation cover and include an emergency flight home if something goes really wrong. If you are likely to do something that might be classified as risky (e.g. ski, drive a moped, dive), make sure your policy does not exclude that risk. Annual travel insurance policies are often good value if you're planning more than one trip a year.

LANGUAGE The Thomas Cook European Travel Phrasebook (£4.95/US$7.95) contains over 300 phrases, each translated (with phonetic spellings) into: French, German, Italian, Czech, Hungarian, Polish, Bulgarian, Romanian, Portuguese, Spanish, Greek and Turkish. Phrases cover the everyday needs of a rail traveller, from arriving in a station to booking accommodation, eating out, changing money and coping in an emergency. Keep a pen and paper handy at all times, then you can ask people to write down such figures as times and prices, and so you can write down words if others can't understand your pronunciation.

PASSPORTS AND VISAS Ensure that your identity document is valid well beyond the end of your stay. EU citizens can travel to other EU countries with a National Identity Card instead of a full passport. Those not citizens of western Europe, Australia, Canada, New Zealand, South Africa or the USA should check about visas with the relevant embassies. Anyone planning to stay more than 90 days in a single country may need a visa.

Some countries will refuse entry if you don't have an onward/return ticket and enough money to cover the cost of food, accommodation and other expenses during your stay. A credit card is a practical way of avoiding precise cash requirements. Even if you can theoretically obtain a visa at the border, it may be easier to get it in advance. Allow plenty of time, especially if you need to get several. You'll need a stack of passport photos and may have to pay in cash or by postal order.

SALES TAX Value Added Tax (known as VAT in the UK) is automatically added to most goods in Western European countries. The level is usually 10–20%. In most countries (except Greece), non-residents can reclaim the tax on major spending; each country sets a different minimum. The refund is also intended to apply to only one article, but if you buy several things in the same shop on the same day, the authorities seldom argue. Ask the shop assistant to fill in a tax refund form for you. Show the form, the receipt and the goods to customs on leaving the country and they will give you an official export certificate. This can sometimes be exchanged on the spot (necessary in Scandinavia); alternatively, post the certificate back to the shop (within a month) and they should send the refund. Many shops will send the goods directly to your home, but anything you save in paperwork at the time is likely to be offset by customs formalities in your own country.

SECURITY Things can certainly go wrong for any traveller, but don't get paranoid about it: Europe's still generally safe and fear of crime should not spoil your trip.

Rip-offs are an enduring part of travellers' conversation. You can avoid becoming subject of an anecdote by taking sensible precautions – carry your valuables in a money-belt or concealed in a pouch under your shirt, be extra vigilant in crowded places (even more so if you're travelling solo), don't leave baggage unattended, avoid seedy looking areas at night, try to look confident and purposeful at rail stations and airports (giving the message 'don't even try to rip me off'), avoid flashy-looking luggage and lock it with a padlock if possible, and leave that expensive ring at home. The obvious scam is simple theft. In Italian cities, bag snatchers sometimes operate on motor bikes, so carry your handbag or shoulder bag in a way that it can't be suddenly snatched away. Just about every major rail station or crowded bus is potential pickpocketing territory; rucksack pockets and a camera slung round your neck are particularly vulnerable. Decoys include a child who falls over in front of you and bursts into tears, a thief who 'drops' several coins and waiting for you to bend over and help pick them up, a mother who gives you her baby to hold while other children steal from you, and someone who says 'I've been robbed' and waits for you to put your hand instinctively where your money is.

Conmen and conwomen often try the 'don't you remember me?' approach, purporting to work at your hotel or to have seen you on a bus; it's an opening gambit for any number of scams. Then there's the good Samaritan who magically appears and helps you find accommodation or go sightseeing or a rail ticket (in Paris con artists loiter at ticket machines offering change, then take your money for a train ticket to the airport and give you a métro ticket costing a fraction as much). Or you might find a bogus cop asking to check your banknotes for forgeries or black market cash, with inevitable results; refuse and ask for ID, and suggest you'll walk to the nearest police station, and he may well instantly disappear.

If you're unlucky enough to be confronted with a mugger, stay calm, breathe deeply and slowly to relax; avoid aggression and try to back off – if that's not possible give him/her some money (or throw it in the air and run off the other way shouting loudly – he/she is likely to go after the money rather than a screaming victim) and contact the police as soon as possible. A personal alarm is useful in such situations (hold it near the assailant's ear if possible); even though you're unlikely to need it, it will give you peace of mind.

When you're sleeping in any sort of dormitory or on trains, the safest place for your small valuables is in the centre of your sleeping-bag. In sleeping-cars, padlock your luggage to the seat and make sure the compartment door is locked at night – if necessary, ask the attendant how to lock it.

SMOKING Banned in many public places and, even where it is allowed, there may be a special area for smokers. In some countries, such as France, Italy and Spain, the prohibitions are often ignored by the locals, but play safe if in doubt and ask before lighting up.

TELEPHONES You should have few problems finding a phone in European towns and everywhere is on direct-dial. In the EU countries you have an extra option: ☎112 for all emergency services. Avoid phones in hotel rooms: they invariably cost exorbitantly.

THOMAS COOK BUREAUX AND LICENSEES The Thomas Cook bureaux listed in this book cash any travellers' cheques and offer emergency assistance to holders of Thomas Cook Travellers Cheques if yours are lost or stolen. Details of Thomas Cook Licensees are also given in this book (look out for 'Thomas Cook Worldwide Network' signs in travel shops across Europe): these offer the benefits of the Thomas Cook Worldwide Customer Promise, available to those who have made their travel arrangements through Thomas Cook. The benefits include airline reservations and revalidation, hotel reservations, changes to travel arrangements and emergency assistance – all free of agency service charges.

TIME ZONES United Kingdom: Greenwich Mean Time in winter, and GMT+1 hr in summer. GMT+1 hr in winter, GMT+2 hrs in summer: Austria, Belgium, the Czech Republic, Denmark, France, Germany, Hungary, Italy, the Netherlands, Norway, Poland, Portugal, Slovakia, Spain, Sweden and Switzerland. GMT+2 hrs in winter, GMT+3 hrs in summer: Bulgaria, Estonia, Finland, Greece, Latvia, Lithuania, Romania and Turkey.

TIPPING Not usually necessary in Continental Europe. You can leave small change on bar counters; otherwise tips are generally not expected. In Britain you should tip 10 per cent at restaurants and in taxis (but never in pubs).

WHAT TO TAKE Travel as light as possible is the golden rule.

Luggage: Backpack (not more than 50 litres for women or 60 litres for men; plus day sack; sort your luggage into see-through polythene bags (makes fishing out your socks from the backpack much easier), plus take plastic bags for dirty clothes etc, and elastic bands for sealing them.

Clothing: Lightweight clothing, preferably of a type that doesn't need ironing; smart casual clothes for evening wear, at least three sets of underwear, swimsuit, sun hat, long-sleeved garment to cover shoulders (essential in some churches/temples; women may need headscarves); non-slip footwear. All purpose hiking boots useful for big walks around cities – or rubber sandals with chunky soles good when it's hot; flip flops for the shower etc.

THOMAS COOK PUBLICATIONS

The **Thomas Cook European Timetable (ETT)**, published monthly at *£8.99*, has up-to-date details of most rail services and many shipping services throughout Europe. It is essential both for pre-planning and for making on-the-spot decisions about independent rail travel around Europe. A useful companion to it is the **Thomas Cook New Rail Map of Europe** (£5.95), with scenic lines shown in green. Both of these publications are obtainable by phoning *(01733) 503571/2* in the UK; in North America, contact the **Forsyth Travel Library Inc.** 226 WESTCHESTER AVE, WHITE PLAINS, NEW YORK 10604; ☎ (800) 367 7984.

Thomas Cook Travellers (£7.99), cover a number of European cities and countries. If you plan on going as far as Athens and then seeing some of the Greek islands, you will find the *Thomas Cook Independent Traveller's Greek Island Hopping* invaluable; as well as covering (literally) every island, it provides detailed, essential information on the complex ferry schedules. These guides and the *Thomas Cook European Travel Phrasebook* are available from many book shops in the UK and the USA (publisher: Passport Books) and from UK branches of Thomas Cook.

First Aid/Medical: Insect repellent and antihistamine cream, sun-screen cream, after-sun lotion, water-sterilising tablets, something for headaches and tummy troubles, antiseptic spray or cream, medicated wet-wipes, plasters for blisters, bandage, contraceptives and tampons (especially if visiting Eastern Europe, where they are difficult to get – or try the luxury shop in the city's biggest hotel). Spare spectacles/contact lenses and a copy of your prescription.

Overnight Equipment: Lightweight sleeping-bag (optional), sheet liner (for hostelling), inflatable travel pillow, earplugs, and eyemask.

Documents: passport, tickets, photocopies of passport/visas (helps if you lose the passport itself) and travel insurance, travellers' cheques counterfoil, passport photos, student card, numbers of credit cards and where to phone if you lose them.

Other items: A couple of lightweight towels, small bar of soap, water-bottle, pocket knife, torch (flashlight), sewing kit, padlock and chain (for anchoring your luggage), safety matches, mug and basic cutlery, toothbrush, Travel Wash, string (for a washing-line), travel adapter, universal bath plug (often missing from wash-basins), sunglasses, alarm clock, notepad and pen, pocket calculator (to convert money), a money-belt and a good book/game (for long journeys).

Rail passes represent excellent value for train travellers and, if you are taking a number of journeys, usually allow you to make substantial savings over point-to-point tickets. Passes may cover most of the continent, a specific 'zone' of Europe, or a regional group of countries. Passes for travel within a specific country are detailed within the Directory (pp. 540–569).

As well as giving free or discounted travel on the national rail networks, many passes also give free or discounted travel with privately owned rail companies, buses and ferries. You get details of any extras when you buy the pass.

BOOKING RAIL PASSES

IN THE UK Sources of international rail tickets, passes and information about rail travel include: **Rail Pass Direct**, which can provide UK travellers with Inter-Rail passes, guidebooks and maps, delivered direct to their home address; ☎(01733) 502808, Fax: (01733) 503596, email: railpassdirect-@thomascook.com. **Rail Europe**, 179 PICCADILLY, LONDON W1; ☎08705 848 848. Most major mainline station enquiry offices (no telephone enquiries). **Wasteels Travel**, VICTORIA STATION, LONDON SW1V 1JY; ☎(0171) 834 7066; **USIT/Campus Travel** (Eurotrain), 52 GROSVENOR GARDENS, LONDON SW1W 0AG; ☎(0171) 730 3402 plus offices in most universities around the UK. **Ffestiniog Travel,** PORTHMADOG, GWYNEDD, WALES, LL49 9NF; ☎(01766) 512340. **Connex South East**; ☎0870 603 04 05. **DB** (German Rail); ☎0171 317 0919. **Holland Rail**, CHASE HOUSE, GILBERT STREET, ROPLEY, HANTS. SO24 OBY; ☎01962 773646. **Rail Choice**; www.railchoice.co.uk; **Freedom Rail**; ☎(01252) 728506.

IN THE USA **Forsyth Travel Library Inc.**, 226 WESTCHESTER AVE., WHITE PLAINS, NEW YORK 10604; (800) 367-7984; **Rail Europe Inc**, 500 MAMARONECK AVE, HARRISON, NEW YORK 10528, and 2100 CENTRAL AVE, SUITE 200, BOULDER CO 80301; ☎(800) 4-EURAIL (toll-free) or, for Eurostar, ☎(800) EUROSTAR (toll-free); **DER Tours**, ☎(800) 782 2424.

ELSEWHERE International rail information and tickets in Australia/Canada/New Zealand are obtainable from Thomas Cook branches (and branches of Marlin Travel in Canada). To contact Rail Europe in Canada, ☎(800) 361-RAIL (toll-free). In South Africa, international rail information and tickets are available from branches of Rennies Travel (Thomas Cook licensee).

EUROPEAN RAIL PASSES

Many countries have rail passes valid only for domestic travel. Those most likely to be of interest are detailed in the Directory (pp. 540–569) and can usually be purchased from any branch of the national railway and its appointed agents. Your passport is required for identification, and one or two passport-size photos may be needed. Passes generally cover all the ordinary services of the national rail companies and can be used on most special services if you pay a supplement. A few passes, such as Eurail, cover most supplements. If you are planning a long journey, consider the following international passes, which are common to most of Europe.

NB. Prices quoted in this chapter were correct at time of going to press. However, rail pass prices are liable to fluctuate, so check prices with the organisations listed on page 23.

INTER-RAIL PASSES The Inter-Rail Pass has launched generations of young people into the travelling life. A well-established scheme, it provides a practical and cheap way of seeing most of Europe by train. It can be bought by anyone who will be under 26 on the first day for which it is valid, if they have lived for at least six months in one of the European countries where the pass is valid (see list below), or are a national of that country and hold a valid passport. It can be purchased up to two months before travel begins. The current cost is £259 for a month and you can buy consecutive passes for longer journeys. You will not get free travel in the country where you buy the pass, but you may be eligible for some discount. Inter-Rail provides unlimited second-class rail travel for a month on the national railways of: Austria, Belgium, Bulgaria, Croatia, the Czech Republic, Denmark, Finland, France, Germany, Greece, Hungary, the Republic of Ireland, Italy, Yugoslavia, Luxembourg, Macedonia, Morocco, the Netherlands, Norway, Poland, Portugal, Romania, Slovakia, Slovenia, Spain, Sweden, Switzerland and Turkey. It also includes a free crossing on the Hellenic Mediterranean/Adriatica di Navigazione shipping lines between Brindisi in Italy and Patras in Greece (you will have to pay port tax of approximately L.10,000 from Italy to Greece or Dr.1500 from Greece to Italy). There are free or discounted crossings on other ferries, so check. The Inter-Rail ticket does not include high speed train supplements, 'Global priced trains' (CityNightLine), seat reservations, couchette or sleeper charges. Reductions of between 10 and 50% are available on various ferry services, the discount only applies to the basic ferry fare. Some ferries require compulsory accomodation. If you purchase an Inter-Rail ticket in the UK, you are entitled to 34% reduction on most fares to London. Eurostar offer a special 'Passholder Fare' to Lille, Brussels or Paris. It is possible to obtain discounts on return Rail-Ferry tickets from London to Hoek van Holland (£64), Oostende (£44), Calais (£36) or Boulogne (£40).

Zonal Inter-Rail Passes: These regional variations on the Inter-Rail Pass now apply for those over 26 as well as for those under 26. The same rules about eligibility apply.

For zonal passes, Europe has been divided into eight geographical zones:

- A United Kingdom and the Republic of Ireland.
- B Sweden, Norway and Finland.
- C Denmark, Switzerland, Germany and Austria.
- D Poland, the Czech Republic, Slovakia, Hungary and Croatia,
- E France, Belgium, the Netherlands and Luxembourg.
- F Spain, Portugal and Morocco.
- G Italy, Slovenia, Greece, Turkey (including shipping lines between Brindisi and Patras).
- H Bulgaria, Romania, Yugoslavia and Macedonia.

Passes are available for 1 zone (22 days: £159); 2 zones (1 month: £209); and 3 zones (1 month: £229). If you have a definite route in mind, these can offer savings over the standard Europe-wide pass. For instance, if you bought a 2-zone pass for zones E and G, you could travel through France into Italy and on to Greece and Turkey for only £209, with a side trip through the Benelux countries on the way home. **The Inter-Rail 26+ Pass** offers all the benefits of the Inter-Rail Pass except where the pass is purchased in the UK, you are only entitled to the Eurostar 'Passholder Fare' and reduced fares on Port to Port fares on the ferries. The current cost is £229 for a 1-zone pass, £279 for 2 zones, £309 for 3 zones and £349 for an all-zones pass.

> **CHILDREN**
>
> Although there are exceptions, the norm is for children aged 4–11 to pay approximately 50% of the adult fare and for babies under 4 to travel free – but babies are not entitled to a seat in crowded trains. Childrens fares can vary from country to country, anywhere between 4–6 to 11–17.

EURAIL PASSES These are available only to people living outside Europe and can be obtained from the agents listed (under 'In the USA' and 'Elsewhere') on p.24. You can get the passes once you've arrived (from Rail Europe, see p.24), but at much higher prices. Since you can buy them up to six months in advance, there is no point in waiting until the last minute.

Eurail offers unlimited travel on the national railways of: Austria, Belgium, Denmark, Finland, France, Germany, Greece, Hungary, the Republic of Ireland, Italy, Luxembourg, the Netherlands, Norway, Portugal, Spain, Sweden and Switzerland. They also cover some private railways and a few selected ferries, such as the Hellenic Mediterranean/Adriatica di Navigazione shipping lines between Brindisi in Italy and Patras in Greece (although, as with the Inter-Rail pass, you will have to pay the port tax of approximately L.10,000 from Italy to Greece or Dr.1500 from Greece to Italy. In addition to this, Eurail passholders must pay a high-season (June–Oct) supplement of L.15,000 from Italy to Greece or Dr.2500 from Greece to Italy). A complete list of bonuses is included on the map issued with your tickets.

The basic **Eurail Pass** has no age limit. It provides first-class travel on all services and even covers most of the supplements for travelling on express and de luxe trains. It also gives free or reduced travel on many lake steamers, ferries and buses. There are several versions, valid for 15 days, 21 days, 1 month, 2 months or 3 months. Current prices range from US$538 for 15 days to US$1512 for 3 months. The **Eurail Youth Pass** is much the same, but cheaper, as it is designed for those under 26 and is based on second-class travel. There are versions valid for 15 days (US$376), 1 month (US$605) and 2 months (US$857). The **Eurail Flexipass** is similar to the basic Eurail pass, but allows you to travel (first class) for any 10 days (US$634) or any 15 days (US$836) within a two-month period. The **Eurail Youth Flexipass** allows second-class travel for those under 26 within a two-month period for 10 days (US$444) and 15 days (US$585). **Eurail Saverpass** is designed for groups of 2–5 people travelling together at all times and offers first-class rail travel over a 15-day period for US$458, 21 days for US$594 and 1 month for US$734.

EURO DOMINO PASS This is a catch-all title for a whole series of passes allowing unlimited travel on the national railway of an individual country (but not if you are a resident of that country). Conditions of use are the same everywhere and the options available are for any 3–8 days within a period of one month. The passes can only be purchased by persons who have lived at least 6 months in Europe, Morocco, Algeria and Tunisia. They cover many of the fast-train supplements.

There is no age limit, but the price depends on age. Those under 26 pay less but are restricted to second-class, while those over 26 can opt for either class. The price varies according to the size of the railway network in the country chosen. Conditions of use are the same everywhere. However the number of days of availability are going to change.

Your ticket includes all high speed train supplements (except on certain 'Global Price' trains). Seat reservations, couchettes, and sleepers are extra. If you are travelling overnight or are to connect with an overnight service, you may commence your journey after 1900. The next day's date must be entered on your ticket. Your Euro Domino Pass is valid to the frontier, only in a few cases does your ticket allow you to cross into a different country.

Passes can be purchased up to two months before travel begins. Countries currently offering them are: Austria, Belgium, Bulgaria, Croatia, the Czech Republic, Denmark, Finland, France, Germany, Greece, Hungary, the Republic of Ireland, Italy, Luxembourg, Macedonia, Morocco, the Netherlands, Norway, Poland, Portugal, Romania, Slovakia, Slovenia, Spain, Sweden, Switzerland, Turkey and Yugoslavia.

Prices range from £19 for 3 days' travel (second-class) in Luxembourg, to £339 for 8 days' first-class travel in France. The Euro Domino Pass entitles the holder to a special 25% discount fare from your home country to the country of visitation, however this option is not available from the UK, in which case buy the Eurostar 'Passholder' ticket, but only if you hold a Belgium or France Euro Domino. Other Ferry discounts are also available.

EUROPASS Available in the USA or from Rail Europe, London, Europass is valid for 5 days unlimited second-class rail travel in a 2-month period. You can also purchase up to 10 additional days of rail travel. The 5-day pass costs US$326 and additional rail days cost US$42 each. The basic cost covers France, Germany, Italy, Spain and Switzerland. 'Associate Countries' can be added to extend the geographic reach of the pass. Choose from Austria and Hungary, Belgium, Netherlands and Luxembourg, Greece and/or Portugal. Prices range from US$386 for 5 days rail travel with 1 associate country to US$446 for 5 days rail travel with 4 associate countries. Two people travelling together receive a 40% companion discount.

For those under 26 the Europass Youth is available for second-class travel; for details contact the agents listed (under 'In the USA') at the start of this chapter. Various bonuses are available and listed on the map which accompanies the rail pass.

RAIL EUROP SENIOR CARD This card is for those over 60. It offers a discount of 30% (sometimes more) off the cost of cross-border rail travel (excluding supplements) between the participating countries: Austria, Belgium, Croatia, the Czech Republic, Denmark, Finland, France, Germany, Greece, Hungary, the Republic of Ireland, Italy, Latvia, Lithuania, Luxembourg, the Netherlands, Norway, Poland, Portugal, Romania, Russia, Slovakia, Slovenia, Spain, Sweden, Switzerland, the UK and Yugoslavia.

Most countries have a rail card for their senior citizens, which is needed to buy the Rail Europ Senior Card. In the UK, the Senior Railcard is available to people over 60 (it costs £18 per annum) The Rail Europ Senior Card, available from Rail Europe, costs an extra £5. It becomes valid on the day of purchase and expires on the same date as the domestic card.

REGIONAL EUROPEAN RAIL PASSES

BALKAN FLEXIPASS This pass offers unlimited first-class travel in Greece, Bulgaria, Romania, Macedonia, Montenegro, Yugoslavia and Turkey for any 5 days in one month (US$152), any 10 days in one month (US$264) or any 15 days in one month (US$317).

SCANRAIL PASS This is available in both the UK and the USA and gives unlimited free travel on the national rail networks of Denmark, Finland, Norway and Sweden (includes all local railways except Inlandsbahn and Stockholm Landstrafik) plus ferries between Helsingsor–Helsingborg, Kalundborg–Arhus, Rodby–Puttgarten Mitte See and Trelleborg–Sassnitz Mitte See. Three bus routes in Norway, Sweden and Finland.

Supplements are payable to use the following trains – X2000 (SJ), ICE (NSB), Pendilino S220 and IC+ (VR) services, and the Flam line in Norway. Seat reservations compulsory on most expresses and InterScandinavian services. Couchettes and sleepers are extra. Journeys may commence 1900 for long distance overnight travel. Next days date to be written on the Flexi Pass.

It is available as a consecutive pass, which offers unlimited rail travel over a 21-day period, or a flexi pass, which is valid for either 5 days travel in a 15-day period or 10 days travel within one month. Supplements payable on certain trains.

Scanrail also offers additional discounts on many ferries and boats, long-distance buses and private railways as well as good discounts at over 100 Best Western hotels.

It is possible to get Scanrail for first-class travel, but second-class seating is almost as comfortable and second-class seats are far more likely to be available. There is a Youth version for anyone aged 25 or less and another for seniors (60 years and over).

In the UK Scanrail is available from DB, ☎(0171) 317 0919, and Rail Europe, ☎0990 848848, for any 5 days within a 15-day period Adult (2nd) £132; Senior (2nd)£118, Youth £99. Any 10 days within the period of 1 month Adult (2nd) £177; Senior (2nd) £157, Youth £133. 21 consecutive days Adult (2nd) £210, Senior (2nd) £179, Youth £151. Children (4–11) half price. First class tickets are available at about 30% more.

In the USA Scanrail passes are available for any 5 days in a 15-day period (US$228 for first-class travel, US$182 for second class); any 10 days in a month (US$364 first class, US$292 second class); or for a full month (US$532 first class, US$426 second class). These passes, plus Scanrail passes for young people and for those aged over 55, are available from Forsyth Travel Library (see p. 25).

Scanrail passes are obtainable inside Scandinavia, but the validity is different and the ones bought prior to arrival are far better value.

Benelux Tourrail Pass This is available in the UK and the USA, and from train stations in Belgium and Luxembourg, but not in the Netherlands. It provides unlimited rail travel throughout Belgium, Luxembourg and the Netherlands for any 5 days in a month. Prices – £120/6600 BEF in 1st class, £80/4400 BEF in the 2nd Class and under 26 £56/3100 BEF. A second person can travel for half the adult price (not available to under 26's or if purchased in Belgium or Luxembourg).

If you are under 26, you are restricted to second class, but pay only £60/US$104.

Central Europe Pass This is available in the USA only and provides unlimited rail travel throughout the Czech Republic, Germany, Poland and Slovakia for any 5 days within a month. The pass is available for first-class travel only and costs US$199. There are no youth reductions.

Czech Republic/Slovakia Explorer Pass Available to holders of an ISIC card (see p.18), and under 26s, (from USIT/Campus Travel). Valid for 7 consecutive days unlimited travel on the national railways of the Czech Republic (CD) and Slovakia (ZSR). Priced at £35 (1st Class) and £23 (2nd Class). Supplements, seat reservations, couchettes and sleepers extra.

Youth Passes If you are under 26, there are many other discounted tickets and passes available. Some are to single destinations or for travel in single countries, others (like the examples above) to whole groups of countries. Passes come under many different names, such as Euro-Youth, Explorer Pass and BIJ (Billets International de Jeunesse).

This chapter provides general information about travelling by train around Europe. Information about rail travel for individual countries is given in the Directory, pp. 540–569, towards the back of this book.

TICKETS It's generally safest to buy your ticket before travelling (from a station or travel agent) as passengers found without tickets can face heavy penalties or criminal prosecution; however, if boarding at at station with no ticket office or machine, pay on the train. Always ask about discounts (eg for travel outside the rush hour and at weekends) before you buy a ticket. Most countries have discounts for children; the age limits vary from country to country, but commonly children under 4 travel free and those under 12 at half price.

ADVANCE RESERVATIONS There's no firm rule as to whether it's worth reserving (and it isn't always possible to do so anyway); some trains never get busy (especially many leisurely back-country routes), while others (such as some InterCity expresses) are packed in high season and around public holidays , and you could spend hours standing in a crowded corridor. In some cases, you may be refused permission to board at all if there are no seats available. There's normally a small fee for reservations. If you are travelling during the busy summer period and have no reservation, board your train as early as possible.

Some of the major express trains (usually marked in timetables by an 'R' in a box) are restricted to passengers with reservations, and you can usually make a reservation about two months in advance. You should book if you want sleeping accommodation, though you can chance your luck and just turn up, hoping a couchette will be available and pay the supplement to the attendant.

SUPPLEMENTS If you are travelling with a rail pass you'll be exempt from many routine surcharges made on express trains, but sometimes you'll have to pay a little more (so always travel with some local currency); ask if you're uncertain – there's nearly always a surcharge-free slower service. Some special high-speed services (such as the French TGV, the German ICE, the Swedish X2000, Eurostar Italia, Eurostar trains and Spanish AVE services) invariably require a supplement. Holders of a first-class Eurail Pass can use most of the special services without paying extra, but even they should check its validity if they want to use certain luxury trains, for example, InterCityNight (Germany), Trenhotel (Spain) .

The fee for reserving seats is normally included in the supplementary payments for faster trains. Sleeping accommodation (see p. 31) always attracts charges. Sort out the extras before you start your journey. You may be able to pay the supplements on the train, but it almost always costs more than doing it in advance.

TYPES OF TRAIN Many of the best daytime international trains are now branded EuroCity (or EC). To qualify, trains have to be fast and offer a certain standard of service, such as food and drink during the journey. All have names, and the EuroCity network continues to expand. Eurostar trains are in operation through the Channel Tunnel between Britain and France.

Most overnight services use ordinary trains, but there is a new breed of high-quality night service known as EuroNight (EN) with air-conditioned coaches and extras such as evening drinks and breakfast, which are available even to couchette passengers.

The IC or InterCity label is applied by many countries to the fast long-distance trains, although there are slight variations in what they provide. The ICE (InterCity Express) designation also crops up in several countries, but is mostly applied to the latest high-speed trains in Germany. IR is the classification for inter-regional express services which make more stops than InterCity services; it is used mainly in Germany (where it stands for 'Inter-Regio') and in Italy (where it's short for 'Interregionale'). These names are all used to distinguish the faster long-distance trains from local or stopping trains.

Most longer-distance trains in Europe offer both first- and second-class travel, but second class is the norm for local stopping services. Where overnight trains offer seating accommodation, this is usually second class only. As a rule in Western Europe, second class is perfectly OK for all but the most ardent comfort-seeker. A few Eastern European services still leave a lot to be desired (and information is often hard to obtain), but tickets are very cheap and it's worth paying a little more to upgrade to first class.

FINDING YOUR TRAIN Larger stations have potential for confusion. Look for the electronic departure boards or large paper timetables (often yellow for departures and white for arrivals) which list the routes, the times of departure and arrival, and the relevant platforms; double-check footnotes and symbols – that seemingly ideal train may in fact turn out to run only on the third Sunday in August. In some stations, the platforms are also labelled with details of regular trains or the next departure and may even give the location of specific carriages and the facilities on board. If you have a reservation, board your allocated carriage (they are all numbered, usually on cards by the entrance).

Look for destination boards on each carriage: even if you've found the right platform you might end up in the wrong place. Make sure you board in the right place: some long platforms serve more than one train at a time; and quite a few trains split en route, with only some carriages going the full distance.

First-class coaches usually have a yellow stripe above the windows and large number '1's on the side of the coach, on the door or on the windows. No-smoking coaches (the majority) display clear signs. A sign near the compartment door often gives seat numbers and sometimes indicates which are reserved. In open carriages (without compartments), seats are usually numbered individually (on the back or on the luggage rack) and reserved seats may have labels attached to their head rests (or the luggage racks). In many countries, however, reserved seats are not marked – so be prepared to move if someone who has booked boards the train.

OVERNIGHT TRAINS A night on the train, being rocked to sleep, soothed by the clatter of the wheels, is not to be missed. Sleeping-cars can cost about the same as a hotel but have the advantage of covering large distances as you rest and you won't waste precious time in transit. Couchettes are more crowded bunk-type arrangements, but reasonably comfortable and inexpensive. You can save quite a bit of money if you are prepared to curl up on the ordinary seats (don't do this too often without a break, however, or you will end up exhausted; the chatter of other passengers, and regular checks to make sure you still have all your bags can lead to a disturbed night). Take earplugs and maybe an eyemask and, as there are often no refreshment facilities, plenty of water and a supply of refreshments. In Eastern Europe, you may be woken for Customs and Immigration checks, which can involve a search of luggage or the compartment/berth. Within Western Europe, it's unlikely you'll notice the borders, even if you're awake.

If you have a rail pass and the night train is due to reach your next destination too early in the morning, consider booking to a town an hour or so further along the line; you can then get some extra sleep and backtrack to your intended destination (assuming there's a suitable early train back).

SLEEPING ACCOMMODATION Sleeping-cars have bedroom-style compartments with limited washing facilities (usually just a wash-basin) and full bedding. WCs are located at the end of the coach. An attendant travels with each car, or pair of cars, and there are sometimes facilities for drinks and/or breakfast – but be prepared to pay extra.

First-class sleeping compartments usually have one or two berths and second-class compartments have two or three berths. However, there are some special sleeping-cars (described as 'T2' in schedules) which have only one berth in first class and two in second class. An exception to the norm is Spain: their T2 cars are first class and their Talgo trains have four berths in second class.

Compartments are allocated to a single sex and small unaccompanied children are placed in female compartments. In Estonia, Latvia and Lithuania berths are allocated on a first-come, first-served basis without regard to sex. Claim your berth within 15 minutes of boarding the train or it may be reallocated.

Couchettes are more basic – and much cheaper. They consist of simple bunk beds with a sheet, blanket and pillow. They are converted from the ordinary seats at night and there are usually four berths in first class and six in second class, with washing facilities and WCs at the end of each coach. Males and females are booked into the same compartment and expected to sleep in their daytime clothes. In a few cases (notably Italy), overnight trains have airline-style reclining seats, which are allocated automatically when you make a seat reservation. These are sometimes free if you have a rail pass.

Couchette/sleeping car attendants will often keep your ticket overnight, and return it prior to your stop. Attendants will give you an alarm call if you tell them you are leaving the train before the final destination – specify the stop rather than the time, so you can sleep longer if the train runs late. If you want to go to sleep before other passengers have arrived, switch on their berth lights and switch off the main overhead light. Before boarding, sort out the things you will need for the night and put them somewhere easily accessible (preferably in a small separate bag), as busy compartments don't allow much room for searching through luggage. Sleepers and couchettes can usually be reserved up to three months in advance; early booking is recommended as space is limited. If you don't have a booking, it's still worth asking the conductor once on board. Keep some local currency handy to pay him/her.

WASHING Showers are generally restricted to a few luxury-class compartments (notably Gran Clase cars on the overnight Spanish Talgos; Intercity Natt cars in Sweden; CityNightLine trains in Germany/Austria/Switzerland and InterCityNight trains in Germany). A few large rail stations have showers for public use.

EATING Most long-distance trains in Europe have dining-cars serving full meals and/or buffet cars selling drinks and snacks. There is an increasing tendency for refreshments to be served from a trolley wheeled through the train. Dining-cars are sometimes red or indicated by a red band above the windows and doors. Quite a few services offer full meals only to first-class passengers. In some cases, especially in Spain, the cost of a meal is included in the first-class fare. Dining-cars often have set times for full meals. Buffets are usually open to both classes and serve for longer periods, but even they may not be available for the whole journey. Train food and drink is not generally good value, save money by bringing your own. Even if money is no object it's always sensible to carry a full water-bottle and some food. Long stops at East European frontiers may tempt you to get out and buy food and drink: always get permission from the control officers, and check that you have the right currency and enough time.

BAGGAGE Lockers are invaluable if you want to look round a place without carrying heavy baggage and most stations (and other transport hubs) have them; sometimes it's cheaper to use a manned left luggage office (which is subject to opening hours). The initial payment generally covers 24 hrs, but you are allowed to stay longer (usually up to a week, but check). The newest lockers have display panels and are automatic: you simply pay any excess when you return. With older lockers, you have to pay the excess to station staff (at the left-luggage office, if there is one). Baggage trolleys (where available) are usually free, but often supermarket-style: you need a coin to release them – which you get back when you return them to a stand.

Colour Section

(i) Brick Lane sign, London (p. 47); Eurostar train, Waterloo (p. 49)

(ii) View over port, Monaco (p. 108); inset: Arc de Triomphe, Paris (p. 58)

(iii) Palombaggio, Corsica (p. 112); inset: French Alpine scenery (p. 109)

(iv) View to city across Rio Tajo, Toledo, Spain (p. 141); Guggenheim Museum, Bilbao; inset, Abando railway station, Bilbao (p. 164).

BRICK LANE, E.
ব্রিক লেন
3003
eurostar

F-C DE SANTANDER A BILBAO
TXINA

The following are some suggestions for long rail routes that cross several frontiers; each of them would make a superb holiday in itself. All the main places of interest and many of the lines travelled are covered in this book.

Some routes in the main text of the book also cross international borders, for example Munich to Verona (p. 275) and Copenhagen to Stockholm (p. 446).

Ferry routes are outlined on p. 48.

LONDON–PARIS–MARSEILLE–NICE–PISA–BOLOGNA–VENICE

ETT TABLES

10 · 350 · 360 · 580 · 610 · 614 · 620

The two great cities of London and Paris are the prelude to the trip down to the Mediterranean, for and exploration of the French and Italian rivieras, then through the historic cities of northern Italy to romantic Venice.

BERLIN–DRESDEN–PRAGUE–VIENNA

ETT TABLES

60 · 843 · 1110 · 1160

From Berlin, one of Europe's great cultural centres, through the resurrected city of Dresden in former East Germany, to Prague and Vienna, two wonderfully unspoilt old capitals.

PARIS–BORDEAUX–BURGOS–MADRID–SEVILLE

ETT TABLES

302 · 46 · 680 · 665

Heads down via the castles of the Loire and the Futuroscope theme park near Poitiers to France's south-western corner and into Spain's Basque country, past the cathedral at Burgos and the Spanish capital to end in the heart of Andalucía, with its Moorish monuments as reminders that Africa is not far away.

LONDON–OSTEND–BRUSSELS–BERLIN

ETT TABLES

12 · 400 · 800 · 810

The ferry leaves Dover's white cliffs behind for the Belgian coast, then the train passes the beautiful old cities of Bruges and Ghent, entering Germany near Aachen and passing the great cathedral spires of Cologne; optional diversions to the Harz Mountains before reaching the German capital.

INTERNATIONAL ROUTES

PARIS–MILAN–FLORENCE–ROME

ETT TABLES

44 · 620

Four strongly contrasting cities, with a magnificent scenic experience through the Swiss Alps, via Lausanne and Brig, to Milan, followed by a journey through Tuscany to the Italian capital.

LYON–ZÜRICH–INNSBRUCK–VIENNA

ETT TABLES

372 · 500 · 86 · 950

An Alpine traverse from west to east, passing Geneva and Berne (both convenient for excursions into the Swiss Alps), then virtually through the entire length of Austria to its very different capital city.

STOCKHOLM–COPENHAGEN–HAMBURG–WÜRZBURG–MUNICH–VERONA–VENICE

ETT TABLES

730 · 50 · 900 · 70 · 600

A display of Europe in all its moods, from the watery northern beauty of Stockholm, Copenhagen and Hamburg, through the heart of Bavaria, through the Alps, to the sunny climes of northern Italy, with the Roman amphitheatre at Verona and the canals of Venice.

PRAGUE–MUNICH–ZURICH–MILAN–NICE–MARSEILLE–BARCELONA–MADRID–LISBON

ETT TABLES

57 · 75 · 84 · 90 · 360 · 81 · 650 · 670

An epic voyage from the Czech Republic, through Bavaria and the Alps, across southern France to Perpignan, and over the eastern end of the Pyrénées to Barcelona, the capital of Catalan, then crosses Spain and Portugal to end near Europe's southwestern corner.

(for Directory information, see p. 569).

Made up of **Great Britain (England, Wales and Scotland)** and **Northern Ireland**, this once mighty naval power formerly commanded a huge empire. Ironbridge in Shropshire was the birthplace of the industrial revolution – the world's first railway was built in northern England in the early 19th century, and the first industrial cities and great factories were built. Although its insular qualities are being eroded to an extent by the rapidly growing status of the European Union, there are plenty of features that are quintessentially British or English, and a lot is carefully preserved. Regional variation surprises many visitors, with an eye-opening range of traditional building styles (half-timbered, stone, brick, timber, flint etc.), plus some astonishing changes in scenery – from the flat marshes of **East Anglia** to the rugged cliffs of the south-west, from the domesticated landscapes of the south-east to the remote hills of northern England and the majestic peaks of the Scottish **Highlands**. Even regional accents have survived – voices sound very different in south Wales, north-east England, Glasgow and London, for example.

It does pay to be selective when touring the UK: a lot of the big cities of the Midlands are not holiday territory, the scenery in parts of east and central England is unspectacular, and some seaside resorts are well past their prime.

For a varied sample of the country, visit **London** plus one or two of the great historic cities such as **York, Canterbury, Norwich, Durham, Edinburgh, Glasgow, Oxford, Cambridge, Bath** and **Lincoln**. Seek out the coastal heritage, both in seaside resorts such as **Brighton, Broadstairs** or **Scarborough**, and the naval history chronicled in **Portsmouth**, and look out for the many reminders of early industrialisation (there are many excellent museums on the subject). If it's scenery you're after, head for one of the ten national parks (the **Lake District** is the star of them all, a great place for walking – **Windermere** is a useful rail station to start from), or **western Scotland**.

ACCOMMODATION

Except in some resorts in high summer, there should rarely be a problem finding somewhere to stay. At the cheapest level are **campsites** and **youth hostels**.

Bed and breakfast (or **'B and B'**) is the next level up, and not the cheapest, but often fair value, with prices around £15–£20 per person plus a generous cooked breakfast: smaller places that are effectively a few spare rooms in someone's home or

YOUTH HOSTELS

Head office for England and Wales:
YHA, TREVELYAN HOUSE, 8 ST STEPHEN'S HILL, ST ALBANS, HERTFORDSHIRE, AL1 2DY, ENGLAND, (44) (1727) 845047
http://www.yha-england-wales.org.uk

Scotland:
SYHA, 7 GLEBE CRESCENT, STIRLING, FK8 2JA, SCOTLAND, (44) (1786) 891400
(http://www.syha.org.uk).

farmhouse are often the most comfortable and friendly. **Tourist offices** can usually book in the area, sometimes for a small deposit that is refunded when you pay your bill. Alternatively, in tourist areas it's usually easy to find places to stay just by strolling likely-looking streets. Some pubs have inexpensive accommodation, though they can be noisy.

Large **hotels** are often expensive. There's a wide choice of country-house-style hotels in historic buildings, often in remote locations. The **BTA (British Tourist Authority), AA (Automobile Association), RAC (Royal Automobile Club)** and other organisations each publish guides with different rating systems.

FOOD AND DRINK

Eating out has progressed immeasurably in the last 20 years, with an explosion in variety and quality, with international, specialised ethnic (particularly **Italian, Hong Kong Chinese, Indian and Thai**), **whole food/vegetarian** and **fast food** available in most medium-sized and larger towns. Famously British, **fish and chips** are still going strong, and feature thickly sliced chips (fries). **Pub food** is generally the best-value sit-down fare, though some of it is pre-cooked and frozen by distributors and bought in by the pubs. Naturally conditioned brown 'real ale' is served in pubs from long wooden handpumps that sit on the counter, or is dispensed direct from the barrel. It's slightly less chilled than pasteurised beer or lager, and varies greatly in taste and character and there's an increasing amount of choice. 'Bitter' is the most popular of these brown beers. Many pubs are now open all day. 'Cider' is an alcoholic apple drink, stronger than beer and occasionally available in 'real' draft form, which can be sweet or acidically dry.

Usual eating hours are: **breakfast** 0730–0900, **lunch** 1200–1400, **afternoon tea** 1330–1700, **dinner** 1930–2130.

Its gateway airports and rail links to the Continent, reinforced by the direct **Eurostar** services through the **Channel Tunnel to Paris and Brussels**, make **London** a natural starting point for overseas visitors embarking on a rail tour of Europe. Though it can't compete in terms of sustained physical beauty with, say, **Paris** or **Rome**, London is undoubtedly one of the world's great cities – with a huge amount of indoor attractions, concerts and theatres. It's an expensive place to stay, but this can be offset by visiting the many free museums and exploring on foot.

There's an excellent range of possible day trips by rail, some of which are listed here.

GOOD AREAS FOR WALKING
include St James's/ Westminster, the Inns of Court/City, the South Bank, Hampstead, Richmond and the Regent's Canal between Camden and Little Venice.

Central London is pretty safe (although be wary of thieves in crowded places). Women on their own should avoid the King's Cross area.

ARRIVAL AND DEPARTURE

There are 16 main-line rail stations (all linked by Underground trains) in central London. The most important are **Victoria**, ☎7928 5100, for trains to **Gatwick** and the south coast (Rail Europe centre, Tourist Office and accommodation desk); **Waterloo**, ☎7928 5100, (south-west, including Portsmouth for ferries to France and Spain; Eurostar trains (see p. 49) for Paris and Brussels); **Liverpool St**, ☎7928 5100, (eastern England, including services to Harwich for ferries to the Netherlands and Scandinavia); **Kings Cross**, ☎7278 2477 (north-east and Scotland); Euston, ☎7387 7070 (West Midlands, north-west and Scotland); **Paddington**, ☎7262 6767 (west and Wales); and **St Pancras**, ☎7387 7070 (Sheffield and East Midlands). For information about trains to Continental Europe, contact Rail Europe, ☎0990 848848.

Buses: **Victoria Coach Station**, BUCKINGHAM PALACE RD, ☎7730 3466, is the main London terminal for long-distance buses. **Green Line** coaches, ☎8668 7261, operate within a 40-mile radius of London; other areas are covered by **National Express**, ☎(0990) 808080.

Heathrow Airport, ☎8759 4321, is 24 km west of central London. The **PICCADILLY LINE** UNDERGROUND (£3.20 one-way; journey time 40 mins) and **Airbuses A1/A2**, ☎8400 6690 (£6 one-way) serve all four terminals, from various pick-up points in central London (every 15–30 mins, approximately 0600–2100: journey time 1 hr). The **Heathrow Express** is a more expensive service, at £10 each way, but takes 15 mins to reach Paddington and runs every 15 mins. (0510–2340 approximately). A **taxi** to the centre costs about £35/£40, cheaper if you share with someone in the queue. The **tourist information desk** at Heathrow is located by the underground station for Terminals 1, 2 and 3; open daily 0830–1800.

Gatwick Airport, ☎(01293) 535353, is 43 km south of London. **Gatwick Express** trains (£7.50 one-way) run every 15 mins during the day, and every 30 mins at night from London Victoria, taking 30 mins; other trains (not called Gatwick Express) are slightly slower and

TOURIST OFFICES

The main tourist information centre is in Victoria Station (daily 0800–1900 Apr–Oct; Mon–Sat 0800–1800, Sun 0900–1600 Nov–Mar) and usually very crowded; allow plenty of time; hotel booking service for whole of UK.

The British Travel Centre (BTC), 12 LOWER REGENT ST, LONDON SW1 (UNDERGROUND: **PICCADILLY CIRCUS**; Mon–Fri 0900–1830, Sat–Sun 1000–1600 (Sat extended June–Sept), local **Bed and Breakfast** and **Book a Bed Ahead** services (£5 booking fee, plus redeemable deposit of first night); **booking service for guided tours and theatres; transport passes; and comprehensive multi-lingual information**; last bookings 30 mins before closing.

cheaper. **Speedlink** coach service, **Flightline 777**, ☎(0990) 747777 runs approximately hourly 0500–1740, then 2010 (£7.50 one-way): allow 70–75 mins for the journey. There's a **tourist information desk** on the arrivals concourse of the South Terminal.

Other international airports are: Stansted (trains to London Liverpool Street), **City** (airport shuttle 10 mins to Canary Wharf on the Docklands Light Railway) and **Luton** (shuttle bus to Luton rail station for services to London St Pancras).

INFORMATION

CITY AND TRANSPORT MAP – inside back cover

MONEY

Banks and Thomas Cook bureaux de change on virtually every main street.

POST AND PHONES

The **post office** near TRAFALGAR SQ. (24/28 William IV St, WC2 4DL) has poste restante (Mon–Fri 0830–1830).

London is now covered by the 020 **phone code** followed by an eight-figure number (beginning with 7 for central London and 8 for outer London); this replaced the 0171 and 0181 codes in early 2000, and you still might see the old codes quoted in places. You only need to dial 020 if you're calling from outside London; within London, just dial the eight-figure number, including the initial 7 or 8. This is, amazingly, the third time in recent years that the capital's phone codes have been changed, so everyone hopes that this latest change is here to stay.

PUBLIC TRANSPORT

Travel during rush hour (primarily Mon–Fri 0800–0930 and 1700–1900) is no fun at all. Free bus and Underground maps and other information about London Transport (LT), including tickets, are available in most Underground stations. The main LT office on the ground level of **ST JAMES'S PARK** UNDERGROUND station, ☎222 1234 – 24 hours a day. As for street maps, the *A–Z Map of London* covers the central area, while the full London A–Z or *Nicholson Street Guides* include the whole city and its suburbs.

Underground trains: London Underground ('the Tube'), the world's oldest and deepest **metro** (subway) is extensive, efficient and usually the quickest way to get around, but can be impossibly crowded during rush hours. Most lines operate

REQUEST STOPS

The red signs are request stops and the buses halt at them only if you signal: by raising your arm if you are at a stop or ringing the bell (once only) if you are on board.

Mon–Sat from 0530 to around midnight, Sun 0700–2330. Smoking anywhere in the system is forbidden. Each line is colour-coded and named. Boards on the platforms and the front of the trains show the destination. Keep your ticket handy: there are occasional inspections and it must be passed through the turnstile machine at the beginning and end of your journey.

Buses: London's bright red double-decker buses have become a tourist attraction in their own right, but others run by private companies now vie for business on some routes and single-deckers are fairly common. The roads are often congested and travel can be slow, but some routes (e.g. no.11/12/129) are excellent for sightseeing and the view from the top deck is always great. Most services run Mon–Sat 0600–2400, Sun 0730–2300. Restricted (often hourly) services radiate from TRAFALGAR SQ. throughout the night: night bus numbers are prefixed by 'N'. Keep your ticket until you reach your destination as there are random checks. Buses sometimes cover only part of the route, so check the final destination board on the front or back. There are bus stops every few hundred metres, showing the relevant bus numbers.

Taxis: London's famous 'black cabs' may be painted in other colours, but their shape remains distinctive. Fares are metered and not cheap; there are extra (metered) charges for baggage, for more than one passenger, and for travelling in the evening (after 2000) or at weekends; drivers expect a tip of 10% of the fare (but you don't need to tip minicabs that you order by phone). There are taxi ranks at key positions, but you can also hail them in the street. When a taxi is free, the roof-light at the front is on.

TICKETS

Underground fares depend on the number of zones travelled: zone 1 is the centre and may well be all you need.
Single tickets are purchased in the station (or in books of 10, giving a small saving) and allow you to change lines as often as necessary.
Bus fares are determined by fare stages and not easy to define, but a **single ticket** (purchased when you board) is valid only for that vehicle, so you must get another ticket if you change.
One-day passes are valid at weekends and after 0930 Mon–Fri and do not cover night buses. There are no time restrictions on the longer passes and night buses are covered, but you will need a photo.

TRAVELCARDS

(available from most stations and many newsagents) are much better value than single tickets. They cover all London's public transport systems (except Airbuses), giving you the freedom to hop on and off LT buses, the Underground, the Docklands Light Railway and suburban trains.
One-day Travelcards (covering Zones 1 and 2) cost £3.80. Passes covering only buses are also available. A one-day bus pass covering zones 1–4 is £2.80 and can be used before 0930 but not on night buses.

ACCOMMODATION

London has an enormous range of accommodation, from world-renowned hotels with sky-high prices to bed and breakfast establishments. The best value for **cheap accommodation** are the seven **Hostelling International youth hostels** in London; main office, 373 3400. The **Paddington, Victoria** and **Earls Court** areas, in particular, have a good range of **bed and breakfast** at around £25 per person. **LTB (London Tourist Board),** 604 2890 (for bookings only), will take hotel bookings by phone up to six weeks in advance if you have MasterCard or Visa. Alternatively, for a small fee, you can book at the **Thomas Cook desks** at **Charing Cross, St Pancras, Paddington, Victoria, Euston and King's Cross stations,** and at **Gatwick Airport**.

Camping in central London is not possible. The parks are locked around midnight and patrolled until they reopen. The city spreads for miles in every direction and the nearest campsites are some way out of town. **Tent City**, OLD OAK COMMON LANE, ACTON, ☎(020) 8743 5708 (UNDERGROUND: **EAST ACTON**), is £6 per person, open June–Sept; pitch your own tent or sleep dormitory-style in large tents. **Crystal Palace Camping Site** ☎(020) 8778 7155 is pleasantly placed in the southern suburbs (🚌no. 3 from **Oxford Circus/ Trafalgar Sq.**, or rail to **Crystal Palace station** from Victoria), open year-round, at £1 per tent pitch plus £4 per person.

FOOD AND DRINK

London is a superb hunting ground for food, with restaurants of every conceivable type, from traditional British to those of countries few could pin point on a map. The cost is equally varied: from fast food chains, where you can get something filling for about £3, to places with no prices on the menu that cost more than some would spend on food in a year.

The Covent Garden and Soho districts (there's an endless choice of **Chinese** places in the GERRARD ST/WARDOUR ST area of **Soho**) offer the best array of *West End* restaurants. The **Queensway, Victoria, Leicester Sq., Panton St** and **Earls Court** areas are very lively, especially in the evenings, with innumerable **cheap eateries** of all types, including some of the eat-your-fill variety.

Italian, Chinese, Indian, Greek and Turkish restaurants are common and many are excellent, with a wide range of cheap dishes on offer. Many do **takeaways** and there are still plenty of **fish and chip shops**. Food in **pubs and wine bars** is usually good value though pubs in the centre are often unpleasantly crowded. **Sandwich**

DAY TRIPS FROM LONDON

BATH

(1 hr 20 mins from **Paddington**; ETT table 130): A fine Georgian town, at the height of fashion in the 18th and early 19th centuries, began life as a Roman spa, and the original **Roman baths** are impressively intact next to the **18th-century pump room**, where you can sip tea to the accompaniment of chamber music; adjacent **Bath Abbey** was known as the 'Lantern of the West' for its display of stained glass. Among some of the masterpieces of Georgian town planning are the **Royal Crescent** (No.1 is open as a museum house) and **The Circus**, built like much of the rest in mellow Bath stone. Pick of the museums are the **Museum of Costume** at the Assembly Rooms, the **Building of Bath Museum** (explaining how John Wood transformed the city), the **Industrial Museum** and the **American Museum**. There are **river cruises** from Pulteney Bridge.

BRIGHTON

(1 hr from **Victoria**; ETT table 102): Still the best place to go to experience the English seaside resort, though it's past its prime as a bathing spot. George IV made

bars are a good alternative for a light lunch. For food shopping, visit **Fortnum and Masons**, PICCADILLY, and the Food Hall in **Harrods**, BROMPTON ROAD.

There are **pubs** on virtually every street, including **historic inns** reputed to have been frequented by everyone from Ben Jonson to Charles Dickens.

HIGHLIGHTS

It's possible to take in a lot of the most famous landmarks in a couple of days. From **Big Ben** (UNDERGROUND: **WESTMINSTER**), the famous Gothic clock tower of the **Houses of Parliament** (where you can hear parliamentary debate if you're prepared to queue), there's a splendid walk over **Westminster Bridge**, after which you turn left along the **Thames** embankment, enjoying river views from the **South Bank**, where you'll see the transition from the **West End** to the **City**, with domed **St Paul's Cathedral** rising spectacularly; on the South Bank is the thatched **Globe Theatre**, a faithful 1990s replica of the place where many of Shakespeare's plays were performed in his lifetime. Around **London Bridge** there are some atmospheric (converted) Victorian warehouses, with high catwalks; then comes **Tower Bridge**, the best known Thames span, which is still raised to allow tall ships through; cross to the north bank here to the **Tower of London**, one of Britain's best-preserved Norman castles, where many famous and notorious prisoners of the Crown met a grisly end. It's home to the Crown Jewels and is guarded by Beefeaters attired in medieval uniform.

For the new millennium, London has added a host of attractions. Foremost is the Millennium Dome at Greenwich (p. 44). Along Millennium Mile (the South Bank between Westminster and Tower bridges) are the BA London Eye (a 150m ferris wheel), the Tate Gallery of Modern Art (in the old Bankside power station, with the Millennium Footbridge over the river to St Paul's from 2001), the revamped Hungerford Footbridge, the FA Premier League Hall of Fame (by the London Aquarium in County Hall) and the huge BFI Imax Cinema.

Day Trips from London cont'd.

sea-bathing fashionable when he erected his **Royal Pavilion**, an Indian fantasy Regency mansion sprouting domes and minarets, as astonishing inside as out. Virtually contemporary are the imposing stucco crescents and terraces lining the front; below are numerous booths offering palm-reading and tattooing, and **two magnificent 19th-century piers** – **Palace Pier** very much alive with tacky amusements, and the wrecked **West Pier,** awaiting restoration.

The maze-like old fishing quarter, now full of eateries, boutiques and antique shops, is known as the **LANES** – not to be confused with the **NORTH LAINE**, a line of pedestrianised shopping streets at the heart of trendy, alternative Brighton. You can return to London by way of **Lewes**, a handsome and surprisingly untouristy town on a ridge between the chalky **South Downs**, with views of the rooftops and coast from its **Norman castle**, and lots of **second-hand bookshops** and ancient alleys (known as 'twittens').

Day Trips from London cont'd.

CANTERBURY

(1 hr 25–40 mins from **Victoria**; ETT table 100): Seat of the premier church of England, **Canterbury** has some gems, notably the **cathedral** (with medieval stained glass, Norman crypt and cloister) and its precincts, which miraculously escaped wartime bombing that obliterated part of the centre (unimaginatively rebuilt) but left some old streets intact. You can walk round the remaining city walls past whirling traffic, and pass under the medieval **Christ Church and West gates**; one of the former pilgrims' hostels, **Poor Priests' Hospital** now houses a good museum covering the city's heritage. **St Augustine's Church** is the oldest church in England, in use since the 6th century.

OXFORD

(1 hr from **Paddington**; ETT table 144) and

CAMBRIDGE

(1 hr; quickest service from **Kings Cross**; ETT table 178): Britain's two oldest universities are organised on a collegiate system – with colleges scattered around the city (there are very few university buildings as such). Though the two places

In the other direction from Big Ben you can delve into the best of the **West End**. In **Parliament Square** is **Westminster Abbey**, crammed with memorials and famed as the crowning place of British monarchs. Along WHITEHALL, with its limestone-fronted government buildings, the **Banqueting Hall** is a remnant of the otherwise vanished **Palace of Whitehall**, and the breastplated Horse Guards keep watch in HORSE GUARDS PARADE. TRAFALGAR SQUARE is London's big set piece, with **Nelson's Column** flanked by a quartet of lions and looked over by **St Martin's-in-the-Fields Church** and the **National Gallery**. From the **Admiralty Arch** runs THE MALL, a Parisian boulevard lined by Regency terraces on one side and the greenery of **St James's Park** (a lovely spot with a lake and bandstand) on the other; at the end is **Buckingham Palace** (the Queen's main residence), rather cold and austere (its state rooms are open Aug–Sep: you can also visit the Queen's Gallery and Royal Mews collection of state coaches). In ugly Victoria Street, the 19th-century **Westminster (Catholic) Cathedral** has a cavernous interior. A lift whisks you up the tower for £2, providing one of London's rare high-level views.

The **City of London** (the east part of the centre) houses such venerable and ancient City institutions such as the **Guildhall**, the **Inns of Court** (the heart of legal London) and the **Bank of England**. The 17th-century architect Sir Christopher Wren built numerous City churches, most famously **St Paul's Cathedral**, with its **Whispering Gallery** providing remarkable acoustics. Buildings to look out for near FENCHURCH ST include **Leadenhall Market** (exuberantly Victorian) and the **Lloyd's Building** (provocatively high-tech).

MUSEUMS AND GALLERIES

Most museums and galleries open daily, year round, but check before you go. The following listing is only the briefest indication of the cream.

Of the countless art galleries, three are outstanding – and admission is free, except for special exhibitions. **The National Gallery**, TRAFALGAR SQ., displays 12th–19th-century art, with a superb cross-section of Impressionists and post-Impressionists (try to catch one of the free gallery tours), and the neighbouring

National Portrait Gallery offers a comprehensive display (UNDERGROUND: **CHARING CROSS/LEICESTER SQ.**). The **Tate Gallery** (incorporating the **Clore Gallery**), MILLBANK (UNDERGROUND: **WESTMINSTER/PIMLICO**), is home to more modern works (some controversial) and noted for its collection of Turners. For the Tate Gallery of Modern Art see p. 41.

The **British Museum**, GREAT RUSSELL ST (UNDERGROUND: **RUSSELL SQ.**), is a treasure trove (entrance free); it's daunting in scale – many come in just to see the **Elgin Marbles** (originally the frieze of the **Parthenon** in Athens) and the ancient Egyptian section. The **Museum of London**, LONDON WALL (UNDERGROUND: **BARBICAN/ST PAUL'S MOORGATE**), offers a beautifully displayed history of the city with an excellent Roman section and a reconstruction of a Victorian street of shops. Most visitors enjoy the **London Transport Museum**, COVENT GARDEN. Don't miss the free and wonderfully eccentric Sir John Soane's Museum, Lincoln's Inn Fields (UNDERGROUND: **HOLBORN**) a bizarre Georgian house stashed with Soane's 'museum' objects.

Where there's a charge, it's usually in the region of £5; consider the **London White Card** (£16 for three days), which covers more than a dozen of the major establishments, all of which can supply it.

Clustered together (UNDERGROUND: **SOUTH KENSINGTON**) are three other truly great museums (all free after 4.30pm though they really deserve a day each). The **Science Museum**, EXHIBITION RD, makes science has a big array of hands-on exhibits demonstrating all things scientific. The adjacent **Natural History Museum** has many interactive exhibits, and there's a wonderful section on dinosaurs. Across the road is the **Victoria and Albert Museum**, CROMWELL RD, a vast treasure house of arts and crafts.

Madame Tussaud's (UNDERGROUND: **BAKER STREET**) has the famous waxworks, plus the **Spirit of London** ride through London's history; fun but expensive, and often a big queue to get in.

Day Trips from London cont'd.

maintain an ancient rivalry, they have much in common in the cloistered tranquillity of the colleges themselves, and the loveliness of the walks along the river (popular for punting – an 'Oxbridge' boating tradition). Many colleges charge for entry and some close to the public in term time.

Oxford, built in honey-coloured Cotswold stone, has more and smaller colleges: **Christ Church** and **Magdelene** are among the finest, while in **Cambridge** the architecture is richly varied, with the chapel at **King's** (a superb example of perpendicular Gothic) and the main courtyard and library at **Trinity** among its treasures Both cities have superb free museums of art and artefacts – the **Ashmolean** at Oxford and the **Fitzwilliam** at Cambridge.

The stations in both cities are a 15–20 min walk, but there are frequent bus services from **Victoria Coach Station** in London getting you closer to the centre.

OUT OF THE CENTRE A distinguishing feature of the suburbs are the old villages incorporated into the cityscape but still with attractive old centres. Along the Thames to the west there are delightful riverside walks from

Day Trips from London cont'd.

PORTSMOUTH

(1 hr 30 mins from **Waterloo**; ETT table 104): Not a pretty place, but the historic Dockyard (next to **Portsmouth Harbour** station) has the best of Britain's naval heritage. **HMS Victory** was Nelson's flagship in the Battle of Trafalgar (1805); you're told about the appalling conditions on board and shown the spot where Nelson died. The **Mary Rose** sunk in the harbour in 1545 and was rescued in 1982; the wreck is now kept in special damp conditions to prevent further decay, and its contents form a fascinating display. You can stroll the four decks of **HMS Warrior**, the world's earliest iron-hulled warship, and there's a huge **Royal Naval Museum**. In Apr–Oct **harbour cruises** are on offer.

RYE

(1 hr 45 mins from **Charing Cross**; change at **Ashford**; ETT tables 101, 106): One of the **Cinque Ports**, which in medieval times supplied men and ships to defend the coast and received special privileges, **Rye** has survived as one of the best-preserved small towns in England, though the sea that brought fame and fortune has

Richmond (UNDERGROUND: **RICHMOND**) and up to **Richmond Park**, a huge deer park; within reach are CHISWICK MALL, just west of **Hammersmith Bridge** and with several old waterside pubs and imposing Georgian houses, and **Kew Botanical Gardens**, (UNDERGROUND: **KEW GARDENS**), one of the greatest plant collections in the world. A bit further out is Henry VIII's superb **Hampton Court Palace** (famous for its maze) and **Windsor Castle** (still a royal residence, but parts of it are open); both are accessible by suburban train from **Waterloo** station – these and Kew Gardens can be reached by boat (see Tours, below).

East from the centre, *Greenwich* was once the hub of nautical Britain and is still the definitive *Meridian*, or 0 degrees longitude. In *Greenwich Park* and towards the river are the **Maritime Museum, Naval College, Royal Observatory,** and the refurbished **Queen's House**. All three are covered by a single ticket. The **Millennium Dome** is the big addition for 2000, home to the controversially pricey Millennium Experience: access by tube or by boat from the Millennium Pier near Waterloo Bridge.

From Greenwich a slightly creepy tiled foot tunnel (free) under the Thames leads to **Island Gardens** station on the elevated **Docklands Light Railway**, which gives a futuristic ride north from here, past *Canary Wharf* (London's tallest building) in the heart of redeveloped Docklands to **West India Quay**, where you can carry on to *Tower Gateway* near the **Tower of London** to finish a memorable day at Tower Bridge.

Another great place to explore is **Hampstead** (UNDERGROUND: **HAMPSTEAD**), a haunt of artists, writers and the simply wealthy; it's a knot of old cottages, Georgian terraces, pretty pubs and stately villas fringing **Hampstead Heath**, a surprisingly large and countrified expanse of unkempt woodland and heath; places to seek out are CHURCH ROW (the finest Georgian street), **Fenton House** (Hampstead's oldest house, home to a keyboard instrument collection) and **Kenwood House** (a stately home with an outstanding art collection, free entry).

TOURS

The **Original London Sightseeing Tour**, ☎(0181) 877 1722, runs special tourist buses, some open-topped, which take in the major sights and provide a multi-lingual commentary via headphones during the journey. **Departure points** are PICCADILLY CIRCUS, MARBLE ARCH, VICTORIA and BAKER ST; a day ticket allows you to board and get off as often as you like. Several companies operate daily **themed walking tours**, usually from underground stations; one of the best is **Original London Walks** ☎642 3978; no booking, cost around £4.50.

You can **cruise** east (down-river) to the **Tower of London**, **St Catherine's Dock** and **Greenwich**. **Catamaran Cruisers**, ☎839 3572, depart from **Charing Cross Pier** (UNDERGROUND: **EMBANKMENT**). Most other departures are from **Westminster Pier** (UNDERGROUND: **WESTMINSTER**), including **WPSA**, ☎(0171) 930 2062, for sailings west (up-river) to ***Richmond, Hampton Court*** and **Kew**. You just turn up and get a ticket on the spot.

NIGHT-TIME AND EVENTS

There are several publications listing London's entertainments, of which the best are the weekly magazine *Time Out*, the daily *Evening Standard* and the free *TNT Magazine* (help yourself from special stands in central areas).

CLUBS, DISCOS, PUBS

Almost everything is on offer in terms of nightlife, including **casinos, jazz clubs, discos, straight and gay clubs** and **pub entertainment**. Most clubs offer one-night membership at the door and often have a dress code, which might be a jacket and tie or could just depend on whether

Most of London shuts by midnight. Those places that do stay open late usually increase their entrance charges at around 2200 and many places charge more at weekends.

Day trips from London cont'd.

receded. The town is full of quaint alleys and cobbled lanes, MERMAID STREET being the best-known. Take the train one stop to **Winchelsea** – another lapsed port, laid out as a medieval town but now a handsome, French-looking hilltop village. Further on is the resort of **Hastings**, a bit run down but with a fascinating and extensive hilly old town of former fishermen's cottages, with walks eastward along the tops of sandstone cliffs.

STRATFORD-UPON-AVON

(2 hrs 10 mins from **Paddington**; ETT table 125): famous as Shakespeare's birthplace, the main places connected with the Bard are **Shakespeare's Birthplace Museum** (within a small timber-framed house), the **thatched cottage of his wife Anne Hathaway, Mary Arden's House** (his mother's childhood home) and the **Memorial Theatre** (productions by the Royal Shakespeare Company; RSC Collection of props and costumes). Shakespeare aside, it's an agreeable town but extremely touristy, and if you're not into literary pilgrimage you might want to give it a miss.

YORK

(2 hrs from **King's Cross**; ETT table 170): The most satisfying English medieval city, encircled by impressively preserved walls (with extensive walks along the top of

Day trips from London cont'd.

them), and graced with the magnificent **Minster** (Britain's largest medieval cathedral, renowned for the quality of its stained glass). Close by **Clifford's Tower** (a 14th-century castle) is the **Castle Museum**, with a reconstructed street of shops among its excellent displays of social history, while the **Jorvik Viking Centre** is a remarkable time journey back to 10th-century York. Foremost among the rest of an excellent set of museums is the **National Railway Museum**, with Queen Victoria's royal carriage as well as the record-breaking *Mallard* locomotive. The centre is enjoyably traffic free, and full of buskers and street life; the **Shambles**, with its jettied, overhanging houses, and the **Merchant Adventurers' Hall** are among the best medieval timber-frame survivals.

ROYAL FESTIVAL HALL TICKETS
The cheapest tickets are in the choir, giving a front-on view of the conductor and an exciting feeling of virtually sitting in the orchestra if you're not too bothered about being near the percussion or brass sections; free foyer events during the day)

you look trendy enough. Jeans and trainers are usually out. The larger **rock venues** (such as the **Fridge** in **Brixton** and the **Hammersmith Odeon**) are all a little way from the centre, as are many of the **pubs with live entertainment**.

WEST END THEATRE TICKETS
are expensive, but there is a **half-price ticket kiosk**, LEICESTER SQ. (the south side), for same-day performances.
To book ahead, go to the theatre itself – most agents charge a hefty fee. Seats for big musicals and other hits are hard to get (unless money is no object and, even then, you should beware of forgeries), but it's always worth queuing for returns.

THEATRE AND MUSIC

London is one of the world's greatest centres of theatre and music. In addition to the **Royal National Theatre** (**South Bank Centre** – see next page) and the **Royal Shakespeare Company** (**Barbican Centre**), there are about 50 theatres in central London.

There's a wide range of classical music, from ultra-cheap lunchtime performances in churches to major symphonies in famous venues. **The Proms** are a huge summer-long festival of concerts held at the **Royal Albert Hall**, with the cheapest tickets sold on the day to 'Promenaders' who stand at floor level; the flag-waving 'Last Night' is massively popular.

CINEMAS There are dozens of cinemas in the West End, most offering discounts for the first showing on weekdays, but the same films can usually be found, at a lower price, a little way out of the centre.

ENTERTAINMENT The **South Bank Centre** (UNDERGROUND: **EMBANKMENT**, plus a walk over **Hungerford Bridge**; **Waterloo** station is slightly closer, but with a less pleasant walk) is an outstanding entertainment complex. Attractions include: **National Theatre (NT)** (three different auditoriums and some tickets are sold only on the day); **National Film Theatre (NFT)**; **Museum of the Moving Image (MOMI)** (a must for cinema buffs);

Hayward Gallery (changing exhibitions); **Royal Festival Hall** (musical performances from symphonies to jazz; and **Queen Elizabeth Hall** (solo and small group performances).

EVENTS It's not difficult to see British pageantry if you time your visit to coincide with one of the many traditional annual events. These include **Trooping the Colour** (second Sat June), the **State Opening of Parliament** (early Nov) and the **Lord Mayor's Show** (second Sat Nov). Other free spectacles include: the **London Marathon** (Apr: the world's largest, truly international); the **University Boat Race** (Sat near Easter: a traditional contest between Oxford and Cambridge Universities); and the **Notting Hill Carnival** (which takes over a wide area for two days late Aug – the largest of its type in Europe, noisy and fun, but don't take any valuables).

SHOPPING

The West End is full of famous shopping areas. For serious shopping, including many department stores, try OXFORD ST and REGENT ST (home to Hamleys toy shop). For designer clothes and upmarket window shopping, try BOND ST, SOUTH MOLTON ST, BEAUCHAMP PLACE and BROMPTON RD (home of Harrods; **KNIGHTSBRIDGE** is the UNDERGROUND STATION). For **books**: CHARING CROSS RD. For **trendy boutiques**: Covent Garden and KINGS RD (Chelsea). For **electronic goods**: TOTTENHAM COURT RD. **London-related souvenirs** don't extend much beyond ephemeral tat; a better bet are items on sale at museum shops such as the **Museum of London, National Gallery** and **London Transport Museum**.

Some of London's **street markets** are tourist attractions in themselves. Amongst the best are PORTOBELLO RD (UNDERGROUND: **LADBROKE GROVE** OR **NOTTING HILL GATE**), Mon–Sat (best Sat morning; antiques and junk) and **Camden Lock**, all week, but best on Sun, with antiques and crafts (UNDERGROUND: **CHALK FARM**): you can tie a visit in with a walk westwards along the Regent's Canal, passing **Regent's Park**, the Zoo and leading to a pretty canal basin at **Little Venice**. For sheer East-end atmosphere seek out BRICK LANE on a Sun morning (much better than the touristy PETTICOAT LANE nearby), with some real bargains among piles of cheap junk, and an excellent bagel shop on the site (UNDERGROUND: **SHOREDITCH**).

WHERE NEXT FROM LONDON?

*For connections from **London** to **Amsterdam, Brussels and Paris**, see Crossing to Continental Europe, p. 48.*

Crossing to Continental Europe

This section details how travellers can reach mainland Europe from Britain and Ireland. Frequencies and journey times are given for the summer season. Please note that the services and timings listed below are always subject to alteration as ferry operators alter their routes and services. Refer to the shipping section of the current edition of *The Thomas Cook European Timetable* for the latest details.

From...To	Sailings	Journey Time	Operator	☎ for details
DOVER to				
Calais (catamaran)	5 per day	55 mins	Hoverspeed	(0990) 240241
Calais (hovercraft)	19 per day	35 mins	Hoverspeed	(0990) 240241
Calais	30 per day	75–90 mins	P&O Stena Line	(0990) 980980
Calais	15 per day	1 hr 30 mins	SeaFrance	(01304) 204204
Ostend	5–7 per day	2 hrs	Hoverspeed	(0990) 595522
FOLKESTONE to				
Boulogne (catamaran)	4–6 per day	55 mins	Hoverspeed	(0990) 240241
HARWICH to				
Esbjerg	3 per week	20 hrs	Scandinavian Seaways	(0990) 333111
Hamburg	2–3 per week	20–22 hrs	Scandinavian Seaways	(0990) 333111
Hook of Holland (fast ferry)	2 per day	3 hrs 40 mins	Stena Line	(0990) 707070
HULL to				
Rotterdam Europort	1 per day	13 hrs	P&O North Sea Ferries	(01482) 377177
Zeebrugge	1 per day	13 hrs	P&O North Sea Ferries	(01482) 377177
NEWCASTLE to				
Amsterdam	2–3 per week	14–16 hrs	Scandinavian Seaways	(0990) 333111
Bergen (via Stavanger)	3 per week	21–24 hrs	Fjord Line	(0191) 296 1313
Gothenburg	2 per week	25 hrs	Scandinavian Seaways	(0990) 333111
Hamburg	2–3 per week	21–23 hrs	Scandinavian Seaways	(0990) 333111
NEWHAVEN to				
Dieppe (catamaran)	2–3 per day	2 hrs 15 mins	Hoverspeed	(0990) 240241
PLYMOUTH to				
Roscoff	1–3 per day	6 hrs	Brittany Ferries	(0990) 360360
Santander	2 per week	24 hrs	Brittany Ferries	(0990) 360360
POOLE to				
Cherbourg	1–2 per day	4hrs 15mins	Brittany Ferries Truckline	(0990) 360360
PORTSMOUTH to				
Bilbao	2 per week	29–35 hrs	P&O European Ferries	(0990) 980980
Cherbourg (ship)	3–4 per day	5 hrs	P&O European Ferries	(0990) 980980
Cherbourg (fast ferry)	2–3 per day	2 hrs 45 mins	P&O European Ferries	(0990) 980980
Le Havre	3 per day	5 hrs 30 mins	P&O European Ferries	(0990) 980980
Ouistreham (Caen)	2–3 per day	6 hrs	Brittany Ferries	(0990) 360360
St Malo	1 per day	8 hrs 30 mins –10 hrs 30 mins	Brittany Ferries	(0990) 360360

From...To	Sailings	Journey Time	Operator	☎ for details
ROSSLARE to				
Cherbourg	1–2 per week	17 hrs 30 mins	Irish Ferries	(0990) 171717
Roscoff	1–2 per week	15 hrs 00 mins	Irish Ferries	(0990) 171717

The Channel Tunnel

The idea of a cross-Channel tunnel was first proposed as long ago as as 1802. Early attempts were stopped for fear of invasion and the project finally got the green light in 1985. This extraordinary feat of engineering actually consists of three tunnels (two for trains, one for services and emergency use), each one 50 km long. Eurostar rail services began in late 1994 and by the end of 1997, 11 million passengers had travelled on Eurostar trains.

The advantage Eurostar has over ferry services, for many travellers, is that the journey is from city centre to city centre. Waterloo International is served by the London Underground and by domestic rail services (see p. 37). From Waterloo, up to 18 trains each day take 3 hrs to reach Paris Gare du Nord, whilst 10 services take just vf2 hrs 40 mins to reach Brussels Midi. Some trains stop at Ashford International (for south-east England), Lille (for connections with TGV services across France) or Calais, and there are services direct to Disneyland Paris. Waterloo International is more like an airport than a typical London rail terminus. Facilities at the modern, purpose-built terminal include shops, cafés and bars. There is an automated check-in system at all Eurostar terminals, and passengers have to check in up to 20 mins before departure. Passengers clear customs before boarding; passport and immigration checks take place during the journey.

The sleek Eurostar trains look incongruous amongst London's commuter services. Each train, a quarter-mile long, provide two classes of travel – first-class offers complimentary meals and drinks, and standard-class usually provides an at-seat trolley service. There are also two buffet cars on each train. Discounted tickets are available to most rail pass holders.

The 20-minute trip through the Channel Tunnel seems just like travelling on any metro system. The thrill comes as you emerge in France and the train accelerates to over 180 mph across the Pas de Calais. Both Paris Gare du Nord (p. 53) and Brussels Midi (p. 197) have been altered to accommodate the Eurostar trains and provide facilities for their passengers. For details and bookings, ☎0990 186 186.

Le Shuttle, which runs from Folkestone to Calais, is the car transporter service. Trains run up to 4 times per hour and journey time is about 35 mins during the day. Tickets are bought at the terminal or given in exchange for vouchers. The carriages have toilet facilities, but little by way of refreshments and no seats – passengers remain in or near their car. ☎0990 35 35 35.

(for Directory information, see p. 548). Many people holiday nowhere else but France. It has a lifetime's worth of historic towns, cities and other heritage, food and wine that can verge on the wonderful, and both scenery and architecture of astonishing variety. To top that, **Paris** is one of the world's most romantic capitals, with a streetscape familiar from a thousand movies.

In the north-west, **Normandy** is a land of half-timbered farms and graceful old manor houses; vast war cemeteries and numerous rebuilt towns that suffered massive bombing are sobering reminders of the toll inflicted by the 20th century's two World Wars. **Brittany** has the best scenery on France's Atlantic coast, with fishing villages and sweeping sandy bays, and inland lies the **Loire valley** – scenically undramatic, but remarkable for its Renaissance châteaux.

Despite the impressive legacy of medieval towns and cities (including some superb cathedrals), much of inland northern France is pretty humdrum scenically, with endless cornfields and long straight roads. The **Massif Central**, the great upland covering much of southern central France, is an area to experience the most rustic France has to offer. Heading towards the Spanish border down western France, you encounter the gentle hills of the **Dordogne**, with a good scattering of sights and many pretty (if sometimes over-discovered) villages, before you reach the Pyrénées which offer an excellent range of walks. Between the Massif Central and the Alps, **Provence** is really southern-looking, with red roofs, vineyards and cypress trees under the harsh summer sun. Known as the **Riviera**, the south coast boasts glamorous resorts (good for people-watching) and fine beaches. North of the Alps, the quiet areas of **Burgundy** and **Alsace** – the latter distinctly German in appearance – have attractive landscapes and rewarding territory for pottering round villages and vineyards.

Trains are fast, reliable and comfortable. The French are proud of the **TGV** *(Trains à Grande-Vitesse)*, among the fastest in the world, with speeds of up to 300 kph. Most of the scenic routes are in the south – in the **Massif Central**, through the **Pyrénées**, in **Provence** and through the **Alps**.

AUBERGES DE JEUNESSE

Fédération Unie des Auberges de Jeunesse (Headquarters), 27 R. PAJOL, 75018 PARIS, ☎(33) (1) 44 89 87 27, fax (33) (1) 44 89 87 10.

CAMPING

Michelin and Fédération Française de Camping et Caravanning, 78 R. DE RIVOLI, 75004 PARIS; ☎(01) 42 72 84 08.

REFUGE HUTS

Club Alpin Français, 24 AV. DE LAUMIÈRE, 75019 PARIS; ☎(01) 42 02 68 64.

ACCOMMODATION

HOTELS If you're staying at hotels, it's much cheaper if you share rather than go single, as prices are often per room. Half-board (i.e. breakfast and evening meal included) can be excellent value in smaller towns and villages. As elsewhere in Europe, budget hotels are often clustered near stations. In summer, you may need to book for some larger towns and resort areas. You can get lists of all types of accommodation from tourist boards for a small charge. Accommodation tax (FFr.1 to FFr.6 per day) is charged, depending on the kind of accommodation.

Hotels have five grades which include 1 (basic) to 5 (luxury). Paris is expensive: a comfortable 2-star double room in most places would average FFr.260–380; in Paris and parts of the south it would be FFr.450–500. Hotel prices quoted are invariably for doubles – singles often cost the same – and usually do not include continental breakfast in the total cost; breakfast is usually cheaper in nearby cafés and seldom consists of more than coffee, bread and jam.

CHAMBRES D'HÔTE *Chambres d'hôte* are rooms in private homes, often good value. One useful organisation is **bed and breakfast France** (excellent friendly, family-run hotels, most offering a railway station pick-up service); their '*Bed and Breakfast FRANCE 2000*' guide, published by Thomas Cook (£11.99 plus p&p) is available from **Thomas Cook Publishing**, PO BOX 227, THORPE WOOD, PETERBOROUGH PE3 6PU, UK; ☎01733 503571.

GÎTES D'ÉTAPE These are rural hostels, usually with private rooms as well as dormitories.

YOUTH HOSTELS **Auberges de Jeunesse (AJ)**, are mostly run by HI. They are usually good quality, but no cheaper than many budget hotels (usually costing FFr.30–68 plus bed linen and meals; most have self-catering facilities).

CAMPING This is virtually a national pastime, and you'll have no problem finding a site; most towns and larger villages will have signposts to the nearest site, commonly the *Camping Municipal* (fairly basic but very cheap). High-grade sites can have full entertainment and facilities such as watersports, but can get very crowded in season. **Michelin** and **Fédération Française de Camping et Caravanning** produce guides. Alternatively, local Tourist Offices have lists of farms where camping is possible (after getting the farmer's permission), and also of **farmhouse accommodation**. In mountain areas, a chain of refuge huts is run by **Club Alpin Français**.

France

Food and Drink

France has a gastronomic reputation that frequently lives up to reality, providing you're prepared to look beyond the ubiquitous *steak frites* (steak and chips). The regional variations are vast, and exploring them is part of the French experience. In general, north-west France tends towards butter-based cooking, with meat and cream much in evidence, while the south is dominated by Mediterranean influences such as olive oil, wine and herbs; in the mountainous areas there's more rustic and flavoursome cuisine based on home-cured dry hams and cheeses. In restaurants, *à la carte* is expensive, but the *menu du jour* (set meal) can be superb value; it's generally even better value if you have your main meal at lunch time. Purely **vegetarian** restaurants are rare, but some places will have one or two veggie choices (though may be not more than variations on an omelette).

Lunch typically begins 1200/1300 and **dinner** (the main meal) from around 1900 – after 2100 you could have problems outside tourist centres. In cafés, you usually pay more to sit down.

Coffees and beers can run up your expenses: wine is invariably cheaper – order a *pichet* or larger carafe and you'll get a vessel of house red *(rouge)* or white *(blanc)*, unlabelled but usually palatable. If you ask for *café*, you'll get a small black coffee; *café crême* is a small white coffee – if you want a bigger cup, ask for *un grand crême*. Tea *(thé)* is served American-style, with non-boiling water and a slice of lemon, unless you ask specifically for *thé au lait* (tea with milk). Lime flower *(tilleul)* and mint tea *(thé de menthe)* are widely available. **Beer** is mostly yellow and fizzy, though brown **Pelforth** is darker and sweeter; *bière pression* is draught beer, better value than bottled. Places in the north have the best selection of beers. Ask about the local specialities for **liqueurs** and **apéritifs**. *Baguettes* with a variety of fillings from cafés and stalls are cheap – as are *crêpes* (sweet and savoury pancakes). Markets are excellent for stocking up on picnic items. Buy your food before noon as shops can be closed for hours at lunchtime.

Editor's Choice

Annecy; Bayeux Tapestry; Brittany (including Carnac); Carcassonne; Chartres Cathedral; Corsica; Futuroscope (Poitiers); Nancy; Nice; Paris; Provence (including Avignon; Arles; Nîmes; Orange and Pont du Gard); Strasbourg. Scenic rail journeys: French Alps (especially Lyon or Marseille–Turin via Chambéry; and Aix les Bains–Chamonix–Mont Blanc; ETT tables 44, 362, 363, 364, 367, 572; and Where Next from Sion?, p. 300); Nîmes–Clermont Ferrand; Béziers–Clermont Ferrand (see Where Next from Nîmes?, p. 96); Marseille–Menton (French Riviera; p. 100); Bastia–Ajaccio (p. 111); Toulouse–Barcelona via Perpignan and the Pyrénées (p. 115).

Beyond the Border

London (Eurostar from Paris, ETT table 10; or cheaper options via ferries from Calais and other ports); Paris–Amsterdam via Brussels (table 18); Strasbourg–Zurich (table 40); Nice–Rome via Pisa (table 90); Bordeaux–Madrid via Burgos (table 46); Dijon–Milan (table 44).

Familiar from hundreds of movies and great paintings, and a byword for chic and elegance, Paris still has great romantic lure, with boulevards punctuated by imposing monuments, and the dignified uniformity of its grey-roofed, tall, cream-shuttered houses that compounds the sense of cohesion. The geometrical layout and long vistas make it generally an easy place to get your bearings. Stand at the **Arc de Triomphe** and you can see far along the main axis: in one direction is the modern arch of **La Défense**, while in the other you look past the obelisk in the **Place de la Concorde** to the **Jardin des Tuileries**, where old ladies toss crumbs to plump pigeons within sight of the **Louvre**, one of the world's biggest and best art museums, ensconced on the north bank of the Seine. By contrast the older quarters such as **Le Marais** and **Montmartre** are more intricate and informal. Parisian night views (notably from a **river boat**, the top of the **Eiffel Tower** and from the steps in front of **Sacre Coeur**) are part of the experience too. If Paris has a lifeless moment it's in August, when half the city goes on holiday and much of it looks shut down.

ARRIVAL AND DEPARTURE

RAIL There are six main rail stations in Paris, all with tourist information and left luggage etc. Each has its own métro stop and is also served by RER. SNCF enquiries for the whole country are handled centrally: ☎36 35 35 35. **Paris–Nord** (or **Gare du Nord**): for Scandinavia, Belgium, the Netherlands and the UK (via Boulogne/Calais ferries and Eurostar Channel Tunnel services). **Paris–Est** (**Gare de l'Est**): north-east France, Luxembourg, Germany, Austria and Switzerland. **Paris–St–Lazare**: Normandy and the UK (via Dieppe). **Paris–Montparnasse**: Brittany, Versailles, Chartres and the south-west coast. **Paris–Austerlitz**: Loire Valley, south and south-west France, Spain and Portugal. **Paris–Gare de Lyon**: eastern and south-eastern France, the Auvergne, Provence, the Alps, Italy and Greece.

Travellers by high-speed TGV trains through France do not need to pass through Paris; there's also a TGV terminal at Charles de Gaulle airport.

✈ **Roissy-Charles de Gaulle** is 23 km north-east of the city: flight times, ☎48 62 22 80 (24-hr); three main terminals, bureaux de change (0615–2330), cashpoints, tourist information and hotel booking desk (0700–2300). Links to the city all 0600–2300. **Roissyrail trains** to GARE DU NORD and on to CHÂTELET every 15 mins, taking 35 mins (RER B3); **Roissybus** (☎04 41 56 78 00) to OPÉRA-GARNIER 0540–2300 every 15 mins, taking 45 mins. **Air France coaches** (☎43 23 97 10) from GARE DE LYON and GARE MONTPARNASSE to PL. CHARLES DE GAULLE/ÉTOILE and PORTE MAILLOT, 0700–2100 every 15–20 mins, taking about 40 mins (FFr.65). Regular buses are slower but cost less – 🚌no. 350 serves GARE DU NORD and GARE DE L'EST, and 🚌no. 351 serves PL. DE LA NATION. A taxi to the centre should cost around FFr.220.

Orly is 14 km south; information service (0600–2300), ☎49 75 15 15; two terminals (*Sud* and *Ouest*), each with a tourist information booth (0600–2345) and bureau de change (0630–2300).

Tourist Information

Office du Tourisme et des Congrès de Paris (Paris Convention and Visitors Bureau), 127 AV. DES CHAMPS-ELYSÉES, ☎49 52 53 54 (métro: CHARLES DE GAULLE-ÉTOILE/GEORGE V), daily 0900–2000. Vast amounts of useful information on everything in **Paris** and the surrounding **Île de France**, a booking service for **excursions**, a France-wide **hotel reservation** desk, desks for **SNCF** and **Disneyland Paris**. Further offices at: **Gare du Nord**, ☎45 26 94 82, open Mon–Sat 0800–2100 (May–Oct); Mon–Sat 0800–2000 (Nov–Apr); **Eiffel Tower**, ☎45 51 22 15, daily 1100–1800 (May–Sept). There's a 24-hr **information number** (in English), ☎49 52 53 56.

City transport roughly 0600–midnight (takes about 30 mins): **Orlyrail** (RER C2) to GARE D'AUSTERLITZ every 15 mins (FFr.28); **shuttle service**, OrlyVal, to GARE ANTONY every few mins and on to CHÂTELET-LES-HALLES or DENFERT-ROCHEREAU (FFr.50); **RATP Orlybus** to DENFERT-ROCHEREAU métro station every 15 mins (FFr.25); **Air France coaches** (☎: 01 41 56 78 00) to GARE MONTPARNASSE and GARE DES INVALIDES every 12 mins or so, 0550–2300 daily (FFr.280). A **taxi** to the centre should cost around FFr.280.

Information

City and Metro Map – inside back cover

Money

The exchange office at **Gare de Lyon** stays open until 2330, and there are plenty of late-opening private bureaux de change and also lots of automatic machines (which take credit cards) at transport terminals etc. **Thomas Cook bureaux de change**: throughout the centre, including most main rail stations; money-changing facilities and other services such as phonecards and reservations.

Post and Phones

Main post office, 52 R. DU LOUVRE, open 24 hrs for telephones and poste restante; other services close at 1900. The **telephone code** for Paris from elsewhere in France is 01, just 1 from outside France.

Public Transport

You can see Paris on foot, but it's worth taking advantage of the efficient and well co-ordinated public transport, made up of the **métro** (subway) and **buses of RATP** (*Régie autonome des Transport Parisiens*) and **RER** (*Réseau Express Régional*) **trains**. Free **maps** of the networks from métro and bus stations (plus many hotels and big stores): the *Petit Plan de Paris* covers the centre; the *Grand Plan de Paris* is more extensive.

Métro: The impressive métro system runs every few mins 0530–0100. Lines are coded by colour and number and named after their final destination. Maps of the whole system are at all stations and signs on platforms indicate connecting lines (*correspondances*). To reach the platform, slot your ticket into an automatic barrier, then retrieve it.

RER: This system consists of four rail lines (A, B, C, D – plus the new 'E'), which are basically **express services** between the city and the suburbs. They form a cross through Paris and have a few central stops. The numbers following the letters (usually in the suburbs) indicate a branch from the main line. There are **computerised route-finders** at the RER stations. These give you alternative ways to reach your destination – on foot, as well as by public transport.

RATP, 53 BIS QUAI DES GRANDS-AUGUSTINS, ☎44 68 20 20, have a separate **information line**, manned 0600–2100, ☎43 46 14 14. Bus-stops show the numbers of the routes using them and display route maps. There are on-board announcements of the next stop. **Tickets** must be validated when you board, but **passes** are just shown to the driver. Most buses run 0630–2030/2100, but some lines continue until 0030. Sun services and bank holidays (*jours feriés*) are infrequent. **Night buses** (*Noctambus*) are hourly 0100–0500 and have ten suburban routes fanning out from PL. DU CHÂTELET. Good bus routes for **seeing the city** are nos. 24, 47, 67, 69 and 73.

Taxis: Flagging them down in the street is rarely successful. **Licensed taxis** have roof lights; white indicates that the taxi is free, orange means it is occupied. **Fares** are determined by three time zones and a host of extras, but they are regulated. Major companies include **Taxi Bleu**, ☎49 36 10 10, and **G7**, ☎47 39 47 39. **Avoid unofficial taxis**. **Tips** are expected (say 10%).

TICKETS

The same tickets are used in the métro, bus and RER systems. The network is divided into five zones: green tickets are used in the two central zones, Paris proper; others, usually yellow, are used as you get further out. Outside the central zone, buy a ticket from an automatic machine or the ticket office (*guichet*). Bus tickets are valid for the whole journey in the central zone. Passes are sold at airports, stations, Tourist Offices and some tobacconists (*tabacs*). The best value for a short stay is probably the *carnet* (a book of ten tickets), currently FFr.46 (individual tickets are FFr.8). **Formule 1** cards give one day of unlimited city travel. You can cover zones 1–3 (FFr.38) or opt for extra zones. The **Paris Visite** pass for zones 1–3 is valid for three (FFr.110) or five (FFr.170) consecutive days and can be extended to cover other zones. You can also get a **Carte Orange** (weekly or monthly pass). The **weekly** (*coupon hebdomadaire/jaune*) is valid Mon–Sun (price depends on the number of zones you require). The **monthly** (*coupon mensuel*) is valid from the first day of the month (FFr.208–526).

ACCOMMODATION

Whatever your price range (except rock-bottom), a lot of options are available, and finding suitable accommodation is a problem only in the busiest months (usually May, June, Sept and Oct).

Bureaux d'Accueil at the main Tourist Office and main-line stations offer a room-finding service for hostels as well as hotels. There are also automated room-finding machines at airports. If you can afford it, stay in a hotel on ST-LOUIS-EN-ÎLE.

Very central and fairly quiet **medium-price** options are: **Le Pavillon** (former convent with a peaceful courtyard), and **Thoumieux** (excellent bistro). The cheapest good options for hotels include **Henri IV** and **Castex.**

Cheaper accommodation is not hard to find. **Quartier Latin** (Latin Quarter) and **St-Germain-des-Près**, on the **Left Bank**, have a good range of low- to medium-price hotels; there are a few places in **Le Marais**, a quiet and characterful area in which to stay. Many budget hotels are clustered round FAUBOURG MONTMARTRE, in the 9th *arrondissement* (district). The area around the Gare du Nord is also cheap, but can be fairly sleazy. Self-catering apartments are arranged by **Paris Séjour Réservation**. **Tourisme chez l'Habitant** covers bed and breakfast.

Fédération Unie des Auberges de Jeunesse has a list of **youth hostels** in France. AJF find beds (often cheap ones) for people aged 18-30. **HI** youth hostels: **Le d'Artagnan, Cité des Sciences, Jules-Ferry, Clichy**. The **Woodstock Hostel** has young, friendly staff, 10 mins' walk from Gare du Nord.

Easily the most central **campsite** is **Camping du Bois de Boulogne**, next to the Seine and very popular, so book well in advance.

HOTELS	**Le Pavillon**, 54 R. ST-DOMINIQUE, 7E, ☎45 51 42 87. **Thoumieux**, 79 R. ST-DOMINIQUE, 7E, ☎47 05 49 75. Both moderate.
	Henri IV, 25 PL. DAUPHINE, ÎLE DE LA CITÉ, 1E, ☎43 54 44 53. **Castex**, 5 R. CASTEX, 4E, ☎42 72 31 52. Cheaper.
CAMPSITE	**Camping du Bois de Boulogne**, ALLÉE DU BORD-DE-L'EAU, 16E, ☎45 24 30 00.
HI YOUTH HOSTELS	**Le d'Artagnan**, 80 R. VITRUVE, ☎40 32 34 56 (métro: PORTE-DE-BAGNOLET). **Cité des Sciences**, 1 R. JEAN-BAPTISTE CLEMENT, LE PRÉ ST-GERVAIS, ☎48 43 24 11 (métro: HOCHE, PORTE DE PANTIN); **Jules-Ferry**, 8 BLVD JULES FERRY, tel: 43 57 55 60 (métro: RÉPUBLIQUE); **Clichy**, 107 R. MAITRE, 921100 CLICHY, ☎41 27 26 90.
HOSTEL	**The Woodstock Hostel**, 48 R. RODIER, 75009, ☎48 78 87 76.

FOOD AND DRINK

Paris is still a great place to eat, with many fabulous restaurants, both French and exotic, at relatively cheap prices. Cafés and bars are the cheapest, and brasseries and *salons de thé* are more expensive. The closer to the bar you stand, the less you pay. Self-service restaurants are usually fine, if a little institutional, and a snack at a crêperie will usually keep hunger at bay. Set lunches tend to be much better value than the evening equivalents. A trip to the supermarket and an hour's picnic in the **Tuileries** gardens of the **Palais Royal** are also a lovely way to lunch.

For evening meals, study the set menus outside most restaurants; these often provide a reasonable choice at affordable prices. The **Latin Quarter**, **Marais**, **Montmartre** and **Montparnasse** are good areas for cheap eating and multi-ethnic cuisine, especially Greek, North African, East European and Vietnamese. For kosher food, try R. DES ROSIERS and R. XAVIER PRIVAS. The weekly listings magazine, *Pariscope*, provides a guide to Paris restaurants.

If you fancy eating *al fresco*, make an early evening visit to R. MOUFFETARD (métro: MONGE/CENSIER DAUBETON) or R. DE BUCI (métro: ST-GERMAIN-DES-PRÉS/MABILLON), where a range of mouth-watering delicacies is on offer; or try the organic products market, BLVD RASPAIL, on Sun morning (métro: RENNES). At LA CHAPELLE on Sat morning there is a huge exotic food market.

HIGHLIGHTS

Almost everything in Paris has an entrance fee, and this can be quite steep. Some places give you up to 50% discount if you are under 25 and have an ISIC card. Paris Visite gives discounts on some major attractions. Much more comprehensive is *La Carte Musée* (Museums and Monuments Card), which offers entrance and reductions to some museums: FFr.70 for 1 day, FFr.140 for 2 days or FFr.200 for 3 days. Unmissable freebies include **Père Lachaise Cemetery**, the view from the **Pompidou Centre**, **Notre-Dame** and **Sacré Coeur**; there are **reduced entry fees** on **Suns** to the **Musée d'Orsay**, the **Musée Rodin** and the **Louvre** (which is free on the first Sun of the month and cheaper on other days after 1500).

Most monuments are on the **Right Bank**, while the islands in the middle of the River Seine are where the city began and offer some of the best architecture. The **Left Bank** is more laid-back, traditionally popular with artists and the Bohemian crowd.

THE ISLANDS (LES ÎLES) Take time out just to wander round the largely 17th-century **Île St-Louis**, as well as the major sights on **Île de la Cité**, which is linked to it by a footbridge (métro: CITÉ). The great twin-towered cathedral of **Notre Dame**, built between 1163 and 1345, is one of the world's finest Gothic buildings. The tiny **Ste-Chapelle** (in the courtyard of the Palais de Justice) has acres of stunningly beautiful stained glass – on a sunny day, it's like standing in a kaleidoscope.

THE RIGHT BANK (LA RIVE DROITE) The unmissable **Centre Georges Pompidou** (also known as Beaubourg; 1200-2000) 19 r. Beaubourg (métro: CHÂTELAT-LES-HALLES), is a high-tech metal and glass shopping mall. Outside are humorously eccentric fountains by the modern Swiss sculptor, Tinguely.

Back beside the river, is the **Louvre** (métro: PALAIS-ROYAL; enter via métro PALAIS

INFORMATION

HOSTELS

Fédération Unie des Auberges de Jeunesse, 27 R. PAJOL, ☎46 47 00 01.

AJF (**Accueil des Jeunes de France**), 119 R. ST-MARTIN, ☎42 77 87 80, and 139 BLVD ST-MICHEL, ☎43 54 95 86.

Self-catering apartments: **Paris Séjour Réservation**, 90 AV. DES CHAMPS ELYSÉES, ☎53 89 10 50.

bed and breakfast: **Tourisme chez l'Habitant**, 27 R. RAMBUTEAU, ☎34 25 44 44.

TOURS

Paribus, 3–5 R. TALMA, ☎42 88 92 88, offer **English commentary tours** and nine stops, so you can get off and on at will over the course of two days. **Caisse Nationale des Monuments Historiques et des Sites**, HÔTEL DE SULLY, 62 R. ST-ANTOINE, ☎44 61 21 50, operate **daily walking tours** with specific themes. **Paris by Cycle**, 2 R. DE LA JONQUIÈRE, ☎42 63 36 63, and **Mountain Bike Trip**, 6 PL. ETIENNE PERNET, ☎48 42 57 87, offer **cycling tours** of Paris. **Boat trips**: Most of the boat companies operate **half-hourly departures**, with **multilingual commentaries**, (about FFr.45) and some offer evening **dinner cruises**. The glass-topped **Bateaux-Mouches** have frequent departures from PONT DE L'ALMA, ☎40 76 99 99. For bookings, ☎42 25 96 10. Other companies include **Vedettes de Paris**, ☎47 05 71 29, from PORT DE SUFFR.EN, SQ. DE VERT GALANT, ÎLE DE LA CITÉ and PONT D'IÉNA, and **Bateaux Parisiens**, ☎44 11 33 33, from PORT DE LA BOURDONNAIS, PONT D'IÉNA and QUAI DE MONTEBELLO. Buy a ticket before boarding. The **Batobus** is a water-bus (without a commentary) that operates every 36 mins 1000–1900 (Apr–Oct), stopping at the Eiffel Tower, the Musée d'Orsay, the Louvre, Notre-Dame and the Hôtel de Ville. You can pay **per stop** (FFr.15) or get a **day-ticket**.

ROYAL/LOUVRE to avoid long queues; closed Tues). From here, the formal **Jardins des Tuileries** lead along the river to the PL. DE LA CONCORDE. From PL. DE LA CONCORDE the AV. DES CHAMPS-ELYSÉES leads up towards the **Arc de Triomphe**, PL. CHARLES-DE-GAULLE; open 0930–2300 in summer (Mon, Sun 0930–1830); 1000–2230 in winter (Mon, Sun 1000–1800).

THE LOUVRE

is one of the greatest art museums in the world. Housed in a former palace, it's a sightseeing marathon, with miles of corridors. Its most famous exhibits, the **Mona Lisa** (*La Joconde* in French) and the **Venus de Milo**, are always surrounded by vast crowds. I M Pei's glass pyramid has formed the startling entrance since 1989.

THE LEFT BANK (LA RIVE GAUCHE) Go up the **Eiffel Tower** (métro: CHAMPS-DE-MARS; 0900–2400) – either take the lift to the highest level or (much cheaper) climb 700 steps to the second level.

The Musée Rodin, 77 R. DE VARENNE; (métro: VARENNE), a magnificent house and garden, is full of the sculptor's works (0930–1730; closed Mon).

Continuing along the river, the **Musée d'Orsay**, 1 RUE DE BELLECHASSE (métro: SOLFÉRINO), is a converted railway station that now houses a truly spectacular collection of 19th- and early 20th-century art, including works by Monet, Manet, Van Gogh and Delacroix.

Beyond this are the narrow medieval streets of the Latin Quarter, home of the **Sorbonne University** and two great parks: **Jardin de Luxembourg** and **Jardin des Plantes**, QUAI ST-BERNARD.

FURTHER OUT North of the river **Montmartre**, once the haunt of artists, offers the most accessible views of the city. Topping the hill are the overblown white cupolas of the basilica of Sacré-Coeur, built at the turn of the century.

The city's largest park, **Bois de Boulogne** (métro: PORTE D'AUTEUIL) is a big Sunday strolling ground, fun for observing Parisian life, and looking at some of the most elegant of the city's suburbs; after dark it's very different – famous for its transvestite nightlife and not that safe.

Nearby is the **Marmottan** (R. LOUIS-BOILLY; métro: LA MUETTE; closed Mon), housing a choice collection of Monet paintings.

DAY TRIPS FROM PARIS

Allow time for trips into the suburbs and a little way out of town. Sights include the huge châteaux at both **Versailles** (RER line C to Versailles Rive-Gauche) and **Fontainebleau** (frequent suburban trains from Gare de Lyon to Fontainebleau-Avon). There are massive theme parks **Disneyland Paris**, ☎60 30 60 30 (RER line A to Chessy Marne-la-Vallée) and **Parc Astérix** (RER line B3 to Roissy–Charles de Gaulle).

NIGHT-TIME AND EVENTS

The monthly *Paris Sélection* and annual *Saisons de Paris* listings are available (free) from Tourist Offices. There's also a 24-hr information line, ☎49 52 53 56. Two inexpensive weekly listings are *l'Officiel des Spectacles* and *Pariscope*, the latter of which has an 8-page English language section (*Time Out*), both on sale at newsagents.

Half-price theatre tickets can be purchased for same-day performances from the kiosks at 15 PL. DE LA MADELEINE and RER CHÂTELET-LES-HALLES station. Both open Tues–Sat 1230–2000; the kiosk at PL. DE LA MADELEINE also opens Sun 1230–1600, but credit cards are not accepted.

SHOPPING

You can get everything you may want, but don't expect bargains.

To admire designer styles, head for R. DE FAUBOURG ST-HONORÉ, AV. MONTAIGNE and R. DE RIVOLI. More reasonable prices can be tracked down at **Les Halles**, **St-Germain-des-Près** and the R. DE COMMERCE at Rennes.

The most famous department stores are **Galeries Lafayette**, 40 BLVD HAUSSMANN, **Printemps**, 64 BLVD HAUSSMANN, and, on the Left Bank, and **Au Bon Marché**, 38 R. DE SÈVRES.

Markets (specialist and otherwise) are big business in Paris (both covered and open-air), so the Tourist Office produces a free list.

The best-known flea-market is **St Ouen** (métro: ST OUEN/PORTE DE CLIGNANCOURT), held Sat–Mon 0730–1900, which consists of 16 separate markets, including **Jules-Vallès** (curios, lace and postcards), **Marché Paul-Bert** (second-hand goods), **Marché Serpette** (products from the 1900s–1930s) and **Marché Malik** (second-hand clothes and records).

Bargains are hard to find. You might do better at PORTE DE MONTREUIL (métro: PORTE DE MONTREUIL), held Sat–Mon (0700–1930).

Paris

Paris is famous for the **huge revues** staged (mainly) in Montmartre, notably **Bal du Moulin Rouge**, the **Folies-Bergère**, the **Lido de Paris** and the **Crazy Horse Saloon**, 12 AV. GEORGE V. Be warned – these shows are exorbitantly expensive.

There are regular seasons of both ballet and opera at **Opéra-Bastille**, 120 R. DE LYON, **Opéra-Garnier**, 8 R. SCRIBE (which sells cheap stand-by tickets on the day of the performance), and **Opéra-Comique**, SALLE FAVARD 5, 5 R. FAVARD. There are also numerous concerts, held everywhere from purpose-built auditoria to museums, with a variety of free performances in several churches (including Notre Dame, every Sun evening).

Cimitiere Père Lachaise

The Cimitiere Père Lachaise (Metro: PÈRE LACHAISE) is the most aristocratic of cemeteries, a fantastically atmospheric place both for the quality of the monuments and the people who are buried there (who include Bizet, Chopin, Oscar Wilde, Edith Piaf, Balzac, Corot and, most famously of all, Jim Morrison, whose grave is covered in fans' graffiti.

Jazz is so popular that it has a special information service: **Centre d'Information du Jazz**, 21BIS R. DE PARADIS, ☎44 83 10 30. Other live music (especially rock) is also easy to find, and there's no shortage of discos and other places to dance.

At cinemas, there are often discounts on Wed. VO (*Version Originale*) means the film is in the original language, while VF (*Version Française*) means it's been dubbed.

The most famous annual celebration is **Bastille Day** (13–14 July), when fireworks and parades mark the anniversary of the storming of the city prison in 1789.

Other major events include **Mardi Gras** (Feb); **May Day workers' marches** (1 May); **the French Open Tennis Championships** (late May–early June); **Fête de la Musique** (June); the final stage of the **Tour de France** cycle race along the Champs Elysées (last Sun July); and **Festival de Jazz** (late Oct).

WHERE NEXT FROM PARIS?

Many of the French routes in this book start from or pass through Paris.

Additionally you can take direct services to join routes in other countries, including ***Amsterdam, Barcelona, Basel, Berlin, Brussels, Cologne, Dresden, Frankfurt, Lausanne, Madrid, Milan, Prague, Rome, Vienna;*** *see also International Routes* *(p. 33).*

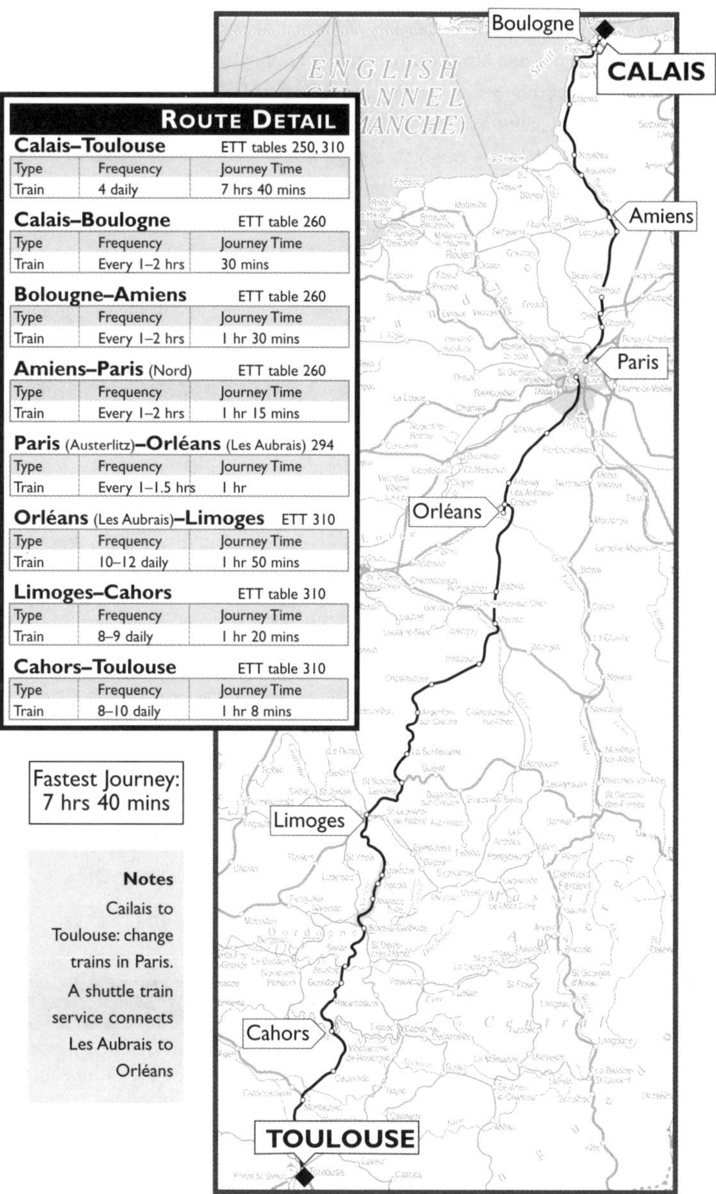

ROUTE DETAIL

Calais–Toulouse ETT tables 250, 310

Type	Frequency	Journey Time
Train	4 daily	7 hrs 40 mins

Calais–Boulogne ETT table 260

Type	Frequency	Journey Time
Train	Every 1–2 hrs	30 mins

Bolougne–Amiens ETT table 260

Type	Frequency	Journey Time
Train	Every 1–2 hrs	1 hr 30 mins

Amiens–Paris (Nord) ETT table 260

Type	Frequency	Journey Time
Train	Every 1–2 hrs	1 hr 15 mins

Paris (Austerlitz)**–Orléans** (Les Aubrais) 294

Type	Frequency	Journey Time
Train	Every 1–1.5 hrs	1 hr

Orléans (Les Aubrais)**–Limoges** ETT 310

Type	Frequency	Journey Time
Train	10–12 daily	1 hr 50 mins

Limoges–Cahors ETT table 310

Type	Frequency	Journey Time
Train	8–9 daily	1 hr 20 mins

Cahors–Toulouse ETT table 310

Type	Frequency	Journey Time
Train	8–10 daily	1 hr 8 mins

Fastest Journey: 7 hrs 40 mins

Notes

Cailais to Toulouse: change trains in Paris. A shuttle train service connects Les Aubrais to Orléans

Calais – Paris – Toulouse

This grand north to south cross-section of France begins from the Channel ports of **Calais** and **Boulogne** and heads through the flat arable lands of the north that formed the focus of some of the fiercest fighting of World War I. **Amiens** is a good centre for seeking out the battlefields and memorials of the time. Allow plenty of time for crossing Paris by métro. **Orléans** is worth a stay, with its cathedral and opportunities for exploring the Loire valley. The porcelain-making town of **Limoges** gives scope for branching into the more out-of-the-way uplands of the Massif Central; meanwhile the main route continues into the Dordogne, a rural region that's much visited by dint of its unspoilt old towns, castles and villages. Cahors has a strong character of the south, while Toulouse is a big, demanding city.

CALAIS

Just under 40 km from the English coast at Dover, this busy cross-channel port is not a place to linger in, though it gets a brisk trade from English daytrippers stocking up with cheap booze at the **Auchun** hypermarket, west of town (buses available). There's also a decent range of shops along the main road from the port, past the famous Rodin statue of the **Six Burghers of Calais**, which stands in front of the Flemish-style **Hôtel de Ville** (town hall), commemorating the English capture of the town in 1347. Opposite, in the PARC ST-PIERRE, is the **Musée de la Guerre**, devoted to a more recent conflict – World War II – and was originally used as a bunker by German forces.

Information

Sea France ☎03 21 34 55 00; **P&O** ☎03 21 46 04 40; **Stena** ☎0232 14 67 868; **Hoverspeed** ☎03 21 46 14 14.

RAIL **Calais-Ville**, the main station, is almost opposite the Hôtel de Ville. The other station, **Calais-Fréthun**, near the mouth of the Channel Tunnel, serves the Eurostar (London–Paris).

All the companies run free shuttles between **Calais-Ville** station and the docks to connect with sailings. **Stena, P&O** and **SeaFrance** sail from **Calais Port**; **Hoverspeed** departs from **Calais Hoverport** (3 km from main port).

i **Tourist Office**: 12 BLVD. CLEMENCEAU; ☎(03) 21 96 62 40.

BOULOGNE

The **Vieille Ville** (Old Town) sits above the largely unremarkable modern part of Boulogne. If you've just stepped off the ferry, the walk around the 13th-century city walls immediately transports you into the real France, and provides views of the harbour. Within these ramparts, the 19th-century **Basilique Notre-Dame** draws together elements from St Paul's in London and St Peter's in Rome. The premier modern addition to Boulogne's tourist attractions is **Nausicaa**, on the seafront at

BLVD STE-BEUVE, one of the largest aquariums in France, equipped with underwater observation tanks. **La Matelote** (opposite Nausicaa), is one of the best fish restaurants in town.

Boulogne-Ville, 1 km south of the centre; all buses stopping here go to the centre.

The **Hoverspeed SeaCat** services linking Boulogne and Folkestone use **GARE MARITIME** and there are free shuttle buses between the dock and the centre of town.

Tourist Office: QUAI DE LA POSTE; ☎21 31 68 38 (Mon–Sat 0900–1900, Sun 1000–1700 July–Aug. Mon–Sat 0900–1230, 1330–1815, Sun 1000–1700 Sept–June). Accommodation booking service free. From the station, turn right on BLVD VOLTAIRE and then left on BLVD DAUNOU.

Boulogne has good value hotels right in the heart of town. Try the reasonably priced 3-star **Hôtel Métropole**, 51 R. THIERS; ☎03 21 31 54 30: convenient, pleasant and with a garden. A good budget bet is the central **Hôtel Faidherbe**, 12 R. FAIDHERBE; ☎03 21 60 93. **Hôtel Sleeping** is convenient and cheap; ☎03 21 80 62 79.

AMIENS

Two world wars inflicted massive damage on this big industrial centre, yet the **Cathédrale de Notre-Dame** survives as the largest in France and arguably the purest example of Gothic architecture in the country. The west doorway will linger in the memory, a 'book in stone' featuring the famous *Beau Dieu* portal.

Restored, but with pockets of its original character, the winding streets of the **St-Leu** district, straddling the *SOMME* just north of the cathedral, date from medieval times.

Amiens-Nord is the main station, about 500 m south-east of the cathedral. The grim concrete **TOUR PERRET** provides a prominent landmark for your return to the station. To reach the cathedral from the station, turn right on BLVD D'ALSACE LORRAINE and then second left on R. GLORIETTE. Buses are allowed into the pedestrianised centre, but it is usually much faster to walk – and certainly the best way to explore.

Tourist Office: 12 R. DU CHAPEAU-DE-VIOLETTES; ☎03 22 91 79 28; fax: 03 22 92 50 58. Open Mon–Sat 0900–1230, 1400–1830 (1900 Apr–Oct). Branch at the **rail station**, ☎03 22 92 65 04 (Mon–Sat 0800–1900, Sun 0930–1900). In midsummer, there's also an information kiosk in front of the cathedral (1000–1900).

PARIS

See p. 46.

Trains from **Calais** arrive at **Paris Nord**; to continue south, cross Paris via Métro to **Austerlitz** for **Orléans** (allow 1 hr; take line 5), or **Montparnasse** for stations between **Poitiers** and **Toulouse** (allow 1 hr; take line 4).

ORLÉANS

Strategically sited and erstwhile capital of France, Orléans has been attacked from Roman times to World War II, yet much of the rather austere historic centre has survived, including a number of Renaissance mansions. Taking pride of place in the spacious PL. DU MARTRO is a statue of **Jeanne d'Arc** (Joan of Arc or the 'Maid of Orléans'), who saved Orléans from the English in 1429 before being burnt at the stake as a witch. The nearby **Maison de Jeanne d'Arc**, PL. DU GÉN. DE GAULLE, is a reconstruction of the house where she stayed, and upstairs there is a museum illustrating the story of the Events of 1429. The annual **Fête de Jeanne d'Arc** (May 7–8) features a 'real' Jeanne riding through the streets.

Jeanne celebrated her triumph at the city's most impressive monument, the **Cathédrale Ste-Croix** (Holy Cross Cathedral), where she is commemorated by a battle scene carved on the altar and a series of 19th-century windows; meanwhile, the crypt gives a view of the Roman and medieval foundations.

RAIL **Gare Orléans** is on the northern edge of the centre, by the *Jeanne d'Arc* shopping complex; R. DE LA RÉPUBLIQUE runs straight ahead to PL. DU MARTROI, in the heart of town. Gare Orléans is actually on a short spur, just off the main rail line and through-services stop only at nearby **LES AUBRAIS**, but a shuttle service (*navette*) links the two stations.

R. M-PROUST, 02 38 53 94 75, a block from Gare Orléans.

Tourist Office: in the **Jeanne d'Arc centre**, PL. ALBERT IER, 02 38 24 05 05 (Mon–Sat 0900–1830, Sun 0930–1200 Oct–Mar. Mon–Sat 0900–1900, Sun 0930–1230, 1500–1830 Apr–Sept). **Youth information**: **Centre Régional d'Information Jeunesse**, 5 BLVD DE VERDUN, 38 54 37 70 (Mon–Sat 1000/1400–1800/1900).

Advance booking is recommended. For reasonably priced places, try around R. DU FG-BANNIER and PL. GAMBETTA. The 2-star **Hôtel Le St-Aignan**, 3 PL. GAMBETTA, 02 38 53 15 35, is good value. Other cheap options include the small **Hotel Saint Martin**, 52 BD ALEXANDRE MARTIN, 02 28 62 47 47, and the economy **Hotel Coligny**, at 80 RUE DE LA GARE 02 38 35 61 60. **Youth hostel** (non-HI): 14 R. DU FG-MADELEINE, 02 38 62 45 75, west of the centre (B). Nearest **campsite**: **St-Jean-de-la-Ruelle**, R. DE LA ROCHE, 02 38 88 39 39, 6 km west (D: ROCHE AUX FÉES), open May–Sept.

WHERE NEXT FROM ORLÉANS?

*The line along the Loire valley joins the **Paris– Bordeaux** route at **Tours** (p. 78; journey time 1 hr, frequent services, ETT table 296). On the way you can stop off at **Blois**, with its superb château (where the Duc de Guise and his brother were murdered on the orders of Henri III in 1588) at the heart of the steeply terraced town.*

LIMOGES

Capital of the Limousin region, Limoges is a large industrial city, renowned for producing high-quality enamel and (to some, often overly frilly) porcelain, but it has a delightful old centre, the **Haut-Cité**, comprising a web of dark, narrow streets, filled with half-timbered houses, small boutiques, antique and china shops. On the eastern edge of the HAUT-CITÉ, surrounded by well-maintained botanical gardens and overlooking the River Vienne, is the Gothic **Cathédrale de St-Etienne** (St Stephen's). One of the world's best collection of Limoges porcelain and faïence is on show at the **Musée Adrien-Dubouché**, PL. WINSTON-CHURCHILL, with over 12,000 pieces.

Gare des Bénédictins, 500 m north-east of the old town. Walk straight along AV. DU GÉN. DE GAULLE, across PL. JOURDAN and into BLVD DE FLEURUS – or take nos. 8/10 to PL. JOURDAN.

Tourist Offices: BLVD DE FLEURUS, 05 55 34 46 87; fax: 05 55 34 19 12, (Mon–Sat 0900–1900, Sun 1000–1400 June–Sept. Mon–Sat 0900–1200, 1400–1830, Sun 1000–1200 Oct–May.) **Regional office** for Haut-Vienne: 4 PL. D-DUSSOUBS, 05 55 79 04 04 (Mon–Fri 0900–1200 and 1330–1730).

Cheap accommodation can be found around the train station.

There are well-priced ethnic restaurants at the southern end of R. CHARLES MICHELS. For an al fresco eating alternative, stock up at the ***Halles Centrales*** (covered market), open daily until 1300. The ***Jardin de L'Eveche*** by the cathedral makes a charming picnic area.

CAHORS

An important Roman base on the tortuously winding river Lot, Cahors became famous for wine that was at times considered to be finer than that of Bordeaux. Its major monument, frequently depicted on wine labels, is the 14th-century **Pont Valentré**, west of the centre – a continuation of R. DU PRÉS-WILSON – a six-arched fortified bridge with three towers, the central one housing a historical display.

10 -mins walk west of the centre: leave PL. GAMBETTA by AV. J-JAURÈS (to the right) and turn left on R. DU PRÉS-WILSON. At BLVD GAMBETTA, turn right for the **Tourist Office**.

Tourist Office: BLVD GAMBETTA/PL. A-BRIAND, 05 65 35 09 56; fax: 05 65 23 98 66 (Mon–Sat, 1000–1200 and 1400–1800, Sun 1000–1200. May–Aug: open until 1830 Sat.

TOULOUSE

Now a lively university city and cultural centre, the capital of the Midi region is one of France's largest cities, not consistently attractive but with a wealth of medieval religious art. The pinky-red brick of many of the grandiose town houses has earned the city the epithet of the *Ville Rose*.

The centre is walkable, but there is also an efficient bus service, run by **SEMVAT** (7 PL. ESQUIROL, ☎61 41 70 70) and a modern métro. Tickets cover both and maps of the network are available from Tourist Offices and ticket booths. The best value ticket is a carnet (strip) of ten.

Many of the main attractions are in the old town, centred on PL. DU CAPITOLE, dominated by the 18th-century **Le Capitole** (town hall); most of the best-value restaurants are here. The town's liveliest part is PL. ST GEORGES, which is usually covered with café tables.

The superb **Basilique St-Sernin** is the sole survivor of an 11th-century Benedictine monastery established to assist pilgrims en route to Santiago de Compostela (p. 162). The **Musée des Augustins** has an exceptional show of medieval sculptures rescued from long-gone city churches.

LA CITÉ DE L'ESPACE

A recent newcomer is **La Cité de l'Espace**, east of **Toulouse** and reached by bus no.19. Situated in a large park, it features exhibitions on a multitude of space themes, with simulations, and the rocket *Ariane 5*, which stands in its own purpose-built garden. Open daily except Mon 0930–1900 (June–Sept), 0930–1800 (Sept–June).

RAIL **Toulouse–Gare Matabiau**, north-east of the city; 15–20- min walk from PL. DU CAPITOLE – or take the métro (the station stop is **MARENGO**). The railway station has baths and showers.

i **Tourist Office**: **Donjon du Capitole**, PL. C-D-GAULLE, ☎05 61 11 02 22; fax: 05 61 22 03 63 (Mon–Sat 0900–1900, Sun 0900–1300 and 1400–1730 May–Sept. Mon– Fri 0900–1800, Sat 0900–1230 and 1400–1800, Sun 1000–1230 and 1400–1700 Oct–Apr). **Branch**: at the station, ☎61 62 50 50, (Mon-Sat 0930–2000, Sun 1000–2000). **Regional** *(**Haute-Garonne**)*: 14 R. DE BAYARD, ☎61 99 44 00, (Mon–Fri 0900–1700).

A wide range of hotels means finding space is seldom a problem. Get the (free) *Hotels Restaurants* booklet from the Tourist Office. Budget places can be found in the centre, around PL. WILSON (R. ST-ANTOINE) and PL. DE CAPITOLE (R. DU TOUR and R. P-ROMIGUIÈRES). There are cheap hotels around the station, but the area is quite unpleasant. In the town centre, the modest **Hôtel Albert I ER**, 8 R. RIVALS, ☎05 61 21 17 91, is excellent value. **Hôtel Grand Balcon**, 8 R. ROMIGUIÈRES, ☎05 61 21 59 98 (closed for most of Aug), is reasonably priced, and noted for its period décor. **Youth hostel**: **Villa des Rosiers**, 125 AV. JEAN RIEUX, ☎61 80 49 93, 3 km from the station (bus no.22: ARMAND LEYGUES). The municipal **campsite** is north of town and rather inaccessible without your own transport.

WHERE NEXT?

*Carry on over the Pyrenees into Spain by taking the **Toulouse–Barcelona** route (p. 115).*

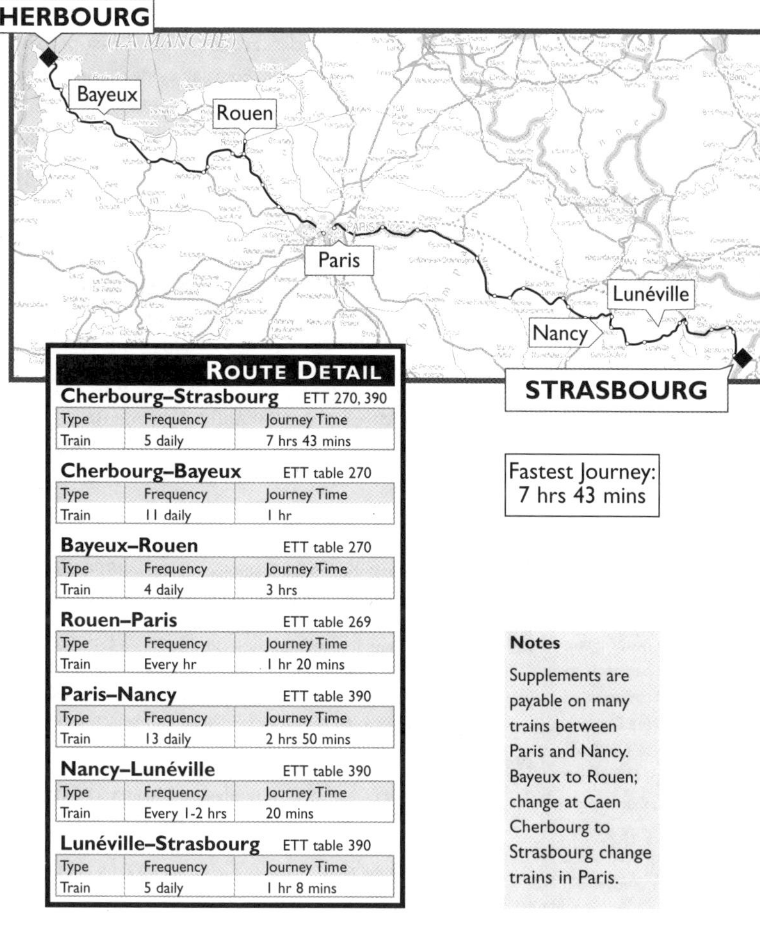

ROUTE DETAIL

Cherbourg–Strasbourg ETT 270, 390

Type	Frequency	Journey Time
Train	5 daily	7 hrs 43 mins

Cherbourg–Bayeux ETT table 270

Type	Frequency	Journey Time
Train	11 daily	1 hr

Bayeux–Rouen ETT table 270

Type	Frequency	Journey Time
Train	4 daily	3 hrs

Rouen–Paris ETT table 269

Type	Frequency	Journey Time
Train	Every hr	1 hr 20 mins

Paris–Nancy ETT table 390

Type	Frequency	Journey Time
Train	13 daily	2 hrs 50 mins

Nancy–Lunéville ETT table 390

Type	Frequency	Journey Time
Train	Every 1-2 hrs	20 mins

Lunéville–Strasbourg ETT table 390

Type	Frequency	Journey Time
Train	5 daily	1 hr 8 mins

Fastest Journey:
7 hrs 43 mins

Notes

Supplements are payable on many trains between Paris and Nancy. Bayeux to Rouen; change at Caen Cherbourg to Strasbourg change trains in Paris.

CHERBOURG – PARIS – STRASBOURG

Cherbourg – Paris – Strasbourg

The prelude to Paris is a trip through Normandy (*Normandie*), named after the invading Norsemen who settled in the Seine valley in the Dark Ages. To the north are some of the most attractive chalklands of the region, dotted with gracious manors and half-timbered farmhouses and culminating in great white cliffs around Dieppe. East of Paris, the route crosses the unspectacular **Champagne** region, Épernay being the industry's headquarters (where you can tour Mercier champagne caves by underground train; free samples afterwards). Next is **Nancy** with its monumental architecture, indisputably the star of Lorraine and on the French side of the Rhineland plain, **Strasbourg** leads you into Germany.

CHERBOURG

Essentially just a commercial and military port, Cherbourg is more a convenient resting place than a base for exploration of the coast. It was liberated by American troops three weeks after the landings on Utah beach to give the Allies a deep-water port for bringing in heavy vehicles. One point of interest is the **Fort du Roule**, which overlooks the town and port. Inside, the Museum of War and Liberation (0930–1730 Apr–Sept) commemorates the Allied landings and the liberation of Cherbourg and the Cotentin peninsula.

RAIL: PL. JEAN JAURÈS, at the south end of Bassin du Commerce (harbour).

Day trip from Cherbourg

A bus service heads down the Cotentin peninsula to the hilltop town of **Coutances** (see Day trip from Bayeux, p. 69), via the villages of Martinvast and Bricquebec, whose ancient fortress has a mighty keep and a museum of local life.

There are cross-channel ferry services to Poole (ETT table 2145), Portsmouth (table 2160) and Rosslare (table 2010).

Tourist Office: 2 QUAI ALEXANDRE III, ☎ 02 33 93 52 02; fax: 02 33 53 66 97 (June–Sept: Mon–Sat 0900–1830. Oct–May: Mon–Fri 0900–1200, 1330–1800). On the far side of Bassin du Commerce, between the lifting bridge and R. MARÉCHAL FOCH.

The area north of the Tourist Office offers some cheap lodging options. **The Grand**, 42 R. DE LA MARINE, ☎ 02 33 43 04 02, is reasonably priced, as is the comfortable **Hotel de la Gare,** 26 PL. DE LA GARE, ☎ 02 31 92 10 70. **Youth hostel:** AV. L. LUMIÈRE, ☎ 33 44 26 31, open mid Apr–mid Oct, 1.5 km from the station by bus no. 5 to stop Jean Moulin.

BAYEUX

One of the first towns to be liberated by the Allies after World War II, Bayeux escaped much damage to its fine medieval centre, which is still dominated by the spires of the magnificent **Cathédrale Notre-Dame**, a marriage of Norman and Gothic styles.

One of the most remarkable historical records in the world is the **Bayeux tapestry**: 70 m of linen embroidered in the 11th century, illustrating the Norman Conquest of England (famously portraying the Battle of Hastings) – thought to have been commissioned by the Bishop of Bayeux from an Anglo-Saxon workshop. Despite the passage of time, the colours are bright and the design is amazingly detailed. Before looking at the real thing, spend some time at the exhibition centre, which will help you to interpret what you'll see.

The **Musée Mémoriale de la Bataille de Normandie 44**, BLVD FABIAN WARE, includes the preparations for D -Day, as well as the action, and is probably the best of several museums in the area that are devoted to the World War II Normandy landings.

RAIL 10–15 mins walk south-east of the centre; turn left on BLVD SADI CARNOT and bear right onto R. LARCHER. Turn left onto R. ST-MARTIN for the Tourist Office. There are also buses into the centre.

i **Tourist Office:** 1 R. ST-JEAN, ☎ 02 31 51 28 28; fax: 02 31 51 28 29 (0900–1200, 1400–1800. Also Sun 1000–1230, 1500–1830 during July–Aug).

DAY TRIP FROM BAYEUX

Low tide at **Arromanches** (about 10 km from Bayeux, bus no. 74), reveals the remains of a Mulberry Harbour – one of the floating landing-stages which crossed the Channel transporting troops and vehicles. Exploration of the region is possible from Le Vallon, a quiet farmhouse outside Bayeux; moderately priced, book through B&B France (see p. 51).

WHERE NEXT FROM BAYEUX?

A neat way of avoiding Paris is by changing at Caen for trains to Le Mans and Tours (ETT tables 270 and 271), both on the Paris–Bordeaux route *(see p. 73)*.

ROUEN

Your first stop in Rouen should be the **Cathédrale Notre-Dame**, the subject of a series of Monet's paintings. An example of his work showing the west front can be seen at the attractively restored **Musée des Beaux Arts**, PL. VERDREL.

The old city was considerably damaged during World War II but has been well restored. Wander from the cathedral down the main street, **r. du Gros Horloge**. Here a 16th-century gatehouse supports the *Gros Horloge* itself, a medieval clock with only one hand. At the end of the road, in PL. DU VIEUX MARCHÉ, a 20-m high memorial marks the spot where Joan of Arc was burned at the stake.

La Tour Jeanne d'Arc, R. DU DONJON, just south of the train station, is where Joan of Arc was imprisoned just before her execution. Entrance is free for students.

DAY TRIPS FROM ROUEN

Dieppe, reached in just over an hour by train (ETT table 269), is an attractive coastal town, with lofty white cliffs rising either side of the resort and bathing beach, and a flint and sandstone château perched up high. Down below in the harbour, a renowned Saturday market (PL. NATIONALE./ GRANDE RUE/R. ST JACQUES) draws people from afar.

You can hike along the coast in either direction on the long-distance path GR21, north to Le Tréport or south to Fécamp and Étrerat (guidebook on local paths from **Tourist Office**, PORT ANGO, ☎02 35 84 11 77). Budget accommodation includes **Au Retour de la Mer** (31 PL. LOUIS VITET, ☎02 35 84 04 81) and **Hôtel de** l'Union (47–49 R. DU HAUT-PAS, ☎02 35 84 35 52). **Youth hostel:** 48 R. LOUIS FROMAGER, ☎02 35 84 85 73 (2.5 km from rail station).

RAIL Rive-Droite (RD), 1 km north of the centre, but linked by buses. At the station you can get a day-pass providing unlimited travel on the city buses and the new métro. The quickest way to the centre is to take the métro from the station to the Théâtre Des Arts. From there, a short walk through the old city up r. Général and left up R. DES CARMES will lead you to the Tourist Office.

i **Tourist Office:** 25 PL. DE LA CATHÉDRALE, ☎02 32 08 32 40; fax: 02 32 08 32 44 (May–Sept: Mon–Sat 0900–1900, Sun 0930–1230 and 1430–1800. Oct–Apr: Mon–Sat 0900–1230 and 1400–1830, Sun 1000–1300).

There are many affordable hotels in town, most in the north, but there are also some in the old city. **Hotel des Carmes**, 33 PL. DES CARMES, ☎02 35 71 92 31, is situated in one of the liveliest squares. The **Hostellerie du Vieux Logis**, 5 R. DE JOYEUSE; ☎02 35 71 55 30, offers reasonably-priced rooms, and the attractive **Hotel Saint Ouen**, 43 R. DES FAULX; ☎02 35 71 46 44 provides a good central base. **Youth hostel:** 118 BLVD DE L'EUROPE, ☎02 35 72 06 45, 4 km from the station (bus no. 12: Diderot).

PARIS

See p. 53

Trains from Cherbourg/Rouen arrive at **Paris St Lazare**, while trains for the Strasbourg direction leave from Paris Est. Allow 1 hr to cross Paris via the Métro: line 3 east to **Opéra** (towards Gallieni), then change for line 7 towards La Courneuve.

NANCY

The capital of Lorraine is a stylish town, though surprisingly little known for its architectural treasures. Three squares, each World Heritage Sites, combine to make one of the greatest architectural set pieces in France: cream stone, ornate gateways and stately arches characterise the 18th-century **place Stanislas**, constructed by ex-King Stanislas Leszcynski of Poland, and with its entire south side taken up by the palatial **Hôtel de Ville** (town hall), behind which is the PL. D'ALLIANCE, and to the north, through the Arc de Triomphe, the 15th-century PL. DE LA CARRIÈRE.

In the early 1900s art nouveau made its mark on the city. You can pick up a walking leaflet from the Tourist Office, while the **Musée de l'École de Nancy**, 36 R. DU SERGENT BLANDAN (bus nos 6/16/26 to Painlevé) displays local examples of the style.

RAIL PL. THIERS; ☎08 36 35 35 35, a 10-min walk from the town centre along R. STANISLAS.

i **Tourist Office:** 14 PL. STANISLAS, ☎03 83 35 22 41 (June–Sept: Mon–Sat 0900–1900, Sun 1000–1700. Oct–May: Mon–Sat 0900–1800, Sun 1000–1300).

If you fancy staying in an official historic monument, **Grand Hôtel de la Reine**, 2 PL. STANISLAS, ☎03 83 35 03 01, fits the bill, but **Le Piroux**, 12 R. R-POINCARÉ, ☎03 83 32 01 10, a Logis de France, is far more affordable. The nearest (non-HI) **hostel** is **Centre d'Accueil de Remicourt**, 149 R. DE VANDOEUVRE, VILLERS, ☎03 83 27 73 67, 4 km west of town (bus no. 26 to Pôle Technologique). **Camping de Brabois,** ☎03 83 27 18 28, close to it (open Apr–Oct).

Try PL. STANISLAS and R. DES MARÉCHAUX for cheap and lively restaurants: don't forget to sample some *macarons* (almond biscuits), the town's speciality.

LUNÉVILLE

Lunéville's chief glory is its massive 18th-century **château,** built by duke Leopold of Lorraine in imitation of Versailles and graced with magnificent gardens. Other curiousities include the **Musée de la Motor et du Vélo**, opposite the château, with its entertaining array of more than 200 motorcycles, and the rococo church of **St-Jacques**, PL. ST-RÉMY, with its unique baroque organ with no visible pipes.

RAIL ☎08 36 35 35 35; a 15-min walk from the centre.

i **Tourist Office:** CHÂTEAU DE LUNÉVILLE, ☎03 83 74 06 55 (1000–1200, 1400–1800); closed Mon.

R. D'ALSACE is a good place to look for cheap hotels like **Hôtel du Commerce** at no. 93; ☎03 83 73 04 17. Or try **Hôtel de l'Europe**, at no. 53; ☎03 83 74 12 34.

STRASBOURG

The old capital of Alsace, which began life as a Celtic fishing village, has grown into a most attractive city, successfully combining old with new, business with tourism. It's best known today as the seat of the **European Parliament**, housed in an imposing new building on the edge of the city. Conspicuously photogenic is the **Petite-France** quarter, a former tanning and milling quarter, with its 16th- and 17th-century houses crowded around narrow alleys and streams. The river itself is spanned by the **Ponts Couverts**, a trio of covered bridges with square towers, remnants of 14th-century fortifications. Boat trips circling the island are operated by **Strasbourg Fluvial**; ☎03 88 84 13 13. Strasbourg also has a fleet of glossy new trams.

With its delicate 142 m spire the **Cathédrale de Notre-Dame** (colourfully floodlit July–Aug), built over three centuries, is a Gothic triumph, with its elaborately carved western façade. Highlights inside include the 13th-century **Pilier des Anges** (Angels' Pillar) and the astonishingly complicated-looking 19th-century **Horloge Astronomique** (Astronomical clock), which strikes noon at 1231 each day (but begins to swing into action at 1215). The tower, a 330-step climb, provides a good view all over the city.

PL. DE LA GARE: 10-min walk to the centre (which is on an island in the River Ill) straight along R. DU MAIRE KUSS or by tram (direction Illkirch); 08 36 35 35 35.

Tourist Office: 17 PL. DE LA CATHÉDRALE; 03 88 52 28 22, with a branch at PL. DE LA GARE; 03 88 32 51 49 (June–Sept: Mon–Sat 0900–1900. Oct–May: Mon–Sat 0900–1230 and 1345–1800). Hotel reservations service, FFr.10. The Tourist Offices sell a 3-day Strasbourg Pass (FFr.56), which covers admission to one museum, the cathedral tower, a cathedral concert, a boat trip and some half-price tours.

There's a good choice of hotels in every grade, including a clutch in the wide semi-circle of buildings around PL. DE LA GARE opposite the station. **Monopole-Metropole**, 16 R. KUHN, 03 88 14 39 14 (moderate) is also handy for it. Or you can stay close to the cathedral, notably at **Hôtel Cathédrale**, PL. DE LA CATHÉDRALE; 03 88 22 12 12 (moderate), which faces its ornate west facade; rooms at the back are cheaper. **Youth hostel: René Cassin**, 9 R. DE L'AUBERGE DE JEUNESSE, MONTAGNE VERTE; 03 88 30 26 46, 2 km from the station (bus nos 3/23: Auberge de Jeunesse). A budget choice is **Ciarus**, 7 R. FINKMATT; 03 88 15 27 88, a 15-min walk from the station (bus nos 10/20: PL. PIERRE).

There are plenty of wholesome restaurants along R. DU MAROQUIN (near the cathedral), R. DES TONNELIERS and in the *Petit France* quarter.

WHERE NEXT FROM STRASBOURG?

Continue east over the border into Germany, to Offenburg or Baden-Baden (table 910) on the Munich–Konstanz route (p. 256). You can also continue through Alsace to enter Switzerland at Basel (p. 287) on the Lausanne–Poschiavo route.

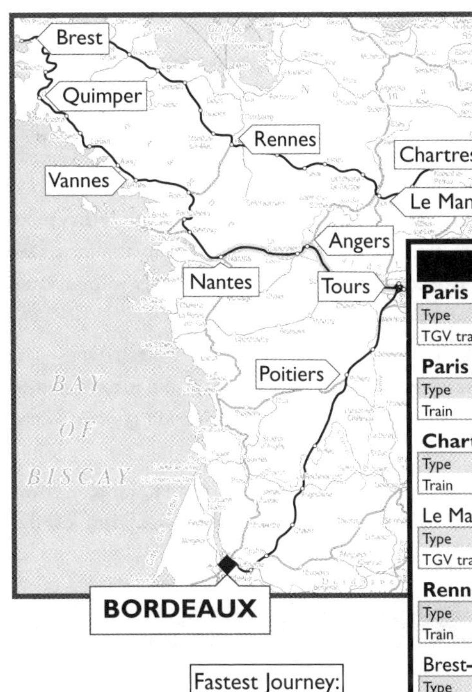

Fastest Journey: 2 hrs 57 mins

Notes
TGV trains require advance seat reservations and an additional supplement to be paid. More services are available between Vannes and Nantes by changing trains at Redon.

ROUTE DETAIL

Paris (Montparnasse)**–Bordeaux** ETT 300

Type	Frequency	Journey Time
TGV train	Every 1-2 hrs	3 hrs

Paris (Montparnasse)**–Chartres** ETT 276

Type	Frequency	Journey Time
Train	Every hr	1 hr 5 mins

Chartres–Le Mans ETT table 276

Type	Frequency	Journey Time
Train	10 daily	1 hr 25 mins

Le Mans**–Rennes** ETT table 280

Type	Frequency	Journey Time
TGV train	10 daily	1 hr 15 mins

Rennes–Brest ETT table 281

Type	Frequency	Journey Time
Train	12 daily	2 hrs 30 mins

Brest**–Quimper** ETT table 286

Type	Frequency	Journey Time
Train	7 daily	1 hr 10 mins

Quimper–Vannes ETT table 285

Type	Frequency	Journey Time
Train	11 daily	1 hr 15 mins

Vannes–Nantes ETT table 285

Type	Frequency	Journey Time
Train	6 daily	1 hr 20 mins

Nantes**–Angers** ETT table 289

Type	Frequency	Journey Time
Train	Every hr	50 mins

Angers–Tours ETT table 289

Type	Frequency	Journey Time
Train	9 daily	1 hr

Tours–Poitiers ETT table 300

Type	Frequency	Journey Time
Train	5 daily	1 hr 5 mins

Poitiers–Bordeaux ETT table 300

Type	Frequency	Journey Time
Train	Every 1-2 hrs	1 hr 46 mins

Paris – Tours – Bordeaux

Western France offers a heady mix of wine, brandy, cathedrals and rocky coastlines. Beyond **Chartres** you enter **Brittany** (*Bretagne*), where regional identity is still strong and in evidence in the Breton dialect (similar to Welsh), the cuisine (featuring crêpes in particular) and numerous summer festivals in which villagers don traditional costumes. The three peninsulas on Brittany's west coast make up Finistère (*Finis Terrae*, the end of the earth), buffeted by the gusts of the Atlantic, which has claimed many shipwrecks; however, the region also abounds in quaint fishing villages, prehistoric remains, resorts and superb beaches – only the fickle climate might dampen your enthusiasm for a sea-side holiday here. Just to the east, **Roscoff** is an attractive Channel port with services to **Plymouth** (England) and links by rail.

At **Nantes** the route joins the **Loire**, famous for its abundant châteaux and high-quality wines. Further south lies **Poitiers**. **Angoulême** stands at the eastern end of the cognac region, while Bordeaux is the capital of one of the world's greatest wine-producing areas.

It's also feasible to shorten the route by omitting the Loire and heading directly down from Nantes to Bordeaux via **La Rochelle**. This journey forms part of the **Paris–Seville** route (p. 33).

CHARTRES

Its spires visible for far around from the cornfields of the Beauce plain, and arguably the world's greatest example of the Gothic style, the **Cathédrale Notre-Dame** replaced an earlier building destroyed by fire in 1194. It's known especially for the quality and brilliance of its 13th-century stained glass, dazzling even on the dullest of days, and the wealth of carved stone, notably around the west doorways.

After the cathedral, the rest of Chartres seems somewhat insignificant, but it's an enjoyable enough place with winding streets and a pleasant riverside area by the **Eure**, which encompasses the old town and gives some choice views of the cathedral.

RAIL PL. PIERRE SERNARD. Walk up AV. J-DE-BEAUCE, cross the square and head towards the cathedral to reach the centre.

i **Tourist Office**: PL. DE LA CATHÉDRALE, ☎02 37 21 50 00; fax: 02 37 21 51 91 (Mon–Sat 0900–1900, Sun 0930–1730; May–Oct Mon–Sat 1000–1800, Sun 1000–1300, 1430–1630, Nov–Apr).

Chartres has a fine selection of hotels: try the lovely **Grand Monarch**, centrally located at 22 PL. DES EPARS, ☎02 27 21 00 72; or for a cheaper option, its neighbour the **Hotel de la Poste**, ☎02 37 21 04 27.

RENNES

Although a useful base for day and longer trips, the commercial and administrative capital of Brittany is not really a place to spend a lot of time in, except for the first week of July, when the **Festival des Tombées de la Nuit** (Festival of Nightfall) takes over the town, with theatre, music and people dressed in medieval costume to celebrate Breton culture. Following a huge fire in 1720, Rennes was rebuilt mostly in reddish granite, though some pretty half-timbering survives.

The 17th-century **Palais de Justice** was one of the few major structures to survive the first fire, but was less lucky when another fire broke out in Feb 1994 and is currently being restored. The nearby 18th-century **Hôtel de Ville** (Town Hall), PL. DE LA MAIRIE, contains some fine Flemish tapestries. The **Musée de Bretagne**, 20 QUAI EMILE-ZOLA, gives an excellent background to Brittany, while the **Musée des Beaux Arts** (above it) houses a collection of French art from the 14th century onwards.

RAIL About 15 mins' walk south-east of the centre (nos.1/20/21/22).

i **Tourist Office**: PONT DE NEMOURS, 02 99 79 01 98; fax: 02 99 79 31 38 (Mon–Sat 0900–1900, Sun 1000–1200 and 1500–1700, June–Sept; Tues–Sat 0900–1230, 1400–1830 Oct–May).

The best place to find hotels is in the area of the station. The only 4-star establishment in town is **Hôtel Lecoq-Gadby**, 156 R. D'ANTRAIN, 02 99 38 05 55. **Central**, 6 R. LANJUINAIS, 02 99 79

DAY TRIPS FROM RENNES

There are regular buses linking Rennes to many other Breton towns. The new long-distance bus station is at BLVD SOLFÉRINO (east of the station), 02 99 30 87 80. Trains run from Rennes to St-Malo (every 1–2 hrs, journey time 1 hr) and then on to Dol, where you should change for **Dinan**.

The romantically named **Côte d'Emeraude** (Emerald Coast) and **Côte de Granit Rose** (Coast of Pink Granite) are fringed with rugged cliffs and unspoilt sandy beaches, interspersed with sheltered fishing ports, many doubling as resorts.

St Malo, beautifully poised at the mouth of the rock-girt Rance estuary and endowed with a fine white sand beach, has been carefully restored since wartime destruction and makes a good base for exploring the coastline by bus; a ferry connects the town with **Dinard**, an appealing resort of turreted villas and with a superb beach.

East of St Malo, the astonishing fortified monastery of **Le Mont St-Michel** perches on a craggy island joined to the mainland by a causeway at low tide; unfortunately, the place gets hideously over-run in high season. Visits to the abbey are only possible by guided tour (some are in English during the summer). The nearest rail station is at **Pontorson**, 9 km away, from which several buses a day run to Le Mont St-Michel; there are also buses from St Malo.

A little way inland, **Dol-de-Bretagne** was built mainly in the 13th century and, although now little more than a village, it has a fine cathedral and streets of tottering medieval arcaded timber-framed houses.

At **Champ-dolent** is one of the finest *menhirs* (prehistoric standing stones) on the north coast, standing 9 m high. Not far away is **Dinan**, with a feudal castle, Romanesque church and cobbled streets of well-preserved 15th-century houses.

DAY TRIPS FROM QUIMPER

Douarnenez (45 mins north-west by SNCF bus) is a working fishing port with plenty of activity to watch on the harbour and quays. The outstanding sight is **Le Port-Musée**, where you can explore a variety of vessels and watch demonstrations of such nautical skills as boat-building and rope-making.

The **Crozon** peninsula, further north, is also reachable by bus. At the tip of the peninsula (forming part of the **Parc Naturel Régional d'Armorique**), **Camaret** is a small resort and lobster fishing port with plentiful fish restaurants; a long sea wall leads to a huge 17th-century tower built by the military architect Vauban.

Boat trips down-river lead to Benodet, a popular small resort from where you can continue by boat to the **Îles de Glénan** (the path round the isle of St Nicolas makes a pleasant walk) – or to **Concarneau**, a busy fishing port with a remarkable medieval *Ville Close* (walled island town), linked to the mainland by two bridges.

12 36, is pleasant and moderately priced, occupying a renovated 19th-century building. **Hôtel d'Angleterre**, 19 R. MARÉCHAL, ☎02 99 79 38 61, is cheap and close to the station. **Youth hostel**: 10–12 CANAL ST-MARTIN, ☎ 02 99 33 22 33, 3 km out of town (🚌nos.20/22: **ST MALO** – no.2 at weekends). **Campsite**: R. DU PROFESSEUR M-AUDIN. COËTLOGON ☎02 99 36 91 22 (🚌no.3), open Apr–Sept.

Two of the prettiest streets in Rennes, ST GEORGES and R. ST MICHEL, are packed with attractive restaurants of a wide variety of cultures. Try the **Palais Gourmand**, which offers open-fire cooking at a reasonable price.

QUIMPER

Brittany's oldest town makes a very attractive base for exploring southern Finistère. The Gothic **Cathédrale St-Corentin** features a strangely off-centre nave. Close by are the well-presented collections of **Musée Breton** and the outstanding **Musée des Beaux-Arts**, which captures the spirit of Brittany on canvas and includes many examples of Quimper's most famous product – faïence porcelain; the factories that make it can be toured.

RAIL East of town, 15 mins' walk to the cathedral (on the north bank): turn right along AV. DE LA GARE, then left to follow the River Odet. The Tourist Office is a bit further along, on the south bank.

i **Tourist Office**: PL. DE LA RÉSISTANCE, ☎02 98 53 04 05; fax: 02 98 53 31 33 (Mon–Sat 0900–1700, Sun 1000–1300, 1500–1800, May–Sept; Mon–Fri 0900–1200, 1330–1800, Oct–Apr).

VANNES

Situated at the top of the **Gulf of Morbihan** – an inland sea strewn with some 300 islands and dotted with yachts – **Vannes** makes a handy base for exploring south-eastern Brittany, with cruises and ferries departing from the port. At the heart of the walled town, near the imposing **Cathédrale de St-Pierre**, the ancient market of **La Cohue** has been restored to form the excellent **Musée de Vannes**, with the old court-house upstairs converted to combine art galleries with exhibits about the Gulf.

Behind the cathedral, at **Porte Prison**, you can climb a short stretch of the old ramparts, giving a view of the long roof of the former wash-house.

RAIL A good 25 mins' walk north of the centre: turn right on AV. FAVREL and left along AV. VICTOR HUGO. Bear right for the Tourist Office, or ahead (on R. BILLAULT) for the centre.

i **Tourist Office**: 1 R. THIERS, ☎02 97 47 24 34; fax: 02 97 47 29 49 (Mon–Sat 0900–1200 and 1400–1800, Sept–June; Mon–Sat 0900–1900, Sun 1000–1200, July–Aug).

ANGERS

Former capital of the Counts of Anjou (the Plantagenet ancestors of the British royal family), this attractive town stands in one of France's major wine-producing areas, and in a land of black schist and slate quarries. It is dominated by the massive stone walls of the 13th-century **Château d'Angers**, the 17 towers of which stand to only half of their original height, while the moat has been converted into formal gardens. Inside is the great series of 14th-century tapestries depicting in astonishing graphic detail the *Apocalypse of St John*.

Across the river, the **Hôpital St-Jean** contains another spectacular tapestry, the 20th-century *Chant du Monde* (inspired by the *Apocalypse*) by Jean Lurçat. The **Cathédrale de St-Maurice** has a medieval façade and Gothic vaulting over an unusually wide nave, lighted by stained glass dating from several different eras.

DAY TRIPS FROM VANNES

Carnac (south-west of Vannes and reachable by bus) is a major resort, with numerous campsites and caravan parks and a long beach that is packed in summer. In the area are some 5000 *menhirs*. The most famous formation is the **Alignements du Ménec**, probably dating from the 3rd century BC and consisting of over 1000 megaliths stretching for more than 1 km. If you have the money, take a helicopter trip over them: sadly they are now fenced off because of the sheer numbers of visitors. There's an informative prehistory museum, explaining how these mysterious structures were erected, and displaying turqouise necklaces and other finds. Several companies offer **boat tours** around the coast and islands, but to explore properly it's better to use the regular ferries – you can reach the various departure points by bus. **Belle-Île** is the largest of the islands and offers everything from fortifications, a citadel and wonderful scenery to beaches, good walking and picturesque villages. Another of Brittany's great ancient sites is the **Île de Gavrinis**, reached by taking a tour from **Larmor-Baden** (south-west of Vannes). The island consists largely of megalithic remains, which are definitely linked to the standing stones at the nearby village of **Locmariaquer**, on the south-west tip of the gulf.

DAY TRIPS FROM ANGERS

Infrequent trains run from Angers (taking 20–25 mins; ETT table 289) to the town of **Saumur**, with its famous cavalry riding school (the ***Cadre Noir***, which mounted a heroic defence of the town in 1940, though greatly outnumbered by the Germans) and a château containing the town museums. The château has a fascinating history: it housed the dungeons of the Plantagenets, was a fortress for Louis VIII, and then a country residence for the Dukes of Anjou.
There are 3–4 English guided tours daily.

Day Trips from Angers cont'd.

Vineyards and mushroom caves surround the town. Like Saumur, the châteaux of the 225-mile long Loire Valley were mostly medieval fortresses converted into luxurious country residences by 16th-century nobles. Trains run along the valley at irregular intervals and connecting buses go to many of the châteaux, but you need a car or bicycle to explore it fully. The most accessible châteaux are along the **Saumur–Tours** line. **Villandry** is famous for its magnificent terraced gardens, which decoratively mix vegetables and flowers in formal box-hedged beds. The fortress-like **Langeais** and the more graceful **Montsoreau** and **Montreuil-Bellay** can be reached by SNCF bus from Saumur. For some serious sampling of the renowned white wine of Anjou, visit **Maison du Vin de l'Anjou**, 5 BIS PL. KENNEDY, in Angers, for details of caves open to visitors, before heading off to the villages of **Savennières** and **La Poissonière**, where some of the best is produced. Both are accessible by local train from **Angers** to **Nantes**. Providing the perfect location for exploration of Angers, the moderate **Malvoisine**, bookable through **B&B France** (p. 51), is an elegantly converted stable block, with comfortable rooms and gourmet cuisine (bike hire nearby; station pick-up service).

TOURS

Founded by the Romans on the banks of the Loire, Tours had, by the 8th century, become an important cultural centre and place of pilgrimage. Home to one of the oldest and most influential universities in France, the city also thrived during the 15th and 16th centuries when the French court and nobility streamed into the region. Today, it is the largest city on the Loire, and much has been sensitively restored after serious damage during World War II.

The city's two main sights stand next to each other, just off R. JULES SIMON. The elaborately ornate **Cathédrale de St-Gatien** dates from the 12th to 16th centuries, with Romanesque, Gothic and Renaissance styles. There's some wonderful 13th-century stained glass, while the **Cloître de la Psalette,** to one side, has 15th- and 16th-century frescos. Next door, in the 18th-century Episcopal Palace, is the **Musée des Beaux-Arts**, with a wide-ranging art collection, including works by Rembrandt, Delacroix and Degas, as well as reconstructed 18th-century rooms.

In the evening, head for the heart of the old town, around the PL. PLUMEREAU, which offers an excellent selection of cheap–moderate restaurants. Also try PL. FLOIRE-LE-ROI on the south bank, which is a maze of narrow streets, mostly pedestrianised, and half-timbered houses, many of which have been carefully restored and turned into boutiques.

RAIL ☎02 47 20 50 50. Near the *Mairie* in the city centre.

i **Tourist Office**: 78–82 R. BERNARD PALISSY (opposite the train station), ☎02 47 70 37 37; fax: 02 47 61 14 22.

Many visitors prefer to stay in the small villages and towns around Tours. However, you can find a reasonable range of cheap hotels in the area around the station and the old town, near the river. There is a **youth hostel** at PARC DE GRANDMONT, ☎02 47 25 14 45, 4 km from the station.

WHERE NEXT FROM TOURS?

There are train services to ***Caen*** *(3 hrs; ETT table 271) on the* ***Cherbourg–Strasbourg*** *route,* *(p. 67)**.*

POITIERS

As one of the earliest Christian centres in France, Poitiers today boasts an impressive array of churches (though for many visitors it is just the nearest place to **Futuroscope** see sidebar). The oldest, first built in 356, is the **Baptistère de Saint-Jean**, R. JEAN-JAURÈS. Almost next door is the 12th–13th-century **Cathédrale de Saint-Pierre**, R. DE LA CATHÉDRALE. Squat from the outside, inside the nave soars high, crowned by some lovely 13th-century stained glass and choir stalls. Behind the cathedral is the **Église de Ste-Radegonde**, R. DE LA MAUVINIÈRE, first built in the 6th century with fine Romanesque and Gothic additions and alterations. With its highly decorated façade, **Notre-Dame-la-Grande** is reckoned to be the finest example of Poitevin Romanesque. Outstanding among the secular buildings is the 13th-century **Salle des Pas Perdus** within the **Palais de Justice**.

DAY TRIPS FROM TOURS

Right in the centre of the most château-laden part of France, Tours is an excellent place from which to explore (with plenty of chartered bus excursions on offer) the adjoining valleys of the Loire, **Loir**, **Cher** and **Indre**, all strewn with such famous castles as **Amboise, Azay-le-Rideau, Chambord, Chenonceaux, Chinon, Langeais, Loches** and **Villandry**. Most are some distance apart, as well as from the city; a car, moped or bicycle will be useful.

DAY TRIPS FROM POITIERS

Futuroscope is a massive theme park 7 km north of the city. Dedicated to the moving image and presented in an amazing series of pavilions – one with a façade of cascading water, another like a giant rock crystal and another resembling organ pipes – it's very expensive (FFr. 140–185, depending on season), with more than anyone could see in a day. The range of cinematic experiences include a 3D projection of a kelp forest that will have you reaching out for the fish as they swim towards you, a stomach-churning car chase through the Vienne as you're strapped in a chair that swerves and jolts in exact time to the movie, and a 'magic carpet' where you apparently fly over forests and cities projected beneath your feet. Every Sat (Apr–Oct) and every evening (July–end Aug), the spectacular sound and light show, the *Water Symphony*, has water jets synchronised with music, images projected onto walls of water, laser and fireworks. There are reduced-rate taxis (FFr. 45 return; hourly or half-hourly) just outside Poiters station, or buses from the town centre.

In the forest of **hotels** around Futuroscope are several offering budget rates from Ffr. 135 (booking agency ☎05 49 49 20 80; fax 05 49 49 30 25; http://www.futuroscope.com).

Poitiers also has a train service to the historic port of **La Rochelle** (ETT table 300), popular with the yachting set; it's an elegant place with gracious old squares, a fine old town hall, arcaded Renaissance houses and a good choice of fish restaurants. Two medieval towers preside over the harbour entrance.

RAIL ☎05 49 58 50 50. About 15 mins' walk from the centre: up a hill and a flight of stairs.

Tourist Offices: 8 R. GRANDES ÉCOLES, ☎05 49 41 21 24, fax: 05 49 88 65 84, and 15 R. CARNOT, ☎49 41 58 22: July–Aug daily 0900–1900; Sept–June Mon–Fri 0900–1200, 1330–1800, Sat 0900–1200, 1400–1800.

Some of the best-value places are south of PL. DE MARÉCHAL.

There are some good-value traditional restaurants around PL. DE MARÉCHAL, LECLERC and R. CARNOT. Poitiers is at the heart of a region noted for the best goats' cheeses in France.

BORDEAUX

Set on the **Garonne** River just before it joins the **Dordogne** and **Gironde** to travel out to sea, **Bordeaux** is the sixth largest port in France, a busy, working city with an 18th-century centre of monumental splendour surrounded by abundant industrial gloom. But primarily the city is the commercial heart of one of the world's greatest wine-growing areas, surrounded by the vineyards of **Graves**, **Médoc**, **Sauternes** and other great names.

To see the best of the city's historic buildings, walk from the Esplanade down the COURS DU 30 JUILLET to the PL. DE LA COMÉDIE, on which stands the majestic neo classical **Grand Théâtre**, stopping off en route at the **Maison de Vin**, 1 COURS DU 30 JUILLET, ☎05 56 52 82 82, to arrange a wine tour and tasting. Take a boat tour on the *Embarcadère Vedettes*, which leave frequently from the ESPLANADE DE QUINCONCES.

From the PL. DE LA COMÉDIE, the COURS DU CHAPEAU ROUGE leads to the PL. DE LA BOURSE, a pleasant square on which stand the **Musée Maritime**, housed in the 18th-century **Customs House**, and the elegant **Hôtel de la Bourse**. Just to the south of this begins the quartier **Saint-Pierre**, the bustling old town filled with small boutiques and cafés.

About 1 km from here, along R. DES TROIS-CANILS, you come to the city's richest gathering of fine buildings and museums, including the 11th–15th-century **Cathédrale de St-André** and the superb 18th-century **Hôtel de Ville** (both on PL. ROHAN), the **Musée des Beaux-Arts**, R. MONTBAZON (nicely varied collection), and the **Musée des Arts Decoratifs**, R. BOUFFARD (furniture, silver, pottery etc.).

Other museums include the archaeological **Musée d'Aquitaine**, COURS VICTOR HUGO/COURS PASTEUR, and the **Musée d'Histoire Naturelle**, tucked into the south-west corner of the grand **Jardin Public**, R. DUPLESSEY.

Most of the greatest sights of interest are within 1 square km, so you should be able to get around on foot.

St Jean, ☎05 36 35 35 35. About 2 km from the south of the centre; you can walk it in about 30 mins, or there are numerous buses. Two other stations, the **Gare St Louis** and the **Gare d'Orléans**, serve local trains.

Bus Tickets

There is also a good bus network and you can buy a one- or three-day pass, the **Carte Bordeaux Découverte**, from the station or Tourist Office.

Bordeaux-Mérignac, 12 km from the city, ☎05 56 34 50 50.

Tourist Office: 12 COURS DU 30 JUILLET, ☎05 56 00 66 00; fax: 05 56 00 66 01; e-mail: otb@mairie-bordeauxfrance. Summer: daily 0900–1900; winter: 0900–1800 with an annexe at the station Mon–Fri 0900–1900.
Thomas Cook bureau de change: **Gare St Jean,** PARVIS LOUIS ARMAND.

The city has a wide range of accommodation, suitable for all pockets. As this is a port, many of the cheapest hotels, scattered around the grimy docks and the red-light district around the railway station, can be rather basic. However, cheap and functional accommodation can be found in a safer area of the city in R. HUGUERIE, near the PL. DE TOURNY. There is a **youth hostel (**the **Foyer des Jeunes)** at 22 COURS BARBEY, ☎05 56 91 59 51, just under 1 km from the St Jean station.

Day Trips from Bordeaux

Probably the main reason for coming to Bordeaux is to visit the great wineries spread out through the surrounding countryside. There are bus tours (ask at the Tourist Office), but also a local rail line to **Pointe-de-Grave** (ETT table 293), whose stations include such redolent names as **Château Margaux** and ***Pauillac*** (for **Château Mouton-Rothschild** and **Château Lafitte**).
There are also services to **La Rochelle** (ETT table 291; takes 1 hr 30 mins; see Where Next From Poitiers, p. 79).

WHERE NEXT FROM BORDEAUX?

*Carry on to **Biarritz** to join the **Biarritz–Marseille** route (p. 90).*
*Alternatively carry on south over the Spanish border to **Seville** (p. 181).*

PARIS – LYON – AVIGNON

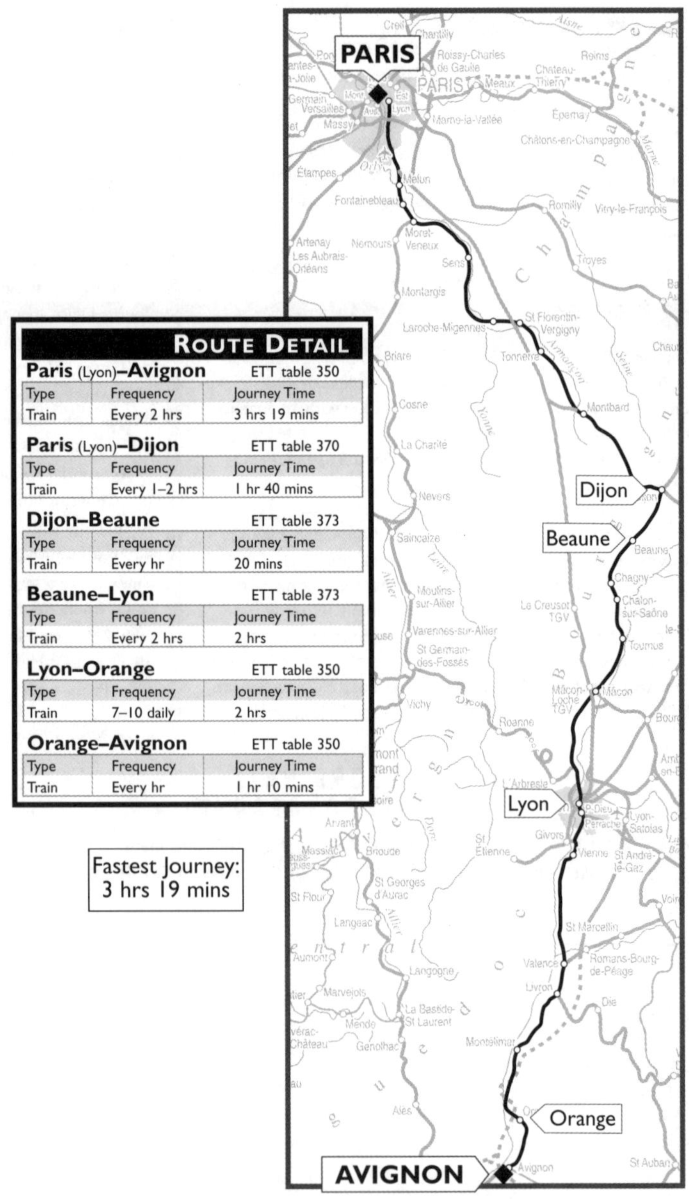

ROUTE DETAIL

Paris (Lyon)**–Avignon** ETT table 350

Type	Frequency	Journey Time
Train	Every 2 hrs	3 hrs 19 mins

Paris (Lyon)**–Dijon** ETT table 370

Type	Frequency	Journey Time
Train	Every 1–2 hrs	1 hr 40 mins

Dijon–Beaune ETT table 373

Type	Frequency	Journey Time
Train	Every hr	20 mins

Beaune–Lyon ETT table 373

Type	Frequency	Journey Time
Train	Every 2 hrs	2 hrs

Lyon–Orange ETT table 350

Type	Frequency	Journey Time
Train	7–10 daily	2 hrs

Orange–Avignon ETT table 350

Type	Frequency	Journey Time
Train	Every hr	1 hr 10 mins

Fastest Journey:
3 hrs 19 mins

The prime interest of this trip is in its southern sections. Paris to Dijon passes uneventfully, though **Dijon**, at the heart of the wine region of **Bourgogne** (Burgundy) is appealing enough for a break of journey. Further south is the captivating town of Beaune. **Lyon**, France's third largest city after Paris and Marseille, is not really a tourist venue, but has a surprising Renaissance quarter and some evocative Roman remains. Meanwhile, the main route continues into Provence, unmistakably southern in character, and harbouring the great Roman remains at **Orange** and the lively, arty city of **Avignon**.

PARIS

See p. 53.

MUSTARD AND CASSIS

In addition to the wines of Burgundy two products spring to mind when Dijon is mentioned: mustard and cassis. The latter is the sweet blackcurrant liqueur that's often mixed with dry white wine to make *kir*, a cocktail named after a French resistance leader whose favourite tipple it was. It's a great way to make a very ordinary bottle of cheap white extremely palatable.

DIJON

Dijon's partly pedestrianised city centre is dotted with attractive squares and 15th and 16th century architecture. A suggested walking tour, which covers all the main sites and takes around 2 hours, is available from the Tourist Office. The highlight is undoubtedly the **Palais des Ducs et des Etats de Bourgogne** which is best viewed from the **place de la Liberation**. Formerly the residence of the Governors of Burgundy, this impressive palace now houses the Musée des Beaux Arts and the town hall. Many of Dijon's museums are free to students and FFr.30 buys a pass giving admission to all of them, available from the Tourist Office or the first museum visited.

The 18th century Gothic **Eglise de Notre Dame**, in R. DE LA CHOUETTE, is celebrated for the three tiers of arches adorning the façade. Numerous gargoyles add to the effect although these were made in 1881 by the sculptor Lagoule who apparently gave his imagination a free reign in their design. There are many attractive half timbered houses in **r. Verrerie** as well as shops selling traditional goods and souvenirs. At the end of R. DE LA LIBERTÉ, one of Dijon's liveliest streets, stands **la Porte Guillaume**, a mini Arc de Triomphe dedicated to Guilluame de Volpiano who founded the abbey of Saint Benigne in the 6th century.

There are lots of lively pizzerias and foreign restaurants around PL. EMILE ZOLA. Around PL. BOSSUET and R. MONGE there are lots of restaurants with outside tables. For more traditional Bourguignon fare try R. MUSETTE or R. DES FORGES.

RAIL Ville, 5 mins west of the centre. The station is at the end of AV. MARÉCHAL-FOCH, which leads to PL. DARCY and the start of the old town.

Tourist Offices: PL. DARCY, ☎03 80 44 11 44. (May–mid Oct: daily 0900–2100; rest of the year: 0900–1300, 1400–1900). At 34 R. DES FORGES, ☎03 80 44 11 44 (Mon–Sat 0900–1200, 1300–1800, closed Sat off-season). Room-finding service FFr.15.

The lowest-priced hotels (mainly 2-star) tend to be in the old town; try R. MONGE. The 4-star **Hostellerie du Chapeau Rouge**, 5 RUE MICHELET, ☎03 80 30 28 10, has old-style graciousness. Moderately priced **Hostellerie 'Le Sauvage'**, 64 RUE MONGE, ☎0380 41 31 21, was once a staging inn. The very central **Hôtel de la Poste** 5 RUE DE CHÂTEAU, ☎03 80 30 51 64 is decorated in a 1930s art deco style. Situated on a lively pedestrian street it is cheap with spacious rooms. **HI: Centre de Rencontres Internationales**, 1 BLVD CHAMPOLLION, ☎ 03 80 72 95 20, 4 km from the centre (bus no. 5: Epirey from PLACE DE LA REPUBLIQUE or night bus no. A). Students could try **Foyer International des Etudiants**, 4-6 R. MARÉCHAL LECLERC, ☎03 80 71 70 00 (bus no. 4: Billardon). **Campsite: Camping du Lac**, 3 BLVD KIR, ☎03 80 43 54 72. By a lake about 1 km from Ville (bus nos. 12/18; no.12 stops closest to the site).

WHERE NEXT FROM DIJON?

4 trains a day run to Nancy (taking 2 hrs 40 mins; ETT table 378), to join the Cherbourg–Strasbourg route (p. 67).

BEAUNE

Beaune is a charming old town of cobbled streets and fine mansions. The magnificent **Hôtel-Dieu**, R. DE L'HÔTEL-DIEU, was originally built in the 15th century as a hospital for the sick and needy. Don't miss its multi-coloured glazed roofs or the 15th-century *Polyptych of the Last Judgement*, showing sinners tumbling to an unpleasant fate. This is also the centre of the Côtes de Beaune vineyards, some of the finest in Burgundy; the Tourist Office lists local caves that offer tastings (*dégustations*). The old ducal palace houses a museum dedicated to the subject; **Musée du Vin**, RUE D'ENFER.

RAIL East of town, just outside the old walls. For the Tourist Office, follow AV. DU 8 SEPTEMBRE/R. DU CHÂTEAU, take the first left onto REMPART ST JEAN/REMPART MADELAINE and right onto R. DE L'HÔTEL-DIEU (15 mins).

Tourist Office: R. DE L'HÔTEL-DIEU, ☎03 80 26 21 30 (May–Sept: Mon–Sat 0900–2000, Sun 0900–1900; Oct–Apr: Sun–Thur 0900–1800, Fri–Sat 0900–1900).

LYON

This big metropolis (population 1.5 million) at the junction of the Saône and the Rhône is not the most conspicuously charming of French cities, but does have merits including its superb gastronomy and thriving nightlife.

The two rivers divide the city into thirds. On the west bank of the Saône is **Vieux Lyon** (Old Lyon), while on the east bank of the Rhône is the business centre, the **Part-Dieu** rail station and high-rise offices and apartment blocks. In between is the partly-pedestrianised centre, running from PL. BELLECOUR to the old silk quarter of **La Croix-Rousse**. Lyon is relatively safe though some care is needed around Perrache station at night.

Lyon is famous for its *traboules* – covered passageways which link streets together and which once served as shortcuts for the silk traders. Most of the traboules are in the preserved Renaissance quarter of Vieux Lyon.

To see Lyon on foot, start at the Tourist Office in PL. BELLECOUR and head north. PL. DES TERREAUX has Lyon's best museum – the **Musée des Beaux Arts** (closed Mon, Tues). South of PL. BELLECOUR is the **Musée des Tissus** (closed Mon), 34 R. DE LA CHARITÉ, a monument to Lyon's textile history, especially silk in the 18th century. Old silk looms are still in use at **Maison des Canuts**, 10–12 R. D'IVRY, (closed Sun). Just across Pont Gallíeni from the station is the poignant **Centre d'Histoire de la Résistance et de la Déportation**, 14 AV. BERTHELOT (closed Mon, Tues).

Julius Caesar was responsible for developing the Roman town of Lugdunum, centred on the hillside of Fourvière above the old town, reached by funicular from near the cathedral. Crowning the hill, from which there are spectacular views of the city, is the **Basilique Notre Dame de Fourvière**, built in the 19th century by the people of Lyon after they had been saved from invasion. The **Musée Gallo-Romain**, 17 R. CLÉBERG (closed Mon, Tues), has mosaics, coins and swords, but the main sight hereabouts is the neighbouring **Théâtre Romain**, 8 R. DE L'ANTIQUAILLE, the oldest Roman amphitheatre in France (open 0700 to dusk, free).

RAIL There are two mainline stations; many trains stop at both. **Lyon-Perrache** is the more central. It provides left luggage facilities, 0530–2030, showers, money exchange offices, a

DAY TRIPS FROM LYON

Pérouges, 35 km east of Lyon, is a charming medieval hill town with narrow cobbled streets lined with 15th-century houses. In the centre of the main square is the Tree of Liberty, planted in 1792 to commemorate the Revolution. (Approx. 15 trains a day, fewer at weekends, taking 40 mins; trains stop at Meximieux-Pérouges, about 2 km from the town; to reach Pérouges, turn left, take the first right after the Gendarmerie and then the right turn opposite the roadside Madonna.) At **Le Puy-en-Velay**, the free leaflet *Historical Visits* outlines two interesting walking routes that pass all the historic sites. Traditional lace-making is still a local industry. Steep climbs make Le Puy hard work to explore. On **Rocher Corneille** (Crow Rock) is a memorably ugly 19th-century red statue of Notre-Dame-de-France (Our Lady of France), a colossal figure fashioned from cannons used during the battle of Sebastopol –18 people can fit inside the chest.

Cathédrale Notre-Dame-de-France is best approached from R. DES

Day Trips from Lyon cont'd.

TABLES, from where 134 steps lead up to the massive arched entrance. The building itself is a major attraction, a vast place notable for its stripes of black and white volcanic rock, mosaics, lovely cloister and carved grand entrance. The most famous feature is a statue modelled from dark cedar that is known as the Black Madonna. Set on the high altar, this is a 19th-century copy of a figure that was reputedly brought back from the Crusades. The cathedral was a major pilgrimage stop in medieval times.

restaurant and bar as well as SOS Voyageurs – an information and practical assistance service for passengers (04 78 37 03 31), open Mon–Fri 0800–2000, Sat 0900–1300, Sun 1530–1930. For the town centre cross PL. CARNOT, then follow R. VICTOR HUGO to PL. BELLECOUR (15 mins). **Lyon-Part-Dieu** is on the east bank of the Rhône and serves the business district. It has similar facilities to Perrache, including **SOS Voyageurs** (Mon–Sat 0800–2000, Sun 0900–2000, 04 72 34 12 16).

Tourist Office: PL. BELLECOUR, 69000, 04 72 77 69 69; Métro: BELLECOUR (summer: Mon–Fri 0900–1800, Sat 0900–1800; winter: Mon–Fri 0900–1800, Sat 0900–1800. Additional branches at PL. ST JEAN, AV. ADOLPHE MAX (Métro: VIEUX-LYON; Mon–Sat 1000–1900), and at Villeurbanne, 3 AV. ARISTIDE BRIAND (Métro: GRATTE-CIEL; Mon–Fri 0900–1800, Sat –1700). **Youth information: Centre Régional d'Information Jeunesse**: 9 QUAI DES CÉLESTINS, 04 72 77 00 66. Open Mon 1200–1900, Tues–Fri 1100–1900, Sat (Sept–June) 1000–1700.

Aéroport Lyon-Satolas: 32 KM EAST OF LYON, 04 72 22 72 21. Buses every 20 mins between the airport and Perrache rail station (via Part-Dieu rail station), FFr.50; takes 45 mins; 0600–2300 (Satolas-Lyon), 0500–2100 (Lyon-Satolas).

There is a huge choice of hotels in every category and finding a room should not be difficult even at the height of summer. Try around the stations or near PL. DES TERREAUX (Métro: HÔTEL DE VILLE) **Grand Hotel des Terreaux** 16 RUE LANTERNE; 04 78 27 04 10 (moderate) is ideally placed with spacious rooms. **HI youth hostels**: 41-45 MONTÉE DE CHEMIN NEUF; 04 78 42 21 88, is more central and attractively situated above Vieux Lyon (no. 31 from Perrache, 28 from Part Dieu or funicular to Minimes); 51 RUE ROGER SALENGRO, 04 78 76 39 23 (no. 35 from R. DE LA CHARTÉ off Bellecour and get off at Auberge de Jeunese. **Camping: Dardilly**, MUNICIPAL SITE, PORTE LYON; 04 78 35 64 55. 10km from city centre, no. 3 from the Hôtel de Ville, direction Ecully-Dardilly to Parc d'Affaires.

Lyon is renowned for its cuisine and boasts some of the best restaurants in France serving fantastic food with prices to match. The most traditional restaurants are bouchons, mainly found in *Les Terreaux* and *Vieux Lyon* (head for R. ST JEAN, R. DU BOEUF and PL. DE LA BALEINE), where simple meals are served.

PUBLIC TRANSPORT IN LYON

Buses, funiculars and subway trains (Métros) are run by **TCL** (*Transports en commun lyonnais*), 04 78 71 70 00. Get the map (*plan de réseau*) from the Tourist Office or any TCL branch. The Métro is modern, clean and safe. There are four lines, A, B, C and D which criss-cross the city. It operates 0500–2400. *Funiculaires* (funicular trains) depart every 10 mins from Vieux Lyon metro station to the Roman theatre at St-Just and the Fourvière Esplanade high above the city. Buses cover every corner of Lyon, generally 0500–2200, but check individual services.

The name dates from the time when inn keepers used to a hang a handful of straw outside so that travellers knew they could eat and drink there while their horses were being rubbed down *(bouchonner)*. Lyon has many specialities: *tablier de sapeur* are slices of tripe fried in breadcrumbs; *melettes* or *frivolités*, lambs testicles cooked in white wine or lemon; *andouillette*, sausages cooked in white wine; and *quenelles de brochet*, souffles made with egg and cheese. It is possible to eat cheaply, although not always very typically. Lyon has some wonderful street **markets**. There are food markets every day except Mon at **Les Halles** and **La Croix Rousse**. On Sun mornings there are a number of interesting markets in Vieux Lyon: the **Marché de la Création** (artists), **Quai Romain Roland**, crafts, **Quai Fulchiron** and the *bouquinistes* market (books) at QUAI DE LA PECHERIE.

NIGHT-TIME IN LYON

The weekly *Lyon Poche* lists the week's events. Lyon is a student city, so clubs and discos abound. The best areas are near the Hôtel de Ville and quai Pierre Scize in Vieux Lyon. Entry including first drink costs up to FFr.100 at weekends. The 1200-seat Lyon Opera House soars up to 18 different seating levels and the company is now one of Europe's finest; 9 QUAI JEAN MOULIN. The roof glows red as it fills up with people. Lyon was birthplace of Guignol, the original 'Mr Punch'. The Guignol de Lyon theatre, 2 R. LOUIS CARRAND in the old town, ☎04 78 28 92 57, puts on shows for kids and adults alike.

WHERE NEXT FROM LYON?

Lyon is handily placed for exploring the Alps by rail. For a superb route into Switzerland, either to Geneva (p. 303) or to Martigny, go via Culoz, Aix-les Bains, Annecy and La Roche sur Foron, where you can either continue to Geneva or take the route via Chamonix-Mont Blanc to Martigny. There's also a (less interesting) direct line from Lyon to Geneva (ETT table 372; takes 2 hrs).

Culoz is a gateway for the Marais de Lavours, a national park noted for its marshland habitats, while beyond the well-heeled lakeside spa of **Aix-les-Bains** (where excursion boats cross Lac du Bourget to the mystical monastery of L'Abbaye d'Hautecombe) is **Annecy**, an outstanding lakeside resort in the heart of the Savoie Alps. Continuing onto Martigny, you switch to a metre-gauge line and climb steadily up into the mountains, with the option of taking the **Tramway du Mont Blanc** from St-Gervais-le-Fayet to the Nid d'Aigle (2372m – from which it's a 15-min stroll to the Bionnassay Glacier). Chamonix is placed beneath snow-capped Mt Blanc, the highest peak in the Alps; the Montenvers rack railway climbs 5 km to a height of 1913 m, looking over the Mer de Glace, Europe's biggest glacier.

A great way of venturing into Italy is by travelling to Turin via Chambéry, Modane and through the 12.8-km **Fréjus tunnel** (or the Mon Cenis Tunnel to the Italians) and past the Italian ski resort of Bardonecchia.

ORANGE

This northern gateway to Provence had a population of some 80,000 in Roman times and several sites have survived from the period. The **Arc de Triomphe**, the third largest Roman arch to have survived, inspired Napoleon to go one better in constructing its namesake in Paris. Orange's most famous sight is its Roman **amphitheatre**, dating from the 1st century AD and with the best preserved back wall in the Roman Empire, standing 37 m tall, a magnificent setting for the town's drama and opera festival in summer. A museum opposite the amphitheatre has some Roman finds as well as works by the Welsh artist Frank Brangwyn showing (intriguingly irrelevant) scenes of British industrial life.

RAIL 1.5 km east of the centre: head along AV. F-MISTRAL/R. DE LA RÉPUBLIQUE and turn into R. ST-MARTIN after PL. DE LA RÉPUBLIQUE (15 mins).

i **Tourist Office:** 5 COURS ARISTIDE BRIAND, ☎04 90 34 70 88 (Apr–Sept: Mon–Sat 0900–1900, Sun 1000–1800; Oct–Mar: Mon–Sat 0900–1800).

AVIGNON

In 1303, troubles in Rome caused the Pope moved his power base to Avignon. Wealth flowed into the town – and remained after the papacy moved back to Rome 70 years later. The city walls, built to protect the papal assets, still surround the city. Jutting from the north-eastern section is **Pont St-Bénézet**, the unfinished bridge famed in song (*Sur le pont d'Avignon*); it's inevitably become a tourist trap (admission payable). The most photographed sight in the city is the huge **Palais des Papes** (Papal Palace), boasting a 45 m-long banqueting hall, where cardinals would meet to elect a new pope.

In the middle of the Rhône lies **Île de Barthelasse**, a favourite picnic island, with its own summer swimming pool. Also try people-watching at **Place d'Horloge**, popular for its street entertainment and relaxed restaurants.

AVIGNON'S SUMMER FESTIVAL

In mid July to mid Aug, Avignon hosts one of Europe's largest drama festivals, and the city packs with people and theatrical events. The atmosphere at this time is highly infectious, with plenty of temptation to hang around and watch what's happening (lots of events are staged outdoors in the square by the Palais des Papes).

RAIL To the south, just outside the city walls: head through porte de la République and straight along COURS JEAN JAURÈS.

i **Tourist Office:** 41 COURS J-JAURÈS, ☎04 90 82 65 11 (Mon–Fri 0900–1300, 1400–1800, Sat 0900–1300, 1400–1700; stays open at lunchtime in summer). At Pont d'Avignon (summer: 0900–1830; winter: 0900–1300 and 1400–1700).

From the station head through the gateway into the old town, where you'll find a large number of reasonably priced pensions and hotels in the backstreets a few minutes away. During the drama festival everywhere gets completely booked up and you'd do better to stay at Tarascon or elsewhere, and travel in. At other times try R. JOSEPH VERNET and r. Agricol Perdiguier (both off J-JAURÈS). To step back in time visit **Cloître St Louis**, a truly unique 4-star hotel. An oasis of calm just off Avignon's main street, it combines tradition and modernity; the old part is housed in original 16th-century cloisters and the new wing was designed by Jean Nouvel. The restaurant, overlooking the impressive courtyard, is particularly stunning in the evening when the cloisters are illuminated. The 2-star Logis de France, **Hôtel d'Angleterre**, 29 BOULEVARD RASPAIL, 04 90 86 34 31, offers a wide price range. There are several **hostels**: **Bagatelle** (Non HI), ÎLE DE LA BARTHELASSE, 04 90 86 30 39; take nos. 10 or 11 from outside the Post Office (opposite station); **Provence Accueil**, 33 AVENUE EISENHOWER, 04 90 25 85 03 and the **YMCA**, 7 BIS CHEMIN DE LA JUSTICE, 04 90 25 46 20 no. 10 or 11. All are open all year.

Île de la Barthelasse also has a number of **campsites** – try **St Benezet**, (4 star) 04 90 82 63 50 (open Mar–Oct) or **Bagatelle** (2 star) 04 90 86 30 39 (open all year): no. 20 takes you all the way there or take 10 or 11 and get off after the bridge.

WHERE NEXT FROM AVIGNON?

Take the train to Tarascon (ETT table 350; 14 services a day; journey time 13 minutes) to join the Biarritz–Marseille route (p. 90).

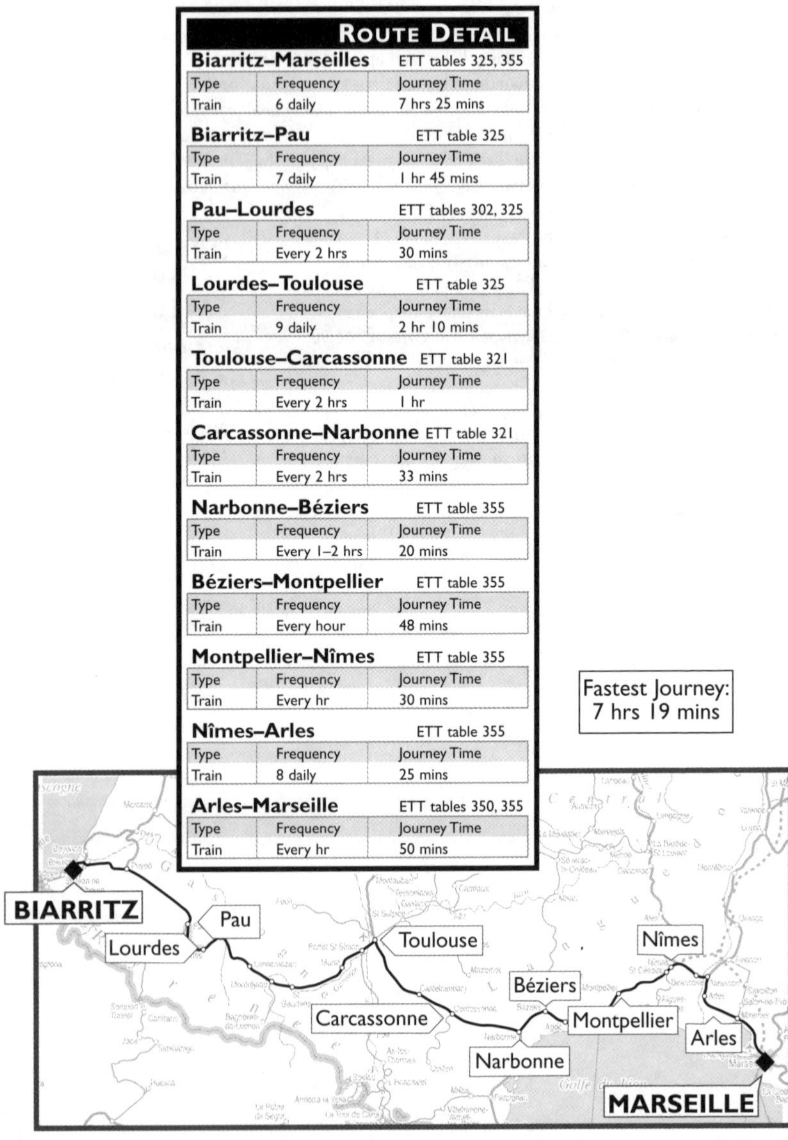

ROUTE DETAIL

Biarritz–Marseilles ETT tables 325, 355

Type	Frequency	Journey Time
Train	6 daily	7 hrs 25 mins

Biarritz–Pau ETT table 325

Type	Frequency	Journey Time
Train	7 daily	1 hr 45 mins

Pau–Lourdes ETT tables 302, 325

Type	Frequency	Journey Time
Train	Every 2 hrs	30 mins

Lourdes–Toulouse ETT table 325

Type	Frequency	Journey Time
Train	9 daily	2 hr 10 mins

Toulouse–Carcassonne ETT table 321

Type	Frequency	Journey Time
Train	Every 2 hrs	1 hr

Carcassonne–Narbonne ETT table 321

Type	Frequency	Journey Time
Train	Every 2 hrs	33 mins

Narbonne–Béziers ETT table 355

Type	Frequency	Journey Time
Train	Every 1–2 hrs	20 mins

Béziers–Montpellier ETT table 355

Type	Frequency	Journey Time
Train	Every hour	48 mins

Montpellier–Nîmes ETT table 355

Type	Frequency	Journey Time
Train	Every hr	30 mins

Nîmes–Arles ETT table 355

Type	Frequency	Journey Time
Train	8 daily	25 mins

Arles–Marseille ETT tables 350, 355

Type	Frequency	Journey Time
Train	Every hr	50 mins

From the Atlantic coast at **Biarritz**, the route edges along the plain to the vast mountain backdrops of the northern Pyrénées. The journey visits Lourdes, with its somewhat surreal, non-stop pilgrimage scene, **Carcassonne** with its massive fortifications, and **Montpellier**, the lively university town in Languedoc–Roussillon.

Nîmes and **Arles** are two of the great Roman sites of the Midi, and the finale, **Marseille**, is a big, bustling port, stronger in atmosphere than in sights. If you have time, stop off en route at **Tarascon** to admire the Château du Roi René, gloriously seated on the Rhône and impressively intact despite the heavy bombing of the surrounding town during World War II.

BIARRITZ

The smart set have been coming to Biarritz since the splendid **beaches** and mild climate were 'discovered' in the mid-19th century by such visitors as Napoleon II and Queen Victoria. Although rather less grand now, it is still essentially a fairly upmarket coastal resort with a string of good sandy beaches, great surfing and a casino.

RAIL **Gare de Biarritz-La Négresse**, 3 km from the centre, along a winding road: about 40-mins walk. Left luggage facilities open daily 0900–1200 and 1415–1800. Take bus no. 2 for a 15-min ride to the town hall – bus no. 9 also goes there, but via a longer route.

i **Tourist Office:** 1 SQ. D'IXELLES, ☎05 59 22 37 00. Open daily 0800–2000 (July–Aug); 0900–1845 (Sept–June). You can get free maps and information on the whole Basque region. There are branches open July–Aug at the station (0700–1330 and 1700–2100) and at PL. CLÉMENCEAU (1000–1300 and 1600–2100).

WHERE NEXT FROM BIARRITZ?

Biarritz is on the Paris–Seville international route *(p. 33).*

PAU

This elegantly prosperous town is perched on a cliff above its river, providing panoramic views of the snow-capped Pyrénées. Pau's attractions are easily walkable and a free map is available from the tourist office. Its **château** (reached via R. HENRI IV from the PL. ROYALE) was the birthplace of the charismatic French monarch, Henri IV, and contains some of his personal possessions, as well as the **Musée Béarnais** (the provincial museum). Soak up more history at the **Musée Bernadotte**, 5 R. TRAN, the birthplace of one of Napoleon's marshals, whose descendants are today's Swedish royal family.

RAIL On the southern edge of town. It's a tough 15-min uphill walk to the centre, but the funicular railway opposite the station will take you to PL. ROYALE for free. It operates Mon–Sat 0645-1230, 1255–1930 and 1955–2140; Sun 1330–1930 and 1955–2100.

Tourist Office: PL. ROYALE, 05 59 27 27 08 (July–Aug: Mon–Sat 0900–1800, Sun 1000–1700. Sept–June: Mon–Sat 0900–1230 and 1330–1800).

LOURDES

In a mountainous riverside setting, Lourdes is surrounded by natural beauty, but is overwhelmed by its status as a pilgrimage centre. The place swarms with visitors (over six million a year), and every other building is a shop overflowing with astonishingly kitsch religious souvenirs of the plastic Virgin genre.

DAY TRIPS FROM LOURDES

There are many regular bus excursions in and around the surrounding area, including **Parc National des Pyrénées**, which follows the Franco-Spanish border for 100 km, providing magnificent views; the Basque country; and the **Grottes de Betharram**, vast underground caverns full of limestone formations.

It all began in 1858, when the 14-year-old Bernadette Soubirous claimed to have seen the Virgin Mary in a local grotto. After 17 further appearances, a spring appeared by the **grotto**, and once word spread that its waters had effected miraculous cures, there was no looking back: the spring still flows and its water supplies local baths and drinking fountains. The 19 baths (rebuilt in 1955) are open to sick and healthy alike and hundreds of people plunge into them daily. To discover more about Bernadette and her life, you can visit various key locations in the centre of town, including **Boly Mill**, where she was born, and the *cachot*, where she lived during the time of the apparitions. Obtain a free map of the grotto from the Forum information centre, St Joseph's Gate, off PL. MGR LAURENCE.

RAIL 10-mins walk north-east of the centre. Bus no. 1 goes to the centre and the Grotto. To reach the tourist office, turn right out of the station down AV. DE LA GARE, and then left at the end along CHAUSSÉE MARANSIN to PL. PEYRAMALE.

Tourist Office: PL. PEYRAMALE, 05 62 42 77 40 (Easter–Sept: daily 0900–1900, Sun 1000–1800. Oct–Easter: Mon–Sat 0900–1200 and 1400–1800). From Easter–end Apr, the office closes for lunch.

Paris aside, Lourdes has more hotels than anywhere else in France, including a huge number of budget and moderate establishments close to the station and around the castle. The tourist office has an excellent list of all types of accommodation. Try the **Albret**, 21 PL. DU CHAMP COMMUN, 0562 94 75 00; or the **Hotel Majestic**, 9 AV. MARANSIN, 05 62 94 27 23 for basic but cheap lodging. Hostel accommodation (non-HI) can be found at **Accueil International**, R. DE L'ARROUZA, 05 62 94 34 54. There are 13 campsites, including two along the rte de la **Forêt: Camping du Loup**, 05 62 94 23 60, and **Camping de la Fôret**, 05 62 94 04 38.

TOULOUSE

See p. 65.

CARCASSONNE

From the 13th century, Carcassonne was the greatest stronghold of the Cathars, a Christian sect ruthlessly annihilated by Albigensian crusaders sent out on the orders of Rome. The great **fortress** held out for only a month, but the structure survived for long afterwards, until being quarried for building materials. Most of what you now see was restored in the 19th century by the architect Viollet-le-Duc.

Today there are two distinct towns. On one side of the River Aude is the **Ville Basse**, (Lower Town), which although modern and grid-like, is in fact of 13th-century origins. The more impressive **Cité** perches on a crag on the other bank of the river and is entered by two gates – Porte d'Aude and Porte Narbonnaise. If you are walking up from Ville Basse, look for the footpath beside St-Gimer, which leads to the 12th-century Château Comtal (Counts' Castle) that dominates the centre – visits inside are by tour only.

RAIL In the Ville Basse, on the north bank of the Canal du Midi. It's a long walk to La Cité – about 30 mins and the last part uphill; cross the bridge and head straight on r. G. CLEMENCEAU. Turn left onto R. DE LA LIBERTÉ and then right along BLVD JEAN JAURÉS. At SQ. GAMBETTa, take R. DU PORT-VIEUX and cross the old bridge, from where La Cité is signposted. Bus no. 4 goes from the station to SQ. GAMBETTA, then change and take Bus no. 2 to just outside the walls of La Cité.

Tourist Offices: In the Ville Basse: 15 BLVD CAMILLE-PELLETAN, ☎04 68 10 24 30 (June–mid Sept: Mon–Sat 0900–1900. Rest of year: Mon–Sat 0900–1200 and 1400–1800). In La Cité: **Tours Narbonnaises,** ☎04 68 10 24 36; fax: 04 68 10 24 38 (June–mid Sept: daily 0900–1900. Rest of the year: daily 0900–1215 and 1345–1830. Off-season opening times may change to 0900–1215 and 1345–1830).

The most picturesque area to stay is in the Cité and there are a couple of cheap options. **Des Remparts,** 3–5 PL. DU GRAND PUITS, ☎04 68 71 27 72; and the moderate **Dame Carcas,** 15 R. ST-LOUIS, ☎04 68 71 37 37. **Youth hostel**: R. DU VICOMTE TRENCAVEL, ☎04 68 25 23 16, in La Cité. **Camping: Camping de la Cité**, RTE DE SAINT HILAIRE, ☎04 68 25 11 77.

NARBONNE

A fine Midi town, lapped by vineyards and good beaches, Narbonne is dominated by the magnificent Gothic **Cathédrale St-Juste-et-St-Sauveur**. It was originally designed to be one of the biggest churches in Christendom, but was never finished as the authorities would not allow the town walls to be pulled down to build the nave. It has some lovely stained glass and the views make it worth climbing the towers. Below ground is **L'Horreum**, 16 R. ROUGET-DE-L'ISLE, a well-preserved Roman granary.

WHERE NEXT FROM NARBONNE?

Frequent trains to Perpignan take 50 minutes (ETT table 355); from there you can join the Toulouse–Barcelona route (p. 115).

RAIL 10-mins walk north-east of the centre: turn right along BLVD F-MISTRAL to the river, and left along R. J-JAURÈS, ☎04 67 62 50 50.

Tourist Office: PL. SALENGRO, ☎08 49 84 46; fax: 04 67 60 60 61 (Mon–Sat 0830–1900, Sun 0930–1230 (summer) Mon–Sat 0830–1200 and 1400–1800 (winter). Guided tours run four times a day (FFr. 30).

BÉZIERS

Vineyards spread from the outskirts of Béziers at the heart of the Languedoc wine country. Rising from the Pont-Vieux over the river Orb, the old town climbs to the 13th-century Gothic **Cathédrale de St-Nazaire**, which replaces an earlier cathedral that was burned down with 20,000 citizens locked inside during the Albigensian Crusade of 1209.

DAY TRIP FROM BÉZIERS

West of town, the **Canal du Midi** leads from the Mediterranean to the Atlantic and there are day cruises through the locks and vineyards, while buses offer a way to reach the long, sandy beaches not far from town.

As an antedote to that bleak episode, the **Musée du Vieux Biterrois et du Vin**, a wine/local history collection, is recommended for its entertainingly diverse exhibits.

RAIL For the centre of town, head straight up through the charming Plateau des Poetes to ALLEES PAUL RICQUET.

Tourist Office: Palais des Congrès 29, av Saint-Saëns, ☎04 67 76 47 00; fax: 04 67 76 50 80. Open Mon–Sat 0900–1900 Sun and holidays 1000–1200 (July–Aug); Mon–Fri 0900–1200 and 1400–1830 (Mon 1400–1800 only), Sat 0900–1200, 1500–1800 (Sept–June). Details of local wine festivals are available here.

WHERE NEXT FROM BÉZIERS?

The line up to Clermont Ferrand slices through the picturesque Cévennes; for more of this glorious scenery, take a bus out from Millau to the spectacular ***Gorges du Tarn*** *to the north-east.* ***St Flour*** *is positioned near the volcanic summits of the Cantal, and makes a pleasant stopover, with plenty of cheap hotels near the station in the low town, and a high town perched on massive volcanic crags. From Clermont, you can return south to Nîmes* *(see Where Next From Nîmes? on p. 96).*

MONTPELLIER

High-tech, young and trendy, Montpellier's attraction is that it's simply fun to spend time in. As a university town, with 55,000 students to feed, Montpellier abounds with inexpensive eating places, bars and hotels.

The **Vieille Ville** (old town) mixes cobbled streets with many 17th- and 18th-century mansions (free guides from tourist office). To the west side, the **Promenade**

de Peyrou leads to an impressive monumental group, with a triumphal arch, a water tower in the form of a hexagonal pavilion and an equestrian statue of Louis XIV, all looking out to the Mediterranean. Just to the north is **Jardin des Plantes**, France's oldest botanical garden.

5-mins walk south-east of the Tourist office. Head north, along R. MAGUELONE.

Tourist Office: PL. DE LA COMÉDIE, ☎: 04 67 60 60 60; FAX: 04 67 60 60 61 (Mon–Fri 0900–1300, 1400–1800, Sat 1000–1300, 1400–1800, Sun 1000–1300, 1400–1700 (Mid June–mid Sept 1500–1800). Branch at the station, : ☎67 92 90 03 (June–Aug, Mon–Thur 0900–1300, 1400–1800, Fri 0900–1300, 1400–1700).

NÎMES

Nîmes has effectively become a household word, by virtue of being the origin of the **Serge de Nîmes**, now known as denim, which was manufactured here in the 18th Century and imported to California for Levi Strauss. However, its history stretches back as far as Roman times, and though much of the town is undistinguished there are several superb Roman buildings. A three-day pass from the tourist office allows access to all sights.

Les Arènes is one of the great surviving Roman amphitheatres, still used for **ferias** (bullfights). The only meetings are in Feb, May and Sept, though in summer it also stages jazz and opera. Maison Carrée, an outstandingly well-preserved 1st-century AD temple, is now an exhibition centre. Next door is the futuristic **Carré d'Art**, designed by Norman Foster and containing wide-ranging displays of contemporary art forms.

To the west, the 18th-century **Jardin de la Fontaine** (Garden of the Fountain), off AV. J-JAURÈS, features a romantic Temple of Diana.

DAY TRIPS FROM NÎMES

The **Pont du Gard** is a spectacular Roman aqueduct 48 m above the Gard river (at a popular swimming spot), accessible by bus eight times a day. The site attracts two million visitors a year. Water was brought to the aqueduct from Uzès, a medieval village centred on a formidable castle, where today waxworks and holographic ghosts entertain visitors.

10-mins walk south-east of the centre: head down AV. FEUCHÈRES to ESPLANADE C DE-GAULLE, then along BLVD VICTOR HUGO, ☎04 36 35 35 35.

Tourist Office: 6 R. AUGUSTE, ☎04 66 67 29 11; fax: 04 66 21 81 04 (Open Mon–Fri 0800–2000 (Thur –2100), Sat 1000–1800, Sun 1000–1800 (July–Aug). Mon–Fri 0800–1900, Sat 0900–1900, Sun 1000–1200 (Sept–Jun). Branch: in the station, ☎04 66 84 18 13, (daily 0930–1230 and 1400–1800). There are free maps and a 24-hr information line for current events, ☎04 66 36 27 27.

Nîmes offers a very wide range of accommodation and space is seldom a problem, except during the major *ferias*. For budget hotels, try BLVD DES ARÈNES, or around BLVD AMIRAL COURBET. **Hôtel La Couronne**, 4 SQ. DE LA COURONNE, ☎04 66 67 51 73, is cheap and close to the station.**Hotel Audrans Terminus** 23, AV FEUCHERES, ☎04 66 29 20 14. Youth hostel: chemin de la cigale, ☎04 66 23 25 04, ischeap and close to the station. **Campsite: Domaine de la Bastide,** RTE DE GÉNÉRAC, ☎04 66 38 09 21, 5 km to the south; cheap (bus no. 4:Valdegour).

WHERE NEXT FROM NÎMES?

Four trains a day head up through some of the best of the Massif Central to Clermont Ferrand, two of which go through to Paris (ETT table 333). From Clermont you can return south by the line to Béziers (see Where Next From Béziers? on p.94).

ARLES

Ancient Rome meets Van Gogh and black bulls in Arles, the spiritual heart of Provence and a great place to relax and absorb history. Most major sights and museums are tucked into a tiny old town and are easily accessible on foot.

DAY TRIPS FROM ARLES

Hourly buses run between Arles and **Les-Stes-Maries-de-la-Mer**, on the coast. This is the site of an annual gypsy pilgrimage in late May and the main base for visiting the Camargue. The **Camargue** is now a nature reserve, an area of marshland and rice fields where semi-wild white horses and black bulls roam free and lagoons, often pink with flamingos in summer. Horseback is the best way to get around, and the Stes-Marie tourist office (AV. VAN-GOGH, ☎04 90 97 82 55, open daily 0900–1300 and

Arles is one of the best-preserved Roman towns in the world. **Les Arènes** is a mini Colosseum, less intact than the Roman amphitheatre at Nîmes but still used for bullfights (Easter-Sept). Summer theatrical productions are still staged at the **Théâtre Antique**, and assorted Roman finds, including mosaics, are exhibited at the Musée Lapidaire Paien.

Art buffs should seek out the **Musée Réattu**, R. DU GRAND PRIEURÉ, which houses a collection of Picasso sketches, and **Alyscamps** (Elysian Fields), an ancient burial ground painted by Van Gogh and Gaugin. Unfortunately none of Van Gogh's works are still in the town where he famously cut off his ear, but the tourist office runs Van Gogh tours to some of the places that inspired his paintings.

Arles parties through the summer: in late June–early July, the *Fête de la Tradition* fills the streets with music, dance and theatre. In mid–July, the lively festival *Mosaique Gitane* celebrates gipsy music and way of life.

RAIL A few blocks north of Les Arènes: walk down AV. TALABOT and along R. LACLAVIÈRE, ☎04 36 35 35 35.

Tourist Office: ESPLANADE CHARLES DE GAULLE (bus no. 4 from rail station), 04 90 18 41 20; fax: 04 90 18 41 29 (Open Mon–Sat 0900–1900, Sun 0900–1300 (Apr–Sept);. Mon–Sat 0900–1800, Sun 1000–1200 Jan–Mar and Oct–Dec). Branch: at the station, 04 90 49 36 90 (Apr–Sept: Mon–Sat 0900–1300, 1400–1800 (Apr–Sept);. Mon–Sat 0900–1300, 1330–1700 (Jan–Mar, Oct–Dec). Differently themed walking tours and self-guided tours use symbols embedded in the pavement. The *Petit train d'Arles* departs every day from Apr–15 Oct between 1000–1200 and 1400–1900 from BLVD DES LICE and Sat 1000–1200 from LES ARENES (FFr.30) 04 90 18 41 20.

For budget hotels look around PL DU FORUM and PL VOLTAIRE (also good for cafés and restaurants). Two elegant upmarket hotels are **Jules César**, 5 BLVD DES LICES 04 90 93 43 20, and **Arlatan**, 26 RUE DU SAUVAGE; 04 90 93 56 66 (both expensive). **Hôtel Gauguin**, 5 PL. VOLTAIRE, 04 90 96 14 35, is one of the better moderate places. **HI** (budget), 20 AV. FOCH; 04 90 96 18 25, is 1.8km south-east of town, a 15-min walk from town centre or bus No. 8: FOURNIER. Camping at **Camping City**, 67 ROUTE DE CRAU; 04 90 93 08 86, or **Les Rosiers** PONT DE CRAU; 04 90 96 02 12. Both to the south of the town

Day Trips from Arles cont'd.

1500–1900 in summer, daily 0930–1200 and 1430–1800 in winter) can supply a list of some thirty farms who have the animals for hire – by the hour, day or week. Cycling is the best alternative: bikes can be hired either from Stes–Maries or from Arles (the tourist office, train station (04 90 96 43 94, or **Dall'Oppio**, 10 R. PORTAGNEL, 04 90 96 46 83).

MARSEILLE

France's second city is hectically vibrant, the busiest port in France; its residents eat, sleep and breath to the rhythm of the sea. The grubby, run-down character of Marseille appeals to some, while others will want to move on swiftly, but it's a hard to remain indifferent. The **Vieux Port** (old port) is the hub of Marseille life and is guarded by the forts of St Jean and St Nicholas on either side of its entrance. From the Quai des Belges, the main boulevard of **La Canebière** extends back into the city.

Across the port from the dark, narrow streets of **Le Panier** – the oldest part of Marseille – is the Notre Dame de la Garde and impressive 19th century Roman Byzantine basilica (take bus 60 or the tourist train). Affectionately known to the Marseillais as *'la Bonne Mère'* the golden virgin watches over all sailors and travellers and the interior decoration features paintings of their ordeals and models of the ships that went down.

MARSEILLE'S MUSEUMS

The streets of Le Panier lead up to the **Vieille Charité**, 2 RUE DE LA CHARITÉ, an erstwhile sanatorium now housing a science and arts centre and two museums covering African and American Indian art and medieval archaeology. Try **Musée Cantini** 19 RUE GRIGNAN (métro: ESTRANGIN PASTRE) which houses a considerable collection of modern art, or the fascinating **Musée des Docks Romains**, (Roman Docks museum) pl. Vivaux (métro Vieux Port). All museums are open daily 1000–1700, 1100–1800 in summer closed Mon.

GETTING AROUND MARSEILLE

The central (Vieux Port) area is walkable. Elsewhere, use the métro and buses, both run by **RTM** *(Réseau de Transport Marseillais)*. Plan du Réseau (from the Tourist Office and RTM kiosks) covers the routes: the map looks complicated but the system is easy to use. Buses stop running at around 2100 and there is a reduced night service, Fluobus, until midnight. 11 lines cover most of the city and most depart from La Canebière. Most of the city centre is safe but avoid wandering too far off the main streets at night particularly in the 6th arrondissement and around St Charles.

DAY TRIP FROM MARSEILLE

Aix-en-Provence, the capital of Provence, and 30–40 mins from Marseille by train (ETT table 362), is a university town of culture, grace and charm; in term time, the distinctly well-groomed students are a feature of the town's street and café life.

Cours Mirabeau, flanked by plane trees and dotted with ancient fountains, forms

There are regular boat trips to the Iles de Frioul just outside the harbour. According to legend the Count of Monte Cristo was imprisoned in Chateau d'If on one of the smallest islands: the well-preserved prison can be visited Contact GACM, 1 QUAI DES BELGES, ☎04 91 55 50 09.

RAIL Gare St-Charles is the main station, 15-mins walk north-east of **Vieux Port** (Old Port): head down the steps and straight along BLVD D'ATHÈNES and BLVD DUGOMMIER to LA CANEBIÈRE, then turn right; or métro: VIEUX PORT – HÔTEL DE VILLE. Facilities include showers, baths, left luggage; open daily 0800–2200 and **SOS Voyageurs**, ☎04 91 62 12 80; Mon–Sat 0900–1200 and 1300–1900. Gare Maritime is west of the old port: follow R. DE LA RÉPUBLIQUE.

For information on ferries to Corsica, Sardinia and North Africa, contact **SNCM**, 61 BLVD DES DAMES, ☎04 91 56 30 10.

Marseille–Provence Airport, ☎04 42 14 14 14; at Marignane, 25 km north-west. (Terminal 1 handles international flights.) An airport bus runs between Provence and St-Charles approximately every 20 mins 0615–2315, taking 25 mins (FFr.44). Buses run every 20 mins 0600–2150 in the other direction. Taxis to the centre cost between FFr.250–300 (more at night and on Sun and holidays).

Tourist Office: 4 LA CANEBIÈRE, ☎04 91 13 89 00, (July–Aug: Mon–Sun 0900–2000; Sept–June: Mon–Sat 0900–1900, Sun 1000–1700). Branch: Gare St-Charles, ☎04 91 50 59 18. (Mon–Fri 1000–1300 and 1330–1800). Student and youth information: **Centre d'Information Jeunesse**: 96 LA CANEBIÈRE, ☎04 91 24 33 50. Walking tours taking in the main sights depart from LA CANEBIÈRE at 1000 (June–Sept) 1400 (Oct–May). Tourist trains visit Notre Dame de la Garde and Vieux Marseille at weekends and during holidays (FFr.30/45 for both circuits), ☎04 91 54 26 58.

The tourist office has a free accommodation booking service. For cheap, functional and tranquil hotels, try around ALLÉES L-GAMBETTA and RUE MONTGRAND, but avoid the dodgy streets south-west of the station (roughly the area bordered by BLVD D'ATHÈNES, BLVD CHARLES NÉDÉLEC, COURS BELSUNCE and LA CANEBIÈRE). **Hôtel St Louis**, 2 RUE DE RÉCOLLETTES, ☎04 91 54 02 74 is just behind the port, inexpensive and air-conditioned. A good budget hotel is **La Pilote**, 9 RUE DU

THEATRE FRANÇAIS, ☎04 91 33 11 15 (rooms from FFr.50–100). Nearer to the port, rooms tend to be pricier. Youth hostel: the more attractive and less expensive hostel is **Château de Bois Luzy**, 76 AVE DE BOIS LUZY, ☎04 91 49 06 18, bus no. 8. You can also camp here Mar–Oct; **Bonneveine hostel,** 47 AV. JOSEPH VIDAL, ☎04 91 73 21 81, is 5 km south in a residential district near the beaches. (Take métro no. 2 to rond pont du Prado or bus 41, then bus 44 toward Roy d'Espagne, get off at Borely).

The harbour and the streets leading from it are lined with fish restaurants: try PL. THIARS and PL. AUX HUILES. More opulent restaurants are found along CORNICHE J F KENNEDY. Specialities of Marseille include *bouillabaisse* (literally meaning to boil slowly): the authentic version of this fish stew contains rascasse, an ugly red Mediterranean species and is served with rouille, potatoes and croutons. Sample the best at **Chez Fonfon**, 140 RUE DU VALLON DES AUFFES, ☎04 91 52 14 38 (open evenings only). **La Daurade**, 36 RUE SAINT SAENS, ☎04 91 33 82 42 is also good but much more reasonable.

WHERE NEXT FROM MARSEILLE?

Marseille is a major rail junction, from which run some of the most scenic lines in France. In addition to exploring the Marseille–Menton route (p.100) and perhaps continuing from Menton over the Italian border, you can take the slow train to Paris via the Allier gorge (see Where Next From Nîmes?, p.95). The line through Aix-en-Provence continues round the hills of the ***Lubéron*** *(the subject of Peter Mayle's book A Year in Provence), and then through increasingly dramatic limestone scenery as you enter the foothills of the Alps. Beyond* ***Gap****, you're really into the Alps proper; you can continue on to Briançon, a major centre for the mountains, with a hilltop quarter fortified by the military architect Vauban. Alternatively, stop at* ***Montdauphin-Guillestre*** *(between Gap and Briançon); from here there are connecting minibuses to the Parc Régional de Queyras, one of the least developed and most rural parts of the French Alps. Good bases are St-Véran (at 2425 m, Europe's highest permanently inhabited village), and Ceillac.*

Day Trip from Marseille cont'd.

the southern boundary of Vieil Aix, the old town, a maze of lively streets with elegant 17th–18th-century houses. The **Cathédrale St Sauveur** is an architectural mishmash, ranging from the 5th to the 17th century, but it has lovely Romanesque cloisters and contains some worthwhile medieval artefacts. The best of the museums is **Musée des Tapisseries** (Tapestry Museum).

Aix was the birthplace of Cézanne and inspired some of his work, although he despised the town, which ridiculed him and his art. Later it came to its senses and his studio, *Atelier Cézanne*, has been lovingly preserved, exactly as it was at the time of his death. Using studs embedded in the pavement and a tourist guide you can follow a tour of the main stages of Cézanne's life.

Aix is also renowned for its thermal springs and a thermal centre is open to the public, ☎04 42 23 81 81.

The station is 5 mins south of the centre: take AV. V-HUGO to La Rotonde; the tourist office is on the left, at 2 PL. DU GÉNÉRAL DE GAULLE, ☎04 42 16 11 61.

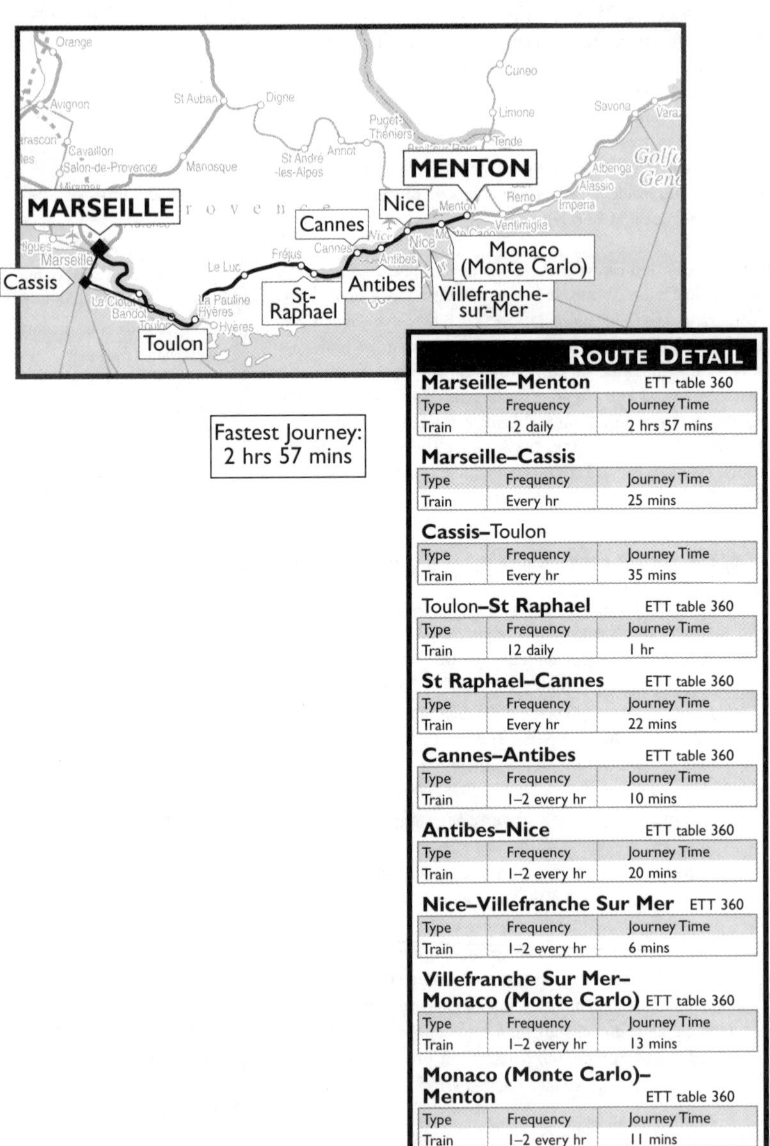

Fastest Journey: 2 hrs 57 mins

ROUTE DETAIL

Marseille–Menton ETT table 360

Type	Frequency	Journey Time
Train	12 daily	2 hrs 57 mins

Marseille–Cassis

Type	Frequency	Journey Time
Train	Every hr	25 mins

Cassis–Toulon

Type	Frequency	Journey Time
Train	Every hr	35 mins

Toulon–**St Raphael** ETT table 360

Type	Frequency	Journey Time
Train	12 daily	1 hr

St Raphael–Cannes ETT table 360

Type	Frequency	Journey Time
Train	Every hr	22 mins

Cannes–Antibes ETT table 360

Type	Frequency	Journey Time
Train	1–2 every hr	10 mins

Antibes–Nice ETT table 360

Type	Frequency	Journey Time
Train	1–2 every hr	20 mins

Nice–Villefranche Sur Mer ETT 360

Type	Frequency	Journey Time
Train	1–2 every hr	6 mins

Villefranche Sur Mer–Monaco (Monte Carlo) ETT table 360

Type	Frequency	Journey Time
Train	1–2 every hr	13 mins

Monaco (Monte Carlo)–Menton ETT table 360

Type	Frequency	Journey Time
Train	1–2 every hr	11 mins

This stretch of coast, the Côte d'Azur, became the haunt of British aristocrats in the 19th century, heralding its new status as a sophisticated playground for the famous, beautiful or just plain rich. Grand hotels and casinos sprung up to cater for their tastes, and although parts have declined into untidy sprawls there's still an enticing mix of ostentatious villas, pretty waterside towns and fine beaches. Sophisticated **Monaco**, a tiny country within France, and **Cannes** (marking the westward bounds of the glamorous Riviera) are hot spots for night life, while **Nice** is large and cosmopolitan. Inland the land rises abruptly and you're into a different world, of rugged mountains and ancient perched villages; much of it is difficult to reach without your own car.

MARSEILLE

See p. 97.

DAY TRIP

Hyères makes a pleasant excursion; it is a charming old resort with a medieval walled core, first attracted winter visitors in the late 19th century: Tolstoy, Queen Victoria and Robert Louis Stevenson enjoyed its mild climate.

From Hyères you can catch a ferry to offshore islands – **Île de Porquerolles, Île de Port-Cros and Île du Levant** – which offer some of the most beautiful beaches in the Mediterranean. Take a bus from the town to the port at La Tour Fondue for the ferry to Île de Porquerolles (ferry information: ☎04 94 58 21 81), Port d'Hyères for Port-Cros and Île du Levant, ☎04 94 57 44 07 (ferries depart

CASSIS

Centred around a pretty, traditional fishing harbour and making an easy day trip from Marseille via bus or train, the town makes a handy base for seeing the spectacular *calanques*, rocky inlets that cut into the limestone cliffs. Coastal walks (including the long-distance path GR98 west to Cap Croisette) offer stunning views.

RAIL 3.5km from town centre, on foot or by taxi (no buses from the station). Go along AV. DES ALBIZZI to AV. AUGUSTE FAVIER then AV. AUGUSTIN ISNARD which leads into town.

i **Tourist Office**: PLACE BARAGNON, ☎04 42 01 71 17 (July–Sept: 0900–1930; Oct–June: Mon–Sat 0900–1300 1400–1800 Sun 0900–1230).

FRÉJUS AND ST-RAPHAËL

The two communities almost merge and, although each has its own station and tourist office, they are effectively one place with three areas. St-Raphaël is the upmarket end and the main transport hub, with spacious beaches, though it lacks real style. Fréjus-Plage is a strip of tacky bars and restaurants that lies between the sea and Fréjus town, the historic area.

Fréjus was a Roman port, created by Julius Caesar in 49 BC and there are quite a few Roman remains scattered around the town. The smallish amphitheatre, **Arènes**, R. HENRI-VADON, is still used for bullfights and rock concerts.

Day Trip cont'd.

hourly in summer). Hyères **Tourist Office**: **rotonde Jean Salusse**, AV. DE BELGIQUE, ☎04 94 65 18 55. St Tropez, is a famously chic resort accessible by Sodetrav bus (eight a day in summer, from St-Raphaël), 'St-Trop' ('Saint Too Much') can be a disappointment. The best way to get around the area (more rewarding than the town) is to cycle and you can hire bikes locally – or mopeds if you don't fancy the exercise. There are two small beaches in town; the closest real beach is the Plage des Graniers, reached by a path from the base of the Citadelle. Tahiti-Plage is the jet-set hang-out and is at one end of Pampelonne, a 5-km stretch of sand that draws most of the crowds and is credited with starting the fashion for topless bathing. **Tourist Office**: PL. BLANQUI, ☎04 94 97 45 21; fax: 04 94 97 82 66.

Fréjus Cathedral, PL. FORMIGÉ, was the first Gothic church in Provence, built around the time the Romans lost power – though little building from that time survives.

RAIL Gare de St-Raphaël is central: for the sea, head down R. JULY BARBIER to PROMENADE DE LA LIBERATION, ☎04 36 35 35 35.

St-Raphaël bus station: behind the rail station, av. VICTOR HUGO, ☎04 94 95 16 71.

i **Tourist Offices**: **St-Raphaël**, R. W-ROUSSEAU, ☎04 94 19 52 52; fax: 04 94 83 85 40, opposite the station (July–Aug: daily 0830–1900. Sept–June: 0830–1200 and 1400–1830). **Fréjus-Ville**, 325 R. J-JAURÈS, ☎04 94 51 83 83 (daily 0900–1200 and 1400–1830) dispenses a guide to the (widespread) Roman sites.

Youth hostel: at CHEMIN DE COUNILLIER, ☎04 94 53 18 75, in a large park 2 km from Fréjus town along the RN7 road towards Cannes. Campsites: 50 km from beach is **Le Val Fleury**, RN98; ☎04 94 95. **St-Aygulf**, ☎04 94 17 62 49, is 4 km from Fréjus station; no. 9 from St-Raphaël bus station to St-Aygulf.

CANNES

Cannes proudly upholds the Riviera's reputation as an overpriced, overcrowded fleshpot. Entertainment here consists of looking good, spending money and sleeping little. Orientation is easy: the town stretches around the **Baie de Lérins**, the promenade being called **La Croisette**. Everything is within walking distance and virtually all the cultural activities (including the film festival) centre on the hideous concrete Palais des Festivals.

Cannes' nightlife can be fun. Twinned with Beverley Hills, glitzy Cannes is surprisingly welcoming to those without MGM contracts or family jewels, especially if they take the trouble to wander away from La Croisette to the small winding streets and hidden squares inland: try R. MACÉ and R. F-FAURE for some reasonably-priced bars.

Cannes specialises in second-hand glamour. Begin at the Palais des Festivals, built in 1982 and christened 'the bunker'. It is here that the red carpets are unrolled and the Rollers glide up, disgorging world-famous faces (and many that seem vaguely or not-at-all familiar), while the world of cinema pats itself on the back. Glimpses of stars are frequent (practise climbing lampposts) and, when it's all over, you may find your favourite's handprint cast in the concrete around the festival hall.

There are few specific sights, but try climbing R. ST-ANTOINE to the hill of Le Suquet, the oldest quarter. The **Musée de la Castre**, housed in the old citadel here, displays antiquities from around the world and gives a history of the town.

EVENTS IN CANNES

With towns all along the coast competing for custom, Cannes keeps ahead of the game by organising an ever-increasing number of special events: barely a week goes by without some kind of conference or festival – concerts, jazz and blues galas, even chess tournaments.

'The' event, of course, is the prestigious **Cannes Film Festival**, which begins during the second week in May. Public tickets for films outside the main competition are sold daily from a special office next to the tourist office.

250 m from the sea and the Palais de Festivals: head straight (south) down R. DES SERBES, ☎04 36 35 35 35.

Tourist Offices: Palais de Festivals, ESPLANADE GEORGES POMPIDOU, ☎04 93 39 24 53 (July–Aug: daily 0900–2000. Sept–June: Mon–Sat 0900–1830). At the station, 1 R. J-JAURÈS, ☎04 93 99 19 77 (July–Aug: Mon–Sat 0830–1200, 1400–1900. Sept–June: Mon–Sat 0900–1215, 1400–1845).

Some of the most exclusive hotels in the world overlook the Croisette. Try the streets leading from the station towards the sea front for more reasonably priced rooms: RUE DES SERBES, RUE DE LA REPUBLIQUE or RUE MARÉCHAL JOFFRE. Advance reservations recommended; during the festival rooms in Cannes are a highly prized commodity often booked from year to year. For celebrity spotting try **The Carlton**, 50 LA CROISETTE; ☎ 04 93 06 40 06 or **The Majestic**, 14 LA CROISETTE, ☎ 04 92 98 77 00 (both very expensive). If your budget won't stretch this far the **Atlantis,** 4 RUE DU 24 AOÛT; ☎ 04 93 39 18 72 or the **Bourgogne**, 11 RUE DU 24 AOÛT; ☎ 04 93 38 36 73. Otherwise consider making one of the other towns along the coast your base. **HI Centre International de Séjour de Cannes**, 35 AV. DE VALLAURIS; ☎ 04 93 99 26 79 is 20 mins walk from the Palais de Congrés. Camping at **Cannes La Bocca** (reached by train from Cannes) is convenient for the wide sandy beaches to the west of the town but not really for the centre. **Parc Bellevue Camping**; ☎ 04 93 47 28 97 (nos. 2/10/11)

DAY TRIPS FROM CANNES

Off Cannes, the Îles de Lérins are an antidote to chic. **Île de Ste-Marguerite** is the larger of the two, and boasts the better beaches. At the north end, Fort Royal is an impressively stark fortress built by Vauban in 1712 – and the legendary home of the Man in the Iron Mask (whose identity is debated to this day). There are daily ferry departures from the quay next to the Palais des Festivals casino.

ANTIBES

Mixing chic and tackiness, Antibes is still home to the obscenely rich, but the town has a relaxed atmosphere. Take a walk along the port; the biggest boats in the northern Med moor here. Do not miss the **Musée Picasso**, looking over the sea from its

DAY TRIPS FROM ANTIBES

Juan-les-Pins, the playground of the coast, is where the Côte d'Azur originated one summer in 1921; it has beaches (many are private, but there is still some public space), bars, discos and in July, a jazz festival. Accessible by train from Antibes, it is a pleasant place to while away a few days.

Just inland, to the west of Antibes and reachable by bus, Vallauris, meaning 'Valley of Gold', is pottery capital of the Riviera, famous for ceramics since 1500. Picasso came here in 1946 (to make pots) and was commissioned to paint a huge fresco, War and Peace, in a chapel which has become the small Musée National Picasso, pl. de la Libération.

home in the **Château Grimaldi**, PL. MARIJOL. Picasso worked here in 1946 and this excellent museum displays some of his most entertaining creations from that period.

RAIL For the centre, head down av. Robert Soleau to PL. DE GAULLE. From here BLVD ALBERT IER leads to the sea.

Tourist Office: 11 PL. DU GÉN-DE-GAULLE, ☎04 92 90 53 00; fax: 04 92 90 53 01 (July–Aug: Mon–Sat 0830–1930, Sun 1000–1300. Sept–June: Mon–Fri 1000–1200 and 1400–1800, Sat 1000–1200). Free minibuses run between all the main sites 0700–1900, but most are within walking distance.

NICE

Undisputed Queen of the Riviera ever since Russian princes and British royalty began to grace its opulent hotels in the middle of the last century, Nice still pulls in the visitors and is now France's fifth largest city.

Standing apart from the pastel-coloured villas of the rich, **Vieux Nice** (the old town) seems more Italian than French (which it was until 1860), and is one of the best places to shop at the outdoor markets.

Nice boasts some of the best museums in France. Some are free; you can also purchase a pass from the Tourist Office. Most are easily accessible by local bus. Best of the bunch is the **Musée Matisse**, 164 AV. DES ARÈNES DE CIMIEZ, wonderfully set in a 17th-century villa amongst the Roman ruins of Cimiez. It houses Matisse's personal collection of paintings (bus nos. 15, 17, 20, 22 from PL. MASSÉNA; 1000–1800 Apr– Sept; daily except Tues 1000–1700 Oct–Mar). Next door **Musée Archéologique**, 160 AV. DES ARÈNES DE CIMIEZ, exhibits the copious finds dug up while excavating the Roman arenas in Cimiez (bus nos. 15/17/20/22 to Arènes; 1000–1200, 1400–1800 or 1700 in winter; closed Mon). Matisse and fellow artist Raoul Dufy are buried in the neighbouring Couvent des Frères Mineurs.

NICE'S BEACHES

The beaches of Nice are pebbly, but this does not deter sun-worshippers from crowding onto the Baie des Anges, below the Promenade des Anglais. Whilst private beach clubs cover some of the central section, charging around FFr.90 for a day's hire of lounger and umbrella, most of the long beach is free. For less hectic sun-bathing, seek out the long beach between Cagnes-sur-Mer and Antibes to the west. However, the prettiest beaches are to the east, at Villefranche (young, lively crowd), Beaulieu (elderly and sedate) and St-Jean Cap Ferrat (well-heeled and laid-back).

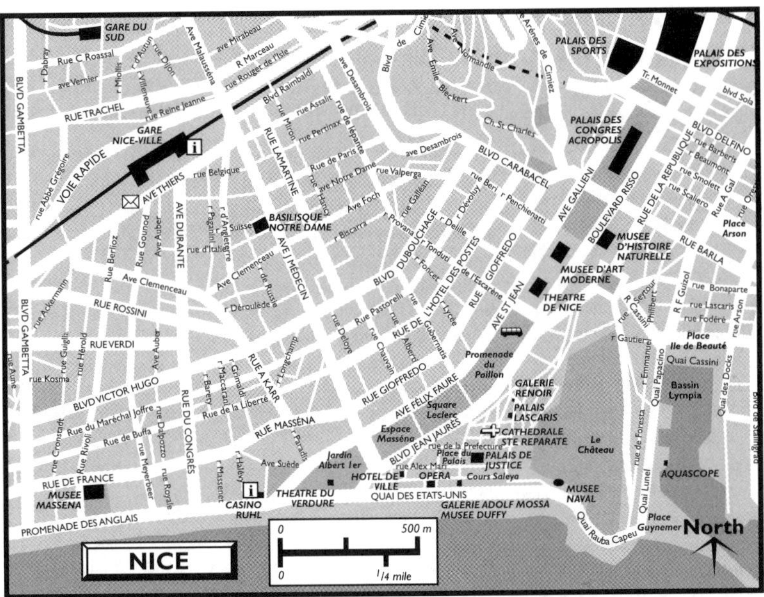

Also in Cimiez, the **Musée Marc Chagall**, AV. DU DR. MÉNARD, is a graceful temple to Chagall's genius – beautifully lit to display his huge biblical canvases (🚌 no. 15, July–Aug 1000–1800; Sept–June 1000–1700; closed Tues).

In the centre of town, the **Musée d'Art Moderne et d'Art Contemporain** (1100–1800, 1100–2200 Fri, closed Tues), PROMENADE DES ARTS, is unmistakable: a white marble cliff rising above the street, and filled with striking pop art. The **Musée d'Art et d'Histoire** in PALAIS MASSÉNA (summer: 1000–1200, 1400–1800, closed Mon), 65 R. DE FRANCE, is in a splendid

WHERE TO SHOP

Vieux Nice with its outdoor markets and small shops is a good place to start: head for the pedestrian area around RUE MASSENA. **Cours Saleya** is the main market place and there is a colourful flower market here everyday except Mon when an antique and flea market replaces it. All the big department stores line AV. JEAN MÉDECIN, while luxury goods and designer boutiques are on R. PARADIS and R. SUÈDE.

GETTING AROUND NICE

The Old Town quarter is manageable on foot, but to get between the various museums and sights requires transport. Bus services are good, most radiating from PL. MASSÉNA. **Information**: 10 R. FÉLIX FAURE, ☎04 93 16 52 10.

Renting a car or motor bike is a popular option, but the traffic is hectic and parking difficult. Rent motorbikes from **Nicea**, 9 AV. THIERS, near the station, ☎04 93 82 42 71.

Taxis are expensive; expect to pay FFr.50 for even the shortest trip (☎04 93 13 78 78).

DAY TRIPS FROM NICE

Renoir spent the last years of his life in **Cagnes sur Mer**, buying an isolated house overlooking the sea. Today this is **Musée Renoir**, CHEMIN LES COLETTES, ☎04 93 20 61 07 (1000–1200, 1400–1700, closed Tues; FFr.20), a tour of the artist's life, with rooms as he kept them 80 years ago (from the rail station, take the bus to Beal-Les Colettes). Above the town, the medieval citadel is now a museum: Montée de la Bourgade; Haut-de-Cagnes, entrance PL. GRIMALDI, (1000–1200 and 1430–1700; summer until 1800; closed Tues).

There are hourly buses from Nice to St Paul-de-Vence, a picturesque village which houses one of the most interesting modern art museums in France, the Fondation Maeght, built by the Maeght family, friends of Matisse. ☎04 93 32 81 63; open 1000–1230, 1430–1800 winter, 1000–1900 July, Aug; FFr.25. The garden is a quirky sculpture park designed by Miró.

Vence, 3 km further up the valley, is another delightful little town. Here Matisse was nursed by local nuns and repaid them by designing a simple yet

old Italianate villa adorned with antiques and decorated with paintings by Renoir and local artists. A Tourist Train visits the flower market, old town and castle hill during summer, from 1000–1900, in a tour lasting 40 mins.

RAIL **Nice-Ville**, AV. THIERS, ☎04 93 82 63 68. Information office open Mon–Sat 0830–1830, Sun 0830–1115, 1400–1700. Frequent services to all resorts along the Côte d'Azur. Station closed 0130–0530. Left luggage 0630–2330; baths and showers 0800–1900 in the basement. For the town centre, turn left from station to AV. JEAN MÉDECIN, the main thoroughfare, right down to PL. MASSÉNA (300 m), right again to the sea, a 15-min walk. Bus to the airport from outside the station, every 30 mins (FFr.20).

SNCM, QUAI DU COMMERCE (on the east side of the port), ☎04 93 13 66 66. Regular crossings to Corsica (from FFr. 229 one way, students from FFr.181).

Airport: Nice Côte d'Azur: PROMENADE DES ANGLAIS, 7 km west of the city. Information: ☎04 93 21 30 12, fax: 04 93 21 31 81. Taxis to the centre cost about FFr.150, but airport buses run along Promenade des Anglais to the Gare Routière (bus station) every 20 mins, and the 20-min journey costs only FFr.21. Bus no. 23 to the rail station (marked 'Gare SNCF') takes 20 mins and costs FFr.20.

i **Tourist Offices**: AV. THIERS, 06000 Nice (on the left just outside the station), ☎04 93 87 07 07, fax: 04 93 16 85 16 (summer: 0730–2000; winter: 0800–1900). Also 5 PROMENADE DES ANGLAIS, ☎04 92 14 48 00, fax: 04 92 14 48 03 (July–Aug: Mon–Sat 0800–2000, Sun 0900–1800; Sept–June: Mon–Sat 0900–1800). Airport, Terminal 1, ☎04 93 21 44 11, fax: 04 93 21 44 50, (Mon–Sun 0800–2200); Ferber, near the airport; ☎04 93 83 32 64, fax: 04 93 72 08 27, (summer: Mon–Sat 0800–2000, Sun 0900–1800; winter: Mon–Sat 0800–1900). Free hotel reservations.

Post Office: 23 AV. THIERS, ☎04 93 82 65 00, with poste restante, money transfer and fax. Open 0800–1900, 0800–1200 Sat.

For the budget conscious, good-value accommodation is available near the station – R. DE SUISSE, AV. DURANTE, R. D'ALSACE-LORRAINE – and in Old Nice, around PL. ST FRANÇOIS. Nice has three youth hostels, all far from the centre. **Mt-Alban**: RTE DE MONT-ALBAN, ☎04 93 89 23 64,

4 km out of town, uphill! (🚌 no. 5 from the station to blvd Jean Jaurès, then no. 14 to hostel.) No reservations; open from 1000. **Clairvallon Youth Hostel**: AV. SCUDÉRI, ☎93 81 27 63, is up in Cimiez, north of the centre (bus nos 15 or 22, stop at Scudéri), located in a park with a pool. **Les Collinettes**, 3 AV ROBERT SCHUMANN, ☎04 93 89 23 64, fax: 04 92 04 03 10, is open July–Aug only. The nearest campsite is at **St Laurent du Var Camping Magali**, 1814 RTE DE LA BAVONNE ☎ 04 93 31 57 00 open Feb-Oct. (take train towards Plan du Var get off at Saint Sauveur – last train 1915). Sleeping on the beach is not recommended; it can be dangerous and is definitely uncomfortable.

Day Trips from Nice cont'd.

breathtakingly beautiful chapel – that he considered his masterpiece – **La Chapelle du Rosaire,** AV. HENRI MATISSE; ☎04 93 58 03 26; open Tues and Thur, 1000–1130, 1430–1700. A mosaic by Chagall enlivens the dark Romanesque church.

Something of a culinary paradise, Nice is influenced by its neighbour – Italy, and by the Mediterranean. The city has many specialities. *Pissaladière* is a Niçois onion tart, garnished with anchovies and olives; socca, a traditional lunchtime snack of flat bread made from crushed chick peas, served piping hot; and of course *salade niçoise*. Vieux Nice (the old town) is best for eating out – particularly COURS SALEYA, which is covered with open-air tables in summer, R. STE RÉPARARTE and the other narrow side-streets around the cathedral. North of the old town, PL. GARIBALDI boasts the best shellfish, notably at the inexpensive **Café de Turin**, and good socca. **Café Puccini**, PL. ROSSETTI, ☎04 93 13 92 73, is cheap with a great view and atmosphere. **Moderate Le Quai**, 13 COURS SALEYA, ☎04 93 92 45 95, offers traditional cuisine.

WHERE NEXT FROM NICE?

A superb route through the Alps to Lyon can be taken via a private narrow gauge line to Digne-les-Bains; see Where Next From Lyon? on p.87.

NIGHT-TIME Nice is the cultural and social capital of the South of France, offering a choice of opera, concerts and plays. **FNAC (Fédération Nationale d'Achats des Cadres)** in the Nice Etoile shopping mall, AV. JEAN MÉDECIN, supplies tickets, ☎04 93 92 09 09.

In summer, Nice grinds on long after midnight, thanks to its many piano bars and nightclubs, though the younger generation gravitate to the beach. For many it is entertainment enough simply to stroll along the Promenade des Anglais or sit on the cours Saleya and watch the world go by.

VILLEFRANCHE-SUR-MER

The incredibly steep little resort of precariously tall ochre houses has one of the deepest ports on the coast, so it's a major stop for cruise ships and also has the liveliest beach in the region.

From Villefranche beach you can walk up to St-Jean Cap-Ferrat, a peninsula with gorgeous beaches plus some of the world's most expensive properties, where second-home owners include the likes of Elizabeth Taylor, Joan Collins and Mick Jagger. The port is lined with restaurants, tranquil even in high season and surprisingly inexpensive. If you make it to St-Jean Cap-Ferrat, don't miss the Villa Rothschild. Once owned by Beatrice de Rothschild, the house is a visual delight, but the exotica-filled gardens are stunning, with views down to Villefranche and Beaulieu. Open 1000–1900 summer, 1400–1800 winter, 1000–1800 weekends.

RAIL Access platform 2 to PROMENADE DES MARINIERES, turn right and follow signs to **Vieille Ville** (uphill).

i **Tourist Office: Jardins François Binon**, ☎04 93 01 73 68; fax: 04 93 76 63 65 (July–Sept: daily 0830–2000; Oct–June: Mon–Sat 0830–1200 and 1400–1900).

DAY TRIP FROM MONACO

La Turbie, just above Monaco, is accessible by bus (six times a day, but doesn't run Sun) – or a steep bicycle ride. The culminating point of the Roman road *Via Aurelia*, and marking the boundary between Italy and Gaul, La Turbie is renowned for the restored remnants of a huge statuesque tower of 6BC known as the Trophée des Alpes (in Latin: Tropaea Augusti). The only other Roman monument of its kind is in Romania. During the 13th century it was converted into a fortress, but was later blown up.

BEAULIEU-SUR-MER

'Beautiful place' (the name was bestowed by Napoleon) is a tranquil spot full of affluent retired people, and palms flourish profusely in its mild climate. Don't miss the **Villa Kérylos** – built by an archaeologist at the turn of the century, this is a faithful replication of a 5th-century BC Athenian home, complete with furnishings.

RAIL A few mins' walk north of the centre.

i **Tourist Office**: PL. G-CLÉMENCEAU, ☎04 93 01 02 21; fax: 04 93 01 44 04 (July–Aug: Mon–Sat 0900–1230 and 1400–1900, Sun 0900–1230; Sept–June: Mon–Sat 0900–1215 and 1430–1800).

MONACO (MONTE CARLO)

Covering just a couple of square km this tiny principality has been a sovereign state ruled since 1308 by the Grimaldis, a family of Genoese descent. Later it grew rich on gambling and banking, and now high-rises crowd round the harbour, some built on man-made platforms that extend into the sea. Whatever the geographical and aesthetic limitations of the place, its curiosity value is undeniable.

Old Monaco is the extra-touristy part, with its narrow streets, the much-restored **Grimaldi Palace**, and the 19th-century **Cathédrale de Monaco**, containing the tombs of the royals, including Princess Grace. In AV. ST-MARTIN is the stimulating **Musée Océanographique**, in the basement of which is one of the world's great aquariums, developed by Jacques Cousteau.

The **Monte-Carlo Rally** (Jan) includes exciting stages in the hills behind Monaco, while the second week in May is a good time to avoid the town unless you are interested in watching the **Grand Prix** – which takes over the city streets.

04 36 35 35 35 or (377) 93 10 60 15: head straight down past PL. D'ARMES to the port (with the palace off to the right), then turn left for the tourist office and casino (500 m); or take no. 4.

Tourist Office: 2A BLVD DES MOULINS; (377) 92 16 61 66, fax: (377) 92 16 60 00, open Mon–Sat 0900–1900, Sun 1000–1200 (all year).

Budget accommodation is scarce but there are a number of 2 star establishments around the station RUE DE LA TURBIE being the best place to look for it – otherwise, make your base elsewhere. The **Hôtel de Paris**, PL. DU CASINO (377) 92 16 30 00, charges upwards of FFr.2000 a night. Just round the corne is its belle époque rival, **Hôtel Hermitage**, (377) 92 16 40 00 – it's worth wandering through the public rooms just to look at the décor. **Hôtel de France**, 6 RUE DE. LA TURBIE (377) 93 30 24 64, is a 2-star establishment that is relatively cheap. **Hôtel Helvetia**, 1 BIS RUE GRIMALDI (377) 93 30 21 71 is also reasonable. The (non HI) **Centre de la Jeunesse Princesse-Stéphanie,** 24 AV. PRINCE-PIERRE; (377) 93 50 83 20 (100 m from the station) is open all year to 16-26 year olds and students up to the age of 31.

Eating out in Monaco ranges from simple bistros and pizzerias (try around the station or the port) to some of the most decadent restaurants in the world. Expect to pay big money in any of the restaurants around the casino. There are also a number of take away establishments, particularly around LA PLACE D'ARMES from which you can sample typical snacks such as *socca* and *tourte*.

MENTON

Looking into Italy, Menton is a retirement town of ample Italianate charm, endowed with long stony beaches and full of lemon, orange and olive trees. Wander around the old town, constructed by the Grimaldis in the 15th-century. The baroque **Église St-**

CASINOS IN MONACO

Monaco is synonymous with gambling and there are several casinos, but you must be over 21 (they check). Granddaddy of them all is the most famous casino in the world, the **Casino de Paris**, PL. DU CASINO, which is worth a look for the interior gilt alone. You can play the slot machines at the entrance, but to get any further costs FFr.50, just for the pleasure of walking into the hallowed gaming rooms – and smart dress is required. The adjoining **Café de Paris** has no entrance fee, but it's definitely less classy.

LONG-DISTANCE WALKS IN THE CÔTE D'AZUR

From Menton you can venture into the Parc National du Mercantour, in the French Alps, by following the waymarked long-distance path GR52. Another route, GR51 (forking from GR52 north of Menton), heads west parallel to the coast and over wild, broken country. Both paths require good levels of fitness.

Michel (St Michael's), built in 1640, is an attractive structure. To the west, **Palais Carnolès** was the summer residence of the princes of Monaco and now houses an interesting art collection (mainly impressionists and modern). **Musée Jean-Cocteau**, 111 QUAI NAPOLÉON-III, was established by Cocteau himself and contains many of his works. In **Musée Municipale de Préhistoire Régionale** (City Museum of Regional Prehistory), R. LORÉDAN-LARCHEY, there are human remains some 80,000 years old.

WHERE NEXT FROM MENTON?

Continue to Ventimiglia in Italy (ETT table 360) and join the ***Ventimiglia–Pisa*** *route* *(p. 357)**.*

RAIL West of the centre. For the sea (about 300 m), head down AV. EDOUARD VII or R. MORGAN.

i **Tourist Office**: **Palais de l'Europe**, 8 AV. BOYER, ☎04 92 41 76 78, fax: 04 92 41 76 78 (July–mid Sept: 0830–1830; mid Sept–June: 0830–1230 and 1330–1830). Turn left from the station for about 100 m, then right.

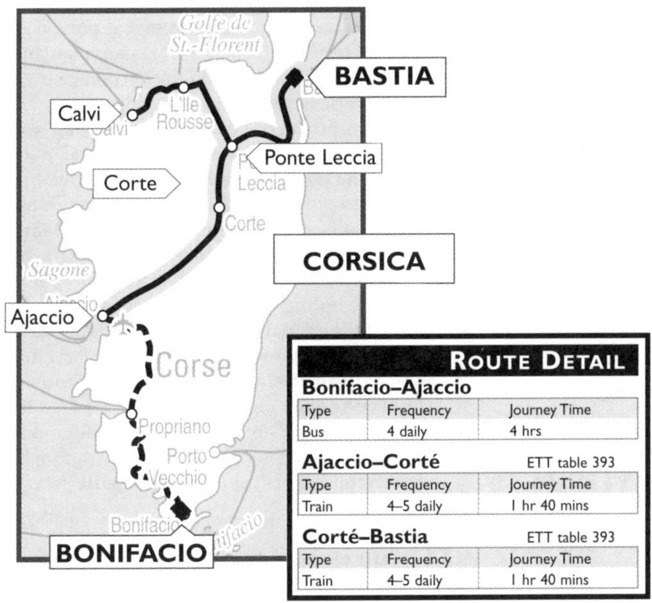

ROUTE DETAIL

Bonifacio–Ajaccio

Type	Frequency	Journey Time
Bus	4 daily	4 hrs

Ajaccio–Corté ETT table 393

Type	Frequency	Journey Time
Train	4–5 daily	1 hr 40 mins

Corté–Bastia ETT table 393

Type	Frequency	Journey Time
Train	4–5 daily	1 hr 40 mins

In French hands since the 18th century, the island of *Corsica* offers an improbably dramatic combination of rugged coastlines, beaches (notably in the south-east) and huge mountains (crossed by the demanding GR20 path, running 180 km from **Conca** in the south-east to **Calenzana** in the north-west). This route uses bus services from **Bonifacio** (the port serving *Sardinia*) to **Ajaccio**, then uses splendidly scenic railways to **Bastia** in the far north. Fish and seafoods are a speciality around the coasts and hearty mountain sausages and strong goat and sheep's cheeses are a local treat.

BONIFACIO – AJACCIO

Four scheduled bus services per day, and 2 on Sunday, taking 4 hrs. Buses are operated by **Eurocorse Voyage**, ☎04 95 70 13 83, and the long, slow bus journey presents an ideal opportunity to discover the vineyards, mountains and valleys of southern *Corsica*.

BONIFACIO

Seen from a ferry or one of the many boat trips that depart from here, **Bonifacio** looks most dramatic, with its characterful upper town and citadel clinging precariously to a spur overlooking the harbour. The hardy can save time climbing to the old city by using the covered stairway inside the *Genoese* walls on the right after leaving the port. Inter-island buses depart from the end of the bay, about a 10-min walk along the

DAY TRIP FROM BONIFACIO

Porto Vecchio, accessible by frequent bus services (the closest being Bonifacio), lies to the South West of the island and has, arguably Corsica's best beaches. Looking more Caribbean than Mediterranean, Rondinara, Santa Giulia, Palombaggio, and Pinarello are protected stretches of white sand and phenomenally clear pale turquoise blue seas.

FERRIES TO CORSICA

Corsica is well served with ferries. For example, **Bonifacio**, at the southern end, has 4–10 sailings daily to **Santa Teresa di Gallura** in Sardinia (p. 386; crossing time 1 hr). Large ferries sail infrequently (not daily) from **Bastia** to **Marseille**. There are many other sailings to **Nice** and **Toulon** from most Corsican ports. Check locally for exact details. Reservations should be made well in advance for the large ferries during July/Aug and French school holiday periods. There's scope for a journey from Sicily, across Sardinia and Corsica and then on to mainland France or Italy. (See ETT tables 2635, 2640, 2645, 2650, 2699).

Note that no rail passes are honoured in Corsica, as the *U Tringhellu* (small train) railway is a privatised service.

quay from the port, past innumerable restaurants and cafés lining the anchorage.

Within the intriguing warren of narrow streets and alleys that makes up the upper town is a seemingly endless number of restaurants. Sights include the **Place du Marché**, the 12th-century Pisan **Eglise Sainte Marie Majeure** with its 14th-century white stone clock tower – the intricate buttresses along both sides contain an ingenious system of rain water canalisation. The 187-step **Staircase of the King of Aragon** is carved into the stone down to the water and is said to have been built one agited night in 1421. The massive 16th-century Genoese Gate with its drawbridge and moat open on to the medieval RUE LONGUE, where the family house of Napoleon Bonaparte faces that of Charles Quint.

Tourist office: at the port is rudimentary, but main office, ☎04 95 73 11 88; fax: 04 95 73 14 97, in upper town at place de l'Europe is very helpful (June–Sept: 0900–2000; Oct–May: Mon–Fri 0900–1200 and 1400–1800). Website: http://www.planetepc.fr/bonifacio.

Moby Lines, ☎(0789) 755 260, **Saremar**, ☎(0789) 754 788.

Hotels of all categories abound. Five **campsites** are located in the brush beyond the car park bounding the bay: **Araguina**, ☎04 95 73 02 96, is the closest to the bay and **Des Îles**, ☎04 95 73 11 89, is closest to the beach.

AJACCIO

Palm trees shade the waterfront cafés of the most French settlement on the island, the birthplace of Napoleon Bonaparte. Like most Corsican cities, **Ajaccio** is compact and all points are easily accessible by foot or by bus from the port side bus station. Bicycles and motorcycles can be rented from **Moto Corse Evasion**, ☎04 95 20 52 05.

The birth of local-boy-made-good (or is it bad?) **Napoleon** is commemorated from 13–15 Aug with parades, dances and pageants.

Foremost among the Napoleon-related sights is **La Maison Bonaparte**, R. SAINT CHARLES at the PL. LETIZIA, the great man's birthplace. His death mask can be seen in a special room in the town hall, while one of the best viewpoints in city is the monumental statue of Napoleon in the PL. D'AUSTERLITZ. looking over the Gulf. Housing works collected by Napoleon's step-uncle, Cardinal Fesch, the **Fesch Museum** (closed Sun and Mon in winter) is Corsica's major art museum with works by Raphael, Titian and Botticelli making it France's best collection of early Italian paintings outside Paris; one wing of the building is the 1868 Public Library, a striking all-teak creation.

Maritime/Bus Station, on the QUAI L'HERMINIER; ☎04 95 29 66 88; also houses kiosks for inter-island buses, ☎04 95 21 28 01. Open daily 0630 until departure of last ferry usually 2000). Rail station, ☎04 95 23 11 03. About 500 m north of the Maritime station along the BLVD SAMPIERO, which is an extension of the QUAI L'HERMINER.

Tourist office: Main Municipal office: next to City Hall *(Mairie)*, PL. DU MAR. FOCH, ☎04 95 21 40 87; open daily 0800–2100 June–Sept; Mon–Fri 0830–1800, Sat 0830–1400 rest of year. A complete tourist desk is in the bus station, open from just before the first to just after the last sailing of the day. Main Corsica Tourism office, 17 BLVD ROI JEROME; ☎04 95 21 56 56, opens daily 0900–1900 June–Sept; Mon–Fri 0900–1300, 1430–1730 Oct–May. **Parc Naturel Regional de la Corse** has its main information centre at 2 R. MAJOR LAMBROSCHINI; ☎04 95 51 79 10.

A plethora of lodging of all categories is available. In the centre between the bus/maritime stations and the rail station are many smaller **hotels**, while slightly further away are the more upmarket **Hotel Imperial**, ☎04 95 21 50 62, fax: 04 95 21 15 20) and the **Hotel Fesch**, ☎ 04 95 21 50 52, fax: 04 95 21 83 36). **Camping Les Mimosas**, ☎04 95 20 99 85, 3 km east of the city, is well equipped. The **Relais regional des gites ruraux** ☎04 95 20 51 34, fax: 04 95 20 28 96 provides information and brochures on rural *gîtes* (self-catering accommodation) in the area.

The full range of Corsican and French cuisine is available and, given the large concentration of Foreign Legion bases in the area, there are numerous Chinese, fast-food and Asian restaurants.

DAY TRIP FROM PONTE LECCIA TO CALVI

From **Ponte Leccia** this exotic rail route takes a curving, mountainous passage through mostly deserted countryside to **l'Île Rousse**, and then hugs the seashore to **Calvi**. Direct narrow-gauge services run, two daily, via **l'Île Rousse**, journey taking 2 hrs. Between **l'Île Rousse** and **Calvi**, 9 additional services operate July–Sept (ETT table 393).

L'Île Rousse takes its name from the nearby red granite isles joined to the mainland by a causeway. The town itself, the warmest place in Corsica, is handsomely compact but lively. The **Oceanographic Museum** deserves a few hours of your time to discover the marvels of the extensive, undersea life of the Mediterranean.

Tourist office: PL. PAOLI, ☎04 95 60 04 35;

Day Trip from Ponte Leccia to Calvi cont'd.

fax: 04 95 60 24 74 (July–Aug: 0900–1300, 1430–1930; Apr–Oct: 0930–1200, 1500–1800). **Rail information**: 04 85 60 00 50; maritime information **SNCM**, 04 95 60 09 56, **Corsica Ferries** 04 95 60 44 11. **Calvi** makes another excellent base, with a lively summer beach and the chance to discover the untouched hinterlands. Treks and camping tours can be organised through the tourist office. **Tourist office**: opposite the station, 04 95 65 16 67; fax: 04 95 65 14 09 (June–Sept: daily 0900–1930; Oct–May: Mon–Sat: 0900–1200, Mon–Fri 1400–1800).

CORTE

Ringed by mountains, Corte perches on a huge outcrop, with cobblestone stairways threading between stone houses to a 15th-century citadel. The town is a good centre for exploring the regional natural park.

RAIL 04 95 46 00 97; left luggage.

Tourist office: Pl. de la Fontaine des Quatre Canons; 04 95 46 26 70 (June–Sept), and 04 95 46 24 20 (Oct–May).

BASTIA

Bastia has a certain allure, especially around the old port and the citadel. Seek out the animated Pl. St. Nicolas and the R. Napoleon that connects it with the atmospherically dilapidated, horseshoe-shaped *Vieux Port* (old port), with fishing boats creaking at anchor and flapping washing-lines strung over dark, shuttered alleys. The evening promenade seems to be the summer activity of many locals. The 17th-century **Église St-Marie** contains a 19th-century silver Virgin said to weigh one ton. Just beyond the Cathedral is the sumptuously baroque **Chapelle St-Croix**, containing the much venerated *Black Christ of Miracles* found in 1428 and now the patron of local fishermen.

RAIL 04 95 32 80 61, luggage storage; close to the centre and port. **Maritime**: in the new port area near the Pl. St Nicolas.

Tourist office: Pl. St. Nicolas, 04 95 31 00 89. Open daily from 0800–1900, July–Aug 0700–2200. **Corsica Loisirs Aventure** 04 95 32 54 34, 3, rue Notre-Dame-de-Lourdes can assist campers and trekkers.

SNCM, 04 95 54 66 88; **Corsica Ferries**, 04 95 32 95 95; **Moby Lines**, 04 95 31 46 29.

Buses: Services for the Cap Corse peninsula – check with the municipal tourist office for details.

A variety of accommodation can be found around the old city between the railway station and the maritime port along the Ave Marechal Sebastiani. **Camping Les Bois de San Damiano** 04 95 33 68 02, fax: 04 95 30 84 10; (open Apr–Oct) is 5 km south on the long Marana beach.

The Old Port area contains a large number of **restaurants** ranging from Corsican seafood speciality to pizzerias to tex-mex establishments. The **daily market** in the square around the City Hall behind the St Jean Baptiste Church offers a delectable array of fresh, local produce.

TOULOUSE – PERPIGNAN – BARCELONA

ROUTE DETAIL

Toulouse–Barcelona ETT tables 11, 47

Type	Frequency	Journey Time
Train	4-5 daily	5 hr 2 mins

Toulouse–Villefranche ETT tables 312, 313

Type	Frequency	Journey Time
Train	4-5 daily	3½ hrs-4½ hrs

Villefranche–Perpignan ETT table 314

Type	Frequency	Journey Time
Train	6-7 daily	50 mins

Perpignan–Collioure ETT table

Type	Frequency	Journey Time
Train	11-13 daily	35 mins

Collioure–Figueres ETT tables 355, 656

Type	Frequency	Journey Time
Train	6 daily	1 hr 40 mins

Figueres–Girona ETT table 656

Type	Frequency	Journey Time
Train	Every hr	30 mins

Girona–Barcelona ETT table 656

Type	Frequency	Journey Time
Train	Every hr	1 hr 20 mins

Notes
Toulouse to Barcelona: change trains at Perpignan. Collioure to Figueras change trains at the border.

Fastest Journey: 5 hrs 2 mins

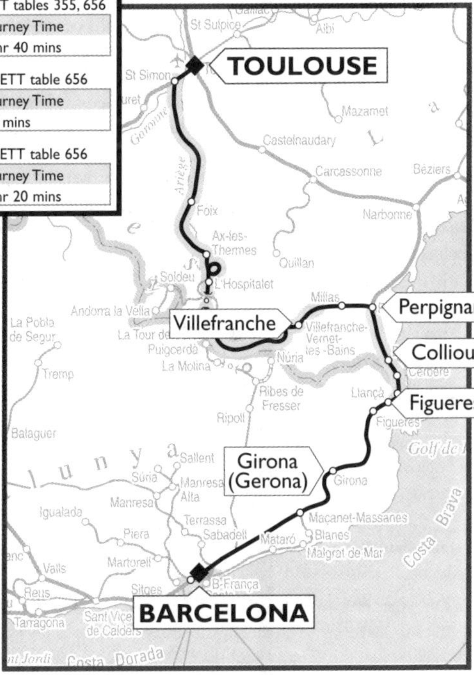

Toulouse – Perpignan – Barcelona

The Pyrénées mountain chain is one of the world's most emphatic national boundaries, a great wall of snow-capped peaks separating France from Spain. Virtually any route over it is a thrilling encounter: here the journey rises up to **La Tour de Carol**, which boasts railways of three gauges. The narrow-gauge **Petit Train Jaune** (Little Yellow Train) twists and turns its way through the mountains to **Villefranche**, with the great summit of Canigou rising to the south; open carriages are used on some services in summer, giving even better views. From **Perpignan** you are firmly in Catalunya (Catalonia), a distinctive region that strongly holds on to its regional identity, even though up to the death of Franco in 1975 the Catalan language was officially banned.

Beyond **Collioure**, the route heads close to the Mediterranean and into Spain, where the rugged, rocky coast of the Costa Brava (reached by bus from Gerona or **Figueres**) has been much developed for the package holiday industry, but has some pleasantly tranquil coves. Barcelona is covered on p. 123–129.

Toulouse

See p. 65.

Day Trip from Villefranche

If you stay in the area, consider a trip by jeep to the base of **Canigou,** one of the most majestic of the Pyrénéan peaks (2784 m) and dominating the view to the south; from the Chalet Hotel it's about a 2-hr climb, requiring no special equipment though obviously it should be undertaken in settled conditions. Contact **Jean-Paul Bouzan**, 17 BLVD DES PYRÉNÉES, 66820 VERNET-LES-BAINS, ☎05 68 05 62 28.

Villefranche

The little town of Villefranche is riddled with narrow streets and seems almost to have been transported from the Middle Ages. It is dominated by the enormous stone-built **Fort Liberia**, built in 1681 by the military engineer Sebastien Vauban.

To get to the fort, take a minibus from the gate, Porte de France; the more athletic can climb 750 steps upwards via an underground staircase that leads from R. ST-PIERRE, The fort is open daily 0900–1900 (Apr–Oct), 1000–1800 (Nov–Mar).

RAIL Villefranche-Vernet-les-Bains: ☎05 68 96 34 74 11.

i **Tourist Office**: PL. DE L'EGLISE, ☎05 68 96 22 96 (open daily 1000–1800).

Prades

The next stop on from Villefranche, Prades is another pleasant base and jumping-off point for walks up Canigou. There's a summer music festival here, begun by the Catalan cellist Pablo Casals. The chief sight is the 10th-century abbey church, which has more than a hint of Arab influence in its architecture.

PERPIGNAN

Unmistakably Spanish in character though unfortunately overrun in summer, Perpignan was formerly the mainland capital of Majorca and is now a vibrant, large city at the heart of French Catalonia. Catalan is spoken hereabouts, and the sardana, Catalonia's national dance, is performed a couple of times a week in summer to the accompaniment of pipes and tambourines in the 14th-century PL. DE LA LOGE, Perpignan's main square and still the hub of the city's life. A 15th-century fortified gatehouse, **Le Castillet**, QUAI SADI-CARNOT, houses Casa Pairal (a Rousillon museum), while the **Cathédrale St-Jean**, PL. GAMBETTA, is Gothically grand. The imposing Citadelle, to the south, guards the 13th-century **Palais des Rois de Majorque** (Palace of the Kings of Majorca).

600 m from the centre: walk along AV. GÉN-DE-GAULLE to PL. CATATOGNE, or take bus nos 2/3/12.

Bus station: AV. DU GÉN-LECLERC; ☎04 68 35 29 02 (north of train station, off PL. DE LA RÉSISTANCE). There are regular services to the beaches (no. 1 or Car Inter 66).

Tourist Offices: Municipal, PL. ARMAND-LANOUX; ☎04 68 66 30 30; fax: 04 68 66 30 26 (30-mins walk from the station. June–Sept: Mon–Sat 0900–1900, Sun 0900–1300, 1500–1900. Oct–May: Mon–Sat 0830–1200, 1400–1830). Regional office for Pyrénées–Roussillon: 7 QUAI DE LATTRE DE TASSIGNY, ☎04 68 34 29 94, (daily 1000–1200, 1400–1730).

COLLIOURE

Easily visited as a day trip from Perpignan, this is the most picturesque of the local ex-fishing villages and is overlooked by a 12th-century château, on a knob of land between two bays. Matisse, Braque, Dufy and Picasso discovered Collioure, and artists still set up their easels here. The domed church belfry looks distinctly Arabic.

300m west of the centre.

Tourist Office: PL. 18 JUIN ☎04 68 82 15 47.

FIGUERES (FIGUERAS)

The much-visited **Teatre-Museu Dalì**, signposted from near the station, is the only real attraction, honouring the town's most famous son. Whether you consider Dalì a genius or a madman (or both), the museum is likely to confirm your views of the surrealist artist. Appropriately enough, it's a bizarre building, parts of which Dalì designed himself (including his own grave), a terracotta edifice sporting giant sculpted eggs. Inside are displays of his works (though don't expect to see the most famous ones), including the Mae West room and the Abraham Lincoln mural.

PLAZA DE LA ESTACIÓN; ☎(972) 50 46 61. Central.

Tourist Offices: PLAZA DEL SOL S/N, ☎(972) 50 31 55, fax: (972) 67 31 66. There is also a branch at the bus station across the Plaza from the train station.

GIRONA (GERONA)

The medieval part of the town stands on the east side of the River Onyar, connected by the Pont de Pedra to a prosperous new city in the west. From the bridge you can see the **Cases de l'Onyar** – a line of picturesque houses overhanging the river. In the heart of the labyrinthine old town the superlative Gothic cathedral is approached by a 90-step 17th-century stairway. Its interior has a single-naved vault with a 22 m span (the largest ever constructed). Buy a ticket for entry to the Romanesque cloister and the museum within the chapterhouse, containing the 15th-century **Tapis de la Creació** (Tapestry of the Creation).

Also seek out the **Banys Arabs** (Arab Baths) are Romanesque with Moorish touches and dating from the 13th century. **Museu d'Art**, housed in a splendid Renaissance bishop's palace, displays a wealth of paintings and carvings from the Romanesque period to the 20th century. In the narrow streets of the **El Call** (old Jewish quarter) is the **Bonastruc ça Porta Centre** (Centre Isaac el Cec), soon to become a Museum of Jewish Culture, but worth a look for the magnificence of the building alone in addition to any temporary exhibitions. The 11th–12th-century Benedictine **Monastery Sant Pere de Galligants** now houses the archaeological museum. The **Palau des Agullana** is a 14th–17th century town palace which, together with Sanxt Marti Sacosta Church, forms an attractive baroque group.

☎(972) 20 70 93. In the new town; 10-min walk from the river and Pont de Pedra.

Bus station: ☎(972) 21 23 19 (there is a linking door from the train station).

Tourist offices: Rambla de la Llibertat 1, ☎(972) 22 65 75; fax: (972) 22 66 12 (Mon–Fri 0800–2000, Sat 0800–1400, 1600–2000, Sun 0900–1400). There's also an office at the train station in summer; ☎(972) 21 62 96 (Mon–Fri 0900–1400).

There is plenty of cheap accommodation, with all the best places in the old town – try around the cathedral and C. SANTA CLARA. Alternatively, head for the streets around PLAÇA DE LA CONSTITUTIÓ. From Oct–June it may be harder to find rooms because lodgings are full of students. Youth hostel: **Cerverí de Girona**, CARRER DELS CIUTADANS 9; ☎(972) 21 80 03; fax: (972) 21 20 23.

BARCELONA

See p. 123.

(for Directory information, see p. 564 and 560). Inexpensive to travel in and blessed with a warm climate, **Spain** is astonishingly varied, ranging from the fashion-conscious sophistication and pulsating atmospheres of Madrid and Barcelona to rural scenes that look as if they might belong to another continent, or another century. It's not consistently beautiful – views from the train might take in hideous high-rise developments or uneventful cereal plains, whilst much of the coast is taken up with concrete resorts that sprang up in the 1950s and 1960s to provide cheap package holidays. But the classic Spanish elements are there too – parched, empty landscapes dotted with cypresses and cacti and backed by rugged sierras, lines of poplars receding to hazy horizons, red-roofed fortified towns clustered round castles – the list goes on. Some scenes are peculiarly local: the lush greenness of Galicia, the spectacular snowy pinnacles of the Picos de Europa, or the canyon-like badlands of Aragon on the southern fringes of the Pyrenees.

Although surrounded on the landward sides by Spain, **Portugal** contrasts strongly from its Iberian neighbour, with a different language and customs; indeed for centuries the two countries were at war with each other. Portugal prospered as a great maritime power and ruled a far-flung empire across Africa, the Far East and South America. For some 500 years the Arabs held sway over country. You'll see Moorish buildings with low domes and flat roofs, while some of the architecture is uniquely Portuguese, such as the *Manueline* style (a flamboyant transition between Gothic and renaissance).

Landscapes look positively lush (especially compared to Spain), with rolling hills dotted with orange, lemon and olive groves. Inland rises a chain of lowish mountains with some timeless fortified towns.

Away from the touristy Algarve, there are plenty of smaller places awaiting discovery, and much of it is amazingly untouched and little-developed – you'll still see peasants with donkeys, and find communities rich in rural customs. Low prices make it tempting to linger, and distances are small.

INFORMATION

PARADORES

Central booking service in Madrid for *Paradores* throughout the whole country ☎(1) 559 00 69.

CAMPING

Book locally or through the **Federación Española de Empresarios de Campings**, San Bernardo, 97/99. Building Colomina, 5. 28015 Madrid, ☎(91) 448 1234, fax: (91) 448 1267.

SPAIN

ACCOMMODATION

There's generally no problem finding somewhere to stay, outside major festivals and other peak periods; however, some large cities (notably Madrid) can be problematic, with virtually everywhere booked up by 0900; accordingly book ahead, for example through the **Hostelling International Booking Network (IBN).**

BUDGET ACCOMMODATION By strolling around, you'll often find budget places congregated near the station and around the main square. Thanks to a useful hierarchy imposed by regional tourist authorities, accommodation is graded according to facilities. Cheapest are the basic **boarding houses** known variously as *fondas* (look for plaques marked F), *Pensionei* (P), *Posadas, Ventas* and *Casas de Huéspedes;* then come *Hostales* (HS) and *Hostales Residencias* (HR); generally higher in the pecking order are *hotels* (H), ranging from one- to five-star. Note that there can be an overlap between different types of accommodation, e.g. the best *Hostales Residencias* are often better value than the low-grade (one- to two-star) hotels. If there is also an 'R' on the plaque, do not expect a full dining service.

HISTORIC ACCOMMODATION There's also scope for staying in a number of castles, old monasteries and other historic buildings, which are government-run hotels called *Paradores Nacionales* (or *paradors*); these tend to be very expensive, but the standard is very high.

PRIVATE HOMES Private homes that offer rooms are known as *Casas Particulares*. They seldom have much in the way of facilities, but are usually central and almost invariably very cheap. *Casas Rústicas* are farmhouses and *Refugios* are mountain huts.

Tourist Offices will give you information about accommodation, but they are not allowed to make hotel reservations. In major cities, there are often hotel booking agencies at the airports and railway stations. Prices away from major resorts start at about Pta2500 for a double room (Pta1500 for a single). Double beds are rare (double rooms usually have twin beds), so ask for *matrimonio* if you want a double bed. By law, places that officially provide accommodation must place a notice (updated every year) in every bedroom stating the maximum amount payable for that room. The price includes all taxes and service charges (but seldom breakfast), and you should pay no more than the stated amount (which is for the room, not per person). When paying for your room, it is a good idea to keep a copy of the quoted price or a copy of the accommodation guide handy as some places have a tendency to put the prices up for tourists. All hotels and hostels are listed in the *Guía de Hoteles*, an annual publication available from Tourist Offices.

YOUTH HOSTELS There are dozens of **HI** youth hostels around the country, and some universities offer accommodation in student dormitories *(Colegios Mayores)* when students are not in residence.

CAMPING There are over 500 **campsites** (some open all year, others just in summer) and the Spanish Tourist Office issues a list of the approved ones *(Guía de Campings)*, which are classified as luxury, first, second and third class. You can camp 'rough' in most suitable places, but not on tourist beaches.

FOOD AND DRINK

The pattern is to have a light **breakfast:** coffee or hot chocolate with rolls or fritters *(churros)*. The main meal is **lunch** (1330–1500 – nearer 1500 on Sunday). Dinner is a little lighter, but can still consist of three courses, and is eaten at around 2200. Restaurants are open only for lunch and dinner, so go to *cafeterías* (usually open 0800–midnight) for breakfast and light meals/snacks. *Platos combinados* and *menú del día* are both good value. If you want an inexpensive light meal, ask for *raciones*, a larger portion of *tapas* (little more than nibbles, intended as aperitifs). The best-known Spanish dish is *paella*, which originated in Valencia; it is at its best when made to order – which takes about half an hour. Another famous dish is *gazpacho* (cold tomato soup), which originated in Andalucía and is found mainly in the south.

Choose your drinking-place according to what you want to consume. For **beer**, you need a bar or *cervecería*, for wine a *taberna* or *bodega*. For **cider** (in the north), you need a *cidreria*. The custom is to pay for all your drinks at the end of the evening, although this is changing in some resort areas. Many drinking-places have a dining-room *(comedor)* at the rear if you want a full meal, or you can go to a proper restaurant *(mesón)*. It is claimed that water is safe to drink, but check for a *'potable'* (drinking) notice above the tap. Mineral water is available everywhere. Coffee tends to be strong. There are some excellent **wines** (notably from the *Rioja* and *Penedés* regions) and Jerez is, of course, the home of sherry. *Sangría* is a very palatable drink based on wine and fruit juice. Beer is generally yellow and weak, but amply thirst-quenching.

PORTUGAL

ACCOMMODATION

A good bet in most places is to find a room *(quartos or domidas)* in a private house, or in a pension *(pensão* – more of a business than a house, and graded from one to three stars). Other inexpensive places are boarding houses *(hospedarias/ casas de hóspedes)* and one-star hotels.

INFORMATION

Tourist offices will be able to give details of many of these, and can make bookings.

YOUTH HOSTELS

Hostels are mostly open 24 hrs and cost Esc.1200–2900 including bed linen and breakfast; for details, contact **Movijovem**, AVDA DUQUE D'ÁVILA 137, 1050 LISBON; ☎(1) 313 88 20, fax: (1) 352 86 21.

CAMPING

for a national coverage of **campsites** contact the **Portuguese Camping and Caravan Association**, AV. CORONEL EDUARDO GALBARDO 24, 1000 LISBON; ☎(1) 812 68 90.

POUSADAS

Advance reservations are essential. For further information or to make a reservation, contact **Enatur**, AVDA. SANTA JOANA A PRINCESA 10, 1700 LISBON; ☎(1) 848 12 21/848 90 78

Pousadas are state-run establishments in three categories. Some are converted national historic monuments, others are modern buildings in historic locations: both these types are four- to five-star standard. The third category is composed of comfortable modern inns or lodges, built in locations chosen for their wild remoteness and fabulous views: these are three- to four-star.

FOOD AND DRINK

The Portuguese pattern of eating is to have a fairly frugal breakfast and two big main meals: **lunch** (1200–1500) and **dinner** (1930–2230). Places that have evening entertainment may stay open until around midnight and, if so, tend to offer a late supper. The **cafés** and **pastry shops** usually stay open all day.

Eating is not expensive but, if your budget is strained, go for the meal of the day *prato do día* or *menú*. Eating is taken seriously, the cuisine flavoured with herbs rather than spices and rather heavy on olive oil. There is lots of delicious seafood such as grilled sardines and several varieties of *caldeirada* (fish stew). Other local dishes are *bacalhau* (dried salted cod in various guises) and *leitão* (roasted suckling pig). The most popular pudding is a sweet egg custard.

Portugal is, of course, the home of **port**, but there are also several excellent (and often inexpensive) wines, such as the *vinho verde* whites and the rich reds of the *Dão* and *Bairrada* regions. Do not be surprised if you are charged for pre-dinner bread, olives, or other nibbles that are brought to your table unordered. If you don't want them, say so.

EDITOR'S CHOICE

Ávila; Barcelona; Bilbao (Museo Guggenheim); Burgos Cathedral; Cáceres; Cádiz; Córdoba; Cuenca; El Escorial; Évora; Granada; Lisbon; Madrid (especially the Prado); Óbidos; Oporto; Picos de Europa; Salamanca; Santiago; Segovia; Seville; Sintra; Toledo. Scenic rail journeys: Madrid–Lisbon (p. 144); Lisbon–Santiago and on via Ourense to León (pp. 156, 162); Douro valley from Oporto (see panel, p. 158); Málaga–Ronda (p. 172); Granada–Almeria (see Where Next from Granada?, p. 179); Madrid–Burgos (ETT table 680).

BEYOND THE BORDERS

Algeciras–Tangier (Morocco) by ferry (ETT table 2502); Madrid–Paris via San Sebastián (table 46); Barcelona–Paris (table 11); Barcelona–Milan via Montpellier and Nice (table 90).

Spain's second city, metropolis of the revolutionary and energetic Catalan people, Barcelona, has real style and demands at least a couple of days. The city is home to remarkable organic-looking Modernist (or Spanish art nouveau) buildings of Antoni Gaudí and wonderful specialist galleries displaying works by Picasso and Miró.

One less appealing aspect of the city is its appreciable crime rate. In particular, beware of muggers at night in the Barri Gòtic and the red-light district in the lower part of the Ramblas.

ARRIVAL AND DEPARTURE

RAIL There are two main stations: the central **Estació de França**, AVDA MARQUÈS DE L'ARGENTERA (metro: **BARCELONETA**), for long-distance national and direct international services, and **Estació de Sants**, PLAÇA PAÏSOS CATALANS, about 3.5 km from the old town (metro: **SANTS-ESTACIÓ**), for suburban, regional and international trains as well as those to the airport. RENFE information: ☎(93) 490 02 02.

Estació de Autobuses Barcelona Nord, CALLE ALI-BEI 80, ☎(93) 265 65 08, is the main coach station; metro: **ARC DE TRIOMF**.

From the port, virtually next door to Estació de França, ferries leave for the Balearics and Sicily. For details contact **Transmediterránea**, ☎(93) 443 02 62 or 443 25 32.

Aeroport del Prat is 12 km south-west of the city. Expanded and refurbished for the 1992 Olympic Games, it now has three terminals. Airport information, ☎(93) 478 50 00. RENFE trains, ☎(93) 490 02 02, run every 30 mins, between about 0600 and 2230, to and from Estació de Sants (journey time: 16 mins) and Estació Plaça de Catalunya (21 mins). The **aerobus** runs to and from Plaça de Catalunya every 15 mins. The service operates from the airport Mon–Fri 0600–2300, Sat and Sun 0630–2250; in the other direction, Mon–Fri 0530–2215, Sat and Sun 0600–2220. Additional stops are shown on the city map available from Tourist Offices. For information, ☎(93) 412 00 00.

TOURS

From the quay below the Columbus monument, **Las Golondrinas** (pleasure boats) ferry visitors around the harbour or across to the Olympic Port. Round trips last half an hour or 2 hours.

INFORMATION

There are three **tourist information centres**: ESTACIÓ DE SANTS offers information on the city. The other two, run by the Catalan state government *(Generalitat)*, give information on Catalunya and the whole of Spain.

For an English telephone information service run by Generalitat, dial 010.

From June–Sept information bureaux can be found at ESTACIÓ DE FRANÇA, in PLAÇA CATALUNYA, near the port, and in PLAÇA DE LA SAGRADA FAMÍLIA. The Tourist Office also runs street information services during summer. Look for staff in red and

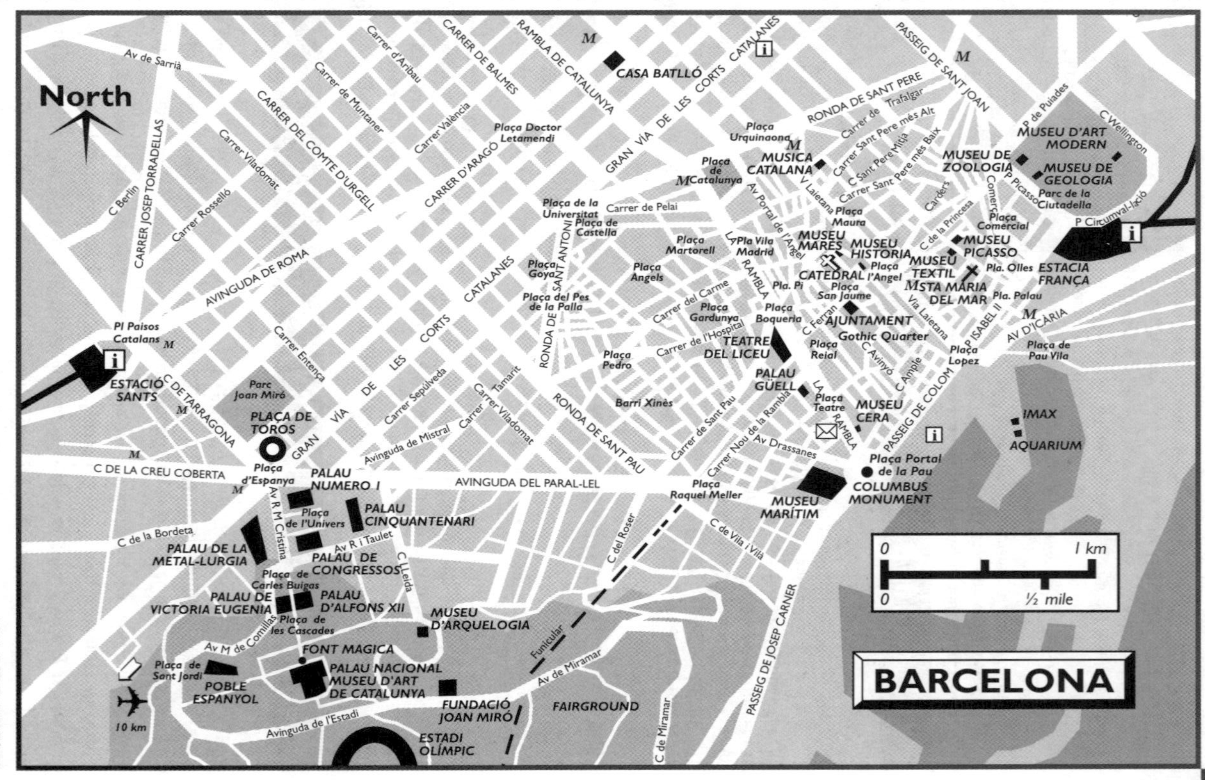
BARCELONA
North
0 1 km
0 ½ mile
ESTACIÓ SANTS
Pl Paisos Catalans
C DE TARRAGONA
PLAÇA DE TOROS
Parc Joan Miró
Plaça d'Espanya
C DE LA CREU COBERTA
C de la Bordeta
PALAU DE LA METAL-LURGIA
PALAU DE VICTORIA EUGENIA
PALAU D'ALFONS XII
PALAU DE CONGRESSOS
PALAU NUMERO I
PALAU CINQUANTENARI
Plaça de l'Univers
Plaça de Carles Buigas
Plaça de les Cascades
Av R M Cristina
Av R i Taulet
C Lleida
Av M de Comillas
Plaça de Sant Jordi
POBLE ESPANYOL
FONT MAGICA
PALAU NACIONAL MUSEU D'ART DE CATALUNYA
MUSEU D'ARQUELOGIA
Avinguda de l'Estadi
ESTADI OLÍMPIC
FUNDACIÓ JOAN MIRÓ
FAIRGROUND
Funicular
Av de Miramar
C de Miramar
10 km
AVINGUDA DEL PARAL-LEL
Avinguda de Mistral
AVINGUDA DE ROMA
GRAN VÍA DE LES CORTS CATALANES
CARRER JOSEP TORRADELLAS
C Berlin
Av de Sarrià
Carrer Rosselló
Carrer Viladomat
CARRER DEL COMTE D'URGELL
Carrer de Muntaner
Carrer d'Aribau
Carrer València
CARRER D'ARAGÓ
CARRER DE BALMES
RAMBLA DE CATALUNYA
CASA BATLLÓ
Plaça Doctor Letamendi
Carrer Entença
Carrer Sepúlveda
Carrer Tamarit
Carrer Viladomat
RONDA DE SANT ANTONI
RONDA DE SANT PAU
RONDA DE SANT PERE
PASSEIG DE SANT JOAN
Plaça de la Universitat
Plaça de Castella
Carrer de Pelai
Plaça Goya
Plaça del Pes de la Palla
Plaça Angels
Plaça Martorell
Plaça de Catalunya
Plaça Urquinaona
MUSICA CATALANA
Av Portal de l'Angel
V Laietana
Carrer de Trafalgar
Carrer Sant Pere més Alt
C Sant Pere Mitja
Carrer Sant Pere més Baix
Plaça Maura
Pla Vila Madrid
LA RAMBLA
Carrer del Carme
Plaça Gardunya
Carrer de l'Hospital
Plaça Pedro
Barri Xinès
Carrer de Sant Pau
Carrer Nou de la Rambla
TEATRE DEL LICEU
PALAU GÜELL
Plaça Boqueria
Pla. Pi
MUSEU MARES
MUSEU HISTORIA
CATEDRAL
Plaça l'Angel
Plaça San Jaume
AJUNTAMENT
Gothic Quarter
C Ferran
Plaça Reial
C Avinyó
C Ample
Via Laietana
Plaça Teatre
MUSEU CERA
Av Drassanes
Plaça Raquel Meller
MUSEU MARÍTIM
Plaça Portal de la Pau
COLUMBUS MONUMENT
PASSEIG DE COLOM
C de Vila i Vilà
C del Roser
PASSEIG DE JOSEP CARNER
Plaça Lopez
P ISABEL II
MUSEU TEXTIL
STA MARIA DEL MAR
Pla. Palau
MUSEU PICASSO
Pla. Olles
C de la Princesa
Carders
Comerç
Plaça Comercial
ESTACIA FRANÇA
AV D'ICÀRIA
Plaça de Pau Vila
IMAX
AQUARIUM
MUSEU DE ZOOLOGIA
MUSEU D'ART MODERN
MUSEU DE GEOLOGIA
Parc de la Ciutadella
P Picasso
P de Puiades
C Wellington
P Circumval-lació

white uniforms, with the standard 'i' symbol on their shirt sleeves.

There are two main youth information offices. **Centre d'Informació i Assessorament per a Joves** CALLE FERRAN 32, ☎(93) 402 78 00/1 (weekdays 1000–1400, 1600–2000), CALLE CALÀBRIA 147, ☎(93) 483 83 78 (Mon–Fri 1000–2000, Sat 1000–1330), gives information and assistance on cultural, sports and leisure facilities in the city. **Oficina de Turisme Juvenil** gives advice on the best travel prices and issues IYHF cards, amongst other services.

MONEY There are several **Ultramar Express** locations acting as Thomas Cook Licensees around the city.

POST AND PHONES The main **post offices** are at PL. ANTONI LÓPEZ 1 (Mon–Fri 0800–2200, Sat 0800–1400 for most services); RONDA UNIVERSITAT 23; and GRAN DE GRÀCIA 118. **Telephones** are available at ESTACIÓ DE SANTS (Mon–Sat 0800–2230, Sun 0900–2230), and at ESTACIÓ DE AUTOBUSES BARCELONA NORD (Mon–Fri 0800–2300). The dialling code for Barcelona is 93.

TOURIST INFORMATION CENTRES

ESTACIÓ DE SANTS, ☎(93) 491 44 31 (summer: daily 0800–2000; winter: Mon–Fri 0800–2000, Sat, Sun and holidays 0800–1400)

GRAN VÍA DE LES CORTS CATALANES 658, ☎(93) 301 74 43 (Mon–Fri 0900–1900, Sat 0900–1400)

INTERNATIONAL TERMINAL, BARCELONA AIRPORT; ☎(93) 315 13 13 (Mon–Sat 0930–2000, Sun and holidays 0930–1500)

BUREAUX

ESTACIÓ DE FRANÇA, ☎(93) 319 57 58 (daily 0800–2000)

PLAÇA CATALUNYA

PLAÇA DE LA SAGRADA FAMÍLIA (daily 0900–2100)

PUBLIC TRANSPORT

Maps of the city's public transport system are available from PLAÇA UNIVERSITAT.

For **general information** ☎(93) 412 00 00.

There are two fast and clean metro services. The **Metro**, run by the city *(Ciutat)*, has five colour-coded lines. Trains are designated by the name of the last stop. The **Ferrocarrils de la Generalitat de Catalunya,** ☎(93) 205 15 15, run by the Catalan State, serves fewer places in the centre, but can take you out into the suburbs and beyond. The same tickets are valid on Metro and Generalitat lines and there is a flat rate for all journeys, regardless of distance or location, of Pta130. You have to pay again if you transfer between the two lines.

The metro runs Mon–Thur 0500–2300, Fri, Sat and the day before holidays 0500–0100, Sun 0600–midnight.

The metro runs daily 0500/0630–2130/2230, with some lines continuing until 0400.

Passes: There are two types of card, both valid for ten metro journeys: T1 and T2. T1 cards are also valid on buses. Travel cards are also available which allow unlimited travel by bus and metro for 1, 3 or 5 days.

Tourist bus: The **Bus Turístic** (tourist bus) runs every day from 0900–2130 for most of the year, usually from late Mar to the following Jan. There is a maximum wait of 30 mins at any of the 18 stops and a full tour lasts 2 hrs 30 mins. A tourist information officer accompanies every bus, and your ticket includes discounts at several attractions.

Taxis: Yellow and black cabs can be hailed in the streets. Make sure you have change as drivers

FURTHER INFORMATION

Barcelona Hotel Association, VIA LAIETANA 47 ☎(93) 301 62 40.

Youth Hostels ☎(93) 483 83 63.

Camping
For more details: **Associació de Campings de Barcelona** ☎(93) 317 44 16.

often seem not to. To order a taxi, ☎(93) 357 77 55, 300 38 11 or 284 88 88. For information about prices or to make a complaint ☎(93) 263 12 06.

ACCOMMODATION

Barcelona has as wide a range of hotels as any major European city. They are graded in stars from one to five. Prices (excluding VAT) vary with the season from Pta43,000 (five-star) to Pta6000 (one-star) for a double room. **Pensiones** come as two- and one-star accommodation (both priced between Pta4000 and Pta6000 for a double with shared facilities). Most are located in the old part of the town, and demand is high in peak seasons. It is difficult to find a room for under Pta4000 except in the most basic of hostels.

PLAÇA DE CATALUNYA, at the top of **Las Ramblas**, is one of the best places to stay, but accommodation can be pricier than in the *Barri Gòtic*. The *Eixample* is further from the action but the wide, open avenues make it pleasant and safe.

Approximately 15 student halls of residence become hostels for young people in the summer. For details, contact a youth information centre (see Information, p. 125). There are also six **youth hostels**, all members of IYHF; it is advisable to book in advance.

Catalunya has 70% of all Spain's **campsites** and there are 12 within easy reach of Barcelona, mostly on the coast to the south of the city.

PENSIONS

Pensión Noya, RAMBLAS 133; ☎(93) 301 48 31.
Pensión Mont Thabor, RAMBLAS 86; ☎(93) 317 66 66.

HOSTELS

Hostal Residencia Lausanne, AVDA PORTAL DE L'ANGEL 24; ☎(93) 302 11 39.
Hostal Palacios, GRAN VÍA DE LES CORTES CATALANES 629; ☎(93) 301 37 92.
Hostal Windsor, RAMBLA DE CATALUNYA 84; ☎(93) 215 11 98.

YOUTH HOSTELS

Kabul, PLAÇA REIAL 17; ☎(93) 318 51 90 (metro: LICEU/DRASSANES).
Palau, CALLE PALAU 6; ☎(93) 412 50 80 (metro: LICEU/JAUME).
Hostal de Joves, PASSEIG PUJADES 29; ☎(93) 300 31 04 (metro: ARC DE TRIOMF).

CAMPING

El Toro Bravo, AUTOVÍA DE CASTELLDEFELS, ☎(93) 637 34 62, bus no.95 from RONDA UNIVERSITAT or RAMBLA CATALUNYA.
Filipinas ☎(93) 658 28 95.
La Ballena Alegre ☎(93) 658 05 04.

FOOD AND DRINK

Catalan cooking is known as good peasant fare, made from ingredients such as cuttlefish, serrano ham and salt cod. *Crema catalana* is a delicious local dessert, similar to crême caramel. Catalunya is also famous for its champenoise sparkling wine, *Cava*. It is the speciality of establishments known as *Xampanyeríes*, especially around **Gràcia**.

In the evenings, there are some good restaurants and tapas bars along CARRER DE AVINYÓ and the streets leading off it or along CARRER DE LA MERCÈ; iced sherry and local *Penedés* wine are widely on offer. For seafood specialities, try around the PASSEIG DE COLUM, at the bottom of LAS RAMBLAS. Away from the old town, the OLYMPIC VILLAGE is packed with bars and restaurants. The *Guía del Ocio*, published weekly, has a good coverage of restaurants. It is available from most news-stands. Off LAS RAMBLAS is **Boqueria** covered market, with an excellent selection of fruit, vegetables and meats.

HIGHLIGHTS

Art goes hand in hand with architecture in Barcelona. In this deeply style-conscious city, there is always a brave juxtaposition of old and new. Further-flung sights can easily be reached using the efficient metro system.

Best seen on foot, the **Barri Gòtic** is an enchanting, if disorienting, Gothic quarter inhabited from Roman times. A web of tiny dark streets radiate from **La Seu Cathedral**, a magnificent Gothic edifice, started in 1298 but only finished in 1892. The small Romanesque chapel of **Santa Llúcia** opens off the cathedral cloister, which encloses a lush central garden with palm trees, ducks and magnolias; on Sun mornings and Wed evening, the *sardana*, a distinctively Catalan dance, is performed in the square outside the cathedral. Nearby, in **La Ribera**, is the 14th-century **Basilica of Santa Maria del Mar**, often regarded as one of the finest examples of Catalan Gothic.

THE AQUARIUM AND THE ZOO

Barcelona has two notable animal collections: the **Aquarium**, on the harbour (by the cable car to Montjuïc), where a moving walkway conveys you through a tunnel of tropical and Mediterranean marine life; and the **Parc Zoològic**, Spain's foremost zoo.

DAY TRIP FROM BARCELONA

The best way to reach **Montserrat monastery** is by taking the train and then an exciting cable car. Trains depart from under the Plaça de Espanya, and connect at Monserrat Aeri with a cable car (leaves every 15 mins). Alternatively take one of the regular tour buses that leave from the Plaça de la Universitat. For the devout, the attraction is the 12th-century Virgin of Montserrat, in the cavernous basilica, but despite the crowds the setting is in any case interestingly surreal, with formidable crags of the Montserrat ('serrated mountain') dwarfing the scene. Twice daily a boys' choir sings in the basilica itself. A funicular climbs the mountain to a lofty hermitage and gains sublime views, and there are museums with religious work by Catalan, Italian and other artists.

For Free

Basílica de Santa Maria del Mar
Olympic Stadium
Parc de la Ciutadella
Parc Güell
Cathedral del Plaça de Sant Jaume

Barcelona is famed for its Modernist architecture, the most eye-openingly innovative being in the hundred or so blocks around the PASSEIG DE GRÁCIA, the so-called **Quadrat d'Or** (Golden Square) in the **Eixample**. At the fore was Antoni Gaudí (1852–1926), who used the city as his canvas, leaving such extraordinary, swirling masterpieces as the wave-like **Casa Milà** (PASSEIG DE GRÀCIA), with its twisted chimneys and weird ducts best seen by taking a tour of the roof, and the **Temple Expiatori de la Sagrada Família**, the astonishing cathedral to which he dedicated the last 43 years of his life, but which remains as yet unfinished. It's a synthesis of all his architectural styles that incorporates complex religious symbolism and visual representations of the mysteries of faith. Since Gaudí's death in 1926, work has continued on the building, but progress has been slow and hampered by controversy. Those with a head for heights can climb up the 400-step winding staircases of the spires (of which a couple have lifts), rising to over 100 m; for an idea of what the final structure should look like, visit the cathedral museum in the crypt.

Camp Nou

This vast 115,000-seater stadium is home to FC Barcelona, one of Spain's most successful soccer teams, whose arch rivals are Real Madrid. Fans unable to go to a match can visit the club museum and souvenir shop. (Metro: MARIA CRISTINA)

The recommendable tourist pamphlet *Gaudí* details other buildings by the architect and there is a museum dedicated to him, the **Casa-Museu Gaudí**, in the PARC GÜELL, an area he designed himself as a decidedly eccentric residential garden city. Inside the park, a flight of steps, guarded by a brightly coloured salamander, lead up to a large pavilion supported by over 80 columns – the original market place of the development. Above the pavilion, a colourful mosaic twists and curves its way around the perimeter of an open terrace, from which there are superb views.

Another classic panorama of Barcelona is from **Montjuïc Castle**, now a military museum, which is reached by cable car from AVDA MIRAMAR in PARC DE MONTJUÏC. The cable car stops halfway up at the **PARC D'ATRACCIONS** fun fair; you can reach the cable car station by funicular railway from AVINGUDA DEL PARAL-LEL (Metro: PARAL-LEL), and there's also a cable car to **Montjuïc** from the harbour.

Also near here is the Olympic stadium, while just across the hillside is **Poble Espanyol** (Spanish village), with mini-replicas of famous Spanish buildings and monuments.

Museums are closed on Mondays

The **Picasso Museum**, CARRER DE MONTCADA, is formed from two Gothic palaces on a street just 3 m wide. The collection is largely made up of his early work, but does include *Las Meninas*, a series of paintings inspired by Velázquez's famous work.

In Montjuïc, is one of a number of museums in the city to merit a visit for the architecture alone: the **Fundació Joan Miró** has paintings, sculptures, ceramics and tapestries by Miró, one of Catalonia's cultural giants, who died in 1983. Within a short walk, the **Museu d'Art de Catalunya** displays a superb collection of Romanesque art, much of it brought from country churches and now housed in the ***Palau Nacional***, a former exhibition hall of the 1929 Universal Exhibition. Another Catalan artist, Antoni Tàpies, is given place of honour in a Modernist building housing the **Fundació Tàpies**, C. ARAGÓ 225 in the *Eixample*.

SHOPPING

Barcelona is rapidly gaining ground as one of the great European centres of fashion and design. The main shopping streets are PASSEIG DE GRÀCIA, RAMBLA DE CATALUNYA and AVINGUDA DIAGONAL. Wandering off these streets sometimes pays dividends, and if you don't mind not being able to find the shop again the next day, try the streets in the Gothic quarter, near the cathedral. Barcelona's newest shopping centre, the **L'ILLA DIAGONAL**, is in an attractive white building designed by Rafael Moreo, who won the Pritzeker Prize for architecture in 1996.

NIGHT-TIME

Barcelona offers a superb range of clubs, bars and discos, catering for all musical tastes from rock to jazz; the busiest nights are Thur–Sat. Clubbing, however, is very expensive and there is often a high minimum drinks charge.

The *Guía del Ocio* has comprehensive listings of what's on in the city. The ***Eixample***, particularly the streets off AVDA DIAGONAL and PLAÇA REIAL, is reputedly the fashionable area for bars and clubs.

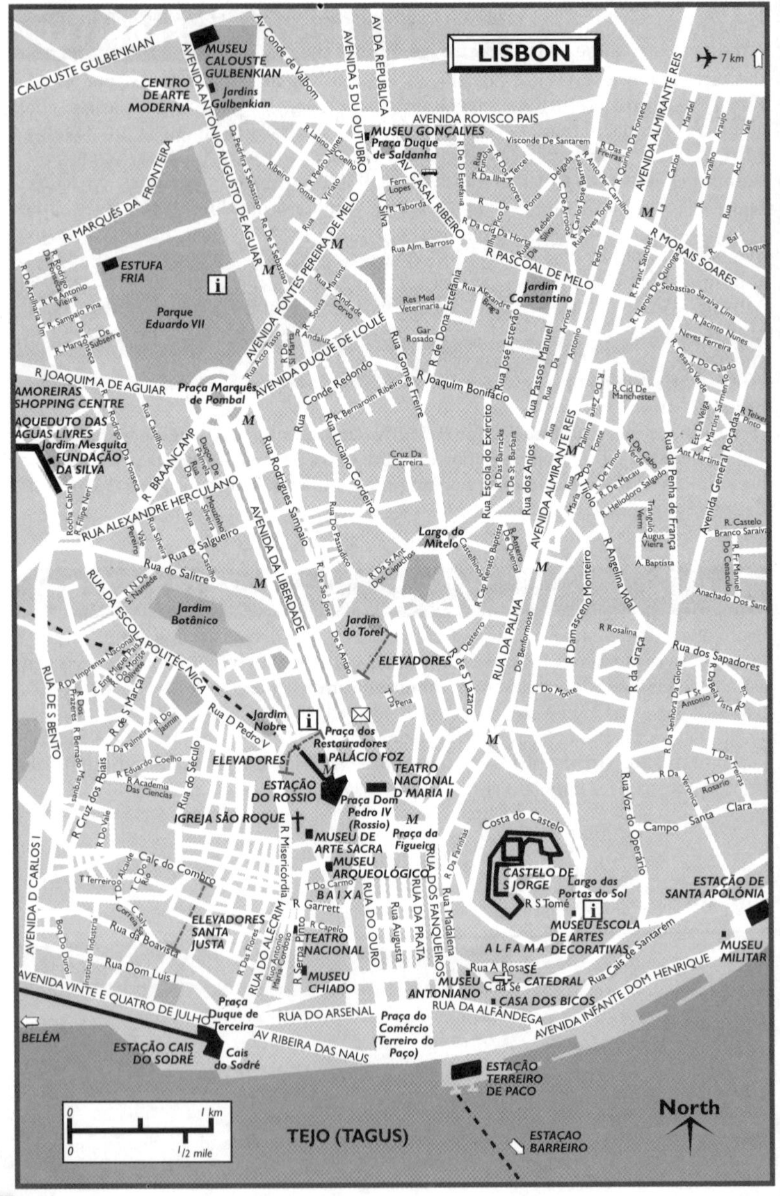
LISBON
7 km
CALOUSTE GULBENKIAN
MUSEU CALOUSTE GULBENKIAN
CENTRO DE ARTE MODERNA
Jardins Gulbenkian
AVENIDA ANTÓNIO AUGUSTO DE AGUIAR
Av Conde de Valbom
AVENIDA 5 DU OUTUBRO
AV DA REPUBLICA
AVENIDA ROVISCO PAIS
MUSEU GONÇALVES
Praça Duque de Saldanha
AV CASAL RIBEIRO
AVENIDA ALMIRANTE REIS
R MARQUÊS DA FRONTEIRA
ESTUFA FRIA
Parque Eduardo VII
AVENIDA FONTES PEREIRA DE MELO
R PASCOAL DE MELO
R MORAIS SOARES
Jardim Constantino
AVENIDA DUQUE DE LOULÉ
R de Dona Estefânia
Rua Gomes Freire
R Joaquim Bonifácio
R JOAQUIM A DE AGUIAR
AMOREIRAS SHOPPING CENTRE
Praça Marquês de Pombal
AQUEDUTO DAS AGUAS LIVRES
Jardim Mesquita
FUNDAÇÃO DA SILVA
R. BRAANCAMP
RUA ALEXANDRE HERCULANO
Rua Rodrigues Sampaio
Rua Luciano Cordeiro
AVENIDA DA LIBERDADE
Rua Escola do Exercito
Rua dos Anjos
AVENIDA ALMIRANTE REIS
Rua da Penha de França
Avenida General Roçadas
Largo do Mitelo
Rua B Salgueiro
Rua do Salitre
RUA DA ESCOLA POLITÉCNICA
Jardim Botânico
Jardim do Torel
ELEVADORES
RUA DA PALMA
R de S Lázaro
R Damasceno Monteiro
R Angelina Vidal
R da Graça
Rua dos Sapadores
RUA DE S BENTO
Jardim Nobre
Rua D Pedro V
Praça dos Restauradores
ELEVADORES
PALÁCIO FOZ
TEATRO NACIONAL D MARIA II
ESTAÇÃO DO ROSSIO
Praça Dom Pedro IV (Rossio)
Praça da Figueira
IGREJA SÃO ROQUE
MUSEU DE ARTE SACRA
MUSEU ARQUEOLÓGICO
Costa do Castelo
CASTELO DE S JORGE
Largo das Portas do Sol
R S Tomé
Rua Voz do Operário
Campo Santa Clara
ESTAÇÃO DE SANTA APOLÓNIA
MUSEU MILITAR
AVENIDA D CARLOS I
Calç do Combro
Rua da Boavista
ELEVADORES SANTA JUSTA
R Garrett
BAIXA
TEATRO NACIONAL
MUSEU CHIADO
RUA DO ALECRIM
RUA DO OURO
RUA DA PRATA
RUA DOS FANQUEIROS
Rua Augusta
Rua Madalena
MUSEU ESCOLA DE ARTES DECORATIVAS
ALFAMA
SÉ CATEDRAL
MUSEU ANTONIANO
CASA DOS BICOS
Rua Cais de Santarém
AVENIDA INFANTE DOM HENRIQUE
RUA DA ALFÂNDEGA
RUA DO ARSENAL
Praça do Comércio (Terreiro do Paço)
AVENIDA VINTE E QUATRO DE JULHO
Praça Duque de Terceira
AV RIBEIRA DAS NAUS
BELÉM
ESTAÇÃO CAIS DO SODRÉ
Cais do Sodré
ESTAÇÃO TERREIRO DE PACO
0
1 km
0
1/2 mile
TEJO (TAGUS)
ESTAÇAO BARREIRO
North

The Portuguese capital lies on seven low hills at the estuary of the River Tagus (Tejo). A massive earthquake in 1755 destroyed most of the city, but spared the Alfama quarter – a flower-bedecked labyrinth of cobbled alleys and balconied whitewashed houses – and, remarkably, the ancient 11-mile-long aqueduct. The rest of Lisbon was redesigned on a grid system and rebuilt on a grand scale, with classical squares and wide esplanades paved with mosaics. It's a relatively small capital by European standards, but you need at least two to three days to explore it.

Lisbon has an excellent range of day trips by rail, notably to the historic cities of **Évora** and **Óbidos**, and the palaces at **Sintra**.

ARRIVAL AND DEPARTURE

For general rail enquiries, ☎888 40 25. **Santa Apolónia Station** on the banks of the Tagus near Alfama, ☎888 41 81, is the main station, handling all international trains and those to east and north Portugal; accommodation desk, luggage lockers. **Rossio Station** serves the west. **Cais do Sodré Station** doubles as the quay for the Tagus ferries and as the station handling the local coastal services. **Terreiro do Paço Station** is the terminal for the ferries across the Tagus to **Barreiro**, the station for trains to southern Portugal. The 30-min ferry crossing costs Esc.170 (single) (free with some rail passes and tickets).There are ferry departures whenever trains are scheduled from Barreiro.

Express **bus services** to the Algarve and Porto are run by **Renex**, ☎887 48 71, departing from CAIS DAS CEBOLAS near Terreiro do Paço. **Terminal Rodoviario Do Arco Do Cego**, AV. DUQUE DE AVILA 12, ☎352 33 84. **Taxis**: Inexpensive; ☎793 27 56 or 815 50 61.

Portela de Sacavém Airport (☎80 20 60) is 7 km north of the city, with no train link; Tourist Office. Bus nos.44/45/83 go to the centre, or take the Aero-bus (☎363 93 43; every 20 mins; daily 0700–2100; buy tickets from driver, Esc.430; tickets valid for any bus, tram or funicular that day) that stops at various points in the city, including Cais do Sodré station, Rossio and Restauradores.

TOURIST INFORMATION

The main **Tourist Office** is in **Palácio Foz** (PRAÇA DOS RESTAURADORES), ☎346 63 07 (daily 0900–2000); commission-free accommodation service.) **Branch**: RUA JARDIM DO REGEDOR 50, ☎343 36 72. **Municipal office**: AV. 5 DE OUTUBRO 293, ☎799 61 00 (Mon–Fri 0930–1130, 1400–1700; metro: CAMPO PEQUENO).

INFORMATION

Thomas Cook Licensees: **Star Viagens S.A.**, TRAVESSA ESCOLA ARAUJO 31, ☎314 24 25.

POST AND PHONES

Main post office: PRAÇA DO COMÉRCIO (poste restante Mon–Fri 0830–1830). **International telephone calls**: from PRAÇA DOM PEDRO IV 68. The telephone code for Lisbon is 01.

PUBLIC TRANSPORT

Public transport in Lisbon is cheap, efficient and varied, consisting of buses, trams, the metro and funiculars *(elevadores)* between different levels of the city. Make a point of getting a walking map of the labyrinthine Alfama district.

TICKETS

Train: available from travel agencies or the **Rossio** and **Santa Apolónia** stations. **Buses and trams**: *Carris*, the Lisbon public transportation company for buses and trams, has kiosks which sell **1-day** (Esc.430), **3-day** (Esc.1000), **4-day** (Esc.1640) or **7-day** (Esc.2320) **city transport passes** (1 and 3-day tickets cover buses and trams but not the metro). Alternatively you can buy **books of ten tickets**.

Taxi-boats: If you are in a rush to cross the *Tagus* ☎0936 58 78 03.

Metro (underground) and trams: The **Metro**, ☎355 84 57, is fast and frequent, but operates only from Rossio to the north of the city. Lisbon's metro system is currently being extended.

For intensive sightseeing, the **Lisboacard** gives unrestricted metro access and free travel on most buses, funiculars and trams, as well as free or discounted entry to 25 museums and monuments. Available from RUA JARDIM DO REGEDOR 50, **Jeronimos Monastery** and the **Museum of Ancient Art**. **Prices**: 1 day, Esc.1700; 2 days, Esc.2800; 3 days, Esc.3600.

Trams are still an integral part of the city and are easy to use. **Carris** offer tram and bus tours: a slow and picturesque way to see the city. Tours leave from PRAÇA DO COMÉRCIO and cost Esc.2800. For **information**: ☎363 93 43 or 363 20 21; buy tickets from the driver.

ACCOMMODATION

Accommodation is scarcest and priciest at Easter and in summer; out of season you may be able to find something for around Esc.3000. The vast majority of cheap places are in the centre of town, on and around AVDA LIBERDADE or the **Baixa**. In the latter, head for the three squares PRAÇA DA FIGUEIRA, PRAÇA DOS RESTAURADORES and PRAÇA DOM PEDRO IV.

HOTELS

Pensão Ibérica, PRAÇA DA FIGUEIRA 10, ☎886 74 12.
Pensão Beira Minho, PRAÇA DA FIGUEIRA 6, ☎ 346 18 46; fax: 886 78 19.
Pensão Residencial Restauradores, PRAÇA DOS RESTAURADORES 13, 4TH FLOOR, ☎347 56 60.

YOUTH HOSTELS

RUA ANDRADE CORVO 46, ☎353 26 96 (metro: PICOAS).

CAMPSITES

PARQUE DA CÂMARA MUNICIPAL DE LISBOA–MONSANTO (on the road to **Benfica**), ☎ 760 20 61, fax: 760 74 74, has a pool (bus no.43 from **Rossio** to PARQUE FLORESTAL MONSANTO).
Clube de Campismo de Lisboa, COSTA DA CAPARICA, ☎290 01 00, is 5 km out of town, with a beach (bus from PRAÇA DE ESPANHA, **metro**: PALHAVÃ).

FOOD AND DRINK

Lisbon's restaurants are inexpensive and offer a wide choice. The bohemian **Bairro Alto** area is patronised by locals and particularly good value, as are the restaurants in **Alfama**. **Baixa** is aimed at tourists and more expensive, but still worthwhile. If you're really into cheap eats, there are food stalls in the market behind Cais do Sodré station. Students can also use the *cantinas* on the university campus.

HIGHLIGHTS

Alfama (metro: ROSSIO) is the old Moorish quarter, little changed since the 12th century, with winding cobbled streets overhung with washing lines and flanked by whitewashed houses, leading to lots of dead ends. One of the few areas to survive the earthquake of 1755, it's a marvellous place to explore on foot.

The medieval **Castelo de São Jorge** (🚌 no. 37 from PRAÇA DA FIGUERA) has ten towers linked by massive battlements and stands on one of the seven hills, giving superb views over the city. A royal residence for four centuries, later it served as a prison and houses the **Olissiponia Museum** covering the history of Lisbon.

Most attractions are closed Mon, but free on Sun morning.

The **Sé Patriarchal** (Cathedral), LARGO DA SÉ, was once a fortress. It contains some notable 14th-century tombs, a magnificent Romanesque screen and a fine collection of religious art, and exquisite cloisters.

DAY TRIPS FROM LISBON

ÓBIDOS

An enchanting medieval walled town (formerly a coastal settlement, but the sea has receded 10 km) and designated a national monument, Óbidos has winding streets and small whitewashed houses, their balconies brimming with flowers. The many places of interest include the 12th–13th-century **castle** (now a hotel), the 15th–18th-century **Church of the Misericórdia**, the Renaissance **Church of Santa Maria** and the 18th-century **town gate**. There are trains from Lisbon (Santa Apolónia or Rossio stations) and the journey takes about 2 hrs (ETT table 692). **Tourist Office**: RUA DIREITA, ☎(062) 95 92 31. **Accommodation**: **Pensao Martim de Freitas**, ESTRADA NACIONAL 8, ☎(062) 95 91 85.

Most museums are closed Tues morning as well as Mon.

Adjoining the **Museum de Arte Sacra** is the **Church of São Roque**, with its marvellous 18th-century chapel dedicated to St John the Baptist, which was constructed in Rome, then shipped in its entirety to Lisbon.

The **Parque Eduardo VII** (metro: PARQUE/ROTUNDA) is a landscaped park with a lake, a good view of lower Lisbon and some attractive tropical plants in its greenhouses.

The **Mosteiro dos Jerónimos** (Jerónimos Monastery) began life as a chapel for Henry the Navigator's seamen. Vasco da Gama was royally received in the chapel

Day trips from Lisbon cont'd.

QUELUZ AND SINTRA

The trains to Queluz continue to Sintra (the full journey taking 45 mins, ETT table 691), so both can be visited in one day trip. **Queluz** is the home of an exquisite small, pink rococo palace that was inspired by Versailles, built in the 18th century for Dom Pedro III. It became the summer residence of the Bragança kings; the interior and the formal gardens have scarcely changed since; closed Tues. **Sintra** (**Tourist Office**: PRAÇA DA REPUBLICA, No.23, ☎923 11 57; the station is a 15-min walk from town) is a small town built up against the luxuriantly vegetated granite upland of the Serra de Sintra, whose beauties inspired Southey and Byron. In town is the **Palácio Real**, the royal summer palace – a mixture of architectural styles, which has two remarkable conical chimneys.

The **Torre de Belém**, with its lace-like loggia, is an exquisite example or Manueline architecture. This tower was built during 1512–21 to protect the harbour entrance, and the fifth floor has a great view across the estuary. The tower was restored in 1845 and is furnished in period style.

when he returned from his triumphant voyages. The present building was designed by Boytac, the best of the Manueline architects, and construction began in 1502; its magnificent south door is often cited as the finest example of the style.

The foremost museum, with a delightful park, is the **Calouste Gulbenkian Museum** (metro: PALHAVÃ), housing the private collection of oil magnate Calouste Gulbenkian, with a superlative and all-embracing collection of art and applied art – from all ages and parts of the world, from Ancient Egypt to the French Impressionists. Next door is the **Centro de Arte Moderna Calouste Gulbenkian**, with exhibits by 20th-century Portuguese painters and sculptors.

The **Museu Nacional de Arte Antiga** on RUA DAS JANELAS VERDES is home to a 15th-century polyptych, which is a masterpiece of Portuguese art. Other exhibits include tapestries, ceramics, ancient sculptures and oriental rugs.

The **Museu Nacional do Azulejo** (National Tile Museum), RUA DA MADRE DE DEUS 4, is in a 16th-century convent which was badly damaged in the earthquake, but restored in the original Manueline style. The cloister survived and the *azulejos* (decorative tiles) include a huge depiction of Lisbon before the earthquake.

SHOPPING

The **Baixa** and **Chiado** districts are good for shopping of all kinds, while RUA DO OURO is a centre for jewellery. The neo-modern **Amoreiras** shopping centre on AVENIDA ENGENEIRO DUARTE PACHECO is a huge complex with over 300 shops.

There's a dawn fish and flower market daily opposite **Cais do Sodré** station. **Feira da Ladro** flea market takes place in the CAMPO DE SANTA CLARA on Tues and Sat.

NIGHT-TIME

Up-to-date entertainment listings are contained in the English-language magazine *What's On in Lisbon* (available from Tourist Offices, hotels etc).

There are many bars, discos and nightclubs, the streets around RUA DIÁRIO DE NOTICIAS (in the **Bairro Alto**) being a particularly lively area. Lisbon also has a lot of bars which feature *fado* singing (a uniquely Portuguese melancholy chant) and guitar playing. The best places are in the **Bairro Alto**; there may be an entrance fee or cover charge. Performances usually begin around 2200 and it's quite usual for them to stay open until 0230 or later.

ÉVORA

This is a stupendous walled city south-east of Lisbon (ferry from Lisbon to Barreiro for train to Évora; ETT table 698; 2 hrs 45 mins). It's best known for the 2nd-century AD **Templo Romano** (Roman Temple; its Corinthian columns standing to their original height) in the square in front of the magnificent 12th–13th century façade of the cathedral, while the cathedral museum's collection of sacred art is noted for its 13th-century ivory statue of the Virgin of Paradise. The **Museu de Évora** houses an all-embracing collection of art from Roman to modern. Other highlights include the **Paço dos Duques de Cadaval** (Palace of the Dukes of Cadaval) and the **Igreja de São João Evangelista** (Church of St John the Evangelist), with its splendid painted *azulejo* tiles. **Tourist Office**: RUA DE AVIZ 90, 7000 ÉVORA, ☎(066) 74 25 34.

THE ALGARVE

TThe Algarve (Portugal's south-west coast), is served with trains to **Lagos**, **Albufeira** and **Faro** (ETT table 699), plus a good bus network. The area is renowned for the quality of its beaches, as well as sports facilities and nightlife, but some of the resorts are hideously over-developed; June and Sept are less busy than July and Aug, and the climate's more bearable then. Some places, such as **Carvoeiro**, **Luz** and **Ferragudo**, have kept their old fishing village character, while **Albufeira** and **Lagos** are busy night spots. There are fine coastal walks from **Lagos** to **Salema** and from **Carvoeiro** to **Armação de Pêra**. **Faro**, the capital of the Algarve, has an international airport (5 km west of **Faro**; 🚌 nos. 14/16). **Tourist Offices**: (regional) AVDA 5 DE OUTUBRO 18,8000, ☎(089) 80 04 00; (municipal) RUA DA MISERICÓRDIA 8, ☎(089) 80 36 04.

TOMAR

On a wooded hill above the old town of cobbled streets is the fortified **Convent of Christ**, one of the architectural pearls of Portugal. The structure was erected in 1160 for the master of the Knights Templar (responsible for keeping open pilgrim routes to the Holy Land during the Crusades), but from the 1320s became the seat of the royally created Order of the Knights of Christ. Highlights include the Templars' Rotunda (the round chancel), modelled on the Holy Sepulchre in Jerusalem, and the magnificent Manueline-style window between the west end of the nave and Santa Barbara cloister. Trains take just over 2 hrs from Lisbon Santa Apolonia (ETT table 694). **Tourist Office**: AV. DR. CANDIDO MADUREIRA. ☎(049) 32 24 27.

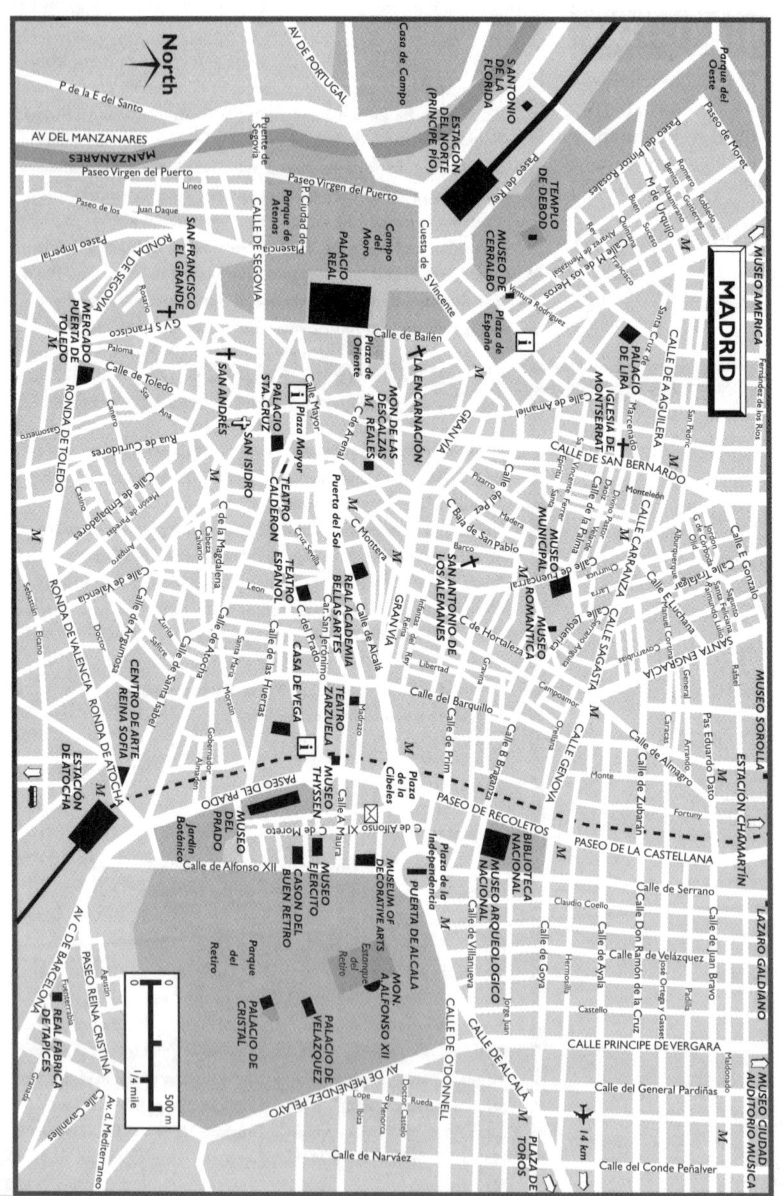
MADRID
North
Parque del Oeste
Paseo de Moret
Paseo del Pintor Rosales
SANTONIO DE LA FLORIDA
Casa de Campo
AV DE PORTUGAL
ESTACIÓN DEL NORTE (PRINCIPE PIO)
P de la E del Santo
AV DEL MANZANARES
MANZANARES
Paseo Virgen del Puerto
Puente de Segovia
TEMPLO DE DEBOD
Paseo del Rey
MUSEO DE CERRALBO
Plaza de España
Campo del Moro
PALACIO REAL
Cuesta de S Vincente
CALLE DE SEGOVIA
Parque de Atenas
RONDA DE SEGOVIA
SAN FRANCISCO EL GRANDE
Paseo Imperial
MERCADO PUERTA DE TOLEDO
GV S Francisco
Calle de Bailén
Plaza de Oriente
LA ENCARNACIÓN
MON DE LAS DESCALZAS REALES
Calle Mayor
Plaza Mayor
PALACIO STA. CRUZ
SAN ANDRÉS
SAN ISIDRO
Calle de Toledo
RONDA DE TOLEDO
Rua de Curtidores
C de Arenal
Puerta del Sol
TEATRO CALDERON
TEATRO ESPAÑOL
GRAN VIA
Calle de Amaniel
PALACIO DE LIRA
IGLESIA DE MONTSERRAT
CALLE DE SAN BERNARDO
CALLE DE A AGUILERA
MUSEO AMERICA
MUSEO MUNICIPAL
MUSEO ROMANTICA
SAN ANTONIO DE LOS ALEMANES
C de Hortaleza
CALLE CARRANZA
CALLE SAGASTA
Calle E Luchana
SANTA ENGRACIA
MUSEO SOROLLA
C Montera
REAL ACADEMIA BELLAS ARTES
Calle de Alcalá
C del Prado
CASA DE VEGA
Calle de las Huertas
Calle de Atocha
CENTRO DE ARTE REINA SOFIA
RONDA DE VALENCIA
RONDA DE ATOCHA
ESTACIÓN DE ATOCHA
TEATRO ZARZUELA
MUSEO THYSSEN
PASEO DEL PRADO
MUSEO DEL PRADO
Jardín Botánico
Plaza de la Cibeles
Calle del Barquillo
CALLE GENOVA
Calle de Almagro
ESTACIÓN CHAMARTÍN
PASEO DE RECOLETOS
BIBLIOTECA NACIONAL
PASEO DE LA CASTELLANA
MUSEO ARQUEOLOGICO NACIONAL
Plaza de la Independencia
PUERTA DE ALCALA
Calle de Alfonso XII
MUSEO EJERCITO
CASON DEL BUEN RETIRO
MUSEUM OF DECORATIVE ARTS
MON. A. ALFONSO XII
Estanque del Retiro
Parque del Retiro
PALACIO DE CRISTAL
PALACIO DE VELAZQUEZ
AV C. DE BARCELONA
PASEO REINA CRISTINA
REAL FABRICA DE TAPICES
AV DE MENENDEZ PELAYO
CALLE DE O'DONNELL
CALLE DE ALCALA
PLAZA DE TOROS
14 km
Calle de Serrano
Calle de Velázquez
Calle de Goya
CALLE PRINCIPE DE VERGARA
Calle del General Pardiñas
Calle del Conde Peñalver
Calle de Narváez
LAZARO GALDIANO
MUSEO CIUDAD AUDITORIO MUSICA
0
1/4 mile
500 m

MADRID

Chosen by Philip II in 1561 to avoid inflaming regional jealousies, the Spanish capital lies right in the geographical centre of Spain; indeed the PUERTA DEL SOL is the point from which all distances in the country are measured. Beyond the compact old quarter, most of it looks 19th century or later, the grand boulevards punctuated with triumphal arches and lavish fountains; elsewhere, there's pretty much relentless high-rise, most of it pretty drab. Architecturally, it must be admitted, the city dwindles into insignificance besides the likes of Barcelona or Seville. What Madrid does score for is its street and nightlife. The city keeps going late into the night.

With so many railways fanning out from Madrid, the city makes a good base for trips to such places as Toledo (p. 141), El Escorial (p. 154) and Segovia (p. 153).

ARRIVAL AND DEPARTURE

RAIL **Chamartín Station**, AUGUSTÍN DE FOXÁ, ☎(91) 314 0924, is in the northern suburbs. It is Madrid's main station (a modern place with a full range of facilities) and handles trains to the north, north-east and north-west, including those for France.

It is also the terminal for some of the south-bound trains, but most of those stop at **Atocha** en route. All *cercanías* (commuter trains) stop at Chamartín. There are accommodation services and a currency exchange that charges no commission. There are no showers at this station.

Part of **Atocha Station**, AVDA CIUDAD DE BARCELONA, ☎(91) 506 69 99, is the main terminal for the southern, eastern and western services, and also for trains to Portugal. The older part of the station, **Puerta de Atocha**, GLORIETA EMPERADOR CARLOS V, ☎(91) 534 05 05, is now the terminal for the AVE express service via Córdoba to Seville.

There are also two intermediate stations, **Recoletos**, PASEO DE RECOLETOS 4, and **Nuevos Ministerios** (on the corner of C. RAIMUNDO FERNÁNDEZ VILLAVERDE and PASEO DE LA CASTELLANA), but no trains originate from these. **El Norte Station**, also known as **Príncipe Pío**, is to the west of town, south of PLAZA DE ESPAÑA, and has suburban services only. All the mainline railway stations are connected to the Metro. 🚌no.5 leaves the station every 5 mins until 2330 (Pta135). Luggage lockers are available from 0730–2330 (Pta300–600).

✈ **Madrid Barajas Airport,** ☎(91) 305 83 43/4, is 16 km north-east of town. There is a Tourist Office in the international arrivals hall, ☎(91) 305 86 56, open Mon–Fri 0800–2000 and Sat 0900–1300. A **bus** operates every 10–15 mins between the airport and LA PLAZA DE COLÓN in the centre of town. The journey takes about 30 mins, ☎(91) 431 61 92, and costs Pta370.

INFORMATION

MONEY Thomas Cook licensees, **Ultramar Express**, are located around the city.

If you have a peseta shortage late in the day, **Western Union** has a currency exchange office in CARRERA DE SAN JERONIMO, which is open until 2200.

RAIL INFORMATION

The main **RENFE office** is at C. ALCALÁ 44; ☎(91) 563 02 02. For general RENFE information: ☎(91) 328 90 20.

TOURIST INFORMATION

Regional/provincial office: **Mercado Puerta de Toledo**, RONDA DE TOLEDO 1, ☎(91) 364 18 76 (Mon–Fri 0900–1900, Sat 0930–1330). **Branch office**: DUQUE DE MEDINACELI 2, ☎(91) 429 49 51 or 91 429 44 87 (Mon–Fri 0900–1900, Sat 0900–1300). **Municipal office**: PLAZA MAYOR 3, ☎(91) 366 54 77, (Mon–Fri 1000–2000, Sat 1000–1400). **Chamartín station** (opposite platforms 10/11), ☎(91) 315 99 76 (Mon–Fri 0800–2000, Sat 0800–1300). **Viajes TIVE**: C. FERNANDO EL CATÓLICO 88, ☎(91) 543 02 08. In summer, there are temporary tourist stands around the city.

POST AND PHONES

The main **post office** is in the **Palacio de Comunicaciones**, PLAZA DE LA CIBELES, ☎(91) 537 64 94 (Metro: BANCO DE ESPAÑA), and is worth a visit just to see the building; opening times vary according to the different services, generally Mon–Fri 0800–2130/2200 and Sat 0830–1400.

The main **Telefónica** office (for international calls) is at GRAN VÍA 30; open daily 0930–2330. There are branches at PALACIO DE COMUNICACIONES and PASEO DE RECOLETOS 41. The area code for Madrid is 91.

INTERNET CAFÉS

are springing up all over Madrid and seem to be all the rage at the moment. Try **La Cibertéca**, C. GENERAL PERÓN 32 (Metro: LIMA), ☎(91) 556 56 03, or **Laser**, C. ROSARIO 21 (Metro: PUERTA DE TOLEDO); ☎(91) 365 87 91.

PUBLIC TRANSPORT

Metro: With services every 5 mins (0600–0130) and colour-coded lines marked according to the destination, the Metro (subway), ☎(91) 552 59 09, is easy to use. Free maps are available from ticket offices, Tourist Offices and many hotels.

The bus system is comprehensive, efficient and the same price as the Metro, but not as easy to master. You can get a map of the whole system *(Plano de los Transportes)* from Tourist Offices, bookshops and the EMT booths on PLAZA DE LA CIBELES, PLAZA CALLAO or PUERTA DEL SOL. There are also route plans on the bus stops *(paradas)*. The regular city buses mostly operate 0600–midnight (there are a few night services from PUERTA DEL SOL and PLAZA DE LA CIBELES, with stops marked 'N', which run every 30 mins to 0200 and then every hour until 0600, but late at night it's safer to use taxis). Metrobus from Metro Stations, Pta670. All long-distance buses use the brand new state-of-the-art terminal at MÉNDEZ ALVARO (Metro: MÉNDEZ ALVARO). This has good facilities, including hot showers.

Taxis: An inexpensive way of getting around late at night; ☎(91) 547 82 00, or 445 90 08.

METROBUS TICKETS

There's a flat fare (Pta135), but you save by buying **Metrobus tickets** (books of ten tickets) for Pta670. These give access to buses and the Metro, but can only be bought in the Metro.

ACCOMMODATION

Madrid is full of budget accommodation, generally well-kept, with the basic necessities, but rarely distinctive or charming. Air-conditioning is not the norm and you may have to pay extra for showers in shared bathrooms.

C. ARENAL is virtually lined with reasonably priced accommodation. To the east of PUERTA DEL SOL, good deals can be found on CARRERA DE SAN JERÓNIMO and its side streets.

The GRAN VÍA is a hectic and noisy thoroughfare with a not unjustifiable reputation for prostitution; however, together with side streets such as C. DE FUENCARRAL, the area offers plenty of accommodation. C. DE LA MONTERA runs from GRAN VÍA to SOL. Although fairly seedy, it has a number of acceptable lodgings. There's also cheap accommodation around Atocha station, but it's a rather creepy area at night.

Madrid's campsites are both out of town, but compensate by having enough facilities to be self-contained.

ACCOMMODATION SERVICE

Brujula is an accommodation service with offices at the **airport bus station**, ☎(91) 575 96 80; **Atocha station**, ☎(91) 539 11 73; **Chamartín station**, ☎(91) 315 78 94; **Torre de Madrid**, 6TH FLOOR (above the Tourist Office) ☎(91) 559 97 05.

It covers the whole of Spain and costs Pta300.

HOTELS

Hostal-Residencia María del Mar, C. MARQUÉS VIUDO DE PONTEJOS 7, 2ND AND 3RD FLOORS, ☎(91) 531 90 64.
Hostal Victoria, CALLE CARRETAS, ☎(91) 522 99 82.
Hostal Amaika, C. ESPARTEROS 11, 3RD AND 4TH FLOORS, ☎(91) 531 52 78.
Hostal Aguilar, CARRERA DE SAN JERÓNIMO 32, 2ND FLOOR, ☎(91) 429 59 26.
Hostal Biarritz, C. DE LA VICTORIA 2, 2ND FLOOR, ☎(91) 521 92 12.
Hostal París, C. DE LA MONTERA 15, 2ND AND 4TH FLOORS, ☎(91) 531 91 52.
Hostal-Residencia Eureka, C. DE LA MONTERA 7, 3RD FLOOR, ☎(91) 531 94 60.

YOUTH HOSTELS

Santa Cruz de Mercenado, C. SANTA CRUZ DE MARCENADO 28, ☎(91) 547 45 32 (Metro: ARGÜELLES).
Richard Schirrmann, CASA DE CAMPO, ☎(91) 463 56 99 (Metro: LAGO).

CAMPING

Camping Madrid, 11 km from town on the N1 road to **Burgos** (Metro: PLAZA CASTILLA, then bus no.151 to IGLESIA DE LOS DOMINICOS) ☎(91) 302 28 35.
Camping Osuna, 15.5 km from town on the Ajalvir-Vicálvaro road (Metro: CANILLEJAS, then bus no. 105 to AVDA LOGROÑO) ☎(91) 741 05 10.

FOOD AND DRINK

Madrid offers a full range of regional dishes from all over Spain; local items include roast lamb and *sopa castellana*, a garlicky soup with poached egg in it. Restaurants don't really get going until well after 2200, late even by Spanish standards.

The old town, south-west of PLAZA MAYOR, is full of 'typical' Spanish bars and restaurants built in cellars and stone-walled caves, where *Madridleños* tend to head for after the evening *paseo* (stroll). However, as with the *tapas* bars surrounding PLAZA MAYOR, some of these tend to be touristy and over-priced.

Pork lovers can't leave Madrid without visiting the **Museo del Jamón**. A restaurant, not a museum, its walls are covered in huge slabs of meat, and diners can feast on Iberian ham in any conceivable shape or form. There are several branches throughout the city, including **Carrera de San Jerónimo 8** (near PUERTA DEL SOL).

A better area is around PLAZA SANTA ANA: CALLES ECHEGARAY, VENTURA DE LA VEGA and MANUEL FERNÁNDEZ GONZÁLEZ all host a number of quality budget restaurants, and PLAZA SANTA ANA itself is great for tapas. On C. DE ECHEGARAY, **La Caserola** is a lively bar with a restaurant at the back and **Taberna D'a Queimada** has a home-from-home atmosphere, in part induced by the painted jugs and dried peppers that adorn every conceivable surface. On the same street is **Taberna D'a Queimada II**, under the same ownership and just as good. **La Trucha** is a superb fish restaurant at C. MANUEL FERNÁNDEZ GONZÁLEZ 3. Nearer PUERTA DEL SOL, PASAJE DE MATHEÚ, which links C. ESPOZ Y MINA and C. DE LA VICTORIA, has several restaurants with outside tables, for example **Manacor. El Duero**, C. ESPOZ Y MINA 4, may lack ambience and charm, but serves good set meals at reasonable prices.

HIGHLIGHTS

PLAZA MAYOR (Metro: SOL) is a stately square surrounded by neo-classical buildings dating from the 17th century, at which time it was a centre of Spanish society, where such dubious entertainments as bullfighting and the Inquisition's *autos-da-fé* were staged. Today's pleasures are more civilised: you can sit at a pavement café, admire the equestrian statue of King Philip III and watch the world go by. The old **Hapsburg** area to the south-west of PLAZA MAYOR is the most attractive in Madrid.

FOR FREE

Campo del Moro, Catedro de San Isidro, Centro de Arte Reina Sofía (free on Sun), **Congreso de los Diputados** (parliament building; Sat morning).

The **Parque del Retiro** (Metro: RETIRO/ATOCHA) is a park laid out in the 17th century as the grounds of Felipe IV's palace; it's a cooling retreat from the summer heat of the city, with wooded corners, formal avenues, brilliant flowers and a large boating lake. Adjoining it is the **Jardín**

Botánico (Metro: ATOCHA), with three separate terraces, some of which feature vegetables as well as shrubs, herbs and flowers, including many exotic species.

Bear in mind that practically all museums close all day on Mon, except (if there's a special event) the **Centro Reina Sofia** (also closed Tues), and the **Palacio Real**. The **Museo del Prado** (Metro: ATOCHA/BANCO DE ESPAÑA) is one of the world's greatest art galleries, with admission a bargain at just Pta500. Many of its paintings were collected by Spanish monarchs between the 16th and 18th centuries. Today there are individual sections devoted to Goya, Velázquez, Murillo, Zurbarán and El Greco. The Italian and Flemish schools are also well represented.

Picasso's masterpiece *Guernica* – showing the misery of a small Basque town bombed by the Germans during the Spanish Civil War – hangs in the art museum **Centro de Arte Reina Sofia** (Metro: ATOCHA), also home to a fabulous collection of other 20th-century Spanish works, including paintings by Miró and Dalí.

The **Museo Arquelógico Nacional** (National Archaeological Museum) (Metro: SERRANO or COLÓN) contains a major collection of artefacts from all over Spain, including stone-carved Iberian mother-goddesses from the 4th century BC. In the grounds is a full-scale reproduction of the **Altamira Caves**: they contain one of the world's greatest sets of early cave paintings.

The late-Renaissance **Palacio Real** (Metro: OPERA), or Royal Palace, is a vast 18th-century Italianate pile, with colonnaded arches and some 2,800 rooms; the Spanish Royal Family now live in **Zarzuela Palace** outside the city. The state rooms were decorated in the 18th and 19th centuries and are full of priceless treasures.

The 16th-century **Convento de las Descalzas Reales** (Metro: SOL) was a convent for noblewomen and handsomely endowed by their families. It still houses a closed order, but parts of it are open: it has a superb collection of 16th- and 17th-century religious art (fittingly displayed in a series of shrines) and many other treasures, including a magnificent set of tapestries with Rubens designs.

DAY TRIP FROM MADRID

Toledo (ETT table 671; 8–9 trains a day from Madrid (Atocha), taking about 1 hr 15 mins; there are also buses every 30 mins from Méndez Alvaro bus station, taking 1 hr 30 mins).

A sense of history permeates every street of this famous and memorably sited walled city, perched on a hill and with the gorge of the Río Tajo (River Tagus) forming a natural moat on three sides. Over the centuries, Christian, Moorish and Jewish cultures have each left their mark on Toledo, which was a source of inspiration to El Greco, who lived and worked here for nearly 40 years.

Although possible as a day trip, it's highly recommended that you stay longer. Only the sheer number of tourists detract from the atmosphere.

As you walk from the station and cross the Tagus, you soon reach the ***Alcázar*** (old fortress). Aptly home to a military museum and on a site that's been fortified from Roman times, it has been repeatedly rebuilt, most recently following its near-total destruction in the Spanish Civil War.

Built over some 250 years, the heavily buttressed

Day trip from Madrid cont'd.

cathedral is one of the wonders of Spain for its stained glass, for the sculpture in the choir, for the tombs within its chapels and for its works of art, notably the *Transparente* – an extravagant baroque creation of paintings and marble sculptures, which catches the light in a most dramatic way. In the sacristy hang paintings by El Greco, Van Dyck, Goya and Velázquez, whilst in the treasury is a huge16th-century monstrance of gold and silver, which is still paraded through the town during the Corpus Christi celebrations.

The ***Iglesia de San Tomé*** (Church of St Thomas) dates from the 14th century and houses El Greco's famous masterpiece *The Burial of Count Orgaz*. The ***Casa del Greco*** is a small museum dedicated to the artist (though he didn't live there), with a number of his paintings, as well as some of his personal effects.

RAIL **Paseo de la Rosa**, ☎(925) 22 30 99, just east of the centre (a pleasant 20-min walk in, or take bus nos.5/6 to the PLAZA DE ZOCODOVER); bus no.5 runs from the bus station.

i **Tourist Offices**: the main office is at PORTE DE BISAGRA; ☎(925) 22 08 43. There is an information booth on PLAZA DE ZOCODOVER.

It can be difficult to find somewhere to stay at summer weekends. The best cheap lodgings are in the old town: try around C. DE JUAN LABRADOR or C. DE DESCALZOS. There is a **youth hostel** on the outskirts of town in a medieval castle (near the station), the **Castillo San Servando**; ☎(925) 22 45 54. The university sometimes has rooms available.

Campsites: **Circo Romano**, AVDA CARLOS III 19, ☎(925) 22 04 42, not very comfortable but only a 10-min walk from PUERTA DE BISAGRA; and **El Greco**, ☎(925) 22 00 90, which has much better facilities, but is 1.5 km out of town, on CTRA. TOLEDO-PUEBLA DE MONTALBÁN bus no.7 from PLAZA DE ZOCODOVER.

The **Museo Thyssen-Bornemisza** (Metro: BANCO DE ESPAÑA) is one of Madrid's newer attractions. After lending the city his priceless 800-piece art collection for a limited period in 1992, Baron Thyssen decided it should be on permanent view and so gave it to the nation; it represents a complete chronology of Western art, from the Italian primitives and medieval German masters to 20th-century pop art.

SHOPPING

For window shopping, try any of several of the main upmarket shopping streets off, or parallel to, C. SERRANO, which is the Spanish equivalent of Knightsbridge or Fifth Avenue.

Foodstuffs, including wine, hams, sausages, cheese and olive oil, are good value and high quality, with some splendid food emporia in Old Madrid. **El Rastro** (Metro: LA LATINA) is a huge flea-market that is something of a Sunday-morning institution. It's best to go early because it can be impossibly crowded by midday and begins to pack up around 1400. Around **Plaza Mayor** is a huddle of specialist craft shops selling such items as fans, ceramics, lace and leather. The PLAZA MAYOR hosts a collectors' market (coins, stamps, books, badges etc.) on Sunday mornings.

NIGHT-TIME

Madrid has a pulsating nightlife, centred on the numerous restaurants, bars and dance venues. Live music can be found easily. At weekends, many bars stay open until 0300 and some close much later than that. Discos tend to have a cover charge, but bars with dance floors don't.

The **Malasaña** area (Metro: BILBAO/TRIBUNAL) is good for music and bars and popular with a wide range of age groups. It centres on PLAZA DOS DE MAYO, C. DE VELARDE and C. DE RUIZ. Although flamenco guitar playing, dancing and singing belong to Andalucía, Madrid is said to have the best performers around, though some of it is aimed firmly at tourists with prices to match.

Huertas (Metro: ANTÓN MARTÍN) is the area around PLAZA SANTA ANA and has a huge variety of bars that stay open pretty much through the night. **Paseo del Prado** (Metro: ATOCHA/BANCO DE ESPAÑA) is rather more upmarket, with smart and expensive café-bars. The **Chueca** area has a lively gay scene, particularly along C. DE PELAYO.

The *Guía del Ocio* is a weekly Spanish language publication with listings of what's on in Madrid, including details of theatre, opera and clubs; it is sold at newsstands. Useful free handouts from Tourist Offices and hotels include *Enjoy Madrid*, *En Madrid* and *What's On in Madrid*. The free magazine, *In Madrid*, in English, gives a monthly low-down on Madrid youth culture, including pubs, clubs and gigs, aimed at young travellers.

SAFETY

Madrid has most of the crime problems common to any large city, but in many areas you are just as safe by night as by day since the *Madrileños* are sociable people and most of the streets are crowded in the evenings. Lone women should avoid lingering around the seedier parts of **Huertas**, **Malasaña** or **Chueca**

TOURS

Ask at the Tourist Office about hop-on and hop-off **bus tours** of the central attractions.

Prices vary: expect to pay Pta750–1600 for half a day, Pta1000–2000 for a full day and Pta2000–2600 for 2-day passes.

Tours are offered by **Madrid Municipal Tourist Board** *(Discover Madrid)*, CALLE MAYOR 69, ☎(91) 588 29 06 (Metro: SOL).

A leaflet, *Conozcamos Madrid* (available from the municipal Tourist Office) lists walking tours for Spanish speakers.

CELEBRATIONS IN TOLEDO

Toledo is famed for its processions, none more than **Corpus Christi** (May/June), when the route is decked out with awnings, embroidered shawls, flags, lanterns and tapestries, and the cathedral monstrance is paraded. **Holy Week** sees more processions, with the *Procession of Christ the Redeemer* on Wed, while on Thur and Good Friday the 'men in armour' represent the Roman legion and there's a *Burning of Judas*. On May 1 is a pilgrimage to the shrine of the *Virgen del Valle*, while the **Festival of the Patroness**, in mid Aug, features sports, bullfights and shows.

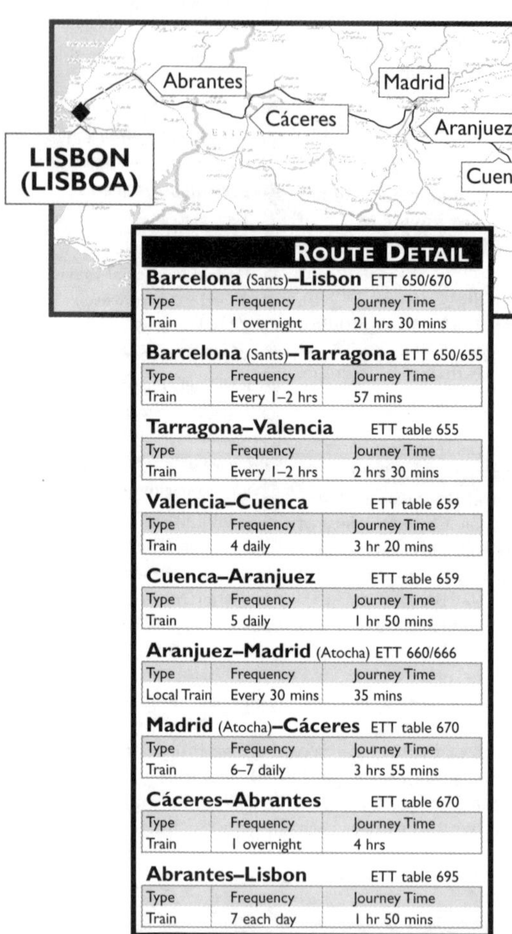

ROUTE DETAIL

Barcelona (Sants)**–Lisbon** ETT 650/670

Type	Frequency	Journey Time
Train	1 overnight	21 hrs 30 mins

Barcelona (Sants)**–Tarragona** ETT 650/655

Type	Frequency	Journey Time
Train	Every 1–2 hrs	57 mins

Tarragona–Valencia ETT table 655

Type	Frequency	Journey Time
Train	Every 1–2 hrs	2 hrs 30 mins

Valencia–Cuenca ETT table 659

Type	Frequency	Journey Time
Train	4 daily	3 hr 20 mins

Cuenca–Aranjuez ETT table 659

Type	Frequency	Journey Time
Train	5 daily	1 hr 50 mins

Aranjuez–Madrid (Atocha) ETT 660/666

Type	Frequency	Journey Time
Local Train	Every 30 mins	35 mins

Madrid (Atocha)**–Cáceres** ETT table 670

Type	Frequency	Journey Time
Train	6–7 daily	3 hrs 55 mins

Cáceres–Abrantes ETT table 670

Type	Frequency	Journey Time
Train	1 overnight	4 hrs

Abrantes–Lisbon ETT table 695

Type	Frequency	Journey Time
Train	7 each day	1 hr 50 mins

Fastest Journey: 21 hrs 30 mins

Notes

Most trains in Spain need advance reservations.

Barcelona to Lisbon: change trains at Madrid

BARCELONA – MADRID – LISBON

This trip across central Spain and Portugal links the three largest cities on the Iberian peninsula – Barcelona (p. 124), Madrid (p. 136), and Lisbon (p. 130). From the heart of Catalan-speaking Spain you head along the Costa Dorada – not Spain's most beautiful stretch of coast, but endowed with impressive Roman remains at **Tarragona** (where you can opt to head inland direct to Madrid via **Zaragoza**). Further down at the centre of the orange-and vegetable-growing Levante region is **Valencia** – big, untidy-looking, but still rewarding to visit. Beyond the wine-making town of **Requena**, with its Moorish castle, extend the excitingly rugged sierras of the north-east corner of New Castile, where you encounter **Cuenca**, with its precariously perched houses beside a precipice.

Madrid (p. 136) and **Toledo** (p. 141) give good reason for lingering in the very centre of Spain. Extremadura (meaning 'the land beyond the Douro') is the name given to west central Spain, a deeply rural region of vast rolling sierras, forests and landscapes rich in wildlife; there are also some deeply atmospheric settlements virtually untouched by the passage of time, notably **Cáceres**. Over the border into Portugal, **Abrantes** provides a base for visiting **Marvão**, an enchanting hilltop town in the wild Alentejo region.

TARRAGONA

With its ancient walled town above the modern settlement, Tarragona has dual attraction: its glorious cliff-top position and its rich heritage of Roman sites, including the remains of temples, a substantial amphitheatre and the Roman forum, which now abuts modern housing. There is also a necropolis, where early Christians were buried, and a well-preserved aqueduct a little way out of town. Along the foot of the 3rd-century BC Roman walls extends the **Passeig Arqueològic**, an archeological walkway. Catalonia's foremost collection of Roman sculptures, temple friezes, bronzes and mosaics is housed in the high-tech **Museu Arqueològic**, PLAÇA DEL REI, while the neighbouring *Pretori*, a Roman palace, contains the **Museu de la Romanitat**, with historical displays ranging from Roman to medieval finds. **La Seu** (the cathedral) exemplifies the transition from Romanesque to Gothic and has a fine cloister.

DAY TRIP FROM TARRAGONA

Port Aventura is one of Spain's best adventure theme parks (Apr–Oct). There are at least eight trains a day from Tarragona, taking about 10 mins. For further details ☎(977) 77 99 00.

RAIL PLAZA DE LA PEDRERA S/N; ☎(977) 24 02 02; centrally located.

i **Tourist Office**: (Regional) CARRER FORTUNY 4; ☎(977) 23 34 15. (**Municipal**) CARRER MAJOR 39; ☎(977) 24 19 53 (near the cathedral).

VALENCIA

Lush parks and gardens and a sprinkling of orange trees redeem the general modernity of Spain's third city, known as the home of *paella* (traditionally eaten for lunch, not dinner) as well as a place of effervescent outdoor life. Many historical structures were destroyed by inept town planners; the Spanish Civil War put paid to most of the rest, but two medieval gateways survive (**Torres de Serranos** and **Torres de Quart**) and there is a large old quarter with some pleasant squares, characterful if run-down backstreets and crumbly baroque mansions. There's a sizeable student population, based on the university on the north bank of the dried-up river; nightlife tends to focus hereabouts.

The old town (containing the main sights) is easily walked. EMT buses operate throughout the city; most can be boarded in PLAZA AYUNTAMIENTO (tickets from tabacos and kiosks), a traffic-ridden triangle overlooked by the copper-domed town hall. Two towers preside over the PLAZA DE LA REINA: the baroque spire of **Santa Catalina** and the **Miguelete**, which is the bell tower of the cathedral; climb the spiral staircase to the top for a magnificent view. Valencia's key building is the cathedral, a mixture of styles ranging from Romanesque to Baroque. A 1st-century agate chalice adorned with gold and pearls is said to be the Holy Grail and is displayed behind the altar in a side chapel.

The Gothic **Lonja de la Seda,** PLAZA DEL MERCADO, with its exquisite interior, is a legacy of the heady

LAS FALLAS IN VALENCIA

Las Fallas, a week-long festival in mid March, centres on a competition to produce the best *ninot* (papier mâché doll). The whole city celebrates as the entries are paraded through the streets and (on the last night) ritually burned, to the accompaniment of a huge firework display.

HORCHATA

In summer, many cafés and bars in Valencia offer *horchata*, a sweet milky drink made from *chufas*, or earth almonds, and bread sticks (either the chewy, sweet *fartons*, or the more brittle *rosquilletas*). The place to drink it is the **Horchatería Santa Catalina**, in the PLAZA DE LA REINA, which has been serving it for some 200 years.

ZARAGOZA

Although flanked by immense tower blocks and traffic-ridden *paseos*, the old town reveals a lively, historic centre. The station (where you can pick up a city map) is 3 km out; to avoid the 25-min walk, take 🚌 no. 21 into the centre.

There are two cathedrals: **La Seo** is Romanesque and Gothic, and contains fine Flemish tapestries and a Gothic reredos; more famous is the mosque-like 18th-century **Basilica de Nuestro Señora del Pilar**, with its domes of coloured tiles, named after the pillar bearing a tiny, much-venerated statue of the Virgin within the church (where the Virgin Mary is said to have descended from heaven in a vision of St James in AD 40). You get a good view from the tower (reached by lift, then stairs). The **Plaza del Pilar** features an interesting water monument of South America: stand at the closest point of the pool to the Basilica, crouch down, and you will see a clear outline of the continent. The **Museo Camón**

days of the 15th-century silk trade, while the nearby **Mercado Central** is a vast art nouveau market hall with a stained-glass ceiling and *azulejos* (coloured tiles).

The **Palacio del Marqués de Dos Aguas** is a baroque pile with an eye-catching alabaster door-way and home to the **Museo Nacional de Cerámica** (National Ceramics Museum; closed Sun and Mon), its displays ranging from ancient Greek vases to 20th-century creations by the likes of Picasso.

The main station is **Estació del Nord**, (96) 352 93 62, centrally located, 10 mins by rail from **Cabanyal** station, (96) 356 21 67, which serves the ferries. For RENFE rail information (96) 352 02 02. There is also an **FGV** station across the river from Torres Serranos, from which a network of narrow gauge railways radiate; (96) 348 46 26.

Tourist Offices: (Regional) C. de la Paz 48, (96) 394 22 22, Mon–Fri 1000–1800, Sat 1000–1400 and at Estacio del Nord, (96) 352 85 73. Mon–Fri 0900–1800 **(Municipal)** Plaza Ayuntamiento 1, (96) 351 04 17, and Avda Cataluña 1, (96) 369 79 32; Mon–Fri 0830–1415, 1615–1815; Sat 0915–1245.

Good budget areas are around Plaza Ayuntamiento and Plaza del Mercado. **Hostal Moratín**, C. Moratín 15, (96) 352 12 20, is comfortable and cheap, if slightly airless. **Hostal-Residencia El Cid**, C. Cerrajeros 13, (96) 392 23 23, gives special deals for groups and, they say, *Independent Traveller* readers. **Youth hostel**: **La Paz**, Avda del Puerto 69, (96) 369 01 52 (no.19 from Plaza Ayuntamiento), is open July–mid Sept. The most convenient **campsite** is **El Saler**, (96) 183 00 23; buses every 30 mins from Gran Vía Germanías.

Cuenca

Finely carved wooden balconies, armorial bearings, impressive doorways and breathtaking views over two river gorges are keynotes to this delightful town. Especially striking are the **Casas Colgadas**, the 13th-century tiered houses that hang over a sheer chasm and form the city's emblem. Level ground is in pretty

Zaragoza cont'd.

Aznar, C. Espoz y Mina 23 (closed Mon), has a fine art collection assembled by a devotee of Goya.

A modern attraction is the theme **Parque Zaragoza**, 1 km north from the station on Duque Alba. Open Mar–Oct, there are ferris wheels, rollercoasters and houses of horror.

The **Tourist Office** is on Plaza del Pilar, (902) 20 12 00; fax: (902) 20 06 35, and offers guided walking and bus tours. May–Sept: daily 1000–2000; Oct–Apr: Mon–Sat 0930–1330, 1630–1930; Sun 1000–1400.

The **Hotel Las Torres**, 11 Pl. del Pilar, (976) 39 42 50, gets a superb view of the Basilica. Alternatively, try the cheap **Hostal Milmarcos**, C. Madre Sacramento 40, (976) 28 46 18; or the **Poseda de las Almas**, C. San Pablo 22; (976) 43 97 00.

Visiting the Balearic Islands from Valencia

Trasmediterranea on Avda Manuel Soto, (96) 367 10 62, operate ferries to the Balearic Islands – Majorca, Minorca and Ibiza – from **Estación Marítima**, (96) 367 07 04. (ETT table 2510.)

short supply, a notable exception being the arcaded PLAZA MAYOR, flanked by the cathedral, which dates from the 12th century. It's more refined inside than its unfinished exterior suggests, and houses an absorbing treasury with paintings by El Greco. The best museums are the **Diocesan Museum** and the **Museo de Arte Abstracto**, the latter within one of the hanging houses and displaying Spanish abstract art.

RAIL (969) 22 07 20. The road leads straight up to the old town, but it is a hard climb and most prefer to take a bus nos. 1 or 2.

i **Tourist Office**: PLAZA MAYOR (969) 23 21 19 (Mon–Fri 0930–1400, 1600–1900; Sat and holidays 0930–1400, 1600–1830); GLORIETA GONZÁLEZ PALENCIA 2, (969) 17 88 00 (Mon–Fri, 0900–1400).

Several cheap places are found between the station and the old town, including **Pensión Adela**, RAMÓN Y CAJAL 53, 1ST FLOOR, (969) 22 25 33, and (more expensive) **Hostal El Pilar**, RAMÓN Y CAJAL 29, (969) 21 16 84; another pension closer to the old town is **Tintes**, C. DE LOS TINTES 7, (969) 21 23 98.

Meaty variations occur on Cuenca's menus, most famously *morteruelo*, a spicy dish combining a multitude of meats, including game, chicken, pig's lard, cured ham and grated pig's liver, with the odd walnut thrown in for good measure. Something of an acquired taste, *zarajos* is roast lamb's guts, one of a number of local concoctions that are rolled on vine shoots, while *ajoarriero* is a more generally palatable dish of cod, eggs, parsley and potato; trout and crayfish are also on offer. *Resolí* is a liqueur made of orange peel, cinnamon and coffee.

Day trips along the coast from Valencia

Flanked by long sandy beaches, the flat coastal strip from Valencia to Castellon (Castelló), named the **Costa del Azahar** after the orange blossom that grows there, has generally suffered the consequences of mass tourism. **Sagunto** (Sagunt), famed for its heroic resistance to Hannibal in the 3rd century BC, has a much-restored 2nd-century Roman amphitheatre (later covered in marble). Further north, the little seaside town of **Peñíscola** has considerably more charm (as well as more tourists), with whitewashed houses and winding streets huddled on a crag beneath a spectacular 14th-century castle. Valencia to Benicarto-Peñíscola takes around 1½ hrs; ETT table 655; Valencia to Sagunto takes 30 mins – infrequent service.

ARANJUEZ

Situated on the south bank of the Tagus, Aranjuez has just one major attraction: the spectacular **Royal Palace** (closed Mon). This started life as a country house that was presented to Ferdinand VI and Isabella, but the present structure dates from the 18th century and is a succession of opulently furnished rooms with marble mosaics, crystal chandeliers, ornate clocks and the like. In the gardens are the **Casa del Labrador** (Farmer's Cottage; more like the *Petit Trianon* at Versailles than a humble workman's dwelling) and the **Casa de Marinos**, housing royal barges.

(91) 891 02 02. 1 km outside town and 10-min walk from the palace. As you exit the station, take the road to the right and then turn left at the end.

Tourist Office: PLAZA DE SAN ANTONIO 9, (91) 891 04 27; (Mon–Sat 1000–1400, 1600–1900).

WHERE NEXT FROM ARANJUEZ?

Trains from here go to ***Toledo*** *(p. 141). Takes 20 mins (ETT table 671).*

CÁCERES

Despite its abundant charms, huge concentration of monuments and World Heritage site status, the golden stone town of Cáceres is less known than it deserves to be, and visitors are still almost outnumbered by the storks that have built nests on every conceivable perch. In medieval times it prospered as a free trade town, and was largely rebuilt in the 15th and 16th centuries; thereafter, it fell into decline and very little was added, hence the time-warp quality. Ancient city walls surround a largely intact old town, with its Jewish quarter and numerous gargoyle-embellished palaces, displaying the heraldic shields of the status-conscious families who built them; the place particularly comes into its own after dark, when it's dramatically floodlit.

The obvious starting point is the cobbled, partially arcaded PLAZA MAYOR, from which the gateway of 1726 known as the **Arco de la Estrella** (Arch of the Star) leads into the compact old town (easily explored on foot). You immediately reach the PLAZA DE SANTA MARÍA, abutted by the **Iglesia de Santa María** (with an interesting cedarwood retable), the **Palacio Episcopal**, and the **Casa de los Golfines de Abajo** (one of the two mansions of the Golfine family)

The **Palacio de Carvajal**, with its Moorish tower, houses the tourism and craft council, but you can visit the chapel and the first floor gallery (decorated in 19th-century style). On the top of the town's hill, the **Church of San Mateo** has a fine array of nobles' tombs, while the nearby **Casa de las Cigüeñas** (House of the Storks) was the only noble's house exempted from a royal decree and allowed to keep its fortifications. Home to a small

DAY TRIP FROM CÁCERES

Trujillo (47 km east of Cáceres; reached by bus, departing at 1315, 1500 and 1730; journey 40 mins), overlooked by a 10th-century Moorish castle, was built largely from the proceeds of the Peruvian conquests and known as the *'Cradle of the Conquistadores'*. From the bus station, a 15-min walk uphill leads to the **Plaza Mayor**, built on two different levels, connected by steps, and lined with once-magnificent palace-mansions, arcades and whitewashed houses. It is dominated in one corner by the **Iglesia de San Martín**, at the foot of which stands a bronze statue of conquistador Francisco Pizarro (who conquered the Inca empire in Peru), mounted and in full regalia. The Plateresque-style **Palacio de los Marqueses de la Conquista** was built by Hernando Pizarro (the elaborate window grilles and corner balcony are particularly attractive), and there are many other 16th- and 17th-century seigneurial mansions with lavish armorial bearings. From PLAZA MAYOR, C. DE BALLESTEROS leads up to the old walls, in which there is a gateway to the 13th-century

Day trips from Cáceres cont'd.

Romanesque-Gothic church of **Santa María la Mayor**, which contains Roman sarcophagi as well as the tombs of the Pizarros and other Spanish heroes, and a winged retable by Fernando Gallego. A short distance away is the **Casa-Museo de Pizarro**, with a reconstruction of a 15th-century *hidalgo* (nobleman's house) and an exhibition of the life of Pizarro.

Tourist Office: PLAZA MAYOR, ☎(927) 32 26 77 (Mon–Fri).

Accommodation: **Pensión Boni**, DOMINGO RAMOS 11, ☎(927) 32 16 04; **Hostal Nuria**, PLAZA MAYOR 27, ☎(927) 32 09 07; **Hostal Trujillo**, FRANCISCO PIZARRO 4, ☎(927) 32 26 61.

DAY TRIP FROM ABRANTES

Marvão, a captivating and remote-feeling, tiny walled town, has a terrific natural position, on a lofty ridge amid a terrain of imposing cliffs, and is well worth the complicated journey. Soaring over its ancient streets is a hilltop 13th-century castle, which from its impregnable

provincial museum, the **Casa de las Veletas** (House of the Weathervanes) stands on the foundations of a Moorish citadel and contains an *Almohade* water cistern *(aljibe)*, with a vaulted ceiling supported by horseshoe arches. The **Casa-Museo Yusuf Al Burch**, CUESTA DEL MARQUÉS, is a faithful recreation of a 12th-century Arabian residence.

RAIL AVDA ALEMANIA; ☎(927) 23 50 61. **Bus Station**: CARRETERA DE MERIDA, S/N, ☎(927) 23 25 50. The bus and train stations are together, about 3 km from the centre. Bus no.1 goes to PLAZA OBISPO GALARZA, near the PLAZA MAYOR. Luggage lockers Pta400.

i **Tourist Office**: PLAZA MAYOR 33; ☎(927) 24 63 47 (0900–1400, 1700–1930). From the rail station, walk up AVDA DE ALEMANIA. Cross PLAZA DE AMERICA, continue along AVDA DE ESPANA until SAN PEDRO. Walk through PLAZA DE SAN JUAN and down either PINTORES or GRAN VÌA to PLAZA MAYOR, where the tourist information office is on the right.

There's a good choice of hotels; the best area for both staying and eating cheaply is in the vicinity of **PLAZA MAYOR**. Cheapies include **Hostal Princesa**, CAMINO LLANO 34, ☎(927) 22 70 00; **Hostal Almonte**, GIL CORDERO 6, ☎(927) 24 09 25 (handy for the station); and **Pensión Carretero**, PLAZA MAYOR 22, ☎(927) 24 74 82. **Campsite**: CIUDAD DE CÁCERES, ☎(927) 23 04 03 or 23 01 30, on the N-630 to **Mérida**.

ABRANTES

Sited high above the Tagus, the small hillside town of Abrantes originally defended the old Portuguese province of Beirã.. Above the town, approached through a maze of flower-bedecked alleys, are the remains of a castle of uncertain, pre-12th-century origins, re-built by King Denis in the 14th century. The keep has been partially restored and is now a belvedere offering panoramic views of the town, the Tagus Valley and the mountains.

The 13th-century **Church of Santa Maria do Castelo** (in the castle grounds) was restored in the 15th century and houses a museum containing Gothic works of art and *azulejos* (decorative blue and yellow tiles), and is also home to a trio of superb tombs of the Counts of Abrantes (the *Almeidas*).

ROSSIO AO SUL DO TEJO, (041) 314 06. No luggage lockers, but the Tourist Office sometimes lets visitors leave bags. The station is about 4 km south of the town centre, on the other side of the River Tagus. nos.3/4/5 run from the station car park approximately every 30 mins (Esc.120).

Tourist Office: LARGO 1, E DE MAIO, (041) 225 55 (daily 0900–1800). Turn left out of the small street at the station. Cross the bridge over the Tejo, follow the road round, then take the turning on your left-hand side and continue up the winding steep hill, past the hospital, to Abrantes; the tourist information office is near the town's market and car park.

Pensão Alianca, LARGO DO CHAFARIZ 50, (041) 223 48 (single Esc.2200, double Esc.3800); **Pensão Central**, PRACA RAIMUNDO SOARES 15, (041) 224 22 (single Esc.2200, double Esc.3800); **Pensão Vera Cruz**, AV. DR AUGUSTO SILVA MARTINS, ROSSIO AO SUL DO TEJO, (041) 312 50 (single Esc.3000, double Esc.5000).

Budget places are around O PELICANO, RÚA NOSSA SENHORA DE CONCEICAO and PRACA RAIMUNDO SOARES (pleasant for sitting outside one of the cafés by the fountains).

Day trips from Abrantes cont'd.

865-m perch gives a 360-degree view, looking across the border into Spain.

From Abrantes, take the train to **Torre das Vargens** and change; Marvão's own station, **Beirã**, is some 6 km out from the town, so it's better to get off at **Castelo de Vide**, about 13 km away, and take a taxi to Marvão – there are no buses. (ETT table: 670, 40 mins Abrantes to Torre das Vargens; 4 trains a day. Torre das Vargens to Castelo de Vide: two trains a day, journey time 45 mins).

If you want to stay, ask the Tourist Office (RÚA DO DR MATOS DE MAGALHÃES, (045) 931 04) about rooms or houses to rent.

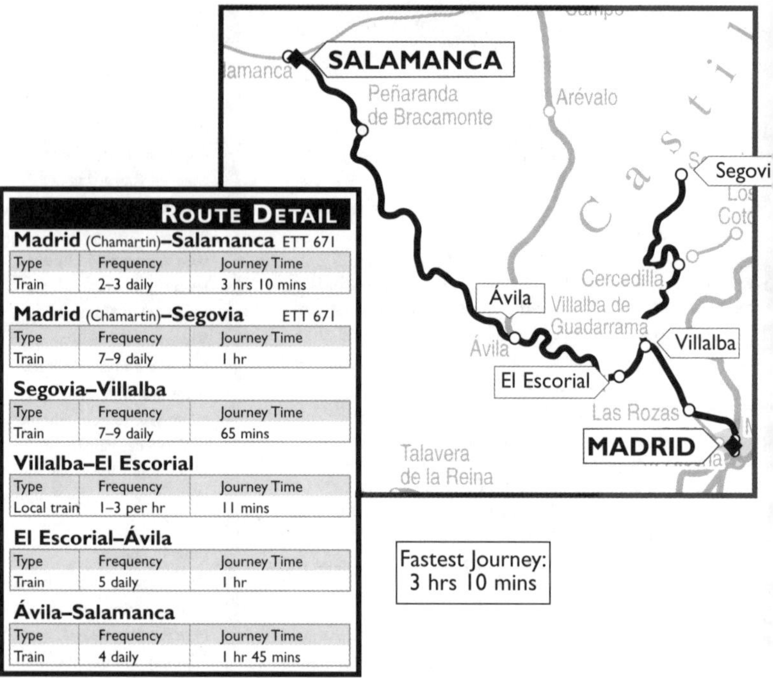

Route Detail

Madrid (Chamartin)**–Salamanca** ETT 671

Type	Frequency	Journey Time
Train	2–3 daily	3 hrs 10 mins

Madrid (Chamartin)**–Segovia** ETT 671

Type	Frequency	Journey Time
Train	7–9 daily	1 hr

Segovia–Villalba

Type	Frequency	Journey Time
Train	7–9 daily	65 mins

Villalba–El Escorial

Type	Frequency	Journey Time
Local train	1–3 per hr	11 mins

El Escorial–Ávila

Type	Frequency	Journey Time
Train	5 daily	1 hr

Ávila–Salamanca

Type	Frequency	Journey Time
Train	4 daily	1 hr 45 mins

From Madrid (p. 136) an incongruously suburban-looking train climbs onto the **Sierra de Guadarrama** to **Segovia**, one of the most exciting places in Spain. At Segovia station there is no hint of the nearby old city. But it soon comes into view after a short bus journey. From here retrace the route over the Sierra to the junction at Villalba de Guadarrama (or else take the bus from Segovia to Salamanca), and change trains, soon passing close to the vast complex of **El Escorial**, seen on the right-hand side of the train. Beyond the walled pilgrimage town of **Ávila** lies **Salamanca**, an elegant old university city built in a gorgeous yellow stone.

Segovia

This romantic walled hilltop city has a tremendous situation, perched above the **Rio Eresma** and looking out to the heights of the **Sierra de Guadarrama**.

The **cathedral**, which towers majestically above the rest of the town, dates from the 16th century and was the last Gothic church to be built in Spain. It's huge inside; one side chapel has great metal dragons supporting censers each side of a ceramic altar.

Scene of the coronation of Isabelle and the marriage of Philip II to Anne of Austria, the **Alcázar** is an entertaining visit, with quaintly undersize suits of armour dotted around rooms and dizzying views from the tower. From just below the castle there's a delightful semi-rural riverside walk.

The perfectly intact granite Roman **aqueduct** was built without mortar and continued to supply the city with water until recent times. The PLAZA DEL AZOGUEJO is the main viewing point, but you can follow the structure as it runs along more obscure streets, where the arches get increasingly wonky and amateurish.

The train station is in the new town; take no.3 (it's much too far to walk) to the PLAZA MAYOR in the old town, or get off just outside the walls. The **bus station** is a 15-min walk from the centre, or you can take the bus.

Tourist Office: PLAZA MAYOR 10; (921) 46 03 34, fax (921) 46 03 30. Another Tourist Office (in summer) is PLAZA DEL AZOGUEJO, (921) 44 03 02 or 44 02 05.

Stay in the old town. **Hostal El Hidalgo**, JOSÉ CANALEJAS 3–5, (921) 42 81 90 has a pleasantly old-fashioned restaurant (serving local specialities such as *judiones*, or huge white beans, and roast suckling pig). Slightly cheaper are the **Mary**, JOSE ZORILLA 102, (921) 42 00 03; the **Montero**, CTRA. VILLACASTIN 2, 2ND FLOOR, (921) 42 08 63; and the **Tagore**, SANTA ISABEL 11, (921) 42 00 35 or 42 42 82. The **youth hostel** is at AVDA. CONDE DE SEPÚLVEDA S/N, (921) 42 00 27, open July and Aug only.

EL ESCORIAL

Although it's some way from the station, you can easily see this vast grey palace and monastery, set beneath a hillside, from the railway. El Escorial is a magnificent 16th-century complex that includes a monastery, where the kings of Spain are buried, and a library with nearly 3000 5th–18th-century documents. Many notable works of art are on display in the complex, some forming an intrinsic part of the décor. The **palace** is of particular interest. Closed Mon; half price on Wed for EC nationals only.

About 2 km from town and it's a long uphill walk, so it's better to take a local shuttle bus to the centre.

Tourist Office: C. FLORIDABLANCA 10; (91) 890 15 54.

ÁVILA

The highest city in Spain, Ávila is encircled by medieval walls in a perfect state of preservation. Pilgrims are drawn to Ávila, which is indelibly associated with its native mystic and reformer Santa Teresa de Jesús (now the city's patron saint), canonised in 1622, who spent 30 years in a convent in the city. The **Sala de Reliquias** contains a variety of relics associated with the saint, including her finger, the sole of her sandal and the walking stick she used.

RAIL (920) 25 02 02.

i **Tourist Office**: PLAZA DE LA CATEDRAL 4; (920) 21 13 87, fax (920) 25 37 17. The bus and train stations are about 2 km from the centre. nos. 1/3 run from AVDA DE JOSÉ ANTONIO (opposite the train station) to within the city walls.

Hostal Continental facing the cathedral and next to the Tourist Office, is thick in faded grandeur, the rooms a strange blend of modern and antiquated, with period plumbing arrangements.

SALAMANCA

Salamanca is beautifully built in yellow stone and home to one of Spain's oldest universities. Virtually throughout the year there's a generous offering of concerts, exhibitions and other cultural events, many of them free.

Echoing to hundreds of footsteps, the PLAZA MAYOR is one of Spain's finest squares, a strikingly unified example of the baroque style. Walk south from here, past the

Casa de las Conchas (House of Shells), a 15th-century mansion named after the carved shells embellishing its exterior, the motif of the Santiago pilgrimage. Dating from 1243, the main part of the **university** (at the south end of RÚA MAYOR) is the country's prime instance of the plateresque style, seen on the ornamental façade, with its carvings of floral themes, royal heraldry, children, women and beasts.

The two cathedrals stand side by side – the **Romanesque Catedral Vieja** (old cathedral), with wonderful frescos, cloisters and a 15th-century retable, and the **Catedral Nueva** (new cathedral), displaying ornate relief carvings in the so-called churrigueresque style. Nearby, the **Monastery of St Esteban** is highly atmospheric.

Just below the cathedrals, the **Casa Lis** is a striking modernist edifice of glass and filigree ironwork, restored and now home to the city's collection of art nouveau, art deco and (for some reason) dolls. From here, you can walk down to the river and the 26-arch **Puente Romano**; the 15 arches on the city side are Roman.

Estacion de RENFE de Salamanca, PLAZA DE LA ESTACION; ☎(923) 12 02 02.

Tourist Office: CAMPAÑIA 2, ☎(923) 26 85 71, or PLAZA MAYOR 1; ☎(923) 28 13 42.

Accommodation is plentiful; head for the PLAZA MAYOR, around which numerous pensions are signposted at the foot of staircases. The **youth hostel** is at C. ESCOTO 13–15, ☎(923) 26 91 41, 1 km from the rail station.

ROUTE DETAIL

Lisbon (Santa Apolonia)–**Santiago de Compostela** ETT 695, 696

Type	Frequency	Journey Time
Train	1 daily	12 hrs 12 mins

Lisbon (Sta Apolonia)–**Coimbra** (B) ETT 695

Type	Frequency	Journey Time
Train	Every 1–2 hrs	2 hrs 35 mins

Coimbra (B)–**Oporto** ETT table 695

Type	Frequency	Journey Time
Train	10 daily	1 hr 15 mins

Oporto–Viana do Castelo ETT 696

Type	Frequency	Journey Time
Train	Every 2–3 hrs	1 hr 30 mins

Viana do Castelo–Valenca do Minho ETT table 696

Type	Frequency	Journey Time
Train	7 daily	1 hr 20 mins

Valenca do Minho–Tui (Túy) ETT 696

Type	Frequency	Journey Time
Train	3 daily	1 hr 10 mins

Tui (Túy)–Vigo ETT table 696

Type	Frequency	Journey Time
Train	3 daily	47 mins

Vigo–Pontevedra ETT table 672

Type	Frequency	Journey Time
Train	Every 1–2 hrs	30 mins

Pontevedra–Santiago de Compostela ETT table 672

Type	Frequency	Journey Time
Train	Every 1–2 hrs	1 hr

Notes
Lisbon to Santiago: change trains at Porto and Vigo.
Fast trains call at Coimbra B station.
A frequent rail shuttle connects to Coimbra A station few mins. later.

Fastest Journey: 12 hrs 12 mins

From the Portuguese capital the route heads northwards through a sequence of photogenic towns such as the old university town of **Coimbra**, the port-producing city of Oporto and the delightful coastal resort of Viano do Castelo, lying close to sweeping golden beaches. You can add on Tomar (to visit the fortified **Convent of Christ**, one of the architectural pearls of Portugal) by changing at Lamarosa. From **Oporto** it's worth spending a few days exploring the scenic and deeply rural Douro valley. Between Valença do Minho and Tui, you cross the border into Spain, and enter Galicia, with its wild coastal inlets known as the Rías Bajas; the journey ends in the breathtaking pilgrimage city of Santiago.

Remember Portugal's time zone is 1 hr behind Spain's.

COIMBRA

Coimbra was a centre of the Portuguese Renaissance and is the seat of one of the oldest universities in the world. Set on a hillside above the River Mondego, the town is packed with medieval character; in term time it has a lively, youthful air. Coimbra has its own version of the *fado*, a melancholy, monotonous and sentimental chant originally sung by sailors in the 18th century.

Although founded in 1290, the old university building is baroque, with a magnificent library resplendent in painted ceilings and gilded wood; you can also visit the grand **Graduates' Hall** and a small museum of sacred art (Esc.500; free to students with ISIC cards). The 12th-century **Sé Velha** (cathedral) is a striking Romanesque building with a fine altarpiece and Gothic cloisters, while the **Monastery of Santa Cruz** contains a 16th-century Manueline cloister, an elaborately carved stone pulpit and the tombs of the first two kings of Portugal. **Machado de Castro Museum**, a choice display of medieval and Renaissance art, is housed in a former bishop's palace, which still retains access to the old Roman forum underneath the building.

BOAT TRIPS

along the Mondego start from **Parque Doctor Manuel Braga** (about Esc.1000; 75 mins) ☎(039) 404 135.

RAIL **Coimbra A**, ☎(039) 82 46 32, 10-mins' walk from centre or 🚌 nos.1, 7, 11, 24. **Coimbra B**, 3 km north-west of town, handles long-distance trains, including those from Lisbon ☎(039) 83 49 98; 🚌 nos. 5/33. Frequent trains between A and B. For luggage lockers go to the bus station; cold showers at PATIO DA INQUISICAO near CAMERA MUNICIPAL.

i **Tourist Office**: (Regional) LARGO DA PORTAGEM (Mon–Sun and holidays 0900–1800), ☎(039) 82 38 86 or 83 30 28. (Municipal) Praça Don Dinis, ☎(039) 83 25 91 (Mon–Fri 0900–1800, weekends and holidays 0900–1230, 1400–1730). PRAÇA DE REPUBLICA, ☎(039) 83 32 02 (Mon–Fri 1000–1830).

DAY TRIPS FROM OPORTO

Allocate time to explore the mountain-backed **Douro valley** east of Oporto (ETT table 697), with its many vineyards as well as some enchanting places accessible by train. **Amarente**, memorably placed by the River Tâmega, has photogenic houses of wooden balconies and iron grilles, and a monastic church with gilded baroque woodwork. **Vila Real**, placed on Corgo Gorge, has a host of 16th–18th-century patricians' houses. North-east of Oporto, **Guimarães** was once the Portuguese capital and contains a rewarding medieval core within its industrial outskirts; **Paço dos Duques** (still used as the president's residence when visiting) includes a museum charting the town's former status, and there's a fine wooden ceiling within the Banqueting Hall. **Braga** (Tourist Office: Avda da Liberdade 1, ☎(053) 225 50, the nation's religious capital, has more than 300 churches as well as Portugal's oldest cathedral; it's the site of massive celebrations in Holy Week,

Near the station, the RUA DA SOTA area has cheap, very basic lodgings. **Youth hostel**: RUA ANTÓNIO HENRIQUES SECO 14, ☎(039) 82 29 55 (🚌nos.7/8/29 from LARGO DA PORTAGEM). **Campsite**: the **Municipal Sports Complex** ☎(039) 870 14 97 (🚌no.7 from LARGO DA PORTAGEM).

Plenty of centrally placed cheap eateries, for example in the University Gardens and in BECO DO FORNO and RUA DOS GATOS (alleyways between LARGO DA PORTAGEM and RUA DO SOTO). **Café Santa Cruz**, PRAÇA 8 DE MAIO, in part of an old cathedral, is a great place for coffee.

OPORTO (PORTO)

Portugal's second city dates from Roman times, when the twin settlements of **Portus** and **Cale** (after which the country is named) were built at the mouth of the River Douro and later gave their name to the whole country. Oporto gives its name to the fortified wine the British know as port; home of the port trade, its port lodges in the suburb of Vila Nova de Gaia, linked to the city centre by the double-decker coathanger-shaped Dom Luis I Bridge, are a major attraction, offering tastings and some explaining the maturing process too (often free; Sandeman's is the most popular tour). Moored on the river, small barrel-laden sailing craft *(barcos rabelos)* advertise the port houses such as Croft, Graham's and Cockburn.

The characterfully shabby old town, with its pastel shades and changes in level, is strongly atmospheric, notably in the **Ribeira** riverside area; there are cruises from here (much cheaper in the week than at weekends). The **Sé** (Cathedral), has baroque adornments, but more rewarding is the **Church of São Francisco**, a fine example of the Manueline style, with a dazzling baroque interior.

The **Soares dos Reis Museum**, housed in the **Carrancas Palace**, is acclaimed for its collection of the decorative arts, including Portuguese faïence. The **Torre dos Clérigos** is Oporto's symbol, an 18th-century granite bell-tower that gives a magnificent view. For an astonishing temple to money-making, take the guided tour of the **Palácio da Bolsa** (Stock

Exchange), which includes the **Arabian Hall**, a 19th-century pastiche of the Alhambra in Granada (p. 178).

To the west of the town ands set amidst magnificent gardens is the **Casa de Serralves**, an art deco mansion housing a fine collection of modern art.

Day Trips from Porto cont'd.

and 5 km east is the pilgrimage site of **Bom Jesus do Monte**, with a 116-m climb up the monumental 'Staircase of the Five Senses' to its Chapel of Miracles and massive reliquary. Some trains from Oporto to Braga require a change at Nine; there are also direct trains and buses from Lisbon.

Campanhã, Rua da Estação, (02) 56 41 41, near the south-east edge of town, serves Lisbon trains (no. 35 to centre); luggage lockers and cash machine. **São Bento**, near Praça da Liberdade, (02) 200 27 22, much more central (wonderful tiling makes it a sight in itself; Sun market), handles local/regional services. Frequent connections between the stations, taking 5 mins. Leave **São Bento** Station and turn right up Praça da Liberdade then Avda dos Aliados; tourist information office is on your left.

Tourist Offices: Praça Dom João I, 25, (02) 205 75 14, (Mon–Fri 0900–1700, Sat and Sun closed) and Rua Clube dos Fenianos 25, (02) 205 27 40 (Mon–Fri 0900–1900, Sat, Sun and Holidays 1000–1700, summer; Mon–Fri 0900–1730, weekends and holidays 1000–1700, winter).

Francisco Sá Carneiro, (02) 941 31 50/60 (no. 56 from Praça de Lisboa); **Tourist Office**, (02) 941 25 34.

Tourist passes and day tickets, from **STCP** kiosks, are valid for buses, trolley-buses and trams.

For cheap lodgings, try the central area around Avda dos Aliados. Avoid the dockside Ribeira. **Pensão Residencial Monumental**, Avda dos Aliados 151, 4th floor, (02) 200 39 64. **Pensão Europa**, Rua do Almada 396/398, (02) 200 69 71. **Pensão Franca**, Praça Gomes Teixeira 7, 2nd floor, (02) 200 27 91. **Campsites: Parque de Prelada**, Rua Monte dos Burgos, (02) 81 26 16 (no.6 from Praça da Liberdade); two in Vila Nova de Gaia (**Salgueiros**, (02) 781 05 00, and **Marisol**, (02) 713 59 42).

VIANA DO CASTELO

This old fortress town doubles as the Costa Verde's most pleasant resort, with the beach on one side of the River Lima and the charming little town (noted for its Renaissance and Manueline architecture, which appeared when trade began with the great Hanseatic cities of northern Europe) on the other. It's also a centre of Portuguese folklore and famous for its handicrafts.

With the exception of **Santa Luzia** on the top of the **Monte de Santa Luzia** (accessible by funicular from Avda 25 de Abril; excellent view), interesting sights are walkable. The central square, **Praça de República**, has a 16th-century fountain that has been copied all over the region. Some choice examples of *azulejos* (tiles) can be seen in **Misericórdia Church** and the **Municipal Museum** (also showing glazed earthenware and furniture). Viana do Castelo's **Romaria** (in Aug) is the biggest festival in the country.

There are several spectacular sandy beaches accessible by train within half an hour, on the line to **Valença**.

RAIL AVDA DOS COMBATENTES, ☎(058) 82 22 96; near the town centre.

i **Tourist Office**: RUA DO HOSPITAL VELHO, ☎(058) 82 26 20.

Pensions are easy to find, but not that cheap; rooms in private houses are often a better bet (look for cards in windows). **Campsites: Orbitur**, ☎(058) 32 21 67, and **Inatel**, ☎(058) 32 20 42 (both by Cabedelo beach, about 2 km away; buses from AVDA 25 DE ABRIL and main bus station, plus seasonal ferry from LARGO 5 DE OUTUBRO).

VALENÇA DO MINHO

Unsightly modern sprawl has marred the approaches to this ancient town by the Minho river, but it still has its fortress-with-a-fortress guarding the border with Spain. Much survives of the 17th–18th-century walls and there are narrow old streets of white houses.

RAIL ☎(051) 82 41 55 or 55 35 36; on the east side of the new town.

i **Tourist Office**: AVDA DE ESPANHA, ☎(051) 233 74/5/6.

TUI (TÚY)

A bridge connects this tiered Spanish town to Portugal. Tui has grown around the lichen-encrusted **Cathedral of San Telmo**. This impressive, austere Romanesque and Gothic building has a 13th-century cloister, carved choir stalls, an ornate 14th-century porch and fine Gothic sepulchres. Visit the churches of **Santo Domingo** and **San Bartolomé** if time permits.

RAIL ☎(986) 60 08 13; central.

i **Tourist Office**: **Puente Internacional** (PUENTE TRIPES) S/N, ☎(986) 60 17 89 (summer only).

Argentino, BO DE BANOS S/N, CALDELAS, ☎(986) 62 90 11; **Generosa**, CALVO SOTELO 37, ☎(986) 60 00 55.

YOU ARE LEAVING
THE AMERICAN SECTOR
ВЫ ВЫЕЗЖАЕТЕ ИЗ
АМЕРИКАНСКОГО СЕКТОРА
VOUS SORTEZ
DU SECTEUR AMÉRICAIN
SIE VERLASSEN DEN AMERIKANISCHEN SEKTOR

VIGO

Spain's major fishing port lies on a beautiful sheltered bay guarded by the Islas Cíes archipelago. It's a clamorous, busy place; in particular, the seafront is a hive of activity early in the morning, when there's a lively fish market *(pescadería)*. There are some attractive arcaded houses near the harbour, and **Castro Castle**, the ruined fort on a hill behind the town, provides a magnificent view.

The *Islas Cíes* are reached by ferry from Vigo. One of them is a bird sanctuary, but the other two can be visited. If you book ahead, ☎(986) 43 83 58, it is possible to camp there in summer.

PLAZA DE LA ESTACIÓN, ☎(986) 43 11 14 (central).

Tourist Office: C. ESTACIÓN MARÍTIMA DE TRANSATLANTICOS, ☎(986) 43 05 77. Also **Tourist Offices** near the station and the port in summer.

La Nueva Cubana, C. LEPANTO 15, ☎22 20 20. **Orensano**, C. LEPANTO 9, ☎43 51 12. **Martinez**, C. URUGUAY 25, ☎43 73 32.

PONTEVEDRA

This typical old Galician town on the River Pontevedra began life as a port, but its importance dwindled as the old harbour silted up. Although surrounded by a new city, the compact old town is pretty much intact, with parts of the original walls still visible around a maze of cobbled streets, arcaded squares with carved stone crosses and low houses with flower-filled balconies. **La Peregrina**, an unusual chapel in the shape of a scallop shell, is situated by the partly arcaded main square, PLAZA DE LA FERRERÍA, on the boundary between the old and new towns. The Gothic façade of the **Convent of San Francisco** looks onto the Herrería. **Iglesia de Santa María la Mayor** has an impressive Plateresque façade, which is floodlit at night. The 13th-century Gothic **Convent of Santo Domingo** by the **Jardines de Vincenti** is now largely in ruins but still evokes a certain splendour. The surviving wing holds part of the **Provincial Museum**, other sections of which are at PLAZA DE LEÑA.

AVDA ALFÉRECES PROVISIONALES, ☎(986) 85 13 13, about 1 km from the centre.

Tourist Office: C. DEL GENERAL MOLA 1, ☎(986) 85 37 16.

Budget accommodation is limited; there are some *fondas* and *pensiones* in the streets around C. DE LA PEREGRINA and PLAZA DE GALICIA, for example at C. DE ANDRÉS MELLADO 7 and 11. **Casa Alicia**, AVDA DE SANTA MARIA 5, ☎(986) 85 70 79, is welcoming. Others include **Casa Maruja**, AVDA SANTA MARIA 2, ☎(986) 85 49 01, and **Pensão Michelena**, C. MICHELENA 11, 3RD FLOOR, ☎(986) 86 32 91.

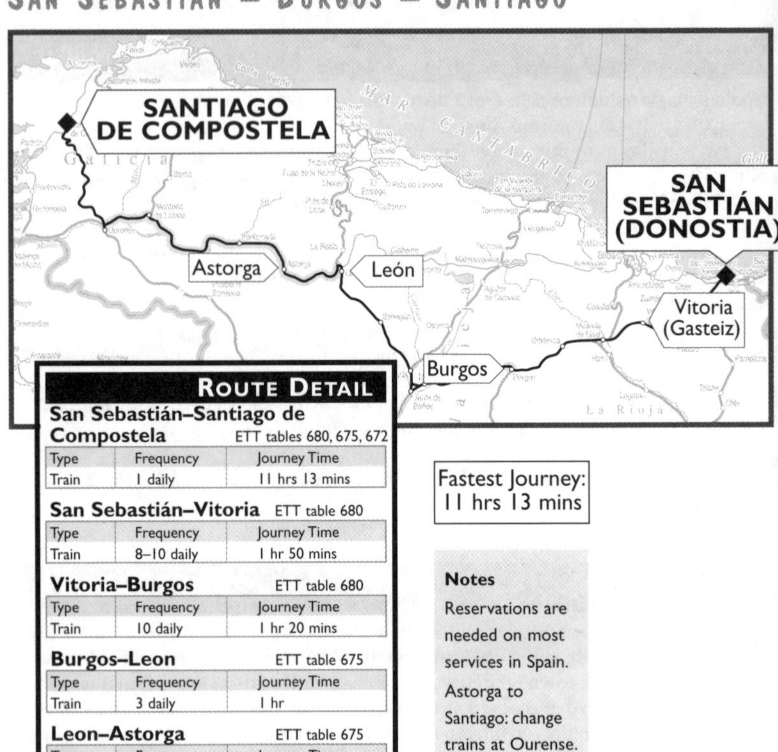

Route Detail

San Sebastián–Santiago de Compostela ETT tables 680, 675, 672

Type	Frequency	Journey Time
Train	1 daily	11 hrs 13 mins

San Sebastián–Vitoria ETT table 680

Type	Frequency	Journey Time
Train	8–10 daily	1 hr 50 mins

Vitoria–Burgos ETT table 680

Type	Frequency	Journey Time
Train	10 daily	1 hr 20 mins

Burgos–Leon ETT table 675

Type	Frequency	Journey Time
Train	3 daily	1 hr

Leon–Astorga ETT table 675

Type	Frequency	Journey Time
Train	6 daily	38 mins

Astorga–Santiago de Compostela ETT tables 675, 672

Type	Frequency	Journey Time
Train	3 daily	6–7 hrs

Fastest Journey: 11 hrs 13 mins

Notes

Reservations are needed on most services in Spain. Astorga to Santiago: change trains at Ourense.

San Sebastián – Burgos – Santiago

If it were ever possible to make a pilgrimage by rail, this is it, for **Santiago de Compostela** (or just plain Santiago to most) has been the objective for millions of pilgrims over many centuries, walking the routes from France and across northern Spain that have come to be known as the 'Camino de Santiago'. San Sebastián stands on the coast beneath the green, rainy foothills of the Pyrénées in the Basque province, known to the assertively independent Basque people as *Euskadi.* Never conquered either by the Romans or the Moors, the Basques suffered appalling repression during the Franco period and their language, one of Europe's oldest, was banned. This area has a reputation for the best cuisine in Spain.

Burgos and **León,** both with superlative cathedrals, lie in the great *meseta* (high plain) of Castilla y León (formerly known as Old Castile). To the north rise the Picos de Europa, not that well served by public transport, but offering some of the best mountain scenery in the country. By contrast, Galicia, comprising Spain's north-west corner, is lushly verdant and intricately hilly, with a complicated coastline buffeted by Atlantic gusts and characterised by fjord-like scenery.

This forms part of the Paris–Seville route (p. 33); for Madrid and Seville, change at Burgos.

SAN SEBASTIÁN (DONOSTIA)

Known as San Sebastián to the Spanish and as Donostia to the Basques, this is now an elegant resort, with tamarisks gracing the promenade that runs along a crescent-shaped bay. Formerly a whaling and deep-sea fishing port doubling as a stopover for pilgrims en route to Santiago de Compostela (p. 168), San Sebastián really came into its own in the mid 19th century, when someone recommended sea-bathing as a cure for Queen Isabella II' s herpes. She arrived, along with a great retinue, and San Sebastián became fashionable.

Take time to wander the streets of the 'old' town, or *parte vieja*, nestled at the foot of Monte Urgull. Although mainly rebuilt in the 19th century, it retains a characterful maze of small streets, tiny darkened shops and bars, arcaded plazas like the PLAZA DE LA CONSTITUCIÓN, which used to serve as a bull ring, and churches such as the beautiful baroque **Basilica of Santa María del Coro**. Fishing is still much in evidence, with the daily catch on show on stalls in the fish market. The **Museum of San Telmo** occupies a former Dominican monastery, with archaeological displays in the cloister and a changing exhibition in the church. At the far end of the quay are the **Naval Museum** and the renovated **Aquarium**.

For superb views, climb **Monte Urgull** itself, topped by a much-rebuilt fort (the **Castillo de la Mota**; free tours in summer). Standing proudly near the top of the hill is the statue of the **Sagrado Corazón de Jesús**, which watches over the city.

DAY TRIPS FROM SAN SEBASTIÁN

From San Sebastián, the narrow-gauge coastal railways lead west, through a series of charming, if increasingly touristy, villages, to the ports of Bilbao and Santander. **Bilbao** (**Tourist Office**: PLAZA ARRIAGA 1, (94) 416 00 22) has a lively old centre, but is primarily a sprawling industrial city, recently redeemed by the opening of the **Museo Guggenheim Bilbao** (Tues–Sun, 1100–2000; on the river, west of the rail station), a stunning modern art gallery that's rapidly emerged as one of the world's most talked about works of contemporary architecture. There's a full programme of changing exhibitions in its 19 galleries – 1999 events include the *Art of the Motorcycle* and an Andy Warhol retrospective (for details (94) 435 90 00 or fax (94) 435 90 10). **Santander** is a mostly modern resort town with a good beach, with ferries to Plymouth (England), and buses to the superb mountain scenery of the **Picos de Europa** (p. 167).

FESTIVALS IN SAN SEBASTIÁN

In September, the international San Sebastián Film Festival, which has been going strong ever since 1953, draws thousands into town; the best star wins the coveted Donostia Prize. July sees a pulsating jazz festival, while classical music is thick in the air in late August.

RAIL (RENFE) **Estación del Norte**, PASEO DE FRANCIA; (943) 28 30 89. Cross the ornate Maria-Cristina bridge, turn right, and it is a few minutes' walk through the 19th-century area to the Old Town. (FV) **Estación Amara**, PLAZA DE EASO; (943) 47 08 15. Beware of being hounded by unregistered hotel owners who group outside the station. Luggage lockers, Pta400 (buy token from counter).

Tourist Offices: **Regional**: PASEO DE LOS FUEROS 1, 20004; (943) 42 62 82, fax (943) 43 17 46. Outside each of the Tourist Offices are touch-screen kiosks that give print-outs of town information. **Municipal**: CALLE DE LA REINA REGENTE 8; (943) 48 11 66, fax (943) 48 11 72 (summer opening times: 0800–2000; Mon 1000–1300). Leave the station by walking over the Maria Christina Bridge, then turn right and walk alongside the river up PASEO DE LOS FUEROS. The regional office is on the corner of the PLAZA DE ESPAÑA, on the left where PASEO DE LOS FUEROS reaches the Santa Catalina Bridge. The municipal office is a little further on: walk along PASEO DE LA REPUBLICA ARGENTINA then left at Zurriola Bridge.

For budget accommodation head for the old town: hidden amongst the narrow streets are many pensiones. Try **Pensión Amaiur**, c. 31 DE AGOSTO, which offers spotless, comfortable rooms and a friendly welcome, or **La Perla**, LOIOLA 10, (943) 42 81 23. Rooms can be difficult to find during July and August. **Youth hostel**: **Albergue La Sirena**, PASEO DE IGUELDO 25; (943) 31 02 68. There is a **campsite**, **Camping Igueldo**, on the fringes of the city at PUEBLO DE IGUELDO; (943) 21 45 02 (no.6 from ALAMEDA DEL BOULEVARD).

For the best small **restaurants**, try the old town and the fishing harbour at the north end of PLAYA DE LA CONCHA.

VITORIA (GASTEIZ)

Known by the Spanish as Vitoria and by the Basques as Gasteiz, the Basque capital is surprisingly little visited. Known for making playing cards and chocolate truffles, it also has considerable charm. Within ugly outskirts, the almost perfectly preserved medieval hill town focuses on handsomely arcaded squares; at the centre of **Plaza de la Virgen Blanca,** a monument commemorates a nearby battle of 1813 in which Napoleon's army was defeated by the Duke of Wellington. From here you can explore a tangled web of narrow dark streets, filled with inexpensive eateries as well as several fine churches and Renaissance palaces. Look out for the **Church of San Miguel**, beside the steps at the top of the large and open Plaza de la Virgen Blanca, and the 16th-century **Palacio de Escoriaza-Esquibel**, with its fine Plateresque-style patio. The **Catedral de Santa María** is currently closed for renovations until further notice; its unfinished 20th-century replacement, the huge neo-Gothic **Cathedral of María Immaculada** (open 1100–1400), stands amid parkland in the flat new town; from here you can stroll Calle Correria, a tree-lined promenade where a mansion houses the **Museo de Bellas Artes** (Museum of Fine Art), with sculpture lurking among the topiary outside, and the rooms containing works by Picasso and Miró.

(RENFE); ☎(945) 23 02 02. Off the Calle Eduardo Dato, about two blocks from the cathedral and Tourist Office. Left luggage lockers Pta400.

Tourist Office: **Regional**: Parque de la Florida, s/n; ☎(945) 13 13 21, fax: (945) 13 02 93 (Mon–Sat 0900–1300, 1500–1900). **Municipal**: Avda Gasteiz s/n, Esquina c. Chile; ☎(945) 16 15 98/9.

Carlos Abaitua Aterpetxea, Escultor Isaac Diez ☎(945) 14 81 00.

The San Pedro Festival in Burgos

The annual festival in Burgos, celebrating **San Pedro**, is held on the last Sun in June, when the old town is transformed with glorious floral displays, a procession with marching bands and street entertainment and fireworks in the evening. Watch out for ladies in traditional dress who tell you your fortune as you are walking along the street – and then try to remove it from you in reward for their efforts!

BURGOS

In medieval times Burgos grew rich on the wool trade, and in the 11th century the city became the capital of Christian Spain as well as home of Rodrigo Díaz de Vivar, better known as El Cid, the romantic mercenary. During the Civil War in the 1930s, it again rose to fame as the Nationalist headquarters. It was here that Franco formed his Falangist government and (18 months later) declared a ceasefire that ended the war.

Burgos has now grown into a large and busy modern city, but its heart is the atmospheric old town around the ruined castle (itself of little interest apart from the views from it). The grand entrance to old Burgos is formed by the **Arco de Santa María**, a fortified 14th-century gateway, altered and decorated in 1536 to pacify Charles V, depicting his figure and those of the founder (Diego Porcelos) and El Cid (whose equestrian statue stands near the **Puente de San Pablo**). From here, it's a short walk to the bulk of the main attractions, eating places and hotels. Foremost is the **cathedral**, consecrated in 1260 but not completed until the 18th century, making it the third largest cathedral in Spain (after Toledo and Seville), and also probably the richest. Amidst the splendour of the 19 chapels and 38 altars, positively dripping in gold leaf, is El Cid's unobtrusive tomb and a grotesquely real-looking crucifix, made in the 13th century with human hair, finger nails and a body of buffalo hide.

WHERE NEXT FROM BURGOS?

4 trains a day make the 5-hr journey from Burgos southwards to Madrid (ETT table 680), a beautiful route over the ***Sierra de Guadarrama****, rising to over 1400 m. Alternatively, services to Salamanca (2 hrs 45 mins; ETT table 680) join the* ***Madrid–Salamanca*** *route* *(p. 152)**.*

Evening sees everyone promenade along the **Paseo del Espolón**, graced with fountains and statues and stretching along the river, with cafés and restaurants making the most of the atmosphere.

Outside the old town, the 16th-century **Casa de Miranda** houses one of Spain's best archaeological museums, exhibiting finds from the Roman city of Clunia.

RAIL Plaza de la Estación; ☎(947) 20 35 60. About 1 km south-west of the cathedral on the far side of the Arlanzon river.

i **Tourist Office**: Plaza de Alonso Martínez 7, 09003 Burgos; ☎(947) 20 31 25; fax: (947) 27 65 29.

LEÓN

Nestling between the Bernesga and Torío rivers and surrounded by rolling *meseta* (plains), León was founded by the Romans (the *Legio Septimo,* or Seventh Legion, gave its name to the city), and over the years was ruled by Visigoths, Moors and Christians. In 1188, Alfonso IX summoned his first *Cortés* (parliament) here – one of the earliest democratic governments in Europe – but the court moved away permanently in the 13th century, and León became little more than a trading centre until 1978, when it was made the capital of the province of León. Today it's thriving once again. The major monuments are within easy walking distance of each other in the old city.

Of all the city's buildings, the most spectacular from the outside is the 16th-century, Plateresque-style **Hospital de San Marcos** (now an upmarket *parador*, or state-run hotel), which was founded by Ferdinand and Isabella as a pilgrim hostel and was later rebuilt as the headquarters for the Knights of Santiago. What is left of the old city is still bounded by fragments of the 14th-century city walls, which followed the line of the original Roman (and medieval) fortifications. Thirty-one of the original

80 bastions are still standing, and are best seen around the cathedral and the **Royal Basílica of San Isidoro**. Much influenced by the cathedrals of France, the **cathedral** has some of the very finest medieval stained glass in Europe (even rivalling Chartres in brilliance), with 125 windows dappling the interior with coloured light. Meanwhile, the Royal Basílica possesses a magnificent Romanesque pantheon, where some 20 monarchs are laid to rest.

RENFE: **El Norte**, AVDA DE ASTORGA 2; ☎(987) 27 02 02, on the west bank of the river. **FEVE**: AVDA DEL PADRE ISLA 48; ☎(987) 27 12 10, near the Basilica de San Isidoro. Luggage lockers.

Tourist Office: PLAZA DE LA REGLA, 4, next to the cathedral (turn right out of the station to reach it); ☎(987) 23 70 82, fax (987) 27 33 91 (Mon–Fri 0900–1400, 1700–1900, Sat, Sun and holidays 1000–1400, 1700–2000).

The city has a wide range of hotels and guesthouses, ranging downwards from the ultra-luxurious **San Marcos** (see above). The **Tourist Office** has a list of places to stay. A good area to find budget accommodation is on and around AVDA DE ROMA and AVDA DE ORDOÑO II. Budget places include **Pensión Avenida**, AVDA DE PALENCIA 4, 3RD FLOOR, ☎(987) 22 37 63. There's a **youth hostel** at SAN PELAYO 15, ☎(987) 23 30 11, fax: (987) 23 32 03.

ASTORGA

Described by the Roman historian Pliny in the 1st century AD as a 'magnificent city', this is now a small, gracefully decaying country town, capital of the bleak moorland region of La Maragatería. Sections of the 6-m Roman walls survive around the old town. Towering over it all, the 15th–17th-century **cathedral** displays an intriguing hotchpotch of late Gothic, Renaissance, baroque and Plateresque styles, with motley towers, one grey and the other pink (there wasn't enough stone to complete it all in the same material). It's a frequent visit for pilgrims on their way to Santiago; next door, the flamboyant **Palacio Episcopal** (Episcopal Palace), designed by Gaudí in 1889, now houses the **Museo de los Caminos**

THE PICOS DE EUROPA

From León you can head north by bus (to **Pasada de Valdeón** via **Riaño**; other approaches include from **Santander** to **Potes** and **Fuente Dé**; services are infrequent and you should check with Tourist Offices what's running) into the high mountains of the ***Picos de Europa***, a stunning (often snow-capped) cave-riddled karst limestone wilderness that still shelters a few wolves and bears. Said to have been the first sign of European land seen by sailors returning from the New World, the peaks rise almost vertically from the Bay of Biscay and offer magnificent views and walking, notably through gorges (such as the ***Cares Gorge***). The scope for longer hut-to-hut walks is more limited, unless you're extremely fit and experienced in mountain walking; the area isn't huge (roughly 40 km across) but it's very easy to get lost in if you stray from the waymarked paths, and there are numerous sink holes and other hazards. Unreliable weather is a further drawback: for much of the time the peaks are swathed in mist. Summer is obviously the time to go, though rooms get heavily booked up from late July to the end of August.

(Museum of the Pilgrims' Way). Smaller buildings of interest centre on the PLAZA MAYOR.

RAIL PLAZA DE LA ESTACIÓN, ☎(987) 61 64 44, about 1 km east of the town centre. Lockers Pta400 (buy token from luggage or information offices).

i **Tourist Office**: PLAZA EDUARDO CASTRO; ☎(987) 57 91 91 (summer: 1000–1400 and 1600–2100). From the station head straight on up PEDRO DE CASTRO, across to ENFERMERAS, then right through PLAZA OBISPO ALCOLEA and up LOS SITIOS. The tourist information office is on your left near the Episcopal Palace.

Budget options include **Delfin**, AVDA MADRID CORUNA, ☎(987) 61 50 16; **Pensión Garcia**, BAJADA DEL POSTIGO, ☎(987) 61 60 46; and **Ruta Leonesa**, CTRA ASTORGA – LEÓN, ☎(987) 61 50 37.

SANTIAGO DE COMPOSTELA

GETTING AROUND SANTIAGO

The old city is tiny and everything of interest is easily accessible on foot. A tourist train tours the sights of interest, leaving C. SAN FRANCISCO every 20 mins. Cost: Pta400 (July and Aug only).

A magnet for millions of pilgrims for the last thousand years, Santiago de Compostela hit the big time when the tomb of St James (*Sant Iago*, Spain's patron saint) was discovered in AD 813, supposedly by a shepherd who was guided to the site by a star. Destroyed in 997 by the Moors, the town was rebuilt during the 11th century and began its golden age. In the 12th century, the Pope declared it a Holy City: for Catholics, only Jerusalem and Rome share this honour. The newer sections of the city do not have a great deal of charm, but the old town (contained within the medieval walls) is one of the most beautiful urban landscapes in Europe. It's not entirely given over to the pilgrimage, endowed as it is with a theatre, a concert hall and plenty of bars and clubs offering dancing and late-night drinking. Around the old town, free entertainment in the form of music and singing is provided by *tunas* – groups of buskers dressed in medieval clothes. Souvenir shops do a roaring trade.

The 12th-century Colegiata de Santa María del Sar, about 2 km from the old town, has a beautiful Romanesque cloister with wild flowers sprouting from its crumbling stone walls; the pillars inside the church lean at such precarious angles that it's a wonder the building still stands. Alameda is a delightful park, with shady walkways, ancient oak trees and superb views of the cathedral and the surrounding countryside.

The old town contains a host of fine churches and monasteries as well as notable secular buildings tucked down the narrow side streets. The **cathedral** (started in 1075) is the obvious centre of attention. Its existing 18th-century baroque façade covers the original 12th-century façade, the *Pórtico de la Gloria* by Maestro

A tree of knowledge

There is a tree for bemused students on the corner of Rúa do Franco and Rúa de Fonseca, on the left towards the Cathedral. The tree is made of iron and set behind glass. It is said that any student who does not know what to study should turn their back to the tree and reach behind them, and whichever of the tree's branches they touch (history, philosophy etc.) should be the branch of academia they study.

Mateo, said to be the greatest single surviving work of Romanesque art in the world, with 200 exceptionally imaginative and detailed sculptures. To celebrate their arrival in the Holy City, pilgrims traditionally touch the base of the *Jesse tree* on the central column, accordingly known as the 'Pilgrim Pillar', and deeply worn down by millions of fingers over the centuries. On the other side of the pillar, facing the altar, is a figure of the sculptor Mateo, popularly known as the 'Saint of bumps on the head', as people knock heads with him in the belief that his talent is contagious. Pilgrims mark the end of their journey by climbing up behind the shiny statue of St James and kissing the scallop shell (the symbol of the pilgrimage) on the back of his gown. The interior is dominated by a silver Mexican altar and a dazzling 17th-century baroque altarpiece. The **museum** contains a valuable collection of tapestries, including a series based on cartoons by Goya, manuscripts from the *Codex Calixtus* and a huge silver *botafumeiro* (incense burner) that is spectacularly swung through the transept on special occasions, with eight men clinging on to it.

Atlas the ball boy

In the **Praza Do Toral,** a little statue of **Atlas** stands on top of one of the buildings. Legend has it that if any female student in Santiago is still a virgin at graduation time, Atlas will drop his ball!

Four plazas surround the cathedral, each architectural gems in themselves. On the largest, the pigeon-populated Plaza del Obradoiro, stand the impressive **Hotel de los Reyes Católicos** (the former hospital for pilgrims) and the classical **Pazo de Raxoi** of 1772 (now the town hall). Along one side of Plaza de la Quintana is the austere façade of the **Monasterio de San Pelayo de Antealtares**. Entrance to the church and the monastery's **Museum of Sacred Art** are via the steps at one end of the square. Another landmark is the 16th-century **Monastery of San Martín Pinario**, (whose monks used to give new clothes to pilgrims who looked worse for wear after their journey), though the interior is no longer open to the public.

The Feast of St James in Santiago

The city's main fiesta, the feast of **St James**, takes place in the three weeks leading up to 25 July. The entertainment becomes ever more riotous until the eve of the feast itself, which begins with a massive firework display in the Pl. del Obradoiro. The following day the statue of St James is processed through the streets in a haze of incense, followed by *gigantes*, vast masked figures representing the Christians and Moors.

Day trip from Santiago

La Coruña (frequent rail services, taking about 1hr 15 mins), a large maritime city, with its old town on an isthmus between the beach and the harbour. The town's main attractions (after its beaches) are the **Castelo de San Antón**, which now houses an Archaeology Museum, and the **Torre de Hércules**, a 2nd-century Roman lighthouse, restored in the 18th century and still in use today, standing at the extreme north of the isthmus. There are also a number of fine churches and gardens. The rail station is 45 mins' walk from the centre; nos.1 and 1A go to the Tourist Office. The municipal office is at Jardines de Méndez Núñez; (981) 20 00 00.

Budget accommodation includes **Muinos**, Santa Catalina 17, (981) 22 28 79; **Palacio**, Plaza de Galicia 2, (981) 12 23 38; and **Roma**, Rúa Nueva 3, (981) 22 80 75.

Rúa Do Horreo, 1 km south of the old city; (981) 52 02 02. no. C2 goes into the centre, but it's quicker to walk. Luggage lockers (Pta400) and cash machine. The accommodation services are open 1000–1400, 1600–2000.

Bus station: **Estación Central de Autobuses**, C. de San Cayetano, (981) 58 77 00, 30-min walk from the old town; no.10 runs every 20 mins from Plaza de Galicia. There is a good local bus system and route plans are posted at most stops.

Bus tickets

Bus fares cost Pta90, or you can get a **Bonobus ticket**, giving 10 trips and saving a few pesetas.

Taxis: There are taxi ranks at the bus and train stations, (981) 59 59 64, 58 24 50 or 59 84 88, and at Plaza de Galicia; 56 10 28 (24 hrs).

Tourist Offices: **Regional office**: Rúa del Villar 43; (981) 58 40 81, fax (981) 56 51 78 (Mon–Fri 1000–1400, 1600–1900 and Sat 1100–1300). **Municipal office**: Plaza de Galicia; (981) 57 39 90. From the station turn right along Avenida De Lugo then left up Rúa do Horreo, to Plaza de Galicia.

Post and phones: The main **post office** is at Travesía de Fonseca, (981) 58 12 52 (Mon–Fri 0830–2030 and Sat 0930–1400) for most services, including poste restante *(lista de correos)* facilities. **International telephone calls** can be made from several places in the old town, including C. de los Bautizados 13 and C. del Franco 48.

During the three weeks leading up to the feast of St James on 25 July, the town is absolutely packed and you should book well in advance. Accommodation ranges from the five-star **Hotel de los Reyes Católicos**, a magnificent 16th-century pilgrim hostel built by Ferdinand and Isabella, to an array of small, relatively inexpensive guesthouses in both the old and new parts of the city. For budget accommodation in the old town, try around Rúa del Villar and C. Raiña. **Hospedaje Ramos**, C. Raiña 18, 2nd floor, (981) 58 18 59, is very central, with small, basic rooms. Other good-value places are **Hospedaje Sofia**, C. del Cardenal Paya 16, (981) 58 51 50; **Hospedaje Santa Cruz**, Rúa del Vilar (laundry service Pta500); **Barbantes**, Rúa do Franco, (981) 58 10 77; **Casa Enrique Pensión**, Rúa do Franco 28, 1st floor, (981) 58 32 60. C. de Montero Ríos (just outside the old town) has a number of reasonably priced **hostels**.

There are three large **campsites** outside the city. **Cancelas**, C. DEL 25 DE XULIO 35, (981) 58 02 66, is the best option, being only 2 km from the centre (no.6 from PLAZA DE GALICIA). **Santiago de Compostela**, (981) 88 80 02, is about 6 km away on the N550 road to La Coruña, while **Las Sirenas**, ROXIDO-PEDRO RUBIA, (981) 88 25 05, is 10 km from the town.

There are plenty of **budget restaurants** around the old town, especially on the streets leading south from the cathedral. **Restaurante-Bar Los Caracoles** is a small and popular place on C. RAIÑA. **Bodecon de Xulio**, C. DEL FRANCO 24, has a restaurant at the back which serves reasonably priced menús. CAMPO DE SAN CLEMENTE, on the edge of the old town, has two good restaurants: **La Trinidad** and **San Clemente**, both with outside seating areas. Slightly further out of town, the PRAZA ROXA area, near the university, is very cheap.

WHERE NEXT FROM SANTIAGO?

*Carry on to **Lisbon** by taking the **Lisbon–Santiago** route in reverse* *(p. 155)*.

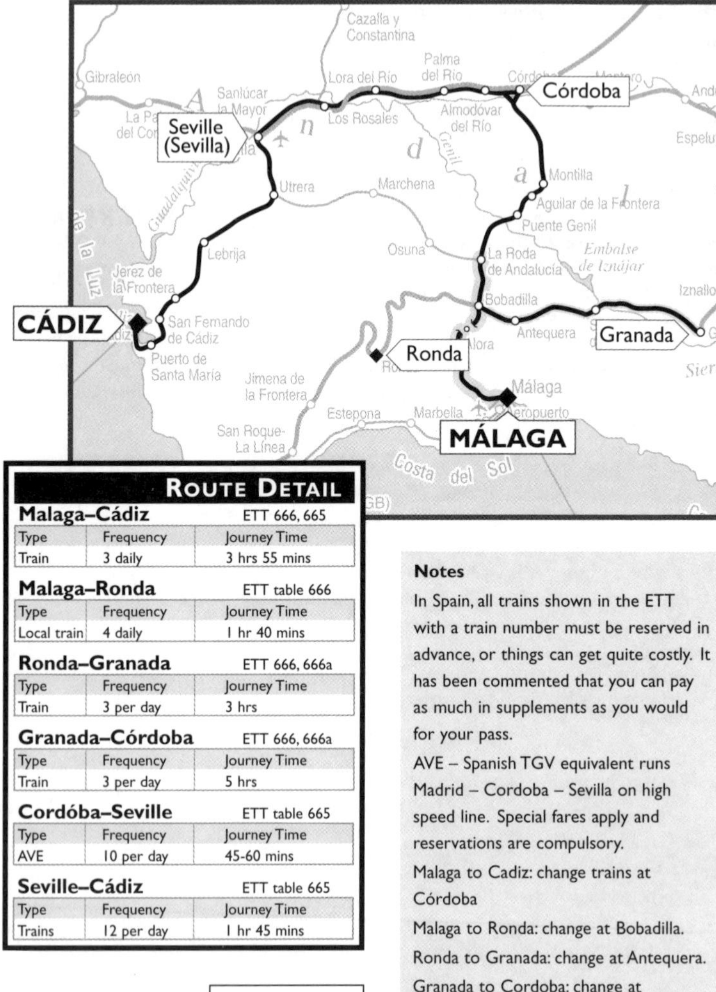

Route Detail

Malaga–Cádiz ETT 666, 665

Type	Frequency	Journey Time
Train	3 daily	3 hrs 55 mins

Malaga–Ronda ETT table 666

Type	Frequency	Journey Time
Local train	4 daily	1 hr 40 mins

Ronda–Granada ETT 666, 666a

Type	Frequency	Journey Time
Train	3 per day	3 hrs

Granada–Córdoba ETT 666, 666a

Type	Frequency	Journey Time
Train	3 per day	5 hrs

Cordóba–Seville ETT table 665

Type	Frequency	Journey Time
AVE	10 per day	45-60 mins

Seville–Cádiz ETT table 665

Type	Frequency	Journey Time
Trains	12 per day	1 hr 45 mins

Fastest Journey: 3 hrs 55 mins

Notes

In Spain, all trains shown in the ETT with a train number must be reserved in advance, or things can get quite costly. It has been commented that you can pay as much in supplements as you would for your pass.

AVE – Spanish TGV equivalent runs Madrid – Cordoba – Sevilla on high speed line. Special fares apply and reservations are compulsory.

Malaga to Cadiz: change trains at Córdoba

Malaga to Ronda: change at Bobadilla.

Ronda to Granada: change at Antequera.

Granada to Cordoba: change at Bobadilla

Málaga – Granada – Cádiz

Andalucía (Andalusia) conjures up the classic images of Spain – with great parched plains dotted with cypresses and groves of olive trees, backdrops of rugged sierras, flamenco music, lively fiestas and timeless hilltop castles. The Moors left evidence of their occupation in the form of spectacular monuments such as the Alhambra in **Granada** and Mezquita in **Córdoba**, but there's also a rich Christian heritage.

Sit on the left-hand side of the train as you leave the port of **Málaga**, for the views soon become stupendous as you snake along the Garganta del Chorro, a huge chasm 180 m deep, and only visible from the train or by a rather dodgy-looking catwalk for walkers with a lot of nerve.

Eastwards lies **Ronda**, one of the finest of the aptly named 'white towns' of Andalucía, perched improbably above a precipice.

Continue to **Cádiz**, an atmospheric old port, or Gibraltar, a British colonial curiosity, worth a few hours; you could stop at Jerez de la Frontera, Spain's main sherry town.

Málaga

The fourth largest city in Spain and a busy working port, Málaga is the communications centre for the holiday coasts on either side. At first sight it isn't exactly pretty, with high-rise modern apartment blocks built up close together within close range of a dismal-looking canalised river. But the centre is a hundred times more cheerful and resolutely Spanish in character, with a tree-lined main boulevard, dark back alleys, a covered market, antique-looking pharmacies and dazzling flamenco dress shops; restaurants are inexpensive and lively, and the city has a real sense of place far removed from the tourist excesses of much of the rest of the Costa del Sol.

Theatre in the Open

At **Paseo del Parque** there is an open-air theatre, which sometimes stages free productions in summer (ask at the tourist information office for details).

Málaga's past is most evident in the area near the port. The long, shady walks of PASEO DEL PARQUE are overlooked by the **Alcazaba** (0930–2000; 🚌 no. 35 from PASEO DEL PARQUE), a fort built by the Moors on Roman foundations; it's rather neglected, but you can walk around for free, and the views extend over the city to the coast (do be careful if you're by yourself here though, as it's something of a crime hotspot). **Gibralfaro castle** (now a *parador*), further up the hill, is of Phoenician origin, but was later reconstructed by the Moors.

Moorish influence can also be seen in the city centre, where the **Museo Arqueológico**, with its collection of neolithic pottery, is located. Just off the PASEO is the Cathedral, set in a secluded square and built between the 16th and 18th centuries. **Museo de Bellas Artes** houses a fine collection of mosaics, sculptures and paintings, including works by Picasso, Málaga's most famous son, as well as Murillo

HORSE AND TRAP TOURS OF MÁLAGA

An unusual way to see the town is in a horse and trap from PASEO DEL PARQUE. Although a little too expensive for lone travellers, at Pta3000 for 40 mins or Pta4000 for 1 hr, it's feasible for a group of four.

DAY TRIPS FROM MÁLAGA

A frequent train service runs west from Málaga (Centro-Alameda and RENFE stations) along the **Costa del Sol**, connecting it to the airport and the busy resorts of Torremolinos, Benalmádena and Fuengirola. If you're driving, be warned that the N340 here has the highest accident rate in Europe.

Once a fishing village, **Torremolinos** is a tacky, exuberant, fun-oriented, concrete high-rise resort, with a plethora of discos, fish and chip shops and bars, much of it run by a huge expatriate population. There are abundant beach facilities along the expansive stretch of grey sands. To the east, **Fuengirola** is another sun and sand haunt, more family-oriented and slightly calmer than Torremolinos,

and Ribera. You can visit the house Picasso was born in for free; it's now the **Museo Casa Natal**, on the PLAZA DE LA MERCED (1000–1400, 1800–2100). The Picasso Museum **(Museo Picasso)** is in POSTIGO SAN AGUSTIN.

RAIL C. CUARTELES, ☎(95) 236 02 02 (luggage lockers and accommodation services; for currency exchange go to the nearby bus station), a boring 20–30 min walk from the main part of town. Bus no.3 goes to ALAMEDA PRINCIPAL and PASEO DEL PARQUE near the centre for Pta115. Local trains for the coastal resorts leave from here as well (at a different level), and this line is also served by another more centrally located station, CENTRO ALAMEDA.

✈ 8 km from the city, ☎(95) 204 88 04 or 204 88 44. There is a Tourist Office in the main hall, ☎(95) 224 00 00 ext 2098. Trains to Málaga run every 30 mins, taking about 10 mins. There is also a bus every 20 mins (bus no.19), which stops near the cathedral and takes 20–25 mins.

i **Tourist Offices**: PASAJE DE CHINITAS 4; ☎(95) 221 34 45, fax: (95) 222 9421, open Mon–Fri 0900–1900, Sat 1000–1900, Sun 1000–1400. CENTRAL AVDA, CERVANTES 1; ☎(95) 260 4410. There is a small municipal office in the bus station, PASEO DE LOS TILOS; ☎(95) 235 0061 ext 260.

There is a good choice of hotels, including a small *parador* set in the gardens of the Gibralfaro castle (bus no.35 from PASEO DEL PARQUE) above the town. Budget accommodation is functional, but lacking in any obvious regional charm. Good areas to try for cheap lodgings are around the PLAZA DE LA CONSTITUCIÓN (north-west of the cathedral) and immediately off either side of the ALAMEDA PRINCIPAL (although the south side is less salubrious). In high season, central Málaga is lively at night (all night); the only solution is to ask for a room away from the street, or buy earplugs. The **Pensión Rosa**, C. MARTÍNEZ 10, ☎(95) 221 27 16, has reasonably sized rooms, some of which have balconies, and there are several other hostels on this street. **Hostal Andalucía**, ALARCÓN LUJÁN 12, ☎(95) 221 19 60, has more charm than most. **Pensión Juanita**, ALARCÓN LUJÁN 8, 4TH FLOOR, ☎(95) 221 35 8 has a number of small, basic rooms, all with wash-basins. South of ALAMEDA PRINCIPAL, and slightly more expensive, are **Hostal-Residencia El Ruedo**, TRINIDAD GRUND 3, ☎(95) 221 58 20, and **Hostal Castilla y Hostal Guerrero**, CÓRDOBA 7, 2ND

FLOOR, ☎(95) 221 86 35. **Youth hostel**: PLAZA PÍO XII 6; ☎(95) 230 85 00 (🚌no.18). **Campsite**: the nearest is 12 km away in **Torremolinos**, CTRA CÁDIZ-BARCELONA km 228; ☎(95) 238 26 02.

There are several good **restaurants** around the cathedral, especially along C. CAÑÓN; **Cafetería El Jardín** is particularly good value. Seafood and *gazpacho* are good bets. You do need to trawl through the usual tourist fare to find the really good places. **Paseo Marítimo** and the seafront in PEDREGALEJE are the best areas for bars and seafood restaurants. Málaga gives its name to an inexpensive sweet fortified red wine. *Convent dulces* are cakes made by nuns throughout Andalucía: in the morning nuns of **Santa Clara** at C. CISTER 11 (just east of the cathedral) sell their goodies.

RONDA

Ronda is a small town of pre-Roman origin set in the rugged Serranía de Ronda, and split in two by a dizzying gorge, with white houses clinging to the rim, and spanned in quite spectacular fashion by an 18th-century bridge known as the **Puente Nuevo**. The view from the bridge is hair-raising, even more so when you realise that it was from here that in 1936 during the Civil War 512 prisoners of the Republicans were hurled to their deaths, an incident adapted by Ernest Hemingway in *For Whom the Bell Tolls*. It was in Ronda that Pedro Romero invented the modern style of bull-fighting – on foot rather than from horseback – and the bullring is one of the oldest in Spain. Near the bullring is the **Alameda**, a public garden beside the gorge, getting breathtaking views of the surrounding area, with olive groves stretching into the hilly distance.

On the other side of the bridge is the old Moorish quarter, with the attractive **Casa del Rey Moro** (House of the Moorish King), an early 18th-century mansion, now a hotel; you can visit the gardens, designed in 1912, and the mines, which provided Ronda with water as early as the 14th century and include the room of secrets, where it is fabled that what is said from one corner of the room to another cannot be heard in the centre (entrance Pta500). A path from this side of the bridge leads into the gorge for another

Day trips from Málaga cont'd.

but equally ugly. Málaga is also at the centre of a bus network reaching out further west to many smaller resorts, and to **Marbella** (self-consciously marketed as a sophisticated resort, but with small, crowded villages, and little to recommend it), **Estepona** and as far as **Gibraltar**. Eastwards, it is possible to reach Nerja and other assorted seaside towns all the way to Almeria.

Nerja is a relatively peaceful resort, built around an old town that still feels distinctly Spanish, about 50 km from Málaga. Buses run approximately every hour, the journey taking 1 hr 30 mins and costing Pta485. It is noted for its panoramic views of the coast, especially from the promenade known as the **Balcon de Europa**. Just east of the town is the **Cueva de Nerja**, a series of large caverns full of breathtaking rock formations (Tourist Office: PUERTA DEL MAR 2; ☎(95) 252 15 31).

You can sail round trip from Málaga to **Benalmádena**. There are three departures daily and the trip costs Pta1300. For details ☎(95) 241 60 68.

DAY TRIP FROM RONDA

Setenil, reached by a handful of buses per day from Ronda bus station, is a bizarre village crammed into a gorge with houses built into overhanging rock ledges, a great place to walk round with a camera, or picnic on the hillside above. Other tourists are unlikely to be much in evidence.

interesting view (the whiff of sewage down there can be a bit of a turn-off though).

The *Baños Arabes* (Arab Baths) near **Puente San Miguel** were constructed in the late 13th and early 14th centuries and are thought to be the best-preserved baths in the Iberian peninsula. They are open free (Tues–Sat 0930–1400, 1600–1800, Sun 1030–1300).

Ronda is at its most charming during one of the many fiestas which occur throughout the year.

RAIL 10–15 min walk to centre. Luggage lockers and accommodation service.

Tourist Office: PLAZA DE ESPAÑA, 9; (95) 287 12 72.

You'll inevitably pass plenty of inexpensive places as you walk in from the station. Options include **Hostal San Francisco**, CALLE MARIA CUBRERA 18, (95) 287 32 99 (singles Pta2000; doubles Pta4000), **Hostal Virgen del Rocio**, CALLE NUEVA, (95) 287 74 25 (doubles Pta4000 with breakfast), and **Hostal Biarritz**, CALLE CRISTO 7, (95) 287 29 10 (doubles Pta2500).

Restaurante/Pizzeria El Capricho, in the PLAZA EL SOCORRO, serves mainly pizzas and pasta dishes, but is cheap and does sometimes offer the odd local dish such as Ronda-style rabbit. For better service and a guarantee of local cuisine, go to **Restaurante Flores**, JESUS FLORES AVILES, VIRGEN DE LA PAZ 9.

GRANADA

Founded, according to legend, either by Noah's or Hercules's daughter, Granada was the last of the great Moorish cities to succumb to Ferdinand and Isabella's ferocious Christian Reconquest, in 1492. The main reason for visiting the city is to see the fortress-palace, the **Alhambra**, resplendent on its lush hilltop, and reachable by bus from PLAZA NUEVA (every 12 mins) if you don't fancy the pleasant but often hot walk up.

Most of the exterior of the Alhambra (see sidebar) dates from rebuilding in the 13th–14th centuries and is reasonably simple, giving no hint of the wealth of decoration inside. There are three sets of buildings: the **Alcazaba** (Fortress), the **Alcázar** (Palace) and the **Generalife** (Summer Palace and Gardens), with a combined entrance fee of just Pta750, or a hefty Pta3500 for an English language tour (summer hours: Mon–Sat 0900–2000, Sun and holidays 0900–1800; late opening Tues, Thur, Sat 2200–2400). The number of visitors to some areas of the Alhambra is now being limited to 8400 per day with timed tickets, so it is advisable to arrive in the morning (or reserve by fax: (958) 21 05 84, at least two days in advance) if you don't want to face a 2-hr wait to get in. The **Generalife** shelters a stunning garden with patios and running water; the Moors used their irrigational expertise to divert the River Darro to supply the pools and fountains. The main Christian edifice in the complex is the 16th-century **Palace of Charles V**, which houses the **Museum of Fine Arts** and the **National Museum of Hispano-Islamic Art**. Sat evenings see a surreal parade of newly married couples being photographed beside the ramparts.

HIGHLIGHTS OF THE ALHAMBRA

The ***Alcazaba*** was predominantly used as a military outpost and is the oldest part of the present site. Its ***Torre de la Vela*** (watchtower), from where the Catholic flag was hoisted in 1492, commands panoramic views of Granada and the Sierra Nevada. The ***Alcázar*** was the main palace. Richly decorated and stunningly beautiful, with brilliant use of light and space, it was largely built in the 14th century. Of particular note are: the ***Mexuar*** (council chamber); the ***Patio de los Arrayanes***, with an incredible honeycomb cupola made up of thousands of small cells; and the ***Patio de los Leones***, so-named for the famous fountain in its centre. The ***Sala de Embajadores*** is the largest and most sumptuous room, its walls covered with inscriptions from the Koran, ornamental motifs, and brilliantly glazed tiles that glint metallically in light.

In the city below the Alhambra, the **Capilla Real** (Royal Chapel) deserves a visit for the tombs of the Catholic monarchs, Ferdinand and Isabella, and their daughter and her husband; displayed in the Sacristy are some notable paintings from the private collection of Queen Isabella. Next door, the Cathedral was completed in the early 18th century, and has rather cold, gloomily impressive classical grandeur.

BEING PAMPERED IN GRANADA

If you're willing to splash out Pta1400 for the experience, **Al Andalus Baths,** CALLE SANTA ANA 16, ☎(958) 22 99 78, provide the chance to bathe in therapeutic waters for 2 hrs in Alhambra-like surroundings; massages are on offer at a very reasonable Pta1000.

The **Albaicín** quarter, on the hill opposite the Alhambra, retains some Moorish atmosphere and is a rewarding and tranquil place for a stroll in its disorientating maze of stepped alleys, out from the hectic whirl of the city centre. Beware of bag-snatchers here. Close by you might stumble on CALLE CALDIERA NUEVA and CALLE CALDIERA VIELLA, a narrow street with rug-hung Moroccan teashops and eateries. Nearby, on the edge of town, are the gypsy cave-dwellings of **Sacromonte** (buses from GENERALIFE or PLAZA NUEVA; every 15 mins, Pta120); note that the widely touted evening gypsy entertainments are a gross tourist trap.

AVDA DE ANDALUCES; ☎(958) 27 12 72. Lockers cost Pta400–600 depending on size. No currency exchange or showers, but you can get information on accommodation. **Agencia Guiamundo,** ☎(958) 26 65 15, CAMINO DE RONDA 63, can provide cheap young-persons' rail passes.

From the station it's a 20-min walk to the centre. Walk straight out of the station and up AVENIDA ANDALUCES. Turn right onto AVENIDA DE LA CONSTITUCIÓN, which becomes GRAN VÍA DE

Bus Tickets

Single fares are Pta120; **Abono Dia**, a 24-hr bus ticket, costs Pta325. **Titulo 1000** tickets cost Pta1000 and are good for 15 trips; **Titulo 2000** tickets cost Pta2000 for 30 trips. *All can be bought from tobacconists or on the bus.*

Day trip from Granada

Guadix (east of Granada) is an old walled town with a sandstone cathedral, and remarkable for its cave district, the **Barrio Santiago**. Some 10,000 live-in cave dwellings have been cut into pyramids of red rock – and electricity installed. Some inhabitants may demand rip-off fees to show you round their homes; you can find some deserted caves, and there's a **cave museum** near St Miguel Church. Frequent buses run from Granada to the town centre; there's a less good train service (with the station some way out). The journey by bus or train takes about 1hr 15 mins.

COLON. Turn off by REYES CATOLICOS on your right; at PLAZA DEL CARMEN follow CALLE MARIANA PINEDA behind REYES CATOLICOS. **Tourist Office** is by the cathedral.

nos.3/4/6/9 go to the GRAN VÍA and the centre (Pta120) from the main road up the hill from the station; they run every 20 minutes.

17 km from Granada on CTRA MÁLAGA S/N; (958) 44 70 81.

Tourist Offices: **Regional**: PLAZA DE MARIANA PINEDA 10; (958) 22 66 88 (Mon–Fri 0930–1900, Sat 1000–1400). **Municipal**: CORRAL DEL CARBÓN, C. MARIANA PINEDA (by the cathedral); (958) 22 59 90, fax (958) 22 39 27. There is also a small Tourist Office in the Alhambra complex itself, (958) 22 04 4, (0900–1700).

Budget accommodation is plentiful, especially off PLAZA NUEVA, PLAZA DE LA TRINIDAD, GRAN VÍA DE COLÓN and on the streets north of PLAZA MARIANA PINEDA. CUESTA DE GOMÉREZ leads directly up to the Alhambra and is lined with hostals. **Hostal Gomérez**, CUESTA DE GOMÉREZ 10, (958) 22 44 37, must be one of the cheapest places in town, and nearby is **Britz**, CUESTA DE GOMÉREZ 1, (958) 22 36 52. GRAN VÍA is a busy street, so traffic noise may be a problem, but try **Hostal Gran Vía**, GRAN VÍA 17; (958) 27 92 12. Around PLAZA MARIANA PINEDA, **Hostal Roma**, NAVAS 1, (958) 22 62 77, has beautifully furnished rooms and spotless bathrooms. Near the university, **Almöhada Hospedaje**, (958) 20 74 46, is cheap, clean and homely.

At the top end of the scale, the *parador* is located in the former **Convent of San Francisco** within the Alhambra complex. Also here is the small but commendable one-star **Hotel America**, REAL DE LA ALHAMBRA 53; (958) 22 74 71. **Youth hostels**: CAMINO DE RONDA 171, (958) 27 26 38 (nos. 10/11 from ACERA DE DARRO in the centre); AVDA RAMON Y CAJAL 2, (958) 28 43 06, fax: (958) 28 52 85 (no. 11 from the station). **Campsite**: **Sierra Nevada**, AVDA DE MADRID 107; (958) 15 00 62, is the nearest (no. 3 from ACERA DE DARRO). **Granada campsite** is 4 km away at CERRO DE LA CRUZ, PELIGROS; (958) 34 05 48 (bus to PELIGROS).

PLAZA NUEVA and the streets around it are where the locals eat: not always cheap, but fair value. **Restaurante Torres Bermejas**, PLAZA NUEVA 6, has reasonably priced set menus

WHERE NEXT FROM GRANADA?

The rail connections from Granada to Córdoba are not that good (though there is a direct bus taking 4 hrs, 3 services a day; and you could instead opt to take the train to Linares-Baeza, for the connecting bus to Baeza (ETT table: 666), which has abundant dozy charm in its Renaissance squares and palaces; from there you can take a bus on to Úbeda, another stunning Renaissance town, linked by bus to Córdoba and Seville. You can also head on by train from Linares-Baeza through spectacular desert to Almería, a landscape that's been used for numerous movie locations.

Buses from Granada zigzag up onto the Sierra Nevada, the great mountain mass that looms over the city. A good place to stay here is Capileira, the highest village, with its flat-roofed whitewashed old houses; there are several places to stay, and spectacular views. Walking hereabouts is fun, but hit and miss; you can try following the many irrigation channels built by the Moors.

and outside seating, and **Restaurante Léon**, C. PAN 1–4, can also be recommended, while **Sevilla**, OFICIOS 12, has the best paella in town. A cup of Arabian tea in one of the bars on CALDERIA NUEVA will help capture the Moorish spirit.

CÓRDOBA

Once the capital of the Moorish caliphate and one of the greatest cities in Europe, Córdoba is filled with a harmonious blend of Christian, Jewish and Moorish architecture. The main attraction is undoubtedly the **Mezquita**, the grandest and most beautiful mosque ever built in Spain. There's also a fascinating Jewish quarter.

The huge Mezquita (hours vary; check times with Tourist Office or with staff at the Mezquita; entry Pta800; it's free to attend mass in the cathedral section of the building) was founded in the 8th century by Caliph Abd al Rahman I and was enlarged over the next 200 years. At the foot of the bell tower, the delicately carved **Puerta del Perdón** leads through the massive outer walls to the **Patio de los Naranjos** (Courtyard of the Orange Trees), a courtyard with fountains for ritual cleansing. Inside the mosque, the fantastic forest of 850 pillars, joined by two-tiered Moorish arches in stripes of red brick and white stone, extends over a vast area. The pillars are not identical: materials include alabaster, marble, jasper, onyx, granite and wood; some are smooth, others have ribs or spirals; most are Roman in origin and were shipped in from places as far apart as France and North Africa, then cut to size. The capitals are equally varied. After the Moors departed, the Christians added the cathedral within the complex, incongruous but stunning, and blocking out the light that was an integral part of the design. The Third Mihrab once housed the original copy of the Koran. Unlike the other two, it survived Christian vandalism and its walls are covered in mosaics of varied colours and friezes of texts from the Koran. Its unusual off-centre position in the *qibla* (the south-facing holy wall) is the result of the final enlargement of the mosque in the 10th century, which, because of the proximity of the river in the south and the palace in the west, had to be made on the east side.

CÓRDOBA'S MUSEUMS

The grisly Museo de Arte Taurino on Plaza de Maimónides is devoted to bullfighting. The Museo Arqueológico, Plaza de Jerónimo Páez, is housed in a 16th-century mansion with visible Roman foundations. The Museo Torre de la Calahorra chronicles the occupation of Muslims in Córdoba from the 9th to the 13th centuries. Recorded information is given to you through headphones (various languages available) as you enter each room (summer, daily 1000–1400, 1630–2030; winter 1000–1800).

The ***Puente Romano*** is a bridge of mainly Moorish construction, but the arches have Roman foundations. Downstream are the remains of an Arab waterwheel, which originally transported water to the grounds of the Alcázar. The **Torre de la Calahorra** (on the other side of the river) is a high-tech museum with a model of the Mezquita as it was before the Christians got to work on it.

The **Alcázar de los Reyes Catolicos,** on the north bank, retains the original Moorish terraced gardens and pools. In August, these stay open until midnight, perfect for an evening stroll. Less gloriously, this was the headquarters of the Spanish Inquisition for over three centuries.

The **Judería** is the old Jewish quarter, a maze of lanes surrounding a tiny Synagogue in C. JUDÍOS. Open doorways provide tantalising glimpses of chequered courtyards filled with flowers; to get a better look visit the town in May, when the **Festival de los Patios** (a type of best-kept patio competition) takes place.

RAIL AVDA DE AMÉRICA, ☎(957) 40 02 02, 1 km north of the main area of interest; 20–30 mins on foot, or take bus no.3 (every 15 mins; Pta110). Luggage lockers and cash machine.

i **Tourist Offices**: **Provincial**: C. TORRIJOS 10 (PALACIO DE CONGRESOS Y EXPOSICIONES), ☎(957) 47 12 35, fax (957) 49 17 78 (Mon–Fri 0930–1900, Sat 1000–1900, Sun 1000–1400). **Municipal**: PLAZA DE JUDÁ LEVÍ; ☎(957) 20 05 22 (Mon–Sat 0900–1400, 1730–1930, Sun 0900–1400; closing hours vary seasonally by an hour or so). To reach the municipal office from the station, go down AVENIDA DE AMÉRICA, turn right along it onto AVENIDA DE LOS MOZARABES then cross over to follow PASEO DE LA VICTORIA. Turn left onto CAIRUAN and walk onto CALLE JUDÍOS. Follow the road round, past PLAZA MAIMONIDES and bear left down ALBUCASIS; the information office is on your left at PLAZA J LEVÍ.

Cheap places are near the station, in and around the *Judería* (Jewish Quarter) and off PLAZA DE LAS TENDILLAS. PLAZA DE LA CORREDERA, although cheap, is a less savoury area. **Pensión Bagdad**, FERNÁNDEZ RUANO 11, ☎(957) 20 28 54, has a beautiful central courtyard. **Hostal Luis de Gongora**, Horno de la Trinidad 7, (957) 29 53 99, is lacking in traditional charm, but is clean, quiet and comfortable. Other budget options include **Hostal Los Arcos**, C. Romero Barros 14, (957) 48 56 43; **Mary II**, Horno de Porras 6, (957) 48 60 04; **Maestre**, Romero Barros 16–18, (957) 47 53 95; and **Hostal Las Tendillas**, Jesús María 1, (957) 47 30 29 (can be quite noisy). There is a **youth hostel** at Plaza de Judá Leví, (957) 29 01 66, and a **campsite**, **Campamento Municipal**, at Avda del Brillante 50; (957) 47 20 00 (about 2 km north of the train station; nos. 10/11 from Avda de Cervantes).

There are a number of restaurants around the *Judería*. **Cafeteria-restaurante El Rincon de Carmen**, C. Romero 4, has outside seating in a small and pleasant courtyard. Budget eateries can be found along C. Doctor Fleming or in the *Judería*.

Walking tour of Córdoba

This walk encompasses the main attractions of Córdoba in a couple of hours. Begin at the Plaza del Potro, see the fountain, the **Museo de Bellas Artes** and the inn, **La Posada del Potro**, where Cervantes is thought to have stayed. Walk down Paseo de la Ribera, along the banks of the *Rio Guadalquivir*. Turn right down Cano Quebrado to take in Córdoba's most famous sight, the **Mezquita**. Carry on along to the riverside Ronda de Isasa; on reaching an Arab waterwheel on your left, with the **Alcázar** off to your right, go down Santa Teresa de Jornet. Go back onto Ronda de Isasa/ Avenida de Alcázar and continue alongside the river. Turn left onto Puente San Rafael, cross the bridge, and turn left to head back in the direction you just came, but on the opposite side of the river. Call at the **Museo Torre de la Calahorra** and afterwards cross Puente Romano and continue straight ahead into the little shops and inexpensive cafés of the *Judería*.

SEVILLE (SEVILLA)

The capital of Andalucía is a romantic, theatrical place, with a captivating park, a gigantic cathedral and such fiestas as the **April Feria** and the processions of **Holy Week**. Columbus sailed from Seville to discover the New World, and *Don Juan*, *Carmen*, the *Barber of Seville* and the *Marriage of Figaro* were all set here.

The downside is the high level of petty crime: be on the alert for bag-snatchers and pickpockets, and never leave anything of value in your hotel room or your car.

The prime sights are in a very small area, but the secondary ones are quite widespread. Unless you are a very keen walker you'll probably want to get a few buses along the way.

Most places of interest are in the Barrio de Santa Cruz. A pleasant place for a stroll, it lives up to the idealised image of Spain; white and yellow houses with flower-bedecked balconies and attractive patios. The focal point is the **Giralda**, a minaret that has towered over the old city since the 12th century and which now serves as belfry to the cathedral. Built by the Almohad rulers 50 years before Ferdinand and

DAY TRIP FROM SEVILLE

Itálica (Tues–Sat 0900–1830, Sun and holidays 0900–1500; Pta250, free to EU nationals) is a substantial excavated Roman town at **Santaponce**, about 9 km from Seville, with remains of streets, baths and mosaics. The 25,000-seater amphitheatre is particularly interesting. Itálica was first founded by Publio Cornelio Espicion, and it was thought to be the home of Trajano and Hadrian in the 2nd century AD. Buses leave Seville bus station every 20 mins and cost Pta100.

TOURS OF SEVILLE

Bus tours depart every 45 mins touring the PLAZA DE ESPAÑA, TORRE DEL ORO, MONASTERIO DE LA CARTUJA and ISLA MAGICA. The tours run from 1000–1900. Tickets are a little expensive (around Pta1500) but as they are valid all day you can get on and off as you please; ☎(95) 450 20 99.

Take a **boat tour** along the Rio Guadalquivir to see the sights of Seville. They embark at 1100, 1200, then every 30 mins until 2200; ☎456 16 92. City tours by **horse-drawn trap** leave from outside the cathedral.

Isabella's Christian Reconquest, it consists of a series of gentle ramps designed for horsemen to ride up; it's in excellent condition and worth climbing for the views.

The **cathedral** is the largest Gothic structure in the world (Mon–Sat 1030–1700, Sun 1030–1330; Pta600, students Pta200), simply groaning with gold leaf. The **Capilla Mayor** has a vast gilded retable, which took 82 years to complete. **Sacristía Mayor** houses the treasury and **Sacristía de los Cálices** contains Murillos and a Goya. A huge memorial honours Christopher Columbus, while outside is the pretty **Patio de los Naranjos** (orange-tree courtyard).

The **Alcázar** was inspired by the Alhambra of Granada (see p. 166), but has been marred by later additions (Tues–Sat 0930–1800, Sun and public holidays 1000–1300). Within is the **Salon de Embajadores,** where Columbus was received by Ferdinand and Isabella on his return from the Americas, and there are also shady, interconnected gardens separated by arched Moorish walls. The neighbouring **Casa Lonja** contains a collection of documents relating to the discovery of the Americas.

Hospital de la Caridad, C. TEMPRADO, was commissioned by a reformed rake, reputed to have been the real-life inspiration for Don Juan. The church contains several works by Valdés Leal, depicting death in ghoulishly disturbing ways; there are also paintings by Murillo.

Nowadays, the 18th-century *Fábrica de Tabacos* (on C. DE SAN FERNANDO south of the Alcázar) houses parts of the university, but it was once a tobacco factory, employing over 10,000 women (supposedly including Carmen).

South-east of the factory is **María Luisa Park**, a delightful mixture of wilderness areas and formal gardens laid out for a trade fair in 1929 and shaded by trees from Latin America. It contains PLAZA DE ESPAÑA, which was the central pavilion, and PLAZA DE AMÉRICA, a peaceful place which is home to the **Archaeological Museum,** containing a famously rich Roman section (closed Mon). The Latin American countries that exhibited at the fair each built a pavilion in their own national style, most of which survive.

The **Museo de Bellas Artes** (closed Mon, free for EU nationals), PL. DEL MUSEO (between SANTA CRUZ and CARTUJA), has a collection of 13th–20th-century Spanish paintings, second only to that in the Prado in Madrid. The decorative **Maestranza** (bullring), near the river, dates from the 18th century. Fights are held every Thur Mar–Oct. A short way along the river bank is the 13th-century **Torre del Oro** (Golden Tower), named after the gold-coloured tiles that once covered its twelve sides. It now contains a small **naval museum** (Pta100; free to EU citizens on Tues). **Cartuja Park** (across the river from the old town) was the site of Expo 92 and is due to reopen as a science and technology park, with theatres and concert halls for staging cultural events.

Estación Santa Justa, AVDA KANSAS CITY; ☎(95) 441 41 11. 15-min walk from the centre. Bus no. 27 goes from the station to PLAZA DE LA ENCARNACIÓN; bus no. 70 goes to PLAZA DE ESPAÑA. General RENFE enquiries, ☎(95) 454 02 02. Luggage lockers cost Pta300–600; the locker area is open 0600–2400. Currency exchange and cash machines.

BUS TICKETS

A single ticket costs Pta125, but a **bónobus** ticket is better value (Pta550 for 10 trips), available from news-stands and tobacconists.

There are two bus stations: **Prado de San Sebastián**, MANUEL VAZQUEZ SAGASTAZABAL, ☎(95) 441 71 11, is mainly for buses to Andalucía; PLAZA DE ARMAS, C. MARQUÉS DE PARADAS, ☎(95) 490 77 37, is for buses elsewhere.
City buses: C1 and C2 are circular routes around the town. Many buses pass through PLAZA DE LA ENCARNACIÓN, PLAZA NUEVA and AVDA DE LA CONSTITUCIÓN.

Taxis: There's a rank on PLAZA NUEVA. To order a taxi ☎(95) 462 22 22 or 458 00 00.

San Pablo Airport, 12 km east of town, ☎(95) 444 90 00; tourist information desk, ☎(95) 444 91 28. There are no train links with Seville, but taxis cost about Pta2000. Express buses take 30 mins to the centre (Pta750).

Tourist Offices: **Regional**: AVDA DE LA CONSTITUCIÓN 21B ☎(95) 422 14 04 or 421 81 57, fax: (95) 422 97 53 (Mon–Sat 0900–1900, Sun 1000–1400). **Municipal**: PASEO DE LAS DELICIAS, ☎(95) 423 44 65 (Mon–Fri 0900–1315, 1630–1845). **Centro de Información de Sevilla**, C. DE ARJONA S/N, ☎(95) 450 56 00. There are also tourist information booths in strategic locations, including the rail station.
Post and phones: The main **post office** is at AVDA DE LA CONSTITUCIÓN 32; ☎421 64 76, open Mon–Fri 0800–2100, Sat

Seville is the home of flamenco and it's easy to find, but you should be selective because it is often staged specially for tourists. If you ask around, you should be able to find more genuine (and cheaper) performances. There are various clubs with flamenco evenings, but they can be quite expensive, especially during festival time in the spring. An excellent one to try is **El Gallo** in BARRIO DE SANTA CRUZ.

Seville is packed with lively bars, clubs and discos, notably in the **Los Remedios** district in the south of the city and on C. BETIS next to the river, but little seems to happen until close to midnight. If you're looking for activity and atmosphere a little earlier in the evening, try the other side of the river, where there is a range of tapas bars, some of which have live music. **Patio de San Eloy**, C. SAN ELOY 7, is a good bet, as is **La Carbonería**, C. LESIES in BARRIO DE SANTA CRUZ. Dining out in Spain happens later than in northern Europe and North America, and nightlife doesn't get going until after dining hours.

El Giraldillo, produced monthly, is a free guide to current events in Seville.

0900–1900. The facilities for poste restante *(lista de correos)* close on Sat afternoons. **International phone calls** can be made from PLAZA DE LA GAVIDIA 7, open Mon–Sat 1000–1400 and 1730–2200 or PASAJE SIERPES 11.

Thomas Cook licensee: **Ultramar Express**, LUIS DE MORALES 2; ☎(95) 458 21 01.

Accommodation is very difficult to obtain, unless pre-booked, during Holy Week and the April Fair. It also tends to be expensive. For the least expensive lodgings, try the **Barrio Santa Cruz**: C. ARCHEROS, the streets around PLAZA NUEVA (C. MARQUÉS DE PARADAS or C. GRAVINA), or the area west of PLAZA NUEVA towards the river. **Pensión Fabiola**, C. FABIOLA 16 (in Santa Cruz), ☎(95) 421 83 46, has basic rooms arranged around a central courtyard. **Hostal Aguilas**, C. AGUILAS 15, ☎(95) 421 31 77, has a small number of clean, well-furnished rooms. **Pensión Alcázar**, C. DEAN MIRANDA 12, ☎(95) 422 84 57, is a pension right next to the Alcázar wall. The rooms are beautifully furnished and decorated, with ceiling fans or air-conditioning. **Hotel Simon** (1-star), GARCÍA DE VINUESA 19, ☎(95) 422 66 60, is in a former 18th-century mansion. **Youth hostel**: C. ISAAC PERAL 2; ☎(95) 461 31 50. All three **campsites** are about 12 km out of town. The main one is **Camping Sevilla**, CTRA MADRID-CÁDIZ km 534, ☎(95) 451 43 79, near the airport: take either the **Empresa Casal** bus towards **Carmona** (hourly) or the no.70 to PARQUE ALCOSA (800 m away). The other two sites are at **Dos Hermanas**: **Club de Campo**, AVDA DE LA LIBERTAD 13, ☎(95) 472 02 50, and **Camping Villsom**, CTRA SEVILLE-CÁDIZ km 554.8; ☎(95) 472 08 28, served by buses from PRADO DE SAN SEBASTIÁN every 30–45 mins.

Seville is probably the best place to sample such typical Andalusian dishes as *gazpacho* (chilled tomato and pepper soup) and *pescaíto frito* (deep-fried fish). Eating out can be expensive, but there are a few places with excellent menus for around Pta700, such as **Café Bar El Callejon**, C. ADRIANO 24, and **Café Bar Nipal**, PASAJE DE LAS DELICIAS. For delicious snacks, try **Café Bar Guadalquivir**, C. GARCÍA DE VINUESA. The liveliest bars and restaurants, frequented by students, are in BARRIO SANTA CRUZ. Guinness fans can drop in at

Flaherty's Irish Pub, CALLE ALEMANES 7. For a meal with a view, try restaurants on the other side of the river by the Puente de San Telmo. The **Rio Grande** is particularly good, but expensive. Buying your own food is a cheap option and to be recommended if you go to the **Mercado del Arenal**, C. ARENAL and C. PASTOR, the town's largest market.

CÁDIZ

Like Venice, that other once-great naval city, Cádiz is approached by a causeway and all but surrounded by water. Its tight grid of streets, squares and crumbly ochre buildings exudes an atmosphere of gentle decay, but it's all the better for that, and really comes into its own during the huge **carnival** in Feb (one of the best in Spain) and in the evening, when the promenaders come out and the bars open. Colourful tiling is a feature of the pavements, parks and even the **Catedral Nueva** (new cathedral), which was rebuilt, like much of the rest, in the city's 18th-century heyday. However its origins go back to 1100 BC when it was founded by the Phoenicians; the port was of vital importance at the time of the conquest of the Americas (which was why Sir Francis Drake attacked it). You can get a panoramic view of it all from **Torre Tavira**, both from the top of the tower and in the camera obscura below, via a mirror and lens on the roof.

The **Museo Histórico Municipal** contains an 18th-century ivory and mahogany scale model of Cádiz, while **Museo de Cádiz** has an eclectic display of exhibits from sarcophagi to paintings by Murillo, Van Dyck and Rubens. The chapel of the **Hospital de Mujeres** houses El Greco's *St Francis in Ecstasy* and **Oratorio de la Santa Ceura** has, among other works, three Goya frescos.

RAIL PLAZA DE SEVILLA S/N; (956) 25 43 01. Centrally located, close to PL. DE SAN JUAN DE DÍOS. Luggage lockers; cash machines near the station.

i **Tourist Office**: CALDERÓN DE LA BARCA 1; (956) 21 13 13, fax (956) 22 84 71.

España, MARQUES DE CADIZ 9, (956) 28 55 00 (doubles Pta3500–3700); **La Argentina**, CONDE DE O'REILLY 1, 1ST FLOOR, (956) 22 33 10 (doubles Pta2500–2700); **Hospederia del Mar**, PZA SAN LORENZO 2, EDF. CLUB NAUTICO, (956) 26 09 14 (doubles Pta3200–3800).

(for Directory information, see pp. 541, 556 and 555).

Belgium, The Netherlands & Luxembourg

Also known collectively as the Low Countries, these small nations for the most part live up to their name: the land lies very low and flat. There are bits of pleasant dune-backed coast, notably in the Netherlands, and agreeably hilly terrain in the **Ardennes** of Belgium and Luxembourg, but essentially it's the places rather than the scenery that provide interest. Cycling is a national passion in both Belgium and the Netherlands, with an excellent network of cycle routes making it a feasible way to get around the cities and to tour larger areas. Cycle hire is available at many stations. In Belgium the **Vlaanderen Fietroute** is a well-signposted and varied 750 km cycle route round the entire country, taking in **Bruges**, **Antwerp**, **Lier**, **Ghent, Leuven** and other cities.

Belgium

Belgium has found it hard to shake off a reputation for dullness. Certainly the coast – almost entirely built up – is undistinguished to the point of blandness, but elsewhere there are handsome brick-built cities with a great sense of history. **Bruges** is the most attractive of all, a canal-laced city dubbed the 'Venice of the North', graced with fine old merchants' houses. There's more fine waterside architecture and a notable cathedral at **Ghent**, while **Antwerp** is a lively cultural city with a medieval printing works.

Brussels, the capital, has a magnificent central square as well as some surprises – including a legacy of **Art Nouveau** architecture that by far outstrips Paris.

Accommodation

The Benelux countries have a common hotel–rating system. The lowest is **'O'** (accommodation only, but meeting minimum requirements of hygiene and comfort); the next is **'H'** (moderately comfortable, with at least one bathroom per ten rooms. After that, you're on to the usual star system, one-star places being obliged (as a minimum) to have a washstand in every room and to serve breakfast.

HOTELS

Resotel,
☎(00) 32 2779 3939, fax: (00) 32 2779 3900, offer a free service for hotel reservations, often at preferential rates.

HOSTELS

Hostelling organisations:
Vlaamse JEGDHERBERGCENTRALE, ☎(32) (3) 2327218, fax (32) (3) 2318126.
Les Auberges de Jeunesse ☎(32) (3) 2153100 fax (32) (3) 2428356 (email: auberges.jeunesse@gate7.be; http://www.planet.be/aubjeun).

HOTELS Hotels tend to be pricey and you're unlikely to get anything for less than BFr.1000 (BFr.700 single).

Tourist offices charge a deposit for booking hotels (which is then deducted from your bill), and can often get reduced rates. They sometimes agree to check availability of other accommodation. In summer, accommodation of all kinds can be hard to find and it's sensible to book, especially in Bruges and on the coast.

A **bed and breakfast guide** is available from **Taxistop**, ONDERBERGEN 51, 9000 GHENT, ☎(09) 223 23 10, fax: (09) 223 22 32, but they require stamps (6 x BFr.15) to cover postage.

CAMPING Rough camping is not permitted, but some farmers may give you permission to use their land. A leaflet covering officially rated campsites should be available from your nearest Belgian Tourist Office.

FOOD AND DRINK

Most restaurants have good-value fixed-price menus (*plat du jour, tourist menu, dagschotel*). There's a wide variation in prices; establishments in the main squares can charge two or three times as much as similar places in nearby streets.

Try **waffles** (*wafels/gaufres*) and sweet or savoury **pancakes** (*crêpes*), **mussels** (*moules*) and freshly baked pastries. The most common snacks are *fritures/frites* (french fries with mayonnaise or other sauce) and (delicious) ice cream. Candies are ubiquitous, notably **nougat** and the deservedly famous **chocolates**, but be warned: the ones containing cream have a very short shelf-life.

Tea comes as teabags with lemon unless you specify milk (you'll get cream), the **coffee** and **hot chocolate** are delicious. It's easy (though not cheap) to get freshly squeezed orange and lemon. Many bottled juices are refreshingly low on sugar. Belgium produces literally hundreds of beers (both dark and light); **wheat beer** comes with a slice of lemon in it.

THE NETHERLANDS

Canals and 17th- and 18th-century gabled buildings are abiding memories of a visit to the Netherlands, whose numerous historic towns and cities have a strikingly uniform appearance. In between, the bulb fields and windmills lend the Dutch

INFORMATION

HOSTELS

Dutch Youth Hostels Association (NJHC): PROF. TULPPLEIN 2, 1018 GX AMSTERDAM. ☎(020) 551 3155, fax: (020) 639 0199.

Holiday Link: PO Box 70-155, NL-9704 AD, GRONINGEN, THE NETHERLANDS. ☎ (050) 313 2424.

NRC (Netherlands Reservation Centre): PO Box 404, 2260 AK LEIDSCHENDAM. ☎(070) 317 54 54. (English spoken), fax: (070) 320 4237; Mon–Fri 0800–2000 and Sat 0800–1400.

BED AND BREAKFAST

Bed and Breakfast Holland: THEOPHILE DE BOCKSTRAAT 3, 1058 TV AMSTERDAM. ☎(020) 615 7527, fax: (020) 669 1573.

farmland a distinctive character. **Amsterdam**, sleazy and bustling at the same time, justifiably draws most visitors, and even the red-light area has become a tourist attraction. Elsewhere, **Delft**, **Haarlem**, **Leiden**, **Maastricht** and **Utrecht** are among many places with pretty centres, while **Rotterdam** has striking modern architecture. Cheese addicts should head for **Gouda, Edam** and **Alkmaar**.

ACCOMMODATION

Standards are high; lower prices reflect limited facilities rather than poor quality. Room rates start around NLG65 for a double, but most cost more. Booking is advisable: there's a free centralised booking service: Netherlands Reservation Centre (NRC).

HOTELS VVV offices have listings of bed and breakfast accommodation in their area, where it exists, or you can book nationwide through **bed and breakfast Holland**. **HolidayLink** offers a similar service, with a guide which can be ordered for NLG35.

FOOD AND DRINK

Dutch cuisine is traditionally simple and substantial. Many Indonesian restaurants offer spicy food and in cities a good variety of international cuisine is available. Most eating places stay open all day but restaurants in small places take last orders by 2100.

Look for boards saying *dagschotel* (a very economical 'special'). 'Brown cafés' (traditional pubs) also serve good-value food. **Mensas** are subsidised student canteens in university towns; very cheap and not restricted to students, but open only during term-time.

Specialities include apple pie (heavy on cinnamon and sultanas), herring marinated in brine, steamed eels, *poffertjes* (tiny puff-pancakes with icing sugar) and *pannekoeken* (pancakes: try bacon with syrup). Street stalls for snacks abound, options invariably including *frites/patates* (a cross between french fries and British chips) with mayonnaise or other sauces. In **Limburg**, try the regional (slightly sour) *zurvlees*. Vending machines at stations sell heated croquettes, *bami* and *nasi* being spicy.

Excellent *coffee* and *hot chocolate* are available everywhere, often topped with whipped cream – *slagroom*. *Tea* is hot water with a choice of teabags – ask if you want milk. Dutch beer is topped by two fingers of froth. Most local liqueurs are excellent. The main spirit is *jenever*, a strong, slightly oily gin made from juniper berries.

LUXEMBOURG

The principality of Luxembourg covers some pretty terrain for hiking, with river valleys, forests and hills, and its eponymous capital has a fine setting straddling two gorges.

ACCOMMODATION

The national Tourist Office has free brochures covering hotels (of all grades, plus restaurants), holiday apartments, farm holidays and camping in the Grand-Duchy, plus a bed and breakfast booklet that covers all three Benelux countries.

HOSTELS There are 14 **youth hostels** (bed and breakfast costing Lfr.355–650, plus Lfr.125 for linen hire).

INFORMATION
HOSTELS

Youth Hostelling organisation: **Centrale des Auberges de Jeunesse** LUXEMBOURGEOISES, 2 R. DU FORT OLISY, L-2261 LUXEMBOURG; ☎(352) 225588, fax (352) 463987.

FOOD AND DRINK

Cuisine is pithily described as 'French quality, German quantity', but eating out is expensive. Keep costs down by making lunch your main meal and looking for the special deals: **plat du jour** (single course) or **menu** (2–3 courses). There are take-aways, most pizzerias are good value and light meals are often available in pastry shops. Local specialities are: Ardennes ham, *treipen* (black pudding), *quenelles* (calf's liver dumplings), *thüringer* (the standard local sausage), *gromperekichelcher* (fried potato patties) and (in Sept) *quetschentaart* (a flan featuring dark, violet plums).

Luxembourg produces a variety of lagers, liqueurs and white wines. Sugar may not be added while making wine, so the Moselles are drier and fruitier than their German equivalents.

EDITOR'S CHOICE

Amsterdam; Antwerp; Bruges; Brussels; Delft; Ghent; Gouda; The Hague; Kröller-Müller Museum (near Arnhem); Luxembourg; Maastricht; Rotterdam.

BEYOND THE BORDERS

Amsterdam–Paris via Brussels (ETT table 18), Amsterdam–Berlin (table 22); Amsterdam–Munich via Cologne (table 28); Brussels–Milan via Luxembourg and Strasbourg (table 43); Luxembourg–Cologne (table 79); Luxembourg–Nice via Avignon (table 79).

Amsterdam

The Dutch say that they earn their money in Rotterdam, talk about it in The Hague, and spend it in **Amsterdam**. Romantic and laid-back, it combines the quintessential historic Dutch city features of tree-lined canals, bicycles and elegant gabled brick houses, with a vibrant, emphatically youthful streetlife. There's a strong seasonal contrast: in summer it's full of tourists, while in winter it's often frosty and shrouded in fog, the few visitors huddled in the famous 'brown cafés' over coffee and apple cake. In the 'Golden Age' of the revolutionary Dutch republic (the 17th century) Amsterdam followed only London and Paris in importance – and assumed its present cobweb-like shape with the building of three new canals. Allow a couple of days for casual exploration, plus plenty of time to visit the marvellously varied museums and galleries around the city, and to take in a canal cruise.

The city centre is large, so it's sensible to concentrate on one area at a time: get there by public transport and then explore on foot (VVV suggest walking routes, and these are well signposted and colour-coordinated by a multitude of city maps at strategic points).

The city's layout can be confusing; bear in mind that *gracht* means 'canal' and that the centre follows the horseshoe shape dictated by the canals.

ARRIVAL AND DEPARTURE

RAIL **Centraal (CS)** is the terminal for all the city's trains and 5 mins' walk north of Dam (the central area); beware of opportunistic thieves that hang around there. There's a manned left-luggage facility, as well as lockers, but the baggage area is closed 0100–0500. If you are interested in organised excursions, the NS Reisburo office in the station is less crowded than VVV, but they have no general information.

✈ **Amsterdam-Schiphol**, general info ☎0900 0141, is about 14 km south-west of town. Transfers by train to/from Centraal are the cheapest: every 15 mins 0500–0100 (hourly 0100–0500); journey time 20 mins.

INFORMATION

CITY AND TRANSPORT MAP – inside back cover

A useful brochure for information on museums, tourist attractions, shopping and dining, plus city map and sights outside Amsterdam, is *Your Favourite Capital 'Amsterdam'* (NLG4.50).

Money **Thomas Cook foreign exchanges:** Dam 23–25; Leidseplein 31a; and Victoria Hotel, Damrak 1–5. Outside banking hours, the GWK exchange at Centraal opens 24 hrs a day. Their branch at Schiphol opens Mon–Sat 0700–2100, Sun 0700–1800.

TOURIST OFFICE

VVV, STATIONSPLEIN 10 (immediately opposite Centraal, in a wooden building just beyond the tram terminal); daily 0900–1700: invariably very busy; computerised system for last-minute availability of rooms nationwide.

There's a booth in Centraal (in the international area, open Mon–Sat 0800–2000, Sat 0830–1630) and a branch at LEIDSEPLEIN 1 (open daily 0900–1900).

The general Amsterdam information number is ☎0900 400 4040.

POST AND PHONES The main **post office**, SINGEL 250–256, open Mon, Tues, Wed, Fri 0900–1800, Thur 0900–2000, Sat 0900–1500, has poste restante.
Branch: OOSTERDOKSKADE 3–5 (Mon–Fri 0830–2100, Sat 0900–1200). The telephone code for Amsterdam is 020. At **Telehouse**, RAADHUISSTR. 48–50 (open 24 hrs), you pay for calls after you've finished.

PUBLIC TRANSPORT

MAPS The free *Tourist Guide to Public Transport* shows all the city transport (except boats) and lists the major attractions and how to reach them. Most tourist literature includes a small map of Centrum, the city centre, where everything of major interest is located.

METRO Primarily for commuters; few central stops.

TRAMS The most efficient method of travel in the centre; the network is extensive and services frequent and fast from early morning to midnight. The terminal is just in front of Centraal. Pressure on the lowest step keeps the door open. The circle tram no. 20 runs around all the major tourist attractions, with a tram every 10 mins or so 0900–1900.

TICKETS

VVV and GVB (Amsterdam's public transport company: a few doors from VVV and easily identified by the large yellow signs in the windows; open daily 0800–2230) offer a variety of passes for city travel, some also covering boats and/or museums, so tell them your requirements.

BUSES These begin/end just across the canal in front of Centraal, but not all from the same terminal. They are less frequent than trams, but go further afield; limited night services (indicated by black square on bus-stops).

TAXIS Main ranks at Centraal, DAM, REMBRANDTSPLEIN and LEIDSEPLEIN, ☎677 7777.

ACCOMMODATION

Best to reserve, particularly in peak season: VVV charge per person to make bookings.

The famous 4-star **American Hotel** includes the Café Américain, a former haunt of artists and writers. Cheaper 2-star options are **Agora** and **Acro**, while two good budget establishments are **Bema** and **Ronnie**. HUISSTRAAT and DAMRAK are both recommended for a plethora of cheap hotels.

Amsterdam

Highly recommended are the two **Flying Pig** private **hostels** in Centrum. These are friendly and secure; cheap bars, free e-mail, kitchens and breakfast. Dormitory accommodation is a good bet. There are two **HI** youth hostels, both in Centrum. If you don't mind a bit of religion, a good cheapie is **Eben Haezer Christian Youth Hostel**.

Avoid the touts at Centraal. They are illegal and many of the places they represent are in the red-light district and/or unlicensed because (among other things) they do not conform with fire regulations.

Hotels

American Hotel, Leidsekade 97, ☎624 5322. Expensive.

Agora, Singel 462, ☎627 2200.

Acro, Jan Luykenstr. 44, ☎662 5538. Moderate.

Bema, Concertgebouwplein 9, ☎679 1396.

Ronnie, Raadhuisstr. 41B, ☎624 2821. Budget.

Hostels

Flying Pig, Nieuwendijk 100, ☎420 6822, 50 m from Centraal, and Vossiusstr. 46–7, ☎421 0583, by Vondelpark.

HI youth hostels

Vondelpark, Zandpad 5, ☎589 8999 (tram nos. 1/2/5: Leidseplein):

Stadsdoelen, Klonveniersburgwal 97, ☎624 6832 (tram nos. 4/9 are most frequent: Muntplein).

Eben Haezer Christian Youth Hostel, Bloemstr. 179, ☎624 4717 (tram nos. 13/17: Marnixstr).

Campsite

Vliegenbos, Meeuwenlaan 138, ☎8855 (10 mins from Centraal on bus no. 32).

Food and Drink

Amsterdam is a good place to eat, with restaurants in every price range and a wide choice of international cuisine (especially Indonesian). Cheap food is easy to find, even in Centrum: the international fast-food chains are well represented and there are plenty of other takeaways, so you can get by perfectly well without ever setting foot in a restaurant. If you want to buy your own groceries there's a good **Albertheijn** supermarket on the corner of Singel and Koningsplein (nicely situated for picnics next to the floating flowermarket). For a sit-down meal at a reasonable price, try one of the many traditional 'brown cafés'. Some of the city's trendiest cafés are around **Spui**, while the areas around **Nieuwmarkt**, **Dam** and **De Pijp** (especially along Albert Cuyperstr.) are the best for Eastern cuisine. Amsterdam has two *mensas* (student canteens): **Atrium** and **De Weesper**.

Student canteens

Atrium, Oude Zijds Voorburgwal 237, open Mon–Fri 1200–1400 and 1700–1900.

De Weesper, Weesperstr. 5, open Mon–Fri 1700–1925.

HIGHLIGHTS

Amsterdam has nearly 200 museums and art galleries. *Amsterdam City of Museums* is a helpful free leaflet (available from VVV and some museums). Particularly unmissable are **Rijksmuseum**, the **Van Gogh museum**, and the **Anne Frank house.**

THE CENTRE: DAM From Centraal, DAMRAK leads directly to **Dam**, site of the original dam, with its distinctive **war memorial**. **Koninklijk Paleis** (the Royal Palace) dominates the square. The interior reflects the glory of the Golden Age and much Empire furniture remains from the time of Louis Bonaparte. The Gothic **Nieuwekerk** (New Church) is used for state functions: the investiture of the Dutch rulers has taken place here since 1814. Also in DAM is the **Madame Tussaud Scenerama** (DAM 20), where audio-animation techniques bring many waxworks to life.

AMSTERDAM CULTURE AND LEISURE PASS

If you don't have a museum card (see p. 557), consider the Amsterdam Culture and Leisure Pass (NLG36.75, or NLG25 for under-25s), giving free or discounted admission to many attractions.

WEST OF DAM **Anne Frank Huis**, PRINSENGRACHT 263 (boat: PRINSENGRACHT; tram nos. 13/14/17: WESTERMARKT), is where a Jewish family hid from the Nazis for two years. They were betrayed in 1944 and only the father survived the concentration camps. Thirteen-year-old Anne recorded the family's ordeal in a moving diary that was discovered after the war: you can see the rooms she described.

THE OLD CITY: EAST OF DAMRAK Across the canal from Centraal is **Nicholaaskerk**, with its largest dome featuring a cross donated by the prostitutes of the area. The notorious red-light district (*De Walletjes* – Little Walls) is (roughly) the area between WARMOESTR. and GELDERSKADE.

CANAL TRIPS

The canals are an integral part of Amsterdam and provide an excellent way to appreciate the city: **boat trips** can be very cheap and have multilingual commentaries. Most people embark at Centraal, but you can board at any stop; there are quays in each area of interest – get tickets at any quay where Rondvaart/Rederij boats are moored. **Museumboats** (STATIONSPLEIN) every 30 mins, 1000–1700, with five intermediate stops convenient for museums; day tickets NLG20 (includes several discounts); boats are turquoise and the stops have turquoise signs. **Watertaxis** are available (STATIONSPLEIN 8, ☎622 2181), but not cheap. **Canal buses** (WETERINGSCHANS) operate 1000–1800 (every 20 mins or so) and issue day tickets (NLG16.50), allowing you to get on or off as often as you like at the six stops – indicated by red, white and blue signs. There are regular (free) **ferries** across the River Ij, linking Centrum with northern Amsterdam: departures from RUYTERKADE (behind Centraal). For individual exploration, you can hire **canal bikes** (WETERINGSCHANS), pedal-boats for two or four people.

THE FRINGE

Amsterdam is renowned for its libertarian views on, among other things, marijuana and homosexuality, and there is a nationwide gay and lesbian organisation (☎623 6565; manned 1000–2200) that gives information about gay venues nationwide.

The city has many 'smoking' coffee-shops where hash and pot can be purchased and smoked (usually to the accompaniment of ear-shattering music). Though it's not legal, the police usually turn a blind eye. One reason for this tolerance is that it contains the problem, so do not assume it's OK to smoke elsewhere.

The red-light district, in and around OUDE ZIJDSACHTERBURGWAL, is always an eye-opener in the evening, with prostitutes posing in windows; the **Erotic Museum** makes the experience that much more memorable if you don't mind the sleazy exterior (well, you probably wouldn't be here if you did!). This area is supposedly a den of thieves, so be warned. Many habitués do not appreciate being photographed and your last sight of your camera might well be as it sinks into the nearest canal. Stick to the well-lit and crowded main streets.

SOUTH OF DAM The most notable museum here is the **Historisch Museum**, KALVERSTR. 92 (boats: HERENGRACHT; tram nos. 1/2/4/5/9/11/14/16/24/25: SPUI), where you can not only view, but also try your hand at bell-ringing. Turn right as you leave and signs lead to the **Begijnhof**, with its old almshouses (once home to pious upper-class women) surrounding a peaceful square and 15th-century church.

The highly fragrant **floating flower market**, SINGEL (between MUNTPLEIN and KONINGSPLEIN), takes place Mon–Sat 0900–1700/1800. The backs of the stalls are on barges, but the fronts are squarely on terra firma.

HERENGRACHT was the city's grandest canal and one stretch (between VIJZELSTR. and LEIDSESTR.) is known as the 'Golden Bend'. This typifies the old architecture, when buildings were tall and thin (to minimise taxes based on width) and had protruding gables (still used) to winch up furniture too big for the narrow staircases.

THE MUSEUM QUARTER This district, south-west of the centre, contains museums of international status, well worth the short tram ride.

Rijksmuseum, STADHOUDERSKADE 42 (boat: SINGELGRACHT; tram no. 16: MUSEUMPLEIN), ranks as one of the world's great museums. See the museum guide (p.193) for full details.

THE JEWISH QUARTER This lies south-east of DAM (metro: WATERLOOPLEIN; boats: MUZIEKTHEATER). The Jews played a very important part in the development of Amsterdam and formed 10 per cent of the pre-war population.

DAY TRIPS

Trips to **Edam** (visit the cheese market), Marken (unspoilt attractive harbour town) and elsewhere, can be made by bus: check numbers at the Tourist Office (see p. 191).

SHOPPING

LEIDSESTRAAT, KALVERSTRAAT, NIEUWENDIJK, DAMRAK and ROKIN are the main shopping streets. For fun shopping, explore the small specialist shops in the alleys linking the main canals, especially in the area between LEIDSEGRACHT and RAADHUISSTRAAT. The whole **Jordaan** area is scattered with second-hand shops and boutiques that offer the creations of up-and-coming designers. For antiques and art, look around the SPIEGELKWARTIER. Amsterdam's great store is the enormous **De Bijenkorf**, DAMRAK. For designer labels, try along PC HOOFTSTR, BEETHOVENSTR. and VAN BAELESTR. **Magna Plaza**, N.Z. VOORBURGWAL 182, is a shopping gallery just behind Koninklijk Paleis. Most shops in the centre of Amsterdam are open on Sunday.

The city has so many **markets** that VVV produces a leaflet about them, *Markstad*. The general market, ALBERT CUYPSTR., is the largest in the country, held Mon–Sat 0930–1700 (tram nos. 4/16/24/25). The flea market, WATERLOOPLEIN (surrounding the **Muziektheater**), takes place Mon–Fri 0900–1700, Sat 0830–1730.

Amsterdam has been a major diamond centre since the 16th century and prices are comparatively low, but it's worth shopping around. Most diamond merchants lay on free tours (explaining cutting and polishing) and hope you will buy. One of the oldest is **Coster Diamonds**, PAULUS POTTERSTR. 2–6 (tram nos. 2/3/5/15: MUSEUMPLEIN).

NIGHT-TIME AND EVENTS

The English-language magazine *What's On in Amsterdam* (published every three weeks), is the most comprehensive guide to events and useful addresses. You can buy it from VVV and bookshops, but it's sometimes free from good hotels. **AUB Uit Buro**, LEIDSEPLEIN 26 (open Mon–Sat 1000–1800), also distributes information about the city's entertainments. It and VVV make bookings, but there is a charge.

The nightlife is both varied and affordable, with bars, live music, cinemas and classical concerts; use the *What's On* magazine to suit your taste. Lively areas include, **Leidseplein**, **Rembrandtsplein** and **Nieuwezijids Voorburgwal**. The Jordaan area is less hectic, and pleasant for a quiet evening.

Amsterdam has several water-related events and music festivals in the course of each year. The major arts event is the **Holland Festival** (June), which covers all the performing arts.

LIVE BANDS

Live music (including jazz and dance – Jon Spencer Blues Explosion and Faithless both played there recently) can be heard at **Paradiso**, WETERINGSCHANS 6, ☎626 4521, and **De Melkweg** (The Milky Way), LYNBAANSGRACHT 234A, ☎624 1777. Both often include club nights after a gig.

Brussels

Headquarters of the EU and NATO, Brussels is an exceptionally cosmopolitan city, as well as home to a sizeable number of immigrants from around the Mediterranean. Though it's not the most glamorous or romantic of European capitals – its two most famous monuments are a statue of a urinating boy (the **Manneken-Pis**) and an out-sized 1950s atomic model (the Atomium). It can be a fun city with some great art galleries, abundant greenery, a majestic central square and many excellent restaurants. There's also a wealth of art nouveau architecture which, for the most part, you have to look at from the outside. Streets to head for include the Square Ambiorix and Square Marie-Louise (both just north of Schuman station) and Av. Louise, with several houses by the great Victor Horta, whose wonderfully stylish house is open to the public.

Brussels is well placed for journeys by rail into the **Netherlands**, **Germany**, **France** and the **UK**, and the most interesting Belgian cities are all within a day trip (with **Antwerp** particularly near). The city is officially bilingual and there's often little similarity between the two versions of street names (e.g. French *Arts-Loi* is Flemish *Kunst-Wet*). This chapter uses the French ones.

ARRIVAL AND DEPARTURE

Airport: Bruxelles Zaventem Airport, ☎753 39 13, is 14 km north-east of the centre; exchange offices, tourist information desk (daily 0600–2200). An express rail link operates until nearly midnight (every 20 mins or so to all three main stations; journey time15–30 mins; BFr.85). A taxi should cost around BFr.1200.

Stations: Virtually all long-distance trains stop at both **Midi** and **Nord** (metro no. 23: change at ROGIER from no. 2 or at DE BROUCKÈRE from no. 1), but many omit **Central** (metro no. 1: CENTRALE, 5-min walk from GRAND-PLACE). The facilities at all three include baggage lockers, eating-places and newsagents selling English papers. Other main-line stations are for local journeys only. For all rail enquiries, ☎203 3640 (French) or ☎203 2886 (Flemish).

Midi/Zuid (metro nos. 2/23) is the most important station, the terminal for Eurostar services, although it's in an area best avoided at night; train information office (daily 0630–2230) with a hotel booking desk (open Mon–Fri 0930–2130, Sat–Sun 1100–2030); few other tourist facilities except bureau de change. Your best bet, unless just transferring, is to hop on a train to **Central** as fast as possible.

INFORMATION

CITY AND TRANSPORT MAP – inside back cover

It's worth buying *Brussels Guide & Map*, easily the most comprehensive and entertaining tourist leaflet; cheaper from the Tourist Office than from bookshops. The English-language weekly *Bulletin* has a useful *What's On* supplement.

MONEY **Thomas Cook** bureaux de change at 4 GRAND-PLACE and at 19 R. DES BOUCHERS. **Midi** station: currency exchange, daily 0700–2200; cash machine. Currency exchange offices at **Nord** (0700–2000) and **Central** (0700–1900).

TOURIST OFFICE

Hôtel de Ville, GRAND-PLACE, ☎513 89 40 (summer: Mon–Sat 0900–1800, Sun 0900–1800; winter 1000–1400). If you make a hotel booking you will get a free map, but the only other thing they give away is the transport map. Better is the **National Tourism Centre**: R. DU MARCHÉ-AUX-HERBES 61, ☎504 03 90 (from GRAND-PLACE, take the road to the right of the Museum, opposite the Hôtel de Ville): daily 0900–1900 (summer); Mon–Sat 0900–1800, Sun 1300–1700 (winter). It has information about the whole country (including a free city map with points of interest marked); ask about the **Brussels Tourist Passport** (BFr.220), which offers free city transport and a wide range of discounts (also available from museums, metro stations and hotels). **Info-Jeunes**: R. DU MARCHÉ-AUX-HERBES 27, ☎512 32 74 (Mon–Fri 1200–1730), has information about special deals for young people.

POST AND PHONES

Main post office: Centre Monnaie, PL. DE BROUCKÈRE (upstairs); Mon–Fri 0800–2000, Sat 0900–1500. There's a 24-hr post office at **Midi** (AV. FONSNY 48), plus branches at **Central** and **Nord**, (Mon–Fri 0900–1700). **Telephone centre**, R. DU LOMBARD 30 (daily 1000–2200). The telephone code for Brussels is 02.

PUBLIC TRANSPORT

The city centre is smaller than it looks on maps and walking is the best way to get around, though it can be confusing initially. Away from the centre, the metro and bus network is efficiently run by **STIB**. For all city transport information, ☎515 20 00.

MAPS

Free route maps from STIB kiosks, metro stations and Tourist Offices.

METRO

Primarily for commuters; few central stops. The terms 'tram' and 'metro' are interchangeable here. Metro stations are indicated by a square white 'M' on a blue background. *Loket/guichet* booths for tickets are in all stations and the trams run 0600–midnight. The system is comprehensive, efficient and easy to use: study the map before setting out. Lines are identified by number and colour (nos. 1/red and 2/orange being central). Routes of the relevant line are shown on all platforms and trams, and every platform has a city map with the metro system superimposed. Doors close automatically (don't use them after the warning buzzer sounds), but you have to open them yourself: usually by exerting a little pressure on the handle and letting the hydraulics take over, sometimes by pressing a thin strip by the door. Smoking is prohibited throughout the system. Watch the escalators: they're pressure-activated, which is pretty smart until you miss the sign and try to walk up the down one.

TICKETS

Individual tickets (BFr.50) can be purchased from drivers and multi-ride tickets from STIB kiosks, Tourist Offices, metro stations and some newsagents; 10-trip tickets cost BFr.330. There's also a one-day travelcard for unlimited travel on all city transport for one calendar day. Stamp your ticket in the machine by the metro entrance or on board buses before travelling.

BUSES

Buses also have a comprehensive network (approximately 0600–2200), and there's a very limited night service. If stops show *sur demande*, raise your hand to the driver as the vehicle approaches. If you want to get off, ring the bell.

TAXIS

Ranks are strategically positioned at all the stations and main squares. Don't tip the drivers.

BIKE HIRE

The streets are a bit crowded, but bikes can be hired from R. E. SOLVAY 32A, ☎502 73 55.

ACCOMMODATION

There's a good choice of hotels in every grade, including plenty of budget establishments in the areas of IXELLES and PL. STE-CATHERINE, several hostels (HI and otherwise) and a number of bed and breakfasts. Advance booking is recommended in peak periods.

Youth hostels: **Jacques Brel**, (METRO no. 2: MADOU, direction SIMONIS, i.e. away from the centre). A sign in the ticket hall indicates the exit. **Bruegel** is 300 m from Central (behind Notre-Dame-de-la-Chapelle) and very modern. **Generation Europe**, 2 km from Central (METRO: COMTE DE FLANDRE – 500 m). **Centre Vincent Van Gogh** is the oldest youth hostel in Brussels and has the largest capacity.

The nearest official **campsite** is **Beersel**, 9 km south (tram no. 55: Uccle). Another is at CHAUSSÉE DE WAVRE 205, ☎264 41681.

HOTELS	**Amigo**, R. D'AMIGO 1–3, ☎547 47 47, fax 513 52 77 Expensive.
	Arenberg, R. D'ASSAUT 15, ☎501 16 16. **Arlequin**, R. DE LA FOURCHE 17–19, ☎514 16 15, fax: 514 22 02. Both moderate.
	Madou, R. DU CONGRÈS 45, ☎217 32 74. **Sabina**, R. DU NORD 78, ☎218 26 37. **Espace du Marais**, R. DU DARNIER 23, ☎218 50 50. **Pension Bosquet**, R. BOSQUET 70, ☎538 52 30. Budget.
HOSTELS	**Jacques Brel**, R. DE LA SABLONNIÈRE 30, ☎218 01 87. **Bruegel**, HEILIG GEESTSTRAAT 2, ☎511 04 36. **Generation Europe**, R. DE L'ÉLÉPHANT 4, ☎410 38 58. **Centre Vincent Van Gogh**, R. TRAVERSIÈRE 8, ☎217 01 58.
CAMPSITES	75 STEENWEG, OP URREL 1650, BEERSEL, ☎331 05 61. CHAUSSÉE DE WAVRE 205, ☎264 41681.

FOOD AND DRINK

The Belgians enjoy eating and there's a huge choice of restaurants serving excellent food, but prices tend to be high and it's advisable to book for the more upmarket restaurants. Many bars sell food and give better value than the restaurants. In the area surrounding GRAND-PLACE you can find every imaginable type of eating-place, including fast-food chains.

AV. DE LA COURONNE offers several inexpensive establishments. One of the many bars is **La Fleur en Papier Doré**, once a favourite of the artist Magritte. **Wittamer** is a renowned patisserie and tea room. There are up to 200 varieties of beer available in some bars – for something local ask for *gueuze* or *kriek*. You can sample *gueuze* at the brewery museum in R. GHEUDE 56, ANDERLECHT, south-west of the centre.

RESTAURANTS AND BARS

Comme Chez Soi, PL. ROUPPE 23. Expensive.

La Charlotte aux Pommes, PL. DU CHÂTELAIN 40.
Aux Armes de Bruxelles, R. DES BOUCHERS 13.
Chez Léon, R. DES BOUCHERS 18–20.
Blues Corner, RUE DES CHAPELIERS 12.
Le Grand Mayeur, PL. DU GRAND SABLON 42.
Chez Flo, RUE AU BEURRE 25. All are moderate choices.

Campus, AV. DE LA COURONNE 437.
Le Picotin, AV. DE LA COURONNE. 443.
Le Loup Voyant, AV. DE LA COURONNE. 562.
Falstaff, R. HENRI MAUS 17–23. Stays open until 0500.
La Fleur en Papier Doré, R. DES ALEXIENS 53–55.
La Dolce Vita, R. MIDDLEBURG 13.
Bombay Inn, 38 R. DE LA FOUSCHE. All inexpensive.

Wittamer, PLACE DU GRAND-SABLON 12. Renowned patisserie.

HIGHLIGHTS

Grand-Place, with its ornate guild houses, remains the heart of the city. The most imposing building is the Gothic **Hôtel de Ville** (Town Hall). The neighbouring brewers' house now contains the **Maison des Brasseurs** (Brewery Museum). Across the square, the **Maison du Roi** houses **Musée de la Ville**, covering the city's history. Don't miss the top floor: along with a selection of puppets is the extensive wardrobe of the **Manneken-Pis**, the famous fountain in R. DE L'ÉTUVE that was designed by Jerome Duquesnoy in 1619.

Centre Anspach stretches between BLVD ANSPACH and PL. DE LA MONNAIE. An escalator leads up from the shopping area to **Historium,** which consists of a series of wax tableaux depicting scenes from Roman times to the present.

At opposite ends of PARC DE BRUXELLES are the **Palais de la Nation** (Belgian Parliament) and the **Palais Royale** (Royal Palace), which is open from late July (after the national day on 21 July) for about six weeks and full of rich decorations, including Goya tapestries. At the nearby **Musées Royaux des Beaux-Arts**, R. DE LA RÉGENCE 3, ☎508 32 11 (Royal Museums of Fine Arts), two separate museums (ancient and modern) are linked by an escalator: the **Musée d'Art Ancien** showing Flemish works, and the **Musée d'Art Moderne** housing modern paintings.

SOUTH OF THE CENTRE

Musée Victor Horta, R. AMÉRICAINE 25, IXELLES (tram nos. 81/92), was once the home of the noted Belgian architect, and the interior is typical of his flowing art nouveau style, notably the famous staircase.

The Belgian Comic Strip Centre, RUE DES SABLES 20, offers a different aspect of local history, depicting the history of one of Belgium's more contemporary art forms in an art nouveau warehouse de-signed by Horta. The star is, of course, Hergé's Tintin.

SHOPPING

Much of the lace on offer is actually made in the Far East, so check that it's Belgian before buying. **Louise Verschueren**, R. WATTEAU 16, ☎511 04 44, is a good place to get local lace. Of the many delicious chocolates, **Godiva** and **Leonidas** are popular. Around R. NEUVE are many affordable shopping malls. **Galeries Royales St-Hubert** (off R. DES BOUCHERS) is a vaulted arcade with lots of sculptures and a mixture of shops.

Brussels has several markets. **Midi Market** (near the station, Sun 0600–1300), resembles an African *souk* and is the place for food and clothes bargains. There's a **flower market** in GRAND-PLACE, Tues–Sun 0800–1800.

From Brussels **Waterloo** battlesite is 30 mins by train, or 40 mins by bus from PL. ROUPPE.

NORTH WEST OF THE CENTRE The 102 m high **Atomium**, BLVD DU CENTENAIRE (metro nos. 1/19/81: HEYSEL), is a gigantic model of an iron atom, built in 1958. Several modules are linked (escalators up, easy stairs down) to form a series of exhibits about the human body and medicine. Don't miss **the view from the top module**, to which there's a high-speed lift (keep the ticket to get into the museum).

NIGHT-TIME AND EVENTS

The Bulletin, a weekly English-language paper, has a comprehensive 'What's On' supplement, and the Tourist Office publishes a free list of musical performances that includes clubs and discos, jazz, opera, films etc. Clustered around FERNAND COCQ and the lower end of CH. D'IXELLES are lots of **bars** with music, many staying open until the early hours. The area around GRAND-PLACE is lively at night.

All major events centre on **Grand-Place**. These include several jazz festivals, **Ommegang** (a historical pageant at the end of June/early July) and the **Tapis de Fleurs** (mid August biennial; even years), when the whole square is carpeted with flowers. The **National Holiday** (21 July) offers varied entertainments.

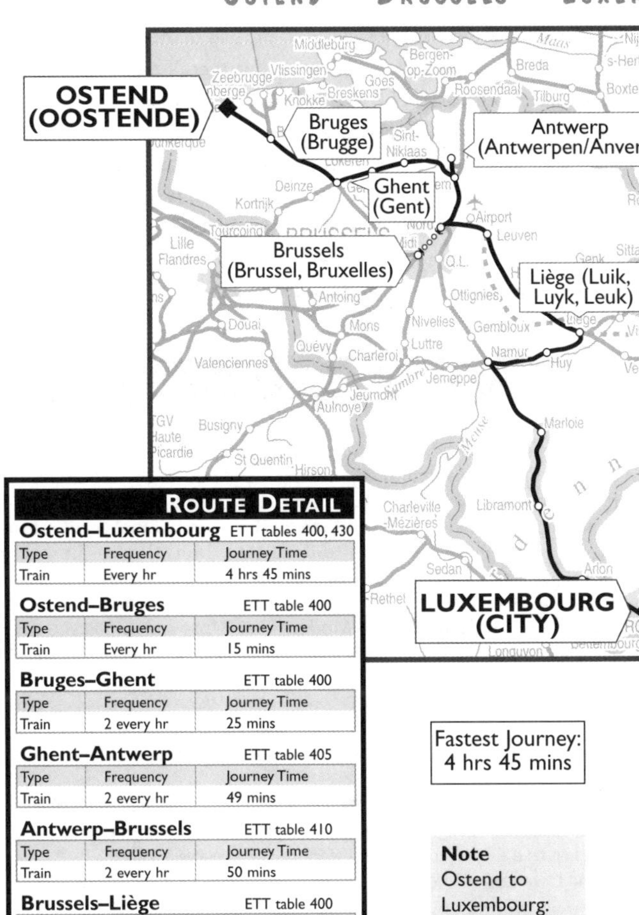

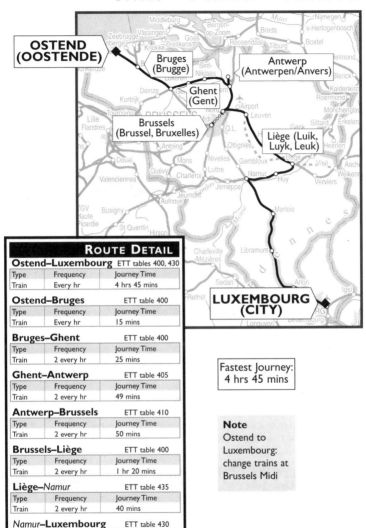

ROUTE DETAIL

Ostend–Luxembourg ETT tables 400, 430

Type	Frequency	Journey Time
Train	Every hr	4 hrs 45 mins

Ostend–Bruges ETT table 400

Type	Frequency	Journey Time
Train	Every hr	15 mins

Bruges–Ghent ETT table 400

Type	Frequency	Journey Time
Train	2 every hr	25 mins

Ghent–Antwerp ETT table 405

Type	Frequency	Journey Time
Train	2 every hr	49 mins

Antwerp–Brussels ETT table 410

Type	Frequency	Journey Time
Train	2 every hr	50 mins

Brussels–Liège ETT table 400

Type	Frequency	Journey Time
Train	2 every hr	1 hr 20 mins

Liège–*Namur* ETT table 435

Type	Frequency	Journey Time
Train	2 every hr	40 mins

Namur–**Luxembourg** ETT table 430

Type	Frequency	Journey Time
Train	Every hr	1 hr 53 mins

Fastest Journey: 4 hrs 45 mins

Note
Ostend to Luxembourg: change trains at Brussels Midi

Not a hill in sight for most of the way, until you cross the hills of the Ardennes in southern Belgium and the Grand Duchy of Luxembourg, but there's plenty of man-made interest, notably the handsome cities of **Bruges**, **Ghent** and **Antwerp**, each boasting impressive legacies of medieval prosperity, and deserving at least a night's stay; Luxembourg itself has a remarkable natural site, perched on two deep gorges. The side trips to **Maastricht** (just over the border in the Netherlands) is recommended, while the journey from **Ostend** to **Brussels** makes a useful link for those starting a European journey from London via the Dover–Ostend sea crossing and venturing on to Germany (see International Routes, **London–Ostend**, p. 33).

OSTEND (OOSTENDE)

A fishing port, ferry port and seaside resort rolled into one, Ostend is not likely to detain you for long, but there are excellent seafood restaurants (oysters are a local speciality). The three-master **Mercator**, a training vessel in authentic style, now houses a maritime museum, **Noordzeeaquarium** (on the front), which displays the flora and fauna of the North Sea. The studio where the expressionist painter James Ensor worked has become a museum devoted to him (James Ensorhuis, VLAANDERENSTRAAT 27), and many of his possessions are among the exhibits in **Museum voor Schone Kunsten** (Fine Arts Museum), CULTUURPALEIS, WAPENPLEIN. **PMMK (Museum voor Moderne Kunst**–Modern Art Museum), ROMESTRAAT 11, contains modern paintings and sculptures.

RAIL (059) 70 15 17. Adjacent to the port.

The ferries and trains share a building, 10 mins' walk from the Tourist Office (or no. 5).

i **Tourist Office**: MONACOPLEIN 2, (059) 70 11 99. Open Mon–Sat 0900–1900, Sun 1000–1900 (June–Sept); Mon–Sat 1000–1800, Sun 1100–1800 (Oct–May): walk right from the station and along the sea front, then take the last turning left before the front curves. Sells the A–Z brochure (BFr.10) and town map (BFr.5).

BRUGES (BRUGGE)

A powerful trading city 500 years ago, Bruges became an economic backwater and the industrial age largely passed it by. It has survived as one of northern Europe's most impressive medieval cities and, despite the throngs of tourists, you still get the feeling of stepping back in time in its cobbled streets. A boat trip on the extensive canal system is a good introduction to the town, with frequent departures from quays along **Dijver,** which, along with **Groene Rei** and **Rozenhoedkaai**, provide some of the vintage views of Bruges. After that, explore on foot – the Tourist Office has an English 'Walkman' guide. Most places of interest are in a small area around

Markt and **Burg**, and much of it is tranquil and traffic-free. Seek out the windmills on the old city ramparts near **Kruispoort** (east of the centre).

Markt, Bruges' main square, is surrounded by guild buildings. **Belfort**, an octagonal 88-m belfry and a useful landmark, is mainly 13th century, but the top storey was added in the 15th century. There are 366 steps to the top, and regular concerts take place on the 47-bell carillon (including Sun 1415 all year).

The Burg, the other main square, features monumental buildings, notably the **Baziliek van Het Heilig Bloed** (Basilica of the Holy Blood), with an atmospheric early 12th-century stone chapel below a magnificent 16th-century chapel. Other buildings around the square include the renaissance **Civiele Griffie** (recorder's house) and the neo classical **Gerectshof** (Court of Justice). The Gothic **Stadhuis** (Town Hall) has a magnificent hall with a polychrome vaulted ceiling and historic murals.

DAY TRIP FROM BRUGES

Quasimodo Tours, POORTERSSTRAAT 47, ☎(050) 37 04 70, fax (050) 37 49 60, runs an English-language day-trip in a minibus, which includes **Damme**, two castles, **Zeebrugge** harbour, waffle sampling waffle, a visit to Chocolate World and a guided tour of a brewery and beer tasting. Departs Mon, Wed and Fri. Pick-ups at various hotels or the rail station. The same company also organises a World War I battlefield tour.

Dijver is the central canal; DIJVERSTRAAT (scene of a weekend antiques and flea market) is home to several museums. **Groeningemuseum** houses a fine collection of Flemish art from the 15th century to date, notably **primitive** and **expressionist**. **Gruuthusemuseum**, on the opposite side of the street, was a 16th-century palace and the décor reflects that time. **Brangwyn Museum** is noted for its **collection of lace**, among other items. **Onze-Lieve Vrouwekerk** (Church of Our Lady), MARIASTRAAT, has Belgium's highest spire (122 m). Among its treasures are a beautiful white marble **Madonna and Child by Michelangelo**. Not far away, the **Kathedraal St-Salvator**, ZUIDZANDST., contains **Gobelin tapestries**, a rood-loft organ, 15th-century carved stalls and a Louis-XVI-style pulpit.

BEGIJNHOF

A visit would not be complete without a walk around the walled convent community of the Begijnhof. The houses where the Beguines once lived are neatly arranged near the **Minnewater**, a tranquil, swan-populated water known as 'Love Lake'.

☎(050) 38 23 82, 20 mins' walk south of the centre; buses stop in front (tickets and a free route map from the De Lijn kiosk, Mon–Fri 0730–1800, Sat 0900–1800, Sun 1000–1800). To the right as you leave the station is a branch of the Tourist Office, open Mon–Sat 1445–2100 (Mar–Oct); Mon–Sat 1345–2000 (Nov–Mar).

Tourist Office: **Municipal**, BURG 11, ☎(050) 44 86 86. Open Mon–Fri 0930–1830, Sat–Sun 1000–1200, 1400–1830 (Apr–Sept); Mon–Fri 0930–1700, Sat 0930–1300, 1400–1730 (Oct–Mar). **Provincial** (West Flanders): KASTEEL TILLEGEM, ☎(050) 38 02 96, open Mon–Fri 0830–1200,

1315–1645. **Brugge** (BFr20), a comprehensive brochure (in several languages), includes walks and a map.

 Book ahead. **Youth hostel: Europa, Assebroek**, BARON RUZETTELAAN 143, (050) 35 26 79, is about 1.5 km east of the station (2 km south of MARKT); no. 2 stops 100 m away: WANTESTRAAT. **Private hostel: Bauhaus**, LANGESTRAAT 135–137, (050) 34 10 93 (nos. 6/16: KRUISPOORT). **Campsite: St-Michiel**, TILLEGEMSTRAAT 55, (050) 38 08 19, 3 km south-west of the station (no. 7).

GHENT (GENT)

Ghent is a deeply Flemish town, steeped in culture, yet very lively during the university year. For ten days in July, **Gentse Feesten** (traditionally a holiday for factory workers) dominates the town, with lots of cheap food, high beer consumption and street entertainments, as well as a variety of more formal performances. The **12th–17th-century guildhouses** along the Graslei quay and the old houses by the Kraanlei quay provide two of the city's classic views.

Sint-Baafskathedraal (cathedral), resplendent with marble statuary and a baroque organ and pulpit, contains Van Eyck's multi-panelled masterpiece *The Adoration of the Mystic Lamb*, painted in 1432 and considered to be the most important work of church art in Belgium (separate entry payable); you can ascend the 90-m **Belfort** (belfry) by lift.

Gravensteen, SINT-VEERLEPLEIN, the 12th-century 'Castle of the Counts', has a museum that displays a selection of gruesome instruments of torture, with illustrations of how they were used. You can also walk round the ramparts and explore the castle grounds.

Allow plenty of time for the fascinating **Museum Voor Volkskunde** (Museum of Folklore), KRAANLEI 65, which spreads through three converted almshouses. It portrays the town's lifestyle at the turn of the century and is crammed with pleasingly unrelated everyday items – toys, flat irons, hats, hurricane lanterns.

CARRIAGE TRIPS

These can be made through the city during summer holidays, weekends and public holidays, 1000–1800 (Easter–Oct). Depart from **Baafsplein**. There are summer boat trips on the River Leie, destinations including Bruges.

RAIL **Gent-St-Pieters**, (09) 222 44 44, 2 km south of the centre (tram nos. 1/10/11/12: KORENMARKT). De Lijn bus/tram information to the left as you exit.

i **Tourist Offices**: **Municipal**, PREDIKHERENLEI 2 (in Stadhuis crypt), (09) 225 36 41 or 226 52 32. Daily 0930–1830 (Easter–Oct); 0930–1630 (Nov–Easter). **Provincial** (East Flanders), WOODROW WILSONPLEIN 3, (09) 267 70 20. Mon–Fri 0830–1200, 1315–1645.

ANTWERP (ANTWERPEN/ANVERS)

Belgium's second city, Antwerp has enough for at least a couple of days' sightseeing, including an extensive old Flemish quarter, plus views over the River **Schelde** (or Scheldt), on which boat tours are available.

The medieval **Steen** (Castle), STEENPLEIN 1, houses the **National Scheepvartmuseum** (Maritime Museum), ☎(03) 232 08 50, while the **Diamantmuseum**, LANGE HERENTALSESTR. 31–33 (walkable from Centraal station), covers all aspects of the diamond trade, one of the cornerstones of Antwerp's appreciable fortunes.

The **cathedral** is Belgium's largest (free multilingual tours; entrance on HANDSCHOENMARKT), built 1352–1521. Its 123-m tower would have been one of a pair had the money not run out. Highlights here are four enormous masterpieces by **Rubens** and some recently revealed 15th-century frescos.

PLANTIN-MORETUS MUSEUM

Perhaps Antwerp's most astonishing survival is the unique **Plantin-Moretus Museum/Stedelijk Prentenkabinet**, VRIJDAGMARKT 22, a perfectly preserved 16th–18th-century printer's works and home built by the famous printer Plantin; don't spend too long on the first few rooms – the most interesting parts come later on.

GROTE MARKT is home to the 19th-century **Brabo Fountain** (which depicts the legend of the city's founding), elaborately gabled guild houses and the Renaissance **Stadhuis** (Town Hall). Not far away is the striking **Vleeshuis** (Butchers' Hall), VLEESHOUWERSTR. 38/40, now an applied arts museum with wood-carvings, antique china, old musical instruments and lots of ticking grandfather clocks.

On Sun mornings, **Vogelmarkt** (bird market), OUDE VAARTPLAATS, sells birds – plus almost everything else. The **Openluchtmuseum Voor Beeldhouwkunst** (Open-Air Sculpture Museum), MIDDELHEIM PARK (🚌nos 18/17), is dotted with sculptures, notably by **Rodin** and **Moore**.

RAIL **Antwerpen-Centraal**, ☎(03) 204 20 40, 2 km east of the centre, linked by metro-tram. The marble and gold-decorated station is worth a visit in its own right. The bookstand stocks UK newspapers and there's an exchange office. De Lijn's office is in Centraal's metro-tram stop, DIAMANT, ☎(03) 218 14 06, open Mon–Fri 0810–1230, 1330–1600. You can get (free) transport maps and tickets from them. Some international trains stop at **Bechem**, 2 km to the south; local services link it to Centraal.

i **Tourist Office**: GROTE MARKT 15, ☎(03) 232 01 03. Open Mon–Sat 0900–1745, Sun 0900–1645. From Centraal, take metro nos. 2/15 to **Groenplaats** (direction: LINKEROEVER), go past the cathedral and continue along the street ahead.

The Tourist Office gets good discounts. Some cheap places near Centraal (beware that some rent by the hour). Bed and breakfast is scarce. **Alfa de Keyser**, DEKEYSERLEI 66–70, ☎(03) 234

01 35, is a 4-star hotel only 100 m from Centraal. **Youth Hostel**: PROVINCIE STRAAT 256, (03) 230 05 22 located only 10 mins' walk from the station. **Campsite: Vogelzanglaan**, (03) 238 57 17.

BRUSSELS

See p. 196.

LIÈGE (LUIK/LUYK/LEUK)

The ancient capital of an independent principality for eight centuries, Liège is now a large industrial city, but retains some noteworthy churches, among which is the Gothic Cathédrale St-Paul which has a fine treasury. Pick of museums are the **Musée de la Vie Wallonne** (Museum of Walloon Life – in a former monastery; local life, art and folklore); **Musée d'Art Religieux et d'Art Mosan** (craftsmanship of the Meuse region) and **Musée de Verre** (**glass items**, many ancient, from around the world. Take the 373 steps up to the citadel for a view of the town.

RAIL **Liège-Guillemins**, (041) 229 2610, 2 km south of the centre (nos 1/4).

i **Tourist Offices**: at the station, (041) 252 4419. Open Mon–Sat 0900–1730, Sun 1000–1600 (Apr–Sept); Mon–Sat 1000–1600 (Oct–Mar). **Municipal**: FÉRONSTRÉE 92, (041) 21 92 21, open Mon–Fri 0900–1800, Sat 1000–1600, Sun 1000–1400 (Apr–Oct); Mon–Fri 0900–1700 (Nov–Mar). **Provincial**: BLVD DE LA SAUVINIÈRE 77, (041) 22 42 10, open Mon–Fri 0830–1730, Sat 0900–1300 (Apr–Sept); Mon–Fri 0830–1700, Sat 0900–1300 (Oct–Mar).

Youth hostel: R. GEORGES SIMENON 9–11, (041) 344 5689.

LUXEMBOURG (CITY)

The city was founded in Roman times and is dramatically sited on a gorge cut by the rivers **Alzette** and **Pétrusse**. It falls naturally into three sections: the old centre (north of the Pétrusse gorge and home to most

DAY TRIP FROM LIÈGE

Maastricht (28 mins; hourly trains, ETT table 417 station 10 mins' walk east of centre; VVV Tourist Office, KLEIN STRAAT 1, (043) 325 2121, plus at station. Tucked into the southern, mildly hilly corner of the Netherlands, the provincial capital of Limburg and busy university town has a captivating, even exciting atmosphere in its lively squares and precincts and Mosan-style stone houses, and its ebullient Lent carnival. You can get a good view from the tower of **St Janskerk**. If you want to stay in Maastricht, there are cheap options round the station and in the **Markt** area.

Youth hostel: City Hostel, DOUSBERG PARK, DOUSBERGWEG 4, (043) 34 66 777, 4 km from the station (nos 55/56 to Dousberg, the last stop, beside a swimming pool, which is free to hostellers).

Campsite: **De Dousberg**, DOUSBERGWEG 102, (043) 34 32 171, 1 km from the hostel.

of the sights); **the modern** city and station (south of the gorge); and **Grund** (the valley settlement).

As well as conventional conducted tours, you can 'Walk with a Walkman' (Apr–Oct) or take the Pétrusse Express (a misnomer: it's slow-moving) from PL. DE LA CONSTITUTION. Both are worthwhile for the commentary alone: a highly dramatised account mingling history and legend, with martial music and cannon fire.

The **Cathédrale Notre-Dame**, a 17th-century Jesuit church, contains the simple stone crypt that is the tomb of Duke John the Blind, backed by statues of mourners. Bronze lions flank a gate through which can be seen the burial chapel of the Grand-Ducal family. From PL. DE LA CONSTITUTION, there is access to the **Pétrusse casemates**: the underground passages that formed part of the city's original defences. Tours take about 45 mins and you need to be reasonably fit. If you're in any doubt, opt for the similar casemates at **Rocher du Bock**, which are easier. The entrance is on R. SIGEFROI, the site where Count Siegfried built the **original fortress**. It was expanded by later rulers, especially the French, who made it one of the most strongly defended cities in 17th-century Europe.

DAY TRIPS FROM LUXEMBOURG

About 30 mins by train north of the capital, Ettelbrück is the base for visiting (by bus) **Echternach,** a 7th-century Benedictine abbey founded by St Willibrord, an English missionary monk.
One wing of the basilica houses the **Musée de l'Abbaye**, with its wide-ranging display of **illuminated manuscripts**, including Codex Aureus, the gospels decorated in gold and bound in a superb 10th-century gold cover encrusted with enamel and gems.

Gare Centrale, ☎49 24 24, about 15 mins' walk south of the centre; showers and baths. The CFL office opens daily 0700–2100, and sells phonecards and tickets for all transport.

Tourist Office: **Municipal**: PL. D'ARMES, ☎22 28 09, in the old town (Mon–Sat 0900–1900, Sun and public holidays 1000–1800); pick up a street map, a route guide for city buses and *A Walk Through the Green Heart of Europe* (two routes through the capital). **National**: 1 R. DU FORT THÜNGEN, ☎42 82 821. Open Mon–Sat 0900–1900, Sun 0900–1200 and 1400–1830 (July–mid Sept); daily 0900–1200 and 1400–1830 (mid Sept–June, except Sun Nov–Mar).

Most of the cheaper hotels are near the station. Two good budget options: **Bristol**, 11 R. DE STRASBOURG, ☎48 58 29, and *Carlton*, 9 R. DE STRASBOURG, ☎48 48 02, fax 48 64 80. **Youth hostel**: 2 R. DU FORT OLISY (3 km from the station), ☎22 68 89, fax 22 33 60. Bus no. 9: VALLÉE **d'Alzette** (150 m from the stop, down a steep hill). **Kockelscheuer campsite**, RTE DE BETTEMBOURG 22, ☎47 18 15, is south of the centre, 4 km from Centrale and 500 m from the bus no. 2 stop; open Easter–Oct.

Avoid the tacky eating places in the station area, there are much better middle-range ones in the old centre. PL. D'ARMES is full of eateries, with open-air entertainment on most summer evenings. There's a regular food market in PL. GUILLAUME (Wed and Sat 0800–1200).

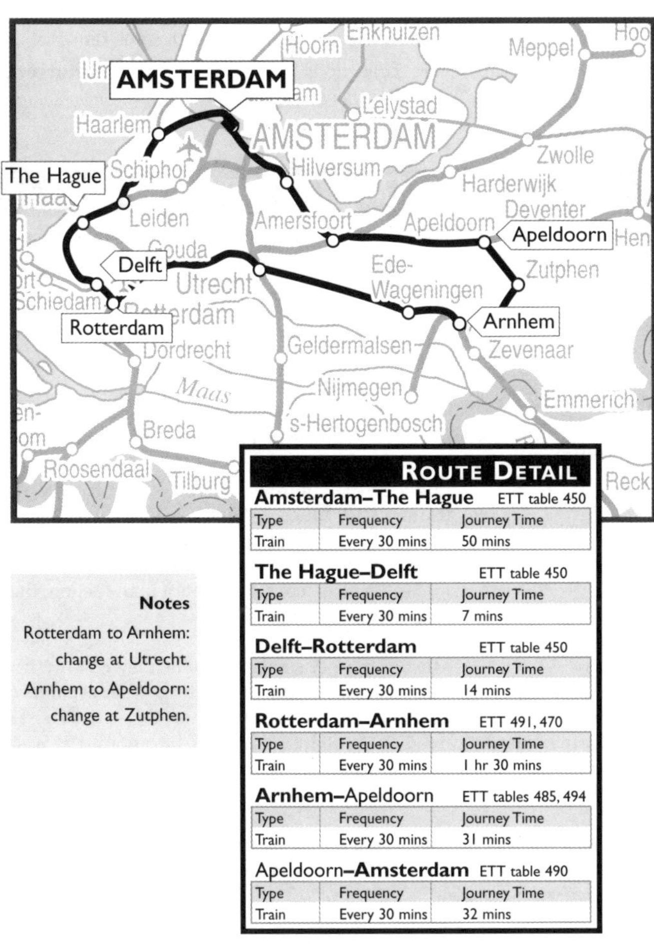

Notes

Rotterdam to Arnhem: change at Utrecht.

Arnhem to Apeldoorn: change at Zutphen.

ROUTE DETAIL

Amsterdam–The Hague ETT table 450

Type	Frequency	Journey Time
Train	Every 30 mins	50 mins

The Hague–Delft ETT table 450

Type	Frequency	Journey Time
Train	Every 30 mins	7 mins

Delft–Rotterdam ETT table 450

Type	Frequency	Journey Time
Train	Every 30 mins	14 mins

Rotterdam–Arnhem ETT 491, 470

Type	Frequency	Journey Time
Train	Every 30 mins	1 hr 30 mins

Arnhem–Apeldoorn ETT tables 485, 494

Type	Frequency	Journey Time
Train	Every 30 mins	31 mins

Apeldoorn–**Amsterdam** ETT table 490

Type	Frequency	Journey Time
Train	Every 30 mins	32 mins

Amsterdam – Rotterdam – Amsterdam

This is a tour of much of the best of the Netherlands, through such classic canal-laced towns as **Delft** and **Gouda** (famous for porcelain and cheese respectively), across the **Bulb** District between **Haarlem** and the university town of **Leiden**, and past **Arnhem**. There's an impressive show of past and present, with some remarkable modern architecture, magnificent art collections and such oddities as **Rotterdam's** vertigo-inducing **Euromast**.

THE HAGUE (DEN HAAG, 'S-GRAVENHAGE)

The administrative capital of the Netherlands is a pleasant town, spread over a wide area of parks and canals and centred around **Binnenhof**, the home of the **Dutch parliament** (tram nos. 2/3/7/8/9; bus nos. 4/5/22). The 13th-century **Ridderzaal** (Knights' Hall) hosts official ceremonies.

Gallery

One of the great galleries of the world, the **Mauritshuis**, Korte Vijverberg 8 (tram nos. 7/8/9/12; bus nos. 4/5/10/22), is a Renaissance mansion on a lake, housing much of the royal collection, with paintings by the major Flemish masters, including Rembrandt and Vermeer.

Installed in a rotunda, the remarkable **Panorama Mesdag**, Zeestr. 65 (tram nos. 7/8, bus nos. 4/5/13/22) consists of a realistic circular view of the North Sea resort of **Scheveningen** painted by Hendrik Mesdag, his wife and some friends in 1881. The 1999 equivalent might be the **Omniversum**, President Kennedylaan 5 (tram no. 10, bus nos. 4/14/65/66 – or through the small garden to the rear of **Gemeentemuseum**), is a stunning spectacle with a wrap-around movie screen that makes you feel like a participant in the action: there are English headphones.

Most of the city's palaces can be viewed only from the outside. An exception is the huge **Vredespaleis** (Peace Palace), Carnegieplein 2 (tram nos. 7/8; bus nos. 4/13), which houses the International Courts of Justice and Arbitration; it is a strange architectural mishmash, with a display of items donated by world leaders. There are tours when the Court is not in session.

RAIL **Centraal/CS** is 5 mins' walk from the centre and serves most Dutch cities. Fast services for Amsterdam and Rotterdam use **Hollandse/HS**, Holland's Spoor station (1 km south). CS and HS are linked by frequent trains and by tram nos. 9/12.

i **Tourist Office**: Kon. Julianaplein 30, ☎(06) 340 350 51, outside the station. Mon–Sat 0830–1730 (Jan–June and Sept–Dec); Mon–Sat 0830–1730, Sun 1100–1500 (July–Aug). *Den Haag Info* is a free monthly covering everything of interest; the free weekly *Over Uit* covers films, theatres and music. Buy a proper street map, as the free small ones are deceptive in scale.

There is an excellent bus and tram network.

If money is a consideration, base yourself at **Scheveningen** or ask VVV about private rooms. **NJHC Hostel** at SCHEEPMAKERSSTRAAT 27, (070) 315 7878. **Youth hostel** (HI): MONSTERSEWEG 4, (070) 397 0011, 10 km west of CS near **Kijkduin** beach: nos. 122/123/124 from CS, then 10 mins' walk: tell the driver you want the hostel. Close to it are a small cheap hotel and a **campsite**.

DELFT

Long-famed for Delftware porcelain and birthplace of the artist Vermeer, **Delft** is an elegant old town with old merchants' houses lining the canal. It has a number of porcelain factories where you can watch the traditional processes in action; the oldest is **De Porceleyne Fles** (ROTTERDAMSEWEG 196, (015) 256 9214), but more central is **Atelier de Candelaer** (KERKSTR. 14, (015) 213 1848).

Stedelijk Museum/Het Prinsenhof (the Prince's Court), ST AGATHAPLEIN 1, (015) 260 2358, includes silverware, tapestries, paintings and Delftware. Across the road is **Nusantara Museum**, with a collection of art from the former Dutch East Indies.

Nieuwekerk (New Church) houses the huge black-and-white marble mausoleum of Prince William, and its 109 m spire provides great views.

A nice way to see Delft is by horse-drawn tram from MARKT, or by canal cruise.

5 mins' walk south of the centre or no. 16 to MARKT.

Tourist Office: MARKT 83, (015) 212 6100. Open Mon–Fri 0900–1800, Sat 0900–1730, Sun 1000–1500.

ROTTERDAM

The city was virtually flattened in World War II, but much of its modern architecture is strikingly innovative (**Lijnbaan** was the European pioneer of shopping precincts for example). Situated at the delta of the Rivers **Rhine**, **Maas** and **Waal**, **Europoort** is the world's largest container port (**harbour tours**, lasting 1 hr 15 mins, operated by Spido, WILLEMSPLEIN, (010) 413 5400; metro: LEUVEHAVEN, tram no. 5).

The **Museum Boymans-Van Beuningen**, MUSEUMPARK 18/20 (tram no. 5), is massive and high quality, with applied art and art (including clocks, lace and paintings by Dali, Magritte, Rembrandt, Van Gogh and Bosch). Maritiem Museum Prins Hendrik, LEUVEHAVEN 1 (metro: BEURS/CHURCHILLPLEIN; tram nos. 3/6/7), is the oldest and biggest maritime museum in the country.

The 185 m **Euromast**, PARKHAVEN 20, (010) 436 4811 (tram no. 6: EUROMAST), towers over the trees in **Central Park**. This is the highest structure in the Netherlands.

Even from the first platform you have panoramic views of the 37-km-long waterfront, but go right to the top on the **Space Adventure**, a simulated rocket flight: after blast-off you go into 'orbit' and have breathtaking views as the capsule ascends and revolves slowly to the top. **Abseiling** is available in summer.

Around **Oude Haven**, the old harbour, is where the most striking modern buildings are located, notably the complex of **Kijk Kubus** futuristic cube houses (metro: BLAAK; tram nos. 3/13/17; nos. 32/49). One, at OVERBLAAK 70, (010) 414 2285, is open to the public.

RAIL **Centraal/CS**, on the northern edge of the centre (blue/green metro).

i **Tourist Office**: COOLSINGEL 67 (5 mins' walk from Centraal; follow the signs), (010) 402 3200; Infoline: 0900 403 4065. Open Mon–Thur 0930–1800, Fri 0930–2100, Sat 0930–1800; also Sun 1200–1700 (Apr–Sept). Kiosk in the **station**: Mon–Sat 0900–2200, Sun 1000–2200. *Inside Out* is a free monthly listing.

RET (STATIONSPLEIN and ZUIDSPLEIN) and VVV sell good-value tickets for unlimited city travel over 1, 2 or 3 days. Metro stations are indicated by a large yellow M. Only two lines matter for the centre: blue/green (north–south) and red/yellow/mauve (east–west), and they intersect at only one station, where you walk from Beurs platform to Churchillplein platform (or vice versa). Trams fill the gaps in the metro; buses are more useful away from the centre.

Plenty of middle-range options. Cheap hotel areas: about 1 km south-west of CS (try GRAVENDIJKWAL and HEEMRAADSINGEL) and just north of CS (try PROVENIERSSINGEL). Youth hostel: ROCHUSSENSTR. 107/109, (010) 436 5763 (metro: DIRECTION MARCONIPLEIN: DIJKZIGT; tram no. 4; take the Nieuwbinnen exit, U-turn at top of steps and you're on ROCHUSSENSTR. – turn left and the hostel is 30 m away). **Campsite: Stadscamping Rotterdam**, KANAALWEG 84, (010) 415 3440, west of CS (no. 33), is open all year. Usually cheap dormitory accommodation (mid June–mid Aug) is at **Sleep-In**, MAURITSWEG 29, (010) 412 1420, 5 mins' walk south of CS.

Where Next from Rotterdam?

Head south to ***Antwerp*** *(ETT table 450) to join the* ***Ostend–Brussels*** *route (p. 201).*

Gouda

This quaint place exemplifies small-town Holland, with a ring of quiet canals around ancient buildings. The 15th-century *Staduis* (Town Hall) is the oldest Gothic municipal building in Holland, while Sint Janskerk is famed throughout the country for its 70 superb stained-glass windows.

Waag

The old weigh-house opens for trading on Thur morning (July–Aug); Gouda cheese comes in several grades (the extra-mature is hard, dry and deliciously strong), while syrup waffles (or *goudse*) are another speciality.

10-mins walk north of the centre.

Tourist Office: MARKT 27, (0182) 513 666. Mon–Sat 0900–1700.

ARNHEM

The attractions are scattered, but there's an excellent network of buses and reaching them is not difficult.

Attractions include **Burgers**, SCHELMSEWEG 85 (no. 3; no. 13 in summer), a zoo with safari park, pride of place going to a giant greenhouse, and **Nederlands Openlucht**, SCHELMSEWEG 89, an extensive and delightful open-air museum.

The **Airborne Museum**, Hartenstein, UTRECHTSEWEG 232, at **Oosterbeek** (8 km west of the centre – no. 1), is devoted to Operation Market Garden, the Allied débâcle of Sept 1944 that was immortalised in the film *A Bridge Too Far*. You can find photographs, film footage, and weapons and equipment from both sides.

On the north-western edge of town.

Tourist Office: STATIONSPLEIN 45, 0900 202 4075. Open Mon 1300–1700, Tues–Fri 0900–1730, Sat 0900–1300. *Rekreatie Krant* is a free newspaper which includes listings.

The 2-star **Hotel-Pension Parkzicht**, APELDOORNSESTR. 16, (026) 442 0698, is walkable from the station. A good budget place is **Pension Warnsborn**, SCHELMSEWEG 1, (026) 442 5994 (bus no. 2). **Youth hostel**: DIEPENBROCKLAAN 27, (026) 442 0114, 4 km north of the station (no. 3 towards ALTEVEER: GEMEENTE ZIEKENHUIS). You'll see a sign with the HI logo; 30 m further on steps climb a forested hill to the hostel. Three **campsites**: **Camping Warnsborn**, BAKENBERGSEWEG 257, (026) 442 3469, Apr–Nov (north-west of the centre, no. 2); **Camping Arnhem**, KEMPERBERGERWEG 771, (026) 443 1600, open all year (no. 2 towards Schaarsbergen); and **Kamperceentrum De Hooge Veluwe**, KONINGSWEG 14, (026) 443 2272, Apr–Oct, by the Hoenderloo entrance to the park.

DAY TRIP FROM ARNHEM

The Kröller-Müller Museum, HOUTKAMPWEG 6 (closed Mon; a good 35 mins' walk from the Otterlo entrance, but nos. 12/107/110 stop there), has one of Europe's best modern art collections, notably 278 paintings by Van Gogh (including *The Potato Eaters* and *Café Terrace at Night*), although only fifty or so are on show at any one time. The adjacent **Sculpture Garden** and **Sculpture Forest** contain works by Rodin, Epstein, Moore, and Dubuffet's *extraordinary Jardin d'Email.*

(for Directory information, see p. 549). Germany has an immense historic heritage boasting such greats as Beethoven and Goethe. Famously, there's a wealth of castles, while church architecture ranges from the superb Gothic cathedrals of the north to the frothy baroque creations of **Bayern** (Bavaria). Even today, much of Germany is surprisingly little-frequented by outsiders.

All the major cities were bombed in World War II, but have been reconstructed with varying degrees of success, and showing very different characters. A plethora of small medieval towns escaped bombing and have survived the centuries impressively intact: **Rothenburg-ob-der-Tauber** is the touristy showpiece, but there are scores of lesser-known spots. You'll also find health resorts (often prefixed by 'Bad', denoting 'bath') where many Germans go for a *Kur* (spa).

Walking is a national pastime, whether in the **Harz Mountains** of central Germany, in the **Alps** near **Garmisch-Partenkirchen** or **Mittenwald,** or in the **Black Forest** *(Schwarzwald)*, with its rolling forests and neat pastures, dotted with huge-roofed old farmhouses.

The excellent network and services make it feasible to tour much of the country by train. It's easy to link the great historic cities and many smaller towns. Scenic routes proliferate in the south-west and the east. Rail travel is much less spectacular in central and northern Germany.

ACCOMMODATION

Prices vary enormously according to demand. The differences between west and east have steadily been eroded since reunification, but it's still cheaper in the east. Though there's no identifiable low season as such, rates are highest between Christmas and mid March in ski resorts and July and August nationwide. As a very rough guide, a budget room in the west might be around DM30 in more remote areas, or DM60 in cities. Try to avoid major trade fairs at such cities as **Frankfurt** and special events, such as Munich's **Oktoberfest,** when prices are at their highest; consult the events calendar published by the **DZT** (German tourist board – see p.550).

PENSIONS *Pensionen* or *Fremdenheime* and **private rooms** *(Zimmer)* represent particularly good value: they're nearly always meticulously kept, and many of the family-run establishments in the country and in small towns are very welcoming and comfortable. You may be required to stay at least two nights at pensions. Less wonderful in general are city hotels, which frequently border on the characterless; the cheapest places tend to be clustered near main railway stations. *Zimmer frei* and *zu vermieten* (posted in a window) indicate availability, while *besetzt* means a place is full. You can usually book through **Tourist Offices** (many of which have lists of places to stay posted in their windows, often with an indication of which places have rooms free). Note that many establishments don't supply soap. Be prepared to pay for pensions and private rooms in German cash, as credit cards and cheques are seldom accepted by small establishments.

YOUTH HOSTELS There are around 620 *Jugendherberge* (**DJH**) in Germany (mostly affiliated with **Hostelling International**). You should book well ahead in peak season (cost DM15.50–29 for under-27s and DM19–34 for over-27s; reductions for those staying more than one night); self-catering is not usually available. Hostels have the emphasis firmly on youth (with an age limit of 26 in Bavaria, and preferential treatment given to under 27s elsewhere): they're often used by school parties. This has resulted in the introduction of a new category of accommodation, *Jugendgästehaus*, aimed more at young adults and mostly with 2–4-bedded rooms, costing DM25–45 including breakfast and bed linen.

CAMPING The cheapest form of accommodation is camping and site facilities are generally excellent, though few sites are conveniently close to stations. **Deutscher Camping-Club (DCC)** publishes an annual list of 1600 sites (DM34.80). **DZT** (the German tourist board) publishes a free list and map showing more than 600 of the best sites nationwide. There are fewer sites in the east. Most sites open only May–Oct and it is advisable to book a few days in advance. A few are open all year and usually have space out of season.

INFORMATION

Hostels

Bookings can be made through: **DJH Service GmbH**, POSTFACH 1462, 32704 DETMOLD, GERMANY; ☎(49) (5231) 7401-0, fax (49) (5231) 7401-49.

Camping

Deutscher Camping-Club (DCC), MANDLSTR. 28, MUNICH.

FOOD AND DRINK

Breakfast is any time from 0630 to 1000. Lunch is around 1200–1400 (from 1130 in rural areas) and dinner 1800–2130 (earlier in rural areas). Breakfast is often substantial (and often included in the price of a room), consisting of a variety of bread, cheese and cold meats and a boiled egg. Germans eat their main meal at midday, with a light supper in the evening, but restaurants and pubs also offer light lunches and cooked evening meals. For lunch, the best value is the daily menu

(*Tageskarte*) in the country there's often a snack menu (*Vesperkarten*) from mid-afternoon onwards.

Traditional German cuisine is widespread, both in towns and rural areas, and age-old recipes are produced with pride. A lot of it tends towards the hearty, with satisfying portions, and often not pricey for what you get: home-made soups, high-quality meat, piquant marinated pot roasts (known as *Sauerbraten*) and creamy sauces commonly turn up on the menu. Service is included, but a 2–3% tip is normal. Regional variations are quite striking. In the south-west, cherries turn up famously in *Schwarzwalderkirschtorte* (the so-called Black Forest gateau found in Britain and elsewhere is a very distant relative), and in *Kirchwasser* (cherry brandy), while *Spätzle* are home-made flour noodles, delicious in soup or with meat. Bavarian cooking is emphatically wholesome and peasanty, with *knödel* (dumplings) and sausages such as *Nürn-berger Bratwürst* (a dark, grilled sausage) and *Münchner Weisswürst* (a white sausage eaten with sweet mustard) making frequent appearances on the menu. In Lower Saxony (around Hannover and Bremen), eel is popular, and there's a tasty local mutton known as *Heidschnucken*. In the north, during the soft fruit season, look for *Rote Grütze*, a wonderful blend of vanilla cream and red fruits such as redcurrants and sour cherries – one of the best German desserts.

For really cheap but generally appetising eats, there are roadside *Imbisse* (stalls) serving a variety of snacks, especially *Kartoffelsalat* (potato salad) and *Wurst* (sausage) in its numerous variations, plus fish in the north.

German **beer** is famously varied in strength, sweetness, colour and character, with dozens of breweries in the great brewing centres like Dortmund and Cologne alone. At the lighter end of the scale are *Hell*, *Weizenbier* (wheat beer, usually served with a slice of lemon in it) and *Berliner Weisse* (served with a dash of fruit syrup); darker beers are *Dunkel* and the malty *Malzbier*. Draught beer is known as *vom Fass*, and is normally a hoppy lager. Medium and medium-sweet white **wines** from the Mosel and Rhine regions are abundant; there are also dry *(trocken)* and semi-dry *(halbtrocken)* whites from Baden and Franconia, plus light reds from Baden and the Ahr Valley.

EDITOR'S CHOICE

Aachen (Schatzkammer); Augsburg; Berlin; Bodensee (Konstanz area); Bonn (Beethoven's birthplace); Bremen; Cologne; Dachau; Dresden; Eisenach; Freiburg im Breisgau; Hamburg; Heidelberg; Lübeck; Mittenwald and Garmisch areas (German Alps); Munich; Neuschwanstein; Rothenburg ob der Tauber; Stuttgart (Staatsgalarie); Trier (Porta Nigra); Weimar. Scenic rail journeys: narrow-gauge lines in Harz Mountains (p. 240); Bonn–Mainz (Rhine gorge; p. 245); Offenburg–Konstanz (via Black Forest; p. 256); Stuttgart-Konstanz via Rottweil (see Where Next from Stuttgart?; p. 260); Munich–Verona via Innsbruck (p. 275).

BEYOND THE BORDER

Hamburg–Copenhagen via Lübeck (ETT table 50); Berlin–Warsaw (table 56); Berlin–Prague (table 60); Nuremburg–Vienna via Regensburg (table 66); Stuttgart–Milan via Zurich (table 84); Cologne–Brussels (table 20); Cologne–Amsterdam (table 28). Cologne–Nice via Avignon (table 79). See also Where Next from Munich (p. 234) and Where Next from Frankfurt (p. 251).

Once famous for being divided, Berlin is now just as renowned for being reunited. With the collapse of the Iron Curtain in 1989, West Berlin ceased to be an island of the capitalist West within the Communist DDR (East Germany), as that most hated symbols of the post–war period, the notorious Berlin Wall, was torn down.

Many newcomers are surprised by the amount of open space within the city limits, with a third of Berlin made up of parkland, forest and water. Berlin is always an exciting place to visit: assured by the city's delight in dabbling with whatever is innovative and experimental, and as the capital of the new Germany, it is embarking on a forward-looking era.

TOURIST OFFICES

The two main offices are the **Europa Centre**, BUDAPESTER STR. 45 (Mon–Sat 0800–2200, Sun 0900–2100), 5 mins from **Zoologischer Garten** (Zoo) station (walk towards the Kaiser Wilhelm Memorial Church with its war-damaged spire), access only from BUDAPESTER STR; and near the south wing of the **Brandenburg Gate**, PARISER PL., (daily 0930–1800), 2 mins from UNTER DEN LINDEN.

ARRIVAL AND DEPARTURE

RAIL Berlin's two major stations for long-distance main line trains are **Berlin Zoo**, HARDENBERGPL. 11, in the western part of the city, and **Berlin Ostbahnhof**, STR. DER PARISER KOMMUNE 5, in the east. Zoo lands you right in the centre of former West Berlin. KURFÜRSTENDAMM (often shortened to Ku'damm), one of the main shopping streets, is a 2-mins walk. Ostbahnhof is quieter, more spacious with a distinctly 1950s feel. There is little to do or see near to Ostbahnhof, so head instead to the S-Bahn platforms – any of four lines take you to the centre of the old east, ALEXANDERPL., just two stops away. Both Zoo and Ostbahnhof have a good range of facilities, including left-luggage lockers (from DM2; up to 72 hrs). Some main-line trains also stop at **Berlin Friedrichstrasse**, FRIEDRICHSTR. 142, midway between the two larger stations; **Berlin Alexanderplatz**, DIRCKSENSTR., 5 mins' walk from Ostbahnhof; and **Berlin Lichtenburg**, WEITLINGERSTR., 22 km east of Ostbahnhof. For rail information, ask at the **Deutsche Bahn Information Office** within Zoo station; (030) 297 49350/1 (daily 24 hrs) or (030) 19419 (0600–2300). **EurAid** also provides train and tourist information in English: (030) 49241 (0800–1100, 1300–1800).

Most flights from the West are to **Berlin-Tegel Otto Lilienthal Airport**, (030) 41011, 10 km from the centre of town. For west city destinations, catch nos.109 or X9, which connect with the U-Bahn at JAKOB-KAISER-PL. and the X9 also at ERNST-REUTER-PL. For east city destinations catch no.128, which connects with the U-Bahn at KURT-SCHUMACHER-PL. Allow about 1 hr. **Taxis** to the centre cost around DM25–30. **Schönefeld Airport** (19 km south-west) serves destinations in the East. For **enquiries**, (030) 60910. The S-Bahn and regional trains *(Regionalverkehr)* run to the main rail stations: **Ostbahnhof** – this may appear as **Hauptbahnhof** on older maps – 29 mins by S-Bahn, 15 mins by the half-hourly AirportExpress train, **Zoo** (47 mins by S-Bahn, 29 mins by AirportExpress) and **Lichtenberg** (17 mins by regional train and 34 mins by S-Bahn).

Long-distance buses: These are run by **ZOB (Zentraler Omnibusbahnhof)**, (030) 301 80 28. The main station is at **Kaiserdamm**, MESSEDAMM 8, CHARLOTTENBURG. Buses run daily to all major cities and smaller towns.

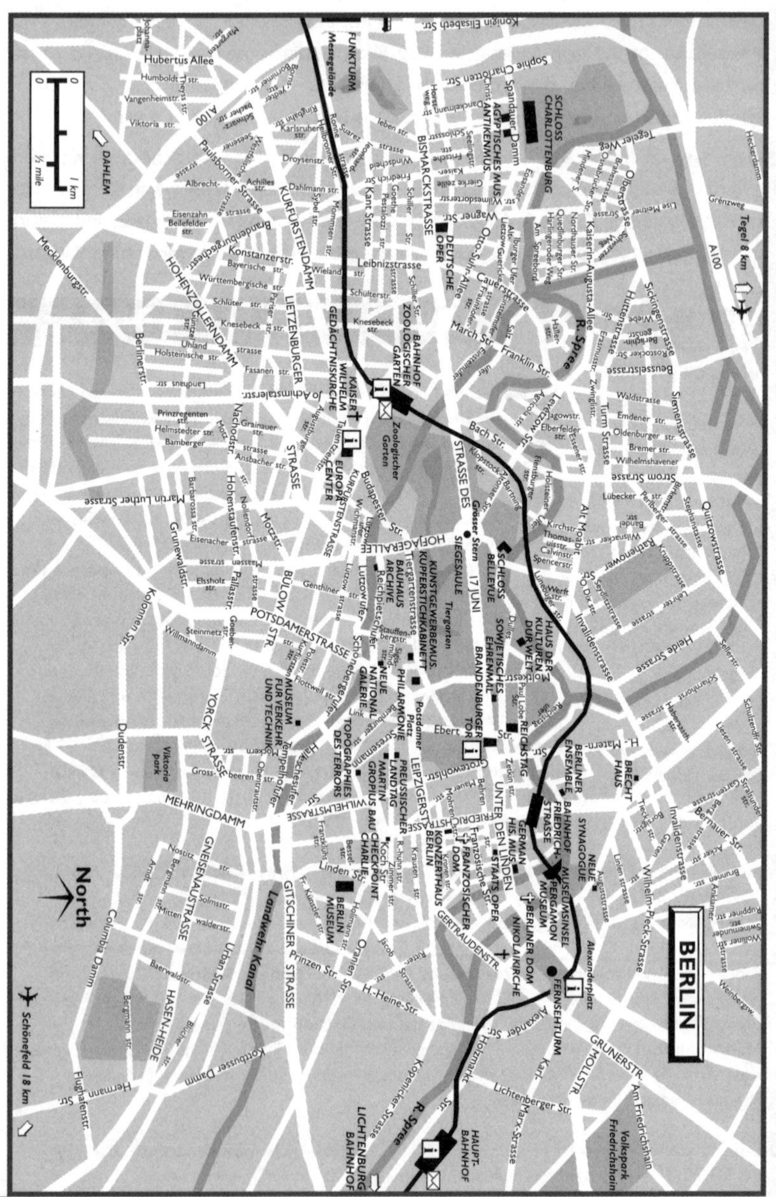
BERLIN
North
1 km
½ mile
DAHLEM
Tegel 8 km
Schönefeld 18 km
SCHLOSS CHARLOTTENBURG
FUNKTURM
Messegelände
BISMARCKSTRASSE
DEUTSCHE OPER
KURFÜRSTENDAMM
LIETZENBURGER STRASSE
HOHENZOLLERNDAMM
BAHNHOF ZOOLOGISCHER GARTEN
KAISER WILHELM GEDÄCHTNISKIRCHE
EUROPA CENTER
Zoologischer Garten
STRASSE DES 17 JUNI
SIEGESÄULE
Grösser Stern
SCHLOSS BELLEVUE
Tiergarten
HAUS DER KULTUREN DER WELT
SOWJETISCHES EHRENMAL
BRANDENBURGER TOR
REICHSTAG
KUNSTGEWERBEMUS.
KUPFERSTICHKABINETT
BAUHAUS ARCHIVE
PHILHARMONIE
NEUE NATIONAL GALERIE
Potsdamer Platz
MUSEUM FUR VERKEHR UND TECHNIK
TOPOGRAPHIES DES TERRORS
MARTIN GROPIUS BAU
PREUSSISCHER LANDTAG
CHECKPOINT CHARLIE
BERLIN MUSEUM
POTSDAMERSTRASSE
BÜLOW STR.
YORCK STRASSE
Viktoria park
MEHRINGDAMM
GNEISENAUSTRASSE
Landwehr Kanal
GITSCHINER STRASSE
LEIPZIGERSTR.
FRIEDRICHSTR.
UNTER DEN LINDEN
KONZERTHAUS BERLIN
FRANZÖSISCHER DOM
STAATS OPER
GERMAN HIS MUS
PERGAMON MUSEUM
MUSEUMSINSEL
BAHNHOF FRIEDRICH-STRASSE
BERLINER ENSEMBLE
BRECHT HAUS
NEUE SYNAGOGUE
BERLINER DOM
NIKOLAIKIRCHE
FERNSEHTURM
Alexanderplatz
GRUNERSTR.
MOLLSTR.
Karl-Marx-Strasse
HAUPT-BAHNHOF
LICHTENBERG BAHNHOF
Volkspark Friedrichshain
R. Spree
HASEN-HEIDE
Columbia Damm
Invalidenstrasse
Alt Moabit
Turm Strasse
Bernauer Str.
Wilhelm-Pieck-Strasse

INFORMATION

For all **tourist information enquiries**, ☎(030) 250025, fax (030) 2500 2424 (Mon–Fri 0800–2000, Sat–Sun 0900–1800). Written enquiries: **Berlin Tourismus Marketing**, AM KARLSBAD 11, 10785 BERLIN. Accommodation and ticket reservation services are available at Tourist Offices. Smaller **Infopoint offices**, run in conjunction with other organisations, are at **Tegel Airport**, opposite the main hall at Gate 0 (daily 0500–2230); **Dresdener Bank**, UNTER DEN LINDEN 17 (weekdays 0830–1400; Tues and Thur 1530–1800); and the **KaDeWe** department store in the travel centre, TAUENTZIENSTR., 21–24 (weekdays 0930–2000 and Sat 0900–1600).

From these offices you can pick up a colour **city map** (DM1; free from some hotels/campsites) and the quarterly *Berlin Magazine* (DM3.50), with information and listings in English.

MONEY Cashpoints and **Thomas Cook bureaux de change** are found throughout the city.

POST AND PHONES There is a **post office** at Zoo station, open Mon–Sat 0600–2400, Sun 0800–2000, where you can also collect mail. The post office at **Tegel Airport** is open Mon–Fri 0700–2100, Sat–Sun 0800–2000. **Post offices** are usually open Mon–Fri 0900–1800; Sat 0900–1200.

To phone **Berlin**, ☎49 (Germany) + 30 (Berlin) + number; to phone Berlin from inside Germany, ☎030 + number.

PUBLIC TRANSPORT

Berlin's efficient public transport network combines buses, trams, underground and surface trains. Free photocopied maps showing public transport routes can be picked up from the Tourist Offices. More comprehensive versions, some with street indexes, cost DM5–10 from newsagents. Train maps are easy to find, but for **bus maps** you must go to the **BVG information centre**, in a separate building outside Zoo station ☎(030) 256 2462 (daily 0800–2000); here you can get the *Region Berlin Linienplan* (DM2) and free smaller transport maps. A public transport information office in **Zoo station**, ☎(030) 2974 9227, covering the S-Bahn, is open Mon–Fri 0600–2100, Sat–Sun 0700–2100.

BOAT TRIPS

For daily boat trips along the **River Spree** ☎(030) 394 4954.

TICKETS AND PASSES

Get **tickets** for buses, trains and trams from automatic machines on station platforms, from bus drivers or from ticket offices; validate your ticket by punching it on the special machine once on board or on the platform.

A **single** (DM3.90) allows travel on any bus, train or tram for a period of 2 hrs.

A **1-day bus and underground pass**, valid until 0300, costs DM7.80, and is available from Tourist Offices and Zoo station.

The **Berlin Welcome Card** costs DM29 and allows you unlimited free use of public transport throughout the city and its suburbs for 72 hrs. The card also entitles you to reductions on city tours, museums, theatres and tourist attractions in Berlin and Potsdam. Buy Welcome Cards at stations, bus ticket offices, hotels, or the Tourist Offices.

Taxis are plentiful, especially in the west, and relatively inexpensive; they can be flagged down on the street or from ranks at stations, the airport and other key points.

Metro: The 20 lines of the U-Bahn (underground) and S-Bahn (suburban surface trains) offer quick transport to most spots within the 40–km diameter of Berlin. The stations are easily recognised by the white U on a blue square or white S on a green circle and lines are colour-coded and numbered. Direction is indicated by the name of the final destination.

Buses: Buses are also a convenient way to see the city. A good sightseeing route is no. 100, which runs from Zoo station through the **Tiergarten**, the **Brandenburg Gate** and along **Unter den Linden**; pick up a free guide brochure to this route from the BVG information centre. Bus-stops are indicated by a green H on a yellow background.

ACCOMMODATION

It is worth booking well in advance if possible. Most upmarket tourist accommodation is in the west, especially in the environs of **Zoo**, **Kurfürstendamm** and **Charlottenburg**, though more deluxe and tourist-standard hotels are opening in the east of the city. The **tourist information offices** will make reservations and give advice, addresses and telephone numbers. Thomas Cook network member **Reisecenter**, FRIEDRICHSTR. 56, (030) 201 7220, also makes hotel reservations. Ask at Tourist Offices for the *Hotels und Pensionen* booklet, which has information (including prices) in English, for *Accommodation for Young Visitors,* which lists cheap hotels and hostels (again including prices) and for a list of campsites and Youth Hostels (most campsites are out of town). Guest rooms in private quarters can be booked through **Privatzimmervermittlung**; (030) 49 56 56.

HOTELS

One of the latest additions is the **Hotel Grand Hyatt Berlin**, which opened in Oct 1998 in the POTSDAMER PL. area. The most exclusive hotel is the **Schlosshotel Vier Jahreszeiten**, BRAHMSSTR. 10, BERLIN-WILMERSDORF, (030) 89 58 40, in the elegant Grünewald residential district and set in a beautiful palace. Both over DM200.

Moderate hotels (DM200-300) include:
Hotel Berliner Hof, TAUENTZIENSTR. 8, BERLIN-CHARLOTTENBURG; (030) 25 49 50.
Hotel Kurfürstendamm am Adenauerplatz, KURFÜRSTENDAMM 68, BERLIN-CHARLOTTENBURG; (030) 88 46 30.

Apart Hotel Hanse, JENAER STR. 2, BERLIN-WILMERSDORF, (030) 211 9052.
BCA Hotel Lichtenberg, RHINSTR. 159, BERLIN-LICHTENBERG, (030) 54 93 50 are two cheaper options (under DM200).

HOSTELS

There are three HI hostels in Berlin. The most central is **JGH Berlin**, Klukstr. 3 (030) 261 1098, 3 km from the centre, no. 129.

CAMPSITES

One of the nearest sites to the centre is **Campingplatz DDC-Kohlhasenbruck**, NEUE KREISSTR. 36, (030) 805 1737.

FOOD AND DRINK

Around **Zoo** station, **Ku'damm** and the **Europa Centre** are plenty of fast-food snackeries and cafés. Just off KU'DAMM is MEINEKESTR., which is much quieter and has a good selection of brasseries and German pubs. In the east of the city, head for GENDARMENMARKT, where the adjoining streets feature smart brasseries and cafés with pavement tables. For a treat, try the cakes at **coffee shops**, while for cheap food and a happy evening's drinking head for the *Kneipe* (pubs) around PRENZLAUER BERG – particularly the side streets around KOLLWITZPL., SAVIGNYPL. and KREUZ-BERG. ORANIENBURGER STR. has dozens of relatively inexpensive restaurants, with food from a wide range of cultures, for a meal out in a trendy, anarchic setting.

CAFÉS & PUBS

Bamberger Reiter, REGENSBURGER STR. 7; ☎(030) 218 4282. is the place for a special meal out (expensive)

Hard Rock Café, MEINEKESTR. 21, ☎(030) 884620.
Café Kranzler, KURFÜRSTENDAMM 18, ☎(030) 882 6911 (at the Charlottenburg end), has Berlin's finest coffee and cakes.
Café am Neuen See, a classic German beer garden, is in the Tiergarten by the Leichtenstein bridge.

Try German pubs such as **Meineke X**, MEINEKESTR. 10, ☎(030) 882 3158.
Wilhelm Hoeck, WILMERSDORFERSTR. 149, ☎ (030) 341 8174, has a real Berlin meal of beer, pickles, pork hocks or meat rissoles.

HIGHLIGHTS

Running roughly westward from the Zoo intersection, 3.5 km long **Kurfürstendamm** is a glitzy showcase of high-rise and neon, lined with shops, restaurants, cafés and cinemas; it is still Berlin's main shopping street. Opposite Zoo station is the **Gedächtniskirche** (Kaiser Wilhelm Memorial Church), with its war-damaged tower left unrepaired as a symbol of World War II. The church, which is free to enter, is open daily 0900–1900, with **concerts** on Saturdays at 1800. BUDAPESTER STR. leads to **Tiergarten**, with lakes and the English Garden: this was the former hunting ground of the kings of Prussia. To the west is **Schloss Bellevue**, residence of the Federal President, and to the east the 1960s **Kongresshalle**.

All that remains of **Checkpoint Charlie**, the Berlin Wall crossing point, is a small area of rubble-strewn wasteland and the nearby **Checkpoint Charlie**

TOURS

Among the numerous sightseeing tours are **Berolina**, ☎(030) 8856 8030, with various routes departing from KU'DAMM 220/225, and other bus stops around the city; **BBS Sightseeing**, ☎(030) 3519 5270, and **BVB Bus**, ☎(030) 885 9880, also leave from Ku'damm. **Walking tours** leave from Zoo station, led by **Berlin Walks**, ☎(030) 301 9194. **Velotaxis**, ☎(030) 328 8888, like covered rickshaws, are another way to see the sights, and can be picked up at Brandenburg Gate,

Tours cont'd.

Zoo station and ADENAUERPL. Various companies provide **boat tours** on the city's waterways; **BWTS**, ☎(030) 6588 0203.

Museum, FRIEDRICHSTR. 44 (U-Bahn: KOCHSTR.; DM8, concessionary rate DM5; daily 0900–2200). You can buy your own genuine piece of the Wall in the museum shop.

Sections of the Wall can still be seen in a number of places including: MUHLENSTR., a 1300m section along the **River Spree**, BERNAUER STR. at the corner of EBERSWALDER STR., where you will find the entrance to **Berlin Wall Park,** and NIEDERKIRCHNERSTR. at the **Martin Gropius Building,** where one of the most sensational escapes took place.

Two free **exhibitions** tell the story of the Wall and divided Berlin. The **Museum of Forbidden Art** (U-Bahn: SCHLESISCHES TOR, S-Bahn: TREPTOWER PARK; Wed–Sun and holidays 1200–1800) and the **Allied Forces Museum**, CLAYALLEE 135 (U-Bahn: OSKAR-HELENE-HEIM; closed Weds). Nearby is the statue *The Day The Wall Came Down*, which commemorates the 50th anniversary of the Berlin airlift.

The towering **Brandenburger Tor** (Brandenburg Gate), PARISER PLATZ, which stands between STR. DEN 17 JUNI and UNTER DEN LINDEN, was built in 1788–91 as a triumphal arch for Prussia's victorious armies. The Gate became a symbol of the divided Germany and was reopened in Dec 1989. Another powerful symbol stands just to the north: the **Reichstag**. Built in 1871 to house the imperial parliament, it reopened in 1999 after a stunning restoration by Norman Foster and is now the seat of the *Bundestag*, the Lower House of Parliament for the reunited Germany.

Rapidly regaining its status as Berlin's principal thoroughfare, **Unter den Linden** features monumental public buildings, most of which were restored after World War II. Since reunification, it has been increasingly flanked by smart shops, restaurants and cafés, government buildings and the offices of international corporations.

A three-day ticket (available only from main Tourist Offices) costing DM15 is valid for all state museums.

Just beyond the eastern end of UNTER DEN LINDEN is the **Berliner Dom,** the city's baroque cathedral (DM5; concessionary rate DM3). From here take the **RATHAUSBRÜCKE**, past **Palast der Republik** to RATHAUSSTR. On the right is the restored 15th-century twin-towered **Nikolaikirche**, Berlin's oldest building. The **Rotes Rathaus** (Red Town Hall, so-called on account of its bricks; Mon–Fri 0700–1800) leads to the base of the **Fernsehturm** (TV tower). This 365m spike, Berlin's tallest building, includes a globe-shaped revolving restaurant and viewing gallery at 200 m (daily 1000–2400; DM8, concessionary rate DM4).

A **day pass** to all palaces in Potsdam and Berlin's Charlottenburg costs DM20; concessionary rate DM15.

'Museum Island' or **Museuminsel**, on the **River Spree**, is home to outstanding museums: the **Pergamonmuseum**, **Germäldegalerie**, **Egyptian Museum and**

Papyrus Collection, SCHLOSSSTR. 70. All open Tue–Fri 1000–1800, Sat–Sun 1100–1800.

Potsdam, a World Heritage Site, 30 km southwest of Berlin, is full of architectural treasures. For details contact the Tourist Office (p.217) for information and travel/ ticket concessions.

SHOPPING

Berlin is becoming much better for shopping, though prices are generally high. The West still has greater variety and includes Berlin's chief shopping boulevard **Ku'damm**, 3.5 km of boutiques, department stores, cafés, shopping malls and the **Europa Centre** shopping complex. Some of the most expensive and chic fashion houses can be found on KU'DAMM between BLEIBTREUSTR. and OLIVAER PL. The giant **KaDeWe** on WITTENBERGPL. is the ultimate temple of Berlin's consumer society. FRIEDRICHSTR. in the former East, historically the city's premier shopping street, is rapidly regaining its former status.

The central food market is at **Winterfeldtplatz**, SCHÖNEBERG (Wed and Sat, 0800–1400; U-Bahn: ZOO). Covered markets can be found on **Marheinekeplatz**, KREUZBERG; **Ackerstr.**, **Mitte** and **Arminiusstr.**, TIERGARTEN.

NIGHT-TIME AND EVENTS

Berlin has a well-deserved reputation for diverse and non-stop entertainment. There are two listings magazines: *Zitty* and *Tip*, available from newsagents for about DM4.50. The quarterly *Berlin Magazine*, available from tourist information offices and newsagents, also covers entertainment and events.

Oranienstr., in the **Kreuzberg** district, is the heart of a busy **club and music bar scene**. **Wintergarten–Das Variete**, POTSDAMERSTR. 96, ☎(030) 2308 8230, is a variety theatre with up to nine shows a week. Classical concerts are held at **Philharmonie and Kammer-Musiksaal,** MATTHAIKIRCHSTR. 1, ☎(030) 2548 8132, and **Konzerthaus Berlin**, GENDARMENMARKT 2, ☎(030) 2090 2101.

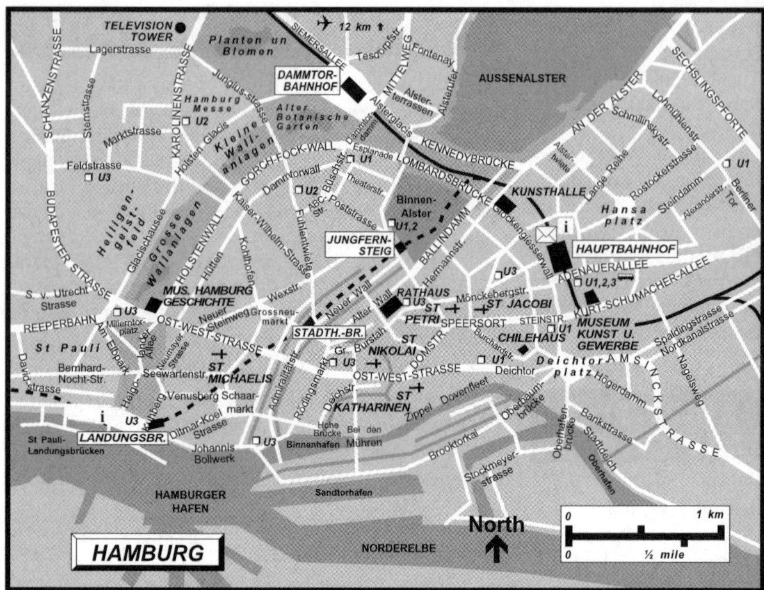

Germany's largest seaport and the country's media capital, Hamburg is one of the most sophisticated and cosmopolitan German cities. Although comprehensively destroyed in turn by fire in 1842 and by World War II bombing, it has a special watery character of its own, with some enjoyable boat trips on offer. One of the main streets, the Jungfernstieg, resembles something of a seaside promenade, while six soaring green copper spires impose themselves on the skyline over the rebuilt historic centre, the numerous parks and the canals. Entertainment and nightlife ranges from the famously sleazy Reeperbahn to the musical offerings of the opera company and the city's resident orchestras.

Hamburg is Germany's second largest city, after Berlin, and also a federal state with its own Parliament. The city's importance as a port dates from the 12th century, with Hamburg becoming a member of the Hanseatic League in 1321, making it one of the most powerful and wealthy free cities in Europe.

The **Hamburg Card** includes free travel on public transport, free admission to museums, and reductions of up to 30% on sightseeing, lake and harbour tours.
A **one-day card** costs DM12.50; a **three-day card** costs DM26.

ARRIVAL AND DEPARTURE

RAIL The **Hauptbahnhof** (Hbf) handles most long-distance trains. It's central and on the U-Bahn. Hbf also houses the main post office. The station's main exit is on KIRCHENALLEE. **Altona**, in the west of the city, is the terminal for most trains serving **Schleswig-Holstein**. **Dammtor**, north of the centre, is mostly for convention traffic and is therefore unlikely to be of much interest to tourists. **Rail information:** ☎(040) 19 419. Frequent S-Bahn trains link the three stations.

Landungsbrücken, BRÜCKE 9, ☎(040) 38 90 71 (2 km from St Pauli), is the terminal for ferries from the UK and Scandinavia.

Hamburg-Fuhlsbüttel, ☎(040) 50 750, is 8 km from town centre. A bus to the city centre takes 25 mins and costs DM8. Buses run every 20 mins between 0540 and 2300, including the **Airport Express,** which terminates at the KIRCHENALLEE exit of the Hauptbahnhof. **Taxi** fare to the city centre is approximately DM30.

TOURIST OFFICES

The main office for written enquiries is STEINSTR. 7, HAMBURG 20095; ☎(040) 30 05 10 (http://www.hamburg-tourism.de; info@hamburg-tourism.de).
Other Tourist Offices are at **Hauptbahnhof** (by the KIRCHENALLEE exit), ☎(040) 30 05 12 00, daily 0700–2300, and at the Port, between Pier 4 and 5 on the **St Pauli Landungsbrücken**; ☎(040) 30 05 12 00, daily 0900–1900.
A special **hotline** for information, hotel reservations, tickets etc. operates daily throughout the year from 0800–2000; ☎(040) 30 05 13 00.

INFORMATION

Get the free city map and tips from *A–Z* and *Top Info* magazine, which include a map of the city rail system, full details of Hamburg travel cards and an outline guide to the city's attractions from the **main Tourist Office**.

MONEY **Thomas Cook bureau de change**: IM METRO-MARKT, PAPENREYE 33; MITTELWEG 126; WAITZSTR. 19; WIESENHOEFEN 3. There are **bureaux de change** at the airport and Hbf.

POST AND PHONES **Hbf** houses the main post office, with international phones on the second floor; open 0700–0200.

PUBLIC TRANSPORT

The main area of interest is small enough to be walkable. **HHV** run efficient buses, U-Bahn (underground) and S-Bahn (urban trains), as well as a limited night bus service in the central area. For all **transport enquiries**, ☎(040) 19 449, daily 0700–2000.

ACCOMMODATION

Accommodation can be booked through the Tourist Office booking service: **Tourismus-Zentrale Hamburg Gmbh**, POSTFACH 10 22 49, 20015 HAMBURG; ☎(040) 30 05 10. Rooms in private homes can be booked through **Privatzimmer**, **Vermittlung-Witt u Hildebrecht,** METHFESSELSTR. 49, HAMBURG 20257, ☎(040) 49 15 666, and **Agentur Zimmer Frei**, SEMPERSTR.16; ☎(040) 27 87 77 77.

HOTELS

Central Hotel-Pensions (cheap) include:

Riedinger, ST GEORGESTR. 8; ☎(040) 24 74 63.

Sarah Petersen, LANGE REIHE 50; ☎(040) 24 98 26.

Schmidt, HOLZDAMM 14; ☎(040) 28 02 119.

Zentrum, BREMER REIHE 23; ☎(040) 28 02 528.

Selig, BREMER REIHE 23; ☎(040) 24.46.89.

Meyn, HANSAPL. 2; ☎(040) 24 53 09.

Kohler, ST GEORGESTR. 6; ☎(040) 24 90 65.

Kieler Hof, BREMER REIHE 15; ☎(040) 24 30 24.

YOUTH HOSTELS

Jugendherberge auf dem Stintgang, ALFRED-WEGENER-WEG 5; ☎(040) 31 34 88, central (U/S-Bahn: LANDUNGSBRÜCKEN).

Jugendgastehaus Hamburg, **'Horner Rennbahn'**, RENNBAHNSTR. 100; ☎(040) 65 11 671, in the eastern suburbs (S-Bahn: HORNER RENNHAHN).

Hamburger Jugendpark Langenhorn, JUGENDPARK 60; ☎(040) 53 13 050, central (U-Bahn: LANGEHORN MARKT).

Beherbergergetrieb Schanzenstern, BARTELSSTR.12, ☎(040) 14 39 84 41.

FOOD AND DRINK

Hamburg's cosmopolitan nature is reflected in its restaurants, with some of the best fine dining in Germany. Seafood and fish are, of course, a speciality. Prices tend to reflect the areas in which they are located, but the places in **Rathausmarkt** are not exorbitant and it's a good place to watch the world go by. **Kirchenallee, Altona, Univiertel** and **Schanzenviertel** are cheap eating areas.

RESTAURANTS

The Ratsweinkeller, ☎(040) 36 41 53, is an atmospheric basement restaurant in the **Rathaus**, serving regional and German cuisine.

Friesen Keller, JUNGFERNSTIEGT, ☎(040) 35 76 06 20, specialises in north German cuisine and has tables on a pontoon moored on a canal.

Kartoffelkeller, DEICHSTR. 21, ☎(040) 36 55 85, is in a historic merchant's house and boasts 56 different kinds of potato recipe.

Brauhaus Joh. Albrecht, ADOLPHSBRÜCKE 7,

☎ (040) 36 77 40, is a canalside guesthouse and brewery with its own landing stage and dishes designed to go well with the beer.
Groninger Braukeller, OST-WEST STRASSE 47, ☎(040) 33 13 81, is a typical Hamburg beer-cellar and restaurant with a good-value menu and beer brewed on the premises.
Bavaria Blick, BERNARD NOCHT STRASSE 99, ☎(040) 31 16 31 16, is a smart, modern restaurant with good German food and a great view of the Elbe river, being on the eighth floor.

HIGHLIGHTS

The oldest part of the city, which survived the great fire of 1842 and carpet bombing by the Allies in World War II, is around the harbour, where two **museum ships** are moored: the tall ship **Rickmer Rickmers** at **Pier 1** and the more modern **Cap San Diego** at the **Uberseebrücke**.

The neo-Renaissance **Rathaus** (Town Hall), MARKTPL. (U-Bahn: RATHAUS), is a magnificent sandstone building constructed 1886–97. Some of its 647 rooms, which can be toured when government is not in session, are adorned with tapestries, chandeliers and paintings. Tours are conducted in English daily; for details ☎(040) 36 81 24 70. The **Rathaus Tower** is one of six towers dominating the city's skyline, the others belonging to churches, the most impressive of which is **St Michaelis**, KRAYENKAMP 4C (U- or S-Bahn: LANDUNGSBRÜCKEN), a 132-m high baroque structure with a crypt and a viewing level at 82 m, which gives panoramic views. This is the city's symbol and a trumpet solo is played from the tower every day.

Hamburg has a good range of museums, some of which are usually closed on Mon, with late night opening on Thur. Foremost is the **Kunsthalle**, GLOCKEN-GIESSERWALL 1 (U- or S-Bahn: HBF) with a superb international art collection that dates from the Gothic period to the present day. This is complemented by the modern works in the next-door **Kunstverein** (Tues–Sun). **Museum für Kunst und Gewerbe**, STEINTORPL. 1 (U- or S-Bahn: HBF), is the museum of arts and crafts with an excellent range

TOURS

The city is dominated by water and a boat-trip is part of the experience. **Hadag**, ☎(040) 35 74 240, is one of the companies that run daily English-language harbour tours Mar–Oct/Nov, departing from the JUNGFERNSTIEG QUAY; ☎(040) 34 11 41. For trips around the harbour and further afield, boats depart from LANDUNGSBRÜCKEN PIERS, daily every 30 mins from 0900–1800 (Apr–Oct), and hourly from 1030–1530 (Nov–Mar).
The **Hummeltrain** is a 1920s-style train with multilingual guides that covers the major sights; ☎(040) 79 28 979.

of art from ancient Egypt, Greece and Rome, along with medieval works, art nouveau and modern art (Tues– Sun).

Hamburg's tallest building, the 280-m **TV Tower**, LAGERSTR. 2–8 (U-Bahn: MESSEHALLEN) has a viewing platform (open daily 1000–2300) and a revolving restaurant. Just below is **Planten un Blomen** (U-Bahn: STEPHANPL.; S-Bahn: DAMMTOR), the city's largest park, with a vast Japanese garden and illuminated fountain displays and concerts on summer nights (May– Sept).

SHOPPING

Style and flamboyance are very much the name of the game, for Hamburg is not a city to hide its prosperity, with a big range of department stores and boutiques, particularly for fashion, interiors, china, glass and antiques. Moreover, there are 10 elegant shopping arcades with cafés and restaurants between RATHAUSMARKT and GÄNSEMARKT – this being the **main shopping area**, easily covered on foot. Shops along NEUER WALL specialise in furniture and interiors, while the **Quartier Satin**, on the ABC-STRASSE, is the place for designer names and antiques. **Colonnaden**, a delightful pedestrianised colonnade just off JUNGFERNSTIEG, has pavement cafés alongside designer shops, together with specialist tobacco, tea and coffee shops.

NIGHT-TIME AND EVENTS

Local nightlife is cosmopolitan, to say the least. In the **St Pauli** quarter, north of the Elbe riverfront, raunchy sex-show clubs tout their delights next to casinos, discos, tattoo parlours and some of Hamburg's best restaurants. The REEPERBAHN, St Pauli's main drag, has been going strong for generations, though there is now an element of gentrification, with a growing number of bars popular with the bohemian and media set. The **DOM Amusement Fair** is open three times a year in the HEILIGENGEISTFELD, from mid Mar to mid Apr, mid July to mid Aug, and early Nov to early Dec.

THEATRES

St Pauli Theater, SPIELBUDENPL. 29, ☎(040) 31 43 44, with musicals and international guest performances.
Hansa-Theater, STEINDAMM 17, ☎(040) 24 14 14, is Germany's oldest classical musical hall.
English Theatre, LERCHENFELD 14, ☎(040) 22 77 089, for English-language productions.

JAZZ CLUBS

Cotton Club, ALTER STEINWEG 10; ☎(040) 34 38 78.
Birdland, GÄRTNERSTR. 122; ☎(040) 40 52 77.

Although there's virtually nothing medieval remaining in the centre, Bavaria's sophisticated and cosmopolitan capital is many people's favourite German city. It's easy to see why: the city exudes a sense of space and greenery, and you soon get caught up in its laid-back approach to life, noticeable particularly among the crowds of all ages out enjoying themselves in its many beer halls, pavement cafés and gardens, and in the student haunts and fringe theatres of the Schwabing area. Only the *Föhn*, a dry wind blowing from the mountains, tempers the local sense of fun.

ARRIVAL AND DEPARTURE

RAIL **Hauptbahnhof München** (Hbf), BAHNHOFPL. (about 15 mins' walk straight ahead to MARIENPL. in the centre) is Munich's main railway station, and southern Germany's most important rail junction, with connections into southern, central and south-east Europe. Timetable information: ☎(089) 19419; fare information: ☎(089) 2333 0256.

Munich's ultra-modern **Franz Josef Strauss Airport** is Germany's second international hub (after Frankfurt). Flight information: ☎(089) 9752 1313. S-Bahn line S8 runs every 20 mins from the rail station via the Ostbahnhof and city centre to the airport 0320–0055. For the city centre, get off at MARIENPL. Journey time is 36 mins; single ticket DM13.60. Buses also run every 20 mins 0650–1950 between the airport and the rail station; journey time about 45 mins.

TOURIST OFFICES

Administrative Office: **Fremdenverkehrsamt München**, 80313 MÜNCHEN; ☎(089) 233 0300 (http://www.munich-tourist.de; e-mail: 100711.1505@compuserve.com). **Main Tourist Office**: BAHNHOFPL. 2, outside the main railway station, ☎(089) 2333 0256, (Mon–Sat 1000–2000, Sun 1000–1800). *Branches:* At the **Airport** (Central Building, ☎(089) 9759 2815; Mon–Fri 1000–2100 and Sat–Sun 1100–2000). **City centre** in the **Rathaus**, MARIENPL. (Mon–Fri 1000–2000, Sat 1000–1600) ☎(089) 2333 0272/3.

INFORMATION

The main Tourist Office offers a free accommodation service, hotel listing (DM1), city map (DM0.50) and theatre bookings. Useful publications include *In München*, a free fortnightly listings magazine, *Monatsprogramm*, a monthly listings and *Munich English Information* leaflet containing answers to the 21 questions most frequently asked by visitors.

MONEY

Thomas Cook bureau de change is at PETERSPL. 10; ☎(089) 2351 0920. Other **Thomas Cook licensees** are located around the city.

POST AND PHONES

The **main post office** is at BAHNHOFSPL., just across from the the main rail station, ☎(089) 5459 7820, with poste restante, money exchange and long-distance telephone calling facilities, all open 24 hrs. To phone Munich from abroad the code is 49 (Germany) + 89 (Munich) + number. To phone Munich from elsewhere in Germany the code is 089 + number.

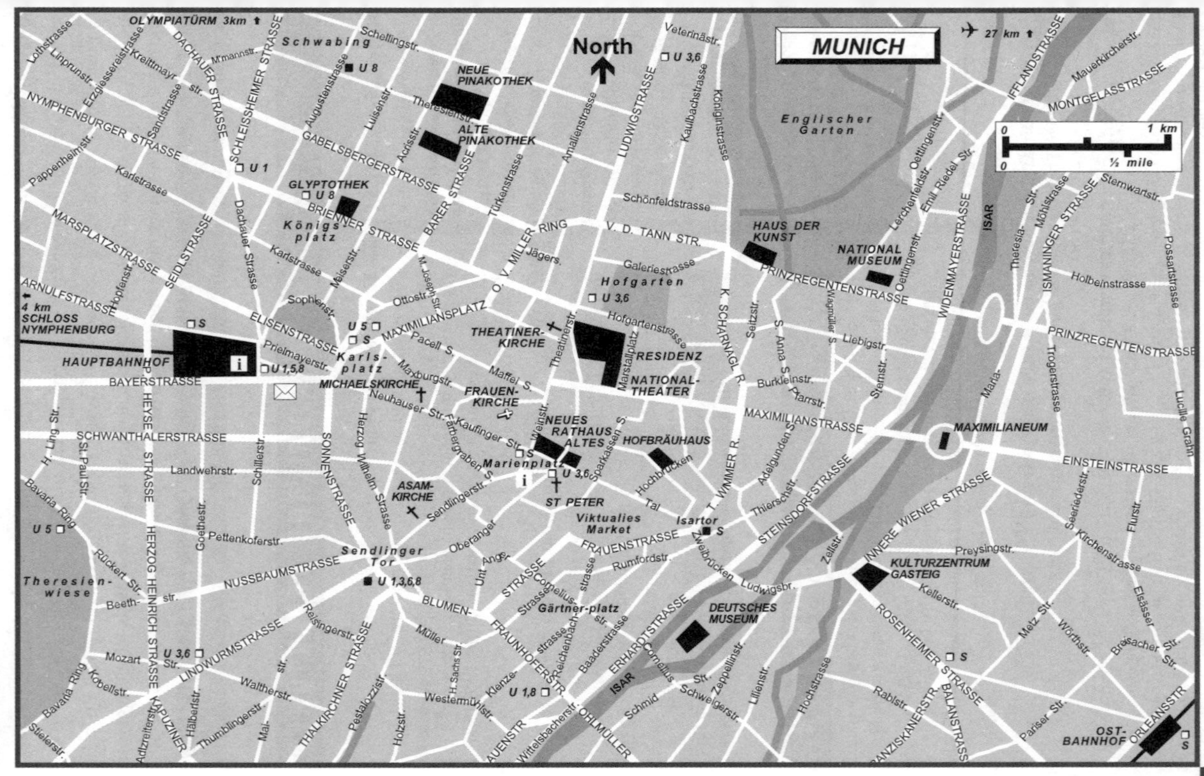
MUNICH
North
OLYMPIATÜRM 3km
27 km
4 km SCHLOSS NYMPHENBURG
Schwabing
NEUE PINAKOTHEK
ALTE PINAKOTHEK
GLYPTOTHEK
Königsplatz
HAUPTBAHNHOF
Karlsplatz
MICHAELSKIRCHE
FRAUEN-KIRCHE
THEATINER-KIRCHE
RESIDENZ
NATIONAL-THEATER
Hofgarten
NEUES RATHAUS
ALTES
Marienplatz
HOFBRÄUHAUS
ASAM-KIRCHE
ST PETER
Viktualies Market
Isartor
Sendlinger Tor
Theresienwiese
Gärtner-platz
DEUTSCHES MUSEUM
KULTURZENTRUM GASTEIG
MAXIMILIANEUM
HAUS DER KUNST
NATIONAL MUSEUM
Englischer Garten
OST-BAHNHOF
ISAR
0
1 km
½ mile

Tourist Offices sell the **Münchner Schlüssel** (Key to Munich), a book of coupons which allows reduced entrance charges to museums, theatres and special attractions, together with a hotel booking, city transport ticket and suggestions to help you plan your visit. Price DM63–DM240 per night depending on hotel.

PUBLIC TRANSPORT

The city centre, pedestrianised apart from trams and cycles, is easy to explore on foot, being only a 20-min walk across. For trips further afield, use the excellent public transport system of buses, trams and trains: S-Bahn (overground) and U-Bahn (underground). Nowhere is more than a few mins' walk from a stop or station; all transport runs 0430–0200. Further information from **MVV** (city transport authority), THIERSCHSTR. 2; ☎2191 3322.

TICKETS

City transport tickets can be used on trains, buses or trams; they must be validated in the blue box the first time you board, or you are liable to be fined DM60 on the spot. Buy them at stations, newsagents, hotel desks and campsites. Singles cost DM8 (inner zone only) or DM16. A **Streifenkarte** is the best value (DM15 for a strip of 10 tickets). A **Tageskarte** (day trip ticket offering unlimited use of the system) costs DM8.50 for inner Munich and is valid from the time it is stamped till 0600 the following morning.

Obtain information on S-Bahn routes, tickets and timetables from **Deutsche Bahn** (German Railways); ☎557 575. The city also has an impressive 11,000 km of cycle paths. Bicycle hire at **Radius Radverleih** at the rail station (platforms 30–36); ☎596 113. Daily walking tours (in English) start from the rail station at 1000 (DM15).

Official taxis are cream-coloured, usually a Mercedes, and are plentiful and reliable; ☎21610.

ACCOMMODATION

Finding accommodation is rarely a problem except during **Oktoberfest** and **Fasching** (see p. 233).

The biggest choice of hotels is around the rail station in streets like SCHILLERSTR. and SENEFELDERSTR; it's a rather drab area but handy for the centre. Budget accommodation in Munich is in plentiful supply, with several youth hostels. There are also several hostels outside the city limits easily accessible by public transport (check *Infopool)*.

HOTELS

Hotel Rafael, NEUTURMSTR. 1, ☎290 980, is a modern but stately luxurious hotel, which occupies a former art gallery.

Moderate accommodation includes:

Hotel Haberstock, SCHILLERSTR. 4; ☎ 557 855.
Hotel Senefelder, SENEFELDERSTR. 4; ☎ 551 540.
Hotel Andi, LANDWEHRSTR. 33; ☎ 552 5560.
Hotel Arosa, HOTTERSTR. 24; ☎267 087.

YOUTH HOSTELS	**Jugendherberge München**, WENDL-DIETRICH-STR. 20, ☎131 156, with 380 beds (U-Bahn 1 to ROTKREUZPL.). **DJH-Jugendgästehaus**, MIESINGSTR. 4; ☎723 6560.
BUDGET AND CAMPING	**Das Zelt** ('The Tent'), KAPUZINERHOZL, IN DEN KIRSCHEN, ☎(089)1414 300, a marquee in the **Botanischer Garten**, where DM10 gets you floor space. Facilities include washing machines, lockers, bicycle rental and an open-air cinema. **München Thalkirchen**, ZENTRALLANDSTR. 49, ☎723 1707, open Mar–Oct (U-Bahn 3 to THALKIRCHEN) is the city's biggest campsite.

FOOD AND DRINK

Good eating areas include SCHWABING, GÄRTNERPL. and, across the River Isar, HAIDHAUSEN. An entertaining place for cheap snacks is the open-air **Viktualienmarkt**, a food market where a score of traditional taverns dispense beer, schnapps, sausage and soup – look out particularly for the tasty *Schwarzwaldschinken* (Black Forest smoked ham), black on the outside and red inside. The city's favourite titbit, particularly popular for mid-morning second breakfast washed down with beer, is the *Weisswurst*, a boiled white sausage flavoured with herbs and spices.

Munich is famous for its bread, but even more for its **beers**, produced by six major breweries. The main varieties are *Helles* (normal), *Dunkeles* (dark) and the cloudy orange-coloured *Weissbier* made from wheat instead of hops. There are beer halls and gardens all over the city; the touristy **Hofbräuhaus**, MARIENPL., is where Hitler launched the Nazi party in 1920. **Augustiner Gaststätten**, NEUHAUSERSTR. 16, is home of Munich's oldest brewery. In traditional beer gardens, you can bring your own food.

MODERATE	**The Ratskeller** (Town Hall cellar), MARIENPL. 8, ☎219 9890, is a traditional restaurant. **Donisl**, WEINSTR. 1, ☎220 184, is a centuries-old beer hall.
CHEAP	**Berni's Nudelbrett**, PETERSPL. 8, ☎264 469, specialises in pasta, steak and seafood with a cheap three-course menu. **Dimitri's**, HOHENZOLLERNSTR. 13, ☎333 837, is a cheap and cheerful Greek eatery.
VEGETARIAN	**Prinz Myshkin**, HACKENSTR. 2; ☎265 596. **Buxs**, FRAUNENSTR. 9, ☎293 684, an inexpensive self-service restaurant serving fresh and delicious salads.

HIGHLIGHTS

Right at the hub of the pedestrianised city centre, the **Glockenspiel** (with its host of jousting knights, among others) of the clock of the **Neues Rathaus** (New Town Hall) performs (at 1100, 1200 and 1700) to the shoppers, buskers and sightseers on the MARIENPL. (U and S-Bahn: MARIENPL.), Munich's main square. And across MARIENPL., the less prominent medieval **Altes Rathaus** (Old Town Hall) houses a small toy museum, while just to the west rise the twin onion domes of the 15th-century **Frauenkirche** (cathedral), FRAUENPL. Facing the Altes Rathaus is **Alter Peter** (Old St Peter's church), inside of which is the strange skeleton of St Munditia, wearing a jewel-laden shroud and bearing a quill pen.

From here, it's a very short stroll northwards into MAX-JOSEPHPL., to the vast **Residenz** (U-Bahn: ODEONSPL.), the baroque palace of Bavaria's Wittelsbach rulers – faithfully rebuilt after bomb destruction. Different parts of the building are open in the morning and in the afternoon. A few steps on from here, ODEONSPL. is Munich's stateliest streetscape, an admirable example of post-war reconstruction. Beside ODEONSPL. are the manicured lawns and flowerbeds of the **Hofgarten** park. To the north-east, the **Englischer Garten** (named because of its informal landscaping – dandelions grow profusely in the long grass) is Europe's biggest city park, popular for the beer garden at its **Chinesischer Turm** (Pagoda) and the nudist meadow beside the **River Isar**, the surprisingly clean and swimmable river that the Englischer Garten flanks for some 7 km.

MUNICH'S EVENTS

The world-famous **Oktoberfest** actually begins in September, and lasts 16 days, with beer and barbecued chicken the accompaniment to Bavarian band music, amusements and sideshows. It takes place in the THERESIENWIESE, south-west of the rail station (U-Bahn 4/5 to THERESIENWIESE). The year begins with a lively carnival known as the **Fasching**, with masked balls as well as processions through the streets.

West of the city centre is **Schloss Nymphenburg** (U-bahn: ROTKREUZPL. then change to tram 17), the summer palace of the Wittelsbachs. The wonder of is its parkland, with numerous lakes, varied gardens, pavilions and hunting lodges, including the **Magdelenklause**, a folly built in the form of a hermit's grotto.

The collection of art in Munich's leading museum, the **Alte Pinakothek**, BARER-STR. 27 (U-Bahn: THERESIENSTR.), is among the world's top six. It includes 65 paintings by Rubens, a small but priceless collection of Italian works and an unrivalled collection of great German masters.

SHOPPING

The main shopping area is the wide traffic-free-roadway from KARLSPL. to MARIENPL., a mixture of department stores, supermarkets and fashion shops, but the city's most elegant designer boutiques are along THEATINERSTR. and MAXIMILIANSTR.

A busy flea market is held in ARNULFSTR. on Fri and Sat. From late Nov to Christmas Eve, the **Christkindlmarkt** (Christ-Child Market) is held on MARIENPL.

NIGHT-TIME AND EVENTS

The monthly *Monatsprogramm* lists all kinds of events, from live music to art exhibitions. An English-language magazine *Munich Found*, published monthly (DM4) primarily for expatriates living in Munich, contains up-to-date news on entertainment, restaurants and the like.

The many **rock, jazz and blues bars** provide a venue for and visiting bands. **Atomic Café**, NEUTURMSTR. (near the Hotel Rafael) is a popular 1960s club, good value at DM10. The city's liveliest area is **Schwabing**, north of the university. Streets there such as LEOPOLDSTR., AMALIENSTR. and TÜRKENSTR. are famous for their many bars, cafés and jazz cellars. Plenty of discos can be found around **Gärtnerpl.**, which is also the city's gay area. At the **Kunstpark Ost**, near OSTBAHNHOF, old warehouses have been converted into bars and nightclubs with names like *Babylon, Incognito* and the *Nachtkantine*.

Several cinemas show English-language films which are subtitled in German; these are advertised in newspapers as *OmU* films. The **Bavarian State Opera** performs at the **Nationaltheater**, MAX-JOSEPH-PL. 2; ☎2185 1919. **Staatstheater**, GÄRTNERPL. 3; ☎201 6767, stages opera, ballet and classical concerts. The ultra-modern **Gasteig Kulturzentrum**, ROSENHEIMSTR. 5, ☎480 980, is three concert halls high on the right bank of the Isar. Students give free lunchtime or early evening concerts.

WHERE NEXT FROM MUNICH?

In addition to following the routes to ***Berlin*** *(p. 217),* ***Verona*** *(p. 368) and* ***Frankfurt*** *(p. 219), you can take direct international services to* ***Ostend*** *via* ***Brussels*** *(ETT table 21),* ***Amsterdam*** *(table 28),* ***Paris*** *(table 32),* ***Budapest*** *(table 61),* ***Bucharest*** *(table 61),* ***Belgrade*** *(table 61),* ***Llubljana*** *(table 62),* ***Vienna*** *via* ***Salzburg*** *(table 67),* ***Rome*** *(table 70) and* ***Geneva*** *via* ***Zürich*** *(table 75).*

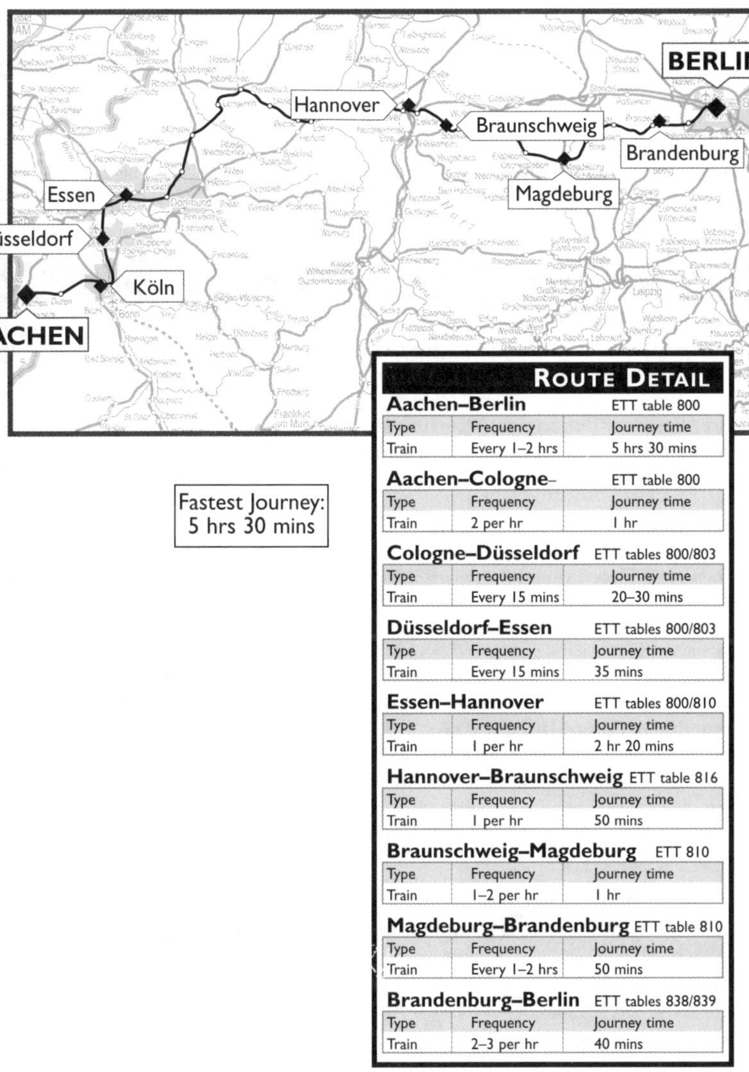

Fastest Journey: 5 hrs 30 mins

ROUTE DETAIL

Aachen–Berlin ETT table 800

Type	Frequency	Journey time
Train	Every 1–2 hrs	5 hrs 30 mins

Aachen–Cologne– ETT table 800

Type	Frequency	Journey time
Train	2 per hr	1 hr

Cologne–Düsseldorf ETT tables 800/803

Type	Frequency	Journey time
Train	Every 15 mins	20–30 mins

Düsseldorf–Essen ETT tables 800/803

Type	Frequency	Journey time
Train	Every 15 mins	35 mins

Essen–Hannover ETT tables 800/810

Type	Frequency	Journey time
Train	1 per hr	2 hr 20 mins

Hannover–Braunschweig ETT table 816

Type	Frequency	Journey time
Train	1 per hr	50 mins

Braunschweig–Magdeburg ETT 810

Type	Frequency	Journey time
Train	1–2 per hr	1 hr

Magdeburg–Brandenburg ETT table 810

Type	Frequency	Journey time
Train	Every 1–2 hrs	50 mins

Brandenburg–Berlin ETT tables 838/839

Type	Frequency	Journey time
Train	2–3 per hr	40 mins

Aachen – Hannover – Berlin

For the most part, it's the man-made aspects that lend this journey its character, as for much of the way you're travelling over the flat farmlands of the north German plain. From the Belgian border to the German capital, the route heads out from the frontier post of Aachen, past Cologne with its great cathedral and through the industrial heartland of the Ruhr. At Osnabrück there is the option of striking out northwards to Bremen, Hamburg, Lübeck and into Denmark; otherwise carry on east through Hannover, diverting southwards to the old towns of Goslar and Wernigerode in the Harz Mountains – with the chance to ride the area's narrow-gauge railways.

AACHEN

Now important only as a frontier town between Belgium and Germany, Aachen was a great city more than 1000 years ago, when the Emperor Charlemagne the Great enjoyed the thermal springs and made it the capital of his revived empire. His octagonal chapel is now the heart of the Dom (cathedral), built on the site of the imperial palace. Some of the original structure survives and his successors added many embellishments. Charlemagne's gilded tomb is here and you can see the imperial throne by joining a guided tour.

The **Schatzkammer** (Treasury) is one of Europe's most dazzling, with such priceless objects as a gold bust of Charlemagne and a jewel-encrusted 10th-century cross. Statues of 50 Holy Roman Emperors adorn the façade of the 14th-century **Rathaus** (Town Hall), which incorporates two of the original palace towers. Inside are replicas of Charlemagne's crown jewels (the originals are in Vienna).

Three other indoor sights to seek out are the **Ludwig Forum für Internationales Kunst** (JULICHERSTR), with its excellent collection of **East European art**; the unique **International Press Museum** (PONSTR. 13) that acts as the 'registry office' of the world's press (in that it contains not only specimen copies, but also first, jubilee and final editions from every publication if the international press): and the **Aachen Computer Museum** (SOMMERFELDSTR. 32; free entry) charts the evolution from the earliest data processing to modern PCs.

> A spa town, Aachen also has several places to unwind in the thermal waters, including the **Reha-Klinik Schwertbad**, BENEDEKTINERSTR. 23, ☎(0241) 60 020, and the **Kubad Quellenhof**, MOHEIMSALLEE 52, ☎(0241) 80 29 22.

RAIL At REUMONTSTR. 1; ☎(0241) 19 419, about 1 km from the city centre.

i **Tourist Office**: in the centre at ELISERBRUNN, FRIEDRICH WILLEM PLATZ, ☎(0241) 180 2960/1, incoming@aachen-tourist.de. Open Mon–Fri 0900–1800 and Sat 0900–1400. Daily guided tours throughout the year start from the Tourist Office.
The **youth hostel** is out of town at MARIA-THERESIA ALLEE 260, ☎(0242) 75 972, bus no. 2 from Aachen Central station,

direction PREUSWALD, stop RHONHEIDE. The nearest campsite is at **Camping Prall,** north of the centre at **Wintersberg,** ☎(0241) 158 502. Medium priced hotels include **Hotel-Restaurant Forthaus Schontal**, KORNELIMUNSTERWEG 1, ☎(0241) 608 305, with singles beginning at around DM60, and the **Hotel Braun**, LUTTICHERSTR. 517, ☎(0241) 74 535, rooms starting at DM70. Private rooms are also offered: details from the Tourist Office.

COLOGNE (KÖLN)

See p.245.

The 60,000-year-old skeleton of what has come to be known as **Neanderthal man** was found in the **Düssel Valley** (also known by the local name of Neandertal) outside Düsseldorf. The city has recently opened a **Neanderthal Museum**, TALSTRASSE 300, ☎(02104) 979 797, (http://www.neanderthal.de.) – a communications and documentation centre delving into the early history of mankind.

DÜSSELDORF

Originally a centre of heavy industry, Düsseldorf is now decidedly upmarket, its transition exemplified by the KÖNIGSALLEE (generally termed the **'Kö'**), one of the most elegant shopping streets in Germany. Primarily Düsseldorf breathes money, and is aptly dominated by three modern monuments as testament to its commercial success: the **Thyssen Skyscraper**, **Mannemann Haus** and the **TV Tower**.

The Romantic poet **Heinrich Heine** is Düsseldorf's most famous son, and his works are commemorated in the **Heinrich-Heine-Haus**, BILKERSTR. 12–14; ☎899 5571.

Most of the areas of interest are along the Rhine, itself spanned by the graceful **Rheinkniebrücke** (bridge) and with the **Rhine Tower** prominent on the skyline. Marked by the **SCHLOSSTURM**, all that remains of the original 14th-century castle, the **Altstadt** (Old Town), is small and walkable, covering no more than 1 square km. Almost wholly demolished during World War II, it has been skilfully reconstructed. Within it is **FLINGERSTR.,** a quaint pedestrianised shopping precinct, somewhat more affordable than KÖNIGSALLE. One of the most attractive corners is the **MARKTPLATZ,** brimming over with outdoor cafés and restaurants. A pedestrian zone that's a hive of entertainment around the clock, Altstadt has more than 200 bars crammed into its busy streets and claims to be 'the longest bar in the world'. At GRABBEPLATZ 5, ☎(0211) 838 910 is the **Kunstsammlung Nordrhein-Westfalen,** a museum of modern art with nearly 100 works by Paul Klee.

☎(0211) 19419: about 2 km from the east bank of the **Rhine**, where most places of interest are concentrated.

Main Tourist Office: IMMERMANNSTR. 65B; ☎(0211)172 020 (opposite Hbf). Mon–Fri 0830–1800 and Sat 0900–1230, http://www.duesseldorf.de. Room booking service Mon–Sat 0800–2200, Sun 1600–2200.

The **Düsseldorf Tourist Association (Verkehrsverein der Stadt Düsseldorf)**, KONRAD 041, is in the **Oberkassel** district, just over RHEINKNIEBRÜCKE (no. 835). The **campsite** is located cycling distance from town on a lake with a surprisingly resort-like atmosphere: **Lake Unterbach**, UNTERBACHER SEE, KLEINER TORFBRUCH.

ESSEN

Largely modern, Essen's spacious but compact centre has its pedestrianised areas enlivened by fountains. It's not a mega-sight: half a day will suffice to skim the highlights. Look into the **Essener Münster** (cathedral), founded in 852, for its splendid **Schatzkammer** (treasury). The **Alte Synagogue**, was the largest synagogue in northern Europe before being burned out in 1938. It is now a memorial and historical site, with a permanent and free exhibition on the Jewish persecution and the resistance in Essen. Pulling in the crowds is the artistic/scientific encounter known as **Meterorit**, in the **RWE Park**, (0201) 3206 7555, founded by the Austrian artist Andre Heller, who has set up an 'underground chamber of wonders, magical attractions and energy room'. The **Folkwang Museum**, GOETHESTR. 41, (0201) 884 5314, specialises in art of the 19th and 20th century. The **Design Zentrum Nordrehin Westfalen**, GELSENKIRCHENER STR 181, (0201) 301 040, designed by the British architect **Sir Norman Foster**, is a showplace for modern design.

RAIL (0201) 19 419; central, two blocks from the Münster.

Tourist Office: AM HAUPTBAHNHOF 2, (0201) 19 433. Mon–Fri 0900–1730 and Sat 1000–1300, directly north over the Ring from the main station; touristikzentrale@essen.de.

As this is a convention city, hotels are expensive, especially close to the centre. **Hotel Kessing**, HACHESTR. 30, (0201) 239 988, and **Hotel Lindenhof**, LOGENSTR. 18, (0201) 233 031 are more reasonable than most, at around DM60 per person. The Tourist Office can make reservations. **Youth hostel**: PASTORATSBERG 2, (0201) 491 163. **Campsite**: **Stadtcamping Essen Werden**, IM LOWENTAL 67, (0201) 492 978.

HANNOVER (HANOVER)

Ancestral home of the first four King Georges of England and capital of Lower Saxony, Hannover is the site of **Expo 2000,** and construction and reorganisation proceeds apace in preparation. The best way of getting to know the city is to follow the '**Der Rote Faden**' ('the Red Thread', a red line painted on the pavement that goes along a 4200-m (2-hr) path through the city centre and can be followed on foot; free maps of it from the Tourist Office. A huge **Schützenfest** (archery festival), featuring fireworks and parades, takes place in July.

From the station, BAHNHOFSTR. leads to the KRÖPCKE PIAZZA, in the heart of the largely reconstructed **Altstadt**; the **Kröpcke clock** is the most popular rendezvous in town. For shopping, head for GEORGSTRASSE, GALERIE LUISE and KRÖPCKE-PASSAGE.

The high-gabled, carefully restored **Altes Rathaus** is a splendid edifice with elaborate brickwork. Alongside is **Marktkirche**, with 14th–15th-century stained glass and a bulky tower that is the city's emblem.

Across town, over the FRIEDRICHSWALL, is the high-domed **Neues Rathaus** located in a pleasant garden and reflected in a small lake . Next door, the **Kestner Museum,** TRAMMPLATE 3; ☎168 2120, contains 'Hannover's most expensive head' (a 3000-year-old Egyptian bust). The wide-ranging **Landesmuseum**, AM MASCHSEEPARK 5, ☎98075, includes a fascinating archaeological section.

The absolute must-see is the **Royal Herrenhausen Garden**, 10 mins from Kropcke (U-bahn: HERRENHAUSERGARTEN; ☎0511 168 7576). It consists of four once-royal gardens, two of which are the English-style landscaped **Georgengarten** and the formal **Grosser Garten**, the scene of spectacular fountain displays in summer. Frequent musical and theatrical performances are staged in the palace and gardens.

☎(0511) 19419. Central location; follow the red line to the information office, open Mon–Sat 0900–1800. The Ernst-August Statue in front is a well-known landmark and meeting place.

Tourist Office: In the **Post Building**, ERNST-AUGUST-PLATZ 2 (next to Hbf (0511) 30140,
Hotline: ☎(0511).19433, fax: (0511) 301414, Mon–Fri 0830–1900; Sat 0830–1500 (closed Sun).
Also at the **Hannover Tourism Center**, THEODOR-HEUSS-PLATZ 1–3,
☎(0511) 811 3502 http://www.hannover.de/, hcc@hannover.de

DAY TRIPS FROM HANNOVER

Overlooked by a magnificent 16th-century castle, **Celle** (41 km north-east; hourly trains, taking 20 mins) rates among the best-preserved medieval towns in northern Germany.

The **youth hostel** is at WEGHAUSTR. 2, ☎(01541) 53208, while other room reservations can be made through the **Tourist Office**, MARKT 6, ☎(051) 411 212, fax: (051) 411 2459. **Hildesheim** (18 trains a day; 30 mins by train), 36 km south-east of Hannover, has the 11th-century **Dom** and **Michaelskirche** (St Michael's Church), both UNESCO World Heritage sites. The **Tourist Office** is at AM RATSBAUHOF, ☎(051 21) 19433.

The Tourist Office can make room reservations at all budget levels and also via the '**Hannover CitySoft**' booking system, at the Hannover Tourism Centre. Because so many conventions take place here, cheap accommodation is hard to find, although prices drop further away from the centre.

Youth hostels include **Stadheim der Naturfreunde**, HERMANN-BAHLSEN-ALLEE 8, ☎(0511) 691493, Line 3 direction LAHE or Line 7, towards FASANENKRUG; bus stop SPANNHAGENGARTEN. There's another branch at AM FAHRENHORSTFELDE 50, ☎(0511) 580537, Line 4, direction RODERBRUCH, bus stop MISBURGER STRASSE then 🚌no.124 to the end station (WALDFRIEDHOF). Both of these are around DM35, including breakfast. The **youth hostel** (reservations advisable) is at FERDINAND-WILHELM-FRICKE-WEG 1; ☎(0511) 131 7674 (U-bahn: 3/7/9 to FISCHERHOF)

DAY TRIPS FROM BRAUNSCHWEIG AND MAGDEBURG

Both of these cities are relatively characterless, but they make good starting points for a number of day trips.

Goslar (58 km south; 70 mins, hourly train services; ETT table 960) has a handsome, labyrinthine centre characterised by half-timbered and stone houses, its sheer architectural diversity being the key to its appeal. It gained its prosperity through silver and lead mining in the Middle Ages, and is now a UNESCO World Heritage site.The **Tourist Office** is open Mon–Fri 0915–1800, Sat 0930–1600; Sun 0930–1400 May–Oct; Mon–Fri 0915–1700, Sat 0930–1400 Nov–Apr.

Goslar is also the centre of the **Harz,** one of Germany's most scenic mountain regions. Until reunification, these hills – whose highest peak, the **Brocken,** rises to 1142 m – formed part of the border between the two Germanies and travel was restricted. The heart of the region is the **Hochharz National Park**, a 14,500-acre region of wooded slopes with some 10,000 miles of marked hiking trails.

WHERE NEXT FROM HANNOVER?

You can join the ***Hannover–Lübeck*** *route (p.241) here. Express* ***trains*** *(ETT table 900, 1 per hr) from Hannover to* ***Munich*** *enable you to stop off at* ***Würzburg*** *and join the route to* ***Passau*** *(p. 245) or travel up the* ***Rhine*** *via* ***Mainz*** *and* ***Koblenz***

THE HARZ MOUNTAIN RAILWAYS

Wernigerode is the northern terminus of Europe's most extensive narrow-gauge steam railway network. The **Harzer Schmalspurbahnen**: 131 km of scenic lines winding through the picturesque Harz mountains. The longest section of the network is the **Harzquerbahn**, 61 km of track between Wernigerode and Nordhausen, traversed by three trains in summer, two in winter. Some are drawn by 1950s steam locomotives, but some older engines are used for special trips.

The Harzquerbahn connects at Eisfelder Talmühle with the 52 km of the **Selketalbahn**, which runs through the scenic Selke valley. A branch line, the **Brockenbahn**, reopened in 1992 for the first time since World War II, and connects with the Harzquerbahn at Drei-Annen-Hohne, from which it ascends 19 km to the summit of Brocken mountain.

For timetables and fares, contact: **Harzer Schmalspurbahnen GmbH**, FRIEDRICHSTRASSE 151, D-38855 WERNIGERODE; ☎(3943) 558143, fax: (3943) 558148.

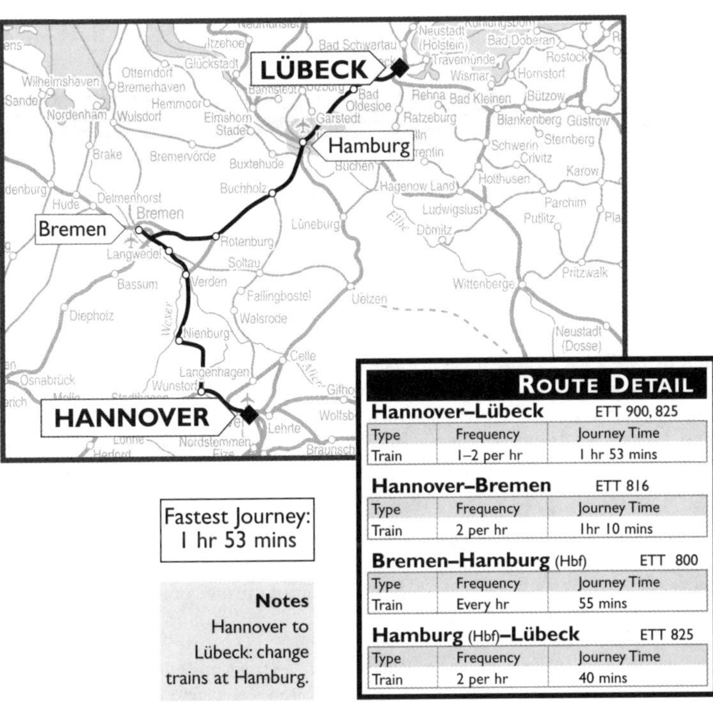

ROUTE DETAIL

Hannover–Lübeck ETT 900, 825

Type	Frequency	Journey Time
Train	1–2 per hr	1 hr 53 mins

Hannover–Bremen ETT 816

Type	Frequency	Journey Time
Train	2 per hr	1hr 10 mins

Bremen–Hamburg (Hbf) ETT 800

Type	Frequency	Journey Time
Train	Every hr	55 mins

Hamburg (Hbf)**–Lübeck** ETT 825

Type	Frequency	Journey Time
Train	2 per hr	40 mins

Fastest Journey:
1 hr 53 mins

Notes

Hannover to Lübeck: change trains at Hamburg.

HANNOVER – HAMBURG – LÜBECK

Hannover, easily accessible from Amsterdam and on the **Aachen–Berlin** route (p. 235), is the starting point for a tour of three great cities that were members of the great 14th- to 16th-century trading association known as the Hanseatic League – **Bremen, Hamburg** (p. 224) and **Lübeck**. Beyond Lübeck you can continue by a train that boards a ferry for a memorable entry into Denmark.

BREMEN

Bremen was a Hanseatic city and much of its 15th- and 16th-century structure survives – much of it quite Dutch-looking. Together with **Bremerhaven**, its outer harbour at the mouth of the Weser river, Bremen is one of the Länder (states) which make up Germany, continuing a proud tradition of self-government which dates back to the Middle Ages.

The **Altstadt**, on the north-east bank of the river, is the main area of historical interest. MARKTPLATZ is dominated by the **Rathaus**, a 15th-century structure overlaid with a Renaissance façade. It's worth joining a tour to see the splendid interior. In MARKTPLATZ are two notable statues. One is a 15th-century, 10-m-high portrait of **Roland** (Charlemagne's nephew), which is a symbol of the town's independence; legend has it that Bremen will remain free as long as he is standing. The other (which is modern and much smaller) illustrates the Grimm Brothers' fairy-tale about the **Four Musicians of Bremen** – a donkey, a dog, a cat and a rooster.

The 11th-century twin-spired **St Petri Dom**, SANDSTR. 10–12, is beautiful in a sombre way. In the **Bleikeller** (basement: open May–Oct) are some perfectly preserved corpses, believed to be of men who fell from the roof during construction, and saved from corruption by the lack of air.

To the south side of MARKTPLATZ is **Bottcherstr.**, a street that is an art deco fantasy from the 1920s. It houses craft workshops, restaurants, a casino and a musical clock that chimes three times a day: at 1200, 1500 and 1800.

The **Schnoorviertel** area (between the Dom and the river) consists of well-preserved 16th–18th-century buildings, many of which are now **craft shops**. Just to the east is **Kunsthalle**, AM WALL 207 (Tues 1000–2100, Wed–Sun 1000–1700), which has an eclectic collection of paintings and sculptures dating from the Renaissance to the present day.

Company tours, from businesses as varied as **Beck's Brewery,** ☎(0421) 5094 5555, to **Mercedes Benz,** ☎(0421) 419 2254, are available. Advance notice is required, and it is worth contacting the Tourist Office for times.

RAIL ☎(0421) 19419. Quite central, north of the main area of interest.

Tourist Office: HILLMANNPLATZ 6; (0421) 308 0038. Close to the station; open Mon–Thur 0930–1830, Fri 0930–2000, Sat 0930–1600, Sun 0930–1600.

Apartment Hotel Remberting, REMBERTING 49, (0421) 339 8676, offers rooms beginning at DM55. Prices at the **Haus Hanseatic Apartments**, FLEETRADE, (0421) 498 9280, start at DM45.The **youth hostel**, KALKSTR. 6, (0421) 171369, is on the western side of Altstadt; no. 26 or tram no. 6 to BRILL. **Campingplatz Bremen** is at AM STADTWALDSEE, (0421) 212002.

The Ratskeller (in the Rathaus) has been a bar since the early 15th century and offers 600 different wines, although it is quite pricey. Cheap eating places can be found on and around OSTERTORSTEINWEG. **Internet café**: HOHENTORSTR. 86, open 1000–0100, m_doerre@netwave.de. lines 24, 61–64 to HOEHNSTROPLATZ.

The **Bremer Kärtchen** gives two days' unlimited travel on all the city's buses and trams. With the exception of some museums, the places of interest cluster around **Markt-platz**. The **TouristCARD Bremen**, available for 2 days (DM19.50 for 1 person, DM35 for up to 5) or 3 days (DM26 and 46), provides free bus travel as well as significant discounts on the city's attractions. A **TouristCARD**, at DM9.50 for 2 adults and 2 children, offers the same without public transport.

LÜBECK

What's really impressive about **Lübeck** is the virtually seamless restoration of a large chunk of the old town: it's amazingly hard to spot what's rebuilt and what's original. Capital of the Hanseatic League, Lübeck has a striking range of architectural styles, but it's the stepped gables and tranquil, concealed courtyards that stay in the memory – there are fine old buildings on the waterfront. There's an excellent bus network, but most places of interest are in the 12th-century **Altstadt**, the moated old city.

Between the main station and Altstadt is Lübeck's emblem, the twin-towered **Holstentor**, which appears in motif form on the ubiquitous marzipan, the town's gastronomic speciality. It's a 15th-century structure, and now museum, that was one of the four city gates. The Altstadt, perched on an oval island, is a World Heritage Site. Get your bearings by taking the lift up the 50-m spire of the Gothic **Petrikirche** (itself now an art gallery). Nearby, **Museum für Puppentheater**, KLEINE PETERSGRUBE 4–6, is devoted to theatrical puppets from all over the world, while behind the façades of 22 handsome houses in GROSSE PETERSGRUBE is the **Music Academy**. Both places give regular public performances.

The Marktplatz is dominated by the striking L-shaped 13th- to 16th-century **Rathaus**, typical of Lübeck's architectural style of alternating red unglazed and black glazed bricks, a style copied by the Dutch and more common in Holland. Opposite the east wing is **Niederegger Haus**, BREITESTR., renowned for displays of **marzipan** (the town has been producing it since the Middle Ages and sells the sweet in an endless number of varieties). Opposite the north wing is the 13th-century **Marienkirche**, a brick-built Gothic church with square towers that was the model for many in the area. Later embellishments were damaged in the war and ignored in the restoration. It contains a magnificent gilded altarpiece dating from 1518.

Buddenbrookhaus, the inspiration for Thomas Mann's Lübeck-based saga of the same name, is a museum at MENGSTR. 4.

To the south of Altstadt is the large brick-built **Dom**, which contains an allegorical triumphal arch and ornate rood screen.

WHERE NEXT FROM LÜBECK?

Carry on north-east into Denmark (ETT tables 720, 825), crossing the border in spectacular style bey-owherend Puttgarden, where the trains follow the tracks onto ferries; continue on to Copenhagen (p. 408).

RAIL (0451) 19419. 10 mins' walk west of Altstadt.

Tourist Offices: There's a small office in the station which offers a room-booking service, (0451) 864675; open Mon–Sat 0900–1300, 1500–1800. There is another office at HOLSTENTOR PASSAGE (0451) 72339, open Mon–Fri 1030–1830, Sat–Sun 1000–1400.

There are several reasonably priced hotels around the main station **(Hbf)**. Private rooms are also available, e.g. **Frau Nickel** at **Historiches Altstadt-Ferienhaus**, ENGELSGRUBE 61, (0451) 593139, with all facilities, starting at DM80 for a double, or **Frau Andresen** G. ALTEFAHRE 17, (0451) 74395, from DM35 per person. **HI**: AM GETRUDENKIRCHOF 4, (0451) 33433, north-east of **Burgtor** (nos. 1 / 3 from HBF). The YMCA (CVJM) runs a **Sleep-In**, GROSSE BURGSTRASSE 9–11; (0451) 71920.

Route Detail

Cologne–Passau ETT table 920

Type	Frequency	Journey Time
Train	4 per day	6 hrs 35 mins

Cologne–Bonn ETT tables 910, 912

Type	Frequency	Journey Time
Local Train	Frequent	30 mins

Bonn–Koblenz ETT tables 910, 912

Type	Frequency	Journey Time
Train	3 per hr	1 hr

Koblenz–Frankfurt ETT table 910

Type	Frequency	Journey Time
Train	Every hr	1 hr 20 mins

Frankfurt–Würzburg ETT table 920

Type	Frequency	Journey Time
Train	Every hr	1 hr 10 mins

Würzburg–Nuremburg ETT table 920

Type	Frequency	Journey Time
Train	Every hr	57 mins

Nuremburg–Regensburg ETT table 920

Type	Frequency	Journey Time
Train	1–2 per hr	1 hr 10 mins

Regensburg–Passau ETT table 920

Type	Frequency	Journey Time
Train	Every hr	1 hr 10 mins

Fastest Journey:
6 hrs 39 mins

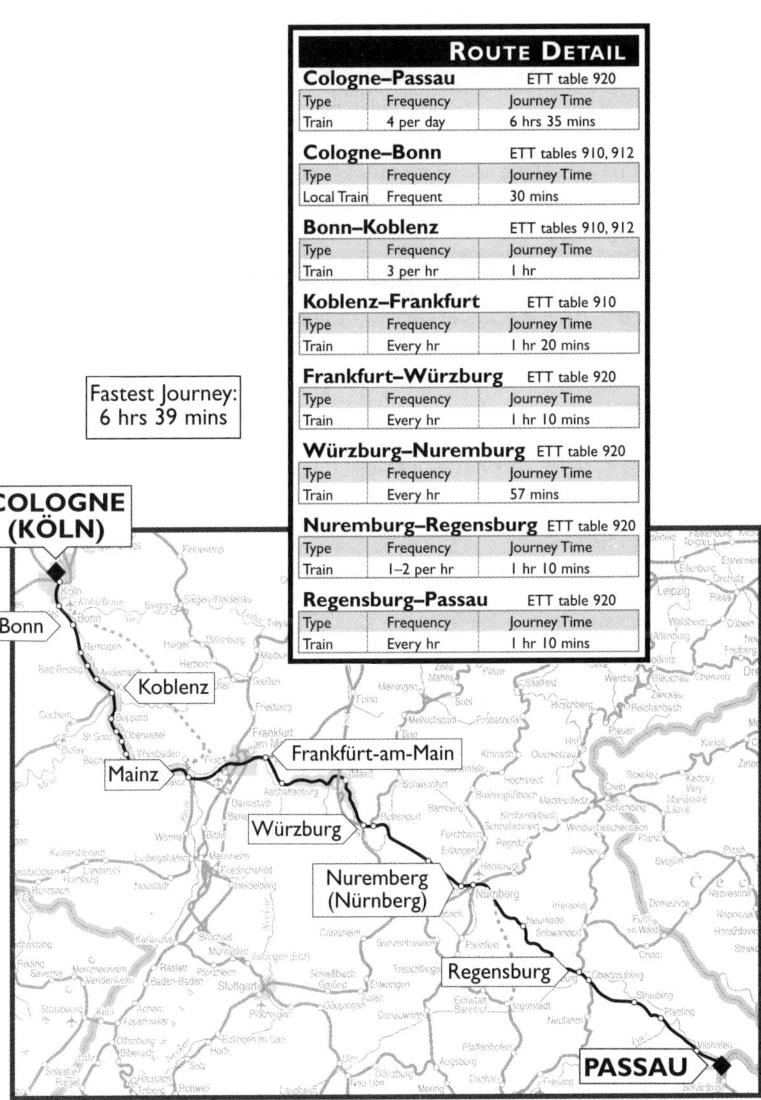

COLOGNE – WÜRZBURG – PASSAU

Leaving **Cologne**, Germany's fourth city, the train takes you past **Bonn**, Beethoven's birthplace, and along the best of the **Rhine valley**, one of the country's classic rail journeys, with castles clinging to the slopes and a series of waterside towns and villages. Sit on the left (east) side for the best views. Beyond **Mainz** the scene briefly becomes less appealing, taking in the high-rise commercial centre of **Frankfurt**. This route enters **Bayern** (Bavaria) – Germany's south-eastern state – at **Aschaffenburg**. South-eastern Bavaria is a relatively little-visited corner of the country; **Passau** stands on a neck of land between two rivers, the **Il** and the **Danube,** and at the threshold of **Austria**.

COLOGNE (KÖLN)

During World War II, nine-tenths of what was Germany's largest *Altstadt* (old town) was flattened by bombing, and the quality of reconstruction has been patchy.

KARNEVAL

During early spring, Cologne hosts Karneval, one of Europe's greatest street celebrations. This week-long festival precedes Lent.

The twin spires of one of the world's greatest gothic cathedrals soar over the Rhineland capital, Germany's fourth city and busiest railway junction. For DM3, you can climb the tower and look down on the city.

The city's Roman traces include remnants of the original, 5th-century-AD city wall. The superlative **Romisch-Germanisches Museum**, RONCALLIPL. 4, holds many of the finds of the ancient town, including an arched fortress gate and the famous **Dionysus Mosaic**.

From 321 until 1424, the city was home to one of the most important Jewish communities in Germany. The remains of a *mikvah* (a Jewish ritual bath) dating from 1170 are preserved under a glass pyramid in the middle of the square of the City Hall. Nearby, in BISCHOFSGARTENSTR., is a modern complex incorporating a trio of outstanding museums: Agfa-Foto-Historama, covering all things photographic, with cameras and a large collection of photos; the **Wallraf-Richartz-Museum**, with superb 14th–16th century paintings by the Cologne school; and the **Museum Ludwig**, housing 20th-century works.

NIGHT-TIME

Nightlife ranges from the latest dance clubs to cool jazz spots (the Altstadt is the best area for music). Cologne also has a strong reputation for classical music and opera, with hundreds of performances a year in top venues, including the modern Opera House and the fine Philharmonie concert house close to the cathedral.

RAIL ☎(0221) 19419, centrally placed, right by the cathedral; currently being converted into a huge shopping centre. Information desk and a 24-hr service point; station closes 0100–0400; coffee shop, snack bar and left luggage.

✈ **Flughafen Köln–Bonn**, south-east of the city. **Information** ☎(02203) 40401/404605. 🚌no. 170 connects the airport with the rail station in 20 mins, running every 15 mins 0700–2000 (every 30 mins earlier and later), fare DM7.70.

Tourist Office: UNTER FETTENHENNEN 19; ☎(0221) 221 3345, fax: (0221) 221 3320, by the Dom. May–Oct: Mon–Sat 0800–2230, Sun 0900–2230; Nov–Apr: Mon–Fri 0800–2100, Sun 0930–1900 (http://www.koeln.de or www/cologne.de).
Main post office: BREITER STR., in the WDR ARCADEN.
Money: **Thomas Cook foreign exchange**: IM METRO MARKT, OTTO-HAHN-STR. ☎2236 942424; KOMOEDIENSTR. 7 ☎(0221) 202080; **City-Center Chorweiler**, MAILUENDER PASSAGE 1; ☎(0221) 9700 300.

GETTING AROUND COLOGNE

The comprehensive public transport system includes U-Bahn (underground/ subway),
S-Bahn (surface suburban trains), trams and buses.
A **24-hr ticket** costs around DM15–16.

Central rooms are almost always at a premium and the cheap hotels are very scattered. Book ahead. The **Tourist Office** has a separate advance booking number, ☎/fax: (0221) 33 20, and charges DM6 for a reservation. **Cheaper hotels** include: **Am Rathaus**, BURGERSTR. 6, ☎(0221) 257 7624; **Ariane**, HOHE PFORTE 19/21, ☎(0221) 236033, and **Brandenburger Hof**, BRANDENBURGER STR. 225, ☎(0221) 122889, all with single rooms beginning at DM50. The more central of the two **youth hostels** is SIEGESSTR. 5A; ☎(0221) 814711, 15-min walk from the station, over the HOHENZOLLERNBRÜCKE, a couple of blocks south of Deutz station. The second hostel is at **Köln-Riehl**, ANDER SCHANZ 14, ☎(0221) 767081. The most accessible **campsite** is **Camping an der Stadt**, POLL; ☎(0221) 083 1966, south-east of ALTSTADT (tram 16: MARIENBURG) or a pleasant 30-min walk along the Rhine from the cathedral.

Balanced between the beer-drinking north and the wine lands of the south, Cologne has the best of both worlds. The renowned food and drink of this area of the Rhineland are distinctive. A typical dish is *Sauerbraten*, a 'sour roast', with beef soaked in vinegar and stewed, served with *Reibekuchen* (potato pulp) and apple sauce. The local sweet Rhine wine is *suuren Hungk* ('sour dog'). *Blootwoosch* (blood sausage) makes a snack served with mustard on a bread roll, known as 'Cologne caviar'. This could be washed down with *Kölsch* (also the name of the local dialect), the local surface-fermented beer made with a special yeast, no less than 8% alcoholic content: it's produced at all of the city's 24 breweries – no other German city has so many. The **Kvartier Lateng** (BARBAROSA PLATZ), Underground line 12 and 16, and the **Südstadt** are where most of the student hangouts are.

BAD GODESBURG

south of Bonn city centre on the same side of the Rhine, is dominated by **Godesburg**, the most northerly of the Rhine castles. The old keep is intact and provides panoramic views. This suburb is where most of the diplomats used to reside; you can sneak good back-garden views from the river.

BONN

Now that the capital status has reverted to Berlin, musical pilgrims beating a path to Beethoven's birthplace are likely to become the town's mainstay. The great composer is also remembered in the modern **Beethovenhalle**. The **Geburtshaus** (house of birth), where he spent the first 22 years of his life, is at BONNGASSE 20 (Mon–Sat 1000–1700, Apr–Sept; 1000–1600, winter; and contains his instruments and a rather sad collection of ear trumpets as testament to his irreversible decline towards total deafness.

On the other side of the rail station, the **Rheinisches Landesmuseum,** COLMANTSTR. 14–16, exhibits a 60,000-year-old Neanderthal skull, discovered in 1856, near a village close to Düsseldorf, as well as Celtic gold from the La Tene era.

The **Museum Meile** (Museum Mile) is a complex outside the city centre, easily reached by Underground lines 16, 63 or 66 (stop HEUSSALLE/MUSEUMMEILE) or nos. 610 or 630 (stop BUNDESKANZLERPLAT). It includes the **Kunsthalle** (for art exhibitions), the **Städtisches Kunstmuseum** (the city art gallery), the **Zoological Institute** and the **Haus der Geschichte**, ADENAUERALLEE 250, a new hi-tech museum on the history of Germany (free entry).

RAIL (0228) 19419, beside the bus terminal and right in the centre, on the edge of the pedestrian precinct.

i **Tourist Office**: CASSIUS PASSAGE, MÜNSTERSTR. 20; (0228) 773466 or 19433, fax (0228) 690368. Open Mon–Fri 0900–1830, Sat 0900–1700, Sun 1000–1400. There is a hotel booking service: (0228) 910 4160 (http://www.bonn-region.de, e-mail: info@tourcon-bonn.de).

Beethoven, RHEINGASSE 26, (0228) 631411, and **Bergmann**, KASERNENSTR. 12, (0228) 633891, both offer rooms from DM60. Nearby **Bad Godesberg** can be cheaper, with **Gästehaus Scholz**, ANNETTENSTR. 16, (0228) 379363, starting at DM40. **Youth hostel**: **Jugendgasthaus Bonn-Venusberg**, HAAGET WEG 42, (0228) 281200.
The **campsites** are outside Bonn, although **Campingplatz 'Genienaue'** is in Bad Godesberg, IM FRANKENKELLER 49, (0228) 344949.

KOBLENZ

The Mosel and Rhine rivers meet here at the **Deutsches Eck** (the German Corner), marked by a massive, heavy-handed monument to Kaiser Wilhelm I. Although originally a memorial to the Kaiser erected by his wife, the edifice was later to become a symbol of German unity. The significance increased at the time of reunification in 1989. The pleasant gardens along both rivers combine to provide an attractive 8 km stroll.

Ehrenbreitstein (across the Rhine, ferries in summer) is dominated by an enormous fortress, the **Festung**. Its earliest fortifications date from the 12th century, but it grew to its present size during the 16th century. The **Sesselbahn** (cable car) operates May–Oct. As well as providing a fantastic view, the fortress contains two regional museums and a youth hostel (see below). A big firework display (**Rhein in Flammen**) is staged here on the second Sat in Aug.

RAIL BAHNHOFPLATZ 2; ☎(0261) 19419. South-west of the centre, 25-min walk downhill (or 🚌no. 1) to the riverside area from which cruises (*Rheinfähre*) depart.

i **Tourist Offices**: opposite rail station; ☎(0261) 31304. Mon–Fri 0900–2000, Sat–Sun 1000–2000, May–Sept; Mon–Fri 0900–1800, Sat–Sun 1000–1800, Oct; Mon–Fri 0900–1800 (closed weekends), Nov–9 April; and Mon–Fri 0900–1800, Sat–Sun 1000–1800, 10–30 Apr (http://www.koblenz.de). It provides boat schedules and a city map that includes listings. There is another **Tourist Office** by the docks, KONRAD-ADENAUER-UFER (Tues–Sat 1200–1800, June–Sept,).

Jan van Werth, V.-WERTH-STR. 9, ☎(0261) 36500, has rooms from DM35–60 per person per night, while the **National**, ROONSTR. 47, ☎(0261) 14194, begins at DM55. The **youth hostel** is housed in the **Festung** (see above), ☎(0261) 73737, and is popular, so book well ahead. The downside is that the ferry and chair lift both stop very early so, after taking a bus (🚌nos. 7/8/9/10) to CHARLOTTENSTR., you end the day with a long uphill climb. An alternative is the nearby **Mockler**, HELFENSTEINSTR. 63–65, ☎(0261) 73725, which has rooms at a comparable price (DM30).
The **campsite** is at **Lutzel**, across the Mosel: CAMPINGPLATZ RHEIN-MOSEL, ☎(0261) 802489. There's a ferry across during the day.

Some of the best bargains for food are to indulge in the *Stehcafés* (standing cafés) and *Biergartens* on the banks of the Rhine, directly at the **Deutsches Eck**.

FRANKFURT-AM-MAIN

Frankfurt, the country's financial capital as well as a major convention centre, is not a pretty place, with massive office blocks asserting their presence, and the crime rate is relatively high; but traffic-free boulevards of shops, parks and the leafy banks of the River Main, which flows through the centre, make the city surprisingly pleasant for strolling around.

Affectionately known as the *gut Stubb* (front parlour), ROEMERBERG, a square of half-timbered and steeply gabled buildings, is at the heart of the *Altstadt* (old town). Along one side is the **Röemer,** the city's town

DAY TRIP FROM KOBLENZ

TRIER

ETT table 915.

Worth a substantial detour for its Roman and early Christian remains, Trier is Germany's oldest city, dating back to 16 BC. The focal point is the **Porta Nigra** (Black Gate), one of the most impressive Roman structures in northern Europe and standing to its original height. You can also see Emperor Constantine's throne room and part of a Roman street in the huge **Konstantin-Basilika**, KONSTANTINPL., part of the imperial palace, and the largest surviving single-hall structure of the ancient world. Backing onto it is the picture-perfect pink, white and gold rococo **Kurfürstliches Palais** in gardens with fountains (and a café). This area leads directly to the **Rheinisches Landesmuseum**, OSTALLEE 44 (at the southern end of the pleasant and well-tended **Palastgarten**), which contains Roman remains. Close by are the **Kaiserthermen**, a huge complex of well-preserved imperial baths, and the **Amphitheatre** (c. AD100), where crowds of up to 20,000 watched gladiatorial

Day trips from Koblenz cont'd.

combat. The **Bischofliches Museum**, WIND-STR., has medieval statuary, sacred art, models of the Roman cathedral and Roman frescos.

The **Karl-Marx-Haus Museum**, BRÜCKENSTR. 10, gives an exhibition on Marx's work and life, in the house in which he was born. Trier's Renaissance **Marktplatz** is outstanding even by German standards.

hall, meticulously restored as it was in the Middle Ages.

A short walk to the east leads to **Kaiserdom,** DOMSTR., the red-sandstone Gothic cathedral, with its dome and lantern tower, where the emperors were crowned.

Frankfurt was the birthplace of Germany's most famous writer, Goethe. The **Goethe Haus,** GROSSE HIRSCHGRABEN 23, is a careful post-war reconstruction of the house where he was born in 1749.

It is furnished in period style and has a museum with manuscripts and documents next to it.

A recent addition to Frankfurt's famous zoo, **Zoologischer Garten,** ALFRED-BREHMPL (U-Bahn 6 to ZOO), which was founded in 1858, is the **Grzimek-Haus,** where nocturnal animals can be observed in daytime.

To the north (U-bahn 7/8 to WESTEND) are the extensive botanical gardens, **Palmengarten**, ZEPPELIN ALLEE, with lily ponds and conservatories of orchids and cacti.

Eleven of the city's forty museums are gathered on the south bank of the river along SCHAUMAINKAI, known as **Museumsufer** (Museum Bank).

RAIL **Hauptbahnof** (Hbf), Europe's busiest rail terminus, opens 24 hrs and has good cafés and shops. There's an airport-style lounge, with bar, armchairs and toys. S-Bahn and U-Bahn services. ☎(069) 19419. The city centre is a 15-min walk straight ahead along KAISERSTR.

✈ **Flughafen Frankfurt-Main** (9 km south-west of the city) is central Europe's busiest airport. ☎(069) 6901 (http://www.frankfurt-airport.de). S-Bahn suburban trains (service S8) to Frankfurt Hbf, the city's main station, leave every 10 mins from 0430 to 0030; the journey takes 11 mins and costs DM5.80. InterCity rail services to Cologne, Dortmund, Hamburg and Nuremberg stop at the airport station hourly; ☎(069) 19419.

NIGHT-TIME AND EVENTS

Frankfurt's entertainment spans everything from the latest dance craze to the best of classical concerts, opera, theatre, cinema and cabaret. For detailed information on the city's cultural scene consult the Info-Hotline: ☎(069) 2123 8800.

The **Main Fair** (usually the first week in Aug) takes over the streets UNTERMAINKAI and MAINKAI, along the north bank of the river from the RÖEMERBERG to UNTERMAINKAIBRÜECKE. Its centrepiece is a big funfair surrounded by beer and wine stalls, and it ends with a huge firework display over the river. In Apr and Sept the **Dippemess**, a traditional folk fair, is in RATSWEG and FESTPL. Open-air concerts are part of the **Museumsuferfest** at the end of Aug.

Tourist Office: **Tourismus + Congress GmbH** is at FRANKFURTER HAUPTBAHNHOF (Hbf) station, ☎(069) 2123 8800 (Mon–Fri 0800–2100, Sat–Sun 0900–1800; http://www.tcf.frankfurt.de; e-mail: info@tcf.frankfurt.de). Hotel booking service, ☎(069) 2123 0808. **Other branches**: in the city centre at RÖMERBERG 27 (Mon–Fri 0900–1730, Sat–Sun 1000–1600), and in **Zeil** at BROCKHAUSBRUNNEN, (Mon–Fri 1000–1800, Sat 1000–1600).

Cheap, no-frills **pensions** are found around the rail station. Inexpensive accommodation includes Europe's biggest **youth hostel**, **Haus der Jugend**, by the river at DEUTSCHERMUFER 12, ☎(069) 619058. Mid-range accommodation can be in short supply during the main trade fairs. The **Aller**, GUTLEUSTR. 23, is near the rail station and has rooms from DM67.50. The **Am Berg**, GRETHENWEG 23, is further away near the Sudbahnhof (on the U-bahn). **Campsite**: **Hedderheim**, near the Hedderheim U-Bahn station (lines 1–3).

A range of national cuisines are represented; the city also has a plentiful choice of *Lokale* (taverns) serving local and regional treats like *Eisbein* (stewed pork knuckle), *Handkäse mit Musik* (sour cheese garnished with chopped onions and caraway seeds) and *Sauerkraut*. Above all, of course, there's the original **frankfurter** – long, thin and at its tastiest eaten at a *Schnell Imbiss* (street stall) in a really fresh roll. You'll find a good selection of restaurants along FRESSGASSE and the narrow streets running north off it. For the more informal *Lokale*, head south of the river to the **Sachsenhausen** district, particularly streets like SCHWEITZERSTR., or the cobbled GROSS RITTERGASSE and KLEINE RITTERGASSE. The city's own beverage is apple wine, called *Apfelwein* (nicknamed *Stoeffche)* a deceptively strong variety of cider. *Hocheimer* (hock) is wine from municipal vineyards.

GETTING AROUND FRANKFURT

Travel within Frankfurt is easy, with an efficient combination of S-Bahn (overground) and U-Bahn (underground) trains, trams and buses all run by **RMV**, the regional transport authority. Directions to the system, in six languages, including English, are on the blue automatic ticket machines at all bus stops, tram stops and stations. **Transport information**: ☎2130.

Buy **tickets** (valid for all RMV transportation) at newspaper booths and blue automat machines. A single ticket costs DM2.80 for short distances (longer trips are DM3.50), or DM8 for a day pass. The **Frankfurt Card**, available from Tourist Offices, gives unlimited travel on all public transport, including local and S-Bahn trains to the airport, as well as half-price admission to fifteen museums and the zoo; DM10 for one day, or DM15 for two.

To book a taxi, ☎230001, 250001, 230033 or 545011. A short city-centre ride costs about six times as much as a single RMV ticket. Bikes can be hired at the rail station.

WHERE NEXT FROM FRANKFURT?

Frankfurt is a major international rail junction and has direct services to ***Amsterdam*** *(ETT table 28),* ***Vienna*** *(table 28),* ***Paris*** *(table 30),* ***Prague*** *(table 30),* ***Moscow*** *(table 55),* ***Warsaw*** *via* ***Kraków*** *(table 56) and* ***Ventimiglia*** *via* ***Avignon, Marseille*** *and* ***Nice*** *(table 79).*

WÜRZBURG

See p. 270.

NUREMBERG (NÜRNBERG)

Tragically Hitler chose Nuremberg, one of the greatest historical cities in all Europe, to hold his mass rallies. Post-war reconstruction has been piecemeal. Some of the most historic sites were re-created with meticulous care, and it's hard to tell that they're not original. However, much of the remaining infill is dully modern.

Heading north from the station, you immediately enter the old town, which is surrounded by a 5km **Stadtbefestigung** (city wall). Beyond the much-photographed **Schöner Brunnen** (Beautiful Fountain), the spacious **Hauptmarkt** (market square) makes a perfect setting for one of Germany's liveliest Christmas markets during December.

For a good view of the whole city, seek out the terraces of the **Kaiserburg** fortifications above the north-west corner of the old town. Just below it nestles Nuremberg's prettiest corner, including the gabled **Dürerhaus**. Here the artist Albrecht Dürer lived from 1509 until his death in 1528; it's now furnished in period style and contains several of his woodcuts.

Hitler's mass rallies in the 1930s were held in the vast **Reichsparteitagsgelände**, a huge area with a vast parade ground, stadium and the shell of a massive congress hall which was never completed. One of the parts that remain, the Zeppelin grandstand, ZEPPELINSTR. (S-Bahn to FRANKENSTADION, a 15-min ride), contains a moving exhibition called *Faszination und Gewalt* (Fascination and Terror).

After World War II, the surviving Nazi leaders were put on trial in the city's court, FÜRTHERSTR. 110, on the western outskirts (S-Bahn 2 or tram no. 4). The Tourist Office has a free brochure describing the *Nazionalsozialismus Movement* in Nuremberg in 1933–45.

RAIL ☎(0911) 19419, on the southern edge of the old town centre, 5 mins to HAUPTMARKT via the underpass.

i **Tourist Office**: In the station, ☎(0911) 233 6132, Mon–Sat 0900–1900. **Branch**: HAUPTMARKT 18, ☎(0911) 233 6135, Mon–Sat 0900–1800; also Sun 1000–1300, 1400–1600 (May–Sept); http://www.virtualnuernberg.de. **Accommodation booking service**, DM5.

Gasthof Zum Schwanlein, HINTERE STERNGASSE 11, ☎(0911) 225 1620 and **Vater Jahn**, JAHNSTRASSE 13, ☎(0911) 440507, both offer rooms beginning at DM40–60. **Youth hostel**: BURG 2; ☎(0911) 230936, in the castle (U-Bahn to PLÄRRER, then tram no.4). Booking advisable. **Campsite**: **Dutzendteich**, HANS KALBSTR. 56; ☎(0911) 811122; (tram no. 12).

WHERE NEXT FROM NUREMBERG?

*Join the **Munich–Berlin** route (p. 267) by taking the scenic line north via **Jena**; through trains from **Nuremberg** to **Berlin** via **Leipzig** take 8 hrs 15 mins (ETT table 850), and run every 2 hrs.*

The TIERGARTENPLATZ is a good place to go in the evenings, with music, night life and drinking. Don't forget to taste some *Lebkuchen* (spiced honey cakes), a local speciality that although imported throughout the world, is still best here (try **Dull-Spezialtäten**, BERGSTR. 23, near the **Dürerhaus**). *Bratwurst* and cod typically appear on the menu in the city's restaurants.

REGENSBURG

Above the Danube, with the knobbly twin towers of the grey stone **cathedral** dominant on the skyline, and a cheerful huddle of stone houses and red roofs, Regensburg claims to be the largest city in Germany to have escaped bombing in World War II. Rather less manicured than the German norm, it has preserved its medieval character particularly well. Pretty pastel plasterwork, in pinks, yellows and greens, and decorative towers on many of the former patrician houses in the narrow streets lend it a southern feel. Originally the city was divided into three areas where, respectively, the princes, churchmen and merchants lived.

The town had strong trading links with Venice in the 13th century, when its merchants grew rich from the selling of silk, spices and slaves. They competed to have the biggest house (often incorporating its own chapel) in the style of an Italian fortified palace with the highest tower on top – these were never defensive, just status symbols. The most striking of the 20 surviving towers is the **Baumburger Turm,** WATMARKT, though the highest is the 9-storey **Goldener Turm,** WAHLENSTR. Some of the chapels have been turned into restaurants but the tiny **Maria-Läng Kapelle,** PFARRGASSE, is still in use.

Domstadt, the church area, centres on ***Dom St Peter,*** the magnificent gothic cathedral; started in the 13th century, its 105-m spires were completed six centuries later. It has fine stained-glass, medieval and modern, and its own interior well. Look out for quirky details such as the tiny stone carvings of the devil and his grandmother just inside the main entrance – a warning to those stepping outside – and a laughing angel near the transept.

(0941) 19419, 10 mins' walk from the historic centre, or take nos.1/2/6.

Tourist Office: ALTES RATHAUS, KOHLENMARKT; (0941) 507 4410. Located in a 14th-century building; open Mon–Fri 0830–1800, Sat 0900–1600; also Sun 0930–1430 (0930–1600, Apr–mid Oct): (http://www.regensburg.de; e-mail: tourismus@infor.regensburg.baynet.de).
Accommodation booking service: 24-hr room vacancy information, (0941) 19414.

Müenchnerhof, TAENDLERGASSE 9, (0941) 58440 (moderate), is centrally located near the cathedral. Cheaper alternatives include **Dioezesanzentrum Obermunster**, OBERMUNSTERPL. 7, (0941) 568 1249, and **Apollo**, NEUPRULL 17, (0941) 91500, both around DM50–55. **Youth hostel**: WOHRDSTR. 60, (0941) 57402, on an island in the Danube, 5-min walk from the centre (no.5 to WEISSENBURGSTR). **Campsite**: **Azur**, WEINWEG 40, (0941) 270025.

The town claims to have the highest proportion of restaurants and bars per head of population in Germany. Thanks to the presence of several student residences in the centre (a deliberate policy by the town council), many are reasonably priced. The 850-year-old **Historische Wurstküche**, WEISSELAMMGASSE 3, beside the Danube, is Germany's oldest sausage house and sells nothing else; note the awesomely high flood-marks on the walls. **Alte Linde Biergarten**, MULLERSTR. 1, on an island in the river, is a lovely beer garden overlooking the old town.

PASSAU

'Living on three rivers' at the point where the Danube, Inn and Ilz come together, this captivating cathedral city on the Austrian border has plenty of scope for waterside walks and cruises on the Danube. With the exception of the **Veste Oberhaus**, a castle high on a hill across the Danube, everything of interest is within close range.

The oldest part lies between the Danube and Inn; most of it postdates a major 17th-century fire and is an enjoyable jumble of colour-washed stone walls, assorted towers, and baroque, rococo and neoclassical styles. Like Regensburg, it's rather Italian in feel. The lofty onion-domed **Stephansdom** (St Stephen's Cathedral) is home to the world's largest church organ (over 17,000 pipes); try to catch a concert (weekdays 1230, May–Oct).

Veste Oberhaus, the former palace of the bishops and a prison for their enemies, is on a peninsula between the Danube and the narrower River Ilz. To avoid the steep walk up, use the regular bus services from the rail station and RATHAUSPL. The stronghold, which offers good photo opportunities over the confluence of the rivers, now contains the **Cultural History Museum** (54 rooms of art and artefacts spanning two millennia) as well as changing exhibitions. Another, more accessible viewpoint is the **Fünfersteg** footbridge, looking over the Inn towards the **Innstadt** on the opposite bank.

RAIL (0851) 19419, west of the centre, a 10-min walk to the right along BAHNHOFSTR., or take nos. 7/8/9 (Mon–Fri 0630–1830).

Tourist Offices: **Main office:** RATHAUSPL. 3; (0851) 955980. Open Mon–Fri 0830–1800, Sat–Sun 1000–1200, 1230–1400 (Easter–mid Oct); Mon–Thur 0830–1700, Fri till 1600 (mid Oct–Easter). **Branch**: opposite the rail station: turn left and cross the road. Open Mon–Fri 0900–1700 and Sat–Sun 1000–1400 (Easter–mid Oct); Mon–Thur 0900–1700, Fri till 1600 (mid Oct–Easter); e-mail: http://www.passau.de; tourist-info@passau.de.

The inexpensive **Hotel Deutscher Kaiser**, BAHNHOFSTR. 30, (0851) 955 6615, from about DM50, is opposite the station. The **Pension Rossner**, BRÄUGASSE 19, (0851) 931350, about DM60, is much more interestingly sited, near the confluence

WHERE NEXT FROM PASSAU?

Continue into Austria from Passau to Linz (10 trains, taking 1 hr 15 mins; ETT table 920), joining the ***Innsbruck–Vienna*** *route* *on p. 318.*

with a pleasant terrace facing the castle across the Danube. There are also cheaper **guesthouses** and **private rooms** available (see Tourist Office brochure).
Youth hostel: **Auf der Veste**, OBERHAUS 125; ☎(0851) 41351, is in the castle across the Danube. Cross the bridge by the docks and be prepared for a steep climb, or take the bus from RATHAUSPL. to the door. **Campsite**: HALSERSTR. 34, ☎(0851) 41457, by the River Ilz (🚌 nos. 1/2/3/4).

Reasonably-priced restaurants spill out onto the promenades beside the Danube in summer, particularly around RATHAUSPL.

ROUTE DETAIL

München–Konstanz ETT tables 935, 939

Type	Frequency	Journey Time
Train	Every 2 hrs	5 hr 10 mins

München–Augsburg ETT table 900

Type	Frequency	Journey Time
Train	3-4 every hr	35 mins

Augsburg–Ulm ETT tables 900, 930

Type	Frequency	Journey Time
Train	2-3 every hr	42 mins

Ulm–Stuttgart ETT table 930

Type	Frequency	Journey Time
Train	2-3 every hr	1 hr

Stuttgart–Heilbronn ETT table 921

Type	Frequency	Journey Time
Train	Every hr	46 mins

Heilbronn–Heidelburg ETT table 924

Type	Frequency	Journey Time
Train	2 per hr	55 mins

Heidelburg–Karlsruhe ETT table 910

Type	Frequency	Journey Time
Train	1-2 per hr	32 mins

Karlsruhe–Baden-Baden ETT table 910

Type	Frequency	Journey Time
Train	1-2 per hr	20 mins

Baden-Baden–Offenburg ETT table 910

Type	Frequency	Journey Time
Train	Every hr	25 mins

Offenburg–Triberg ETT table 916

Type	Frequency	Journey Time
Train	Every hr	40 mins

Triberg–Konstanz ETT table 916

Type	Frequency	Journey Time
Train	Every hr	1 hr 20 mins

Fastest Journey:
5 hrs 10 mins

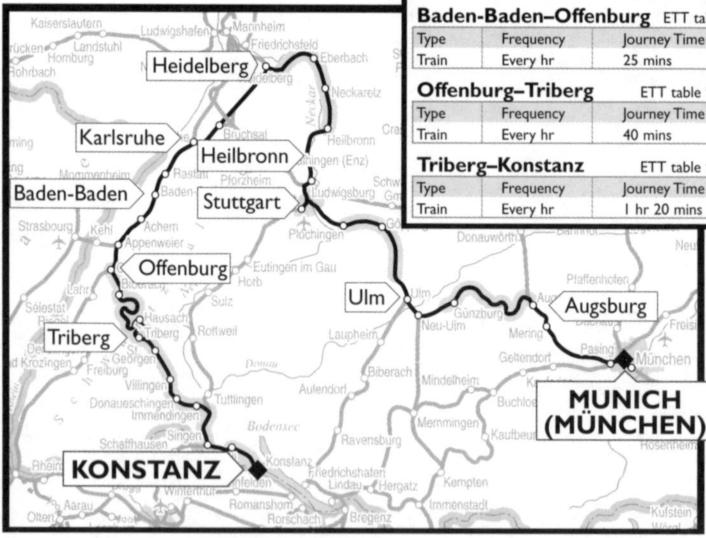

The scenic highpoint of this excursion to Germany's south-western corner is the Schwarzwaldbahn, the railway that crosses the lofty massif of the Black Forest, eventually reaching Konstanz, on the Lake (*Bodensee*) Constance at the border with Austria and Switzerland. The prelude is no less distinguished, leading out to the beautifully sited old university town of **Heidelberg** via **Augsburg** and **Ulm**. You can shorten the route by going directly from **Stuttgart** to **Konstanz**, taking in the perfect-looking hill town of **Rottweil**.

AUGSBURG

Within sprawling industrial outskirts is the attractive old heart of the city, originally fashioned in the 16th century by two wealthy trading and banking families, the Welsers and Fuggers. The main sights are within walking distance of the central pedestrianised RATHAUSPL, with its distinctive onion-domed **Rathaus** (painstakingly rebuilt after World War II). There's a great view from the adjoining **Perlachturm** (70 m), the tower of the **Peterskirche,** beside it.

A short stroll east down narrow alleys and over three small canals leads to the **Fuggerei,** a pioneering 'village' that the Fugger brothers built in 1516 as accommodation for the poor, who were requested to pray for the Fuggers in lieu of paying rent. You can see inside one small house that's been set up as a museum with furnishings of the period. The Fuggerei retains its four original gateways, which are still closed each night. By contrast, the city burghers lived in style in the stately mansions that still set the tone of MAXIMILIANSTR., where the **Schaezler Palace**, an 18th-century rococo edifice with a sumptuous ballroom, now houses the state art gallery.

On the hilly north side of the city centre, the lofty Gothic cathedral is striking for its imposing south doorway, 12th-century stained glass (the earliest in Germany), and paintings by Hans Holbein the Elder on the nave's four altars.

RAIL ☎(0821) 19419, 10 mins west of the city centre.

i **Tourist Offices**: BAHNHOFSTR. 7, 5 mins from the rail station; open Mon–Fri 0900–1800. Also RATHAUSPL; open Mon–Fri

DAY TRIPS FROM AUGSBURG

From the rail station, Europabus services (on which train tickets are valid) run to **Schwangau**, on the **Romantic Road**. **Tourist Office**: **Rathaus**; ☎(08362) 819825; open Mon–Fri 0730–1230 and 1330–1700; also Sat 0900–1200 (May–Oct) and Sun 1000–1200 (May–Sept). An alternative approach is from **Füssen** (served by trains from Augsburg; 2 hrs), with frequent buses making the short trip from there to the castles; Füssen's a particularly appealing place to stay (**youth hostel**: MARIAHILFENSTR. 5, ☎(8362) 7754). However, it's Bavaria's three *Königsschlösser* (Royal Castles), where resided the fabulously over-extravagant and eccentric Ludwig II, that steal the show. Just over the road from Schwangau (and 4 km from Füssen), ***Hohenschwangau*** and

Day Trips from Augsberg cont'd.

Neuschwanstein are within walking distance of each other (involving a modest climb). Tudor-style **Hohenschwangau,** built in the early 19th century by Maximilian II, was an attempt to recreate the romantic past and was adorned with Wagnerian references by his son, 'mad' King Ludwig II. It was Ludwig who surpassed his father by building the fairy-tale neo-Gothic **Neuschwanstein** on a rocky outcrop high above; it is best seen from the dizzying heights of the **Marienbrücke**, a bridge spanning a huge gorge. This most famous of his castles was never finished – hence the Throne Room without a throne, and doorways leading to suicidal drops. The third castle, **Linderhof**, 20 km east, is a small French-style château, modelled on the Petit Trianon at Versailles. The outstanding oddity is the king's dining table, engineered to be lowered to the kitchens and then raised again for him to dine entirely alone.

0900–1800, Sat 1000–1600, Sun 1000–1300. ☎(for both): (0821) 502070, tourismus@augsburg.btl.de. There are four 'town walks' colour coded on the *Augsburg and its Sights* map available from the Tourist Office.

Two places within 0.5 km of the rail station are the **Iris**, GARTENSTR. 4, ☎(0821) 510981 (rooms from DM70) and the **Lenzhalde**, THELOTTSTR. 2, ☎(0821) 520745 (from DM38). **Youth hostel**: BEIM PFAFFENKELLER 3, ☎(0821) 33909 (tram no. 2 to STADTWERKE). **Campsite**: CAMPINGPLATZ AUGUSTA, ☎(0821) 707575, 7 km from city centre (bus 301/302/305 to AUTOBAHNSEE).

There's no shortage of places to eat in the old town centre, mostly offering hearty local Swabian or Bavarian dishes. Plenty of jolly beer cellars too.

ULM

This endearing old town on the Danube has a quaint quarter known as **Fischer-und-Gerberviertel,** the old fishing and tanning district, with half-timbered houses beside the Blau, a rushing tributary. Most places of interest are on the north bank of the Danube and the main attractions are easily walkable.

You can hardly fail to notice the soaring spire of the **Münster** (cathedral), all 161 m of it, the tallest such structure in the world. Dominating a huge traffic-free square, the cathedral represents gothic architecture at its mightiest. Climb the 768 steps up the tower to survey the terrain, on a clear day, from the Black Forest to the Alps.

Ulm was the birthplace of Einstein, marked by a memorial opposite the rail station. It was also the place where Albrecht Ludwig Berblinger, the 'Tailor of Ulm', made man's first attempt to fly. In 1811, he took off from the Adlerbastei (town wall), but didn't make it across the Danube.

Many buildings that were hit in the bombing raid in 1944 have been carefully restored, including the 16th-century **Rathaus**, RATHAUSPL., with its intricate astronomical clock. One notably fine Renaissance building houses the **Ulmer Museum**, MARKTPL. 9, notable for its early Ulm paintings and an outstanding 20th-century collection.

Towards the Danube, the **Metzgerturm** (Butchers' Tower), formerly a prison, is known as the leaning tower of Ulm (36 m high) as it's about 2 m off the vertical. Paths lead from it to a pleasant riverside walk dotted with sculptures or up onto a stretch of the old city walls.

(0731) 19419. 5 mins to centre through pedestrian zone.

Tourist Office: **Stadthaus**, MÜNSTERPL. 50; (0731) 161 2830. Open Mon–Fri 0900–1800, Sat 0900–1230, Sun 1100–1400 (summer only), http://www.ulm.de/tourismus, unt@tourismus.ulm.de. There is a free accommodation booking service.

INTERNET ACCESS
Albert's Café, KORNHAUSPL.; or at the public library, **Weinhof** in the '**Schworhaus**'.

There are several reasonably priced central hotels, including **Münster-Hotel**, MÜNSTERPL. 14 (0731) 64162 (opposite the cathedral), and **Hotel Schwarzer Adler**, FRAUENSTR. 20, (0731) 27735. **Youth hostel**: GRIMMELFINGERWEG 45; (0731) 384455, 4 km south-west of the centre (no. 9 from the rail station or no. 4 from Rathaus, both to SCHULZENTRUM).

The old fishermen's quarter near the Danube has a selection of restaurants in picturesque spots. The wood-panelled **Allgäuer Hof**, 'Ulm's First Pancake House', FISCHERGASSE 12; (0731) 67408, features traditional pancakes on large platters, with a choice of over 40 toppings.

STUTTGART

Surrounded by green hills, the capital of Baden-Württemberg is probably best known for its vibrant cultural activities and as the home of the Daimler-Benz and Porsche motor factories. But the traffic-free centre, radiating from the huge SCHLOSSPL. – with its pavement cafés, buskers, fountains and gardens – is an inviting place to stroll.

The British architect James Stirling has firmly put the city on the map with his **Neue Staatsgalerie**, the post-modern wing of the **Staatsgalerie,** KONRAD- ADENAUER-STR 30, with its audacious use of materials. It's the setting for one of the world's largest Picasso collections, as well as a comprehensive survey of 20th-century art. The adjoining **Alte Staatsgalarie** has earlier works, notably the superb *Herrenberg Altar* by Jorg Ratgeb.

Motor enthusiasts can head for the Daimler-Benz Museum, MERCEDESSTR. 137, Bad Cannstatt (S1 to GOTTLIEB-DAILER STADION), where 100 historic models are on show. Racing cars make up the bulk of the exhibits in the smaller Porsche-Museum, PORRSCHESTR. 42, in the northern suburb of *Zuffenhausen* (S6 to NEUWIRTSHAUS).

(0711) 19419. 5 mins' walk from the centre, along SCHLOSSPL.

Tourist Office: Directly on coming out from the rail station underpass, at KONIGSTR. 1A;

WHERE NEXT FROM STUTTGART?

You can go south to Singen (2 hrs; ETT table 940) and change trains there to Konstanz. This is a very pretty line through the Neckar valley. On the way, ***Rottweil*** *deserves a pause. It's a delightful fountain-embellished little market town, squeezed on a spur of the Neckar between the Black Forest and the Schwäbische Alb (Swabian Jura), and revealing tremendous views. Punctuated by the medieval* ***Schwarzes Tor*** *(Black Tower), the pedestrianised Hauptstrasse has a striking array of colourful Renaissance and baroque houses displaying a wealth of carvings and murals, and sprouting projecting oriel windows. The town is also the provenance of the ferocious Rottweiler dog, descended from Roman guard-dog stock and formerly used by local butchers to pull carts (hence the German name of Metzerhund - butcher's dog). Tourist Office: RATHAUSSEG. ☎(741) 494280. Youth hostel: LORENZGASSE 8; ☎(741) 7664; fax (741) 7604.*

☎(0711) 222 8240, opposite the rail station. Mon–Fri 0930–2030, Sat 0930–1800, Sun 1100–1800 (from 1300 Nov–Apr). 24-hr Fax Info-Service; ☎(0711) 957680-4200. Free accommodation booking service. They sell theatre tickets and the good value **City Pass**, DM27.50, for 3 days' travel and museum discounts, and **Night Pass**, DM12, free entrance to discos and bars.

INTERNET ACCESS

No internet cafés yet, but it's possible to go on-line at **Karstadt** department store.

Hotel prices around the station tend to be high as it is so central. Small **pensions**, such as the **Theaterpension**, PFIZERSTR. 12, V ☎(0711) 240722, **Schwarzwaldheim**, FRITZ-ELSAS-STR 20, ☎(0711) 296988 and **Alte Mira**, BUCHSENSTR. 24, ☎(0711) 295132, begin at around DM60, but without private bath or toilet. **Youth hostel**: HAUSMANNSTR. 27; ☎(0711) 241583, a 15-min uphill walk from the rail station (or U-Bahn 15/16: EUGENSPL). **Campsite**: **Cannstatter Wasen**, MERCEDESSTR. 40; ☎(0711) 556696, is beside the River Neckar (tram nos. 1/2). Open all year.

HEILBRONN

Ensconced beside the River Neckar, **Heilbronn** is at the centre of one of Germany's largest wine-producing areas. The town itself is mainly modern with traffic-free streets around **Kilianskirche,** the Gothic church which is the town's symbol. Tasting of the local wines is available at the **Haus des Handwerks** in town. During the second week of Sept, the **Heilbronner Herbst** wine festival takes over the town centre. The local Swabian wines - over 200 of them - can be sampled at stalls at knock-down prices to the sound of 'oompah' bands.

RAIL ☎(07131) 19419, a good 10-min walk to the centre. Frequent bus services.

Tourist Office: (next to the Rathaus), MARKTPL; ☎(07131) 562270-71. Mon–Fri 0900–1800 and Sat 0900–1300, (http://www.HNOLINE.de). They also offer room vacancy advice.

Gasthof Anker, BRUCKENSTR. 6, ☎(07131) 21345 and **Gasthof Rossle**, SAARBRUCKENER STR 2, ☎(01731) 91550, both offer inexpensive rooms starting at DM48. **Youth hostel**: SCHIRRMANNSTR. 9, ☎(07131) 172961 (🚌no. 1). **Campsite**: **Heilbronn Camping**, ☎(07130) 8558 is at Löwenstein, south-east of the town by the *Breitenauer See*, one of the best and most scenic sites in Germany. Open all year. 🚌 no. 7829 from the rail station, direction SCHWÄBISH HALL, to OBERSULM/WILLSBACH (on the B39); bus stop SEEMHLE, ABSWEIGUNG BREITENAUSER SEE; 500 m to campsite.

HEIDELBERG

Heidelberg's romantic setting, beneath wooded hills along the banks of the River Neckar and overlooked by castle ruins, makes it a magnet for tourists and movie-makers. The town has a long history and is home to Germany's oldest university, founded in 1386, but there's little that's ancient in the centre, as most of it was rebuilt in the 18th century following wholesale destruction by Louis XIV's troops in 1693. In high summer, there's pretty much a non-stop procession of tourists through the central streets.

The city's most famous sight is the part-ruined pink sandstone castle, high above the town. From its terraces, you get a beautiful view over the red rooftops and gently flowing river.

Many fine old mansions are scattered around the old town *(***Altstadt***)*. The buildings around MARKTPL. include the Renaissance **Haus zum Ritter,** and the 14th-century **Heiliggeistkirche** (Church of the Holy Spirit). UNIVERSITÄTSPLATZ, which has the **Löwenbrunnen** (Lion Fountain) in the centre, is the location of both the 'old' and 'new' universities. Until 1914, students whose high spirits had got out of hand were confined in the special students' prison round the corner in AUGUSTINERSTR. 2. Incarceration was regarded as an honour and self-portraits are common in the graffiti on the walls.

Across the river, over the *Alte Brücke*, the steep **Schlagenweg steps** zig-zag up through orchards to the **Philosophenweg** (Philosophers' Path). This is a scenic

DAY TRIP FROM HEILBRONN

Cruises on the **River Neckar** from **Friedrich-Ebert-Brücke** near MARKTPL. (May–Oct) go downstream to **Bad Wimpfen** and **Gundelsheim** twice a day. Bad Wimpfen, which can also be reached by train (20-min journey) is a gem of a fortified town above the river, its cobbled streets full of crooked half-timbered houses. The Tourist Office is in the old station, ☎(0763) 97200.

HEIDELBERG'S CASTLE EVENTS

The highlight of summer is the castle festival throughout August, when opera performances are staged outdoors in the cobbled courtyard; Romberg's romantic operetta 'The Student Prince' is the permanent fixture. For tickets, ☎(06221) 583521. Grand fireworks displays are held on the first Sat in June, July and Sept.

lane across the hillside, so-called because the views inspired philosophic meditation.

RAIL (06221) 19419, a good 10-mins walk to the edge of the pedestrian district, or take no. 1 or 2; or 20 mins to the heart of the old Altstadt (or no. 33).

i **Tourist Office**: WILLI-BRAND-PLATZ 1, directly in front of the rail station; (06221) 19433. Open Mon–Sat 0900–1900; also Sun 1000–1800 (Apr–Oct), (http://www.germany.eu.net/shop/Heidelberg; info.cvb, cvbhd@info.hd.eunet.de). Accommodation booking service costs DM5. The **Heidelberg Card** is valid for city travel, castle admission and various discounts, DM25 (1 day) or DM34 (3 days). Guided walking tours in English, Mon–Fri at 1400 (Apr–Oct) from UNIVERSITÄTSPL., DM10. There are also themed guided tours, such as *Heidelberg in the Time of Romanticism*, or *Student Life in Heidelberg*: check with the Tourist Office for details

A network of buses and trams serve the pedestrianised Altstadt, where a funicular ride (DM7) saves the 300-step climb up to the Schloss. It's also possible to tour by bike (rentals available from BERGHEIMER STR, (06221) 181108), particularly pleasant for exploring the banks of the Neckar.

Heidelberg is a prime tourist destination, so the later you book during the summer, the further from the centre you will find yourself staying. The **Goldener Hirsch**, KLEINGEMUNDER STR 27, (06221) 800211, is a bit away from the Altstadt, but has simple rooms beginning at DM45. **Burgfreiheit**, NEUE SCHLOSSSTR. 52, (06221) 22062, is a bit pricier at DM60, but is right next to the castle. **Youth hostel**: TIERGARTENSTR. 5, (06221) 412066. **Campsite**: **Camping Neckartal**, HEIDELBERG-SCHLIERBACH; (06221) 802506, between *ZIEGELHAUSEN* and *NECKARGEMUND* (no. 35).

The **Altstadt** is very touristy and its restaurants lively with a student atmosphere. Many spill out onto the traffic-free streets. This is also where most of the nightlife goes on. You are spoilt for choice along HEILIGGEISTR. and UNTERE-STR. For good value, try **Im Perkeo**, HAUPTSTR. 75, where you serve yourself freshly cooked hot dishes, salads and pastries. *Kneipen* (taverns) are an important part of Heidelberg life and in term-time they fill up with students. Try **Knosel**, HASELPG. 20; **Schnookeloch**, HASELPG. 8; **Zum Roten Ochsen**, HAUPTSTR. 217, or **Zum Sepp'l**, HAUPTSTR. 213.

WHERE NEXT FROM HEIDELBERG?

Heidelberg is served by trains to ***Frankfurt*** *(55 mins, ETT table 910), where you can join the* ***Cologne–Passau*** *route* *(p. 245)*.

KARLSRUHE

A major industrial and university city, Karlsruhe's most interesting sight is the huge **Schloss**, home of the Grand Dukes of Baden until 1918. Built in 1715 by Margrave Karl Wilhelm, it's an enormous neo-classical pile with extensive formal gardens. From the tower, you see clearly how he designed the city to spread out from it like a fan, with 32 streets.

Inside the Schloss, the wonderfully eclectic **Badisches Landesmuseum** covers pre-history to the present day. The Orangerie (free entry), merits a look for its 19th- and 20th-century European art.

Marktplatz, the enormous central square near the *Schloss*, is dominated by a pyramid of red sandstone, under which Karl Wilhelm is buried.

The ZKM (*Zentrum furKunst und Medientechnologie Karlsruhe*: Centre for Art and Media Technology), LORENZSTR. 19, (no. 55 from the rail station; alight at BRAUERSTR.), is an experience-oriented centre, media museum and interactive art gallery. There's enough for a full day's visit (entry DM10).

(0721) 19419, a 25-min walk south of the centre (tram nos. 3/4).

Tourist Office: BAHNHOFPL. 6; (0721) 35530, (http://www.karlsruhe.de, vv@karlsruhe.de), opposite the rail station. Open Mon–Fri 0900–1800 (to 1230 Sat). Free room-booking service. There are good bus and tram services. Rhine cruises operate Easter–Nov from the western edge of town.

Pension Stadtmitte, ZAHRINGER STR. 72, (0721) 389637 and **Pension am Zoo**, ETTLINGERSTR. 33, (0721) 33678, both offer rooms from around DM65. **Youth hostel**: MOLTKESTR. 24; (0721) 28248, west of Schlossgarten (tram nos 3/4 to EUROPAPL.).

INTERNET CAFÉS

webSPIDERcafé, MOLTKESTR. 28, (0721) 292 3745.

BADEN-BADEN

Fashionable in the 19th century for gambling, particularly among Russian aristocrats, Baden-Baden soon became a major spa resort, thanks to its health-promoting hot mineral springs. The spa continues to this day, and it's extremely upmarket, with elegant promenades surrounding the pedestrian shopping area.

A long, manicured park with an avenue of plane trees known as the **Lichtentaler Allee** forms the heart of the resort. You can sip the warm saline waters at the art nouveau **Trinkhalle** (pump room), KAISERALLEE 3, whose walls are adorned with Romantic murals of maidens and Germanic heroes depicting the town's history as a spa.

The Casino in the neo-classical **Kurhaus**, KAISERALLEE 1, is Germany's oldest and biggest. Redecorated in French style in 1853, it is promoted as one of the world's most beautiful casinos. Guests no longer have to wear formal attire, but jackets and ties are required (available for hire); you'll be turned away if you're in jeans or trainers. Entrance DM5; minimum stake DM5 (DM10 Fri–Sun); maximum stake DM50,000.

(07221) 19419. This is at **Oos**, 12 km north-west of town, but there is a bus (no. 201) every 10 mins 0500–0100.

Tourist Office: SCHWARZWALD 52 (at the entrance to the city); **Haus des Kurgastes**, AUGUSTAPL. 8; (07221) 275202 (bbm.sales@baden-baden.de). Open 0930–2000 (summer), till 1900 (winter); AUGUSTAPL., daily 0930–1800.

As the baths and casino attract many wealthy visitors, most hotels are glossy and expensive. Two cheaper options, are **Hotel Deutscherkaiser**, LICHTENDALER HAUPTSTR. 35; (07221) 72152 (no. 201 to ECKERLESTR. from the rail station or town centre) and **Schutzenhof**, BALDREITSTR. 1, (07221) 24088, in the pedestrian area, both offering rooms beginning at DM53–60. There are also **private rooms** available. **Youth hostel**: **Jugenherberger**, HARDBERGSTR. 34; (07221) 52223 (no. 201 to GROSSE DOLLENSTR., then a 7-min walk.). The closest campsite is at **Campingplatz Adam**, 77815 BUHL-OBERBRUCH, (07223) 23194, approximately 12 km from Baden – the site also does bike rentals.

For eating inexpensively in the centre, **Le Bistro**, SOPHIENSTR. 4; (07221) 32494, is a small bar-restaurant whose tables spill onto the pavement in summer.

WHERE NEXT FROM BADEN-BADEN?

It is easy to get to Switzerland *or* France *from here, with hourly train services taking 40 mins to both Basel and Strasbourg (ETT table 910), at the end of the Cherbourg–Strasbourg route across central* France *(p. 67–72); it's also easy to get to Switzerland, with hourly services to Basel (40 min).*

DAY TRIP FROM OFFENBURG

Freiburg in Breisgau (30 mins; hourly trains), at the western edge of the Black Forest, spreads around its Gothic cathedral. With most sights in the **Altstadt** (old town), it's very walkable so long as you don't fall into the numerous Bächle (gulleys) that run along the streets; these formed part of the old drainage system and were used for watering livestock, and often have water flowing along them. Freiburg's famously easy-going atmosphere is immediately apparent; the university is very much the life and soul of the city.

OFFENBURG

Change here for trains to **Basel** (p. 290) via Freiburg.

TRIBERG

Cuckoo-clock shops have arrived here with a vengeance. At the heart of the **Schwarzwald** (Black Forest) and known for the purity of its air, the touristy spa town has been a centre for cuckoo clock-making since 1824, when Josef Weisser started his business in the **Haus der 1000 Uhren** (House of a Thousand Clocks). The **Schwarzwaldmuseum** is full of wood-carvings, some splendid local costumes and inevitably clocks. Apart from clocks, **Triberg** is an appealing centre for walking; one walk is to the waterfall of the **Gutach,** which cascades down 162m in seven stages and is floodlit at night.

Station: (07722) 4552. 1.5km north-east of the town.

Tourist information: KURVERWALTUNG TRIBERG, LUISENSTR 10, 78098 (07722) 953 230. Open Mon–Fri 0900–1700, Sat 10–1200 (May–Sept).

Youth hostel: ROHRBERGERSTR 35, (7722) 4110.

KONSTANZ

The Swiss border cuts through the southern part of this town on the Lake (*Bodensee*) Constance. Leafy gardens extend along the water's edge and there's a pleasant old quarter, **Niederburg**, where alleys wind between half-timbered buildings with decorated façades. The harbour is the departure point for lake cruises and ferries. At the mouth of the marina is the 9-m high Imperia, a controversial statue built in 1993, allegedly depicting a famous courtesan of the past. In one hand she holds the king (representing the state) and in the other, the pope (representing the church), thus questioning who has the real power.

In the MARKTSTÄTTE (Market Place), elaborate frescos on the Renaissance **Rathaus** depict the town's history, and children clamber on the bronze beasts of a decidedly jolly 19th-century fountain.

(07531) 19419, between BAHNHOFPL., the eastern boundary of Altstadt, and the *Bodensee* (Lake Constance).

Tourist Office: BAHNHOFPL. 13; (07531) 131330. Open Mon–Fri 0900–1830 (May–Sept), Sat 0900–1300 (Apr–Oct), Mon–Fri 0900–1200 and 1400–1800 (Oct–Apr), (http://www.bodensee-info.com, info@touristinformation.stadt.konstanz.de).
Bicycles can be hired at **Aktiv-Reisen**, MAINAUSTR. 34; (07531) 98280. Accommodation service: DM5.

The centre of town is more expensive than the (very pleasant) outlying villages, with,for example **Zur Linde**, RADOLFZELLERSTR. 27, (07351) 97420, and **Sonnenhof**, O.-RAGGENBASS STR 3, (07351) 22257, beginning at the DM75–85 level. Nearby in **Dingelsdorf**, 30 mins away via no.4, is the **Gasthaus Seeschau**, ZUR SCHIFFLANDE 11, (07533) 5190 and **Gasthaus Pension Rose**,

Day Trip from Offenburg cont'd.

Topped by a 116-m spire, the red sandstone **Münster** (cathedral) has a Romanesque-Gothic interior illuminated by 13th- to 16th-century stained glass – many sections depicting the guilds who paid for them. From the tower, 331 steps up, you get a vertigo-inducing panorama On MUNSTERPL., the **Historisches Kaufhaus**, an arcaded merchants' hall, is flanked by tow handsome baroque palaces, **Erzbischofliches Palais** and **Wenzingerhaus**. The latter was the house of the 18th-century artist Christian Wenzinger. A short stroll away, RATHAUSPL. is notable for the **Neues Rathaus,** two Renaissance mansions linked by a bridge. They face the red and gold **Haus zum Walfisch**, a recreation of the elegant house (bombed in World War II) where Erasmus lived for two years. The **Augustiner**, SALZSTR., the town's best museum, contains religious and folkloric art from the Upper Rhine area, as well as old master. Station: (0761) 19419, a good 10-min walk west of the centre.

Day Trip from Offenburg cont'd.

The **Tourist Office**, ROTTECKRING 14 ☎(0761) 290 7447, is two blocks down EISENBAHNSTR. (http://www.freiburg-online.com or www.uni-freiburg.de). Open Mon–Fri 0930–2000 (to 1800 Oct–May), Sat 0930–1700 (to 1400 Oct–May), Sun 1000–1200. Accommodation booking service DM5.

Accommodation: **Zum Roten Bären**, OBERLINDEN 12, ☎(0761) 387870, is expensive, but is allegedly the oldest inn in Germany, dating back to 1120. There are plenty of cheaper places to stay (and restaurants too) around the **Altstadt**, such as **Hotel Löwen**, HERRENSTR. 47, ☎(0761) 33161, and **Hotel Schemmer**, ESCHOLZSTR. 63, ☎(0761) 207490, with rooms from DM55–65. **Youth hostel**: **Jugendherberge**, KARTAUSERSTR. 151; ☎(0761) 67656, at the extreme east of town (tram no. 1 to HASEMANN-STR.). **Campsite**: **Hirzberg**, KARTAUSERSTR. 99; ☎(0761) 35054, near the youth hostel.

WALLHAUSERSTR. 12, ☎(07533) 97000, offering rooms with bath/shower and toilet at DM50–70. **Private rooms** are available at a similar price. **Youth hostel**: **Otto-Moericke-Turm**, ZUR ALLMANNSHOHE 18; ☎(07531) 32260, (🚌 no. 4). **Campsite**: **Litzelstetten-Mainau**, GROSSHERZOG-FRIEDRICHSTR. 43; ☎(07531) 943030, on **Mainau island,** which is linked by a footbridge to the north-east corner of the town (🚌no. 4 or ferry).

INTERNET CAFÉS

Schultze & Schultze, HUSSENSTRASSE (across from K9).

WHERE NEXT FROM KONSTANZ?

The Bodensee ferries link Konstanz *with Lindau (journey 3½ hrs), from which there are services to Ulm (2 hrs 15 mins) and* **Augsburg** *(3 hrs); ETT table 935.*

AROUND THE BODENSEE (LAKE CONSTANCE)

Linked by a footbridge to to the mainland, and reached by boat services from Konstanz, **Mainau** is a delightful 110-acre island, where a lushly colourful garden surrounds an inhabited baroque palace that was used by the Teutonic Knights for more than five centuries.

Ferry destinations include **Meersburg**, an atmospheric hillside town with a picturesque *Markt* and old inhabited castle; **Unteruhldingen**, which has an open-air museum (with re-creations of Neolithic dwellings) and a basilica that's fully worth the 20-min uphill walk; **Überlingen**, a strikingly attractive town with a Gothic ***Münster*** and a fine Moat Walk; and the island of **Reichenau**, which has three 9th-century monasteries, each surrounded by a village.

The quay on the *Bodensee* (Lake Constance), behind the rail station, offers a wide choice of boat trips and cruises on the lake and the Rhine (into which it flows nearby). The service is seasonal. The main operator is **Bodensee-Schiffsbetriebe**, HAFENSTR. 6; ☎(07531) 281398. DB rail passes are valid.

MUNICH – WEIMAR – BERLIN

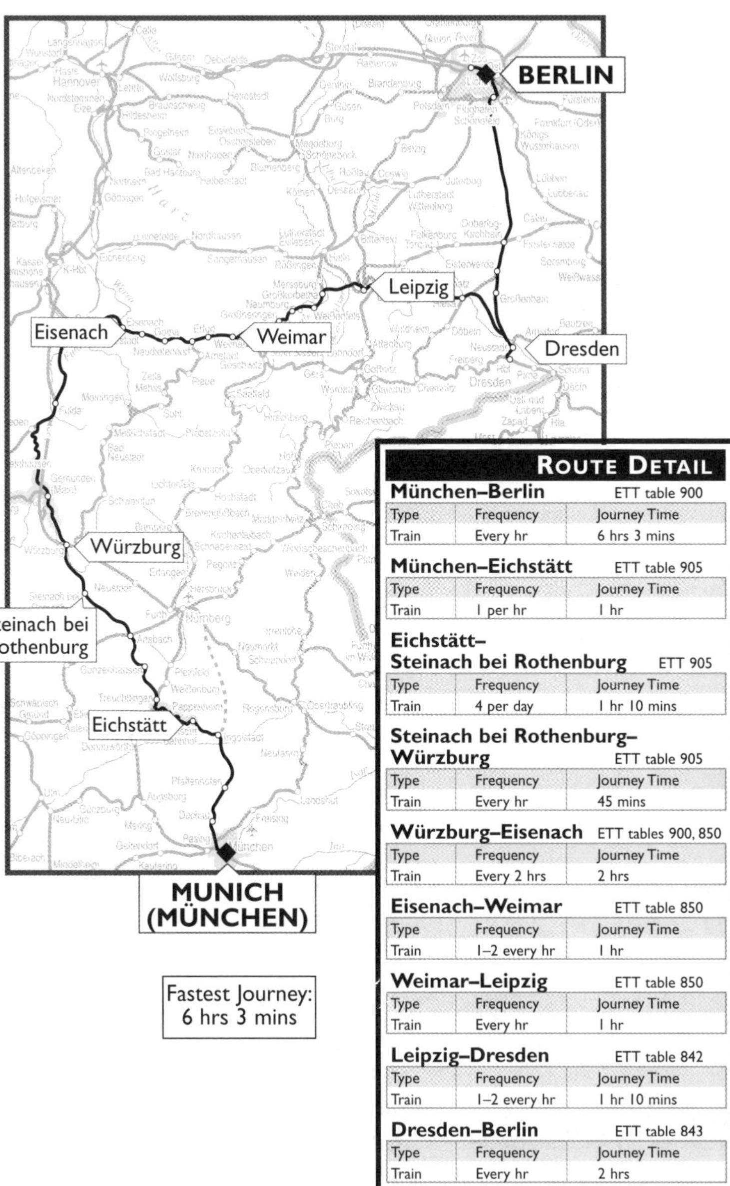

Fastest Journey:
6 hrs 3 mins

Route Detail

München–Berlin ETT table 900

Type	Frequency	Journey Time
Train	Every hr	6 hrs 3 mins

München–Eichstätt ETT table 905

Type	Frequency	Journey Time
Train	1 per hr	1 hr

Eichstätt–Steinach bei Rothenburg ETT 905

Type	Frequency	Journey Time
Train	4 per day	1 hr 10 mins

Steinach bei Rothenburg–Würzburg ETT table 905

Type	Frequency	Journey Time
Train	Every hr	45 mins

Würzburg–Eisenach ETT tables 900, 850

Type	Frequency	Journey Time
Train	Every 2 hrs	2 hrs

Eisenach–Weimar ETT table 850

Type	Frequency	Journey Time
Train	1–2 every hr	1 hr

Weimar–Leipzig ETT table 850

Type	Frequency	Journey Time
Train	Every hr	1 hr

Leipzig–Dresden ETT table 842

Type	Frequency	Journey Time
Train	1–2 every hr	1 hr 10 mins

Dresden–Berlin ETT table 843

Type	Frequency	Journey Time
Train	Every hr	2 hrs

Munich – Weimar – Berlin

This route passes through northern **Bavaria**, and includes the appealing old town of **Eichstätt** in the delightful **Altmühl** valley, and equally pretty Ansbach (not included here), and the university town of Würzburg. The picture-book **Rothenburg ob der Tauber** is a major tourist attraction, while the rail route takes you into former East Germany, visiting **Weimar**, **Leipzig** and **Eisenach**. Elsewhere you can take your pick of lesser-known gems such as **Fulda**, **Gotha** (not included here) and **Erfurt** (not included here). There's a lot to take in during this trip, and if you don't have time for all of it, take the detour to Rothenburg, then cut across from Ansbach to **Dresden**.

EICHSTÄTT

For a great view of the town, make the steep but pretty 15-min climb from the station up a wooded hillside to the **Willibaldsburg**, a splendid white palace built between the 14th and 18th centuries. A recent addition to this is the **Hortus Eystenttensis**, a garden based on the plants documented in the definitive 16th-century illustrated horticultural work. The Burg also houses the **Jura-Museum** of natural history, with a notable collection of fossils from the Altmühl valley.

The bustling market square consists of pretty gabled buildings, shops and pavement cafés, while nearby the **Residenzplatz** is a serene complex of pale green and white 18th-century mansions in a semi circle around the imposing **Residenz**, the former bishops' residence, now used by the town council as offices and reception rooms (free guided tours Mon–Sat). The adjoining light and airy Gothic **Dom** (cathedral) is notable for its stained-glass windows by Hans Holbein and intricately-carved 500-year-old Pappenheim altar.

RAIL **Eichstätt Stadt**, ☎(0841) 19419, is served by a shuttle train from **Eichstätt Bahnhof** on the main line, a 9-min journey. The Tourist Office is a 5-min walk across the town.

i **Tourist Office**: KARDINAL-PREYSINGPL. 14; ☎(08421) 98800. Mon–Sat 0900–1830, Sun 1630–1830 (Apr–Oct); Mon–Sat 0900–1200, 1300–1700 (Nov–Mar); http://www.bH.de/eichstatt; email:tourismus@eichstatt.bh.de. Information on the **Altmühl National Park**, the surrounding area, is available next door: NOTRE-DAME 1, ☎(08421) 6733, Mon–Sat 0900–1800, Sun 1000–1800 (Easter–mid Sept), Mon–Sat 0900–1700, Sun 1000–1700 (mid Sept–Oct), Mon–Fri 0800–1200, 1400–1600 (Nov–Easter); tourismus@naturpark-altmuehltal.btl.de.

Spaces in guesthouses are easy to find. **Gasthof Zum Griechen**, WESENSTR. 17, ☎(08421) 2640, has rooms from DM37 while the **Gasthof Ratskeller**, KARDINAL-PREYSINGPL. 8–10, ☎(08421) 1258, begins at around DM47. **Private rooms** are also available (pick up a brochure at the Tourist Office). **Youth hostel**: REICHENAUSTR. 15; ☎(08421) 98040, 10 mins from the rail station (closed Dec–Jan).

STEINACH BEI ROTHENBURG

Change here for the 15-min train journey to **Rothenburg ob der Tauber**.

ROTHENBURG OB DER TAUBER

This little town probably justifies the title 'the Jewel of the Romantic Road' – the **Romantische Strasse** being the best known of Germany's themed routes, running from Würzburg to Füssen. Situated on a rocky outcrop surrounded by medieval walls, its pastel-coloured steep-gabled houses – some half-timbered – are the stuff of picture-books, especially in summer, when window boxes trail with flowers.

A great area for nightlife is the **Bermuda Dreieck** ('Bermuda Triangle)', between ANSBACH-, ADAM- and HORBERSTRASSE, with two discos, a cocktail bar and a couple of *Kneipen* (pubs).

As early as 1902, the local council, showing commendable foresight, imposed a preservation order, so physically not much has changed since the 15th century – if you ignore all the tourist shops, galleries and restaurants (of which there were 110 at the last count). One of the best walks is around the intact (and roofed) town walls, which are long enough for you to lose most of the hordes of visitors.

On **Marktplatz**, there is usually some entertainment, whether a musical concert or a theatrical performance. The glockenspiel on the 15th-century **Ratstrinkstube** (Councillors' Tavern), now the Tourist Office, re-enacts on the hour (1100–1500 and 2000–2200) the historic scene in 1631, during the Thirty Years War, when Mayor Nusch rose to the challenge of knocking back a gallon of wine to save the town from destruction. The **Meistertrunk** festivities at Whitsun commemorate his feat.

Climb the 200 steps (very steep and narrow at the top) onto the **Rathaus tower's** roof for a dizzying view. Then walk down SCHMIEDGASSE to the **Burggarten**; graced by a remarkable 15th-century backdrop of the town, these shaded gardens were the site of a castle destroyed in an earthquake in 1356.

Hbf; ☎(09861) 47611, the centre a 10-min walk straight ahead, then follow *'Stadtmitte'* signs.

Tourist Office: MARKTPL. 2; ☎(09861) 40492 (http://www.rothenburg.de; email:info@rothenburg.de). Open Mon–Fri 0900–1230 and 1300–1800, Sat–Sun 1000–1500. Accommodation reservations DM5 and 24-hr hotel freephone. **Guided tours** in English at 1400 from MARKTPL. Apr–Oct and Dec (during Christmas Market time).

There is plenty of choice, including **private houses**, both inside and outside the old town walls. These include **Blasi**, ALTER STADTGRABEN, ☎(09861) 5198, and **Hedwig Gartner**, KREBENGASSCHEN 2, ☎(09861) 3248, both with prices beginning from around DM40. **Youth hostel**: **Rossmühle**, MUHLACKER 1, ☎(09861) 94160, located in a former horse mill in the old town; opens at 1700. **Campsite**: **Tauber-Romantik**, DETWANG; ☎(09861) 6191, a steep 30-min walk down the valley.

There are some inexpensive, yet still typical **restaurants** in the town, including **Nusch**, SPITALGASSE 1, ☎(09861) 8964, and the **Altfränkische Weinstube**, AM KLOSTERHOF 7, ☎(09861) 6404. Also, try the *schneeball* (snowball), a local pastry speciality which has a different – and secret – recipe from each baker. **Internet café**: PARADIESENWEG 4–7, ☎(09861) 91541.

WÜRZBURG

Würzburg is a university town where in autumn the *Winzerfest*, a traditional annual harvest festival, celebrates the (justly famous) Franconian wines.

The rebuilt domes, spires and red roofs are seen at their best from the terrace battlements of **Festung Marienberg**, an impressive white fortress on a wooded hill above the River Main. Converted to baroque style in the 17th century, little remains inside, though the **Mainfränkisches Museum** displays a large collection of works by Franconian artists, including superb 16th-century wood carvings by one of the city's most famous sons, Tilman Riemenschneider. The Festung is best reached by no. 9, a 10-min ride, otherwise it's a 40-min walk.

The market place is notable for the **Marienkapelle**, a 14th-century church with more Riemenschneider carvings, and the richly decorated 18th-century **Haus zum Falken**, which houses the Tourist Office.

The town's main sight is the massive sandstone **Residenz**, RESIDENZ-PL. Built as the new palace of the Prince-Bishops in the 18th century by Balthasar Neumann, it has been given World Heritage Site status. Statues line the roof façade, symbolising the church's wealth and power. The rooms are sumptuously decorated with frescos and sculptures by leading artists of their day, including the Venetian master Tiepolo. Nightlife revolves around SANDERSTR., popular with students.

WHERE NEXT FROM WÜRZBURG?
Würzburg is on the ***Cologne–Passau*** *route* *(pp. 245–255).*

RAIL (0931) 34326; at the foot of vineyards on the northern edge of the town centre, a 15-min walk.

Tourist Offices: In front of the rail station, (0931) 373436 (http://www.wuerzburg.de;-email:infor@wuerzburg.de). Open Mon–Sat 1000–1800. **Haus Zum Falken**, MARKTPLATZ; (0931) 372398. Mon–Fri 1000–1800, Sat–Sun 1000–1400 (Apr–Dec), but closed Sun Nov–Dec. Two-hour guided walks around the town in English start from the Haus Zum Falken Tourist Office at 1100, Tues–Sun (Apr–Oct); DM12.

There is no shortage of hotels in all categories. Handy for the station and moderately priced is **Pension Spehkuch**, RONTGENRING 7, (0931) 54752, starting around DM50; the **Pension Siegel**, REISGRUBENGASSE 7, (0931) 52941, is slightly cheaper. **Youth hostel**: BURKARDERSTR. 44, (0931) 42590, on the bank of the Main, below Festung. **Campsite**: **Camping Canoe Club**, MERGENHEIMERSTR. 136; (0931) 72536 (tram no. 3 to JUDENBÜHLWEG).
Internet cafés: **Café Cairo** (near the youth hostel); **Café Franz**, FRANZ LUDWIGSTR. 6.

EISENACH

Though still a bit run-down as a legacy of its recent East German past, there are plentiful splashes of modern architecture as the town undergoes a facelift. The glory of the town is the splendid **Wartburg** on a hill on its south-west edge (12 mins by 🚌 no. 10 from the rail station, and then 227 steps), the seat of the Landgraves of Thuringia. A medieval castle dating from 1067 with many later additions, it's an attractive complex where half-timbered buildings surround two courtyards. Wagner stayed there and used it as the setting for his opera *Tannhäuser,* and Martin Luther translated the New Testament into German there – in just 10 weeks – while being held in secret for his own protection in 1521–22 after being excommunicated.

The 15th-century **Lutherhaus**, LUTHERPLATZ, is where Martin Luther lodged as a boy; the present half-timbered structure encloses the original house. **Bachhaus,** FRAUENPLAN (Mon 1330–1630, Tue–Fri 0900–1630, Sat–Sun 0900–1200 and 1330–1630), the former Bach family home as well as the birthplace of J. S. Bach in 1685, is furnished in period style with documents and old musical instruments. A large statue of Bach stands just inside the big triple-galleried **St Georgenkirche**, MARKT, where he was christened.

☎(03691) 19419, Mon–Fri 0600–2400. Turn right outside for the town centre, a 5-min walk.

Tourist Office: MARKT 2; ☎(03691) 19433 (http://www.eisenach-tourist.de; email: tourist-info@eisenach-tourist.de).Mon 1000–1230 and 1315–1800,Thur–Fri 0900–1230 and 1315–1800, Sat–Sun 1000–1400.

There is a reasonable selection of both **Pensionen** and **Gasthofe** around DM30–50, such as **Pension 'Schlutter'**, PLANSTR. 39, ☎(03691) 213344, and **Gasthof 'Storchenturm'**, GEORGENSTR. 43, ☎(03691) 215250. The **youth hostel, Artur Becker**, MARIENTAL 24, ☎(03691) 743259, is about 1 km from the city centre. The **campsite, Altenberger See**, WILHELMSTHAL, ☎(03691) 215637, is some 10 km away, but is accessible by bus to BAD LIEBENSTEIN, from the bus station next to the rail station. It is on a lake, in the middle of the Thuringian Forest.

Eisenach was where East Germany's second most famous car (after the notoriously unrobust Trabant), the **Wartburg**, was manufactured, until 1991. The **Automobilbau-museum** (the Museum of Car Building), RENNBAHN 6–8 (in SPARKASSENGEBAUDE), ☎(03691) 743232, commemorates 100 years of its production (together with the occasional BMW).

WEIMAR

Smart shops, pavement cafés and a lively **Onion Fair**, which takes over the town for a weekend in October, are outward signs of **Weimar's** vitality. But, famously, Weimar is steeped in German culture, having been the home of two of the country's greatest writers, Goethe and Schiller, as well as the composers Bach, Liszt and Richard Strauss, the painter Lucas Cranach and the philosopher Nietzsche. It was also where the ill-fated pre-Nazi Weimar Republic was founded. Horse-drawn carriages offer 45-min rides (Apr–Oct) round the main centre of interest, **Altstadt**.

The entire town centre, with its wide tree-lined avenues, elegant squares and fine buildings, is officially listed as a historical monument. After decades of neglect, extensive renovation for its role as European City of Culture in 1999 – coinciding with the 250th anniversary of the birth of Goethe – has revived its gracious character.

The baroque mansion where Goethe lived, **Goethehaus**, FRAUENPLAN 1, displays furniture, personal belongings and a library of 5400 books. A stroll across the little River Ilm in the peaceful **Park an der Ilm** leads to the simple **Gartenhaus**, his first home in town and later his retreat (closed Tues). Goethe himself became a tourist attraction: people travelled from afar to glimpse the great man.

In the **Marktplatz** a plaque marks the house in the south corner where Bach lived when he was leader of the court orchestra. Close by, the spectacularly ornate **Cranachhaus** was where the painter Cranach spent the latter part of his life and produced the bulk of his work.

The **Liszthaus**, on the town side of the park, is the beautifully maintained residence of the Austro-Hungarian composer Franz Liszt. He moved to Weimar in 1848 to direct the local orchestra and spend the last 17 summers of his life: his piano and numerous manuscripts are on display.

Schiller spent the last three years of his life at **Schillerhaus**, SCHILLERSTR., and his rooms are much as they were then. Statues of Schiller and Goethe stand in the nearby THEATERPLATZ outside the imposing **Deutsches National Theater**, where many of their plays were first performed.

North of Weimar by 10 km is the memorial museum and site of Buchenwald, a grim reminder of the horrors of the Nazi regime during the Second World War.

The **Classic-Card Weimar**, at DM25, gives 3 days' worth of free transport, admission to the 12 most important museums in the city, a 50% reduction on City Tours and a 10% discount on tickets for the German National Theatre.

RAIL (03643) 903330 is 15 mins' walk north of the centre (nos. 1/7)

Tourist Office: MARKT 10; (03643) 24000 (http://www.weimar.de; email: tourist info@weimar.de) Mon–Fri 1000 – 1900, Sat–Sun 1000–1700 (Mar–Oct); Mon–Fri 1000–1800, Sat 1000–1500 (Nov–Apr).

The Café, Restaurant, Pension 'Hainfels', BELVEDERER ALLEE 65, (03643) 850116, and **Zum Alten Gasthof**, WOHLSBORNER STR. 2, (03643) 437300, are some of the cheaper guesthouses in town (prices are lower at weekends). There are 5 **youth hostels**, including **Germania**, CARL-AUGUST-ALLEE 13, (03643) 850490, 2 mins from the rail station, and the new **Am Poseckschen**, HUMBOLDTSTR. 17, (03643) 850792, in the centre.

LEIPZIG

Leipzig has been a cultural centre for many centuries, famous particularly for its music: numerous great 19th-century works were premiered at the **Gewandhaus**. AUGUSTUS-PLATZ, beside the broad ring road encircling the **Innenstadt**, makes a good starting point for a stroll around the pedestrianised centre, whose streets of long-neglected buildings and arcades are fast acquiring rows of smart shops and offices – yet Leipzig retains some of the grace of an old European city.

In 1989, the mass demonstrations and candlelit vigils in **Nikolaikirche,** NIKOLAISTR., were the focus for the city's brave peaceful revolt against communism. The **Stasi 'Power and Banality' Museum**, DITTRICHRING 24, in the former Ministry of State Security, covers the years of communist oppression.

Marktplatz is the centre for many of Leipzig's outdoor activities, including free concerts and impromptu beer fests. The fine Renaissance **Altes Rathaus** has survived and now houses the **Stadtgeschichtliches Museum**, covering the city's history.

From Leipzig a trip can be made to Colditz, an attractive little town dominated by its castle – made notorious as a prisoner-of-war camp in the Second World War.

Leipzig is second only to Vienna for its musical tradition, being the home of Bach, Mendelssohn and Schumann. The **Gewandhaus Orchestra**, **Opera House** and **Thomaner-chor** (St Thomas's Church Choir), which was conducted by Bach for 27 years, have a worldwide reputation. Performances of all kinds of music take place throughout the year.

RAIL (0341) 7240, on the edge of the Innenstadt (city centre), a 10-min walk to the middle. Known as the **Promenaden Hauptbahnhof Leipzig** and built in 1915, the station is an attraction in its own right, and is one of Europe's biggest and most impressive, recently refurbished and attired with a glossy shopping mall, with its restaurants, cafés and supermarkets. Also part of the facelift is the magnificent *Deutsche Bahn* waiting room, complete with bar, stained-glass overhead ceiling and rich wooden interior.

i **Tourist Office**: RICHARD-WAGNERSTR. 1; (0341) 704260. Just inside the Innenstadt, a 2-min walk from the rail station. Open Mon–Fri 0900–2000, Sat 1000–1600, Sun 1000–1400. Brochures are provided free (lipsia@aol.com). Local hotel and restaurant information, (0190) 588008 (http://www.Inn-line.com; email: inn-line@t-online.de).

There's a good tram network from the rail station, but most things of interest are within the pedestrianised Innenstadt, which is encircled by a ring road. A **day card**, including travel and museum discounts, costs DM9.90 (DM21 for 3 days).

Ask the Tourist Office for a list of local pensions; these include **Elster Pension Plagwitz**, GIESSERSTR. 15, (0341) 479 8039, starting at DM44 (without breakfast), and **Pension Britte**, GETZLAUER STR. 32, (0341) 338 1834, single room price from DM40. **Youth hostel**:

Jugendherberge Leipzig-Centrum, VOLKSGARTENSTR. 24, (0341) 245 7011, and **Am Ausensee**, GUSTAV-ESCHESTR. 4, (0341) 461 1114, on the north-west edge (tram nos.10/11/28), with a nearby campsite: **Am Ausensee**, GUSTAV-ESCHESTR. 5, (0341) 465 1600.

Restaurants crowd the pavements around KLEINE FLEISCHERGASSE, such as **Zill's Tunnel**, BARFÜSSGASSE 9, (0341) 960 2078, a typical Saxon beerhouse serving traditional dishes. Famed because Goethe featured it in *Faust*, having dined there as a student, is the 16th-century wood-panelled **Auerbachs** cellar restaurant in the exclusive Mädler shopping arcade off GRIMMAISCHESTR; (0341) 21600. Lots of cafés crowd around the MARKTPLATZ, with music spouting out of most of them. **Spizz** does jazz nights, as well as an excellent breakfast. **Internet café**: **Lebit**, KURGARTENSTR. 2, (0341) 9982020 (http://wilder,osten.de/le-bit; email: le bit@img-net.de).

DRESDEN

Capital of Saxony for four centuries, **Dresden** was one of Europe's most beautiful baroque cities until the British and American air raids of 1945. Much of the rebuilding is uninspired, but what survived was meticulously restored. To the west lies Dresden's best-known feature, the **Zwinger palace**, with its range of baroque buildings, including the **Orangery** and the exceptional **Old Master Picture Gallery** (Tues–Sun 1000–1800). A reconstruction of the **Semper Opera House** was unveiled in 1985. The same will eventually happen to the bombed **Dresden palace**, where work continues – you can view this free of charge.

RAIL Most trains serve the the rail station: (0351) 471 0600. Left luggage (PASSAGE 4, 0600–2200 Mon–Fri, 0600–2100 Sat, 0600–2200 Sun, DM2–4), exchange facilities, hotel information (main hall). Follow signs for PRAGER STR. – the old town is directly at the end of this street. **Neustädt station** is to the north; (0351) 471 0600.

The excellent value 48-hr **Dresden Card** allows free public transport, admission to 11 main museums, and bus, boat and tram city tours. **Travel passes**: DM2.70/hour; DM24 weekly; DM59 monthly.

Tourist Offices: PRAGER STR. (caravan near the rail station), Mon–Fri 0900–2000, Sat 0900–1600, Sun 1000–1400; SCHINKELWACHE, THEATERPLATZ, Mon–Fri 0900–1800 (–1600 Sat), Sun 1100–1600; NEUSTÄDTER MARKT (in tunnel), Mon–Fri 0900–1800 (–1600 Sat), Sun 1100–1600. All (0351) 491920.
Hostels include **Jugendgastehaus Dresden**, MATERNISTRASSE 22 (0351) 492 620; **Mondpalast**, KATHERINENSTRASSE 11–13, (0351) 804 6061, and cheap, central **hotels** include the **Stadt Rendsburg**, KAMENZER STR. 1, (0351) 804 1551.

WHERE NEXT FROM DRESDEN?

Trains to Prague (p. 492) take 3 hrs for the 191 km journey; there are eight services a day. ETT table: 60.

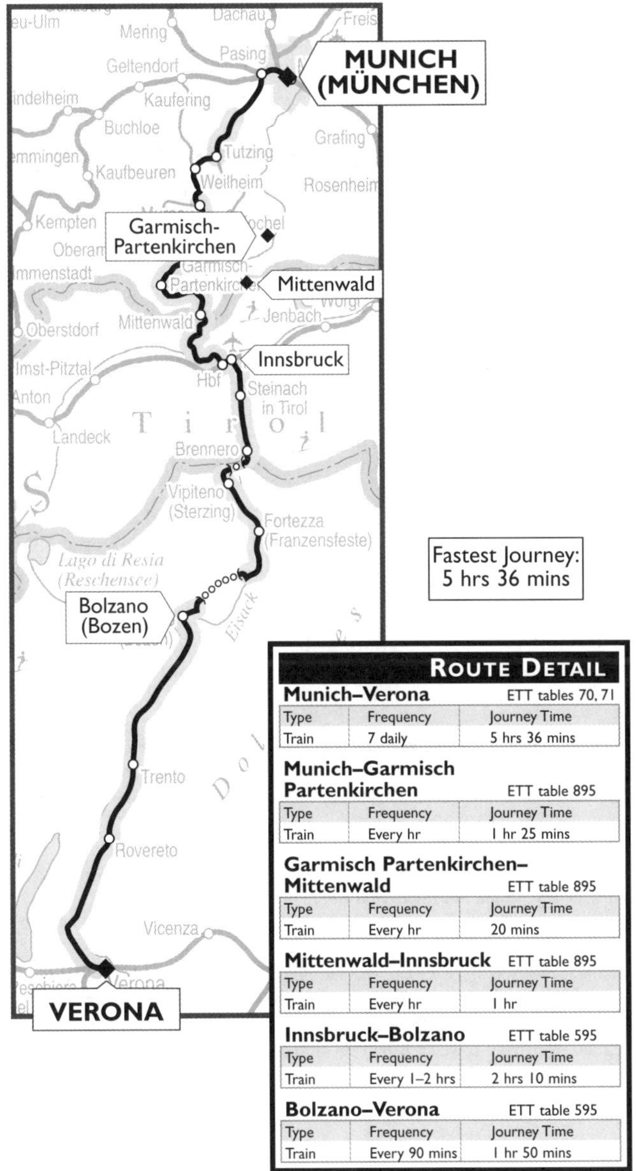

Fastest Journey:
5 hrs 36 mins

ROUTE DETAIL

Munich–Verona ETT tables 70, 71

Type	Frequency	Journey Time
Train	7 daily	5 hrs 36 mins

Munich–Garmisch Partenkirchen ETT table 895

Type	Frequency	Journey Time
Train	Every hr	1 hr 25 mins

Garmisch Partenkirchen–Mittenwald ETT table 895

Type	Frequency	Journey Time
Train	Every hr	20 mins

Mittenwald–Innsbruck ETT table 895

Type	Frequency	Journey Time
Train	Every hr	1 hr

Innsbruck–Bolzano ETT table 595

Type	Frequency	Journey Time
Train	Every 1–2 hrs	2 hrs 10 mins

Bolzano–Verona ETT table 595

Type	Frequency	Journey Time
Train	Every 90 mins	1 hr 50 mins

Munich – Innsbruck – Verona

Despite its relatively short distance, this journey through **Germany**, **Austria** and **Italy** and across the **Alps** packs in astonishing variety. Munich (p. 229) and Verona (p. 360), each worth at least a few days to explore, could hardly be more different, and the Alps change in character almost from one valley to the next.

GARMISCH-PARTENKIRCHEN

Once two quiet Bavarian villages at the foot of the 2962-m **Zugspitze**, Germany's highest mountain, **Garmisch** and **Partenkirchen** were officially united to host the 1936 Winter Olympics. Though now separated only by the railway line, they retain individual personalities. **Garmisch** is more expensive and upmarket while **Partenkirchen** has much more of a traditional Bavarian character – the most appealingly rustic part is around FRÜHLINGSTR.

Garmisch is Germany's most popular ski resort and has 52 lifts (12 open in summer), with downhill and cross-country skiing on offer. In summer, it's a centre for mountain walking, climbing and biking. The **Olympic Ice Stadium**, OLYMPIASTR., built in 1936, stays open virtually year-round.

The **Zugspitzbahn** cog railway goes from beside the main rail station to a point near the summit of the Zugspitze, a 75-min journey. On the way, it stops at **Eibsee**, an idyllic mountain lake, where you can transfer to the **Eibseebahn** cable car (often appallingly crowded) to reach the summit; alternatively, take the easy 7-km path round the lake itself, which has a pleasant beer garden. Meanwhile, the train continues up through a winding 4.5-km tunnel to **Sonnalpin** (2600 m), from where the **Gletscherbahn** cable car goes the final stage to the summit. The views are impressively far-ranging in decent weather.

RAIL ☎(08821) 19419, centrally located between Garmisch and Partenkirchen.

i **Tourist Office**: RICHARD-STRAUSS PL., ☎(08821) 1806 (http://www.garmisch-partenkirchen.de). Mon–Sat 0800–1800, Sun 1000–1200.

This is a popular ski resort, with plenty of pensions and hotels. The least expensive options are private rooms, which include **Hildegard Huber**, SCHWALBENSTR. 4, ☎(08821) 3443, and **Martin Maurer**, TORLENSTR. 5, ☎(08821) 2994, both with rooms between DM25 and DM30.

Partenkirchen has plenty of typically Bavarian bar-restaurants. **Gasthof Fraundorfer**, LUDWIGSTR. 24, ☎(08821) 2176, and **Gasthof Werdenfelser Hof**, LUDWIGSTR. 58, ☎(08821) 3621, both offer folklore evenings (thigh-slapping and *Lederhosen*). **Youth hostel**: JOCHSTR. 10, ☎(08821) 2980, 4 km from town, in **Burgrain** (nos. 3/4/5). **Campsite**: ZUGSPITZE, ☎(08821) 3180, west, near **Grainau** village.

MITTENWALD

Close to the Austrian border, **Mittenwald** is perhaps the most attractive town in the German Alps, with an abundance of character. Elaborate outside murals are another striking feature, but the town's main claim to fame is in its violins. Matthias Klotz (1653–1743), a pupil of the great Amati, began Mittenwald's tradition of high-quality violin-making that continues to this day.

Youth hostel: BUCKELWIESEN 7, (8823) 1701.

INNSBRUCK

See p. 319.

BOLZANO (BOZEN)

Although in Italy and with street names in Italian, **Bolzano** looks decidedly Austrian, with its pastel-coloured baroque arcades and Austrian menu items; from the 14th to 19th centuries Bolzano was mostly in the possession of Austria. Set beneath Alpine slopes in a deep valley, it's a pleasant enough stopover, handy for exploring the **Dolomites**. PIAZZA WALTHER is the focus of the town's outdoor life.

RAIL (0471) 974 292; 5 mins from the town centre. Buses stop from an area by a small park, reached by crossing the main road outside the station and turning left.

Tourist office: Municipal: PIAZZA WALTHER 8, (0471) 970 660 (Mon–Fri 0830–1800; Sat 0900–1230). **Regional**: PIAZZA PARROCHIA 11/12, (0471) 993 808.**Mountaineering**: **Club Alpino Italiano (CAI)**, PIAZZA DELL'ERBE, (0471) 971 694.

Reasonable range, starting from moderately priced.

WHERE NEXT FROM BOLZANO?

Buses from Bolzano climb eastward into the Dolomites for some of the most stunning scenery in the Alps. It's a virtually unbeatable region for walking, with paths to suit all abilities. A good centre to head for is ***Ortisei*** *(St Ulrich in German), reached by direct bus twice daily from Bolzano. Famed for its woodcarving tradition, this pleasantly set small town at the meeting of valleys has plenty of accommodation and walkers are spoilt for choice. A cable car takes you onto the* ***Seiseralm****, said to be the largest of all Alpine pastures, and abundant in very easy strolls punctuated with strategically sited cafés.*

SWITZERLAND

(for Directory information, see p. 567).

Even by European standards, Switzerland packs a lot into a small space, and, even with its admirable transport system, it can take a surprisingly long time to explore thoroughly, though it's predominantly scenery rather than sights that attracts the appreciable crowds. For once, reality lives up to the common preconception: the **Swiss Alps** have idyllically unspoilt Alpine pastures, grazed by bell-wearing cattle and backed with improbably perfect snow-topped pointy mountains, and the Swiss are still into traditions of the likes of alpenhorn-blowing, yodelling and folk music, as well as regional specialities, festivals (including classical music and jazz) and local pageantry. Costs can deter budget travellers from lingering, though it's not too bad if you use the hostels and mountain huts. Don't expect to find dazzling nightlife: a lot of it is decidedly peaceful after dark, although there's quite a bit happening in **Zürich**. Souvenir shopping can be rewarding, with numerous items special to certain areas, such as hand-woven linen, country crafts, painted pottery and wood carving.

There are marked regional differences, and four separate languages. Although most of the population lives outside the Alps in cities such as **Geneva** and **Basel**, you can still find pockets of rustic and architecturally varied picture-book charm, with quaint wooden chalets and traditional farmhouses scattered around the landscape (to a much greater extent than you'll find in neighbouring Austria). The best areas include the dramatic valley of the **Engadine** (where ski resorts such as Davos and St Moritz double as summer centres for walking) and in the side valleys of the **Valais** region (in the south-west).

INFORMATION

Switzerland Tourism (**ST**) can provide information on accommodation, but does not make bookings.

HOSTELS

The hostelling headquarters is **Schweizer Jugendherbergen**, SCHAFFHAUSERSTR. 14, POSTFACH 161, CH 8042 ZÜRICH, SWITZERLAND, ☎(41) (1) 360 14 14, fax (41) (1) 360 14 60 (http://www.youthhostel.ch; bookingoffice@youth-hostel.ch).

CAMPSITES

Guides are available from specialist bookshops or **Schweizer Camping und Caravanning Verband**, HABSBURGERSTR. 35, 6004 LUZERN, ☎(041) 23 48 22, or **Verband Schweizer Campings**, SEESTR. 119, 3800 INTERLAKEN; ☎(036) 23 35 23.

Some of the most majestic scenery is in the **Bernese Oberland**, around the relaxed, provincial-feeling capital, **Berne,** and on the doorsteps of **Interlaken** and **Grindelwald**. Less of a scenic jaw-dropper, central Switzerland does have some delicious lake scenery, notably around **Lake Lucerne** and **Lake Geneva** *(Lac Léman)*. **Lugano**, in the south, is unmistakably Italian in feel.

ACCOMMODATION

Swiss hotels have high standards but are expensive, and you'll be very lucky to get anything for less than SFr50 for a single or SFr80 for a double. In rural areas and Alpine resorts, it is often possible to get rooms in **private houses** (look for *Zimmer frei* signs posted in windows and gardens), but these are few and far between in cities. Budget travellers (unless they are camping) rely heavily on **youth hostels** – so book these as far ahead as possible. Every major town and major station has a **hotel-finding service**, sometimes free and seldom expensive. If you want a double bed, you must ask for a 'matrimonial' or 'French' bed. Prices vary widely according to season.

YOUTH HOSTELS These cost SFr17.50–30, including linen and breakfast (but excluding breakfast at the cheapest hostels), with a second night reduction of SFr2.50; self-caterers pay a small fee for use of fuel. Most hostels have family rooms.

BACKPACKERS' ACCOMMODATION Mountain backpackers can stay at **Swiss Alpine Club** (**SAC**) huts; these are primarily climbing huts based at the start of climbing routes, but walkers are welcome. There are also (in more accessible locations) mountain inns known as *Berghotels* or *Auberges de Montagne,* with simple dormitory accommodation as well as private rooms ranging from basic to relatively luxurious.

CAMPING There are hundreds of **campsites** in Switzerland (most open summer only). They are graded on a one to five star system. International *carnets* are required at many campsites. 'Rough' camping is not officially permitted, though it does happen.

FOOD AND DRINK

Portions tend to be ample, and pork and veal are common menu items, but in the lake areas you'll also find fresh fish. Swiss cheese is often an ingredient in local dishes; the classic *Swiss fondue*, for instance, is bread dipped into a pot containing melted cheese, garlic, wine and kirsch. *Raclette*, a speciality of the canton of Valais, is simply melted cheese, served with boiled potatoes, gherkins and silverskin onions. The ubiquitous meal accompaniment in German-speaking areas is *Rösti*, fried potatoes and onions, while French Switzerland goes in for stronger tastes, such as smoked sausages. In the Grisons, *Bündnerfleisch* is a tasty raw smoked beef, sliced very thin. Swiss wines are also excellent and very difficult to get in other countries.

There is a wide range of both food and eating-places. The cheapest are supermarket or department store cafeterias, such as those housed in the ubiquitous **Migros** outlets. Look out too for **EPA**, **Co-op** and, in Ticino, **Inova**. At lunch time (and quite often in the evenings), most resturants have a fixed-price dish-of-the-day menu *(Tagesteller, plat du jour, piatto del giorno),* which is good value. Tipping in Swiss restaurants is not the norm.

EDITOR'S CHOICE

Berne; Château de Chillon (near Montreux); Interlaken; Lucerne; Lugano; Sion; St Moritz; Zermatt; Zurich. Scenic rail journeys: Chur–St Moritz (Bernina Express, p. 286); Berne–Geneva via Interlaken (p. 294); St Moritz–Zermatt (Glacier Express; see Where Next from Brig?, p. 299); Jungfraujoch and other funiculars from Interlaken (see panels, pp. 297, 298); Gornergrat mountain railway from Zermatt (see panel, p. 299); Lucerne–Lugano (p. 304).

Virtually any list of the world's top ten rail journeys would include at least one trip in Switzerland. As well as the breathtakingly engineered routes over countless viaducts and through scores of tunnels, such as the **Glacier Express** from Zermatt to St Moritz, rack railways edge their way up improbable gradients to stunning viewpoints such as the **Jungfraujoch**.

BEYOND THE BORDER

Basel–Brussels via Strasbourg (ETT table 43); Basel–Milan (table 84); Zurich–Vienna (table 86); Zurich–Stuttgart (table 84); Basel–Hamburg via Cologne (table 73); Geneva–Avignon via Lyon (tables 14, 81); Sion–Chamonix Mont Blanc (see Where Next from Sion?, p. 300).

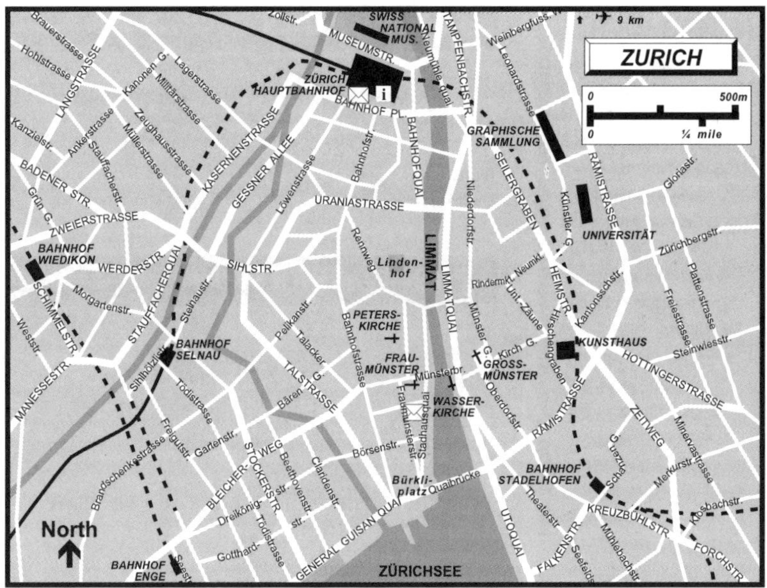

Switzerland's largest city (though not its capital), publicised as the 'little big city', comes as a surprise. Despite a stern reputation as one of the world's major financial centres, it has a picturesque setting on the River Limmat beside Lake Zürich, a mountain backdrop, immaculate quayside parks, smart shops, open-air cafés, chic shopping and ancient squares. With its sizeable immigrant population, the city wears a distinctly cosmopolitan air. The best view of the lake and city is from Quaibrücke, which crosses the Limmat where the lake flows into it.

ARRIVAL AND DEPARTURE

RAIL **Zürich Hauptbahnhof** (HB), ☎(01) 157 22 22, is on the west side of River Limmat and leads out onto BAHNHOFSTR., the main shopping street.

✈ **Zürich-Kloten Airport** is 12 km north-east of the city centre; information, ☎(01)157 10 60. Trains run every 10–15 mins from the rail station; journey time 10 mins.

TOURIST OFFICE

On the station concourse, BAHNHOFPL. 15, ☎(01) 215 40 00; Mon–Fri 0830–2030, Sat–Sun 0830–1830 (May–Sept), Mon–Fri 0830–1900, Sat–Sun 0900–1830 (Nov–Mar) (http://www.zuerich.ch; zhtourismus@access.ch). This efficient, well-stocked office sells a street map (SFr. 1, or SFr. 3 with index), provides a free accommodation service and the free 2-week listing, *Zürich News*, and monthly *Zürich Guide*.

INFORMATION

PHONES To phone **Zürich from abroad**: ☎ 41 (Switzerland) + 1 (Zürich); to phone **Zürich from elsewhere in Switzerland**: ☎01.

INTERNET CAFÉ

Cybergate (rail station), open daily 1130–2300, SFr. 5 for 20 mins, includes up to 20 pages printed free.

PUBLIC TRANSPORT

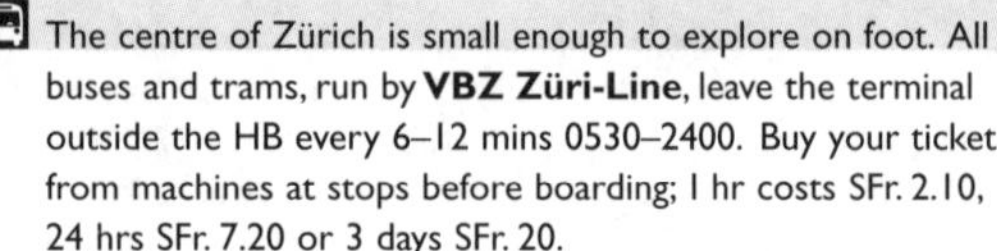

The centre of Zürich is small enough to explore on foot. All buses and trams, run by **VBZ Züri-Line**, leave the terminal outside the HB every 6–12 mins 0530–2400. Buy your ticket from machines at stops before boarding; 1 hr costs SFr. 2.10, 24 hrs SFr. 7.20 or 3 days SFr. 20.

Taxis: ☎(01) 222 22 22, or hail one in the street. **Bikes** can be hired at the rail station.

ACCOMMODATION

HOTELS

The **Aparthotel**, KARLSTR. 5, ☎(01) 422 11 75, is central and near the lake, with rooms beginning at SFr. 78.

The **St Josef**, HIRSCHENGRABEN 64–68, ☎(01) 251 27 57, is located between the rail station and University, prices from SFr. 70.

Hotel Biber, NIEDERDORFSTR. 5, ☎251 90 15, is in the lively Niederdorfer area and has dormitories and private rooms from SFr. 65.

HOSTELS

HI: MUTSCHELLENSTR. 114, ☎(01) 482 35 44, south of the city in Wollishofen (tram no.7 to MORGENTAL, then 5-min walk).

CAMPSITES

Campingplatz Zürich-Seebucht, SEESTR. 559, ☎(01) 482 16 12 (bus nos.161/165 from BÜRKLIPL.)

FOOD AND DRINK

Zürich has a large selection of restaurants of most nationalities, as well as its own local cuisine. The Tourist Office issues a restaurant guide, *Gastro Zürich-City*, which includes many affordable places among the 196 listed. Local specialities include *Kalbgeschnetzeltes* (veal in cream sauce) and the less expensive pork version,

Schweingeschnetzeltes. There are numerous fast-food and conventional restaurants around the huge station complex. The largest selection of eating places is on or just off NIEDERDORFSTR., the main nightlife area, which stretches for about 1 km on the east side of the river, a block back from it. Fierce competition keeps prices at a relatively reasonable level, even in the smarter roads and squares that lead off it to the east. For a novel experience that combines sightseeing and dining, board the **Chuchi Chäschtli tram**, which serves typical Swiss dishes on the move. It runs May–Oct and covers a loop around both banks of the Limmat starting at BELLEVUEPL., which is where you should board if you wish to dine (see Tourist Office for details).

RESTAURANTS

Walliser Kanne, LINTHESCHERG. 21, ☎211 31 33, a 2-min walk from the station complex, serves fondue, raclette and dishes from the Valais area, in a dark wood-panelled setting.
Rheinfelder Bierhalle, 76 NIEDERDORFSTR., ☎251 54 64, is one of the best value establishments for hearty local food.
Adler's Swiss Chuchi, part of **Hotel Adler**, ROSENG. 10, ☎266 96 96, serves local dishes. Moderate.
Le Dézaley, RÖMERGASSE 7, ☎251 61 29, is slightly more expensive but excellent for fondues.
Hiltl Vegi, SIHLSTR. 28, ☎221 38 70, which opened in 1898, serves the best vegetarian food in town but is not cheap.

HIGHLIGHTS

On the west bank of the Limmat, just behind the station, is the **Schweizerisches Landesmuseum** (Swiss National Museum), housed in a 19th-century mock castle, and giving an excellent cross-section of Swiss history. Reconstructed rooms depict different periods and there are impressive displays of costumes, weapons and medieval art. A stroll away, the city's highest spot, **LINDENHOF**, is a wide terrace of lime trees with good views overlooking the river. It's a favourite with local people who come to grapple with chess – three sets of giant pieces are there for anyone to use. The nearby 13th-century **Peterskirche** is remarkable for its 16th-century clock tower, the largest in Europe; each of the four faces is 8.7 m wide.

Near MÜNSTERBRÜCKE, the 13th-century **Fraumünster** has five outstanding stained-glass windows by Marc Chagall. Across the bridge, the twin towers of the Romanesque **Grossmünster** (cathedral), offer great

TOURS

Various daily city coach tours and guided walks are organised by the Tourist Office, departing from the main station. Glass-roofed cruisers offer circular 1-hr trips along the Limmat from outside the rail station by the *Schweizerisches Landesmuseum*. Lake cruises and other touring options, such as steamboat parties and dance/fondue cruises, are offered by **Zürichsee-Schiffahrtsgesellschaft**, ☎(01) 487 13 13, leaving from BÜRKLIPL. at the tip of the lake.

views from the top, daily 1330–1700. It has stained glass by the Swiss artist Giacometti and a statue of Charlemagne in the crypt. Nearby, **Wasserkirche** (Water Church), on LIMMATQUAI, is attached to the 18th-century **Helmhaus**, cloth market hall, where contemporary art exhibitions are staged.

Other old **Zunfthäuser** (guild halls) line LIMMATQUAI, some now converted to restaurants. **Kunsthaus** (Fine Arts Museum), HEIMPL., has a major collection ranging from late Gothic to contemporary, including Giacometti sculptures. On the east bank, in the heart of the **Niederdorf** area, take a stroll along the quiet and narrow *Spiegelg* to see the house where Lenin once lived (no. 14).

Reached by tram no. 2 or 4, at ZOLLIKERSTR. 172, the **Sammlung Bührle** (Bührle Collection) is a wonderful treasure-trove of art displayed in the villa of the industrialist who collected it; Emil Bührle had a taste for Impressionist paintings, and the means to acquire them, resulting in a rich show of works by Manet, Sisley and Van Gogh, as well as earlier masters such as Delacroix and Hals.

Day trip from Zürich

Just within the Swiss side of the German border is the 150-m wide and 23-m high **Rheinfall** – the dramatic start of the same Rhine that ends in the North Sea, having wound its way gently through the castles of middle Germany from Basel. Taking 45–50 mins from Zürich to Schaffhausen (ETT table 940), the train then continues to the base of the falls themselves, a journey of only 3 mins. The walk down from **Schloss Laufen** (which is a youth hostel, ☎(052) 360 14 14) skirts the water, leading to dramatic views. Halfway down, a tunnel opens out directly into the middle of the cascade, granting a spectacular, if a bit damp, prospect. Continuing along the cliff walk, and down to the water level, it's possible to take a boat trip to the tiny Swiss-flag adorned island in the middle of the stream (for boat information: **Rhyfall Mandli** ☎(052) 672 48 11).

SHOPPING

The main shopping street is BAHNHOFSTR. Look out particularly for **Franz Karl Weber** at no. 62, which sells toys of all sorts, including a big selection of model trains, and cuckoo clocks. **Sprungli** is arguably the best *Konditorei* in town and sells superb chocolate, some not sold outside of Zürich. AUGUSTINGASSE, off it, is charming and has buildings dating from the 14th century as well as several very smart boutiques. **Jermoli Department Store**, just off BAHNHOFSTR. has the best selection and prices for Swiss souvenirs. They also have a '**Gourmet Garage**', which stocks British and American items. Shopping hours are Mon–Fri 0800–1830, Sat 0800–1600, though a few stay open until 2100 on Sat. Shops in the rail station open daily 0800–2000. The **Apothek** (pharmacy) here is open daily 0700–midnight.

NIGHT-TIME AND EVENTS

The **Zürich Night Card** (SFr. 20), is good for 3 consecutive nights, offering free transport (after 1700) as well as significant discounts and offers at many of the city's centrally located restaurants, bars and clubs.

There's no shortage of bars, clubs and street performers on and around NIEDERDORFSTR., a lively – and safe – area for tourists, despite its reputation as the city's red light district.

Zürich's acclaimed opera company performs at the **Opernhaus Zürich**, THEATERPL., ☎(01) 268 66 66; concerts are given at the **Tonhalle**, CLARIDENSTR 7 (☎206 34 34), which was inaugurated by Brahms in 1895.

In mid-April is the **Sechseläuten**, the city's spring festival, when its guild members celebrate the end of winter by parading in historic costumes before burning Böögg, a huge snowman, on an enormous bonfire. July sees the Zürich **Festspiele**, a 3-week music festival inaugurated in 1997; box office, ☎215 40 82. In Aug there is a **Street Parade** of young people and deafening music to celebrate love, peace and tolerance.

WHERE NEXT FROM ZÜRICH?

*Hourly trains to **Lucerne** (45 mins; ETT table 555) join the **Berne–Lugano** route* *(p. 304).*

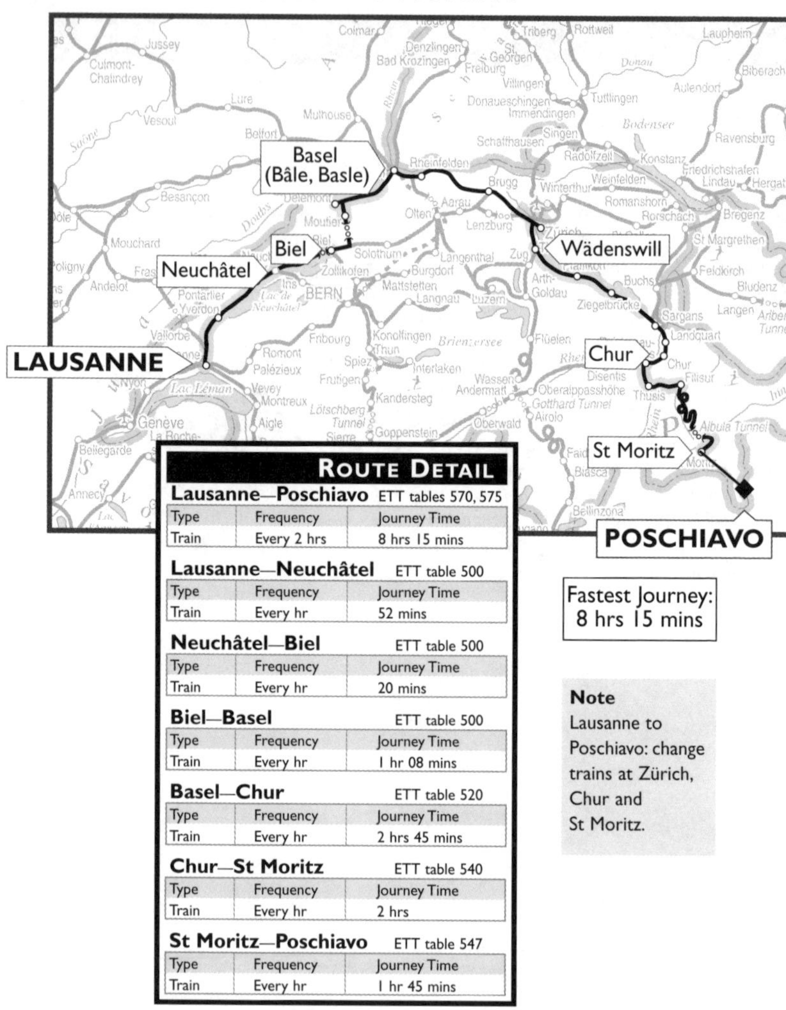

ROUTE DETAIL

Lausanne—Poschiavo ETT tables 570, 575

Type	Frequency	Journey Time
Train	Every 2 hrs	8 hrs 15 mins

Lausanne—Neuchâtel ETT table 500

Type	Frequency	Journey Time
Train	Every hr	52 mins

Neuchâtel—Biel ETT table 500

Type	Frequency	Journey Time
Train	Every hr	20 mins

Biel—Basel ETT table 500

Type	Frequency	Journey Time
Train	Every hr	1 hr 08 mins

Basel—Chur ETT table 520

Type	Frequency	Journey Time
Train	Every hr	2 hrs 45 mins

Chur—St Moritz ETT table 540

Type	Frequency	Journey Time
Train	Every hr	2 hrs

St Moritz—Poschiavo ETT table 547

Type	Frequency	Journey Time
Train	Every hr	1 hr 45 mins

Fastest Journey:
8 hrs 15 mins

Note

Lausanne to Poschiavo: change trains at Zürich, Chur and St Moritz.

Vineyards cling to the hilly shores of **Lac Neuchâtel**, where **Yverdon** and **Neuchâtel** are pleasantly set lakeside towns, and lake views are a feature from the right (south) side of the train as far as **Biel**. Beyond the watch-and clock-making town of **Delmont**, the scenery is less remarkable between the cities of **Basel** and **Zürich**. Thereafter, things step up a couple of gears, with **Lake Zürich** and the **Walensee** immediately on the left, and beyond **Sargans** you pass within a stone's throw of the tiny prinicipality of **Liechtenstein**. **Chur** lies at the foot of an astonishing climb high up into the **Alps**, a section covered by the **Bernina Express** service (reservation compulsory and supplement payable), where the finely set resort of **St Moritz** is at the heart of the **Engadine**, the huge straight valley of the **Inn** that cuts across the **Grisons** (Grishun) Switzerland's canton in Romansch-speaking south-eastern corner. **Poschiavo**, on the other hand, is distinctly Italian both in character and language, and from there you can cross into Italy via the **Bernina Pass**.

LAUSANNE

Half Alpine and half Riviera, this university town, both a commercial centre and resort, has a hilly setting, with some of the best views from the cathedral and old town, perched 130 m above **Lake Geneva**. The steepness of the place is part of its appeal, and if you don't fancy the trudge up from the lakeshore suburb of **Ouchy**, with its grand hotels and large park, to the station and up to the old town, there's a useful Metro (actually a funicular) linking all three in a few mins; from the old town it costs SFr.1.30 to the station and SFr.2.20 to Ouchy. The partly pedestrianised old town is small enough to be explored on foot.

The upper Metro terminal is at **Sainfe**, PL. ST-FRANÇOIS, just south of the main area of interest and dominated by the 15th-century steeple of the 13th–14th-century **Église St-François** (St Francis' Church). The **Cathédrale de Notre-Dame**, a 10-min walk up into the town, was consecrated in 1215. Italian, Flemish and French craftsmen all had a hand in its construction, and it is accepted as a perfect example of Burgundian Gothic. The watch is still called from the steeple every hour from 2000 to 0200.

The **Musée Historique de Lausanne**, PL. DE LA CATHÉDRALE 4 (closed Mon), in the **Ancien-Evêché** (the bishops' palace until the early 15th century), exhibits a large-scale model of 17th-century Lausanne. Also by the cathedral is another fortified bishops' residence, the **Château St-Maire**, now the seat of the cantonal government (part open to the public). **Escaliers-du-Marché**, a wooden-roofed medieval staircase, links the cathedral square to PL. DE LA PALUD, an ancient square surrounded by old houses.

LAUSANNE – BASEL – POSCHIAVO

DAY TRIP FROM LAUSANNE

Frequent **SBB** service links the waterfront towns. **Compagnie Générale de Navigation (CGN),** AVE DE RHODANIE 17, (021) 617 06 66, operate ferries from Ouchy (and paddle-steamers in summer) to **Geneva** (western end of the lake), **Evian** (in France, southern shore), **Montreux** and **St Gingolph**.

West of the cathedral, the Florentine-style **Palais de Rumine**, PL. DE LA RIPONNE, was built by a Russian family at the turn of the century. It now houses the modern university, as well as several museums. Take a 10-min walk north-west (or no.2) to the **Collection de l'Art Brut**, AV. DES BERGIÈRES 11, housed in the **Château de Beaulieu**. This compelling post-war gallery was founded by a local collector, who sought the works of anyone who was not a trained or formal painter, from amateur dabblers to the criminally insane.

North of the centre is the **Fondation de l'Hermitage**, ROUTE DU SIGNAL 2, an early 19th-century villa full of period fixtures and fittings, which hosts top-quality touring exhibitions of contemporary art. The view from the villa gardens, over the city and the lake to the Alps, is magnificent. For more lake views, take no.16 to the **Forêt de Sauvabelin**, 150 m above the city centre. This 140-acre beech forest offers a choice of walking paths and encompasses a deer reserve around a small lake (a natural skating rink in winter). Paths lead to **Vivarium**, CHEMIN DE BOISSONNET, a reptile zoo.

The **quai de Belgique** is a shady, flower-lined, waterside promenade, looking towards the Savoy Alps. The 13th-century keep of **Château d'Ouchy** is now a hotel. Baron Pierre de Coubertin, founder of the modern Olympics in 1915, chose Lausanne as the headquarters of the International Olympic Committee. The unique **Musée Olympique**, QUAI D'OUCHY 1 (Mon–Sun, 0900–1900, Thur till 2000) is a large modern complex, cleverly designed to retain the natural beauty of its surrounding park. Subsequently, in 1994, the city was named the official Olympic headquarters and the IOC is still located here. Boats can be hired near the 'cruise' pier.

RAIL (021) 320 80 71, between the centre and Ouchy, connected by the Metro. Left luggage facilities and bike rental available.

i **Tourist Office**: AVE DE OUCHY 60, (021) 613 26 26 (Mon–Sun 0900–1800; http:www.region-du-leman.ch; email:info@lake-geneva-region.ch). Pick up a free copy of *Lausanne: Useful Information*. A walking tour (not always in English) of the old town leaves from the Town Hall at 1000, Mon–Sat.

There's plenty of budget accommodation. The new **Jeunotel**, CHEMIN DU BOIS-DE-VAUX 36, (021) 626 02 26, on the lakeside west of Ouchy, offers simple modern rooms and dormitories, with prices starting at SFr.76–80. The one-star **La Croisee**, AV. M. DUFOUR 15, (021) 321 09 09, is in the middle of town, not far from the station, with rooms from SFr.88. **Youth hostel**: CHEMIN DE MUGUET 1, (021) 616 57 82, near Ouchy, by the lakeside. **Campsite**: **Camping de Vidy,** CHEMIN DU CAMPING 3, (021) 624 20 31.

Colour Section

(i) The Jungfraujoch from Interlaken (p. 298); inset: Highest open-air railway station in Europe at Gornergrat (p. 299)

(ii) Roof spire, duomo, Milan, Italy (p. 334)

(iii) A narrow street in Siena, Italy (p. 364)

(iv) Old town square, Poznan, Poland (p. 484); Auschwitz Prison Camp, Poland (p. 487).

33

MUZYCZNA
MUZYCZNA
ARBEIT MACHT FREI

NEUCHÂTEL

Set steeply beside the 38-km-long lake of the same name, **Neuchâtel** slopes down from its castle to its old town, and down to the busy quays. At the heart of the old town, itself characterised by Renaissance fountains and defensive towers, is **Place Pury**; markets are held in the adjacent **Place des Halles**. It's well worth the walk up to the top of town, past the **Tour des Prisons** (prison tower), used as a dungeon until 1848, for the views from the town's monumental set pieces: the imposing **Château**, built from the 12th to 16th centuries, now functions as the cantonal office; free guided tours take you inside, though there's not much of historical interest inside nowadays. A walkway leads from there to the **Église Collégiale** (collegiate church), founded in the 12th century and featuring a splendid 14th-century monument to the Counts of Neuchâtel. The town's museums include the **Musée d'Art et d'Histoire**, boasting three fascinatingly intricate 18th-century automata – a draughtsman, a writer and a musician – the latter representing a lady harpsichordist.

(032) 157 22 22; 1 km north of the centre.

Tourist office: *Hotel des Postes* (032) 889 68 90. Open Mon–Fri 0900–1200, 1330–1730; Mon–Sat 0900–1700, Sun 1600–1900 (July–Aug).

WHERE NEXT FROM NEUCHÂTEL?

Twice-hourly trains, taking 36 mins, link Neuchâtel with ***Berne****, where you can join the* ***Berne–Geneva*** *(p. 294) or* ***Berne–Lugano*** *(p. 304) routes.*

BIEL (BIENNE)

Beside **Lake Biel**, the busy clock-making town (home to Omega watches since 1879) is unique in Switzerland in that French and German share equal billing – you can even hear one person talking in French and the other answering in German; French speakers know it as Bienne. Its old town has a wealth of medieval architecture, with turrets and arcades characteristic of the Bernese style, and prettily painted wrought-iron signs. Some of the best of it is along BURGGASSE and the RING, a fine old square with a 16th-century fountain in the middle.

Hauptbahnof, (032) 157 22 22, town centre. The old town is a 10-min walk via BAHNHOFSTR. and NIDAUGASSE, while the lake is 5 mins away, behind the station via BADHAUSSTR.

LAKE BIEL AND ST PETERSINSEL

Lake Biel *(Bielersee* or *lac de Bienne)* has a nearby bathing beach, but its chief interest derives from ***St Petersinsel*** (St Peter's Island), a nature reserve reached by a 50-min boat trip from SCHIFFLÄNDE, just west of Biel station.

A monastery on the island has been tastefully converted into the **Restaurant-Hotel,** ST PETERSINSEL ((032) 88 11 14); here in 1765 the Swiss-born French philosopher Jean-Jacques Rousseau spent a blissful time, which he recorded in his *Confessions* and in the *Reveries of the Solitary Walker*.

Tourist Office: INFO CENTER AM BAHNHOF, ☎(032) 322 75 75. Open Mon–Fri 0800–1230, 1330–18, Sat 0900–1500, May–Oct.

BASEL (BÂLE, BASLE)

Wedged into the corners of Switzerland, France and Germany, this big, working city (the second largest in the country after Zürich) has long been a crossroads for European culture, with many museums and other sights.

Of the six bridges across the River Rhine, **Mittlere Brücke** offers the best views. The medieval centre is on the south bank, in GROSSBASEL. KLEINBASEL is the small modern area on the north bank. Admission to most museums generally costs around SFr.6/7, with some, such as the **Basel Museum of Ancient Art** and the **Historisches Museum**, offering free entry on the first Sun of the month.

BASEL'S CARNIVAL

The **Basel Fasnacht** is the country's most riotous carnival, taking over the town at 0400 on the Mon after Ash Wednesday and lasting for three days of noisy colourful fancy-dress fun.

Just south of the Rhine, MÜNSTERPLATZ is dominated by the 12th-century red sandstone **Münster** (cathedral), which has decorative twin towers, a Ro-manesque portal surrounded by elegant carvings, and a rose window featuring the wheel of fortune. Housed within a Gothic church in BARFÜSSERPL., the **Historisches Museum** (closed Tues) has 13th–17th-century artefacts, including Luther's chalice; the 18th–19th-century sections of the collection are in the **Haus zum Kirschgarten**, ELISABETHENSTR. 27, about 300 m north of the SBB station.

TINGUELY IN BASEL

Tinguely is the Basel-born sculptor whose works typically resemble parodies of machines, manically juddering into action, seemingly against the odds. His **Fasnacht-Brunnen/Tinguely-Brunnen**, THEATERPL., is an extraordinary fountain (1977) that resembles a watery scrapyard. A museum dedicated to Tinguely, the **Museum Jean Tinguely**, GRENZACHERSTR. 210, celebrates his life and work (closed Mon, Tues).

The one sight not to miss is the world-class **Kunstmuseum** (Fine Arts Museum; closed Mon; tram no.2 from the SBB rail station), ST-ALBAN-GRABEN 16, in a building constructed in 1932–36 to house the art treasures the town had been accumulating since the 17th century, including important works by the 15th-century Basel master Konrad Witz, the world's largest collection of works by the Holbein family, and modern contributors such as Van Gogh, Picasso, Braque and Dalí.

GETTING AROUND BASEL

Most of the old centre is pedestrianised. Elsewhere a frequent tram service is supplemented by buses. Information and tickets (SFr.1.20) are available from machines at every stop.

The permanent collection of the **Museum für Gegenwartskunst** (Museum of Contemporary Art), ST-ALBAN-RHEINWEG 60, ☎(061) 272 81 83, includes pieces by Stella, Warhol and Beuys.

The recently restored 16th-century **Rathaus** (Town Hall) has an ornate and very picturesque red façade that includes an enormous clock. It towers over MARKTPLATZ, the long-standing heart of Basel. Of the two main surviving medieval city gates, **St-Alban-Tor**, ST-ALBAN-GRABEN, takes second place to the splendid 14th-century **Spalentor**, SPALENGRABEN. Near here, on SPALENVORSTADT, is the pick of the town's older fountains, the **Holbeinbrunnen**, based partly on a Holbein drawing and a Dürer engraving.

The **Zoologischer Garten**, BINNINGERSTR. 40, west of the SBB station, has gained a reputation for breeding armoured rhinos, but is also known for its collections of pygmy hippos, gorillas and penguins.

Basel is a frontier town for both France and Germany. The main station, **Bahnhof SBB**, ☎(061) 157 22 22, is a 10-min walk south of the city centre (5 mins on tram nos. 1/8 from the terminus in front of the station), and handles Swiss and principal German services. Facilities include left luggage (SFr.5 per day), bike rental (SFr.20 per day), showers, a post office and a supermarket with extended opening hours. The **SNCF** station, ☎36 35 35 35, provides French services and boasts a large, suspended and animated Tinguely sculpture. Both stations evoke the heady old days of train travel, owing to the city's location at the 'Triangle' of Europe.

Tourist Office: SCHIFFLÄNDE 5; ☎(061) 268 68 68, near the MITTLERE BRÜCKE (Mon–Fri 0830–1800, Sat 1000–1600). At the SBB rail station, ☎(061) 271 36 84 (Mon–Fri 0830–1800, Sat 1830–1230; longer hours in summer), the staff are extremely helpful. E-mail: office@baseltourismus.ch.

Moderate hotels in the old town include the **Stadthof**, GERBERGASSE 84, ☎(061) 261 87 11, with prices beginning around SFr.120–150 (without private facilities), and the **Steinschanze**, STEINGRABEN 69, ☎(061) 272 53 53, at SFr.150–250, including shower. The **youth hostel** (**Auberge de Jeunesse Bâle**) is at ST ALBAN-KIRCHRAIN 10, ☎(061) 272 05 72, a 15-min walk from the SBB station or tram no.2, then a 5-min walk. **Camping Place Waldhort**, is 20–30 mins' south of the Bahnhof SBB rail station, via tram no. 11 to LANDHOF.

INTERNET CAFÉS

CYBERZONE, GERBERGASSE 43, PFLUGGASSELIN; Mon–Fri 1100–2300, Sat 1000–2400, Sun 1300–1900.

CHUR

A cathedral city as well as capital of the canton of Grisons (population 32,000), **Chur** (pronounced Koohr) has an appealing old town. Green and red footprints mark recommended walking tours of the town (details from Tourist Office). With a fair range of places to eat and stay, it makes a feasible stopover.

DAY TRIP FROM CHUR TO DAVOS

Retrace the route back to **Landquart**, and change for Davos (two stations: **Davos Dorf** and **Davos Platz**, the latter being the main place for activity, 67 mins by narrow-gauge railway, hourly (ETT table 545). This ski resort (**Tourist Office**: PROMENADE 67, DAVOS PLATZ, ☎(081) 45 21 21.) is on yet another scenic line, between Landquart and **Filsur** – both ends connecting with the main **Lausanne–Poschiavo** route. **Davos** is the highest town in Europe (1560 m), and though it's rather dominated by modern purpose-built blocks and lacking in genuine Alpine atmosphere, it is an excellent centre for walking: a favourite easy excursion is to take the funicular up to the Alpine Garden at **Schatzalp**, where 800 plant species flourish. Schatzalp has a summer toboggan run and toboggans are for hire. Alternatively, take the cable car to **Jakobshorn** for superlative views along waymarked paths from the top. There's a **youth hostel** at **7625 Davos-Wolfgang**, ☎(081) 416 14 84.

Its Romanesque-Gothic cathedral, built 1150–1272, has a dark, impressive interior with an exceptional Gothic triptych of carved and gilded wood, made by Jakob Russ 1486–92. In POSTPLATZ in the **Kunstmuseum** has works by artists associated with Grisons.

RAIL In the town centre; cycle hire and left-luggage facility; ☎(081) 157 22 22.

i **Tourist Office**: GRABENSTR. 5, ☎(081) 252 18 18.

LIECHTENSTEIN

The Principality of **Liechtenstein**, independent since 1719, is a green, mountainous little country covering just 158 square km; the train passes very close to it at **Sargans**, from where buses go to the capital, **Vaduz** (Swiss Passes valid). Apart from giving the chance to pick up a passport stamp of an obscure country, there isn't much to attract visitors, though the **Liechtensteinische Staatliche Kunstsammlungen** (State Art Collection) has some fine works (including a dazzling golden carriage) from the private collection of the Prince, who lives with his family in **Schloss Vaduz** (not open). Liechtenstein issues its own postage stamps, and philatelists may like to pay a visit to the **Briefmarkenmuseum** (Postage Stamp Museum).

ST MORITZ

Even in the face of opposition from the likes of Zermatt and Davos, **St Moritz** still pretty much leads the way as a Swiss sports resort, with a breathtaking location and a sunshine record (322 sunny days a year) unrivalled elsewhere in the country.

St Moritz divides into **Dorf** (village) on the hill, and **Bad** (spa) 2 km downhill around the lake; in St Moritz-Dorf lie the main hotels, shops and museums (including the **Engadine Museum**, offering an absorbing look at the furniture and house interiors of the Engadine). The centre for downhill skiing is

Corviglia (2486 m), but even if you're not skiing it's worth the 2-km funicular trip for the views and a glimpse of the 'beautiful people' at play. From there, it's worth taking the cable car up to **Piz Nair** (3057 m) for a panorama of the Upper Engadine.

(081) 157 22 22. Near the centre of the town.

Tourist Office: VIA MAISTRA 12, (081) 837 33 33.

Accommodation and food are generally less expensive in St Moritz Bad than in St Moritz Dorf. **Youth hostel**: VIA SURPONT 60, 7500 ST MORITZ BAD, (081) 833 39 69.

WHERE NEXT FROM ST MORITZ?

Take the ***Glacier Express****, one of the great scenic rail journeys of the Alps from* **St Moritz** *to* ***Zermatt*** *via* ***Andermatt*** *and Brig* *(p. 299).*

POSCHIAVO

Tucked just inside the Swiss-Italian border, **Poschiavo** is distinctly southern in appearance, with a lovely central piazza surrounded by dignified Italianate houses. A wander round town reveals the 17th-century **town hall**, the Lombardian-style Gothic **church of San Vittore** and the 17th–18th-century **church of Santa Maria Presentata**, with its glorious ceiling. Spanish settlers in the 19th century built colourful houses in the SPANIOLA quarter.

(081) 157 22 22. In the town centre.

Tourist Office: PIAZZA COMMUNALE, (081) 844 05 71. Open Mon–Fri 0800–1200, 1400–1800, Sat 0900–1200 (summer); Mon–Fri 0900–1200, 1400–1700 (winter).

WHERE NEXT FROM POSCHIAVO?

Continue southwards over the **Bernina Pass** *and into Italy, passing the shore of* **Lake Lecco***, the eastern part of* **Lake Como** *and ending at* ***Milan*** *(p. 334).*
See ETT tables 547 and 593.

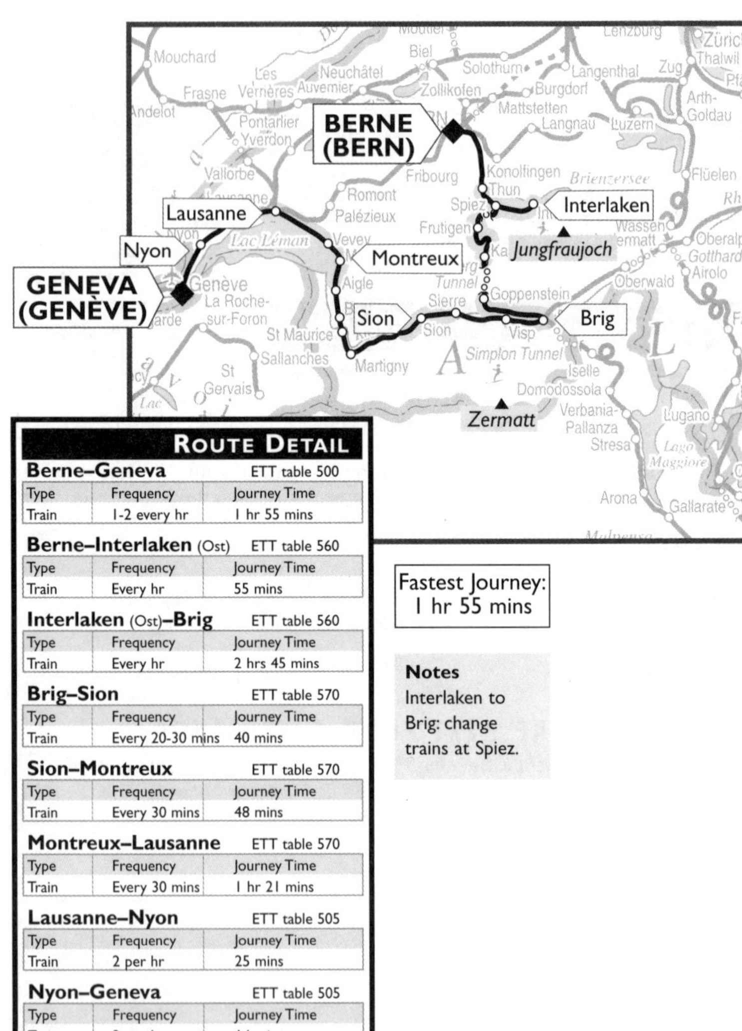

ROUTE DETAIL

Berne–Geneva ETT table 500

Type	Frequency	Journey Time
Train	1-2 every hr	1 hr 55 mins

Berne–Interlaken (Ost) ETT table 560

Type	Frequency	Journey Time
Train	Every hr	55 mins

Interlaken (Ost)**–Brig** ETT table 560

Type	Frequency	Journey Time
Train	Every hr	2 hrs 45 mins

Brig–Sion ETT table 570

Type	Frequency	Journey Time
Train	Every 20-30 mins	40 mins

Sion–Montreux ETT table 570

Type	Frequency	Journey Time
Train	Every 30 mins	48 mins

Montreux–Lausanne ETT table 570

Type	Frequency	Journey Time
Train	Every 30 mins	1 hr 21 mins

Lausanne–Nyon ETT table 505

Type	Frequency	Journey Time
Train	2 per hr	25 mins

Nyon–Geneva ETT table 505

Type	Frequency	Journey Time
Train	2 per hr	14 mins

Fastest Journey: 1 hr 55 mins

Notes
Interlaken to Brig: change trains at Spiez.

Berne, an easy-going city that has been the seat of Swiss government since 1848, is the prelude to the dramatic heights of the Berner Oberland, a long-established area for tourism, with the best of it around Interlaken and Grindelwald. Highly recommended is the day trip by rack railway up Jungfraujoch, Europe's highest railway station and a stupendous trip for views. From Brig you follow the Rhone Valley, which gives its name to the canton of Valais, and, although partly industrialised, has a string of towns with old centres built round castles; you can leave the route here and go eastwards on the spectacular Alpine Express route (which in its entirety is Zermatt to St Moritz), or carry on and take the optional detour into Zermatt, a wonderfully placed mountain resort, where it's worth allocating time to try the local walks. Thereafter comes the transition from German- to French-speaking Switzerland; Sion is the best-preserved town in the vicinity. At Martigny you have the choice of venturing into France and taking an exciting route past Chamonix and Mont Blanc, or dropping past the pilgrimage church at St Maurice to Lac Léman (Lake Geneva), the largest of all the Swiss lakes, with Geneva itself at its far end.

Montreux is a major festival town, and can get very busy. In late spring–early summer is the Silver Rose TV Festival, while the famous Jazz Festival occupies the first two and a half weeks in July (book well ahead). There are also festivals of choral music (week after Easter) and of classical music (autumn).

BERNE (BERN)

One of Europe's more relaxed capitals and much less international than Zürich or Geneva, Berne is pleasant for wandering around, with its harmonious medieval houses of yellow sandstone, its irregular roofscape, its ancient arcaded streets that make up Europe's largest covered shopping promenade (all 6 km of it) and its numerous fountains. The Alps are often visible in the distance, though the immediate surroundings are unremarkable.

> Berne was founded in 1191 by Berchtold V, Duke of Zähringen, who supposedly declared he would name his new city after the first creature he killed while hunting. The unfortunate victim, a bear, thus became the town's mascot.

From the main station, the first of 11 monumental fountains is the **Pfeiferbrunnen,** on SPITALGASSE, a flamboyant 16th-century creation with technicolour carvings and flowers around the base.

MÜNSTERPL. is home of the Gothic **Münster** (cathedral), originally built in 1200. Today's outlook started in 1421, continuing through the Reformation. Although many decorative touches were removed, it retains a magnificent depiction of the *Last Judgment* above the main entrance, elaborate carvings on the pews and choir stalls, and superb 15th-century stained glass. The 100-m steeple (Switzerland's highest) gets a good view if you feel like climbing its 270 steps.

Back on the main street (by now GERECHTIGKEITSGASSE), you pass GERECHTIGKEITSBRUNNEN, where the blindfolded Goddess of Justice stands over the severed heads of historical figures. Cross the river by the 15th-century **Nydeggbrücke** and climb the hill facing you to look back on the picture-postcard view of the city.

ZYTGLOGGETURM CLOCK TOWER

The clock tower, which was the original western gate, was first built in the 12th century. In the 16th century, an astronomical clock was added to the **Zytgloggeturm** on its KRAMGASSE face. At exactly 4 mins to each hour, a mechanical jester summons a lion, a rooster and a procession of bears.

The **Kunstmuseum** (Fine Art Museum), HODLERSTR. 8–12 (near LORRAINEBRÜCKE, north of the station), has a fine display of works by the Swiss artists Ferdinand Hodler and Paul Klee (of whom this is the world's largest collection). Look too for exhibits by such diverse artists as Fra Angelico, Matisse, Kandinsky, Cézanne and Picasso. The other major museums are around HELVETIAPL., south of the River Aare, across the KIRCHENFELDBRÜCKE (tram nos. 3/5). **Kunsthalle**, HELVETIAPL. 1, hosts temporary exhibitions of contemporary art. Opposite, **Schweizerisches Alpines Museum** contains an interesting assemblage of items connected with the history of mountaineering. The apartment and workplace of Albert Einstein, a resident of Berne, is at KRAMGASSE 49. Close by, the **Naturhistorisches Museum** (no. 15) features Barry, the St Bernard dog, that rescued over 40 people, as well as African animals and the inevitable bears.

GETTING AROUND BERNE

Berne's main thoroughfare runs east–west through the town centre, linking the station and Nydeggbrücke, and changes name four times: SPITALGASSE, MARKTGASSE, KRAMGASSE, GERECHTIGKEITSGASSE. Other than the museums, much of interest is on or just off this street. There's an excellent tram and bus network. **Buses** 9A and 15 and trolleybus 12 cover this street, as well as the BÄRENGRABEN, on the other side of the river. Departures from track 1 in the VORPL. outside the station. The Tourist Office has details of city tours.

RAIL **Hauptbahnhof (Hbf)**, (031) 311 22 52, is at the western end of the old centre.

Tourist Office: *Verkehrsbüro*, in the station complex; (031) 311 66 11 (http://www.bernetourism.ch; info-res@bernetourism.ch). Daily 0900–2030 (June–Sept); Mon–Sat 0900–1830 and Sun 1000–1700 (Oct–May). Its brochure *Bern Information* covers almost everything you're likely to need to know.

Cheap accommodation is not plentiful but at least most of it is quite central. The two-star **Arabelle**, MITTELSTR. 12, (031) 301 03 05, offers rooms with a shower beginning at SFr.75 (no.2, MITTELSTR.). **The Landhaus**, ALTENBERGSTR. 4–6, (031) 331 41 66, has rooms from SFr.78 (no.12, BÄRENGRABEN). **Youth hostel**: WEIHERG. 4, (031) 311 63 16,

10-min walk from the rail station, just below BUNDESHAUS. **Campsites**: **Eichholz**, STRANDWEG 49, ☎(031) 961 26 02, 3.5 km south-east of centre (tram no.9 to WABERN), also **bungalows**: **Eymatt**, HINTERKAPPELEN, ☎(031) 901 10 07, 5 km north-west of the centre (Postbus from rail station).

The area around SPITALGASSE, BÄRENPL. and ZEUGHAUSGASSE is good for menu browsing. The best-value lunch is at the pleasant self-service restaurant of the **EPA** department store, which straddles ZEUGHAUSGASSE and MARKTGASSE. **Café Aarberghof**, AARBERGERG 40, ☎(031) 311 08 70, is a popular meeting-place just off the main street, with reasonably priced Italian food. Three characterful establishments are to be found on GERECHTIGSKEITG: at no. 62 is the **Klötzlikeller**, Berne's oldest wine cellar (dating from 1635) serving snacks and full meals, ☎(031) 311 74 56; at no. 18, **Belle Époque** is a popular small daytime café serving pastries and snacks in period surroundings, ☎(031) 311 43 36; and at no. 51 is **Arlequin**, offering national and local dishes at reasonable prices; ☎(031) 311 39 46. Vegetarians should try **Menuetto**, HERRENGASSE 22; ☎(031) 311 14 48. For a picnic with a view, cross the NYDEGGBRÜCKE and walk to the lovely **Rose Garden**, or cross the LORRAINEBRÜCKE to the **Botanical Gardens**.

INTERLAKEN

This distinctly lively resort boomed in the 19th century when it became popular with British visitors as a base for exploring the mountains, and fanciful hotels sprang up along the HÖHEWEG, the town's principal avenue (which links the two stations). It's still virtually unrivalled in the country as a centre for scenic excursions. You don't need transport for getting around town, but hiring a bike to explore the adjacent lakesides can be fun. Horse-drawn carriages (at a price) are available for hire outside both stations.

One of the period pieces in town is the distinctive 19th-century **Kursaal** (Casino), which in addition to gambling (high rollers should note that the ceiling for bets is only SFr.5) stages concerts and folklore evenings. Across the River Aare is the old part of town known as **Unterseen**, with the oldest buildings in the region. Cross the bridge and walk along the river to

DAY TRIPS FROM INTERLAKEN

As well as the spectacular **Jungfraujoch train trip** (see p. 298) there are other, cheaper funicular rides up **Harder Kulm** (1320 m) and **Heimwehfluh** (669 m); both are close to town. A **boat or bus ride** will take you to the **Beatushöhlen** – dramatic cliff caves along the Thunersee. For the best views of **Interlaken** and the **lakes of Thun and Brienz**, from which the towns take their names, catch a train to **Wilderswil** for the rack railway to **Schynige Platte**, its summit adorned with an Alpine garden. Beyond **Lauterbrunnen**, a bus ride to **Trummelbach waterfalls** (actually inside the mountain face) is a good afternoon's trip. The cliff steps are not for the infirm, though. Also from Lauterbrunnen, it's possible to take a cable car up to the revolving restaurant on the 2970 m **Schilthorn**, better known for its James Bond film connections, *(On Her Majesty's Secret Service)* and which offers views of more than 200 Alpine peaks.

THE JUNGFRAUJOCH

Interlaken's most popular excursion is the 2hr 30-min journey – each way – to **Jungfraujoch**, the highest railway station in Europe (3454 m). The narrow-gauge railway rack is operated by the **Berner Oberland Bahn** (BOB) consortium. Services are hourly, and changes of train are necessary in **Lauterbrunnen** or **Grindelwald** and **Kleine Scheidegg**. The earlier you start the better to increase the chance of clear views. Ostbahnhof has weather reports (see right). It's best to dedicate a whole day to the trip, if the weather warrants it, as stops can be made en route. This trip is undeniably breathtaking, but also very expensive (currently SFr.159), although you can save about a quarter by taking the (very early) first train. (0635; ETT Table 564). On a good day, you'll see the best of Switzerland, including phenomenal glaciers. At **Kleine Scheidegg**, the stop is directly in front of the magnificent triumvirate, the **Eiger**, the **Mönch** and the **Jungfrau**. The little rack-and-pinion railway then goes into the face of the Eiger, emerging from the long tunnel at the 3454-m summit. The views are incomparable.

Marktplatz, with its 17th-century town hall and palace, 14th-century church and **Touristik Museum** (charting the rise and rise of Interlaken's tourist industry).

RAIL **Ostbahnhof**, (033) 828 73 19, is on Lake Brienz, a 10–15-min walk from the centre. **Westbahnhof**, (033) 826 47 50, by Lake Thun, is central. The two stations are 15 mins apart on foot, 5 mins by rail. It is the Ostbahnhof that connects with the railway to Jungfraujoch. From Berne, Westbahnhof is the first stop and the journey, by hourly trains, averages 50 mins – sit on the left as you head south.

Tourist Office: HÖHEWEG 37; (033) 822 2121, http://www.InterlakenTourism.ch, mail@InterlakenTourism.ch. Mon–Fri 0800–1200,1400–1800 (1330–1830, July–Aug), Sat 0800–1200 (till 1700, July–Aug), Sun 1700–1900 July–Aug.

There's no shortage of hotels, many catering largely for tour operators, but private rooms are better value. **Villa Margaretha**, AARMUHLESTR. 13, (033) 822 1813, has rooms from SFr.37–75, while the prices at **Frau Ritschard**, HAUPSTR. 31, (033) 822 7093, are SFr.30–80. **Youth hostel**: AAREWEG 21, (033) 82 24 53, 20-mins walk east from **Ostbahnhof**, in the village of **Böningen** on Lake Brienz (no. 1). There's also an excellent private **hostel**: **Balmer's Herberge**, HAUPTSTR. 23, (033) 822 19 61, 15-mins walk from both stations, in the suburb of **Matten** (nos. 5/15). Seven **campsites** are within easy walking distance, so ask the Tourist Office for details.

Interlaken doesn't offer a wide choice of interesting cheap eats, with the usual fast food outlets (including McDonald's). In the summer, spontaneous outdoor restaurants and grills sprout, offering cheaper fare. **Bernerhof**, BAHNHOFSTR., (036) 23 16 10, is conveniently central and relaxed with a fairly extensive menu, while vegetarians should try **Vegetaris**, downstairs in the **Hotel Weisses Kreuz**.

INTERNET CAFÉS

Yeti's Belvedere Bar, HÖHEWEG, http://www.quicknet.ch, surfpoint@Yeti's Belvedere-Bar (they also do DIY pizzas).

BRIG

The town stands at a major meeting of rail routes, where you can change for trains to Zermatt. Now home to municipal offices, the vast Italianate palace of **Stockalper Castle** is the largest private building ever erected in Switzerland. It was constructed 1658–1668 by Kaspar Stockalper, a merchant who made a fortune controlling the flow of goods between France, Lombardy and Switzerland and was dubbed the 'uncrowned king of the Valais'.

Station: ☎(081)157 22 22. Near the town centre.

Tourist Office: VERKEHRSVEREIN, ☎(027) 923 19 01; Mon– Fri 0830–1200, 1330–1800, Sat 0900–1200 (and 1400–1730 summer).

WHERE NEXT FROM BRIG?

From Brig you can continue south through the ***Simplon Tunnel*** *(one of the world's longest rail tunnels at 20 km) and into Italy, proceeding along the shores of* ***Lake Maggiore*** *(p. 309) to* ***Milan*** *(p. 334) (a 2–3 hr trip – see ETT table 590).*

One of the great scenic Alpine routes is east on the ***Glacier Express*** *(narrow-gauge line) to* ***St Moritz****; the full Glacier Express route begins from Zermatt. There are some through services; for others you must change at* ***Andermatt*** *(takes 4 hrs 30 mins; ETT table 575; reservations required). At St Moritz you can join the* ***Lausanne–Poschiavo*** *route (p. 286). In its entirety, from Zermatt to St Maurice, the route crosses 291 bridges and passes through 91 tunnels and innumerable hairpin bends. Reservations obligatory.*

SION

Though the area's a bit marred by industrial development, the attractive old centre of Sion looks terrific from a distance, with two hills popping up beside it, both excellent viewpoints in themselves. One is crowned by the scant ruins of **Château Tourbillon**, the

DAY TRIP FROM BRIG TO ZERMATT

Served by narrow-gauge railway (1hr 30 mins from Brig, hourly; ETT table 576), **Zermatt** is a major, car-free ski centre and a superb place for mountain walking. The little town's popularity largely rests on its proximity to the 4477-m **Matterhorn**, one of the best-known mountain shapes in the world, best appreciated by walking a little out of town. Zermatt is very touristy, but nothing (except the frequent clouds) can detract from the glory of its magnificent jagged peak. The **Gornergrat mountain railway** and a network of cable cars provide superb views of the whole area. The **Kleiner Matterhorn Cable Car** makes a three-stage ascent up to 3828 m, giving an extremely dramatic, and very different, view of the Matterhorn, as well as the Alpine range; Mont Blanc in France is prominent on a clear day.

The journey to Zermatt is the westernmost stage of the famous **Glacier Express** route (see *Where Next from Brig?*).

Tourist Office: by the station, ☎(027) 967 01 81 (http://www.zermatt.ch; zermatt@wallis.ch).

other by a strange fortified church called the **Basilique de Valère**. As capital of the Valais canton, the town has provincial **museums** covering fine arts, archaeology and natural history.

ST MAURICE

Maurice, the Roman commander of the Theban legion, gives the town its name; he refused to worship the gods of Rome and was killed in a massacre here in AD303. Two centuries later, an abbey was founded in his name, and by the Middle Ages St Maurice had become a pilgrimage centre. The restored abbey church has a fine 11th-century belfry and a wonderful treasury with pieces from the early Christian era.

DAY TRIPS FROM MONTREUX

Take the funicular up to the 2042-m summit of **Rochers de la Naye** (55 mins), or about 3 hrs' walk. There are a couple of wonderfully sited restaurants at the top.

Reached by no.1 train or a pleasant walk of 3 km south from Montreux, **Château de Chillon** is as impressive and well-preserved a medieval castle as you could hope to see. Famously, the Reformationist Bonivard was chained to a pillar in the dungeon here for four years, an event immortalised in verse by Byron; the poem itself brought the castle to public notice, and it's become the most visited attraction in Switzerland. A computer-aided display in the chapel projects representations of icons of the saints on the walls, giving an idea of how the original must have appeared.

RAIL (027) 157 22 22. Near the town centre.

Tourist Office: **Sion Tourisme**, (027) 322 85 86 (www.siontourisme.ch,info@siontourisme.ch). Open Mon–Fri 0830–1200, 1400–1730; Sat 0900–1200.

Youth hostel: RUE DE L'INDUSTRIE 2, (27) 323 74 70, 350 m from station. There is a riverside **campsite** 4 km west at LES ÎLES 36 43 47.

WHERE NEXT?

*Cross into **France** in style by taking the route via Chamonix–Mont Blanc and St Gervais, and re-entering **Switzerland** to end at **Geneva**, getting stunning mountain views most of the way. ETT Tables 572, 367 and 368.*

*The **Mont Blanc Express** train grinds up an incredible one-in-five gradient to the French border village of **Vallorcine**; here you change trains to the less sleek orange-pale grey French railcars. At **Chamonix Mont Blanc**, you have the option of taking the **Montenvers** rack railway up to Europe's biggest glacier.*

MONTREUX

The best-preserved of the **Lake Geneva** resorts, Montreux is blessed with a mild climate, with palm trees, magnolias and cypresses along its 10-km waterside promenade – a lovely place for strolling. Smart hotels make the most of the views, while the rest of the

WHERE NEXT?

You can turn north-eastward here by joining the ***Lausanne–St Moritz*** *route* *(p. 286).*

town rises in tiers up the hillside. The effect is slightly spoiled by a garish casino.

RAIL Station: (021)157 22 22. In the centre of town.

Tourist Office: AV. DU THEATRE 5, MONTREUX, ☎(021) 962 84 84 (www.montreux.ch; tourism@montreux.ch). Mon–Fri 0900–1800, Sat 0900–1200, (Oct–Mar); Mon–Sat 0900–1800, Sun 0900–1200 (Apr–Sept).

LAUSANNE

See p. 287.

NYON

The lakeside town has flower gardens by the water's edge. The 1st-century basilica of the great Forum is now an underground **Roman Museum** showing a rich haul of finds from excavations, including lamps, coins and chunks of mosaic. The five-towered castle, begun in the 12th century and modified 400 years later, and the arcaded houses on the PLACE DU MARCHÉ are characteristically Bernese style. Try to visit on Wed or Sat morning when the market is on.

Station: (022)157 22 22. Near the town centre.

Tourist Office: ☎(022)361 62 61 (www.nyon.ch, tourism@nyon.ch). Open Mon–Fri 0830–1200, 1330–1730; Sat–Sun 0830–1200, 1330–1730 (June–Sept).

GENEVA (GENÈVE)

With a dual role as a banking centre and a base for many international organisations, Geneva is a cosmopolitan, comfortably prosperous place, with promenades and parks beautifying the shores of **Lac Léman** (**Lake Geneva**). The River Rhône splits the city into two distinct sections, with the international area on the *Rive Droite* (right bank, to the north) and the compact old town on the *Rive Gauche* (left bank, to the south).

On *Rive Droite* (nos. 5/8/14/F/Z) is **place des Nations**, near which most of the international organisations are grouped. The **Musée International de la Croix-Rouge**, AVENUE DE LA PAIX 17, is a stern building with high-tech exhibits tracing the history of the Red Cross and its Islamic offshoot, the Red Crescent. Profoundly moving, it covers man's inhumanity to man and natural disasters. Close by, the **Palais des Nations**, AVENUE DE LA PAIX 14, is home of the European headquarters of the United Nations, which replaced the League of Nations in 1945; there are guided tours. Between here and the lake is the lovely **Jardin Botanique**, a perfect place for a quiet stroll (once you're away from the main road) and featuring a rock garden, a deer and llama park, and an aviary.

GETTING AROUND GENEVA

Geneva's sights are fairly scattered and a bit of route-planning is worthwhile. There is a good network of buses and one tram route. From May to Sept, Compagnie Générale de Navigation de Lac Léman (CGN) operate regular lake ferries from quai du Mont-Blanc and Jardin Anglais, 10 mins' walk straight ahead out of the station subway down Rue des Alpes; ☎(022) 311 25 21. Tramway and little train tours through the city operate in season.

West of the cathedral, ***Parc des Bastions*** *houses the university (founded by Calvin in 1599) and the vast* ***Monument de la Réformation*** *(erected in 1917), a 90-m-long wall featuring four central characters – Farel, Calvin, Bèze and Knox – each over 4.5 m high.*

On *Rive Gauche*, south of the centre, the **Jardin Anglais**, on the waterfront, is famous for its **Horloge Fleurie** (floral clock), while the city's trade mark, the 140-m high fountain known as **Jet d'Eau**, spouts from a nearby pier.

At the heart of the old town is the lively Place du Bourg-de-Four, Geneva's oldest square. Take rue de l'Hôtel de Ville to the 15th-century Hôtel de Ville (town hall), where the first Geneva Convention was signed in 1864. Adjacent is the former arsenal and the 12th-century **Maison Tavel**, Geneva's oldest house and now an evocative museum, with several period rooms and exhibits covering the 14th–19th centuries.

The original 12th–13th-century Gothic façade of the **Cathédrale de St-Pierre** has incongruous 18th-century additions. Most interior decorations were stripped out in the Reformation, but there are some frescos in the neo-Gothic Chapelle des Maccabées. Calvin preached here and his chair has been saved for posterity. The north tower, reached by a 157-step spiral staircase, offers a great view of the old town. Beneath the cathedral is the **Site Archéologique**, where catwalks allow you to see the result of extensive excavations, including a 4th-century baptistery and a 5th-century mosaic floor.

Two blocks south, the vast marble **Musée d'Art et d'Histoire**, RUE CHARLES-GALLAND 2, has several rooms in period style, Hodler landscapes and the famous painting *The Fishing Miracle*, by Witz, which portrays Christ walking on the water – of Lake Geneva.

The 19th-century **Petit Palais**, TERRASSE ST-VICTOR 2, has an impressive array of modern art and includes works by Cézanne, Renoir and the Surrealists. Nearby, the **Collection Baur**, RUE MUNIER-ROMILLY 8, contains some lovely Japanese and Chinese objets d'art, ranging from Samurai swords to jade and delicate porcelain.

RAIL **Gare de Cornavin,** ☎ (022) 157 22 22, is the main terminal, 10-min walk north of the centre (🚌 nos. 5/6/9). **Gare Genève Eaux-Vives,** ☎(022) 736 16 20, on the eastern edge of the city, is the terminal for SNCF trains from Annecy and St Gervais (30-min walk from Cornavin station or 🚌no. 12). **Metro Shopping**, a large complex that includes the *'Alimentation Automatique'*, is open Sun. The Aperto supermarket is open 0600–2200 every day.

Tourist Office: In **Gare de Cornavin** (022) 909 70 50, and at RUE DE MONT-BLANC 3, (022) 909 70 00; Mon–Sat 0900–1800. A smaller central office is at PL. DU MOULARD 4, (022) 311 98 27, Mon 1230–1830, Tue–Fri 0900–1830, Sat 1030–1630. *Genève Guide pratique* and *Info-Jeunes* are free guides definitely worth picking up. *Genève Agenda* is the city entertainment guide.

Most hotels are expensive, but there are plenty of hostels and private rooms. Ask at the Tourist Office for a copy of *Info-Jeunes*, which lists useful information. From 15 June to 15 Sept, the **CAHJ** *(Centre d'Accueil d'Herbergement des Jeunes)*, located in a trailer in the pedestrian area opposite the station, offers accommodation and other advice to young people. There are at least a dozen hotels listed which are within walking distance of the centre, offering a room with shower for around SFr.30–50 including **Beau-Site**, PLACE DU CIRQUE 3, (022) 328 10 08, and **De la Cloche**, RUE DE LA CLOCHE, (022) 732 94 81. Just as cheap are the many university and religious institution lodgings on offer. Those with the most attractive and central location are the **Logements Universitaires**, RUE DE CANDOLLE 4, (022) 705 77 20, in the beautiful Parc des Bastions, adjacent to the old town. **Campsites**: **Camping Sylvabelle**, CHEMIN DE CONCHES 10, (022) 347 06 03, 3 km south-east (nos. 8/88) also **bungalows**; **Camping de l'Abarc**, ROUTE DE VERNIER 151, (022) 796 21 01, 6 km west (no. 6); **Camping Pointe-à-la-Bise**, VÉSENAZ, (022) 752 12 96, 7 km north-east, close to Lac Léman (no. E).

Because of its French influence and cosmopolitan nature, Geneva claims to be the culinary centre of Switzerland. The majority of places, however, cater for international business people. Good places to look for reasonably priced restaurants are on the RUE DE LAUSANNE (turn left out of Gare de Cornavin) and around PLACE DU CIRQUE (BOULEVARD GEORGES-FAVON), where you'll find the **Cave Valaisanne et Chalet Suisse** for all things Swiss, (022) 328 12 36, and, close by, the simple café-style **Grappe Dorée**, BOULEVARD GEORGES-FAVON 14, (022) 29 77 98, offering local cheese specialities. Consult *Info-Jeunes* (see Accommodation) for a list of University restaurants (the most central is the **Cafétéria UNI-Bastion** at PLACE DE L'UNIVERSITÉ by the Parc des Bastions) and for other cheap eats. **Parc des Bastions** is also great for picnics.

INTERNET CAFÉS

Café Nomade, ROUTE DU BOUT-DU-MONDE 6, (022) 789 55 77, open Mon–Thur 1100–2030, Fri–Sat 1100–2200, Sun 1300–2030, http://www.geneva-link.com; SFr.5 for 1 hr. Also **Escape Internet Café**, QUAI DU MONT-BLANC 19, (022) 900 12 91, http://mygale.org/09/point6, SFr.6 for 1 hr.

WHERE NEXT FROM GENEVA?

Trains cross the border to France, with TGV services to ***Paris, Mâcon*** *and* ***Lyon*** *(ETT table 372) and to* ***Grenoble*** *(table 363) continuing to Marseille, Nice and Montpellier (table 355). Geneva to Paris takes 3 hr 40 mins, Lyon 2 hrs and Grenoble 2 hrs 15 mins.*

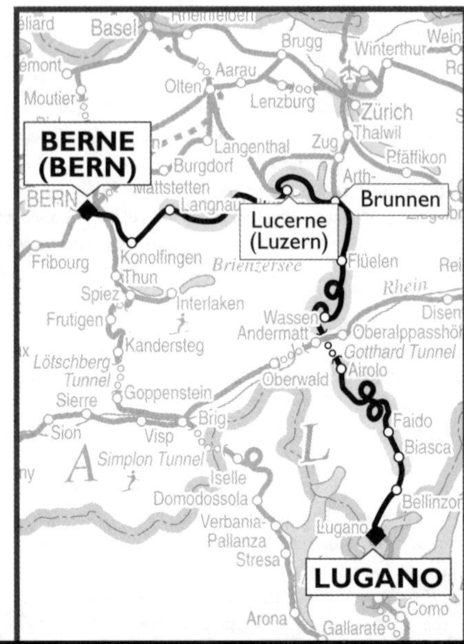

Fastest Journey:
4 hrs

ROUTE DETAIL

Berne–Lugano ETT tables 515, 550

Type	Frequency	Journey Time
Train	Every 2 hrs	4 hrs

Lucerne–Brunnen ETT table 550

Type	Frequency	Journey Time
Train	Every 2 hrs	1 hr

Berne–Lucerne ETT table 515

Type	Frequency	Journey Time
Train	Every 1-2 hrs	1 hr 15 mins

Brunnen–Lugano ETT table 550

Type	Frequency	Journey Time
Train	Every hr	1 hrs 20 mins

Lake Lucerne is the outstanding scenic feature of central Switzerland, an irregularly shaped body of water encompassed by flattish land around the dignified old resort of Lucerne itself, as well as picture-book snowy mountains dotted with wooden chalets to the south. Beyond the Gothard Tunnel, the landscape changes abruptly, as you enter the canton of Ticino, to an emerald-green valley dotted with rustic granite houses and tall campaniles as you head towards the Italian border. Lugano has the atmosphere of a smart Italian provincial town, and makes a good base for excursions.

LUCERNE (LUZERN)

This major resort straddles the River Reuss, itself crossed by quaintly roofed medieval footbridges, at the end of Lake Lucerne. Old-fashioned hotels attest to the town's long standing as a busy holiday place, which hosts a major music festival mid-Aug to Sept.

Old Lucerne is characterised by its many elaborately painted houses, its cobbled squares, its fountains, its Renaissance town hall by the KORNMARKT, and the two bridges over the Reuss. As you cross the 14th-century **Kapellbrücke**, a wooden-roofed footbridge that straggles crookedly over the river, you pass under a succession of 111 triangular-shaped paintings depicting local and national history. Thirty date back to the 17th century, but the remainder are reproductions following a disastrous fire which destroyed most of the bridge in 1993. Halfway across, the bridge goes through a sturdy 13th-century octagonal **Water Tower**, which has undergone several changes of function over the centuries, including use as a prison. A short distance further down the river is the other medieval roofed bridge, the **Spreuerbrücke**, also lined with 17th-century paintings, in this case depicting the macabre *Dance of Death*.

> The **Luzern Museum Pass**, SFr.25, is good for one month and gives free entry to all the museums in town, including the **Verkehrshaus** (transport museum), which is SFr.16–18 on its own.

Near the south end of KAPELLBRÜCKE, the **Jesuit Church** looks plain from the outside, but has a gorgeous pink-and-white baroque interior dating from 1677. **Nolliturm**, on the riverbank near the north end of SPREUERBRÜCKE, is a fortified gate that marks one end of a well-preserved stretch of **Musegg Wall**, the old fortifications. You can follow this all the way (and climb three of its nine surviving towers) as it curves eastwards to end just off LÖWENPL.

The graceful twin-spired **Hofkirche**, (Cathedral), off SCHWEIZERHOFQUAI, near the lake, has an organ with 4950 pipes and a 10-ton bell. The city's mascot, the **Löwendenkmal** (Lion Memorial), LÖWENSTR., is a massive but movingly portrayed dying lion carved out of the cliff-side, commemorating the Swiss Guards massacred at the Tuileries in Paris during the French Revolution. Nearby is the **Gletschergarten** (Glacier Garden), DENKMALSTR. 4, a bed of smooth rocks pitted with holes, created by glacial action. There's an ingenious mirror-maze here too.

Anyone with an interest in transport in all its guises and vintages should make for the **Verkehrshaus** (Swiss Transport Museum), LIDOSTR. 5, 2 km east of town (near the campsite), reached by a pleasant lakeside walk (or bus no.2); it's one of Europe's leading museums on the theme, with exhibits covering locos, vintage cycles, space rockets and more, plus an IMAX movie theatre (with a huge, almost vertigo-inducing screen), a 360-degree cinema.

PICASSO AND WAGNER IN LUCERNE

The Picasso Museum, AM RHYN-HAUS, FURRENGASSE 21, just off the old KORNMARKT square, contains a small collection of his later paintings and photographs of the great man. The local Rosengart family commissioned Picasso to paint a portrait of their daughter; they were so pleased with it that they bought several of his paintings, eight of which they donated to set up this museum.

The **Richard Wagner Museum**, WAGNERWEG 27, by the lake, 1.5 km south-east of the centre (bus nos. 6/8 or walk east along the lake from the station), occupies the house where the German composer lived during the time he wrote the scores for *Siegfried* and *Die Meistersinger von Nürnberg*. There's a collection of his memorabilia and original scores.

RAIL On the south bank of the River Reuss, where it meets Lake Lucerne, ☎(041) 157 22 22, a few mins' walk over the bridge to the old town. In the basement is the '24-hr shopping' automat, for emergency rations.

Tourist Office: FRANKENSTR. 1; ☎(041) 410 71 71 (by station), luzern@luzern.org. Open Mon–Fri 0830–1800, Sat 0900–1700 (Apr–Oct); Sun 0900–1300 (mid May–Oct); Mon–Fri 0830–1200 and 1400–1800, Sat 0900–1300 (Nov–Mar). Also in the station basement: open 1100–1800 (mid Mar–mid Oct).
Accommodation booking service costs SFr.2, but this will be credited to your hotel bill. The *Luzern City Guide* is free and full of useful information.

Lucerne is a popular tourist destination, so advance booking is advisable for its limited range of cheap options, especially in summer; some of the19th-century hotels surrounding the old town can be noisy.
The **Tourist Hotel**, ST KARLIQUAI 12, ☎(041) 410 24 74, touristhotel@centralnet.ch, has rooms beginning at SFr.45, The **Pickwick**, RATHAUSQUAI 6, ☎(041) 410 59 27, and the **Alpha**, ZAHRINGERSTR. 24, ☎ (041) 240 42 80, both have prices starting at SFr.55. **Backpackers Lucerne**, ALPENGASSE 42, ☎ (041) 360 04 20, offers student-style accommodation by the south shore of the lake (10-min walk from the station).
Youth hostel: SEDELSTR. 12, AM ROTSEE, ☎(041) 420 88 00, by the lake north-west of town (bus no.18 to **GOPPLISMOOS**; after 1930, tram no.1 to SCHLOSSBERG plus 15-min walk).
Campsite: **LIDO**, LIDOSTR. 8; ☎(041) 370 21 46 (bus no. 2 to VERKEHRSHAUS), on the north shore of the lake.

There are reasonably priced restaurants and cafés all round Lucerne's many squares and waterside promenades. The town's speciality is *Kügelipasteti*, a large meat and mushroom vol-au-vent covered in rich sauce.
There are several good places to hang out in the evenings, including the **Opus vinothek**, next

to Jesuit Church, **CUCARACHA**, PILATUSSTR., the **Penthouse** bar and disco, **Hotel Astoria** and the **Adagio**, a medieval-themed disco.

INTERNET CAFÉ
RESTAURANT PARTERRE, CAFÉ LOAS, GMBH, MYTHENSTR. 7, ☎(041) 210 40 93.

BRUNNEN

You may like to pause here to enjoy the site, at the meeting of **lakes Uri and Lucerne**. The bustling resort is well set-up for most water sports, as well as walking on Lake Uri's shores. Brunnen can claim to be the cradle of the nation's history. Here the forest states of Unterwalden, Uri and Schwyz were sworn together as the Confederation in a declaration on Aug 1 1291 on the Rütli Field by the lake, an event immortalised in the legend of William Tell as told by Schiller in 1804; Aug 1 is Swiss National Day, celebrated nationwide with bonfires lit on high spots and the **Rütli Field** floodlit. The **Swiss Way** is a 22-km walkers' route round the lake, divided into 26 sections; each section represents a canton or half-canton, with the length of each determined by the proportionate populations of each canton.

Station: ☎(041)820 10 66, close to the town centre.

Tourist Office: BAHNHOFSTR. 32, ☎(041) 825 00 49.

LUGANO

Lugano, the largest town in the Italian-speaking canton of Ticino, is a handsome, sophisticated resort of Lombardic arcades and piazzas beside **Lake Lugano**. It climbs the hillside around a horseshoe bay surrounded by verdant mountains, so is an ideal base for walking as well as watersports. The lakeside promenade becomes a popular place to stroll or roller-blade after 2000 in July and Aug, when vehicles are banned from it. At its eastern end is the **Parco Civico** (Municipal Park), the pleasant setting for summer concerts and graced with fountains, statues and trees.

DAY TRIPS FROM LUCERNE

You can get to most of the settlements around Lake Lucerne, which covers 114 square km, by regular local boat services, as well as excursion cruises in summer; for information contact **Schiffahrtgesellschaft des Vierwaldstattersees**, ☎(041) 367 67 67, http://www.lakelucerne.ch (or book through the Tourist Office). These boats combine nicely with walks as well as rack railway and cable car trips.

From **Alpnachstad** (reached by steamer), south of Lucerne, take the world's steepest rack railway (climbing a 48% gradient) up **Mt Pilatus** (2132 m). Supposedly haunted by the spirit of Pontius Pilate, the summit is also accessible by cable car from **Kriens** (🚌 no.1), on the southern outskirts of Lucerne – giving scope for a circular tour of the mountain.

From Vitznau, on the eastern shore, Europe's oldest rack railway ascends **Mt Rigi** (1800 m), where the summit view from **Rigi-Kulm** at sunrise (including the Jungfrau and Titlis) has attracted generations of tourists, including Victor Hugo.

Day trips from Lucerne cont'd.

There's also a cable car from the sunny waterside resort of **Weggis**; if you prefer to walk, there's a 4-hr route from Weggis, or you can take the cable car up from **Küssnacht** to within a 2-hr hike of the summit. At **Engelberg**, 16 km south of the lake and 1 hr from Lucerne by train (hourly; ETT table 552), the huge **Rotair**, the world's first rotating cable car, gives an unparalleled view of the permanently snow-capped **Mt Titlis** (3020 m).

By boat from Lugano

Navigazione Lugano, ☎(091) 971 52 23, operate a wide choice of boat trips from the central landing stage to picturesque villages on the lake, such as **Gandria**. This charming town near the Italian border is more reminiscent of the Riviera, with its winding passages and narrow houses, which eventually emerge onto the lake. There are several restaurants, cafés and even small hotels where you can stay and admire the turquoise blue water and the mountain views. In **Melide**, you can hire a pedalo or visit **Swissminiatur**, a model version of Switzerland.

Swimmers can head for the lido (to the east of the river), with its pool and sandy beaches.

Funiculars climb the two mountains guarding the bay: up **Monte Brè** (930 m) from **Cassarate** and up **San Salvatore** (912 m) from **Paradiso**, both 20-min walks from the centre or take bus no. 1. The former provides magnificent views over the town, while the latter offers a panoramic sweep into Italy.

The arcaded VIA NASSA is the main pedestrianised shopping street, where you can take your pick of such Swiss specialities as expensive wristwatches or chocolate in all its national varieties.

On the hillside immediately below the station is the 16th-century **Cattedrale San Lorenzo**, while the other notable church is the lakeside **Santa Maria Degli Angioli**, with its fine Renaissance frescos by Bernardo Luini.

There's more worthwhile art in **Thyssen-Bornemisza**, a collection of 19th- and 20th-century paintings and watercolours housed in the **Villa Favorita**, RIVIERA 14 (Fri–Sun, Easter–Oct), while the **Cantonal Art Museum**, VIA CANOVA 10, also has many 20th-century works.

RAIL ☎(091) 923 75 01, at the top of the town. From it a funicular descends to the middle (otherwise a 6-min walk), half-way down to the lake.

i **Tourist Office**: **Palazzo Civico**, RIVA ALBERTOLLI, ☎(091) 921 46 64; on the lakeside opposite the central landing stage. Open Mon–Fri 0900–1830, Sat 0900–1230 and 1330–1700, Sun 0930–1300. Accommodation booking service: SFr.4.

The **Rosa**, V. LANDRIANI 2–4, ☎(091) 922 92 86, and the **Selva,** V. TESSERETE 36, ☎(091) 923 60 17, offer rooms beginning at SFr.46–47. **Youth hostel**: **Lugano-Savosa**, V. CANTONALE 13; ☎(091) 966 27 28 (bus no. 5 from station to CROCIFISSO). Generally, **Paradiso** (the southern part of Lugano) is slightly better value.

There are several restaurants along the lakeside, as well as around the main square, the PIAZZA RIFORMA. Good nightspots are the **Café Tango**, PIAZZA RIFORMA, **La Salsita**, V. G. VEGEZZI and **Ethnic,** QUARTIERE MAGHETTI (which also has music).

INTERNET ACCESS

City Disk Music Store, VIA P. PERI, SFr.4 for 20 mins, and **Biblio Café Tra**, V. VANONI 3, ☎(091) 923 23 05, which, as well as having exhibitions and a library, is a good meeting point; SFr.8 for 1hr, open 0900–2400.

DAY TRIPS FROM LUGANO

Locarno on **Lake Maggiore** is an hour by train from Lugano (changing at Bellinzona) (ETT tables 550, 548). From it, the scenic **Centovalli** (Hundred Valleys) route crosses the border to **Domodossola** in Italy. The 53-km line clings to dramatic hillsides, soars across dozens of steep valleys (hence its name) over spectacular bridges and viaducts to **Santa Maria Maggiore**. Afterwards, continue exploring Switzerland via the major rail junction at **Brig**, 42 km north of Domodossola through the Simplon Tunnel.

North-east of Lugano, just beyond Gandria, is the Mediterranean-flavoured **Menaggio**. Already in Italy, this Lake Como town provides lovely views over the water. To get to the other bank, there are frequent trains from Lugano to Como (taking about 50 mins). Continuing on the Italian side, the train skirts the shore, providing views of Italian villages on both sides of the lake.

WHERE NEXT FROM LUGANO?

*Hourly trains to **Milan** (p. 334) take 1 hr (ETT table 84), for connections with **Florence**, **Rome** and other Italian cities.*

(for Directory information, see p. 540).

Sharing borders with Germany, Switzerland, Liechtenstein, Italy, the Czech Republic, Slovakia, Slovenia and Hungary, Austria feels very much at the centre of Europe. Yet its capital, **Vienna**, a greyish, stately affair of boulevards, parks and palaces, has a poignant air of once being at the centre of bigger things – harking back to the era of the great Habsburg empire. The rest of the country is quite different. **Salzburg**, the city indelibly associated with Mozart (though he hated the place), has bags of charm with its baroque squares. The Alps, which dominate the map of Austria, cover much of the country, and, though not as consistently dramatic as the Swiss Alps, have enough diversity to make them well worth exploring. There's little in the way of old-fashioned rural buildings in the mountain areas, though: the ubiquitous item is the immaculate white chalet with balconies full of geraniums, and onion-domed church towers preside over postcard-pretty scenes. Some may find the neat, groomed appearance of Austria almost verges on the monotonous.

Tyrol and **Vorarlberg**, in western Austria, include the country's highest mountains and are stirring stuff, with villages to match, with **Innsbruck** and **Kitzbühel** among the larger places worth seeing. The **Salzkammergut** is the obvious upland to venture into from Salzburg, pleasant resorts scattered beside lakes beneath miniature limestone mountains. Further south are the lesser known areas of **Carinthia**, with more lake resorts, and the peaks of **Styria**, not quite as breathtaking as the Tyrol but very fine in their own right.

YOUTH HOSTELS

Head office: **Österreichischer Jugendherbergsverband,** HAUPTVERBAND, 1010 WIEN, SCHOTTENRING 28, AUSTRIA, ☎(43) (1) 533 5353, fax: (43) (1) 535 0861 (email: öejhv-zentrale@ öejhv.or.at; website:http://www.oejhv.or.at).

ACCOMMODATION

Hotels are graded on the usual five-star system, but even one-star establishments are pricey. *Gasthaus/Gasthof* indicates an **inn** and *Frühstückspension* a **bed and breakfast** place. The best value is usually **a private room** (look for signs), but many require stays of several nights and some charge extra for short stays. *Jugendherberge* is the word for a **youth hostel**; few have self-catering but most serve meals. In summer, some universities let rooms.

GUEST CARDS

Several resorts, indicated by **GC** next to Tourist Office details, issue a guest card to visitors in higher quality accomodation. The cards entitle holders to anything from free escorted mountain hikes to discounts for ferries or museums. The cards are generally issued by *Gasthofs* or **hotels**.

Camping is popular and there are lots of sites, mostly very clean and well run, but pricey. Many sites are open summer only. In Alpine areas, there are also **refuge huts** – details from the local Tourist Office. For all accommodation it is advisable to book ahead for July, Aug, Christmas and Easter.

FOOD AND DRINK

Food tends towards the hearty, with wholesome soups and meat-dominated main courses (famously *Wiener Schnitzel* – a thin slice of veal fried in egg and bread-crumbs), while *goulasch* (of Hungarian origin) and dumplings are also prevalent. Cakes are sinfully cream laden and high-cholestorol, including the amazingly rich *Sachertorte*, an iced chocolate cake invented in Vienna. A filling snack, sold by most butchers, is *Wurstsemmel* – slices of sausage with a bread roll.

Lunch is usually more expensive in cafés than in restaurants. Drinks in bars and clubs cost more than in eating-places.

The Austrian pattern is: continental breakfast, lunch (1200–1400), coffee and cake mid-afternoon, then dinner (1800–2200). Beer is the most popular drink, but Austrian wine is good and there are multiple *Schnapps* varieties. A service charge of 10–15% is included in restaurant bills. It is the custom to leave a further 5% if you're happy with the service.

EDITOR'S CHOICE

Innsbruck; Salzburg; Tyrol Alps around Kitzbuhel; Vienna. Scenic rail journeys: Swiss border–Vienna via Innsbruck and Salzburg (p. 318 and Where Next from Innsbruck, p. 320); Innsbruck-Spittal Millstättersee via Fortezza (Italy; ETT tables 596, 970).

BEYOND THE BORDERS

From Vienna to: Budapest (ETT table 61); Munich (table 67); Cologne via Würzburg (table 66); Prague (table 96); Bratislava (table 94b); Rome via Venice (table 88); Warsaw (table 94a). From Innsbruck to: Munich (table 70); Rome via Verona (table 70); Zurich (table 86).

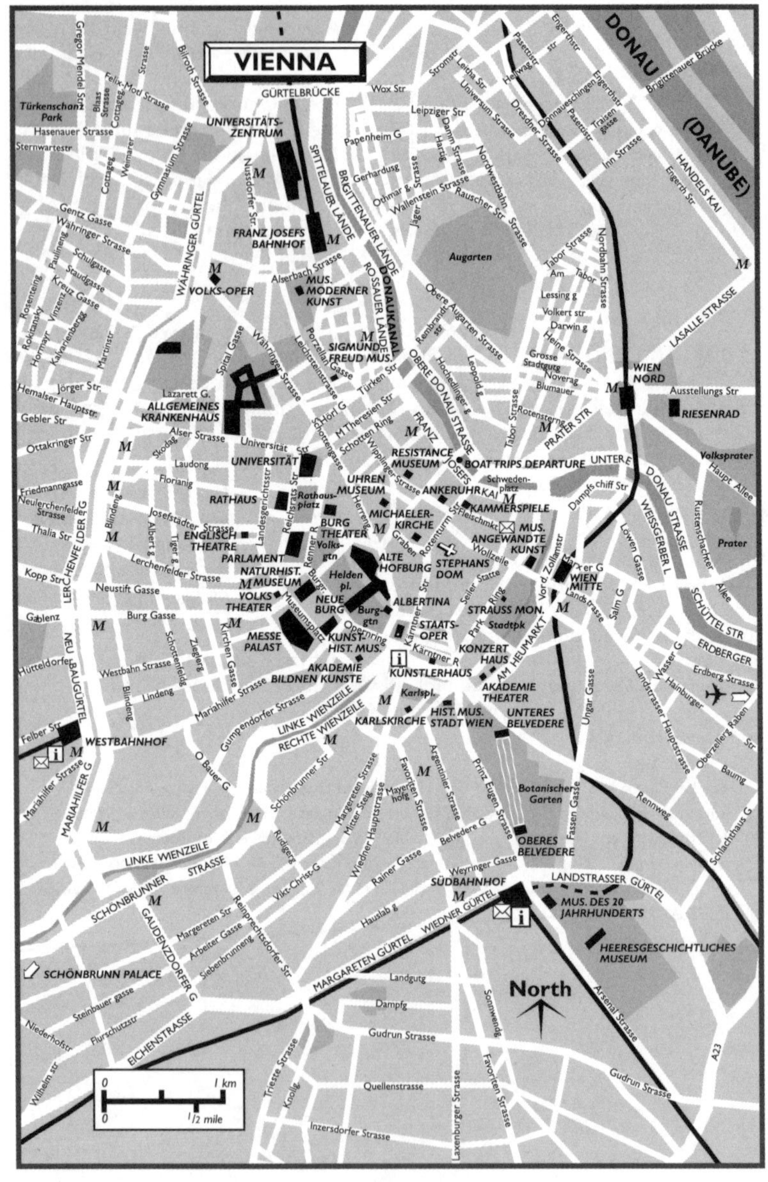
VIENNA
North
0
1 km
0
1/2 mile

Austria's capital is one of Europe's great cultural centres, revered the world over for its music (the waltz was born here in 1820). Much of it wears a grand, old-fashioned air, evoking its heyday as the centre of the Habsburg empire for 600 years. Around a hundred years ago, Vienna became a leading architectural exponent of *Jugendstil* – the Austrian art nouveau – examples of which dot the city.

ARRIVAL AND DEPARTURE

RAIL Vienna has three main stations; for information: ☎ 17 17 for all stations. All three are 3–4 km outside the RINGSTR, connected to the centre by underground or tram, and have left-luggage and accommodation services. **Westbahnhof**, MARIAHILFERSTR./EUROPAPL., serves the west, Germany, Switzerland and Hungary; money exchange (0700–2200), post office (0400–0100). **Südbahnhof**, WIENER GURTEL/ARSENALSTR., serves the south and east, including Italy, former Yugoslavia, the Czech Republic and Hungary; money exchange (0630–2200 May–Oct, 0630–2100 Nov–Apr). **Franz-Josefs-Bahnhof**, JULIUS-TANDLER-PL., serves the north, plus Berlin and the Czech Republic.

Vienna International Airport is 19 km south-east of the city at ***Schwechat*** (taxi fare around ÖS480). Flight information, ☎ 70072233. Express bus transfers (ÖS70) run from the airport to City Air Terminal and back (every 20 mins) and to WESTBAHNHOF and SÜDBAHNHOF and back every 30 mins.

TOURIST OFFICE

Main office: KÄRNTNERSTR. 38, ☎ (1) 2111 40 (0900–1900). Accommodation booking service, ☎ (1) 2111 4444, Mon–Sat 1000–1800.

Phone cards available from tobacconists and post offices for ÖS100 and ÖS50.

INFORMATION

Pick up the free *The Young Vienna Scene* brochure from the tourist information office (useful information, accommodation, great ideas for walks), the *Vienna Scene* and the monthly *List of Events*. Information and accommodation bureaux also at WESTBAHNHOF, SÜDBAHNHOF and SCHWECHAT AIRPORT.
Thomas Cook licensee: **Papageno Reisen** at GENTZG. 177, ☎ (1) 478 5511, and ESSLINGER HAUPTSTR. 81–87, ☎ (1) 774 8872.

POST AND PHONES

The **central post office**, FLEISCHMARKT 19, has poste restante facilities (open 24 hrs), money exchange.
To phone Vienna from abroad, ☎ 43 (Austria) +1 (Vienna) + number; to phone the city from elsewhere in Austria: ☎ 01 + number.

PUBLIC TRANSPORT

The **U-Bahn** has five lines, operating 0500–2400. The **trams** run on 33 radial routes as well as in both directions round the RINGSTR., 0500–2400. **Buses** include 22 night routes (0030–0430), marked by a green N symbol. **Taxis**: not cheap; hail one with a *'frei'* sign, or ☎31 300, 40 100, 60 160 or 81 400. **Cycling**: fun, as the city is largely flat and has leafy boulevards and 500 km of marked cycle paths.

The Tourist Office has a free booklet, *Wien von Sattel* (Vienna from the Saddle), with route maps. Hire bikes from stations: **Westbahnhof** 0400–2400, **Wien Nord** 0715–2200 and **Südbahnhof** 0500–2400 (ÖS90 per day on production of a rail ticket for the same day, otherwise ÖS150). **Pedal Power** bring hire bikes to your hotel, ☎729 7234. Or try the **Miracle Tour** electric moped hire, ÖS120 per hr, SCHWEDENPL./CAPRICORNI-GARAGE, daily 0800–2100. **Vienna Bike**, WASAG. 28/2/5, ☎319 1258, offers daily tours by bike; ÖS200 for 2–3 hrs.

TICKETS

U-Bahn (underground trains), **trams** and **buses** all use the same tickets, with transfers allowed. Single tickets, sold in blocks of 5, for one journey, cost ÖS17 each (under-15s travel free at weekends and school holidays).

A **24-hr Tageskarte Wien** costs ÖS50 and **72-hr excursion ticket** ÖS130. Tickets must be validated on the bus or tram or at the U-Bahn entrance.

Another option is the **Vienna Card** (ÖS180 from hotels, Vienna Transport ticket offices and Tourist Offices), valid for 72 hrs' transport, plus reduced entry to popular museums, tourist sights, shopping/restaurant discounts.

ACCOMMODATION

There are lots of options – and takers – so book ahead for May–Oct. Expect to pay ÖS300–680 per person for a cheap hotel, including breakfast. For a moderately priced stay, try guesthouses or youth hostels. Campsites are across the Danube Canal. If you need a wash, try one of the *Jugendstil* or art deco baths, such as **Amalienbad**, REUMANNPL. 23, ☎607 4747 (baths, showers, saunas, steam rooms, swimming pools).

GUESTHOUSES

Pension Sacher, ROTENTURMSTR. 1, ☎533 3238, on a central 7th floor next to the cathedral.

YOUTH HOSTELS

Jugendherberge Wien, MYRTHENG. 7, ☎523 6316 (U2 to LERCHENFELDER STR., then short walk).

Jugendgastehaus Brigittenau, FRIEDRICH-ENGELS-PL. 24, ☎3328 2940.

Jugendgastehaus Hutteldorf-Hacking, SCHLOSSBERGGASSE 8, ☎877 1501.

Schlossherberge am Wilhelminenberg, SAVOYENSTR. 2, ☎4858 503-700.

CAMPSITES

Aktive Camping Neue Donau, AM KLEEHAÜFEL, ☎202 4010 (mid May–mid Sept).

FOOD AND DRINK

Vienna has given the gastronomic world *Wiener Schnitzel* (veal in breadcrumbs), *Sachertorte* (rich chocolate cake) and *Kaiserschmarrn*, the dessert of emperors. You'll find typically Viennese dishes in low-priced *Beisel*, which are pubs-cum-brasseries, or *Kellern*, wine cellars. *Konditoreis* (cake shops/cafés) offer a tempting array of home-made cakes and pastries. Coffee also comes in many varieties, from *melange* to *grosser Brauner*. Every *Kaffeehaus* serves hot dishes too. Don't miss the sausages on sale from street vendors! The wide pedestrianised GRABEN near the cathedral is just one source of cafés, while the area around the university (U2/4 to SCHOTTENTOR) is good for budget meals. BÄCHERSTR. is a good place to look for a moderately priced traditional meal, as at **Oswald & Kalb**, which looks rather gloomy, but is full of atmosphere. There are also plenty of *Würstelstände* (hot-dog stalls), sandwich bars like **Trzesniewski**, DOROTHEERGASSE 1, and fast-food stalls at the NASCHMARKT.

HIGHLIGHTS

The Tourist Office runs specialist walking tours (approximately ÖS110), but finding your own way around the compact city centre is easy.

An ornately carved spire soars over **Stephansdom**, U1/3 to STEPHANSPL., Austria's greatest Gothic building. Its colourful roof, tiled in jazzy stripes, is best seen floodlit at night. The magnificent 14th-century **Südturm** (south tower), known locally as the *Steffl*, is climbed by 343 steps for a terrific city view, while a lift whisks you up the (considerably lower) north tower, the **Pummerin**. Interior highlights include the Albertine Choir, the pulpit and organ loft by Anton Pilgrim, and the tomb of Friedrich III.

The **Hofburg**, the Habsburg's winter residence until 1918, occupies a prime position on the edge of the RING overlooking formal gardens. Altogether, it comprises 18 wings, 54 stairways and 2,600 rooms, and now houses several museums. The **Imperial Apartments** have been preserved as they were in Emperor Franz Josef I's time, while the **Schatzkammer** (treasury) displays the crown of the Holy Roman Empire.

The **Burgkapelle** is the chapel where the **Vienna Boys' Choir** sing on Sun (Sept–June, ÖS60–280, standing room free; for tickets write to **Hofmusik Kapelle**, HOFBURG, A-1010 WIEN). The choir also performs Fri, 1530 at the **Konzerthaus**, ÖS390/430 (tickets: **Reisebüro Mondial**, FAULMANNGASSE 4, A-1040 WIEN, ☎588 04141).

SPANISH RIDING SCHOOL

The famous Lippizaner horses perform on Sat and Sun (except July–Aug, U1/3: STEPHANSPLATZ). **Tickets** (ÖS250–900) can be booked by writing to **Spanische Reitschule**, HOFBURG 1, A-1010 WIEN, ☎535 0186. Or queue at the door of the **Redoute**, JOSEFSPL., to see 'morning training' without music, Tues–Sat 1000–1200, ÖS100.

TOURS

A sedate 20-min tour by *Fiaker* (horse-drawn carriage) costs ÖS440 from HELDENPL. (next to the cathedral) and outside the Hofburg and Albertina.

Bus tours of the city are operated by several companies, including **Vienna Line**, ☎712 46830, whose hop-on-hop-off service stops at 13 places of interest; hourly from 0900–1700 Apr–Oct, 2-hourly Nov–Mar. A **2-day ticket** costs ÖS220.

For a 90-min boat trip on the River Danube/ Danube Canal, start from SCHWEDENPL./ SCHWEDENBRÜCKE (May–Oct; **DDSG-Blue Danube**, ☎727 50222; fare ÖS170, depart 1000 and 1400).

Vienna has roughly 100 museums (most Tue–Sun, 1000–1800; some open late on Thur). The major museum, the **Kunsthistorisches Museum** (Museum of Fine Arts), MARIA-THERESIEN-PLATZ 1, is based on the Habsburgs' collection. The superb 18th-century baroque **Belvedere Palace**, PRINZ-EUGEN-STR. 27, has two galleries and delightful gardens; its **Österreichische Galerie** (Austrian Gallery) contains important works by Klimt, Schiele and 19th-century artists. The **Academy of Fine Arts**, SCHILLERPL. 3, includes Flemish works, while museums with a distinctive local flavour include the **Historisches Museum der Stadt Wien** (Historical Museum of the City of Vienna), KARSLPL. The original entrance to KARLSPLATZ station is one of the city's finest examples of *Jugendstil*.

The **Pasqualati Haus**, MÖLKER BASTEI 8, is one of Beethoven's many lodgings; there's a museum at the **Heiligenstadt Testament Haus**, PROBUSGASSE 6, in HEILIGENSTADT. Mozart's lodging, the **Figaro House**, DOMGASSE 5, contains memorial rooms. The **Schubert Museum** is at his birthplace, NUSSDORFERSTR. 54 (tram nos. 37/38).

The **Sigmund Freud Museum**, BERGGASSE 19; (tram nos. D, 37, 38, 40, 41, 42, 0900–1800 July–Sept, 0900–1600 Oct–June) is where the great psychoanalyst lived and worked from 1891 until his expulsion by the Nazis in 1938.

An architecture leaflet from the Tourist Office highlights interesting 20th-century buildings, including the anarchic, ecological **Hundertwasserhaus** (LOWENGASSE/KEGELGASSE), named after the painter-architect who redesigned this municipal housing estate in 1985, transforming the vicinity into an astonishing riot of colours and textures that has to be seen to be believed.

Further out, the palace of **Schönbrunn**, SCHÖNBRUNNER SCHLOSSTR. 13 (U4: SCHÖNBRUNN, tram nos.10, 58, 60; daily 0830–1700 Apr–Oct, daily 0830–0430 Nov–Mar), is a grand palace with fabulously baroque decoration, built as the Habsburgs' summer residence (guided tours of 40 rooms, or see 20 on your own).

The legendary **Prater park** (U-Bahn 1 to PRATERSTERN, tram nos. O/5/21) was originally the imperial hunting grounds. Riding the giant ferris wheel (famously filmed in the movie *The Third Man*), which has been turning there since 1897, provides a great view – but take care in the park at night.

SHOPPING

KÄRNTNERSTR. is the busiest shopping street and, together with GRABEN, the place to promenade. The nearby **Ringstrasse Galerien**, MAHLERSTR., is a modern mall with over 70 smart shops, open until 1900 (1700 Sat). Department stores are in MARIAHILFERSTR., outside the RING leading to the WESTBAHNHOF. Flea market: **Flohmarkt**, U4: WIENZEILE/KETTENBRUCKENGASSE, by station, Sat (except public holidays) 0630–1800. *'The Young Vienna Scene'* leaflet (free from Tourist Office) contains tips on the latest stores.

NIGHT-TIME AND EVENTS

Wien Magazin (monthly), listing all entertainment except cinemas (for which see newspapers), is free from Tourist Offices. Festivals abound, often with free Events: the May–June festival features classical music and jazz, while the **Danube Island Festival** (June) is an open-air event with rock, pop and fireworks. In July–Aug, the **Mozart in Schönbrunn** festival features open-air Mozart concerts in front of the Roman ruins. In July–Aug, there's the free **Festival of Music Films**, shown on a giant screen in RATHAUSPLATZ, which also hosts a great **Christmas market** from mid-Nov to Christmas.

To avoid high agency commissions, apply for tickets (ÖS50–5000) to **Bundestheaterverband**, HANUSCHGASSE 3, A-1010 WIEN, ☎513 1513; standing tickets sold 1 hr before the performance.

Night owls focus on the **'Bermuda Triangle'**, an area of lively bars, discos and pubs around RUPRECHTSPL., particularly JUDENGASSE and STERNGASSE. The famous **Staatsoper** (Vienna State Opera), OPERNRING 2, stages operas Sept–June. The **Volksoper**, WAHRINGERSTR. 78, offers operettas and musicals.

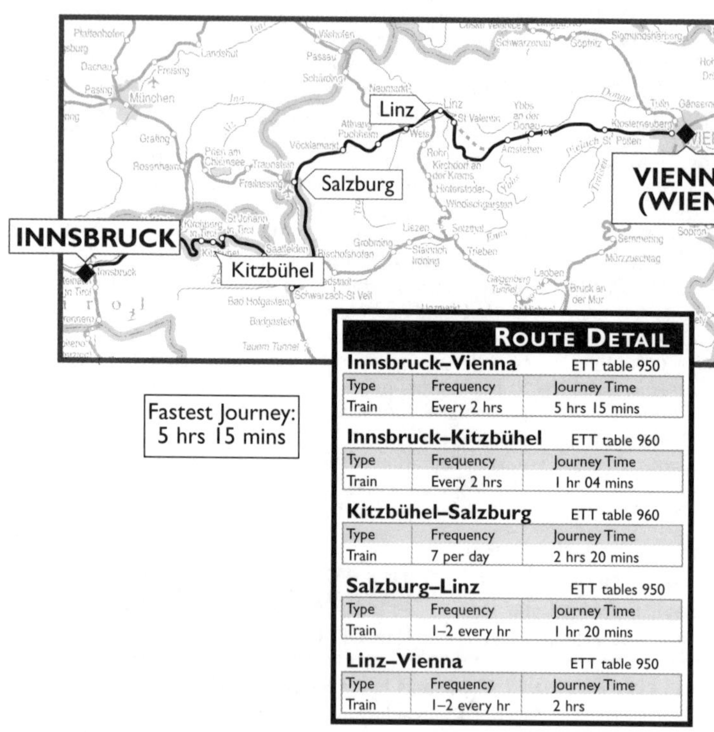

ROUTE DETAIL

Innsbruck–Vienna ETT table 950

Type	Frequency	Journey Time
Train	Every 2 hrs	5 hrs 15 mins

Innsbruck–Kitzbühel ETT table 960

Type	Frequency	Journey Time
Train	Every 2 hrs	1 hr 04 mins

Kitzbühel–Salzburg ETT table 960

Type	Frequency	Journey Time
Train	7 per day	2 hrs 20 mins

Salzburg–Linz ETT tables 950

Type	Frequency	Journey Time
Train	1–2 every hr	1 hr 20 mins

Linz–Vienna ETT table 950

Type	Frequency	Journey Time
Train	1–2 every hr	2 hrs

Austria's elongated shape permits few long journeys within its borders, but this is one well worth seeking out, making a trans-Alpine experience from the heart of the Tyrol to Salzburg, famed as Mozart's birthplace, before ending up at the Austrian capital (see p. 312). The most scenic route between Salzburg and Linz is via Bischofshofen and Selzthal (effectively three sides of a square).

INNSBRUCK

The 800-year-old Tyrolean capital on the River Inn is a bustling, amiable city overlooked by the Karwendel mountains to the north and the Patscherkofel mountains to the south – making it an excellent starting point for walks and other activities in the Alps (free guided hikes start daily June–Oct, meeting 0830 outside the Congress Hall).

The **Altstadt** area is dotted with 15th- and 16th-century buildings, many with elaborate stucco decorations and traditional convex windows to catch extra light on the narrow streets. Its most famous sight is the 15th-century **Goldenes Dachl**, HERZOG-FRIEDRICHSTR. 1, a roof of 2,657 gilded copper tiles covering a balcony, which Emperor Maximilian I (the subject of an exhibition inside) added in 1500 to the **Neuhof**, the residence of the Tyrolean princes. The **Stadtturm** (city tower) opposite the balcony offers views across the rooftops to the mountains. Nearby is the **Dom zu St Jakob**, a striking baroque cathedral.

The **Hofburg** (Imperial Palace), RENNWEG, has a sumptuous ballroom lined with portraits of Empress Maria Theresa's family, who also feature in 28 larger-than-life bronze statues on Emperor Maximilian's grand tomb in the 16th-century **Hofkirche**, the court church. Wander round the **Hofgarten** (court gardens) for outdoor chess, elegant flower-beds and pavilions (free). The neighbouring **Tiroler Volkskunst Museum** concentrates on Tyrolean culture, displaying traditional costumes and wood-panelled rooms. The **Ferdinandeum**, MUSEUMSTR. 15, is more diverse, with beautiful old stained glass, medieval altars and works by Cranach and Rembrandt.

RAIL SUDTIROLER PL. 7, ☎(0512) 503 5000. Left luggage, showers, tourist information. Walk down SALURNER STR. and then right at the 1765 triumphal arch into MARIA-THERESASTR. (10 mins).

✈ ☎ (0512) 22525, 4 km west (🚌F from the station).

i **Tourist Office**: BURGGRABEN 3, ☎(0512) 5356, on the edge of Altstadt (0800–1900, Sun 0900–1800). At station: ☎(0512) 583766 (0800–2100 Oct–May, 0900–2200 June–Sept). Accommodation booking service, ÖS40 deposit; money exchange, concert tickets, ski/cable car passes and Innsbruck cards.

INNSBRUCK CARD

All-inclusive **Innsbruck Card**, covering local transport (including cable cars) and entrance to 18 museums and attractions: 24-hr card ÖS230, 48-hr ÖS300, 72-hr ÖS370, from Tourist Offices and museums.

24-hr ticket for **tram, bus** and **trolley bus** system costs ÖS45 (single ÖS21). Bikes from the station, ÖS90 per day.

WHERE NEXT FROM INNSBRUCK?

Innsbruck is on the ***Munich–Verona*** *route (p. 275). You can also continue west to* **Liechtenstein***, then enter Switzerland at* ***Sargans*** *to join the* ***Lausanne–Poschiavo*** *route (p. 286; ETT tables 530, 950).*

Budget rooms are scarce in June, when only three hostels are open, but 'summer hotels' usually open in university accommodation July and Aug. The family-run **Sailer**, ADAMGASSE 6–10, (0512) 5363, notable for its Tyrolean restaurant and décor, is handy for the station (moderate). Relatively central **youth hostels** are **Glockenhaus**, WEIHERBURGGASSE 3, (0512) 286515, and **St Nikolaus**, INNSTR 95, (0512) 286515 (K from the station to St Nikolaus, then walk up hill).
Campsite: **Camping Innsbruck Kranebitten**, KRANEBITTER ALLEE 214, (0512) 284180, is west of town (O).

The **Altstadt** area is generally expensive. Moderate alternatives include **Schwarzer Adler**, KAISERJAGERSTR. 2, (0512) 587109, which serves traditional meals. **Café Munding** is the oldest Tyrolean café and pastry-shop, with fabulous cakes. Try the young, friendly pub, **Elferhaus**, HERZOG-FRIEDRICH-STR. 11, (0512) 582875.

KITZBÜHEL

Graced with a mountain backdrop, this pleasant old town with its tree-lined streets of steeply-gabled pastel-coloured buildings is one of Austria's prettiest and largest ski resorts (though the snow's not that reliable; main season Christmas–Easter). The **Heimatmuseum**, HINTERSTADT 34, occupies the town's oldest house and displays Klimt paintings (Mon–Sat 0930–1230). Don't miss the **Kitzbuheler Horn** cable car to the summit of the Horn; near the top, some 200 flowers and grasses bloom in an **Alpine flower garden**, 1880 m high.

The ski elite arrive in Jan for the **Hahnenkamm Ski Competition**, a World Cup leg down one of the world's trickiest ski runs. At the top of the Hahnenkamm lift, the **Bergbahn Museum** reveals the history of skiing in Kitzbühel since 1893 (free, daily 1230–1800).

LIFT PASSES

In summertime, hikers can buy lift passes valid for any three days in a week (ÖS390).

The Tourist Office organises free guided bike and mountain bike trips (register one day before). A 2.5-km walk leads to the **Schwarzsee**, a good bathing lake.

RAIL BAHNHOFPL. 2, (05356) 64055. 10-min walk to town centre; go straight across the River Ache, left along ACHENPROMENADE, then follow signs right for centre. Bike hire at station: ÖS150 per day (ÖS90 with rail ticket).

Tourist Office: HINTERSTADT 18, (05356) 621550, next to the **Rathaus** (town hall). Open Mon–Sat 0830–1830, Sun 1000–1200 and 1600–1800 (July–Sept, Christmas–New Year and Feb–mid Mar); Mon–Fri 0830–1200 and 1430–1800, Sat 0830–1200 (rest of year). Free accommodation service, free street and hiking maps.

The *Frühstuck pensionen* (bed and breakfast) are cheap, such as **Pension Hörl**, JOSEF-PIRCHL-STR. 60, (05356) 63144. **Youth hostel**: **Skiheim Rote Teufel**, EHRENBACHGASSE 48, (05356) 65669; **Seereith**, KIRCHBERGER STR. 67, (05356) 62360. **Campsite**: **Camping Schwarzsee**, REITHERSTR. 24, (05356) 62806, near Schwarzsee station.

Keep hold of **guest cards** or the **orange 'holiday' slip** from your accommodation, as these give discounts on lifts, cable cars, etc.

Chizzo, JOSEF-HEROLD-STR.2, is relaxed and good value. During the ski season, restaurants up on the ski slopes are open too. **Café Kortschak**, HINTERSTADT 13, (05356) 62643, has the best cakes in town (moderate).

SALZBURG

Wonderfully sited between the Alps and the lakes of the Salzkammergut, Salzburg is renowned as Mozart's birthplace and is where *The Sound of Music* was filmed in 1964. Much of the city's appearance dates from the 17th century, when most of the old buildings were pulled down to make way for Italian-style squares with spectacular fountains. In 1997, Salzburg's entire **Old City** (Altstadt) was designated a UNESCO World Heritage Site.

The main shopping street is narrow GETREIDEGASSE, always oozing tourists and bordered by elegant old houses, decorative wrought-iron signs and medieval arcades. **Mozarts Geburtshaus**, NO.9, where the composer was born in 1756 and spent most of his first 17 years, is now a museum. The family subsequently lived in the **Mozart-Wohnhaus**, MAKART-PL. 8, across the river, recently rebuilt in its original style following World War II destruction, its rooms furnished in period style; concerts are held there. In nearby RESIDENZPL. is the **Residenz** (hourly tours), the former Prince Archbishop's palace, built after the need for fortification had passed. Mozart conducted in its grand rooms.

The **cathedral**, in the adjacent DOMPL., is considered to be the finest early baroque church north of the Alps. A magnificent light-filled building, it has four domes and space inside for 10,000 people. Mozart worked there as *Konzertmeister* and court organist.

On **Mönchsberg** (Monk's mountain), high above the Altstadt, looms the formidable **Festung Hohensalzburg**, MÖNCHSBERG 34, once the stronghold of the Archbishops of Salzburg. Built over six centuries, it's almost perfectly preserved, with medieval torture chambers, early Gothic state rooms, and a 200-pipe barrel organ that booms out once the 7th-century 35-bell carillon of the **Glockenspiel**, MOZARTPL., has pealed

DAY TRIPS FROM SALZBURG

Just south of town (5 km) is the ornate 17th-century **Schloss Hellbrunn** (no. 55 from station or MIRABELLPL.). The gardens of this Italian-designed pleasure-palace are famous for their lovely sculptures and fountains, especially those that squirt unexpectedly from stone stools to surprise drunken guests (guided tours, 0900–1630; Apr–Oct, evening tours, July–Aug).

(at 0700, 1100 and 1800). The castle can be reached on foot from FESTUNGSGASSE behind the cathedral, or by the Festungsbahn (cable railway, May–Sept). Alternatively, the Mönchsberglift operates from GSTÄTTENGASSE 13 (by MUSEUMPL.) and takes you to the **Café Winkler**, where paths lead across to the castle.

Across the river is **Schloss Mirabell**, MIRABELLPL., originally built in the 17th century for Prince-Archbishop Wolf Dietrich's mistress Salome Alt, who bore him 15 or 16 children. It houses the **Marble Hall**, a magnificent venue for chamber music concerts; its Angel Staircase sports marble cherubs. The **Mirabellgarten**, former royal pleasure gardens, is an oasis of late baroque gardens, terraces and statuary (free).

RAIL SUDTIROLER PL. 1, (0662) 8887 3161; 20 mins' walk from the old centre (nos. 1/2/5/6/51 to STAATSBRÜCKE, the main bridge). Tourist information, accommodation service, left luggage (by platforms 4 and 5, daily 0600–2200), money exchange, shops.

4 km west of the city; (0662) 851223. no. 77 every 15–30 mins connects station with airport; journey time about 15 mins. Taxis to the city centre (about ÖS150) (0662) 8111.

i **Tourist Offices**: **City centre**: MOZARTPL. 5, (0662) 8898 7330. Open 0900–1900 June–Sept (to 2000 July–Aug); Mon–Sat 0900–1800 Oct–May; **station**, PLATFORM 2A, (0662) 8898 7340. Open 0845–2030 May–June and Sept; 0800–2130 July–Aug; 0845–1945 Oct–May. Accommodation service (ÖS30).

Most of the centre is pedestrianised and within walking distance.

Salzburg cards
ÖS200 – 24 hrs, ÖS270 – 48 hrs, ÖS360 – 72 hrs provide free admission to all of Salzburg's attractions.
Salzburgerland Summer Joker card for free access to over 130 attractions in the region from ÖS495, 16 days (10 May–26 Oct).
Bus and trolley tickets: ÖS15 from automatic vending machines or tobacconists; more expensive from driver (punch immediately after boarding).
Day passes: ÖS32.

During festivals, it pays to book early as accommodation often gets very scarce. Cheaper options, near the rail station, include **Hotel Sandwirt**, LASTENSTR. 6A, (0662) 874351; **Pension Elisabeth**, VOGELWEIDERSTR. 52, (0662) 871664. **Youth hostels** (both about 5 mins' walk from station): HAUNSPERGSTR. 27, (0662) 875030 (July–Aug), and **Youth Hotel Obermair**, PARACELSUSSTR. 9, (0662) 879649 (year-round). **Campsites** include **Nord Sam**, SAMSTR. 22A, (0662) 660494 (no. 33).

Traditional Salzburg fare is served in the **Zum Mohren**, JUDENGASSE 9, ☎(0662) 842387, where the Mozart family liked to eat. Less expensive is **Der Wilde Mann**, GETREIDEGASSE 20. **Café Tomaselli**, ALTER MARKT 9, is where the elegant have sipped coffee for the last two centuries. Also worth trying are beer gardens, especially the **Augustiner Brau**, AUGUSTINERG. 4, where beer is brewed by the monastery.

NIGHT-TIME AND EVENTS

The big event is the **Salzburg Festival**, late July–end Aug. For major performances, tickets must be booked months ahead from **Kartenbüro der Salzburger Festspiele**, A-5010 SALZBURG, POSTFACH 140; ☎(0662) 844501, fax: (0662) 846682. Last-minute standing tickets sometimes available in the **Kleine Festspielhaus**. Events linked to the festival include an opening *Fackeltanz* (torch-dance) in the RESIDENZPL. and performances of *'Jedermann'* ('Everyman'); standing tickets only sold at the DOMPL. door one hour before start. Other events include **Mozart Week** in late Jan, a Nov **Jazz Festival** and an Easter **Music Festival**. In addition, there's always a concert on somewhere in the city. The **Marionetten Theater**, SCHWARZSTR. 24, ☎(0662) 872 4060, presents operas 'performed' convincingly by puppets which 'sing' to recordings.

WHERE NEXT FROM SALZBURG?

*From here it's a short ride over the border to Germany, with services to **Munich** (p. 229; ETT table 890) taking just under 2 hrs.*

LINZ

As Austria's third city, Linz's prosperity is based on its position as a Danube port. **HAUPTPLATZ**, a huge 13th-century closed square just off the river, blends colourful baroque and rococo façades around the baroque marble **Trinity column**. In 1938, Hitler stood on the balcony of no. 1 (now the Tourist Office) to inform the Austrians that the Nazis had annexed their country.

Starting from HAUPTPL., the dinky yellow 'road-train' provides a 25-min city introduction (1000–1800 May–Sept, ÖS50); alternatively follow the free *'Linz geht rund'* guided walk brochure from the Tourist Office. Every Sept/Oct, Linz hosts the 3-week **International Bruckner Festival** and **Klangwolke** (Cloud of Sound), a stunning multimedia spectacle, but there are also 'cultural summer' festivals, Advent markets and many other free events throughout the year.

MUSEUM OF THE FUTURE

The city's hottest attraction is the 21st-century **Museum of the Future** (Wed–Sat 1000–1800, ÖS80), ARS ELECTRONICA CENTER, HAUPTSTR 2.

The 17th-century **Alter Dom**, DOMGASSE, one of the city's two cathedrals, is simple outside but restrained baroque within. The other, the huge neo-Gothic **Neuer Dom**, BAUMBACHSTR., can hold 20,000 people. **Landhaus**, KLOSTERSTR. 7, is where the astronomer Johannes Kepler developed the third law of planetary motion.

DANUBE STEAMBOAT

Trips and cruises are operated from the quay, ERNST-KOREF-PROMENADE, (0732) 783607.

The Linz City Ticket (ÖS299) gives unlimited travel on public transport, the road-train and *Postlinberg* tram, free admission to one museum and to the **Museum of the Future** plus a restaurant voucher worth ÖS150.

Public transport day ticket: ÖS36; **single:** ÖS9.

Across the river, the **Postlingbergbahn**, Europe's steepest rack railway, chugs from the tram no. 3 terminus at LANDGUTSTR. to a fortress and pilgrimage church (ÖS48).

BAHNHOFPL. 8, (0732) 6908 3170 or 1717. Electronic information service, left-luggage lockers (24 hrs, ÖS30–50), shops. For centre, take tram no. 3 to HAUPTPL. (10 mins).

Tourist Office: HAUPTPL. 1, (0732) 7070 1777 (Mon–Fri 0800–1900, Sat 0900–1900, Sun and holidays 1000–1900 May–Sept; Mon–Fri 0800–1800, Sat 0900–1800, Sun and holidays 1000–1800 Nov–April). **Branch**: URFAHRMARKT 1, (0732) 7070 2939.

Near the station is the (moderate) **Hotel Zur Locomotive**, WEINGARTSHOFSTR. 40, (0732) 654554. More central is the **Goldenes Dachl hotel**, HAFNERSTR. 27, (0732) 675480 (cheap). **Youth hostels**: KAPUZINERSTR. 14, (0732) 778777; STANGLHOFWEG 3, (0732) 664434, just west of station; **Landesjugendherberge**, BLUTENSTR. 23, (0732) 737078. The nearest **campsite** is **Campingpl. Pleschingersee**, WIENER BUNDESSTR., 937, (0732) 305314 (tram no. 3 from station to RUDOLFSTR. across the river, then no. 32).

The pedestrian zone around HOFGASSE is busy at night and has plenty of reasonable eateries. **Klosterhof**, LANDSTR. 30, boasts Austria's biggest beer garden. Tuck into fabulous sausages from the **Zum warmen Hans** sausage stand, HAUPTPL., and don't forget to sample *Linzer Torte* (almond cake topped with redcurrant jam).

WHERE NEXT FROM LINZ?

*Join the **Cologne–Passau** route (p. 245) by taking the train over the German border to **Passau** (ETT table 920; 1 hr 30 mins).*

(for Directory information, see p. 552). The cornerstone of Western civilisation, **Italy** has been firmly on the tourist map since the days of the 18th-century 'Grand Tour'. There is so much to experience that it isn't necessary to make a literal grand tour of the entire country at one go. You can get a good sample by, for instance, keeping to the hills and medieval cities of Tuscany, or heading down from **Rome** to **Sicily**, or combining **Lake Como** and **Lake Garda** with the **Dolomites** – which include some of the most astonishing mountain shapes in the Alps – plus maybe **Verona** and **Venice**. The rail network covers all of this, except for the Dolomites, which can be visited by taking a bus from Bolzano.

Although an absolutely unmissable cocktail of man-made and natural beauty, Italy does have notable shortcomings. The sheer quantity and quality of historic stuff can be hard work, and great showpieces like the Renaissance art in Florence's **Uffizi** gallery and the Roman ruins of **Pompeii** can make it a laborious traipse, with oppressive crowds (and debilitating heat in high summer) and often incessant traffic too. You'd be better off mixing the major attractions such as **Florence** and **Rome** with some less hectic spots such as **Lucca** or **Orvieto**.

Although virtually surrounded by sea, Italy lacks decent mainland beach resorts: the Neapolitan Riviera has great scenery around **Sorrento**, but no beaches to speak of, while the Adriatic (eastern) coast has the best beaches but the resorts are anonymous, dull high-rise concrete affairs. By contrast, the islands of **Elba**, **Ischia** and **Sardinia** have much more scope for a beach holiday, though they do get packed in summer.

Drop into any street café for a snapshot of Italian life, where locals discuss the news or the football.

Around dusk the whole town meets during the evening stroll, or *passeggiata*, in the main street or square, and the Italian knack of chic dressing and looking good comes to the fore.

YOUTH HOSTELS

The youth hostel headquarters is the **Associazione Italiana Alberghi per la Gioventù**, V. Cavour 44, 00184 Roma, (6) 4871152, fax (6) 4880492 (email: aig@uni.net; website: http://www.travel.it/hostels).

INFORMATION

Touring Club Italiano (TCI), Corso Italia 10, 20122 Milano; (02) 85 261 or 852 6245, publish an annual guide. Alternatively, you can get a list from **Federcampeggio**, Casella Postale 23, 50041 Calenzano (Florence), (055) 88 2391, who can also make bookings.

These two organisations produce a detailed directory of campsites, *Campeggi e Villagi Turistici in Italia*, available from bookshops in Italy (L.30,000).

Agriturismo, Corso V Emanuele 101, Roma, (06) 6852 342, has information about staying in rural cottages and farmhouses.

Club Alpino Italiano, Via Fonseca Pimental 7, 20121 Milan, (02) 26 141 378, can supply details of mountain refuge huts.

ACCOMMODATION

All **hotels** are classified according to a five-star system and inspectors set a maximum (seasonal) rate that must be displayed in each room. It does not necessarily include showers or breakfast, but extras must be listed separately, so complain (to the Tourist Office if all else fails) if your bill does not agree with the rates listed. You must, by law, obtain a receipt from all hotels. **Venice** and **Capri** are particularly expensive for accommodation. Prices are often for rooms rather than per person.

Most establishments now term themselves **hotel** or *albergo*, but some are still called *pensione* (one-, two-, or three-star) or *locande* (one-star). There are many private rooms, unofficial and otherwise. You can find the unofficial ones by looking for signs saying *affitta camere*, often in shop windows. It's worth trying to bargain, but you will usually pay about the same as for a one–star hotel. *Alberghi diurni*, near stations or in the centre, are essentially day rooms: you can have a wash without taking a room for the night. **Cheaper hotels** may require you to stay at least three nights and take half board (covering breakfast and evening meal).

There is no shortage of **youth hostels**, but relatively few are members of the **HI** and the standard varies considerably; expect to pay L.18,000–30,000 including sheets and breakfast for HI hostels. It is often just as cheap and more convenient to stay at a one-star hotel.

Camping is popular and there are over 2000 sites (all **Tourist Offices** have information about their area), but they are often fairly expensive and/or difficult to reach without a car. There are few places where you can rough camp without asking permission.

FOOD AND DRINK

Mealtime is an important social event for Italians, and there's a wide variety of food available everywhere, with pasta just one of many options. A full meal will consist of *antipasta* (cold meats etc.), *pasta*, a main course, and fruit or cheese. Italian ice-cream *(gelato)* is among the world's best. Much of the pleasure of eating in Italy is derived

Look for **cover charges** *(coperto)* and **service** *(servizio)*, both of which will be added to your bill. Prices on **Menu Turistico** include taxes and service charges.

from the sheer freshness and quality of the ingredients.

Trattorie are simple establishments which are cheaper than *ristoranti*. Most *osterie* are trendy and expensive. *Alimentari* stores often prepare excellent and interesting sandwiches. *Rosticerrie* sell good hot takeaways, while *tavole calde* are cheap self-service, sit-down places. Smaller establishments seldom have menus: just ask for the dish of the day if you want something reasonably priced. Menus are displayed by the entrance.

Dishes vary enormously from region to region. For example in the **Trentino Alto Adige** up in the Alps the fare is Austrian, with smoked hams and sausages perhaps followed by fruit strudel, while in **Liguria** fish and shellfish predominate in such soups as *zuppa di datteri* and in a Genoese fish and vegetable salad known as *cappon magro*.

Coffee *(caffe)* takes many forms, from *espresso* to *liqueur*. It tends to come in small shots of *espresso*; if you want a larger cup of white coffee ask for *cappuccino* or *caffe-latte*. There are various types of Italian beer and many fine wines. Bars are good places to get a snack, such as a roll or toasted sandwich, as well as to sample the local 'fire waters' such as grappa.

If you're gathering picnic items, beware that food shops close for a lengthy lunch break.

EDITOR'S CHOICE

Assisi; Bologna; Dolomites (bus from Bolzano to Ortisei; or train to Toblach); Florence; Milan; Naples; Orvieto; Pisa; Pompeii and Herculaneum; Ravenna; Rome; San Gimignano; Sardinia; Sicily (Palermo, Taormina etc); Siena; Venice; Verona. Scenic rail journeys: Ventimiglia–Pisa (p.357); Arezzo–Assisi (p. 373); Messina–Palermo (p. 381); Circumetna railway around Etna (see Day Trips panel, p. 383) lines in Sardinia to Arbatax, Nuoro and Palau (pp. 386, 388, 389); Cosenza–Castiglione–Cosentino (ETT table 642).

BEYOND THE BORDER

Ventimiglia–Marseille (p. 100); Verona–Munich (p. 275); Milan–Stuttgart via Zurich (ETT table 84); Milan–Paris (table 44); ferry Livorno–Bastia (table 2580); ferry Genova–Bastia (table 2540). See also Where Next? panels for Milan (p. 339); Naples (p. 344); Rome (p. 350); Venice (p. 356); Trieste (p. 372); Palermo (p. 385).

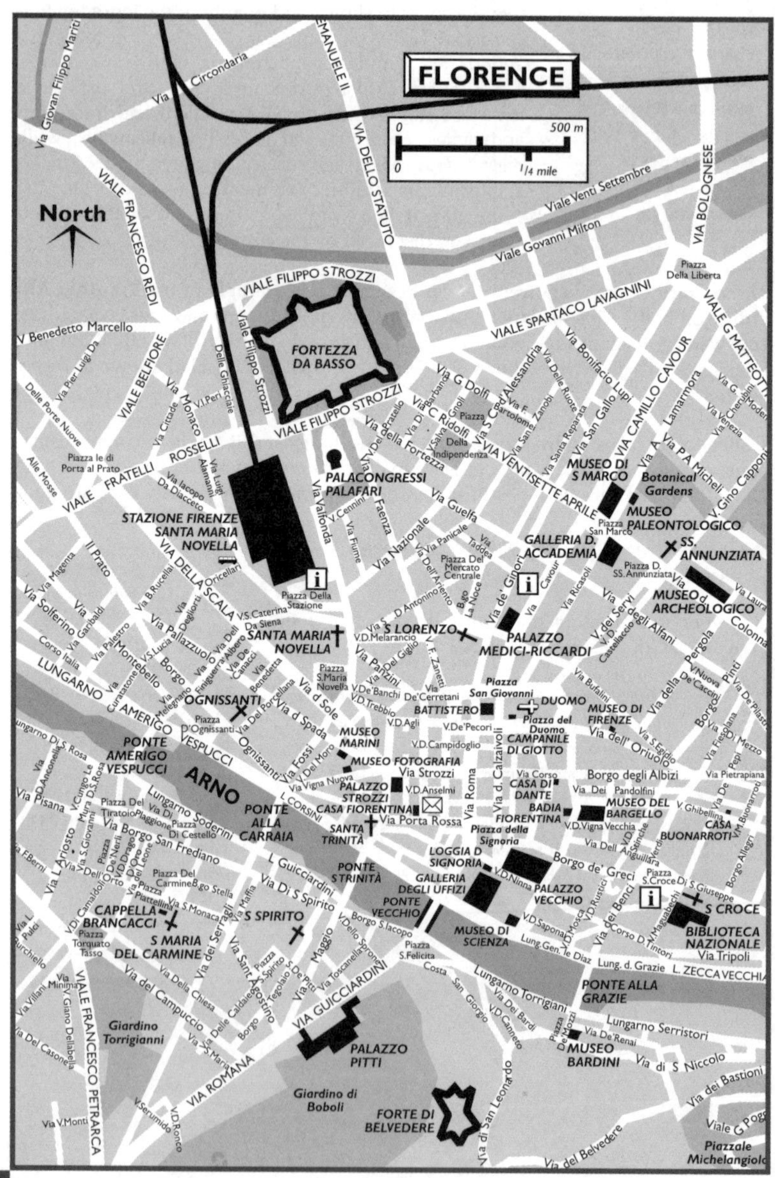
FLORENCE
North
0 500 m
0 1/4 mile
FORTEZZA DA BASSO
PALACONGRESSI PALAFARI
STAZIONE FIRENZE SANTA MARIA NOVELLA
Piazza Della Stazione
SANTA MARIA NOVELLA
S LORENZO
PALAZZO MEDICI-RICCARDI
MUSEO DI S MARCO
Botanical Gardens
MUSEO PALEONTOLOGICO
GALLERIA D. ACCADEMIA
SS. ANNUNZIATA
MUSEO ARCHEOLOGICO
OGNISSANTI
BATTISTERO
DUOMO
Piazza del Duomo
CAMPANILE DI GIOTTO
MUSEO DI FIRENZE
MUSEO MARINI
MUSEO FOTOGRAFIA
PALAZZO STROZZI
CASA FIORENTINA
SANTA TRINITÀ
CASA DI DANTE
BADIA FIORENTINA
MUSEO DEL BARGELLO
CASA BUONARROTI
Piazza della Signoria
LOGGIA D SIGNORIA
GALLERIA DEGLI UFFIZI
PALAZZO VECCHIO
MUSEO DI SCIENZA
PONTE VECCHIO
PONTE STRINITÀ
PONTE ALLA CARRAIA
PONTE AMERIGO VESPUCCI
ARNO
S CROCE
BIBLIOTECA NAZIONALE
PONTE ALLA GRAZIE
CAPPELLA BRANCACCI
S MARIA DEL CARMINE
S SPIRITO
PALAZZO PITTI
Giardino di Boboli
Giardino Torrigianni
FORTE DI BELVEDERE
MUSEO BARDINI
Piazzale Michelangiolo
Piazza Della Liberta
VIALE FILIPPO STROZZI
VIALE SPARTACO LAVAGNINI
VIALE FRATELLI ROSSELLI
VIA DELLO STATUTO
VIA BOLOGNESE
VIALE FRANCESCO REDI
VIALE FRANCESCO PETRARCA
VIA GUICCIARDINI
VIA ROMANA
LUNGARNO AMERIGO VESPUCCI
VIA DELLA SCALA
VIA CAMILLO CAVOUR
VIA VENTISETTE APRILE
VIALE G MATTEOTTI
Viale Venti Settembre
Viale Govanni Milton
Via Circondaria
Via Nazionale
Via Guelfa
Via Faenza
Via Strozzi
Via Porta Rossa
Borgo degli Albizi
Borgo de' Greci
Lungarno Torrigiani
Lungarno Serristori
Via di S Niccolo
Via del Belvedere
Via di San Leonardo
Lungarno Soderini
Via Borgo San Frediano
Via Di S Spirito
Via Maggio
Via dei Serragli
Via del Campuccio
Via Tripoli

One of the greatest of Italy's old city-states, Florence has one of the richest legacies of art and architecture in Europe. It is so popular that its narrow streets are tightly crammed from Easter to autumn and major sights get extremely crowded during this period. Be prepared to wait in line to enter the **Galleria Uffizi** – Italy's premier art gallery – or to see Michelangelo's David in the **Galleria dell'Accademia**. Nevertheless, few would omit Florence from a tour of Tuscany, and it's supremely rewarding providing you don't overdo the sightseeing, have an afternoon siesta and keep your valuables well out of the reach of pick-pockets and bag-snatchers. There are plenty of other galleries of world status if you don't feel able to cope with the Uffizi crowds. Try for example the **Museo dell'Opera del Duomo** or the **Bargello**. Enjoy the city by walking around: take in the **Ponte Vecchio**, the **Duomo** (cathedral), or the huge piazza by the Gothic church of **Santa Maria Novella**.

You pay an entrance fee for every building you visit in Florence – apart from the churches. **Combined entrance tickets** are available for some museums. Most museums close on Mon, and some are closed Sun as well. The **Uffizi** is quietest an hour or so before it closes at 7pm.

ARRIVAL AND DEPARTURE

Santa Maria Novella (SMN), PZA DELLA STAZIONE; ☎ 1478 88088, is Florence's main rail hub. It is a short walk from the city centre; facilities include left luggage, currency exchange and an accommodation service. The main station, ☎ (055) 565 0222, is next door. The fast **ETR 450** Milan/Florence/Rome express service stops at **Rifredi** station, 3 km north of the city centre. There is an ATM on the station platform.

Amerigo Vespucci Airport, 4 km north-west of the city, ☎ (055) 373 498, handles mainly domestic and some European services. The airport bus is operated by **SITA**, V. SANTA CATERINA DA SIENA 157, ☎ (055) 214 721. Pisa's **Galileo Galilei Airport** (84 km) is the main regional hub for international flights, ☎ (050) 500 707. Hourly trains run between the airport and Florence's **Santa Maria Novella** rail station (1 hr). A terminal for this airport is within the station, ☎ 1478 88088 (toll-free).

INFORMATION

MONEY Eurocheques are widely accepted, but credit cards are useful only in the more expensive shops and restaurants. Banks that change money usually display the sign *Cambio* (Exchange). There are also exchange kiosks at **SMN** station and at numerous city centre locations. **Thomas Cook bureau de change** is located at PONTE VECCHIO, LUNGARNO ACCIAIOLI 6R; ☎ (055) 289 781. They will cash Thomas Cook travellers' cheques free of

TOURIST OFFICES

The **Azienda Promozione Turistica (APT)** has its head office at V. MANZONI 16, fax: (055) 234 6286.

The **City of Florence** has tourist information offices at BORGO SANTA CROCE 29R, ☎(055) 234 0444, and at PZA DELLA STAZIONE (arrival end), ☎(055) 212 245. There is a combined **City and Province of Florence** office at V. CAVOUR 1R, ☎(055) 290 832/3; BORGO S. CRUCE 29R (Mon–Sat 0830–1915, Sun and holidays 0830–1345); PZA DELLA STAZIONE (Mon–Sat 0830–1915, Sun and holidays, closed; closes 1345 Oct to Apr).

commission and can offer emergency assistance for lost or stolen travellers' cheques.

POST AND PHONES The main **post office** is at V. PELLICCERIA 53, open Mon–Fri 0815–1800, Sat 0815–1230. There are usually long queues. You can buy stamps from tobacconists and from stationers. You can also make calls from the V. PIETRAPIANA office, open 0800–1745 daily, and at the **SMN** station office, open 0800–2145, closed Sun and holidays. To phone **Florence from abroad**: ☎39 (Italy) + 55 (Florence) + number; to phone **Florence from elsewhere in Italy**: ☎(055) + number.

PUBLIC TRANSPORT

Most sights are in the compact central zone and the best way to see them all is on foot. You can cover much of the city in two days. You can also rent bicycles from the municipal rental location at PZA DELLA STAZIONE, next to the SMN station, and at several other outlets around the city. Town maps are available from Tourist Offices and from ATAF (see below).

Buses: Florence's **Azienda Trasporti Autolinee Fiorentine (ATAF)** municipal buses run from 0515 to 0100. There is an **ATAF information office** opposite the main entrance of **SMN** rail station, ☎(055) 565 0222. Buy your tickets singly from machines at main bus stops, in books of four from tobacconists or bars: cancel them in the machine on boarding.

Tickets last for one hour from the time the machine stamps them, and you may change buses on the same ticket. You can also buy an all-day *turistiche* (tourist ticket) which costs less than five times the price of a single. Various other tickets are available.

Taxis: Licensed taxis are white with a yellow stripe. Prices are high (minimum fare is about six times the cost of a one-hour bus ticket). Avoid unlicensed cabs, which can be even more expensive.

ACCOMMODATION

Europe's busiest tourism city as well as a major venue for trade fairs and for business travel, Florence has some magnificent luxury properties, such as the exquisite **Villa Cora** and the elegant **Excelsior**. At the other end of the scale, accommodation for the budget traveller is limited. Whichever you choose, try to book well ahead. Very near the station is the family run **Hotel Nuova Halia**.

The cheapest accommodation, though not always the most appealing, is near the **SMN** station. Elsewhere, lodgings outside the city centre and south of the **Arno** are cheaper than those in the city's historic heart. The *Informazione Turistiche Alberghiere* **(ITA)** booth at the **SMN** station may be able to find you a room if you arrive without a booking (small commission charged); open 0830–2030 – prepare to wait in a long queue.

CAMPSITES

A further list of campsites in and around Florence is available from **Federazione Italiane per Campeggio e Caravanning,** VIA V EMANUELE II M1, ☎(055) 882 391, which also handles campsite bookings.

Florence has three **youth hostels**: advance booking is recommended at all three. They are: **Ostello Villa Camerata**, **Ostello Santa Monaca** and **Archi Rossi**.

There are **campsites** at: **Italiani e Stranieri**, and in the grounds of the **Villa Camerata** youth hostel (see below).

HOTELS	**Villa Cora**, V. MACHIAVELLI 18; ☎(055) 229 8451. **Excelsior**, PZA OGNISSANTI; ☎(055) 264 201. Both expensive **Hotel Nuova Halia,** Via Faenza 26, ☎(055) 268 430. Moderate
YOUTH HOSTELS	**Ostello Villa Camerata**, VLE A. RIGHI 2/4, ☎(055) 601 451. **Ostello Santa Monaca**, V. SANTA MONACA 6, ☎(055) 268 338. **Archi Rossi**, VIA FAENZA 94R, ☎(055) 290 804.
CAMPSITES	**Italiani e Stranieri**, VIALE MICHELANGELO 80, ☎(055) 681 1977 (Apr–Oct). **Villa Camerata youth hostel** – in the grounds (see above).

FOOD AND DRINK

Florence has a good supply of reasonably priced eating-places. You can cut costs by opting for fixed-price *(prezzo fisso)* meals which give you a choice of first courses, a choice of main courses, and fruit or cheese. Since one of the first course choices is always pasta, this makes a filling meal. **S. Spirito**, and **S. Frediano** are good regions to get inexpensive food in **Altrarno**, south of the river. An even cheaper option is the *tavola calda*, a buffet-style self-service restaurant where you can choose a single dish or a full meal. These are found all over town and cover and service charges are included in the price displayed for each dish.

As in other Italian towns, drinks taken standing or sitting at the bar are a great deal cheaper than those consumed at a table, and restaurants outside the main sightseeing semi circle are usually cheaper than those close to the main sights. For picnic ingredients try an *alimentari* (grocery shop) – but remember that they shut for lunch.

HIGHLIGHTS

The city is divided by the **River Arno**, with most of its glorious medieval heart on the north bank. South of the river, the **Altrarno** district is packed with artisans' workshops; this is the traditional 'working' Florence, largely untouched by the major tourist sights at its heart across the river. Five bridges cross the Arno. The most central, the **Ponte Vecchio**, is lined with shops specialising in jewellery. Built in 1345, it is Florence's oldest bridge.

NORTH OF THE ARNO

Most of the important sights lie in a semi circle north of the Arno, within a 2-km radius of the **Uffizi**. These include Florence's 'musts'. The **Galleria Uffizi** itself, PZLE DEGLI UFFIZI 6, contains works by many of the Renaissance greats such as Giotto, Cimabue, Botticelli, Michelangelo and Raphael. The **Duomo** (Cathedral) of **Santa Maria del Fiore** is topped by Brunelleschi's dome. At the base of the **Campanile** (Bell Tower), designed by Giotto in 1334, are sculpted relief panels by Andrea Pisano.

The **Museo dell'Opera del Duomo**, PZA DEL DUOMO 9, houses works taken from the **Duomo** for safe-keeping. Highlights are Michelangelo's *Pietà* and sculptures by Donatello and Della Robbia. The **Bargello**, V. DEL PROCONSOLO 4, possesses Italy's finest collection of Renaissance sculpture, including works by Michelangelo, Donatello and Cellini.

SOUTH OF THE ARNO: THE OLTRARNO

Cross the **Arno** by the Ponte Vecchio to reach the main attractions south of the river: the grandiose 15th-century **Palazzo Pitti**, PZA PITTI, housing the wealth of the Medicis, a fine gallery of modern art and the huge collection of painting from the Renaissance and the Baroque in the Palatine Gallery. The home of Elizabeth Barrett Browning and Robert Browning, *Casa Guide*, is on PZA SAN FELICE 8 (Mon, Wed and Fri, 1500–1800). Further south, behind the Palazzo Pitti, lies the city's landscaped green gardens, the **Giardino di Boboli**, a park laid out for the Medici in the 16th century with vistas, avenues and fountains.

SHOPPING

Florence offers some of the finest quality products in leatherwork (particularly shoes and accessories), linen and jewellery. Cheaper souvenirs include hand-made paper and pottery. See where the supremely wealthy shop, on V. TORNABUONI and V. DELLA VIGNA NUOVA, where prices range from unaffordable upwards. Then visit the PZA CIOMPI flea-market (open daily, go early), the **Mercato Nuovo** on V. CALIMALA, the daily market in the PZA DI SAN LORENZO (for cheap clothing, silks, belts and food), or the vast Tuesday-morning market in the **Cascine** park for more affordable buys. Hand-made perfumes, herbal remedies and soaps can be had from the frescoed **Farmacia di Santa Maria Novella**, V. DELLA SCALA 16R; prices vary from inexpensive to outrageous. In general, olive oil, aromatic vinegars, cheese and dried mushrooms, neatly packaged, are good buys.

NIGHT-TIME AND EVENTS

Florence offers plenty to do and see, especially out on the street. On summer evenings, street performers and fortune-tellers take over the PZA DELLA SIGNORIA, the PZA DEL DUOMO and the V. CALZAIUOLI, which connects them. Alternatively, opera is as popular as anywhere in Italy, though an expensive way to spend an evening. The English-language listings guide *Florence: Concierge Information* can be picked up at most hotel desks. If you can read Italian, the monthly listings *Firenze Spettacolo* can be bought at most bookstalls.

OPERA TICKETS

The box office, V. Alananni, (055) 242 361, has information and sells tickets.

A lively, local youth culture boosted by a large, summer, floating population ensures that there are plenty of clubs and discos. There is often an admission fee, and drinks are usually very expensive.

There are numerous theatres, the most important of which is the **Teatro Comunale**, the venue for most opera and classical concerts. There is a big music and opera festival in May–July. At **Fiesole**, 8 km to the north-east, the July–Aug **Estate Fiesolana** is an annual festival of concerts and films. **Cinetia Astro**, PIAZZA S SIMONE, shows films in English every evening; closed Mondays.

VIEWS OF FLORENCE

Despite the crowds, the view of the old city straddling the banks of the **Arno** from the **Ponte Vecchio** is still much as the Florentines' ancestors knew it, while from the top of the cathedral dome there's a magnificent view across the city's rooftops. A wider view of the city can be had from **San Miniato al Monte**, the church facing the city from the hill to the south, behind the **Boboli Gardens**. Alongside it, the wide PIAZZALE MICHELANGELO is a popular place for night views of the city.

DAY TRIP FROM FLORENCE

Fiesole, set on a hill 8 km north-east, makes a handy escape from summertime heat of Florence (no.7 from city centre) and provides excellent views of its larger neighbour. Also founded by the Etruscans, **Fiesole** was once an independent city-state at war with Florence. Its main sights are the **Roman Theatre** and its attendant museum, and the **Monastery of San Francesco**: both are a short walk from the main square, the PZA MINO.

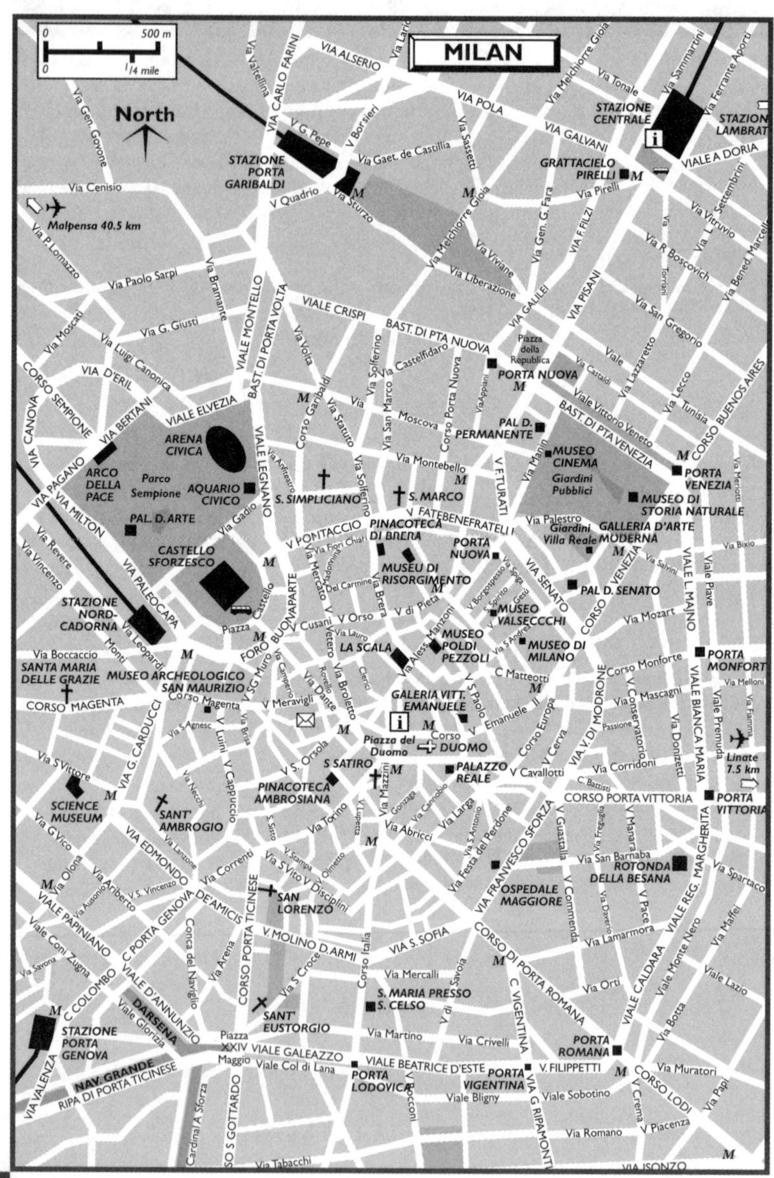
MILAN
0 500 m
0 1/4 mile
North
Via Valtellina
VIA CARLO FARINI
VIA ALSERIO
Via Lario
Via Melchiorre Gioia
Via Sammartini
Via Ferrante Aporti
Via Tonale
VIA POLA
STAZIONE CENTRALE
STAZIONE LAMBRATE
VIA GALVANI
VIALE A DORIA
GRATTACIELO PIRELLI
Via Pirelli
Via Gen. Govone
V G. Pepe
V Borsieri
Via Gaet. de Castillia
Via Sassetti
STAZIONE PORTA GARIBALDI
Via Cenisio
V Quadrio
Via Sturzo
Via Melchiorre Gioia
Via Gen. G. Fara
Via F. FILZI
Via Vitruvio
Via L. Settembrini
Malpensa 40.5 km
Via P. Lomazzo
Via Viviani
Via R Boscovich
Via Torriani
Via Bened. Marcello
Via Liberazione
Via Paolo Sarpi
Via Bramante
VIALE MONTELLO
BAST. DI PORTA VOLTA
VIALE CRISPI
VIA GALILEI
VIA PISANI
Via San Gregorio
Via G. Giusti
Via Moscati
BAST. DI PTA NUOVA
Piazza della Repubblica
Via Lazzaretto
Viale
Via Luigi Canonica
Via Volta
Via Solferino
Via Castelfidardo
Corso Porta Nuova
Via Appiani
PORTA NUOVA
Via Castaldi
Via Lecco
CORSO BUENOS AIRES
CORSO SEMPIONE
VIA D'ERIL
Viale Vittorio Veneto
Via Tunisia
VIALE ELVEZIA
Corso Garibaldi
Via Statuto
Moscova
PAL. D. PERMANENTE
BAST. DI PTA VENEZIA
VIA CANOVA
VIA BERTANI
ARENA CIVICA
VIALE LEGNANO
Via San Marco
Via Manin
MUSEO CINEMA
Via Montebello
Via F.TURATI
Giardini Pubblici
PORTA VENEZIA
Via Menotti
VIA PAGANO
ARCO DELLA PACE
Parco Sempione
AQUARIO CIVICO
Via Anfiteatro
S. SIMPLICIANO
S. MARCO
MUSEO DI STORIA NATURALE
VIA MILTON
PAL. D. ARTE
Via Gadio
V FATEBENEFRATELLI
Via Palestro
Giardini Villa Reale
GALLERIA D'ARTE MODERNA
Via Revere
V PONTACCIO
PINACOTECA DI BRERA
Via Vincenzo
CASTELLO SFORZESCO
Via Fiori Chiari
PORTA NUOVA
MUSEO DI RISORGIMENTO
VIA SENATO
Via Salvini
Via Bixio
VIALE L. MAJNO
Viale Piave
VIA PALEOCAPA
Via Mercato
Via Madonnina
Del Carmine
Via Brera
Via Borgospesso
Via Spiga
Via Gesù
PAL D. SENATO
STAZIONE NORD-CADORNA
Castello
V Cusani
V Orso
V di Pietà
V S. Spirito
MUSEO VALSECCCHI
CORSO VENEZIA
Via Mozart
Piazza
Via Leopardi
FORO BUONAPARTE
Via Lauro
Via Vetero
MUSEO POLDI PEZZOLI
Via S. Andrea
MUSEO DI MILANO
Monti
LA SCALA
Via Aless. Manzoni
Via Boccaccio
VIA G. CARDUCCI
SANTA MARIA DELLE GRAZIE
MUSEO ARCHEOLOGICO SAN MAURIZIO
V S G Muro
Via Camperio
Rovello
Via Dante
Via Broletto
Clerici
C Matteotti
Corso Monforte
PORTA MONFORTE
VIALE BIANCA MARIA
Via Melloni
CORSO MAGENTA
Corso Magenta
V Meravigli
GALERIA VITT. EMANUELE
V S Paolo
Emanuele II
Via Mascagni
Via Conservatorio
Viale Premuda
Via S Agnese
V Luini
Via Brisa
Piazza del Duomo
Corso DUOMO
Corso Europa
VIA V. DI MODRONE
Passione
Via Donizetti
Via Fiamma
Linate 7.5 km
Via S Vittore
V S. Orsola
S SATIRO
PALAZZO REALE
Via Cerva
V Cavallotti
Via Corridoni
C. Battisti
Via Necchi
V Cappuccio
Via Mazzini
PINACOTECA AMBROSIANA
SCIENCE MUSEUM
SANT' AMBROGIO
Via Lupetta
Gonzaga
Via Cannobio
Via Larga
CORSO PORTA VITTORIA
PORTA VITTORIA
VIALE REG. MARGHERITA
Via G Vico
S. Sisto
Via Torino
Via Abricci
Via S. Antonio
V Guastalla
Via Freguglia
V Manara
VIA EDMONDO
Via Lanzone
V. Stampa
Ometto
Via Festa del Perdono
VIA FRANCESCO SFORZA
Via San Barnaba
ROTONDA DELLA BESANA
Via Spartaco
Via Olona
Via Correnti
Via S Vito
V Disciplini
OSPEDALE MAGGIORE
V Commenda
Via Daverio
V Pace
Via Maffei
Via Ariberto
V.S. Vincenzo
Via Ausonio
C. PORTA GENOVA
DE' AMICIS
SAN LORENZO
VIALE PAPINIANO
Conca del Naviglio
CORSO PORTA TICINESE
V. MOLINO D. ARMI
VIA S. SOFIA
CORSO DI PORTA ROMANA
Via Lamarmora
Via Monte Nero
Viale Coni Zugna
Via Savona
VIALE D'ANNUNZIO
Via Arena
Via S. Croce
Corso Italia
Via Mercalli
Via Savoia
C. VIGENTINA
Via Orti
VIALE CALDARA
Viale Lazio
C COLOMBO
DARSENA
Viale Gorizia
S. MARIA PRESSO S. CELSO
V di
STAZIONE PORTA GENOVA
SANT' EUSTORGIO
Via Martino
Via Crivelli
Via Botta
Piazza XXIV Maggio
VIALE GALEAZZO
PORTA ROMANA
VIA VALENZA
NAV. GRANDE
RIPA DI PORTA TICINESE
Viale Col di Lana
VIALE BEATRICE D'ESTE
PORTA VIGENTINA
V. FILIPPETTI
CORSO LODI
Via Muratori
Via Papi
PORTA LODOVICA
V Bocconi
Viale Bligny
Viale Sobotino
V Crema
VIA G RIPAMONTI
Cardinal A Sforza
CORSO S GOTTARDO
Via Romano
V Piacenza
Via Tabacchi
VIA ISONZO

Italy's second largest city is Italy's first commercial, industrial and banking city. With much of its centre rebuilt after bombing in 1943, Milan is not as architecturally attractive as Florence, Rome and Venice but is cosmopolitan, with a rich legacy of art and architecture including Romanesque churches, neo classical boulevards, Renaissance treasures (notably in the **Pinacoteca di Brera**) and one the the most majestic cathedrals in Christendom. A street network of concentric circles radiates outwards: within the central circle are the main sights.

Milan is the commercial hub of Italy: exciting, fashionable and prosperous, its industrial and commercial acumen played a major role in the Italian post-war miracle. Today the city is deeply style-conscious, as befits one of Europe's top fashion centres, and its shops are strikingly upmarket. Be prepared for correspondingly inflated prices.

A Celtic and Roman settlement, Milan gained importance during medieval times. The Visconti and Sforza families ruled Milan between the 13th and 16th centuries. The Viscontis started construction on the **Duomo** (cathedral) while the Sforzas built the **castle** and brought to Milan many of the talented artists and thinkers of the time, including Leonardo da Vinci.

ARRIVAL AND DEPARTURE

RAIL The vast majority of trains serve the monumental and fully equipped **Stazione Centrale**, PZA DUCA D'AOSTA, ☎(02) 6707 0958 (metro lines 2/3). Some trains stop instead at **Stazione Porta Garibaldi**, ☎(02) 655 2078, served by metro line 2. Milan's prime position in the heart of northern Italy always helped its trade; now the city acts as the key node in Italy's railway system. For **national rail information**, ☎1478 88088.

✈ **Malpensa**, about 50 km north-west of Milan, handles intercontinental and charter flights. **Linate**, 7 km from Milan, handles domestic and European flights. **Buses** to and from both airports depart from the bus terminal: PZA LUIGI DI SAVOIA, ☎(02) 6698 4509, beside STAZIONE CENTRALE. For information on flights from either airport, ☎(02) 7485 2200.

TOURIST OFFICES

Main **APT** office: **Palazzo del Turismo**, VIA MARCONI 1, ☎(02) 7252 4300, to the right of the cathedral; free maps and guides to Milan in English (summer: Mon to Fri 0830–2000, Sat 0900–1300, 1400–1900, Sun 0900–1300, 1400–1700; winter: closes 1 hr earlier Mon–Sat).

Branch: **Stazione Centrale**: ☎(02) 7252 4360/370.

INFORMATION

MONEY There are many **bureaux de change** in Milan. At weekends, exchange facilities are available in PZA DUOMO and **Stazione Centrale** and in both airports. Automatic machines that convert cash are located in the town centre and in **Stazione Centrale**. Thomas Cook Licensee: **CIT Viaggi**, GALLERIA VITTORIO EMANUELE, ☎(02) 863 701.

POST AND PHONES The **central post office**, V. CORDUSIO 4, ☎(02) 869 2069, is open 24 hrs for telexes, faxes and telegrams. **Public telephone offices** can be found at **Galleria V Emanuele II**, 4 V. CORDUSIO, and **Stazione Centrale**. Public phones take either coins or phonecards, the latter available from automatic cash dispensers and kiosks.
The dialling code for Milan is 02. To phone **Milan from abroad**: ☎39 (Italy) 02 (Milan) + number; to phone **Milan from elsewhere in Italy**: ☎02 + number.

PUBLIC TRANSPORT

Metro: **Metropolitana Milano (MM)**, is clean, efficient and easy to use. There are three colour-coded lines. Stamp tickets in the gates at station entrances.

Buses and trams: The bus and tram systems are more comprehensive and more complicated, but stops have details of each route serving them. Buy tickets in advance and validate them in the machines on board.

Taxis: Milan's taxis are yellow or white and can be expensive. There's a substantial flat fare to start with and extra charges are applied for baggage and travel on holidays or late at night. There are large ranks at **Stazione Centrale** and PZA DUOMO and cabs can also be booked by phone or hailed on the street. Avoid touts offering unofficial taxis.

TICKETS

The same tickets are used for all public transport. **Single tickets** (L.1500) are good for one journey on the metro or 1¼ hrs' travel on buses.

Tickets are available from machines in metro stations or from *tabacchi* (tobacconists) and newspaper kiosks. **Passes for one day** (L.5000) or **two days** (L.9000) are sold at underground stations.

ACCOMMODATION

Accommodation in Milan is not cheap, but there are plenty of *pensione* around the station and the town centre. The Tourist Office will provide a full list of accommodation.

YOUTH HOSTEL V. MARTINO BASSI 2, ☎(02) 3926 7095 (metro line 1 to QT8 station).

CAMPSITE V. G AIRAGHI, ☎(02) 4820 0134 (open all year).

HOTEL RESERVATIONS

Contact **'Centro Prenotazioni Hotel Italia'** at the following numbers: ☎1478 88088 from Italy, ☎+ 39 02 2953 1605 from abroad.

FOOD AND DRINK

The Milanese take their food seriously and are prepared to pay substantial sums for their meals, so restaurants are generally expensive. Better value eateries include the lunch spots catering for office workers, with many reasonable self-service restaurants around the centre. Away from the city centre, there are family-run *trattorie* and a variety of other inexpensive places. At lunch time, customers often eat standing up. *Pizzerie* and *Chinese* restaurants offer reasonably priced evening meals. Bars tend to serve more coffee than alcohol, along with *panini* – rolls with a multitude of fillings.

Regional specialities include *cotoletta alla milanese,* an Italian version of *Wiener schnitzel, risotto alla milanese* (rice dish) and the filling vegetable and pork soup minestrone. Despite being inland, Milan has excellent fish, fresh from the coast. Inexpensive pizzerias include: **La Cucuma**, **Grand'Italia** and **Malastrana**.

PIZZERIAS

La Cucuma, V. PACINI 26, ☎(02) 2952 6098.
Grand'Italia, V. PALERMO 5, ☎(02) 877 759.
Malastrana, RIPA PORTA TICINESE 65, ☎(02) 837 8984.

HIGHLIGHTS

If a city can have such a thing as a 'signature building', then Milan's is undoubtedly the **Duomo** (Cathedral), in the pigeon-populated PZA DUOMO (Metro: DUOMO). Work started in 1386, at the behest of Gian Galeazzo Visconti. Wanting a son, and finding his prayers granted, he built this remarkable edifice as a tribute to the Virgin Mary.

Note that museums (including the Brera) are closed on Mondays

On the north side of PZA DUOMO is the **Galleria Vittorio Emanuele II**, a monumental 19th-century iron and glass shopping arcade known as the **Salon de Milan** where there are elegant cafés.

The **Pinacoteca di Brera**, 28 VIA BRERA, is Milan's finest art gallery. Its collection concentrates on Italian artists of the 14th–19th centuries, although foreign schools of the 17th–18th centuries are also represented. Notable works here are Raphael's *Marriage of the Virgin*, Mantegna's *Dead Christ* and works by Bramante, Carpaccio, Bellini and Veronese. The gallery is housed in part of the **Palazzo di Brera**.

THE DUOMO

The **Duomo** is a magical and extravagant Gothic structure, overflowing with belfries, statues and 135 pinnacles in white marble. It shimmers in the sunlight and glows in the winter fog. The stark interior contains fine stained glass and works of art dating back to before the cathedral's construction. Stairs (73 to the dome; 139 to the tower) lead up to the roof, from which there are fine views.

In the **Pinacoteca Ambriosiana**, 2 PZA PIO XI (Metro: DUOMO OR CORDUSIO), you will see works by Leonardo da Vinci, including the portrait of the musician Caffurio. Caravaggio's *Basket of Fruit* and Raphael's cartoons for the Vatican are other star attractions.

LA SCALA

The Galleria leads through to PZA SCALA, home of **La Scala** (more properly the **Teatro alla Scala**), probably the most famous opera house in the world. The opera season starts on 7 Dec. Book well in advance for a good seat; please contact the following number in order to have information about prices and seats: ☎(02) 7200 3744.

In summer the repertoire extends to ballet and concerts as well. **La Scala Theatre Museum**, in the building, exhibits a huge array of opera memorabilia. It also provides the opportunity to see into the opera house itself.

Milan's most famous painting, and one of the great works of the Renaissance, is Leonardo da Vinci's *Last Supper* (1495–1497), painted, in tempera, on a wall in the old Dominican monastery refectory next to **Santa Maria Delle Grazie** (Metro: CADORNA). It attracts large crowds and a hefty entrance fee, and has been restored after years of deterioration.

The **Basilica di Sant'Ambrogio** (Metro: SANT'AMBROGIO) was built in the late 4th century by St Ambrose, patron saint of the city and former Bishop of Milan. So eloquent and smooth in speech was St Ambrose that his name was given to honey liqueur. Most of what is standing today dates from the 12th century. A festival commemorates **St Ambrose**, on 7 Dec. It includes a street fair which takes place near the **Basilica di Sant'Ambrogio**.

Sforza Castle, PZA CASTELLO, at the end of V. DANTE (Metro: CAIROLI), is a distinctive, heavy fortress, built by Francesco Sforza, Duke of Milan in the 15th century, on top of an earlier Visconti fortress. The castle now houses an encyclopaedic collection of galleries and museums, displaying everything from arms to furniture, from Egyptian art to musical instruments, and including the **Museum of Antique Art**, with some valuable works by Michelangelo. It also houses the **Museum of Musical Instruments**, which contains a spinet on which Mozart played.

Behind the castle is **Sempione Park**, the largest green space in central Milan. At the far end is the **Arco Della Pace** (Arch of Peace).

SHOPPING

Milan is the prime place in Italy to buy clothes, accessories, modern furniture or jewellery – not necessarily practical or affordable! The image the Milanese present to the outside world is that of *la bella figura* (looking good), and the most chic shop in V. DELLA SPIGA, V. S. ANDREA, V. MONTENAPOLEONE and V. BORGOSPESSO. Those with smaller bank accounts shop in V. TORINO and department stores La Rinascente and Coin.

Window-shop for Milanese furniture at Artemide, CORSO MONFORTE 19, in the centre of town. A good, less expensive general shopping street is CORSO BUENOS AIRES. Otherwise, the VLE. PAPIANO market (Sat) in the Navigli district is good for cheap clothes and other bargains. In the Brera district there is a Mon market at the PZA PIRABELLO, while NAVIGLIO GRANDE is the scene of the monthly Antiques Fair (last Sun of each month).

Also see the **Poldi-Pezzoli Museum**, VIA MANZONI 12 (Metro: MONTENAPOLEONE), which includes Botticelli and Mantegna paintings.

The **Leonardo da Vinci National Museum of Science and Industry**, VIA SAN VITTORE 21 (Metro: SANT'AMBROGIO), exhibits displays of Leonardo's own ideas, including a model of his famous air-screw, the precursor of the helicopter. In the western suburbs, the **San Siro Stadium** stands – a futuristic construction of steel lattices and huge concrete cylinders – visible for miles around.

NIGHT-TIME AND EVENTS

Milan's daily newspapers, *La Repubblica* and *Corriere della Sera* produce weekly supplements detailing Milan's entertainment, Events and nightlife.

The city's most famous institution is the grand **La Scala** opera house. Tickets are extremely elusive, but you may be able to get them on Mondays, for performances of classical music rather than opera. The **Conservatorio** also hosts concerts.

Cinemas cluster around CORSO VITTORIO EMANUELE, near PZA DUOMO. **Nightclubs** tend to close around 0200–0300. **Le Scimmie** (Monkeys) is one of the most famous. Two of the more trendy areas of town are **Porta Ticinese** and **Brera**. The **Porta Ticinese** and the **Navigli** (canals) district are home to a high concentration of bars and venues (the actual Porta Ticinese is a remnant of the 14th-century city ramparts). **Cafés and bars** also dot the small streets around **Brera**.

V. BRERA is the showcase of Milan's fashion industry. The Milanese care about their clothes and smart dress is the norm for almost all nightlife throughout the city, even informal promenading.

WHERE NEXT FROM MILAN?

*Join the **Milan–Trieste** route (p. 367), or head south-east to **Bologna** (ETT table 630) for the **Bologna–Rome** route (p. 373). Alternatively head west through Turin (Torino) and the Alps into France and take the scenic mountain route via **Modane** and **Aix-les-Bains** to **Lyon**. There's an equally stunning ride northwards into Switzerland via **Como** on Lake Como (Lago Como) to **Lugano**, from where you can take the **Berne–Lugano** route (p. 304) in reverse.*

Naples

There's nowhere quite like **Naples** – the unruly, raucous, run-down capital of the South. It might have a notorious reputation as a city of crime and incredible traffic jams but its ebullience, history, cuisine and sheer range of treasures make it a compelling place to visit on a southern Italian journey. The highlights are the **National Archaeological Museum** whose main glories are its Greek sculptures, mosaics and artefacts, while for many the abiding memory will be the dark, crumbling, medieval alleys with washing lines strung over and assorted cooking smells emanating from within, where housewives haul up bucketfuls of shopping by ropes linked to high tenement windows. Out on the streets, you can wander for hours in the city's various districts, such as the **Sanita**, and be entertained by the ebullience of daily life. Behind the PZA DEL PLEBISCITO is the ironically named V. SOLITARIA, a long, busy, local street.

Originally the Greek colony of Neapolis, Naples became a desirable winter resort for wealthy Romans. Of the many families that later ruled Naples, the Anjou and Aragon dynasties of the 13th–16th centuries were among the most influential, and many remains from that era dot the city.

Naples is somewhat upstaged by its surroundings, notably the Neapolitan Riviera – with the ultra-scenic resorts of **Sorrento**, **Positano** and **Amalfi**, within a boat trip of the island of **Capri** – and the astonishing Roman remains of **Herculaneum** and **Pompeii**. All can be reached in a day trip from Naples, though you might prefer to base yourself on the Riviera for exploring the area fully.

ARRIVAL AND DEPARTURE

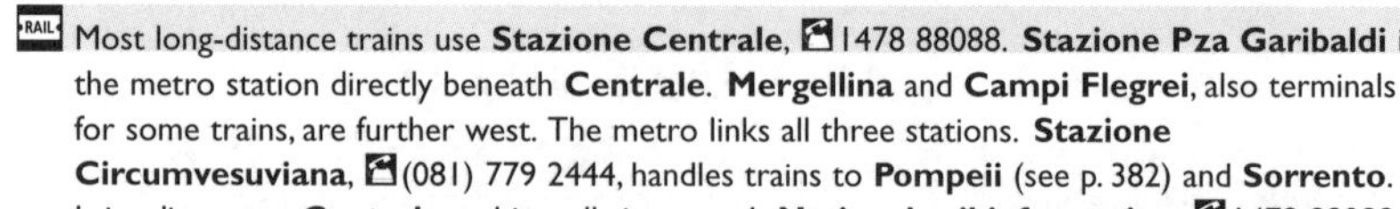

RAIL Most long-distance trains use **Stazione Centrale**, ☎ 1478 88088. **Stazione Pza Garibaldi** is the metro station directly beneath **Centrale**. **Mergellina** and **Campi Flegrei**, also terminals for some trains, are further west. The metro links all three stations. **Stazione Circumvesuviana**, ☎ (081) 779 2444, handles trains to **Pompeii** (see p. 382) and **Sorrento**. It is adjacent to **Centrale** and is well signposted. **National rail information**: ☎ 1478 88088.

Capodichino, to the north, is reasonably close to the centre, so taxi fares are not exorbitant. There is a daily bus service to **Stazione Centrale**. For **airport information**, ☎ (081) 780 5761.

INFORMATION

Pick up a town map at the city Tourist Office and a copy of the monthly listing *Qui Napoli. Ente Provinciale per il Turismo* **(EPT)** has a free hotel reservation service; it maintains a spartan but helpful office in the **Stazione Centrale**, ☎ (081) 268 779, and in the **Stazione di Mergellina**,

TOURIST OFFICES

The city Tourist Office is at **Palazzo Reale**, PZA PLEBISCITO, ☎(081) 418 744, with branches in PZA DEL GESÙ, ☎(081) 552 3328 (Mon–Sat 0900–1900 and Sun 0900–1500; it may be closed in the afternoon despite the official opening hours), and at V. PARTENOPE, by **Castel dell'Ovo**, ☎(081) 764 5688.

☎(081) 761 2102. **Youth information**: (not always helpful) V. MEZZOCANNONE 25, ☎(081) 552 7960 (Mon–Fri 0930–1330, 1500–1830, Sat 0930–1230).

There is a special 'Hello Napoli' freecall number for tourists, ☎167 251 396, though it is not always reliable.

PUBLIC TRANSPORT

The metro runs west to **Pozzuoli** and **Solfatara**. Trains can be infrequent and stations quiet out of peak hours. **Buses** are more frequent and more extensive. For those arriving between Friday and Sunday, there is a **free bus tour** with guide. Frequent **hydrofoils and ferries** ply across the bay and out to the islands. Most leave from **Molo Beverello** (by **Castel Nuovo**) but some go from Mergellina. Three funicular railways link the old city with the cooler **Vomero Hill**. All three (**Funicolare Montesamo**, **Centrale** and **Chaia**) have recently been rebuilt and the 19th-century stations have been beautifully renovated.

TICKETS

Trains: Buy tickets at kiosks and cancel them in the machines by the entrances.

Buses: Buy tickets from street kiosks.

Day passes are available.

A local **transit ticket** valid for 90 mins, and good for one bus, one funicular and one metro ride, costs L.1500.

ACCOMMODATION

The **Tourist Office** has a list of hotels and can occasionally help in finding a place to stay, but confirm prices with the hotel before committing yourself. Cheap hotels cluster in and around the noisy, and not particularly salubrious, PZA GARIBALDI. Better areas to look are near the waterfront in **Mergellina** and **Santa Lucia**, where there are some cheapish options, and around PZA DANTE in the centre. The **youth hostel** is close to the **Stazione Mergellina**. **Campsites** are mainly in Pozzuoli (on the metro), west of Naples. **Vulcano Solfatara** is the nearest. The **Royal Continental Hotel** is more expensive, but worth the great view of the **Castel Dell'Ovo**.

HOTELS: **Royal Continental Hotel**, V. PARTENOPE 38/44; ☎(081) 764 4800.

YOUTH HOSTEL: SALITA DELLA GROTTA A PIEDIGROTTA 23, ☎(081) 761 2346.

CAMPSITES: **Vulcano Solfatara**, V. Solfatara 16, ☎(081) 526 7413.

DAY TRIPS FROM NAPLES

In some ways, the glorious **Bay of Naples** offers more than the city itself and **Sorrento** is one of the finest and most romantic resorts, perched by a ravine. There are regular train services daily from **Napoli Circumvesuviana** to **Sorrento**, taking 55–65 mins. Alternatively, catch a ferry from **Beverello** (or **Mergellina**). There are about 8 sailings daily, journey time is about 25 mins (see ETT table 2520). The equally captivating and similarly near-vertical resorts of **Positano** and **Amalfi** have good bus services; all three have ferries to **Capri**. None of the resorts have beaches to speak of. The island of **Capri** is renowned for its wonderful setting, mild climate, Greek and Roman remains, the **Villa San Michele** (the fascinating home of the Swedish doctor and author Axel Munthe) and **Blue Grotto** (though you might like to give the rip-off boat trip a miss). The fertile island of **Ischia**, less well known than Capri, also has a remarkable setting, with spa resorts offering cures in radioactive waters, and some excellent beaches

FOOD AND DRINK

Naples is the birthplace of the *pizza*, the city's main contribution to the culinary world – authentically served with a fresh tomato sauce. The city's food is among Italy's best, healthiest and cheapest. Pasta is the staple ingredient, as are deep-fried vegetables and seafood. There are plenty of inexpensive places to eat – try just to the west of V. TOLEDO or the many open-air food stalls around the station and PZA MERCATO.

HIGHLIGHTS

Modern Naples is hectic, crowded and noisy. Petty crime is rife, notably pickpocketing and bag-snatching, so be very careful, especially after dark.

Do not miss the world-class **Museo Archeologico Nazionale** (National Archaeological Museum), PZA MUSEO (METRO: PZA CAVOUR; free for under 18s and over 60s), which contains an unparalleled collection from Pompeii and Herculaneum: bronzes, sculptures, mosaics, glass and, most interesting of all, mundane everyday objects. Here too is a huge, intricate model of Pompeii and some important Roman sculpture – most notably the so-called *Farnese Bull*.

A NIGHT AT THE OPERA

The best entertainments in Naples are culinary, operatic, or just strolling the streets. If you like opera, the Teatro San Carlo is well worth the ticket price.
For this and other cultural pursuits, enquire at the Tourist Office.

South of the museum is the heart of medieval Naples, SPACCANAPOLI, centred around V. BENEDETTO CROCE and PZA GESÙ NUOVO, where you'll find the GESÙ NUOVO, a 16th-century church whose façade, originally part of a palace, is studded with peculiar basalt diamond-shaped extrusions. Within, it is one of the extreme expressions of the ebullient Neapolitan baroque style. Not far away, **Santa Chiara**, V. BENEDETTO CROCE, dates from the 14th century. In it are some exceptionally fine medieval tombs. Attached to it and bright with roses, marguerites and geraniums, the gently decaying **Cloister of the Clarisse** is notable for its walks lined with decorative majolica tiles dating from the 18th century. Further east, the cavernous **Duomo** (Cathedral), V. DUOMO, is dedicated to Naples's patron saint, San Gennaro. Housed here is a phial of his blood which allegedly liquefies miraculously twice every year.

Down by the waterfront, the new **Museo Ferroviario Nationale** (National Railway Museum), CORSO GIOVANNI/TEDUCCIO, is located in old railway facilities and is a real treat for rail fans. The massive **Castel Nuovo** (or *Maschio Angioino*) guards the port. The castle, begun in 1279, is chiefly recognisable for its massive round towers. The nearby **Palazzo Reale** was the seat of the Neapolitan royalty. Vast and handsome, within it are acres of 18th- and 19th-century rooms. The adjacent **Teatro di San Carlo**, begun in 1737, ranks second only to **La Scala** (Milan) in the Italian opera league.

Day trips from Naples cont'd.

for lingering. There are about nine sailings daily to Capri and Ischia departing from **Molo Beverello** (40 mins to Capri, 80 mins Ischia). Hydrofoils depart hourly from **Mergellina** (journey time 35 mins for both islands).

The **Circumvesuviana railway** has stops at the great Roman cities of **Herculaneum** (station: **Ercolano**) and **Pompeii**: see p. 382.

Santa Lucia, the waterfront district to the south, is where **Castel dell'Ovo**, built by Frederick II, sticks out into the bay. The third major castle in Naples, **Castel Sant'-Elmo**, occupies a peak high above the city – alongside the **Certosa di San Martino**. Inside the latter, whose courtyard is one of the masterpieces of the local baroque style, is **Museo Nazionale di San Martino** which contains an important collection of Neapolitan paintings and Christmas cribs, the *presepi*. The **Museo Principe di Aragona Pignatelli**, RIVIERA DI CHIAIA, contains salons decorated entirely in **local ceramics**. This gallery houses one of the greatest of European art collections.

SHOPPING

Shopping in Naples is rather specialised. Crib figures and accessories are available in the streets around the church of **S. Gregorio Armeno**, while **Capodimonte** figures and miniature tableaux are available citywide, particularly in the centre. Shopping for unfamiliar herb-infused oils and vinegars, salamis and other easily portable foodstuffs in the markets and delicatessens is a must. The shopping mall **Galleria Umberto I**, a real showcase, was built in 1887.

WHERE NEXT FROM NAPLES?

*You can take the train via **Foggia** to **Brindisi**; a change of train is needed in **Caserta** or **Bari** unless the overnight service is used. Journey time 5 hrs 40 mins–8 hrs 35 mins; ETT table 626. An alternative (and extremely attractive) route goes via **Battipaglia** to **Taranto** (table 635). Despite the heavy industry when approaching **Taranto**, there is an archaeological museum, **Museo Nazionale**, which is beginning to rival **Naples** with its excellent collection of ancient Greek artefacts. From **Taranto**, continue on to **Bari** or **Brindisi**.*

*From **Brindisi** you can take ferries to **Corfu** and **Patras**.*

*There is also a nightly ship from **Naples** to **Palermo** (table 2625) and a weekly ship to **Cagliari** (table 2620).*

The 'Eternal City', dominated by its seven hills (Aventine, Capitoline, Celian, Esquiline, Palatine, Quirinal and Vimial), is cut by the fast-flowing river **Tiber** and suffused with the sound of running fountains. Filled with museums and galleries, churches and ruins redolent of the Caesars and the creative genius of Michelangelo, Rome spans 2000 years. There's an immense amount here: don't try to see too much, and make plenty of stops for ice cream and espresso coffee. Heading most people's list of attractions are likely to be the **Colosseum**, the **Forum**, **St Peter's Cathedral**, the **Sistine Chapel** in the Vatican and the **catacombs** on either side of the VIA APPIA ANTICA, and the PZA NAVONA.

In August, the town empties a little as the Romans escape the heat and go on holiday;consequently the city is rather lacking in atmosphere at that time. Be extra vigilant with your belongings, as thieves are abundant.

ARRIVAL AND DEPARTURE

There are four main railway stations. **Termini**, PZA DEI CINQUECENTO, ☎(06) 4775 seat reservations, ☎(06) 48 84 069, is Rome's largest, handling all the main national and international lines; bureaux de change, tourist and hotel information; well served by taxis, buses and night buses, and at the hub of the metro system. **Ostiense**, ☎(06) 57 58 748, serves some long-distance north–south trains. **Roma–Nord**, ☎(06) 36 10 441, serves **Viterbo** (2 hrs), **Bracciano** (90 mins) and other parts of northern **Lazio**. **Tiburtina**, ☎(06) 43 42 39 72, serves some long distance north–south trains. Trains arriving after midnight stop here. There are **ATM**s in the stations. The national toll-free number for **rail information** is: ☎1478 88088.

Leonardo da Vinci (FIUMICINO) is 36 km south-west of Rome, ☎(06) 65 951. **Taxis** into the centre are hassle-free, but expensive (L.60,000–70,000). Less expensive is the 45-min train service, every 20 mins, 0600–0100, to **Tiburtina** station (for further information ☎(06) 65 951). A new express rail link to **Termini** opened in 1998. **Aeroporto Ciampino,** ☎(06) 794 921, is closer to town, 16 km to the south-east. A bus service (**ACOTRAL** or **ATAC**) runs every 10–20 mins to ANAGNINA METRO STATION (services to **Termini** every 30 mins between 0530 and 2230). Expect to pay at least L.50,000 by metered taxi.

CITY AND TRANSPORT MAP – inside back cover

INFORMATION

MONEY **Banks** open 0830–1330 and 1500–1600, and **bureaux de change** generally open 0830/0900–1300 and 1530/1600–1930/2000; **hotels** will also change money. Major credit cards and Eurocheques are widely accepted (though not in all cheaper restaurants and places to stay; check beforehand). **Thomas Cook Italia** have **bureaux de change** at V. DELLA CONCILIAZIONE 23/25, V. DEL CORSO 53 and PZA BARBERINI 21A/21D.

TOURIST INFORMATION

Main tourist information office, **EPT** (Rome Provincial Tourist Board): V. PARIGI 5 (near V. XX SETTEMBRE), ☎ (06) 488 991 or 482 4078 (metro: REPUBBLICA; Mon–Sat 0815–1915); hotel listings, maps and itineraries.

Other tourist and hotel information desks: **Leonardo da Vinci Airport**, ☎(06) 595074; **Stazione Termini**, ☎(06) 48 71 270 (0815–1915; closed Sun Oct–May).

POST AND PHONES

The main **post office**, PZA SAN SILVESTRO, ☎(06) 679 5530 (open Mon–Fri, 0800–2100; Sat 0800–1200; Sun 0900–1800), has 24-hr phones, fax and poste restante (address letters c/o **Palazzo delle Poste**, ROMA CENTPO, FERMO POSTA – put the surname first, underlined). Stamps are available from post offices and tobacconists displaying a black and white T. Letters posted at the main post office, or anywhere within the **Vatican City** (use Vatican stamps in blue post boxes), arrive faster than those posted in the red pavement boxes.

To phone **Rome from abroad**: ☎39 (Italy) + 6 (Rome) + number. To phone **Rome from elsewhere in Italy**: ☎06 (Rome) + number.

PUBLIC TRANSPORT

The *centro storico* (historic centre) is fairly compact, traffic-free and easy to see on foot. However, many of the most important sights lie outside this area. The main arteries are well served by buses, but stick to those and you miss Rome's ebullient street life, medieval alleys and baroque squares. Most hotels supply a basic street map. For more detail, and bus and metro maps, ask at news-stands, tobacconists and tourist information offices. Romans are usually helpful to a point of glowing enthusiasm when you ask for help with directions.

METRO: The Metropolitana has only two lines – A and B – and is not much use in the centre. Line A (red) is open 0530–2400; Line B (blue) is open 0530–2100, Mon–Fri. Tickets are for a single journey.

Buses and trams: Rome's excellent bus service is centred on PZA DEI CINQUECENTO, with major stops *(fermate)* in PZA VENEZIA, LARGO ARGENTINA and PZA DEL RISORGIMENTO. Buses are orange, the number is at the front and they generally stop without your having to flag them down. Only one (🚌no.119, a small electric bus) is able to enter the narrow streets of the *centro storico*. For **bus and tram information**: ☎(06) 43 17 84.
Night buses run from 2400–0800. Buy tickets from the conductor on board. For information, look in the *Tuttocittà* supplement of the telephone directory.

Taxis: There are plenty of metered taxis, available from ranks or by phone: **Radiotaxi**, ☎(06) 3570; **Roma Sud**, ☎(06) 3875; **Capitale**, ☎(06) 4994; or **Cosmos**, ☎(06) 8433. There are surcharges for luggage, at night (2200–0700) and on Sun and holidays.

METRO TICKETS

You must purchase your ticket before travelling. Tickets are on sale at all metro stops, bus termini with green ACOTRAL kiosks, and at news-stands and tobacconists displaying ATAC (bus and tram) and ACOTRAL (metro) signs. You can also get tickets from the **ATAC Information Booth**, PZA DEI CINQUECENTO (metro: TERMINI). Tickets and passes covering all forms of public transport include **monthly passes**, a ticket valid for **75 mins** or **1 subway trip** (L.2000), and the **24-hr BIG ticket** (L.6000); these are valid on all forms of public transport.

BUS AND TRAM TICKETS

Time-stamp your ticket in the machine as you enter (heavy on-the-spot fines if you are caught ticketless). The **basic ticket** is valid for one journey, but a block of ten (red) tickets saves money, as does a **half-day ticket** *(biglietto orario)*, valid from either 0600–1400 or 1400–2400. Passes include a **one-day pass**; a **seven-day tourist pass**, the *Carta Settimanale per Turisti*; and a **one-month pass**.

ACCOMMODATION

There are plenty of **hotels**, from the opulent, mainly located close to the **Spanish Steps** and the V. VENETO, to the basic, largely clustered around the V. NAZIONALE and Termini station. Moderately priced centrally located hotels are generally very popular, and you should book up to two months ahead in high season. For the cheaper hotels, expect to pay around L.70,000 per night, even without a private bathroom. Some do not take credit cards.

Tourist Offices will provide lists of residential hotels and make bookings. **International Services**, V. DEL BABUINO 79, ☎(06) 36 00 18, has a list of self-catering studios and apartments.

If you don't mind a night-time curfew and pilgrims, several religious institutions offer cheap accommodation: try **Domus Mariae**, ☎(06) 663 88 23, and **Istituto Madri Pie**, ☎(06) 63 19 67 – both near the Vatican.

Youth hostels: **Associazione Italiana Alberghi per la Gioventù (HI)**. Only holders of **AIG** or **HI** cards can use the **Ostello del Foro Italico**. The **Protezione della Giovane** will locate accommodation for women under 25. There are no **campsites** in central Rome, though there are ten within a 45-min bus ride away.

YOUTH HOSTELS

Associazione Italiana Alberghi per la Gioventù (HI), V. CAVOUR 44–47, ☎(06) 48 71 152.
Ostello del Foro Italico, VLE DELLE OLIMPIADI 61, ☎(06) 32 42571/3.
YWCA, V. C. BALBO, 4, ☎(06) 48 83 917.
Protezione della Giovane, V. URBANA 158, ☎(06) 48 81 489.

FOOD AND DRINK

Italian **cafés and bars** have hefty seating charges, so most Romans have their breakfast, and often lunch, standing up at the bar. You generally pay first and take your receipt to the counter. **Picnics** are a good alternative. Some **delicatessens** will fill a roll with the ingredients of your choice (try the delicatessen in the CAMPO DEI FIORI vegetable market).

Restaurants are more expensive than *trattorie*, which offer substantial amounts of simple, robust Roman-style food, washed down with local wine. Some have no name, their purpose defined only by cooking smells, loud chatter and paper table cloths. Some don't even have menus, so just point to whatever seems delicious on the next table. In these, expect to pay around L.25,000 per head for three courses, bread (*coperta*, cover charge) and wine. *Pizzerie* are a cheap alternative, while you can taste different wines and have delicious tiny snacks at an *enoteca*. **Vegetarian** restaurants are rare but most Italian menus are adaptable.

The CAMPO DEI FIORI neighbourhood is best for alfresco dining, while the streets off the nearby PZA FARNESE have stylish but reasonably cheap venues. **Trastevere** has boisterous, crowded, rough-and-ready eateries, which may involve queuing but are worth the wait. Other popular places are around PZA NAVONA and the **Pantheon**, while the **Ghetto** and the old slaughterhouse area of **Testaccio** offer some of the best traditional Roman cooking. Read the menu in the window to gauge price.

HIGHLIGHTS

Most places charge an entrance fee; some are free on Sundays. The **EPT** publishes *Musei e Monumenti di Roma*, giving details of current changes and closures as well as information about exhibitions. Museums are closed on Mon.

The **Capitoline** hill was once the sacred heart of the Roman Empire and seat of its principle temple, devoted to Jupiter. Today it is occupied by Michelangelo's PZA DEL CAMPIDOGLIO, which is dominated by Rome's town hall, the **Palazzo Senatori**. On either side of this, the magnificent Capitoline Museums in **Palazzo Nuovo** and, opposite it, **Palazzo dei Conservatori** constitute the world's first public museum. They house important collections of classical sculpture. In addition, the **Palazzo dei Conservatori** also contains the **Pinacoteca Capitolina**, an art gallery with paintings by, amongst others, Rubens, Caravaggio and Titian.

The great basilica of **Santa Maria Maggiore**, PZA DI SANTA MARIA MAGGIORE, dominates the **Esquiline** hill. Nearby, **San Pietro in Vincoli**, PZA SAN PIETRO IN VINCOLI, houses the chains with which St Peter was imprisoned, and Michelangelo's superb statue of Moses. Beyond it,

EXPLORING THE VATICAN

The **Vatican City**, a state within a city and home of the Pope and the Catholic Church, houses numerous treasures. The **Basilica di San Pietro** (St Peter's Cathedral), worked on by, amongst others, Bramante, Michelangelo and Bernini (whose immense colonnade precedes it), dominates the Vatican. The vast and elaborate **Vatican Museum,** VIALE VATICANO, and the recently cleaned **Sistine Chapel** (enter from the museum), with Michelangelo's *Last Judgment*, considered his masterpiece, and his ceiling frescos depicting scenes from the Old Testament, draw in the crowds. Nearby is the **Castel Sant' Angelo**, built as a Roman tomb, converted into a fortress, used as a palace, and now a museum, **Lungotevere Castello**.

Trajan's Market (the world's first shopping mall; V. 4 Novembre) and **Trajan's Column** face the **Forum**, site of the temples and basilicas of Imperial Rome.

The **Celian** hill is quiet, covered mainly by the gardens of the **Villa Celimontana**, Pza della Navicella. In front of it, the formal **Farnese Gardens** on the **Palatine** are filled with the ruins of Imperial palaces. Below lies Rome's most famous landmark, the **Colosseum**, Pza del Colosseo, built by Emperor Vespasian in AD 72. It held over 55,000 spectators and was the scene of the Roman Games and gladiatorial combats.

At the base of the **Quirinal** hill is the **fountain di Trevi** Pza Fontana di Trevi – into which, to ensure your return, you must throw a coin, while on its summit sits the President of Italy's residence, the **Palazzo del Quirinale**. Also on the Quirinal is the **Palazzo Barberini**, V. delle Quattro Fontane 13, which contains the **Galleria Nazionale d'Arte Antica** housing important works of the Renaissance and baroque periods.

The **Campo dei Fiori's** vegetable market adds life and colour to the district near **Palazzo Farnese**, Pza Farnese, and **Santa Andrea della Valle**, Corso Vittorio Emanuele. The **Palazzo Spada**, V. Capo di Ferro 13, houses paintings – including those by Reni, Titian and Rubens – collected in the 17th century by Cardinal Spada.

The old Jewish **Ghetto** is one of Rome's quaintest neighbourhoods. It faces the district of Trastevere, on the far side of the Tiber. On the **Janiculum**, the hill which dominates Trastevere, **San Pietro in Montorio**, Pza San Pietro in Montorio, is adjacent to Bramante's *Tempietto* – one of the greatest buildings of the High Renaissance. Below it is the riverside **Villa Farnesina**, Via della Lungarna 230, which was decorated in part by Raphael. The **Porta Portese** is Trastevere's Sunday flea market.

The **Spanish Steps** link the Pza di Spagna with the **Pincio** hill and the **Villa Borghese** gardens, which contain the **Villa Giulia Etruscan Museum** (Museo Nazionale Etrusco), Pzale di Villa Giulia 9, and the

Tours

Sightseeing tours are provided by **ATAC.**
Tickets and information:
ATAC, Pza dei Cinquecento, CIT,
☎(06) 479 11;
American Express,
☎(06) 67 641;
Green Line Tours,
☎(06) 482 74 80; and
Carrani Tours,
☎(06) 47 42 501.
Expect to pay about L.100,000 for a full day's tour.
A ride in a *carrozzella* (open carriage) can be fun, but expensive: agree a price with the driver beforehand.

Day trips from Rome

The **EUR** complex (monumental architecture of the Fascist era, but also a funfair and a good Museum of Roman Civilisation) is on metro line B, as is **Ostia Antica** (24 km south-west) with the sizeable remains of the ancient Roman port.
Trains from **Termini** run south-east to the **Castelli Romani** (Alban Hills), which include the wine areas of **Frascati** and **Castelli Romani,** and the papal residence of **Castel Gandolfo**. One of the highlights of this area is the little town of **Tivoli**, with the charmingly eccentric **Villa d'Este,** its garden flowing with fountains.

Galleria e Museo Borghese, VILLA BORGHESE – unmissable if you like Bernini. At the base of the Pincio, **Santa Maria del Popolo** contains important Caravaggio paintings.

SHOPPING

Best buys are from the **delicatessens and grocery stores** – olive oil, fragrant vinegars, dried *funghi* (mushrooms), packets of dried herbs – in and around VIA DELLA CROCE and the CAMPO DEI FIORI. In VIA DEL CORSO you can buy cheaper versions of the designer clothing, from hats to shoes, on sale in the VIA DEI CONDOTTI (big names like Gucci and Prada) and its parallel streets, while cheaper still are the clothes stalls of the PORTA PORTESE and VIA SANNIO markets (metro: SAN GIOVANNI) with their astonishing arrays of second-hand hand-me-downs and ex-army tackle. Rome has a strong artisan goldsmith and silversmith tradition here (Ghetto, VIA DEI CORONARI, VIA DELL'ORSO), and is fairly well served by antique shops (VIA DEI CORONARI, VIA GIULIA, VIA DEL BABUINO). Take-home items might include terracotta from southern Italy, kitchen equipment made by Alessi, chunks of *parmesan* or *peccorino* cheese, ex-reliquaries from the flea market or bottles of heart-stopping grappa from a liquor store.

NIGHT-TIME AND EVENTS

Trovaroma (published with *La Repubblica* on Thursdays) and *Metropolitan* (published fortnightly in English) are very comprehensive 'what's on' guides, available from news-stands.

Nightlife is limited. Most Italians like nothing better than to while away the evening in a restaurant. However, there are good venues for dancing, vibrant clubs (jazz, salsa, African, Latin) and overflowing, noisy bars. There is also a thriving gay scene.

The summer is Rome's liveliest season for **theatres and concerts**, with many performances set beneath the stars, possibly within some ancient ruin or Renaissance garden. The **Teatro dell'Opera** moves out to the ruins of the **Baths of Caracalla** in July and Aug. As a rule, tickets for these Events (apart from opera) cannot be booked in advance. There are also many choral concerts in the churches – watch the billboards outside for details.

WHERE NEXT FROM ROME?

*Join the **Rome–Palermo** route (p. 381) or head north on the **Bologna–Rome** route (p. 373), branching off if desired at **Orte** to pick up the **Pisa–Orvieto** route. You can also head northwards to **Pisa** to take the **Ventimiglia–Pisa** route (p. 357) in reverse to the French border, from where you can head on through the **French Riviera** (see **Marseille–Menton**, p. 100).*

Few places merit the description 'unique', but **Venice** – as romantic a spot for a get-away as anywhere in the world – is definitely one of them. Built on 118 tiny islands, with gondolas and boats providing the only transport and endowed with a stunning legacy of notable architecture, it formerly commanded an empire stretching from northern Italy to Cyprus. Rising dreamily out of the Lagoon, it looks magnificent at any time of year and any time of day. No matter that the plasterwork has faded and the paint is peeling off many of the tall terracotta buildings or that the canals can look dark and dirty. Sadly Venice is gradually sinking, and no one knows how to solve the problem; in the meantime the mild sense of doom only adds to the poignancy of this marvellous place. As the city is very compact, the highlights can be absorbed in two or three days, though there's enough to fill a lifetime of sightseeing.

As Europe's only roadless city, Venice is a joy to explore, with its great public buildings and magnificent palaces bordering canals and narrow alleys and tiny squares, much of it exuding a village-like calm once you're away from the main tourist drags such as the **Rialto**, **St Mark's Square** and the **Accademia.** Prepare yourself for plenty of walking – there are 400 bridges over 177 canals – and expect to get lost fairly often (it must rank among the world's most confusing places; a compass is useful). However, you're never far from the **Grand Canal**, which snakes through the centre.

The best way to sightsee is simply to wander the narrow streets and canalsides at random, popping into churches as you pass and pausing to window-shop or sit at a pavement café whenever the whim takes you.

ARRIVAL AND DEPARTURE

RAIL To get to Venice itself, take a train to **Santa Lucia** station as some terminate 10 mins earlier at **Mestre** on the mainland. A frequent local service operates between **Mestre** and **Santa Lucia**. **Santa Lucia** has its own *vaporetto* (waterbus) stop, right outside it, at the north-east end of the Grand Canal. **Train information**: ☎785570.

✈ **Marco Polo International Airport** is 13 km north-east of Venice; **flight information,** ☎260 9260. **Buses**: ACTV 🚌no. 5 and blue ATVO operate half-hourly (hourly in winter) between the airport and PZLE ROMA. To continue into Venice, transfer onto a **waterbus**. The regular motorboat service of **Alilaguna** operates from the airport (daylight hours in summer) via the Lido to the PZA SAN MARCO in the heart of Venice.

INFORMATION

CITY MAP
– inside back cover

Santa Lucia Station, ☎529 872, open Mon–Sun 0800–1900, and at **Lido di Venezia**, VIALE S. M. ELISABETTA; ☎526 5721. The free *Guest in Venice* guide lists what's on.
For **youth information**, contact **Comune di Venezia Assessorato al Gioventù**, SAN MARCO 1529; ☎2704 7650. A Rolling Venice Card, costing L.5000, allows 14–29-year-olds discounted entry to museums, theatres, cinemas and cultural Events, maps, cut-price shopping guide and reductions on public transport. Available from **Santa Lucia Station** (daily 0800–2000 July–Sept), or **Assessorato al Gioventù**, SAN MARCO, CORTE CONTARINA 1529; ☎274 7651 (Mon–Fri 0930–1300; also Tues and Thur 1500–1700).

MONEY

When changing money, always ask for a supply of small denomination bills as every shop and café always seems to be short of change. There are exchange offices everywhere.

POST AND PHONES

Main post office: **Poste Centrali**, RIALTO, FONTEGO DEI TEDESCHI; ☎522 0606. To phone **Venice from abroad** the code is 39 (Italy) + 41 (Venice); to phone **Venice from elsewhere in Italy**, it is 041.

PUBLIC TRANSPORT

Vaporetto (waterbus): Other cities have the bus, train, tram or metro, but Venice has the vaporetto. These sturdy waterbuses, operated by the ACTV transport authority, run at 10–20 min intervals in daytime and approximately hourly from midnight to 0600. Lines 1 and 82 run the length of the **Grand Canal** connecting **Santa Lucia** station to PZA SAN MARCO. Piers bear the line numbers – but make sure you go in the right direction. Line 52 is a round-the-islands service taking in **Murano** and handy if you are staying at the youth hostel on **Isola del Giudecca**, which has its own stop, line 82. **Information**: ACTV, PZLE ROMA, ☎528 7886.

Water Taxis: These are sleek but expensive. L.27,000 buys you a ride of up to 7 mins.

Radio Taxi; ☎522 2303.

Gondolas: The city's 400 gondolas, which can take up to 6 passengers each, provide a costly, but definitely the most romantic, means of getting around. Rates are fixed, starting at L.120,000 for 50 mins in a 'procession'. If you decide to treat yourself, go in the evening when the canals are at their most magical. There are 'stands' on several canals.
The cheapest gondola ride in Venice is on the *traghetto* (ferries), which cross the Grand Canal at eight points (signposted **Traghetto**) and only cost L.700.

TICKETS

A 24-hr *turistiche* (tourist ticket), price L.18,000, enables you to use all *vaporetto* routes, and is especially useful if you plan to explore some of the city's outlying islands; **3-day tickets** cost L.35,000, **7-day** L.69,000. Tickets are sold singly or in booklets of ten from kiosks at main stops, open 0600–2100 (later at the station), and have to be validated in the machines on the piers before boarding.

ACCOMMODATION

Don't expect to find cheap accommodation. The city boasts some of Europe's grandest **luxury hotels**, like the legendary **Cipriani, Danieli** and **Gritti Palace**. There are slim pickings for those on a tight budget, especially in spring and autumn, when booking ahead is strongly advisable. In summer, many visitors come for the day by ferry from the Lido. **Less expensive hotels** include **Hotel Remedio**, tucked away in a 15th-century building at the back of a tiny courtyard, and **Hotel Ai Do Mori**.

The main youth hostel **Albergho per la Gioventù** is on ISOLA DEL GIUDECCA.

The nearest **campsites** are on the mainland or on the beach **Litorate del Cerallino**.

HOTELS

Hotel Remedio, C. DEL REMEDIO 4412; ☎520 623 262.
Hotel Ai Do Mori, C. LARGA ST MARCO 658; ☎520 4817.

YOUTH HOSTELS

Albergho per la Gioventù, ISOLA DEL GIUDECCA; ☎523 8211 (vaporetto line 82).

INFORMATION

HOTEL RESERVATIONS

AVA (Venetian Hotel Association) has reservation desks at **Santa Lucia** station, ☎715 016 or 715 288, open daily 0800–2200 (Apr–Oct) and 0800–2130 (Nov–Mar) and at **Marco Polo International Airport**.

HOSTELS

Azienda Promozione Turistica (APT) (Tourist administration): CASTELLO 4421, 30122 VENEZIA; ☎529 8711.
Information offices:
S Marco – PALAZZINA DEL SANTI (GIARDINETTI REALI); ☎522 6356.

For further hostel information, contact **Associazone Alberghi per la Gioventù**, PALAZZO DELLA CIVILTÀ DEL LAVORO, QUADRATO DELLA CONCORDIA, 00144 ROMA, ☎(06) 593 1702.

FOOD AND DRINK

Like all Italian cities, Venice takes pride in its distinctive regional cuisine which, as you would expect, leans heavily towards seafood. Rice and beans are also staple ingredients of local dishes.

Many of the **restaurants** around touristy areas like PZA SAN MARCO and RIALTO charge premium prices, but you only have to stroll a bridge or two away to find quieter streets and more affordable *trattorie* and *pizzerie*. Several atmospheric restaurants of varying price ranges are clustered around **La Fenice** (the opera house), like **Al Theatro** (moderate). For reasonably priced canal-side eating, try **Da Gianni**, which has a tasty selection of *pizzas*.

Bacari, the typically Venetian **wine-bars**, are ideal for budget travellers as they sell plates of *pasta* or *risotto* as well as sandwiches. **Cafés** sell delicious slices of *pizza* and if you want to save money as well as time, stand at the bar where drinks cost a third as much as at a table. **Bar Foscarini**, RIO TERRA FOSCARI, tucked beside the Grand

Canal near the **Accademia** gallery, is well placed for people-watching and for gazing over the water.

The city's most atmospheric bar is **Florian** in one of the arcades around PZA SAN MARCO. It occupies a series of small, beautifully decorated 'drawing rooms', which are still just as they were in the 18th century when Floriano Francesconi opened it. Expect to pay as much for a *cappuccino* as for a *pizza* elsewhere, but it's worth every lira for the surroundings and the opportunity to listen to the orchestra which strikes up in the square outside in the evenings.

The **Rialto** market is a great place to pick up picnic items.

RESTAURANTS	**Al Theatro**, CAMPO ST FANTIN; ☎522 1052. **Da Gianni**, ZATTERE 918; ☎523 7210.
WINE-BARS/CAFÉS	**Bar Foscarini**, RIO TERRA FOSCARI. **Florian**, PZA SAN MARCO; ☎528 5338.

HIGHLIGHTS

Most of the major sights charge a steep entrance fee, but many of the city's art treasures can be seen free, adorning church walls and altars.

A *vaporetto* ride along the Grand Canal – sit at the front – is probably the greatest sightseeing journey in the world. Dodging gondolas, water taxis and delivery boats, it takes you past a succession of grand palaces and churches, and under the decorative white arch of the famous **Rialto** bridge.

PZA SAN MARCO (ST MARK'S SQUARE) This piazza is the hub of the city, close to the mouth of the Grand Canal. Surrounded by arcades of exclusive shops and cafés, the huge square echoes with the chatter and footsteps of crowds of tourists while pigeons flap at their feet. Begin by taking the lift up the Campanile di San Marco for a panoramic view of the city and lagoon. The slender red brick tower itself is a 20th-century reconstruction of a 1000-year-old bell tower which fell down in 1912.

Next to the Campanile di San Marco, the **Museo Correr**, occupying the south side of the square, traces the history of Venice and displays 14th- to 19th-century paintings.

The **Basilica di San Marco**, consecrated in 1094, was built to house the bones of St Mark the Evangelist. It has five impressive domes, each heavily encrusted with gold mosaics, best seen from the narrow catwalks which run round an upper rim – though to appreciate them you need a good head for heights. The floor, too, is elaborately patterned in marble.

Its museum, in the galleries above the church, contains sculpture and carvings from all over the medieval Venetian empire. One of the highlights is the gilded bronze *Horses of St Mark*, believed to date from the 4th century and stolen from Byzantium by the Venetians in 1204.

Next to the Basilica along the waterfront stands the icing-white **Palazzo Ducale** (Doge's Palace). It contains important Venetian works of art, which provide a glimpse of the lifestyles of the city's former rulers. Stairs from it lead down to the **Ponte dei Sospiri** (Bridge of Sighs), which crosses a narrow canal to the **Palazzo delle Prigione**, the former prison for petty offenders. Prisoners were led across it – hence the name. However, the best view of it is from another bridge, **Ponte de la Paglia**, on the busy promenade between the Lagoon and ST MARK'S SQUARE.

CANALE GRANDE (GRAND CANAL): EAST BANK Following the canal around from St Mark's, you come to the handsome white **Ponte di Rialto** (Rialto Bridge) at the geographic heart of the city. Beyond it, the **Ca'd'Oro**, the most lavish of all Venice's aristocratic palaces, now houses **Galleria Franchetti**, a magnificent collection of paintings (including Mantegna and Guardi), renaissance bronzes and medallions.

THE ISLANDS

Organised sightseeing tours of the outlying **Murano** island and its neighbours, **Burano** and **Torcello**, are mainly trips to see the glass factories; Murano also has a fine church, **Santissimi Maria e Donato**, with Byzantine paving and 13th-century mosaics, while *Burano* is generally more pleasant, with a lively little fishing community and brightly coloured houses. You can visit these and other islands just as easily – and much more cheaply – on an ordinary *vaporetto* no.12. The **Lido** is a swimming and sun-bathing haunt.

CANALE GRANDE: WEST BANK Standing guard at the beginning of the canal's west bank is the domed **Santa Maria della Salute**, the greatest baroque church in Venice. Nearby the **Palazzo Venier dei Leoni**, the palace that Peggy Guggenheim bought specially in 1919, houses her remarkable cubist, abstract and surrealist collection. Yet another of the city's great art galleries, **Galleria dell' Accademia**, is only a short stroll away; it features Venetian artists like Bellini, Canaletto, Carpaccio, Guardi, Titian, Tintoretto and Veronese, as well as Florentine Renaissance artists such as Piero della Francesca.

A short walk west of the canal, between the RIO DELLA FRESCADA and the CAMPO DI SAN PAOLO, the **Scuola di San Rocco** guildhall contains a magnificent collection of Tintoretto's works. Nearby, the huge red-brick Gothic church of **Santa Maria Gloriosa dei Frari** looks almost like a factory from the outside but contains paintings by Bellini, Donatello and Titian, amongst others. Both Titian and the composer Monteverdi are buried there.

NIGHT-TIME AND EVENTS

The entertainment calendar is busier in summer than winter, with Events like the annual 10-day **Venice Film Festival** (in Sept). **Palazzo Grassi** is the venue for many of the exhibitions that the city stages, including its major one, the **Biennale di Venezia**, which is the largest modern art show in the world (June–Oct in even years).

The city's biggest event is **Carnival**, ten days of masked balls and street celebrations immediately before Lent. **La Vogolonga** – the long row – on Ascension Sunday is a marathon regatta around the Lagoon – any sort of oar-powered craft can take part. Historic **Regata Storica** (first Sun in Sept) begins with a magnificent procession of veteran boats rowed by costumed crews along the Grand Canal. The main venue for opera, **La Fenice**, now being rebuilt after a serious fire in 1996, may reopen in 2000. Meanwhile, performances take place in a marquee erected on the parking area of **Tronchetto** island. Numerous concerts are held in the city's churches. The **Palazzo del Cinema** on the Lido is the venue for the annual film festival and shows international films year-round. Throughout the city, bars and clubs offer live music and late-night drinking, but the streets are safe for quiet strolls throughout the night and there's no obvious red light area.

SHOPPING

The Venetians' aptitude for commerce has been sharpened by more than eleven centuries of international trade and 200 years of tourism. The main shopping streets are between PZA SAN MARCO and the **Rialto**, particularly **Mercerie**. However, bargains are thin on the ground, except in the Rialto open-air market, though many of its stalls sell little but souvenirs. Manufacturers of the city's famous glass include **Cenedese** and **Salviati**, both of which have shops on PZA SAN MARCO. More affordable, and uniquely Venetian, are the painted papier-maché carnival masks sold in many small stores.

Colourful marbled paper printed from old blocks is the most inexpensive local souvenir. Typical Venetian jewellery is made from thin gold chain called *la manina*, but plenty of imitations are on sale as well as the genuine article, particularly around PZA SAN MARCO. Visitors to the neighbouring islands in the Lagoon, such as Murano where the glass is made, are invariably disappointed to find prices much the same as in the city centre.

WHERE NEXT FROM VENICE?

***Venice** is on the **Milan–Trieste** route (p. 367). Ferries to **Patras** via **Corfu** take 33 hrs (ETT table 2875). A scenic route over the* Alps *into* Austria *via **Villach** (table 88) joins the **Innsbruck–Vienna** route (p 318) at **Linz**, or you can change at **Villach** and join the same route further west at **Schwarzach-St Veit** (table 970).*

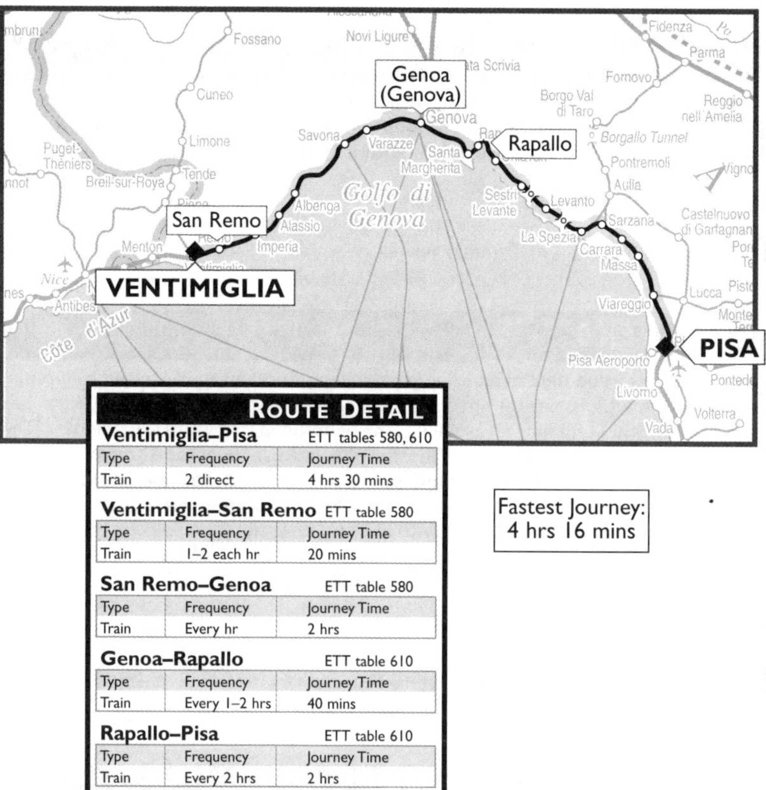

ROUTE DETAIL

Ventimiglia–Pisa ETT tables 580, 610

Type	Frequency	Journey Time
Train	2 direct	4 hrs 30 mins

Ventimiglia–San Remo ETT table 580

Type	Frequency	Journey Time
Train	1–2 each hr	20 mins

San Remo–Genoa ETT table 580

Type	Frequency	Journey Time
Train	Every hr	2 hrs

Genoa–Rapallo ETT table 610

Type	Frequency	Journey Time
Train	Every 1–2 hrs	40 mins

Rapallo–Pisa ETT table 610

Type	Frequency	Journey Time
Train	Every 2 hrs	2 hrs

Fastest Journey:
4 hrs 16 mins

VENTIMIGLIA – GENOA – PISA

From the French border (you can join this journey on to the **Marseille–Menton** route on p. 100) the line along the **Italian Riviera** has a wonderful sequence of coastal views. Against mountain backdrops the vineyards, olive trees and palms flourish in the mild climes that attracted English visitors to the **Liguria** region in the 19th century. **Genoa** is less pretty but has its fascinations, and **Pisa** (see p. 362) is a fine introduction to **Tuscany**.

VENTIMIGLIA

The railway runs between the town and the beach of this resort right on the French/Italian border. It's rather untidy and traffic-ridden, but there's a Roman theatre and a steeply built old town, with a 12th-century cathedral. The olive oil industry generates *lire* for the local economy.

RAIL ☎1478 880888.

i **Tourist office**: V. CAVOUR 61, ☎(0184) 351 183.

SAN REMO

The prime resort on the Italian Riviera stretches around an 8 km bay. It has a pleasant old town, with its narrow streets, steep steps and arches, while the new town has a casino and yachting marina as well as the palm-lined CORSO DELL' IMPERATICE. The **Nobel Villa**, C. CAVALOTTI 112, the house of the Swedish inventor Alfred Nobel who established the series of international prizes named after him open to the public. Early risers can visit the incredible flower market that takes place every morning from June to October from 0600 to 0800 in C. GARIBALDI.

RAIL ☎1478 880888.

i **Tourist Office**: CORSO NUVOLONI 1, ☎(0184) 571 571.

Modest rooms can be found at **hotels** like the **Morandi**, CORSO MATUZIA 51, ☎(0184) 667 641 and the **Villa Maria**, CORSO NUVOLONI 30, ☎(0184) 531 422.

GENOA (GENOVA)

Noisy, sprawling and demanding to visit, **Genoa**, *La Superba*, is Italy's foremost seaport and was once, like Venice, a proud maritime republic ruled by a Doge or elected ruler. The city's grandeur has faded, but there is an interesting old town, with a maze of tiny alleys and many old palaces and mansions. It is centred on the port, to the south and south-west of the modern city, where stands the **Lanterna** (1544), the nation's oldest lighthouse.

The old part of town centres on the docks and is easily explored on foot (during the day: it's not safe at night). Elsewhere, there's a good bus service. There is also a funicular from PZA DEL PORTELLO to SANT'ANNA, high on the hill on which the town is built. There's a great view from the top and the journey is worthwhile in itself.

BUS TICKETS

Automatic kiosks sell tourist tickets providing unlimited travel for one day (price L.5000)

The **Palazzo Ducale**, PZA MATTEOTTI, was once the seat of the Doge. Across the street is the **church of the Gesù,** which contains two Rubens and a Guido Reni. The nearby **Cattedrale di San Lorenzo** has some unusual artefacts: the reliquary of John the Baptist on which his severed head is reputed to have rested and a dish said to have been used at the Last Supper.

PZA CARICAMENTO is on the waterfront, and always a hive of activity with market stalls and many cafés. On one side is the **Palazzo San Giorgio**, which has housed various government departments for several centuries and has two rooms that are open to the public. PZA BANCHI was the heart of the old city and is now the commercial centre. To the north is V. GARIBALDI, home to several Renaissance palaces. Two of these, **Palazzo Bianco** (no.11) and **Palazzo Rosso** (no.18) are now galleries with excellent collections, including Flemish and Dutch masterpieces. Both palaces are worth a visit to see the incredible décor.

If you fancy a swim, the suburb of **Albaro** (take 🚌 no. 41 from **Principe**) has a beach with showers.

Genoa's **Aquarium**, PORTO ANTICO, is the largest in Europe and truly mesmerising – the harbour seals are absolutely the definition of adorable. **Nervi**, a few stops from **Brignole** station, has a beautiful promenade on a dramatic coast.

Stazione Principe, ☎ 1478 88088, handles trains to the west; take 🚌 no. 41 from here to get to the city centre. **Stazione Brignole,** ☎ 1478 88088, is further east and serves trains to the south and east take 🚌 no. 40 from here to get to the city centre. Trains to the north use both stations; use 🚌 no. 37 to transfer between them.

DAY TRIP FROM GENOA

Pavia, north of **Genoa** on the line to **Milan**, is reached by train in about 1 hr 30 mins (hourly; ETT table 610; station 10-min walk from centre, or take 🚌 nos. 3/6). It's a quietly attractive old town, known for its medieval towers, churches and peaceful squares. The pick of the churches is the 12th-century Romanesque **church of San Michele**, VIA CAVALLOTTI, with its yellow sandstone façade and friezes depicting mythical creatures and symbolising the struggle between good and evil. It contains 14th-century bas-reliefs and a 7th-century silver cross. The huge 14th-century **Castello Visconteo** (Castle of the Visconti), STRADA NUOVA, houses the **Museo Civico**, which contains an absorbing archaeological section and some Venetian paintings (including works by Bellini). The highlight of the area and one of the great buildings of Italy is the **Certosa di Pavia**, a Carthusian monastery, 8 km north of town. It has an incredible façade, including Carrara marble transported from 250 km away.

Cistercian monks now live there and maintain a vow of silence. The interior of the church is Gothic, filled with paintings, statues and tombs and as elaborately decorated as the flamboyant exterior. The rest of the monastery

Day Trip from Genoa cont'd.

can be seen by joining a guided tour. Buses from **Pavia** are frequent (from PZA PIAVE), then there's a 1.5-km walk to the entrance. **Tourist Office**: V. FABIO FILZI 2, ☎(0382) 22 156 (near station). Mon–Sat 0830–1230 and 1400–1800. There's a shortage of budget accommodation. Try the **Hotel Aurora** 23664, V. VITTORIO EMANUELLE II. **Camping** (May–Sept): **Ticino**, V. MASCHERPA 10, ☎(0382) 527094 (bus no. 4).

Tourist Offices: **City centre**: PORTO ANTICO-PALAZZINA S. MARIA, ☎(010) 248 711, fax: (010) 246 76 580, (daily 0800–1830). There are also offices at **Stazione FS Principe**, PIAZZA ACQUAVERDE, ☎(010) 246 26 33 (Mon–Sat 0800–2000, Sun 0900–1200), at **Aeroporto** C. COLOMBO-SESTRI PONENTE, ☎(010) 601 52 47, and at **Stazione Marittima–Terminal Crociere**, ☎(010) 246 36 85 (Apr–Sept only). The PIAZZA DE FERRARI often has a stand.

Cheap accommodation is easy to find, but some of it is very tacky. Try the roads on the outskirts of the old town and (near **Brignole**) V. XX SETTEMBRE and PZA COLOMBO. **Youth hostel**: V. COSTANZI, ☎(010) 242 24 57 (bus no. 40 from **Brignole**); it has (deservedly) been voted one of the top ten hostels in the world.

The cheapest eating places for lunch are in the dock area, but most close in the evening. Street stalls all over the city sell fried seafood and chickpea pancakes.

RAPALLO

A once-beautiful resort haunted by writers, **Rapallo** is now hectically chic and expensive, with a large marina, but there is an attractive old area with cobbled streets and a castle. Menus offering fresh fish are everywhere. Walkers can enjoy the scenery by following footpaths up to the hill village of **Montallegro** (600 m above sea level), with its 16th-century **San-tuario**, while the less energetic can ride the cable-car up from V. CASTEGNETO.

RAIL ☎1478 88088.

Tourist Office: V. DIAZ 9, ☎(0185) 51 282 (daily 0930–1230 and 1600–1900).

WHERE NEXT FROM PISA?

*Either venture into **Tuscany** on the **Pisa–Orvieto** route (p. 361) or carry on along the coast to **Rome** (p. 345) –see ETT table 610.*

*On the way to Rome you can visit the island of **Elba**; change at **Campiglia** for **Piombino** (table 609), then take the 25-min ferry crossing to **Elba** (table 2699). **Elba** has clear waters, fine beaches and a ragged coastline of capes and bays, though in summer it gets impossibly tourist-ridden; there are paths and attractive villages to explore, plus Napoleon's villa and a cable car up to a 1019-m summit. **Buses** serve the island's villages and resorts. **Accommodation** is plentiful (with lots of campsites), but it gets heavily booked in July and August; contact the **Tourist Office** at CALATA ITALIA 26, PORTOFERRAIO (in the dilapidated ten-storey block near the ferry port), ☎(0565) 914 1.*

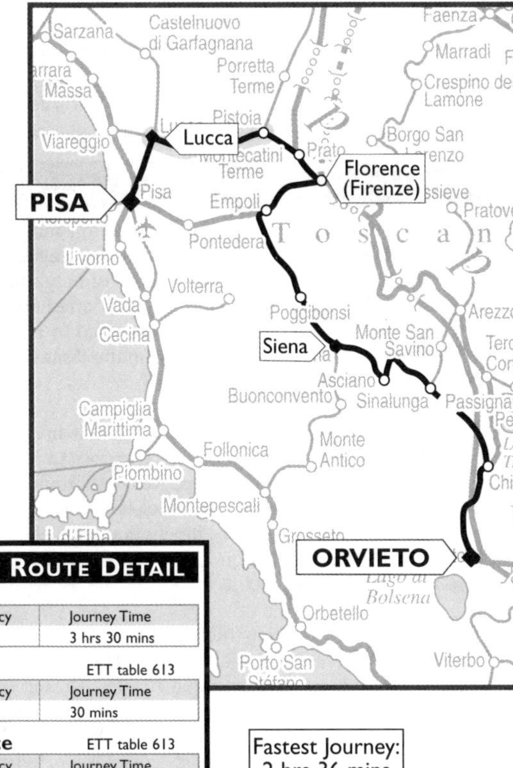

ROUTE DETAIL

Pisa–Orvieto

Type	Frequency	Journey Time
Train	10 daily	3 hrs 30 mins

Pisa–Lucca ETT table 613

Type	Frequency	Journey Time
Train	10 daily	30 mins

Lucca–Florence ETT table 613

Type	Frequency	Journey Time
Train	Every 1-2 hrs	1 hr 20 mins

Florence–Siena ETT table 616

Type	Frequency	Journey Time
Train	Every hr	1 hr 45 mins

Siena–Orvieto

Type	Frequency	Journey Time
Train	Every 2 hrs	2 hrs 5 mins

Fastest Journey:
2 hrs 36 mins

Notes

Pisa to Orvieto change at Florence

Siena to Orvieto: change at Chiusi

PISA – SIENA – ORVIETO

This trip encounters the heart of **Tuscany**, one of the culturally richest and most unspoilt parts of Italy, with its green hills striped with olive groves and vineyards, as well as historic towns and cities with astonishingly rich legacies of Renaissance art and architecture.

PISA

The **Leaning Tower of Pisa** rates among the world's most familiar landmarks, part of a magnificent triumvirate of buildings around the **Campo dei Miracoli** (Field of Miracles), by the Cathedral and Baptistry. Some of Italy's finest medieval sculptures are here, many by Nicola and Giovanni Pisano (father and son) and other Pisanos (unrelated). The unusual architecture, characterised by distinctive stripes of marble and blind arcades, is thought to emanate from the Pisans' contact with the Moslems of North Africa and Spain.

The 11th-century, four-tiered **Duomo**, one of Italy's finest cathedrals, was the first Tuscan building to use marble in horizontal stripes (a Moorish idea). The original bronze entrance, **Portale di San Ranieri**, was cast around 1180 and is by Bonanno, one of the designers of the Leaning Tower itself. A 16th-century fire destroyed much of the interior but some of Cosmati's lovely floor survived, as did the 14th-century mosaic of Christ Pantocrator by Cimabue, in the apse, and a magnificent sculpted pulpit by Giovanni Pisano (*c.*1300).

SAVING PISA'S LEANING TOWER

The famous Tower is now 5 m off true, visitors can no longer go inside and the architects continue to spend their days arguing about how to prop it up. Collapse of the campanile at **Pavia** has prompted serious concern about its future, and proposed remedies have included an elaborate refrigeration of the foundations, and enclosure of the entire tower within a superstructure.

Construction of the circular **Baptistery** stopped when money ran out. The three lower storeys consist of Romanesque arcades. The top half, in Gothic style, with pinnacles and a dome, was added later (again by the prolific Pisanos, in the 1260s). It has a pulpit superbly carved by Nicola Pisano, whose design produced a whole series of similar pulpits during this period.

The **Leaning Tower** *(Torre Pendente)* began life in 1173, as a campanile for the Duomo. When it was 10 m high it began to tilt and the architect fled. Construction continued, however, with successive architects trying unsuccessfully to restore the balance.

RAIL **Centrale**, ☎ 1478 88088 (national number), south of the River Arno and 20 mins' walk from the Leaning Tower, or **CPT** 🚌 nos. 1 & 3, ☎ (050) 505511; L.1500 one-way and L.300 return.

🚌 **Buses: APT**, PZA SANT'ANTONIO, ☎ (050) 505511, and **Lazzi**, PZA VITTORIO EMANUELE, ☎ (144) 801161, between them cover all Tuscany.

Pisa's **Galileo Galilei Airport** is the main regional hub for international flights, (050) 500 707. Frequent buses run to the city centre and rail station.

Tourist Offices: **Cathedral** (0930–1300, 1500–1900; closed holidays and Sun), (050) 42291. Free booking service, (050) 83 0253. Station (same hours but closes 1830), (050) 560464.

There are several good budget hotels around CAMPO DEI MIRACOLI, but they are popular and in term-time students fill the best. **Hostel**: **Centro Turistico Madonna del qua vie Pietrasantina N15**, (050) 890622, no.3. **Campsite**: **Campeggio Torre Pendente**, VLE CASCINE 86, (050) 561774, 1 km west of the Leaning Tower, signposted from PZA MANIN.

DAY TRIP FROM PISA

Certosa di Pisa

(12 km to the east and served by regular APT buses) is an enormous 14th-century Carthusian monastery with a frescoed church where all eleven chapels are painted in pastel colours. Each three-room cell has its own little patch of garden.

LUCCA

Despite its considerable beauty, the city never feels overrun with tourists, and bicycles are more in evidence than cars. The tranquil streets are dotted with palaces, towers and handsome early churches, most of them dating from **Lucca's** heyday (11th–14th centuries). Start with a stroll around part of the 4 km of ancient walls – the most complete in Italy – that enclose the old city and are themselves encircled by a green belt, a buffer between the medieval and modern towns. Some bastions have been restored and you can get a good idea of the town's original layout.

The Romanesque **Duomo di San Martino**, in the south of the centre, has individually designed columns and loggias: look out for an exquisite early 15th-century **Tomb of Ilaria del Carrett** (by Jacopo della Quercia) and Tintoretto's *Last Supper*.

The central **church of San Michele** in FORO, which takes its name from its position in the midst of what was once the ancient Roman forum, has a multi-tiered façade of striped marble loggias with a diversity of supporting pillars, either inlaid with mosaic or carved and twisted, and, at the top, a huge bronze of Archangel Michael. Funds ran out before the interior could be completed.

Near the western city wall is the **Pinacoteca Nazionale**, housed in **Palazzo Mansi**, V. GALLI TASSI 43. The 17th-century palace is of rather more interest than the pictures it displays, the over-decorated interior including a particularly spectacular gilded bridal suite.

Further south-east is **Palazzo Guinigi,** V. SANT' ANDREA, a rambling complex of interconnected

LUCCA'S AMPHITHEATRE

The PZA ANFITEATROL is an oval of medieval tenements clustered round the site of a Roman amphitheatre. Parts of the original arches and columns are visible in the buildings themselves, and the shape of the oval is effectively a fossilisation of the theatre itself.

medieval buildings. A climb of 230 steps leads up a turreted tower with an oak sprouting from the top, giving a fascinating view over the city's rooftops.

The city's main museum, **Museo Nazionale Guinigi**, east of the centre on V. DELLA QUARQUONIA, contains a huge and varied collection of local romanesque and renaissance art.

RAIL ☎ 1478 88088 (national rail information). Just outside the city walls, an easy walk to the centre. There are frequent trains from **Pisa, Viareggio** or **Florence**, taking about 30 mins.

Tourist Offices: PZA VERDI (just inside western city walls), ☎ (0583) 419 689 (March–Oct: 0930–1830; Nov–Feb 0930–1530).

Finding space is always a problem, so book ahead. An accommodation service is provided by **Hotel Reservation**, ☎ (0583) 312 262. **Youth hostel**: V. DEL BRENNERO 673, ☎ (0583) 341 811. Open Mar–Oct. **Camping** is possible behind the hostel.

The **Ristorante Giglio**, PZA DEL GIGLIO 2, has a splendid interior, with painted ceiling and gilt mirrors, and huge marble fireplace; it looks pricey but has a very reasonable *menu turistica*.

FLORENCE (FIRENZE)

See p. 328.

SIENA

Spread over low hills and filled with robust terracotta-coloured buildings, **Siena** is not much changed since medieval times. Indeed this most beautiful of Tuscan cities has contracted inside its walls in places – look out from just behind the **Campo**, the main square, and there's a vista down a green, rural valley, as pretty as a wine label. The city was Florence's most tireless enemy for much of the Middle Ages, competing with it for supremacy politically, economically and artistically. Now it's a delightful place to visit, for its artistic treasures as well as just for the pleasures of discovering its myriad sloping alleys.

The fan-shaped Campo dates from 1347 and is regarded as the focus of the city's life. The arcaded and turreted **Palazzo Pubblico**, on the south side, still performs its traditional role as the town hall, and its belltower, the 102 m **Torre del Mangia**, soars above the town. The views from the top are dizzying in the extreme. Part of the **Palazzo Pubblico** houses the **Museo Civico**, where the *Sala dei Pace* and *Sala del Mappamondo* contain treasures of Lorenzetti and Martini amongst others.

To the west stands the **cathedral,** its striped marble exterior featuring notable Renaissance sculpture by masters. Inside, the floor comprises 56 separate sections, on which over 40 artists worked for nearly two centuries, including an elaborate pulpit of Nicola Pisano's and a notable Donatello bronze. The **Museo dell' Opera del Duomo** contains many Sienese masterpieces of painting and sculpture.

SIENA AND THE PALIO RACE

In the past, the city was divided into 60 *contrade* (wards named after animals), of which 17 remain, each with its own church, museum and central square with a fountain featuring the relevant animal. Rivalry between wards is strong, reaching a head in the famous twice-yearly **Palio**, no-holds-barred horse race around the *Campo* (which is regarded as neutral territory). Only 10 horses can participate, so lots are drawn to decide which wards will be represented; the whole event is regarded as a matter of honour by the locals, with rehearsals for days beforehand and excitement mounting to fever-pitch. Races last only 70 seconds or so, but are preceded by a two-hour procession. Get there early if you want to watch – standing in the centre is free, if crowded.

Terzo di Città (south-west of the CAMPO), has some of the city's finest private palaces, such as the **Palazzo Chigi-Saracini**, V. DI CITTA 82.

RAIL ☎ 1478 88088 (national rail information); 2 km north-east (in valley below town). It is a tedious 45-min walk uphill to the centre, but there are regular shuttle buses (tickets from machine by entrance).

Long-distance buses (covering all Tuscany), run by **Lazzi and Train**, leave from PZA SAN DOMENICO bus station, ☎ (0577) 204 246.

Tourist Office: PZA DEL CAMPO 56, ☎ (0577) 280 551. Mon–Sat 0830–1930 (summer); Mon–Fri 0830–1300 and 1530–1830, Sat 0830–1300 (winter). This office has good maps and the useful booklet *Tourist Information*. There are also booths in the train and bus stations.

Private rooms are best value, but you often have to stay at least a week and they can be full of students in term-time. The relatively few hotels are often full. For the **Palio** (early July and mid Aug), either book well ahead or stay up all night (many do). At other times, if the Tourist Office can't help, try the **Cooperativa Siena Hotels** promotion booth opposite **San Domenico**, V. CURTATONE, ☎ (0577) 288 084; Mon–Sat 0830–2000 in summer (closes 1900 in winter). **Private hostel**: V. FLORENTINA 89, ☎ (0577) 52 212, 2 km north-west of centre (bus nos. 15, 35, 36, 4, 10. The cheapest hotel is **Tre Donzelle**, V. DELLE DONZELLE 5, ☎ (0577) 280 358. **Campsite**: **Campeggio Colleverde**, STRADA DI SCACCIAPENSIERI 47, ☎ (0577) 280 044, 2 km north (bus nos. 8 or 3, both from PIAZZADE/SALE).

ORVIETO

Orvieto's setting on a raised plateau of volcanic tufa makes a striking impact amid a valley of vines. Dominating the town is the vividly striped **Duomo,** PZA DUOMO, built in honour of a 13th-century miracle. With its triple-gabled exterior of gilded mosaics, bronze doors and bas reliefs by Louis Maitani as well as outstanding interior frescos by Luca Signorelli depicting the *Last Judgement* (in the **Cappella di San Brizio** in the right transept), it is one of the great

DAY TRIPS FROM SIENA

San Gimignano (32 km north-west, half-hourly buses from **Siena**, via **Poggibonsi**) is a typical medieval hill town, which originally sported 70 towers, partly defensive and partly status symbols, of which 14 survive. PZA DEL DUOMO has some of the

Day trips from Siena cont'd.

finest medieval buildings, while the frescos by Gozzoli in the **church of Sant'Agostino** and the four fresco cycles in the **Collegiata** (cathedral) stand out among the town's notable art heritage. The Tourist Office is on the main square.

churches of Umbria. Several grand buildings near the Duomo now contain museums.

The **Pozzo di San Patrizio**, PZA CAHEN, near the funicular terminal, is an astonishing cylindrical well with a diameter of 13 m and a depth of 62 m. A double-helix mule-ramp runs around the interior. It was completed in 1537 to provide an emergency water supply for the city.

COMBINED ENTRY TICKETS IN ORVIETO

A combined ticket, the **Carta Orvieto Unica**, allows access to four sights: the **Cappella di San Brizio**, the **Museo Claudio Faina**, **Orvieto Underground** and the **Torre del Moro** (a clock tower on CORSO CAVOUR). It can be bought at any of the sights, or at the Tourist Office. Another cumulative ticket includes entrance to the **Pozzo di San Patrizio** and the **Museo Greco**.

RAIL By the bus station and connected by funicular to PZA CAHEN in the old town (takes 2 mins; every 15 mins weekdays 0715–1230, Sun and public holidays 0800–2030), from where you can then walk or take any of the frequent buses (Line A or B) to the centre.

i **Tourist Office**: PZA DUOMO 24, ☎(0763) 341 772 or 341 911 (Mon–Fri 0800–1400 and 1600–1900; Sat 1000–1300 and 1600–1900, Sun 1000–1200 and 1600–1800). Local bus tickets and the combined sightseeing ticket, **Orvieto Unica**, can be purchased here. Pick up the current version of *Welcome to Orvieto* for useful listings. The Tourist Information Point on V. DUOMO is privately run and charges for most of its services.

If you want to experience the atmosphere of Orvieto at night, best-located central hotels (both inexpensive) are **Virgilio**, PZA DEL DUOMO 5, ☎(0763) 341 882 (only a few rooms have views), or **Duomo**, V. MAURIZIO 7, ☎(0763) 341 887. The **Maitani**, V. MAITANI 5, ☎(0763) 342 011 offers more luxury in a 17th-century palace with a garden.

Orvieto is famous for its wines: best-known are the crisp fruity whites made from *Trebbiano* grapes, but reds and sweet wines are also produced. *Orvieto Classico* wines come from a specific area immediately around the city. They are fermented and stored in the underground passages and caves which honeycomb the soft local tufa, and are widely on sale throughout the region, many under the *Cardeto* label (the largest Umbrian wine cooperative). Bars and *enotecas* offer a chance to taste before you buy. **La Bottega del Buon Vino**, V. DELLA VACA 26, ☎(0763) 42373, is an atmospheric place with good prices. Orvieto is full of good eating places, though prices are on the high side. A cheaper option is **Al San Francesco**, V. CERRETTI 10, ☎(0763) 43302, a popular self-service cafeteria and evening pizzeria. There are picnic facilities in the **Parco delle Grotte** near the PZA DUOMO (entrance L.2000); the public gardens of the **Rocca,** near the funicular terminal, can be enjoyed free, and have fine views over the **Paglia Valley**.

WHERE NEXT FROM ORVIETO?

*Carry on to **Rome** (p. 350); this route goes via **Orte**, where you can change for trains to **Spoleto**. See ETT tables 615 and 625.*

ROUTE DETAIL

Milano (Centrale)**–Trieste** ETT 600, 605

Type	Frequency	Journey Time
Train	3 daily	5 hrs

Milano (Centrale)**–Verona** ETT table 600

Type	Frequency	Journey Time
Train	1–2 every hr	1 hr 30 mins

Verona–Vicenza ETT table 600

Type	Frequency	Journey Time
Train	1–2 every hr	42 mins

Vicenza–Padua ETT table 600

Type	Frequency	Journey Time
Train	1–2 every hr	22 mins

Padua–Venice (Sta Maria) ETT table 600

Type	Frequency	Journey Time
Train	1–2 every hr	30 mins

Venice (Sta Maria)**–Trieste** ETT table 605

Type	Frequency	Journey Time
Train	Every 1–2 hrs	1 hr 45 mins

Fastest Journey:
4 hrs 42 mins

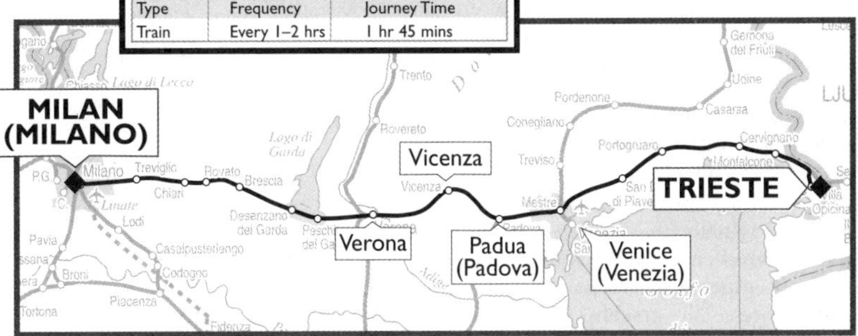

MILAN – VENICE – TRIESTE

The places rather than the views are of primary interest on this trip from **Lombardy**, Italy's busiest and most prosperous region, to **Trieste** in the east, with the foothills of the **Alps** to the north. **Verona** and **Venice** are among Europe's most romantic cities.

MILAN (MILANO)

See p. 334.

VERONA

ARENA TICKET OFFICE

☎(045) 800 5151 (the cheap seats are unreserved and you sit on the stone terraces; bring or hire a cushion, and plenty of fluid); or contact: **Liaisons Abroad** in London ☎(0171) 384 1122.

Placed on an S-bend of the river **Ádige** and best explored on foot, this beautiful city of pastel-pink marble thrives on the story of *Romeo and Juliet* (see below), but the real attractions are its elegant medieval squares, fine Gothic churches and massive Roman amphitheatre, the **Arena**, which comes alive during the annual opera festival in July and August. Dominating the large PZA BRA, it has 44 pink marble tiers which can accommodate 20,000 people – incredibly the singers and orchestra are perfectly audible.

ROMEO AND JULIET IN VERONA

A delicate bronze statue of Juliet stands in the small cobbled courtyard beneath the famous balcony of her supposed house, VIA CAPPELIO 27. This restored 13th-century building was once an inn but the balcony was not added until 1935. The Montagues and Capulets on which Shakespeare's play was based were real Veronese families.

VIA MAZZINI, which leads off PZA BRA, is one of Italy's smartest shopping streets. This leads to PZA DELLE ERBE, which is surrounded by renaissance palaces, their burnt-orange façades now rather worn. Originally the Roman forum, the square is now covered each day by market stalls under giant white umbrellas. An archway leads to a much serener square, PZA DEI SIGNORI, centre of medieval civic life. Among its treasures is the graceful 15th-century **Loggia del Consiglio** and the **Palazzo del Capitano**, which has a crenellated tower. Be sure to pause too for coffee at the Dante, the most celebrated café in town.

The ornate Gothic tombs of the Scaligeri family are in the grounds of the small Romanesque **church of Santa Maria Antica**. They ruled Verona when the city was at its peak in the 13th century and commissioned many of its finest buildings. An equestrian statue that once topped one of them stands outside their castle beside the river, now the **Castelvecchio Museum**, which displays weapons, jewellery and religious paintings. Beyond it, **San Zeno Maggiore**, a superb Romanesque church, has a notable Madonna altarpiece by Mantegna and magnificent 11th–12th-century bronze doors.

Verona's striped red and white marble **cathedral**, PZA DUOMO, is a blend of Romanesque and Gothic styles. Among its treasures is Titian's *Assumption*. Across the river, there are good views from the terraces of another Roman theatre on a wooded hillside.

1478 88088, 15–20 min walk south of the centre (nos.11/12/13/14 from stop A). Bike hire available.

Tourist Office: V. LEONCINO 61; (045) 806 8680 (Mon–Sat 0900–2000 and Sun 1000–1300, 1600–1900). Also at the station (045) 800 0861(Tue–Sat 0800–1930, Sun and Mon, 1000–1600).

There is plenty of **budget** hotel and student accommodation (booking essential for the opera season, July–Aug). **Youth hostel**: **Della Gioventù**, SALITA FONTANA DEL FERRO 15, (045) 590 360, 3 km from the station, no. 73 (no. 90 on Sun) to PZA ISOLO, from which the hostel is a short walk; camping in the grounds. **Campsite**: CASTEL SAN PIETRO 2, (045) 592 037, open mid June–mid Sept, is walkable from the centre (no. 41).

For reasonably priced **restaurants**, look around PZA DELLE ERBE; *polenta* with sauce (including such ingredients as mushrooms and gorgonzola) is a filling and inexpensive meal. Places to see and be seen, as well as eat, are lined along LISTON. The PZA DELLE ERBE'S **food market** is useful for gathering picnic items.

WHERE NEXT FROM VERONA?

Venture north into the Dolomites from Bolzano, or head via Innsbruck to Munich; see Munich–Verona, p. 275. Services (ETT table 595; 1 hr 30 mins) to Bologna link with the Bologna–Rome route (p. 373) via Florence, where you can join the Pisa–Orvieto route (p. 361).

VICENZA

CORSO PALLADIO, the long straight main street, is lined with palaces. The **Teatro Olimpico** at the eastern end was Palladio's last work. Based on the design of ancient Roman theatres and opened in 1585, it is the oldest indoor theatre in Europe and still in use during the summer months. The acoustics are superb. **Palazzo Chiericati**, PZA MATTEOTTI, houses the well-stocked **Museo Civico** which contains paintings by such masters as Tintoretto and Memling.

Palladio's most famous villa, **La Rotonda**, is on a hillside about 1.5 km south-east of the centre (nos. 8/13). It has a round interior under a dome set in a cube of classical porticoes, a design often copied. Nearby is the **Villa Valmarana**, an 18th-century country house notable for its Tiepolo frescos and dwarfs on the garden wall.

1478 88088. 10-min walk south of the centre (nos. 1/7).

Tourist Office: PZA MATTEOTTI 12; (0444) 320 854 (Mon–Sat 0900–1300 and 1430–1800; Sun 0900–1300); branch at rail station (0444) 540 355 (0900–1400).

The cheapest **hotels** are away from the centre or in noisy locations, so it's worth considering two-star places like **Hotel Vicenza**, STRADA DEI NODARI 5; (0444) 321 5121. Book ahead for summer and autumn. **Campsite**: **Campeggio Vicenza**, STRADA PELOSA 241; (0444) 582 311, 20 mins by (no.1) from the station.

For eating out, look around PZA DEI SIGNORI. **Malvasia**, CONTRÀ DELLE MORETTE 5; (0444) 543 704, specialises in local dishes.

PALLADIO

This prosperous city was largely rebuilt in the 16th century to designs by Andrea di Pietro della Gondola, better known as **Palladio**, who had moved there from Padua at the age of 16 to become an apprectice stone mason. He gave his name to the **Palladian** style of architecture which applied elegant Romanesque concepts to classical forms. His first public commission was the imposing Basilica, on Pza dei Signori, hub of the city. This medieval palace was in danger of collapsing but he shored it up brilliantly with Ionic and Doric columns.

PADUA (PADOVA)

Home of one of Europe's oldest universities, **Padua** is a busy, down-to-earth town with plenty of shops and several large daily markets, while an abundance of artistic treasures fill its churches and museums. Though the northern parts are modern, following World War II destruction, the old town has attractive arcaded streets and squares, now traffic-free. South of the centre is PRATO DELLA VALLE, the largest square in Italy. A market is held there on Saturdays.

One work of art alone is reason enough to visit Padua – the glorious depiction of the lives of Mary and Jesus in the **Cappella degli Scrovegni** (Scrovegni Chapel), CORSO GARIBALDI. This Giotto masterpiece, which took three years to complete, has 38 panels in three tiers and is in virtually perfect condition.

In the **University**, V. VIII FEBBRAIO, founded in 1222, you can see the wooden desk used by Galileo, who taught natural philosophy there, and visit the old anatomical theatre.

Padua's other major attraction is **Il Santo** – the **Basilica di Sant' Antonio**, PZA DEL SANTO, which is visited by some five million pilgrims each year, St Anthony being one of Italy's best loved saints. The building is a mixture of styles (with a distinctly oriental flavour). The chapel contains 16th-century panels about the saint's life, but more notable are Donatello's bronze sculptures on the high altar and marble reliefs by Lombardo. Donatello's superb monument to Gattamelata, a famous medieval *condottiere* or mercenary leader, is the central point of the square, the first major bronze of the Renaissance.

The **Oratorio di San Giorgio** is home to some fine frescos, while the works in the nearby 15th-century **Scuola del Santo** include early Titians. Just to the south is the

Orto Botanico (Botanic Garden). Established in 1545, it was originally the university's herb garden and has changed little since.

PZA DEI SIGNORI has some attractive 15th–16th-century buildings, while to the south an unexciting cathedral adjoins the Romanesque Baptistery, lined with lovely 14th-century frescos.

Stazione Ferroviaria, 1478 88088, is at the northern edge of town, 15-min walk to centre or nos. 3/8/12/18.

Tourist Office: **APT** in the station; (049) 27767 (Mon–Sat 0900–1900 and Sun 0900–1230). *Padova Today* is a monthly mini-guide to what's on.

There is a wide choice of places to stay (try around PZA DEL SANTO), though booking is advisable. Two-star **Hotel Al Cason**, V. FRA PAOLO SCARPI 40, (049) 662 636, is handy for the station. **Youth hostel**: **Centro Ospitalita**, CITTÁ DI PADOVA, V. ALEARDI 30; (049) 875 2219 (nos.3/12/18). **Campsite**: **Montegrotto Terme**, STRADA ROMANA APPONESE; (049) 793 400 (15 mins by train, then 1-km walk). It has a pool and thermal baths.

PASSES

If you're aged 14–29 you can get a **'Rolling Padova'** pass (L.7.000), which gives a number of worthwhile discounts.

You should soon find a reasonably priced *trattoria* around PZA DEL SANTO, where the local specialities include *piperata* (mutton in wine sauce). Don't miss **Caffè Pedrocchi**, PZA CAVOUR, one of Italy's most famous cafés, where writers and artists used to meet during the last century when it stayed open all night. A grand staircase leads to a series of fabulous rooms for sipping your *cappuccino*.

VENICE (VENEZIA)

See p. 351.

TRIESTE

This city, on the border with Slovenia, once the chief port of the Austro-Hungarian Empire (up to 1918), is also the **Istrian** hinterland's window on the western world. Rebuilt in the 19th century, it is today a stately, solid place that relishes its role as a crossroads between east and west.

At **Trieste's** heart, the BORGO TERESIANO is a stately grid of regular streets which identify this city more with its central

The **Capitoline hill** formed the heart of Roman and medieval Trieste, and it is here that its oldest surviving buildings are to be found. Apart from the surviving remains of the ancient **Forum** (ancient Trieste was called Tergeste), there is the 11th-century Cathedral of San Giusto (beside the Forum), founded in the 5th century on the site of a Roman temple; there are splendid early medieval mosaics and frescos. Still on the Capitoline, the 15th-century Venetian-built **Castello** houses the Museo Civico in which can be seen a collection of weaponry and armour. Still close to the cathedral, the Museo di Storia ed Arte houses important Roman artefacts, as does the Orto Lapidario. In V. TEATRO ROMANO are the ruins of a Roman theatre.

European counterparts than with anything Italian. Here, the CORSO CAVOUR straddles the **Canal Grande**, an urban waterway where boats are moored. Beside it, in PZA PONTEROSSO, is the daily market. Trieste's civic heart lies in PZA DELL'UNITA D'ITALIA: you can't miss the vast **Palazzo del Comune del Governo** beside it, aglow with its mosaic ornamentation. Also in the *piazza* is one of Trieste's oldest cafés (1839), the **Caffè degli Specchi**. There is another, **Caffè San Marco**, on the other side of town, at VIA CESARE BATTISTI 18.

RAIL **Stazione Centrale**, PZA DELLA LIBERTÀ 8; ☎ 1478 88088.

i **Tourist Office**: the central office is at V. SAN NICOLO 20, ☎(040) 67961, and there is a second, smaller one in the station, ☎(040) 420 182. The regional information office is at V. ROSSINI 6; ☎(040) 363 952.

WHERE NEXT FROM TRIESTE?

Continue over the border into Slovenia to the caves at ***Postojna****, and to* ***Llubljana****; see the* ***Llubljana–Dubrovnik*** *route on p. 393–397.*

BOLOGNA – ASSISI – ROME

Route Detail

Bologna–Rome ETT table 620

Type	Frequency	Journey Time
Train	Every 2 hrs	2 hrs 45 mins

Bologna–Florence ETT table 620

Type	Frequency	Journey Time
Train	Every hr	1 hr

Florence–Arezzo ETT tables 615, 620

Type	Frequency	Journey Time
Train	Every hr	55 mins

Arezzo–Perugia ETT table 615

Type	Frequency	Journey Time
Train	Every 2 hrs	1 hr 5 mins

Perugia–Assisi ETT table 615

Type	Frequency	Journey Time
Train	Every hr	20 mins

Assisi–Spoleto ETT tables 615, 625

Type	Frequency	Journey Time
Train	9 daily	40 mins

Spoleto–Rome ETT table 625

Type	Frequency	Journey Time
Train	Every hr	1 hr 20 mins

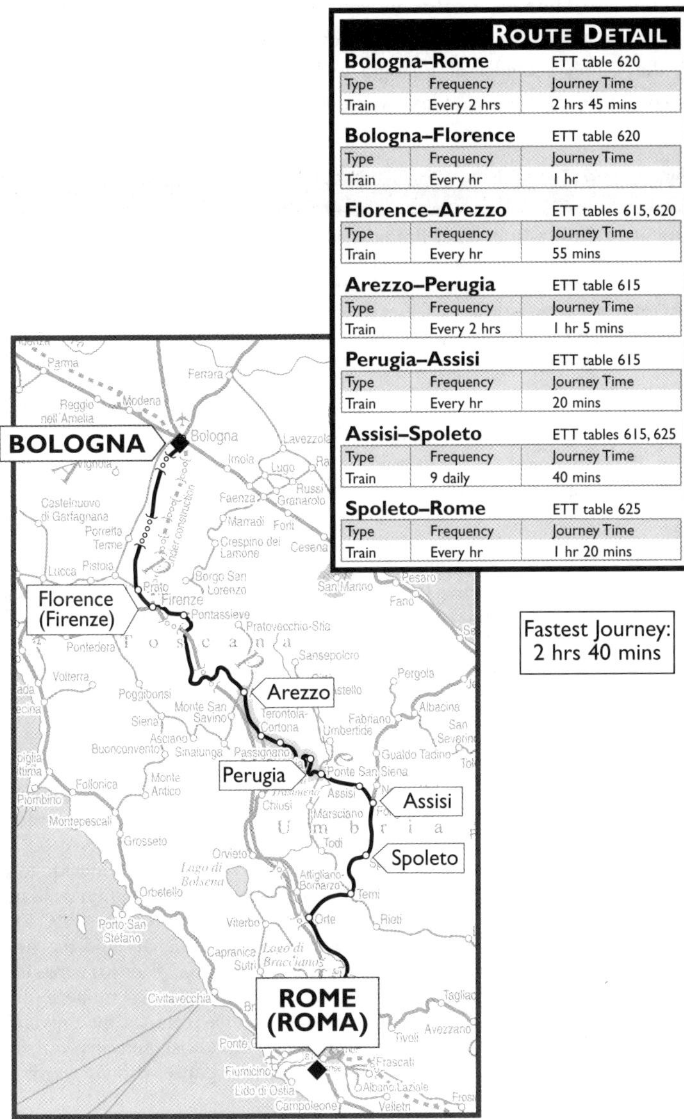

Fastest Journey: 2 hrs 40 mins

Bologna – Assisi – Rome

From the graceful old university town of **Bologna** at the threshold of the **Apennines**, you venture into **Umbria**, with its ancient hilltop towns – the garden of Eden to Dante. Art and history are intermingled in such places as the great pilgrimage city of **Assisi**, the Umbrian capital of **Perugia** and the old Roman town of **Spoleto**. **Florence** and **Rome** demand at least a few days each.

BOLOGNA

The capital of **Emilia-Romagna**, **Bologna** is home to Europe's oldest university, founded in 1088. It has all you'd expect of a civilised, affluent university seat: the streetscape has real dignity in its arcades, red- and ochre-coloured buildings, stucco façades, greatly varied porticoes, church spires, palaces and medieval towers, the latter built as status symbols by the city's wealthy nobles.

Bologna, Italy's foodie capital

Bologna has a gastronomic reputation in Italy second to none. Even a sandwich is likely to be noticeably high quality. For good cheaper restaurants *(trattorie, pizzerie)*, try around the small streets near PZA VERDI, the hub of student life.

The university's first permanent home is today in **Palazzo Poggi**, VIA ZAMBONI. The two adjoining 13th-century squares, PZA MAGGIORE and PZA NETTUNO, make the obvious central starting point. Around them lie the **Palazzo Comunale** (the town hall, which now houses Bologna's modern art collection), the 15th-century **Palazzo del Podestà, the Palazzo dei Banchi** and the **Basilica of San Petronio**. The Fountain of Neptune (1564) spouts in the north-west corner. At PZA SAN STEFANO, the churches of **San Stefano** (**Crocifisso**, **Santo Sepolcro**, **Trinità**, **San Vitale** and **Sant'Agricola**) make up a complex, complete with cloisters and courtyards, that has retained its ancient atmosphere.

Getting around Bologna

Central **Bologna** can be seen on foot. The bus system covers the suburbs (route maps from Tourist Office). **Tickets**, sold at tobacconists' kiosks, are good for 1 hr once validated on board. [illegible] pass is available.

The two most distinctive towers still standing are the 98-m **Asinelli** (with a wonderful, if dizzying, panorama from the top; 486 steps up) and its inferior partner the **Garisenda**, by PZA DI PORTA RAVEGNANA. A row of 666 arcaded porticoes ascends a hillside to the 18th-century **Basilica de San Luca**, a 35-min walk from **Meloncello** (reached by 🚌 no. 20 from PZA MAGGIORE), for a splendid vista of the city and the Apennines that adjoin it. Another great place for views is the PARCO DE VILLA GHIGI, an area of Apennine foothills given to the city by a former rector of the university. Walk up from the PZA MAGGIORE and step out from city centre to a wild, open expanse with vineyards and cattle.

Stazione Centrale, 1 km north of PZA MAGGIORE; walk along VIA DEL'INDIPENDENZ (bus nos.25/30). A memorial to casualties of the 1980 station bombing stands by the renovated station entrance.

Tourist Offices: **railway station**, ☎(051) 246 541, fax: (051) 25 19 47 (Mon–Sat 0900–1900); **airport**, ☎/fax: (051) 647 203 (Mon–Sat 0900–1300 and 1400–1600); and 6 PZA MAGGIORE, ☎(051) 239 660, fax: (051) 231 454 (Mon–Sat 0900–1900 and Sun 0900–1400).

The Tourist Office has a wide-ranging list of **hotels** and **pensione** in all categories. **Youth hostel**: 5 VIA VIADAGOLA, ☎(051) 501 810, and 14 VIA VIADAGOLA, ☎(051) 519 202, 6 km from the centre. **Camping**: **Città di Bologna**, ☎(051) 325 016, fax: (051) 325 318, open all year.

WHERE NEXT FROM BOLOGNA?

__Bologna__ is on the line from __Naples__ (p. 340) to __Venice__ (p. 351), via __Florence__ (p. 328); see ETT table 620.

You can also take the line along the Adriatic coast to __Brindisi__, though this trip isn't Italy at its best. On the way you could pause at __Rimini__, a somewhat charmless resort but with an excellent beach and a 20-mins bus trip from the tiny independent republic of __San Marino__ (just 60 sq km of it), memorably perched on the slopes of __Monte Titano__. Other worthwhile detours include __Peschici Calenella__, east of __San Severo__ on the __Gargano massif__ (a rugged limestone coast), and the area around __Monópoli__ (notable for its Trulli *– curious dry-stone, white domed structures of feudal origins). __Brindisi__, the port near the 'heel' of Italy, has a useful ferry from __Rimini__ to __Patras__ in Greece (ETT table 2770).*

The __Bologna__ to __Milan__ service (tables 611, 620, 630; approx 2–3 hrs) runs via __Modena__ (a quietly attractive old town with a Romanesque cathedral and with a fine collection of art and illuminated manuscripts within the Palazzo dei Musei*) and __Parma__ (a household name for its ham and cheese, worth a stop for the frescos by Correggio in the cathedral and the church of San Giovanni Evangelista).*

DAY TRIP FROM BOLOGNA

Ravenna (just over 1 hr; ETT table 621), a quiet place today, was the centre of Byzantine rule in Italy during the 6th and 7th centuries AD. The most impressive reminders of these periods, and the major reason for visiting the town, are Ravenna's famed **mosaics** (the major sights cluster in the north-west corner of the old town). The 6th-century octagonal **Basilica of San Vitale** features depictions of the Byzantine Emperor Justinian and Empress Theodora. **Sant'Apollinare Nuovo** dates from the same period; its walls are lined with green and gold mosaics showing processions of saints (on the men's side of the church) and virgins (on the women's side). In the grounds are the **Mausoleum of Galla Placidia**, lined with richly coloured mosaics, and the **National Museum**. The station is about 500 m east of town; walk down VIALE FARINI and V. DIAZ. **Tourist Office**: 8 V. SALARIA, ☎(0544) 35 404; in the centre of town.

FLORENCE (FIRENZE)

See p.328.

AREZZO

Arezzo was a major settlement in Etruscan, Roman and medieval times. Always a wealthy city, today its economy rests on jewellers, goldsmiths and antiques. Much of the centre is modern, but there are still attractive winding streets in the hill-top old town, with its Renaissance houses and the handsome Pza Grande.

One of the masterpieces of Italian Renaissance painting and the city's major attraction is Piero della Francesca's brilliant fresco cycle of the *Legend of the True Cross* (1452–66), on display in the 14th-century **church of San Francesco**, V. della Madonna del Prato, in the centre of the old town.

The spacious **cathedral**, begun in 1278, lit by 16th-century stained glass, is adorned by Piero della Francesca's fresco of Mary Magdalene, near the organ. The **Galleria e Museo Medioevale e Moderno**, Via di San Loretino 8, contains an exceptional collection of majolica as well as sculpture dating from the 10th to the 17th centuries. **Santa Maria delle Grazie**, Via di Santa Maria, is a particularly fine 15th-century church which contains a high altar by Andrea della Robbia.

Arezzo's Antiques Fair

Don't expect to find a bargain by attending the **Fiera Antiquaria** (Antiques Fair), in Pza Grande on the first Sun of every month. Hugely popular with an ever more international clientele, it's the place to buy serious antique furniture, terracotta, linen and of course jewellery. Accommodation gets very heavily booked up.

There's less to detain you in the lower town, though you may like to pause at the **Museo Archeologico**, V. Margaritone 10, in an old monastery not far east of the station; it has a collection of Roman Aretine ware (50 BC to AD 60–70 terracotta with a shiny red glaze and adorned with bas-reliefs), Etruscan bronzes and 1st-century-BC vases. Nearby is a ruined Roman amphitheatre, the **Amfiteatro Romano**.

RAIL ☎ 1478 88088. In the modern sector, west of the centre: walk up the hill to the old town.

i **Tourist Office**: by the station, ☎(0575) 377 678. Open daily 0915–2000, Apr–Sept; Mon–Fri 0830–1800, Sat 0830–1300, Oct–Mar. The latest information on accommodation is posted outside the **APT office**, Pza Risorgimento 116, ☎(0575) 23 952.

Rooms are difficult to find over the first weekend of every month, but you should have few problems at other times. There are several budget options near the station. **Private hostels**: **Villa Severi**, V. F. Redi 13, ☎(0575) 299 047 (bus no.4).

PERUGIA

Warlike and belligerent, the splendid capital of Umbria was smitten by strife almost until the 19th century and has a host of monuments bearing an undeniably martial face. Ignore the unattractive modern suburbs and head straight for the almost intact medieval centre, by bus or escalator. From PZA ITALIA the pedestrianised CORSO VANNUCCI, lined with fortified palaces, cafés and shops – the centre of activities for a cosmopolitan crowd almost around the clock – runs north to the city's heart in PZA IV NOVEMBRE, where the **Duomo** (cathedral) is located. All the other major sights are within easy walking distance of here.

The **Duomo**, PZA IV NOVEMBRE, is a large plain medieval building, supposedly home to the Virgin Mary's wedding ring. In the centre of the square, but undergoing restoration, is the 13th-century Fontana Maggiore, a fountain that's a triumph of decoration by Nicola and Giovanni Pisano. Facing the fountain, the somewhat forbidding **Palazzo dei Priori**, CORSO VANNUCCI, Perugia's civic headquarters since 1297, has a great Gothic portal and long rows of windows. Fan-like steps lead up to the *Sala dei Notari*, covered with an entertaining array of frescos. **The Galleria Nazionale dell' Umbria**, on the 4th floor, contains works notably by Pinturicchio and Perugino, and is Italy's most important repository of Umbrian art; it also has a few Tuscan masterpieces, including Piero della Francesca's *Madonna and Saints with Child* and a triptych by Fra Angelico.

DAY TRIP FROM PERUGIA

Gúbbio (10 buses a day run from Perugia's PZA DEI PARTIGIANI, by the FCU station) is a typical Umbrian hill town, largely medieval, with steep narrow streets, grey and tiered. The huge PZA GRANDE DELLA SIGNORIA, home of the turreted **Palazzo de Consoli**, provides superb views, while the **Museo Civico** contains the most complete extant record of the ancient Umbrian language, in seven bronze tablets – the **Tavole Eugubine** (300–100 BC).

A funicular climbs to the pink-brick **Basilica of Sant'Ubaldo** from Porta Romana, wherein lies St Ubaldo, Gúbbio's bishop saint.

Tourist Office: PZA ODERISI 6, ☎(075) 922 0693.

See also **Collegio della Mercanzia** with its magnificent 15th-century carvings, while the restored frescos of the **Collegio del Cambio, the Bankers' Guild** , are considered to be Perugino's finest works.

Authorship of the well-preserved 14th-century Tomb of Pope Benedict XI is unknown, but it's clearly the work of a master sculptor. Here too is a magnificent 15th-century, stained-glass window. The **Museo Archeologico Nazionale dell'Umbria**, in the monastery alongside San Domenico, includes Etruscan artefacts as well as Roman sculpture.

Don't miss the 10th-century **church of San Pietro**, south-east from the centre (BORGO XX GIUGNO). The decorations, dating from the Renaissance, are unbelievably rich, with scarcely an unadorned patch. The paintings were executed by a host of artists, including Perugino. A highlight is the magnificently carved choir.

FS (State Railway), 1478 88088 (toll free); 4 km south-west of the centre (an uphill walk) or 15 mins by bus (nos. 6/7/8/9/11/27/29/32/36) to PZA ITALIA. Tickets from a forecourt booth or machine by the entrance. The private **FCU** (Ferrovia Centrale Umbria) railway terminal is **Stazione Sant'Anna**, (075) 572 3947, from which you can get a *scala mobile* (escalator) to PZA ITALIA. There is an ATM in the station.

Tourist Office: **Palazzo dei Priori**, PZA IV NOVEMBRE, (075) 572 3327 or 573 6458. Mon–Sat 0830–1330 and 1530–1830, Sun 0900–1300. Get the monthly listing *Perugia What, Where, When* for detailed information.

There is plenty of cheap, central accommodation, but book ahead if you're coming during the international jazz festival (10 days every July). **Youth hostel**: 2 mins from the **Duomo**: **HI**: V. BONTEMPI 13, (075) 5722 880 11 **Rocolo**, COLLE DELLA TRINITÀ STR. FONTANA, 517 8550, or you can rough camp by **Lago Trasimeno**, reached by bus and train.

ST FRANCIS AND THE BASILICA DI SAN FRANCESCO

San Francesco (St Francis) expressed the wish to be buried simply, but the news of his death (in 1226) brought a flood of donations from all over Europe and construction of the **Basilica di San Francesco**, at the western end of the old town, began in 1228. It has a choice collection of masterpieces, making it something of an art gallery in itself; several great artists were employed, inspiring each other into innovative forms of painting that departed from the rigid Byzantine conventions. The basilica consists of two churches: the **lower church**, designed for peaceful meditation by the saint's tomb, and the soaring **upper church**, intended to mollify the faction who wanted a glorious monument.

The upper church suffered severe damage during the 1997 earthquake, and is closed for restoration.

ASSISI

One name is irrevocably linked with **Assisi** – St Francis. Born there in 1182, he practised what he preached: poverty, chastity and obedience, leading to love of God and appreciation of all living things. He founded the Franciscan order, and his home town became (and remains) a major pilgrimage centre, with the action concentrated around the Basilica di San Francesco, erected in his memory at the western end of the old town and adorned with some of the most magnificent frescos in Italy.

St Francis's life initiated a wealth of art and architecture in Assisi. Still largely medieval, and clinging to a side of **Monte Subasio** high above the green Umbrian countryside, the town is instantly familiar from the landscapes in the frescos of the Umbrian painters.

The PZA DEL COMUNE, in the centre of the old town, is dominated by the 1st-century-AD **Tempio di Minerva** – a Roman temple partly incorporated into what is now the church of Santa Maria.

To the east of the centre, below the cathedral, is the **Basilica di Santa Chiara**. Santa Chiara (St Clare) was an early friend of St Francis and, with his guidance, established the Order of the Poor Clares, the female equivalent of the Franciscans.

The old fortress, known as **Rocca Maggiore,** towers dramatically above the northern edge of the city, providing panoramic views of the town and surrounding countryside.

The **Basilica di Santa Maria degli Angeli**, near the station, surrounds a chapel used by St Francis and the spot where he died. Much more evocative, if you fancy a 4-km forest walk to the north-east, is **Eremo delle Carceri**, on the slopes of Monte Subasio. It was here, in caves, that the original Franciscans lived. You can see the cell later used by St Francis and the altar from where he addressed the birds.

Day trip from Assisi

Spello (10 mins by train) is the epitome of an Umbrian hill town, with tiers of pink houses, cobbled alleys and churches, and Roman gateways. The 13th-century **church of Santa Maria Maggiore** contains a chapel full of brilliantly restored frescos by Pinturicchio and a 15th-century ceramic floor. Despite the quiet beauty of the town, it's far from overrun with tourists and is generally much quieter than **Assisi**. From the station it's a short walk up to the old town.

Tourist Office: Pza Matteotti 3. Open only in summer, ☎(0742) 301 009.

☎(075) 804 0272. This is not in Assisi proper, but in **Santa Maria degli Angeli**, about 5 km south-west and uphill all the way. Buses run to the centre every half hour.

Tourist Office: Pza del Comune 12, ☎(075) 812 532. Mon–Fri 0800–1400 and 1530–1830, Sat 0900–1300 and 1530–1830, and Sun 0900–1300. It provides a map in English and has information about accommodation, including pilgrim hostels.

There is plenty of accommodation of every grade, but booking is advisable – essential for Easter, the **Feast of St Francis** (3–4 Oct) and **Calendimaggio** (a medieval celebration of spring held in early May). **Youth hostel**: V. Valecchi, ☎(075) 816 767, 10-min walk from Pza San Pietro. **Campsite**: **Fontemaggio,** ☎(075) 813 636, 4 km east of town and uphill. Take a taxi or follow the signs from **Porta Cappuccini**.

Spoleto

Founded by Umbrians in the 6th century BC, **Spoleto** has an interesting mix of Roman and medieval sights, the most spectacular being the cathedral, adorned on its entrance façade with eight rose windows of differing sizes. Its campanile, propped up by a flying buttress, was constructed from various bits of Roman masonry and other un-medieval elements – and yet still manages to present itself as a perfect blend of Romanesque and Renaissance. Within, a baroque makeover rather ruined the effect, though Fra Filippo Lippi's magnificent frescos depicting the life of the Virgin are timeless. Also of interest is **Cappella Erioli**, with a *Madonna and Child* by Pinturicchio, and the Cosmati marble floor.

MONASTIC TIME WARP

For a glimpse of a little-changed monastery in Spoleto, seek out **San Salvatore**, in the lower town's cemetery. Built by 5th-century monks, it has something of a pagan look.

After several centuries of power the town fell into obscurity until being chosen (in 1958) to host Italy's leading performing arts festival in June/July, the **Festival dei Due Mondi**, which transforms tranquil Spoleto into an unrecognisably invigorated place; prices, inevitably, soar.

Part of the small **Roman Amphitheatre**, PZA LIBERTÀ at the southern end of the old centre, has been carefully restored and is now used for festival performances. Another section is occupied by the **convent of Sant'Agata**, which houses a small collection of Roman artefacts. A walk through the **Arco di Druso** (AD 23), 100 m north, leads to PZA DEL MERCATO, which was the Roman forum and is still a marketplace and the hub of Spoleto's social life. It's a great place to linger, surrounded by attractive old streets and overlooked by the huge hulks of medieval buildings.

Nearby, the small **Pinacoteca Comunale** is housed in the **Palazzo del Municipio**, a visit to which requires a guide. The décor is magnificent and some of the paintings outstanding, especially in the Umbrian section. **Sant'Eufemia**, above the **Duomo**, is a lovely 12th-century Romanesque church remarkable for its early capitals and columns, and for the matroneum, the upper gallery where the women worshipped, segregated from the men below.

The **Rocca**, a huge 14th-century castle to the south-east of town, guards one of the finest engineering achievements of medieval times, the **Ponte delle Torri**: a bridge 240 m long, supported by ten arches 80 m high. From it there are magnificent views of the gorge it spans and there's a pleasant 2-km walk (turn right) leading to **San Pietro**, with a façade adorned by some of the region's finest Romanesque sculpture.

RAIL ☎ 1478 88088. In the lower town, with a long uphill walk south to the medieval town (or orange bus to PZA LIBERTÀ – tickets from the station bar). Free city map from the station newsstand.

i **Tourist Office**: PZA LIBERTÀ 7, ☎(0743) 220 311. Open Mon–Fri 0900–1300 and 1400–1700, Sat–Sun 1000–1300 and 1630–1930.

Book well ahead during the **summer arts festival**. At that time accommodation can be very pricey. At other times, look in the lower town. Alternatively, try **Foligno**, 26 km north-east and linked by trains that run until late; it has a **youth hostel** at PZA SAN GIACOMO 11, ☎(0742) 52 882. **Campsites**: **Camping Monteluco**, ☎(0742) 220 358, 15-min walk south from PZA LIBERTÀ, is very small and opens only in summer. **Il Girasole**, ☎(0742) 51 335, in the village of **Petrognano**, is larger and has a pool (hourly bus from station).

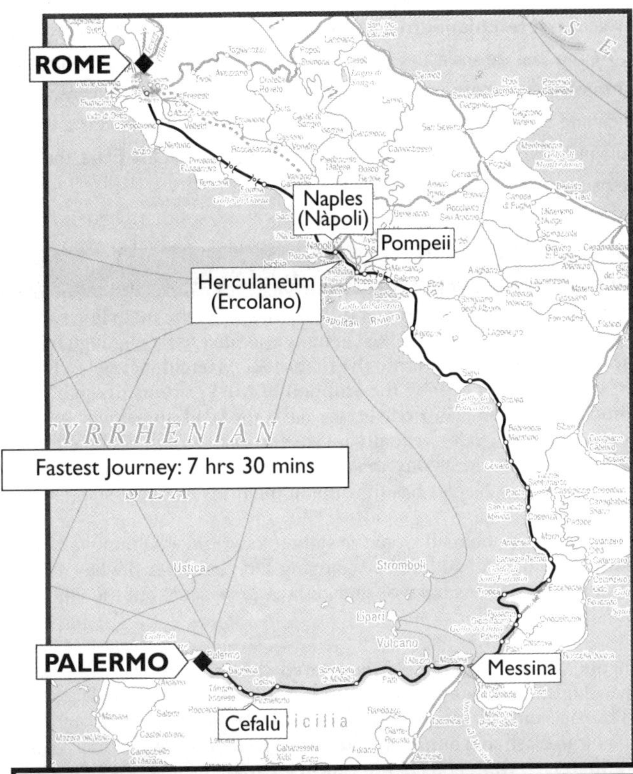

ROUTE DETAIL

Roma–Palermo ETT tables 620, 640

Type	Frequency	Journey Time
Train	4 daily	12 hrs

Roma–Napoli ETT table 620

Type	Frequency	Journey Time
Train	Every hr	1 hr 45 mins

Napoli–Ercolano

Type	Frequency	Journey Time
Train	1-2 every hr	10 mins

Ercolano–Pompeii

Type	Frequency	Journey Time
Train	1-2 every hr	20 mins

Pompeii–Messina ETT table 640

Type	Frequency	Journey Time
Train	3 per day	6 hrs 10 mins

Messina–Cefalu ETT table 640

Type	Frequency	Journey Time
Train	8 daily	2 hrs 40 mins

Cefalu–Palermo ETT table 640

Type	Frequency	Journey Time
Train	8 daily	50 mins

This coastal tour of southern Italy really gets going at **Naples**, a worthy stop in its own right, beyond which are **Herculaneum** and **Pompeii**, two of the greatest sites in the ancient world. At the 'toe' of mainland Italy, you board a train ferry from **Villa San Giovanni** to **Messina**, on the isle of Sicily. Successive invasions of Romans, Arabs, Normans, French and Spanish have shaped the Sicilian character; the land is a strange mixture of fertile plains, volcanic lava fields and virtual desert, while **Mt Etna**, the great volcano, threatens to erupt within the next ten years.

THE CIRCUMVESUVIANA

Although both **Herculaneum** (Ercolano) and Pompeii are on the main line south of Naples, both can be reached by taking the Circumvesuviana narrow-gauge railway which runs between Naples and Sorrento (ETT table 623). **Herculaneum** is a Roman settlement that was buried in AD 9 by the eruption of **Mt Vesuvius**, though it was engulfed by mud rather than ash. Excavations have revealed an astonishing time capsule, with many house façades virtually intact: you can see half-timbered buildings and even the balconies. In its day this was a wealthy subtopia. The **National Archaeological Museum** in Naples has the bulk of the finds from the site.

Five buses a day zigzag up the road from the station to within a 30-min walk of the summit of **Vesuvius**, where in addition to enjoying the view over the bay you can peer into the crater. There's no smoke or molten lava to be seen, but the volcano is still active.

Like Herculaneum, most of the objects discovered during excavations are in the National Archaeological Museum in Naples, but **Pompeii** is much the larger (and more touristy) site, its ruins mesmeric and eerie. This substantial Roman town, excavated from the volcanic ash that buried it, gives a real feel for life at the time: you can see original graffiti on the walls and chariot ruts in the road, wander into houses and courtyards, and even lose the crowds in some of the more remote areas. Highlights include the **Forum**, the **Forum Baths**, the **Villa of the Mysteries**, the outdoor and indoor theatres, and the house of I Ceius Secundus and the house of the Vettii (both have marvellous wall paintings), and, the Lupunar (a brothel complete with beds).

MESSINA

Throughout its history **Messina**, Sicily's nearest port to the mainland, was the victim of a massive earthquake in 1908 that shook for two months and claimed 84,000 lives and a massive attack by US bombers in 1943, though even those Events can't take away its glorious setting beneath the mountains. Much has been rebuilt in a stable, squat style. The well-reconstructed **cathedral**, PZA DEL DUOMO, has an ornate Gothic central entrance portal and mosaics in the three apses: try to catch the moving figurines on the clock as it chimes at midday, and climb the tower for the view.

Trains from the mainland arrive on **FS** ferries at **Stazione Marittima**, a short walk to the city's **Stazione Centrale** in PZA DELLA REPUBBLICA, – departure point for city and long-distance buses. National information number: ☎ 1478 88088.

Tourist Office: PZA DELLA REPUBBLICA, ☎(090) 674 236, Mon–Sat 0800–1400, closed Sun.

There is limited accommodation, and the only youth hostel is at Ali (25 km) – PZA SPIRITO SANTO, open May–Oct. The nearest **campsite**, DELLO STRETTO, is remotely situated on the city's northern edge at PUNTO DEL FARO.

CEFALÙ

Crammed between a rocky promontory and the sea, this idylically attractive little fishing port and beach resort is a great place to rest, with plenty of restaurants, walks and views, and a variety of characterful corners and buildings, particularly in CORSO RUGGERO.

The Arabo-Norman **cathedral**, a twin-towered, fortified medieval structure dominates the town from its position just beneath the **Rocca**, the rock which protects it. It contains some of Sicily's best preserved – and earliest (1148) – mosaics. Dating from the time of the Norman kings, these are the work of Byzantine craftsmen. See the *Christ Pantocrator* in the main apse: it's one of the great works of medieval Sicily.

The **Museo Mandralisca**, V. MANDRALISCA 13, contains, along with a variety of artifacts including some Greek ceramics, an important painting by Antonello da Messina, *Portrait of an Unknown Man* (c1460). Above the town, on the *Rocca* – ascend from PZA GARIBALDI – a ruined medieval fortification provides magnificent views out over **Cefalù** and the coast. The attractive beach offers shallow bathing.

V. MORO, 10-min walk from CORSO RUGGERO, ☎(1478 88088).

Tourist Office: CORSO RUGGERO 77, ☎(0921) 421 050, Mon–Fri 0800–1400 and 1600–1900, Sat 0800–1400. (Oct–May); Mon–Sat 0800–1400, 1530–2030 (June–Sept).

DAY TRIPS

MT ETNA

The chief scenic interest of this stretch of coast is **Mt Etna**, the 3223-m active volcano that threatens to engulf the towns in the ultra-fertile plain beneath it.

For a superb scenic route round the mountain, take the *ferrovia circumetna* from Catania's station on Corso Italia (not the same station as you stop at on the line from Messina and Taormina) and ride 2 hrs 30 mins to Randazzo and back (same trains continue to join the main line at Riposto).

Further down the east coast is **Siracusa** (Syracuse), the power base in Sicily from the 5th century BC up to the year 878. Notable sites to visit are **Neapolis** with its supremely preserved Greek and Roman theatres, early Christian catacombs by the church of San Giovanni, and, on the finest square in the town, a cathedral built out of an ancient Doric temple. The **Museo Archeologico National** is a treasure house of Greek antiquities, including vases and statuary.

There is a variety of **hotel** accommodation here in all categories. **Campsites: Costa Ponente**, (0921) 420 085 and, beside it, **Sanfilippo**, (0921) 420 184 – both about 3 km west of town.

PALERMO

With huge **Monte Pellegrino** to the north and an arc of mountains behind the city to the west, this somewhat undervisited and picturesquely decaying port looks tremendous from the ferries that arrive from **Naples**, **Genoa** and **Sardinia**. Wartime bombing, severe neglect and a bad criminal record have left their mark on **Palermo**, but it has great atmosphere, with a ancient-feeling labyrinth of narrow alleys and streets, hidden squares and ancient *souk*-like markets. More North African than Italian, the **Vucciria** in V. MACCHERONAI, or the excellent **Ballaro** in PZA BALLARO (near the station), signal Palermo's status as a meeting of two continents.

The rich legacy of the ancient Greeks can be studied in one of southern Italy's best museums, the **Museo Archeologico Regionale**, at PZA OLIVELLA; highlights include the panels of relief sculpture from temples at **Selinunte**.

Deep inside the **Palazzo dei Normanni**, are the lavishly ornamental mosaics by Arab and Byzantine craftsmen (1150). Its ceiling is the finest surviving example of **Fatamid** architecture anywhere. Other mosaics in the city can be seen in the **Martorana** in PZA BELLINI (12th century).

The other great milestone of Sicilian style is the baroque: the local Palermitan baroque is ornate and ebullient. The richest examples of it can be seen in the interiors of the little oratories of **Rosario di San Domenico** at V. BAMBINAI 2, and of Santa Zita, behind the **church of Santa Zita** at V. VALVERDE 3. In both, the stuccatore Giacomo Serpotta (1656–1732) unleashed the full throttle of his exuberant style. His remarkably realistic stucco figures run riot around the walls. The QUATRO CANTI of 1611 is Palermo's finest piazza, with a statue of a Spanish king in each corner and a fountain in the middle.

GETTING AROUND PALERMO

A good way to get around **Palermo** is by bus. The **Palermo City Pass** costs L1500 for an hour or L5000 for a day pass. For information, tel: 167 018 378 (toll-free), although only broken English is spoken.

Stazione Centrale, in PZA GIULIO CESARE, is at the southern end of the city – rail information: 1478 88088). Located in the same square, and in the streets around it, are some of the termini of local, provincial and long-distance bus services. **Stazione Marittima**, V. FRANCESCO CRISPI, (091) 602 1111) in the east, by the port, is the focus of ferry services **(Tirrenia Shipping Line)** from **Naples**, **Cagliari** (Sardinia), **Genoa, Ustica** and occasional hydrofoil connections to the *Aeolian Islands*. There is an ATM in the station.

Tourist Office: in the station, (091) 616 5914 – The main office is at PZA CASTELNUOVO 34, ☎(091) 583 847 or 605 8351, Mon–Fri 0830–1400, 1500–1800, Sat 0830–1400 (both offices). Ask for *Un Mese a Palermo*, the local monthly entertainment guide. Otherwise look at the daily newspaper, *L'Ora*, for listings.

Cheap accommodation is easy to find, though much of it tacky. The mid-range is well catered for. Away from the city, at **Sferracavallo** near the sea, are two **campsites** – **Camping Trinacria**, V. BARCARELLO, ☎(091) 530 590, and **Camping dell'Ulivo**, V. PEGASO, ☎(091) 533 021. The only youth hostel is open from the end of July through August. **Pensionato San Saverio**, V. DI CRISTINA. Call in at **Albergherie Viaggi**, PIAZZA SAN SAVERIO 3 ☎(091) 6518576 to make a reservation and to get directions. The **Hotel Cortese**, V. SCARPARELLI 16 ☎(091) 331722 is a central and clean alternative.

WHERE NEXT FROM PALERMO?

Ferries (ETT table 2655; once a week; 14 hrs 30 mins) depart to ***Cágliari*** *(**see p. 386**), capital of the island of* Sardinia, *as well as to* ***Naples*** *(table 2625; once a week),* ***Livorno*** *(table 2588; three days a week; 17 hrs) and* ***Genoa*** *(table 2547; weekly; 20 hrs).*

Served by the ferry from ***Palermo*** *to* ***Naples*** *as well as shorter 50-min hydrofoil crossings from* ***Milazzo*** *(west of Messina), the* Aeolian Islands *(also known as the* Eolian Islands *or the* Lipari Islands*) rise dramatically from warm, azure waters north of Sicily. Thought by the ancients to be the home of Aeolus, the God of the Winds, the volcanic archipelago has wonderful scenery and rich marine life including turtles, hammer-fish and flying-fish.* ***Lipari****, the main island, has an old walled town, while the isles* Vulcano *and* Strómboli *each have extremely active volcanos.*

STRÓMBOLI

Strómboli provides a terrific display almost constantly (it's the world's most active volcano). Enquire locally about day cruises.

DAY TRIPS FROM PALERMO

Mondello (about 10 km), is Palermo's beach resort, while **Monreale** (about 8 km to the south-west), is the focus of a splendid medieval cathedral containing a great series of Byzantine-style mosaics. **Monreale** also affords a **stunning view** over the city. At **Segesta** (about 65 km), to the north west, a near-complete Greek temple survives, while at **Bagheria** (about 14 km), in the south-east, the quirky baroque **Villa Palagonia** is an oddity in an area once renowned for the holiday homes of the 17th- and 18th-century nobility.

All of these places are accessible by bus.

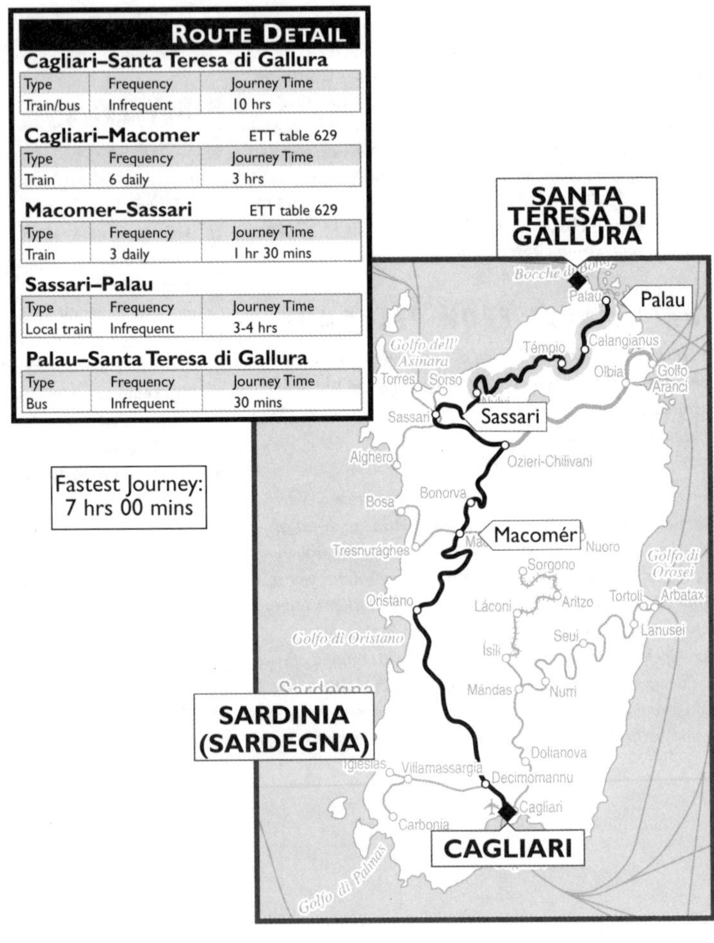

ROUTE DETAIL

Cagliari–Santa Teresa di Gallura

Type	Frequency	Journey Time
Train/bus	Infrequent	10 hrs

Cagliari–Macomer ETT table 629

Type	Frequency	Journey Time
Train	6 daily	3 hrs

Macomer–Sassari ETT table 629

Type	Frequency	Journey Time
Train	3 daily	1 hr 30 mins

Sassari–Palau

Type	Frequency	Journey Time
Local train	Infrequent	3-4 hrs

Palau–Santa Teresa di Gallura

Type	Frequency	Journey Time
Bus	Infrequent	30 mins

This trip through the Mediterranean island of **Sardinia** enables some rewarding side visits to such coastal gems as **Alghera**, and to **Arbatax** via a railway that twists through the mountains. Resorts here are low-key, and nightlife is not that busy, except in July and August, when half of Europe seems to converge on it: June and September are much better. Some 7,000 ancient **Nuraghic** fortress houses (or *nuraghis*), dating back to 1600 BC, dot the island.

CAGLIARI

The largest and most modern-looking city on the island, **Cagliari** is nevertheless thought to be of Phoenician origin. Much was rebuilt following wartime bomb damage, but there's a compact old city, inside the imposing 13th-century **Pisan** walls, with a warren of brick-paved lanes leading to the tree-lined piazzas. Seek out the two Pisan towers – the **Torre San Pancrazio** and **Torre delle Elefante** – and stroll the medieval quarter around the BASTIONE DE SAINT-REMY and the PORTE DI LEONI. The **National Archaeology Museum** in the PZA ARSENALE contains an expansive and well-documented collection of **Nuraghi** artefacts. The Romanesque **cathedral**, built by Pisa, is inside the massive walls. On the north-west side of the citadel is the Roman **amphitheatre**, hewn from the rock in the 3rd century AD; it stages summer performances. The 5th-century Byzantine **church of San Saturno** is just off the busy VLE CIMITERO. Visit the beach at **Poette** and the **Sella del Diavolo** stone formation in the bay, and wander to the salt marshes beyond the dunes to observe cranes and pink flamingos.

ENTERTAINMENT AND EVENTS IN CALIARI

The free bilingual monthly *By Night* magazine (available at most Tourist Offices) provides listings for cinemas, concerts and cultural Events.

The annual **Festival of Sant'Efisio** (from 1 May), honouring the saint martyred under the Emperor Diocletian, features a solemn procession with horse-borne participants attired in traditional red costumes.

FERRIES TO CAGLIARI

There are overnight ferries, two weekly (12-hr passage) to **Cagliari**: one from **Palermo** and one from **Trápani** (both operated by **Tirrenia Lines**). Other ferries operate to Cagliari from **Naples, Civitavecchia** and **Genoa** (ETT International Shipping pages).

The modern **FdS Railway Museum** (at Monserrato in the northern suburbs) should interest railway enthusiasts, while the **botanical gardens**, V. IGNAZIO, make a pleasant retreat from the summer heat.

Maritime Station, PZA MATEOTTI, for all ships. **Tirennia** bookings at 1 V. CAMPIDANO C/O AGENAVE, (070) 666 065. The **FS** stately 19th-century marble station, served by mainline trains to **Sassari** and the northern ports of **Porto Torres** and **Olbia**, is on PZA MATTEOTTI, V. SASSARI side. The **Cagliari FS** station has a bank (Mon–Fri 0830–1330,

BRANCH LINE TO ARBATAX

The **FdS** narrow-gauge train runs once daily to **Arbatax** on the east coast. It allows access to the following towns, as well as spectacular mountain views from both sides of the train.

Inland, **Seui** gives access to the **Barbagia** and some of Sardinia's highest and wildest peaks through the **Gennargentu** mountain range. Accommodation (Hotel Moderno, ☎(0782) 54 621) and tourist services are available in the compact little mountain town.

Arbatax has bright red (porphyry) cliffs and many isolated coves with sandy beaches.

Tourist information is available through the **FdS office**, ☎(0782) 667 285.

This tortuous rail line includes a unique full circle as it descends from **Barbagia** through tunnels and stone viaducts into the plateau town of **Tortoli**. Note the many large prickly pear cactuses along the rail line after **Tortoli**. Their fruit is cherished as a delicacy by locals. From **Tortoli**, an **ARST** bus runs to **Nuoro**, to make a very scenic link (check connections) back to the mainline.

1430–1530) with ATM inside the main information/ticketing lobby. **FdS** tiny corner station is 3 km away at the PZA REPUBBLICA on V. DANTE side. Information through **ESIT** or at the station, ☎(070) 580 076. Local rail schedules will be shortened as massive rail work begins.

Buses: **ARST** ☎(1678) 65042 intercity and **Cagliari** city transit buses use the newish station on PZA MATTEOTTI. All main urban sights within a 20-min walk, but some steep hills could be an incentive to taking a city bus. Local buses terminate at bus station on PZA MATTEOTTI (L.1200 for a single trip). Urban buses are necessary for beaches (no. P to **Poetto**).

Tourist Office: Most immediate **Cagliari AAST** *(Azienda Autonoma di Soggiorno e Turismo)* office is on the V. ROMA side of the PZA MATTEOTTI near the maritime, **FS** rail and bus stations, ☎(070) 669 255. Free maps and brochures in English (Mon–Sat 0830–1945, July–Sept; winter 0800–1400, closed Sun). Main **AAST** office: 97 V. MAMELI, ☎(070) 60231 (0800–1930). Five blocks up V. SASSARI then right along V. GOFFREDO MAMELI two blocks. It has a more complete selection of material. There's also a branch at the airport (Mon–Fri 0900–1300 and 1600–1900). Sardinia-wide **ESIT** office is situated next door to main **AAST**.

A wide range of accommodation exists but prices rise in July and Aug. Budget **hotels** and **pensione** cluster on the V. ROMA between the PZA MATTEOTTI and the **Palazzo Consiglio Regionale**, but similar and much quieter places line the V. SARDEGNA paralleling V. ROMA one block behind it. Near the **Poetto** beach try the **Calamosca Sul Mare**, ☎(070) 371 628, fax: (070) 370 346. **Camping**: 45 mins east on the **Costa Rei** at **Villasimius** is **Spiaggia Del Riso** (Apr–Oct and Christmas holidays), ☎(070) 791 052, fax: (070) 797 150. 1 hr to the west on the Costa del Sud at **Teulada** is the PORTO TRAMUTZA, ☎(070) 928 3027.

As the capital of Sardinia, **Cagliari** offers the greatest opportunity to sample the fine cuisine and wines specific to the island. Excellent and inexpensive seafood restaurants are located on the V. SARDEGNA and V. CAVOUR just off the port. Try the PZA YENNE for relaxed cafés and [illegible] of panini and focaccia.

MACOMÉR

Macomér is the mainline junction with **FdS** lines for **Nuoro** and the **Barbagia** to the east and **Bosa** and its coast to the west. Occasional **FdS** steam excursions operate from **Macomér** towards the sea at **Tresnuraghes**.

The **FdS Station**, (0785) 70 001, is 200 m across the railway square from the **FS** station, but many **FdS** rail cars shuttle around the square to meet **FS** trains.

SASSARI

Sardinia's second city, founded in the 12th century, **Sassari** is the capital of the province of the same name and a busy modern commercial, administrative and university town. While it's not exactly a tourist hot spot you can experience real Sardinian life here in the knot of medieval streets. Near the station are the 13th-century **cathedral** on PZA DE DUOMO and the PZA ITALIA, the town's most lively evening spot, with its monumental statue of Vittorio Emanuele II as well as **Palazzo Giordano** and **Palazzo del Governo**.

DAY TRIPS FROM MACOMÉR

The recently rebuilt **FdS** line to **Nuoro** (east of **Macomér**; up to seven trains daily, taking 1 hr 20 mins) passes many groves of cork trees with their trunks characteristically stripped of bark. Cork has proven to be a valuable export for Sardinia. The small town of Nuoro set on a high granite plateau on the slopes of Mt Ortobene (itself bearing a vast statue of *Christ the Redeemer*) is disappointingly ugly with high-rise development, but is a useful starting point for the exploration of the villages and rough country in the **Barbagia**. All bus lines fan out from the railway station, (0784) 30 115, on V. MARMORA. A compact, attractive old quarter radiates out from the pedestrianised CORSO GARIBALDI. Traditional Barbagia costumes and masks are on display in the town's best sight, the wonderful **Regional Ethnographic Museum**, V. ANTONIO MEREU 56; some 3000 of the costumes on display are used during the 29 Aug **Festival del Redontore**. **Tourist Office**: PZA ITALIA 19, (0784) 30 083 or 32 307, fax: 33 432.

The Genoese **Rosello fountain** near the **Rosello Bridge** in the northern part of the centre is the symbol of the city. The **Cavalcata** on Ascension Day and the 14th of August **I Candelieri** are two occasions where participants dress in traditional costumes to commemorate events that are important locally.

The combined monumental **FS/FdS** rail station, (079) 243 587, is on V. XXV APRILE, about 15 mins from the old city around the PZA CASTELLO.

Tourist Office: VLE CAPRERA 36, (079) 299 544 or 299 579.

PALAU

This peaceful little port serves the small islands of **Capprera** – where the hero of Italian unification, Guiseppe Garibaldi, lived out his life – and **Maddalena**, the resort and naval base island.

DAY TRIP FROM SÁSSARI

Alghero (up to 12 trains daily; 35 mins) is a bewitching, bustling and unsophisticated west coast seaside resort. Much of the present city (as well as the local dialect) within the sturdy Genoese walls dates to the Catalan era: the **cathedral** (1552) in PZA DUOMO, the **churches of San Francesco** (late 14th-century) in the V. CARLO ALBERTO, **Misericordia** (1662), V. MISERICORDIA, and **San Michele** (1612), V. CARLO ALBERTO, and the entire PIAZZA CIVICA contain striking Catalan influences. An active fishing fleet based near the **Porta a Mare** and several local markets – one directly in the PZA CIVICA attest to the living city and assure a constant supply of fresh seafood. Souvenir shops do a brisk trade in coral jewellery. Though walking along the narrow, cobblestone paved streets around the three bastions or in the centre is the best way to soak up the ambience, bicycles can be rented through **Cicloexpress**, V. LAMARMORA 39, in the port, (079) 980 238. Excursion boats make the trip to the towering cliffs of **Capo Cáccia**, beneath which is the **Grotte di Nettuno**, bristling with stalagmites and stalactites.

The most appealing accommodation within the city is the restored **convent of San Francesco**, V. MACHIN 2, (079) 980 330. **Camping**: **La Mariposa**, (079) 950 360, is 2 km away and **Giuliani Youth Hostel**, (079) 930 353, is 6 km away. Both open Apr–Oct. **Tourist Office**: PZA PORTA TERRA 9, 07041 ALGHERO (Sassari), (079) 979 054, fax: 974 881 (Mon–Sat 0800–2000 May–Sept, and Sun 0800–1200 July–Aug; Mon–Sat 0800–1400, Sun 0800–1200 Oct–Apr). The **FdS** railway station, (079) 950 785, is in the **Lido** area 3 km from the centre, but **ARST** buses call in at the city park on V. CATALOGNA.

Tourist Office: **(Maddalena)** (0789) 736 321. **Palau**, V. NAZIONALE 94, (0789) 709570.

There are occasional ferries to **Genoa**, check with the local travel agency on V. NAZIONALE 97, (0789) 709 570.

SANTA TERESA DI GALLURA

A pleasantly uneventful town on the northern tip of the island, cited by the Romans and still called *Portolongone* by locals, sits on a rocky promontory, with a 16th-century Spanish tower looking out to the white cliffs of **Corsica**. It is a discreet summer tourism resort with all the expected facilities (ATM, bureau de change, hotels and pensione) and a wide variety of isolated beaches accessible by foot or the phalanxes of small motor boats anchored in the harbour. The small town's limited hotels tend to fill in July–Aug.

Tourist Office: PZA VITTORIO EMANUELE 24, 07028 SANTA TERESA GALLURA, (0789) 754 127, a helpful office in the main square.

It will respond to written queries in English and offers a free booklet on accommodation.

(for Directory information, see pp. 543 and 563).

Croatia and **Slovenia**, having emerged as new independent states following the break up of Yugoslavia, are now in the process of restructuring their economies and affirming their respective national identities. Slovenia is finding this transition somewhat easier than Croatia, where the political situation remains uncertain.

CROATIA

Croatia now takes up a vast stretch of the Adriatic Coast. Travelling southwards the landscape becomes increasingly dramatic, culminating in Dalmatia with spectacular rugged mountains, sea and islands. Coastal towns such as Split, Hvar and Korčula spent several centuries under Venetian rule: traces remain in local architecture, customs and dialects. Inland Croatia is more Central European. The rather austere buildings, food and manners of the capital, Zagreb, remind one of the other grand cities that passed under Austro-Hungary. The recent war has left a shadow of depression over the city, but prejudices are gradually being cast aside.

Youth Hostels

The booking/travel section of the **Croatian Youth Hostel Association**: HFHS Travel Section, Deźmanova 9, 10000 Zagreb, Croatia, ☎(385) (1) 435781, fax (385) (1) 278239.

Accommodation

Massive amounts of money have already gone towards revitalizing Croatian tourism since the recent war, with hotels and youth hostels gradually being refurbished. Private accommodation is generally the best-value option and can be arranged through local Tourist Offices. Owners usually live on the ground floor and let rooms or apartments upstairs. Prices vary depending on location and season: expect to pay between 70 Kn and 170 Kn per person per night. For stays of less than 3 nights you may have to pay a 30% surcharge. **Youth hostels** as yet are very few in number.

Food and Drink

Along the Dalmatian coast, fish and seafood predominate. Many dishes are prepared Mediterranean-style, using large amounts of olive oil, garlic and parsley. Locals say that fish should swim three times: in the sea, in olive oil and in wine. Specialties include *lignje* (squid), *crni rižot* (rice in cuttlefish ink), and *škampi* (scampi). Inland, meat and dairy produce are more popular. Some of the best restaurants have gardens, where they serve *janjetina* (lamb) roast whole on a spit. Another traditional method of preparing meat is in a *peka*, a large iron pot with a dome shaped lid, which is buried to cook under glowing embers.

Tap water is safe and drinkable throughout both countries.

Top of the range wines are pricey. The cheapest solution is to buy wine 'on tap': look for the sign '*točno vino*' and bring an empty bottle with you. When staying on the coast try a herb brandy, **Travarica**; when staying inland ask for a grape brandy, **Lozova Ča**. Coffee (*kava*) is often served as espresso or cappuccino in bars, though most families prepare it Turkish style at home. Tea (*čaj*) is normally made from rosehip (*šipak*) and served with sugar and lemon.

SLOVENIA

Economically and spiritually, Slovenia was barely affected by the fighting. In the riverside cafes of Ljubljana people discuss music rather than politics. This is a university town of learning and culture. Gardens are neat and ordered. Politicians aspire to join the European Union. Slovenes love mountains and Triglav National Park is their pride. This alpine landscape of peaks, valleys and lakes offers an exhilarating challenge to walkers in a rather idyllic setting.

ACCOMMODATION

Bookings for all types of accommodation can be made through Tourist Offices. Many hotels are currently being upgraded, standards are high and prices comparable to those of EU countries. Prices are higher in July and Aug, when accommodation may be in short supply. Tourist offices have lists of private rooms for rent, categorized I and II – category I having private shower and toilet, while you have to share the bathroom and toilet for category II. A 30% surcharge is sometimes made for stays of less than 3 nights. There is still a shortage of youth hostels, however, in **Ljubljana** and **Maribor** it is possible to stay in **university halls of residence** during the summer break (details from Tourist Offices). There are numerous mostly small but well equipped **campsites**, many with sports facilities.

YOUTH HOSTELS

Head office: Poćitniśka Zveza Slovenije, Parmova 33, 1000 Ljubljana, Slovenia, (386) (61) 312156, fax (386) (61) 1332219).

FOOD AND DRINK

Places to eat go by many different names in Slovenia. A restaurant where you are served by a waitress is a *restauracija,* while a *gostilna* is an inn which typically serves national dishes in a rustic setting. Both sometimes have a set menu (*dnevno kosilo*) at lunch, which is usually the most inexpensive option. There are also a variety of self service places (*samopostrezna restauracija*) where you can eat standing up. Slovenian cuisine reflects historic ties with Vienna. Meat and dairy products predominate: *Wiener schnitzel* (veal in breadcrumbs) is a speciality, as is *pohana piska* (breaded fried chicken). There's a tasty range of smoked sausages, salamis and cured hams. Coffee shops offer a wide range of pastries, cakes and ice-creams. A *zavitek* is a light pastry filled with cream cheese, either sweet or savoury.

EDITOR'S CHOICE

Dubrovnik; Ljubljana; Postojna Caves; Slovenian Alps (around Bled); Split; Zagreb. Ferry trips: Rijeka–Split (ETT table [illegible]); Split–Dubrovnik (p.393).

BEYOND THE BORDERS

Ljubljana–Venice via Trieste (ETT table 89b); Ljubljana–Schwarzach (table 62) to join Innsbruck– Vienna route (p. 318); Zagreb– Budapest (table 92).

Route Detail

Ljubljana–Zagreb ETT table 1320

Type	Frequency	Journey Time
Train	5 daily	2 hrs 20 mins

Zagreb–Split ETT table 1330

Type	Frequency	Journey Time
Train	2 per day	7 hrs 55 mins

Split–Dubrovnik ETT table 2855

Type	Frequency	Journey Time
Ship	Twice weekly	9 hrs 30 mins

Fastest Journey: 36 hrs 50 mins

This is a route with many alternatives, giving a choice between rail, ferry and bus. From Llubljana, at the heart of Slovenia, you can either go via **Zagreb** or by **Postojna** (home to some of Europe's finest caves) to the Adriatic coast at **Rijeka** for ferries to **Split**, or carry on by train from Zagreb to Split (be sure to go via Karlovac and avoid Bosnia, where lines are closed). Split itself has a roman palace and is a good base for ferry excursions to islands; from here take the bus or the ferry to the wonderfully preserved town of Dubrovnik, one of the wonders of the Adriatic. Alternative starting points leading to Llubljana include Venice/Trieste (see Milan–Trieste, p. 367; 3 hr from Trieste to Llubljana, ETT table 1300); or Vienna via Graz and the old university town of Maribor

980, 1315; or from Villach via Bled, an attractive lake resort in the Slovenian Alps (ETT table 1320).

LJUBLJANA

DAY TRIPS FROM LJUBLJANA

Postojna (1 hr; ETT table 1300); station is 1 km from town is notable for its tremendous cave system; tours hourly 0900–1800 (May–Sept), less frequent out of season, one of the largest in Europe, extending 27 km into the surrounding hills. About 2 million years old, the tunnels and caverns are adorned with strange rock formations, stalactites and stalagmites. When the British sculptor Henry Moore came here, he wrote in the visitors' book, 'the best exhibition of nature's sculpture I have ever seen'. A miniature railway guides visitors through this magical array of chambers; within these are the hideous amphibian human-fish, found nowhere else in the world. Buses make the 9 km trip from Postojna to Predjama Castle, a fantastic 16th-century construction high up on a rocky cliff, and built over an under-world cave (which can also be visited 0900–1800 in high season). Postojona Tourist Office has details on buses and is at JAMSKA CESTA 30, ☎(067) 25 041.

The capital of Slovenia, Ljubljana is where the West meets Mittel Europa. Dominated by a hilltop fortress, it is a lively university city with an important historic core.

The river Ljubljanica divides the city into two parts, joined in the city centre by a triple bridge, the **Tromostovje**. This links the city's old heart, **Stari Trg**, on the right bank, built below the hilltop castle, to **Novi Trg** on the left bank.

On the right bank, baroque St Nikolas's Cathedral, **Ciril-Metodov Trg**, abuts the Bishop's Palace. Beyond, on **Vodnikov Trg**, lies the **central food market** (Mon–Sat 0600–1800), good for picnic shopping. Going south from the cathedral, a baroque fountain by the Italian architect and sculptor Francesco Robba stands opposite the Magistrat (Town Hall) on MESTNI TRG.

On the river's left bank, the 17th-century Franciscan **church dominates Prešernov Trg**. Within, the high altar is the work of Robba. The **left bank of the city** also contains a conglomeration of museums. The **National Museum, Trg Herojev 1**, houses archaeological artifacts and a natural history section whose key exhibit is a complete mammoth skeleton. The National Gallery, CANKARJEVA 20, contains works from the 13th–20th centuries. The Museum of Modern Art, CANKARJEVA 15, provides an interesting cross-section of 20th-century Slovenian art. The Architectural Museum, KARUNOVA 4, highlights the work of Jože Plečnik, one of the pioneers of modern architecture, who altered much of Ljubljana, as well as completing important works in Vienna and Prague. Antique enthusiasts may want to visit to the flea market at Cankarjevo Nabrežje, Sun 0800–1300.

SUMMER FESTIVAL

The annual International Summer Festival takes place in Plečnik's open air Križanke Theatre, attracting well known musicians, actors and dancers from all over the world, (July–Aug).

Trg Osvobodline Fronte (TRG OF); (061) 1315 167, a 15-min walk from the main street, Slovenska Cesta.

Tourist Office: Mačkove 1, (061) 133 01 11 (Mon–Fri 0800–1900, Sat 0900–1700); branch in station (daily 0800–2100 high season, 1000–1800 low season). Guided tours of the city meet at the Magistrat, Mestni Trg 1, every day 1700 (June–Sept), Sun 1100 (Oct–May).

Private rooms are available for rent through the Tourist Office, but may be in short supply during the summer. Expect to pay 3500 SIT for a double. Although there is no official Youth Hostel at present, rooms can be taken in student halls of residence during the summer break through Jul–Aug. **Dijaški Dom Bežigrad**, KARDELJEVA PLOŠČAD 28, (061) 342 864, and **Dijaški Dom Tabor**, VIDOVDANSKA CESTA 7; (061) 321 067 – ask at the Tourist Office for further details. Camping is the best cheap option and Ljubljana's site is located by the Sava River: Autocamp Ježica, Dunajska 270; tel: (061) 371 382. Bungalows also available.

The riverside zone between Stari Trg and Novi Trg is the centre for friendly bars and reasonably priced eating places.

ZAGREB

Head for **Gornji Grad**, the upper town. From **Trg Bana Jelačića** follow **Ilica**, to reach **Tomičeva**, where you can take the funicular up to Strossmayer promenade for one of the **best vantage points for views** over the city. From Lotrsčak Tower a cannon is fired daily at 1200. Next take éirilometodska to St Mark's Church, noted for its extra-ordinary red, white and blue tiled roof, and follow Kamenita to pass through the archway, which has become a shrine, with a small altar, flowers and burning candles. Turn left up Radićeva, and take one of the series of steep wooden stairways to your right, which link the upper town to Kaptol. In the cathedral look for the inscription of the ten commandments on the northern wall, written in 12th-century Glagolithic characters, unique to the old Slavic language.

Zagreb's fine art collection is in the **Mimara Museum,** ROOSEVELTOV TRG 4 (closed Mon). Outdoor strolling grounds include **Maksimir Park** (tram nos 11/12 from the main square), and the Mirogoj Cemetery (frequent bus service from Kaptol in front of the Cathederal). The city is served by a fine tram network. Single ticket 5 Kn, day ticket 12 Kn.

Day Trips from Ljubljana cont'd

Private accommodation can be arranged through **Kompas**, (067) 24 549. Camping: **Pivka**, 4 km from Postojna, has one of the area's only campsites (May–Sept; bike hire).

Bled (45 mins; ETT table1320; alight Lesce-Bled), on the lake of the same name, lies on the edge of Triglav National Park, and is the main resort in the Slovenian Alps, popular for boating (boat hire available), walking and golf in summer, and ice skating (on the lake) and skiing in winter.

Tourist Office: CESTA SVOBODE 15; (064) 741 122. There is an excellent youth hostel, GRAJSKA CESTA 17; (064) 74 52 50, just a 5-min walk from the lake.

From Bled Jezero station you can head on to Bohinj Lake (Bohinjska Bistrica station; ETT table 1305) is less commercial than Bled, but the serene landscape is incomparable.

(064) 723 441. **Tourist Office**: RIBČEV LAZ 48; (064) 72 33 70.

Glavni Kolodvor, (01) 9830, in the centre of town, overlooking the first of three squares dating back to the Austro-Hungarian era, TRG KRALJA TOMISLAVA. The station is well equipped with toilets, left luggage, exchange offices, newspaper kiosks and a bar.

Tourist Offices: TRG BANA JELAČIĆA 11, (01) 48 14 051 or 48 14 052. Open Mon–Fri 0830–2000, Sat 1000–1800, Sun and holidays 1000–1400. A 10-min walk from the station, over the three squares, keeping to Praska on the left, to arrive in TRG BANA JELAČIĆA, the main town square. Alternatively, take tram nos 6 or 13 which follow the same route. TRG NIKOLE SUBICA ZINJSKOG 14, (01) 4552 867. Mon–Fri 0900–1700 only. On the third square in front of the station, responsible for guided tours. Pick up a copy of the free monthly pamphlet, Events and Performances, published in English.

Generally expensive (around 170 Kn for a single); private rooms can be booked through the Tourist Office or various agencies. **Youth hostel**: PETRINJSKA 77, (01) 484 1261, out of the station turn right off the square and take the first road to the left. Just a 100 m walk from the station, but this hostel is in very poor condition and needs to be upgraded; 70 Kn.

The best area for eating and drinking is TKALČIĆEVA, a lively street leading from Trg Bana Jelačica up to Gornji Grad. The nearby market at Dolac is the best place to shop for a picnic.

SPLIT

A useful transit point for ferries, Split is also a delightful coastal town. Its historic seafront area known as Grad lies within the walls of the **roman palace** built in the 2nd century by Emperor Diocletian, and consists of narrow paved alleys, opening onto ancient piazzas, is only accessible to pedestrians. From here the Tourist Office's self-guided walk leads through town; there are well illustrated information boards scattered around, highlighting the town's roman roots, the Cathedral of St Duje, the various buildings dating back to the Venetian times, and the Austro-Hungarian facades. Climb the bell-tower (open 0900–1200, 1600–1900) for a good overview.The Split Summer Festival runs mid July to mid Aug. The programme includes concerts, opera and theatre, set against a backdrop of the city's most beautiful ancient buildings.

OBALA KNEZA DOMAGOJA, (021) 48 588. The train station, bus station (021) 345 047) and ferry port are all next to each other, overlooking Gradska Luka, the town harbour. Left luggage; supermarket. The historic centre is just 100 m away.

Tourist Offices: OBALA HRVATSOG NARODNOG PREPORODA 12, (021) 342 142 (0730–2100, closed Sun). Situated on the seafront, better known by locals as the RIVA. PERISTIL 1, (021) 40 685 (0900–1400, 1700–2000); guided tours on request.

Accommodation is scarce, especially in Aug. Try the Tourist Office for private rooms. Expect to pay 135 Kn single, 210 Kn double.

Locals eat out primarily at **merenda**, a hearty fisherman's brunch served between 0900–1130. Simple eating places offer a fixed menu at budget prices. For typical Dalmatian food try **Kod Jose**, SREDMANUSKA 4, behind the market. For a cheap stand-up lunch with locals try **ribice**, tiny fishes deep fried and served with a glass of white wine, in a canteen style establishment opposite the fish market (**Ribarnica**), KRAJ SV. MARIJE 8. To shop for a picnic visit **Pazar**, the colourful open air market held just outside the main walls, Mon–Sat 0700–1330. Just across the road from here the all-night bakery provides for midnight snacks. Split is packed with bars, which are busy the year through. Café life centres around Luxor on PERISTIL, amid a theatrical setting of roman ruins floodlit by night.

Day Trips from Split

Trogir: The tiny city stands on a small island with a 13th century cathederal. Easily reached by bus.

Brač (13 ferries a day in summer, journey time 1 hr, 16 Kn): best known for the spectacular sandspit, Zlatni Rat, near Bol; expensive and crowded in summer. **Tourist Offices**: (in Supertar), P. JAKSIĆA 17, (021) 630 551; (in Bol) UZ PJACU 4, (021) 635 122.

Hvar (two ferries a day, journey time 2 hr, 24 Kn; the more regular service, Split–Stari Grad, involves a bus transfer to Hvar town): an island famed for its wines, lavender, pretty fishing villages and unspoilt coastline. Hvar town is one of the finests island settlements, with buildings dating back to the 15th century planned around the harbour, backed by hills and a castle. **Tourist Office**: (in Hvar town), TRG SV STJEPANA 16; (021) 741 059.

DUBROVNIK

With its walls enclosing a basin of traffic-free streets and steeply dropping, stepped alleys, Dubrovnik is one of the most impressive medieval fortified cities on the Mediterranean. There's an entry charge for walking the walls (open daily 0900–1830), which give a series of vantage points over the terracotta rooftops, the churches, the sea and the islands. For centuries Dubrovnik was a refined and prosperous trading port, which managed to keep its independence by paying off various would-be conquerors. The city as it stands today still bears witness to this glorious past. There's a major festival, mid July to mid Aug, with outdoor theatre, opera, jazz and classical music.

PUT REPUBLIKE 19; (020) 423 088, with 24 hr left luggage.

Gruž Port, OBALA S. RADIĆA, (020) 418 000. The Jadrolinija coastal service runs Split-Dubrovnik, 4 times per week in summer, journey time 7–10 hrs depending on number of stops, 72 Kn.

Tourist Office: PLACA 1, (020) 426 354 or 426 355, daily 0800–2000. Pick up a copy of the free monthly city guide, Dubrovnik, available at the Tourist Office.

Youth Hostel, ULICA BANA JELAČICA 15–17, (020) 412 592. 100 m from the coach station and 300 m from the city walls. Clean and friendly; 60 Kn a night.

Try along PRIJEKO, a picturesque narrow street running parallel to the central street, Placa, is the main area for eating out within the city walls.

(for Directory information, see pp. 544, 546, 557, 566).

DENMARK, FINLAND, NORWAY, SWEDEN

Scandinavian countries have much in common, with histories dominated by Viking exploits and political upheavals, as Denmark and Sweden sought to impose their authority over the Baltic and national boundaries changed many times.

English is widely spoken, making communication easy, aided by the natural friendliness of Scandinavians. All these countries are expensive by European standards, with costs particularly high in Norway. Scandinavian towns and buildings tend to have a neat, tidy look that's appealing to some, and dull to others.

SCANDINAVIA

FOOD AND DRINK

While each country has its own specialities, the Scandinavians share a love of fish – herring, sole and dried cod in particular. Meat can include reindeer or elk, and there is the open sandwich *smørrebrød* which, topped with meat, fish or cheese, can be a meal in itself. Eating out is quite expensive but there are good supermarkets where you can buy sandwiches and pastries. Coffee, tea and hot chocolate are widely available: a second cup of coffee is often free or half price. Alcohol is expensive, and you have to be over 18 or in some cases over 20 to buy it. See country specialities below. *Dagens ret* is the day's special menu which is generally good value.

DENMARK

Protruding between the Baltic and Atlantic, **Denmark** incorporates some 400 islands, 90 of which are inhabited, as well as the peninsula of **Jutland**. It's low-lying and undramatic terrain, where you sense you're never far from the sea. With its 7000 km of coast, it has a long maritime tradition going back to the Vikings. Along the coast you'll also find quaint centuries-old fishing communities. **Copenhagen** is the brightest, liveliest spot in the nation, accounting for more than a quarter of the country's 5 million population. The island of **Fyn** (Fünen) has some of the most attractive of Danish landscapes, and its main city, **Odense**, is celebrated as the birthplace of Hans Christian Andersen. Some of the nearby islands, such as **Æro,** have an aptly fairy-tale prettiness and are tailor-made for exploring on foot or by cycle. **Århus**, in Jutland, is the most vibrant place outside Copenhagen.

ACCOMMODATION

The **Danish Tourist Board** produces a brochure on hostels and camping. Local Tourist Offices have lists of rooms in private homes, which are usually very clean and acceptable, and cheaper than hotels.

HOTELS Branches of the Danish Tourist Board have the free annual *Denmark Hotels* guide. This covers **hotels**, **pensions**, **inns** and **motels**, together with details of various discount schemes. In Copenhagen, expect to pay DKr.335–500 for a double, without facilities but including breakfast. Elsewhere expect to pay DKr.275–390. In rural areas the old inns, known as *kros*, are characterful places to stay. Hotel standards are good and the choice and price range are wide. Hotels affiliated to Horesta, the Danish hoteliers' association, are classified by one to five stars.

HOSTELS

Hostelling headquarters: **Danhostel** at Vesterbrogade 39, DK-1620, Copenhagen V, Denmark; ☎(45) 31 31 36 12; fax (45) 31 31 36 26. e-mail ldv@danhostel.dk; http://www.danhostel.dk).

CAMPING

Campingrådet, Hesseløgade 16, DK-2100 Copenhagen Ø; ☎39 27 88 44.

HOSTELS There are more than 100 hostels, graded one to five stars, and the general standard is excellent; most have private rooms (sleeping 2–6; DKr.120–540) as well as dormitories (sleeping bags usually not allowed; about DKr.100 including bedding).

CAMPING You'll need an **International Camping Card** from your own country, plus a Visitor's Pass, available from any campsite. Many camps also have attractive self-catering cabins. Wild camping and camping on beaches is illegal, and wrongdoers can be fined.

SLEEP-INS For rock-bottom sleeping (almost literally), there are temporary **Sleep-Ins** set up by local municipalities for a few weeks in summer, and usually there's no more than mattresses; you'll need your own sleeping bag.

FOOD AND DRINK

Look for *Dagens Ret* (today's special), which is cheaper than à la carte. A choice of fish might include flounder or halibut; the smorrebrod are served on *rugbrod* (rye bread) or frankskbrod (wheat bread). *Frikadeller* are pork meatballs and *wienerbrod* are real, flaky Danish pastries. The local spirit is akvavit.

FINLAND

Tucked up into Scandinavia's north-eastern corner and stretching well into the Arctic, **Finland** is a relatively new country, having gained independence in 1917, and is probably the least-known Scandinavian nation. It formerly belonged to its neighbours, first Sweden in the Middle Ages, then after 1808 it became an autonomous Grand Duchy of tsarist Russia. There are cultural overtones to be found from both these countries, but Finland also has a strong identity of its own.

The south-western corner is the most populous region by far and includes **Turku**, the country's long-standing spiritual and cultural hub, as well as the rewarding industrial city of **Tampere**. The capital, **Helsinki**, is especially striking for its 19th– and 20th–century architecture. Glaciers gouged out huge trenches that became thousands of lakes, making up the **Finnish Lake District** that, together with the vast forests, covers much of southern Finland. Comfortable trains link the major towns, which, like the lines themselves, are virtually all confined to the south. For scenic rail routes, head for the lake regions, notably from **Helsinki** to **Oulu**, and from **Pieksämäki** to **Tampere**.

Like the rest of Scandinavia, Finland is an easy place to meet people and the Finns are friendly and receptive to outsiders.

ACCOMMODATION

Some Tourist Offices **book accommodation** for a small fee.

You can mitigate the cost by buying vouchers on the **Finncheque discount hotel scheme** from the Finnish Tourist Office in your own country.

HOTELS Hotels tend to be quite luxurious and expensive. Better for budget travellers are **kesähotelli** (summer hotels in student accommodation) and **matkustajakoti** (the relatively cheap tourist hotels). Ask at Tourist Offices for the free brochures *Finland Hotels* (not graded, but standards are high) or *Finland Budget Accommodation*.

As is traditional in Scandinavia, **saunas** are pretty universal, even on ferries and in hostels; **M** is for men, **N** for women.

HOSTELS The 130-plus **hostels** (*retkeilymajat*; pronounced ret-kay-loo-mayat) are well spread across the country and open year-round. They're graded from two to four stars, all with dormitories sleeping 5–10 as well as singles, doubles and family rooms; prices are around FIM45–150 without sheet sleeping bag (FIM25–30 extra). It's advisable to book ahead in July and August, and to warn if you will be arriving after 1800; booking is mandatory in winter. Many hostels have activity programmes, plus canoes, skis, boats and cycles.

HOSTELS

The **Finnish hostelling association headquarters** is **Suomen Retkeilymajajärjestö-SRM,** Yrjönkatu 38 B 15, 00100 Helsinki, Finland; ☎(358) (9) 6940377/ 6931347; fax (358) (9) 6931349 (e-mail: info@srm.inet.fi).

CAMPING Campsites are widespread too (about 350; 70 open all year), and are graded from one to three stars; three-star sites typically have **camping cottages** sleeping up to five and are sometimes very well appointed (maybe including a sauna). Rough camping is generally allowed providing you keep 150 m from residents and remove any trace of your stay.

FOOD AND DRINK

Fixed-price menus in a *ravintola* (upmarket restaurant) are the best value, or you may want to try a *grilli* (fast-food stand), *kahvila* (self-service cafeteria) or a *baari* (snack bar). For self-caterers, try **Slepa, Siwa, Saastari** or **Valintatalo** supermarkets. Some specials are *muikunmati* (a freshwater fish roe served with onions and cream and accompanied by toast or pancakes) and for dessert *kiiseli* (berry mousse). **Alko** is the state-owned outlet that sells alcohol.

NORWAY

Stretching 1800 km, far above the Arctic Circle, **Norway** is one of Europe's great natural wonderlands. Its majestic fjords – massive watery corridors created by glacial action – make up one of the finest coastlines in the world, among a wild mountainous terrain that includes **Jostedalsbreen**, mainland Europe's largest glacier. **Bergen** makes the ideal access point for taking a cruise or a ferry to see the fjords at close range. The majestic scenery continues far north beyond the Arctic Circle and into **Lappland**, where at Easter there are colourful Sami festivals.

The downside of visiting Norway is the cost: prices are just about double what they are in the rest of Europe, and even by camping or hostelling and living frugally, you'll inevitably notice the difference. Be sure to stock up on things like camera film before going.

ACCOMMODATION

Because Norway is so expensive, the **youth hostel** network is indispensable if you don't want to break the bank. There are 90 hostels (*vandrerhjem*), many of which unfortunately open only mid June–mid August. The standard of hostel accommodation is very high, with singles, doubles and dormitories, and there's a good geographical spread. Booking ahead is highly recommended, and mandatory Oct 1–Apr 30. The Norwegian **HI** logo is a variation on the usual theme: a stylised green tree and blue hut with a yellow sun. The charge is NKr.70–165, excluding linen. **Private houses** offering rooms can be quite good value, and in some cases almost the same price as hostels, with the advantage of greater privacy. Moving up the price scale, there are **guesthouses** and **pensions**.

HOTELS

Generally very pricey, but many cut rates at weekends and in summer. Advance booking is important, especially in **Oslo**, **Bergen** and **Stavanger,** which are popular towns for conferences as well as tourists. Local Tourist Offices provide lists of all types of accommodation; most will make bookings for a small fee.

CAMPING

Many of the 1500 official **campsites** (with 5-star classification) have pre-bookable **log cabins** for two or four people. Campsites nearly always have cabins (*hytter*), sleeping 2–4 people and equipped with kitchen and maybe a bathroom. Rough camping is permitted as long as you don't intrude on residents (you must be 150 m from them) or leave any trace of your stay. Never light fires in summer.

HOSTELS

The hostelling headquarters, **Norsek Vandrerhjem**, are at DRONNINGENSGATE 26, N-0154, OSLO; ☎(47) 23 13 93 00; fax (47) 23 13 93 50 (http://www.vandrerhjem.no, e-mail: hostels@sn.no).

CAMPSITES

The *Norwegian Camping Guide* is available from the **NTB** (Norwegian Tourist Board) and **NAF** (Norwegian Automobile Association), STORGT 2, N-0155 OSLO; ☎22 34 14 00. The **Tourist Board** also produces *Norway Accommodation*, a free brochure listing hotels, cabins, hostels and hotel discount passes. **DNT: Den Norske Turistforening** (the Norwegian Mountain Touring Association), STORGATE 3, N-0125 OSLO.

If you are venturing into the wilds, contact **DNT: Den Norske Turistforening**, who provide information for campers and walkers. They have branches in gateways to wilderness areas and run the network of mountain huts (open at Easter and in summer); you must join DNT in order to use their huts. Trails are marked by their logo, a large red 'T'.

You can also join **DNT** in the UK through **Mountain and Wildlife Venture**, COMPSTON ROAD, AMBLESIDE, CUMBRIA LA22 9DJ, ☎(015394) 33285; fax (015394) 34065.

FOOD AND DRINK

Specials here include *gravetlaks* (marinated salmon cured in dill) and *fiskesuppe* (a satisfying fish and vegetable soup. Meat can be hearty stew, sausages or meatballs. You may see heads of fish and animals – these are eaten by the locals. State-owned shops for wines and spirits are known as **Vinmonopol** but lagers are sold inexpensively in supermarkets. Bars may restrict the drinking age to over 21. Mulled wine – *glogg* – is good for a warm up.

SWEDEN

Scandinavia's largest country includes huge tracts of forest and thousands of lakes, with mildly rolling, fertile terrain to the south, and excitingly rugged uplands spilling over the Norwegian border and beyond the Arctic Circle into **Lappland**. The sheer amount of space is positively exhilarating. The beaches (including naturist ones) compare with the finest in Europe, and in summer the climate of the south is much like that of Central Europe, except with longer days. Mosquitoes can be a problem, so take a strong repellant.

Sweden has a conspicuously comfortable standard of living: owing to its tax and social welfare system you won't see much poverty – conversely, few are ostentatiously rich either; equality is the buzz word. For all their sophistication, Swedes are very aware of their country origins, and walking, nature and village life are close to their hearts. National costume is accepted as formal wear, and there's a thriving tradition of handicrafts, particularly woodcrafts. Anything with a *Svensk Slöjd* token is approved by the national handicrafts organisation. Authentic Sami crafts carry a circular *Duodji* tag.

accommodation. It's a good idea to warn your hosts if you plan to arrive at any accommodation after 1800. The **Swedish Travel and Tourism Council** can provide a limited national list of hotels. Local Tourist Offices have listings for their area, including a range of farmhouse accommodation. You can also get brochures issued by individual chains, such as **Sweden Hotels**, which offers hotels with individual character. **Bed and breakfast Service Stockholm** can provide rooms and flats in the capital. Look for details of **hotel passes**, giving the option of paying for vouchers up front and getting discounts.

HOTELS Hotel standards are high and the cost usually includes a sauna and breakfast. SKr.400–600 for a single/SKr.700–900 for a double is at the cheap end of the scale.

HOSTELS There's a network of some 280 hostels *(vandrarhem)* about half of which open only in summer (most do not allow sleeping bags); some are extremely characterful places and include castles and boats. Family rooms are available. Most hostels are shut 1000–1700, and charges are about SKr.75–150. Hostels are run by **Svenska Turistföreningen** (**STF**). Room-only accommodation in **private houses** is a good budget alternative.

CAMPING **Sveriges Campingvärdars Riksförbund** (**SCR**, Swedish Camping Association) lists 650 campsites. As in Norway, you can rough camp for one night, as long as you keep more than 150 m from the nearest house and leave no litter.

FOOD AND DRINK

Hearty help-yourself-buffet breakfasts are a good start to the day. Some cheap eateries for later on are the **konditori** (cafés) and fast-food outlets. *Pytt i panna* is a hearty fry-up and other traditional dishes are pea soup served with pancakes, and **Jansson's temptation** (potatoes, onions and anchovies). Food in towns is quite cosmopolitan and Chinese food is popular. The local spirit is aquavit and the Swedish vodka called *Absolut*. **Systembolaget** is the state-owned outlet for alcohol – shoppers must be over 20.

Sweden Hotels, SVEAVÄGEN 39, BOX 3377, S-103 67 STOCKHOLM; ☎(020) 77 00 00

Svenska Turistföreningen (STF), STUREPLAN 4C, PO BOX 25, 101 20 STOCKHOLM, SWEDEN; ☎(46) (8) 46 32 100; fax (46) (8) 67 81 958 (http://www.stf-turist.se).

Bed and Breakfast Service Stockholm,
PO BOX 26175, S-100 41 STOCKHOLM; ☎ (08) 66 05 565.

Sveriges Campingvärdars Riksförbund (SCR, Swedish Camping Association), PO BOX 255, S-45117 UDDEVALLA; ☎(0522) 393 45.

EDITOR'S CHOICE

Bergen (and surrounding fjords); Copenhagen; Geirangerfjord from Åndalsnes (panel, p. 444); Gothenburg; Helsinki; Kuopio (Orthodox Church Museum); Legoland (near Århus); Linköping (museum village); Lofoten Islands (near Bodø); Lund; Malmo; Odense (Hans Christian Andersen museum); Oslo; Savonlinna; Stockholm; Turku; Uppsala. Scenic rail journeys: Oslo–Bergen (p. 436); Stavanger–Kristiansand (p. 436); Oslo–Boden (p. 442); Norway in a Nutshell (via Flåm, p. 440); Stockholm–Gällivare (Inlandsbanan; p. 444, ETT table 762); Helsinki–Oulu (p. 456).

BEYOND THE BORDERS

See Where Next? panels for Copenhagen (p. 409) and Helsinki (p. 414).

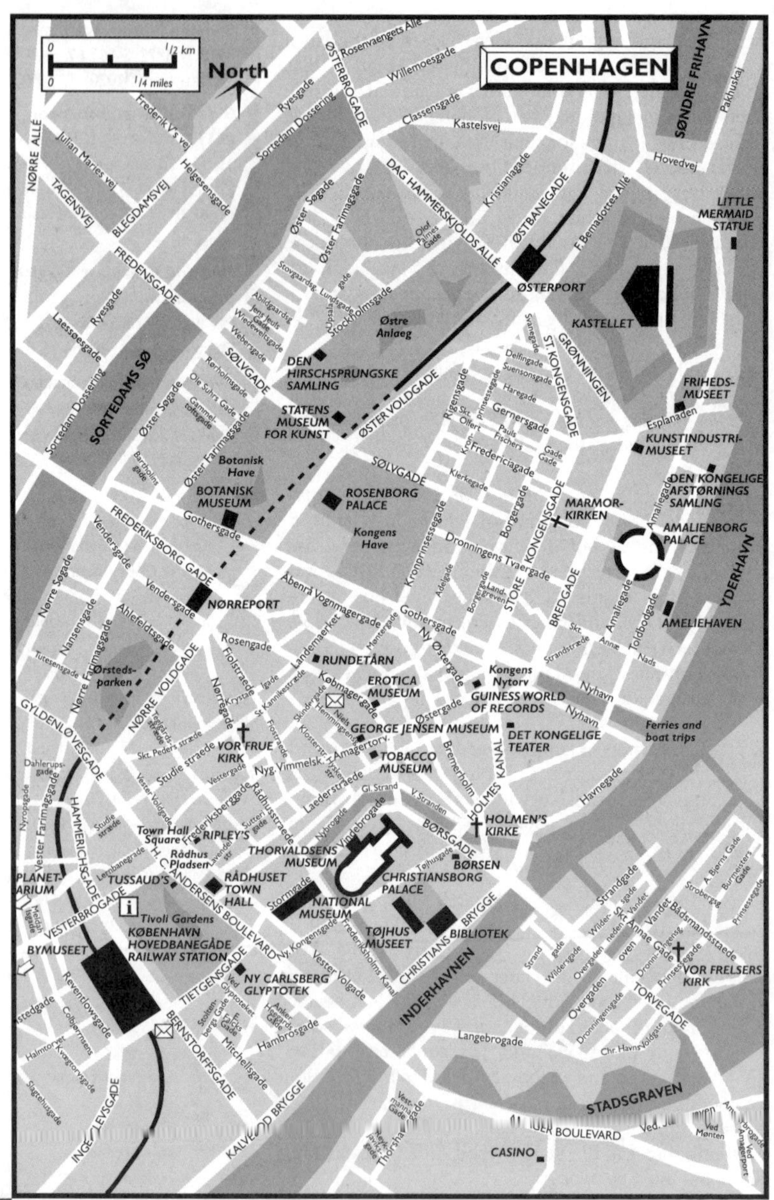
COPENHAGEN
0 1/2 km
0 1/4 miles
North
Rosenvaengets Allé
Willemoesgade
Classensgade
Kastelsvej
ØSTERBROGADE
Ryesgade
Sortedam Dossering
Frederik V's vej
Julian Maries vej
NØRRE ALLÉ
TAGENSVEJ
BLEGDAMSVEJ
Helgesensgade
SØNDRE FRIHAVN
Pakhuskaj
Hovedvej
DAG HAMMERSKJOLDS ALLÉ
Kristianiagade
ØSTBANEGADE
F. Bernadottes Allé
LITTLE MERMAID STATUE
Øster Søgade
Øster Farimagsgade
Olof Palmes Gade
ØSTERPORT
KASTELLET
FREDENSGADE
Stockholmsgade
Østre Anlaeg
Ryesgade
Laessøesgade
SORTEDAMS SØ
Sortedam Dossering
SØLVGADE
DEN HIRSCHSPRUNGSKE SAMLING
STATENS MUSEUM FOR KUNST
ØSTER VOLDGADE
GRØNNINGEN
ST. KONGENSGADE
FRIHEDS-MUSEET
Esplanaden
KUNSTINDUSTRI-MUSEET
Botanisk Have
BOTANISK MUSEUM
ROSENBORG PALACE
SØLVGADE
Fredericiagade
DEN KONGELIGE AFSTØRNINGS SAMLING
MARMOR-KIRKEN
AMALIENBORG PALACE
Gothersgade
FREDERIKSBORG GADE
Kongens Have
Dronningens Tvaergade
YDERHAVN
Vendersgade
NØRREPORT
Åbenrå
Vognmagergade
Gothersgade
Kronprinsessegade
STORE KONGENSGADE
BREDGADE
Amaliegade
Toldbodgade
AMELIEHAVEN
Nørre Søgade
Ahlefeldtsgade
Rosengade
RUNDETÅRN
Ørsteds-parken
Nørre Farimagsgade
NØRRE VOLDGADE
Fiolstraede
Nørregade
Købmagergade
EROTICA MUSEUM
Kongens Nytorv
GUINESS WORLD OF RECORDS
Nyhavn
Ferries and boat trips
GYLDENLØVESGADE
VOR FRUE KIRK
Studie straede
GEORGE JENSEN MUSEUM
DET KONGELIGE TEATER
Østergade
Amagertorv
TOBACCO MUSEUM
Bremerholm
HOLMENS KANAL
Havnegade
Laederstraede
Gl. Strand
HAMMERICHSGADE
Vester Farimagsgade
Town Hall Square
RIPLEY'S
Rådhus Pladsen
HOLMEN'S KIRKE
BØRSGADE
BØRSEN
THORVALDSENS MUSEUM
CHRISTIANSBORG PALACE
PLANET-ARIUM
TUSSAUD'S
RÅDHUSET TOWN HALL
H. C. ANDERSENS BOULEVARD
VESTERBROGADE
Tivoli Gardens
NATIONAL MUSEUM
KØBENHAVN HOVEDBANEGÅDE RAILWAY STATION
TØJHUS MUSEET
CHRISTIANS BRYGGE
BIBLIOTEK
BYMUSEET
Strandgade
A. Bjørns Gade
Burmeisters Gade
Strøbergsg
Prinsessegade
Bådsmandsstaede
VOR FRELSERS KIRK
INDERHAVNEN
TIETGENSGADE
NY CARLSBERG GLYPTOTEK
Vester Voldgade
Reventlowsgade
Colbjørnsens
Halmtorvet
Kvægtorvsgade
Slagtehusgade
BERNSTORFFSGADE
Mitchellsgade
Hambrosgade
Langebrogade
TORVEGADE
Overgaden
Chr. Havns Voldgate
STADSGRAVEN
INGERSLEVSGADE
KALVEBOD BRYGGE
Vestmannagade
Thorshavn
BOULEVARD
CASINO
Ved Mønten

Copenhagen manages to be civilised, refined and vibrant, all at the same time: its easy-going, friendly atmosphere is perhaps its greatest draw. Cruise boats tour the canals that thread through the historic core, which reveals an appealing diversity of open spaces, spires, towers and statuary. Cycling is encouraged here, and the outdoor, almost Mediterranean, feel is compounded by an effervescent street life.

ARRIVAL AND DEPARTURE

RAIL The main rail station is **København Hovedbanegård (København H)**, ☎33 14 17 01, with a metro station of the same name. There are dozens of shops and cafés in the large bright foyer, including a supermarket, a **bureau de change** and a kiosk that stocks English-language newspapers. The **Inter-Rail Centre** in the station, daily 0600–2200 (June–Sept), provides showers and information. Buses to just about anywhere in town stop right outside.

Several competing companies run ferries to Malmö in Sweden, leaving from HAVENGADE by NYHAVN. All have ticket offices on the quay; for advance booking try **Pilen,** ☎33 32 12 60, or **Flyvebådene,** ☎33 12 80 88. A cheaper option is to get the train to **Helsingør** and get the 25–min ferry (which leaves every 20 mins) to **Helsingborg** on the Swedish side. DKr32 return; ☎33 15 15 15.

Copenhagen Airport, ☎31 54 17 01, is at **Kastrup**, 8 km south-east of town, and is sometimes called Kastrup Airport. There is a tourist information desk and a hotel reservations desk in the arrival hall and banks in all areas. The SAS bus runs between Kastrup and København H rail station every 15 mins, taking 15–25 mins.

INFORMATION

The Tourist Office has information covering all of Denmark. Get the *Wonderful Copenhagen* map and a copy of *Copenhagen This Week* (published monthly; also at http://www.ctw.dk), both of which are free and incorporate masses of useful information. Also try to get hold of the *Copenhagen Post*, a weekly newspaper in English, for recent news and more listings.

THE LITTLE MERMAID

The city's most enduring symbol is to the north of the centre. The statue of Hans Christian Andersen's **Little Mermaid (Den Lille Havfrue)** sits staring towards a less than fairy–tale backdrop of cranes and wind generators.

For budget travellers, the first port of call should be the youth tourism service **USE IT** (RÅDHUSSTRÆDE 13; ☎33 15 65 18; e-mail: useit@ui.dk), which provides youth-oriented information and advice of all kinds, and can find you a place in a hostel for no fee – and you will probably have less of a wait than at the Tourist Office. Open daily 0900–1900 (1 June–30 Sept); Mon–Fri 1000–1600 (Oct–May). Make sure you get a copy of *Playtime* magazine, which contains more than you could ever want to know about seeing Copenhagen on a tight budget.

MONEY In København H are **Den Danske Bank** (open 0800–2000) and **Forex** (open daily 0800–2100).

TOURIST OFFICE

BERNSTORFFSGADE 1 (☎ 33 11 13 25, e-mail: woco@woco.com), opposite the station, by Tivoli's main entrance. Open daily 0900–2100 (May–mid Sept); Mon–Sat 0900–1630 (mid Sept–May).

TOURS FOR FREE

There's no admission charge to **Statens Museum for Kunst** and **Nationalmuseet** on Wednesdays, or to the **Carlsberg Glyptotek** on Wed and Sun. **Carlsberg Brewery** tours are free. Devotees of the philosopher Søren Kierkegaarde and the fairy–tale writer Hans Christian Andersen can seek out their graves in **Assistens Cemetery**.

POST AND PHONES

The **City Centre Post Office** is open Mon–Fri 0930–1800, Sat 1000–1400. Unless some other post office is specified, poste restante mail goes to the **Main Post Office**, TIETGENSGADE 39 (☎33 33 89 00; open Mon–Fri 1100–2000, Sat 1000–1300).
Phone Home, RADHUSET 4, ☎33 36 86 00, is open Mon–Fri 1000–1700, Sat 1100–1700, Sun 1300–1800.

PUBLIC TRANSPORT

USE-IT (see Information, above) provides excellent information on walking, cycling and seeing the city by bus. Buses and trains all form part of an integrated system in the Copenhagen area and tickets are valid on both. Fares are calculated by the number of zones travelled, but since most attractions are central, for a single journey you will probably only need the cheapest ticket, DKr.11, which covers travel in two zones for one hour. Alternatively, buy either a 24-hr transport pass from the Tourist Office (DKr.70), or a **klippekort** ten-ride ticket covering 2 or 3 zones (DKr.75 or 105). These tickets must be validated in the machines on board buses and on metro platforms.
The **Copenhagen Card** can be valid for 24 hrs (DKr.140), 48 hrs (DKr.255) or 72 hrs (DKr.320). It provides free public transport in Copenhagen and the surrounding region, gives free entrance to most attractions (including Tivoli), discounts on ferries to Sweden and a useful colour guide. It is on sale at the airport, DSB stations, hotels, travel agents and Tourist Offices.

ACCOMMODATION

Book ahead for June–Aug, but otherwise there are masses of places to stay; the accommodation service in the Tourist Office (opening hours see above) has a booking service (small fee, but can save you 25% on hotel prices if you book for the same day). Be prepared for a wait if it's busy. Advance booking phone service, ☎33 25 38 44, fax 33 25 74 10, Mon–Fri 0900–1600. **USE IT** (see p. 405) makes no charge for reservations, even in advance, and has an external noticeboard indicating room vacancies in hostels.

Cheaper hotels are clustered in **Istedgade** (to the side of the station, away from the centre). Although not beautiful, it is quite safe. In the summer months, when demand is high, Copenhagen offers a good choice of hostel accommodation, but you must arrive early if you have not booked. **HI** has three hostels, all a fair distance out.

HOTELS	**Copenhagen Admiral**, TOLDBROGADE 24–28, ☎ 33 11 82 82; old and new mingle harmoniously in what used to be a granary.
HOSTELS	**Copenhagen Hostel**, VEJLANDS ALLÉ 200, ☎ 32 52 29 08; 4 km south-east of the centre, but right beside the stops for the airport bus and 🚌 nos.37 and 46. **Bellahoj Vandrerhjem**, HERBERGVEJEN 8, ☎ 31 28 97 15, is 5 km from the centre in the opposite direction – 20 mins on 🚌 no.2 or 11, or nightbus 82N. **The City Public Hostel,** ABSALONSGADE 8, ☎ 31 31 20 70; open May–Aug.
SLEEP-INS	132 BLEGDAMSVEG, ☎ 35 26 50 59; open July–Aug; 🚌 nos.1, 6 or 14, or nightbus 85N or 95N. 18 RAVNSBORGGADE, ☎ 35 37 77 77; open June–Sept; 🚌 nos.5 or 16; nightbus 81N or 84N.
INTER POINT CENTRES	STORE KANNIKESTRŒDE 19, ☎ 33 11 30 31; open July. VALDEMARSGADE 15, ☎ 31 31 15 74; open July–early Aug. YMCA/YWCA: join on the spot if you are not a member
CAMPSITES	**Bellahøj Camping** 66 HVIDKILDEVEJ; ☎ 31 10 11 50, open June–Aug; bus 11; the most central campsite.

FOOD AND DRINK

Copenhagen This Week and *Playtime* have listings for all sorts of eating; the latter is full of tips for doing so on a budget. **Nyhavn** is pretty at night and has loads of bars and restaurants, but is a bit touristy and on the expensive side.

Traditional Danish fare tends to be a bit more expensive, but it's worth visiting one of the cellar restaurants (off STRØGET). These are a traditional part of life in Copenhagen and serve mainly Danish specialities.

Try *pølser* (sausages) from street stalls and open sandwiches: as well as being very Danish, fast-food such as this is cheap. Otherwise, stock up at an all-you-can-eat buffet, often to be found in Turkish, Greek and Italian restaurants on or just off the main pedestrian streets. Another cheapish option is ethnic restaurants, particularly Chinese: (red-light) districts **Halmtorvet** and **Istedgade** have many. **Frederiksberg** is a good area for budget eateries. **Cap Horn** in NYHAVN is an enticing place and serves organic food. Inexpensive food is easy to come by in **Christiania** (p. 408).

HIGHLIGHTS

Punctuated with pretty squares and invariably full of shoppers and strollers, **Strøget** is the city's pedestrian-only zone at the heart of the city.

On the far side of GOTHERSGADE, the green-roofed Dutch Renaissance-style **Rosenborg Slot** (Rosenborg Palace) sits majestically in the **Rosenborg Have** (Rosenborg Garden), ØSTER VOLDGADE, adjacent to the **Botanisk Have** (Botanical Gardens). The palace, no longer home to the royals, is now a museum of sumptuous 17th-century interiors. From here, beaver-hatted soldiers march east for the **Changing of the Guard** at the current royal domicile, **Amalienborg** (accompanied by a band when the Queen is in residence). This consists of a quartet of rococo palaces near the river, framing a courtyard that's overlooked by an equestrian statue of Frederick IV. The adjacent **Ameliehaven** is a narrow strip of densely planted garden, ideal for picnics.

CYCLING

Thanks to an inspired cycle policy, Denmark's cycle paths are widespread. In Copenhagen, bicycles are a sensible alternative to public transport: hire per day is cheaper than a 24-hr transport pass. Use the commendable City Bikes scheme: deposit a DKr20 coin and pick up one of 1,500 bicycles from 120 racks in the city centre. On replacing the bike in any of the racks, the coin is returned.

City Safari (ISTEDGADE 114; ☎31 24 04 07) organise several cycle tours of the city. For straightforward hire, try Københavens Cykler Reventlowsgade 11; ☎33 33 86 13 at København H station. Expect to pay around DKr50 per day.

Especially photogenic is the small 300-year-old **Nyhavn** (new harbour), bordered by picturesque 18th-century townhouses, cafés and masts of restored sailing vessels.

Most museums are closed on Mondays. The recently renovated **Statens Museum for Kunst** (State Museum of Fine Arts), SØLVGADE 48–50, houses Danish art from the 17th century and works by such masters as Matisse, Picasso and Munch.

By contrast, in south-east Copenhagen lies **Christiania** – a self-Governing, alternative society of about 1,000 citizens, and almost as many large but friendly dogs. It's a fun place to wander in: a maze of graffiti-encrusted alternative housing, cafés, bars and workshops – very laid-back and quite safe (though wild during concerts); not at all salubrious, but that's the point. There are several lively bars and cheap places to eat: 15mins walk or 🚌 no. 8 from the centre.

SHOPPING

Prices are somewhat higher than in other western European capitals. Design plays an important part in Danish living and many ordinary household objects, such as kitchenware, candlesticks and clocks, are worth buying for that alone. Streets around **Vesterbro**, **Norrebro** and **Studiestrœde** have many trendy boutiques and shops for second-hand books, records and so forth. Nevertheless, **Strøget**, home to the two biggest department stores (**Illum**, OSTERGADE 52, and **Magasin**, KONGENS NYTORV 13), is still the essential area for serious shoppers.

24-HOUR PHARMACY **Steno Apotek**, VESTERBROGADE 6C.

NIGHT-TIME AND EVENTS

There are comprehensive listings in *Copenhagen This Week* and *Playtime*.

Copenhagen's night scene is lively, and dress is almost always informal. There is no shortage of cafés and bars with live music, notably jazz. Discos and clubs tend to get lively around midnight and stay open until 0500 (when the breakfast bars open). The admission charge is usually not very much and prices for drinks are seldom loaded – but alcohol is always expensive.

Alternatively the city has a long theatrical tradition. Among some 160 stages, **Det Kongelige Teater** (The Royal Theatre), KONGENS NYTORV, reigns supreme (red lights outside mean it's sold out). The **Mermaid Theatre**, SKT PEDERSTRŒDE 27, presents English-language productions. The **Nørreport kiosk**, by NØRREPORT S-TOG, sells same-day discounted theatre tickets. Films are almost invariably shown in the original language and subtitled.

The major **annual events** are the ballet and opera festival in May and an international jazz festival in July. Out of town, the July rock festival in Roskilde (p.427) is gaining in international stature.

LIGHTING UP THE TIVOLI

Best seen at night, when 100,000 fairy lights are switched on, the 155-year-old Tivoli amusement park is Copenhagen's playground, with everything from fairground rides to ballet – and dozens of eateries. Three nights a week (ask on arrival), fireworks are let off just before midnight. For information, ☎33 15 10 01; http://www.tivoli-gardens.com).

INTERNET CAFÉS

USE IT, RÅDHUSTRÆDE 13; **PC-Café,** AMAGERBROGADE 22; **Nethulen,** ISTEDGADE 114, 1ST FLOOR.

WHERE NEXT?

*Southwards to **Hamburg** (p.224) via the train ferry between Rødby and Puttgarten (5 a day: 4½-hour journey time) ETT table 50. Catamarans cross in 45 mins to **Malmø** in Sweden (ETT table 2362), where you can join the route into Norway and on to **Oslo** (p. 415).*

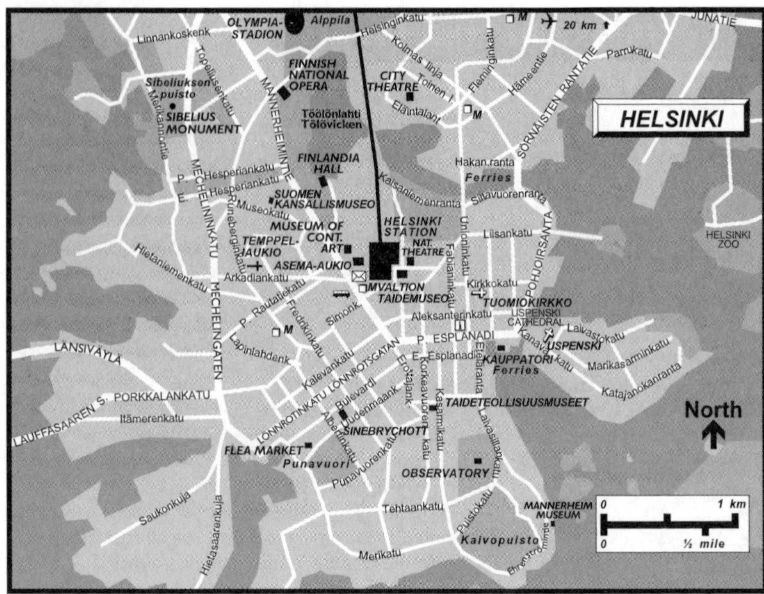

Built on a series of peninsulas and distinctly a city of the sea, Helsinki is perhaps something of an acquired taste, with a gritty, northern flavour, and both small and relatively modern as European capitals go. It became the capital of Finland in 1812 while under Russian influence and was rebuilt in a grand grid in the 19th century. With its public buildings standing proud on great granite steps, it has a distinctively Russian air, having been modelled on St Petersburg. The streets exude an exhilarating sense of space, while in the midst of it all rears the onion dome of the Russian Orthodox cathedral. Many buildings have sunny yellow walls, countering the slightly forbidding look.

ARRIVAL AND DEPARTURE

RAIL **Helsinki**, ☎707 5700, open Mon–Fri 0515–0130; Sat–Sun 0515–0100. An amazingly innovative art nouveau structure of 1916 by Eliel Saarinen, a sight in itself, foreshadowing the art deco style that was to emerge later; as a station it is central and reasonably well-equipped. English newspapers are available at R-kioski, a Forex office converts currency, the **VR** (Finnish Railways) information offices open 0635–2200 daily, and there are several eateries. Lockers and a lost-property office are in the wing near platform 11 (open 1630–2200). The station is linked to the labyrinthine metro stop at **Rautatientori** (Railway Square) and is the terminal for many local buses, while a number of trams have stops in front of the station.

TOURIST OFFICE

POHJOISESPLANADI 19; ☎169 3757; http://www.hel.fi (5 blocks from the station: south on KESKUSKATU, left on POHJOISESPLANADI), open Mon–Fri 0900–1900, Sat–Sun 0900–1500 (May–Sept); Mon–Fri 0900–1700, Sat 0900–1500 (Oct–Apr). Most leaflets are free and include a street map. Get the very useful free leaflet *Helsinki on Foot*, which describes six separate walks and *Helsinki This Week*,(http://www. helsinkiepert.fi). For nationwide information, cross the road to the **Finnish Tourist Board**: **MEK (Matkailun edistmiskeskus)**, ETELÄESPLANADI 4; ☎4176 9300; (http://www.mek.fi); Mon–Fri 0830–1700 (Wed till 1800), Sat 1000–1400 (June–Aug); Mon–Fri 0830–1600, Wed till 1700 (Sept–May).

There are many **cruises**, both within Scandinavia and to **Tallinn, Estonia** and **Germany**: check whether a visa is needed for your destination. The big companies are: **Silja Line**, MANNERHEIMINTIE 2, ☎9800 745 52, and **Viking Line**: MANNERHEIMINTIE 14, ☎123 577. **Tallink**, EROTTAJA 19, ☎2282 1277, has the cheapest ferries and catamarans to Tallinn (see p. 472).

Long-distance buses: ☎9600 4000 (premium rate). The main terminal is off MANNERHEIMINTIE, just west of the post office. Tickets can be purchased at the terminal or on board.

Helsinki–Vantaa, ☎9600 8100, 20 km north; has a Thomas Cook exchange bureau. **Finnair buses** depart (every 20 mins 0500–2400) from their office, ASEMA–AUKIO 3 (Station Yard); ☎818 7750. The journey takes about 30 mins and costs FIM25. Bus no. 615 (from the opposite side of the station) costs FIM15, takes an hour and operates 0520–2220. Taxis cost around FIM120, but special airport taxis cost around FIM50 if you book at least 2 hrs in advance, ☎700 800.

INFORMATION

Budget travellers should drop in at **Kompassi**, the **youth information centre**, MIKONKATU 8, 2ND FLOOR, ☎612 1863 (http://www.hel.fi/nk/kompassi); Mon–Thur 1100–1700, Fri 1100–1600 (May–July), Mon–Thur 1100–1800, Fri 1100–1600 (Aug–Apr).

Get *Helsinki Guide* and *Helsinki This Week*, for every conceivable listing and event. *Helsinki Helps* (students wearing green and carrying green bags with an 'i') wander round the centre 0800–2000 (June–Aug) to provide general guidance. They know more about youth activities than Tourist Officers.

The **Helsinki Card** is available from the Tourist Office, **Hotellikes-kus** and travel agents, and provides free public transport (including some ferry trips), free or discounted museum entrance and many other discounts: 24 hrs (FIM110), 48 hrs (FIM140) or 72 hrs (FIM170). **TourExpert**, in the City Tourist Office, ☎622 69 90, sells boat, bus, train and concert tickets. **Thomas Cook licensees**: **Travel House Tournee Ltd**, SILTASAARENKATU 4A, ☎7740 480; **Tournee Elemamatkat Oy**, FREDRIKINKATU 33; ☎6801 717.

MONEY

Banks open Mon–Fri 0915–1615. **Forex** in the station (daily 0800–2100); cash exchange counter at the airport (daily 0600–2300).

POST AND PHONES

The **main post office**, MANNERHEIMINAUKIO 1, ☎02045 14400 (open Mon–Fri 0900–1800), has a poste restante section that's open Mon–Fri 0900–2100, Sat 0900–1800, Sun 1100–2100 (entrance ASEMA-AUKIO), and phone and fax services. **Helsinki telephone code**: 9 (09 from within Finland).

PUBLIC TRANSPORT

Many of the sights are in the area between the station and KAUPPATORI, and trams are a quick way of reaching most of the others.

METRO The Metro was designed primarily for commuters. The only line serves the north and east, but it is spreading. It operates 0545–2320 (0230 at weekends) and tickets are obtained from vending machines. Single tickets for city centre travel cost FIM10 tram/bus and a ten-trip ticket (from R-kiosks and HKL offices) is FIM75. Tickets are valid for one hour.

PUBLIC TRANSPORT A good network of **buses** and **trams** runs approximately 0600–2300 (a few continue until 0130). The public transport company is **HKL** (*Helsingin Kaupungin Liikennelaitos*), with offices in ASEMATUNNELI/RAUTATIENTORI, **Hakaniemi** station. For information, ☎010 0111 (premium rate), Mon–Fri 0700–1900, Sat–Sun 0900–1700. The best way to get around is by tram. Tram no. 3T is frequent, 0600–0130, and has a figure-of-eight route, going to, or near, most of the city's main attractions. Many tram numbers are followed by a letter that denotes the direction. For taxis try **Helsinki Taxi Center,** ☎700 700, or the station, ☎651 766.

City tourist tickets (from the Tourist Office and HKL offices) give unlimited city travel on buses and trams for one day (FIM25), three days (FIM50) and five days (FIM75).

FERRIES Most local **cruises and ferries** leave from **Kauppatori**. Ticket kiosks on the quays indicate the time of the next departure.

ACCOMMODATION

The hotel booking service, ☎171 133, is off platform 11 at the station, open Mon–Sat 0900–1900, Sun 1000–1800 (June–Aug); 0900–1700 (Sept–May). They charge FIM20 for same-day bookings.

HOTELS

Satakuntatalo, LAPINRINNE 1A, ☎695 85231, is a cheap hotel, open summer only.

HOSTELS

Eurohostel (open all year), LINNANKATU 9, ☎622 0470; 2 km east of the station (tram no. 4 goes within 100 m: EUROHOSTEL).

Erottajanpuisto, UNDENMAANKATU 9, ☎642 169, is part HI hostel, part cheap hotel.

Omapohja, ITÄINEN TEATTERIKUJA 4, ☎666 211, is central. Slightly up the scale, the small **Anna**, ANNANKATU 1, ☎616 621, and **Arthur**, VUORIKATU 19, ☎173 441, are good value, the latter 200 m from the station.

CAMPSITES

Rastila, VUOSAARI, ☎316 551, opens all year and also has cottages for 2–6 people. It's 14 km east (metro: RASTILA).

FOOD AND DRINK

Helsinki This Week gives a comprehensive listing of eating places. Students can take advantage of the exceptionally low-priced **university cafés**: FABIANINKATU 33 and **Porthania,** HALLITUSKATU 6. Fried fish is available in abundance around the port. You can also pick up smoked salmon and reindeer sandwiches here, at the **Kauppahalli**. For fast food try the MANNERHEIMINTIE area – **Forum** offers a good choice.

HIGHLIGHTS

Finland's remarkably numerous 20th-century architects of international stature have graced the city with some of the most elegant modern architecture you could find anywhere.

The **harbour** is a good place to start, with pleasant views and a market selling trinkets. To the east is the Byzantine **Uspenski Cathedral**, KANAVAKATU 1, a magnificent reminder of Finland's Russian past, which still serves the Orthodox community.

To the west, **Esplanadi** is a boulevard busy with street musicians in summer. To the north, grand-scale **Senaatintori** (Senate Square) is dominated by **Tuomiokirkko**, the domed Lutheran Cathedral designed by Engel. The recently renovated interior is plain but elegant. Also flanking the square are the **Government Palace**, **Helsinki University** and the **University Library**: an impressive group. The new **City Museum**, just south of SENATE SQUARE, is a high-tech survey of Helsinki's growth from a seaside village to the national capital.

Valtion taidemuseo (Finnish National Gallery), KAIVOKATU 2–4, incorporates the **Ateneum** (Museum of Finnish Art), Finland's largest collection of paintings, sculptures and drawings from the 18th century to the 1960s, with **Nykytaiteen museo** (Museum of Contemporary Art) under the same roof – this will soon be moved next to the post office at MANNERHEIMAUKIO.

In MANNERHEIMINTIE is the 1970s **Finlandia Hall**, whose designer, Alvar Aalto, plays on his surname, which means 'wave', in the asymmetrical pattern. Further north is the **Olympic Stadium**, worth the traipse out, if only to take in the immense view from the stadium tower; there's also a sports museum here.

Other attractions include the Sibelius monument in **Sibeliuksen puisto** (Sibelius Park), 🚍no. 18, and the wonderful **Temppeliaukiokirkko** (Church in the Rock), LUTHERINKATU 3, blasted out of solid rock. The highly worthwhile **Taideteollisuusmuseo** (Museum of Applied Arts), KORKEAVUORENKATU 23, shows off the design by which Finland sets such high standards.

Four main islands hug the Helsinki peninsula, linked to Helsinki, and each other, by

TOURS

Boat trips and **bus tours** are available, and for the **walking tour** – get the free leaflet *See Helsinki on Foot* from the Tourist Office.

ferries and/or bridges. The first is **Suomenlinna** (15-min ferry trip from the South Harbour), endowed with a fine fortress and a World War II U-boat, *Vesikko*. There are good beaches – ideal for a picnic on a fine day. The island of **Korkeasaari** is home to **Helsinki Zoo**, which specialises in species from the Arctic. **Seurasaari** is the site of Finland's largest and oldest **open-air museum**, with 80 historic buildings, including peasant huts and Same (Lapp) tents; the island has several naturist beaches (emphatically single sex). **Pihlajasaari** is a recreation centre, popular with walkers and home to the area's best beaches.

NIGHT-TIME AND EVENTS

The Tourist Office has free entertainment guides and some hotels dispense copies. *Helsinki This Week* contains monthly listings. For recorded programme information in English, ☎058. Reservations for all events are handled by **Lippupalvelu**, MANNERHEIMINTIE 5; ☎9700 4700 (premium rate). Cultural events can also be booked with **Tiketti**, YRJÖNKATU 29C, ☎9700 4240 (premium rate). Better still is **TourExpert** in the City Tourist Office, ☎622 69 90.

SHOPPING

Mannerheimintie, Helsinki's main artery, is home to countless shops, including the vast **Stockmann** department store (good selection of English-language publications) and **Forum**, a complex with over 150 shops. The tree-lined **Esplanadi** is busy, but the park separating the north (POHJOISESPLANADI) from the south (ETELÄESPLANADI) makes it more strollable. In the **Tunneli** (the tunnel underneath the station), shops open until about 2200 and many open Sun.

Kauppatori (Market Square), by the port, has colourful waterside displays of freshly caught fish. This is where you get the best food buys. In season, look for *suomuuraimet* (cloudberries), which grow under the midnight sun.

Finlandia Hall, KARAMZININKATU 4, is the main centre for classical music. It's next door to the new **Opera House**.

Evenings are lively; options range from discos to sophisticated nightclubs – more and more now open till 0400, and are often linked to big hotels, such as the **Sokos Vaakuna**. Most have a minimum age of 20 or 24. The best areas for bars are around the station, or further south around UUNENMANKATU and ISO ROOBERTINKATU. Travellers tend to congregate at **Mulligan's Irish Bar**, MANNERHEIMINTIE 2. **Soda**, nearby, is lively. In summer there's a tram carriage converted into a pub which travels around town: you can hop on, have a beer and hop off again after a pleasant tour.

WHERE NEXT?

Ferries serve ***Stockholm*** *(p. 420),* ***Tallinn*** *(p. 472) and* ***St Petersburg*** *(p. 461).*

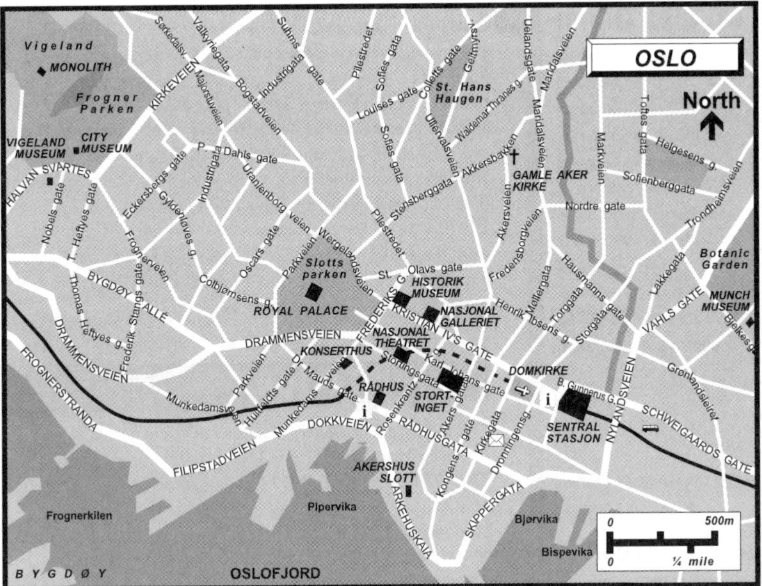

Hemmed in by water, mountains and forests, the former Viking capital is now a pleasant and laid-back modern-looking city. It is not a big place, more somewhere to look in on be-fore venturing to the wilds of Norway, rather than a destination in its own right. There are watery views from the fortress of Akershus, while the harbour area merits a brief exploration, and there are some enjoyable boat trips. An outstanding list of museums offers the best possible insight into Norwegian culture.

ARRIVAL AND DEPARTURE

RAIL The main rail station is the very central **Oslo Sentralstasjon** (known as **Oslo S** and open daily 0430–0130), ☎815 00 888. All long-distance trains stop here, as well as some local services. Crammed with facilities of every kind, it's an interesting design – the old half is of traditional cast-iron construction; the new half is airport-lounge-style steel and glass. The long-distance ticket office opens daily 0630–2300. The T-bane (metro) is to the right as you leave the station.

There are daily sailings by **Color Line,** ☎22 94 44 70, to Germany (**Kiel**) and Denmark (**Hirtshals**); **DFDS Scandinavian Seaways,** ☎22 41 90 90, to Denmark (**Copenhagen**); and **Stena Line,** ☎22 33 50 00, to Denmark (**Frederikshavn**).

Long-distance buses: these use **Bussterminalen**, SCHWEIGARRDSGT 8, ☎23 00 24 40, which is linked to Oslo S by overhead walkway.

TOURIST OFFICE

VESTBANEPLASSEN 1 (at the west end of the harbour), ☎22 83 00 50 (or 820 60 100, cheap rate, from within Norway); http://www.osloprp.no, oslo@oslopro.no. Open Mon–Fri 0900–1600 (Dec–Jan); Mon–Sat 0900–1600 (Feb–Apr, Oct–Nov); Mon–Sat 0900–1800 (May, Sept); Mon–Sat 0900–1800, Sun 0900–1800 (June); daily 0900–1900 (July–Aug). This is the Tourist Office for the whole of Norway as well as Oslo city.

✈ Oslo's main airport was at **Fornebu** (7 km west) until Oct 1998, when a new airport opened at **Gardermoen** (50 km north). The new airport will gradually take over all flights from the old one. **Flybussen SAS** airport buses between Fornebu and Oslo central station (also stopping at Natjonalteatret) run every 10/15 mins, 0550–2300, cost NKr.35, and take 20 mins. Transport arrangements for Gardermoen were not finalised at time of press, but there will be a similar airport bus. ☎67 59 62 20 for **airport bus** info. The express train link from the central station takes 33 mins (2–4 trains per hour) but this should be reduced to 19 mins. ☎815 32 019 for **express train** info, or see ETT tables 771/785.

INFORMATION

Get *The Official Guide for Oslo*, *What's On* and a map, all free. A small information office in Oslo S station opens daily 0700–2300 in summer, 0900–1700 in winter.

The youth tourism information service **USE IT** is at MØLLERGT 3; ☎22 41 51 32, http://www.unginfo.oslo.no, open Mon–Fri 0730–1800, Sat 0900–1400 (July–Aug), Mon–Fri 1100–1700 (Sept–June); it has free internet access. Make sure you get their (free) *Streetwise* magazine – an excellent guide to Oslo on a shoestring, and probably the most up-to-date guide you'll get.

Hikers should visit **DNT**, STORGATE 3; ☎22 82 28 00, open Mon–Fri 0830–1600.

The widely available **Oslo Card**, valid for 24 hrs (NKr.150), 48 hrs (NKr.220) or 72 hrs (NKr.250), provides free city transport, free admission to most attractions and various discounts. The **Oslo Package** provides hotel room and breakfast and the Oslo Card at NKr.370 per person in a double room – including children under 16 in their parents' room. Valid early June–mid Aug and weekends year-round.

MONEY **Post offices** (most open Mon–Fri 0900–1700, Sat 1000–1400) take least commission. The **bank** in Oslo S opens Mon–Fri 0800–1930, Sat 1000–1700. The airport bank opens Mon–Fri 0630–2000, Sat 0700–1700, Sun 0700–2000.

POST AND PHONES **Oslo Sentrum Postkontor** (the main post office), DRONNINGENSGT/ PRINSENSGT, opens Mon–Fri 0800–1800, Sat 1000–1500. The post office in Oslo S opens Mon–Fri 0700–1800, Sat 0900–1500.

PUBLIC TRANSPORT

The centre's small and it's easy to reach outlying attractions on the excellent public transport system.

Trafikanten (the tower-like construction outside Oslo S), JERNBANETORGET, ☎22 17 70 30 (open Mon–Fri 0700–2000, Sat–Sun 0800–1800), handles transport queries, timetables and

Colour Section

(i) View from the Oslo–Bergen route (p. 436); Christiania hippy commune, Copenhagen, Denmark (p. 404)

(ii) View across the Bosphorus, Istanbul (p. 520)

(iii) Anichkov Bridge, St Petersburg (p. 461)

(iv) Olympia, Greece (p. 535); Restored theatre, Epidavros, Greece (p. 513).

CHRISTIANIA
VÆR SØD:
RESPEKTER
CHRISTIANIAS
INGEN VÅBEN
INGEN RYGMÆR-KER
JUNKFRI BY

tickets. Get the (free) public transport map, *Sporveiskart for Oslo*. Single tickets, valid for 1 hr, cost NKr.18. Multi-ride tickets include day cards (*Dagskort*; NKr.40) and 7-day cards (*Syv-Dagerskort*; NKr.140).

Metro: T-lines converge at STORTINGET. There are maps on the platforms and trains have a destination board. Most trams converge at Oslo S and most city buses at Oslo M (on VATERLAND, by Oslo S). Most westbound buses (including those to **Bygdøy** and **Vigelandsparken**) stop at the south side of Nasjonalteatret.

Taxis: ☎22 38 80 90, or use the strategically positioned ranks. If you use an unregistered 'pirate taxi', agree a price beforehand and don't go alone.

Ferries to **Bygdøy** leave (Apr–Sept) from quay 3 on RÅDHUSBRYGGE, near the Tourist Office, as do sightseeing boats. Ferries to **Hovedøya**, **Langøyene** and other islands in Oslofjord leave from VIPPETANGEN (bus no.29).

ACCOMMODATION

The Tourist Office at Oslo S supplies a list of pensions and will book accommodation, including rooms in private houses (fee NKr.20 per person). **USE IT** book rooms for no fee. Book in advance in high season (July–early Aug).

Hotels

Grand Hotel, KARL JOHANSGT 31, ☎22 42 93 90, was built in the 1870s and is hard to beat for period character.

City Hotel, SKIPPERGT 19, ☎22 41 36 10, is more reasonably priced and central (two blocks from Oslo S), with comfortable old-style furniture and décor.

Hostels

Haraldsheim, HARALDSHEIMVN 4, GRENSEN, ☎22 22 29 65, is 5 km from Oslo S: tram 10/11or bus no.31/32 to SINSENKR.YSSET.

The **YMCA** (next door to USE IT in MØLLERGT) is really central. Bring a sleeping bag for both these.

Sleep Safe Church Hostel is probably the cheapest place in town (also claims to be open 25 hrs): ☎22 15 20 99; tram 11/12/17 to GREFSENVEIEN.

Campsites

Bogstad Camping, ANKERVEIEN 117; ☎22 50 76 80, open all year (bus no.2 from Oslo S, 30 mins).

Ekeberg Camping, EKEBERGVN 65, ☎22 19 85 68, is closer (about 3 km: 10 mins on tram no. 19: Ekeberg), but open only mid May–Aug.

You can camp in the forest north of town if you avoid public areas (head into the trees for about 1 km). Camping is also free on **Langøyene island**, which has good beaches, but ferries operate only 1015–1930 (June–Aug).

FOOD AND DRINK

Eating out in Oslo is expensive and many places close Sun. For restaurant listings, see *The Official Guide for Oslo*. There are a number of pricey options for good Norwegian food: **Restaurant Blom**, KARL JOHANSGT 41B, is something of an institution and has been frequented by many famous figures; the slightly more affordable **Gamle Rådhus**, NEDRE SLOTTSGT 1, is Oslo's oldest restaurant, specialising in fresh shrimps and mussels. Eating on a budget is tricky but possible. Stock up on hotel buffet breakfasts. Shop at a supermarket (e.g. **Kiwi**, STORGATEN 33, open until 2300) or cheap delis on the east side of town, and picnic in one of the parks. Try fresh (boiled) prawns from the harbour, on a fresh roll, with a dash of mayonnaise.

HIGHLIGHTS

A pleasant boat trip across the bay is to the mostly boat-related attractions at **Bygdøy** (pronouned Big-duh). Ferries leave from quay 3 every hour (half-hourly at peak times in summer); they take 10 mins and cost NKr.50 return. There are also beaches and picnic spots.

Twenty mins' walk up the hill (bear right) is a group of museums. The breathtaking **Vikingskiphuset** (Viking Ship Museum) houses three 9th-century ships, once buried fully equipped for the voyage to Valhalla, now resurrected and reassembled. Many beautifully worked and well-preserved iron, wood and leather artefacts are on display. Some 150 Nordic buildings, including an ancient stave church, have been collected to form the nearby **Norsk Folkemuseum**, worth allocating a day to see to the full.

Back at Oslo harbour, the fortress-palace complex of **Akershus** looms to the east; entry from AKERSGT or over a drawbridge from KIRKEGT. Several museums are in the extensive grounds, notably **Hjemmefrontmuseet**, a fascinating place devoted to the history of the Norwegian Resistance. The huge **Forsvarsmuseet** (Defence Museum) goes back as far as the Vikings.

Domkirke, STORTORGET 1, dates from 1697, but only the baroque carved altarpiece and pulpit survive from the original cathedral. The stained-glass windows are by Vigeland, but the most striking feature is the vast ceiling painting.

Nasjonalgalleriet (National Gallery), UNIVERSITETSGT

Day trip from Oslo

Viking Landet, NORGES PARKEN, VINTERBRO (20 mins south by shuttle bus from the centre), is a theme park that recreates every aspect of daily life in a Viking community.

For free

Botanisk Hage (botanical gardens), **Nasjonalgalleriet** (National Gallery), **Domkirke** (Cathedral), **Sculpture Park** in VIGELANDSPARKEN, **National Museum of Contemporary Art**, park around Askerhus, university **museums** of geology, palaeontology and zoology (by Munchmuseet), Post Museum (in main post office).

13 (metro: NASJONALTEATRET), houses a huge collection of Norwegian art and includes a room dedicated to Edvard Munch.

Vigelandsparken/Frognerparken, in north-west Oslo (main entrance from KIRKEVN) – bus no.20; tram no.12: FROGNERPARKEN – is a lush city park and sculpture garden. Some two hundred of Gustav Vigeland's life-size statues line the central avenue, culminating in the phallic 15m column of writhing bodies, which form the monolith of life.

SHOPPING

The most attractive buys are those reflecting Norwegian craftsmanship, such as crystal, leather goods, silver and knitwear, but nothing is cheap. **Karl Johans Gate** is the city's main street – part pedestrian and loaded with shops, restaurants, bars and street performers. **Basarhallene** (behind the cathedral) is an art and handicraft boutique centre, while the **Aker Brygge** complex stays open late and is a good place to browse. Other major complexes are **Paléet**, KARL JOHANSGT 37–43, and **Oslo City**, across from the station.

24-HOUR PHARMACY	**Ernbanetorgets Apotek**, JERNBANETORGET 4B.
LAUNDRETTE	**A-Snarvask**, THORVALD MEYERSGT 18.

Edvard Munch gave much of his art to the city, most of it housed in the **Munchmuseet** (Munch Museum), TØYENGT 53 (metro: T-YEN/MUNCHMUSEET), east of the centre. The display almost always includes his most familiar work, *The Scream*. The museum adjoins the extensive **Botanisk Hage** (botanical gardens).

NIGHT-TIME AND EVENTS

See *Streetwise, The Official Guide for Oslo* and *What's On* for listings. Oslo has a well-developed café culture, rather than big bars and clubs. The focus is the stretch between the station and the palace. The current trendy area is the **Grünerløkka** suburb to the north-east; a bit yuppie, but still atmospheric and lively. The scene is rapidly evolving. **Aker Brygge**, by the harbour, has waterfront bars, but is more touristy and expensive. Drinking anywhere in Oslo is expensive; alcohol is cheaper from supermarkets, but they can't sell it after 2000 and you can only get wine and spirits from special **Vinmonopolet** shops, e.g. MØLLERGATA 10/12. The drinking age is 18, but bars only serve 21+, and check ID rigorously. Most places stay open until 0300 or 0330.

Well-known operas are performed at **Den Norske Opera**, STORGT 23C, while the **Konserthus**, MUNKEDAMSVN 14, stages folklore Events in midsummer. Most movies are shown in their original language.

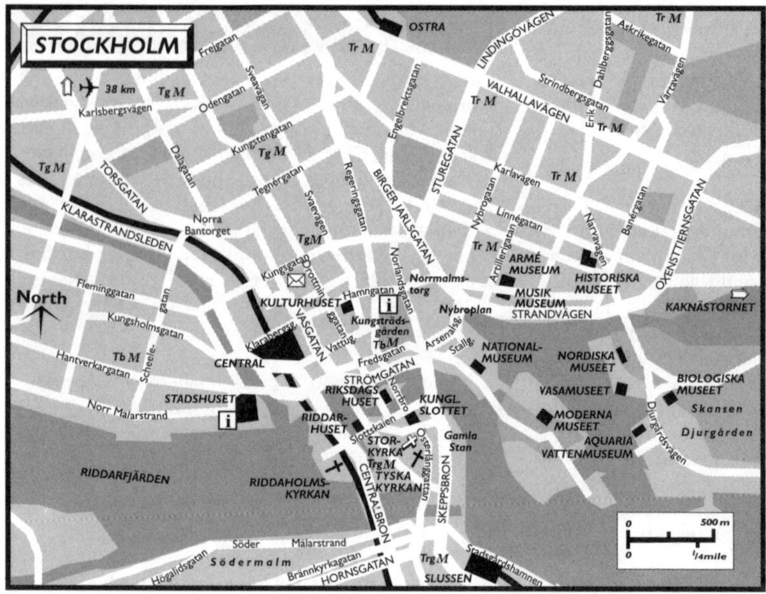

Spread over fourteen islands with countless inlets, Stockholm has a stunning waterfront setting on a par with the likes of San Francisco and Sydney, and most visitors would probably rate it the most rewarding of the Scandinavian capitals. At the heart of it is the impressively intact original part of the city, **Gamla Stan**, with an enticing blend of dignified old buildings, cafés, and craft and designer shops. In contrast, the **Djurgården** is a huge natural park where the city comes to swim, canoe, fly kites, visit the zoo and the superb outdoor museum, or just admire the views.

ARRIVAL AND DEPARTURE

RAIL The labyrinthine **Stockholm C** – or Stockholm Centralstation (0400–midnight) – has showers (on the lower level), a bus information/ticket office and the city's longest opening hours for postal services and currency exchange. Anything you need should be in (or adjoining) the main hall. If not, try the nearby Cityterminalen (see Buses, below). For domestic train information, ☎(020) 75 75 75 (24 hrs); for international information, ☎762 28 21 (0800–2200).

Cityterminalen (long-distance bus station), KLARABERGSVIADUKTEN: across the road from Stockholm Centralstation, but linked by tunnels. **Swebus (Intercity),** ☎(020) 64 06 40, open Mon–Fri 0830–1800/1900, Sat 0830–1330, Sun 1100–1800.

TOURIST OFFICE

SVERIGEHUSET (SWEDEN HOUSE), HAMNG. 27; ☎789 24 90; http://www.stoinfo.se; e-mail: info@stoinfo.se; open Mon–Fri 0800–1900, Sat–Sun 0900–1700 (June–Aug); Mon–Fri 0900–1800, Sat–Sun 0900–1500 (Sept and May); Mon–Fri 0900–1800, Sat–Sun 1000–1500 (Oct–Apr).

Ferries from Helsinki: the overnight ships to Finland (see feature, p. 425) are run by **Silja Line**, with offices at KUNGSGATAN 2, ☎22 21 40, and **Viking Line**, office at the CITYTERMINALEN, ☎452 40 00.

Stockholm Arlanda, ☎797 60 00, is 45 km north of Stockholm. The **Flygbuss** (airport bus), ☎(08) 600 10 00 takes about 40 mins from **Cityterminalen** and runs every 10–15 mins 0425–2200; SKr.70.

INFORMATION

From Centralstation, walk up KLARABERGSG. to SERGELS TORG (marked by an oddly-shaped pillar), then right on HAMNG for the Tourist Office.

Small city maps are freely available, but a larger-scale one is useful. A wealth of free English-language literature includes the useful *Stockholm This Week*. *Discover Stockholm* (SKr.49) is a 150-page illustrated guide that makes an excellent souvenir.

The **Stockholm Card** (**Stockholmskortet**, SKr.199 for 24 hrs, SKr.398 for 48 hrs or SKr.498 for 72 hrs) from Tourist Offices, stations, **Pressbyrån** and most hotels, provides free public transport, free entrance to many attractions and wide-ranging discounts.

MONEY

Forex branches include CENTRALSTATION (ground level), daily 0800–2100; CITYTERMINALEN, Mon–Fri 0800–2000, Sat 1000–1500; SWEDEN HOUSE (Tourist Information Centre), Mon–Fri 0900–1800. **Valutaspecialisten**, KUNGSGATAN 30, opens Mon–Fri 0800–1900, Sat 0900–1600.

POST AND PHONES

The main post office, DROTTNINGGATAN 53, opens Mon–Fri 0930–1830, Sat 1000–1300. Centralstation branch opens Mon–Fri 0700–2200, Sat–Sun 1000–1900.

Telecenter, CENTRALSTATION, opens daily 0800–2100. Buy phonecards here or from vending machines in the station. The telephone code for Stockholm is 08.

PUBLIC TRANSPORT

Storstockholms Lokaltrafik (SL) runs the excellent bus and metro network. Main office: lower level of SERGELS TORG; ☎600 10 00; Mon–Fri 0700–1900, Sat–Sun 1000–1700. There's a branch in CENTRALSTATION, open Mon–Sat 0630–2330, Sun 0700–2330.

Single tickets (from drivers: SKr.7 to board, plus SKr.7 per zone) are valid for 1 hr. **Rabattkuponger** provide 20 tickets for SKr.95 and **Turistkorten** provide unlimited travel for 24 hrs (SKr.60) or 3 days (SKr.120). There are reductions for students and seniors. Multi-ride tickets are available from **SL**, **Pressbyrån** and the **Tourist Centre**.

The metro, **Tunnelbanan (T-banan)**, has three lines (red, green and blue). Trains are fast and frequent, 0500–0100. Metro stations display a blue 'T' on a white background. The décor on some lines is among the most imaginitive in Europe: walls are moulded to look like caves and painted strident colours, with original murals.

DAY TRIPS FROM STOCKHOLM

Björkö (an island in Lake Mälaren) is the site of the **Birka Vikingstaden** (Birka Viking Town), Sweden's oldest city, accessible by ferry from Stadhusbron. Excavations have unearthed remains of ancient houses and a cemetery. The island has good beaches for swimming.

City buses are frequent, 0500–midnight, and there's a night service *(nattbus)*.

The larger taxi companies, **Taxi Stockholm,** 15 00 00, **Taxi Kurir,** 30 00 00, and **Taxi 020,** (020) 93 93 93, are usually cheapest and have fixed rates from the airport (about SKr.350). If you take an independent 'Fritaxi' cab, make sure you agree the fare before setting out.

The main local operator is **Waxholmsbolaget**, STRÖMKAJEN; 679 58 30. A **Båtluffarkort** allows 16 days of travel (SKr.260 from the Excursion Shop or Waxholmsbolaget offices). Single tickets can be purchased when you board. See also Tours, p. 424.

ACCOMMODATION

Hotellcentralen, the official accommodation booking service, is in the main hall of Centralstation; 789 24 25; e-mail: hotels@stoinfo.se; open daily 0800–1900 (May, Sept, 0900–1800 (June–Aug); Mon–Fri 0800–1700, Sat–Sun 0800–1400 (Oct–Apr). Advance bookings are free, but there's a fee for same-day bookings. Pick up a (free) copy of *Stockholm Hotel Guide*. A useful booking service for private rooms is **BBA** (bed and breakfast Agency Sweden), MARIATORGET 8; (08) 643 80 28, fax (08) 643 80 78; http://www.torget.se/ftg/bedandbreakfastagency.

HOTELS

Grand Hotel, BLASIEHOLMSHAMNEN 8, 679 35 00, has been voted one of the best in the world (for people with SKr.3500 per night to spend).

Hotel Winn, HOTELLGATAN 11, 705 95 00, is comfortable and surrounded by good shops.

HI

AF Chapman, SKEPPSHOLMEN, 679 50 15 (no.65), is a tall ship moored in the harbour.

Långholmen, GAMLA KRONOHÄKTET, 668 05 10, was once a prison (nearest metro: HORNSTULL).

CAMPSITES

Östermalm City Camping, FISKARTORPSVÄGEN, ÖSTERMALM, 10 29 03, is the most central campsite, open mid June–mid Aug. **Bredäng**, 97 70 71, 10 km south-west of the city (metro: BREDÄNG), opens all year; there's a **youth hostel** here too.

FOOD AND DRINK

Although not exactly the culinary capital of Europe, Stockholm has a good range of cuisine. Budget options are limited: by eating a main meal at lunchtime you can take advantage of the best offers. Small, inexpensive places are more abundant south of the water.

For a real splurge offering the best of Swedish fare, try **Den Gyltene Freden**, ÖSTERLÅNGGATAN 51, which has been going strong since the 1770s. **Operakällaren**, at the Opera House, was *the* place for so long that Stockholmers often refer to it as 'the café'. It consists of several restaurants, from gourmet to **Bakfickan** (good for a cheap lunch). **Stadshus Källoren**, basement of STADSHUSET, has a great atmosphere; dishes range from a cheap lunch to the Nobel Prize banquet menu. **Kungshallen**, KUNGSGATAN 44, offers a wide choice.

HIGHLIGHTS

Many museums are closed on Mon; most are open 1100–1600, with longer hours in summer. See *Stockholm This Week* for details.

GAMLA STAN

Joined to the mainland by bridges, **Gamla Stan** is the immaculately preserved old quarter of Stockholm, with old merchants' houses, boutiques and craft shops to browse in. Seek out the main square, **Stortorget**, with its colourful façades, gabled roofs and rococo **Börsen** (Stock Exchange), and the timewarp street of **Prästgatan**. Conspicuous both for its size and its splendour is **Kungliga Slottet** (metro: GAMLA STAN), the former royal palace of 1760, whose royal apartments, treasury, armoury and palace museum can be visited (separate entrance for each), and where the royal palace guard changes at noon each day.

DAY TRIPS FROM STOCKHOLM

For details get the leaflet *Run Away For A Day* from the Tourist Office. Probably the most impressive is **Drottningsholms Slott** (Drottningsholm Palace), home of the royal family and sometimes called 'Sweden's Versailles'. It is 11 km west of the city, and best reached by boat, taking an hour. Several rooms are on view and there are tours of the 18th-century theatre. **Kina Slott** (the Chinese pavilion and a World Heritage Site), at the far end of the gardens, was a summer cottage.

In the 1970s, the remains of the old town wall were discovered and incorporated into **Stockholms Medeltidsmuseet** (Museum of Medieval Stockholm). On a small island accessible from NORRBRO (one of the bridges linking Norrmalm and Gamla Stan, nos.43/62), it presents an imaginative reconstruction of medieval life. In front of the museum stands the **Riksdagshuset**, where the Swedish parliament meets; there are free guided tours from the rear of the building in early afternoon (weekdays in summer; weekends Jan–May and Sept).

North of the centre (metro: UNIVERSITETET), the **Bergianska Botaniska Trädgården** (the Botanical Gardens) includes **Victoriahuset**, home of the world's largest waterlily, while at **Fjärilsa Fågelhuset** (Butterfly House), HAGAPARKEN, you can see tropical butterflies and birds in a natural environment created by a 400 square m hothouse.

TOURS

Strömma Kanalbolaget, SKEPPSBRON 22; ☎(08) 587 140 00, operate summer tours. **Cinderella Boats**, (08) 20 88 25, offer archipelago transport and guided tours.

FOR FREE

Tours of **Riksdagshuset** (Swedish parliament); Changing the Guard at **Kungliga Slottet** (Royal Palace); **Postal Museum** in Gamla Stan; **Storkyrkan** (main church in Gamla Stan); art shows at **Kulturhuset**.

NORRMALM AND BLASIEHOLMEN

Norrmalm is the bland centre of modern Stockholm, an area of 1960s office blocks and shopping malls near the main rail station, with the glass obelisk of **Sergels Torg** (where the **Kulturhuset** is home to changing exhibitions of Swedish contemporary arts and crafts; free). Things get better around the leafy park of **Kungsträdgården**, the foremost meeting place in the city, lined with cafés and full of street life. There are museums at nearby **Blasieholmen** and **Skeppsholmen**.

DJURGÅRDEN

🚌 nos. 44/47 stop near each of the main attractions in the city's island pleasure garden. There are ferries from NYBROPLAN (in Gamla Stan) year-round, and from SKEPPSBRON (east of Kungsträdgården) in summer, as well as a private tram.

The eastern section of this large island, together with **Ladugårdsgärdet** (to the north), forms **Eko Park**, a 56 square km nature reserve.

Along the western side are various attractions. Don't miss **Vasamuseet**, built to house *Vasa*, a 17th-century warship that was well preserved in mud dredged up in 1961 from the harbour where she sank on her maiden voyage.

Aquaria Vattenmuseum (Water Museum) is a high-tech complex that enables you to experience 24 hours in a rain-forest and get close to marine creatures (entrance fees help to save endangered rain-forest).

SHOPPING

The main areas are HAMNGATAN, DROTTNINGGATAN, SERGELS TORG and GAMLA STAN. **NK**, HAMNG. 18–20, and **Åhléns**, KLARABERGSG. 50, are well-stocked department stores. Specialities include Swedish crystal, handmade paper, textiles and ceramics. **Æter & Essencefabriken**, WALLINGATAN 14, is a highly fragrant spice shop, while **Stockholms Läns Hemslöjdförening**, DROTTNINGG., is one of a number of places for Swedish handicrafts, which can also be found at numerous places in Gamla Stan. The most popular markets, a mixture of stalls and indoor food halls, are **Östermalmstorg**, **Hötorget** and **Søderhallarna**.

24-HOUR PHARMACY — **C. W. Scheele**, KLARABERGSG. 64; ☎454 81 30.

LAUNDRETTE — VÄSTMANNAGATAN 61, ☎34 64 80 (just north of the main rail station).

For something more frivolous, **Gröna Lund Tivoli** offers live entertainments and rides.

NIGHT-TIME AND EVENTS

Stockholm This Week carries listings. There are around seventy theatres and concert halls and, in summer, you can enjoy free concerts in the parks. Most films are shown in the original language. **Cosmonova Omnitheatre** (in Naturhistoriska) offers highly advanced planetarium performances and Omnimax films.

INTERNET CAFÉS
Café Access, KULTURHUSET, SERGELS TORG; **NK IT-Center,** HAMNGATAN 18–20.

Södermalm, south of the water, is the best area for pubs (open till 0100), and is more bohemian and cheaper than the glitzy north side – a good place to wander around too. Clubs are centred around **Stureplan** and **Norrmalm**; some stay open till 0500, but some don't admit under-25s.

EVENTS

The major annual event is the **Stockholm Water Festival** (ten days in Aug), with varied celebrations, including many water-oriented activities. Other regular events include a **kite festival** (May), **National Day** (6 June) and a **beer festival** (late Sept). **Regattas** are held frequently in the summer.

WHERE NEXT? FERRIES TO HELSINKI

Departing at 1800 from each port, the immense Viking and Silja ferries (ETT table 2465) that make the journey across the Baltic are a popular institution with the locals. There's a great view of the archipelagos at each end as the sun goes down, and the food and drink are tax-free, a difference you are certain to notice in Scandinavia. Each has pubs and clubs which stay open and distinctly active until 0500, especially at weekends; some say it's the best night out around. This journey is surprisingly cheap: four sharing a cabin can pay as little as SKr.150 each including the ticket – less still if you don't take a cabin. The boats arrive around 0830, and you can sleep off your night's entertainment for a while before getting booted off. Travellers have been known to spend all their nights on the boat, touring Helsinki and Stockholm on alternate days. The operators sometimes run even cheaper 20-hr sailings which just cruise out of harbour, drop anchor and open the bar.

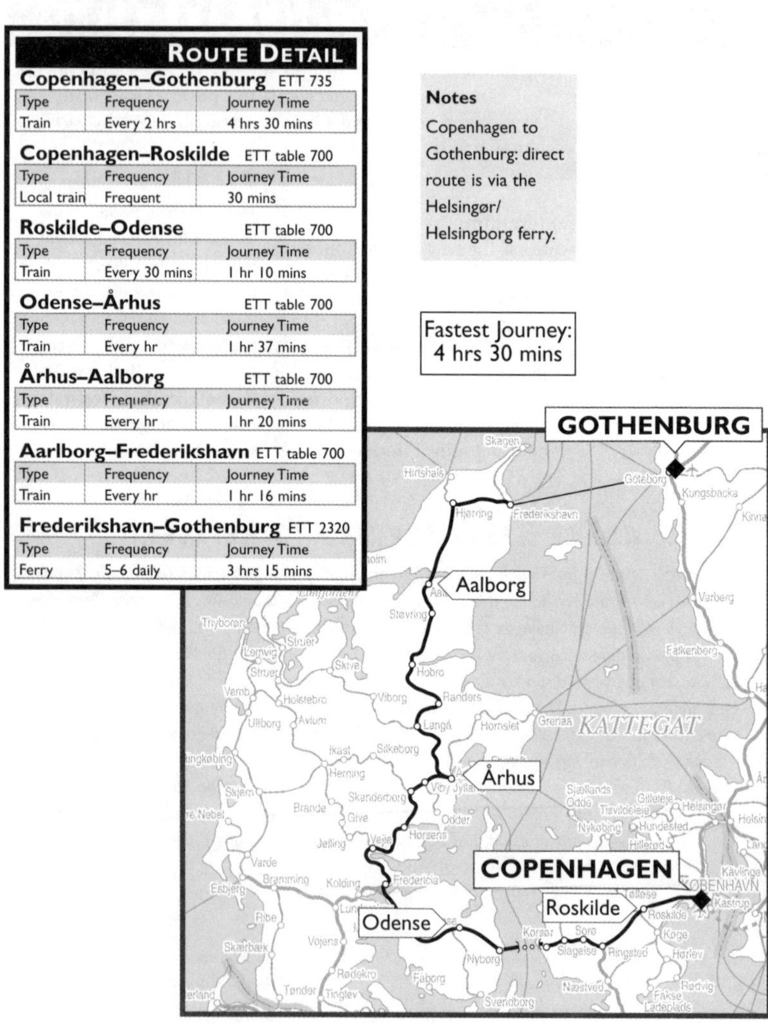

ROUTE DETAIL

Copenhagen–Gothenburg ETT 735

Type	Frequency	Journey Time
Train	Every 2 hrs	4 hrs 30 mins

Copenhagen–Roskilde ETT table 700

Type	Frequency	Journey Time
Local train	Frequent	30 mins

Roskilde–Odense ETT table 700

Type	Frequency	Journey Time
Train	Every 30 mins	1 hr 10 mins

Odense–Århus ETT table 700

Type	Frequency	Journey Time
Train	Every hr	1 hr 37 mins

Århus–Aalborg ETT table 700

Type	Frequency	Journey Time
Train	Every hr	1 hr 20 mins

Aarlborg–Frederikshavn ETT table 700

Type	Frequency	Journey Time
Train	Every hr	1 hr 16 mins

Frederikshavn–Gothenburg ETT 2320

Type	Frequency	Journey Time
Ferry	5–6 daily	3 hrs 15 mins

Notes

Copenhagen to Gothenburg: direct route is via the Helsingør/ Helsingborg ferry.

Fastest Journey: 4 hrs 30 mins

This journey takes in the dramatic 18-km **Great Belt** tunnel and bridge combination linking Denmark's two largest islands – **Zealand** and **Funen** – as well as the opportunity to visit some of northern Denmark's lesser-known yet highly attractive towns. **Odense** makes a particularly useful base for exploring the area. The sea crossing from **Frederikshavn** to **Gothenburg** – soon to be made obsolete by a huge bridge – is a convenient way to enter Sweden.

ROSKILDE

Roskilde, south-west of Copenhagen, was Denmark's first capital. Its cathedral is the traditional burial place of Danish royalty.

Late June/early July sees the Roskilde major open-air rock festival (special campsite and a shuttle bus from the station). Many international stars are now appearing at this event, likely to be attended by more than 100,000 people in 1999.

ODENSE

Odense, a busy manufacturing city, is the largest settlement on the island of **Fyn** *(Funen)* and the third largest in the country. Throughout Denmark it's known as the birthplace of Hans Christian Andersen, who turned to writing fairytales after failing in his ambitions to be an actor and playwright.

Hans Christian Andersen's childhood home from the age of two, **Barndomshjem**, has a couple of rooms crammed with his belongings, but there's far more material in the **HC Andersen Hus** (HC Andersen Museum), HANS JENSEN STRÆDE 37–45, the tumbledown cottage where he was born in 1805, including manuscripts and his celebrated top hat. Another cultural shrine is the only museum outside the USA dedicated entirely to **Elvis Presley**: GRØNLØKKEN 3, ☎ (66) 19 16 40.

Two excellent art museums are **Fyns Kunstmuseum** (Art Museum of Funen; free Wed evenings), a superb collection of Danish art, and the **Museum of Photographic Art**, featuring permanent and temporary exhibits.

Carl Nielsen, Denmark's greatest composer, was born near Odense in 1865, and is commemorated by the **Carl Nielsen Museet**, a museum at CARL BERGS GADE 11 (by the concert hall).

☎(70) 13 14 15. This forms the northern boundary of the city centre.

Tourist Office: RÅDHUSET, JERNBANEGADE; ☎(66) 12 75 20; otb@odenseturist.dk; http://www.odenseturist.dk. Open Mon–Sat 0900–1900, Sun 1100–1900 (mid June–Aug); Mon–Fri 0930–1630, Sat 1100–1300, closed Sun (Sept–mid June).

An **Odense Adventure Pass** is available for 24 hrs (DKr.50) or 48 hrs (DKr.90), giving free public transport and large reductions on attraction admission fees. If you're using buses without a pass, be aware that Odense is unique in Denmark in that you pay your fare at the end of the trip.

Youth hostel, KRAGSBJERGVEJ 121 ☎ (66) 13 04 25, (mid Feb–Dec); **InterRail Point**, RØDEGÅRDSVEJ 91 ☎ (66) 14 23 14.

ÅRHUS

Denmark's second city is a large port and commercial and cultural centre, but even so most places are within walking distance.

Old Århus has the monopoly of nightspots and several museums, including three on one site – the **Kvindemuseet** (Woman's Museum), examining the lot of modern women, the **Besttelsesmuseet**, paying homage to the Danish Resistance in World War II, and the free **Vikingemuseet** (Viking Museum). Close by, the vast **Domkirke** (cathedral) has a 93 m nave – Denmark's longest – and contains several restored, pre-Reformation frescos as well as an altar triptych by Bernt Notke.

DAY TRIP FROM ÅRHUS

An hour's journey away in **Billund** is the **Legoland** park, a showpiece of this Danish invention: ☎75 33 13 33 (http://www.legoland.dk).

Set in **botanical gardens** to the west of the centre, the city's major attraction is **Den Gamle By**, Denmark's national museum of urban living. This delightful open-air complex consists of some 70 houses from around Denmark, depicting 400 years of life in the city.

Located 5 km south of the city the superb **Mosegård Prehistoric Museum** is home to the 2000-year-old **Grauballe man**, discovered in a bog in 1952; 🚌 no. 19 passes by.

The station, ☎(86) 12 37 77, is just south of the centre.

Tourist Office: RÅDHUSET, PARK ALLÉ; ☎(86) 12 16 00; aarhconv@inet.uni-c.dk; http://www.aarhus-tourist.dk. Open Mon–Fri 0930–1800, Sat 0930–1700, Sun 0930–1300 (23 June–14 Sept); Mon–Fri 0930–1630, Sat 1000–1300 (15 Sept–30 Apr); Mon–Fri 0930–1700, Sat 1000–1300 (1 May–22 June). An **Århus Passet** gives free bus travel and entry to all attractions.

AALBORG

The humble herring brought prosperity to the town in the 17th century, and the legacy of that boom is the handsome old quarter, with fine old merchants' houses, such as the spectacularly ornate **Jens Bangs Stenhouse**. **Aalborg Historiske Museum** displays finds from **Lindholm Hoje** – the largest Viking burial ground in

Scandinavia – with the peat-preserved 1600-year-old skeleton of a woman the highlight (closed Mon; no. 6). **Nordjyllands Kunstmuseum** (Museum of Modern and Contemporary Art) is home to one of the nation's foremost collections of 20th-century art – and has a sculpture garden. The **Zoo** AT MOLEPARKVEJ 63 contains animals in a near-natural environment.

After the sun goes down, JOMFRU ANE GADE is the street for bars (maybe to sample the eponymous local *schnapps*), nightlife and eateries.

(98) 16 16 66, a short walk south down Boulevarden from the town centre.

Tourist Office: ØSTERÅGADE 8; (98) 12 60 22; http://www.tourist-aal.dk; email: tourist@pip.dknet.dk. Open Mon–Fri 0900–1800, Sat 0900–1700 (mid June–mid Aug); Mon–Fri 0900–1630, Sat 1000–1300 (mid Aug–mid June).

GOTHENBURG (GÖTEBORG)

The huge cranes and shipyards that greet visitors arriving at Scandinavia's prime port mask Sweden's second largest and most attractive old city.

To get your bearings, go up **Göteborgs Utkiken**, a striking red and white skyscraper, 86 m, which has a lookout and a small café near the top, giving superb harbour views. It's situated in **Lilla Bommen**, itself a charming area, with shops and craft workshops. Dominating the whole scene here, however, is the spectacular waterside **Opera House,** (031) 13 13 00. The resident company is the **Göteburg Operan** and performances of opera, ballet and concerts are held from Aug–May.

In summer there are English-language tours on **Lisebergslinjen** *(a vintage open-air tram: July) and* **Göteborgståget** *(a miniature train: May–Aug).* **Paddan sightseeing boats,** *(031) 60 96 70, depart from* KUNGSPORTPLATSEN *(May–Oct): their harbour cruise is recommended, but be prepared to duck low under one or two of the bridges. Paddan also run dry-land tours on a 'convertible bus'. A range of summer cruises are also available, around the harbour and further afield. Ask the Tourist Office for details.*

Kungsportsavenyn, usually known simply as **'Avenyn'** (The Avenue), is the hub of the city, a 50-m wide boulevard lined with lime trees and endowed with shops and eateries, further enlivened by buskers and impromptu street stalls. It leads up to **Götaplatsen**, the city's cultural centre, fronted by the fountain of **Poseidon** by the Swedish sculptor Carl Milles. Just off AVENYN is **Trädgårdsföreningen**, NYA ALLÉN, a park full of fragrance, flora and birdsong, dotted with works of art and other attractions.

The city's oldest secular building (1643) is **Kronhuset** (Crown Arsenal), POSTGASSE 6–8. Around it is **Kronhusbodarna**, a courtyard bounded by handicraft boutiques in 18th-century artisans' dwellings. Other good places for browsing are the **Antikhallarna** antique market in VÄSTRA HAMNGATAN, and **Haga Nygata**, a renovated historical area of cobbled streets, lined with craft, second-hand, antique, and design shops, as well as cafés and restaurants. Opposite, the **Feskekörkan** resembles a 19th-century church, but is a thriving fish market, open Tues–Fri 1000–1800, Sat 1000–1400, and has a good fish restaurant.

Most city museums open Tues–Sun 1100–1600 (Sept–Apr) and daily 1100–1600 (May–Aug), but some open earlier and close later. Details, including those of special exhibitions, are given in the multi-lingual leaflet, *Göteborgs Museer*. Of special interest are the **Göteburgs Maritima Centrum** (Gothenburg Maritime Centre), PACKHUSKAJEN, the **Konstmuseet** (Art Museum) and the **Ethnografiska Museet** (Museum of Ethnography).

In the large nature park of **Slottskogen** (outside the city: tram nos. 1/2: LINNÉPLATSEN) are an observatory, a children's zoo and the **Naturhistoriska Museet** (Natural History Museum).

BOCKKRANEN ERIKSBERG

Bungee jumping takes place from the huge gantry crane visible from the ferry on the way into Gothenburg, ☎(031) 779 11 11.

The popular ***Liseberg Amusement Park****,* ÖRGRYTEVÄGEN *5 (tram no. 5), is dominated by the 150 m high* ***Spaceport****, which offers panoramic views. Among the 30 or so gut-wrenching rides is one of Europe's longest roller-coasters.*

RAIL **Göteborg C (Central),** ☎(031) 10 44 45; at the north-east edge of the centre, compact and with many amenities. Open Mon–Fri 0430–0030, Sat 0530–0030, Sun 0630–0030; the ticket/information office opens Mon–Fri 0700–1900, Sat 0900–1800, Sun 0800–1900. Facilities include **Forex** foreign exchange (open daily 0800–2100), **Narvesen** (a chain selling papers, snacks etc.), lockers, showers (daily 0700–2100) and reasonably priced eateries. Most buses stop at NILS ERICSONSPLATSEN, in front of the station. There's a branch of **Nordstan** (eateries etc.) in the centre of the huge complex opposite the station, to which it's linked by a foot tunnel. Open Mon–Fri 0930–1800, Sat 0930–1500.

To/from the UK (**Harwich/Newcastle**), **Oslo** and **Amsterdam**, **Scandinavian Seaways**, ☎(031) 65 06 50, sail from SKANDIAHAMNEN, 20 mins west of the centre by bus. The bus leaves from stop U on NILS ERICSONSPLATSEN 1hr 30mins before each ferry departs. **Stena Line**, ☎(031) 704 00 00, to/from Germany (**Kiel**) sail from MANJABBEHAMNEN, 15 mins west of town; Stena ships to/from Denmark sail from MASTHUGGSKAJEN, at the west end of the centre. **Sea Cat**, ☎(031) 775 08 00, catamarans to/from Denmark (**Frederikshavn**), sail from FISKEHAMNEN, 10 mins west of town.

i Main **Tourist Office**: KUNGSPORTSPLATSEN 2; ☎(031) 10 07 40; http://www.gbg-co.se; e-mail: info@gbg-co.se. Open Mon–Fri 0900–1700, Sat 1000–1400, closed Sun (Sept–Dec); Mon–Fri 0900–1800, Sat–Sun 1000–1400 (May); daily 0900–1800 (2–21 June and 17–30 Aug); daily 0900–2000 (22 June–16 Aug).
Pick up the *Göteborg Guide*, a booklet containing listings and tips, and with a good town map. Also get a copy of *What's On*, a monthly guide to culture and events.

ENTERTAINMENT AND EVENTS

There is a wide selection of lively bars and clubs, centred around **Avenyn**; things hot up around midnight, and keep going until 0500. At the Gothenburg **annual festival** in mid August the town goes mad and there is all-night partying in the streets.

The centre's attractions are quite close together, but there's an excellent **tram** network if you don't feel like walking. Lines are colour-coded, so it's easy to see the stop and vehicle you need. Tram and bus stops show the numbers and destinations of lines using them. A single ticket is SKr.16, but you can save by buying a multi-ride **Magnet Kort** (SKr.100; must be purchased in advance at **Pressbyrån**), giving ten city rides on trams, buses and city boats. **TidPunkten** supply information about routes, times and fares; ☎(031) 80 12 35. **Main office**: NILS ERICSONSPLATSEN, open Mon–Thur 0700–2200, Fri 0700–0230, Sat 0900–0230, Sun 0900–1800. Others: DROTTNINGTORGET (Mon–Sat 0600–2000, Sun 0700–2000) and BRUNNSPARKEN (Mon–Fri 0700–1900, Sat 0900–1900).

The Tourist Offices will book private rooms, as well as hotels, for a small fee. **Hotel Lorensberg**, BERZELIIG 15, ☎(031) 81 06 00, is much more reasonably priced – a central and friendly place where imaginative use of murals depicting exterior scenes gives the interior an unusual feeling of space. For something a little different, try **M/S Seaside**, a hostel on a boat semi-permanently docked at PACKHUSKAJEN 8; ☎(031) 10 59 70. It offers 2–4-berth cabins and private cabins, and supplies equipment for evening deck barbecues. There are four **HI hostels** (and dozens of others). **Torrekulla Turiststation**, KÅLLERED, ☎(031) 795 14 95; **Slottsskogens**, VEGAGT 21, ☎(031) 42 65 20; and **Kårralunds**, OLBERGSG, ☎(031) 84 02 00. This last hostel is near the closest **campsite** to town: **Kårralunds Camping**, OLBERGSG (same ☎), which has **cottages** as well as camping and is open all year.

Göteborgskortet (Gothenburg Card) is obtainable from Tourist Offices, kiosks, hotels and campsites: SKr.125 for 24 hrs, SKr.225 for 48 hrs, SKr.275 for 72 hrs. It gives free use of the city's public transport and parking meters as well as free or discounted entrance to most museums and attractions (including **Liseberg amusement park** and the ferry to Frederikshavn).

There's a wide range of food on offer, much of it cosmopolitan or ethnic. The **seafood** is excellent, most restaurants clustering along the waterfront. For other types of cuisine, try around AVENYN. The further down sidestreets you go, the cheaper the restaurants. The Nordstan complex offers a lot of eateries, including familiar fast-food outlets and a good supermarket, **Hemköp**, which has a deli section in the basement of the big store known as **Åhléns City**. Virtually all the other shopping malls have heaps of inexpensive places to eat. For picnic items, the indoor **Storr Saluhallen market**, KUNGSTORGET, has a tempting range of goodies, particularly the cheeses.

WHERE NEXT?

*The **Copenhagen–Oslo** (p. 432) route passes through Gothenburg. Services run north-east to **Stockholm**; for a longer route to the Swedish capital via the southern shore of Lake Vänern use the **Herrijunga–Hallsberg** service via **Mariestad** (ETT table: 741).*

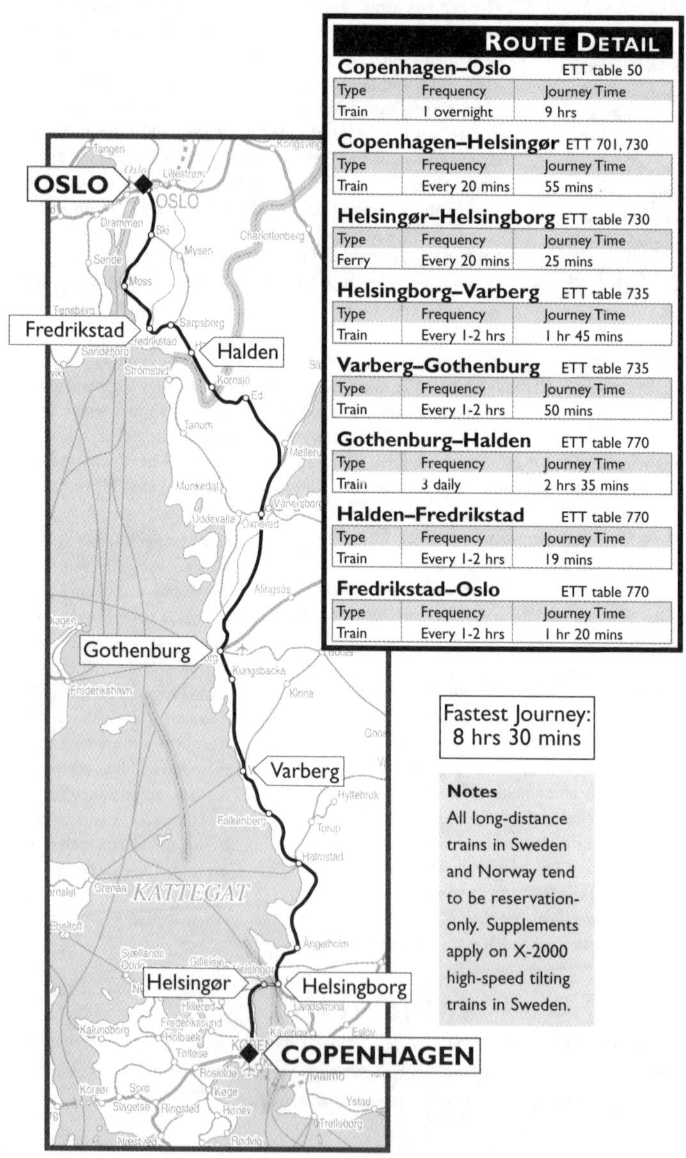

Route Detail

Copenhagen–Oslo ETT table 50

Type	Frequency	Journey Time
Train	1 overnight	9 hrs

Copenhagen–Helsingør ETT 701, 730

Type	Frequency	Journey Time
Train	Every 20 mins	55 mins

Helsingør–Helsingborg ETT table 730

Type	Frequency	Journey Time
Ferry	Every 20 mins	25 mins

Helsingborg–Varberg ETT table 735

Type	Frequency	Journey Time
Train	Every 1-2 hrs	1 hr 45 mins

Varberg–Gothenburg ETT table 735

Type	Frequency	Journey Time
Train	Every 1-2 hrs	50 mins

Gothenburg–Halden ETT table 770

Type	Frequency	Journey Time
Train	3 daily	2 hrs 35 mins

Halden–Fredrikstad ETT table 770

Type	Frequency	Journey Time
Train	Every 1-2 hrs	19 mins

Fredrikstad–Oslo ETT table 770

Type	Frequency	Journey Time
Train	Every 1-2 hrs	1 hr 20 mins

Fastest Journey: 8 hrs 30 mins

Notes

All long-distance trains in Sweden and Norway tend to be reservation-only. Supplements apply on X-2000 high-speed tilting trains in Sweden.

Starting in **Copenhagen** (p. 404) this journey takes an alternative route to **Gothenburg**. This route takes the ferry over the **Sound of Öresund** from the castle at **Helsingør** to the Swedish port of **Helsingborg**. You now head along Sweden's western seaboard, with its superb sandy beaches, through the impressive historic city of **Gothenburg** (see p. 429). There is plenty of potential to stop off at lesser known but imposing fortress towns, further reminders of times when the neighbouring countries were at war with each other.

HELSINGØR

The prominent feature of this busy ferry port is **Kronberg Slot**, the castle strategically sited on a knob of land that juts into the Sound. Hordes come here on the trail of the semi-legendary prince of Denmark – this being the Elsinore of Shakespeare's *Hamlet*, though the Bard himself never came here. It is an interesting fortress and can be tied in with an amble round the medieval part of the town. Also worth a peek is the (free) **town museum**, a former poorhouse in a monastic hospital, with displays on the times when brain operations of a stomach-churning nature were carried out.

RAIL Next to the ferry terminal.

i **Tourist Office**: opposite the station and ferry terminal, ☎(49) 211333; open Mon–Fri 0930–1900, Sat 1000–1800 (June–Aug) Mon–Fri 0930–1700, Sat 0900–1300.

HELSINGBORG

During much of the Middle Ages, Helsingborg was Danish and functioned as an important garrison town. With 4 m thick walls and measuring some 60 m across, the massive fortified keep, the **Kärnan**, still dominates the place. With a decent range of accommodation and eateries, the bustling port is a pleasant enough base, with an old quarter to explore, as well as the rewarding 15th-century **church of St Maria** and an entertainingly eclectic **Stadssmuseet** (town museum).

RAIL Next to the ferry terminal.

i **Tourist Office**: Mon–Fri 0900–2000, Sat 1000–1700, Sun 1100–1700 June–Aug; Mon Fri 0800–1800, Sat 1000–1400 Sept–May, ☎(042) 12 03 10.

Villa Thalassa Youth Hostel: 4 km north (bus nos. 7 or 44), ☎11 03 84042.

WHERE NEXT?

*Continue southwards for **Lund**, joining with the **Copenhagen–Stockholm** route (p. 446).*

VARBERG

Varberg was discovered in the late 19th century as a **bathing station**, and has some appealing period survivals, notably the **wooden pavilion** (Societeshuset) in the **park**, and the rectangular bathing section of 1903, with changing rooms and sun-loungers ranged around a tamed expanse of sea water. The dominant feature of this spa-like port is the moated 13th-century **castle**, which doubles as a youth hostel, with plenty of idyllic beaches (including naturist ones) within close range. In the **castle's museum** is the **Bockstén Man**, a remarkably preserved 14th-century corpse found in a peat bog nearby, and the only instance yet unearthed of a figure wearing a complete medieval costume.

WHERE NEXT?

*Links to **Stockholm**, either via the direct line, or via **Mariestad**.*

Tourist Office: (0340) 887 70, Mon–Sat 0900–1900, Sun 1500–1900, mid June–mid Aug.

Youth hostel: (0340) 41173. 7 km south of the centre.

GOTHENBURG

See p. 429.

HALDEN

Halden is another old border post, on the attractive **Iddefjord** and overlooked by **Fredriksten Fort**, a huge star-shaped 17th-century castle just south-east of the town. Other historical highlights include the **Frederikshalds Theater**, with its fully restored baroque stage and old scenery, and **Rød Herregard**, a furnished 18th-century manor house with a weapon collection. The **Gjesthavn** (Marina) offers day trips to Sweden.

RAIL 69 18 11 23, on the south bank of the river.

Tourist Office: GJESTHAVN (Visitors' Marina), south of the station; 69 18 01 02, open daily 0800–2000 (1 June–17 Aug), Sat–Sun only 0800–1400 (May); LANGBRYGGE 3, north of the station in the main town (over the bridge); 69 17 48 40, Mon–Fri 0900–1600 (rest of the year).

FREDRIKSTAD

With three sides still bordered by fortified walls, Fredrikstad guarded the southern approaches to Oslo and has survived as one of the best-preserved fortress towns in Scandinavia, owing to its continuous military use. It's conducive for wandering, particularly around the walls and along the cobbled alleys of the **Gamlebyen** (old town) over on the east bank. **Fort Kongsten**, perched on a bluff, is a pleasant 15–20-min stroll and contains a warren of rooms and underground passages.

RAIL ☎69 31 26 03, 5 mins' walk south-east of the centre.

i **Tourist Office**: BROHODET ØSTSIDEN; ☎69 32 03 30, http://www.travel.expo.no/Oes/Borgdest. Mon–Fri 0800–1600, Sat 1000–1600, Sun 1200–1600 (summer); Mon–Fri 0900–1600 (winter).

WHERE NEXT?

Follow the routes to ***Malmö*** *(p. 446) or* ***Stockholm*** *(p. 420), or the* ***Oslo–Bergen–Oslo*** *circuit (p. 436).*

Route Detail

Oslo–Voss ETT table 780

Type	Frequency	Journey Time
Train	5 daily	5 hr 30 mins

Voss–Bergen ETT table 780

Type	Frequency	Journey Time
Train	10–12 daily	1 hr 12 mins

Bergen–Stavanger ETT table 2270

Type	Frequency	Journey Time
Ship	2–3 daily	4 hrs

Stavanger–Kristiansand ETT table 775

Type	Frequency	Journey Time
Train	6 daily	2 hrs 52 mins

Kristiansand–Kongsberg ETT table 775

Type	Frequency	Journey Time
Train	6 daily	3 hrs 30 mins

Kongsberg–Oslo ETT table 775

Type	Frequency	Journey Time
Train	9 daily	1 hr 20 mins

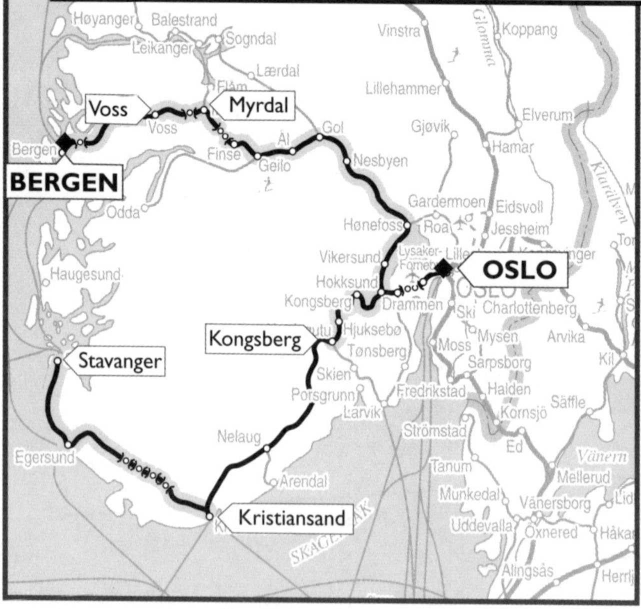

Undoubtedly one of Europe's most spectacular train journeys, this circuit encounters some of the most stunning of Norwegian landscapes. The trip incorporates two lines, connected by a catamaran voyage between Bergen and Stavanger. From Oslo the route steadily climbs, past the year-round resorts of **Gol** and **Geilo**, and up to the holiday centre of Ustaoset (990 m), followed by a bleak but magnificent mountainscape of icy lakes and rocky, snow-capped ridges. Shortly after leaving Finse, the train enters a 10–km tunnel to emerge near Hallingskeid. The next stop is **Myrdal**, where you can divert to the the hugely popular loop via train, boat and bus to the north via **Flåm** dubbed *Norway in a Nutshell* and offering a glimpse of a superb fjord. The main line then descends to the lakeside town of **Voss**. Thereafter, the scenery's a little less wild, although still impressive.

After you've had a look around the quaint harbour city of Bergen, the catamaran to Stavanger is fast and enjoyable. Even the last leg back to Oslo passes consistently pleasant countryside, lakes and forest, and gives access to the cities of **Kristiansand** and **Kongsberg**. If the Oslo–Bergen train is booked up, make Bergen–Oslo reservations and do the circuit in reverse, which has the advantage of saving the really dramatic stuff for later on.

VOSS

Mountains rise straight out of the lakeside resort, itself just 56 m above sea level. Sights are pretty much limited to the 13th-century baroque-embellished **church**, as most of the town is modern and geared towards winter sports; its après-ski atmosphere is distinctly lively. A cable car, **Hangursbanen**, runs up to 1100 m, covering a height difference of about 570 m in 4 mins. For water sports, contact the Voss Rafting Centre, voss.rafting@online.no, ☎56 51 05 25.

RAIL ☎56 51 12 22 5-mins' walk from town centre

Tourist Office ☎56 51 00 51, **Uttrågata** has plenty on hiking.

Youth Hostel ☎56 51 20 17; fax 56 51 22 05; Jan–Oct; 10 min from centre.

Bergen has plenty of nightlife. **Ole Bulls Plass**, south-east of the quay, is good for bars, as is the area behind TORGET. There are more student-frequented bars and cafés up towards the university. Look out for events at the **Kulturehuset**, on an old wharf to the south.

BERGEN

An old Hanseatic port, Norway's extremely appealing second city is the gateway to some of the country's most magnificent fjords. Placed on a peninsula and

WALKING TRIPS

You can get almost everywhere on foot in Bergen, but take the **Fløibanen** (funicular) from the centre up Mt Fløyen (320 m), for a panoramic view. At the top there's scope for pleasant picnics and walks in the woods.

surrounded by mountains, Bergen has meandering cobbled streets lined with gabled weatherboard houses and dignified old warehouses.

The city centres on the waterfront **Fisketorget** open Mon–Fri 0800–1600, Sat 0800–1500, a working fish (and various other things) market.

At the centre of the old quarter, **Bryggen** contains a fine row of medieval houses deemed worthy of UNESCO World Heritage Site listing.

Tiny **Theta Museum**, ENHJØRNINGSGÅRDEN BRYGGEN, was the clandestine one-room centre for Resistance operations in World War II, until it was discovered by the Nazis in 1942. When the **Bryggens Museum** was being constructed, the remains of the original city of 1050–1500 were discovered and incorporated.

Other museums in town are the art museums and those housed in the university CHRISTIESGT, which also runs the botanical garden.

Gamle Bergen (Old Bergen), at **Sandviken**, is an open-air museum of some three dozen 18th- and 19th-century wooden houses and shops, many furnished in period style, ranged around cobbled paths and streets. You can wander round for nothing, but have to join a tour if you want to see the interiors. Yellow buses nos. 9/20/22/70 and 80 take 10 mins: from the east side of Vågen, direction **LØNBORG**.

EDVARD GRIEG'S HOME

Classical music lovers may like to pay a visit to **Troldhaugen**, home of Edvard Grieg, Norway's greatest composer. Crammed with memorabilia, it is little altered since his death in 1907, and is open daily in summer; the site includes a museum and concert hall. There are buses from the main bus station to HOPSBROEN, from where it's a walk of 15–20 mins.

RAIL **Strømgt**; 55 96 69 00, 10–mins walk east of the centre; walk straight ahead down MARKEN and keep going.

The **Tourist Office** has details of international and local ferries, most of which leave from **Vågen**, the inner harbour. International sailings use SKOLTEGRUNNSKAIEN, on the east side. **Flaggruten** catamarans to **Stavanger** leave from **STRANDKAIEN**, on the west side. Their office is in STRANDKEITERMINALEN, 55 23 87 80; www.hsd.no; open 0730–1730/1800. Pick up a boarding–pass 30 mins before departure; be certain to book ahead in July. **Hurtigruten** (see p. 445) uses a separate harbour at FRIELENESKAIEN, west of the centre.

177 for transport information, including trains, boats and buses. **Tourist Office**: (the best outside Oslo) VÅGSALMENNING 1; 55 32 14 80; www.bergen-travel.com; bergen@bergen-travel.com; open daily 0830–2200 (June–Aug); 0900–2000 (May and Sept); rest of year Mon–Sat 0900–1600,

closed Sun. Room booking service, charge Nkr.20. There's a mass of free English-language literature. Get the *Bergen Guide*, which includes maps and lists of just about everything. The **Bergen Card** (Nkr.130 for 24 hrs, Nkr.200 for 48 hrs, from Tourist Officess, station, hotels and campsites) offers free local transport, free or discounted admission to most of the attractions, and 'a surprise in the menu' at selected restaurants. If you want to wander further afield on foot, or even on skis, **Bergen Turlag** (Bergen Touring Association), in DNT office, Tverrgt 4–6; ☎55 32 22 30, open Mon–Fri 1000–1600 (Thur until 1800), can provide walking maps for the surrounding mountains.

Advance booking recommended – Bergen is often chock full of tourists and conference-goers. **HI**: **Montana**, Johan Blydttsvei 30; ☎55 29 29 00, is on **Mt Ulriken** (bus no.4: Loegdene); open May–Sept. The **YMCA/Interrail Centre**, 4 Nedre Korskirkealm; ☎55 31 73 32, is conveniently located, within sight of the Tourist Office. The most central **campsite** (open 2 July–end Aug) is **Bergenshallen**, Vilh. Bjerknesvei 24, Landås; ☎55 27 01 80, 10 mins on bus no.90.

There's a cheap **supermarket** next to the YMCA on Nedre Korskirkealm. Buy fruit and cheap (and delicious) smoked salmon or prawn sandwiches from the **fish market**. The large red and white building on Zachariasbryggen contains several mid-market restaurants; **Pasta Basta** ☎55 55 96 65 does large and tasty pasta dishes for under NKr.100.

Day Trips to the Fjords

Three fjords south of Bergen are among the deepest and most popular in the country: **Hardangerfjord** is a major target for tourists, alternating verdant lowlands and precipitous cliffs scattered with waterfalls; **Nordfjord** twists over 100 km to the foot of **Briksdal glacier**; **Sognefjord** is the longest (205 km) and deepest (1300 m) in Norway; in some places the shoreline is gentle, in others it soars straight up to 1000 m. Two of its most spectacular arms are **Nærøyfjord** and **Aurlandsfjord** (see *Norway in a Nutshell*, p. 440). Several boat tours, including day trips, depart from Bergen.

Stavanger

The centre is small and easily walkable, with an excellent pedestrianised cobbled shopping area, and there's a good bus network to reach outlying attractions. The **Stavanger Card** (pick one up from wherever you're staying; NKr.110 for 24 hrs, NKr.190 for 48 hrs, NKr.240 for 72 hrs) provides free bus travel, free admission to the town's museums/mansions and 50% discounts on other attractions. If you pay (NKr.30) to enter a museum, the ticket covers any others you visit the same day (except the **Archaeological Museum** and **Jernadergarden** Iron Age farm).

Gamle Stavanger (the old town) is the area on the west side of the harbour. Lovely for a stroll, with cobbled walkways and rows of early 18th-century wooden houses at crazy angles. The impressive medieval has retained **Domkirke** (St Svithun's), in its medieval atmosphere.

You can also enter **Ledål**, a mansion of 1800 that is used by the royal family when visiting the town, and **Breidablick**, a 19th-century ship owner's house. **Valbergtårnet**, a 19th-century watchtower perched on top of a hill in the centre, provides an excellent view of the harbour.

Jernbanevn; 51 56 96 00, 10 mins from the harbour and Tourist Office; round the left side of the lake and straight on.

Flaggruten, 51 89 50 90, catamarans for Bergen use the **Børevigå Express Terminal**, 5–mins walk north. **Color Line** international sailings, 51 56 65 55, leave from **Strandkaien**, to Newcastle, England, and Hirtshals, northern Denmark.

Tourist Office: ROSENKILDETORGET 1; 51 85 92 00; www.destinasjon-stavanger.no; e-mail: info@destinasjon-stavanger.no. Open daily 0900–2000 (June–Aug); Mon–Fri 0900–1600, Sat 0900–1400 (Sept–Mar); Mon–Fri 0900–1700, Sat 0900–1400 (Apr–May). Exchange, cash machine next door.

Essential to book in advance – Stavanger is often booked out for conferences and is short on cheap hotels. The only **youth hostel** is **Stavanger Vandrerhjem Mosvangen**, HENRIK IBSENSGT 21, 51 87 29 00, south of the centre. Otherwise, try **Madlaveien Pensjonat**, MADLAVN. 7, 51 53 43 27 or **Havly Hotel**, VALBERGGT. 1, 51 89 67 00.

NORWAY IN A NUTSHELL

Trip from ***Myrdal*** via ***Flåm*** and the ***Sognefjord.*** This ever-popular circuit uses the main rail line to Myrdal and rejoins it at Voss (or vice versa), combining a **t**rain, bus and ferry to link them. You can do it as a day excursion from Bergen, or en route to or from Oslo; the mainline trains must be booked in advance. It's not an escorted tour: you simply buy a ticket and follow the relevant timetable. The ferry and bus journeys are not covered by rail passes, except for Eurail, but it's worth paying the extra NKr.250 for this experience.

KRISTIANSAND

Ferries from Harwich in England and Hirtshals in Denmark serve this bustling port and resort at the southern tip of Norway. In summer, the town's pleasant beaches get are busy. Much of the town was laid out in the 17th century by Christian IV, after whom it is named. His plan included the **Christiansholm Festning**, STRANDPROMENADEN, built to guard the eastern approach to the harbour; the circular fortress is now the major sight with views to match. Forming the north-eastern part of the old quarter, **Posebyen** has many carefully preserved little wooden houses, while the neo-Gothic **Domkirke** (cathedral), KIRKEGT, of 1885 asserts a massive presence. The **fish market** on the quay is a good place to pick up some smoked salmon or prawns for a picnic lunch.

DYREPARKEN

(15 mins from the centre of Kristiansand by no. 1) is a virtually cageless zoo and Norway's most visited attraction. There is also an amusement park with a special children's area (Cinnamon Town).

RAIL 38 07 75 00. On the west side of the centre, a few blocks from the Tourist Office, along VESTRE STRANDGT.

i **Tourist Office**: DRONNINGENSGT 2; 38 12 13 14; www.sol.no/destinasjon-soerlandet;destsor@-online.no. Open Mon–Fri 0800–1600 (1930 June–Aug); Sat 0800–1500 (June); 0800–1930 (July–mid Aug); Sun 1200–1930 (mid June–July).

KONGSBERG

Silver put the town on the map following the discovery of silver deposits of unique purity in the early 17th century in the nearby mountains. Kongsberg also established Norway's National Mint.

RAIL 32 73 11 78, on the west side of the river, next to the Tourist Office.

i **Tourist Office**: STORGT 35; 32 73 50 00; destination.kongsberg@eunet.no. Open Mon–Fri 0900–1900, Sat–Sun 1000–1700 (26 June–16 Aug); Mon–Fri 0900–1630, Sat 1000–1400 (rest of the year).

Norway in a Nutshell cont'd.

At **Myrdal**, you board a local train for a breathtaking journey down the branch to **Flåm**, taking about an hour. The descent covers 866 m in 20 km (at a gradient of up to 1:18), with superb views of towering cliffs, chasms and cascades. There are 16 tunnels on the route, including one 'turn around', in which the line makes a 360° turn completely within the mountain. The train stops at the particularly spectacular **Kjosfossen waterfall** for photo-graphers to descend.

The railway ends at **Flåm**, a tiny village at the head of **Aurlandsfjord,** accessible by rail on the **Sognefjord**. There are at least a couple of hours to relax, lunch, shop before boarding a 2-hr ferry journey (refreshments available) along Aurlandsfjord and **Nærøyfjord**.

Disembarking at **Gudvangen** (accommodation available here also), the bus back to Voss follows an incredibly steep and breathtakingly dramatic road out of the fjord.

Day Trip from Kongsberg to The Silver Mines

Highly recommended is the trip to the disused **silver mines** at **Saggrenda** (8 km south, no. 11 towards NOTODDEN). **Tours** (mid May–Sept) feature a train ride through the heart of the mountain. The shafts go 560 m below sea-level and it's definitely chilly at 6°C.

Route Detail

Oslo–Boden ETT tables 750, 760

Type	Frequency	Journey Time
Train	Overnight	20 hrs 55 mins

Oslo–Lillehammer ETT table 785

Type	Frequency	Journey Time
Train	9 daily	2 hrs 30 mins

Lillehammer–Dombås ETT table 785

Type	Frequency	Journey Time
Train	5 daily	1 hr 55 mins

Dombås–Trondheim ETT table 785

Type	Frequency	Journey Time
Train	4–5 daily	2 hrs 45 mins

Trondheim–Bodø ETT table 786

Type	Frequency	Journey Time
Train	2 per day	10 hrs

Bodø–Narvik ETT table 786

Type	Frequency	Journey Time
Bus	2 daily	5 hrs 30 mins

Narvik–Gällivare ETT table 765

Type	Frequency	Journey Time
Train	2 Daily	4 hrs

Gällivare–Boden ETT table 765

Type	Frequency	Journey Time
Train	3 daily	2 hrs 20 mins

Notes

The direct service between Oslo and Boden includes a change of train at Stockholm.

Travellers from Trondheim to Narvik not wanting to visit Bodø can connect into the Bodø to Narvik bus at Fauske (55km south of Bodø).

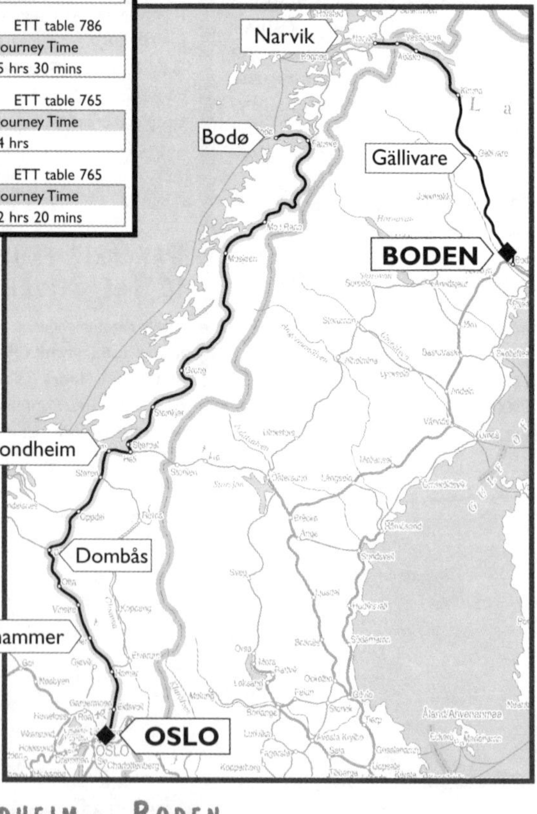

Fastest Journey:
20 hrs 55 mins

Narvik

Bodø

Gällivare

BODEN

Trondheim

Dombås

Lillehammer

OSLO

The real attraction of this extremely popular route into the Arctic Circle is the scenery itself, giving the opportunity to experience the Midnight Sun in summer. Gradually the scene evolves from gentle and bucolic in the area north of Oslo to breathtakingly dramatic in the northern reaches, which are inhabited by reindeer and by the Sami, or Lapps – one of the oldest peoples in Europe. Distances here are serious: Norway is a big country and sections of the route take as long as 10 hours. In particular, the ride from Dombås to Åndalsnes is an epic one, plunging through tunnels, over bridges, and past waterfalls and Europe's highest vertical canyon. From Narvik, you can continue on the scenic Ofoten line to Boden in Sweden, or change at Gällivare and take the equally fine Inlandsbanan to Mora, and then on to Stockholm.

LILLEHAMMER

Lillehammer is a major skiing centre as well as an appealing lakeside town with wooden houses clinging to a hillside. It hosted the 1994 Winter Olympics and many of the facilities can be visited – and in some cases used (see Day Trips). In winter, the downhill and cross-country ski trails and skating rinks runs are open. Many are open in summer too – including chair lifts and summer ski-jumping, and the surrounding area is laced with paths. The Tourist Office has details.

RAIL ☎61 26 41 99, west of the centre. Bus no.177.

i **Tourist Offices**: Turistkontor: Elvegate 19; walk straight out of the station to Storgata and turn left; ☎61 25 92 99; lillehammer@sn.no, Mon–Sat 0900–1900, Sun 1100–1800 (early June–mid Aug); Mon–Fri 0900–1600, Sat 1000–1400 (mid Aug–early June). **Skysstasjon**, in the station, ☎61 26 41 99, Mon–Fri 0730–1630, Sat 1000–1400. The free guide has an unhelpful map – a decent one costs NOK.60. *Lillehammer This Month* lists Events and opening times.

Gjestebu, Gamleveien 110; ☎61 25 43 21, is central and comfortable. **Gjestehuset Ersgaard**, Nordseterveien 201; ☎61 25 06 84, another pension-type. **HI**, Jernbanetorget 2; ☎61 26 25 66.

Day Trips from Lillehammer

At **Hunderfossen**, 15 km north (10 mins by train), you can try out the 1994 Olympic luge and bobsleigh tracks (up to 60 mph; on wheels in summer), or 'play, learn and experience' at the **Hunderfossen Family Park**. Worth it for the highly surreal 12 m model trolls.

Several operators run rafting and canoeing trips in the **Gundbrandsdal valley**, ranging from a half-day taster to an epic two-day voyage down the river Sjoa. Ask for details at Tourist Offices in **Lillehammer** or **Dombås**.

DOMBÅS

The branch line to **Åndalsnes** diverges here.

DAY TRIP FROM DOMBÅS

ÅNDALSNES

The journey itself is one reason for a visit. Another is **Geirangerfjord,** arguably the most stunning of all the fjords. The green-blue water winds for 16 km between cliffs (up to 1500 m) and past cascading waterfalls. Get a bus from Åndalsnes to **Hellesylt** or **Geiranger** (at opposite ends of the fjord) and take the ferry between them (70 mins), then bus back to Åndalsnes – or on to **Ålesund**, a trip offering a mix of architectural styles. **Station**: ☎71 22 10 50, a few mins walk from the centre. **Tourist Office**: in the station; ☎71 22 16 22. Mon–Sat 0930–1830, Sun 1230–1830 (mid June–Aug); Mon–Fri 0800–1530 (Sept–mid June).

INLANDSBANAN

Gällivare is the northern end of the superbly scenic Inlandsbanan, that runs 1067 km through central Sweden from **Mora** (summer-only service; change at Östersund; ETT tables 761, 762). For a 100 km sample, ride from Gällivare to Jokkmokk

TRONDHEIM

Norway's first capital was founded in 997 by the Viking king, Olav Tryggvason, whose statue tops a column in the market square.

Nidaros Domkirke (Cathedral), BISPEGATA, is cavernously Gothic, worth seeing for its decorative stonework and sumptuous stained-glass windows. Northwards from the cathedral lies **Torvet**, the main square, and further on by the water's edge is **Ravnkloa**, home to a fish market. From here there are hourly boats to the island of **Munkholmen**, a monastery turned fortress standing on the site of an execution ground; it's a popular place for swimming.

RAIL ☎72 57 20 20, north of the centre; also the bus station, and contains a Tourist Office; 15-min walk to the Tourist Office (cross the bridge, after three blocks turn right on to OLAV TRYGGVASONSGATA and left down MUNKEGATA).
Taxis: ☎73 50 50 73 (24hrs).

i **Tourist Office**: MUNKEGATA 19; ☎73 92 94 00 (entrance from TORVET (market square)); www.taas.no; firmapost@taas.no; open weekdays only in winter; open Mon–Fri 0830–1800 (mid May–early June), Sat and Sun 1000–1600; Mon–Fri 0830–2000, Sat and Sun 1000–1800 (early June–end of Aug). First two weeks of Aug: Mon–Fri 0830–2200; Sat and Sun 1000–2000.

HI: **Rosenborg,** WEIDEMANNSVEI 41; ☎73 53 04 90, 2 km east (bus no. 63; infrequent Sat–Sun). **Pensjonat Jarlen**, KONGENSGT. 40; ☎73 51 32 18, is the cheapest pension in town. **Munken Hotel**, KONGENSGT. 44; ☎73 53 45 40, is comfortable and cheap (for Norway).

BODØ

The main attraction of Bodø is that it is the departure point for ferries to the spectacular **Lofoten Islands**. These are a chain of improbably jagged glacier-carved mountains sheltering fishing villages, farms and thousands of birds. The main town is **Solvaer**, on Austvågøy. (**Tourist office**: ☎76 07 30 00).

RAIL ☎75 52 25 53.

Tourist office: SJOGATA 21; ☎75 52 60 00.

Inlandsbanan cont'd

(1hr 50 mins). There's only one train a day in each direction, giving you rather longer than you might need there; alternatively, daily buses from Gällivare allow you a 5-hr stay. **Jokkmokk** grew from a Sami mission into a sizeable town and its prime role today is to keep the Sami culture alive.

NARVIK

Narvik is dominated by its port, and there is a guided tour of the dock every day at 1300 from the tourist office. Iin the evening there's a walking tour of the town. For panoramic views towards the Lofoten Islands, take the **gondolbaner** (cable car) up Fagernesfjellet – a popular place for hang-gliding and paragliding; allow at least 2 hrs if you wish to walk up.

☎76 92 31 21, a few mins walk east of the Tourist Office.

Bus station: next to the quay; ☎76 92 35 00. Open daily 0800–1600.

Tourist Office: KONGENSGATA 66; ☎76 94 33 09. Open Mon–Sat 0900–1900, Sat 1000–1600, Sun 1400–1800 (mid June–mid Aug); Mon–Fri 0900–1600 (mid Aug–mid June).

GÄLLIVARE

Iron and copper ore mining dominates the scene, and tours (Mon–Fri mid June–mid Aug) enter the open-cast copper mine and the underground iron mine. Gällivare's also a good place to immerse yourself in the Sami (Lapp) culture. There's a small museum of Sami history in the Tourist Office building, and about 2 km from the centre of town, up the road to Dundret, **Vägvisaren** is a small open-air museum based on Sami culture, with traditional huts (similar to teepees) and live reindeer.

The top of Dundret, the 820-m hill that looms to the south of the town, is a **nature reserve** with panoramic views. It's 7 km to the top and you should allow at least 3 hrs for the full return hike (many people take twice as long), but you can get great views by going only as far as **Bornfällan** (4 km). When the **Midnight Sun** is visible there are special bus tours to the top of Dundret.

☎0970 752 00, on the western edge of town.

Tourist Office: STORGATAN 16, ☎(0970) 166 60; www.gellivare.se; turistinfo@gellivare.se; open Mon–Fri 0900–2000, Sat–Sun 1000–1800 (mid June–mid Aug); Mon–Fri 0900–1600 (mid Aug–mid June).

Try **Gällivare Vandrarhem**, ANDRA SIDAN, ☎(0970) 143 80, or **Gällivare Värdshus**, KLOCKLJUNGSVÄGEN 2, ☎(0970) 162 00 – central and cheap. **HI**, ☎(0970) 143 80. Cross the bridge over the tracks in the station.

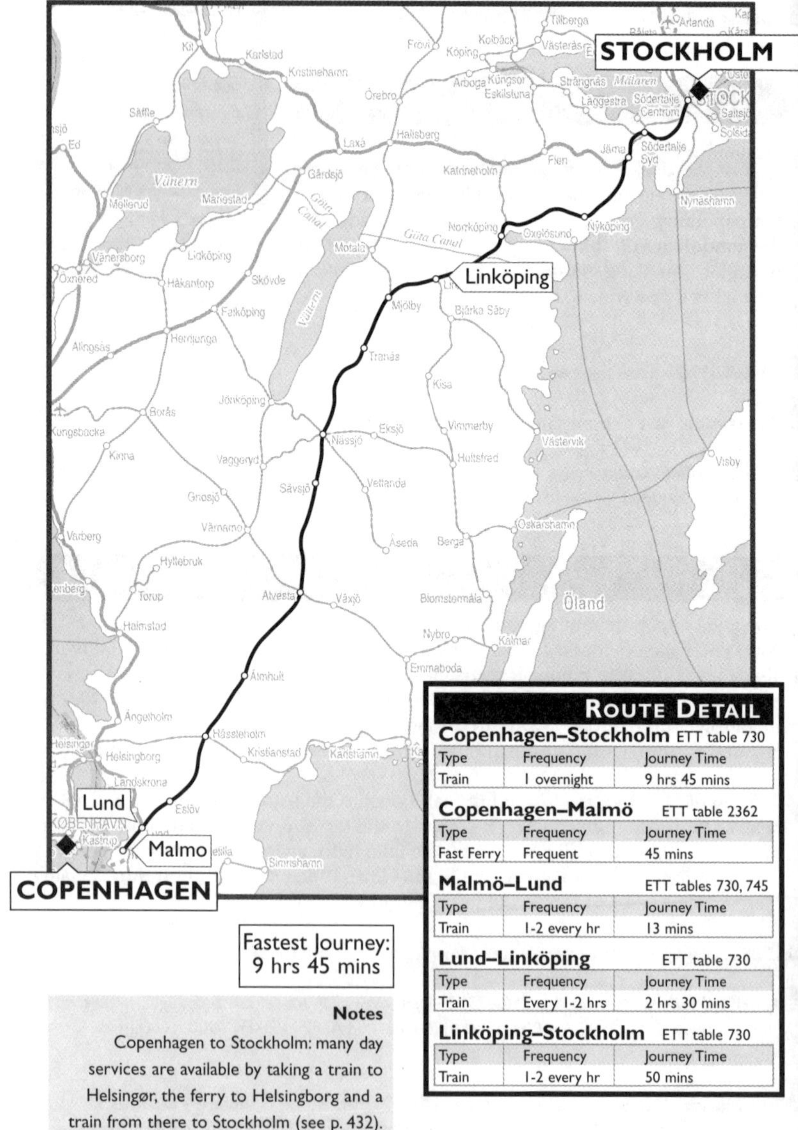

ROUTE DETAIL

Copenhagen–Stockholm ETT table 730

Type	Frequency	Journey Time
Train	1 overnight	9 hrs 45 mins

Copenhagen–Malmö ETT table 2362

Type	Frequency	Journey Time
Fast Ferry	Frequent	45 mins

Malmö–Lund ETT tables 730, 745

Type	Frequency	Journey Time
Train	1-2 every hr	13 mins

Lund–Linköping ETT table 730

Type	Frequency	Journey Time
Train	Every 1-2 hrs	2 hrs 30 mins

Linköping–Stockholm ETT table 730

Type	Frequency	Journey Time
Train	1-2 every hr	50 mins

Fastest Journey:
9 hrs 45 mins

Notes

Copenhagen to Stockholm: many day services are available by taking a train to Helsingør, the ferry to Helsingborg and a train from there to Stockholm (see p. 432).

This route is an excellent introduction to the beauty of the landscape of the southern portion of Sweden, yet it also allows the opportunity to visit three historical Swedish cities. Forests and countless numbers of picturesque lakes are visible on the journey.

MALMÖ

Sweden's fast-growing third city, with a population of around quarter of a million, is a lively place, with plenty of good bars, clubs and coffee houses, and an excellent festival in August. Capital of the Skåne province, Malmö was part of Denmark for much of the Middle Ages and came under Swedish sovereignty in 1658: even today the Skåne accent has something of a Danish tinge. Enclosed by a canal that loops round through a park and doubles as the castle moat, the city's well-groomed historic centre dates back to Danish times and features two fine cobbled squares.

If the weather's set fair, lounge in one of the three great parks, **Kungsparken**, **Slottsparken** and **Pildammsparken**; or head down to the 3 km-long **Ribersborg beach**, within walking distance. You can pick up the basics for a picnic at the excellent **Saluhallen** covered market in **Lilla Torget**.

Leaving the station southwards along HAMNGATAN, you soon reach the huge central square, **Stortorget**, presided over by the statue of Carl X Gustav, who won Skåne back from Denmark. The square is flanked on its east side by the statue-embellished **Rådhus** (town hall) of 1546 (with 19th-century alterations), itself on the line of **Sodergatan**, the main pedestrianised street. Just behind stands **St Petri Kyrka** (St Peter's church) – Sweden's second largest church – its whitewashed Gothic interior showing off its baroque altar and medieval frescos to best advantage. Off STORTORGET'S south-western corner lies **Lilla Torget**, a smaller and infinitely more charming square with medieval, sometimes lopsided, brick and timber façades, outdoor cafés and restaurants; live music adds to the atmosphere on summer evenings. From here a short walk west leads to the formidable 15th-century fortress, **Malmöhus**, open Mon–Sun 1200–1600, with its circular towers and assorted buildings containing a set of museums covering a range of themes – including city history, military exhibits, art and natural history – with real flair.

Consider getting the **Malmö Card** (SKr.125 for 24 hrs) for free local buses and savings on sightseeing, shopping and eating out. It can get you on the **vintage tram tour** round the city, and has two-for-one ticket deals to see **Malmö Symphony Orchestra** and entry to **Malmö Stadium** to watch Sweden's best soccer team in action.

RAIL **Malmö C**, just north of the old town. SJ information; ☎(020) 75 75 75. Local trains; ☎(020) 61 61 61.

INTERNET CAFÉS
Surfers Paradise, AMIRALSGATAN 14; **CyberSpace C@fé,** ENGELBREKTSGATAN 13A.

WHERE NEXT?
Malmö to Gothenburg *X2000 trains taking 3 hrs – supplement payable – and IR (InterRegio) taking 4 hrs run from Malmö to Gothenburg,* *see Copenhagen–Gothenburg (p.420).*

Flygbåtarna Catamarans; (040) 10 39 30 and **Scanlines**; (040) 40 10 39 30, and **Pilen ferries**; (040) 23 44 11, www.pilen.com, all leave from **Skeppsbron** (Just north of Malmö C), providing an hourly service to Copenhagen, taking about 45 mins.

Tourist Office: **Central Station**; (040) 30 01 50; (www.tourism.malmo.com; info@tourism.malmo.com). Open Mon–Fri 0900–1900, Sat–Sun 1000–1500 (June–Aug); Mon–Fri 0900–1700, Sat 1000–1400; closed Sun (Sept–May). Get the useful *Malmö This Month* guide for Events and listings. For information on the August festival contact the website (info@festival.malmo.se).

City Room, S. FORSTADG.31; (040) 795 94 (open Mon–Fri 1000–1700), supply lists of private rooms. **Garden Hotel**, BALTZARSGATAN 20; (040) 10 40 00, is true to its name: the very peaceful garden is on the roof. **Hotel Formule 1**, LUNDVÄGEN 28, 40 93 05 80, is cheap. HI: **Södergården**, BACKAVÄGEN 18; (040) 822 20 (no. 36); another hostel, **City Vandrarhem**, VÄSTERGATAN 9, 40 23 56 40, is only 200 m from the station, but is only open June–Aug.

LUND

The handsome ancient university town is one of the most rewarding places in southern Sweden. A religious centre in the 12th century, much of medieval Lund is still extant. There's a decent range of accommodation and plenty of studenty eating haunts.

RAIL (046) 15 02 20, 5 mins walk west of the centre.

Tourist Office: Stadshuset, KYRKOGATAN 11; (046) 35 50 40; www.lund.se; BitteSaur@lund.se. Open Mon–Fri 1000–1800, Sat–Sun 1000–1400 (June–Aug); Mon–Fri 1000–1700, Sat 1000–1400 (May, Sept); Mon–Fri 1000–1700 (Oct–Apr). Get the free brochure *i Lund* for listings and info.

LINKÖPING

The town's prime attraction is **Gamla Linköping**, MALMSLÄTTSVÄGEN (5 mins on nos 203/205/207, or 20-mins walk), an ambitious lived-in museum village recreating the 19th century Linköping, much of which was painstakingly removed piece by piece and rebuilt here – it includes a small chocolate factory, as well as working craft shops, houses, street lamps and old signs. Try to go when the individual buildings will be open; otherwise you may have to be content with walking round and viewing from the outside.

Linköping's **Domkyrkan** is one of Sweden's oldest cathedrals, with a 107 m green spire visible from far around, and contains fine stone carving around the south doorway and elsewhere; the north doorway is a survival of the original Romanesque building that was later Gothicised.

Domkyrkan (the cathedral), is a magnificent structure with a fascinating crypt resplendent with ancient carved tombstones, and an intricate **astronomical clock** that springs into action twice a day (1200 and 1500; Sun and holidays 1300 and 1500), with an entire miniature theatre's worth of moving figurines. **Kulturen** (Cultural-Historical) **Museum**, TEGNÉRPLATSEN, open daily 1100– 1700, is an assemblage of buildings dating back 300 years: some have furnishings of the period, while others are empty or used for a variety of exhibitions – in particular, don't miss the **burgher's house**; outside stand a group of **rune stones**.

RAIL (013) 24 23 23, 5 mins walk east of the centre.

i **Tourist Office**: KONSISTORIEGATAN 7; (013) 20 68 35; e-mail: turistbyra@linkoping.se. Open Mon–Fri 0900–1800 (all year) plus Sat–Sun 0900–1500 (June–Aug). Get *Next Stop Linköping*.

Hotel Ekoxen (Tourist Spot), KLOSTERGATAN 68; (013) 14 60 70, also supply information: Mon–Fri 1800–2200 (all year) plus Sat–Sun 1500–2200 (June–Aug).

ROUTE DETAIL

Stockholm–Helsinki ETT table 2465

Type	Frequency	Journey Time
Ship	3 per day	15 hrs

Stockholm–Uppsala ETT table 760

Type	Frequency	Journey Time
Train	2 every hr	38 mins

Uppsala–Umeå ETT table 760

Type	Frequency	Journey Time
Train	1 overnight	10 hrs

Umeå–Boden ETT table 760

Type	Frequency	Journey Time
Bus, train	4 daily	5 hrs

Boden–Haparanda ETT table 769

Type	Frequency	Journey Time
Bus	5 daily	2 hrs 10 mins

Haparanda–Torino ETT table 769

Type	Frequency	Journey Time
Bus	6–7 daily	1 hr 10 mins

Torino–Kemi ETT table 769

Type	Frequency	Journey Time
Bus	7–8 daily	45 mins

Kemi–Oulu ETT table 790

Type	Frequency	Journey Time
Train	5 daily	1 hr 10 mins

Oulu–Tampere ETT table 790

Type	Frequency	Journey Time
Train	6 daily	5 hrs 20 mins

Tampere–Turku ETT table 792

Type	Frequency	Journey Time
Train	7 daily	2 hrs

Turku–Helsinki ETT table 791

Type	Frequency	Journey Time
Train	Every 1–2 hrs	2 hrs

Notes

Umea to Boden: By bus to Lulea, thence train to Boden.

Fastest Journey: 14 hrs 30 mins

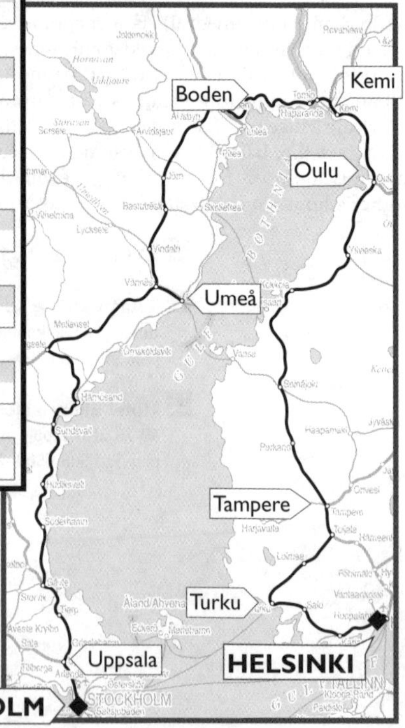

Sweden's coastal towns north of Stockholm offer a variety of attractions. The northern stretch of the route runs above the Arctic Circle, where reindeer roam and local Sami peoples retain their traditional, if modernised, ways. Later, you cross over into the wild northern territories of Finland and head south past the strongly contrasting cities of Tampare and Turku.

UPPSALA

No visitor to Sweden should miss out on the former capital, home of the country's oldest university as well as its religious centre.

Dominating the skyline are the twin towers of Scandinavia's biggest church, the French-Gothic **Domkyrka**. It took 175 years to build and was consecrated in 1435, but there were major restorations in the 18th and 19th centuries.

The 16th-century **Uppsala Slott** (Red Castle), overlooking the town, was built by King Gustaf Vasa, who broke ties with the Vatican and pointed his cannons directly at the archbishop's palace.

Books, manuscripts and maps are on display in **Carolina Rediviva Universitetsbiblioteket** (library), corner ÖVRE SLOTTSG/DROTTNINGG, notably half of a 6th-century Silver Bible – a rare example of the extinct Gothic language, written on purple vellum – and the manuscript of Mozart's *Die Zauberflöte* (the Magic Flute).

The great 18th-century professor of botany, Linnaeus (Carl von Linné), developed the definitive system of plant and animal classification. His former residence is now a museum, **Linnéanum**, in the small **Linnéträdgården** (Linnaeus Gardens), SVARTBÄCKSG 27. His **Botaniska Trädgården** (Botanical Gardens), THUNBERGSV 2–8, are much larger.

Uppsala C, (018) 65 22 10. East of the centre, 10-min stroll to the Tourist Office: walk straight up BANGÅRDSG to the river, turn right and cross the second bridge – the Tourist Office is halfway along the block.

Tourist Office: FYRISTORG 8; (018) 27 48 00; res.till.uppland.nu; info@utkab.se; open Mon–Fri 1000–1800, Sat 1000–1500, also Sun 1200–1600 (July–early Aug). The free leaflet *Worth Seeing in Uppsala* has tourist information; also get the brochure *Uppsala/Uppland* for the map in the back.

Room agency (018) 10 95 33, Mon–Fri 0900–1700, can book private rooms. **Plantan**, DRAGARBRUNNSGATAN 18; (018) 10 43 00, is part hostel/part cheap hotel; turn right out of the station, 100 m away. **Campus**, ULLERÅKERSVÄGEN 17; (018) 711 210, is similar. nos 16/20. **Basic Hotel**, KUNGSGT 27, (018) 480 50 00, is just what it says it is, and cheap. **Grand Hotell Hörnan**, BANGÅRDSGATAN 1; (018) 13 93 80, is old-style classy and more expensive. **HI**: **Sunnersta Herrgård**, SUNNERSTAV. 24; (018) 32 42 20, 6 km south (nos 4/20/50 to **HERRGÅRDSVÄGEN**). **Fyris Camping**, IDROTTSG 2; (018) 27 49 60, by river, 2 km north (nos 4/6/25/50). Open all year.

UMEÅ

Umeå is a rapidly growing university town with a youthful population. You can shoot nearby rapids in rubber rafts (May–Sept). One place really worth lingering is **Gammlia**, a complex with seven museums, including a **Ski Museum** and an excellent **open-air museum** with buildings brought from all over the region; most sections open only in summer. Nightlife revolves around the university campus.

15 58 70, 5-min walk north of the centre. Basic facilities: lockers, toilets and a ticket/ information office.

Silja Line, (090) 71 44 00, dock at **Holmsund**, 16km out of town. A shuttle bus leaves from behind the Tourist Office 1 hr before ferries depart and meets incoming ferries. Journey time 20–25 mins.

Tourist Office: RENMARKSTORGET 15; (090) 16 16 16; www.umea.se; umeturist@bfc.umea.se. Mon–Fri 0800–2000, Sat 1000–1700, (June–Aug); Mon–Fri 1000–1800 (Sept–May).

The Strand, VÄSTRA STRANDGATAN 11; (090) 12 90 20, is budget and has a central riverfront location. It is overshadowed, literally, by the upmarket first **Hotel Grand**, (090) 77 88 70, and the top-market Umeå Plaza, (090) 17 70 00.

BODEN

WHERE NEXT FROM BODEN?

For those with a real taste for epic journeys, carry on far into ***Lappland*** *and the Arctic Circle, by taking the* ***Oslo–Boden*** *route in reverse (p. 442), or by returning to* ***Stockholm*** *via Gällivare and taking the Inlandsbanan. Between Boden and Kemi are* ***Haparanda*** *and* ***Tormo*** *– effectively one town but in two time zones, linked by bridges. There is a border post, as Haparanda is in Sweden and Tormo in Finland, but no formalities to observe.*

Primarily a rail junction and garrison town, Boden is a pleasant enough place to wait between trains. Fearing attack by Russia after the 1809 invasion of Finland, the Swedes erected a mighty fortress, the **Svendjefortet**, whose mighty ramparts date from 1901. Six regiments are based here; the **Garnisonsmuseet** (Garrison Museum), on the south-western edge of town, is chock-full of militaria.

Boden C. (0921) 772 50, 0700–2045, 20-mins walk north-west of centre.

Tourist Office: in summer there's a kiosk at the station; (0921) 624 10. Open daily 0900–2100 (21 June–31 July). A noticeboard outside displays tourist information: if it's closed, try **Naringslivsstiftelsen**, FÄRGAREG 10A; (0921) 623 14. Open Mon–Fri 0800–1600.

Hotell Standard, opposite station; (0921) 160 55; mid-range rooms, plus dorm beds in basement.

KEMI

One thing to head for here is the **Jalokivigalleria** (Gemstone Gallery), at the end of KAUPPAKATU (recognisable by the crown in a glass case on the corner). The ground floor has excellent displays of stones, while upstairs you'll find copies of some famous diamonds and royal regalia, as well as the genuine – but never worn – Finnish royal crown. From Feb–mid April every year the three-storey **Kemi Snowcastle** is open to the public for exhibitions and Events, even restaurants and accommodation. Ask for details at the Tourist Office.

(016) 221 658, 5-min walk east of the centre: straight along KAUPPAKATU.

Asemakatu; 0200 4069. Walk round the post office building in front of the rail station and it's on the far side. It's better equipped than the rail station. **Information office** opens Mon–Fri 0800–1630, ticket office Mon–Fri 0730–1730. When it's closed, get tickets on board – you don't need them if you have a valid rail pass. Booking is not necessary.

Tourist Office: KEMIN KAUPUNGIN MATKAILUTOIMISTO, VALTAKATU 26; www.kemi.fi; kynsijarvim-@kemi.fi; (016) 259 467, 2 streets from the station. Mon–Fri 0800–1800, Sat–Sun 0800–1800 (June–Aug); Mon–Fri 1000–1600 (Sept–May). In the town hall, the tallest building in town (on a clear day you can see Sweden from the roof).

Hotel Cumulus (part of a Finnish chain), HAHTISAARENKATU 3; (016) 22 831, or (youth) **Hostel Turisti**, VALTAKATU 39; (016) 250 876, across from the Tourist Office – an **HI** member, with cheap rooms.

OULU

High-tech industries are in evidence here, and the mostly modern town is home to **Rovia Tietomaa**, NAHKATEHTAANKATU 6, an interactive science and technology centre – completely non-esoteric and great fun. A few older buildings such as the city hall recall the 19th-century tar boom – in which Oulu did pretty well – and there's an assemblage of Sami artefacts and other local miscellania at the absorbing **Pohjois–Pohjanmaan Museo** (North Ostrobothnia Provincial Museum), Ainola Park. The lake shore looks out to the town's islands, joined by bridges.

Rautatienkatu, information: 0200 5000; east of centre. From Kemi there are about 6 trains daily, taking 1 hr.

Tourist Office: **Matkailuneuvonta**, TORIKATU 10, (08) 558 41330; www.ouka.fi. Open 0900–1600 (Sept–May); 0900–1800 (June–Aug). Take ASEMAKATU for six blocks, left on TORIKATU. Get *Oulu This Week* and *Look at Oulu* (plus free map).

WHERE NEXT?

An alternative, but longer, way to Helsinki is by taking the ***Helsinki–Oulu*** *journey (p 456) in reverse.*

Apoppo, ASEMAKATU 31, (08) 374 344, is cheap-moderate, right near the station.
HI: KAJAANINTIE 36; (08) 311 8060, 15-mins walk from the station.

TAMPERE (TAMMERFORS)

Finland's second city is the country's major industrial base, but a surprisingly attractive place, flanked by lakes and graced with abundant green spaces.

A few streets to the right as you exit the station is **Tuomiokirkko** (cathedral), SATAKUNNANKATU, built of granite in 1907 and resplendent with frescos and stained glass. From the station, HÄMEENKATU leads across the **Tammerkoski**, a series of rapids that connect the city's two lakes and provide a source of eco-friendly hydroelectric energy for Tampere.

Two of Tampere's galleries give an excellent survey of Finnish art: earlier works amassed by goldsmith Kustaa Heikka include some of his jewellery, while the lakeside **Sara Hildén Museum** (20 mins walk or no. 16 north-west of the centre) displays some of the nation's finest modern art.

Towards the surreal end of the scale is the **Moomin Museum**, HÄMEENPUISTO 20 (Tampere City Library, separate entrance), dedicated entirely to Moomins, the characters of Tove Jansson's wonderfully innovative children's books.

RAIL 0100 112, 5-min walk east of the centre.

Tourist Office: VERKATEHTAANKATU 2; (03) 3146 6800; www.tampere.fi; touristbureau-@tampere.fi; open Mon–Fri 0830–2000, Sat 0830–1800, Sun 1100–1800 (June–Aug); Mon–Fri 0830–1700 (Sept–May). Walk up HÄMEENKATU and turn left just before the bridge: it's on the riverside. *Tampere and its Surroundings* is a free comprehensive listing that includes a map; there's also a self-guided walking tour.

Tampereen hotellivaraukset (hotel booking centre), VEHN-MYLLYNKATU 6; (03) 356 4800. Open Mon–Fri 0830–1630. The four **HI hostels** include **Uimahallin Maja**, PIRKANKATU 10–12; 222 9460, a hostel and hotel with reasonably priced rooms. Open all year, comfortable and central. 1 km from the station, straight up HÄMEENKATU, turn right and PIRKANKATU is on the left. **Hostel Tampereen**, open June–Aug, 254 4020, at TUOMIOKIRKINK 12A, is also cheap. **Camping Härmälä**; (03) 265 1355, 5 km south of the centre(no. 1 to within 200 m). Open mid May–Aug.

TURKU (ÅBO)

Finland's oldest city and until 1812 its capital, Turku is home to Finland's oldest university and is a vibrant commercial and cultural centre, with a pulsating nightlife. **Museolinja**, a special museum bus, operates June–mid Aug.

Turku's much-rebuilt but impressive **Tuomiokirkko** (cathedral) is easily spotted by the tower's distinctive face, the result of several fires over the centuries, which has become the city's symbol; look out for some intriguing tombs, including those of **Karin Måndotter**, a local flower girl who became Queen of Sweden in 1568.

South of the cathedral, **Luostarinmäki**, VARTIOVUORI HILL, is an 18th-century area of town that has been turned in its entirety into a highly recommendable open-air museum, busy with artisans' workshops. A recent addition to the city's museums is **Aboa Vetus/Ars Nova**, ITÄINEN RANTAKATU 4–6. In 1992, excavations for the **art museum** *(Ars Nova)* revealed extensive remains, parts dating from the 15th century. They were left in situ and form the basis of 'Aboa Vetus', so history and contemporary art rub shoulders.

WHERE NEXT?

__Turku__ is served by ferries to __Stockholm__ (9hrs 30mins), some of which stop at __Mariehamn__ in the __Åland islands__, an archipelago of 6000 low-lying, forested isles belonging to Finland.

Turku, (02) 100 44, is north-west of the centre, 15-min walk from the Tourist Office. Many trains continue to **Satama** (*Hamnen*; the harbour). **Kupittaa** is also fairly central, but not as well equipped as Turku.

Ferries: At the south-west end of town. no. 1 (to the main square) is more frequent than the trains, and also goes to the airport.

City Tourist Office: AURAKATU 4; (02) 233 6366. Open Mon–Fri 0800–1545 (June–Aug), Mon–Fri 0815–1600 (Sept–May). The free full-colour brochure *Turku* has everything you need. **Varsinais-Suomen matkailuyhdistys** (Regional): the **South-West Finland Regional Tourist Office**, at LÄNTINEN RANTAKATU 13; (02) 251 7333, is open Mon–Fri 0900–1500. **InterRail Centre**, LÄNTINEN RANTAKATU 47–49; (02) 253 5749, opens Mon–Sat 0900–2100 (July–Aug).

Arctia Marina Palace, LINNANKATU 32; (02) 336 300, is pricey but has an unbeatable riverside location.
Astro, HUMALISTONKATU 18; (02) 251 7838, between the station and the centre, has the cheapest rooms in town. **HI** is near the Arctia at LINNANKATU 39; (02) 231 6578. **Bed and breakfast**: **Niiranen**, VANHA LITTOISTENTIE 27, 233 0230, is good value, as is **Kultainen Turisti**, KÄSITYÖLÄISENKATU 11, 250 0265.

ROUTE DETAIL

Helsinki–Oulu ETT table 790

Type	Frequency	Journey Time
Train	5 daily	7 hrs 15 mins

Helsinki–Parikkala ETT table 795

Type	Frequency	Journey Time
Train	4 daily	4 hrs

Parikkala–Retretti

Type	Frequency	Journey Time
Train	2 per day	30 mins

Retretti–Savonlinna

Type	Frequency	Journey Time
Train	2 per day	30 mins

Parikkala–Joensuu ETT table 795

Type	Frequency	Journey Time
Train	6 daily	1 hr 15 mins

Joensuu–Kuopio ETT tables 792, 795

Type	Frequency	Journey Time
Train	2 daily	3 hrs 45 mins

Kuopio–Oulu ETT table 795

Type	Frequency	Journey Time
Train	3 daily	4 hrs 30 mins

Notes
Helsinki to Oulu: 3 of the trains run overnight. Parikkala to Retretti to Savonlinna: additional buses run throughout the day. Joensuu to Kuopio: change trains at Pieksämäki.

Fastest Journey: 6 hrs 50 mins

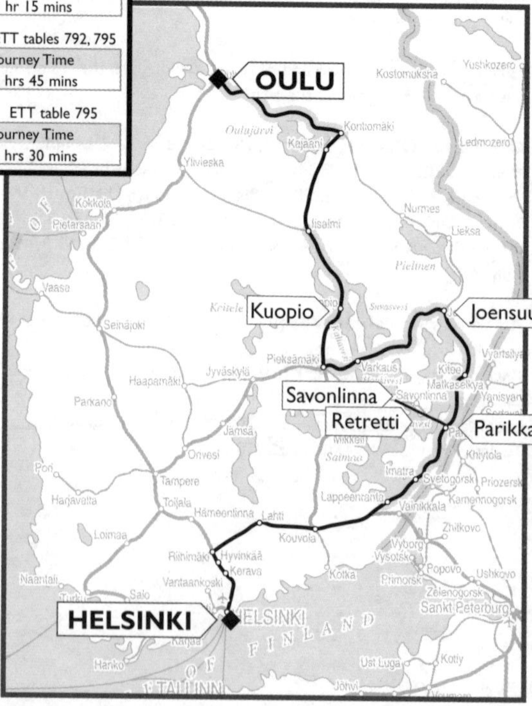

OULU
Kuopio
Joensuu
Savonlinna
Retretti
Parikkala
HELSINKI

This satisfying trip takes in all that is quintessential about Finland, from the rolling farmlands of the south to the untamed swathes of forest and thousands of lakes in the north, with **Kuopio** one of the main highlights. The spur from **Parikkala** to **Savonlinna** via the **Punkaharju** causeway has far from frequent services but is especially rewarding, so it is included as part of the main route.

PARIKKALA

Change here for trains on the spur to **Savonlinna** (buses also available).

The rail spur from **Parikkala** to **Savonlinna** leads on to **Retretti.**

RETRETTI

Retretti, 26 km away from Parikkala (there are buses when the train isn't running and the option of a cruise in summer), is a spectacular arts complex housed partly in man-made caverns in **Punkaharjuesker**, a 7-km-long Ice Age ridge of pine-crowned rocks, but also spreads into the surrounding woodlands. In addition to the many paintings and sculptures, you can attend summer concerts underground – which gives great acoustics.

SAVONLINNA

Sited on a group of bridge-linked lake islands, this spa resort, fashionable with the tsars in the mid 19th century, has a number of attractions, but there are two which make it unmissable. **Olavinlinna**, the best-preserved medieval castle in the northern countries, was built in 1475. It's largely intact and retains a medieval character. The courtyard is the venue for the other major draw, the annual international **opera festival**. It's staged in July: tickets go on sale the previous Nov and it's essential to book months in advance, for accommodation as well as tickets. Contact the Tourist Office for booking information.

RAIL **Savonlinna–Kauppatori** station is the first stop and more central than the main one. Two trains and 2–3 buses make the hour-long trip from **Parikkala**, serving **Retretti** en route, shortly after crossing the **Punkaharju** causeway. Turn left out of the station, then left again onto **Olavinkatu** to get to the centre.

i **Tourist Office**: PUISTOKATU 1, (015) 517 510, http://www.travel.fi/int/Savonlinna; email: savonlinna@tourist-svl.fi); open daily 0800–1800 (June and Aug), 0800–2200 (July), Mon–Fri 0900–1600 (Sept–May).

Vuorilinna, on Vaaarasaari island, just north of the rail

DAY TRIP FROM KUOPIO

On an island in Lake Ladoga, the 800-year-old **Valamon Luostari,** (Monastery of Valamo; ☎(017) 570 1504, 🚌 daily to within 4 km), at Heinävesi is the centre for the Russian Orthodox religion in Finland. You can stay at the hostel on the island ☎017 566 419, but wearing shorts is not acceptable and photographs are not permitted. The Orthodox Lintulan Luostari (Convent of Lintula) ☎(017) 563 106, 20 km away, also offers accommodation. A full-day excursion that operates June–Aug is the easiest way to visit both briefly. If you want to stay longer, there are various options: ask the Tourist Office for details.

WHERE NEXT?

The Stockholm–Helsinki trip (p. 450) passes through Oulu. By following the Stockholm direction to Boden, you can join the Oslo–Boden route (p. 442) at Boden and travel through Norway to Oslo.

station, has fairly cheap rooms and a hostel, ☎(015) 739 5430. Or try **Savonlinnan Kristillinen Opissto**, RITALANMÄMI 1, ☎(015) 537 007.

JOENSUU

Worthy of a few hours' stop, Joensuu has the worthwhile **North Karelia Museum**, an art nouveau **town hall**, Lutheran and Orthodox **churches**, the university's **botanical gardens** and a **tropical butterfly and turtle garden**. Try to be there for the **festival** in mid July.

KUOPIO

The main reason to stop here is the outstanding **Suomen Ortodoksinen Kirkkomuseo** (Orthodox Church Museum), KARJALANKATU 1, on top of a hill about 1 km north-west of the centre (🚌 no. 7). The Russian Orthodox religion once flourished in this area and in 1939, to safeguard them from the Nazis precious 18th-century icons and other sacred objects were gathered together from all over the country. The result is an eclectic and fascinating collection. ther sights include a pretty Lutheran **cathedral**, an open-air ethnographic museum, and a harbour with summer festivals when it's light all night. All are in the centre.

RAIL ☎(017) 211 4245, open Mon–Fri 0800–1700. On the northern edge of town, about 500 m from the central market square.

i **Tourist Office**: HAAPANIEMENKATU 17 (by the market square), ☎(017) 182 584; http://www.travel.fi/kuopio. Open Mon–Fri 0900–1800, Sat 0900–1600 (June–mid Aug), Mon–Fri 0900–1700 (mid Aug–May). In summer, information guides wander round the town.

🛏 **Hermannin Salit**, HERMANNINAUKIO 3A, ☎(017) 364 4961, is 10 mins' walk south of the centre and has both cheap rooms and dorm beds. Other budget options are **Hospitsi**, MYLLYKATU 4, ☎(017) 261 4501, a central boarding house, and **Matkakoti Souvari**, VUORIKATU 42, ☎(017) 262 2144.

(for Directory information, see pp. 546, 553 and 554).

The landscape of the Baltic states belongs to the northern European plain, which some might consider monotonous, but is often very distinctive. Forests of birch give way to low, rolling hills, scattered woods, lakes, great lazy rivers, and rocky outcrops with ruined castles. The coast is often studded with islands, large and small.

All three states are undergoing the transition from a Soviet planned economy (with many relics of the Soviet past in evidence) to a Western market-oriented economy. In many areas the transition is complete, but there may be occasional shortcomings in the quality of service. There are few places in Europe where you can see change at such a pace.

Of the three Baltic states, **Latvia** and **Lithuania** are cheaper than **Estonia.** Although the standard of living is increasing, you may still come across pensioners begging. Please give them something – it will not mean a lot to you, but it will to them. You will at least get a blessing in return.

ESTONIA

YOUTH HOSTELS

The **Estonian Youth Hostel Association**, TATAVI 39–310, ☎(372) (6) 464 14 57 (fax: (372) (6) 461595; email: puhkemajad@online.ee), will make reservations at 15 hostels throughout Estonia from 150EEK.

Throughout the **Baltic States** you should avoid tap water (not safe to drink anywhere) and stick to bottled water. Tea and coffee are widely available.

ACCOMMODATION

Hotels are still fairly thin on the ground. **Home stays** offer accommodation in farmhouses, summer cottages, homes and small boarding houses. There are three **bed and breakfast agencies**. The Estonian Farmers' Union produces a farm holidays brochure. Try to be back at your lodgings/hotel by 2200 (usual lock-out time), unless you've checked that it's OK to return later.

FOOD AND DRINK

Restaurants are generally open noon to midnight. The pattern of eating is to have a large helping of hors d'oeuvres and modest helpings thereafter; fish appears on many menus. The most popular drink is beer *(olu)*, and Estonian beers (both dark and light) have a growing reputation – e.g. **Saku, Tartu** and **Saaremma**. Vodka and brandy are better value and some bars serve mulled wine. Try the Estonian liqueur, **Vana Tallinn**.

BALTIC STATES

Latvian beer *(alus)* is cheap, strong and quite good – try **Aldaris**, **Bauskas** and **Piebalga**. **Kvass** is a mildly alcoholic rye drink.

LATVIA

Accommodation

The more sophisticated accommodation tends to cluster around **Riga** and the seaside resort **Jurmala**, once colonised by Russian holiday makers, including Boris Yeltsin. Most camping facilities are in the area of Jurmala and the coastline. **Latvian Youth Hostels Association**, Laimdotas 2a, Riga LV 1006; ☎ (371) 755 1271.

Food and drink

Latvian cuisine features fish and meat, many dishes accompanied by a richly seasoned gravy. The brown granary bread and sweet pastries are excellent. There are lots of different berries in season and they are often used in ice-cream sundaes.

LITHUANIA

Accommodation

There is a last minute booking service at the **Tourist Information and Hotel Reservation Centre**. If looking away from the capital, book ahead or at least have some names, addresses and phone numbers. There's a small network of hostels; contact **Lithuanian Youth Hostels**.

Food and drink

Local specialities include: *cepelinai* (the national dish – meatballs in potato), *blynai* (mini pancakes) and *kotletas* (pork cutlets). Fish and dairy products are common in all dishes. Lithuanians eat their **evening meal** early and you should aim to order by 2000, even in places that are theoretically open much later; service is leisurely, so relax and make an evening of it. Vodka (the best is **Kvietine**) and very sweet liqueurs are the main spirits. Lithuanian beer (**Vtena** and other brands) is easily available. The beer bars in **Vilnius** are worth a visit if you want to see 'the other side' of Lithuania. They are usually large rooms where snacks and watered-down beer are sold to sometimes belligerent hard drinkers.

Tourist Information

Hotel Reservation Centre Vilnius Airport, ☎(370) (2) 26 08 75. Prices are often listed in DM or US$, suggesting that they bear little relation to local costs.

The **Litinterp Agency**, Bernadinn 7–2, ☎(370) (2) 22 28 50 (for Vilnius and Lithuania), can arrange accommodation with local families.

Lithuanian Youth Hostels PO Box 12, Filaretu 17, 2000 Vilnius-C, ☎/fax: (370) (2) 26 26 60 (email: lyh@jnakv.vno.soros.lt).

Editor's Choice

Kaunas; Riga; St Petersburg (Russia); Tartu; Tallinn; Vilnius.

Beyond the Borders

Vilnius–Warsaw (ETT table 1040); Tallinn–Helsinki ferry (tables 2410, 2412).

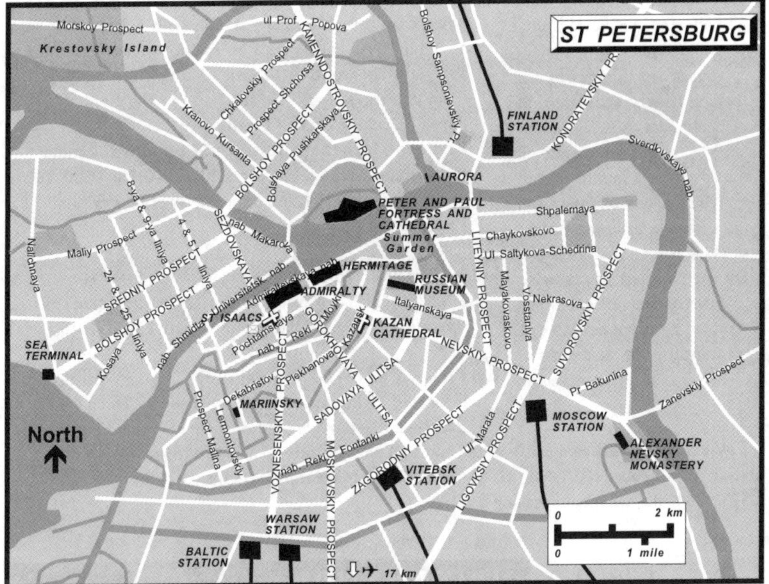

We have included Russia's second city in this chapter on the Baltic States as it's very much dominated by the Baltic itself and a tremendously atmosphere-laden city. You'll need to obtain a Russian visa in advance; the journey from Berlin or Warsaw involves transit through Belarus, but the visa allows for this. There are direct services to *Moskva* (Moscow), 650 km away (shortest journey by high-speed ER200 train, taking just over 5 hrs; ETT table 1900).

St Petersburg (formerly *Leningrad*), the former capital of Russia, is the brainchild of the westernising Tsar, Peter the Great. Almost every other building is a palace or architectural monument of some kind – there are more than 8000 listed for conservation – St Petersburg is still very beautiful, despite the crumbling façades and peeling paintwork.

ARRIVAL AND DEPARTURE

RAIL **Moskovsky Vokzal** (alternative name: **Glavny**), ☎ 168 4597 (METRO: **Ploshchad Vosstaniya**) for trains to Moscow. Varshavsky Vokzal, ☎ 168 2690 (METRO: **Baltiyskaya**) for trains to **Poland** and the **Baltic States. Finlandsky Vokzal**, ☎ 168 7024 (METRO: **Ploshchad Lenina**) for trains to **Helsinki** (in a large glass case on platform 5 you can see Locomotive 293, which carried Lenin into hiding in Finland). The facilities in all terminals are basic, with a left luggage

Tickets for all local transport (buses, trams, trolleybuses and the metro) are sold at **metro stations** and **kiosks**. A *yedinye bilyeti* (110rbs) allows you to use all transport for a month. Punch your tickets on board the vehicle or in the station booking hall to validate them. For metro travel you can also buy **tokens** (*talony*), which should be dropped into one of the turnstiles at the top of the escalator.

office, cheap snack bars and station stalls. Watch your bags at all times. All tickets must be paid for in hard currency and you will have to show your passport. You can buy them at a travel agency or at a hotel or the Central Railway Booking Office (**Tsentralny Zheleznodorozhnye Kassy**), (**Griboedova**) **kanala naberezhnaya** 24 (Mon–Sat 0800–2000; Sun 0800–1600) at windows 100–104, 2nd floor. METRO: **Nevsky Prospekt**.

Sea Terminal, **Morskoy Vokzal**, MORSKOY SLAVY PLOSHCHAD 1; ☎355 1310, trolleybus: 10 and 12. Parom Baltic Line operate ferries to Ökesund (Sweden), ☎355 1616.

Pulkovo, ☎104 34. St Petersburg's international airport is located 17 km south of the city centre. The currency exchange office has limited opening hours and is generally unreliable. The Route Taxi (a 10-seater minibus) links both terminals to **Moskovskaya** metro station from 0700–2200, taking 10–15 mins. **Taxis**: **Matralen**, LYUBOTINSKY PROEZD 5, ☎298 364, offers English-speaking drivers.

INFORMATION

TOURIST OFFICE

No city information office but try a travel agency, the **Ost-West Kontaktservice**, MAJA KOVSKOGO 7; ☎327 3417 or 279 7945; open Mon–Fri 1000–1800, Sat 1200-1800. Organises accommodation, excursions and tours, and can help register visas.

Available from hotels, bookstalls, restaurants etc., the useful publication *The Guide*, provides comprehensive information. The twice-weekly *St Petersburg Times* has events listings every Friday.

POST AND PHONES

Central Post Office, POCHTAMTSKAYA ULITSA 9; ☎312 83 02 (open Mon–Sat 0900–2000, Sun 1000–1800). The most convenient **poste restante** is **St Petersburg 1904**, NEVSKY PROSPEKT 64. The local phone area code is 812. For **local calls** you'll need to buy *zhetony* (tokens) from a metro station. To make an **international call**, go to your hotel desk or the **St Petersburg International Telephone and Telegraph Office**, BOLSHAYA MORSKAYA ULITSA 3–5 (open daily, except 1230–1300).

ATMs are now fairly extensive on NEVSKY PROSPEKT, and within hotels, shops and restaurants.

PUBLIC TRANSPORT

RAIL **Metro**: The metro is cheap and fairly reliable, but far from comprehensive. All four lines are colour coded, but you'll need a basic knowledge of the Cyrillic alphabet. Two stations on the same site but on different lines will have different names. Stations are indicated by a large red M. Indicator boards in the station give exit and transfer information. If you're changing lines, look for a sign with the word *perekhod* and the name of the station you want. To get back to street level, follow the signs *vykhod*.

The public transport system is comprehensive and very cheap. All transport runs 0530–0030, but beware of delays at night as bridges are lifted. There is no official transport map, but most city maps include bus and tram routes as well as a metro plan. Look out for the signs (T) for trams, (A) for buses and (M) for trolley buses. Most vehicles, especially on the Nevsky Prospekt, are extremely crowded and there is a considerable amount of re-routing, often with no notice.

Tours

River

As well as canal and river tours, there is a regular hydrofoil service (0900–2000 in summer, 30-min journey) to Peterhof (Petrodvorets), departing from the Neva Embankment. This involves a highly pleasurable trip along the river Neva and is still cheap (double-check the time of the last hydrofoil back to town).

Taxis: Beware of the unofficial ones; the authorised cabs (☎312 0022 or ☎265 1313) have a chequered pattern and the letter T on the side. It is best to order a cab from a hotel (at least 1 hr in advance). **Never** take a taxi without agreeing a price in advance and **never** get into a cab where there is already another passenger.

Accommodation

There is a shortage of good medium-price and budget accommodation. Several major hotels have been upgraded in recent years, including the Astoria and the Grand Hotel Europe, which featured in the James Bond movie *Goldeneye*.

The St Petersburg is reasonbably priced, and in a nice location across the river from the Cruiser Aurora. It's about 20 mins walk from the Winter Palace, while the Pribaltiyskaya Hotel is further from the centre. The Mir Hotel is good value and convenient for the metro and airport.

Some of the old Soviet hotels are still a bargain if you're prepared to put up with minor inconveniences. The best located is the **Oktyabrskaya** Hotel just across the road from the Moscow station.

The **St Petersburg International Hostel**, 3-ya Rozhdestvenskaya (Sovyetskaya) ulitsa ☎28; 329 8018, metro **Ploshchad Vosstaniya**, is an American venture aimed at backpackers and will help with information and reservations.

Hotels

Astoria, Bolshaya Morskaya ulitsa 39; ☎210 5757
Grand Hotel Europe, Mikhaylovskaya ulitsa 1/7; ☎329 6000. Both expensive.

St Petersburg, Pirogovskaya naberezhnaya 5/2; ☎542 9411 (Metro: Ploshchad Lenina).

Pribaltiyskaya Hotel, Korablestroiteley ulitsa 14; ☎356 0263, (Metro: Primorskaya) then bus.
Mir Hotel, Gastello ulitsa 17; ☎108 5165, metro **Moskovskaya** are competitively priced.

Oktyabrskaya Hotel, Ligovsky prospekt 10; ☎277 6330, (metro: Ploshchad Vosstaniya). Cheaper.

FOOD AND DRINK

There is a wide choice of restaurants, but eating out can be expensive. You'll find eateries of all types in the main shopping street, Nevsky prospekt. If money is no object, you're best advised to head for the major hotels, offering Russian and international cuisines.

Bahlsen Le Cafe, Nevsky Prospekt 142, has a homely atmosphere. The cafe next door is a good place for a snack.

HIGHLIGHTS

State Hermitage The **State Hermitage** is not only one of the world's largest and most magnificent picture galleries, but also the former residence of the Russian imperial family, the **Winter Palace**. A tour of the royal apartments includes the sumptuous ballroom known as the **Nicholas Hall** the **Malachite Hall** where Alexander Kerensky's Provisional Government surrendered to Lenin's Bolshevik forces in 1917. (Open Tues–Sun 1030–1800). Free for students.

St Petersburg's elegant main avenue, **Nevsky Prospekt**, extends 5km eastwards from Palea Square to the River Neva. The elaborate bridges, imposing frontages and stunning palaces combine to make it a principal sight.

Pushkin's house No writer has closer associations with St Petersburg than the 19th century novelist, Fyodor Dostoevsky. Although he is most closely associated with the Haymarket, the setting for Crime and Punishment, it is his last home in the city that has been refurbished as a museum. (Kuznechny pereulok 5/2, Tues–Sun 1100–1730, closed last Wed of each month).

WHERE NEXT?

*Ferries serve **Stockholm** (p. 420), and **Talinn** (p. 466): ETT table 1800.*

ROUTE DETAIL

Vilnius–St Petersburg ETT table 1860

Type	Frequency	Journey Time
Train	2 per day	14 hrs

Vilnius–Riga ETT table 1850

Type	Frequency	Journey Time
Train	2 daily	7 hrs

Riga–Tartu ETT table 1845

Type	Frequency	Journey Time
Bus	1 a day	4 hrs 45 mins

Tartu–Tallinn ETT table 1800

Type	Frequency	Journey Time
Train	5 a day	3 hrs 40 mins

Tallinn–St Petersburg ETT table 1800

Type	Frequency	Journey Time
Train	1 a day	10 hrs 45 mins

Fastest Journey:
15 hrs 00 mins

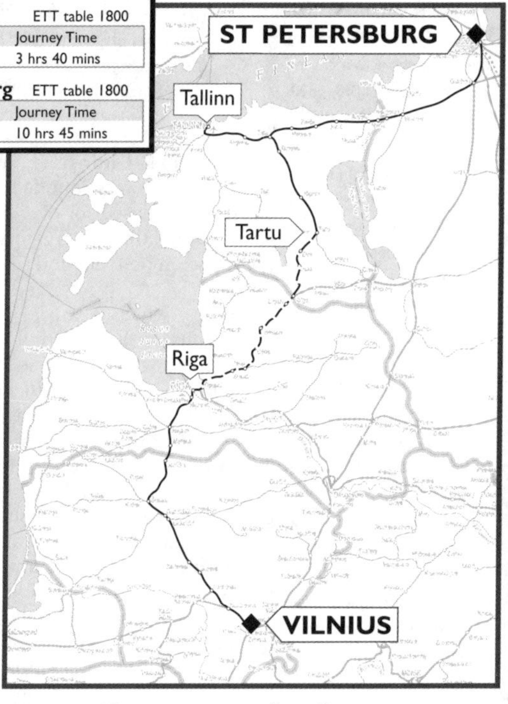

ST PETERSBURG
Tallinn
Tartu
Riga
VILNIUS

Vilnius – Tallinn – St Petersburg

This intriguing route crosses no fewer than four international frontiers, those of the three independent Baltic Republics of **Lithuania, Latvia and Estonia**, and of Russia. The through journey can be performed by bus or a combination of bus and rail, with ample time to absorb a landscape of dense forest of pine and silver birch, gently undulating verdant uplands, and isolated farmsteads. You can extend the journey by beginning from **Warsaw** (p. 477), or omit **St Petersburg** and take the ferry from **Tallinn** across the **Gulf of Finland** to **Helsinki** (p. 410).

Vilnius

Vilnius is a curiosity of history - a Central European city of outstanding baroque architecture translated to Northern Europe. But take your own walking tour!

Avoid the districts of **Uzupio** and **Kalvariju** late at night.

Note that **museums and galleries** are usually closed on Mondays.

The main offices of the **Lithuanian Art Museum** can be found at DIDZIOJU 4, ☎62 80 30, where tickets for all the branch galleries can be purchased (student and other concessions available).

St John's Church is the University Church. The University was founded in the seventeenth century, but was closed for over eighty years in Tsarist times. Look for the **Observatory Tower** (1659) and a small museum of books and scientific instruments.

Pilies, which is full of gift shops, terminates in the vicinity of the cathedral square, the focal point of the city and which witnessed mass anti-Soviet demonstrations in the run-up to independence. The **cathedral** was built on an ancient site dedicated to the God of thunder. Re-built eleven times, it received its classical façade in 1777–1801. Within its **Kazimieris Chapel**, are the splendid tombs of the members of the Polish-Lithuanian royal dynasty. The **Gedimino tower** is all that remains of the royal castle and now contains the **Vilnius Castle Museum**. Adjacent to the cathedral is **Kalnu Park**, a shady streamside sanctuary. T KOSCIUSKOS leads eastwards from the north side of the park to the **Church of St Peter and St Paul**, the finest baroque church interior in Vilnius, with over 2000

Day Trips from Vilnius

Museum of Genocide, AGRASTU (frequent bus services) marks the site where 100,000 people (mostly Jews) were murdered by the Nazis in the Paneriai Forest, 10 km from Vilnius. Grassed over pits in the forest serve as a chilling reminder (1100–1800, closed Tue).

Trakai, the old medieval capital of Trakai (Tourist Office: VYTAUTO 90, ☎51 934) has an impressive (restored) castle, dating from the 14th century, on a picturesque lake (open daily; book English-language tours, ☎51 527. Frequent buses and trains; just under 1 hr.

Kaunas (Tourist Office: SAPIEGOS 4, ☎(370) 7 22 29 83; buy *Kaunas in Your Pocket*) was the pre-war capital, and retains an air of elegance as Lithuania's second city. LAISVES, the city's pride and joy, is a pedestrianised, tree-lined boulevard, bordered with shops and cafés that

stucco figures. The **Tuskulenai Estate** opposite, was a burial place of Stalin's victims. GEDIMINO leads westwards from the square into modern Vilnius, terminating at the Parliament Building. Adjacent to the **Music Academy** may be found the old KGB headquarters, now home to the **KGB Museum**, GEDIMINO 40 (entrance from AVKU 4; conducted tours of the cells, sometimes by former inmates, Tues–Sun).

RAIL ☎63 00 88; 24-hr left luggage office, accommodation bureau, 24-hr currency exchange. **Buses**: Trolleybuses and long-distance/international bus station outside rail station; left luggage office.

RAIL TICKETS

can be purchased by Visa or MasterCard at branches of **Baltic Travel Service** at SUBACIAUS 2, GEDIMINO 21, and UKMERGES 12.

i **Tourist Office**: PILIES 42, ☎62 07 62, (Mon–Fri 1000–1800). They will book accommodation and arrange guides. **Branch**: at VILNIUS 22, ☎62 96 60. Buy *Vilnius in Your Pocket*, an objective guide to the sights, hotels, restaurants and bars.
Lithuanian Student and **Youth Travel**, BASANAVICIAUS 30-13, ☎22 13 73: bargain fares for students, ISIC, ITIC and other discount cards and visas and travel insurance.
Money: **Cash machines**: Visa: GEDIMINO 10-12 and SAVANOVIU 19. MasterCard: VILNIAUS 16, PILIOS 9 and GEDIMINO 56.
Post and phones: The **Central Post Office**, GEDIMINO 7, ☎61 67 59. Some phones accept magnetic strip cards, others chip cards; both kinds will eventually work in all phone boxes; cards from post offices or Spauda kiosks. The **Vilnius area code** is 370 2.
Shopping: Markets (haggling permitted!) may be found at PILIES 23 (souvenirs) and GEDIMINO (general). Gift shops selling handicrafts and amber proliferates in the old town.

Public transport: The most attractive part of the city, the old town, is best explored on foot (easy walking distance from bus and train stations.) Bus and trolleybuses cost 60 centas from kiosks/post office (75 centas on board), but you need different tickets for each. Public transport runs from 0500–0030.

The Lithuanian Youth Centre Hostel, UKMERGES 25, ☎72 22 70, is a modern upmarket hostel, with singles at 80Lt. The **Filaretai Hostel**, FILARETU 17, ☎24 46 27, is run by

Day Trips from Vilnius cont'd.

reflect increasing prosperity. Next to the **Military Museum of Vytantas the Great**, DONELAICIO 64, **MK Cuvlionis State Art Museum**, houses a vast collection of modern Lithuanian and folk art. The famous **Devil's Museum** is a collection of over 2000 devils from all over the world, including Hitler and Stalin dancing upon Lithuania.
A walk eastwards, along **Putvinskio**, leads to the funicular, which ascends the 'green hill' for a fine view over the city; you can pay using a trolleybus ticket. **Pevkunas House** is the finest example of late Gothic architecture in the town, and houses handicraft displays at weekends.
Youth hostel: PRANCAZU 59, ☎74 89 72. **Litinherp Agency**, KUMELIU 15-4, ☎22 87 18, will find you somewhere for bed and breakfast (closed Sun).
Šiaulia, en route north of Vilnius, is worth visiting for its extraordinary **Hill of Crosses** – 80,000 crosses of all sizes, built since 1975, as a symbol of resistance to Soviet power. From Šiaulia, visit **Klaipeda**, the old port city (ETT table 1850) with its aquarium and dolphinarium and the Maritime Museum in the old fort (closed Mon).

Day Trips from Vilnius cont'd.

From **Klaipeda** you can use the frequent taxibus service to visit the pleasant seaside resort of **Palanga** (**Tourist Office**: VYTAUTO 106; ☎+370-36 53 927) – with fine beach and dunes as well as a fascinating amber museum with Jurassic-era insects embedded in orange resin (closed Mon).

DAY TRIPS FROM RIGA

Jurmala is a string of seaside resorts, 20km west of Riga, a popular holiday destination since the 19th century. It's a continuous length of beach, sand dunes, and fragrant pines between the Baltic and the Lielupe river. After a major clean-up programme, the sea is once again safe for swimming, but many of the resorts are struggling to make a living. The best place to visit is **Majovi** and its vicinity. **The Tourist Office** at JOMAS 42 ☎+371-2 76 42 76, has English-speaking staff, and will organise accommodation. **Frequent trains** from Riga, taking less than 1 hr; get off at **Majovi** or **Dubulti**.

Rundale Palace, the Baltic Versailles, designed by the architect of the **Winter Palace** at **St Petersburg**, was completed in 1768; best visited by investing in a coach tour from Riga.

Kuldiga is probably the most perfectly preserved Latvian town; four to six buses a day, taking 4 hrs.

enthusiastic students; 24-32Lt. For the first night, with a discount of 4Lt for each additional night; accommodation booking serves for rest of Baltics (🚌 no.34 from the station). **Litintorp Agency**, BERNARDINU 7-2, ☎22 38 50, books bed and breakfast accommodation from 70Lt.

The cheapest food is from street stalls and the colourful food market at **Hales Turgaviete** on the corner of PYLIMO and BAZILIJONU. Some restaurants close early. If you wish to sample Lithuanian food, try the moderately priced **Ritos Smukle**, IKI COMMERCIAL CENTRE, ZIRMUNU 68, ☎77 07 86. **Medininkai Ausros**, Varta ☎61 40 19, is a relatively inexpensive café and restaurant in the old town. A traditional Lithuanian lunch can be had at **Skanumelis 2**, PYLIMO 4, ☎22 74 50, a café frequented by locals.

RIGA

Riga has two cities – a 17th century Hanseatic town preserved as the historic core and a large monumentally Parisian-feeling quarter of boulevards, parks and art nouveau architecture stretching beyond the old fortifications. You can walk the old town, but might need public transport for the rest.

Adjacent to the rail and bus stations is the eye-opening Central Market on NEGU IELA. Housed in three huge former Zeppelin hangars, it's a mixture of meat, varieties of bread, dairy products, vegetables and anything else edible. The approaches often consist of lines of women selling things like used shoes to make a bit of money.

Cross the road by the subway and proceed up ASPAZIJAS BULV. On the right is the newly restored National Opera, and the old moat, set in a linear park on the site of the old fortifications.

The wide expanse of the **Brivibas** on the right, leads to the **Freedom Monument**. A guard is

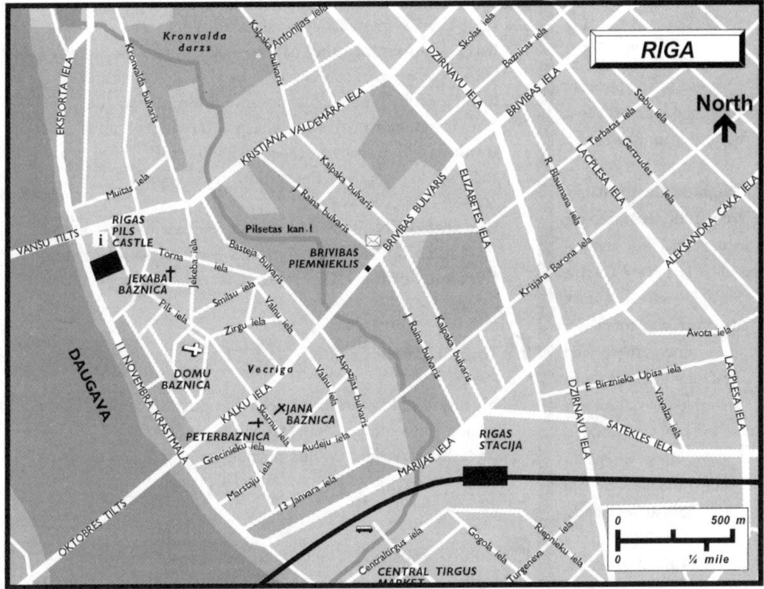

mounted (and changed) every hour by the new Latvian Army. Turn left down TORNA LELA. The **Pulvertonis** (Powder tower) on the left is now part of the **Museum of War**.

The road continues past the surviving (but much restored) section of the old town wall, dating from the 13th-century. It ends with the picturesque **Swedish Gate**, built in 1698.

Riga Castle dates from 1330 and contains the official residence of the President of Latvia and **museums of Latvian history, foreign art** and **Latvian culture**. On the cobbled cathedral square, the **cathedral** is the largest place of worship in the Baltics, and is famous for its organ. In M. PILS IELA, **Three Brothers** are the most famous of Riga's old houses, dating from the 15th century.

For an excellent view of the city, ascend the tower of the **Church of St Peter**, SKARNU 19 (closed Mon).

On *Rifleman Square* (named after the Latvian Red Rifleman who played a heroic part in the first World War and later aided the Bolsheviks) is the medieval **House of the Blackheads**, a lay order of bachelor merchants, being restored in time for the city's 800th birthday in 2001. The **Occupation Museum** (free) displays the sufferings of the Latvian people under the Nazi and Soviet regimes, and tells of the recent struggle to regain independence.

DAY TRIP TO SIGULDA

A visit to the Livonian Switzerland is an excellent day out from Riga. Head straight for the ruins of **Sigulda Castle**, dating from 1207, and including an auditorium for cultural events. The **New Castle** is a nineteenth century structure, and contains a moderately priced restaurant. Continue to the cable-car station and cross the beautiful wooded valley. Bungee jumpers launch themselves from here at weekends; if you'd like to try ☎+371-2 97 25 31. From the far side of the valley, find the path to the right to the ruins of **Kimulda Castle**, where it veers left; then look for the path on the right, signposted for **Gutman's Cave**, dropping steeply via steps to the valley floor, where the path veers to the left (with the river on the right) to reach the celebrated cave. Gutman was a Latvian Robin Hood and his sandstone cave has graffiti dating back to the 17th century. Where the path ends at a roadside picnic area, carry on along the road, looking for a path on the right that ascends steeply up the

RAIL ☎23 30 95; immediate departure tickets from windows 3-9. **International booking office**: walk through the subway, then left across car park; purchases in cash until 2000. Left luggage in the station basement, plus lockers off the subway (0400–0100). **Tourist bureau** arranges cheap international travel. **Pavex Bank** cashes travellers' cheques 0830–2130. There is a 24-hr supermarket opposite the station.

Bus station: Near the rail station, adjacent to the Central Market, ☎721 3611; **Latvian and international routes**; **Eurolines office**, ☎721 4512. Currency exchange and left luggage.

Tourist Office: SKARNU 22, ☎722 1731; buy *Riga in Your Pocket*.
Money: Visa/MasterCard machine at post office next to the station. Riga is a problem (especially on Sundays) if you want to cash a travellers cheque outside banking hours; try **Maviku** 24-hr exchanges at BASTEVA BULV 14, MARIJAS 5 and 14, BRIVIBAS 30 and MERKELA 10.

Public transport: The very crowded buses, trams and trolleybuses operate 0530–0030, with some all-night services. Buy separate tickets for each mode of transport from conductor/kiosk; 80 santimi flat fare. **Taxibuses** charge 15-25 santimi. Avoid **taxis**, except for long distances, and stick to the orange and black vehicles (insist the meter is turned on).
Post and phones: **Main post office**: BRUBAS 19, open 24 hrs. It has a number of phone cabins (pay after call). There are numerous digital phone boxes. Chip cards and magnetic strip cards are available from 2 to 10L at any post office and most shops. The **telephone code** is (371).

Saulite (opposite station) at MERKELA 12, ☎722 4546; Auvova, Marijas 5, ☎ 722 44 79. **Patricia Accommodation Agency**, ELIZABETES 22-6, ☎728 4868, offers rooms in the centre for $15 a night without breakfast. Of the several hostels the **Placis** at LAIMDOTIS IELA 2A, ☎755 1824 is particularly recommended (trolleybus no.4 to **Teika** stop).

The **buffet bars** in the Riga meat market offer bargain price and filling fare. The local speciality is *Rigas Balzam*, a mix of cognac, ginger and oak bark, drunk with vodka or coffee; a shop opposite the station sells a wide variety. Try also the local bread, known as *Rupjmaize*, sometimes used with cream to make tomato soup.

Tartu

Tartu is Estonia's University town, built into a wooded hill, with picturesque views. The concrete river bridge replaces the original stone bridge of 1784 which symbolised Tartu. There is a fund to reconstruct it, hence the donation boxes all over the town. The **Tartu Citizens' Museum**, Jaani 16, is a reconstructed 1830s home (closed Mon, Tue). **St John's Church** is being reconstructed bit by bit, including its remarkable terracotta. The **University** was founded by the King Gustav Adolphus of Sweden in 1632 (statue behind) but the classical university building dates from 1809.

The **Town Hall Square** is probably the most photographed spot in Tartu. At one end is the bridge and at the other, the fine neo-classical **Town Hall**, built in 1778–84. Notice the leaning house (No.18) – one wall is built on the foundation of the town wall, the other isn't.

Take time out to explore **Toomemägi**. You can cross the 'sighing bridge' to ascend 'kissing hill'. Look out for the sacrificial stone upon which Tartu students burn their notes at the end of final exams.

The excellent **Estonian Folk Museum**, Kuperjanov 9, has Estonian customs, traditions and costumes (closed Mon, Tues, free Fri).

RAIL **Vaksali**, ☎439 22 20. Left luggage, international booking office. The simplest way into the town centre is right along Vaksali, and left along Riia.

Bus station: Junction of Riia and Turu, ☎477 227.

i **Tourist Office**: Raekoja plats 12, ☎44 17 56.

Randur, Vasava 25, ☎47 56 91. In a housing block some distance from the centre. **Youth hostel**: **Tartu**, Soola 1, ☎43 20 91. The Tourist Office can arrange accommodation from about 800EEK in the centre and 200EEK out of town.

Day Trips to Sigulda cont'd.

opposite side of the valley and to **Tuvaida Castle**, one of the most attractive in Latvia; there's a great view from the tower. Here you can hire horses, take a carriage ride or use the bobsleigh track at Sveices 13, ☎+371-2 97 20 08; in summer, try a wheeled sledge.

Tourist offices: **Sigulda Tourist Information Centre**, Pils 4a, ☎+371-2 97 13 35. **Gauga National Park Information Centre**, Raina 15, ☎+371-2 97 13 45.

Day Trips from Tartu

Polva Lake (train to **Taerakonu**, then walk), with its sandstone caves and picnic areas, is a popular Sunday outing, when you can join the locals picking berries and mushrooms in the woods.

Otepää (buses from Tartu) is one of Estonia's few a hilly areas with conditions suitable for winter sports including the Tartu Marathon.

Tourist Office: **Lipuvaljak Town Hall**, ☎+372-76 55 364; accommodation and maps of ski trails.

AROUND TALLINN

Kadriorg Palace of 1718 (tram to the **Kadriorg** terminus) was created for Peter the Great and is now the official residence of the President, who hopes to have the park restored to its original condition; the nearby **Peter the Great House Museum** at MAEKALDA 2 is open in summer. In the district of **Pirita** (buses; or, better, walk from **Kadriorg**), where there's a beach and a yacht marina. The graceful **Russalka** (mermaid) monument stands by the sea, commemorating the loss of a Tsarist warship in a storm. Walk along PIRITA TEE, to the great concrete complex built by the Soviets as a war memorial, and known to Estonians as the bridge to Finland; it's now destined to be a national war memorial to all Estonia's war dead. You can continue past **Marjamäe Palace**, home to the modern section of the **Estonian History Museum**, from 1918 to the present day (closed Mon, Tues). The oldest attraction in Pivita is the **Convent of St Bridget**, an impressive ruin. You can also visit the British-built submarine *Lembit* (1936) in the harbour

Rocca-al-Mave, the open-air **Ethnographical Museum**, is beside the sea at VABAOHUMUSEUMI 12, ☎656 02 30. There's a host of reconstructed buildings from all over Estonia, plus folk performances at weekends in summer (🚍no. 21 from the rail station).

TALLINN

Compact, manageable and a delight to explore on foot, **Tallinn** is thick with medieval churches, houses and fortifications. Against a stretch of the medieval wall is a **craft market**, specialising in traditionally patterned fishermen's knitwear. KATARIINA KÄIK is a medieval alley tenanted by craftswomen and is lined with ancient gravestones. **Tallinn Town Museum**, VENE 17, has a section on modern history (English tour available; closed Tues). From here it's a short walk through the **Vana Turg** (Old Market) into the **Raekoja Plats** (Town Hall Square), with its outdoor cafés on the cobbles, and watched over by the Gothic town hall of 1404 (sporting **Vana Toomas**, or Old Thomas, the city guardian, on its tower – which can be climbed).

St Nicholas Church houses medieval art, including a striking 15th-century *Dance of Death*, while the **Orthodox Cathedral of Alexander Nevsky** of 1900 is worth a look if you've never seen the interior of a Russian church. Behind the church is a stretch of wall with the **Virgins Tower** and museum of fortification. Across LOSSI PLATS is **Toompea Castle**, the seat of government: it's not open, but you can walk round its 18th-century façade (hiding the medieval structure) and see **Tall Herman**, the tower from which the Estonian flag now flies.

From here TOOM KOOLI leads to the cathedral, Tallinn's oldest church, founded by the Danes and much rebuilt. It contains fine gravestones and crests of Swedish and German noblemen, plus a memorial to a Scottish admiral in Russian service (closed Mon).

The adjacent **National Art Museum** is currently housed in the **House of Knighthood**; after restoration it will move back to **Kadviag Palace** (closed Tue). Nearby **Tompea Hill** has two good viewpoints, one over the old town and the other looking towards the harbour.

Returning to the **Orthodox Cathedral**, PIKK VALG (long leg) drops between the walls of **Toompea** and

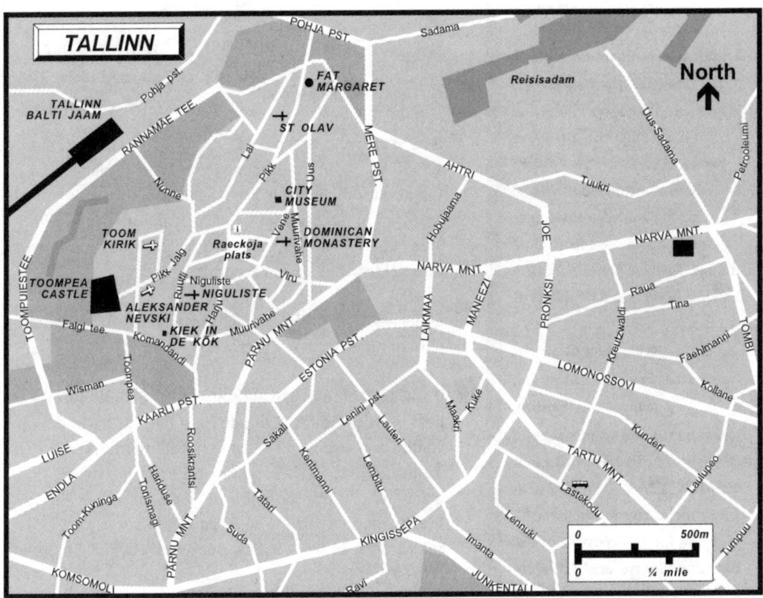

Tallinn proper (the two communities didn't get on). The charming gate leads to PIKK. On the corner is the **Church of the Holy Ghost**, with a beautiful altar piece (1483), while at PIKK 17 is the **Estonian History Museum**, housed in the **Great Guild Hall** (1407–1410) and with captions in English (closed Wed). PIKK terminates at the **Coastal Gate** by the **Three Sisters**, a perfectly preserved range of medieval houses. Alongside the gate is the **Fat Margaret tower**, which contains the excellent **Estonian Maritime Museum** (closed Mon, Tues).

The **Official City Tour** combines a walking tour of the old town, and a bus tour of the environs, operated by **Reisiekspert**, ROOSIKVANTSI 17, ☎6108 600; three daily departures from A Terminal passenger port; **Olümpia Hotel** and the **Viru Hotel**; 150EEK; free with Tallinn Card.

RAIL ☎615 68 51; booking hall at east end for local trains; main building for long distance travel within **Estonia**; upstairs for

DAY TRIPS FROM TALLINN

Pärnu (ETT tables 1805; 3 hrs 45 mins; take bus from station to town centre) is a pleasant and historic resort town (a good break if you're making the journey from **Riga** to **Tallinn** by bus). Within the old town you can explore a stretch of the old fortifications overlooking the former moat. The pre-1914 wooden bandstand and mud baths are features of the sea front; a short walk along RANNA PUISTI reveals two pre-war architectural treasures – the **Rannahoon Beach Pavilion** and the

Day Trips from Tallinn cont'd.

Rannahotel, both art deco gems. Supeluse (bathing street) commences at the mud bath, and runs through the attractive parkland back to town. From **Pärnu** excursions include by local bus to the railway museum at **Lavasaare** (steam days from time to time). **Tourist Office**: Munga 2, ☎(+372-44) 40 639. **Narvu-Joesu** is a (decayed) resort, with a great deal of tourist potential. Frequent buses and trains from **Tallinn**.

Haapsalu is Estonia's second seaside resort (**Tourist Office** at Posti 39, ☎+372 47 33 248; it may move to the rail station). Look for the remains of the **Bishops Castle and Church**. The old resort area and spa building have been restored, although the modern beach is to the west of the town. The old station (specially built to receive the Tsar) is now the home of the **National Railway Museum**, complete with historic locomotives and rolling stock. Estonians regard the islands of **Kuressaare** and **Saavema** (the Western Islands) as the most unspoilt part of their country – the true heartland of the people. Kuressaare is the capital of Saavema, the largest island (**Tourist Office at town hall**, ☎+372-45 33 120). To see the island fully, stay overnight, but book the accommodation ahead from **Tallinn**. The castle at Kuressaare is the best preserved in Estonia, and

international/advance tickets and customs declaration forms for Russian trains. Left luggage, currency exchange, Visa cashpoint.

Bus station: Lastekodu 4, ☎650 95 30, some distance from centre (take a tram). Obtain tickets before travel; destination board is arranged in direction of travel, not alphabetically, with international buses listed last. For Estonia use **Ekspress** buses. Eurolines have a separate office.

Tickets to Russia and the C.I.S are said to be 20% cheaper than in Moscow.

Enquiries ☎631 85 50; main terminal has full facilities, plus summer tourist information desk.

Tourist Office: Raokoja Plats 10, ☎631 39 40; one of best in Baltic States. On sale here (also at harbour, station and airport, plus some hotels and ferries) is the **Tallinn Card**: includes admission to major sights, unlimited city transport journeys, a boat trip in **Pirita Harbour**, a city tour and discounts in some restaurants; 24 hrs, 195EEK per adult, 100EEK per child; also longer periods.

The **Ekspress Hotline**, ☎626 69 00, is a useful source of information in English.

Money: Cash machines in lobby of the Vivru Hotel (Visa), and at several banks.

Post and phones: The main post office is at **Narnu** Mantee 1, ☎641 13 33, closed Sun; telephone office 0800–1900, Sat 0900–1600, closed Sun. Long-distance/ international calls ordered at the counter are 30% cheaper than from the public phone. To **call abroad from a phone box**, dial 8, and then 00. Most public phones are now digital card phones; by cards (from 30EEK upwards) from kiosks. The **area code** is ☎+372-6 (digital) or ☎+372-2 (analogue).

Tickets

Buy tickets from a kiosk (5EEK) or from the driver (7EEK) with the right change (not coins). Cancel tickets on board. Express buses cost 7EEK (kiosk) and 9EEK (driver). White minibuses (10EEK) can be flagged down at stops.

Public transport: Trams connect harbour, rail and bus stations with **Vivu Valjak** (Vivu Square); also buses and trolleybuses.

Eeslitau: DUNKU 4, ☎631 37 55. Centrally located in the old town; singles from 350EEK; popular, so book early. **Bussiterminali Oömaja**, ☎42 51 50, above bus station; shared singles from 80EEK. **Hostels**: **The Barn**, VÄIKE KARJA 1, ☎644 34 65; **Mevevaike**, SOPRUSE 182, ☎52 96 04 (trolleybus from rail station). **Bed and breakfast agencies**: CDS TOURS, RAEKOJA PLATS 17, ☎627 67 97; **Rasastra**, MERE 4, ☎641 22 91.

Day Trips from Tallinn cont'd.

the rest of the island boasts historic churches, windmills and a meteorite crater. Frequent buses from **Tallinn** (which go on the ferries) take about 4 hrs.

Tallinna Eesti Maja; LAUTERI 1; Traditional Estonian fare. Lunch buffet is 75 EEK. Good for a splurge.
Kloostri Alt; VENE 14; inexpensive – live music some evenings. Recommended.
A number of fast-food establishments are open 24 hrs. Try **Lemmik**; VIRU 18, or **Vöireoos;** KARLI 4. There are a number of branches of **Peetri Pizza**.

POLAND

(for Directory information, see p. 560).

With sandy beaches, ancient lakes, dense forests and alpine mountains, Poland is a surprisingly varied country. Don't miss the rich architecture and culture in the many historic towns, castles, shrines and palaces that have managed to survive centuries of strife, but also make time for its sober monuments to the devastation of the last war. There is much that is unique here: the Wieliczka salt cathedral, the Jaskinia Niedźwiedzia caves and Malbork's vast Teutonic fortress.

Although many older folk and 90% of station staff don't speak English, Poles are friendly, good-natured people who are only too happy to help travellers.

Youth Hostels
The hostelling organisation is **Polskie Towarzystwo Schronisk Mlodziezowych**, 00–791 WARSZAWA, UL. CHOIMSKA 28, POLAND, ☎(48) (22) 498128, fax: (48) (22) 498354.

ACCOMMODATION

Orbis runs a chain of international and tourist standard **hotels** across the country, and some less expensive motels. Otherwise, your best bet will probably be a **pension** or **private room**. In popular holiday areas, you may be able to hire a **holiday cottage** for a longer stay. In the summer season, **youth hostels** (priority to children and students under 26; book in by 2100) and **university rooms** are also available.

FOOD AND DRINK

Simple meals and snacks can easily be obtained at cafés and fast-food outlets, while *zajazdy*, reasonably priced roadside inns and cafés, serve typical Polish food and pastries. Restaurants in major cities are usually open between 1200 and 2400. Classic national dishes include beetroot soup, herrings in soured cream, potato pancakes, stuffed cabbage leaves, cabbage and sausage stew, *pierogi* (a large-scale ravioli), baked cheesecake and doughnuts.

A wide variety of Polish mineral waters are drunk in preference to tap water, which is best avoided. The vast range of clear and flavoured vodka is excellent and inexpensive.

EDITOR'S CHOICE
Auschwitz–Birkenau; Kraków; Poznań; Toruń; Wieiliczka Salt Mines; Zakopane (for Tatra Mountains).

BEYOND THE BORDERS
Warsaw–Vilnius (ETT table 93); Poznan–Berlin (table 56); Warsaw–Prague (table 95a); Warsaw–Vienna (table 95a); Kraków–Budapest via Slovakia (table 95b).

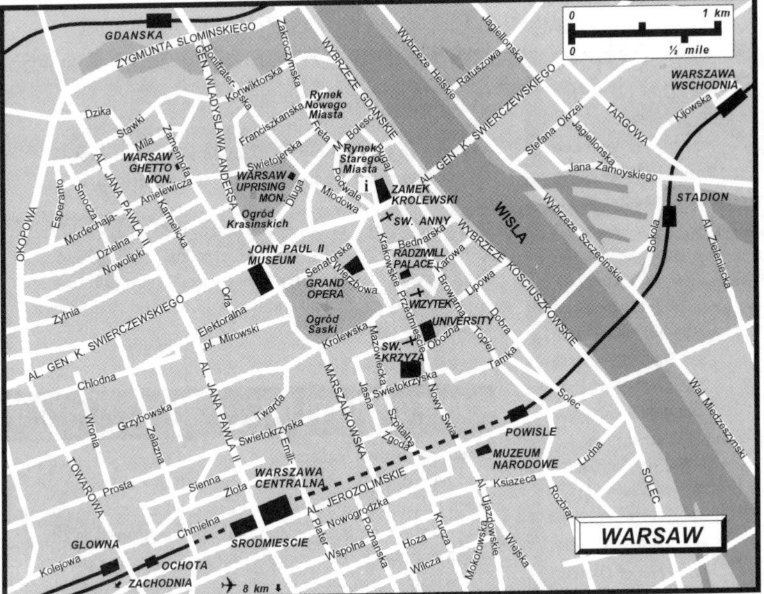

While **Warsaw** has its fair share of post-war concrete blocks, there are also areas of beauty and historic significance, including its parks, palaces and old town that were meticulously rebuilt after complete devastation in the Second World War. Having suffered under communism, Warsaw is now thriving under democracy: entertainment, restaurants and shopping are coming into their own, and fast approaching the standards of major Western cities.

If you're in a hurry, the places to head for are the **Royal Castle, Lazienki Palace and Park,** the **Old Town Square** and **Warsaw Historical Museum**. The **River Vistula** divides Warsaw, with most sights on the west bank. Most attractions are walkable.

ARRIVAL AND DEPARTURE

RAIL **Warszawa Centralna** is the central rail station at AL. JEROZOLIMSKIE 54, ☎(022) 620 5010 (international information), ☎(022) 620 4512 (national), ☎(022) 620 0361–9 (local); a crime hotspot, so avoid at night. Some 30 mins' walk to the old town (with **Hotel Marriott** in front of you turn left along AL. JEROZOLIMSKIE, then the next main left onto UL. MARSZAŁKOWSKA for numerous buses to the old town). Left luggage (counter 0700–2100, lockers 24 hrs); showers

TOURIST OFFICES

Look out for the distinctive yellow and red 'it' logo of **Warsaw Tourist Office** at the following addresses: UL. POWATAŃCÓW, WARSZAWY 2 (summer, Mon–Fri 0800–2000, Sat 0900–1700, Sun 0900–1500; winter, Mon–Fri 0800–1900, Sat–Sun 0900–1500); 100–102 UL. MARSAŁKOWSKA, in the round PKO Bank (Mon–Fri 0800–1900, Sat 0900–1300); RYNEK STAREGO MIASTA 28–42 (daily 1000–2000); and at the arrival hall of **Okecie airport**, UL. ŻWIRKI I WIGURY 1 (daily 0800–2000). **Central number for all offices**: ☎9431 or (022) 827 3864. Central rail station (summer, daily 0800–2000; winter, daily 0900–1900). Private tourist information office: PL. ZAMKOWY 1/13, (022) 635 1881 (summer, Mon–Fri 0900–2000, Sat 1000–2000, Sun 1100–2000; closes 1800 in winter).

(24 hrs; 4zl), rail information (24 hrs), post office, bus information, currency exchange (0800–2200) and ticket office (0600–2000). Other large stations in the city are: **Warszawa Wschodnia**, ☎(022) 618 3497, on the east bank of the **Wisla** (Vistula River), and the western suburban station, **Warszawa Zachodnia**, ☎(022) 36 5742, 3 km west of **Centralna**, opposite the PKS bus station, ☎(022) 36 5500.

✈ **Okecie Airport**, UL. ŻWIRKI I WIGURY 1, ☎(022) 46 1731, lies 10 km south of the city, with two terminals (arrivals and departures). **Airport City Bus** every 20 mins (30 mins on Sat and holidays), stopping at major hotels and **Warszawa Centralna** rail station.

INFORMATION

Good free brown leaflets/maps from the tourist offices, plus monthly magazines *Welcome to Warsaw* (free) and *What, Where, When* (often free), both with maps and information in English. The *Warsaw Voice* is an English language newspaper) is also worth consulting. The pocket-size *Polish Pages For Visitors* is free and available from the information point on the ground floor of the **Marriott Hotel** complex, AL. JEROZOLIMSKIE 65/79. **Thomas Cook licensee: Pegrotours**, EMILI PLATER STR. 47, ☎(022) 624 3676.

MONEY

Cashpoint machines and credit-card facilities are fairly common in most tourist areas. Some **bureaux de change** *(kantor)* will not cash traveller's cheques (try **Orbis Travel**, large hotels or the larger banks instead).

POST AND PHONES

The **Main Post Office**, UL. SWIECTOKRZYSKA, 31/33, is open 24 hrs; counter facilities, poste restante, luggage lockers. **Phone cards** are needed to operate most public telephones – the cards are available from kiosks and other outlets. **To phone Warsaw:** ☎48 (Poland) + 22; **to phone Warsaw from elsewhere in Poland**: ☎022.

PUBLIC TRANSPORT

Trams and buses operate on a grid system. Buses, which are generally crowded, run from 0430–2300 on weekdays. Night buses run every 30 mins and cost three times the normal fare. The useful PPWK-published Warsaw map (about 5zl) shows bus routes. The limited underground service (Metro) runs from the south to the centre of the city (red 'M' on yellow background denotes a Metro station); trains every six minutes, 0430–2330. You can pick up taxis at ranks, outside larger hotels, or ☎919.

TICKETS

Bus and tram tickets (daily, weekly or monthly) are sold at kiosks marked **Bilety MZK**, and at Ruch kiosks. Punch the end that doesn't have a metal strip in a small machine to validate it. Spot checks are frequent.

ACCOMMODATION

Book through the tourist office (or use its leaflet *Hotels, Warsaw and the Environs*). Business hotels often charge in US dollars or German marks. Even if you can't aspire to staying there, take a peek into the **Hotel Bristol**, a beautifully restored art nouveau building that is one of Poland's grandest hotels (very expensive). A good choice in the centre is the **Hotel Forum**. Mid-range choices (both with doubles from 120zl) include **Harctur Hotel** and **Tina Hotel**. Cheaper accommodation can be found at **Annopol Hotel**, (doubles from 42zl) and **Wilenski Hotel**. There are also some **pensions and budget hotels** on KRAKOWSKIE PRZEDMIEŚCIE and UL. NOWY ŚWIAT. For **private rooms** try the accommodation bureaux near the station.

There are five **hostels**, two belonging to **Hostelling International** (prices start from around 7zl for students with PTSM or IYH membership cards). The most central campsite is **Camping Astur Camping;** it is within the city boundary (well sign-posted) and has good facilities.

HOTELS

Hotel Bristol, KRAKOWSKIE PRZEDMIEŚCIE 42/44, ☎(022) 625 2525.
Hotel Forum, UL. NOWOGRODZKA 24/26, ☎(022) 823 0364.

Moderate choices: **Harctur Hotel**, UL. NIEMCEWICZA 17, ☎(022) 822 1913.
Tina Hotel, UL. GORASZEWSKA 212, ☎(022) 664 9720.

Annopol Hotel, UL. ANNOPOL 4, ☎(022) 811 4185.
Wilenski Hotel, UL. KLOPOTOWSKIEGO, ☎(022) 818 5780; both cheaper.

HOSTELS

HI: UL. SMOLNA 30, in the centre; ☎(022) 827 8952.

HI: UL. KAROLKOWA 53A, ☎(022) 632 8829 (tram nos.1/13/20/24 to AL. SOLIDARNOSCI).

CAMPSITES

Camping, NR 34 UL. ZWIRKI I WIGURY 32, ☎(022) 825 4391.
Astur Camping NR 123, UL. BITWY WARSAWSKIEJ, ☎(022) 276 778.

FOOD AND DRINK

Privatisation has revolutionised eating out, with **restaurants** spanning Asian, European and South American food. Traditional Polish food has been joined by 'new wave' Polish, featuring lighter versions of classic dishes. 'New wave' pioneers include the **Malinowa** and **Restauracja Polska**. For traditional Polish food in an Old Town burgher's house, try **Bazyliszek** and **Swiectoszek**. Snacks and fast food can easily be found, with plenty of alfresco cafés, particularly in the Old Town. **Pijalnia Czekolady** (a hot-chocolate café) is an antique paradise. **Karczma Wojtkowice Stara** is a recreation of an 18th-century country inn. Delicatessens are abundant, particularly in NOWY ŚWIAT, KRAKOWSKIE PRZEDMIEŚCIE and the Old Town. Expect to pay around 20zl for a moderately priced two-course meal. For a splurge try **Flik**, **Fukter** or **La Boheme**. For cheaper eats: **Lotos**, **Opus One** or **Emocja**.

RESTAURANTS	**Malinowa** (within the **Hotel Bristol**), FUKIER, RYNEK STAREGO MIASTA 27, ☎(022) 831 1013. **Restauracja Polska**, UL. NOWY ŚWIAT 21, ☎(022) 826 3877. **Bazyliszek**, RYNEK STAREGO MIASTA 3/7, ☎(022) 831 1841. **Swiectoszek**, UL. JEZUICKA 6/8, ☎(022) 631 5634.
CAFÉ	**Pijalnia Czekolady**, UL. SZPITALNA 8.
COUNTRY INN	**Karczma Wojtkowice Stara**, RYNEK STAREGO MIASTA 21, ☎(022) 831 1661.
DELICATESSENS	**Flik**, UL. PULAWSKA 43, ☎(022) 494 434. **Fukter**, RYNEK STAREGO MIASTA 27. **La Boheme**, PL. TEATRALNY 1, ☎(022) 831 1013.
BUDGET EATING	**Lotos**, UL. BELWEDERSKA 2, ☎(022) 841 1301. **Opus One**, UL. E. MLYNARSKIEGO, ☎(022) 827 5100. **Emocja**, UL. MOKOTOWSKA 57, ☎(022) 621 6674.

HIGHLIGHTS

RYNEK STAREGO MIASTA (OLD TOWN MARKET SQUARE) AND AREA Very much a focal point, this square is lined with painstaking reconstructions of the original burghers' houses. At no. 28 is the **Muzeum Historyczne Warszawy** (Warsaw Historical Museum, Tues, Thur 1200–1900, Wed, Fri 1000–1530, Sat–Sun 1130–1630), ☎(022) 635 1625, which chronicles the city's turbulent history. A short film, *Warsaw After All*, includes footage shot by the Nazis, documenting their systematic destruction of the city.

Continue along SWIĘCTOJANSKA to PL. ZAMKOWY, dominated by **Zamek Krolewski** (Royal Castle; Tues–Sat 1000–1800, Sun–Mon 1100–1800, last entry 1700). Restored after the war, the castle's mixed architecture and stylised interiors are a showcase for furniture, tapestries, paintings and more. Tickets (11zl) are sold from the souvenir shop opposite the castle on the corner of SWIĘTOJANSKA.

NORTHWARDS AROUND THE BARBAKAN AND KRASINSKI PARK The 16th-century **Barbakan** (Barbican) was once part of the city walls, but is now a haunt of artists out to make a quick zloty or two. Here you may or may not see the 1855 statue of the **Warsaw Mermaid**, which has become the symbol of the city (under repair at the time of writing; future location uncertain).

From here UL. FRETA leads to 18th-century RYNEK NOWEGO MIASTA (New Market Square), less flamboyant than its Old Town counterpart, with the **Church of the Blessed Sacrament**, founded in 1688 by Queen Maria in memory of her husband (King Jan III Sobieski), who defeated the Turks at Vienna. From RYNEK NOWEGO MIASTA, UL. DLUGA leads to PL. KRASISINSKICH, site of a monument and museum to the 63-day-long Warsaw Uprising, and **Kraśinski Palace** (now a library), fronting the **Kraśinski Park**.

THE ROYAL ROUTE

The city's main thoroughfare is the **Royal Route**, which starts at KRAKOWSKIE PRZEDMIEŚCIE by the **Stare Miasto** (Old Town) and heads south, along NOWY ŚWIAT and UL. UJAZDOWSKIE, 10 km to Wilmanów, the royal summer palace, taking in 15th-century **Kósciól Sw. Anny** (St Anne's Church), the **Adam Mickiewicz Monument** and finally Radzwill Palace, where the Warsaw Pact was signed in May 1955. Just off KRAKOWSKIE PRZEDMIESCIE, in the **Ogrod Saski** (Saxon Gardens), the Tomb of the Unknown Soldier is guarded around the clock. Dominating PL. PITSUDSKIEGO is the neoclassical **National Theatre** (1825–33). Returning to KRAKOWSKIE PRZEDMIEŚCIE, Chopin played the organ in the **Kościól Wizytek** (Church of the Visitation), while **Koscio Sw. Krzyza**, is a masterpiece of baroque, and also the resting place of Chopin's heart (in an urn on the left column by the nave).

MUSEUMS Pride of place amongst the many museums goes to **Muzeum Narodowe** (National Museum; Tues, Wed, Fri, Sat, Sun 1000–1600, Thur 1000–1800, 5zl, students 2.5zl, AL. JEROZOLIMSKIE 3, which has an impressive collection of paintings.

PALACES Surrounded by water, the late-18th-century **Łazienki Palace** (Palace-on-the-Isle, Tues–Sun 0930–1600, 3.5zl, students 2zl); UL. AGRYKULA 1, ☎(022) 625 7944, was the classical summer residence of Stanislaus Augustus Poniatowski, Poland's last king. Its park contains the **Chopin monument**, plus smaller palaces, pavilions, and other unusual buildings.

Some 10 km from the centre of town stands the extravagantly baroque **Wilanów Palace**, UL. WIERTRICZA 1 (Mon, Wed–Sat 0930–1430, Sun 0930–1530 3zl, students 1zl); park open daily until dusk; 🚌no.130.

JEWISH WARSAW Before World War II, Warsaw had one of Europe's largest Jewish communities. During the Nazi occupation, the population fell from 380,000 to just 300. There are two great monuments: to the **Heroes of the Warsaw Ghetto**, UL. ZAMENHOFA, and the white marble monument to Concentration Camp Victims.

Boat trips leave from **Poniatowski Bridge** for a leisurely view of Warsaw.

TOURS

For a more leisurely view of Warsaw, tour the city by boat on the River Vistula: the **WARS** ship sails daily from the passenger marina near **Poniatowksi Bridge** on WYBRZEZE KOSCIUSZKOWSKIE, ☎(022) 628 5883.

SHOPPING

Local specialities include silver, leather, crystal and amber, with **Cepelia** stores having the best selection of folk art. **Desa** is a chain of antique shops (there are restrictions on what can be exported). Some of the best shopping is in the Old Town, KRAKOWSKIE PRZEDMIESCIE, UL. NOWY ŚWIAT and UL. CHMIELNA. Try **Wola antique market**, KOLO BAZAAR, UL. OBOZOWA, for clothes, furniture and books (Sat–Sun 0800–1300; 🚌no.159 or tram nos.13, 20 and 24); it gets crowded by 1000.

NIGHT-TIME AND EVENTS

There is a good range of entertainment, with pubs and discos, and live music, including rock, jazz, and classical music. Chopin concerts are held every Sun at 1200 and 1600 in Jul–Aug by Chopin's monument in **Lazienki Park**. Cinemas often show American films, usually subtitled. The imposing **Palac Kultury i Nauki** (Palace of Culture and Science) houses a **casino, theatres, cinemas, nightclub** and one of the city's best **bookshops**.

There are opera and ballet at the **National Theatre** *(Teatr Narodowy)*, PL. TEATRALNY 1, while the **National Philharmonic** (*Filharmonia Narodowa*) is at UL. JASNA 5. Many of the performances at **Buffo Theatre**, UL. KONOPNICKIEJ 6, ☎(022) 622 9293, have gained cult status with young Poles. **Nightclubs** worth a visit include: **Grand Zero**, UL. WSPLONA 62, ☎(022) 625 4380; **Planeta**, UL. FORT WOLA 22, ☎(022) 634 4891, or **Stereo**, NOWY ŚWIAT 23–5, ☎(022) 826 3575.

WHERE NEXT FROM WARSAW?

Warsaw is on the ***Poznan–Zakopane*** *route (p.483); if you just want to see one Polish city take this to* ***Kraków****. Alternatively head north-east to* ***Vilnius*** *to join the* ***Vilnius–St Petersburg*** *route (p.465).*

ROUTE DETAIL

Poznań–Zakopane ETT tables 1080, 1066

Type	Frequency	Journey Time
Train	3 daily	9 hrs 45 mins

Poznań–Toruń ETT table 1020

Type	Frequency	Journey Time
Train	3 daily	2 hrs

Toruń–Warsaw ETT table 1035

Type	Frequency	Journey Time
Train	3 daily	3 hrs

Warsaw–Kraków ETT table 1065

Type	Frequency	Journey Time
Train	Every 1-2 hrs	2 hrs 35 mins

Kraków–Zakopane ETT table 1066

Type	Frequency	Journey Time
Train	10 daily	2 hrs 45 mins

Fastest Journey:
9 hrs 36 mins

Poznań – Kraków – Zakopane

This succinct exploration of the best of Poland encounters its two finest cities – **Kraków** and **Toruń** – as well as the Polish capital, and ends up at the foot of the majestic **Tatra** mountains. The earlier parts of the journey are low-lying and unspectacular, but the cultural highlights more than compensate. **Poznań** can easily be reached by train from **Berlin**, and from **Kraków** you can venture out to **Auschwitz** – a grim reminder of the atrocities of the Third Reich – or see the extraordinary **Royal Wieliczka Salt Mine**; it's also feasible to extend the journey into **Slovakia**.

Poznań

The provincial capital of **Wielkopolska** became one of the two main centres of Poland as well as the seat of its first bishop in the 10th century. A long-held status as a great trade centre (it's still an important place for trade fairs) has contributed to the architectural heritage of its old town.

All the museums are closed Mon and most are free on Fri.

The city's focal point is STARY RYNEK, a spacious square with gabled burghers' houses and a grand 16th-century Renaissance **Town Hall**, where at midday two mechanical goats emerge from above the clock to lock horns. Inside lie the **Chamber of the Renaissance** with its beautifully painted, coffered ceiling (1555) and the **Historical Museum of the City of Poznań**. Also on STARY RYNEK, at no. 45 is the **Muzeum Instrumentow Muziczrych** (Museum of Musical Instruments), housing some 2,000 instruments, and with a room dedicated to Chopin. In the partly reconstructed **Royal Castle** on Przemyslaw Hill is the **Museum of Applied Arts**, with a wide-ranging collection through the ages, and a cellar full of poster art.

Several churches form an outer ring around the market square. One of the finest can be found on GOLEBIA, south of the square, the baroque **Poznań Parish Church** (Kósciól Frany) dedicated to St Mary Magdalene. The **Jesuit College**, next door, once Napoleon's residence, now hosts Chopin concerts. A short walk to the east is **Ostrów Tumski**, the original part of the city, an island in the middle of the River **Warta**; here stands the **cathedral,** heavily restored after World War II.

Poznań has two zoos and a vast palm house (part of Poland's largest botanical garden). On the edge of the city is the 100 square km **Wielkopolski Park Narodowy** (Great Poland National Park), easily accessible by train.

RAIL The main station, **Poznań Główny**, ☎(061) 852 7221, has a 24-hr rail information office, ☎(061) 866 1212, tourist information, cash machines, currency exchange, left luggage and shops; 10 min walk to centre. Most international trains stop here, although some use **Staroleka Station**, 5 km south-east.

Tourist Offices: The most central is at STARY RYNEK 59, (061) 852 6156 (Mon–Fri 0900–1700, Sat 1000–1400). **National Tourism Promotion Agency**, UL. KRAMARSKA 32E, (061) 852 9805 (Mon–Fri 0800–1600). **Glob-Tour** office at the station, (061) 866 0667 (24 hrs). **City information centre**, ARKADIA SHOPPING CENTRE, UL. RATAJCZAKA 44, (061) 851 9645. Get the blue map of Poznań, plus *Welcome to Poznań* and the bi-monthly *Wielkopolska* magazine (information in English). The PPWK-published map of Poznań is useful for travel outside the centre (shows bus routes).

The central **Tourist Guest House**, STARY RYNEK 91, (061) 852 8893, has rooms and dormitories. Try also the **Lech Hotel**, UL. SW. MARCIN 74, (061) 853 0151; **Rzymski Hotel**, AL. MARCINKOWSKIEGO 22, (061) 852 8121 or **Wielkopolska Hotel**, UL. SW. MARCIN 67, (061) 852 7631. A typical price for a double room in these hotels is about 170zl. There are a number of **motels** on the edge of the city which also offer cheap accommodation, such as **Streszynek**, at UL. KOSZALINSKA 15, (061) 848 3129 (also runs a nearby campsite next to a lakeside recreation centre; buses). The most central **campsite** is **Lake Malta**, KRANKOWA 98, (061) 876 6155. **Youth hostels** at BERWINISKIEGO 2/3, (061) 866 3680; GLUSZYNA 127, (061) 878 8461, and BISKUPINSKA 27, (061) 822 1063.

There are plenty of eateries on STARY RYNEK, many with menus in English. For traditional Polish food in a classic market square setting, try the charming but expensive, antique-style **Stara Ratuszowa**, STARY RYNEK 55, (061) 851 5318. Cheaper places include the **Elite Bistro Café**, UL. STRZELECKA 2/6, (061) 852 4687, and **Casa-Mia Pizzeria Restaurant**, UL. SZPITALNA 27, (061) 847 7194.

TORUŃ

Pomerania's capital is an almost perfectly intact medieval city on the river **Wisla** (Vistula), second only to Kraków in terms of Polish architectural heritage. **Toruń** has two diverse claims to fame: one is its elaborately iced gingerbread, the other the great astronomer Nicolaus Copernicus (1473–1543), who broke new ground in arguing that the Sun, and not the Earth, is the centre of the solar system.

The obvious starting point is the RYNEK STAROMIEJSKI (Market Square). Its main building, the 14th century **Ratusz** (Town Hall) – with 12 halls, 52 small rooms and 365 windows – houses the **Muzeum Okregowe** (Regional Museum; Tues–Sun 1000–1600) and has panoramic views from the tower. Copernicus's house at UL. KOPERNIKA 17 is now the **Nicolaus Copernicus Museum** (Tues–Sun 1000–1600), its interior recreated as it was in his day.

Don't miss the **Leaning Tower of Toruń** on KRZYWA WIEZA.

Toruń hosts many annual international festivals, including **Probaltica** (music festival) early May; **Kontakt** (theatre festival) last week in May; a **June folk festival** and a **street theatre festival** (July–Aug).

BOAT TRIPS

These go along the **Wisla** from the landing stage in BULWARD FILADEFIJSKI.

Main station: **Toruń Główny**, (056) 654 7222; left luggage (main hall, window 10), restaurant; nos. 22 or 27 to old town – get off at 2nd stop; buy tickets at kiosks/on bus. There are two other stations: **Toruń Miasto** is nearest the old town. It is easiest to book train tickets at **Kompas**, KOPERNIKA 5, (056) 621 0016.

Tourist Office: UL. PIEKARY 37/39, 87–100 TORUŃ, (056) 621 0931. Tues–Fri 0900–1800, Mon, Sat 0900–1600 (Sun 0900–1300 May–Aug).

Hotel Polonia, PL. TEATRALNY 5, (056) 622 3028 (moderate, central). **Youth hostels**: **Schronisko Mlodziezowe**, UL. SW. JOZEFA 22/24, (056) 654 4107 (cheap, bring bedding; nos.11 and 6 from main station); **Fort IV**, SCHRONISKO TURYSTYCZNE, UL. CHROBREGO/ROG MLECZNEJ, (056) 623 4562 (18-bed rooms in old fort). **Campsite**: UL. KUJAWSKA 14, (056) 654 7187 (huts available).

Try **Zajazd Staropolski** restaurant for typical Polish food (moderate), ZEGLARSKA 10/14, (056) 6226 061; old-fashioned **Cafe Pod Atlantem** (cheap), UL. DUCHA SW. 3, (056) 622 6739; and **Czarna Oberza students' pub** (cheap), RABIANSKA 9, (056) 621 0963.

WARSAW (WARSZAWA)

See p. 477.

KRAKÓW

Kraków is Poland's cultural and spiritual centre and the most beautiful city in the country. The city entered a golden age in the 14th century but lost its capital status to **Warsaw** in 1596. When Poland was partitioned at the end of the 18th century, Kraków was part of the Austro-Hungarian Empire. During the Nazi occupation, it served as headquarters for the General Government, then was liberated by Soviet forces in 1945.

It's a great place for strolling the old town, looking in designer boutiques, antique shops and old pharmacies that boast original fittings.

The notorious Auschwitz–Birkenham concentration camps are 1 hr 45 mins away by train. Guided tours are available – see panel, p. 487.

RYNEK GŁÓWNY Lively with flower stalls and alfresco cafés, this is one of the largest and most beautiful medieval market places in Europe. While the originally 13th-century RYNEK GŁÓWNY is never entirely swamped by the crowds, try visiting late at night or early in the morning for the full impact. The size of the **Sukiennice** (Cloth Hall), which stands centre-stage, and the surrounding burghers' houses create a unique setting. The Cloth Hall started as a Gothic roof over trading stalls, enlarged during the reign of Casimir the Great. Following a 1555 fire, it was reconstructed in the Renaissance style, and remains a thriving commercial concern, packed with stalls selling amber, silver and upmarket souvenirs. With almost 30 museums, it's worth getting a detailed guidebook from the Tourist Office, as opening times can change. Many are free certain days of the week. A branch of the

SIGHTSEEING TOURS can be arranged through **InterCrac**, RYNEK GŁÓWNY 14, (012) 422 58 40.

National Museum, (1st floor) houses 18th- and 19th-century historical Polish paintings and sculptures (closed Mon).

All that remains of the Gothic town hall is the **Ratusz** (City Hall Tower), RYNEK GŁÓWNY 1 (closed Mon and Tue), which has a fine view from the top and contains a basement café. In the opposite corner of the square, **St Adalbert's**, in Romanesque style, is the oldest and smallest church in Kraków. Within the vaults is the **Historical Museum of the Rynek** (Tue–Sat, 1000–1500).

Further north, **Mariacki** (St Mary's Church) has a wooden Gothic altar, 13 m high and adorned by 200 figures, created by Wit Stwosz, the 15th-century master carver of Nuremberg. Legend has it that a watchman was shot down from the church tower by Tartar invaders. The *hejna*, the melody he trumpeted to sound the alarm, is repeated hourly.

For military architecture explore the **Florianska Gate,** three towers and barbican**.**

THE UNIVERSITY DISTRICT Central Europe's second oldest university was founded in 1364. Distinguished students include the Polish astronomer Nicolaus Copernicus and Pope John Paul II. **Collegium Maius**, UL. JAGIELLONSKA 15, (012) 422 0549 (open Mon–Fri 1100–1430, Sat 1100–1330), is the oldest college, a magnificent example of Gothic architecture in which 35 globes are on display, one dating from 1510 and featuring the earliest illustration of America, marked 'a newly discovered land'. Tours take in the alchemy rooms (supposedly Dr Faustus's laboratory), lecture rooms, the assembly hall and professors' apartments.

WAWEL Kraków's most important sites are the dramatic **cathedral** and fortified **Royal Castle** (both built by King Casimir the Great), high on **Wawel Hill** and bordered by the **Wisła** (*Vistula*) river. The Gothic cathedral of 1320–64 replaced an 11th-century church, whose relics are displayed in the castle's west wing.

DAY TRIPS FROM KRAKÓW

Auschwitz, synonymous with the atrocities of the Holocaust, was the largest Nazi concentration camp. Between 1.5 and 2 million mainly Jewish men, women and children were transported here in cattle trucks from across Europe to meet brutality and death. Piles of spectacle frames, shoe-polish tins, baby clothes and monogrammed suitcases are displayed. Screenings of liberators' films are regularly shown in several languages. Nearby **Birkenau** was an even more 'efficient' Nazi death factory.

National Museum of Auschwitz–Birkenau, UL. WIEZNIÓW OÚWIECCIMA 20, (033) 432 133 (daily, free). **Trains** (1hr 45 mins; ETT table 1099) leave from Kraków, mostly from **Główny station**; frequent buses from **PKS station** (11 daily, take 1hr 40 min). Alternatively, join one of the private guided tours – e.g. **Point Tours, Hotel Continental**, UL. ARMII KRAJOWEJ 11, KRAKÓW, (012) 423 7894, (60–75zl).

Accommodation: 5 hotels, including **International Youth Meeting House**, UL. LEGIONISTOW 11, (033) 432 107.

Day Trips from Kraków cont'd.

WIELICZKA (MAGNUM SAL)

The **Royal Wieiliczka Salt Mine**, PARK KINGI I. Mined for over 700 years, it has 350 miles of tunnelling. It's a dazzling spectacle, with 40 chapels carved entirely from salt, larger-than-life salt statues and an underground lake. Guided tours are offered in English.

Infrequent trains leave Kraków Główny – alternatively, hop on the LUX minibus just right of Główny, departs every 15 mins (very cheap, 30 mins), stops below the mine.

One-day ticket: 5zl; **single journey**: 1.50zl. **Taxis** are quite cheap; ☎(012) 919.

SIGHTSEEING TRIPS

Various agencies offer sightseeing trips to **Auschwitz** and 'Schindler's List' tours: try **Jewish Book Shop**, SZEROKA PL. 2, ☎(012) 421 7166.

The most striking of the 19 side chapels is the gold-tiled, domed Renaissance **Zygmuntowska** (Sigismund's Chapel), built 1519–31. Climb the tower for a great view plus the 2.5 m diameter **Zygmunt Bell**, rung on church or national holidays.

The Royal Castle, chiefly a Renaissance structure of 1502–36, has a superb courtyard with three-storey arcades. Displayed in the Royal Chambers you can see 142 exquisite **Arras tapestries**, commissioned in the mid-16th century. Both are open Tues and Fri 0930–1630, Wed–Thu 0930–1530, Sat 0930–1500 and Sun 1000–1500.

RAIL **Kraków Główny** (main station), ☎(012) 422 2248 or 933 for rail information, is a short walk from the centre. Currency exchange, accommodation information, left luggage (0500–2300), showers, restaurant. Head left from station, turn right down BASZTOWA STREET, enter the large underpass and head for *Planty/Basztowa* exit to right. **Główny** has a service to **Auschwitz**. **Plaszów Station** serves **Wieliczka**, has some night services and is about 30 mins from centre by tram no.13.

i **Tourist Office**: UL. PAWIA 8, ☎(012) 422 60 91, near **Główny** station (Mon–Fri 0800–1800, Sat 0900–1300).

Public transport: The **Stare Miasto** (Old Town), encircled by the **Planty**, is traffic-free. Beyond this lies a network of buses and trams; tickets sold at *Ruch* kiosks. Punch both ends of the ticket on board (once only for concessions). *Kraków Plan Miasta*, a city map with a distinctive red and yellow cover, shows bus and tram routes; on sale at news-stands and bookshops.

For those on a limited budget, finding a bed can be difficult, although private pensions are available in the Old Town. The **Tourist Office** makes reservations. It's common to be approached by individuals at the station – remember to check location and price first. **Hotel Ibis** is modern, two tram stops from **Główny**: PRZY RONDZIE 2, ☎(012) 421 8188 (moderate). **Youth hostels**: **Schronisko Mlodziezowe PTSM**, UL. OLEANDRY 4, ☎(012) 633 8822; six **students' hostels** (July–end Sept) – try: **Bydgoska**, UL. BYDGOSKA 11A-D, ☎636 8000; **Dom Turisty hostel**, WESTERPLATTE 15, ☎(012) 422 9500, on the edge of the old town (cheap). Three **campsites**, including **Krak**, UL. RADZIKOWSKIEGO 99, ☎(012) 637 2122 (summer), with inexpensive motel.

Rynek Główny and the surrounding streets are packed with inexpensive restaurants. For superb, traditional Polish food, try **Wierzynek**, RYNEK GŁÓWNY 15, ☎(012) 422 1035 (expensive). Traditional Jewish cuisine: **Ariel Gallery**, UL. SZEROKA 17, ☎(012) 421 3870 (moderate). One of the best courtyard garden restaurants is **Chimera**, UL. SW. ANNY 3, ☎(012) 423 2178, with live music (traditional, moderate). There are numerous **cafés** with alfresco tables: **Kawiarnia Noworolski**, RYNEK GŁÓWNY l (in the Sukennice), ☎(012) 422 4771, or the Art Nouveau **Jama Michalika**, UL. FLORIANSKA 45 (cakes and cabaret). There are many cellar bars in the Old Town, like **Piwnica pod Baranami**, RYNEK GŁÓWNY 26, ☎(012) 423 0732. **Bar Dworzanin**, UL. FLORIANSKA 43, serves drinks and vegetarian meals (really cheap). **Planty Park** is ideal for picnics (unsafe after dark).

NIGHT-TIME

Evening activities revolve around theatres, concerts, cabaret and nightclubs. Full information, tickets and a monthly listings magazine (English supplement) can be obtained from **Centrum Informacji Kulturalnej** (Cultural Information Centre), UL. ÁW JANA 2, ☎(012) 421 7787, Mon–Fri 1000–1900, Sat 1100–1900.

WHERE NEXT FROM KRAKÓW?

*Join the eastern end of the **Prague–Poprad Tatry** route by travelling to **Poprad Tatry** and changing at **Plaveč** (3 services daily taking 6 hrs; ETT tables 1078 annd 1188).*

ZAKOPANE

This winter sports centre (Dec–April) occupies a national park of rocky peaks rising to over 2,500 m, lakes, forests and 300 km of marked hiking trails in the heart of the **Tatra** mountains. The scenery is outstanding, but it gets crowded. Take the cable car up the mountains to **Kasprowy Wierch** for some great high-level walking near the Slovakian border. **Zakopane** is also a highland folk art centre – the annual **Tatran Autumn Festival** (end Aug-early Sept) includes the **International Highland Folk Festival**.

Muzeum Tatrzanskie (Tatra Museum), UL. KRUPÓWKI 10 (closed Mon), has folklore exhibits. The local architecture features ornate wooden houses and churches (see the 19th-century **Stary Kósciól Parafialny**, UL. KOSCIELISKA).

RAIL **Dworzec Główny**, ☎(0165) 14504. Left luggage (0645–1800, 1.25–1.60zl), currency exchange. Short walk to town centre.

i **Tourist Office**: UL. KOŠCIUSZKI 17, ☎ (0165) 12211, daily 0800–2000 (arranges accommodation).

Book ahead. **Dom Turisty PTTK**, UL. ZARUSKIEGO 5, ☎(0165) 63281. **Youth hostel**: **Szarotka Schronisko PTSM**, UL. NOWOTARSKA 45, ☎(0165) 2013618.

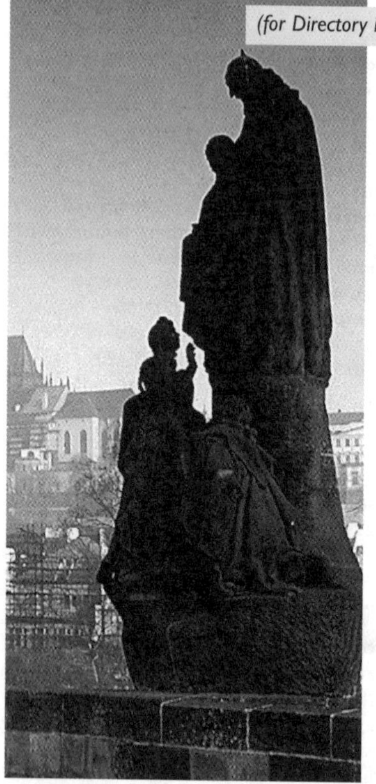

(for Directory information, see pp. 544 and 562).

In the bloodless Velvet Revolution of 1989, Czechoslovakia defiantly broke away from the Soviet bloc, and the **Czech Republic** and **Slovakia** soon went their separate ways. The Czechs fared better economically, and **Prague,** one of the most gracious of old European capitals, a city that survived the world wars virtually unscathed, has emerged as a major tourist destination.

Industrialisation has left its mark on much of the two countries, but there's plenty to enjoy. Acid rain has ravaged large tracts of forest, especially in northern Bohemia, and many towns are often surrounded by unsightly industrialisation and grim tower blocks. But persist and you'll find some extremely pretty hills (laced with trails; walking is very much a national pastime) and delightful old town squares and imposing castles. In the Czech Republic, **Bohemia** conjures up romantic visions but parts of northern Bohemia are heavily industrialised. However, the **Krkonose mountains** harbour some good hiking country and the lesser-known hills of **Beskydy** in **Moravia** have idyllic meadows and woodlands.

Western Bohemia, home to several big spas, is distinctly Germanic in feel. Slovakia (UK nationals should note the recently imposed visa requirements) has a deeply traditional rural hinterland and a characterful capital in **Bratislava**, and though it's not quite as well-endowed with historic buildings has the most dramatic scenery in the **High Tatra** mountains (shared with Poland), a compact range of Alpine-like peaks, the highest summits in the Carpathian Mountains. They get very busy in high season; the less spectacular but rewarding **Low Tatra** and **Fatra** mountains might be better if you want to escape the crowds.

ACCOMMODATION

There is a growing choice of one–five-star **hotels**, **private rooms** and **pensions**, and, at a much more basic level, old-style **tourist hotels**, **hostels** and **inns** with a few spartan rooms, plus *chaty* (cottages) in the mountains. However, quality (once outside the top range) can leave a lot to be desired. Although people are trying to upgrade as fast as possible, it can still make more sense to look at private rooms rather than cheap hotels. Credit cards are accepted in bigger hotels, though some places insist on payment in hard currency. The Czech Republic is the most popular of the former Eastern bloc countries and the deluge of tourists has resulted in a real shortage of beds, so always book ahead (directly or through Tourist Offices). There are plenty of **campsites** (usually May–Oct only), most of which cater for caravans as well. Rough camping is forbidden.

YOUTH HOSTELS

In the **Czech Republic**, the organisation to contact is the **KMC Club of Young Travellers**, KAROLÍNY SVETLÉ, 11000 PRAHA 1, CZECH REPUBLIC, ☎/fax: (420) (2) 24230633.

On arriving at a station, you're often greeted by locals offering rooms. This can be a good way to find somewhere to stay, but be sure to ask the price first.

Note that **youth hostels** are not very common in Slovakia, only in bigger towns.

FOOD AND DRINK

Drink mineral rather than tap water.

Lunch is around 1130–1400 and dinner 1700–2200. Czech cuisine is rich and meat-based, but vegetarian options include fried cheese *(smažený)*, risotto and salads. Pork with cabbage and dumplings *(vepřo)* is on virtually every menu, as is *guláš*, a spicy meat dish served with wine. Try goose *(husa)* and potato soup *(bramborová)*. Slovak food is very similar to Hungarian; pork and dumplings *(knedliky)* are popular; a typical dish is *Brynzové halušky*, gnocchi with grated cheese.

The cost of eating and drinking is reasonable, especially in a self-service *bufet* (where you stand while eating). *Kavárny* and *cukrány* serve coffee (often Turkish-style) and delightful pastries. Pubs *(pivnice)* and wine bars *(vinárny)* are good places to eat. Czech and Slovak beers are excellent, and Moravian wine and the sweet *Tokaj* from South Slovakia are worth a try. Beers include **Pilsner, Budvar** and black beer *(černé pivo)*, spirits include herb-based **Becherovka** or **Fernet**.

EDITOR'S CHOICE

Bratislava; High Tatra mountains near Poprad Tatry; Prague; Trnava.

BEYOND THE BORDERS

Poprad Tatry–Kraków (ETT tables 1188, 1078; Prague–Hamburg via Berlin and Dresden (table 60); Prague–Cologne via Würzburg and Frankfurt (table 57); Prague–Warsaw (table 959); Prague–Vienna (table 96).

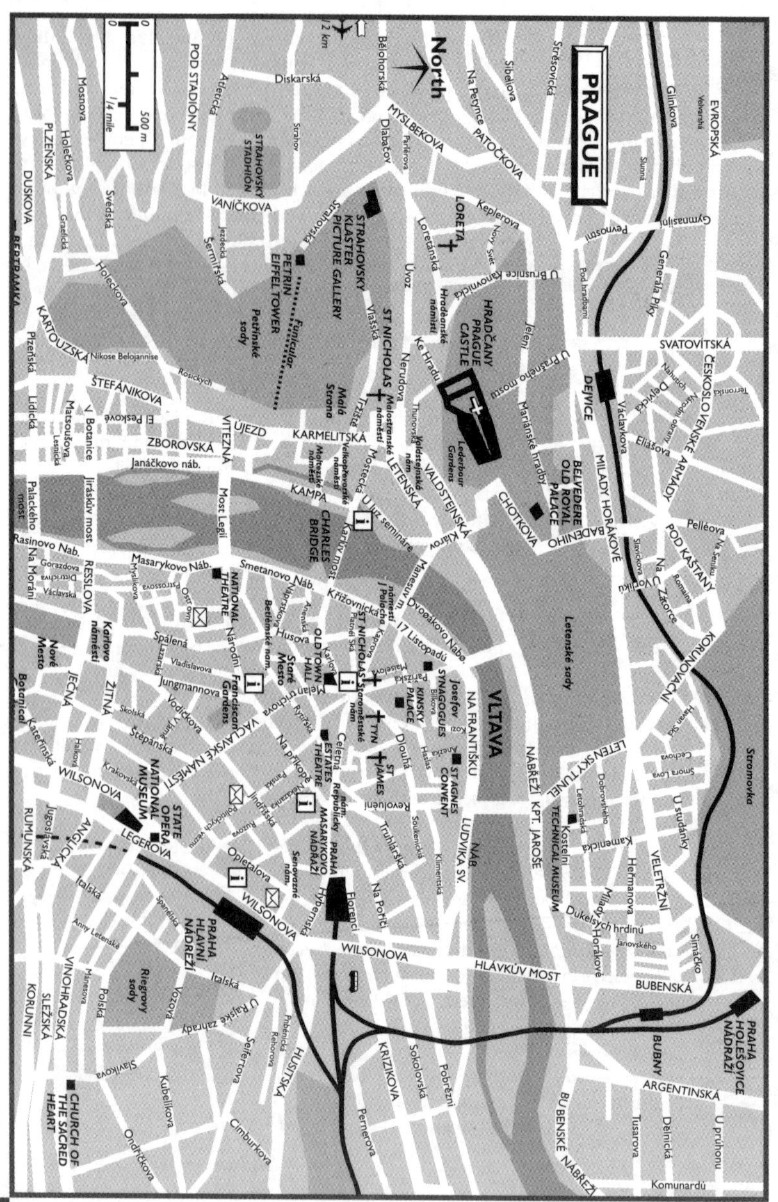
PRAGUE
North
500 m
1/4 mile
STRAHOVSKÝ STADIÓN
STRAHOVSKY KLASTER PICTURE GALLERY
PETRIN EIFFEL TOWER
Funicular
Petřínské sady
LORETA
HRADČANY PRAGUE CASTLE
Hradčanské náměstí
Lederbour Gardens
BELVEDERE OLD ROYAL PALACE
ST NICHOLAS
Malá Strana
Malostranské náměstí
Valdštejnské nám
CHARLES BRIDGE
KAMPA
NATIONAL THEATRE
OLD TOWN HALL
Staré Mesto
ST NICHOLAS
Staroměstské nám
TYN
ST JAMES
KINSKY PALACE
Josefov SYNAGOGUES
ST AGNES CONVENT
VLTAVA
Letenské sady
TECHNICAL MUSEUM
ESTATES THEATRE
Franciscan Gardens
Karlovo náměstí
Nové Mesto
NATIONAL MUSEUM
STATE OPERA
MASARYKOVO NÁDRAŽÍ
PRAHA HLAVNÍ NÁDRAŽÍ
Riegrovy sady
CHURCH OF THE SACRED HEART
PRAHA HOLEŠOVICE NÁDRAŽÍ
BUBNY
Stromovka
DEJVICE
MYSLBEKOVA
PATOČKOVA
VANÍČKOVA
KARTOUZSKÁ
ŠTEFÁNIKOVA
ZBOROVSKÁ
KARMELITSKÁ
ÚJEZD
VITEZNÁ
LETENSKÁ
VALDSTEJNSKÁ
CHOTKOVA
MILADY HORÁKOVÉ
ČESKOSLOVENSKÉ ARMÁDY
SVATOVÍTSKÁ
POD KAŠTANY
KORUNOVAČNÍ
LETENSKÝ TUNEL
NA FRANTIŠKU
NÁBŘEŽÍ KPT. JAROŠE
NÁB. LUDVIKA SV.
VELETRŽNÍ
HLÁVKŮV MOST
WILSONOVA
BUBENSKÁ
ARGENTINSKÁ
BUBENSKÉ NÁBŘEŽÍ
VÁCLAVSKÉ NÁMĚSTÍ
LEGEROVA
RESSLOVA
JEČNÁ
ŽITNÁ
VINOHRADSKÁ
KORUNNÍ
SLEZSKÁ
HUSITSKÁ
KRIZIKOVA
RUMUNSKÁ
ANGLICKÁ
DUSKOVA
PLZEŇSKÁ
POD STADIÓNY
EVROPSKÁ

A major tourist destination since the fall of the Iron Curtain, Prague is one of Europe's most beautiful capitals, with an exceptional and architecturally rich (mostly baroque) centre of cobbled streets, pastel buildings and fine squares, plus abundant green space. In turns, laid back, elegant and charged with creative energy, the city is full of buskers and artists, and notices everywhere advertising meetings and theatrical or musical events. May to August is very touristy; spring sees a wonderful array of cherry blossom.

ARRIVAL AND DEPARTURE

RAIL TICKETS

can only be purchased in Czech currency at the station. Credit card and cheque purchases can be made at **Czech Railways** travel agencies at the stations or at **Čedok**, NA PŘÍKOPĚ 18.

TOURIST OFFICES

Prague Information Service (PIS): in the **Old Town Hall** (STAROMĚSTSKÁ RADNICE), STAROMĚSTSKÉ NÁMĚSTÍ 1 (Mon–Fri 0900-1800, Sat–Sun 0900–1700), at the **Praha Hlavní Nádraží rail station** and, in the summer months, in the **Malá Strana Bridge Tower** (MALOSTRANSKÁ MOSTECKÁVĚZ). Free brochures, accommodation services. **For information:** ☎544 444 (Mon–Fri), reservation service, ☎231 1116.

RAIL **Praha Hlavní Nádraží** (Main Railway Station), WILSONOVA 2, ☎(02) 26 49 30, is the main station (rail reservations 0800–1800; often long queues; English spoken); some long-distance and international services also use **Nádraží Praha-Holešovice**, ☎(02) 80 75 05, in PRAGUE 7 (a little way out). Both stations on Metro Line C and have exchange bureaux, left luggage and accommodation services. **Rail information service**, ☎(02) 24 22 42 00 or ☎24 61 40 30. Avoid **taxis** (extortionate fares). At night, the main station park operates as a red light district and sleeping rough here is dangerous. **Masarykovo** (HYBERNSKÁ, PRAGUE 1) and **Smíchov** (NÁDRAŽNÍ, PRAGUE 5) stations cover many local trains.

Central Bus Station (long-distance services): KŘIŽÍKOVÁ 4, ☎(02) 24 21 10 60 (METRO: **Florenc**).

Ruzyní Airport, 20 km west of the city centre (flight enquiries, ☎(02) 2011 1111). Accommodation desks and 24-hr currency exchange. Bus no.119 (every 10 mins; 12Kč) from Dejvicka metro; **Czech Airlines (ČSA) bus service** every 30 mins 0530–2400 to Dejvická metro and to its terminal in the STARÉ MĚSTO (Hotel Renaissance, near Masarykovo rail station). **Cedaz's** excellent mini-bus service runs door-to-door (0600–2200) and to NÁMĚSTÍ REPUBLIKY, but costs more. Fixed price taxis should charge 450 Kč to the centre, but often demand far more. Alternatively, order a taxi from **Taxi AAA** (English spoken) ☎1080.

INFORMATION

METRO MAP – inside back cover

MONEY **Banks** open Mon–Fri 0900–1700. There are plenty of automatic cash dispensers. **Thomas Cook bureau de change**; KARLOVA ST. 3. Travellers cheques, Eurocheques and credit cards are widely accepted.

TICKETS

A **12Kč single ticket** *(jízdenka)* allows 1hr on all forms of public transport (Mon–Fri 0500–2200) (90 mins all weekend, plus Mon–Fri 2200–0500); a **8Kč single ticket** gives up to 15 mins, no transfers, (30 mins off peak). A better buy are **1, 3, 7 or 15-day** (70Kč, 180Kč, 250Kč or 280Kč) **tourist tickets** *(denní jízdenka)*, valid on all forms of public transport. Tickets from Tabák or Trafika tobacconists/ newsagents or from metro stations. Punch your ticket at the metro station entrances or inside trams and buses. Plain-clothes inspectors often flash their badge and ID – fines are 200Kč. Children aged up to 5 travel free; those aged 6–15 half price.

POST AND PHONES

The **Central Post Office** and Poste Restante are at JINDŘIŠSKÁ 14; nearby, at POLITICKYCH VEZNU 4, is a 24-hr fax, telegram and phone service. Stamps and phone-cards from post offices/ newsagents. The older, coin-operated telephones are unreliable (local calls 3Kč), but modern phone booths accept phone cards and have instructions in English. **English-speaking operator,** ☎(02) 0135. Collect calls, ☎(02) 0132. Prague area code: 02.

PUBLIC TRANSPORT

Metro, trams and buses: All public transport runs from about 0500 to 2400; there are also night services, at approximately 40-min intervals. Efficient metro (3 lines; red, yellow and green) plus good tram network (buses mostly serve suburbs and are little use for visitors); beware pickpockets on popular tourist routes (especially no. 22). Night trams all stop at LAZARSKÁ, just off VODIČKOVÁ. A funicular runs up Petřín hill between 0915 and 2045 daily (trams 9, 12, 22).

A **Prague Card**, from **Čedok travel agency** *(Na příkopě 18)*, or **Thomas Cook** combines a 3-day transport ticket with free entry to major sights.

Taxis: Avoid if possible – over-charging of foreigners is endemic. Always agree a fare before getting in. Reputable services include **AAA**, ☎1080 (English-speaking), PROFI, ☎1035. They should, theoretically, charge 17Kč per km.

ACCOMMODATION BUREAUX

AVE, *Hlavní nádraží*, ☎(02) 2422 33226 or ☎2422 3521 or **reservations**, ☎ 2461 7113; **Čedok**, NA PŘÍKOPĚ 18, ☎2419 7632; PAŘÍŽSKÁ 6, ☎(02) 2314 302; and RYTÍŘSKÁ 16, ☎(02) 26 27 14.

YOUTH-ORIENTED INFORMATION

CKM, JINDŘIŠSKÁ 28, ☎(02) 26 05 32/26 85 07, (daily 0900–1800), or the **Junior Hotel (Youth Hostel) reservation office**, ŽITNÁ 12, ☎(02) 29 29 84, (open 24 hrs).

ACCOMMODATION

Hotels are often pricey. In July, Aug and Sept, **CKM** also lets cheap rooms in student hostels. You can call the **Student Hostel Booking Office**. Accommodation hawkers offering private apartments/ rooms wait for visitors arriving by train – agree a price first. There are several **campsites** within the city boundary (camping rough is forbidden).

HOTELS

Dům" U Krále Jiřího", LILIOVÁ 10; ☎/fax: 242 219 83, in the old town.
U Zlatého Stromu, KARLOVA 6, PRAHA 1, ☎242 213 85, moderate and ideally located.
Hotel Alta, ORTENOVO NÁMĚSTÍ 22, PRAHA 7, ☎800 252-9, clean and friendly.
Hotel Libra Q, SENOVAZNĚ NÁM. 21, ☎2423 1754, central and cheap.

STUDENT HOSTEL BOOKING OFFICE

☎(02) 53 99 51/59.

CAMPSITES

UAMK, MÁNESOVA 20, ☎(02) 74 74 00 or ☎24 22 16 35 (closed weekends).

FOOD AND DRINK

There are three main categories of eating house: *restaurace* (restaurant), *vinárna* (wine-bar/restaurant) and *pivnice* (pub). Prices range from expensive in fashionable old town locations to great value pubs serving locally brewed beer off the beaten track.

PUBS	**U Flekú** beer garden and cellar, KŘVEMENCOVA 11.
BREWERY	**Pivovarský Dům**, LIPOVA 15, PRAGUE 2.
PUBS	**Molly Malones**, U OBECNÍ HO DVORA 4, ☎534 793. **Novomestsky pivovar**, VODIÉKOVA 20 (OFF WENCESLAS SQ.). **U Pinkasů**, JUNGMANNOVO NÁMĚSTÍ 15.
VEGETARIAN	**Radost**, BÉLEHRADSKÁ 120, ☎251 240. **Góvinda**, SOUKENICKÁ 27 (1000–1700).
PIZZERIA	**Pizzeria Felicita**, ŘÍČNÍ 5, ☎533 555.
KOSHER	**Massada**, MICHALSKÁ 16, ☎2421 3418.

HIGHLIGHTS

Old Prague is divided into **Staré Město** (Old Town), **Nové Město** (New Town) and **Josefov** (the Jewish Quarter) to the east, and **Malá Strana** (Lesser Quarter) and **Hradčany** (Castle District) to the west of the River **Vltava**.

STARÉ MESTO, NOVÉ MĚSTO AND JOSEFOV

At the heart of **Staré Město** is the picturesque **Staroměstské náměstí** (Old Town Square), (tram nos.17/18; metro: **Staroměstská**, line A). Here, visit the STAROMĚSTSKÁ RADNICE (Old Town Hall), with its astronomical clock and fabulous views over the Old Town, the baroque **Kostel Sv. Mikuláše** (St Nicholas Church), the baroque **Kinský Palace**, and the Romanesque **Dům U kamenné ho zvonu** (House of the Stone Bell), which hosts art exhibitions.

NATIONAL JEWISH MUSEUM
One timed ticket for all sights; 200 Kč; Sun–Fri 0900–1800 (Apr–Oct) 0900–1630 (Nov–Mar).

The old Jewish ghetto of **Josefov** (METRO: A/tram no.17: STAROMĚSTSKÁ) was cleared in 1893, leaving behind the only functioning medieval synagogue in Central Europe (the Old-New Synagogue) and a haunting **Old Jewish Cemetery**. The surrounding buildings (which include the **Pinkas Synagogue**, with a Holocaust memorial, among others) constitute a **National Jewish Museum**.

Nové Město is a sprawling area with fewer sights, but all visitors spend time in the lively **Václavské náměstí** (Wenceslas Square) (METRO: **MŮSTEK** OR **MUZEUM**), which witnessed the climax of the 'Velvet Revolution' in 1989. At the top end is a shrine to **Jan Palach**, who burned himself to death on 16 Jan 1969 in protest at the Warsaw Pact invasion.

MALÁ STRANA is a picturesque town of narrow cobbled streets of orange/yellow-rendered houses, with diminutive squares. Here, **Malostranské námestí** (Lesser Quarter Square) is particularly worth visiting (TRAM nos.12/22: MALOSTRANSKÉ NÁMESTÍ), dominated by the **Sv. Mikuláše** (Church of St Nicholas) – Prague's finest church – and ringed with baroque palaces. The **Waldštejn gardens** on LETENSKÁ, north-east of the square, contain exquisite gardens (open 1000–1800). Not far away are the even more delightful **Velkopřevorské náměstí** (Grand Prior's Square) and the adjoining **Maltézské náměstí** (Square of the Knights of Malta), which contain churches, embassies and palaces, together with the celebrated John Lennon Wall, a pop-art folly (tram nos. 12/22: HELLICHOVA). Visit the **Church of our Lady Victorious** (Panna Marie Vítězná) on KARMELITSKÁ 9, to see the wax effigy of Baby Jesus, still an object of pilgrimage.

HRADCANY the huge hilltop castle district, is the focal point of Prague (TRAM NO.22: **Malostranské náměstí/Pražský hrad**; METRO: **Hradčanská**, line A). Dominating the whole complex is the magnificent **Katedrála Svatého Víta** (St Vitus Cathedral), the core of which was commenced in 1344, but completed in 1929.

Nearby, much of the **Starý Královský Palác** (Old Royal Palace) was built for King Vladislav Jagello in the 15th century. Don't miss the **Bohemian Chancellery**, where the most famous of Prague's four defenestrations occurred, when Protestant nobles threw Frederick II's ambassadors from the window in 1618. The castle is now the seat of the President of the Republic.

The **Prague castle** area is open daily 0500–2400, castle gardens daily 1000–1800, Changing of the Guard at castle gates, on the hour.

For further information on the **castle district**, ☎2437 3368. You can buy a 100 Kč, **3-day ticket** covering the entire district.

Beyond the Castle area lies an imposing district, beginning with **Hradčanské náměstí** (Hradcany Square). If you walk up LORETÁNSKÁ, you come to **Černín Palace** (no. 5), from whose window Foreign Minister Jan Masaryk plunged to his death in 1948. The **Belvedere** (Summer Palace), Prague's finest Renaissance building (tram no. 22: BELVEDER), houses exhibitions – don't miss the 'singing fountain' in the gardens. South of the castle, wander through ***Petří n Hill*** (Petřínské sady), a traditional lovers' spot with its lush woods, orchards, 1891 model of the Eiffel Tower and funicular to Malá Strana.

The superb National Gallery collection is scattered round four main venues: **Šternberg Palace**, HRADČANSKÉ NÁMĚSTÍ 15, contains a collection of European art; **St George's Convent**, JIŘSKÉ NÁM. 33, houses old Bohemian art; **St Agnes' Convent**, U MILOSRDNÝCH 17 (tram nos. 5/14/26: **REVOLUČNÍ**) is devoted to 19th-century artists of the Czech national revival; and **Zámek Zbraslav** (Zbraslav Castle), ZBRASLAV NAD VLTAVOU (METRO: **SMÍCHOVSKÉ NÁDRAŽÍ**, then 129/241), has a remarkable display of 19th- and 20th-century Czech sculpture.

All museums are open Tues–Sun 1000–1800 unless stated

The beautiful sandstone **Charles Bridge**, commissioned by Charles VI in 1357, is now the standard image of Prague. At each end are high towers, and the parapet is lined by 31 statues (mainly 1683–1714, with a few copies and later works) – some cleaned up, others stained black with pollution.

The free, monthly *'Prague Cultural Events'*, available at all Tourist Offices, lists all museums and galleries.

NIGHT-TIME AND EVENTS

Consult the English-language newspaper *The Prague Post* for weekly listings. *Kultura v Praze* (monthly, also issued in English) details what's on. There's an excellent array of classical music, opera and theatre (in Czech), plus numerous puppet and mime shows.

ADVANCE TICKETS

Try **TicketPro**, SALVÁTORSKÁ 10, Mon–Fri 0800–1800, 2481 4020, or **Bohemia Ticket International**, MALÉ NÁM. 13, Mon–Fri 0900–1200, 1300–1600, Sat 0900–1400, 2422 7832; it's generally cheaper to buy directly from the venue.

SHOPPING

The Czech speciality is crystal glass. (Fiendishly expensive) **Moser**, NA PŘÍKOPĚ 12, (02) 24 21 12 93, and MALÉ NÁM 11, offers a mailing service. In the narrow streets and *pasáže* (passages) of MALÁ STRANA, NOVÉ MĚSTO and STARÉ MĚSTO are small souvenir shops, selling glass, ceramics, wooden toys and puppets; try **Česka lidová remesla** at MELANTRICHOVÁ, for local handicrafts, or the museum shops at Prague Castle, the Jewish Museum and the Decorative Arts Museum. The four main department stores are: **Kotva**, NÁMĚSTÍ REPUBLIKY 8; **Bílá labut'**, NA POŘÍČÍ 23; **Julius Meinl**, VÁCLAVSKÉ NÁMĚSTÍ 21; and **Tesco**, NÁRODNÍ 26.

ROCK AND DISCO
Rock Café, NÁRODNÍ 20, (02) 2491 4414.
Roxy, DLOUHÁ 33, (02) 2481 0951.

DANCE CLUB
Radost FX, BĚLEHRADSKÁ 120, 2425 4776.
Palac Acropolis, KUBELIKOVÁ 27, PRAGUE 3, 697 6411.

JAZZ
Agharta, KRAKOVSKÁ 5, (02) 2421 2914.
Reduta, NÁRODNÍ 20, (02) 2491 2246.
Malostranská Beseda, MALOSTRANSKÉ NÁMESTÍ 21, 539 024.

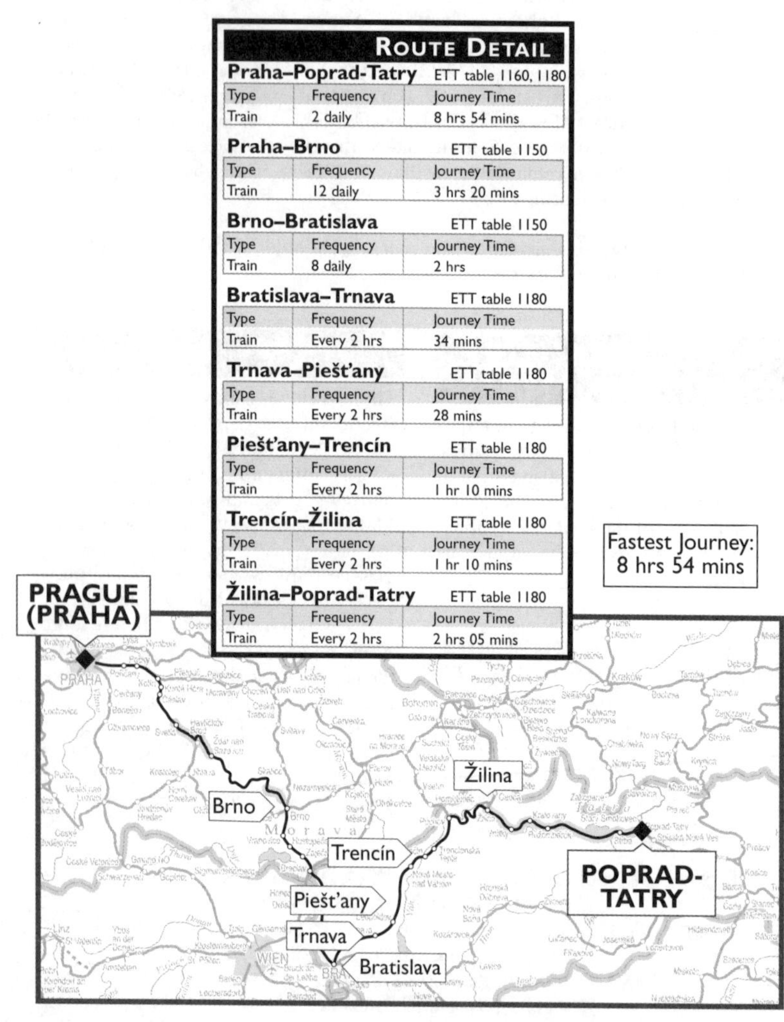

ROUTE DETAIL

Praha–Poprad-Tatry ETT table 1160, 1180

Type	Frequency	Journey Time
Train	2 daily	8 hrs 54 mins

Praha–Brno ETT table 1150

Type	Frequency	Journey Time
Train	12 daily	3 hrs 20 mins

Brno–Bratislava ETT table 1150

Type	Frequency	Journey Time
Train	8 daily	2 hrs

Bratislava–Trnava ETT table 1180

Type	Frequency	Journey Time
Train	Every 2 hrs	34 mins

Trnava–Piešt'any ETT table 1180

Type	Frequency	Journey Time
Train	Every 2 hrs	28 mins

Piešt'any–Trencín ETT table 1180

Type	Frequency	Journey Time
Train	Every 2 hrs	1 hr 10 mins

Trencín–Žilina ETT table 1180

Type	Frequency	Journey Time
Train	Every 2 hrs	1 hr 10 mins

Žilina–Poprad-Tatry ETT table 1180

Type	Frequency	Journey Time
Train	Every 2 hrs	2 hrs 05 mins

Prague – Bratislava – Poprad Tatry

From the Czech capital, the train heads past Kolín, with its old medieval town huddled round a superb Gothic church, through the Bohemian–Moravian uplands to **Brno**, in the centre of South Moravia, a land of rolling forests and karst limestone scenery (notable for its caves).

Bratislava, served by trains to Vienna and Budapest, deserves a few days' exploration; beyond lies the finest part of the route, rounding the spectacular Fatra and **Tatra** mountains, amid the bear and wolf country of the Carpathians. Beyond **Poprad Tatry**, it's feasible to continue into Poland.

BRNO

High-rise blocks and an unmistakably industrial look might tempt you to skip **Brno,** which expanded in the 19th century as a textile making centre, but it does have a scattering of good sights (most close Mon, and are either cheap or free) within 1 km of the station in the largely traffic-free centre. **The Chrám sv. Petra a Pavla**, (neo-Gothic Cathedral of Sts Peter and Paul), crowns Petrov Hill, while the 13th-century **Špilberk Castle** was the most notorious prison in the Austro-Hungarian empire – you can visit the horrifying prison cells (Tues–Sun 0900–1800). A little way south-west is the **Augustinian Monastery**, where in 1865 the monk Mendel studied genetics, breeding pea plants in the garden. Garden and plants remain, and there's also a small museum, the **Mendelianum**, MENDLOVO NÁM.1 (Mon–Fri 0800–1700).

The **Old Town Hall**, RADNICKÁ 8, is Gothic-, Renaissance- and baroque-style and displays a 'dragon', a stuffed crocodile from 1608. Brno's most bizarre sight is the crypt of the **Kapucínsky Klášter** (the Capuchin Monastery), containing 150 mummified bodies, air-dried since 1650 (closed Mon).

En route to Brno is the stunning town of **Kutná Hora** with an ancient silver mine, the lovely Gothic church of **Sv. Barbora**, endless renaissance and mediaeval architecture and also an extraordinary 'bone church' 2 km from the centre in Sedlec (just by the train station) richly and gruesomely decorated with the bones of long-expired nobles.

RAIL (05) 4221 4803 (exchange facilities, left luggage). For town centre, head across the road in front of the station and up MASARYKOVA STREET.

Day Trips from Brno

The **Moravský Kras** *(Moravian Karst)* limestone caves form a series of dramatic underground rivers, stalagmites and stalactites in the middle of a forest (daily 0800–1530, cheap). There are several trains a day to nearby **Blansko** (35 mins). Take the frequent bus from **Zvonarska** central bus station to explore **Mikulov**, a lovely hill-top town with a castle (rebuilt in the 1950s, but it still looks impressive from afar), charming old houses and noted wine-cellars, overlooking the Austrian border (40 mins).

Tourist Office: **Old Town Hall**, RADNICKÁ 4, 8, 10; (05) 4221 1090/3267 (Mon–Fri 0800–1800, Sat–Sun 0900–1700).

Book well in advance. **YMCA**: STAMICOVA 11, 382 651; **Pension Venia**, RIEGROVA 27, (05) 4121 3290.

BRATISLAVA

For four centuries Bratislava was a strategic part of the *Limes Romanus*, the Roman frontier. In the 16th century, when much of Hungary lay under Turkish occupation, it became the Hungarian capital, remaining in this position for almost 250 years. Now, as the Slovak capital since 1993, the city is slowly re-establishing itself.

Within particularly hideous outskirts of grey tower blocks and factory chimneys, it has a charming and relaxed old centre, free from the tourist crowds and peppered with cafés (though it suffers in comparison with Prague). Many of its older and more distinguished buildings and squares have been refurbished. The castle dominates the town – although dating from the 9th century, most of the current structure is 1960s vintage (closed Mon). During Bratislava's period as Hungarian capital, 11 kings were crowned in **St Martin's Cathedral**, across STAROMESTSKA from the castle. The attractive, fountain-filled old centre, largely pedestrianised, contains the glorious **Mirbach Palace**, RADNIČNÁ ST, the **Primacialne Palace**, 1 PRIMACIALNE SQ., and the Gothic **Franciscan Church**, FRANTIŠKÁNSKÉ NÁMESTIE, one of Bratislava's oldest surviving structures. Clamber up the medieval **St Michael's Tower**, MICHALSKA 22 (Wed–Mon), for a bird's-eye view over the old town, and visit the **Town Hall**, 1 HLAVNÉ NÁMESTIE, (Tues–Sun), a gorgeous hotch-potch of buildings housing a surprisingly interesting municipal museum.

DAY TRIP FROM BRATISLAVA

Towering above the Danube and Morava rivers, **Devín castle** is a picturesque ruined fortress at the edge of the Little Carpathian mountains. There are frequent buses (no.29) and boats (from FAJNOROVO NÁBR.; 533 5123, cheap). **Pezinok** (25 mins by bus, ten daily) is a pretty vintner's town in the wine-growing region, boasting a Renaissance castle and centre. Don't miss the **wine festivals** at the end of Aug and early Sept.

RAIL Most trains serve the main station, **Hlavná stanica,** (07) 204 4484, 1.5 km north of old town. **Tourist/accommodation office** (07) 395 906, exchange facilities, café, left luggage and showers. Tram no.1 to old town. **Nové Mesto** station is 3 km north-east of the centre.

Tourist Office: BIS, KLOBÚČNICKÁ 2; (07) 533 3715/4370,

Cheap accommodation is scarce; book ahead through Tourist Offices. **CKM-Slovakia**, 16 HVIEZDOSLAVOVO NÁM; (07) 334 114 or 331 607, for university dorms in the summer and a year-round student hotel. **Hostels**: **Bernolák**, BERNOLÁKOVA 1; 497 721 (July–early Sept); **Belojanis**, WILSONOVA 6 (very basic, no phone); **L'udovít Štúr**: 36 STARÉ GRUNTY, (07) 726 507, or 722 866.

Try the **Slovenska reštaurácia** (Slovak restaurant), HVIEZDOSLAVOVO NÁM. 20, ☎(07) 5334 883 (moderate); **Korzo** (Hungarian specialities), HVIEZDOSLAVOVO NÁM. 11, ☎(07) 5334 974; **Stará Sladovňa – Mamut** (in-house brewery and pub, cheap), CINTORÍNSKA 32, ☎(07) 321 151.

WHERE NEXT FROM BRATISLAVA?

It's just over 1 hr to ***Vienna*** *(ETT table 996), and just over 2½ hrs to* ***Budapest*** *(table 1170).*

TRNAVA

Dubbed somewhat ludicrously the 'Slovak Rome', Trnava is a picturesque walled university town boasting 12 churches and unspoiled, cobbled lanes. It's an easy day trip from Bratislava.

RAIL ☎(0805) 26241/24983. The centre is 10-mins walk up HOSPODÁRSKA ST., then right down BERNOLÁKOVA BRANA ST.

Tourist Office: **TINS**, TROJIČNÉ NÁMESTIE 1; ☎(0805) 186 or ☎511 022.

PIEŠŤANY

Slovakia's biggest, grandest spa, built at the turn of the century, offers cures, elegant cafés and peaceful, riverside parks.

RAIL ☎(0838) 21213, 15-mins walk west of the centre (signposted).

Tourist Office: **Informačné stredisko Piešťany** (in the Hotel Eden), WINTEROVA 60; ☎(0838) 27689.

TRENČÍN

Trenčín, dwarfed by a towering castle on a crag, is a charming old town. There is a branch line from Trenčianska Teplá (8km from Trenčín) to **Trenčianske Teplice spa** (with pseudo-Turkish baths).

RAIL ☎(0831) 419484. Walk 10 mins east through the park for the centre.

Tourist Office: **Kultúrno-informačné centrum mesta Trenčín**, ŠTÚROVO NÁMESTIE 10; ☎(0831) 186 or ☎533 505.

ŽILINA

It's worth taking a look at the Renaissance arcades in the town centre, but Žilina is an ideal base for exploring the Fatra mountain ranges and the **Kysuce Nature Reserve**.

DAY TRIP FROM ŽILINA

Four trains per day make the short run through from Žilina to Martin, taking 45 mins. Plenty more journeys are possible by changing at **Vrútky**. **Martin** is an outstanding base for walking or skiing in the Malá and Velká Fatra mountains, and for visiting the **Slovak Village Museum** (at JAHODNICKE HAJE), 3 km away.

DAY TRIP FROM POPRAD TATRY

From Poprad and Strba, the TEZ railway (ETT table 1192) climbs into the stunning alpine **High Tatra** mountains, stopping at **Starý Smokovec, Štrbské Pleso** and **Tatranská Lomnica** for spas, hiking and skiing.

Buses cover the *Spiš* region – unspoilt Renaissance villages amongst rolling hills, striped fields and tiny white churches: the town of **Levoča** and **Spišský Hrad (Spiš castle)** are unmissable UNESCO World Heritage sites.

RAIL (089) 22226, north-east of the centre, on NÁRODNÁ ULICA.

i **Tourist Office**: **Selinan Travel Agency**, BURIANOVA MEDZIERKA 4; (089) 620 789.

POPRAD TATRY

Poprad, sandwiched between the High and Low Tatra mountain ranges, is undistinguished, but **Spišská Sobota** (3 km east of the station) has Renaissance houses and exquisite church carvings.

RAIL (0969) 225 654 (international) 933 (local), 1 km north of the town centre.

i **Tourist Office**: **Popradská informačná agentúra**, NÁM. SV. EGÍDIA 2950/114; (092) 186 or 721 700.

WHERE NEXT FROM POPRAD TATRY?

It's feasible to continue into Poland *by heading on east to* **Plaveč** *then north to* **Kraków**, *joining the* **Poznan–Zakopane** *route (p. 483).(ETT tables 1192 and 1078)*

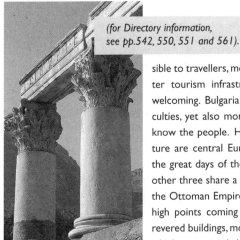

(for Directory information, see pp.542, 550, 551 and 561).

Of the four countires covered in this section, Greece and Hungary are the most accessible to travellers, more cosmopolitan and with a better tourism infrastructure, yet less spontaneously welcoming. Bulgaria and Romania present more difficulties, yet also more opportunities to really get to know the people. Hungary's traditions and architecture are central European, with many reminders of the great days of the Austro-Hungarian Empire. The other three share a history of being subject states of the Ottoman Empire, their architectural and cultural high points coming with liberation, and their most revered buildings, monasteries and towns being those which maintained the national spirit during the long centuries of subjugation.

Nowadays, the young in all these countries are catching up fast with their counterparts in western Europe. Cafés are lively and stimulating meeting places. Head for Hungary for its elegant capital and fine towns; to Greece for its vibrant light and relaxing beach life, with archaeological treasures always within reach, to Romania for a country with rural beauty but dilapidated cities and a capital trying to recapture its role as the Paris of the East, and to Bulgaria for magnificent scenery and wildlife, inexpensive skiing, quality wine at bargain prices, some fine cities and great beaches.

BULGARIA

This small and comparatively little-known country on the eastern side of the Balkan Peninsula has beautiful mountain scenery, rich in wild flowers and birds. There are cities like **Plovdiv** and **Veliko Târnavo** (both accessible by train), with picturesque old quarters built during the 19th century National Revival. Monasteries like Rila and Bachkovo, both on UNESCO's World Heritage List, have stunning frescos and impressive buildings. They can be reached by bus from **Sofia** and **Plovdiv** respectively. The large resorts on the Black Sea coast are gradually being improved, but much of the coast is still largely agricultural, and there are some pretty small villages as well as the more cosmopolitan charms of Varna, the largest port. Folk traditions still play a part especially in rural life, and hospitality to visitors is warm and friendly.

ACCOMMODATION

In **Sofia** (particularly at the airport, railway station and in the city centre) various agencies offer accommodation booking and information. Small private hotels and bed and breakfast type accommodation are increasingly available and good value. The main hotels also have information desks, often useful for maps and a monthly free city information guide in English.

FOOD AND DRINK

Bulgaria produces a wide variety of excellent fruits and vegetables. Soups are popular the year round, with yoghurt-based cold ones on offer in summer. Meat is generally pork or lamb, either cooked slowly with vegetables or grilled. Desserts include seasonal fruit, ice-cream, gateaux and sweet pastries. Vegetarians can go for the varied and generally excellent salads, and dishes such as stuffed peppers or aubergine dishes like *kyopolou*.

Tea is often herbal or Chinese and served without milk. Coffee is normally espresso. Bottled fruit juices are cheap and readily available, as are imported soft drinks in cans. Local beers are European lager style and good value. **Grozdova, slivova** and **mastika** are strong drinks, served in large measures, traditionally accompanying cold starters. Tap water is safe to drink and there are many good local mineral waters. Bulgarian wine is often of high quality, and very good value.

GREECE

Inexpensive, sunny, friendly and beautiful, with a wonderful array of archaeological sites, Greece offers a seductive mix of culture and idling around, with plenty of opportunity to linger in tavernas or relax on a beach as well as visiting ancient ruins. Wild flowers make a colourful spectacle in spring – an ideal time for travelling – while in summer it's often too hot to do more than flop in the shade (August can be really crowded as most Greeks take the month off), and by autumn the landscape is parched and past its prime but is still excellent for swimming and sightseeing.

Most visitors will probably at least pass through **Athens**, and spare more than a fleeting glance at the famous classical remains. From there you can escape the noise and pollution of the capital by taking ferries out to the islands. Close by are the **Cyclades**, while farther east, towards Turkey, lie the **Dodecanese**. Within these archipelagos the islands are strongly contrasting, some ruggedly mountainous such as **Naxos, Santorini** and **Karpathos**, some good for nightlife and beaches such as **Ios** and **Mykonos**, others peaceful and uncrowded such as **Skopelos**. Further afield are

PELOPONNESE PENINSULA

A particularly idyllic area for exploring is the Peloponnese peninsula, with the seaside town of Nafplion and some impressive classical sights and scenic treats. The rail network is sparse, and many services are erratic, but buses are generally efficient and plentiful.

the major resort islands of **Corfu, Rhodes** and **Crete** (the most southerly and largest of all the islands, with superb ancient remains and astonishingly diverse scenery). The islands are covered in great detail in *Greek Island Hopping* by Frewin Poffley (Thomas Cook Publishing).

Accommodation

Greece is over-supplied with accommodation, from five-star hotels to pensions, village rooms, self-catering apartments, dormitories and youth hostels. You should have **no problem finding a bed in Athens, Patras** or **Thessaloniki (Salonika)** even in high summer (though the very cheapest Athens dorms and pensions are often very crowded in July and Aug). Rooms are hardest to find over the Greek Easter period (note this date is different from Easter elsewhere, as it's based on the Orthodox calendar), so try to book ahead. Outside the Easter and July–Sept peaks, accommodation costs up to 30% less. You should also get a 10% discount if staying three or more nights. Cheaper places will keep your passport overnight unless you pay in advance. Youth hostels are not good value and are being phased out by the government. **Campsites** at major sights (including **Delphi**, **Mistra** and **Olympia**) can be good value, with laundries, hot showers, cafés and even swimming pools. You can get a list of sites from the GNTO (see p. 551).

Food and Drink

Greeks rarely eat breakfast (many get up at dawn and start the day with coffee and a cigarette) but cafés in tourist areas advertise 'English breakfast'. Traditional Greek meals are unstructured, with lots of dishes brought at once or in no particular order. Lunch is any time between 1200 and 1500, after which most restaurants close until around 1930. Greeks dine late, and you will find plenty of restaurants open until well after midnight.

The best Greek food is fresh, seasonal and simply prepared. Seafood dishes are usually the most expensive. Veal, chicken and squid are relatively cheap, and traditional salad – olives, tomatoes, onions, peppers and feta cheese drowned in oil, served with bread – is a meal in itself. Most restaurants have a bilingual Greek and English menu. In smaller places, visit the kitchen to choose what you want, or in more expensive establishments choose dishes from a display cabinet.

Coffee is easier to find than tea; iced coffee (**frappé**) is now more popular than the tiny, strong cups of old-fashioned Greek coffee. Aniseed-flavoured **ouzo** is a favourite aperitif. **Retsina** (resinated wine) is an acquired taste; many Greeks mix it with Coke. Greek brandy is on the sweet side. Draught lager is not widely available and is neither as good nor as cheap as bottled beer: Amstel, Henninger and Heineken, brewed in Greece and sold in half-litre bottles. Tap water is safe but heavily chlorinated.

HUNGARY

The **Great Plain** extends across more than half this landlocked country, with the most appreciable hills rising in the far north. Hungary's most scenic moments occur along **Lake Balaton** (much developed with resorts, one of the pleasantest being **Keszthely**) and the **Danube Bend** (or Dunakanyar), north of Budapest, with a trio of fine towns – **Szentendre** (with its ceramics museum), **Visegrád** (with its ruined palace) and **Esztergom** (dominated by a huge basilica). **Budapest** is the obvious highlight, exuding the grace of an old middle European city, memorably placed on the Danube.

ACCOMMODATION

There is a wide range of accommodation, with some superb **hotels** of international standing in the capital. Some castles are being turned into hotels of varying standards. **For the medium to lower price bracket**, **private rooms** are very good value as is the small pension. Steer clear of the old Soviet-style tourist hotels and youth hostels as they are very basic with limited facilities. **Spas** offer good weekend packages. **Campsites** are, on the whole, very good and can be found near the main resorts. Many have cabins to rent, but contact the authorities first in order to book. Camping 'rough' is not permitted and could net a hefty fine. Information on accommodation addresses, phone numbers and services: **Tourinform**.

FOOD AND DRINK

Cuisine has been much influenced by Austria, Germany and Turkey. Portions are generous and most restaurants offer a cheap fixed-price menu. Lunch is the main meal of the day, and a bowl of *gulas* (goulash) laced with potatoes and spiced with paprika is a 'must'. Try smoked sausages, soups (sowcherry soup is superb) and paprika noodles or pike-perch. Dinner is early and you should aim to begin eating well before 2100. In order to avoid the pitfalls of phrase book ordering, try eating in an **Önkiszolgáló** or **ételbár** (inexpensive self-service snack bars). **Csárda** are folk restaurants usually with traditional music, but menus can be limited and slightly more expensive. Still in the moderate range are the **Vendéglő**, where home cooking often features. **Étterem** are larger restaurants with a more varied menu. Leave a tip, generally equivalent to 10–20% of the total. Hungary has some very decent wines, such as **Tokaj** and **Egrí bikavé** (Bulls Blood), while **pálinka** is a fiery schnapps.

ROMANIA

The lofty **Carpathian Mountains** snake through the heart of the country, rising to over 2500 m in the region of **Transylvania**, the terrain of the original Count Dracula. Much of the countryside is rugged and remote, and travel can be a real adventure, though be warned that standards for tourism are not on a par with Western countries'. The brutal dictator Ceauşescu, before his demise and assassination in 1989, destroyed many villages and re-housed large communities in hastily erected apartment blocks; **Bucharest** has many legacies of his era and is not the most appealing of European capitals, and many other towns suffered a similar fate. Yet in the northern provinces of **Moldavia** and **Maramures** much rustic charm has survived. Prices are low and you'll still find places where tourists are rare, and the reception from locals is almost universally warm despite the obvious poverty of the inhabitants.

ACCOMMODATION

Hotels vary a great deal in quality, even within each category (one to four stars). At the bottom end they can be basic and inexpensive, while some match the highest international standards and prices. **Private rooms** may be booked at Tourist Offices in some towns, and in a few tourist areas touts will meet trains at the station to offer their rooms – which may be centrally located in attractive old houses, or far out in grim suburban tower blocks, so make sure you know what you're agreeing to. **Campsites** should generally be avoided, as standards of cleanliness and hygiene can be appalling. Book in advance for **hotels on the Black Sea coast** in summer and in **mountain ski resorts** at winter weekends.

FOOD AND DRINK

There are many restaurants in the main cities, offering a variety of foods, in principle. In practice you often end up with pork, plus potato but without fresh vegetables. Chicken, beef and lamb are also available, and fish can be delicious, especially Danube carp (termed, unfortunately, as *'crap'*). The traditional accompaniment is *mămăligă*, a mush of maize flour. Unsmoked frankfurters *(pariser)* and light liver sausages *(cremwurst)* equal those found in the West. Other local specialities are *sarmale*, stuffed cabbage leaves (sometimes without meat), and *mititei*, small meatballs grilled in beer gardens in summer. There's a plethora of takeaway stalls, some open 24 hours, and some pizzerias which serve a poor version of the real thing. Fresh vegetables and fruit are delicious and easily found in markets in season: imports such as bananas are pricey.

Cafés serve excellent cakes *(prăjitură)*, soft drinks, beer and coffee; *turceasca* is Turkish-style ground coffee, while *Ness* is instant coffee. Wines are superb and very cheap; you should also try the plum brandy known as *tuică* (pronounced 'tswica'), or its double-distilled version *palinca*. Tap water is safe to drink, although highly chlorinated.

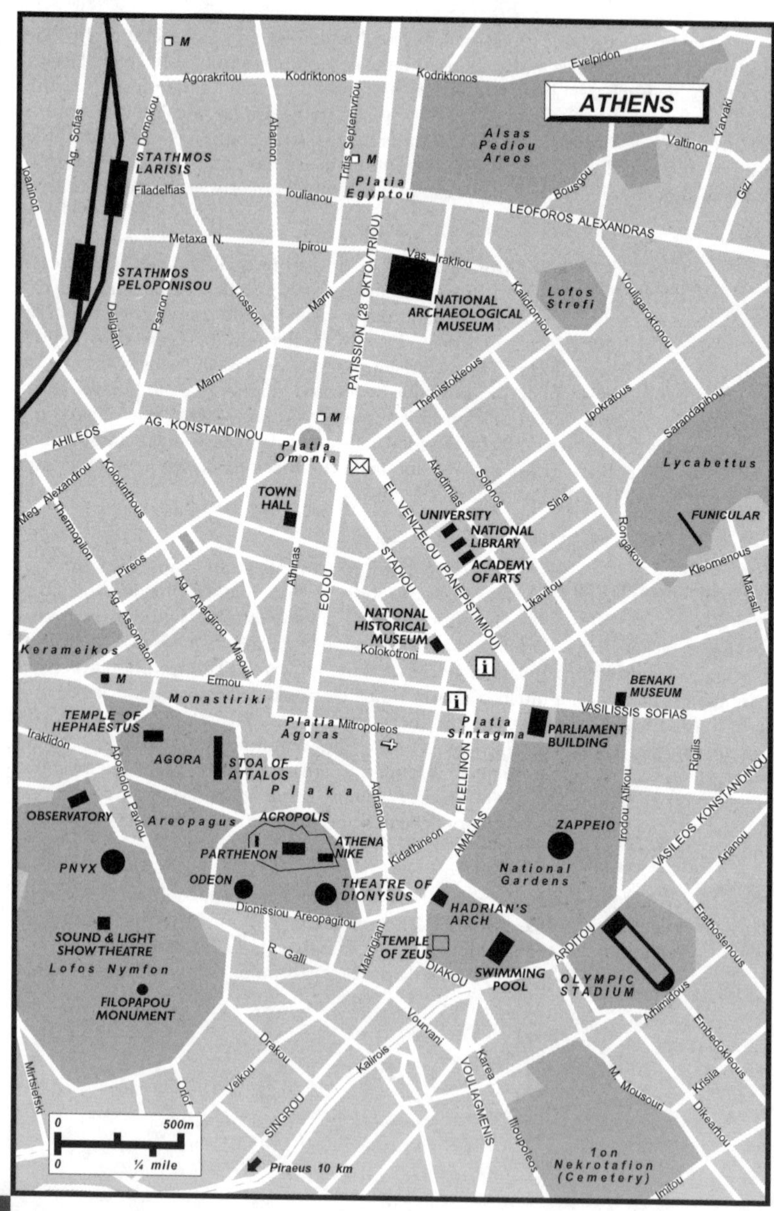
ATHENS
M
Agorakritou
Kodriktonos
Kodriktonos
Evelpidon
Alsas
Pediou
Areos
Varvaki
Valtinon
Bousgou
Gizi
Ag. Sofias
Domokou
Ioaninon
STATHMOS
LARISIS
Filadelfias
Aharnon
Tritis Septemvriou
M
Platia
Egyptou
Ioulianou
LEOFOROS ALEXANDRAS
Metaxa N.
Ipirou
Vas. Irakliou
PATISSION (28 OKTOVRIOU)
STATHMOS
PELOPONISOU
Liossion
Marni
NATIONAL
ARCHAEOLOGICAL
MUSEUM
Kalidromiou
Lofos
Strefi
Vouligaroktonou
Deligiani
Psaron
Marni
Themistokleous
Ipokratous
Sarandapihou
M
AHILEOS
AG. KONSTANDINOU
Platia
Omonia
Lycabettus
Meg. Alexandrou
Kolokinthous
TOWN
HALL
EL. VENIZELOU (PANEPISTIMIOU)
Akadimias
Solonos
Sina
UNIVERSITY
NATIONAL
LIBRARY
ACADEMY
OF ARTS
FUNICULAR
Rongakou
Kleomenous
Thermopilon
Pireos
Ag. Anargiron
Athinas
EOLOU
STADIOU
Likavitou
Marasli
Ag. Assomaton
Miaouli
NATIONAL
HISTORICAL
MUSEUM
Kolokotroni
Kerameikos
M
Ermou
Monastiriki
BENAKI
MUSEUM
VASILISSIS SOFIAS
TEMPLE OF
HEPHAESTUS
Platia
Agoras
Mitropoleos
Platia
Sintagma
PARLIAMENT
BUILDING
Iraklidon
Apostolou Pavlou
AGORA
STOA OF
ATTALOS
Plaka
Adrianou
FILELLINON
Irodou Atikou
Rigilis
VASILEOS KONSTANDINOU
OBSERVATORY
Areopagus
ACROPOLIS
AMALIAS
ZAPPEIO
PARTHENON
ATHENA
NIKE
Kidathineon
Arianou
PNYX
ODEON
THEATRE OF
DIONYSUS
National
Gardens
HADRIAN'S
ARCH
Dionissiou Areopagitou
Erathostenous
TEMPLE
OF ZEUS
SOUND & LIGHT
SHOW THEATRE
R. Galli
Makrigianni
DIAKOU
SWIMMING
POOL
ARDITOU
OLYMPIC
STADIUM
Lofos Nymfon
FILOPAPOU
MONUMENT
Arhimidous
Vourvani
Embedokleous
Drakou
Kalirois
Karea
VOULIAGMENIS
M. Mousouri
Krisila
Mirtsiefski
Orlof
Veikou
SINGROU
Dikearhou
Ililoupoleos
0
500m
0
¼ mile
Piraeus 10 km
1on
Nekrotafion
(Cemetery)
Imitou

Modern **Athens** is a noisy, bustling, exhausting and badly polluted city of more than four million people. Yet many Athenians live a laid-back, village-style life amid the concrete apartment blocks, and hardly a corner is without a tiny café or taverna. Street crime rates are remarkably low and it's a conspicuously friendly place. Its enduring draw are the great sights of the ancient city where the seeds of Western democracy, philosophy, medicine and art were planted. You can visit most of the sights on foot as it is quite compact and best seen early in the morning to avoid the worst of the heat and crowds.

ARRIVAL AND DEPARTURE

Tourist Information

The Greek National Tourist Organisation (EOT) (HQ administration, ☎22 3111/9, fax 322 4148): office off 2 AMERIKIS ST., ☎31 0561/2, fax 325 2895 (Mon–Fri 0900–1700, Sat 1000–1400); sightseeing information leaflets, fact sheets, local and regional transport schedules and up-to-date opening times of sights. There are also **EOT offices** (Mon–Fri 0900–1700, Sat 1100–1700) in the **East Terminal of the airport**, ☎961 2722, and in **Piraeus Zea Marina**, ☎413 5730/411 5716. The **tourist police** in Athens, ☎171, can help with lists of licensed accommodation (DIMITRAKOPOULOU 77, KOUKAKI, ☎922 6393). **International Students and Youth Travel Services**, ☎322 1267.

RAIL Trains from **Thessaloniki (Salonika)**, **Northern Greece**, **Bulgaria** and **Europe** use **Larissa Station** (*Stathmos Larisis*), THEODOROU DILIGIANI, ☎82 37741. Trains from **Patras** and the **Peloponnese** use **Peloponnese Station** (*Stathmos Peloponisou*), ☎513 1601. These small stations are only 200 yards apart: Peloponnese is behind Larisis over the metal footbridge. They are about 2 km north-west of **Syntagma** (tram no. 1). The nearest **metro stop** is VICTORIA, 500 m to the east. **International rail tickets** can be bought at Larisis station or **OSE offices** in Athens: KAROLOU 1, ☎529 7777 (**info** for all stations from 0700 until 2100); 6 SINA ST., ☎362 4404/6; and FILELLINON 17, ☎323 6747. For **domestic rail timetable information**, ☎145; **international services**, ☎147.

The **Piraeus Port Authority** serves the Greek islands, ☎451 1311 or 422 1211. The port itself, 8 km south-west of Athens, is served by **train** and **metro**. The **Tourist Office** has a monthly **all-island ferry timetable**. If you are island-hopping, Thomas Cook's guidebook *Greek Island Hopping* combines a guide to every Greek island with ferry timetable information.

Athens International Airport is 10 km south of the city centre. **Olympic Airways flights** use the **West Terminal**, ☎926 9111. Bus no.19 runs to **Syntagma**, at 30 mins intervals. All other airlines use the **East Terminal**, ☎969 4111. For **international flight information** except Olympic, ☎969 4111; for **Olympic**, ☎936 3363. Bus no.91 links the terminal and Syntagma **every 30 mins** during the day and **every hour** at night. **OA Reservations** ☎966 6666.

INFORMATION

MONEY There is a **Thomas Cook bureau de change** at 4 KARAGEORGI SERVIAS ST., Syntagma Sq.

POST AND PHONES The **main post office** is at EOLOU 100, ☎324 7690, Mon–Sat 0730–2030. One branch is in **Syntagma**, ☎323 7573, Mon–Sat 0730–2030 and Sun 0730–1330. The **Greek Telecommunications Organisation** (*OTE*) has an office open 24 hrs at PATISSION 85. **International calls** can be made. You can make **local calls** from public coin boxes and international calls from those which bear the orange 'international' legend. You can also make calls from **metered phones** at *periptero* street booths all over the city. The **dialling code** for Athens is 301.

PUBLIC TRANSPORT

The Tourist Office's excellent **free map** of Athens shows **trolley-bus routes, metro stations** and details of **bus services**. Central Athens, from OMONIA to SYNTAGMA through the **Plaka** to the **Acropolis**, is increasingly walkable thanks to a ban on traffic in several core blocks.

Metro: There is currently one metro line (in the process of being expanded), which runs from **Piraeus** north to the centre of town, where there are stations at MONASTIRAKI (for the Acropolis and the Plaka), OMONIA (for the Archaeological Museum) and VICTORIA (for mainline stations), then on to KIFISSIA. A cross-town metro line, with stations at SYNTAGMA and Larisis main line stations, is being built. This is quite disruptive, but it has thrown up interesting archaeological finds, such as two Roman wells at SYNTAGMA.

Trolley-buses and **buses**: the network is far more comprehensive than the metro. Most routes pass through either SYNTAGMA or OMONIA.

Metro tickets are available from station kiosks or self-service machines; validate them in the machines at station entrances. **Trolley-buses** and **buses** – buy **tickets** from blue booths near bus stops or from kiosks throughout Athens. Validate tickets on board.

Taxis: Hard to find, especially during the rush hour, around lunch time and early afternoon. Sharing a taxi is normal; all passengers pay full fare. Some airport taxi drivers will overcharge unwary visitors so agree a fare before getting in.

ACCOMMODATION

The **Hellenic Chamber of Hotels** provides a booking service for Athens hotels. They can be contacted before arrival at STADIOU 24, 10564 ATHENS, by correspondence, fax 322 5449 or 323 6962, or upon arrival in Athens at KARAGEORGI SERVIAS 2, off SYNTAGMA, ☎: 323 7193/322 9912, in the National Bank. The Tourist Office has details of class D and E hotels if you are seeking cheaper options. Athens has many private hostels for budget travellers. Standards vary widely.

Hostels cluster in the **Plaka** area, noisy but ideally located for the main sights, or between **Victoria** and the stations (where the tackiest accommodation is found). Some of the cheapest 'hostel' accommodation near the station is extremely overcrowded in high season with tight-budget travellers. However, except in the height of summer, you should have plenty of options. The HI hostel **Athens International Youth Hostel** and **Greek Youth Hostel Organisation** are further out than most of the private hostels. **Campsites** are up to an hour from the centre by bus, dirty, poorly serviced, and not much cheaper than hostels.

INFORMATION

HOSTELS

HI hostel, Athens International Youth Hostel, 16 VICTOROS HUGO ☎523 1095, fax 523 4170.

Greek Youth Hostel Organisation, 75 DAMAZEOS STREET, ☎751 9530, fax 751 0616.

FOOD AND DRINK

On a tight budget, eat on the move: *giros*, slices of veal kebab with onions, tomatoes, yoghurt and fries wrapped in flat bread, is a meal in itself and there are lots of other street snacks to choose from. Try *souvlaki* and *frappé* coffee. **Plaka** restaurants tend to be touristy, but those at PLATEIA FILIKI ETERIAS, off KIDATHINEON on the edge of the Plaka, are a little less so. Around **Dexameni**, there are many *souvlaki* places. For even cheaper eats, head for the **Pankrati** suburb, north of the National Gardens and Stadiou.

HIGHLIGHTS

THE ACROPOLIS Occupied since neolithic times (5000 BC), the 'high city' was Athens's stronghold until it was converted into a religious shrine. What you see today dates from the 5th century BC. It's on a steep hill and can only be reached on foot: smog often limits the otherwise spectacular views.

The Tourist Office has fact sheets on the major sites – highlights are the **Parthenon**, the **Temple of Athena**, the great gateway to the Acropolis, and **Propylaea** – and full details also of the many museums; the **National Archaeological** is most notable.

Pericles built the **Parthenon** (Home of the Virgin), between 447 and 432 BC. Designed by Iktinus and Phidias, it is the finest example of Doric architecture still in existence. Close examination of the temple reveals irregularities: columns are closer together at the corners, where light can shine between them; columns are of differing widths and bulge one third of the way up; the roof line is curved. But it was designed to be seen from afar, giving an impression of perfect symmetry – one of the finest optical illusions ever devised. Most of the dramatic friezes (known as the **Elgin Marbles**) that adorned the Parthenon's exterior are in London's British Museum (and Greece would dearly like them back), although the **Acropolis Museum** to the east of the Parthenon has some fragments.

The **Erechtheum**, north-west of the Parthenon, is most notable for its six caryatids – graceful sculptures of women. Due to the effects of air pollution, the originals have been removed and replaced by the replicas on display today. Four of the originals are on display in the **Acropolis Museum**.

The **Temple of Athena Nike** (Victory), with its eight small columns, stands on the south-west corner of the Acropolis. Built around 420 BC, during a pause in the Peloponnesian War, the temple was once the only place from where you could look out to sea over the defensive walls. It is considered one of the finest Ionic buildings left in Greece.

The bulky **Propylaea**, the great gateway to the Acropolis, takes up most of the western end of the hill and today welcomes thousands of visitors. Arrive early if you want any peace or uninterrupted photo opportunities.

There is a fantastic view of the Acroplis and all of Attica from the **Monument of Filopapou**, though the site itself is unimpressive and sadly defaced by graffiti.

Beyond the Acropolis Most of the city suburbs are anonymous concrete swathes distinguished only by dark green awnings, but in areas close to the Acropolis you can pick out many other ancient ruins. Just below the Acropolis hill, on the south side, are two ancient theatres. Now scant ruins, the **Theatre of Dionysius**, built in the 4th century BC, is the earliest such structure in the Western world. The **Roman Odeon of Herodes Atticus** has been reconstructed and is once again in use.

The remains of the **Temple of Olympian Zeus** are also clearly visible east of the Acropolis. There are only a few surviving columns, but you can still absorb the grandeur of what was the largest temple in Greece. Next to it is **Hadrian's Arch**, constructed by the enthusiastic Roman emperor-builder to mark where the ancient Greek city ended and his new city began.

Museums and Churches Entrance to state-run museums is free on Sun. For an incomparable collection of relics from Athens and many other Greek sites, head to the **National Archaeological Museum**, 44 Patission: allow a full day. Exhibits range through Minoan frescos, Mycenaean gold, a phenomenal collection of over 300,000 coins, sculptures, *kouroi* and much more.

Plenty of other museums offer insights into ancient and modern Greek life. These include the **Museum of Cycladic and Ancient Greek Art**, 4 Neofitou Douka St.; the **Benaki Museum**, Koumpari St.; and Vasilissis Sofias Ave.; and **the Byzantine Museum**, Vasilissis Sofias 22, which houses icons from this later glory of Greek culture.

From **Lycabettus Hill**, the highest in Athens at 278 m, the view surpasses even that from the Acropolis. **Take the funicular railway up** and the path down for the best round-trip.

SHOPPING

For gold and silver jewellery, ceramics, leather goods and fashion with a Greek slant – lots of linen and cotton in bright colours – try **Pandrossou Flea Market**, between **Monastiraki** and MITROPOLEOS SQ. For antiques, junk, army surplus, antique clothing and camping gear, the original flea market on IFESTOU, on the opposite side of MONASTIRAKI, is a better bet. Streets such as ADRIANOU and PANDROSSOU in the **Plaka** quarter have plenty of tourist-oriented shops and stalls, with clothes, leather, pottery and marble on offer. Other crafts include lace making, needlepoint and crochet.

NIGHT-TIME AND EVENTS

The Plaka is where most of the night scene happens. Most **cinemas** show the latest English language movies with original soundtrack and Greek subtitles; see the English-language daily *Athens News* for listings. See traditional music and dance with the **Dora Stratou Dance Theatre** in the Philopappous Theatre; ☎324 4395. The **Sound and Light** show on PNYX HILL, ☎322 1459, is not to be missed. **Absolut Dancing Club**, FILELLINON 23, ☎323 7197, is Athens's most popular dance venue.

During the **Athens Festival** (June–Sept), events staged in the Odeon of Herodes Atticus and Megazon, as well as Lycabettus Hill Theatre, include **ancient Greek drama** plus **classical music** and **ballet**, performed by Greek and international companies and orchestras. For information, ☎322 1459.

WHERE NEXT FROM ATHENS?

*Athens is well placed for beginning a trip to the **Kiklades** (Cyclades) archipelago and other islands. For full descriptions consult **Greek Island Hopping** by Frewin Poffley, published annually by Thomas Cook.*

*The other main area to head for is the **Peloponnese** (south-west of Athens; ETT tables 1450, 1455), a largely unspoilt peninsula ringed by railways, and with limestone peaks, sandy bays and a stunning heritage of ancient and medieval sites. **Korinthos** (Corinth) is the first place across the gorge-like Corinthian Canal; Old Corinth (7 km away) features the columns of the 6th-century BC **Temple of Apollo** – a huge central forum flanked by the odd row of crumbling ancient shop buildings, plus the Fountain of Peirene – and the fortress of Akrokorinth on a crag high above the old city. You can continue by train to **Nafplion** (Nauplia), the prettiest town in the Peloponnese, set on a little rocky peninsula beneath a huge Venetian fortress: a great place to stay. From here and Athens excursion buses visit **Epidavros** (Mikinai), site of the most famous of all ancient Greek amphitheatres – its acoustics as perfect as ever. **Mycenae** (Epidauros) is the other nearby must-see, the 1600-year-old royal residence of the kingdom of Agamemnon.*

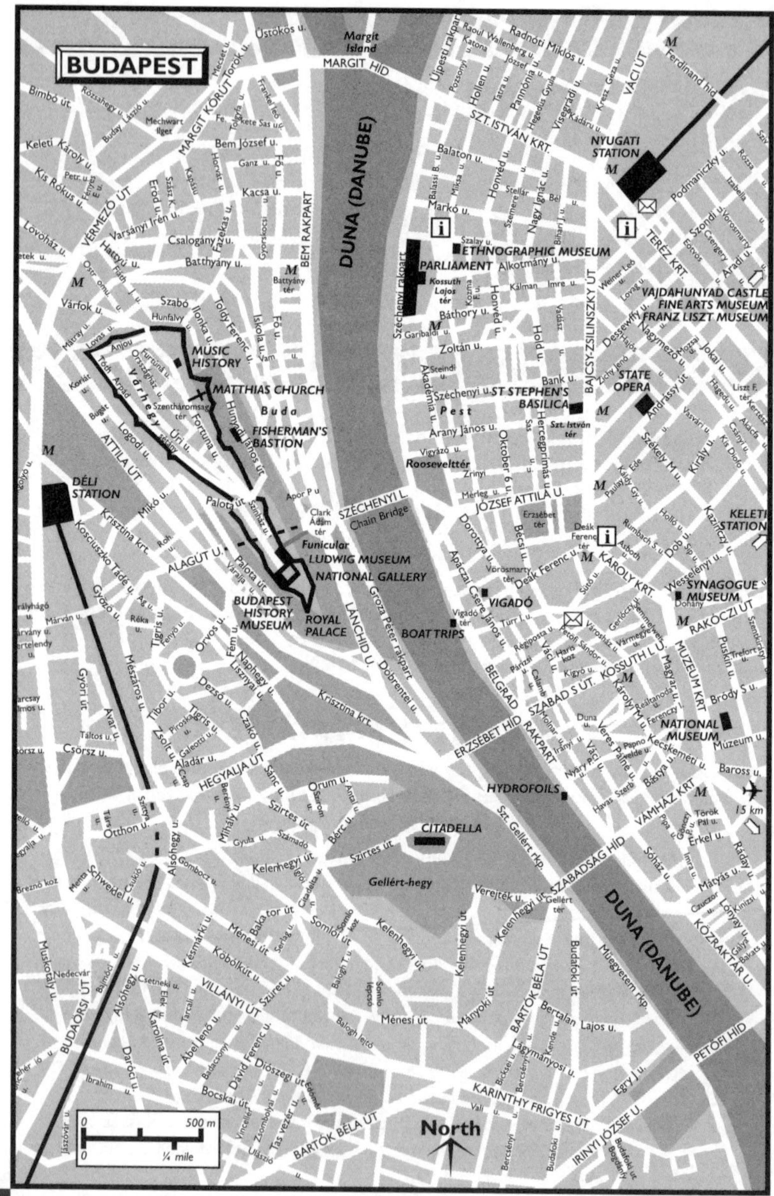
BUDAPEST
Margit Island
MARGIT HÍD
DUNA (DANUBE)
NYUGATI STATION
ETHNOGRAPHIC MUSEUM
PARLIAMENT
Kossuth Lajos tér
VAJDAHUNYAD CASTLE
FINE ARTS MUSEUM
FRANZ LISZT MUSEUM
MUSIC HISTORY
MATTHIAS CHURCH
Buda
Várhegy
FISHERMAN'S BASTION
ST STEPHEN'S BASILICA
Pest
STATE OPERA
Roosevelttér
DÉLI STATION
SZÉCHENYI L.
Chain Bridge
Clark Ádám tér
Funicular
LUDWIG MUSEUM
NATIONAL GALLERY
BUDAPEST HISTORY MUSEUM
ROYAL PALACE
KELETI STATION
SYNAGOGUE MUSEUM
VIGADÓ
BOAT TRIPS
NATIONAL MUSEUM
ERZSÉBET HÍD
HYDROFOILS
CITADELLA
Gellért-hegy
SZABADSÁG HÍD
DUNA (DANUBE)
PETŐFI HÍD
15 km
0
500 m
¼ mile
North
MARGIT KÖRÚT
VÉRMEZŐ ÚT
ATTILA ÚT
BEM RAKPART
ALAGÚT U.
SZT. ISTVÁN KRT.
VÁCI ÚT
TERÉZ KRT.
BAJCSY-ZSILINSZKY ÚT
JÓZSEF ATTILA U.
KÁROLY KRT.
RÁKÓCZI ÚT
MÚZEUM KRT
KOSSUTH L. U.
BELGRÁD RAKPART
VÁMHÁZ KRT
HEGYALJA ÚT
VILLÁNYI ÚT
BUDAÖRSI ÚT
BARTÓK BÉLA ÚT
KARINTHY FRIGYES ÚT
IRINYI JÓZSEF U.
KÖZRAKTÁR U.
Ferdinand híd
Andrássy út

Budapest always was the most westernised of the Warsaw Pact capitals, and with the fall of the Iron Curtain rapidly demolished many of its communist monuments (though the Liberation Monument survives and others have been assembled in a Statue Park) and embraced capitalism. It's a place to indulge yourself in spas, Hungarian cuisine and thriving cultural life. The grey-green Danube splits the city into **Buda**, on the west bank, and **Pest** on the east. Buda is the photogenic, hilly old town, with its pastel-coloured baroque residences, gaslit cobblestone streets and hilltop palace, while Pest is the thriving, mostly 19th-century commercial centre, with the imposing riverside State Parliament building, its wide boulevards and **Vörösmarty tér**, the busy main square. Between Buda and Pest, Margit Bridge gives access to the island of **Margit**, a green oasis and venue for alfresco opera and drama in summer. Note that museums are closed on Monday.

ARRIVAL AND DEPARTURE

RAIL There are 3 major stations: **Nyugati Pályaudvar** (Western Station), ☎ 149 0115, designed in 1877 by the Eiffel firm from Paris (tourist office; accommodation; exchange); **Keleti Pályaudvar** (Eastern Station), ☎ 113 6835 (Ibusz, ☎ 122 5429; Hellas Express car-train to Thessaloniki Tues and Fri 1 June–28 Oct; accommodation; exchange; K&H Bank Mon–Fri 0815–1800, Sat 0900–1600; left luggage 24 hrs); and **Déli Pályaudvar** (Southern Station), ☎ 175 6293, electronic information system; post office with exchange services; accommodation; exchange).

Most **international trains** depart from Keleti. All three stations are fairly central, close to hotels and on the metro: KELETI and DÉLI on line 2, NYUGATI on line 3, trams 4 and 6. International services, ☎ 342 9150, international fares, ☎ 122 8035, local train information, ☎ 322 7860. Rail tickets can also be bought from the MÁV offices, ANDRÁSSY ÚT 35; Mon–Fri 0900–1800, (1 Oct to 31 March: 0900–1700), and at the stations. Information on international ticket prices: ☎ 322 8405. A rail-bus service runs between the stations, ☎ 153 2722.

✈ **Ferihegy Airport** has two terminals. For the centre, there's an extortionate taxi service or the cheap 🚌 no.93 (every 30 mins, 0530–2100) outside both terminal buildings for ERZSÉBET TÉR. Some hotels have collection services. There's also an airport minibus service which takes visitors directly to their destination, ☎ 296 8555.

INFORMATION

MONEY Only change currency in official places such as banks (**Mezibank**, BAJCSY-ZS. ÚT, 74, ☎ 131 6358).

POST AND PHONES Main **telephone office**: PETIFI SÁNDOR ÚT, 17–19, ☎ 117 5500, Mon–Fri 0800–2000, Sat–Sun 0900–1500. The main **post office** is next door to the main telephone office; 24-hr post offices near **Nyugati**, TERÉZ KÖRÚT 51, and **Keleti** stations, BAROSS TÉR 11/C. The code for Budapest is 1.

TOURS

Legenda, VIGADÓ TÉR, ☎117–2203 (Ft 2500), offer river cruises, including a video commentary and champagne. Boats leave Budapest for the charming town of **Szentendre** and follow the Danube bend to **Visegrád** and **Esztergom**. **Mahart tours**, INTERNATIONAL BOAT STATION, BELGRÁD RAKPART, ☎118 1704, run hydrofoils to **Vienna** and **Bratislava.** Book well ahead (at least 3 days).

TOURIST INFORMATION

The nationwide Tourinform tourist bureaux are an excellent source of information. **Tourinform**, SÜTI ÚT 2, ☎317 9800 (metro: Deák tér) are helpful, with multilingual staff (daily 0800–2000 Apr–Oct, 0800–1500 Nov–Mar). **Budapest Tourist Office** has a branch at Nyugati railway station (0800–2000, ☎332 0597). **Ibusz**, the former state-run Hungarian travel company, books accommodation and organises tours. The branch at VIGADÓ ÚT 6, ☎118 6466, is open Mon–Fri 0900–1700 and serves as the **Thomas Cook office**. The central office at PETŐFI TÉR 3, ☎118 5707 (metro: DEÁK TÉR or FERENCIEK TERE) is open 24 hours; branches at **Ferihegy Airport** (open 0700–2100), the **International Pier** (0700–2100) and at the **rail stations**: **Nyugati**, ☎112 3615; **Keleti**, ☎122 5429 and **Déli**, ☎155 2133 (0800–1800/2000).

PUBLIC TRANSPORT

Night lines run 2300–0500 on the most popular routes. There are also 82 km of **cycle lanes**. **Public transport information,** ☎201 9408.

Metro tickets are available from kiosks in stations or from machines requiring exact change. All tickets must be punched: on line M1 this is done on board, but on lines M2 and M3 they must be stamped in the machines at the station entrance. If you change line you need a new ticket. A one-ride fare is Ft60 and a transfer Ft100. One-day and three-day travel passes are available, as are packs of ten tickets for the price of nine. For visitors staying longer, consider weekly passes.

Metro: Fast and inexpensive; runs 0430–2310; just **three lines**, all intersecting at **DEÁK TÉR**. Line M1 was the first continental metro, built in 1896 (original carriages can be seen at DEÁK TÉR metro).

Buses, trams and **suburban trains**: For areas not on the metro, the bus, trolleybus and tram system is very useful as it covers the city extensively. A similar method for ticket stamping exists, with machines on board. Ticket inspectors wearing red armbands can fine Ft 800 on the spot. The suburban network of HÉV trains travel several kilometres out of the city boundary as well as embracing the ruins of **Aquincum** and the old town of **Óbuda**. Maps available at the metro stations cover all suburban routes.

Taxis: Abundant at all times. Remember to check that the meter is running, have the address of where you are going written down and negotiate the fare before setting off. It may be easier to use public transport. Taxis are forbidden in the castle area. Reputable firms include: **City Taxi**, ☎211 1111, and **Fi Taxi**, ☎222 2222.

The **Budapest card**, widely issued, allows free travel, admission and reductions to more than 80 sights over 3 days (Ft 2500).

ACCOMMODATION

The city offers a wide choice of one- to five-star hotels, pensions and hostels (in summer heat air-conditioned rooms are advisable). **Advance booking** is strongly recommended, particularly in early August during the Hungarian Grand Prix. Spa hotels generally offer competitive weekend packages.

Hotel Tanne in the Buda Hills is attractive and comfortable. **Buda Center** is basic but has air-conditioning and is ideally located below Castle Hill. The immaculate **Alba** is smart and efficient.

Inside the Royal Palace, **Hotel Kulturinov** is spartan but inexpensive. **Hotel Citadella** is perched on Géllert Hill. The old-fashioned **Délibáb** is a stone's throw from City Park.

Private rooms are less expensive than hotels. Rooms are usually a few stops away from the centre of town. These, as well as hotel and pension accommodation, are bookable at **Tourinform** and **Ibusz**. Outside the main offices and at railway stations, you may well find people offering private accommodation; make sure you know the price and location – usually the rooms they offer will be safe and clean, as the Hungarians are excellent hosts.

Youth hostel and **student accommodation** is plentiful. Hostel organisations advertise widely at the stations and often offer free transport to hostels. **Camping** is mainly limited to the Buda hills, accessible by bus (listed in tourist information leaflets). Camping at unregistered sites is forbidden.

HOTELS

Hotel Tanne, 2092 BUDAPEST, ESZE TAMÁS UTCA 6, ☎ 176 6144.
Buda Center, 1027 BUDAPEST, CSALOGÁNY U. 23, ☎ 201 6333.
Alba, 1011 BUDAPEST, APOR PETER UTCA 3, ☎ 175 9244.
Moderate.

Hotel Kulturinov, SZENTHÁROMSÁG TÉR 6, ☎ 155 0122.
Hotel Citadella, 1118 BUDAPEST, CITADELLA SÉTÁNY, ☎ 166 5794. .
Délibáb, 1062 BUDAPEST, DÉLIBÁB UTCA 35, ☎ 342 9301.
Cheaper.

FOOD AND DRINK

Rich, spicy and meat- or fish-based, Hungarian cuisine is delicious. Cold fruit soups make wonderful starters, followed by game, goose, pike-perch or pork dishes, goulash soup or paprika chicken, washed down with sour cherry juice, *palinka* spirit or **Tokaji aszú** wine. Budapest's elegant coffee houses offer irresistible cakes, pastries and marzipans.

HIGHLIGHTS

BUDA The Buda hills offer marvellous views of the city and the Danube. To the west lie woods and paths, circumnavigated by a cogwheel railway from **Városmajor** to **Széchenyi** hill. On **Gellért-hegy** (Gellért Hill), surveying the city and the Royal Palace, is the gigantic **Liberation Monument**, which commemorates the Soviet liberation of Budapest (nos. 27 or 127). **Várhegy** (Castle Hill) was first built in the 13th century and is the prime historic feature in Budapest; its streets have retained their medieval form. **Budavári Palota** (Buda Palace), a vast neo-baroque edifice, was originally built as part of the fortifications of the city during the Middle Ages and remained a royal residence for 700 years, but was virtually destroyed by during World War II and then rebuilt. There are three museums in the palace: **Budapest History Museum**; **Museum of Contemporary History** and **Hungarian National Gallery** (Tues–Sun 1000–1800, free concerts every Tues). Walk up the hill from DÉLI or MOSKVA metro stations, or catch the **Budavári Sikló** funicular (0730–2200 daily, Ft150) from CLARK ÁDÁM TÉR at the foot of the Chain Bridge. There is also a shuttle bus service from MOSZKVA TÉR. It's possible to visit the **Castle caverns** at the corner of DÁRDA and ORSZÁGHÁZ ÚT. (open daily).

SPAS

Budapest boasts ten spas, offering mixed and segregated bathing, endless treatments and often stunning architecture at affordable prices. Just south of Buda Palace, the art nouveau **Gellért** has a much-photographed 'champagne' bath, (KELENHEGYI ÚT 2–4, 185 3555), and nearby the **Rudas Baths** (DÖBRENTEI TÉR., 156 1322), are an amazing time warp (men only). Further north the **Király Baths** (FI UTCA 84, 202 3688) were built in the 16th century – their green cupolas are a reminder of the Turkish occupation. For further details, 117 8992 at **Tourinform**, or see the booklet *Medicinal Baths* (Hungarian National Tourist Office).

Look out for **Halász bástya** (Fisherman's Bastion), with its seven conical turrets connected by a walkway, built mainly for decoration and presents a perfect river panorama, and the nearby square (SZENTHÁROMSÁG TÉR), always filled with tourists, street entertainers and market stalls.

The **statue to St Stephen** (Szent István), legendary King of Hungary, is overlooked by the neo-Gothic **Mátyás Templom** (Matthias Church), the coronation church of Hungarian kings, and resplendent with its multicoloured roof tiles. The surrounding streets are cobbled, below fine baroque and Gothic buildings and façades. It's worth wandering down TÁNCSICS MIHÁLY UTCA, TÁRNOK UTCA, TÓTH ÁRPÁD SÉTÁNY and ÚRI UTCA to explore.

Do visit the picturesque **Margit Island** (Margit-sziget). Vehicles are only allowed as far as the Thermal and Grand hotels: the miles of walks along the river are delightful, as are the Japanese garden, open-air theatre, cinema and two 13th-century ruins (trams 1, 4, 6 or no. 26).

PEST This is the busy commercial sector, built in two semicircular avenues with broad tree-lined boulevards radiating from it, and home to the elegant shopping street VÁCI UTCA, and the street cafés of VÖRÖSMARTY TÉR, the artists' haunt. The imposing **Parliament**, KOSSUTH LAJOS TÉR, built in 1904, has a richly ornate interior and was built in 1904 in Gothic style (highly reminiscent of London's Palace of Westminster), and can be visited by pre-arranged guided tour (book through the Tourist Office).

One thousand years of Hungarian existence are commemorated by statues of rulers and princes in the **Millenary Monument** in Hisök tere (Heroes' Square). This opens onto leafy **City Park** (Városliget), with its zoo, boating lake-cum-ice rink and the romantic **Vajdahunyad vára** (Vajdahunyad castle) replicating sites from pre-Trianon Hungary and built at the end of the 19th century. Don't miss ANDRÁSSY ÚT., Budapest's most famous avenue, home of the **Opera House** (tram 22). Close by is the **Liszt Museum**, 35 VÖRÖSMARTY UTCA (open Mon–Fri 1000–1800, Sat 0900–1700), where the composer lived. There are also museums to the Hungarian composers Bartók and Kodály.

SHOPPING

The main shopping streets are VÁCI UTCA for boutiques, including **folk art** and **black ceramics** at VÁCI UTCA 14, PETIFI SÁNDOR UTCA and ANDRÁSSY UTCA. Best buys include **records** and **CDs**, Zsolnay and Herend **porcelain** (SZENTHÁROMSÁG U. 5), and **glass**, **antiques**, **wine**, Pick and Herz **salami** and **leather**. Try the **Wine Society**, BATTHYÁNYI U. 59 (Mon–Fri 1000–2000, Sat 1000–1800) and the **Hungarian Wine Shop**, RÉGIPOSTA UTCA 7–9. **Markets** abound, some open air, others flea markets (NAGYKIRÖSI ÚT. 156).

NIGHT-TIME AND EVENTS

There is always plenty for all tastes in Budapest. Check monthly listings guides and English-language newspapers such as the *Budapest Sun*, for the latest information.

Music has always been popular in Hungary. Opera, recitals and cinema shows can be checked from the *Budapest Sun*. The stunning neo-Renaissance **Opera House**, ANDRÁSSY ÚT. 22, ☎131 2550, now 112 years old, was the first modern theatre in the world (Sat–Sun 1300–1500). Operetta, too, has its place, and the less ornate building at VIGADÓ U. 2, ☎117 0869, is usually packed for patriotic programmes of light music. Seats are not reservable, so arrive in good time. Organ recitals are often given at **Matthias Church**, VÁRHEGY, and at **St Stephen's Basilica**. The **Academy of Music**, LISZT FERENC TÉR 8, ☎142 0179, and the **Vigado Concert Hall**, VIGADÓ TÉR 2, ☎118 9903, frequently host classical concerts.

Many cinemas show English-language movies. Bars are to be found all over the city; the nightclubs in the red-light area in district VII are only for the extremely broad-minded.

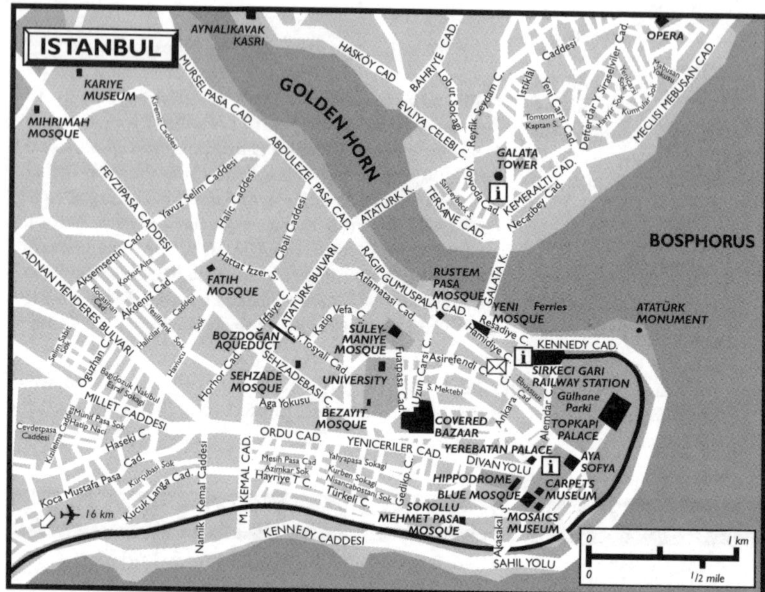

Istanbul is unique in being a city in two continents, with the Bosphorus dividing Europe from Asia. A noisy, hectic and vibrant place, and in turns beautiful and drably modern, it is full of atmosphere in its congested streets and haunting skyline of minarets and domes.

To the ancient Greeks it was Byzantium. The Emperor Constantine christened it Constantinople, relocating his capital here from Rome in AD 330. Constantinople it remained until renamed by Kemal Atatürk, father of modern Turkey, in 1923. In 1453 it fell to the Ottoman Sultan Mehmet II, and became the glittering, cosmopolitan capital of an even greater empire stretching from the Danube to the Red Sea – the city was as much Greek, Armenian and Balkan as Turkish.

The Asian side is usually called **Anadolu Yakasi**. The European side is itself split by the Golden Horn (Haliq), an inlet of the Bosphorus. Most of the historic tourist sights are in **Sultanahmet**, south of the Golden Horn. Places not to be missed include **Topkapi Palace**, **Aya Sofya museum** and the **Covered Bazaar**; also try to visit one of the mosques (such as the **Suleimaniye**) and to take a boat trip on the Bosphorus.

Nationals of Ireland, the UK and the USA need visas for Turkey; these can be obtained on entry.

TOURIST OFFICES

Main Office: 57 MESRUTIYET CAD., BEYOGLU; ☎(0212) 243 3731 or 243 2928, fax (0212) 252 4346. **Branches**: **Atatürk Airport**, ☎(0212) 663 0793; **Karakoy Maritime Station**, ☎(0212) 249 5776; **Hilton Hotel,** CUMHURIYET CAD., HARBIYE, ☎(0212) 245 6876; and **Sultanahmet Meydani;** ☎(0212) 518 8754, fax (0212) 518 1802; **Taksim Meydani Maksem**, ☎(0212) 245 6876; and **Sirkeçi Station**, ☎(0212) 511 5888. Open Mon–Sat 0900–1700, they distribute free **maps** and **guides** to Istanbul (in English) and have details on **local transport**.

The **tourist police**, ☎(0212) 527 4503 or 528 5369, can be recognised by their beige uniforms and maroon berets.

ARRIVAL AND DEPARTURE

RAIL There are two rail terminals. **Sirkeçi Station** ☎(0212) 527 0050 or 520 6575, near the waterfront at Eminönü (express tram or 10 mins. walk beside tram line to SULTANAHMET) serves trains to **Europe via Greece or Bulgaria**. The bureau de change in the station will exchange only cash, but there are others immediately outside and automatic cash dispensers in the forecourt. Rail services to **Asian Turkey** and beyond use **Haydarpasa Station** ☎(0216) 336 0475, across the Bosphorus (by ferry). Note that in **Greek rail timetables**, Istanbul is still referred to (in Greek script) as **Constantinopolis**.

Atatürk Airport, ☎(0212) 663 6400, fax (0212) 663 6250, is in **Yeşilköy**, 15 km west of Istanbul. **Buses** run every hour between Atatürk and the Marmara Hotel in TAKSIM SQ. between 0600 and 2400.

INFORMATION

MONEY

There are plenty of bureaux de change around Istanbul, especially in Sultanahmet and in the covered market. These Dövis bureaux have almost exactly the same rates. Banks usually have poor exchange rates. Traveller's cheques are difficult to cash – some banks and post offices accept them. Owing to extremely high inflation, exchange rates date rapidly, although prices stay reasonably constant in terms of Western currencies. Automatic cash dispensers are becoming more common and are convenient.

POST AND PHONES

The **main PTT office** is at 25 YENI POSTANE CAD., near Sirkeçi Station. However, there are many branches throughout Istanbul which generally have shorter queues, both for postal services and for making telephone calls. You can make **international calls** at all the major PTT offices. Pay phones require *jetons* (tokens), which come in small, medium and large sizes and can be bought from kiosks. Few pay phones seem to work. A small *jeton* should suffice for a local call; long-distance attempts require many large ones. **Card phones** are more common (cards available from PTT offices). The **dialling code** for Istanbul is 0212 (European side of the Bosphorus), or 0216 (Asian side of the Bosphorus).

PUBLIC TRANSPORT

Trams: There is one express tram line, running from **Sirkeci station** west along **DIVAN YOLU** and **MILLET CAD.**, out to the **old city walls**. Buy tickets from kiosks by the stops: place them in the metal containers at the entrance to the platforms. Istanbul's oldest trams and tramline, dating from the turn of the century, have been reprieved and refurbished, and run down the 1.2km length of ISTIKLAL CAD., the Beyoglu district's fashionable pedestrianised shopping street. They connect with the *Tünel*, a short, steep, underground railway built in 1875 to connect the hilltop avenue – then the main thoroughfare of the smart European quarter called Pera – with the warehouses and docks of the Golden Horn waterfront.

Buses: Large fleets of buses cover most of Istanbul, but routes can be confusing and there is no bus map, so ask for details at major stops or Tourist Offices. The major departure points are TAKSIM SQUARE, EMINÖNÜ (near the Galata Bridge) and BEYAZIT.

Taxis: The yellow taxis offer a simpler alternative to the buses. Fares are cheap, but ensure that the driver starts the meter when you get in. Fares double between midnight and 0600. The unique *dolmus* (communal taxis) run on set routes and cram remarkable numbers of passengers into huge, refurbished American cars or Japanese minibuses.

Ferries: These run regularly across the Bosphorus, between **Karaköy** on the European side and **Haydarpasa** and **Kadiköy**; and between **Eminönü** on the European side and **Üsküdar**. Schedules can be confusing and piers chaotic, so ask for details at the Tourist Office, or consult Thomas Cook's *Greek Island Hopping*.

Bus tickets are sold from kiosks or from street vendors and are surrendered into machines on board. Depending on the route taken, one or two tickets may be required.

ACCOMMODATION

Most **budget accommodation** lies in the *Sultanahmet* district, in the back streets between SULTANAHMET SQUARE and the water and especially in YEREBATAN CAD. There is a **youth hostel** (see right), and a collection of similarly priced **private hostels**. Although basic and often crowded, these are cheap and marvellously placed for Istanbul's main sights. There are often a few people hawking rooms to arriving rail passengers, but they are usually touting for establishments far from the centre. Make sure you know where they are and how to get there before accepting.

Most of Istanbul's **top-range hotels** congregate north of the Golden Horn around *Taksim* and *Harbiye*, rather characterless areas a considerable distance from the main sights. There are, however, plenty of hotels south of the Golden Horn, so it is possible to stay in this more atmospheric part of the city without having to rough it, with a particular concentration of hotels of all categories in **Beyazit**, **Laleli** and **Aksaray**.

Arguably the nicest hotel in Istanbul is the **Ayasofya Pansiyonlari**, a refurbished row of traditional wooden homes, prettily painted and furnished in Ottoman style, immediately behind the Aya Sofya church. Rooms cost around US$75 double. The Ayasofya has spawned a host of cheaper imitators in traditional wooden mansions: there are several in the streets just east of Aya Sofya and *Topkapi*.

A cheaper option on the other side of Sultanahmet is **Hotel Antique**, where rooms are around US$35 double.

On *Büyük Ada*, an island in the Sea of Marmara some 40 mins away by fast catamaran, is the magnificently ramshackle **Splendid Otel**, in a domed 19th-century wooden building.

There are four **campsites** around Istanbul, all a long way from the centre and offering no advantages to campers without vehicles.

HOTELS

Ayasofya Pansiyonlari, SOGUKCESME, 34400 SULTANAHMET–ISTANBUL; ☎(0212) 513 3660, fax (0212) 513 3669

Hotel Antique, K. AYASOFYA CAD., OGUL SOK NO. 17; ☎(0212) 516 4936/516 0997, fax (0212) 517 6370),

YOUTH HOSTEL

6 CAFERIYE SOK; ☎(0212) 513 6150.

FOOD AND DRINK

Istanbul's eating options are as varied and colourful as the city itself. Surprisingly, though, Sultanahmet is a restaurant desert. In the daytime, head for the **Grand Bazaar**, where there are lots of indoor and outdoor cafés, or the **Laleli** district around the university.

Located near two seas, Istanbul is naturally a great place for **seafood,** though it is relatively expensive. It's also a great place for vegetarians, with plenty of meat-free dishes and wonderful fresh fruit. The best place to eat is in **Çiçek Paşaji** (Flower Passage), off pedestrianised ISTIKLAL CAD., where a covered arcade and the alleys around it are packed with restaurant tables. The cheapest places are in the lane behind the arcade.

When you visit **Topkapi Palace**, stop at **Konyali**, ☎(0212) 513 9696, on the grounds. Lunch only – traditional fare. Two seating areas have different prices (one is self-service – no tablecloths). Breathtaking view.

HIGHLIGHTS

Memorable landmarks surround **Sultanahmet**, where the **Aya Sofya museum** and the **Blue Mosque** sit squarely opposite one another, with the **Topkapi Palace** nearby. These, with many others, create a memorable skyline, best seen from the Bosphorus at dawn, or from the top of the **Galata Tower**, north of the Golden Horn (daily 0800–2100), built in 1348 by the Genoese, and now a club and bar.

TOPKAPI

This is a sightseeing 'must', spectacular both outside and in, with glowing displays of jewels and cloth. If you see nothing else in Istanbul, see the amazing contents of *Topkapi Palace* (closed Tues), seat of the Ottoman Sultans from the 15th to the 19th centuries. The complex, at the tip of the old city peninsula, has now been converted into an all-embracing collection of the Imperial treasures, stretching through three courtyards. Allow at least a half day to take in the cream of the exhibits, which include Islamic armour, imperial robes, jewellery and precious objects, porcelain and miniatures.

AYA SOFYA Aya Sofya (closed Mon) was the largest domed structure in the world until St Peter's in Rome was built. Inside, massive marble pillars support a vaulted dome 31 m in diameter and 55 m high, and around the gallery (up the sloped flagstone walkway) are some outstanding mosaics. The interior is an uneasy mixture; the Christian frescos which adorned the dome in Byzantine times were covered by abstract patterns while Aya Sofya was a mosque; the décor that remains is an intriguing harmony of religions.

MOSQUES AND MUSEUMS Undoubtedly the most beautiful of Istanbul's many mosques is the **Suleimaniye**, built between 1550 and 1557 for Sultan Suleiman the Magnificent by his court architect Mimar Sinan. Seen from the banks of the Golden Horn, the complex of domes and spires is the most striking sight in the old city.

All mosques are open daily except during prayer times. Take your shoes off when you enter, and dress modestly.

DAY TRIP FROM ISTANBUL

Take a ferry from Sirkeci or Kabatas to the **Princes' Islands,** an archipelago of nine islands, where princes were sent into exile by paranoid Ottoman sultans. **Büyükada** is the largest, and is distinctive as it has outlawed all cars. Transport is by horse carriage. If you want a day on the beach, try **Kilyos** on the European side of the Black Sea coast. One of the most fascinating parts of the Topkapi is the extensive **Harem** area, which housed the concubines and children of the sultans, with their attendant eunuchs. The harem can only be seen on tours. Book as soon as you get to Topkapi.

West of the Blue Mosque are the remains of the **Hippodrome,** with three columns dating from the early centuries of the Byzantine era: the 4th-century Column of Constantine, the 6th-century Obelisk of Theodosius, and the bronze Serpentine Column. A few fragments of the Hippodrome wall can be seen nearby. Across from the Hippodrome, the *Ibrahim Paşa Palace* houses the **Museum of Turkish and Islamic Art** (closed Mon), including some priceless ancient Persian carpets.

On the other side of the Blue Mosque are the *Mosaic Museum* (closed Tues), with some Byzantine mosaics, and the plainly named **Turkish Carpets Museum** (closed Sun and Mon.)

The **Yeni Mosque** (meaning 'new', although built between 1597 and 1633) is unmissable to those arriving at Eminönü or crossing the *Galata Bridge*. There are a miserly two minarets here.

Some distance west of Sultanahmet, the **old city walls,**

now partially restored, stretch across the landward end of the peninsula from the Sea of Marmara to the Golden Horn. Built at the command of the 5th-century Emperor Theodosius, they protected all the land approaches to the ancient city.

The **Bosphorus strait**, leading north from the Sea of Marmara to the Black Sea, is sprinkled with impressive imperial palaces and pavilions built by a succession of sultans. The best way to see them is by boat; popular excursion trips run up to RUMELI KAVAGI and ANADOLU KAVAGI from Eminönü, pier 3. Three boats run each way Mon–Sat; on Sun and bank holidays there are five each way and prices are halved.

The most prominent palace en route – and the one not to miss – is the **Dolmabahce** (closed Mon, Thur), which has a 600 m water frontage. Built in the 19th century, this served as the final seat of the Ottoman sultans – a compromise between what the sultans thought of as modern European style and their age-old love of lavish adornment. In the enormous reception room, the 4.5 ton chandelier is supported by 56 columns and glitters with 750 bulbs. Atatürk died here in 1938.

NIGHT-TIME AND EVENTS

Istanbul's thriving nightlife is to be found in the side streets off ISTIKLAL, in the **Beyoglu** area, and in **Ortaköy**, which has a huge number of bars and restaurants, with the benefit of a Bosphorus view. At weekends, the streets are bursting with stalls selling jewellery, books and trinkets.

If you prefer to have a leisurely walk, try a **Bosphorus walk** along from **Bebek** to **Rumeli Hisari** or the ancient city walls.

The **International Arts Festival** is in June and July. Its main venues are the Cemal Resit Rey Hall, Harbiye, and the Atatürk Cultural Center, Taksim.

SHOPPING

The most famous of the markets is the **Kapali Carşi** (Covered Bazaar), Beyazit: go along DIVAN YOLU from SULTANAHMET, with around 5 km of lanes, streets and alleys. Keep moving, because you'll be pressurised to buy if you pause to browse. There are thousands of shops and stalls here, roughly grouped according to merchandise, with whole alleys selling gold, silver, brass or leather.

If you are going to buy anything, bargain: this is a sport in itself.

Akmerkez, in Etiler, is a huge modern shopping mall where you can find high quality clothing for reasonable prices. The ultimately chic shopping district is **Nisantasi**, around VALI KONAGI ST.

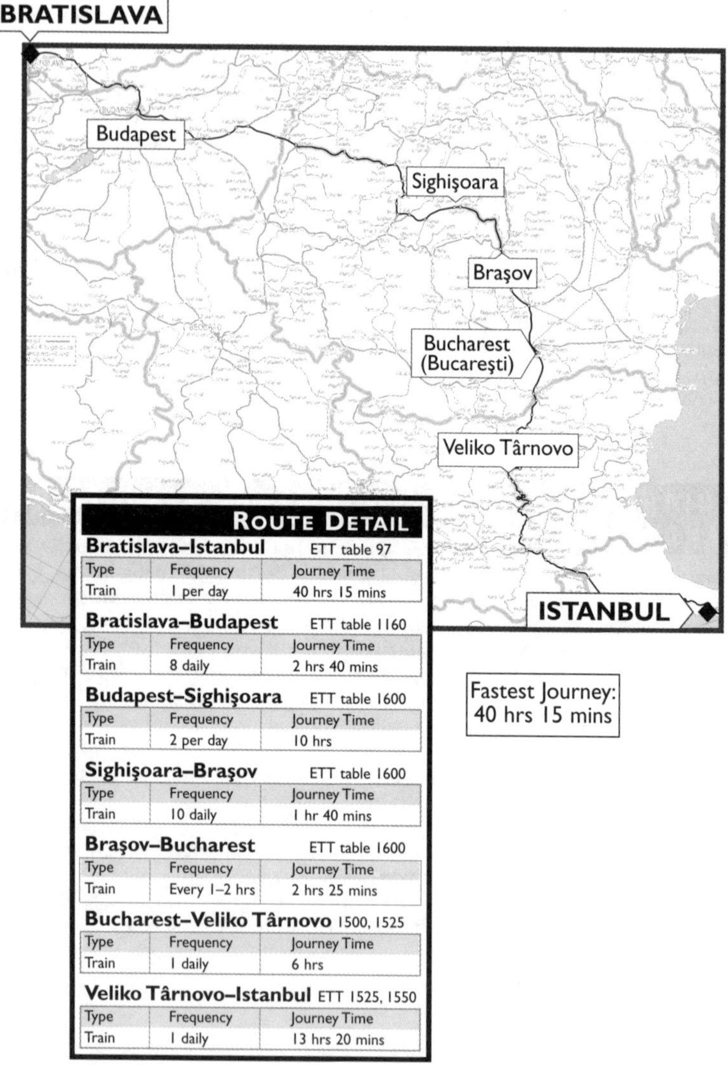

ROUTE DETAIL

Bratislava–Istanbul ETT table 97

Type	Frequency	Journey Time
Train	1 per day	40 hrs 15 mins

Bratislava–Budapest ETT table 1160

Type	Frequency	Journey Time
Train	8 daily	2 hrs 40 mins

Budapest–Sighişoara ETT table 1600

Type	Frequency	Journey Time
Train	2 per day	10 hrs

Sighişoara–Braşov ETT table 1600

Type	Frequency	Journey Time
Train	10 daily	1 hr 40 mins

Braşov–Bucharest ETT table 1600

Type	Frequency	Journey Time
Train	Every 1–2 hrs	2 hrs 25 mins

Bucharest–Veliko Târnovo 1500, 1525

Type	Frequency	Journey Time
Train	1 daily	6 hrs

Veliko Târnovo–Istanbul ETT 1525, 1550

Type	Frequency	Journey Time
Train	1 daily	13 hrs 20 mins

Fastest Journey:
40 hrs 15 mins

This winding route through Slovakia, Hungary, Bulgaria, Romania, easternmost Greece and ending in the western tip of Turkey gives a fascinating insight into parts of Eastern Europe still unfamiliar to most Westerners.

In Romania the route includes the capital, Bucharest, another rapidly changing city, beautiful old towns and stunning mountain scenery, particularly in Transylvania, one of the most colourful and multi-ethnic areas in Europe – the land of Dracula (real and legendary), with Bran Castle the must-visit Dracula sight near **Braşov**. Sit on the west side of the train (the right side, heading south) for spectacular mountain views between Braşov and the Romanian capital, **Bucharest** (itself a bit blighted by petty crime, and dominated by a charmless Communist palace, though for some it has great curiosity value). Soon after, you're into Bulgaria, where the fortified town of Veliko Târnovo is worth leaving the train for; the bus from Gorna Orjahovitza can be more convenient than the through train (buses nos 10 and 14 leaving every 20 mins or so).

Facilities in many places en route are not up to western standards yet, though they are changing fast, but tourists are still something of a novelty and get a correspondingly warm welcome.

BRATISLAVA

See p. 500.

BUDAPEST

See p. 514.

SIGHIŞOARA

Sighişoara is a wonderful Transylvanian town set in some of the most spectacular medieval fortifications you'll see anywhere. It was one of the strongholds of the Saxon community, and also has large populations of Hungarians and Gypsies.

From the commercial centre, you enter the old town by the redoubtable Clock Tower, now a history museum. Beyond this is an ancient house where Vlad the Impaler (Dracula) was reputedly born about 1431, and to the right, the 15th-century church of the Dominican monastery, PIAŢA MUZEULUI 8, is famous for its bronze baptismal fonts dating back to 1440. At the highest point of the citadel and reached by a roofed wooden stairway is the **Bergkirche** (Church on the Hill), STR. SCOLII 7, built in Gothic style 1345–1525, adorned with some remarkable frescos.

RAIL ☎(065) 77 18 86, about 1 km north of the centre. **CFR Agency**, STR. I DECEMBRIE 2, ☎(065) 77 18 20.

i **Tourist Office**: STR. I DECEMBRIE 10.

The state hotel, the **Steaua**, STR. I DECEMBRIE 12, ☎(065) 77 15 94, is the only central one; new private hotels include the **Chic**, STR. LIBERĂŢI 44, ☎77 59 01, opposite the station. **Bobby's Youth Hostel**, STR. TACHE IONESCU 18, ☎(065) 77 22 32, operates in the summer holidays only.

BRAŞOV

Baroque buildings dominate much of the centre of Romania's second city, while imposing gates guard the road into the Schei quarter to the southwest. In central PIAŢA SFATULUI (Council Square) stands the Town Hall, now the local History Museum; from its tower trumpeters sounded the warning of impending attack, by Tatars or Turks, for many centuries. Nearby, the Black Church overshadows the same square with its Gothic pinnacles. Dating from the 14th century, this is one of the greatest monuments of Transylvania's saxon (German) community, and displays historic prints and fine carpets brought by merchants from Turkey.

DAY TRIP FROM BRAŞOV

The ski resorts of **Sinaia** and **Predeal** lie on the main rail line from Bucharest to Braşov, and most trains call here, making it easy for you to break your journey. One of the best hotels in Romania, although hardly expensive, is the **Palace**, STR. OCTAVIAN GOGA 4, SINAIA, ☎ 31 20 51; there are plenty of other places to stay. **Bran Castle** has been associated by the tourist industry with **Count Dracula** and is visited by every coach tour to the area. Although there's no factual connection with Vlad the Impaler, the castle looks the part, bristling with medievalism (though it's largely renewed inside). It's 26 km from Braşov, with regular buses from **Livada Postei**, as well as tours laid on by the Tourist Office. There is a wealth of excellent private **accommodation** in Bran, easily found once you're there.

You can **get great views of the city** and surrounding mountains from the summit of **Mt Tîmpa**, reached by a cable car or by footpaths; the base of the hill is fortified with a wall and bastions.

RAIL ☎(068) 952, about 2 km north of the old town. Bus no. 4 runs from the station to PIAŢA SFATULUI and PIAŢA UNIRII in the old town. **CFR Agency**, STR. REPUBLICII 53, ☎(068) 14 29 12.

i **Tourist Office**: BLVD EROILOR 9, in the lobby of the **Hotel Carpaţi**, ☎(068) 14 11 96.

Hotels in the centre are expensive, and your best bet is either a private room (from people who meet trains at the station), or through the **EXO office**, STR. POSTĂ VARULUI 6, ☎(068) 14 27 73; or try the **Hotel Stadion**, STR. COCORULUI 12, ☎(068) 18 74 35, 100 m from the *Autocamione* bus terminal.

BUCHAREST (BUCUREŞTI)

Bucharest was once known as 'The Paris of Eastern Europe', for its decadent lifestyle and for the elegant mansions lining its 19th-century boulevards. However, the city has been vandalised over the years, above all by communist planners, perversely for many people and the city's main sight is the so-called **Ceauşescu's Palace**, now officially known as the Palace of Parliament, a huge edifice whose construction required the demolition of a quarter of the city's historic centre. BLVD UNIRII, lined with fountains and trees, leads from PIAŢA UNIRII (hub of the Metro system), which offers the major vista of the Palace. Tours of the interior start from the south door; these pass through a succession of grandiose public halls with

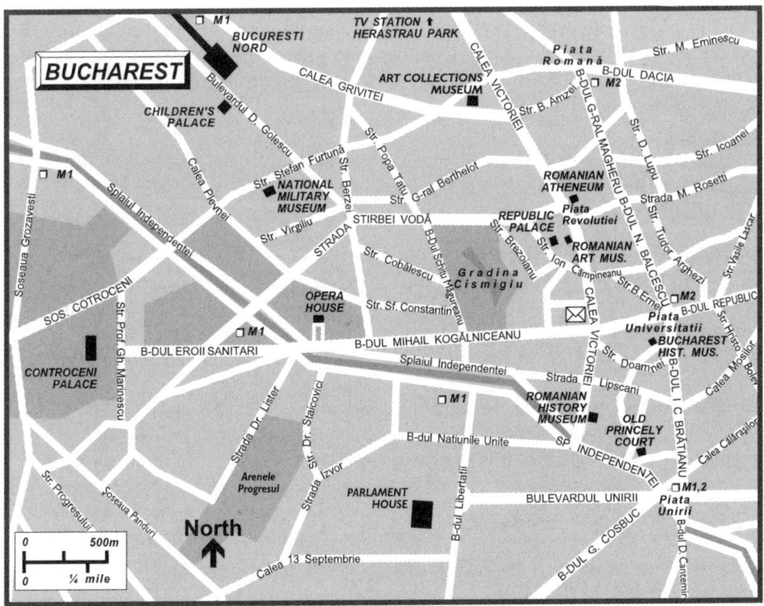

chandeliers, marble and mirrors. Its construction costs almost bankrupted the country.

Most other sights are along CALEA VICTORIEI, the historic north–south axis, which is also lined with the smartest shopping street. Near its mid-point is PIAȚA REVOLUȚIEI, scene of the most dramatic Events of Ceauşescu's overthrow during Christmas 1989; here the newly refurbished Atheneum concert hall faces the former Royal Palace, now the National Art Gallery (which may be closed for restoration). To the south along CALEA VICTORIEI, is the National History Museum, which houses Romania's finest archaeological collection and National Treasury. To the north of PIAȚA REVOLUȚIEI are the Museum of Ceramics and Glass, the Museum of Arts Collections and the George Enescu Museum of Music, all in former palaces.

The **History Museum** of Bucharest on PIAȚA UNIVERSITAP II forges some links with the legend of

DAY TRIP FROM BUCHAREST

Only 40 km from the city, lies **Snagov**, the playground of Bucharest. Imposing villas surround the attractive lake, and on an island is a monastery which probably houses the body of Vlad the Impaler, the original Dracula. Unfortunately, trains only come here at summer weekends, but buses and tours operate at other times. The Romanian Railways-owned Complex CFR Snagov Sat, ☎(0179) 40460, has rooms and camping space directly on the lake. CFR Snagov Sat, ☎(0179) 40460, has rooms and camping space directly on the lake.

Dracula, in fact the local prince **Vlad Tepeş** (Vlad the Impaler). Protests against the hijacking of the 1989 revolution by the functionaries of the communist regime were centred on PIAŢA UNIVERSITAP II. You can still see political graffiti here, as well as memorials to those killed.

To the west of the city in a pleasant leafy suburb is **Cotroceni Palace**, home of the president of Romania. There is a medieval art collection here, and occasionally concerts are held.

Bucharest has a large number of pleasant parks: to the north in the largest, Herăstrău Park, is the **Village Museum**, OS. KISSELEFF 28. This fascinating collection of re-erected buildings brought from all over the country includes churches, houses, watermills and windmills. Elsewhere, the quintessential Bucharest experience is to be had walking through backstreets, visiting the tiny Romanian Orthodox churches.

RAIL Virtually all trains use the **Gara de Nord**, northwest of the city centre on CALEA GRIVIŢEI (☎952 for **general information**). This is chaotic and crowded, and it's teeming with pickpockets. It is served by the **Metro**, although you'll have to change trains to reach the city centre. Other stations are mostly for local or seasonal trains. The **Gara de Nord** currently has the only computerised ticket office in Romania, allowing you to join any queue and buy any ticket virtually until departure time. **Tickets and reservations** can also be purchased from one to ten days in advance at **agencies** (in Bucharest at: STR. DOMNIŢA ANASTASIA 10, ☎(01) 613 26 42; and CALEA GRIVITŢEI 139, ☎(01) 650 72 47.

Otopeni, ☎(01) 212 01 38, 16 km north of the centre, handles almost all international flights. There is a good **bus service** (no. 783) to the city centre (PIAŢA UNIRII), costing about $1. **Taxis** prefer US dollars or occasionally Deutschmarks, and charge at least $25. Negotiate before you travel!

Tourist Office: **ONT-Carpati**, BLVD MAGHERU 7, ☎(01) 613 07 59 or ☎614 51 60; Metro: PIATA ROMAN, (Mon–Fri 0800–2000, Sat 0800–1500, Sun 0800–1300). There's a branch at **Otopeni Airport**, and major hotels, such as the **Intercontinental** and **Bucureşti**, also have tourist information desks. ONT-Carpati can arrange tours and car hire, book hotels and private rooms, exchange money and supply maps.

Money: Always change your money at official exchange offices or banks and keep the **receipts**, as the more expensive hotels may require proof of legitimate exchange.

Post and phones: The main telephone and post office, CALEA VICTORIEI 37, is around the corner from the *poste restante* office at STR. MATEI MILLO 10.

The **metro** is efficient and fast, linking central Bucharest to the **Gara de Nord** and the **suburbs**. There are three main lines and most city maps carry a metro plan. **Magnetic tickets** (for a minimum of two trips) must be bought as you enter a station and passed through a turnstile.

Buses, trams and **trolley-buses** run throughout the city, although it can be hard to work out their routes, as maps are rare. They are rundown and crowded, but very cheap. Buy any number of tickets before boarding from the **grey kiosks** by most stops. **Express buses**, including those to the airports, require special magnetic tickets.

Taxis are plentiful and inexpensive by Western standards. State-run cabs should have and use meters, but this is unlikely with the private ones; **agree on a price** before travelling. These cars may also be old and in poor condition. You may prefer to phone ☎953 to order a cab; waiting time is usually 5–10 mins. Have a **street map** to hand and show the driver exactly where you want to go.

ONT can arrange both hotel and private rooms, for a hefty commission. Private rooms usually come with breakfast, but check first. Expect to pay US$15 (in dollars) a night for a double. Some hosts will also offer an evening meal, for about US$5. You may be offered a room by a tout at the Gara de Nord, but you should be very careful, as these will often be in outlying suburbs and of very poor standard. Hot water may only be available morning and evening, or less frequently, and even cold water may be cut off at times.

Hotels are more central and have fewer problems with water supply, and those around the Gara de Nord are barely more expensive than those in the rest of the country. The cheapest of these is the Griviţa followed by the Dunărea and Cerna; the best in the area is the Astoria. Nearer the city centre, the best hotels in the budget price range are the **Veneţia,** and **Strada C;** the **Hanul lui Manuc** costs remarkably little and is one of the most attractive hotels in the country, a former *caravanserai*. Good central hotels that match Western standards include the Ambasador, the Capitol, and Dorobanţi,

There are no convenient **campsites** near Bucharest; **student hostels** can be used during the summer holidays; the most convenient is at the N. Balescu Agronomic Institute on BLVD MĂRĂŞTI (no. 105 from the Gara de Nord, or tram 41/42 from the centre). There's also a youth hostel, Villa Helga, (no. 785 east from STR. ŞTEFAN FURTUNŞĂ near the Gara de Nord, trams 5 or 16 from the centre).

HOTELS

Veneţia, PIAŢA KOG, INICEANU 2, ☎615 91 48.
Ambasador, BLVD MAGHERU 10, ☎615 90 80.
Capitol, CALEA VICTORIEI 29, ☎615 80 30.
Dorobanţi, CALEA DOROBANŢILOR 1, ☎211 54 90. Expensive.

Astoria, BLVD GOLESCU 27, ☎637 73 36. Moderate.

Griviţa, CALEA GRIVIŢA 130, ☎(01) 650 23 27.
Dunărea, at CALEA GRIVIŢA 140, ☎(01) 22 98 20.
Cerna, BLVD GOLESCU 29, ☎637 40 87. All cheaper.

HOSTELS

N. Balescu Agronomic Institute, BLVD MĂRĂŞTI.
Villa Helga, STR. SALCIMILOR 2, ☎610 22 14.

You can afford to eat well in Bucharest, or opt for pizzas/hamburgers, or patisseries/cafés. *Panipat* is a chain of good if pricey takeaway bunshops, found all over the city. The area around PIAŢA UNIVERSITĂTII has several cafés frequented by students and young people.

WHERE NEXT FROM BUCHAREST?

About 260 km east of Bucharest, (2 hrs 30 mins by train, ETT table 1670; book ahead in summer), ***Constanţa*** *on the Black Sea coast is a long-standing port dating from the 6th century* BC *(an excellent collection of Roman statues and mosaics, plus a display on the exiled poet Ovid in its archaeology museum), with a pleasant waterfront graced by 19th-century buildings, an elegant promenade and a casino. There's ready access to sandy beaches and a choice of resorts. Costinesti and Neptun are the favoured beaches for young Romanians, and these have the liveliest discos and nightlife.*

NIGHTLIFE English-language newspapers and magazines, distributed free in the better hotels, list what's on. Discos include **Vox Maris**, CALEA VICTORIEI 155; **Why Not?** STR. TURTURELELOR 11; and **Martins**, BLVD IANCU DE HUNEDCARA 61. Bars such as **Sidneys**, PIATA VICTOREI 224 and the **Dubliner Irish Pub**, BLVD N. TITULESCU 18 are also very popular. There are no language difficulties at classical music concerts or the **Opera**, BLVD REGINA ELISABETA 70 (Metro: EROILOR). Many films are shown in English, for example at the **Cinematheca**, STR. EFORIE 2; there's live jazz in the bar here at weekends, and also at the **Green Hours Bar**, CALEA VICTORIEI 120.

VELIKO TÂRNOVO

Former capital 1185–1393, this spectacular fortified medieval town perches on three steep hills above the River Yantra. At the heart of its enchanting historic district the hilltop ruin of **Tsarevets** (Tsar's Castle), floodlit at night, was the royal and patriarchal centre of the town. Beside the river, the **Samvodska Charsiya** (Bazaar District) is a pretty quarter of workhops and cafés, though it has lost much of the bustle of an old bazaar nowadays.

RAIL Both rail and bus stations are inconvenient. From the rail station (2 km out) take bus no 4; from the bus station (4 km out) take bus no 12.

Often booked up as the town is popular with Bulgarians. The **Hotel Itur**, UL, IVAILO 2, ☎2 68 61, is reasonable and houses the **Tourist Office** ☎(062) 24 195.

WHERE NEXT FROM VELIKO TÂRNOVO?

Tulovo, south of Veliko Târnovo, is served by trains to Plovdiv and Sofia – the latter a particularly scenic journey through the mountains; both places are on the Athens–Plovdiv route *(p. 533)**.*

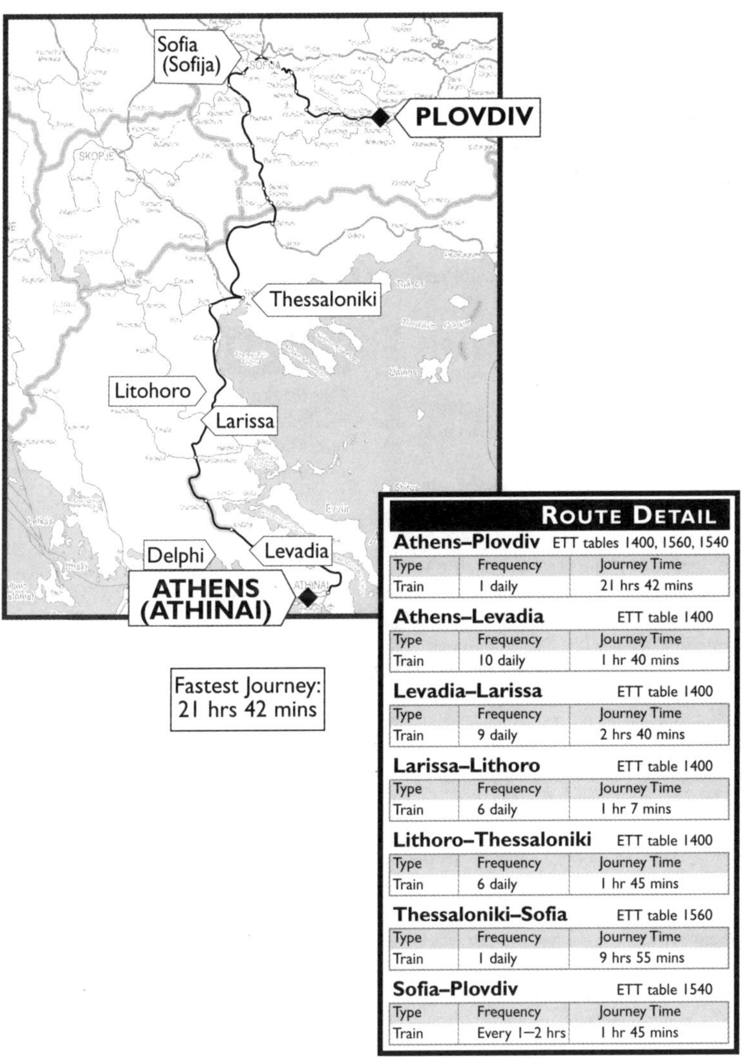

Fastest Journey:
21 hrs 42 mins

ROUTE DETAIL

Athens–Plovdiv ETT tables 1400, 1560, 1540

Type	Frequency	Journey Time
Train	1 daily	21 hrs 42 mins

Athens–Levadia ETT table 1400

Type	Frequency	Journey Time
Train	10 daily	1 hr 40 mins

Levadia–Larissa ETT table 1400

Type	Frequency	Journey Time
Train	9 daily	2 hrs 40 mins

Larissa–Lithoro ETT table 1400

Type	Frequency	Journey Time
Train	6 daily	1 hr 7 mins

Lithoro–Thessaloniki ETT table 1400

Type	Frequency	Journey Time
Train	6 daily	1 hr 45 mins

Thessaloniki–Sofia ETT table 1560

Type	Frequency	Journey Time
Train	1 daily	9 hrs 55 mins

Sofia–Plovdiv ETT table 1540

Type	Frequency	Journey Time
Train	Every 1–2 hrs	1 hr 45 mins

Athens – Thessaloniki – Plovdiv

From **Plovdiv**, you can head east to join the **Bratislava–Istanbul** route (p. 526).

It's worth allocating time to take some of the diversions from the main route. North of **Athens**, the towns on the railway tend to be modern and unprepossessing, but nearby are some of the most wonderful ancient sites in Greece, including **Delphi**, near **Levadia** (itself a town in the cornfields of the Thessalian plain) and the extraordinary **Meteora** monasteries perched on crags beneath mountains near **Larissa**. Near **Litohoro** rises **Mt Olympus**, marking the border between **Thessaly** and **Macedonia**, and its lofty summit, a demanding two-day hike. Beyond **Thessaloniki** (worth a stop for its archaeology museum), the route enters Bulgaria, passing through its fast-changing capital, **Sofia**, and ending at **Plovdiv**, its more appealing second city.

Day Trip from Levadia

Delphi (buses from Levadia and Athens) is synonymous with its Oracle, the greatest spiritual power in ancient Greece, said to be situated over the centre of the world. This belief was aided by leaking volcanic gases which induced lightheadedness and trance-like stupors. People came from far and wide to seek wisdom; prophecies were given so ambiguously that they could never be proved wrong. The most dramatic aspect of the **Temple of Apollo** (the Oracle), however, is its location, perched on the cliffs of **Mt Parnassus** and reached by the paved, zigzagging **Sacred Way**. Delphi is one of the largest remaining ancient sites in Greece, with a host of other ruins, notably a **Stadium** and an **Amphitheatre**. The famous bronze of a charioteer is among many beautiful artefacts in the outstanding **Delphi Museum**. Thousands of visitors make for Delphi, so come early (or out of season). **Accommodation** is a frequent problem: in high season hotels and pensions are often full, while many of them are closed off season. The **Stadion Hotel**, ☎(0265) 82 251, just up from the tourist office, has great views. **Tourist office**: Pavlou St, ☎(0265) 82 900. Open Mon–Fri 0800–1430.

LEVADIA

Overlooked by a 14th-century sandstone castle tower, the modern town is a common stopping point for travellers en route to Delphi, 56 km west. In ancient times those heading to the Oracle at Delphi could stop at Levadia's Oracle of Zeus Trofonios on top of **Profitis Ilias**, one of the two hills overlooking the town, on which the **castle** now stands.

RAIL ☎(0261) 28 661, 3 km from the centre, but **taxis** are available.

i **Tourist Police**: ☎(0261) 28 551.

LARISSA

Larissa is the starting point for some outstanding day trips (see opposite page).

RAIL ☎(041) 236 250, 1 km from the centre of the town.

i **Tourist office**: **EOT**, 18 Koumoundourou St. ☎(041) 250 919. **Tourist Police**: 86 Papanastasiou St. ☎(041) 623 158.

LITOHORO

Litohoro is the access point for **Mt Olympus** (2917 m), home of the ancient gods: it actually has nine peaks. You don't need any special equipment (other than suitable footwear) for the full ascent, but it does demand real fitness and takes two days – and treat it with respect, as more people die here than on any other Greek mountain. Book a bunk in one of the mountain refuge dormitories (hot meals and drinks available) through the EOS office. Getting to the top involves taking a taxi or hitching a lift to the car park 6 km from Litohoro, at the 1000 m level; then hiking through wooded ravines to the refuge at around 2000 m. It is best to spend the night here before making the demanding trek to the tops. The final 100 m traverse to **Mitikas**, the highest peak, requires strong nerves.

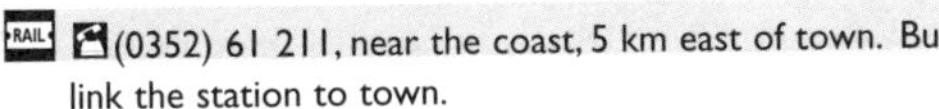

RAIL (0352) 61 211, near the coast, 5 km east of town. Buses link the station to town.

Tourist Office: ODOS AG. NICOLAOU 15, (0352) 83 100/84 701/81 111 (in the Town Hall), plus mountain refuges in Litohozo – **Olympus**, ZOLOTES 81 800, **Szavzis**. (0352) 84 519/093/293 511 **Kazalos** 83 442. Open Mon–Sat 0900–1400, 1700–2100, Sun 0900–1400. The **youth hostel**, 2 ENIPEOS ST, SEO, (0352) 84 200, has information on the various climbs. More reliable information is available from the **Greek Alpine Club (EOS) office**, KENTRIKI PLATIA, 60200 LITOHORO, (0352) 84 544. **Police**: (0352) 81 100

DAY TRIP FROM LITOHORO

Dion: This is a comparatively uncrowded archaeological site, not as spectacular as the likes of Delphi but still impressive. There are several **buses** daily from Litohoro village and station to Dion village, 8 km north of Litohoro and 2 km west of the site. Highlights are the **marble** and **mosaic floors**, the **Sanctuary of Isis**, the extensive **public bath complex**, and a length of the **paved road** which led to Olympus. The **museum**, in the centre of the village, has a fine collection of finds from the site.

DAY TRIPS FROM LARISSA

Volos: Apart from the waterfront **Archaeological Museum** there's little of note in this ugly industrial port (where Jason set sail in the Argo in search of the Golden Fleece), but it's the main base from which to explore the lush forests and charming old villages of the mountainous **Pilion peninsula** to the east (best done by hired car, or take either of two bus routes from Volos); or you can take a ferry to the **Sporades islands** (of which **Skiathos** is the most beautiful and most touristy). There are **trains** every 1–2 hrs from Larissa, taking about 1 hr. **Station**: ODOS PAPADIAMANDIS, (0421) 24 056, **bus station info**, (0421) 25 527. **EOT Office**: PLATIA RIGA FEREOU, (0421) 36 233, fax: (0421) 24 750. **Tourist Police**: 217 ODOS ALEXANDRAS, (0421) 72 421.

Kalambaka and the **Meteora monasteries**: The major tourist attraction in northern Greece, **Meteora**, is reached by **bus** from Kalambáka, to which there are five **trains** a day from Larissa, with a change in **Paleofarsalos**. The journey takes about 2 hrs 30 mins. Paleofarsalos is on the main rail route between **Athens** and **Salonika**, if you want to visit Meteora without going to Larissa.

THESSALONIKI (SALONIKA)

The second largest city in Greece was founded in 315 BC; many of the interesting sights are within 10–15 mins walk of the Tourist Office. The old town was destroyed by fire in 1917 and suffered a severe earthquake in 1978. Thessaloniki today is a modern, busy city, laid out along a crescent bay – yet it's a worthwhile place to stop over, with some elegant corners and a lively night scene. A good area to eat and go out at night is **Ladadika**.

Buses cover the city comprehensively. Buy bus tickets from the conductor, who sits at the rear.

Thessaloniki (Salonika) became strategically vital to the romans, straddling the Via Egnatia, their highway between Constantinople and the Adriatic, and later to the Byzantines and their Turkish conquerors. It was one of the greatest cities of the Ottoman Empire, rejoining Greece only in 1913.

A **Museum of Byzantine Art and History** is housed in the White Tower, the most prominent surviving bastion of the Byzantine-Turkish city walls. Opposite, the **Archaeological Museum** – the **city's top sight** – houses the contents of Macedonian Royal Tombs discovered at **Vergina** in 1977. The **Folklore Museum**, VASSILISSIS OLGAS 68, has a fine series of exhibits on the vanished folkways of northern Greece. The city's Roman heritage includes remains of the **Forum**, ODOS FILIPOU, the **Palace of Galerius**, PLATIA NAVARINOU, the **Baths**, next to **Agios Dimitrios church**, and the **Arch of Galerius**, beside ODOS EGNATIA, near PLATIA SINTRIVANIOU. The city also has a fine collection of Byzantine churches the most notable of which are **Agios Georgios** and the restored 4th-century **Agios Dimitrios rotunda.**

RAIL (031) 517 517, 1 km west of town centre. no. 3 from the station to the centre, via PLATIA ARISTOTELOUS.

i **Tourist Office**, 34 MITROPOLEOS ST., (031) 271 888 or 222 935, fax: (031) 265 504 (Mon–Fri 0800–2000 and Sat 0830–1400). **Information desk** at the station. **Tourist Police**: ODOS DODEKANISSOU, near PLATIA DIMOKRATIAS, (031) 554 870/554 871.
Main post office: 26 ARISTOTELOUS ST., (031) 268 954. **Phone office**: 27 KAROLOU ST. (ERMOU ST.).

Accommodation: The cheaper D and E class hotels mostly cluster along EGNATIA ST. – the continuation of MONASTIRIOU ST., east of the station. There's a fairly central **youth hostel**: 44 AL. SVOLOU ST., (031) 225 946.

SOFIA (SOFIJA)

When Bulgaria was liberated from the Turks in 1878, Sofia became its capital but is one of the least known capitals in Europe. Traces of Thracians, Romans, Byzantines, Slavs and Ottoman Turks can all be seen here, although Sofia nowadays is a lively, changing city with many new cafés, bars, restaurants and small family-run hotels.

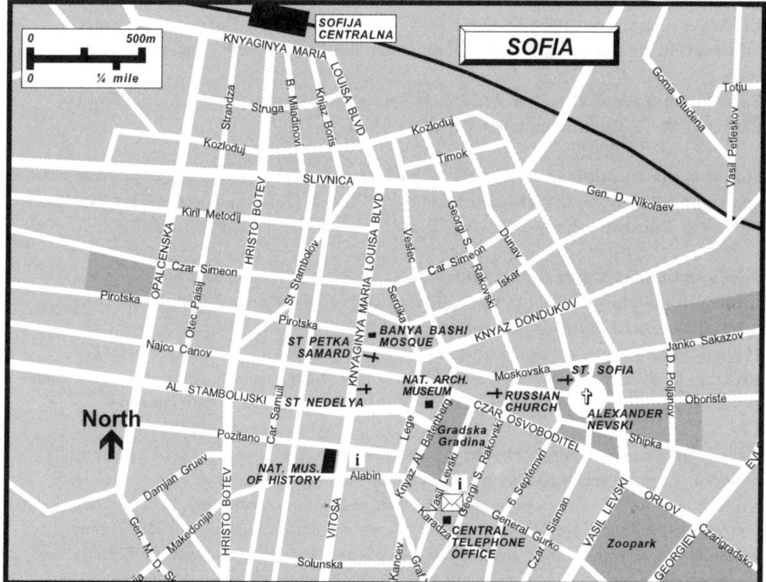

Its excellent museums, art galleries and concerts, and the proximity of **Mt Vitosha** (about 30 mins from the centre by public transport) deserve a visit.

The **Alexander Nevski Memorial Church**, with its neo-Byzantine golden domes dominating the skyline, is the most photographed image of Sofia: don't miss the superb collection of Bulgarian icons in its crypt. Nearby, the tiny **Russian Church** is an exuberant, vividly decorated gem, its gold domes contrasting with its emerald-green spire.

If you only have time for one museum, visit the **National History Museum** which has the richest collection, including fabulous Thracian gold treasures. In the foothills of Mount Vitosha, **Boyana Church**, with its sophisticated 13th-century frescos, is on UNESCO's World Heritage list.

NIGHT-TIME Some clubs and discos are expensive and aimed at businessmen, but others are for students and young people. There is live music at **Swingin Hall**, 8 DRAGAN TSANKOV; **Cocaracha**, 10 LEGUE ST.; and **Funky's Pub**, 24A SHANDOR PETYOFI. Discos include **Chervilo, Army Club**, TSAR OSVOBODITEL BLVD.; **Bibliotekata**, under the National Library; **Nero,** at the National Palace of Culture; and near the University, **Yalta** and the gay club **Spartacus**. Good pubs include **Beer Hall Schweik,** 1A VITOSHA BLVD.; **Jazz Café,** 13 GRAF IGNATIEV ST.; and **Luciano Rock Café,** at the corner of LEVSKI BLVD. and GURKO ST. Cinemas are inexpensive and show current films in the original language, with subtitles.

Central rail station, (02) 31 111; 1.5 km north of the centre. **Buses, taxis, tourist information, currency exchange**. Be extra cautious here, as petty crime is not uncommon.

Sofia International, (02) 88 44 33, is 11 km from the centre. **International flights** (02) 72 06 72; **domestic flights** (02) 72 24 14.

National Information and Advertising Centre, 1 SV. SOFIA ST., (02) 987 97 78, is a useful first stop for information. **Tickets** are sold by the **Travel Centre**, underneath the **National Palace of Culture,** 1 BULGARIA SQUARE. Expect to pay for printed information.

Post and phones: **Central Post Office**: 2 GURKO ST, opposite the **Rila** agency. **International phone calls** can be dialled directly from the **Central Telephone Office** on STEFAN KARADZA ST., diagonally behind the post office.
Money: Some bureaux de change open 24 hrs on VITOSHA BLVD, and there are plenty of exchange facilities in the central station. Bureaux may give a better deal than banks (but check rates/commission). Changing money on the street is risky and should be avoided.

Central Sofia is fairly compact and most areas of interest can be reached on foot. Good network of **trams, trolleybuses** and **buses**; stops display the routes of each service using them. Buy **tickets** from kiosks or street vendors near stops. A **one-day pass** is good value if you are planning more than three rides, but tickets are extremely cheap anyway. **Trams** (nos.1/7) run from the station along KNYAGINYA MARIA LOUISA BLVD and VITOSHA BLVD through the town centre.

Various agencies offer accommodation booking, information and exchange facilities. **Balkan Travel** has branches at the airport (02) 72 01 57, and at 7 SUBORNA ST (02) 89 98 77. **Balkantourist** is at 1 VITOSHA BLVD; (02) 43 331. Information on **youth hostels** and **hiking** is handled by **Pirintourist**, 12 POSITANO, (02) 87 06 87. **Rila**, 5 GURKO ST, (02) 87 07 77, can also make **international train reservations** and sell **tickets**. Holders of **ISIC cards** can often get discounts. **Private rooms** are good value (£10–£15 per person in a twin-bedded room), as are the many small **family-run hotels** in the foothills of **Mount Vitosha** at **Simeonovo** and **Dragalevtsi**.

WHERE NEXT FROM SOFIA?

Join the ***Bratislava–Istanbul*** *route by taking the train east to* ***Tulovo*** *(ETT table 1520).*

Sofia's restaurants have increased in number and quality, but prices (for foreign visitors) remain low. Side streets off VITOSHA BLVD, particularly to the east, have a mixture of western fast-food outlets and **Bulgarian, Italian, Chinese** and **Indian** restaurants. In the foothills of **Mount Vitosha** are several traditional style **taverns** serving **local specialities**. Some of the more popular restaurants need to be booked ahead. Bulgarian food is generally the best value, and good, but moderately priced. Pizza restaurants are very popular, some of which are excellent. **Street kiosks** have excellent coffee, very cheap fast food, sandwiches, cakes, pastries, nuts and seasonal offerings like corn on the cob.

PLOVDIV

Plovdiv (**Philippopolis** to the Macedonians and **Trimontium** to the Romans) was described by Lucian in the 2nd century AD as 'the largest and most beautiful of all cities in Thrace'. The unification of Bulgaria was announced here in 1885: Sofia became capital of the unified state and Plovdiv's influence slowly declined. As Bulgaria's second city, Plovdiv has uninspiring suburbs of industrial buildings and tower blocks, but the characterful **Old Town** is a different world, with coarsely cobbled streets full of National Revival period houses and dotted with Roman remains: it has a charm that Sofia lacks.

Buses and trolleybuses run throughout Plovdiv, but much of the hilly **Old Town** is only accessible on foot. It's a 10–15 mins walk north-east along tree-lined IVAN VAZOV ST., diagonally across from the station, to the central square. Here you will find **Hotel Trimontium** and the main **post office** and telephone building. TSAR BORIS III OBEDINITEL ST., the pedestrianised main street, leads north towards the Old Town.

ETHNOGRAPHIC MUSEUM

Don't miss the Ethnographic Museum, Argit Koyumdjioglu House, with its wonderful wooden ceilings and interior; it also has interesting local history exhibits.

Archaeological finds date Plovdiv to around 4000 BC, and the city was occupied by Thracians and Macedonians before the Romans took over in 72 BC. Remains of Trimontium, the city of the three hills, include the partially restored 2nd-century marble **Roman Theatre**, one of Bulgaria's most notable archaeological sites. The remains of the **Roman Forum**, including marble floors, can be seen in the central square near Hotel Trimontium.

The city's most important contribution to recent Bulgarian culture is the National Revival period house. This refers not to a single house, but to many, scattered around the Old Town: The **Balabanov House** now hosts recitals and exhibits works by contemporary Bulgarian painters.

RAIL (032) 22 27 29, about 1 km south-west of the centre on HRISTO BOTEV BLVD. No exchange facilities. The city's two **bus stations** are immediately to the east.

i **Puldin Tours** is at 34 MOSKVA BLVD (032) 55 28 07. **Hotel Trimontium**, (032) 23 491, in the central square, is helpful with **tourist information** and sells reasonable **city maps** (0700–2200). The **Hotel Bulgaria**, EVTIMI ST., (032) 22 55 64, also has **maps**.

Puldin Tours at 34 MOSKVA BLVD arrange **private rooms**. Other commercial **accommodation agencies** operate along TSAR BORIS III OBEDINITEL ST. Plovdiv has six major hotels, but even the cheaper ones cost more than a private room. You may also find locals offering **private accommodation**.

WHERE NEXT FROM PLOVDIV?

*Join the **Bratislava–Istanbul** route by taking the train east to **Tulovo** (ETT table 1520).*

Abbreviations

IR	Inter-Rail Pass
EP	Eurail Pass
ED	Euro Domino Pass
Eu	Europass
Aus	Australia
Can	Canada
Ire	Republic of Ireland
SA	South Africa
NZ	New Zealand
UK	United Kingdom
USA	United States of America

Austria

Capital	**Vienna** (Wien).
Climate	Moderate Continental climate. Warm summer; high winter snowfall.
Customs allowances	EU nationals may import tax and duty paid items for personal use. Non-EU residents from outside Europe: 200 cigarettes or 50 cigars or 250g tobacco, 1 litre spirits and 2 litres wine or 3 litres beer plus other commodities to a value of ÖS2500 (ÖS1000 from the Czech or Slovak Republics or Slovenia).
Embassies in Vienna	**Aus**: Mattiellistr. 2-4, ☎512 85 80. **Ire**: Hilton Center, Landstr./ Hauptstr. 2, ☎715 4246. **SA**: Sandg. 33, ☎326 493. **UK**: Jauresg. 12: ☎716 13-0. **USA**: Botzmanng. 16, ☎313 39-0.
Embassies overseas	**Aus**: 12 Talbot St, Forrest, ACT 2603, Canberra ☎(62) 951376. **Can**: 445 Wilbrod St, Ottawa, Ontario KIN 6M7, ☎789 1444. **Ire**: 15 Ailesbury Court Apts, 93 Ailesbury Rd, Dublin 4, ☎(1) 2694577. **SA**: 1109 Duncan St, Momentum Office Park, 0011 Brooklyn, Pretoria, ☎(12) 463361. **UK**: 18 Belgrave Mews West, London SW1X 8HU, ☎(020) 7235 3731. **USA**: 3524 International Court N.W., Washington DC 20008, ☎(202) 895 6700.
Language	**German**; English is widely spoken in tourist areas.
Currency	**Schilling** (ÖS); 1 Schilling = 100 Groschen.
Opening hours	**Banks**: mostly Mon, Tues, Wed, Fri 0800–1230 and 1330–1500, Thur 0800–1230 and 1330–1730. **Shops**: Mon–Fri 0800–1830, Sat 0800–1300 (in larger towns often until 1700 on Sat). **Museums**: check locally.
Post offices	Indicated by golden horn symbol; all handle poste restante *(postlagernde Briefe)*. Open mostly Mon–Fri 0800–1200 and 1400–1800. Stamps *(Briefmarke)* also sold at Tabak/Trafik shops.
Public holidays	1, 6 Jan; Easter Mon; 1 May; Ascension Day; Whit Mon; Corpus Christi; 15 Aug; 26 Oct; 1 Nov; 8, 25, 26 Dec. Many people take unofficial holidays on Good Fri, Easter Sun, Whit Sun, 2 Nov, 24 Dec and 31 Dec.
Public transport	Long-distance: bus system run by Bundesbus; usually based by rail stations/ post offices. City transport: tickets cheaper from Tabak/Trafik booths; taxis: metered; extra charges for luggage (fixed charges in smaller towns).
Rail travel	Run by Österreichische Bundesbahnen (ÖBB); ☎(00) 43 1 1717 (Vienna 24 hrs). Mostly electrified; fast and reliable, with IC trains every 1–2 hrs and regional trains connecting with IC services. Other fast trains: D (ordinary express trains); E (semi-fast or local trains); EC and EN (with stops only in larger cities). Most overnight trains have sleeping-cars (up to three berths) and couchettes (four or six berths), plus 2nd-class seats. Seat reservations: 2nd class ÖS30, 1st class free. Most stations have left luggage facilities.
Rail passes	IR, ED, EP valid (p. 23–28). Visitor Card: unlimited travel on local transport, discounted museum entry; Vienna (ÖS210; 3 days), Salzburg (ÖS290; 2 days), Innsbruck (ÖS230; 1 day). 1-Plus Ticket: 2–5 persons; journey over 101 km; 25–40% discount. Das Gruppen: 6 or more persons; discounts of 30–40%.
Telephones	Cheapest to phone long distance 1800–0800 and public holidays. Dial in: ☎ 00 43. Outgoing: ☎00. International enquiries and operator: ☎08. National enquiries and operator: ☎1611. Police: ☎133; Fire: ☎122; Ambulance: ☎144.
Tourist information	Staff invariably speak some English. Opening times vary widely, particularly restricted at weekends in smaller places. Look for green 'i' sign; usually called a *Fremdenverkehrsbüro*.
Tourist offices overseas	**Aus**: 1st Floor, 36 Carrington St, Sydney NSW 2000, ☎(2) 9299 3621.

Can: 2 Bloor St E./Suite 3330, Toronto, Ontario M4W 1A8, ☎(416) 9673381. **SA**: Private Bag X18, Parklands 2121 Jo'burg, ☎(11) 4427235. **UK**: National Tourist Office and Railways, PO Box 2363, London W1A 2QB, ☎(020) 7629 0461. **USA**: National Tourist Office, PO Box 1142 New York NY 10108–1142, ☎(212) 944 6880.

VISAS — An EU National Identity Card is sufficient. Visas are not needed by nationals of Australia, Canada, New Zealand or the USA.

BELGIUM

CAPITAL — **Brussels** (Bruxelles/Brussel)

CLIMATE — Rain prevalent at any time; warm summers, cold winters (often with snow).

CURRENCY — **Belgian Francs** (BFr.)

CUSTOMS ALLOWANCES — Standard EU regulations apply (see p. 17–18).

EMBASSIES IN BRUSSELS — **Aus**: r. Guimard 6, ☎: 231 05 00. **Can**: av. de Tervuren 2, ☎735 60 40. **Ire**: r. du Luxembourg 19, ☎513 66 33. **NZ**: blvd du Régent 47, 512 10 40. **SA**: 26 r. de la Loi, ☎230 68 45. **UK**: r. Arlen 85, ☎287 62 11. **USA**: blvd du Régent 27, ☎513 38 30.

EMBASSIES OVERSEAS — **Aus**: 19 Arkana St, Yarralumla, Canberra, ACT 2600, ☎ (06) 273 2501. **Can**: 80 Elgin St, Ottawa, Ontario K1P 1B7, ☎(613) 236 7267 **NZ**: Willis Coroon House, 1–3 Willeston St, Wellington, ☎(04) 472 9558. **SA**: 625 Leyds St, Muckleneuk, 0002 Pretoria, ☎(012) 44 3201. **UK**: 103-105 Eaton Sq., Victoria, London SW1W 9AB, ☎(020) 7470 3700. **USA**: 3330 Garfield St N.W., Washington DC 20008, ☎(202) 333-6900.

LANGUAGE — **Flemish** (north), **French** (south) and **German** (east). Most speak both French and Flemish, plus often English and/or German.

OPENING HOURS — Many establishments close 1200–1400. **Banks**: Mon–Fri 0900–1600. **Shops**: Mon–Sat 0900/1000–1800/1900 (often later Fri/Sat). Museums: vary, but most open six days a week: 1000–1700 (usually Tues–Sun or Wed–Mon).

POST OFFICES — *(Postes/Posterijen/De Post)* open Mon–Fri 0900–1700 (some also open Fri evening and Sat morning). Stamps sold by postcard vendors.

PUBLIC HOLIDAYS — 1 Jan; Easter Mon; 1 May; Ascension Day; Whit Mon; 21 July; 15 Aug; 1, 11 Nov; 25 Dec. Transport and places that open usually keep Sun times.

PUBLIC TRANSPORT — National bus companies: De Lijn (Flemish areas), Tec (French areas); few long-distance buses. Buses, trams and metros: board at any door with ticket or buy ticket from driver. Fares depend on length of journeys. Tram and bus stops: red and white signs (all request stop – raise your hand). Taxis seldom stop in the street, so find a rank or phone; double rates outside city limits.

RAIL TRAVEL — SNCB (French) or NMBS (Flemish). SNCB/NMBS Information/Motorail, Blackfriars Foundry, 156 Blackfriars Rd, London E1 8EN, ☎0171 593 2332 (Mon–Fri 0900–1700). Rail information offices: 'B' in an oval logo. Sleeping-cars/couchettes available. Seat reservations for international journeys only. Refreshments not always available. Some platforms serve more than one train at a time; check carefully. Left luggage and cycle hire at many stations. Timetables usually in two sets: Mon–Fri and weekends/holidays.

RAIL PASSES — IR, EP, ED, Benelux Tourrail Pass valid (p. 23–28). Reductie Kaart: BFr.600; half price tickets for one month. Weekend Ticket: 40% discount on return ticket anywhere in Belgium, maximum fare BFr.700; valid for 4 days.

TELEPHONES — Phonecards sold at rail stations, post offices, some tobacconists. Most international calls cheaper Mon–Sat 2000–0800, all day Sun. Dial in: ☎00 32. Outgoing: ☎00. Police: ☎101. Fire/ambulance: ☎100.

TOURIST INFORMATION — *Office du Tourisme* in French, *Toerisme* in Flemish and *Verkehrsamt* in German. Most have English-speaking staff and free English literature, but charge for walking itineraries and good street maps. Opening hours, especially in small places and off-season, are flexible.

TOURIST OFFICES OVERSEAS — **UK**: 29 PRINCES ST, LONDON W1R 7RG, ☎(0891) 887799 (also gives visa information). **USA**: 780 THIRD AVE, SUITE 1501, NEW YORK, NY 10017, ☎(212) 758 8130, fax: (212) 355 7675.

VISAS — Same requirements as The Netherlands (see p. 20).

BULGARIA

CAPITAL — **Sofia** (Sofija)

CLIMATE — Hot summers; wet spring and autumn; snow in winter (skiing popular).

CURRENCY — **Leva** (Lv.); 1 Lev = 100 stotinki, obtainable only in Bulgaria; re-exchanged for hard currency before leaving. Credit cards increasingly accepted.

CUSTOMS ALLOWANCES — 200 cigarettes, or 50 cigars, or 250g of tobacco products, 1 litre of spirits, 2 litres of wine, and 100g of perfume. Declare amounts above $5000. Some goods, such as antiques, liable for export duty; check with vendors. Keep receipts *(borderaux)* for exchange transactions and accommodation.

EMBASSIES IN SOFIA — **UK**: 65 LEVSKI BLVD; ☎(02) 88 53 61. **USA**: UNIT 1335, 1 SABORNA ST; ☎(02) 88 48 01. Citizens of Canada, Australia and New Zealand: use UK embassy.

EMBASSIES OVERSEAS — **Aus**: 1/4 CARLOTTA RD, DOUBLE BAY, SYDNEY NSW 2028, ☎(02) 372 7592. **Can**: 325 STEWART ST, OTTAWA, ONTARIO K1N 6K5, ☎(613) 789 3215. **SA**: TECHNO PLAZA E., 305 BROOKS ST, MELO PARK, PRETORIA, ☎(012) 342 3721. **UK**: 186/188 QUEEN'S GATE, LONDON SW7 5HL, ☎(020) 7584 9433. **USA**: 1621 22ND STREET N.W., WASHINGTON DC 20008-1921, ☎(202) 387 7969.

LANGUAGE — **Bulgarian** (Cyrillic alphabet); English, German, Russian and French in tourist areas . Nodding the head indicates 'no' *(ne)*; shaking it means 'yes' *(da)*.

OPENING HOURS — **Banks**: Mon–Fri 0900–1500. Some exchange offices open weekends. Shops: Mon–Sat 0800–1900, closed 1200–1400 outside major towns. **Museums**: vary widely, but often 0800–1200, 1400–1830. Many close Mon or Tues.

POST OFFICES — Stamps *(marki)* sold only at post offices *(poshta)*, usually open Mon–Sat 0800–1730. Some close 1200–1400.

PUBLIC HOLIDAYS — 1 Jan; 3 Mar; Orthodox Easter Sunday and Monday, dates variable; 1, 24 May; 22 Sept; 25 Dec.

PUBLIC TRANSPORT — Buses (good network) slightly more expensive than trains; both very cheap for hard currency travellers. Sofia: buses and trams use same ticket; punch it at machines inside, get new ticket if you change. Daily/weekly cards available.

RAIL TRAVEL — IR, EP, ED valid Bulgarian State Railways (BDZ) run express, fast and slow trains. Quickest on electrified lines between major cities. Often crowded; reservations recommended (obligatory for express). All medium- and long-distance trains have 1st and 2nd class, plus limited buffet service. Overnight trains between Sofia and Black Sea resorts have 1st- and 2nd-class sleeping cars and 2nd-class couchettes. One platform may serve two tracks, platforms and tracks both numbered. Signs at stations are in Cyrillic.

TELEPHONES — Use central telephone offices in major towns for long-distance calls. Dial in:

☎00 359. Outgoing: ☎00 and the country code. Police ☎166. Fire ☎160. Ambulance ☎150.

TOURIST OFFICES OVERSEAS — **USA**: BALKAN HOLIDAYS, SUITE 508, 41 EAST 42ND ST, NEW YORK, NY 10017, ☎(212) 573 5530.

VISAS — Passports must have 6 months validity remaining. Visas not required for EU nationals for stays up to 30 days, or for nationals of Aus, NZ, Can and SA if on package holidays or if with Travel Agency vouchers on arrival for pre-paid accommodation and tourist services in Bulgaria. Visitors staying with friends or family (i.e. not in paid accommodation) need to register on arrival.

CROATIA

CAPITAL — **Zagreb**

CLIMATE — Continental on the Adriatic coast, with very warm summers.

CURRENCY — **Kuna** (Kn); 1 Kuna = 100 Lipa. Credit cards widely accepted.

CUSTOMS ALLOWANCES — 200 cigarettes, or 50 cigars, or 250 g tobacco products, 1 litre spirits.

EMBASSIES OVERSEAS — **Aus**: 14 JINDALEE CRESCENT, O'MALLEY ACT 2606, CANBERRA, ☎(6) 286 69 88. **Can**: 130 ALBERT ST, SUITE 1700, OTTAWA, ONTARIO, K1P 5G4, ☎(613) 230 73 51. **NZ**: 131 LINCOLN RD, HENDERSON, PO BOX, 83200 EDMONTON AUCKLAND, ☎(9) 83 65 581. **SA**: 1160 CHURCH ST, 0083 COLBYN PRETORIA, PO BOX 11335, 0028 HATFIELD ☎(12) 342 1206. **UK**: 21 CONWAY ST, LONDON, W1P 5HL, ☎(020) 7387 1790. **USA**: 2343 MASSACHUSETTS AVE, N.W. WASHINGTON DC, 20008-2803, ☎(202) 588 5943.

LANGUAGE — **Croatian**. English, German and Italian spoken in tourist areas.

OPENING HOURS — **Banks**: Mon–Fri 0800–1900, Sat 0800–1200, but may vary. Most **food shops**: Mon–Sat 0800–2000, closed Sun. Some shops close 1300–1700. Most open-air **markets** daily, mornings only. **Museums**: vary.

POST OFFICES — Usual hours: 0700–1900. Stamps *(markice)* sold at news-stands *(kiosk)* or tobacconists *(trafika)*. Post boxes are yellow.

PUBLIC HOLIDAYS — Jan 1, Jan 6, Easter Mon, May 1, May 30, Jun 22, Aug 5, Aug 15, Nov 1 and Dec 25–26. Many local saints' holidays.

PUBLIC TRANSPORT — Jadrolinija maintains most domestic ferry lines; main office in Rijeka, ☎(051) 666 100; cheap and efficient. Buses and trams are cheap, regular and efficient.

RAIL TRAVEL — National railway company: Hrvatske Željeznice (HŽ), ☎(01) 9830. Main intersection for international trains at Zagreb. Slow services and limited network, due in part to the war; reconstruction of damage has reopened some lines to passenger traffic. Zagreb–Rijeka and Zagreb–Split lines are efficient. Stations amenities: left luggage and WCs at most.

RAIL PASSES — IR, ED valid. Domestic fares are cheap. (see p. 23–28).

TELEPHONES — Make international calls from booths in post offices (HPT) – pay the clerk after the call; or from public telephone booths (scarce) – phonecards sold at post offices, news-stands and tobacconists. Dial in: ☎385. Outgoing: ☎00. Police: ☎92. Fire: ☎93. Ambulance: ☎94.

TOURIST OFFICES OVERSEAS — **UK**: 2 THE LANCHESTERS, 162–164 FULHAM PALACE RD, LONDON, W6 9ER ☎(020) 8563 7979. **USA**: PARSIPPANY, NJ 07054, 300 LANIDEX PLAZA, ☎(201) 428 0707.

VISAS — South African nationals need a 3-month tourist visa.

CZECH REPUBLIC

CAPITAL	**Prague** (Praha).
CLIMATE	Mild summers and very cold winters.
CURRENCY	**Czech Korunas** or Crowns (Kc); 1 Koruna = 100 Hellers. No restrictions on foreign currencies. Credit cards widely accepted.
CUSTOMS ALLOWANCES	250 cigarettes or equivalent in tobacco, 1 litre spirits and 2 litres wine.
EMBASSIES IN PRAGUE	**Can**: Mickiewiczova 6, 160 00 Praha 6, ☎2431 1108. **Ire**: Trziöte 13, ☎530 911. **SA**: Rusk· 65, 100 00 Praha 10, ☎6731 1114. **UK**: Thunovsk· 14, Praha 1, ☎ 5732 0355. **USA**: Trziöte 15, 110 00 Praha 1, ☎5732 0663.
EMBASSIES OVERSEAS	**Aus**: 38 Culgoa Circuit, O'Malley, Canberra, ACT 2606; ☎2901 1386. **Can**: 541 Sussex Dr., Ottawa, Ontario, KIN 6Z6; ☎(613) 562 3875. **Ire**: 57 Northumberland Rd, Ballsbridge, Dublin 4; ☎(1) 668 1135. **SA**: P.O.B. 3326, 936 Pretorius St, Arcadia, Pretoria 0083; ☎(12) 342 3477. **UK**: 28 Kensington Palace Gdns, London W8 4QY, ☎(020) 7243 1115. **USA**: 3900 Spring of Freedom St N.W., Washington DC 20008; ☎(202) 274 9100.
LANGUAGE	**Czech**. Czech and Slovak are closely related Slavic tongues. English, German and Russian often understood, but Russian is less popular.
OPENING HOURS	**Banks**: Mon–Fri 0800–1700. **Shops**: Mon–Fri 0900–1800, Sat 0900–1200 (often longer in Prague Sat–Sun). **Food shops**: usually open earlier plus on Sun. **Museums**: (usually) Tues–Sun 1000–1800. Most castles close Nov–Mar.
POST OFFICES	Usual opening hours are 0800–1900. Stamps also available from newsagents and tobacconists. Erratic postal services. Post boxes: orange and blue.
PUBLIC HOLIDAYS	1 Jan; Easter Mon; 1, 8 May; 5–6 July; 28 Oct; 24–26 Dec.
PUBLIC TRANSPORT	Good long-distance bus network, run by ČSAD or private companies. You can buy tickets from the driver; priority to those with reservations.
RAIL TRAVEL	National rail company is České Dráhy (ČD). Network cheap and extensive, often crowded. Main lines: IC , EC and expresses (supplement payable), SuperCity (SC) Praha to Ostrava, 1st class, special fare. Some branch lines have been privatised. Other trains: spešný (semi-fast), osobný (very slow). Some dining cars; sleepers and couchettes; reserve seats for express at least 1 hr before departure at counter marked R at stations.
RAIL PASSES	IR, ED, Central Europe, Czech and Slovak Rail Pass (p. 493). Kilometricka banka 2000 (KMB); 2000 km or 6 months travel; minimum journey 100 km, maximum 400 km. Karta Z: Kc590; 20% discount on ČD fares; passport photo required.
TELEPHONES	Dial in: ☎420. Outgoing: ☎00. Police: ☎158. Fire: ☎150. Ambulance: ☎155.
TOURIST INFORMATION	The Czech Tourism Centre, Na547 rodní 37, 110 15 Praha 1, ☎2421 1458. Čedok Travel agency a.s., ☎2419 7350.
TOURIST OFFICES OVERSEAS	**Can**: PO Box 198, Exchange Tower, 2 First Canadian Pl., 14th Floor, Toronto, Ontario M5X 1A6, ☎(416) 367 3432. **UK**: 95 Great Portland St, London W1N 5RA. **USA**: 1109–1111 Madison Ave, New York, NY 10028, ☎(212) 288 0830.
VISAS	Visas needed by nationals of Canada, Australia and New Zealand.

DENMARK

CAPITAL	**Copenhagen** (København)

CLIMATE	Maritime climate. July–Aug is warmest, May–June often very pleasant, but rainier; Oct–Mar is the wettest, with periods of frost.
CURRENCY	**Danish kroner** (crown), DKK DKr.; 1 krone = 100 øre.
CUSTOMS ALLOWANCES	Standard EU regulations apply (see p. 17–18).
EMBASSIES IN COPENHAGEN	**Aus**: 122 STRANDBOULEVARDEN; ☎39 29 20 77. **Can**: 1 KRISTEN BERNIKOWSGADE; ☎39 29 41 41. **Ire**: OSTBANEGADE 21; ☎31 42 32 33. **SA**: GAMMEL VARTOVVEJ 8, HELLERUP; ☎31 18 01 55. **UK**: KASTELSVEJ 40; ☎35 44 52 00. **USA**: DAG HAMMERSKJÖLDS ALLÉ 24; ☎35 55 31 44.
EMBASSIES OVERSEAS	**Can**: 47 CLARENCE ST, SUITE 450, OTTAWA, ONTARIO K1N 9K1; ☎00-1 613 562 1811. **Aus**: 15 HUNTER ST, YARRALUMLA, A.C.T. 2600; ☎00-61 2 6273 2195/96. **Ire**: 121–122 ST. STEPHEN'S GREEN, DUBLIN 2; ☎00-353 1 475 6404. **NZ**: CONSULATE: 18TH FLOOR, MORRISON KENT HOUSE, 105–109 THE TERRACE, PO BOX 10035, WELLINGTON 1; ☎00-64 4 472 0020. **SA**: 8TH FLOOR, SANLAM CENTRE, CNR PRETORIUS AND ANDRIES STS, PO BOX 2942, PRETORIA 0001; ☎00-27 12 322 0595. **UK**: 55 SLOANE ST, LONDON SW1X 9SR, ☎(020) 7333 0200. **USA**: 3200 WHITEHAVEN ST, N.W., WASHINGTON D.C. 20008-3683; ☎00-1 202 234 4300.
LANGUAGE	**Danish**. English is almost universally spoken. *'Ikke'* translates as 'do not'.
OPENING HOURS	**Banks** (Copenhagen): Mon–Fri 0930–1600 (some until 1700; most until 1800 on Thur). Vary elsewhere. **Shops**: (mostly) Mon–Thur 0900–1730, Fri 0900–1900/2000, Sat 0900–1300/1400. **Museums**: (mostly) daily 1000–1500 or 1100–1600. In winter, hours are shorter and museums usually close Mon.
POST OFFICES	Mostly Mon–Fri 0900–1800, Sat 0900–1330. Stamps also sold at newsagents.
PUBLIC HOLIDAYS	1 Jan, Maundy Thursday–Easter Monday; Great Prayer Day (1999: 30 Apr); Ascension Day; Whit Sun–Mon, Constitution Day (5 June), 24–26 Dec.
PUBLIC TRANSPORT	Long-distance travel easiest by train. Excellent regional and city bus services, many dovetailing with trains. Ferries link all the big islands. Taxis: green *'Fri'* sign when available; metered and quite expensive, but no tip required. Many cycle paths and hire costs are quite low. Danish Tourist Board has details.
RAIL TRAVEL	State railway system: Danske Statsbaner (DSB); some private lines. IC trains reach up to 200 kph. Re *(regionaltog)* trains frequent, but slower. IR: slower and less frequent. Refreshment on most trains. Reservations recommended, not compulsory (DKr.15). Special rules apply during holidays. Nationwide reservations ☎70 13 14 15. Baggage lockers at most stations, usually DKr.20 per 24 hrs. Usually free trolleys, but you may need a (returnable) coin.
RAIL PASSES	IR, ED, EP, Scanrail Pass (p. 23–28). Fares based on national zonal system. Pendlerkort: DKr.3500 (1st class) DKr.2200 (2nd); all-zone, 30-day ticket; photo card required. Kobenhavn 24-hr klippekort: DKr.70; trains and buses; also valid in North Zealand; one adult and two children (under 7); from stations or ticket offices. Copenhagen Card: DKr.155 (24 hrs), 255 (48) or 320 (72); free entry to 60 locations, some reductions on trains/buses; 4–11 yrs travel half-price; from stations, HT travel offices, hotels, Tourist Offices.
TELEPHONES	Most operators speak English. Phonecards available from DSB kiosks, post offices and news-stands. Dial in: ☎45. Outgoing: ☎00. Directory enquiries: ☎118. International operator/directory: ☎14. Emergency services: ☎112.
TOURIST INFORMATION	Danish Tourist Board website: www.dt.dk. Danish railways: www.dsb.dk. Local buses: www.ht.dk. Tourist Offices distribute maps, information and advice. Some also book accommodation for a small fee, and change money.
VISAS	Citizens of South Africa need a visa.

ESTONIA

CAPITAL	**Tallinn**
CLIMATE	Warm summers, cold, snowy winters; rain all year, heaviest in Aug.
CURRENCY	**Kroons** or Crowns (EEK); 1 Kroon = 100 Sents. Purchase on entry (tied to Deutschmark at 1DM=8EEK). Exchange facilities limited; carry spare cash.
CUSTOMS ALLOWANCES	Although not a member state, standard EU regulations apply (see p. 17–18).
EMBASSIES IN TALLINN	**Can**: Toomkooli 13, ☎631 79 78. **UK**: Kentmanni 20, ☎631 34 61; **USA**: Kentmanni 20, ☎631 20 21.
EMBASSIES OVERSEAS	**Aus**: 86 Louisa Rd, Birchgrove 2041, NSW 2010, ☎61 2 818 1779.
CONSULATES OVERSEAS	**Can**: 958 Broadview Ave, Toronto, Ontario, M4K 2R6, ☎(416) 461 0764. **UK**: 16 Hyde Park Gate, London SW7 5DG, ☎(020) 7589 3428. **USA**: 2131 Massachusetts Ave N.W., Washington, DC 20008, ☎(202) 588 0101.
LANGUAGE	**Estonian**. Some Finnish is useful, plus Russian in Tallinn and the north east.
OPENING HOURS	**Banks**: Mon–Fri 0930–1730. **Shops**: Mon–Fri 0900/1000–1800/1900, Sat 0900/1000–1500/1700. **Museums**: days vary; hours commonly 1100–1600.
POST OFFICES	Stamps sold at large hotels, post offices, news-stands, Tourist Offices, etc.
PUBLIC HOLIDAYS	1 Jan; 24 Feb (Independence Day); Good Fri; Easter Mon (unofficial); 1 May; 23, 24 June; 25, 26 Dec.
PUBLIC TRANSPORT	Bus services often quicker than rail but getting pricier. Book international services in advance from bus stations. Pay the driver when boarding at rural stops or small towns, where tickets not on sale.
RAIL TRAVEL	Gradual improvements to rail travel taking place; comfortable overnight trains; best to take berth in 2nd-class coupe (compartment of four berths). Trains to Moscow etc carry superior coupe with two berths. Reservations compulsory for all sleepers; Russian-bound ones may require proof of entry visa when booking. Rail pass usually includes hire of bed linen. Very little English spoken at stations. Stations sell timetables for Estonian Railways.
TELEPHONES	Dial in: 372. Outgoing: ☎8 and wait for long, constant tone, then ☎00 + country code + area code + subscriber's number. Local calls: ☎8 + area code + number. Pay phones take phonecards (from hotels, Tourist Offices, post offices, news-stands). Police: ☎02. Fire: ☎01. Ambulance: ☎03.
TOURIST INFORMATION	Eesti Express Hotline is an information service with numbers in most cities. Tallinn: ☎6 313 222 1188. Info is a new information line, ☎8 and then 1188.
TOURIST OFFICES OVERSEAS	**USA**: 630 Fifth Ave (Suite 2415), New York, NY 10111, ☎(212) 247 7634.
VISAS	Visas not needed by nationals of Australia, Ireland, Japan, New Zealand, UK and USA. Estonian visas also valid for Latvia and Lithuania. Regulations change constantly; check with the consulate/embassy. Canadian passport holders can enter with visa for other Baltic States or obtain visa on border.

FINLAND

CAPITAL	**Helsinki** (Helsingfors).
CLIMATE	Extremely long summer days; spring and autumn curtailed further north; continuous daylight for 70 days north of 70th parallel. Late June–mid Aug best for far north, mid May–Sept for south. Ski season: mid Jan–mid Apr.
CURRENCY	**Finnmarks** or **markkaa** (FIM/Mk.); 1 markka = 100 penniä. Forex give the

best exchange rates and have a branch at Helsinki station.

CUSTOMS ALLOWANCES EU regulations apply (p. 17–18), but must be aged 20 or over to buy spirits.

EMBASSIES IN HELSINKI **Can**: POHJOISESPLANADI 25B; ☎171 141. **Ire**: EROTTAJANKATU 7A; ☎646 006. **SA**: RAHAPAJANKATU 1A; ☎658 288. **UK**: ITÄINEN PUISTOTIE 17; ☎2286 5100. **USA**: ITÄINEN PUISTOTIE 14A; ☎171 931.

EMBASSIES OVERSEAS **Aus**: 10 DARWIN AVE, YARRALUMLA, CANBERRA ACT 2600, ☎2-6273 3800. **Can**: 55 METCALFE ST, SUITE 850. OTTAWA, ONTARIO K1P 6L5, ☎613-236 2389. **Ire**: RUSSELL HOUSE, ST. STEPHEN'S GREEN, DUBLIN 2, ☎1-478 1344. **SA**: 628 LEYDS ST, MUCKLENEUK, PRETORIA 00029, ☎(0) 12-343 0275. **UK**: 538, CHESHAM PLACE, LONDON SW1X 8HW, ☎(020) 7235 9531. **USA**: 3301 MASSACHUSETTS AVE, N.W., WASHINGTON, D.C., 20008, ☎202-298 5800.

LANGUAGE **Finnish**, and, in the north, **Lapp/Sami**. Swedish, the second language, often appears on signs after the Finnish. Knowledge of English is scattered, but there's not much problem in Helsinki. German reasonably widespread.

OPENING HOURS **Banks**: Mon–Fri 0915–1615, with regional variations. **Shops**: Mon–Fri 0900–1800, Sat 0900–1400/1500. **Stores/food shops**: Mon–Sat 0900–1800/2000. **Museums**: usually close Mon, hours vary. Many close in winter.

POST OFFICES Most *posti* open at least Mon–Fri 0900–1700. The logo is a posthorn on a yellow background. Stamps also sold at shops and hotels. Yellow postboxes.

PUBLIC HOLIDAYS 1, 6 Jan, Good Fri, Easter Sun–Mon, May 1, Ascension (May 21), Whit Sun, Midsummer Day (June 20), All Saints Day (Nov 1), Independence Day (6 Dec), 25–26 Dec.

PUBLIC TRANSPORT Timetables for trains, buses and boats dovetail conveniently. *Suomen Kulkunevot* (published twice a year in Finnish only; FIM.100) covers all in detail, available at bus and rail stations. Buses: stops are usually a black bus on a yellow background for local services; white bus on a blue background for longer distances. Cheaper to buy tickets from stations or agents than on board. At terminals, look for destination rather than bus number. Taxis: free when the yellow *'taksi'* sign is lit; hailing them in the street is acceptable; metered, with a surcharge after 1800 and at weekends.

RAIL TRAVEL National rail company: VR (www.vr.fi); Pendolinos (up to 220 kph) are being introduced. Reservations compulsory for IC and EP. Sleeping-cars: two or three berths per compartment; single occupancy costs more; 1st-class ticket must be held. Sleeping accommodation costs less Mon–Thur (winter). Long-distance trains have a buffet and/or trolley service. Station: *'Rautatieasema'* or *'Järnvägsstation'*. Many have no trolleys, but virtually all have baggage lockers.

RAIL PASSES IR, ED, EP, Scanrail Pass valid (see p. 23–28). Finnrailpass: unlimited 2nd-class travel on VR for any 3 (FIM.600), 5 (FIM.810) or 10 (FIM.1090) days in a month; 1st class FIM.900, 1215, 1635. Tourist Ticket (Helsinki): 1, 3 or 5 days consecutive travel on public transport, excluding Red Arrow buses; FIM.25, 50 or 75. Helsinki Card: unlimited travel on public transport, City Tour bus, free entry to 46 attractions; FIM.120, 150, 180.

TELEPHONES Phonecards sold by R-kiosks, Tourist Offices, Tele offices (Tele card used nationwide). Dial in: ☎358. Outgoing: ☎999. Emergency services: ☎112.

TOURIST INFORMATION Tourist Office *(Matkailutoimistot)* staff speak English. English literature, mostly free; accommodation listing, direction to booking centres. Most public buildings operate a numerical queuing system.

VISAS National identity cards or passports issued by EU countries, Iceland and Switzerland sufficient. Visas not required by those countries, nor by nationals of Australia, Canada, New Zealand or the USA. South Africans need visas.

FRANCE

CAPITAL	**Paris**
CLIMATE	Cool winters, hot summers (especially in south); south coast best Oct–Mar, Alps and Pyrénées, June and early July. Paris best spring and autumn.
CURRENCY	**French Francs** (FFr.); 1 Franc = 100 Centimes.
CUSTOMS ALLOWANCES	Standard EU regulations apply (see p. 17–18).
EMBASSIES IN PARIS	**Aus**: 4 R. JEAN REY, ☎01 40 59 33 00. **Can**: 35 AV. MONTAIGNE, ☎01 44 43 29 00. **Ire**: 4 R. RUDE, ☎01 44 17 67 00. **NZ**: 7TER R. L-DA-VINCI, ☎01 45 00 24 11. **SA**: 59 QUAI D'ORSAY, ☎01 53 59 23 23. **UK**: 16 R. D'ANJOU, ☎01 44 51 31 00. **USA**: 2 R. ST-FLORENTIN, ☎01 43 12 23 47.
EMBASSIES OVERSEAS	**Aus**: 6 PERTH AVE, YARRALUMLA, CANBERRA, ACT 2600; ☎(06) 270 5111. **Can**: 42 PROMENADE SUSSEX, OTTAWA, ONT. Q1M 2C9; ☎(613) 789 1795. **NZ**: ROBERT JONES HOUSE, 1-3 WILLESTON ST, WELLINGTON; ☎(04) 472 0200. **Ire**: 36 AILESBURY RD, BALLSBRIDGE, DUBLIN 4; ☎(01) 260 1666. **SA**: 807 GEORGE AVE, ARCADIA, PRETORIA 0083; ☎(012) 435 564. **UK**: 58 KNIGHTSBRIDGE, LONDON SW1X 7JT; ☎(020) 7201 1000. **USA**: 4101 RESERVOIR RD N.W., WASHINGTON DC 20007; ☎(202) 944 6000.
LANGUAGE	**French**; many people can speak a little English, particularly in Paris.
OPENING HOURS	**Banks**: Mon–Fri 0900–1200 and 1400–1600/1700. Most close early on day preceding a public holiday. **Shops**: Tues–Sat 0900–1200 and 1430–1830. **Museums**: (mostly) 0900–1600 (later in summer), closed Mon or Tues plus public holidays. Many offer free or discounted entrance on Sun.
POST OFFICES	Most PTT *(Poste et Telecommunications)* open Mon–Fri 0800–1200 and 1430–1900; Sat 0800–1200; in cities often remain open over lunch. Stamps *(timbres)* also sold in cafés or shops with red Tabac signs.
PUBLIC HOLIDAYS	1 Jan; Easter Mon; 1, 8 May; Ascension Day; Whit Sun–Mon; 14 July; 15 Aug; 1, 11 Nov; 25 Dec. If on Tues or Thur, many places also close Mon or Fri.
PUBLIC TRANSPORT	Bus services in rail timetables accept rail passes/tickets – ask if yours is valid. *Guide Régional des Transports* (from SNCF and bus stations) is a free schedule of regional long-distance transport. City bus services infrequent after 2030 and on Sun. Sparse public transport in rural areas. Licensed taxis (avoid others) are metered; white roof-lights when free; surcharges for luggage, extra passengers and journeys beyond the centre.
RAIL TRAVEL	Société Nationale des Chemins de Fer Français (SNCF); ☎08 36 35 35 35 or 00 33 8 36 35 35 39 (English). Overnight trains may carry sleeping-cars *(wagons-lits;* reservation) and couchettes (six berths, mixed sexes); some have Cabine 8 cars (2nd-class compartments, eight semi-reclined bunks). Buffet/trolley service on most long-distance trains. SOS Voyageurs arrange safe meeting points, help disabled/distressed travellers in a number of stations.
RAIL PASSES	IR, ED, EP, Eu valid (p. 23–28). Stamp all tickets (except Inter-Rail) in orange machines *(composteurs)* on platform. Two fare periods: blue (quiet) and white (peak). TGVs require reservations. Carte 12–25: 50% discount in blue periods, 20% in white for 12 months; must be aged 12–25. Discovery fare: 50% discount on main routes. Paris Visite: Fr.50–350; 1, 2, 3 or 5 days consecutive travel on public transport within selected zones in Paris and Ile de France; free or discounted entry to 14 attractions. Regional Weekend Ticket: unlimited travel on local (TER) trains and buses, not TGV; most only valid Sat–Sun July–Aug; contact SNCF for details; Fr.50–200.
TELEPHONES	Phone boxes: most have English instructions. Many post offices have metered

phones: pay when you've finished. Phonecards *(télécartes)* from post offices and some tobacconists; some phones accept coins or credit cards. Dial in: ☎00 33 and knock off the zero from area code. Outgoing: ☎ 00 followed by country code. Emergency services: ☎112.

TOURIST INFORMATION
Full range at *Syndicats d'Initiative* and *Offices de Tourisme* (called *Accueil de France* in some cities); also handle accommodation. Mostly open Mon–Sat 0900–1200 and 1400–1800, plus on Sun in high season. 24-hr leisure information line (English) ☎(1) 49 52 53 56.

TOURIST OFFICES OVERSEAS
Aus: BNP House, 12 Castlereagh St, Sydney, NSW2000; ☎(02) 231 5244. **Can**: 30 St Patrick St (Suite 700), Toronto, Ont. M5T 3A3; ☎(416) 593 6427. **Ire**: 35 Lower Abbey St, Dublin 1; ☎(01) 703 4046. **SA**: Craighall, Johannesburg 2024; ☎(011) 880 8062. **UK**: Maison de la France (MDLF), 178 Piccadilly, London W1V 0AL; ☎(0891) 244123. **USA**: 444 Madison Ave (16th Floor), New York, NY 10020-2452; ☎(212) 838 7800.

VISAS
EU National Identity Card. Visas needed by Australians and South Africans.

GERMANY

CAPITAL
Berlin (the functions of the capital are being transferred from Bonn).

CURRENCY
Deutsche Mark (DM). 1 Mark = 100 Pfennig.

CUSTOMS ALLOWANCES
Standard EU regulations apply; see p. 17–18. Danes must spend at least 24 hrs in Germany before taking their allowances home.

EMBASSIES IN BERLIN
Aus: Kempinski Plaza, Uhlandstr.181-3, ☎(030) 88 00 880. **Can**: IHZ Building, Friedrichstr.95, ☎(030) 261 1161. **NZ**: Bundeskanzlerpl. 2-10, Bonn; ☎(0228) 228 070. **UK**: Unter den Linden 32-34, ☎(030) 201 840. **USA**: Neustadtische Kirchstr. 4; ☎(030) 238 5174.

EMBASSIES OVERSEAS
UK: Embassy, 23 Belgrave Sq., London SW1X 8PZ; ☎(020) 7824 1300. **USA**: Embassy, 4645 Reservoir Rd N.W., Washington DC 20007-1998; ☎(202) 298 8141.

LANGUAGE
German; English and French widely spoken in the West, especially by young people, less so in the Eastern side.

OPENING HOURS
Vary; rule of thumb: **Banks**: Mon–Fri 0830–1300 and 1430–1600 (until 1730 Thur). **Shops**: Mon–Fri 0900–1830 (until 2030 Thur) and Sat 0900–1400. **Museums**: Tues–Sun 0900–1700 (until 2100 Thur).

POST OFFICES
Mon–Sat 0800–1800. Main post offices have poste restante *(postlagernde)*.

PUBLIC HOLIDAYS
1, 6 Jan; Good Fri; Easter Sun–Mon; 1 May, Ascension Day; Whit Sun–Mon; Corpus Christi*, 15 Aug*; 3 Oct; 1 Nov*; Day of Prayer (third Wed in Nov); 25 Dec; 26 Dec (afternoon). *Catholic feasts, celebrated only in the south.

PUBLIC TRANSPORT
Most cities have U-Bahn (U) underground railway and S-Bahn (S) urban rail service. City travel passes cover both and other public transport, including ferries in some cities. International passes usually cover S-Bahn. Local fares are expensive; day card *(Tagesnetzkarte)* or multi-ride ticket *(Mehrfahrkarte)* pays its way if you take more than three rides.

RAIL TRAVEL
Deutsche Bahn (DB); also some privately owned railways. Buy tickets before you board, or pay a small supplement. Long-distance trains: ICE (ultra-modern; up to 174 mph), IC, EC, EN, InterRegio. Regional: RB and RE (modern, comfortable; link with long-distance network). Local services: SE or S-Bahn. Most offer 1st and 2nd class. Supplements charged on IC, EC trains; ICE have special fares. Overnight services: 2nd-class seating and sleeping-cars

with up to three berths and/or couchettes with four or six berths. Seat reservations possible for most express trains, not local ones. Most long-distance trains have refreshments. Stations: well staffed, often with left luggage, refreshments, bicycle hire. Main station is *Hauptbahnhof* (Hbf).

RAIL PASSES

IR, ED, Eu, EP, Central Europe valid (p. 23–28). DB Railcard: half-price 2nd-class tickets; passport photo required. Saver and Supersaver Tickets: discounts on ICE long-distance travel; stay must include Friday night. Welcome Card: selected cities; public transport, free or reduced entry to many attractions. StadtTicket: 24-hr ticket in all cities; all or most public transport; fares usually based on zonal system. Regional Ticket: unlimited travel on DB local trains Mon–Fri off-peak (0900–1600, 1800–0200) in Bavaria and Rheinland-Pfalz. Minigroup Ticket: medium-distance return journeys; 1st adult pays full fare, all others pay half, children pay quarter; minimum of 1 adult, 1 child, maximum 5 adults, 1 child.

TELEPHONES

Kartentelefon boxes take only cards (buy at post office, DM12 or 50). Dial in: ☎00 49. Outgoing: ☎00 (few exceptions, but kiosks give full information). Police ☎110. Fire ☎112. Ambulance ☎112.

TOURIST INFORMATION

Usually near station. English is widely spoken; range of English-language maps and leaflets available. Most offer room-finding service.

TOURIST OFFICES OVERSEAS

UK: PO Box 2695, London W1A 3TN; ☎(0891) 600 100. **USA**: Chanin Building, 122 East 42nd St. (52nd Floor), New York, NY 10168-0072; ☎ (212) 661 7200; gntony@aol.com.

VISAS

EU National Identity Cards and ID cards acceptable for citizens of the Czech and Slovak Republics, Hungary, Iceland, Liechtenstein, Malta, Monaco, Poland, and Switzerland. Visas not needed by nationals of Aus, Can, NZ or the USA.

GREECE

CAPITAL

Athens (Athinai).

CLIMATE

Uncomfortably hot in June–Aug; often better to travel in spring or autumn.

CURRENCY

Drachmae.

CUSTOMS ALLOWANCES

Normal EU regulations apply, see p. 17–18

EMBASSIES IN ATHENS

Aus: 37 D. Soutsou St; ☎644 7303. **Can**: Ioannou Gennadiou 4; ☎725 4011. **Ire**: 7 Vas.Konstantinou Ave; ☎723 2771/2. **NZ**: 24 Xenias St; ☎771 0112. **SA**: 60 Kifissias Ave, Marousi; ☎680 6645/9. **UK**: Ploutarchou 1; ☎723 6211. **USA**: Vassilissis Sofias 91;☎721 2951/9 or 721 8401.

EMBASSIES OVERSEAS

UK: Consulate General, 1A Holland Park, London W11 3TP; ☎(020) 7221 6467. **USA**: 2221 Massachusetts Ave N.W., Washington DC 20008-2873; ☎(202) 667 3169 or 939 5800.

LANGUAGE

Greek; English widely spoken in tourist areas (some German or Italian), less so in remote mainland areas and Athens.

OPENING HOURS

Banks: (usually) Mon–Fri 0800–1400, longer hours in peak holiday season. **Shops** vary; in summer most close midday to early evening. **Sites and museums**: mostly 0830–1500; Athens sites open until sunset in summer.

POST OFFICES

Normally Mon–Fri 0800–1300, Sat 0800–1200; money exchange, travellers cheques, Eurocheques. Stamps sold from street kiosks and general stores.

PUBLIC HOLIDAYS

1, 6 Jan; Shrove Mon; 25 Mar; Easter; May Day; Whit Mon; 15 Aug; 28 Oct; 25, 26 Dec. Everything closes for Easter; Greeks use the Orthodox calendar and dates may differ from western Easter.

PUBLIC TRANSPORT

KTEL buses: fast, punctual, fairly comfortable long-distance services; well-organised stations in most towns. Islands connected by ferries and hydrofoils; see Thomas Cook Guide to *Greek Island Hopping*. City transport: bus or (in Athens) trolley-bus and metro; services are crowded. Outside Athens, taxis are plentiful and good value.

RAIL TRAVEL

Trains run by Organismós Sidiródromon tis Éllados (OSE): limited rail network, especially north of Athens. Sleepers/couchettes. Reservations essential on most express trains. IC trains (supplement payable) are fast and fairly punctual, other services are erratic. Station: often no left luggage or English-speaking staff, but many have restaurants.

RAIL PASSES

IR, EP, Eu, ED valid (p. 23–28). Tourism Card: unlimited 2nd-class rail travel for up to 5 people; 10, 20 or 30 days; Dr.14,850–91,920; only available from OSE Head Office, 1 Karolou St, Athens or International Window at Thessaloniki station. Greek Flexipass Rail'n'Fly: return airline ticket, plus one-way air ticket from Athens to any Greek island served by Olympic Airways.

TELEPHONES

Dial in: ☎30. Outgoing: ☎00. General emergency/police/operator: ☎100. Fire ☎199. Ambulance: ☎150/166. Tourist police (24 hrs; English): ☎171.

TOURIST OFFICES OVERSEAS

Aus: 51–7 Pitt St, Sydney NSW 2000; ☎(2) 92 41 16 63/5. **Can**: 1300 Bay St, Main Level, Toronto, Ontario M5R 3K8, ☎(416) 968 2220. **UK**: 4 Conduit St, London W1R 0DJ; ☎(020) 7734 5997. **USA**: Olympic Tower, 645 Fifth Ave (5th Floor), New York, NY 10022, ☎(212) 421 5777.

VISAS

Not needed for EU citizens; or for nationals of the USA, Canada, Australia and New Zealand for stays of less than three months.

HUNGARY

CAPITAL

Budapest

CURRENCY

Forints (Ft); 1 Forint=100 fillér (fillér are almost worthless and little used). You can buy your currency at banks and official bureaux, but take care not to buy too much. You need an *Ertékbehozatali tanúsìtvány* (export certificate) if exporting more than 100,000Ft or equivalent. Keep all your receipts. Credit cards/Eurocheques/small denomination traveller's cheques widely accepted; Deutschmarks more useful than dollars or sterling. Plenty of cash machines.

CUSTOMS ALLOWANCES

250 cigarettes or 50 cigars or 250 g tobacco; 2 litres wine, 5 litres beer, 1 litre spirits and 250 ml cologne or perfume.

EMBASSIES IN BUDAPEST

Aus: Királyhágó tér 8–9; ☎214 1489. **Can**: Budakeszi út 32; ☎275 1200. **NZ** (Consulate): Teréz krt 38; ☎131 4908. **Ire**: Szabadság tér 7–9; ☎302 9600. **SA**: Rákóczi út 1–3; ☎4566. **UK**: Harmincad út 6; ☎118 2888. **USA**: Szabadságtér 12; ☎112 6450.

EMBASSIES OVERSEAS

Aus: 17 Beale Crescent, Deakin Act., 2600 Canberra; ☎282 3226. **Can**: 299 Waverley St, Ottawa, Ontario K2P 0V9; ☎(613) 230 9614. **Ire**: 2 Fitzwilliam Pl., Dublin 2; ☎(1) 661 2902. **SA**: 959 Arcadia St, Arcadia, Pretoria (PO Box 27077, Sunnyside 0132); ☎(12) 433 030. **UK**: 46 Eaton Pl., London SW1X; ☎(020) 7235 2664. **USA**: 3910 Shoemakers St N.W., Washington DC 20008-3811; ☎(202) 362 6730.

LANGUAGE

Hungarian (Magyar). German is widely understood, plus English in tourist areas.

OPENING HOURS

Food/tourist shops, markets, malls open Sun. **Banks**: National Bank of Hungary: Mon–Fri 1030–1400; commercial banks Mon–Thur 0800–1500, Fri 0800–1300. **Food shops**: Mon–Fri 0700–1900, others: 1000–1800 (Thur until 1900); shops close for lunch and half-day on Sat (1300). **Museums**: usually Tues–Sun 1000–1800, free one day a week, closed public holidays.

Post offices — Mostly 0800–1800. Postal service fairly slow but reliable. Stamps also sold at tobacconists. Major post offices cash Eurocheques and change western currency; all give cash for Visa Eurocard/Mastercard and Visa Electron cards.

Public holidays — 1 Jan; 15 Mar; Easter Mon; 1 May; Whit Mon; 20 Aug; 23 Oct; 25, 26 Dec.

Public transport — Long-distance buses (*Volán busz*, ☎118 2122), slow ferries along Danube.

Rail travel — Comprehensive rail system; most towns on the Hungarian State Railways (MÁV) network; most trains *(személyvonat)* very slow. Express *(gyorsvonat)*, IC, some EC services (reservation; supplement on latter two) connect Budapest with major towns and Lake Balaton. Book sleepers well in advance.

Rail passes — IR, ED, Eu, EP valid (p. 23–28). Hungary Rail Pass (MÁV): holders of ISIC or under 26 years from USIT/Campus Travel; unlimited 1st (£34) or 2nd (£23) class travel for 7 days; supplements extra. MÁV Turistabérlat: 7 days (1st class Ft13,410, 2nd Ft8940) or 10 days (1st Ft19,320, 2nd Ft12,880) consecutive travel at 20% discount; IC supplements/reservations extra. GySev offer similar ticket. Budapest Card: 3 days unlimited travel on public transport, free or reduced entry to many attractions.

Telephones — Phonecards on sale at news-stands, tobacconists, post offices, supermarkets. Payphones take 10, 20 50 and 100 forint coins. Dial in: ☎36. Outgoing: ☎00. Police ☎107. Fire ☎105. Ambulance: ☎104.

Tourist information — **Tourinform** branches throughout Hungary; English-speaking staff. Hungarian Tourist Card, valid for 13 months, Ft2520, provides various concessions.

Tourist offices overseas — **UK**: 46 Eaton Pl., London SW1X; ☎(020) 7823 1032. **USA**: 150 E. 58th St, 33rd Floor, New York, NY 101 55-3398; ☎(212) 355 0240.

Visas — Not required by Nationals of EU (except citizens of Albania and Turkey), Can, SA or USA. Nationals of Aus and NZ must obtain visas before travelling.

Italy

Capital — **Rome** (Roma)

Climate — Very hot in July and Aug; May, June, Sept best for sightseeing. Holiday season ends mid Sept or Oct. Rome crowded at Easter.

Currency — **Lira** (L.). Telephone tokens and sweets sometimes offered as small change.

Customs allowances — Standard EU regulations apply (see p. 17–18).

Embassies in Rome — **Aus**: V. Alessandra, ☎215; (06) 85 27 21. **Can**: V. Zara 30; ☎(06) 445 981. **NZ**: V. Zara, 28; ☎(06) 440 29 28. **UK**: V. XX Settembre, 80A; ☎(06) 482 54 41. **USA**: V. Veneto, 119A/121; ☎(06) 467 41.

Embassies overseas — **UK**: 38 Eaton Pl., London SW1X 8AN; ☎(020) 7235 9371. **USA**: 1601 Fuller Street N.W., Washington, DC 20009; ☎(202) 328 5500.

Language — **Italian**; strong dialectal differences. Many speak English in cities and tourist areas. In the south and Sicily, French is often more useful than English.

Opening hours — **Banks**: Mon–Fri 0830–1330, 1430/1600–2200. **Shops**: (usually) Mon–Sat 0830/0900–1230, 1530/1600–1900/1930; closed Mon AM/Sat PM July/Aug. **Museums/sites**: usually Tues–Sun 0930–1300/1400; last Sun of month free; most refuse entry within an hour of closing. Churches often close lunchtime.

Post offices — Mostly Mon–Fri 0800–1330/1400, Sat 0800–1145. Some counters (registered mail and telegrams) may differ; in main cities some open in the afternoon. Postal service is slow; send anything urgent via express. Stamps *(francobolli)* available from post offices, tobacconists *(tabacchi)*, some gift shops in resorts. Poste restante *(Fermo posta)* available at most post offices; charge payable.

PUBLIC HOLIDAYS All over the country: 1, 6 Jan; Easter Sun and Mon; 25 Apr; 1 May; 15 Aug (virtually nothing opens); 1 Nov; 8, 25, 26 Dec. Regional saints' days: 25 Apr in Venice; 24 June in Florence, Genoa and Turin; 29 June in Rome; 11 July in Palermo; 19 Sept in Naples; 4 Oct in Bologna; 6 Dec in Bari; 7 Dec in Milan.

PUBLIC TRANSPORT Buses often crowded, but punctual; serve many areas inaccessible by rail. Services drastically reduced at weekends; not always shown in timetables. Taxis: metered, can be expensive; extra charges for baggage and journeys out of town, on holidays or late at night; steer clear of unofficial ones.

RAIL TRAVEL National rail company: Ferrovie dello Stato (FS). High-speed express services between major cities. 'Eurostar Italia' requires reservation, plus basic supplement to use train, plus another before you board. Reservations also obligatory for IC and EC. IR trains: semi-fast expresses. Espresso: 1st-/2nd-class long-distance domestic trains; stop only at main stations. Diretto: stop frequently, very slow. Locale: stop almost everywhere. Services reasonably punctual. Some long-distance trains do not carry passengers short distances. Sleepers: single or double berths in 1st class, three (occasionally doubles) in 2nd. Couchettes: four berths in 1st class, six in 2nd. Refreshments on most long-distance trains. Don't drink tap water. Queues at stations often long; buy tickets and make reservations at travel agencies (look for FS symbol).

RAIL PASSES EP, IR, ED, Eu valid (p. 23–28). Biglietto Chilometrico: valid for 2 months; allows up to 20 journeys or 3000 km for up to 5 people; 1st class £150/L338,000, 2nd class £88, L206,000; supplements/reservations extra. Italy Railcard: 8, 15, 21 or 30 days consecutive travel on FS network; prices for 1st/2nd class: £188/£128; £236/£158; £274/£186 or £328/£220. Italy Flexi Railcard: 8, 12 or 14 days consecutive travel on FS network within 1 month; prices for 1st/2nd class: £130/£88; £184/£122 or £234/£156. Available from Wasteels/CITravel.

TELEPHONES Directories may list two numbers: try both. Public phones take coins or phonecards *(carte telefoniche/scheda)*, available from nearby automatic machines, tobacconists, news-stands; good for international calls. Scatti (metered) phones common in bars; pay the operator after use, check for service charge. Dial in: ☎00 39, include first zero in area code. Outgoing: ☎00. English information for intercontinental calls: ☎170; for European and Mediterranean calls: ☎176. Fire: ☎115. Police, ambulance: ☎113.

TOURIST INFORMATION Most towns and resorts have *Azienda di soggiorno* or *Pro Loco*.

TOURIST OFFICES OVERSEAS **UK**: Italian State Tourist Board, 1 Princes St, London W1R 8AY; ☎(020) 7408 1254. **USA**: Italian Government Travel Office (ENIT), 630 Fifth Ave (Suite 1565), Rockefeller Center, New York, NY 10111; ☎(212) 245 4822.

VISAS Visas not needed by commonwealth citizens or nationals of USA.

LATVIA

CAPITAL **Riga**

CLIMATE Similar to Estonia.

CURRENCY **1 Lat=100 Santims**. Credit cards: limited use; some cash machines in Riga.

CUSTOMS ALLOWANCES 200 cigarettes or 200g tobacco products, and 1 litre alcohol.

EMBASSIES IN RIGA **Can**: Doma Laukums 4; ☎(78 30141). **UK**: A Lunana 5; ☎(73 38126). **USA**: Raina bulv 7; ☎(721 0005).

EMBASSIES OVERSEAS **Aus**: PO Box 23, Kew, Victoria 3101; ☎(03) 949 96920. Consulates: **Can**:

	112 KONT ST, PLACE DE VILLE, TOWER B, SUITE 208, OTTAWA, ONTARIO; ☎(613) 238 6868. **UK**: 45 NOTTINGHAM PL., LONDON W1M 3FE; ☎(020) 7312 0040. **USA**: 4325 17TH ST N.W., WASHINGTON, DC 20011; ☎(202) 726 8213/4.
LANGUAGE	**Latvian**, spoken by over half the population. Russian understood in Riga and the east, unpopular with native Latvians. English and German often spoken.
OPENING HOURS	**Banks**: mainly Mon–Fri 0900–1600, some Sat 0900–1230. **Shops**: Mon–Fri 0900/1000–1800/1900 and Sat 0900/1000–1700. Many close on Mon. Food shops usually open earlier and close later. 24-hr supermarkets in Riga. **Museums**: days vary, but usually open Tues/Wed–Sun 1100–1700.
POST OFFICES	Mon–Fri 0900–1800, Sat 0900–1300. In Riga (BRIVIBAS) open 24 hours.
PUBLIC HOLIDAYS	1 Jan; Good Fri; Easter Mon (unofficial); 1 May; Mothers' Day (second Sun in May); 23, 24 June (Midsummer); 18 Nov; 25, 26, 31 Dec.
PUBLIC TRANSPORT	Very cheap for Westerners. Taxis generally affordable (agree fare first if not metered). Beware of pickpockets on crowded buses and trams. Long-distance bus network preferred to slow domestic train service.
RAIL TRAVEL	See Estonia, p. 459–460.
TELEPHONES	Phone cards for 2, 5 or 10 Lats sold at post offices. Dial in: ☎371. Outgoing: ☎8 + 00 + country code. Police: ☎02. Fire: ☎ 01. Ambulance: ☎03.
VISAS	Visas (not needed by Ire, UK, USA) obtainable by Australian, Canadian and most European nationals at airport and Riga passenger ports (not train border crossings), valid 10 days. Check at least 21 days before travelling.

LITHUANIA

CAPITAL	**Vilnius**
CLIMATE	Similar to Estonia.
CURRENCY	**Litai**; 1 Litas = 100 Cents. Travellers cheques and credit cards widely accepted. Cash machines in Vilnius and Kaunas.
CUSTOMS ALLOWANCES	Allowances constantly changing; always check first. Currently: 200 cigarettes or 50 cigars or 250g tobacco, and 1 litre wine or 2 litres champagne or 1.5 litres beer.
EMBASSIES IN VILNIUS	**Can**: GEDIMINO 64; ☎22 08 5. **UK**: ANTAKALNIO GATVE 2; ☎22 20 70. **USA**: AKEMNU 6 ☎22 27 37.
EMBASSIES OVERSEAS	**Aus**: 26 JALANGA CRESCENT, ARANDA, ACT 2614, ☎(062) 53 2062. **Can**: 130 ALBERT ST, SUITE 204, OTTAWA, ONTARIO; ☎(1613) 567 5458. **UK**: 84 GLOUCESTER PL., LONDON W1; ☎(020) 7486 6401. **USA**: (CONSULATE-GENERAL), 420 FIFTH AVE, NEW YORK, NY 10018, ☎(212) 354 7849.
LANGUAGE	**Lithuanian**. Lithuanian and Latvian are both Indo-European in origin. Russian is helpful but unpopular.
OPENING HOURS	**Banks**: mostly Mon–Fri 0900–1700, some Sat 0900–1300. **Shops**: (large shops) Mon–Fri 1000/1100–1900; many also open Sat until 1600. Some close for lunch 1400–1500 and also on Sun and Mon. Food shops: Mon–Sat 0900–1400 and 1500–2000, Sun 0800–1400. Grocery shops: Mon–Fri 0800–2000. **Museums**: days vary, most close Mon and open at least Wed and Fri; often free on Wed; hours usually at least 1100–1700, check locally.
POST OFFICES	All towns have post offices with an international telephone service.
PUBLIC HOLIDAYS	1 Jan; 16 Feb; 11 Mar; Easter Sun and Mon; 1 May; the first Sun in May

(Mothers Day); 6 July; 1 Nov; 25, 26 Dec.

PUBLIC TRANSPORT See Estonia, p. 459–460.

RAIL TRAVEL See Estonia.

TELEPHONES Phone cards sold at news-stands. Dial in: ☎370. Outgoing: ☎8 10 + country code. Police: ☎02. Fire:☎01. Ambulance:☎ 03.

VISAS Not required by Nationals of Aus, Can, Ire, UK, USA. EU nationals can obtain visa at the airport. Lithuanian visas valid in Latvia and Estonia; check first.

LUXEMBOURG

CAPITAL **Luxembourg City** (Ville de Luxembourg).

CLIMATE Similar to Belgium.

CURRENCY **Luxembourg Francs**. Belgian and Luxembourg francs are co-rated: Belgian francs accepted. Try not to get left with Luxembourg francs when you leave.

CUSTOMS ALLOWANCES Standard EU regulations (p 17–18). No checks at land borders (by train).

EMBASSIES OVERSEAS **UK**: 27 WILTON CRESCENT, LONDON SW1X 8SD, ☎(020) 7235 6961. **USA**: 2200 MASSACHUSETTS AVE N.W., WASHINGTON DC 20008,☎(202) 265 4171.

LANGUAGE **Lutzebuergesch** is the national tongue, but almost everybody also speaks fluent French and/or German, plus often at least some English.

OPENING HOURS Many establishments take long lunch breaks. **Banks**: usually Mon–Fri 0800/0900–1600 or later. **Shops**: Mon 1300/1400–1800; Tues–Sat 0900–1800. **Museums**: most open six days a week (usually Tues–Sun).

POST OFFICES Usually open Mon–Fri 0800–1200 and 1400–1700.

PUBLIC HOLIDAYS 1 Jan, Feb (Carnival), Easter Mon, 1 May, Ascension, Whit Mon, 23 June (National Day), 15 Aug, 1 Nov and 25 Dec. When holidays fall on Sun, the Mon usually becomes a holiday but only twice in one year.

PUBLIC TRANSPORT Good bus network between most towns. Taxis not allowed to pick up passengers in the street; most stations have ranks.

RAIL TRAVEL National rail company: CFL, also runs long-distance buses; these and city buses covered by multi-ride passes. Stations: most are small, few facilities.

RAIL PASSES IR, EP, ED, Eu Benelux Tourrail Pass valid (p. 23–28). Billet Réseau: day card LFr.160; unlimited 2nd-class travel on all public transport; *carnet* of 5 day cards costs LFr.640; from CFL offices. Luxembourg Card: free transport on all trains and buses, free entry to many attractions within the Duchy of Luxembourg; 1 day (LFr.350); 2 days (LFr.600), 3 days (LFr.850), family pass for 2–5 people at twice one person rate; available from Tourist Offices, hotels, stations etc.

TELEPHONES *Télécartes*, available from post offices. Dial in: ☎352. Outgoing: ☎00. Police ☎113. Emergency services: ☎112. Emergency operators speak English.

TOURIST INFORMATION Literature covering all of Luxembourg from any Tourist Office.

TOURIST OFFICES OVERSEAS **UK**: 122-4 REGENT ST, LONDON W1R 5FE; ☎(020) 7434 2800. **USA**: 17 BEEKMAN PL., NEW YORK, NY 10022; ☎(212) 935 8888.

VISAS Visas are not needed by nationals of Australia, Canada, EU, New Zealand or the USA. South Africans do need visas.

Directory

The Netherlands

Capital
Administrative capital: **Amsterdam**. Legislative capital: **The Hague** (Den Haag).

Climate
Can be cold in winter; rain prevalent all year. Many attractions close Oct–Easter, while Apr–May is tulip time and the country is crowded; June–Sept is pleasantly warm.

Currency
Guilders; 1 Guilder = 100 cents. Guilders abbreviated to 'f', 'fl'or NLG.

Customs allowances
Standard EU regulations apply (see p. 17–18).

Embassies in The Hague/Amsterdam
Aus: Carnegielaan 4, The Hague; ☎(070) 310 8200. **Can**: Sophielaan 7, The Hague; ☎(070) 311 1600. **NZ:** Carnegielaan 10, The Hague; ☎(070) 346 9324. **Ire:** Dr. Kuyperstr. 9, The Hague; ☎(070) 363 099. **SA**: Wassenarseweg 40; ☎(070) 392 4501. **UK**: Koningslaan 44, Amsterdam; ☎(020) 676 4343. **USA**: Museumplein 19, Amsterdam; ☎(020) 664 5661.

Embassies overseas
Aus: 120 Empire Circuit, Yarralumla, Canberra, ACT 2600; ☎(06) 273 3111. **Can**: Suite 2020, 350 Albert St, Ottawa, Ontario K1R 1A4; ☎(613) 237 5030. **Ire**: 160 Merrion Rd, Dublin 4; ☎(01) 269 3444. **NZ**: PO Box 840, Wellington; ☎(04) 477 6390. **SA**: PO Box 117, Pretoria 0001; ☎(012) 344 3910. **UK**: 38 Hyde Park Gate, London SW7 5DP; ☎(020) 7540 3200. **USA**: 4200 Linnean Ave N.W., Washington, DC 20008; ☎(202) 244 5300.

Language
Dutch; English widely spoken.

Opening hours
Banks: Mon–Fri 0900–1600/1700 (later Thur). **Shops**: Mon–Fri 0900/0930–1730/1800 (until 2100 Thur or Fri), Sat 0900/0930–1600/1700. Many close Mon morning and one afternoon a week. **Museums**: vary, but usually Tues–Sun (or Mon–Sat) 1000–1700. In winter many have shorter hours.

Post offices
Logo is 'ptt post' (white on red). Most open Mon–Fri 0830–1700 and some Sat 0900–1600. Stamps also sold in many postcard shops. Post international mail in slots marked *overije*.

Public holidays
1 Jan; Good Fri; Easter Sun–Mon; 30 Apr; 5 May (Liberation Day); Ascension Day; Whit Sun–Mon; 25, 26 Dec. You won't go far wrong by assuming that Sun hours/timetables apply.

Public transport
Centralised (premium rate) numbers for all rail and bus enquiries (computerised, fast and accurate): national, ☎0900 9292; international, ☎ 0900 9296. Most vehicles/carriages have yellow buttons inside and out for passengers to open doors. Taxis best boarded at ranks or ordered by phone as they seldom stop in the street. In many cities (not Amsterdam), shared Treintaxis have ranks at stations and yellow roof signs (NLG.6 for anywhere within city limits; tickets from rail ticket offices). *Strippenkaarten* (from stations, city transport offices, post offices and sometimes VVV) are strip tickets valid nationwide on city trains, metros, buses and trams; zones apply; validate on boarding; valid 1 hr; change of transport allowed.

Rail travel
National rail company: **Nederlandse Spoorwegen** (NS). Sneltreins call at principal stations and stoptreins at all stations. Seat reservations only for international journeys. Credit cards not accepted at rail stations. Most stations have GWK banks (daily; credit cards accepted), plus cycle hire and baggage lockers.

Rail passes
Benelux Tourrail Pass, IR, ED, EP, Eu valid (see p. 23–28). Netherlands Rail offer range of tickets. Normal fares based upon distance travelled: day return costs about 25% less than two singles; Weekend Return gives 50% reduction – valid from Fri afternoon, return before Sat 1800. Zomertoer: July–Aug;

3 days unlimited travel within 10-day period; 1st or 2nd class; if 2 people travel together, price is only a third more. Dagkaart/Day Rover: NLG.114/£35.50 (1st class), NLG.73.50/£23 (2nd class); unlimited travel around Holland. OV Dagkaart: NLG.122.50 (1st class), NLG.82 (2nd); rail, bus, tram and Metro day rover; use in conjunction with Dagkaart; purchase in Holland. Meermanskaart: unlimited travel for group of 2–6 people; 1st and 2nd class; valid any day, including public holidays; must be used after 0900 Mon–Fri, except in July or Aug. Holland Rail Pass: 3 or 5 days unlimited 1st or 2nd class travel on Netherlands Rail; adult, senior, under 26 and child tickets; 3 days – £55, £44 or £27 1st class, £36, £29 or £18 2nd class; 5 days – £82, £66 or £41 1st class, £55, £44 or £27 2nd class; if 2 people travel together, 2nd person travels half price; purchase in UK (more details from Netherlands Rail).

TELEPHONES Booths have instructions in English. Cash booths are green, blue booths take only *telefoonkaarten* cards – available from post offices, VVV and NS. International calls cheapest Mon–Fri evenings and all day Sat, Sun. A few numbers prefixed 06 are free, but most are at premium rates. Dial in: ☎31. Outgoing: ☎00. Operator: ☎06 0410. International directory: ☎06 0418. National directory ☎06 8008. Emergency services: ☎06 11.

TOURIST INFORMATION Tourist bureaux are VVV *(Vereniging voor Vreemdelingenverkeer)*: signs show a triangle with three Vs. All open at least Mon–Fri 0900–1700, Sat 1000–1200. Museumjaarkaart (NLG.45 from VVV and participating museums) is valid for one year; free entry to most museums nationwide; Kortingkaart is less comprehensive; CJP (Cultureel Jongeren Paspoort), for those under 26.

TOURIST OFFICES OVERSEAS **Can**: Suite 710, 25 Adelaide St E., Toronto, Ontario M5C 1Y2; ☎1 888 GO HOLLAND. **UK**: Egginton House, 25/28 Buckingham Gate, London SW1E 6NT / PO Box 523, SW1E 6NT; ☎(020) 7828 7900. **USA**: Suite 1854, 225 N. Michigan Ave, IL 60601, Chicago; ☎188 GO HOLLAND.

VISAS Visas are needed by nationals of South Africa, but not of Australia, Canada, EU, New Zealand or USA.

NORWAY

CAPITAL **Oslo**.

CLIMATE Surprisingly mild considering it's so far north; can be very warm in summer, particularly inland; the coast is appreciably cooler. May and June are driest months, but quite cool; summer gets warmer and wetter as it progresses, and the the western fjords have high rainfall year-round. Days are very long in summer: the sun never sets in high summer in the far north. July and Aug is the busiest period; Sept can be delightful. Winter is the time to see the Northern Lights *(Aurora Borealis)*. Excellent snow for skiing Dec–Apr.

CURRENCY **Norwegian kroner** (Nkr./NOK); 1 krone = 100 øre. On slot machines, *femkrone* means a NKr.5 coin and *tikrone* a NKr.10 coin.

CUSTOMS ALLOWANCES EU residents aged 18 or more: 200 cigarettes or 250g tobacco, 2 litres of beer, 1 litre of spirits (up to 60% and only if aged over 20) 1 litre of wine etc (up to 22%), or 2 litres wine if no spirits. All limits doubled for non-EU residents.

EMBASSIES IN OSLO **Can**: Wergelandvn 7; ☎22 46 69 55. **SA**: Drammensvn 88C; ☎22 44 79 10. **UK**: Thomas Heftyesgt 8; ☎22 55 24 00. **USA**: Drammensvn 18; ☎22 44 85 50.

EMBASSIES OVERSEAS **Aus**: 17 Hunter St., Yarralumla, Canberra ACT 2600; ☎(06) 273 3444. **Can**: Royal Park Center, 90 Sparks St (Suite 532), Ottawa, Ont. K1P 5B4;

☎(613) 238 6570. **Ire**: 34 MOLESWORTH ST, DUBLIN2; ☎(01) 662 1800. **NZ**: 70 SHORTLAND ST. (3RD FLOOR), AUCKLAND; ☎(09) 377 1944. **SA**: 524 CHURCH ST (7TH FLOOR), ARCADIA, PRETORIA 0083; ☎(012) 323 4790. **UK**: 25 BELGRAVE SQUARE, LONDON, SW1X 8QD; ☎0171 591 5500. **USA**: 2720 34TH ST N.W., WASHINGTON D.C. 20008-2799; ☎(202) 333 6000.

LANGUAGE

Bokmål and **Nyorsk** are both variants of Norwegian. Almost everyone speaks English; if not, try German. Norwegian has three additional vowels: æ, ø and å, which (in that order) follow z.

OPENING HOURS

Banks: Mon–Wed and Fri 0815–1500 (1530 in winter), Thur 0815–1700. In Oslo, some open later, in the country some close earlier. Many have mini-bank machines that accept Visa, MasterCard (Eurocard) and Cirrus. **Shops**: Mon–Fri 0900–1600/1700 (Thur 0900–1800/2000), Sat 0900–1300/1500, many open later, especially in Oslo. **Museums**: usually Tues–Sun 1000–1500/1600. Some open Mon, longer in summer and/or close completely in winter.

POST OFFICES

Usually Mon–Fri 0800/0830–1700, Sat 0830–1300. Postboxes: red posthorn and crown on yellow boxes for local mail; reversed colours for elsewhere.

PUBLIC HOLIDAYS

Jan 1; Maundy Thur–Good Fri; Easter Sun–Mon; May 1; Ascension Day (May 13); Constitution day (May 17) Whit Sun–Mon; 25–26 Dec.

PUBLIC TRANSPORT

Train, boat and bus schedules linked to provide good connections. Often worth using buses or boats to connect two dead-end lines (e.g. Bergen and Stavanger), rather than retracing your route. Rail passes sometimes offer good discounts, even free travel, on linking services. NorWay Bussekspress, BUSSTERMINALEN, GALLERIET, SCHWEIGAARDSGT 8, N-0185 OSLO; 23 00 24 49 40, fax: 23 00 24 49, has the largest bus network, routes going as far north as Kirkenes. Long-distance buses: comfortable, with reclining seats, ample leg room. Tickets: buy on board, booking not required. Taxis: metered, can be picked up at ranks or by phoning; treat independent taxis with caution.

RAIL TRAVEL

National rail company: Norges Statsbaner (NSB). Fast trains: ICE, IC, IN (InterNord: daytime international services) and Et (Expresstog). 2nd-class seating is comfortable and far more plentiful than 1st-class. Sleepers: one berth in 1st class, two or three in 2nd. Couchettes: three berths. Long-distance trains carry refreshments. Reservations required for express and many other fast trains. Reserved seats not marked, but your confirmation specifies carriage and seat/berth numbers. Carriage numbers are shown by the doors at the ends, berth numbers outside compartments, seat numbers on seat-backs or luggage racks. Stations: most have baggage lockers, larger stations have baggage trolleys. Narvesen chain (at most stations; open long hours) sells English-language publications and good range of snacks. Inter-Rail Centres (in Oslo and Trondheim stations July–Aug) offer cheap showers, cooking facilities and free baggage storage (albeit at your own risk).

RAIL PASSES

Scanrail, IR, ED, EP valid (p. 23–28). Norway Rail Pass: 3 (NKr.1100, 2nd class), 4 (NKr.1364, 2nd) or 5 (NKr.1540, 2nd) days travel within one month; 1st class prices about 33% more than 2nd, senior fare about 33% less than adult fare; seat reservations and Flam line supplement extra; not valid on Oslo airport trains; available from major NSB stations. Oslo Kortet/Card: free transport on buses, trams, underground and NSB local trains (up to Zone 3), free entry to attractions, discounts on sightseeing buses/boats; 1 day NKr.150, 2 days NKr.220, 3 days NKr.250, 1 day family card (2 adults, 2 children) NKr.350; available from most hotels, campsites and Tourist Offices.

TELEPHONES

Telekorten (phonecards) available from Narvesen and post offices. Card phones spreading fast, some accept credit cards. Coin and card boxes usually together, green marking the ones for cards. Free information service;

☎80 03 10 32. Overseas calls cheapest 2200–0800 and weekends. Dial in; ☎47. Outgoing; ☎00. Directory enquiries; ☎180 for Nordic countries, ☎181 for other countries. Local operator; ☎117. International operator; ☎115. Operators speak English. These are all premium rate calls. Emergencies: Police: ☎112. Fire: ☎ 110. Ambulance: ☎113.

TOURIST INFORMATION www.tourist.no. Tourist Offices: *Turistinformasjon;* tourist boards: *Reiselivslag*. To be found in virtually all towns; free maps, brochures etc available.

VISAS National identity cards issued by EU countries, Iceland and Switzerland are sufficient. Visas not needed by Nationals of Australia, Canada, New Zealand and the USA. South Africans need visas.

POLAND

CAPITAL **Warsaw** (Warszawa).

CLIMATE Temperate, with warm summers and cold winters; rain falls throughout year.

CURRENCY Zloty (Zl.). British pounds, American dollars and German marks are useful. Kantor exchange offices sometimes give better rates than banks and opening hours are longer. Credit cards increasingly accepted but not universal.

CUSTOMS ALLOWANCES 250 cigarettes or 50 cigars or 250 g tobacco, 1 litre wine, and 1 litre any other alcoholic beverage.

EMBASSIES IN WARSAW **Aus**: ul. Estonska 3/5; ☎(022) 617 60 81. **Can**: ul. Matejki 1/5 (door on ul. Pieknej); ☎(022) 629 80 51. **NZ**: Migdalowa 4; ☎(022) 645 14 07. **UK**: Al. Roz. 1; ☎(022) 628 10 15. **USA**: Al. Ujazowskie 29/31; ☎(022) 628 30 41-9.

EMBASSIES OVERSEAS **Aus**: 7 Turrana St, Yarralumla ACT, 2600 Canberra; ☎(02) 62 73 12 11. **Can**: 443 Daly Ave, Ontario K1N 6H3, Ottawa 2; ☎(613) 789 04 68. **Ire**: 5 Ailesbury Rd, Dublin 4; ☎(1) 283 08 55. **NZ**: 17 Upland Rd, Kelburn, Wellington; ☎(4) 475 94 53. **SA**: 14 Amos St, Colbyn, Pretoria 0083; ☎(12) 43 26 31. **UK**: 47 Portland Pl., London W1N 3AG; ☎(020) 7580 4324. **USA**: 2640 16th St N.W., Washington DC 20009; ☎(202) 234 3800.

LANGUAGE Polish; many older Poles speak German; younger Poles (particularly students) may understand English. Russian widely understood, but unpopular.

OPENING HOURS **Banks**: Mon–Fri 0800–1500/1800. **Shops**: Mon–Fri 0800/1100–1900, Sat 0900–1300. **Food shops**: Mon–Fri 0600–1900, Sat 0600–1300. **Museums**: usually Tues–Sun 1000–1600; often closed public holidays and following day.

POST OFFICES Known as *Poczta*; Mon–Sat 0700/0800–1800/2000 (main offices). City post offices are numbered (main office is always 1); number should be included in the post restante address. Post boxes: green (local mail), red (long-distance).

PUBLIC HOLIDAYS 1 Jan; Easter Sun–Mon; 1, 3 May; Corpus Christi; 15 Aug; 1, 11 Nov; 24, 25, 26 Dec.

PUBLIC TRANSPORT PKS buses: cheap and often more practical than trains. Tickets include seat reservations (seat number is on back), bookable from bus station. In rural areas, bus drivers often halt between official stops if you wave them down.

RAIL TRAVEL Cheap and punctual, run by Polskie Koleje Panstwowe (PKP). At stations, departures *(odjazdy)* are on yellow paper, arrivals *(przyjazdy)* on white. IC, express *(ekspres* – prefixed Ex) and semi-express trains *(pospieszny)* are printed in red (all bookable). Black *osobowy* trains are the slowest. About 50% more for 1st class, but still cheap by Western standards and probably worth it. Overnight trains usually have 1st/2nd-class sleepers, plus 2nd-class couchettes and seats. Most long-distance trains have refreshments. Left luggage and refreshments in major stations. Few ticket clerks speak English.

RAIL PASSES Central Europe, IR, ED valid. Polrail Pass: unlimited 1st and 2nd class travel on PKP network for 8 (£61/£42), 15 (£71/£49) or 21 (£84/£55) days, or 1 month (£103/£71); available from Wasteels. Poland Rail Pass: unlimited 1st and 2nd class travel for 7 (£30/£23), 14 (£47/£32) or 21 (£63/£45) days; available to students with an ISIC card and those under 26 from USIT/Campus Travel.

TELEPHONES Older public telephones take tokens (from post offices, Ruch kiosks). Newer (more efficient) telephones take phonecards. Dial in: ☎48. Outgoing: ☎901. English-speaking operator: ☎903. Police: ☎997. Fire: 998. Ambulance: ☎999.

TOURIST INFORMATION IT tourist information office can usually help with accommodation. Also Orbis offices, for tourist information, excursions and accommodation.

TOURIST OFFICES OVERSEAS **UK**: Remo House, 310–312 Regent St, London W1R 5AJ; ☎(020) 7580 8811. **USA**: Polish National Tourist Office, 275 Madison Ave, Suite 1711, New York, NY 10016; ☎(212) 338 9412.

VISAS No visas needed for citizens of Ireland, UK or USA (but passports must be valid for at least six months after planned departure date from Poland). Nationals of Australia, Canada, New Zealand and South Africa need visas.

PORTUGAL

CAPITAL **Lisbon** (Lisboa).

CLIMATE Hotter and drier as you go south; parts very hot in summer; spring and autumn milder, but wetter. Mountains are very cold in winter.

CURRENCY **Escudos** (Esc.). 1 Escudo = 100 Centavos. In written form, the "$" sign comes between Escudos and Centavos in place of a decimal point.

CUSTOMS ALLOWANCES Standard EU regulations apply (see p. 17–18).

EMBASSIES IN LISBON **Aus**: R. Marquês da Bandeira 8; ☎353 07 50. **Can:** 4th Floor, Avenida da Liberdade 144-156; ☎347 48 92. **Ire**: R. da Imprensa à Estrella 1–4; ☎396 15 69. **NZ**: UK Embassy handles New Zealand business. **UK**: Rua S. Bernado 33; ☎392 40 00. **USA**: Avenida das Forças Armadas; ☎726 66 00.

EMBASSIES OVERSEAS **Aus**: 33 Culgoa Circuit, PO Box 92, Deakin Act, 2600 Canberra; ☎6262 901 733. **Can**: 645 Island Park Dr., Ottawa, Ontario, K1Y OB8; ☎(613) 729 0883. **Ire**: Knocksinna House, Knocksinna, Foxrock, Dublin 18; ☎(1) 289 4416. **NZ**: Deleite Touche Tohmatsu, 61 Molesworth St, Wellington; ☎644 472 1677. **SA**: 599 Leyds St, Muckleneuk, 0002 Pretoria; ☎(012) 341 2340. **UK**: 11 Belgrave Sq., SW1X 8PP; ☎(020) 7235 5331. **USA**: 2125 Kalorama Rd N.W., Washington, DC 20008-1619; ☎(1202) 328 8610.

LANGUAGE **Portuguese**; English, French, German in some tourist areas. Older people often speak French as second language, young people Spanish and/or English.

OPENING HOURS **Banks**: Mon–Fri 0830–1445/1500. **Shops**: Mon–Fri 0900/1000–1300 and 1500–1900, Sat 0900–1300. City shopping centres often daily 1000–2300 or later. **Museums**: Tues–Sun 1000–1700/1800; some close for lunch and some are free on Sun. Palaces and castles usually close on Wed.

POST OFFICES *Correio* indicates both post boxes and post offices. Most post offices open Mon–Fri 0900–1800, Sat 0900–1300; smaller ones close for lunch and Sat. Most large post offices have poste restante. Stamps *(selos)* on sale at places with sign depicting red horse or white circle on green background.

PUBLIC HOLIDAY 1 Jan; National Carnival – end Feb/beginning March; Shrove Tues; Good Fri; 25 Apr; 1 May; 10 June; Corpus Christi; 15 Aug; 5 Oct; 1 Nov; 1, 8, 25 Dec. Many local saints' holidays.

PUBLIC TRANSPORT Usually buy long-distance bus tickets before boarding. Bus stops: *paragem;* extend your arm to stop a bus. Taxis: black with green roofs or beige; illuminated signs; cheap, metered in cities, elsewhere fares negotiable; drivers may ask you to pay for their return journey; surcharges for luggage over 30 kg and night travel; 10% tip. City transport: can buy single tickets as you board, but books of tickets or passes are cheaper; on boarding, insert 1–3 tickets (according to length of journey) in the machine behind driver.

RAIL TRAVEL National rail company: Caminhos de Ferro Portugueses (CP); cheap (rail passes probably not worth it), but not punctual; 1st/2nd class on long-distance. Trains: Suburbano or Regional (local, slow); IR, IC and Serviço-Alfa (modern, fast; supplement payable; seat reservations compulsory for IC and Alfa, which have buffet cars). CP information in Lisbon; ☎(1) 888 40 25. Lockers in most stations.

RAIL PASSES IR, EP, ED, Eu valid (p. 23–28). Heavy fines if you board train without ticket bought in advance. Bilhetes turisticos: unlimited 1st and 2nd class travel on CP network; 7 (Esc.18,00), 14 (Esc.30,000) or 21(Esc.42,000) days; available from major stations. Portugal Railpass: 1st or 2nd class travel for 7, 14 or 21 days; 2nd class prices – £37, £62 or £97; available from USIT/Campus Travel to holders of ISIC cards and those under 26.

TELEPHONES Phonecards (from post offices and some tobacconists), plus coin-operated and (erratic) credit card phones. Surcharge for phones in hotels etc. International calls best made at post offices; pay after the call. Dial in: ☎351. Outgoing: ☎00. Operator: ☎118. Emergency services: ☎115.

TOURIST INFORMATION Multi-lingual telephone information service for tourists, based in Lisbon, ☎(01) 70 63 41. The police (dark blue uniforms in towns, brown in rural areas) wear red arm bands if they are bi-lingual.

TOURIST OFFICES OVERSEAS **Can**: 60 Bloor St W., Suite 1005, Toronto, Ontario, M4W 3B8; ☎(613) 921 7376. **Ire**: 54 Dawon St, Dublin 2; ☎(1) 670 9133. **SA**: Diamond Corner, 8th Floor, 68 Eloff St, Johannesburg 2000; ☎(11) 33 74775. **UK**: 22/25A Sackville St, London W1X 1LY; ☎(020) 7494 1441. **USA**: 590 Fifth Ave (4th Floor), New York, NY 10036-4704; ☎(212) 354 4403/4.

VISAS Visas required by Nationals of South Africa. Nationals of Canada and USA may stay for up to 2 months without a visa.

ROMANIA

CAPITAL **Bucharest** (Bucureşti).

CLIMATE Hot inland in summer, coast cooled by breezes; milder in winter, snow inland.

CURRENCY **Lei**. Carry dollars or Deutschmarks, plus traveller's cheques; change cash at exchange kiosks: avoid black market exchange (risk of theft). Credit cards needed for car rental, accepted in better hotels and restaurants. Bancomats (automatic cash dispensers; accept most cards at good rates) in most cities.

CUSTOMS ALLOWANCES 200 cigarettes or 300 g of tobacco, 2 litres of spirits and 4 litres of wine or beer, one video, two cameras. On departure: maximum food and medicine for 24 hours only, and 100,000 lei in cash.

EMBASSIES IN BUCHAREST **Aus**: c/o Liviu Buzila, Str. Dr E. Racota 16–18 #1; ☎666 69 23. **Can**: Str.

NICOLAE IORGA 36; ☎222 98 45. **UK**: STR. JULES MICHELET 24; ☎312 03 03. **USA**: STR. TUDOR ARGHEZI 7; ☎32 40 40.

EMBASSIES OVERSEAS
UK: ARUNDEL HOUSE, 4 PALACE GREEN, LONDON W8 4QD; ☎(020) 7937 9667. **USA**: 1607 23RD ST N.W., WASHINGTON DC, 20008-2809; ☎(202) 232 4747.

LANGUAGE
Romanian; English understood by younger people, plus some German.

OPENING HOURS
Banks: Mon–Fri 0900–1200/1300; private exchange counters open longer. **Shops**: usually 0800/0900–1800/2000, plus Sat morning or all day; often close 1300–1500. Local food shops often 0600–late. Few open Sun. **Museums**: usually 0900/1000–1700/1800; open weekends, closed Mon (and maybe Tues).

POST OFFICES
Mail usually takes five days to reach Western Europe and up to two weeks to reach North America. Post offices in every town.

PUBLIC TRANSPORT
Buy bus/tram/metro tickets in advance from kiosks (as a rule) and cancel on entry. Taxis inexpensive; if meter not in use agree a price first. Trains are best for long-distance travel, although bus routes are expanding.

RAIL TRAVEL
Rail company: Căile Ferate Române (CFR). Network links major towns; main lines mostly electrified and quite fast, but branch lines very slow. Service fairly punctual and very inexpensive. Buy tickets in advance from Agenţia de Voiaj CFR, or at the station from 1 hr before departure. Except local trains, reserve and pay a speed supplement in advance (tickets issued abroad include supplement): cheapest are *tren de persoane* (very slow), then *accelerat* (still cheap), rapids and finally IC trains (prices approaching Western levels). Food usually only available on IC and some rapids; drinks sold on other trains. Couchette *(cuşeta)* or sleeper *(vagon de dormit)* inexpensive.

RAIL PASSES
Balkan, IR, ED valid (see p. 23–28).

TELEPHONES
Operator-connected calls by telephone offices in post offices, or use Direct Acess number to reach operator at home, or buy telephone card (L20,000) for use in orange phones in some towns. Calls through hotel operators/ domestic phones: ☎971 (international), ☎991 (long-distance). Dial in: ☎40. Outgoing: ☎00. Police: ☎955. Fire: ☎981. Ambulance: ☎961.

TOURIST INFORMATION
UK: 83A MARYLEBONE HIGH ST, LONDON W1M 3DE; ☎(020) 7224 3692. **USA**: 342 MADISON AVE, SUITE 210, NEW YORK, NY 10173; ☎(212) 697 6971.

VISAS
Cheapest to obtain on entry; $33. Required by most, except USA and a few other countries, eg former Eastern bloc, Cyprus, Mexico, Tunisia, Turkey.

SLOVAKIA

CAPITAL
Bratislava.

CLIMATE
Similar to Czech Republic.

CURRENCY
Slovak Korunas or Crowns (SK.); 1 Koruna = 100 Hellers. Credit cards becoming more widely accepted.

CUSTOMS ALLOWANCES
200 cigarettes, or 50 cigars, or equivalent in tobacco, 1 litre spirits and 2 litres wine.

EMBASSIES OVERSEAS
Aus/NZ: 47 COLGOA CIRCUIT, O'MALLEY, CANBERRA ACT 2606; ☎(6) 2901 516. **Can**: 50 RIDEAU TERRACE, OTTAWA, ONTARIO K1M 2AL; ☎(3) 749 4442. **Ire**: 107 THE SWEEPSTAKES, BALLSBRIDGE, DUBLIN 4; ☎(1) 660 0270. **SA**: 930 ARCADIA ST, ARCADIA 0083, PRETORIA; ☎(12) 342 2051-2. **UK**: 25 KENSINGTON PALACE GARDENS, LONDON W8 4QY; ☎(020) 7543 0803. **USA**: 2201

Wisconsin Ave, N.W., Suite 250, Washington DC 20007; ☎(202) 965 5160-5.

LANGUAGE
Slovak, a Slavic tongue closely related to Czech. Some Russian (unpopular), German, Hungarian, plus a little English and French.

OPENING HOURS
Banks: Mon–Fri 0800–1700. **Shops**: Mon–Fri 0900–1800, Sat 0800–1200. Food shops usually open 0800 and Sun. **Museums**: (usually) Tues–Sun 1000–1700. Most castles close national holidays and Nov–Mar.

POST OFFICES
Erratic post service. Usually post office hours: 0800–1900. Stamps also available from newsagents and tobacconists. Post boxes are orange.

PUBLIC HOLIDAYS
1, 6 Jan; Good Fri; Easter Mon; 1 May; 8 May; 5 July; 29 Aug; 1, 15 Sept; 1 Nov; 24–26 Dec.

PUBLIC TRANSPORT
Comprehensive long-distance bus network, often more direct than rail in upland areas. Buy tickets from driver; priority given to those with bookings.

RAIL TRAVEL
Zeleznice Slovenskej Republiky (ZSR). Trains cheap, but often crowded. Fastest trains *expresný; rychlík* cost as much as express; cheaper are *speöný* (semi-fast) and *osobný* (very slow). At stations, departures *(odjezdy)* are on yellow posters, arrivals *(prijezdy)* on white. Sleeping cars/couchettes (reserve at all main stations, well in advance in summer) on most overnight trains. Seat reservations recommended (at station counters marked R) for express trains. Reservation agency: MTA, Párièkova 29, Bratilava; ☎(07) 526 9311.

RAIL PASSES
Central Europe, Czech and Slovak Railpass, ED, IR valid (see p. 23–28). Fares based upon distance travelled; supplements for travel on R, EC/IC and IC air-conditioned trains. Kilometrica Banka (KMB): you purchase 2000 km of travel (small discount); minimum journey 100 km; 1st class travel 1½ times 2nd class price.

TELEPHONES
Poor phone connections. Dial in: ☎421. Outgoing: ☎00. Bratislava code: ☎07. Information: ☎120 (national), ☎0149 (international). Police: ☎158. Fire: ☎150. Ambulance: ☎155.

TOURIST INFORMATION
Bratislava Information Service (BIS), Klobucnicka 2, ☎(07) 533 3715/4370; staff speak English and can arrange accommodation. SACR (Slovak Tourist Board) Head Office: Banska Bystrica: SACR, Nam. Slobody 2, PO Box 497, 974 01 Banska Bystrica, ☎(088) 742 860, fax: (088) 746 626. Satur (Slovak Tours and Travel Company), Mileticova 1; 824 72 Bratislava, ☎542 2828.

TOURIST OFFICES OVERSEAS
USA: Victor International Travel Services, 10 East 40th St, 3604 New York, NY 10016; ☎(212) 6800 730.

VISAS
Not needed by nationals of EU, South Africa or USA. Nationals of Canada, Australia and New Zealand need visas and passports valid for at least six months.

SLOVENIA

CAPITAL
Ljubljana.

CLIMATE
Warm summers, cold winters; Mediterranean climate along coast; snow in the mountains in winter.

CURRENCY
Tolar (SIT); 1 SIT = 100 stotins.

CUSTOMS ALLOWANCES
200 cigarettes, or 50 cigars, or 250g tobacco products, 1 litre spirits.

EMBASSIES OVERSEAS
Aus: Level 6, Advance Bank Center, 60 Marcus Clarke St, Canberra ACT 2601, PO Box 284; ☎(6) 243 48 30. **Can:** 150 Metcalfe St, Suite 2101, Ottawa, K2P 1P1; ☎(613) 565 57 81. **UK**: Suite One, Cavendish Court,

	11–15 WIGMORE ST, LONDON, W1H 9LA; ☎(020) 7495 77 75. **USA**: 1525 NEW HAMPSHIRE AVE N.W., WASHINGTON DC 20036; ☎(202) 667 53 63.
LANGUAGE	**Slovenian**; English, German and Italian often spoken in tourist areas.
OPENING HOURS	**Banks**: vary, but mostly Mon–Fri 0090–1200 and 1400–1630, Sat 0900–1100. **Shops**: mostly Mon–Fri 0700–1900, Sat 0730–1300. **Museums**: larger ones 1000–1800, many smaller ones 1000–1400; some close Mon.
POST OFFICES	Mon–Fri 0800–1800, Sat 0800–1200. Ljubljana's main post office, TRG OSVOBODILNE FRONTE 5, by station, open 24 hrs. Efficient postal service.
PUBLIC HOLIDAYS	1–2 Jan; 8 Feb; Easter Sun–Mon; 27 Apr; 1–2 May; 25 June; 15 Aug; 31 Oct; 1 Nov; 25–26 Dec.
PUBLIC TRANSPORT	Long-distance bus services frequent and inexpensive; usually buy ticket on boarding. Information: TRG OSVOBODILNE FRONTE 5, next to Ljubljana station; ☎(061) 1336 136. City buses have standard fare, paid with correct change into box by driver; cheaper to buy tokens from news-stands/post offices. Daily or weekly bus passes in main cities.
RAIL TRAVEL	National rail company: Slovenske Železnice (SŽ). Information: Ljubljana station; ☎(061) 1315 16, or SLOVENIJATURIST, SLOVENSKA 58, LJUBLJANA; ☎(061) 311 851.
RAIL PASSES	ED, IR valid.
TELEPHONES	International calls best made in post offices (pay afterwards). Phone booths: buy phonecards from post offices or tokens from post offices/news-stands. Dial in: ☎386. Outgoing: ☎ 00. Police: ☎113. Fire/ambulance: ☎112.
TOURIST INFORMATION	SlovenianTourist Board, DUNAJSKA 156, SI-1000 LJUBLJANA; ☎386 61 189 18 40.
TOURIST OFFICES OVERSEAS	**UK**: 49 CONDUIT ST, LONDON W1R 9FB; ☎(020) 7287 71 33. **USA**: 345 E. 12TH ST, NEW YORK, NY 10003; ☎(212) 358 96 86.
VISAS	South Africans need 3-month tourist visa and return ticket.

SPAIN

CAPITAL	**Madrid**.
CURRENCY	**Pesetas** (Pta).
CUSTOMS ALLOWANCES	Standard EU regulations apply (see p. 17–18).
EMBASSIES IN MADRID	**Aus**: PASEO CASTELLANA 143; ☎(91) 579 04 28. **Can:** C. NÚÑEZ DE BALBOA 35; ☎(91) 431 43 00. **Ire**: PLAZA DE LA CASTELLARA, 46; (4th FLOOR); ☎(91) 576 35 00. **NZ**: PLAZA LEALTAD 2 (3RD FLOOR); ☎(91) 523 02 26. **SA**: C. CLAUDIO COELLO 91; ☎(91) 435 66 88. **UK**: C. FERNANDO EL SANTO 16; ☎(91) 319 02 00. **USA**: C. SERRANO 75; ☎(91) 577 40 00.
EMBASSIES OVERSEAS	**Aus**: LEVEL 24 ST MARTIN'S TOWER, 31 MARKET ST, SYDNEY NSW 2000; ☎(612) 261 24 33. **SA**: 169 PINE ST, ARCADIA, PRETORIA 0083; ☎(21) 22 23 26. **UK**: 20 DRAYCOTT PL., LONDON SW3 2RZ; (020) 7589 8989; **USA**: 2700 15TH ST N.W., WASHINGTON, DC 20009; ☎(202) 265 0190.
LANGUAGE	**Castilian Spanish** most widely spoken. Three other official languages: Catalan, spoken in the east; Galego, spoken in Galicia (north-west), and Basque,common in the Basque country, Navarra, even across the Pyrénées into France. English is fairly widely spoken in tourist areas. In Spanish listings

'CH' comes at the end of the 'C' section, 'LL' at the end of the 'L' section.

OPENING HOURS

Banks: Mon–Thur 0930–1630; Fri 0830–1400; Sat 0830–1300 (winter); Mon–Fri 0830–1400 (summer). **Shops**: Mon–Sat 0930/1000–1400 and 1700–2000/2030; major stores do not close for lunch, food shops often open Sun. **Museums**: vary; mostly open 0900/1000, close any time from 1400 to 2030. Few open Mon and some also close (or open half day) Sun. Expect to find most places closed 1300–1500/1600, esspecially in the south.

POST OFFICES

Most *correos* open 0800–1400 and 1700–1930. Larger ones offer poste restante *(lista de correos)*. Stamps *(sellos)* also sold at tobacconists *(estancos)*. Post boxes: overseas mail in slot marked *extranjero*. Postal system very slow.

PUBLIC HOLIDAYS

1, 6 Jan; several days at Easter; 1 May; Corpus Christi; 24 June; 25 July; 15 Aug; 12 Oct; 1 Nov; 6, 8 Dec and several days at Christmas. Not of all of these are official holidays, but many places close anyway. Each region has at least four more public holidays, usually local saints' days.

PUBLIC TRANSPORT

Numerous regional bus companies *(empresas)* provide fairly comprehensive, cheap (if confusing) service. City buses are very efficient. Taxis: easily available, when free display green light on roof at night or *Libre* sign in windscreen by day; metered and cheap; surcharges on Sun or late at night, for luggage placed in the boot and travel outside town (including to airports and stations). If you feel you've been overcharged, ask the driver for a receipt *(recibo)* when you pay and take note of the route taken and the driver's licence number. Take the receipt and details to the Town Hall.

RAIL TRAVEL

National rail company: Red nacional de los Ferrocarriles Españoles (RENFE). FEVE and a number of regionally-controlled railways operate lines in coastal regions. Long distance: AVE (Alta Velocidad Española: high-speed line) and Largo Recorrido (all other express services). RENFE offer money back if their AVE trains arrive more than 5 mins late! Premier Largo Recorrido services include Talgo (light articulated train) and IC expresses. *Diurno:* ordinary long-distance day train; *Estrella* is night train (including sleeper and/or couchette cars). Pricier alternative for night travel is the *Trenhotel* (train-hotel), offering sleeping compartments with their own shower and WC. All convey 1st- and 2nd-class accommodation *(Preferente* and *Turista;* AVE also have a 'super-first' class: *Club)* and require advance reservation. *Regionales:* local stopping service; *Cercanías:* suburban trains. *Regional Exprés* (not express in English sense of word) is gradually being introduced. In remoter parts of country, services may be very infrequent. If sleeping berths/couchettes are fully booked, particularly in the middle of the night, ask if you can sleep in the train's cafeteria; supplement may still be payable.

RAIL PASSES

IR, ED, EP, Eu valid (p. 23–28). Fares based upon date and time of travel. Tarjeta Tursita: 3–10 days unlimited 2nd-class travel within 2-month period; Pta18,000–42,000; sold by RENFE; holders must purchase another discount ticket to travel on AVE, Talgo or Euromed trains. ISIC card holders and under 26s (from USIT/Campus Travel): Spain Explorerail Pass – unlimited 2nd-class travel on long-distance trains, excluding International, AVE, Talgo 200, Euromed, suburban trains; 7 (£80), 14 (£97) or 30 (£126) consecutive days; and Spain Rail Pass – 5 consecutive days travel on cercanias in and around Madrid, Barcelona or Malaga; £9 for any *one* area. Spain Rail'n'Drive: any 5 days travel (3 rail, 2 car) within 2-month period.

TELEPHONES

At least one Telefónica office (state telephone company) in every large town: use a booth to make a call and pay the clerk afterwards. Public telephone booths *(teléfono publico* or *locutorio)* usually have English instructions. Accept credit cards, money or *Teletarjeta* (phonecard – sold in tobacconists, post offices, some shops). Pay phones in bars are usually more expensive. Dial in:

☎00 34. Outgoing: ☎07. Police: ☎091 everywhere. Fire: ☎080 in most towns, can vary. Ambulance: numbers vary, check locally.

TOURIST INFORMATION *Oficinas de Turismo* (Tourist Offices) can provide maps and information on accommodation and sightseeing, and generally have English-speaking staff. Regional offices stock information on the whole region, municipal offices cover only that city; larger towns have both types of office.

TOURIST OFFICES OVERSEAS **UK**: 22 MANCHESTER SQ., LONDON W1M 5AP; ☎(020) 7486 8077. **USA**: 666 FIFTH AVE, NEW YORK, NY 10103; ☎(212) 265 8822.

VISAS EU National Identity Cards and those issued to nationals of Andorra, Austria, Liechtenstein, Malta, Monaco and Switzerland sufficient. Visas not needed by nationals of Aus, Can, NZ, USA for visits of up to 90 days. Non-EU nationals must hold onward or return tickets plus a minimum of £25 (sterling) per day of their intended stay, or a minimum of Pta50,000.

SWEDEN

CAPITAL **Stockholm**.

CLIMATE Often warm (especially in summer; non-stop daylight in far north). Huge range between north and south; it can be mild in Skåne (far south) in Feb, but spring comes late May in the north. Winter generally very cold everywhere.

CURRENCY **Kronor** or crowns. (SEK or SKr.); 1 krona = 100 öre. Växlare machines give change. The best exchange rate is obtained from Forex, which has branches at many stations. Keep receipts so that you can re-convert at no extra cost.

CUSTOMS ALLOWANCES EU regulations apply (p. 17–18); must be aged 20 or over to import alcohol.

EMBASSIES IN STOCKHOLM **Aus**: BLOCK 5, SERGELS TORG 12; ☎613 29 00. **Can**: TEGELBACKEN 4; ☎453 30 00. **SA**: LINNÉGATAN 76; ☎24 39 50. **UK**: SKARPÖGATAN 6-8; ☎671 90 00. **USA**: STRANDVAGEN 101; ☎783 53 00.

EMBASSIES OVERSEAS **Aus**: 5 TURRANA ST, ACT 2600, YARRALUMLA, CANBERRA; ☎(2) 6270 2700. **Can**: 377 DALHOUSIE ST, OTTAWA, ON K1N 9N8; ☎: (613) 241 8553. **Ire**: SUN ALLIANCE HOUSE, 13-17 DAWSON ST, DUBLIN 2; ☎(1) 671 5822. **NZ**: (see Australia); Consulate: VOGEL BUILDING 13TH FL. AITKEN ST. WELLINGTON; ☎(4) 499 9895. **SA**: OLD MUTUAL BUILDING, ANDRIES ST 167, 9TH FLOOR, PRETORIA; ☎(12) 321 1050. **UK**: 11 MONTAGU PL., LONDON W1H 2AL; ☎(020) 7917 6413. **USA**: 1501 M ST N.W., WASHINGTON, D.C., 20005-1702; ☎(202) 467 2600.

LANGUAGE **Swedish**. English is widely spoken. Useful rail/bus/ferry words include *daglig* (daily), *Vardagar/Vard* (Mon–Fri) and *helgdagar* (holidays).

OPENING HOURS **Banks**: Mon–Fri 0930–1500, Thur 1600–1730. Some, especially at transport terminals, have longer hours. **Shops**: mostly Mon–Fri 0900/0930–1700/1800, Sat 0900/0930–1300/1600. **Museums**: vary widely. In winter, many attractions close Mon and some close altogether.

POST OFFICES Generally Mon–Fri 0900–1800, Sat 1000–1300. Stamps also sold at news-agents and tobacconists. Post boxes: overseas mail are yellow; blue are local.

PUBLIC HOLIDAYS 1 ,6 Jan; Good Friday; Easter Sun–Mon; Labour Day (1 May); Ascension Day; Whit Sun–Mon; Midsummer's Eve–Day; All Saints Day; 24-26 and 31Dec. Many places close early the previous day, or Fri if it's a long weekend.

PUBLIC TRANSPORT Transport system is highly efficient; ferries covered (in whole or part) by rail passes and city transport cards. Biggest operator of long-distance buses is Swebus. Advance booking is required on some routes and always advisable in summer; bus terminals usually adjoin train stations.

RAIL TRAVEL

National rail company: Statens Järnvävar (SJ); some local lines run by regional authorities. Central information line (local rates): ☎(0498) 491 455. Supplement required on X2000 train (up to 200 kph); smaller supplements for CityExpress trains. Sleeping-cars: one or two berths in 2nd class; couchettes: six berths; female-only compartment available. 1st-class sleeping-cars (ensuite shower and WC) on many overnight services; 2nd-class have ensuite wash-basins, shower, WC at end of carriage. Long-distance trains have refreshment service. Many trains have family car, with a playroom, and facilities for the disabled. Seat reservations compulsory on X2000, night trains and journeys over 150 km on other services. Better to use local trains for short journeys. A big town's main station shows 'C' (for Central) on platform boards. Stations: *Biljetter* is the rail ticket office. Large, detailed timetables are displayed for long-distance trains: yellow for departures, white for arrivals. CityExpress services often use the same platforms; there's usually a diagram of the train. Pressbyrån (at most stations): sell English-language publications and snacks.

RAIL PASSES

IR, ED, EP, Scanrail valid (p. 23–28). Sweden Rail Pass: unlimited 1st or 2nd class travel on SJ network; 3 days out of 7 (£194/£143); 5 out of 14 (£233/£177) or 7 (£268/£216) and 14 (£364/£273) consecutive days; seat reservation extra; 2 children under 15 travelling with 1 adult go free, reduced rates for other children; purchase outside Sweden from Deutsche Bahn. 1 dynskort, SKr.60, and 3 dynskort, SKr.120: unlimited travel on all public transport in Greater Stockholm from 0000–0430 the next morning.

TELEPHONES

Coin-operated phones decreasing in number; most card phones accept both credit cards and *Telia* phonecards *(telephoncarten,* from most newsagents, tobacconists, Pressbrån kiosks). Dial in: ☎46. Emergency services: ☎900 00.

TOURIST INFORMATION

Swedish Tourist Board: info@stoinfo.se; www.visit-sweden.com. Tourist offices called *Turistbyrå*'. Often a numerical queuing system in public places.

TOURIST OFFICES OVERSEAS

UK: 11 MONTAGU PL., LONDON W1H 2AL; ☎(020) 7724 5868.

VISAS

National identity cards issued by EU countries, Iceland and Switzerland are sufficient. Visas not required by citizens of Australia, Canada, New Zealand and the USA. South Africans need visas.

SWITZERLAND

CAPITAL

Berne.

CLIMATE

Rainfall spread throughout the year. May–Sept are best in the mountains. June or early July best for the wild flowers. Snow at high altitudes even in midsummer. Season in the lakes: Apr–Oct. July and Aug get very busy.

CURRENCY

Swiss Francs (SFr.); 1 Franc = 100 Centimes.

CUSTOMS

Visitors aged 17 or over: 200 cigarettes or 50 cigars or 250 g tobacco, 2 litres alcohol up to 15% volume, and 1 litre over 15% volume. Residents outside Europe are entitled to twice the tobacco allowance.

EMBASSIES IN BERNE

Aus: ALPENSTR. 29; ☎(031) 351 01 43. **Can**: KIRCHENFELDSTR. 88; ☎(031) 352 63 81. **UK**: THUNSTR. 50; ☎ (031) 352 50 21. **USA**: JUBILÄUMSSTR. 93; ☎(031) 357 70 11.

EMBASSIES OVERSEAS

UK: 16/18 MONTAGU PL., LONDON W1H 2BQ; ☎(020) 7616 6000. **USA**:

2900 CATHEDRAL AVE N.W., WASHINGTON, DC 20008-3499; ☎(202) 745 7900.

LANGUAGE	**German, French, Italian** and **Romansch** are all official languages. Most Swiss people are at least bilingual. English is widespread.
OPENING HOURS	**Banks**: Mon–Fri 0800–1200 and 1400–1700. Money change desks in most rail stations, open longer hours. **Shops**: Mon–Fri 0800–1200 and 1330–1830, Sat 0800–1200 and 1330–1600. Many close Mon morning. In stations, shops open longer hours and on Sun. **Museums**: usually close Mon. Hours vary.
POST OFFICES	Usually Mon–Fri 0730–1200 and 1345–1830, Sat 0730–1100; longer in cities. Poste restante *(Postlagernd)* facilities available at most post offices.
PUBLIC HOLIDAYS	1 Jan; Good Fri; Easter Mon; Ascension Day; Whit Mon; 1 Aug (Swiss National Day); 25, 26 Dec. 2 Jan; 1 May; Corpus Christi in some areas.
PUBLIC TRANSPORT	Swiss buses are famously punctual. Yellow postbuses stop at rail station; free timetables from post offices. Swiss Pass valid (see below), surcharge (SFr.5) for some scenic routes. Best way to get around centres is on foot.
RAIL TRAVEL	Principal rail carrier is Swiss Federal Railways (SBB),CFF in French, FFS in Italian; plus many small, private lines. Services are fast and punctual, trains spotlessly clean. All express trains stop only at major cities. *Regionalzüge,* slow local trains, stop more frequently on same routes. Some international trains have sleepers (3 berths) and/or couchettes (up to 6 people). Sleepers can be booked up to 3 months in advance, couchettes/seats up to 2 months ahead. Reservations required on sightseeing trains (e.g. Glacier Express). Information: ☎157 22 22, English-speaking operator. All main stations have information offices (and usually Tourist Offices), shopping and eating facilities. Provincial stations display train schedules. Cycle hire at most stations.
RAIL PASSES	IR, ED, EP, Eu valid (p. 23–28). Swiss Pass: 4, 8, 15 days or 1 month; 1st and 2nd class; £90–260; Swiss Flexi Pass: 3 days in 15-day period; 1st (£136) or 2nd (£90) class; both include Swiss rail, postbuses, boats, 35 municipal tranports, 25% discount on Jungfraubahnen, Rigibahnen. Swiss Transfer Ticket: 1-day transfer from any airport/border station to any other station and return; valid for 1 month; 1st class £64, 2nd £42; from Swiss Tourism. Swiss Half Fare Card: £38; half-price tickets for 1 month; includes mountain rail, bus, boat. Regional Pass: unlimited travel on train, bus, boat in 9 areas; 2, 3 or 5 days out of 7- or 15-day period; 50% discount on other days in period; 50% discount in adjoining areas, not region 6; reduced price for holders of above cards. Urban Areas: special fares in 15 tarif zones. Jungfraubahnen Pass: 25% discount on Jungfraubahn, discounts on other public transport.
TELEPHONES	Swisscom offices sell phonecards *(taxcard;* also available from most rail stations) and you can make international calls from them; pay when you have finished. All operators speak English. Dial in: ☎00 41. Outgoing: ☎00. Police: ☎117. Fire: ☎118. Ambulance: ☎144 (most areas).
TOURIST INFORMATION	Tourist Offices in almost every town or village. The standard of information is excellent.
TOURIST OFFICES OVERSEAS	**Can**: Switzerland Tourism, 926 THE EAST MALL, ETOBICOKE, TORONTO, ONT., M9B 6K1; ☎(416) 695 2090. **UK**: SWISS CENTRE, SWISS COURT, LONDON W1V 8EE; ☎(020) 7734 1921. **USA**: Switzerland Tourism (ST), SWISS CENTER, 608 FIFTH AVE, NEW YORK, NY 10020; ☎(212) 757 5944.
VISAS	Valid passport required. Visas required for stays of more than 3 months, For shorter stays, visas not needed by nationals of EU, Australia, countries of the American continents (except Belize, Dominican Republic, Haiti and Peru), Japan and New Zealand.

UNITED KINGDOM

CAPITAL	**London**.
CLIMATE	Cool, wet winters, mild spring and autumn, winter can be more extreme. Wetter in the west. Aug and Bank Holiday weekends busiest in tourist areas.
CURRENCY	**Pounds Sterling** (£). 1 Pound = 100 Pence.
CUSTOMS ALLOWANCES	Standard EU regulations apply (see p. 17–18).
EMBASSIES IN LONDON	**Aus**: Australia House, Strand, WC2B 4LA; ☎(020) 7379 4334. **Can**: 1 Grosvenor Sq., W1X 0AB; ☎258 6600. **Ire**: 17 Grosvenor Pl., SW1X 7HR; ☎235 2171. **NZ**: New Zealand House, 80 Haymarket, SW1Y 4TQ; ☎(020) 7930 8422. **SA**: South Africa House, Trafalgar Sq., WC2N 5DP; ☎(020) 7451 7299. **USA**: 24 Grosvenor Sq., W1A 1AE, ☎(020) 7499 9000.
EMBASSIES OVERSEAS	**Aus**: Commonwealth Ave, Yarralumla, Canberra, ACT 2600, ☎(06) 270 6666. **Can**: 80 Elgin St, Ottawa, Ontario K1P 5K7; ☎(613) 237 1530. **Ire**: 31–33 Merrion Rd, Dublin 4; ☎(01) 269 5211. **NZ**: 44 Hill St, Wellington 1; ☎(04) 472 6049. **SA**: 255 Hill St, Pretoria 0002; ☎(021) 433 3121. **USA**: 3100 Massachusetts Ave N.W., Washington, DC 20008, ☎(202) 462 1340.
LANGUAGE	**English**, plus, in a very small way, Welsh and Gaelic.
OPENING HOURS	**Banks**: Mon–Fri 0930–1530. Some open Sat morning. **Shops**: Mon–Sat 0900–1730. Many supermarkets and some small shops open longer, plus Sun. **Museums**: usually Mon–Sat 0900/1000–1730/1800, half-day Sun.
POST OFFICES	Usually Mon–Fri 0930–1730, Sat 0930–1300; stamps sold in newsagents etc.
PUBLIC HOLIDAYS	England and Wales: 1 Jan; Good Fri; Easter Mon; May Day (first Mon May, may change): Spring Bank Holiday (last Mon May); Summer Bank Holiday (last Mon Aug); 25, 26 Dec. Variations in Scotland and Ireland.
PUBLIC TRANSPORT	Inter-city buses are cheaper, but slower, than trains. Main operator: National Express. Most town networks are good, but rural services patchy.
RAIL TRAVEL	Passenger services run by private sector companies; booking office staff must give cheapest fare. IC trains: comfortable, fast and frequent; 1st and standard class. Other long- and medium-distance regional services, usually standard class only. Refreshments available on board. Sleepers: cabins are two-berth or (higher charge) single. Reservation (essential for sleepers) available for most long-distance services; usually free on busiest trains, others £1–£2. Weekend travel often interrupted by engineering works, buses replace trains.
RAIL PASSES	(p. 23–28). Rover/Ranger Ticket: almost unlimited travel within defined area; All-Line Rail Rover covers whole country; rovers valid 3–15 days, rangers 1 day. Saver/SuperSaver: reduced fare tickets; some time restrictions; purchase day of travel or shortly before.
TELEPHONES	Phonecards sold at newsagents; pay phones take coins, phonecards or credit cards. Dial in: ☎44. Outgoing: ☎00. Emergency services: ☎999.
TOURIST INFORMATION	Best to contact local Tourist Offices.
TOURIST OFFICE OVERSEAS	**Aus**: 210 Clarence St, Sydney, NSW 2000; ☎(02) 261 6034. **Can**: 111 Avenue Rd (Ste 450), Toronto, Ontario M5R 3J8; ☎(416) 961 8124. **Ire**: 18–19 College Green, Dublin; ☎(01) 670 8000. **NZ**: Ste 305, 3rd Floor Dilworth Building, Customs/Queen St, Auckland 1; ☎(09) 303 1446. **SA**: Lancaster Gate, Hyde Park Lane, 2196-Johannesburg, ☎ (011) 325 0343. **USA**: 551 Fifth Ave (7th Flr), New York, NY 10176-0799 ☎(212) 986 2266.
VISAS	Visas not needed by EU citizens, or by tourists from Aus, Can, NZ, SA, USA.

DISTANCES (approx. conversions)

1 kilometre (km) = 1000 metres (m) 1 metre = 100 centimetres (cm)

Metric	Imperial/US	Metric	Imperial/US	Metric	Imperial/US
1 cm	3/8 in.	10 m	33 ft (11 yd)	3 km	2 miles
50 cm	20 in.	20 m	66 ft (22 yd)	4 km	2½ miles
1 m	3 ft 3 in.	50 m	164 ft (54 yd)	5 km	3 miles
2 m	6 ft 6 in.	100 m	330 ft (110 yd)	10 km	6 miles
3 m	10 ft	200 m	660 ft (220 yd)	20 km	12½ miles
4 m	13 ft	250 m	820 ft (275 yd)	25 km	15½ miles
5 m	16 ft 6 in.	300 m	984 ft (330 yd)	30 km	18½ miles
6 m	19 ft 6 in.	500 m	1640 ft (550 yd)	40 km	25 miles
7 m	23 ft	750 m	½ mile	50 km	31 miles
8 m	26 ft	1 km	5/8 mile	75 km	46 miles
9 m	29 ft (10 yd)	2 km	1½ miles	100 km	62 miles

24-HOUR CLOCK

(examples)

0000 = Midnight	1200 = Noon	1800 = 6 pm
0600 = 6 am	1300 = 1 pm	2000 = 8 pm
0715 = 7.15 am	1415 = 2.15 pm	2110 = 9.10 pm
0930 = 9.30 am	1645 = 4.45 pm	2345 = 11.45 pm

TEMPERATURE

Conversion Formula: °C × 9 ÷ 5 + 32 = °F

°C	°F	°C	°F	°C	°F	°C	°F
-20	-4	-5	23	10	50	25	77
-15	5	0	32	15	59	30	86
-10	14	5	41	20	68	35	95

WEIGHT

1kg = 1000g 100 g = 3½ oz

Kg	Lbs	Kg	Lbs	Kg	Lbs
1	2¼	5	11	25	55
2	4½	10	22	50	110
3	6½	15	33	75	165
4	9	20	45	100	220

FLUID MEASURES

1 ltr.(l) = 0.88 Imp. quarts = 1.06 US quarts

Ltrs.	Imp. gal.	US gal.	Ltrs.	Imp. gal.	US gal.
5	1.1	1.3	30	6.6	7.8
10	2.2	2.6	35	7.7	9.1
15	3.3	3.9	40	8.8	10.4
20	4.4	5.2	45	9.9	11.7
25	5.5	6.5	50	11.0	13.0

MEN'S SHIRTS

UK	Europe	US
14	36	14
15	38	15
15½	39	15½
16	41	16
16½	42	16½
17	43	17

MEN'S SHOES

UK	Europe	US
6	40	7
7	41	8
8	42	9
9	43	10
10	44	11
11	45	12

LADIES' CLOTHES

UK	France	Italy	Rest of Europe	US
10	36	38	34	8
12	38	40	36	10
14	40	42	38	12
16	42	44	40	14
18	44	46	42	16
20	46	48	44	18

MEN'S CLOTHES

UK	Europe	US
36	46	36
38	48	38
40	50	40
42	52	42
44	54	44
46	56	46

LADIES' SHOES

UK	Europe	US
3	36	4½
4	37	5½
5	38	6½
6	39	7½
7	40	8½
8	41	9½

AREAS

1 hectare = 2.471 acres

1 hectare = 10,000 sq meters

1 acre = 0.4 hectares

This index lists places and topics in alphabetical sequence. All references are to page numbers. **Bold** numbers refer to map pages. To find routes between cities, see pp. 8–9.

If you enjoyed using this book, or even if you didn't, please help us improve future editions by taking part in our reader survey. Every returned form will be acknowledged, and to show our appreciation we will give you £1 off your next purchase of a Thomas Cook guidebook. Just take a few minutes to complete and return this form to us.

When did you buy this book? ______________________________

Where did you buy it? (Please give town/city and if possible name of retailer)

____

____

When did you/do you intend to travel in Europe? ______________________________

____

For how long (approx.)? ______________________________

How many people in your party? ______________________________

Which cities and other locations did you/do you intend mainly to visit?

____

____

____

____

Did you/will you:

- Make all your travel arrangements independently?
- Travel on an Inter-Rail pass?
- Travel on a Eurail Pass?
- If you purchased a rail pass, where did you buy it? ______________________________
- Use other passes or tickets, please give brief details: ______________________________

____

Did you/do you intend to use this book:

- For planning your trip?
- During the trip itself?
- Both?

Did you/do you intend also to purchase any of the following travel publications for your trip?

- *Thomas Cook European Timetable*
- *Thomas Cook European Timetable Independent Traveller's Edition*
- *Thomas Cook New Rail Map of Europe*
- *Thomas Cook European Travel Phrase book*
- Other guidebooks or maps, please specify

____

____

Have you used any other Thomas Cook guidebooks in the past? If so, which?

____

____

Reader Survey

Please rate the following features within this guide for their value to you
(Circle vu for 'very useful', u for 'useful', nu for 'little or no use'):

The 'Travelling around Europe' section on pages 14–22	vu	u	nu
The 'Rail pass' section on pages 23–28	vu	u	nu
The 'Rail travel' section on pages 29–32	vu	u	nu
The 'Directory' section on pages 540–569	vu	u	nu
The recommended routes throughout the book	vu	u	nu
Information on towns and cities	vu	u	nu
The maps of towns and cities	vu	u	nu

This book will be updated annually, which allows us to amend and enhance the information we include within it, but we need our readers to tell us what they would like to see changed and improved. Please use this space to make any comments you have concerning this book.

Your age category: under 21 21-30 31-40 41-50 over 50

Your name: Mr/Mrs/Miss/Ms
(First name or initials)
(Last name)

Your full address: (Please include postal or zip code)

Your daytime telephone number:

Please detach this page and send it to: **The Editor, Independent Traveller's Europe, Thomas Cook Publishing, PO Box 227, Peterborough PE3 6PU, United Kingdom.**

We will be pleased to send you details of how to claim your discount upon receipt of this questionnaire.

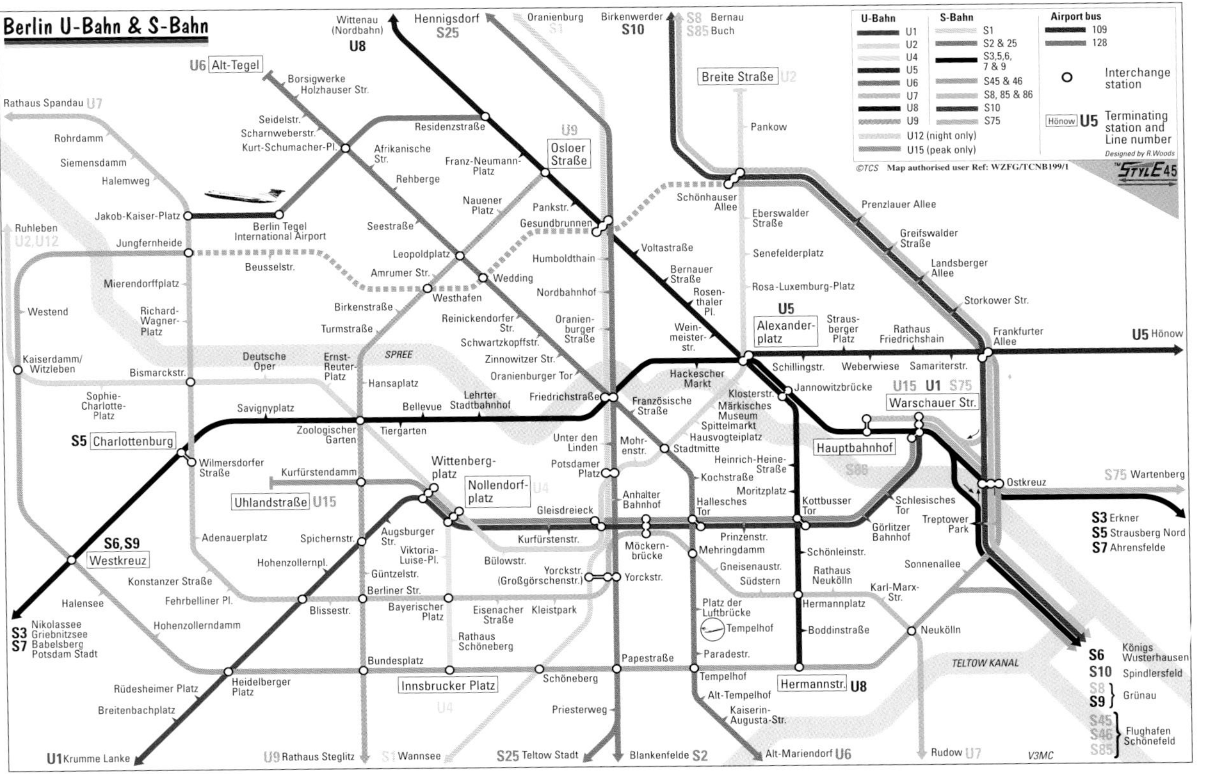

Berlin U-Bahn & S-Bahn
U-Bahn
U1
U2
U4
U5
U6
U7
U8
U9
U12 (night only)
U15 (peak only)
S-Bahn
S1
S2 & 25
S3,5,6, 7 & 9
S45 & 46
S8, 85 & 86
S10
S75
Airport bus
109
128
Interchange station
Hönow U5 Terminating station and Line number
Designed by R.Woods
©TCS Map authorised user Ref: WZFG/TCNB199/1
STYLE45
Wittenau (Nordbahn) U8
Hennigsdorf S25
Oranienburg S1
Birkenwerder S10
S8 Bernau
S85 Buch
U6 Alt-Tegel
Borsigwerke
Holzhauser Str.
Rathaus Spandau U7
Rohrdamm
Siemensdamm
Halemweg
Jakob-Kaiser-Platz
Berlin Tegel International Airport
Seidelstr.
Scharnweberstr.
Kurt-Schumacher-Pl.
Residenzstraße
Afrikanische Str.
Rehberge
Franz-Neumann-Platz
U9
Osloer Straße
Breite Straße U2
Pankow
Ruhleben U2,U12
Jungfernheide
Beusselstr.
Seestraße
Nauener Platz
Pankstr.
Gesundbrunnen
Schönhauser Allee
Eberswalder Straße
Prenzlauer Allee
Greifswalder Straße
Landsberger Allee
Storkower Str.
Leopoldplatz
Amrumer Str.
Wedding
Humboldthain
Voltastraße
Senefelderplatz
Mierendorffplatz
Westend
Richard-Wagner-Platz
Westhafen
Birkenstraße
Turmstraße
Nordbahnhof
Bernauer Straße
Rosenthaler Pl.
Rosa-Luxemburg-Platz
Reinickendorfer Str.
Schwartzkopffstr.
Oranienburger Straße
Weinmeister-str.
U5
Alexanderplatz
Strausberger Platz
Rathaus Friedrichshain
Frankfurter Allee
U5 Hönow
Kaiserdamm/ Witzleben
Deutsche Oper
Ernst-Reuter-Platz
SPREE
Zinnowitzer Str.
Oranienburger Tor
Bismarckstr.
Hansaplatz
Lehrter Stadtbahnhof
Friedrichstraße
Hackescher Markt
Schillingstr.
Weberwiese
Samariterstr.
Sophie-Charlotte-Platz
Savignyplatz
Bellevue
Französische Straße
Klosterstr.
Märkisches Museum
Spittelmarkt
Jannowitzbrücke
U15 U1 S75
Warschauer Str.
Zoologischer Garten
Tiergarten
Unter den Linden
Mohrenstr.
Hausvogteiplatz
Hauptbahnhof
S5 Charlottenburg
Wilmersdorfer Straße
Kurfürstendamm
Wittenberg-platz
Nollendorf-platz U4
Potsdamer Platz
Stadtmitte
Heinrich-Heine-Straße
S86
Ostkreuz
S75 Wartenberg
Uhlandstraße U15
Anhalter Bahnhof
Kochstraße
Moritzplatz
Gleisdreieck
Hallesches Tor
Kottbusser Tor
Schlesisches Tor
Treptower Park
S3 Erkner
S5 Strausberg Nord
S7 Ahrensfelde
S6,S9
Westkreuz
Adenauerplatz
Spichernstr.
Augsburger Str.
Kurfürstenstr.
Prinzenstr.
Görlitzer Bahnhof
Viktoria-Luise-Pl.
Bülowstr.
Möckernbrücke
Mehringdamm
Schönleinstr.
Hohenzollernpl.
Güntzelstr.
Yorckstr. (Großgörschenstr.)
Yorckstr.
Gneisenaustr.
Sonnenallee
Konstanzer Straße
Berliner Str.
Südstern
Rathaus Neukölln
Karl-Marx-Str.
Halensee
Fehrbelliner Pl.
Blissestr.
Bayerischer Platz
Eisenacher Straße
Kleistpark
Platz der Luftbrücke
Hermannplatz
Hohenzollerndamm
Tempelhof
Boddinstraße
Neukölln
S3 S7 Nikolassee Griebnitzsee Babelsberg Potsdam Stadt
Rathaus Schöneberg
Paradestr.
TELTOW KANAL
S6 Königs Wusterhausen
S10 Spindlersfeld
Bundesplatz
Papestraße
Rüdesheimer Platz
Heidelberger Platz
Innsbrucker Platz
Schöneberg
Tempelhof
Hermannstr. U8
S8 S9 Grünau
Alt-Tempelhof
Breitenbachplatz
U4
Priesterweg
Kaiserin-Augusta-Str.
S45 S46 S85 Flughafen Schönefeld
U1 Krumme Lanke
U9 Rathaus Steglitz
S1 Wannsee
S25 Teltow Stadt
Blankenfelde S2
Alt-Mariendorf U6
Rudow U7
V3MC

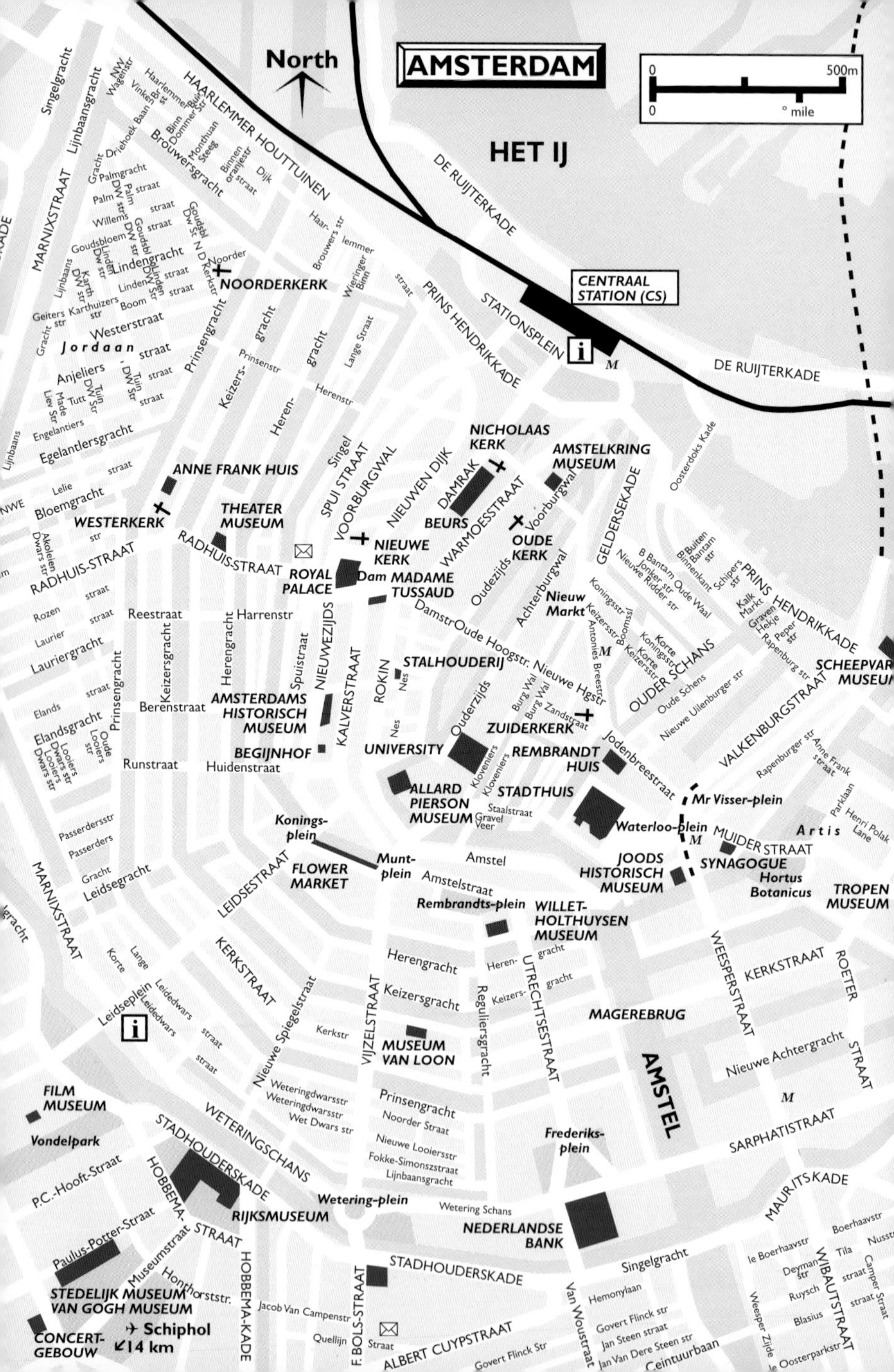
North
AMSTERDAM
0
500m
0
° mile
HET IJ
Singelgracht
Lijnbaansgracht
MARNIXSTRAAT
HAARLEMMER HOUTTUINEN
Haarlemmer
Brouwersgracht
Palmgracht
Lindengracht
Westerstraat
Jordaan
Anjeliers
Egelantiersgracht
Engelantiers
Bloemgracht
Lelie
Noorder
NOORDERKERK
Prinsengracht
Keizers-gracht
Heren-gracht
Singel
Herenstr
Prinsenstr
Lange Straat
Brouwers str
Haar-lemmer
Wieringer
DE RUIJTERKADE
PRINS HENDRIKKADE
STATIONSPLEIN
CENTRAAL STATION (CS)
M
DE RUIJTERKADE
Oosterdoks Kade
ANNE FRANK HUIS
WESTERKERK
THEATER MUSEUM
RADHUIS-STRAAT
SPUI STRAAT
VOORBURGWAL
NIEUWEN DIJK
DAMRAK
NICHOLAAS KERK
AMSTELKRING MUSEUM
WARMOESSTRAAT
BEURS
NIEUWE KERK
ROYAL PALACE
Dam
MADAME TUSSAUD
OUDE KERK
Oudezijds
Voorburgwal
Achterburgwal
GELDERSEKADE
Nieuw Markt
Damstr
Oude Hoogstr.
Nieuwe Hgstr
PRINS HENDRIKKADE
SCHEEPVAR MUSEUI
Rozen
Laurier
Lauriergracht
Reestraat
Harrenstr
Keizersgracht
Herengracht
Spuistraat
NIEUWEZIJDS
KALVERSTRAAT
ROKIN
Nes
STALHOUDERIJ
Berenstraat
AMSTERDAMS HISTORISCH MUSEUM
Elands
Elandsgracht
BEGIJNHOF
UNIVERSITY
ZUIDERKERK
REMBRANDT HUIS
Jodenbreestraat
OUDER SCHANS
VALKENBURGSTRAAT
Runstraat
Huidenstraat
Kloveniers
STADTHUIS
Staalstraat
ALLARD PIERSON MUSEUM
Mr Visser-plein
Waterloo-plein
Artis
MUIDER STRAAT
Konings-plein
Passerdersstr
Passerders
Leidsegracht
LEIDSESTRAAT
FLOWER MARKET
Munt-plein
Amstel
Amstelstraat
JOODS HISTORISCH MUSEUM
SYNAGOGUE
Hortus Botanicus
TROPEN MUSEUM
Rembrandts-plein
WILLET-HOLTHUYSEN MUSEUM
MARNIXSTRAAT
KERKSTRAAT
Herengracht
Keizersgracht
UTRECHTSESTRAAT
Reguliersgracht
WEESPERSTRAAT
KERKSTRAAT
ROETER STRAAT
MAGEREBRUG
Leidseplein
Leidsedwars straat
Nieuwe Spiegelstraat
Kerkstr
VIJZELSTRAAT
MUSEUM VAN LOON
AMSTEL
Nieuwe Achtergracht
FILM MUSEUM
Vondelpark
Weteringdwarsstr
Wet Dwars str
Prinsengracht
Noorder Straat
Nieuwe Looiersstr
Fokke-Simonszstraat
Lijnbaansgracht
Frederiks-plein
SARPHATISTRAAT
WETERINGSCHANS
STADHOUDERSKADE
P.C.-Hooft-Straat
HOBBEMA-STRAAT
RIJKSMUSEUM
Wetering-plein
Wetering Schans
NEDERLANDSE BANK
MAURITSKADE
Paulus-Potter-Straat
Museumstraat
Honthorststr.
HOBBEMA-KADE
STADHOUDERSKADE
Singelgracht
Van Woustraat
Hemonylaan
Govert Flinck str
Jan Steen straat
Jan Van Dere Steen str
Ceintuurbaan
WIBAUTSTRAAT
Weesper Zijde
Oosterparkstr
STEDELIJK MUSEUM
VAN GOGH MUSEUM
Jacob Van Campenstr
Quellijn Straat
F. BOLS-STRAAT
ALBERT CUYPSTRAAT
CONCERT-GEBOUW
✈ Schiphol
↙14 km

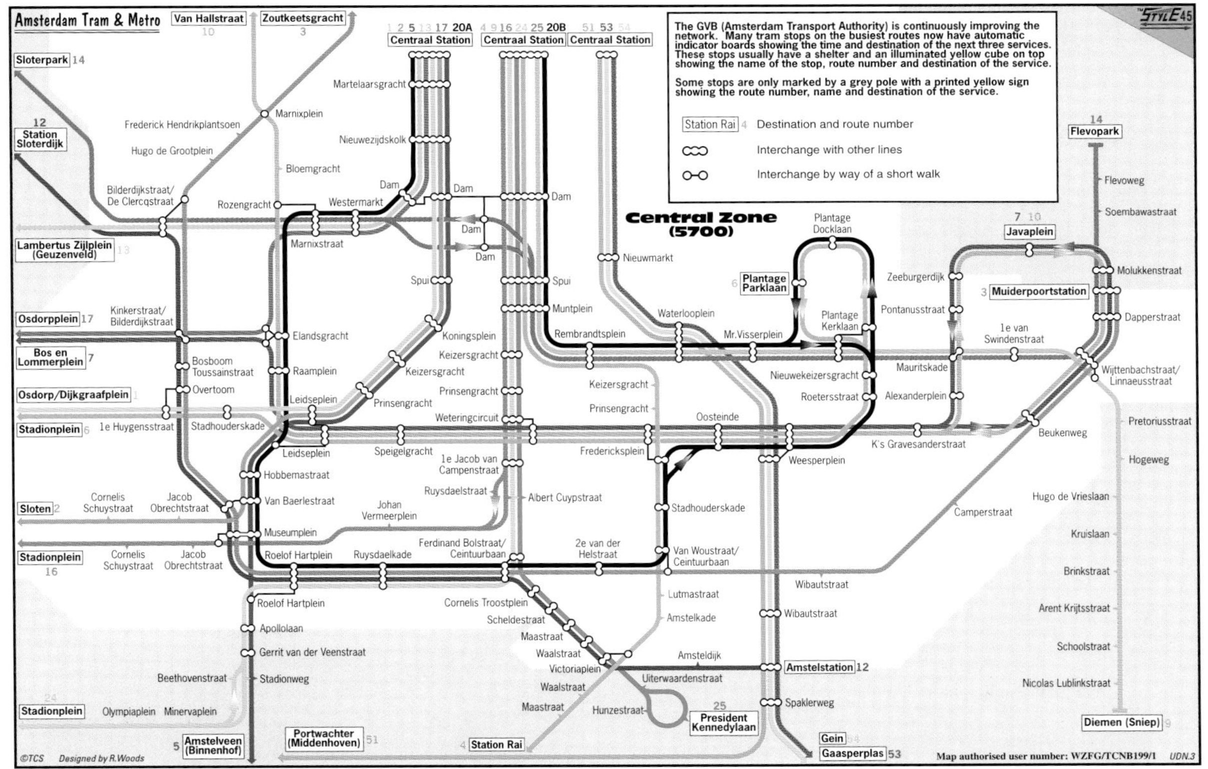

Amsterdam Tram & Metro
Van Hallstraat 10
Zoutkeetsgracht 3
1 2 5 13 17 20A Centraal Station
4 9 16 24 25 20B Centraal Station
51 53 54 Centraal Station
STYLE45
The GVB (Amsterdam Transport Authority) is continuously improving the network. Many tram stops on the busiest routes now have automatic indicator boards showing the time and destination of the next three services. These stops usually have a shelter and an illuminated yellow cube on top showing the name of the stop, route number and destination of the service.
Some stops are only marked by a grey pole with a printed yellow sign showing the route number, name and destination of the service.
Station Rai 4 Destination and route number
Interchange with other lines
Interchange by way of a short walk
Central Zone (5700)
Sloterpark 14
12 Station Sloterdijk
Lambertus Zijlplein (Geuzenveld) 13
Osdorpplein 17
Bos en Lommerplein 7
Osdorp/Dijkgraafplein 1
Stadionplein 6
Sloten 2
Stadionplein 16
24 Stadionplein
5 Amstelveen (Binnenhof)
Portwachter (Middenhoven) 51
4 Station Rai
25 President Kennedylaan
Gein 54
Gaasperplas 53
Amstelstation 12
Diemen (Sniep) 9
14 Flevopark
7 10 Javaplein
3 Muiderpoortstation
6 Plantage Parklaan
Martelaarsgracht
Nieuwezijdskolk
Marnixplein
Frederick Hendrikplantsoen
Hugo de Grootplein
Bloemgracht
Bilderdijkstraat/ De Clercqstraat
Rozengracht
Westermarkt
Dam
Marnixstraat
Spui
Muntplein
Rembrandtsplein
Nieuwmarkt
Waterlooplein
Mr.Visserplein
Plantage Docklaan
Plantage Kerklaan
Zeeburgerdijk
Pontanusstraat
1e van Swindenstraat
Molukkenstraat
Dapperstraat
Mauritskade
Alexanderplein
Nieuwekeizersgracht
Roetersstraat
Wijttenbachstraat/ Linnaeusstraat
Flevoweg
Soembawastraat
Pretoriusstraat
Hogeweg
Beukenweg
K's Gravesanderstraat
Weesperplein
Oosteinde
Frederickspleín
Keizersgracht
Prinsengracht
Kinkerstraat/ Bilderdijkstraat
Elandsgracht
Koningsplein
Raamplein
Bosboom Toussainstraat
Overtoom
Leidseplein
1e Huygensstraat
Stadhouderskade
Weteringcircuit
Speigelgracht
1e Jacob van Campenstraat
Ruysdaelstraat
Albert Cuypstraat
Hobbemastraat
Van Baerlestraat
Johan Vermeerplein
Museumplein
Cornelis Schuystraat
Jacob Obrechtstraat
Roelof Hartplein
Ruysdaelkade
Ferdinand Bolstraat/ Ceintuurbaan
2e van der Helstraat
Van Woustraat/ Ceintuurbaan
Stadhouderskade
Camperstraat
Hugo de Vrieslaan
Kruislaan
Brinkstraat
Arent Krijtsstraat
Schoolstraat
Nicolas Lublinkstraat
Wibautstraat
Lutmastraat
Amstelkade
Amsteldijk
Uiterwaardenstraat
Spaklerweg
Cornelis Troostplein
Scheldestraat
Maastraat
Waalstraat
Victoriaplein
Hunzestraat
Apollolaan
Gerrit van der Veenstraat
Stadionweg
Beethovenstraat
Olympiaplein
Minervaplein
©TCS Designed by R.Woods
Map authorised user number: WZFG/TCNB199/1 UDN.3

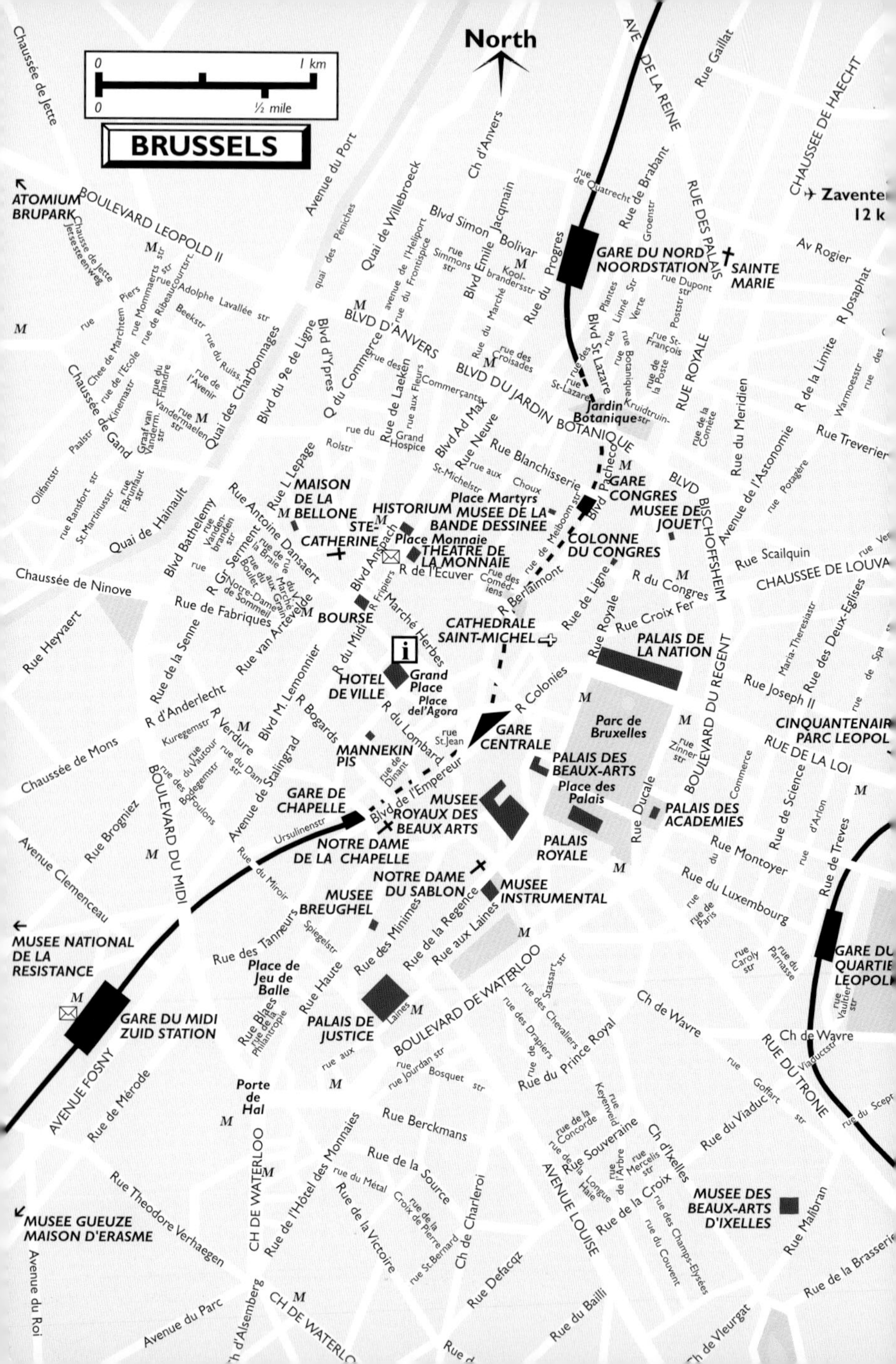

BRUSSELS
North
0
1 km
0
½ mile
ATOMIUM
BRUPARK
BOULEVARD LEOPOLD II
Chaussée de Jette
Avenue du Port
Quai de Willebroeck
Ch d'Anvers
AVE DE LA REINE
Rue Gaillat
CHAUSSEE DE HAECHT
Zaventem
12 km
Blvd Simon Bolivar
Blvd Emile Jacqmain
Rue du Progres
Rue de Brabant
RUE DES PALAIS
GARE DU NORD
NOORDSTATION
SAINTE MARIE
Av Rogier
R Josaphat
BLVD D'ANVERS
BLVD DU JARDIN BOTANIQUE
Jardin Botanique
Blvd St Lazare
RUE ROYALE
Rue du Meridien
R de la Limite
Rue Treverier
Avenue de l'Astronomie
Quai des Charbonnages
Blvd du 9e de Ligne
Blvd d'Ypres
Q du Commerce
Rue de Laeken
Chaussée de Gand
Quai de Hainault
Blvd Bathelemy
Rue Antoine Dansaert
Rue L Lepage
MAISON DE LA BELLONE
HISTORIUM
STE-CATHERINE
Place Monnaie
THEATRE DE LA MONNAIE
R de l'Ecuver
Place Martyrs
MUSEE DE LA BANDE DESSINEE
Rue Neuve
Rue Blanchisserie
Blvd Ad Max
Blvd Pacheco
GARE CONGRES
MUSEE DE JOUET
BLVD BISCHOFFSHEIM
COLONNE DU CONGRES
Rue Scailquin
CHAUSSEE DE LOUVAIN
R du Congres
Rue Croix Fer
Rue de Ligne
R Berlaimont
Chaussée de Ninove
Rue de Fabriques
Rue van Artevelde
R Gr Serment
Blvd Anspach
BOURSE
CATHEDRALE SAINT-MICHEL
Rue Royale
PALAIS DE LA NATION
BOULEVARD DU REGENT
Rue des Deux-Eglises
Rue Joseph II
CINQUANTENAIRE
PARC LEOPOLD
RUE DE LA LOI
Rue Heyvaert
Rue de la Senne
R du Midi
Marché Herbes
HOTEL DE VILLE
Grand Place
Place del'Agora
R Colonies
Parc de Bruxelles
R d'Anderlecht
Blvd M. Lemonnier
R Bogards
R du Lombard
GARE CENTRALE
R Verdure
Chaussée de Mons
MANNEKIN PIS
PALAIS DES BEAUX-ARTS
Place des Palais
BOULEVARD DU MIDI
Avenue de Stalingrad
GARE DE CHAPELLE
Blvd de l'Empereur
MUSEE ROYAUX DES BEAUX ARTS
Rue Ducale
PALAIS DES ACADEMIES
Rue de Science
Rue Brogniez
NOTRE DAME DE LA CHAPELLE
PALAIS ROYALE
Rue Montoyer
Rue de Treves
Avenue Clemenceau
NOTRE DAME DU SABLON
MUSEE INSTRUMENTAL
Rue du Luxembourg
MUSEE BREUGHEL
MUSEE NATIONAL DE LA RESISTANCE
Rue des Tanneurs
Rue des Minimes
Rue de la Regence
Rue aux Laines
GARE DU QUARTIER LEOPOLD
Place de Jeu de Balle
Rue Haute
BOULEVARD DE WATERLOO
Ch de Wavre
GARE DU MIDI
ZUID STATION
PALAIS DE JUSTICE
Rue Blaes
Rue du Prince Royal
RUE DU TRONE
AVENUE FOSNY
Porte de Hal
Rue de Mérode
Rue Berckmans
Rue du Viaduc
Rue de la Source
Rue Souveraine
Ch d'Ixelles
CH DE WATERLOO
Rue de l'Hôtel des Monnaies
Ch de Charleroi
AVENUE LOUISE
Rue de la Croix
MUSEE DES BEAUX-ARTS D'IXELLES
Rue Theodore Verhaegen
MUSEE GUEUZE
MAISON D'ERASME
Rue de la Victoire
Rue Malibran
Avenue du Roi
Rue Defacqz
Rue de la Brasserie
Avenue du Parc
Ch d'Alsemberg
CH DE WATERLOO
Rue du Balli
Ch de Vleurgat

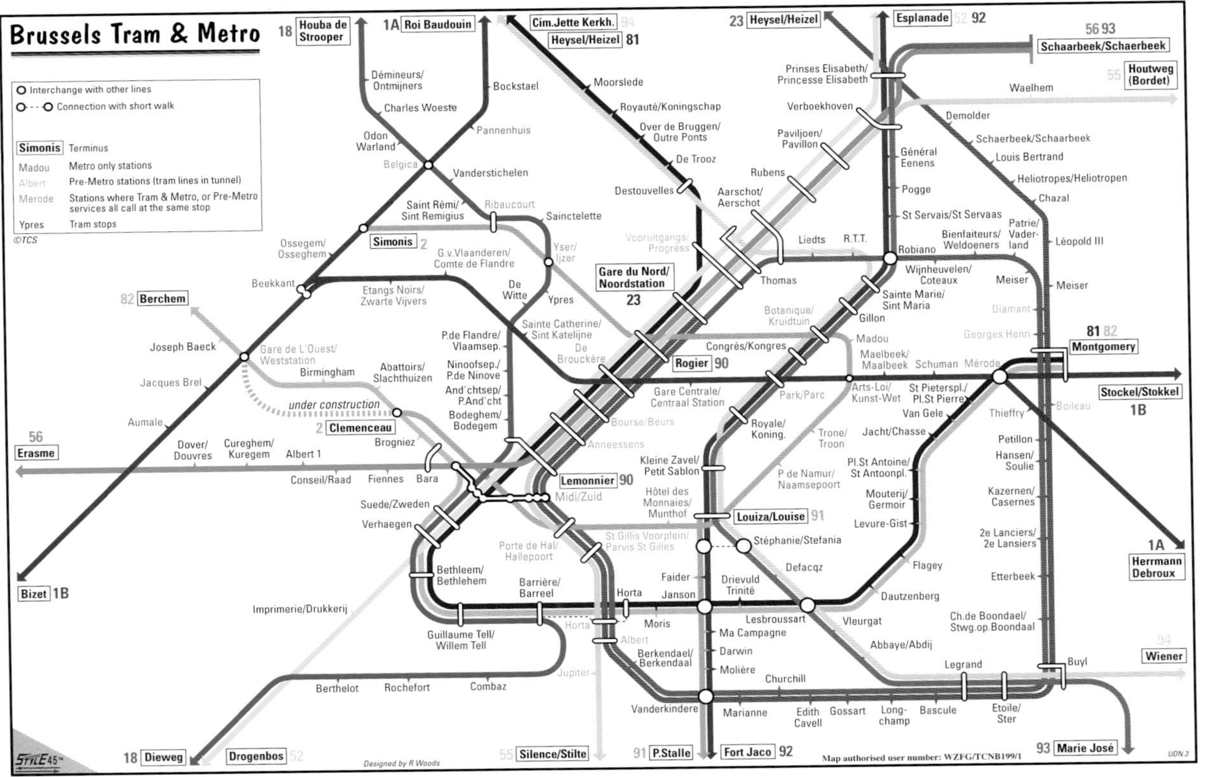

Brussels Tram & Metro
Interchange with other lines
Connection with short walk
Simonis Terminus
Madou Metro only stations
Albert Pre-Metro stations (tram lines in tunnel)
Merode Stations where Tram & Metro, or Pre-Metro services all call at the same stop
Ypres Tram stops
©TCS
18 Houba de Strooper
1A Roi Baudouin
Cim.Jette Kerkh. 94
Heysel/Heizel 81
23 Heysel/Heizel
Esplanade 52 92
56 93 Schaarbeek/Schaerbeek
55 Houtweg (Bordet)
Démineurs/ Ontmijners
Bockstael
Charles Woeste
Pannenhuis
Odon Warland
Belgica
Vanderstichelen
Saint Rémi/ Sint Remigius
Ribaucourt
Sainctelette
Simonis 2
Ossegem/ Osseghem
G.v.Vlaanderen/ Comte de Flandre
Yser/ Ijzer
Beekkant
Etangs Noirs/ Zwarte Vijvers
De Witte
Ypres
82 Berchem
Joseph Baeck
Gare de L'Ouest/ Weststation
Birmingham
Abattoirs/ Slachthuizen
Jacques Brel
under construction
2 Clemenceau
Aumale
56 Erasme
Dover/ Douvres
Cureghem/ Kuregem
Albert 1
Brogniez
Conseil/Raad
Fiennes
Bara
Suede/Zweden
Verhaegen
Bizet 1B
Imprimerie/Drukkerij
Bethleem/ Bethlehem
Barrière/ Barreel
Guillaume Tell/ Willem Tell
Berthelot
Rochefort
Combaz
18 Dieweg
Drogenbos 52
Designed by R.Woods
Moorslede
Royauté/Koningschap
Over de Bruggen/ Outre Ponts
De Trooz
Destouvelles
Vooruitgangs/ Progress
Gare du Nord/ Noordstation 23
Aarschot/ Aerschot
Rubens
Paviljoen/ Pavillon
Verboekhoven
Prinses Elisabeth/ Princesse Elisabeth
Thomas
Liedts
R.T.T.
P.de Flandre/ Vlaamsep.
Ninoofsep./ P.de Ninove
And'chtsep/ P.And'cht
Bodeghem/ Bodegem
Sainte Catherine/ Sint Katelijne
De Brouckère
Rogier 90
Botanique/ Kruidtuin
Congrès/Kongres
Gare Centrale/ Centraal Station
Bourse/Beurs
Anneessens
Lemonnier 90
Midi/Zuid
Porte de Hal/ Hallepoort
St Gillis Voorplein/ Parvis St Gilles
Horta
Albert
Jupiter
55 Silence/Stilte
Faider
Janson
Moris
Berkendael/ Berkendaal
Vanderkindere
91 P.Stalle
Kleine Zavel/ Petit Sablon
Hôtel des Monnaies/ Munthof
Louiza/Louise 91
Drievuld Trinité
Stéphanie/Stefania
Defacqz
Lesbroussart
Ma Campagne
Darwin
Molière
Marianne
Fort Jaco 92
Royale/ Koning.
Trone/ Troon
P de Namur/ Naamsepoort
Park/Parc
Madou
Arts-Loi/ Kunst-Wet
Maelbeek/ Maalbeek
Schuman
Mérode
Gillon
Sainte Marie/ Sint Maria
Wijnheuvelen/ Coteaux
Robiano
Général Eenens
Pogge
St Servais/St Servaas
Bienfaiteurs/ Weldoeners
Patrie/ Vader- land
Meiser
Diamant
Georges Henri
81 82 Montgomery
Demolder
Schaerbeek/Schaarbeek
Louis Bertrand
Heliotropes/Heliotropen
Chazal
Léopold III
Waelhem
St Pieterspl./ Pl.St Pierre
Van Gele
Jacht/Chasse
Pl.St Antoine/ St Antoonpl.
Mouterij/ Germoir
Levure-Gist
Flagey
Dautzenberg
Vleurgat
Abbaye/Abdij
Churchill
Edith Cavell
Gossart
Long- champ
Bascule
Etoile/ Ster
Legrand
Buyl
Stockel/Stokkel 1B
Boileau
Thieffry
Petillon
Hansen/ Soulie
Kazernen/ Casernes
2e Lanciers/ 2e Lansiers
Etterbeek
Ch.de Boondael/ Stwg.op.Boondaal
1A Herrmann Debroux
94 Wiener
93 Marie José
Map authorised user number: WZFG/TCNB199/1
UDN.3

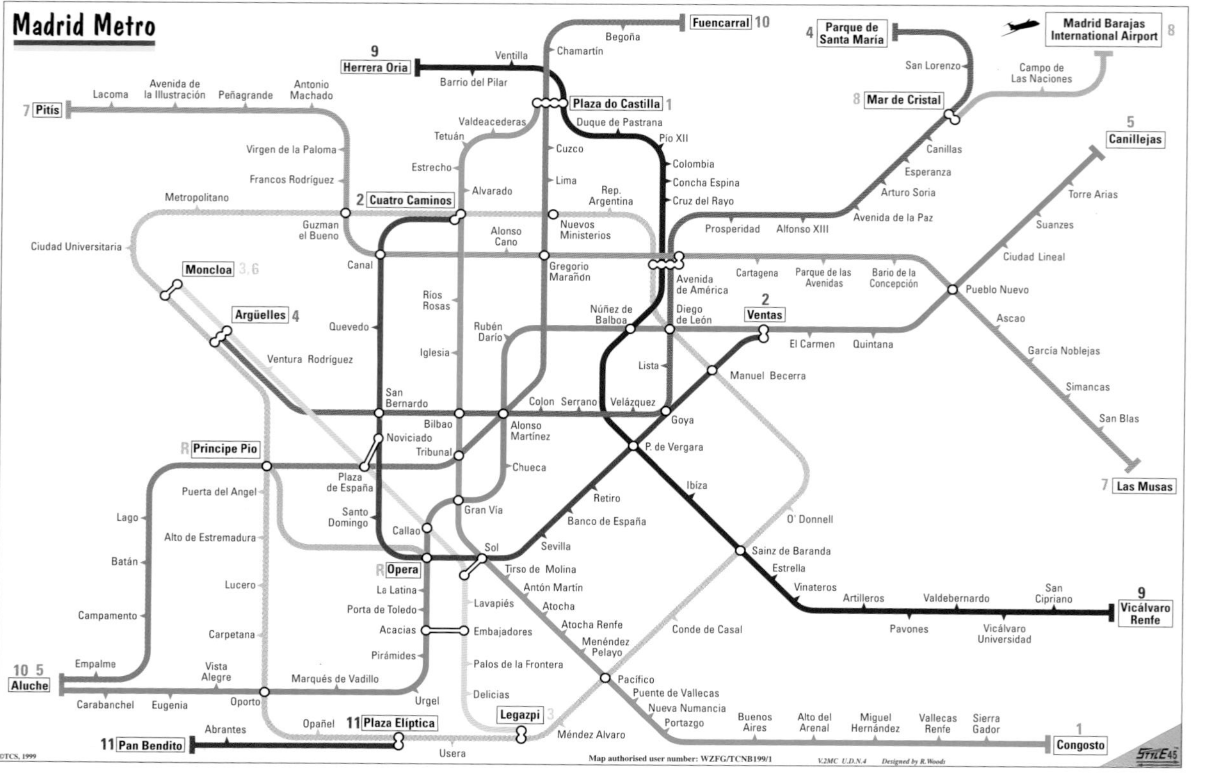
Madrid Metro
9 Herrera Oria
Fuencarral 10
4 Parque de Santa María
Madrid Barajas International Airport 8
7 Pitís
Lacoma
Avenida de la Illustración
Peñagrande
Antonio Machado
Ventilla
Barrio del Pilar
Begoña
Chamartín
San Lorenzo
Campo de Las Naciones
8 Mar de Cristal
Plaza do Castilla 1
Valdeacederas
Tetuán
Duque de Pastrana
Pío XII
5 Canillejas
Virgen de la Paloma
Francos Rodríguez
Estrecho
Alvarado
Cuzco
Lima
Colombia
Concha Espina
Cruz del Rayo
Canillas
Esperanza
Arturo Soria
Avenida de la Paz
Torre Arias
Suanzes
Metropolitano
2 Cuatro Caminos
Rep. Argentina
Nuevos Ministerios
Prosperidad
Alfonso XIII
Ciudad Universitaria
Guzman el Bueno
Alonso Cano
Canal
Gregorio Marañon
Avenida de América
Cartagena
Parque de las Avenidas
Bario de la Concepción
Ciudad Lineal
Pueblo Nuevo
Moncloa 3,6
Ríos Rosas
Argüelles 4
Quevedo
Rubén Darío
Núñez de Balboa
Diego de León
2 Ventas
El Carmen
Quintana
Ascao
García Noblejas
Iglesia
Ventura Rodríguez
Lista
Manuel Becerra
Simancas
San Bernardo
Colon
Serrano
Velázquez
Goya
San Blas
Bilbao
Alonso Martínez
Noviciado
Tribunal
P. de Vergara
R Principe Pio
Plaza de España
Chueca
Ibíza
7 Las Musas
Puerta del Angel
Retiro
Lago
Santo Domingo
Gran Vía
O' Donnell
Banco de España
Alto de Estremadura
Callao
Sol
Sevilla
Sainz de Baranda
R Opera
Tirso de Molina
Estrella
Batán
Lucero
La Latina
Antón Martín
Vinateros
Atocha
Artilleros
Valdebernardo
San Cipriano
9 Vicálvaro Renfe
Porta de Toledo
Lavapiés
Atocha Renfe
Campamento
Acacias
Embajadores
Conde de Casal
Pavones
Vicálvaro Universidad
Menéndez Pelayo
Carpetana
Pirámides
Palos de la Frontera
Empalme
Vista Alegre
Marqués de Vadillo
Pacífico
10 5 Aluche
Puente de Vallecas
Delicias
Carabanchel
Eugenia
Oporto
Urgel
Nueva Numancia
Buenos Aires
Alto del Arenal
Miguel Hernández
Vallecas Renfe
Sierra Gador
Legazpi 3
Portazgo
Abrantes
Opañel
11 Plaza Elíptica
1 Congosto
Méndez Alvaro
11 Pan Bendito
Usera
©TCS, 1999
Map authorised user number: WZFG/TCNB199/1
V.2MC U.D.N.4
Designed by R.Woods
STYLE45

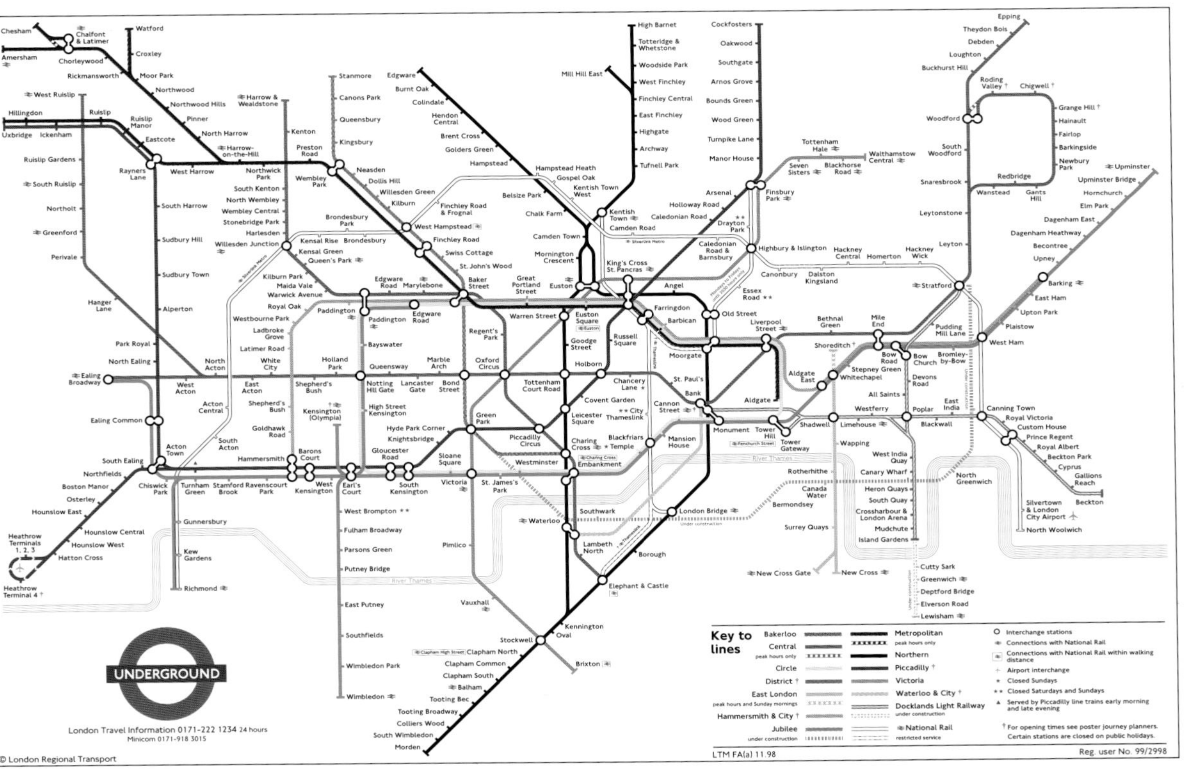

Chesham
Chalfont & Latimer
Amersham
Chorleywood
Rickmansworth
Watford
Croxley
Moor Park
Northwood
Northwood Hills
Pinner
North Harrow
Harrow-on-the-Hill
West Harrow
West Ruislip
Hillingdon
Uxbridge
Ickenham
Ruislip
Ruislip Manor
Eastcote
Rayners Lane
Ruislip Gardens
South Ruislip
Northolt
Greenford
Perivale
Hanger Lane
Park Royal
North Ealing
Ealing Broadway
Ealing Common
South Ealing
Northfields
Boston Manor
Osterley
Hounslow East
Hounslow Central
Hounslow West
Hatton Cross
Heathrow Terminals 1, 2, 3
Heathrow Terminal 4 †
South Harrow
Sudbury Hill
Sudbury Town
Alperton
West Acton
North Acton
Acton Central
South Acton
Acton Town
Chiswick Park
Turnham Green
Stamford Brook
Ravenscourt Park
Gunnersbury
Kew Gardens
Richmond
Harrow & Wealdstone
Kenton
South Kenton
North Wembley
Wembley Central
Stonebridge Park
Harlesden
Willesden Junction
Northwick Park
Preston Road
Wembley Park
Stanmore
Canons Park
Queensbury
Kingsbury
Neasden
Dollis Hill
Willesden Green
Kilburn
Edgware
Burnt Oak
Colindale
Hendon Central
Brent Cross
Golders Green
Hampstead
Hampstead Heath
Gospel Oak
Kentish Town West
Belsize Park
Chalk Farm
Camden Town
Mornington Crescent
Finchley Road & Frognal
West Hampstead
Finchley Road
Swiss Cottage
St. John's Wood
Brondesbury Park
Brondesbury
Kensal Rise
Kensal Green
Queen's Park
Kilburn Park
Maida Vale
Warwick Avenue
Royal Oak
Westbourne Park
Ladbroke Grove
Latimer Road
White City
East Acton
Shepherd's Bush
Goldhawk Road
Hammersmith
Barons Court
West Kensington
Earl's Court
Kensington (Olympia)
Holland Park
Notting Hill Gate
High Street Kensington
Queensway
Bayswater
Paddington
Edgware Road
Marylebone
Baker Street
Great Portland Street
Regent's Park
Lancaster Gate
Marble Arch
Bond Street
Oxford Circus
Hyde Park Corner
Knightsbridge
Gloucester Road
South Kensington
Sloane Square
Green Park
Piccadilly Circus
Victoria
St. James's Park
Westminster
Pimlico
Vauxhall
West Brompton **
Fulham Broadway
Parsons Green
Putney Bridge
East Putney
Southfields
Wimbledon Park
Wimbledon
Stockwell
Clapham North
Clapham High Street
Clapham Common
Clapham South
Balham
Tooting Bec
Tooting Broadway
Colliers Wood
South Wimbledon
Morden
Oval
Kennington
Brixton
Elephant & Castle
Lambeth North
Waterloo
Southwark
Borough
London Bridge
Mill Hill East
High Barnet
Totteridge & Whetstone
Woodside Park
West Finchley
Finchley Central
East Finchley
Highgate
Archway
Tufnell Park
Kentish Town
Camden Road
Caledonian Road
Holloway Road
Caledonian Road & Barnsbury
Silverlink Metro
Euston
Euston Square
Warren Street
Goodge Street
Tottenham Court Road
Holborn
Russell Square
King's Cross St. Pancras
Angel
Farringdon
Barbican
Thameslink
Moorgate
Chancery Lane *
St. Paul's
Covent Garden
Leicester Square
** City Thameslink
Charing Cross
Embankment
Blackfriars
* Temple
Mansion House
Cannon Street *
Bank
Monument
Fenchurch Street
Tower Hill
Tower Gateway
Aldgate
Aldgate East
Liverpool Street
Old Street
Essex Road **
Highbury & Islington
Drayton Park **
Arsenal
Finsbury Park
Manor House
Turnpike Lane
Wood Green
Bounds Green
Arnos Grove
Southgate
Oakwood
Cockfosters
Seven Sisters
Tottenham Hale
Blackhorse Road
Walthamstow Central
Canonbury
Dalston Kingsland
Hackney Central
Homerton
Hackney Wick
Mondays to Fridays until 2030 hours only
Bethnal Green
Shoreditch †
Whitechapel
Stepney Green
Mile End
Bow Road
Bow Church
Pudding Mill Lane
Devons Road
All Saints
Shadwell
Limehouse
Westferry
Poplar
East India
Blackwall
Wapping
Rotherhithe
Canada Water
Bermondsey
Surrey Quays
New Cross Gate
New Cross
West India Quay
Canary Wharf
Heron Quays
South Quay
Crossharbour & London Arena
Mudchute
Island Gardens
Cutty Sark
Greenwich
Deptford Bridge
Elverson Road
Lewisham
Under construction
North Greenwich
Canning Town
Royal Victoria
Custom House
Prince Regent
Royal Albert
Beckton Park
Cyprus
Gallions Reach
Beckton
Silvertown & London City Airport
North Woolwich
Stratford
Bromley-by-Bow
West Ham
Plaistow
Upton Park
East Ham
Barking
Upney
Becontree
Dagenham Heathway
Dagenham East
Elm Park
Hornchurch
Upminster Bridge
Upminster
Leyton
Leytonstone
Snaresbrook
South Woodford
Woodford
Wanstead
Redbridge
Gants Hill
Newbury Park
Barkingside
Fairlop
Hainault
Grange Hill †
Chigwell †
Roding Valley †
Buckhurst Hill
Loughton
Debden
Theydon Bois
Epping
River Thames
UNDERGROUND
London Travel Information 0171-222 1234 24 hours
Minicom 0171-918 3015
© London Regional Transport
Key to lines
Bakerloo
Central
peak hours only
Circle
District †
East London
peak hours and Sunday mornings
Hammersmith & City †
Jubilee
under construction
Metropolitan
peak hours only
Northern
Piccadilly †
Victoria
Waterloo & City †
Docklands Light Railway
under construction
National Rail
restricted service
Interchange stations
Connections with National Rail
Connections with National Rail within walking distance
Airport interchange
* Closed Sundays
** Closed Saturdays and Sundays
Served by Piccadilly line trains early morning and late evening
† For opening times see poster journey planners. Certain stations are closed on public holidays.
LTM FA(a) 11.98
Reg. user No. 99/2998

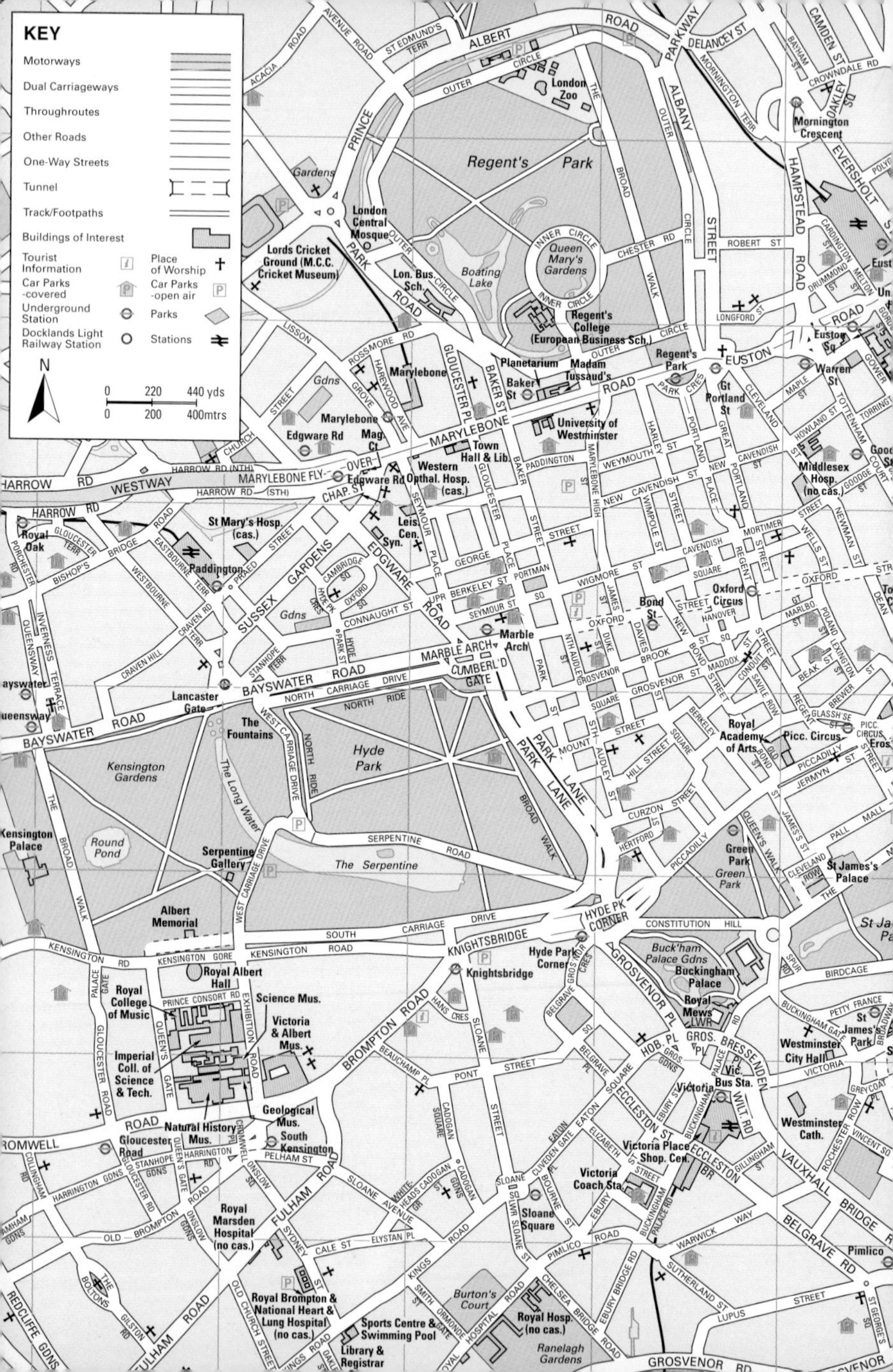

KEY
Motorways
Dual Carriageways
Throughroutes
Other Roads
One-Way Streets
Tunnel
Track/Footpaths
Buildings of Interest
Tourist Information
Place of Worship
Car Parks -covered
Car Parks -open air
Underground Station
Parks
Docklands Light Railway Station
Stations
N
0 220 440 yds
0 200 400mtrs
Regent's Park
London Zoo
Queen Mary's Gardens
Boating Lake
London Central Mosque
Lords Cricket Ground (M.C.C. Cricket Museum)
Lon. Bus. Sch.
Regent's College (European Business Sch.)
Planetarium
Madam Tussaud's
Baker St
Regent's Park
Gt Portland St
Euston Sq
Warren St
Mornington Crescent
Marylebone
Edgware Rd
Mag. Ct
Town Hall & Lib.
Western Opthal. Hosp. (cas.)
University of Westminster
Middlesex Hosp. (no cas.)
St Mary's Hosp. (cas.)
Paddington
Royal Oak
Leis. Cen.
Syn.
Marble Arch
Bond St
Oxford Circus
Lancaster Gate
The Fountains
Kensington Gardens
Hyde Park
The Long Water
The Serpentine
Round Pond
Kensington Palace
Serpentine Gallery
Albert Memorial
Royal Academy of Arts
Picc. Circus
Green Park
St James's Palace
Hyde Park Corner
Buck'ham Palace Gdns
Buckingham Palace
Royal Mews
Knightsbridge
Royal Albert Hall
Royal College of Music
Science Mus.
Victoria & Albert Mus.
Imperial Coll. of Science & Tech.
Natural History Mus.
Geological Mus.
Gloucester Road
South Kensington
Victoria
Vic. Bus Sta.
Victoria Place Shop. Cen.
Victoria Coach Sta.
Westminster City Hall
St James's Park
Westminster Cath.
Sloane Square
Royal Marsden Hospital (no cas.)
Royal Brompton & National Heart & Lung Hospital (no cas.)
Sports Centre & Swimming Pool
Library & Registrar
Burton's Court
Royal Hosp. (no cas.)
Ranelagh Gardens
Pimlico
MARYLEBONE ROAD
EUSTON ROAD
WESTWAY
BAYSWATER ROAD
OXFORD STREET
PARK LANE
PICCADILLY
KNIGHTSBRIDGE
KENSINGTON ROAD
CROMWELL ROAD
BROMPTON ROAD
FULHAM ROAD
KINGS ROAD
EDGWARE ROAD
VAUXHALL BRIDGE ROAD
BELGRAVE RD
GROSVENOR RD

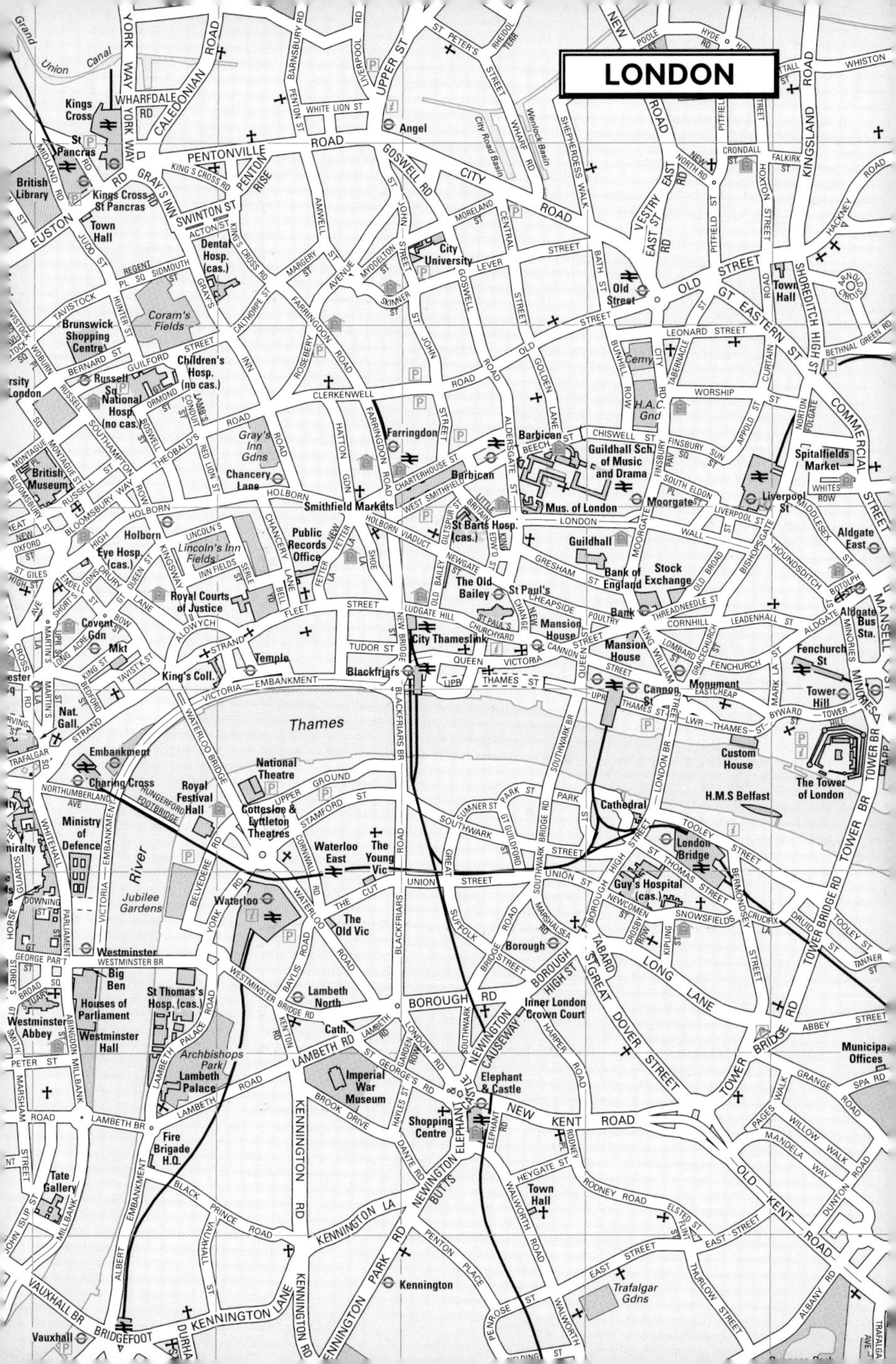

LONDON
Grand Union Canal
York Way
Caledonian Road
Barnsbury Rd
Liverpool Rd
Upper St
St Peter's Street
Rheidol Terr
New North Road
Poole St
Hyde Rd
Whiston
Kingsland Road
Wharfdale Rd
Kings Cross
St Pancras
Midland Rd
British Library
Penton St
White Lion St
Angel
City Road Basin
Wharf Rd
Wenlock Basin
Shepherdess Walk
East Rd
Vestry St
Pitfield St
Hoxton Street
Crondall St
Falkirk St
North Rd
Pentonville Road
Penton Rise
King's Cross Rd
Gray's Inn Rd
Goswell Rd
City Road
Kings Cross St Pancras
Euston Road
Swinton St
Acton St
Judd St
Town Hall
Dental Hosp. (cas.)
Amwell St
John St
Moreland St
Central St
Hackney Rd
Regent Sq
Sidmouth St
Margery St
Myddelton St
City University
Lever Street
Bath St
Old Street
Shoreditch High St
Arnold Circus
Tavistock Pl
Hunter St
Coram's Fields
Calthorpe St
Farringdon Road
Avenue
Skinner St
Goswell Rd
Gt Eastern St
Brunswick Shopping Centre
Woburn Pl
Bernard St
Guilford Street
Rosebery Av
St John St
Golden Lane
Bunhill Row
Leonard Street
Tabernacle St
Curtain Rd
Bethnal Green Rd
Russell Sq
National Hosp. (no cas.)
Children's Hosp. (no cas.)
Ormond St
Lamb's Conduit St
Old Street
Cemy
City Rd
University of London
Southampton Row
Theobald's Road
Clerkenwell Road
Worship St
H.A.C. Gnd
Norton Folgate
Commercial
Montague Pl
British Museum
Gray's Inn Gdns
Red Lion St
Hatton Gdn
Farringdon
Aldersgate St
Barbican
Beech St
Chiswell St
Guildhall Sch. of Music and Drama
Finsbury Pav
Finsbury Sq
Appold St
Sun St
Spitalfields Market
Bloomsbury Way
Russell St
Chancery Lane
Holborn
Charterhouse St
Smithfield Markets
West Smithfield
Little Britain
Mus. of London
Moorgate
South Eldon Pl
Liverpool St
Whites Row
Middlesex
Oxford St
New Oxford St
Holborn
Lincoln's Inn Fields
Public Records Office
Holborn Viaduct
Giltspur St
St Barts Hosp. (cas.)
King Edw'd St
London Wall
Guildhall
Aldgate East
Houndsditch
St Giles High St
Kingsway
Eye Hosp. (cas.)
Drury Lane
Serle St
Bell Yd
Fetter La
Shoe La
Newgate St
Old Bailey
The Old Bailey
St Paul's
Gresham St
Bank of England
Stock Exchange
Old Broad St
Bishopsgate
Botolph St
Shaftesbury Ave
Endell St
Royal Courts of Justice
Fleet Street
Ludgate Hill
Cheapside
Poultry
Bank
Threadneedle St
Aldgate
Mansell St
Covent Gdn
Mkt
Aldwych
New Bridge St
City Thameslink
St Paul's Churchyard
Change
Mansion House
Cornhill
Leadenhall St
Aldgate Bus Sta.
Long Acre
Strand
Tudor St
Queen Victoria St
Cannon Street
King William St
Lombard St
Gracechurch St
Fenchurch St
Minories
King's Coll.
Temple
Blackfriars
Upr Thames St
Cannon St
Monument
Eastcheap
Mark La
Tower Hill
St Martin's La
Bedford St
Victoria Embankment
Lwr Thames St
Byward St
Nat. Gall.
Trafalgar Sq
Thames
Waterloo Bridge
Blackfriars Br
Southwark Br
London Br
Custom House
Tower Br
Embankment
Charing Cross
National Theatre
Upper Ground
Park St
H.M.S Belfast
The Tower of London
Northumberland Ave
Hungerford Footbridge
Royal Festival Hall
Cotteslee & Lyttleton Theatres
Stamford St
Sumner St
Southwark Bridge Rd
Cathedral
Tooley Street
Whitehall
Ministry of Defence
River
Belvedere Rd
Waterloo East
The Young Vic
Southwark Street
Gt Guildford St
London Bridge
Tower Bridge Rd
Horse Guards
Downing St
Jubilee Gardens
Waterloo
The Cut
Union Street
Union St
Borough High Street
St Thomas Street
Guy's Hospital (cas.)
Bermondsey
Parliament St
Cornwall Rd
The Old Vic
Great Suffolk St
Marshalsea Rd
Newcomen St
Crosby Row
Snowsfields
Crucifix La
Druid St
Tooley St
Westminster
George St
Westminster Br
York Rd
Baylis Rd
Waterloo Road
Blackfriars Road
Borough
Tabard St
Kipling St
Long Lane
Tanner St
Storey's Gate
Broad Sanctuary
Big Ben
Houses of Parliament
St Thomas's Hosp. (cas.)
Westminster Bridge Rd
Lambeth North
Borough Rd
Inner London Crown Court
Great Dover Street
Westminster Abbey
Westminster Hall
Lambeth Palace Road
Kennington Rd
Cath.
Lambeth Rd
London Rd
Newington Causeway
Harper Road
Tower Bridge Rd
Abbey Street
Peter St
Marsham St
Abingdon Millbank
Archbishops Park
Lambeth Palace
Imperial War Museum
St George's Rd
Elephant & Castle
Municipal Offices
Lambeth Road
Lambeth Br
Brook Drive
Hayles St
Shopping Centre
New Kent Road
Grange Walk
Spa Rd
Pages Walk
Willow Walk
Mandela Way
Dunton Road
Fire Brigade H.Q.
Kennington Road
Dante Rd
Newington Butts
Elephant Rd
Rodney Pl
Heygate St
Town Hall
Rodney Road
Walworth Road
Elsted St
Flint St
Old Kent Road
Tate Gallery
John Islip St
Millbank
Black Prince Road
Vauxhall St
Kennington La
Kennington Park Rd
Penton Place
East Street
Kennington
Trafalgar Gdns
Thurlow Street
Albany Rd
Albert Embankment
Vauxhall Br
Bridgefoot
Vauxhall
Kennington Lane
Penrose St
Walworth
Durham
Trafalgar Ave

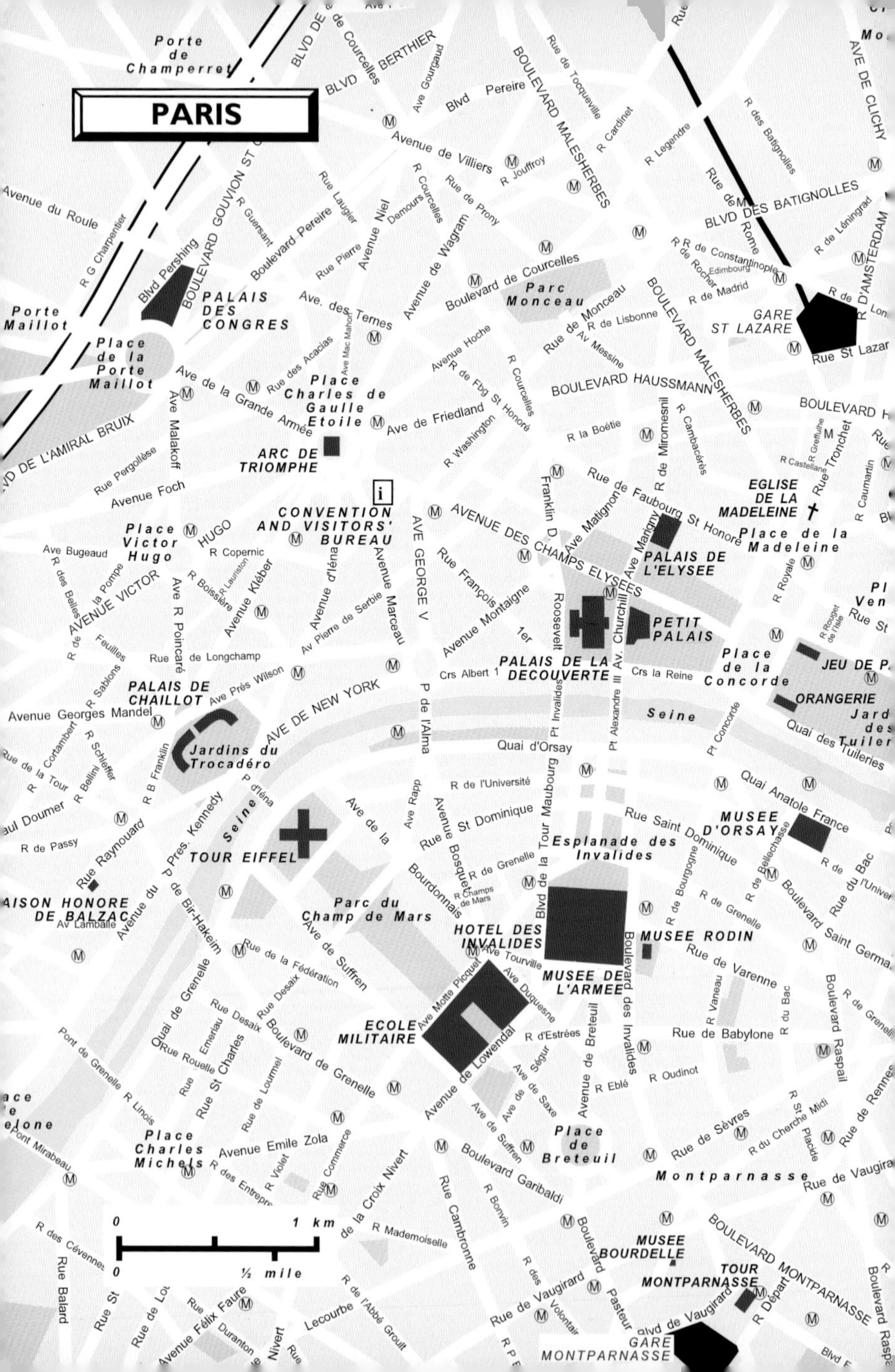
PARIS
Porte de Champerret
Porte Maillot
Place de la Porte Maillot
Palais des Congres
Place Charles de Gaulle Etoile
Arc de Triomphe
Convention and Visitors' Bureau
Place Victor Hugo
Parc Monceau
Gare St Lazare
Eglise de la Madeleine
Place de la Madeleine
Palais de l'Elysee
Petit Palais
Palais de la Decouverte
Place de la Concorde
Jeu de Paume
Orangerie
Jardin des Tuileries
Palais de Chaillot
Jardins du Trocadéro
Seine
Tour Eiffel
Parc du Champ de Mars
Maison Honore de Balzac
Musee d'Orsay
Esplanade des Invalides
Hotel des Invalides
Musee de l'Armee
Musee Rodin
Ecole Militaire
Place de Breteuil
Place Charles Michels
Montparnasse
Musee Bourdelle
Tour Montparnasse
Gare Montparnasse
Blvd Berthier
Blvd Pereire
Boulevard Malesherbes
Avenue de Villiers
BLVD des Batignolles
Ave de Clichy
R d'Amsterdam
Boulevard Gouvion St Cyr
Blvd Pershing
Avenue du Roule
Avenue de Wagram
Boulevard de Courcelles
Ave. des Ternes
Ave de la Grande Armée
Ave de Friedland
Boulevard Haussmann
Rue de Faubourg St Honore
Avenue des Champs Elysees
Ave George V
Avenue Marceau
Avenue d'Iéna
Avenue Kléber
Avenue Foch
Avenue Victor Hugo
Ave R Poincaré
Avenue Montaigne
Avenue Georges Mandel
Ave de New York
Ave Prés Wilson
Crs Albert 1er
Crs la Reine
Quai d'Orsay
Quai des Tuileries
Quai Anatole France
Rue St Dominique
Rue de Grenelle
Boulevard Saint Germain
Rue de Varenne
Rue de Babylone
Boulevard Raspail
Boulevard de Grenelle
Avenue Emile Zola
Rue de la Croix Nivert
Boulevard Garibaldi
Rue Cambronne
Rue de Vaugirard
Boulevard Pasteur
Boulevard Montparnasse
Rue de Sèvres
Rue de Rennes
Avenue de Suffren
Avenue de Lowendal
Avenue de Ségur
Boulevard des Invalides
Avenue de Breteuil
Blvd de la Tour Maubourg
Avenue Bosquet
Ave de la Bourdonnais
Quai de Grenelle
Rue Raynouard
Avenue du Pres. Kennedy
Rue Lecourbe
Rue Balard
0 1 km
0 ½ mile

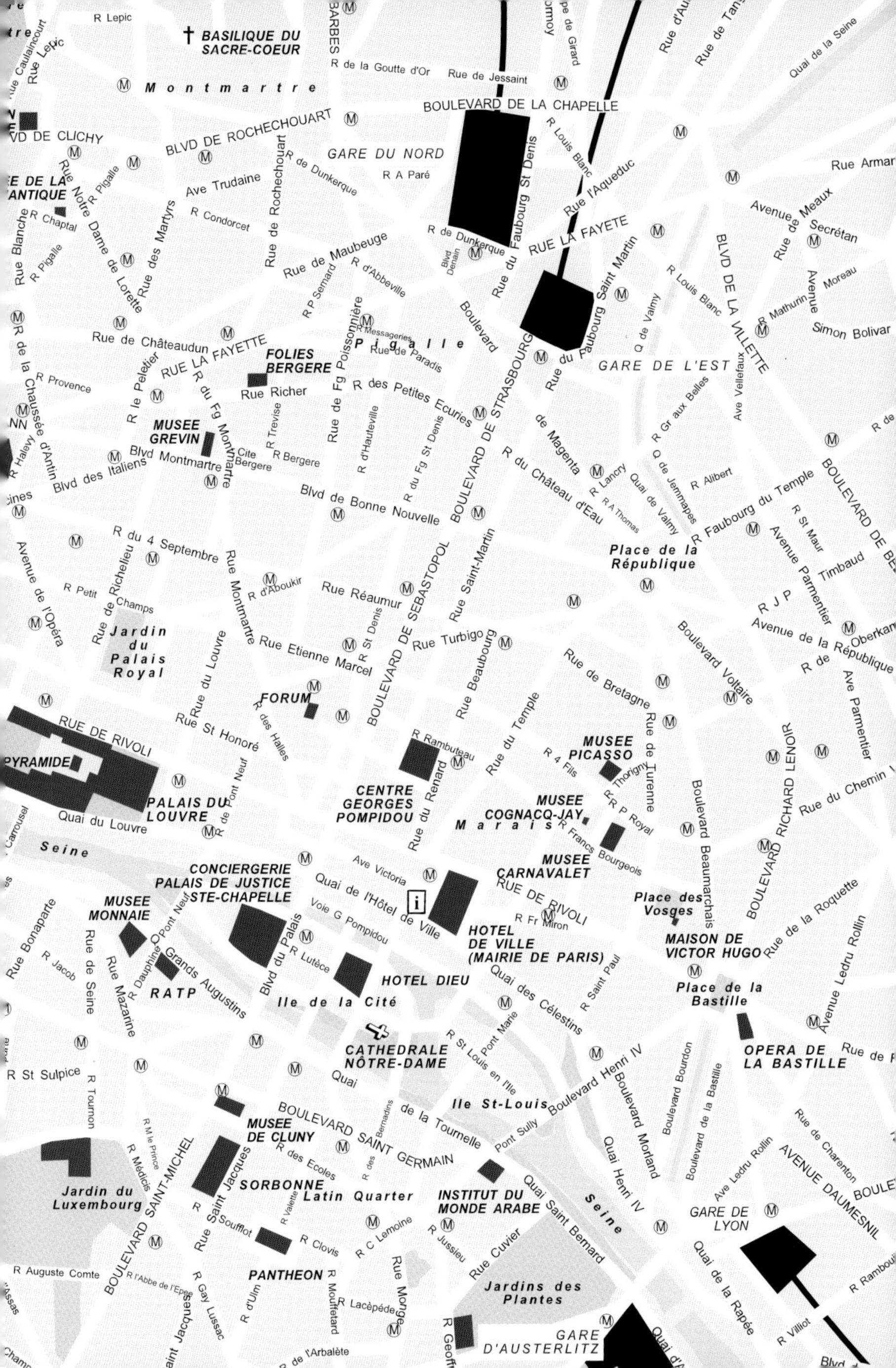

BASILIQUE DU SACRE-COEUR
Montmartre
BLVD DE CLICHY
BLVD DE ROCHECHOUART
BOULEVARD DE LA CHAPELLE
GARE DU NORD
R Lepic
Rue Lepic
Rue Caulaincourt
BARBES
R de la Goutte d'Or
Rue de Jessaint
R de Dunkerque
R A Paré
Ave Trudaine
R Condorcet
Rue de Rochechouart
R Pigalle
Rue Notre Dame de Lorette
R Chaptal
Rue Blanche
Rue des Martyrs
Rue de Maubeuge
R d'Abbeville
R P Semard
Rue de Châteaudun
RUE LA FAYETTE
FOLIES BERGERE
Rue Richer
Pigalle
R Messageries
Rue de Paradis
Rue de Fg Poissonnière
R des Petites Ecuries
R de la Chaussée d'Antin
R Provence
R le Peletier
R du Fg Montmartre
MUSEE GREVIN
R Trevise
Cite Bergere
R Bergere
R d'Hauteville
R du Fg St Denis
Blvd Montmartre
Blvd des Italiens
Blvd de Bonne Nouvelle
Boulevard
BOULEVARD DE STRASBOURG
Rue du Faubourg St Denis
R Louis Blanc
Rue l'Aqueduc
RUE LA FAYETTE
Rue du Faubourg Saint Martin
GARE DE L'EST
Blvd Denain
Q de Valmy
R Louis Blanc
BLVD DE LA VILLETTE
Avenue de Meaux
Secrétan
Rue Armand
Avenue Moreau
R Mathurin
Simon Bolivar
Ave Vellefaux
R Gr aux Belles
Q de Jemmapes
R Alibert
Quai de Valmy
R Lancry
R A Thomas
de Magenta
R du Château d'Eau
R Faubourg du Temple
R St Maur
Avenue Parmentier
BOULEVARD DE BE
Timbaud
Place de la République
R J P
Avenue de la République
Oberkampf
R du 4 Septembre
Avenue de l'Opéra
R Petit Champs
Rue de Richelieu
Jardin du Palais Royal
Rue Montmartre
R d'Aboukir
Rue Réaumur
R St Denis
BOULEVARD DE SEBASTOPOL
Rue Saint-Martin
Rue Turbigo
Rue Etienne Marcel
Rue du Louvre
FORUM
R des Halles
Rue Beaubourg
Rue du Temple
Rue de Bretagne
Boulevard Voltaire
Ave Parmentier
RUE DE RIVOLI
PYRAMIDE
Rue St Honoré
R Rambuteau
CENTRE GEORGES POMPIDOU
Rue du Renard
MUSEE PICASSO
R 4 Fils
Thorigny
Rue de Turenne
Boulevard Beaumarchais
BOULEVARD RICHARD LENOIR
Rue du Chemin Vert
PALAIS DU LOUVRE
R de Pont Neuf
Quai du Louvre
R du Carrousel
MUSEE COGNACQ-JAY
Marais
R P Royal
R Francs Bourgeois
Seine
CONCIERGERIE PALAIS DE JUSTICE STE-CHAPELLE
Ave Victoria
Quai de l'Hôtel de Ville
Voie G Pompidou
MUSEE CARNAVALET
RUE DE RIVOLI
R Fr Miron
Place des Vosges
MAISON DE VICTOR HUGO
Rue de la Roquette
Avenue Ledru Rollin
MUSEE MONNAIE
Pont Neuf
Q Dauphine
Grands Augustins
Rue Bonaparte
R Jacob
Rue de Seine
Rue Mazarine
R Dauphine
RATP
Blvd du Palais
R Lutèce
HOTEL DE VILLE (MAIRIE DE PARIS)
HOTEL DIEU
Quai des Célestins
R Saint Paul
Place de la Bastille
Ile de la Cité
CATHEDRALE NÔTRE-DAME
R St Louis en l'Ile
Pont Marie
OPERA DE LA BASTILLE
Rue de Lyon
R St Sulpice
R Tournon
Quai de la Tournelle
Ile St-Louis
Boulevard Henri IV
Boulevard Morland
Boulevard Bourdon
Boulevard de la Bastille
BOULEVARD SAINT GERMAIN
MUSEE DE CLUNY
R M le Prince
R Bernardins
R des Ecoles
R des
Pont Sully
Quai Henri IV
Rue de Charenton
Avenue Ledru Rollin
AVENUE DAUMESNIL
Jardin du Luxembourg
R Médicis
BOULEVARD SAINT-MICHEL
Rue Saint Jacques
SORBONNE
Latin Quarter
INSTITUT DU MONDE ARABE
Quai Saint Bernard
Seine
GARE DE LYON
R Soufflot
R Valette
R Clovis
R C Lemoine
R Jussieu
Rue Cuvier
Quai de la Rapée
R Auguste Comte
R l'Abbe de l'Epee
R Gay Lussac
PANTHEON
R d'Ulm
R Mouffetard
R Lacèpède
Rue Monge
Jardins des Plantes
R Geoffroy
GARE D'AUSTERLITZ
R Villiot
R Rambouillet
R de l'Arbalète
Rue Saint Jacques
R d'Assas

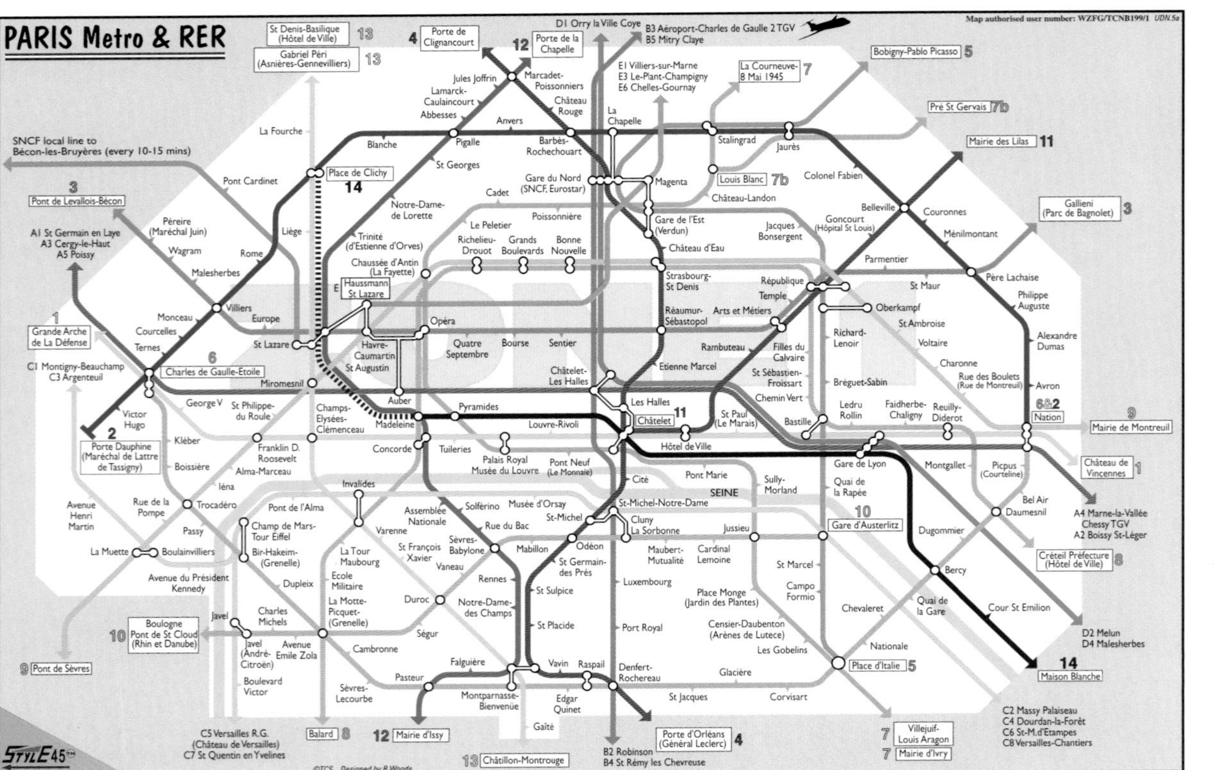
PARIS Metro & RER
Map authorised user number: WZFG/TCNB199/1 UDN.5a
St Denis-Basilique (Hôtel de Ville) 13
Gabriel Péri (Asnières-Gennevilliers) 13
4 Porte de Clignancourt
12 Porte de la Chapelle
D1 Orry la Ville Coye
B3 Aéroport-Charles de Gaulle 2 TGV
B5 Mitry Claye
E1 Villiers-sur-Marne
E3 Le-Plant-Champigny
E6 Chelles-Gournay
La Courneuve-8 Mai 1945 7
Bobigny-Pablo Picasso 5
Pré St Gervais 7b
Mairie des Lilas 11
Gallieni (Parc de Bagnolet) 3
SNCF local line to Bécon-les-Bruyères (every 10-15 mins)
3
Pont de Levallois-Bécon
A1 St Germain en Laye
A3 Cergy-le-Haut
A5 Poissy
1
Grande Arche de La Défense
C1 Montigny-Beauchamp
C3 Argenteuil
La Fourche
Pont Cardinet
Place de Clichy
14
Jules Joffrin
Marcadet-Poissonniers
Lamarck-Caulaincourt
Château Rouge
Abbesses
Anvers
Blanche
Pigalle
Barbès-Rochechouart
La Chapelle
Stalingrad
Jaurès
St Georges
Gare du Nord (SNCF, Eurostar)
Magenta
Louis Blanc 7b
Colonel Fabien
Cadet
Notre-Dame-de Lorette
Château-Landon
Belleville
Couronnes
Péreire (Maréchal Juin)
Wagram
Liège
Le Peletier
Poissonnière
Gare de l'Est (Verdun)
Jacques Bonsergent
Goncourt (Hôpital St Louis)
Ménilmontant
Rome
Trinité (d'Estienne d'Orves)
Richelieu-Drouot
Grands Boulevards
Bonne Nouvelle
Château d'Eau
Malesherbes
Chaussée d'Antin (La Fayette)
Parmentier
Strasbourg-St Denis
République
Père Lachaise
E
Haussmann St Lazare
Temple
St Maur
Philippe Auguste
Villiers
Europe
Arts et Métiers
Oberkampf
Monceau
Opéra
Réaumur-Sébastopol
St Ambroise
Courcelles
St Lazare
Havre-Caumartin
Quatre Septembre
Bourse
Sentier
Rambuteau
Richard-Lenoir
Alexandre Dumas
Ternes
Voltaire
Filles du Calvaire
6
Charles de Gaulle-Etoile
St Augustin
Etienne Marcel
Charonne
Miromesnil
Châtelet-Les Halles
St Sébastien-Froissart
Bréguet-Sabin
Rue des Boulets (Rue de Montreuil)
Avron
Auber
Chemin Vert
Victor Hugo
George V
St Philippe-du Roule
Champs-Elysées-Clémenceau
Pyramides
Les Halles
Ledru Rollin
Faidherbe-Chaligny
Reuilly-Diderot
6&2
Nation
9
Mairie de Montreuil
2
Madeleine
Louvre-Rivoli
Châtelet 11
St Paul (Le Marais)
Bastille
Porte Dauphine (Maréchal de Lattre de Tassigny)
Kléber
Franklin D. Roosevelt
Concorde
Tuileries
Palais Royal Musée du Louvre
Pont Neuf (La Monnaie)
Hôtel de Ville
Gare de Lyon
Montgallet
Picpus (Courteline)
Château de Vincennes 1
Boissière
Alma-Marceau
Cité
Pont Marie
Sully-Morland
Quai de la Rapée
Iéna
Invalides
SEINE
Avenue Henri Martin
Rue de la Pompe
Trocadéro
Pont de l'Alma
Assemblée Nationale
Solférino
Musée d'Orsay
St-Michel-Notre-Dame
10
Gare d'Austerlitz
Bel Air
Daumesnil
A4 Marne-la-Vallée Chessy TGV
A2 Boissy St-Léger
Champ de Mars-Tour Eiffel
Varenne
St-Michel
Cluny La Sorbonne
Jussieu
Passy
Rue du Bac
Dugommier
La Muette
Boulainvilliers
Bir-Hakeim-(Grenelle)
La Tour Maubourg
St François Xavier
Sèvres-Babylone
Mabillon
Odéon
Maubert-Mutualité
Cardinal Lemoine
Créteil Préfecture (Hôtel de Ville) 8
Vaneau
St Germain-des Prés
St Marcel
Bercy
Avenue du Président Kennedy
Dupleix
Ecole Militaire
Rennes
St Sulpice
Luxembourg
Place Monge (Jardin des Plantes)
Campo Formio
Duroc
Notre-Dame-des Champs
Quai de la Gare
Cour St Emilion
Chevaleret
La Motte-Picquet-(Grenelle)
Charles Michels
Javel
Boulogne Pont de St Cloud (Rhin et Danube)
10
St Placide
Port Royal
Censier-Daubenton (Arènes de Lutece)
Ségur
D2 Melun
D4 Malesherbes
Javel (André-Citroën)
Avenue Emile Zola
Cambronne
Les Gobelins
Nationale
Falguière
Vavin
Raspail
Denfert-Rochereau
Glacière
Place d'Italie 5
14
Maison Blanche
9 Pont de Sèvres
Boulevard Victor
Sèvres-Lecourbe
Pasteur
Montparnasse-Bienvenüe
Edgar Quinet
St Jacques
Corvisart
C2 Massy Palaiseau
C4 Dourdan-la-Forêt
C6 St-M.d'Etampes
C8 Versailles-Chantiers
Gaîté
7 Villejuif-Louis Aragon
7 Mairie d'Ivry
C5 Versailles R.G. (Château de Versailles)
C7 St Quentin en Yvelines
Balard 8
12 Mairie d'Issy
Porte d'Orléans (Général Leclerc) 4
B2 Robinson
B4 St Rémy les Chevreuse
13 Châtillon-Montrouge
STYLE45
©TCS Designed by R.Woods

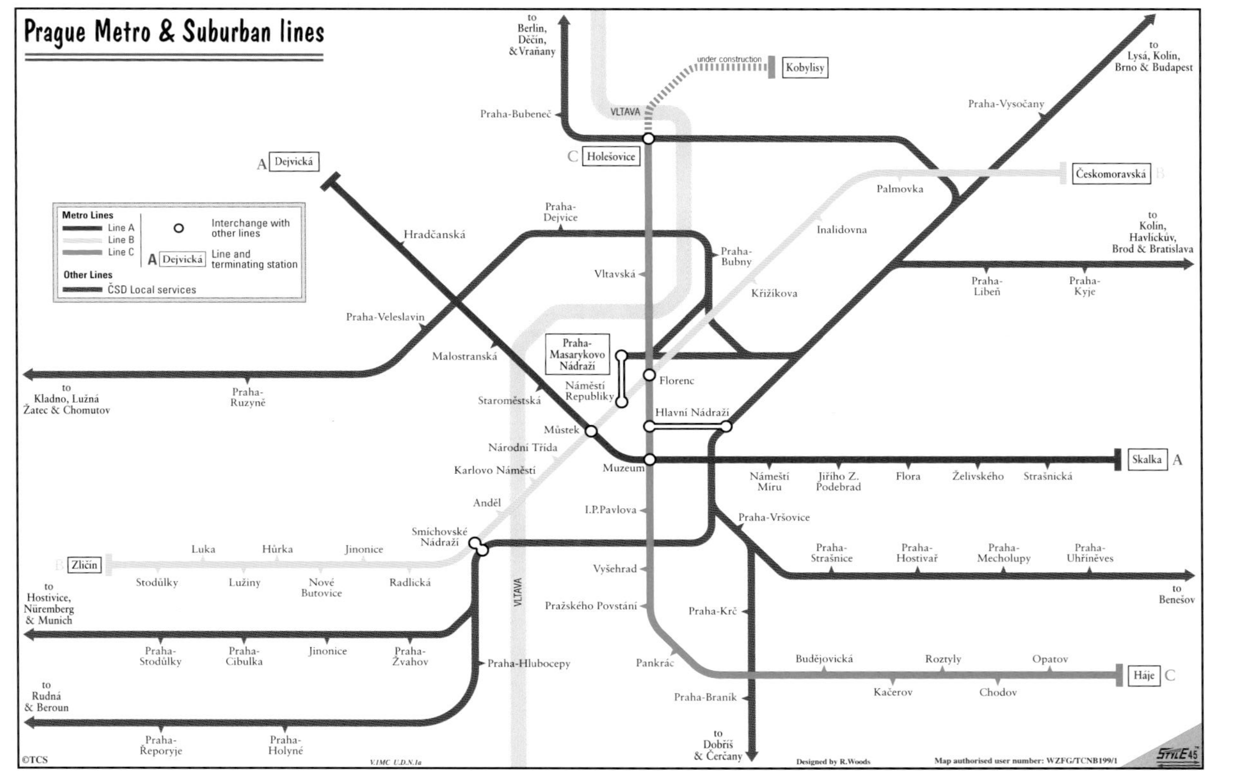

Prague Metro & Suburban lines
Metro Lines
Line A
Line B
Line C
Other Lines
ČSD Local services
Interchange with other lines
A Dejvická Line and terminating station
to Berlin, Děčín, & Vraňany
to Lysá, Kolín, Brno & Budapest
to Kolín, Havlíčkův, Brod & Bratislava
to Kladno, Lužná Žatec & Chomutov
to Hostivice, Nüremberg & Munich
to Rudná & Beroun
to Dobříš & Čerčany
to Benešov
under construction
Kobylisy
VLTAVA
Praha-Bubeneč
C Holešovice
A Dejvická
Hradčanská
Praha-Dejvice
Praha-Bubny
Vltavská
Praha-Veleslavín
Malostranská
Praha-Masarykovo Nádraží
Náměstí Republiky
Florenc
Staroměstská
Můstek
Hlavní Nádraží
Národní Třída
Karlovo Náměstí
Muzeum
Anděl
I.P.Pavlova
Smíchovské Nádraží
Praha-Vysočany
Českomoravská B
Palmovka
Inalidovna
Křižíkova
Praha-Libeň
Praha-Kyje
Skalka A
Náměstí Míru
Jiřího Z. Podebrad
Flora
Želivského
Strašnická
Praha-Vršovice
Praha-Strašnice
Praha-Hostivař
Praha-Mecholupy
Praha-Uhříněves
Praha-Ruzyně
B Zličín
Luka
Hůrka
Jinonice
Stodůlky
Lužiny
Nové Butovice
Radlická
Vyšehrad
Pražského Povstání
Praha-Krč
Praha-Stodůlky
Praha-Cibulka
Jinonice
Praha-Žvahov
Praha-Hlubocepy
Pankrác
Budějovická
Roztyly
Opatov
Háje C
Kačerov
Chodov
Praha-Braník
Praha-Řeporyje
Praha-Holyné
©TCS
V.IMC U.D.N.1a
Designed by R.Woods
Map authorised user number: WZFG/TCNB199/1
STYLE45

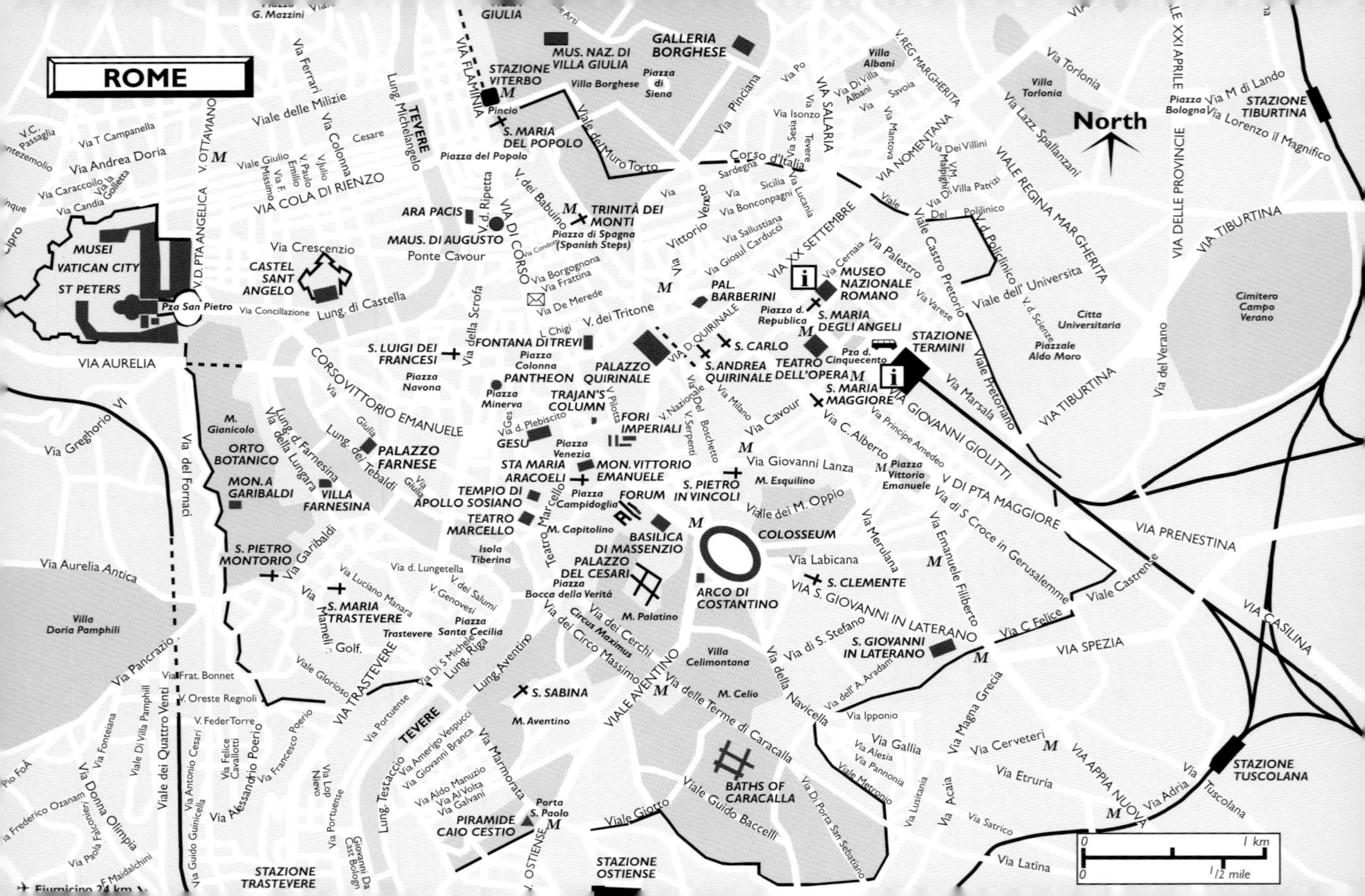

ROME
North
0 1 km
0 1/2 mile
MUSEI
VATICAN CITY
ST PETERS
Pza San Pietro
Via Concillazione
CASTEL SANT ANGELO
Via Crescenzio
Lung. di Castella
Ponte Cavour
MAUS. DI AUGUSTO
ARA PACIS
VIA DI CORSO
V.d. Ripetta
Piazza del Popolo
S. MARIA DEL POPOLO
Pincio
STAZIONE VITERBO
VIA FLAMINIA
GIULIA
MUS. NAZ. DI VILLA GIULIA
Villa Borghese
GALLERIA BORGHESE
Piazza di Siena
Viale del Muro Torto
V. dei Babuino
TRINITÀ DEI MONTI
Piazza di Spagna (Spanish Steps)
Via Condotti
Via Borgognona
Via Frattina
Via De Merede
V. dei Tritone
L. Chigi
FONTANA DI TREVI
Piazza Colonna
PANTHEON
Piazza Minerva
S. LUIGI DEI FRANCESI
Piazza Navona
Via della Scrofa
CORSO VITTORIO EMANUELE
PALAZZO FARNESE
Lung. dei Tebaldi
Via Giulia
PALAZZO QUIRINALE
TRAJAN'S COLUMN
V. Pilotta
FORI IMPERIALI
GESU
Via d. Plebiscito
Piazza Venezia
MON. VITTORIO EMANUELE
STA MARIA ARACOELI
Piazza Campidoglio
TEMPIO DI APOLLO SOSIANO
TEATRO MARCELLO
Teatro Marcello
M. Capitolino
FORUM
BASILICA DI MASSENZIO
PALAZZO DEL CESARI
Piazza Bocca della Verità
M. Palatino
Circus Maximus
Via dei Cerchi
Via dei Circo Massimo
Isola Tiberina
COLOSSEUM
ARCO DI COSTANTINO
Via Labicana
S. CLEMENTE
VIA S. GIOVANNI IN LATERANO
S. GIOVANNI IN LATERANO
Via Merulana
Viale dei M. Oppio
M. Esquilino
S. PIETRO IN VINCOLI
Via Giovanni Lanza
Via Cavour
Via Milano
V. Nazionale
V. Serpenti
Via Del Boschetto
S. ANDREA QUIRINALE
S. CARLO
VIA D. QUIRINALE
PAL. BARBERINI
Piazza d. Repubblica
S. MARIA DEGLI ANGELI
MUSEO NAZIONALE ROMANO
TEATRO DELL'OPERA
Pza d. Cinquecento
STAZIONE TERMINI
S. MARIA MAGGIORE
Via C. Alberto
Via Principe Amedeo
Piazza Vittorio Emanuele
VIA GIOVANNI GIOLITTI
V DI PTA MAGGIORE
Via di S Croce in Gerusalemme
Via Emanuele Filiberto
Via C Felice
Viale Castrense
VIA PRENESTINA
VIA CASILINA
VIA SPEZIA
VIA APPIA NUOVA
Via Adria
Via Tuscolana
STAZIONE TUSCOLANA
Via Latina
Via Satrico
Via Acaia
Via Etruria
Via Cerveteri
Via Magna Grecia
Via Gallia
Via Alesia
Via Pannonia
Viale Metronio
Via Lusitania
Via Ipponio
Via dell' A. Aradam
Via della Navicella
Via di S. Stefano
Villa Celimontana
M. Celio
Via delle Terme di Caracalla
BATHS OF CARACALLA
Viale Guido Baccelli
Via Di Porta San Sebatiano
Viale Giotto
VIALE AVENTINO
S. SABINA
M. Aventino
Lung. Aventino
Via Marmorata
Porta S. Paolo
PIRAMIDE CAIO CESTIO
V. OSTIENSE
STAZIONE OSTIENSE
TEVERE
Lung. Testaccio
Via Amerigo Vespucci
Via Giovanni Branca
Via Aldo Manuzio
Via Al Volta
Via Galvani
Via Portuense
Via Di S Michele
Lung. Ripa
Piazza Santa Cecilia
Trastevere
V. Genovesi
V. dei Salumi
Via d. Lungetella
Via Luciano Manara
S. MARIA TRASTEVERE
Via Mameli
Golf.
VIA TRASTEVERE
Viale Glorioso
Via Garibaldi
S. PIETRO MONTORIO
MON. A GARIBALDI
ORTO BOTANICO
M. Gianicolo
VILLA FARNESINA
Lung. d. Farnesina
Via della Lungara
Via del Fornaci
VIA AURELIA
Via Greghorio VI
Via Aurelia Antica
Villa Doria Pamphili
Via Pancrazio
Via Frat. Bonnet
V. Oreste Regnoli
V. Feder Torre
Via Felice Cavallotti
Via Alessandro Poerio
Via Francesco Poerio
Via Antonio Cesari
Via Guido Guinicella
Viale dei Quattro Venti
Viale Di Villa Pamphili
Via Fonteiana
Via Donna Olimpia
Via Federico Ozanam
Via Paola Falconieri
F. Maidalchini
Pio FoÀ
Via Lop Nievo
Via Portuense
Giovanni Da Cast Bologn
STAZIONE TRASTEVERE
Fiumicino 24 km
V.D. PTA ANGELICA
V. OTTAVIANO
VIA COLA DI RIENZO
Via Andrea Doria
Via T Campanella
V.C. Passaglia
Via Caraccoilo
Via la Golletta
Via Candia
Viale Giulio Cesare
V. Paulo Emilio
V. Julio
Via F. Missimo
Via Colonna
Viale delle Milizie
Via Ferrari
G. Mazzini
TEVERE
Lung. Michelangelo
Via Pinciana
Corso d'Italia
Via Po
Via Isonzo
VIA SALARIA
Via Tevere
Via Sesia
Via Lucania
Via Sicilia
Sardegna
Via Boncompagni
Via Sallustiana
Via Giosul Carducci
Via Vittorio Veneto
VIA XX SETTEMBRE
Via Cernaia
Via Palestro
Via Varese
Viale Castro Pretorio
Via Marsala
Viale Pretoriano
VIA NOMENTANA
Via Mantova
V.REG MARGHERITA
Villa Albani
Via Di Villa Albani
Savoia
Via Dei Villini
V.M. Malpighi
Via Di Villa Patrizi
Via Del Policlinico
V. d. Policlinico
Viale dell' Universita
V. d. Scienze
Citta Universitaria
Piazzale Aldo Moro
VIA TIBURTINA
Via del Verano
Cimitero Campo Verano
VIALE REGINA MARGHERITA
Via Lazz. Spallanzani
Villa Torlonia
Via Torlonia
VIALE DELLE PROVINCIE
VIALE XXI APRILE
Piazza Bologna
Via M di Lando
Via Lorenzo il Magnifico
STAZIONE TIBURTINA

Rome Trams Metro & Suburban lines

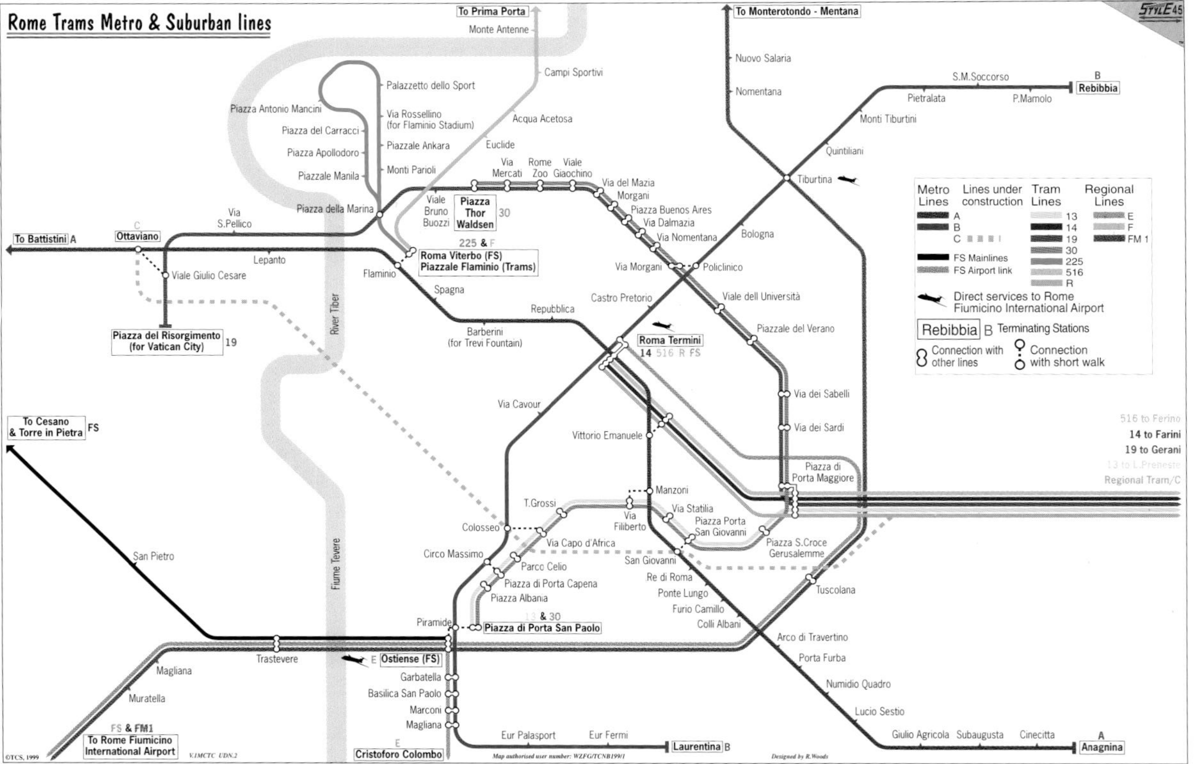

VENICE

North

CANALE DELLE SACCHE
CANALE DELLE NAVI
Isola S Michele
Fond. della Sensa
Fond. Ormesina
Fond. della Misericordia
F.d. Misericordia
Canale di Cannaregio
Canale della C.
S. Leonardo
Sott d. Pegolotto
Maddalena
F. Canal
F. Vendramin
F. Labia
C.d. S. Antonio
PALAZZO VENDRAMIN CALERGI
C. Vendramin
C.d. Olio
C.d. Stua
Rachetta
C. Marco Fosca
Fondamenta Nuove
C.d. Magazin
C.d. Volti
C.d. Fumo
STAZIONE FS SANTA LUCIA
Lista di Spagna
Priuli detta d. Cavalletti
F. Crotta
CANAL GRANDE
Riva di Biasio
Fond. Santa Lucia
L. dei Bari
Gallion
F.d. Turchi
C.d. Megio
PALAZZO CA'PESARO
C. Colombo
C. Tintor
S. Stae
C. d. Forner
C. Pontei
C.d. Spezier
C.d. Rosa
CA' D'ORO
C. Porno
C. d. Vele
Strada Nuova
R.t.d. Barba Fruttarol
Rio t.d. Franceshi
C.d. Oca
C.d. Oca
C.d. Forno
C.I. Berlendis
Birri
R.T. dei
C.d. Squero
Fond. S. Simeone
C. Traghetto
F. Garzotti
C.d. Oche
C.d. P. Storto
F. del Grue
C. Rotta
C.d. Teatro
Corte Michiel
C.d. Beccarie
C.d. Morti
C.d. Donzella
C.d. Posta
S. Chianciano
C. Bag.
C.I.G. Gallina
C.d. Testa
SAN ZANIPOLO
Ponte di Erbe
Bressane
C.d. Morti
AUTORIMESSA (CAR PARK)
Piazzale Roma
Sottop e Corte d C Nuove
Corte Canal
C. Visciga
C.S. Zuane
Sottop e Corte Amai
C. de Lacca
C.d. Chiesa
Calleselle Rampani
C.d. Aseo
C. Scaletta
RIALTO BRIDGE
C.d. Orso
C.d. Stagneri
C.d. Dose
Campo Santa Maria Formosa
C.d. Orbi
C.d. Ospedal
F.d. Tolentini
C.d. Fonderia
Ramo Cimesin
F.d. Gaffaro
C.d. Clero
C.d. Forno
S. Pantalon
Fabbrica dei Tabachi
F.d. Burchielle
Pensieri
SCUOLA D. S. ROCCO
C.d. Volti
Rio Terra C. Corner
S. Polo
S. MARIA GLORIOSA DEI FRARI
C. Madonnetta
C. Barzizza
C.d. Stagneri
C.S. Antonio
Mondo Nuovo
C. Bande
F.d.S. Severo
Calle Molin
C.d. Preti
Rio Nuovo
F. Rizzi Maggiore
F. delle Procratie
C.I. Ragusei
C.C. Contarini
S. Margherita
C.d. Saoneri Saonera
C.del Campaniel
CANAL GRANDE
Riva del Carbon
C. Loredan
C.d. Carbon
Fabbri
C.d. Ballotte
Mercerie
C.d. Spadaria
C.d. Specchier
C.d. Rimedio
Sal Zorzi
C.d. Figher
F.d. Ole
C.d. Guardiani
F. Rossa
C.d. Aseo
C. Giustian
C. Mocenigo
C. Corner
C. Pesaro
C. Vecchia
C. Magazen
C.d. Fuseri
C. Ascensione
BASILICA SAN MARCO
BRIDGE OF SIGHS
Fond. Briati
C.d. Olio
Corte Larga
C. Staffa
CA' REZZONICO
TEATRO LA FENICE
C. Vesta
C. Venier
C. Barcaroli
Piazza S. Marco
R. degli Schiavoni
C. Paziente
F.d. Squero
C.d. Teatro
S. MOISE
22 Marzo
PROCURATIE
PALAZZO DUCALE
Pescaria
C. Rossi
C.d. Vecchi
Calle Lunga S. Barnaba
C.d. Cerchieri
C. Giustinian
F. Morosini
S. MARIA DEL GIGLIO
C.d. 13 Martin
C.d. Pestrin
F. Ostreghe
Corte Barozzi
Molo Riva
Vaporetto line 1
C. Nuova
Sz.d. Chiesa
C.d. Frati
C. Balastro
F.d. Eremite
Ford. di Brogo
C. Lombarda
F. Corner Zaguri
CANAL GRANDE
F. Ognissanti
Corte Canal
Calle Trevisan
Nani
GALLERIE DELL' ACCADEMIA
PALAZZO VENIER DEI LEONI
S. MARIA DELLA SALUTE
CANALE DI SAN MARCO
Zattere al Ponte Lungo
Fondamenta C.d. Frati
C.d. Cristo
F. Foscarini
Pisc S. Agnese
Fond Venier
Fondamenta Bragadin
C.d. Ponte
Ramo dietro gli Incurabili
Corte d. Mende
Corte Nuova
Rio Terra di San Vio
Fondamenta Soranzo della Fornace
Rio Terra dei Catecumeni
Calle d. Squero
Zattere al Saloni
Zattere allo Spirito Santo
S. GIORGIO
Isola di S Giorgio Maggiore
Canale della Grazia
S Bagio
F. San Biagio
CANALE DELLA GIUDECCA
Corte Nuova e C. Montorio
Ponte Piccolo
C.d. Nicoli
C.d. Forno
Ferrando
Ponte Lungo
F. San Giacomo
F. della Croce
Isola della Giudecca

0 500 m
0 400 yds